The *Dictionary of North Carolina Biography*, the most comprehensive state project of its kind, provides information on some four thousand notable North Carolinians whose accomplishments and occasional misdeeds span more than four centuries. Current plans call for six volumes to be published over a period of several years. Volume 4, L–O, includes 592 entries.

The *Dictionary* contains the first compiled biographical information for many of these individuals. Included are native North Carolinians, no matter in what area they made their contributions, and non-natives whose contributions were made in North Carolina. All persons included are deceased.

Explorers, inventors, engineers, writers, chemists, business leaders, architects, artists, musicians, colonial leaders, military figures, national and state officials, and outstanding teachers and clergymen are among those recognized. And there are the infamous and eccentric— pirates, criminals, a hermit, and the man who weighed more than one thousand pounds. Averaging about eight hundred words, each sketch includes the full name of the subject, dates and places of birth and death (when known), family connections, a career description, and a bibliography. Most of the sketches are based on manuscript and contemporary printed sources that are rare or difficult to find. Some research was conducted in Europe.

William S. Powell has been working on the *Dictionary* since 1971 with the help of several hundred volunteer contributors.

DICTIONARY OF NORTH CAROLINA BIOGRAPHY

EDITED BY WILLIAM S. POWELL

VOLUME 4 L-O

DICTIONARY OF NORTH CAROLINA BIOGRAPHY

EDITED BY WILLIAM S. POWELL

VOLUME 4 L-O

The University of North Carolina Press

Chapel Hill and London

© 1991 The University of North Carolina Press
All rights reserved

Library of Congress Cataloging-in-Publication Data

Dictionary of North Carolina biography.
    Includes bibliographies.
        1. North Carolina—Biography—Dictionaries.
I. Powell, William Stevens, 1919–
CT252.D5   920'.0756   79-10106
ISBN 0-8078-1329-X (vol. 1)
ISBN 0-8078-1656-6 (vol. 2)
ISBN 0-8078-1806-2 (vol. 3)
ISBN 0-8078-1918-2 (vol. 4)

The paper in this book meets the guidelines for perma-
nence and durability of the Committee on Production
Guidelines for Book Longevity of the Council on Library
Resources.

Manufactured in the United States of America

95 94 93 92 91   5 4 3 2 1

In Memory of

William Patterson Cumming
31 October 1900–16 August 1989

Dorothy Long
7 October 1912–20 June 1987

Hugh Frank Rankin
17 June 1923–1 July 1989

Mattie Underwood Russell
14 May 1915–4 May 1988

Richard Gaither Walser
23 October 1908–25 November 1988

whose scholarly assistance contributed
to the usefulness of the *Dictionary of
North Carolina Biography*

Acknowledgments

I am grateful to the North Carolina Society of the Cincinnati for a generous grant to The University of North Carolina Press to assist with the publication costs of this volume; to George London for his concern and support in seeing that our work continues; to Claiborne T. Smith, Jr., for his research skills in writing some of the biographies that appear in this work and for his gifts for clerical assistance; to Amanda Upchurch for her work in verifying and alphabetizing many of the bibliographies; to my wife, Virginia Waldrop Powell, for her assistance in reading both manuscript and proof; to Stevie Champion for her skill as a copyeditor and for her interest in this work in numerous ways; and, most important of all, to the many authors of the biographies without whose careful and generous work this volume would never have been possible.

Volume four of the *Dictionary of North Carolina Biography*, like the first three, has been produced without grant money of any kind from the federal government. It is the result of the willing and cooperative scholarly labor of a great many people who contributed their knowledge and ability to its successful completion. I continue to find enormous satisfaction both in their work and in their spirit.

The Department of History at The University of North Carolina very generously permitted me to continue to use an office in Hamilton Hall for three years after my retirement. Eric E. Palo of the University Library then made available space in which I could continue to work on the *DNCB*. To all who have contributed in any way to the progress of this work, I am deeply indebted.

Dictionary of North Carolina Biography

Lacy, Benjamin Rice *(19 June 1854–21 Feb. 1929)*, state treasurer, was born in the old Presbyterian manse in Raleigh where his father, the Reverend Drury Lacy, D.D., was pastor for eighteen years until he accepted the presidency of Davidson College. Benjamin's mother, Mary Rice, like his father, was of Welsh ancestry, a daughter of the Reverend Dr. Benjamin Holt Rice who held pastorates in Petersburg, Hampden-Sydney, and other places in Virginia, as well as in New York City and Princeton, N.J. Dr. Rice became moderator of the General Assembly of the Presbyterian church at its 1829 session in Philadelphia.

Benjamin Rice Lacy was reared in a home where Christian piety and resoluteness of purpose prevailed under the guidance of Christian parents—the father, a great preacher and teacher of preachers; the mother, a daughter of a great preacher. The effect of such training in character was the foundation of his life of probity and civic usefulness. He received his schooling at the preparatory school of R. H. Graves in Graham and at the Bingham School at nearby Mebane. On account of the prevailing poverty during Reconstruction, he was unable to obtain the college education he wanted. Nevertheless, his learning and experience came to be so generally recognized that Davidson College in 1928 awarded him an honorary doctor of laws degree.

Having a natural aptitude for mechanics, Lacy served an apprenticeship in the shops of the Raleigh and Gaston Railroad at Raleigh. After becoming foreman, he entered the operating department of the railroad and for fifteen years ran a locomotive. Because of his innate fairness and rugged honesty, he gained the confidence not only of his fellow railroad workers and executives but also of the state's labor force generally. "Honest Ben Lacy," as he came to be known, took a commanding position in the field of labor in North Carolina. He served as an alderman in Raleigh and in 1894 as commissioner of labor and printing. In 1901 he became state treasurer, winning reelection to the post from 1904 to 1928. He also was prominent in councils of the Freemasons and in various other fraternal organizations.

In 1882 Lacy married Mary Burwell, the daughter of Captain and Mrs. J. B. Burwell; at the time, Captain Burwell was president of Peace Institute in Raleigh. The couple had six children: Mrs. R. Y. McAden, Mrs. Charles G. Rose, Frances, Nan, Dr. Thomas Allen, and the Reverend Dr. Ben R., Jr. Thomas Allen Lacy became a noted New York psychiatrist, and Ben Lacy, Jr., served as president of Union Theological Seminary from 1926 until 1956 and as moderator of the Presbyterian Church of the United States in 1950.

Lacy's concern for the welfare of working people made him a natural leader in the amicable and constructive transition of North Carolina industrial life. While he was state treasurer, and especially during the last eight years of his public service, the state embarked on an unprecedented program of financial expansion in which it became necessary for him to handle hundreds of mil-

lions of dollars for permanent improvements. In that work he enjoyed the friendship and confidence of the nation's leading bankers. Lacy was buried in Oakwood Cemetery, Raleigh. An oil portrait of him hangs in the state capitol.

SEE: Grady L. E. Carroll, Sr., *They Lived in Raleigh: Some Leading Personalities from 1792–1892*, vol. 2 (1977); *North Carolina Manual* (1909–29); *Who's Who in the South and Southwest* (1952).

HOLT MCPHERSON

Lacy, Benjamin Rice, Jr. *(30 July 1886–3 Aug. 1981)*, Presbyterian clergyman, educator, and author, was born in Raleigh. His father was a pioneer in promoting labor organizations in North Carolina and treasurer of the state from 1901 to 1928. His grandfather, Drury Lacy, was also a Presbyterian minister and president of Davidson College. His mother was Mary Burwell Lacy, daughter of the president of Peace Institute in Raleigh. After attending the Raleigh Male Academy, young Lacy entered Davidson College where he was the star quarterback on the football team. Following his graduation with a degree in history, he was awarded a Rhodes Scholarship for study at Oxford University during 1907–10. In 1913 he received a bachelor of divinity degree from Union Theological Seminary in Richmond and was awarded the Hoge Fellowship for the next year. While at the seminary, he taught church history.

During World War I Lacy served as a chaplain with the 113th Field Artillery. Because of his heroism in aiding the wounded before the German lines in France, he became known as the "Fighting Parson." It was later noted that on one occasion a deserted German battery with guns and ammunition was found, but it could not be turned against the enemy because all of the instructions were in German. Chaplain Lacy, who was able to decipher the tables and symbols, took charge and for two hours joined in operating the guns in well-directed fire.

After the war he served briefly as pastor of a church in Johnston County before being named pastor of Central Presbyterian Church in Atlanta. In 1926 he became president of Union Theological Seminary, where he remained until his retirement in 1956. During these years he sat on a number of councils and committees and in 1948 was the U.S. representative to the International Conference on Theological Education in Geneva. In 1950 he was moderator of the Presbyterian Church of the United States. Among other works, Lacy was the author of *Revival in the Midst of the Years*. He received honorary degrees from Davidson College, Duke University, Hampden-Sydney College, the University of Richmond, and The University of North Carolina.

In 1919 Lacy married Emma Elizabeth White, daughter of the pastor of the First Presbyterian Church in Raleigh. They were the parents of two sons and a daughter. A portrait of him hangs in the Nevill Ray House in Richmond.

SEE: Grady L. E. Carroll, Sr., *They Lived in Raleigh: Some Leading Personalities from 1792–1892*, vol. 2 (1977); *Charlotte Observer*, 12 May 1926; *Greensboro Daily News*, 12 May 1926; Raleigh *News and Observer*, 27 Mar. 1934, 27 May 1945, 4 Aug. 1951; Richmond, *Union Seminary Bulletin*, July, August, September 1946.

CAROLYN F. ROFF

Lacy, Drury, Jr. *(5 Aug. 1802–1 Aug. 1884)*, college president, clergyman, and educator of Welsh ancestry, was born at Ararat, Prince Edward County, Va., where his father, the Reverend Drury Lacy, had a school and was a Presbyterian minister; his mother was Anne Smith. After receiving his early education at the classical school conducted by his father, young Lacy attended Washington College for a year and then entered Hampden-Sydney College where he received a degree in 1822. From 1823 to 1828 he taught school in Virginia, and from 1828 to 1831 he studied at Union Theological Seminary. He was pastor of the Presbyterian church in New Bern, N.C., from 1834 through 1836 and then of the church in Raleigh.

Lacy remained in Raleigh until 1855, when he became president of Davidson College. Early in his administration, the college received a magnificent benefaction from the late Maxwell Chambers, making it the wealthiest private college in the South. It was also during Lacy's tenure that the large and handsome Chambers building was erected. In 1860 he left Davidson to enter the home mission field of Orange Presbytery, and in August 1863 he became a chaplain in the Forty-seventh Regiment. The regiment saw action in Virginia, particularly at Spottsylvania Court House, Cold Harbor, and Reams' Station. While in the field, Lacy conducted "a Christian Association and an Educational Institute for the moral and mental improvement of his men." For a time he also was chaplain at the General Military Hospital at Wilson, N.C. After the war he taught school, sometimes at Peace Institute in Raleigh, and served a number of churches in the Orange Presbytery that were temporarily without a regular pastor. In 1882 he became pastor of the church in Jonesboro where he spent the remainder of his life.

In 1839 Lacy received an honorary M.A. degree from The University of North Carolina. In 1852 the university awarded him—along with the Reverend Moses Ashley Curtis—a D.D. degree; on the same occasion, it gave Matthew Fontaine Maury a doctor of laws degree. Two of Lacy's sermons were published: *A Thanksgiving Discourse* (1851) and *Address Delivered at the General Military Hospital, Wilson, N.C., on the Day Appointed by the President as a Day of Fasting, Humiliation and Prayer* (1863).

Lacy was married twice. His first wife was Williana Wilkinson (1806–46), and following her death he married Mary Ritchie Rice in 1849. By his first wife he was the father of Elizabeth, James Horace, Drury, Jr., and William Sterling. By his second wife he was the father of Benjamin Rice.

SEE: Mary D. Beaty, *Davidson: A History of the Town from 1835 until 1937* (1979); Grady L. E. Carroll, Sr., *They Lived in Raleigh: Some Leading Personalities from 1792–1892*, vol. 2 (1977); *Minutes of the Seventy-First Session of the Synod of North Carolina* (1885); A. J. Morrison, *College of Hampden Sydney: Dictionary of Biography, 1776–1824* (1920?); Alfred Nevins, ed., *Encyclopedia of the Presbyterian Church in the United States of America* (1884); E. C. Scott, *Ministerial Di-*

rectory of the Presbyterian Church, U.S., 1861–1941 (1942); L. C. Vass, *History of the Presbyterian Church in New Bern* (1886 [portrait]); Stephen B. Weeks Scrapbook, vol. 8 (North Carolina Collection, University of North Carolina, Chapel Hill).

WILLIAM S. POWELL

Lacy, William Sterling *(25 Mar. 1842–14 Oct. 1899)*, Presbyterian minister, educator, and writer, was born in Raleigh, the son of the Reverend Drury Lacy, Jr., and his wife Williana Wilkinson Lacy. His grandfather was the president of Hampden-Sydney College. Lacy received his early education in Raleigh. When he was thirteen, the family moved to Davidson where his father assumed the presidency of Davidson College. At age seventeen he was graduated from Davidson and entered Union Theological Seminary, then located at Hampden-Sydney, to prepare for the ministry. He was nineteen when the Civil War began, and he volunteered with the company that enlisted from Hampden-Sydney. His father was opposed to secession and withdrew young Lacy and his brother from the military unit. Within a year, as a volunteer private, Lacy served briefly with the Rockbridge Artillery until General Thomas J. (Stonewall) Jackson learned that he had been a ministerial student and had him withdraw in order to be licensed by the Roanoke Presbytery in October 1862. Lacy thereafter became chaplain to the Twenty-sixth North Carolina Regiment and served until the end of the war.

After teaching in Raleigh for several years, he was ordained by the Abingdon (Va.) Presbytery in 1869 and was pastor of Presbyterian churches in Virginia until 1873, when he returned to North Carolina to serve churches in Moore County. From 1878 to 1886 he was stated clerk of the Synod of North Carolina and later of the Abingdon and Norfolk presbyteries in Virginia. He also was a member of the board of trustees of Union Theological Seminary. In 1885 Lacy became pastor of the church in Jonesboro, and there he married Mary Shepherd in 1888 just before becoming pastor of the Second Presbyterian Church in Norfolk, Va., where he remained for eleven years. Ill health dictated his return to Raleigh in August 1899; he died two months later and was buried in Oakwood Cemetery. He had no children.

Lacy was a prolific contributor to both religious and secular newspapers and magazines and was the author of a collection of war reminiscences and a book of sermons and addresses.

SEE: Raleigh *News and Observer*, 15 Oct. 1899; E. C. Scott, *Ministerial Directory of the Presbyterian Church in the U.S., 1861–1941* (1942); James P. Smith, *Memorial, Addresses, Sermons* (1900).

HAROLD J. DUDLEY

Laflin, Byron *(24 Apr. 1829–20 June 1901)*, manufacturer, army officer, and legislator, was born in Lee, Mass., the son of Sophronia Sylvester and Walter Laflin. He was the third of four children; the oldest, Addison Henry, was a New York congressman from 1865 to 1871. Laflin's maternal grandparents were Polly King and George Hall Sylvester of Massachusetts. His paternal grandparents were Lydia Rising and Matthew Laflin of Smithwick, Mass. Byron Laflin's father, a gunpowder and paper manufacturer and a merchant active in the public affairs of Lee, served as a state representative in 1833 and 1834. Little is known of Byron's early life or education.

In 1849 his brother Addison purchased a paper mill in Herkimer, N.Y., and Byron helped to manage it. In 1854 Byron served as a warden of Christ Episcopal Church in Herkimer and aided in the purchase of land and construction of a building for the thirteen communicants. In 1861 and 1864 he served as president of the village of Herkimer.

Laflin rendered his most notable public service during the Civil War as an officer in the Thirty-fourth New York Volunteer Regiment of Infantry. When the six companies of Herkimer County were mustered into service for two years on 8 May 1861, at Albany, Laflin was commissioned a major in the regiment. After serving picket duty in Maryland and Virginia from July 1861 to April 1862, the regiment saw sharp action in the Peninsular campaign at Fair Oaks, the Seven Days' Battle, and Malvern Hill. In September 1862, after twelve days of steady marching, the regiment fought at Antietam and narrowly escaped destruction on an exposed flank. After fighting at Fredericksburg in 1863, the regiment was mustered out of service. It had lost nearly half of its men in two years. Meanwhile, Laflin had been appointed lieutenant colonel on 20 Mar. 1862. On his promotion to colonel on 22 Jan. 1863, he assumed command of the regiment until he was mustered out on 30 June. Briefly at Fredericksburg, he commanded a brigade. For his able leadership and gallant conduct in the field, he was breveted brigadier general of volunteers on 13 Mar. 1865.

Laflin's move to North Carolina was fortuitous. After the Herkimer paper mill went bankrupt in 1865, he accepted a position in the U.S. Army as provost marshal of Virginia. One day Davis Jefferson Rich, a fellow officer from the Thirty-fourth New York, happened into his office in Richmond and expressed a desire for a position or a business. Laflin suggested that Rich go to North Carolina and purchase a plantation for $20,000 or less, and Laflin would buy half interest in it. Following his advice, Rich bought land in Pitt County. When the enemies of President Andrew Johnson said he had "commenced to raise hell," probably in mid-1866, Laflin became disgruntled with national politics and joined Rich in North Carolina. The two men proceeded to help build the Republican party in Pitt County.

Laflin's venture into Tar Heel politics earned him a reputation for venality. As a member of the constitutional convention of 1868, he reputedly received part of $2,500 from General L. G. Estes for his "vote and influence" in securing the passage of an ordinance for the issuance of $1 million in bonds for the Wilmington, Charlotte, and Rutherfordton Railroad. From 1868 to 1871, Laflin served in the legislature as chairman of the house committee on internal improvements, which acted on all railroad legislation. Members of the corrupt "Ring" that was engaged in the misuse of railroad bonds testified that they paid Laflin $785 on one occasion and $20,000 on another for his help in obtaining railroad bond issues. They also let Laflin use the bonds as a margin for speculation in the bond market. Although a legislative committee uncovered these indictable offenses, there is no record of Laflin's indictment or any indication that he amassed a fortune.

His business ventures in North Carolina did not prosper. After Davis J. Rich died in February 1869, Laflin continued the plantation and also entered banking. His financial affairs declined after the panic of 1869, and he was ruined financially when he left North Carolina for Norfolk, Va., in 1871. In Norfolk, he worked briefly for one of his former company commanders, William L. Oswald, who had built up a prosperous steamship line.

But soon Oswald died and Laflin moved to Hudson, N.Y., where he lived out his life as an invalid and a pensioner.

It is unfortunate that most assessments of Laflin's character came from his political opponents. Jonathan Worth called him a "miserable carpet bag fop without property or intelligence and no sympathy with us." According to the Raleigh *Sentinel*, which dubbed him "Laughing Laflin," he was "cynical and dissipated," a "man at loose ends, careless, contemptuous and dissolute," and "the big dog of the concern who lays about loose in the city of Raleigh, laughs, loves, and drinks whiskey." The *Sentinel* also described him as having a "splendid mind" and "an eye among the best and most beaming that was ever set in the head of man."

Laflin's negative qualities are perhaps related to an element of tragedy in his personal life after the war. The evidence indicates that by 1866 Laflin and Fannie Caswell, of Herkimer, his wife of thirteen years and the mother of his four children, were separated. She died on 24 Nov. 1867, at age thirty-four, in Pittsfield, Mass. Her youngest child and namesake died on 18 July 1869 at age three. Apparently none of Laflin's children lived with him after his wife's death. Ada, born in 1854, married Chester Mitchell Dawes in 1881 and moved to Chicago. Dawes was the son of U.S. Senator Henry Laurens Dawes of Massachusetts. Eliza, born in 1858, never married; she lived in Watertown, N.Y. Byron Laflin died in Hudson, N.Y., and was buried in the family plot at Herkimer.

SEE: Louis N. Chapin, *A Brief History of the Thirty-Fourth Regiment* (1903 [portrait]); John L. Cheney, Jr., ed., *North Carolina Government, 1585–1974* (1974); Jonathan Daniels, *Prince of Carpetbaggers* (1958); J. G. de Roulhac Hamilton, *Reconstruction in North Carolina* (1914); J. G. de Roulhac Hamilton, ed., *Correspondence of Jonathan Worth*, 2 vols. (1909); George A. Hardin, *History of Herkimer County, New York* (1893); F. B. Heitman, *Historical Register and Dictionary of the United States Army*, 2 vols. (1965); *History of Berkshire County, Massachusetts*, 2 vols. (1885); *History of Herkimer County, New York* (1879); H. T. King, *Sketches of Pitt County, 1704–1910* (1976); Louis E. Laflin, *Laflin Genealogy* (1930); *New York Times*, 21 June 1901; *Official Records of the Union and Confederate Armies* (1880–1901).

JOHN L. BELL, JR.

Laker, Benjamin (*d. 21 Apr. 1701*), deputy to one of the Lords Proprietors of Carolina, member of the governor's Council, judge, and Baptist leader, was in 1664 a resident of Betchworth Parish, Surrey County, England, and a member of the family of that name living in southern Surrey County in the vicinity of the towns of Guildford, Dorking, and Reigate. The county is remarkable for the number of surnames that later played an important role in eighteenth- and early nineteenth-century General (or Free Will) Baptist history in North Carolina: Arthur, Ayres, Brookes, Burgess, French, Hart, Hearne, Health, Palmer, Purefoy, Roach, and Wingfield.

It is probable that Laker came under the influence of the Baptist polemicist and pamphleteer, Matthew Caffin, an Oxford student who settled at Horsham and gathered and settled General Baptist congregations in Surrey and Sussex during the interregnum. On the restoration of the monarchy, Caffin and thirty-nine others presented to Charles II in 1660 "A Brief Confession or Declaration of Faith" setting forth the religious tenets and peaceableness of the General Baptists, acknowledging the authority of the civil magistracy, and denying that they had insurrectionary aims. The "Confession" was reaffirmed in 1663, at which time Laker added his name to those of the earlier signatories. Laker is not known to have been personally troubled by the Conventicle Act, the mainspring for systematic repression of religious dissent in England from 1664 through 1666. He was, however, presented at the April 1667 term of the Surrey Quarterly Sessions for practicing the trade of a mercer without having first served the mandatory seven years' apprenticeship. Whether or not the complaint to the magistrates that resulted in the indictment was connected to Laker's status as a religious dissenter does not appear. At the October 1667 term, he was found not guilty by a jury from the neighborhood of Betchworth. The revival of a strengthened Conventicle Act in 1671 and the Test Act, which received the royal assent in 1673, gave an added fifteen years of religious repression. The Lords Proprietors of Carolina, cognizant of the situation of the dissenters in England, seriously committed the Proprietary board in London and the government of Carolina to religious liberty (as opposed to mere toleration) as a basic constitutional principle. In 1682 the Proprietors went so far as to publish a number of promotional pamphlets in order to give widespread published assurances of religious liberty in Carolina. At least one of the pamphlets was given for publication to the General Baptist printer, Francis Smith, of the Elephant and Castle, who had printed the "Brief Confession" in 1660.

Laker's decision to emigrate with his family occurred at this time, and he seems to have left England with sufficient funds to begin his life in Carolina as a man of substance. Sometime after 1680 when Richard Bentley secured a new patent for his 1,500-acre tract on Albemarle Sound in Perquimans Precinct (originally held by him under a Virginia patent of 1663), he sold 400 acres of it to Laker. Here Laker settled with his wife Elizabeth and their six children and commenced the life of a planter with a white laborer and slaves Francisco, Maria, and Mingo and Mingo's family. The usual "seasoning" by local fevers appears to have carried off Laker's son and oldest daughter, the latter of whom died in July 1685 (his wife and two other daughters dying at unspecified dates). In November 1685 Laker was obliged by court order to deport Mingo out of the colony after his conviction of theft from a neighboring plantation. Whether Mingo was deported with his wife and children or alone is not clear. Laker, however, continued to add to his landholdings and labor force. In 1688 his daughter Sarah married Thomas Harvey, then a member of the Council and subsequently deputy governor from 1694 to 1699.

Sometime in the 1680s Laker had been made a commissioner of the peace for Perquimans Precinct. Early in 1690 Governor Philip Ludwell gave him a deputation to represent in Albemarle one of the Lords Proprietors, consequently raising him to the governor's Council and to the benches of the highest courts of the colony. Since the records of the Council meeting as the chief executive body do not survive, it is impossible to tell how regular Laker was in his attendance; it is known, though, that he attended sessions in March 1695 and December 1696. Laker seems to have sat regularly as one of the judges in the high court of justice from the beginning of 1691 until the end of 1696, except for the fall session of 1695 and the spring session of 1696. His attendance on the land court was faithful, and he sat on most of the courts of claims held in 1695 and 1696. At the beginning of 1697, Laker stepped down from the Council and lived as a private gentleman until his death.

The evidences for Laker's role as a General Baptist leader in the colony are all circumstantial, and, unfortunately, all postdate his death. His will bequeathed to his daughter Sarah Harvey his copy of Thomas Grantham's monumental treatise on General Baptist doctrine and polity published in 1678 under the title *Christianismus Primitivus*; in view of the fact that the Widow Harvey shortly thereafter married Christopher Gale, an ardent churchman, this was a regrettable bequest. To the husband of Laker's daughter Lydia, George Blighton of Martins Brandon Parish in Virginia, he left his copy of the *Exposition of the First Five Books of Moses*. The remainder of Laker's property was left to his daughter Ruth and his third wife, Juliana Hudson Taylor Laker. The will was witnessed by, among others, Richard French.

On Laker's death, the Carolina Baptists appealed to the General Assembly of General Baptists in London for a minister or books. In June 1702 the London body raised a sum of money for the purchase of books to be sent to "our Brethren of the Baptist perswation and of the General Faith who have their aboad in Caralina." It is presumably of this group in Albemarle that the Reverend John Blair complained to the Society for the Propagation of the Gospel in January 1704, when he wrote of a set of people "something like Presbyterians, which is upheld by some idle fellows who have left their lawful employment, and preach and baptize through the country."

Richard French, one of the witnesses of Laker's will, the son of Richard French of Musbury, Devon, matriculated at St. Alban's Hall (belonging to Merton College), Oxford, in 1685 and claimed to have been ordained by the vice-chancellor of Oxford. He emigrated to North Carolina in the late 1690s and settled near Laker in Perquimans Precinct. As early as 1701, French was performing marriages and terming himself "minister of the Gospel." He was prohibited from performing further marriages by an order of the executive council in 1705 as a result of his having pronounced as man and wife about 1704 a couple whose marriage was later declared to be bigamous (though, in fact, records suggest that the bride did no more than give birth to a child out of wedlock by another man early in 1703). That French continued baptizing and celebrating marriages is borne out by the complaints raised against him by the Anglican missionary John Urmston in the summer of 1711; French was ordered at the end of 1712 to appear before the Council to answer the charges. Since, however, French had been appointed to the commission of the peace for Perquimans Precinct and designated one of the quorum by Governor Edward Hyde in July 1712, he had an undoubted authority to perform marriages after that date, and nothing more appears in the council minutes concerning the matter. French's death in 1716 removed him from the scene.

The family of Laker's son-in-law, George Blighton of Martins Brandon Parish in Virginia, seems to have been connected with Baptist activities there. As had been the case with the Carolina Baptists after the death of Laker, the Virginia Baptists appealed for ministers to the General Assembly of General Baptists in London following the death of Blighton in 1703. It is not known in what year the appeal was made, but in 1714 the Assembly ordained Robert Norden (who had joined that body in 1704) as a minister for Virginia. Norden appeared before the court of Prince George County, Va., in June 1715 and subscribed the oaths required of dissenting ministers. At the same time, George Blighton's adjoining neighbor, Matthew Marks, registered his house as a public meeting place for the Baptists; on his death in 1719, Marks further provided a living place for Norden for the duration of his ministry in Virginia. The records of Prince George County further show that Laker's daughter, Lydia Blighton Clements, and grandson, William Blighton, were familiars of Norden's supporter, Dr. John Hammersley, who in 1742 prepared a brief account of the Virginia Baptists for the Rhode Island Baptist leader, Nicholas Eyres. The indictment of Laker's grandson, William Blighton, in 1738 in Prince George County for failure to attend Anglican services may point to his attendance, instead, at a Baptist meeting.

Finally, it must be significant that in 1722, several years after the marriage of Paul Palmer to Laker's stepdaughter, Joanna Taylor Peterson, in 1719, Palmer stopped attending Quaker meetings and soon began his ministry as a Baptist preacher. Although Palmer is generally given the sobriquet "Father of North Carolina Baptists," it seems probable from circumstances that the title properly belongs to Benjamin Laker.

SEE: Robert J. Cain, ed., *Records of the Executive Council, 1664–1734* (1984); Weynette Haun, comp., transcripts of records from the originals in the North Carolina State Archives, Raleigh: Perquimans Precinct Court Minutes (1688–1706), Perquimans Precinct Births, Marriages, Deaths, and Flesh Marks (1659–1820), Perquimans County Record of Deeds (1681–1729), and Secretary of State Record of "Old Albemarle County Book of Land Warrants and Surveys, 1713–1728" (1980–84); Margaret M. Hofmann, comp., *Province of North Carolina, 1663–1729: Abstracts of Land Parents* (1979); Francis Earl Lutz, *The Prince George-Hopewell Story* (1957); Mattie Erma E. Parker, ed., *North Carolina Higher-Court Records, 1670–1696* (1968); Benjamin B. Weisinger, *Prince George County, Virginia, Wills and Deeds, 1713–1728* (1973); Thomas M. Whitley, "General Baptists in Carolina and Virginia," *The Crozer Quarterly* (January 1936); Thomas M. Whitley, ed., *Minutes of the General Assembly of the General Baptists*, vol. 1: 1654–1728 (1909).

GEORGE STEVENSON

Lamb, Gideon (*20 Feb. 1741–8 Nov. 1781*), soldier, was the seventh and last child of Thomas (31 Jan. 1702–ca. 1761) and Sarah Beckwith Lamb (b. 1 July 1701 in Lyme, Mass.). Thomas married Sarah on 5 Nov. 1723 in Springfield, Mass., sold his home in that town on 3 Mar. 1732, and settled in Salisbury, Conn., by 1734. He speculated in land, dabbled in ironworks, and owned a saw- and gristmill. He supposedly left Salisbury in 1746 to become a mariner, after which he resided successively in New Jersey, Maryland, and finally North Carolina.

Gideon Lamb was born in Salisbury, Conn., and eventually moved with his father to Pasquotank County, N.C. Little is known about Lamb's career until he evidenced support for the American cause in the Revolutionary War. In August 1775, at Hillsborough, he represented Currituck County in the Third Provincial Congress, which appointed him a member of the Committee of Safety for the Edenton District. In April 1776 Lamb represented Currituck County in the Fourth Provincial Congress at Halifax. At that time he became major of the Sixth Regiment, North Carolina Continental Brigade.

Lamb, whose reputation rests principally on his contribution to the North Carolina military effort, advanced to colonel of the Sixth Regiment by March 1777. The promotion aroused discontent because other ranking officers in the North Carolina Brigade felt that promotions should come from the state line as a whole. A board of

field officers of the brigade contested the validity of Lamb's promotion and prevailed upon General Francis Nash to submit the matter to General George Washington, who asserted that Lamb's appointment was valid.

The North Carolina Brigade remained in the state until late 1776, when it was ordered to reinforce troops in Georgia. Lamb moved with the brigade as far as Charles Town, S.C., where it remained until March 1777. At that time it was ordered to join Washington's army. Lamb moved north with the North Carolina Continentals, joined Washington, and participated in most of the major battles of 1777 including Brandywine, which again embroiled him in controversy. By order of Brigadier General Jethro Sumner, Lamb was court-martialed for abandoning his regiment on the field at the Battle of Brandywine. A court of inquiry, however, determined that "the Charge is not Supported and that [Lamb] be Acquitted with Honour."

The next three years witnessed Lamb in his best—though most thankless—tasks, which were recruiting and supplying troops. In late 1778 he rallied two hundred Continentals in eastern North Carolina and worked in the Charlotte area, and in April 1779 he led a large contingent of troops from eastern North Carolina to Camden, S.C. In January 1781 Lamb was one of several officers placed on waiting orders at half pay. By July, he had become so exasperated with his situation that he wrote Sumner that he seemed "neither to be in the service nor out of it" and asked the general "to let me know Where, Who, and What I am." But Lamb saw little service after that. He had been troubled by "a low state of health" in early 1781 and almost immediately after writing to Sumner was confined to his home by a "bilious fever" from which he died. Lamb and his wife, Mary Burgess, had at least one child, Abner, who was commissioned lieutenant in the First North Carolina Continental Regiment.

SEE: Samuel A. Ashe, ed., *Biographical History of North Carolina*, vol. 8 (1908); Walter Clark, ed., *State Records of North Carolina*, vols. 12–16, 19, 22 (1895–1907); R. Hooker, *Thomas Lamb* (1947); William L. Saunders, ed., *Colonial Records of North Carolina*, vol. 10 (1890).

ALAN D. WATSON

Lamb, John Calhoun (*21 Dec. 1836–27 May 1864*), businessman, Confederate regimental officer, and a war casualty, was born in Camden County, the oldest child of Wilson Gray and Eliza Williams Lamb. His paternal grandparents, Mary and Gideon Lamb were cousins; Gideon, a former state senator, was the son of Luke Lamb who was a brother of Gideon Lamb, a colonel in the Revolution. After his schooling at the academy near his home in Elizabeth City, John Lamb acquired a hotel in Williamston and established a merchandising business which included West India trade. Several of his vessels were captured by Federal forces during the early part of the Civil War.

When Roanoke Island fell, Lamb enlisted with his father and two of his brothers, Wilson Gray, Jr., and Gideon; the father soon contracted rheumatism from exposure and was sent home, an invalid for the rest of his life. The younger Wilson Gray remained in the army for the entire war, attaining the rank of second lieutenant. Forty years after enlisting with his kinsmen, Wilson wrote the chapter on the Seventeenth Regiment (first called the Seventh Volunteers) for Walter Clark's *Histories of the Several Regiments and Battalions*. He recorded much of his brother John's military career from personal observation or knowledge, including the battle where the "brave and youthful Lieutenant Colonel Lamb fell mortally wounded upon the enemy's works and died a few days therafter."

John C. Lamb rose rapidly in the army. He helped organize the Roanoke Guards as the first company in Martin County, and ten days before the state passed the ordinance of secession, he was commissioned captain. His company, a part of the Seventh Regiment of North Carolina Volunteers, was mustered into service as Company F, Seventeenth Regiment, North Carolina Troops, at Hatteras Inlet on 26 July 1861 and was stationed at Fort Clark with Captain Lamb in command. One mile away, Fort Hatteras under Colonel W. F. Martin completed the defenses of the inlet, with fewer than a thousand men in the two forts; when attacked in late August by seven war vessels and the land forces of the U.S. fleet, both forts fell. The entire regiment was taken first to Fort Columbus, New York Harbor, and then to Fort Warren, Boston Harbor, for imprisonment. Some of Lamb's less unhappy experiences at Fort Warren are reflected in mementos preserved by his family, including an autograph book with the names and addresses of about 135 fellow prisoners from fourteen states and Canada.

Lamb was paroled near the end of January 1862, transferred for an official exchange of prisoners on 20 February, and mustered out of service with his company at Williamston a month later. Early in May, he and some of his men reported to Camp Mangum, about three miles west of downtown Raleigh, for the reorganization of the Seventeenth Regiment; on 16 May he was appointed captain of Company A and then named lieutenant colonel. By the end of the year, Lamb was in command of the force that made the first attack on Plymouth at the mouth of the Roanoke River on Albemarle Sound. His troops captured and destroyed the town without losing a single Confederate. The records of the succeeding twenty-four months include his regiment's capture of the forts and all the artillery at Newport Barracks near Morehead City in February 1864, as well as the costly but successful assault in May at Bermuda Hundred in Virginia where Lamb was mortally wounded. He died one week after entering the North Carolina room at the officer's hospital in Petersburg, Va. His remains were taken home for burial in Williamston, where he had been a vestryman in the Episcopal Church of the Advent. He never married.

SEE: Samuel A. Ashe, ed., *Biographical History of North Carolina*, vol. 7 (1908); Walter Clark, ed., *Histories of the Several Regiments and Battalions from North Carolina in the Great War, 1861–1865*, vol. 2 (1901 [portrait]); Family mementos, papers, and records (possession of Susan and Matilda Lamb, Henderson); Mrs. John Howell Fry (Jacksonville, Fla.), personal contact; Weymouth T. Jordan, comp., *North Carolina Troops, 1861–1865: A Roster*, vol. 6 (1977 [portrait]); Lamb Papers I and Swain Papers (Southern Historical Collection, University of North Carolina, Chapel Hill); Mrs. Matilda Lamb (Rocky Mount), personal contact; *Wilmington Journal*, 2 June 1864.

CLARA HAMLETT ROBERTSON FLANNAGAN

Lamb, William (27 Sept. 1835–23 Mar. 1909), publisher, Confederate soldier, and politician, was born in Norfolk, Va., the son of William Wilson and Margaret Kerr Lamb. He attended the Norfolk Academy, the Rappahannock Military Academy, and the college preparatory Jones School in Bridgeport, Conn., before entering William and Mary College at Williamsburg, Va., in 1852.

At age twenty he was graduated with a bachelor of law degree. As he was too young to practice law, his father purchased for him a half ownership of the newspaper, *Southern Argus*, in Norfolk. While part owner and coeditor of the newspaper, Lamb participated in national as well as local politics. In 1856 he was a delegate to the Democratic National Convention. In 1857 he was instrumental in ensuring the election of a Norfolk city council that would institute a system of public education based on New England models. Finally, in 1860 he was a presidential elector for the Breckinridge Democrats. When Abraham Lincoln defeated John Breckinridge, Lamb felt that the Union could not be preserved.

In 1861 the *Southern Argus* was forced to close due to loss of staff to the Confederate army. On 18 April Lamb himself was appointed captain of Company C of the Sixth Virginia Regiment. This force had formerly been known as the Wood's Rifles, a militia company that Lamb had commanded at Harpers Ferry at the time of the John Brown raid in 1859. On 24 Sept. 1861, he was appointed major and quartermaster for the Wilmington District in North Carolina under Brigadier General Joseph R. Anderson. Lamb served as commander of Fort St. Philip, a minor defense work in the Wilmington area. In 1862 the Thirty-sixth North Carolina Regiment was formed and Lamb was elected its colonel. This regiment, also known as the Second North Carolina Artillery Regiment, was to form the garrison for Fort Fisher, at the mouth of the Cape Fear River, which protected the vital port of Wilmington. Lamb was appointed commander of the fort on 4 July 1862 and remained in that post for two and a half years. Under his direction, the fort's defenses were expanded and it became the largest earthwork fortification on the continent. Colonel Lamb was severely wounded and captured when it fell to Union forces on 15 Jan. 1865 after a heroic defense. Because of his courageous stand against the enemy, he often was referred to in later life as "the hero of Fort Fisher." The wounds he received during the final assault would leave him on crutches for seven years. He was confined to Fort Monroe, Va., and released on 1 May 1865.

Lamb returned to Norfolk and managed the shipping of coal for the Norfolk and Western Railroad, helping to make Norfolk the major coaling station on the Atlantic coast. He designed and used the first bill of lading to aid in shipping coal from cities in the American interior through Norfolk to Europe.

Politically he was again active as a Democrat, serving as a delegate to the Democratic National Convention in 1876. But in 1879 he joined the Readjusters (those who advocated readjusting the state's prewar debts without ruining taxpayers); this plus his high-tariff and other views held by the Republicans caused him to switch parties in 1882. He served three terms as mayor of Norfolk (1880–86) and turned down a fourth. His father and grandfather also had been mayors of Norfolk. Lamb served as Republican state chairman (1895–97) and was a delegate to the Republican National Convention in 1896. He became a consul for Germany and Sweden at Norfolk, and for his services King Oscar of Sweden conferred on him the Royal Order of Vasa.

Committed to the field of education, Lamb helped to establish public education in Norfolk. After the war he advocated education for blacks. He served on the board of visitors of the University of Virginia, was a rector of the College of William and Mary, and was the first president of the Norfolk Public Library. He contributed both time and money to build up the College of William and Mary and the University of Virginia; at the former institution, he helped to reestablish the Phi Beta Kappa fraternity, serving for many years as president. Additionally, he was active in the Virginia Historical Society. In 1899 he received a doctor of laws degree from St. Lawrence University, Canton, N.Y.

In business, Lamb served as president of the Lower Norfolk Coke and Gas Corporation, the Norfolk Chamber of Commerce, and the Board of Trade in Norfolk. He also was president of the Norfolk Seamen's Friend Society and a vestryman of St. Paul's Church. He contributed $50,000 to help Confederate veterans.

Lamb married Sara Ann Chaffee of Providence, R.I., in 1857. She was visiting her parents when the war broke out but, due to the influence of friends, was allowed to pass through Union lines to join her husband. She accompanied him throughout his life; during his two-and-a-half-year stay at Fort Fisher, she lived in a small cottage a short distance from the fort and narrowly escaped capture when it was overrun. The Lambs had three children. He died at home and was buried in Norfolk.

SEE: Bern Anderson, *By Sea and by River: Naval History of the Civil War* (1962); Lester J. Cappon, *Virginia Newspapers, 1821–1935* (1936); "Defense of Fort Fisher and the Account of Colonel William Wilson Lamb," *Southern Historical Society Papers*, vol. 10 (1882); Ralph Donnelly, *The History of the Confederate States Marine Corps* (1976); *Encyclopedia of Virginia Biographies*, vol. 3 (1915); Douglas S. Freeman, *Lee's Lieutenants* (1944); Alfred Guernsey and Henry Alsen, *Harper's Pictorial History of the Civil War* (1866); Louis H. Manarin, comp., *North Carolina Troops, 1861–1865: A Roster*, vol. 1 (1966); *Nat. Cyc. Am. Biog.*, vol. 1 (1892); *New York Times*, 24 Mar. 1909; Oscar M. Voorhees, "Col. Wm. Lamb and Phi Beta Kappa," *Virginia Magazine of History and Biography* 54 (1946); *Who Was Who in America*, vol. 1 (1963); *William and Mary Quarterly* 3 (1896).

JOSEPH EDMUND DEATON

Lamb, Wilson Gray, Jr. *(17 Nov. 1842–22 Feb. 1922),* political leader, merchant, and Confederate soldier, was born in Elizabeth City, one of the four sons and five daughters of W. G. Lamb of Pasquotank and Martin counties and his wife, Eliza Williams. Members of the family moved to the region from New England before the American Revolution. A direct ancestor was Colonel Gideon Lamb of the Sixth Regiment, North Carolina Continental Brigade, during the Revolution. Young Lamb's only formal education was at the school conducted in Elizabeth City by the Reverend Edward M. Forbes, rector of Christ Church. He had been tendered an appointment to the U.S. Naval Academy and had passed the entrance examination when summoned home by his father at the outbreak of the Civil War.

In March 1862 Lamb enlisted as a private in the newly redesignated Seventeenth North Carolina Regiment for service in the company commanded by his older brother, Captain John S. Lamb. He became sergeant-major of the unit on 17 May 1862 and eventually was named regimental adjutant, though never commissioned to the post. In December 1863 he was commissioned third lieutenant. When the regiment was in brigade around Petersburg, Va., in 1864, Lamb commanded a skirmish line and was wounded on 18 June. During the repulse of Union forces along the North East River following the evacuation of Wilmington, he was remembered "as displaying coolness and conspicuous bravery." He also distinguished himself during engagements in the Kinston area, participated in the Battle of Bentonville, and was among the forces of General Jo-

seph E. Johnston surrendering at Centre Church in Randolph County in April 1865.

Conspiring with Abel Thomas to conceal the colors of the Seventeenth Regiment in Thomas's saddle blankets, Lamb helped to smuggle the banner past Federal sentries at Chapel Hill and carried it home to Martin County. There he had it framed and displayed in his Williamston residence for half a century; he donated it to the Hall of History in Raleigh about 1915. Lamb was the author of the history of the regiment published in Walter Clark's history of the Civil War units from North Carolina.

Settling in Williamston after the war, Lamb was the chief manufacturer's representative in the state for Daniel Miller and Company, Baltimore wholesalers. A strong Democrat in politics, he represented the party at the national conventions of 1884, 1892, and 1912. He also was a longtime member of the state Democratic executive committee and of its central committee. On one occasion he declined to become a candidate for governor. As chairman of the State Board of Elections from its founding in 1901, he was complimented several times by Republican leaders for the impartiality of his rulings. "He always hit above the belt," one observer commented, "no matter how bitter the struggle."

Lamb was a member of the Episcopal church, serving as vestryman and senior warden of the Church of the Advent in Williamston from 1868 until 1918 and several times as a delegate to the denomination's General Convention. He resigned as senior warden only after his seventy-sixth birthday. His principal avocation was his membership in the North Carolina Society of the Cincinnati, through descent from Colonel Gideon Lamb. He became a charter member when the society was revived in Raleigh in 1896. Named its first president, he retained that office until his death. In 1913 he headed the society's North Carolina delegation to the White House where he inducted President Woodrow Wilson into honorary membership.

On 7 June 1870 at Hamilton, Lamb married Virginia Louisa Cotten and they became the parents of three sons and five daughters. A portrait of him hangs in the headquarters of the General Society of the Cincinnati in Washington, D.C. He was buried in Woodlawn Cemetery, Williamston.

SEE: Archives of the North Carolina Society of the Cincinnati (Raleigh); Samuel A. Ashe, ed., *Biographical History of North Carolina*, vol. 7 (1908 [portrait]); Walter Clark, ed., *Histories of the Several Regiments and Battalions from North Carolina in the Great War, 1861–1865*, vols. 2, 4 (1901); J. C. Daves, ed., *Minutes of the North Carolina Society of the Cincinnati*, vols. 2–3 (1910, 1922); Curtis C. Davis, *Revolution's Godchild* (1976); *Greensboro Daily News*, 23 June 1920; Weymouth T. Jordan, Jr., comp., *North Carolina Troops, 1861–1865: A Roster*, vol. 6 (1977); Raleigh *News and Observer*, 23 Feb. 1922; Williamston *Enterprise*, 24 Feb. 1922.

CURTIS CARROLL DAVIS

Lambeth, John Walter, Sr. *(25 May 1868–3 July 1934),* pioneer furniture manufacturer, banker, and civic leader, was born in the Fair Grove community, two miles south of Thomasville, the sixth child of David Thomas and Caroline Eliza Simmons Lambeth. His mother was the daughter of Benjamin Whitfield and Eliza Hussey Harris Simmons and was educated at Glen Anna Female Seminary. The Lambeths were of English descent, the first settlement of this family in North Carolina having been made before 1750 in the Craven County area. Later generations moved inland to Guilford and Rowan counties near the end of the century. In 1835 Dr. Shadrach Lambeth (father of David Thomas), his wife, Jane Thomas, and children moved from Guilford to Fair Grove where some of their relatives had been living for many years. In addition to being a farmer, the elder Lambeth was a physician, doctoring principally with herbs. After the passage of the North Carolina Railroad Act in 1849, he joined his brother-in-law, John W. Thomas, and other leaders in its implementation by pledging the construction of a section of the railroad. Although he died before his part was completed, Dr. Lambeth had directed in his will that this important work be finished by his sons.

As an executor of his father's will, David Thomas Lambeth took a leading part in the completion of his contract with the railroad. A year later, he and Caroline Eliza Simmons were married and went to live on their farm east of Fair Grove. Here their eleven children were born and reared. Although he was the father of three at the outbreak of the Civil War, David T. volunteered for service in the Confederate army; entering as a second lieutenant, he was discharged as first lieutenant a short time later. His name appears on the honor roll of his company. A successful farmer, he was the first in his community to try advanced methods of farming. He also owned the largest store in Thomasville. In 1886 the David T. Lambeths moved into the village where he continued to operate his store and later owned a flour mill.

John Walter Lambeth attended I. L. Wright's Academy at Fair Grove and later Trinity College, about seven miles from his father's farm. His special interests were athletics and hunting. After the family moved to Thomasville, he organized an athletic club. Six feet tall with a strong physique, he excelled among the village young men. In later life, he often said that his earliest ambition was to be high sheriff but that as he reached manhood the adventure of private business had more appeal.

In 1890, when the population of the village was less than six hundred and the economic outlook very dark, John W. Lambeth married, bought the Thomasville Hotel, renamed it Lambeth Hotel, and moved into it as manager. Three years later he was appointed postmaster, an office he held four years; then, after selling the hotel, he bought a flour mill.

In 1898, along with three other resourceful men—his brother Frank S. Lambeth, E. W. Cates, and John Pope—he took a business step that started the conversion of Thomasville from a small village to an industrial town. Despite financial limitations, they pooled their resources, organized the Standard Chair Company, erected a building, and bought machinery; with only twelve employees, they began manufacturing chairs. Within a few years this venture was a success, and other factories sprang up all over town. In 1905 Lambeth sold his interest in the chair company and bought the Lambeth Furniture Company, a factory making kitchen safes and cupboards, to which he devoted his full time for many years. After World War I, he was joined by his son, John Walter, Jr.; they changed the line to bedroom furniture and greatly increased the output. It was a successful enterprise, but in their most profitable year, 1928, the Lambeths were persuaded to sell it.

Soon afterwards, the elder Lambeth became president of the First National Bank, a position he held for the remainder of his life. During the depression, this bank stood firm and was among the first in the state to open its doors after the bank holiday declared by presidential proclamation in March 1933. For a time Lambeth was also a director of the High Point branch of Wachovia

Bank and Trust Company as well as a director of the North Carolina Railroad.

In addition to his business interests, Lambeth owned two large farms, one known as the Gray Place and the other as Cedar Lodge Farm, once the home of his great-uncle, John W. Thomas, the founder of Thomasville. Like his father, Lambeth tried new methods of farming and maintained a high level of production.

Although he devoted most of his time to business, Lambeth was vitally interested in the betterment of his community. Early in the twentieth century, with the building of new factories and a fivefold increase in population, Thomasville had an urgent need for better schools. As candidate for mayor in 1901, Lambeth led the campaign for a bond issue of $10,000 to erect a public graded school. The bond issue carried, and he and his ticket won by a large majority. As mayor for six years, he helped lay the foundation of Thomasville's educational system. Later he served on the town school board and on the county board of education. For four years he was a member of the city council.

Lambeth also had a leading role in the Good Roads movement, in popularizing the idea of state-supported roads, and in seeking legislation to that end. He was appointed to the Davidson County Board of Road Commissioners in 1915 and served as treasurer. Under the supervision of this board, Davidson became one of the pioneer counties in good road building.

In 1916 Lambeth was a delegate to the Democratic National Convention from the Seventh Congressional District. He did not desire public office for himself, saying with a smile that he preferred being a "ward heeler." All of his political ambition was centered around his son's career. In the councils of the Democratic party his opinions had great weight, not only in the county but also in the state.

For many years Lambeth was a trustee and steward of the Main Street Methodist Episcopal Church, and in 1928 he became chairman of the board of stewards. He was a charter member of the Thomasville Rotary Club and a member of the Junior Order of United American Mechanics, the National Grange, and the Benevolent and Protective Order of Elks. A Shriner and a Mason, he served as treasurer of the local lodge for twenty-five years.

On 23 Dec. 1890 Lambeth married Daisy Hunt Sumner, the daughter of Captain Julian Everard and Jennie Loftin Sumner. The Sumners had long been prominent in the state and active in Davidson County government for many years. Daisy Lambeth had attended Thomasville Female College. They became the parents of four children: David Sumner, who died at age seventeen; John Walter, Jr., who became a congressman; Ernestine, who married Thomas Austin Finch, Sr., and after his death, Dr. L. K. Mobley, a well-known dentist in New York City; and Julian Hill, who died in infancy.

Lambeth was buried in the Thomasville City Cemetery.

SEE: Mary N. Doggett and Sophie S. Martin, *The Lambeth Family of North Carolina* (1974); Archibald Johnson, "Sketch of Walter Lambeth, Sr." (Manuscript Department, Duke University Library, Durham); J. C. Leonard, *Centennial History of Davidson County* (1927); *Lexington Dispatch*, 2 May 1905; Mary Green Matthews and M. Jewell Sink, *Wheels of Faith and Courage: A History of Thomasville, North Carolina* (1952); *North Carolina Biography*, vol. 5 (1941); Records of the City of Thomasville and Davidson County (Davidson County Courthouse, Lexington); Records and Deeds of the Lambeth Family

(North Carolina State Archives, Raleigh); M. Jewell Sink and Mary Green Matthews, *Pathfinders, Past and Present: A History of Davidson County, North Carolina* (1972).

M. JEWELL SINK

Lambeth, John Walter, Jr. *(10 Jan. 1896–11 Jan. 1961)*, manufacturer and congressman, the son of John Walter and Daisy Hunt Sumner Lambeth, was born in the Lambeth Hotel, Thomasville, at the time owned and operated by his parents. He was graduated from Trinity College in Durham in 1916 and in the fall entered Harvard University to study business administration. Before completing his first year there, however, he volunteered as a private in World War I. As a sergeant in the First Army, American Expeditionary Force, he participated in the St. Mihiel and Meuse-Argonne offensives. At the end of the war he studied for a few months at London University.

After returning home, Lambeth joined his father in the operation of Lambeth Furniture Company, a plant they soon converted to the streamlined manufacture of bedroom furniture. He was secretary-treasurer and later president of the company. Although the factory prospered, the partners sold it in 1928. A few months later the younger Lambeth also resigned as vice-president of the local First National Bank, an office he had held for several years. These steps left him free to pursue a course he had long anticipated. As a boy he had listened to his elders discuss politics, and he studied government and read biographies of noted leaders. In 1921 he took time out from business to serve a term in the state senate. From 1925 to 1929 he was mayor of Thomasville and during that time instituted improvements in city government such as a sinking fund for bonded indebtedness and a study of city planning.

In 1930 Lambeth was elected to the U.S. House of Representatives as a Democrat and continued to win reelection until he retired in 1939. While in Congress, he was unusually attentive to the needs and wishes of his constituents. As chairman of both the House Committee and the Joint Committee on Printing, he endeavored to reduce the cost of public printing and struggled to convince other congressmen to cease the long-standing practice of free distribution of government documents. In many ways, he was able to effect economy and increase efficiency in government printing.

His most important service, however, was on the Foreign Affairs Committee. During the 1930s, no member of Congress was more active and outspoken in defense of Woodrow Wilson and the idea of collective security—the maintenance of the peace of the world by nations acting cooperatively against an aggressor nation. In 1937 Lambeth was one of six members of Congress selected to participate as an official delegate in the dedication of World War I monuments and chapels erected at American battlefields in Europe. He delivered the dedicatory address at Bellicourt (Aisne), where the Thirtieth Division took part in the decisive Battle of the Hindenburg Line in September 1918. In further recognition of his service in the field of foreign affairs, President Franklin D. Roosevelt in 1939 tendered Lambeth the post of minister to Bulgaria, but he declined it.

After his retirement from Congress, Lambeth devoted his time to his investments, including real estate and farming. Under partnership arrangements, he operated Cedar Lodge farm and dairy as well as two other farms, making practical experiments in grass farming and the scientific harvesting of trees. Contributing to the life of his hometown, he was the first president of the cham-

ber of commerce (1949), an organizer of the United Fund efforts, and a leading participant in the celebration of Thomasville's centennial. He also was active in a number of civic clubs, patriotic groups, and fraternal organizations. A member of the Methodist church from childhood, he served on boards of stewards and made significant donations for the erection of two Methodist churches in the community. In addition, he assisted in funding a Thomasville branch of the county library and in his will left the library a large bequest.

In 1949 Lambeth married Helen Urban of Bridgeport, Conn., and they were the parents of one child, Diane Sumner. He died in Washington, D.C., and was buried in the Thomasville City Cemetery.

SEE: *Congressional Directories* (1930–38); *Congressional Record* (1931–38); Mary Green Matthews and M. Jewel Sink, *Wheels of Faith and Courage: A History of Thomasville, North Carolina* (1952); M. Jewel Sink and Mary Green Matthews, *Pathfinders, Past and Present: A History of Davidson County, North Carolina* (1972).

M. JEWEL SINK

Lamon, Duncan *(d. ca. 1798)*, Revolutionary Patriot whose antecedents are not known, appeared in Edgecombe County records in 1749, when he bought a tract of land on Toisnot Swamp. In the same year, Robert West sold him three hundred acres on the north side of Tar River. Lamon settled in that part of Edgecombe that became Nash County in 1777. He represented his county in the colonial Assembly in 1760, 1761, and 1766–68 and in the Provincial Congresses of 1775 and April 1776. On 1 Aug. 1761 Robert Jones, Jr., of Northampton County, one of the agents and receivers of quitrents for Earl Granville, appointed Lamon collector for the lands on the south side of Tar River in Edgecombe. In January 1763 Jones appointed him deputy collector for all of the county.

Lamon became active early in the Revolutionary movement. At the Hillsborough Provincial Congress in August 1775 he was appointed to the Committee of Safety for Halifax District, and at a meeting of the Provincial Council in Johnston County in December he was empowered to purchase materials and to employ proper persons to make and mend guns and bayonets and to purchase good guns, gun barrels, stocks, locks, and flints. He also was a member of the congress that drew up the Halifax Resolves; the congress placed him on a committee to settle rations and the price to be allowed the commissioners for victualing the army. In the act creating Nash County in 1777, he and Arthur Arrington were ordered to contract with workmen to build a courthouse, a prison, and stocks for the new county.

Lamon had established a ferry over Tar River by 1775, when it was shown on the Mouzon map of North Carolina; the name persists to the present time in the form of Lemons Bridge across the river near Easonburg in Nash County. This was on the main north-south route across the province, which was followed by the British army under Lord Charles Cornwallis in May 1781 as it marched from Wilmington to Yorktown. On 8 May General Jethro Sumner wrote that a party of the enemy was seen on each side of the river at Duncan Lamon's ferry.

There are few records pertaining to Lamon after 1777. From deeds, it appears that the name of his wife was Eunice. He left no will, but in several deeds he conveyed land to sons John, Archibald, and Duncan and to daughters Martha and Ann. It is said that another daughter, Mary, married Joseph Clinch of Nash County and was the mother of Duncan Lamon Clinch, a general in the Seminole War in 1835.

SEE: Deeds of Edgecombe and Nash Counties (North Carolina State Archives, Raleigh); William L. Saunders, ed., *Colonial Records of North Carolina*, vols. 6–7, 10 (1888–90).

CLAIBORNE T. SMITH, JR.

Lander, Samuel (*30 Jan. 1833–14 July 1904*), teacher, author, and clergyman, born in Lincolnton, was the son of the Reverend Samuel Lander and his wife, Elizabeth (Eliza) Ann Miller, both natives of Ireland. He began school at age four and after the school day was introduced to Greek and Latin by his uncle, J. W. Murphy, even before he had studied English grammar. Soon afterwards his sisters began to teach him to play the piano and guitar, while a teacher at the local academy taught him sight singing. In 1847 or 1848 he was sent to Lexington to continue his studies under Murphy, who had moved to that town. In 1849 Lander entered the sophomore class at Randolph-Macon College in Virginia; he was graduated in 1852, at age nineteen, with highest honors. While in college he taught himself fine penmanship and developed the habit of taking long walks with friends while discussing scholarly subjects.

Returning home to Lincolnton after graduation, Lander studied civil engineering and participated in the surveying of a new road from Lincolnton to Charlotte. He also began a practice that he continued almost until the year of his death—the study of foreign languages. Although he never learned to speak them, he was able to read German, French, Spanish, Italian, Hebrew, and Portuguese; further, he made considerable progress during a three-year study of Volapük, an artificial international language. Young Lander became tutor to the children in the Michael Hoke family but in 1853 joined the faculty of Catawba College as an instructor. In 1855 he received a master's degree from Trinity College, which also awarded him an honorary D.D. degree in 1878.

From Catawba College, Lander moved for a brief time to Olin Institute in the northern part of Iredell County. He then taught foreign languages at Randolph-Macon College for a year before accepting a post at Greensboro Female College, where he remained for three years. He next became president of the High Point Female Seminary. Returning to his native town, he founded the Lincolnton Female Seminary, but in 1868–70 he was president of Davenport Female College in Lenoir. Late in 1870 Lander moved to South Carolina to become copresident of Spartanburg Female College. However, after less than a year he was persuaded to accept appointment as a Methodist minister in charge of the Williamston Circuit and to establish and direct the Williamston Female College. In February 1872, he began the work that was to occupy him for the remainder of his life at the new school, then in Williamston, S.C., that now bears his name—Lander College. In 1904 the college was moved to Greenwood.

In 1861 Lander was licensed as a local preacher. During the Civil War, to meet the need of Southern schools, he was persuaded by North Carolina educational leaders to write several textbooks. He was the author of *Our Own Primary Arithmetic* and *Our Own School Arithmetic*, both published in Greensboro in 1863, and of *The Verbal Primer*, published in 1865. The latter was a pioneer in teaching reading by the word rather than with the alphabet.

Lander married Laura Ann McPherson in 1853, and

they had eleven children: Lily, Martha, John, William Tertius, Augustus, Nell, Kathleen, Malcolm, Frank, Christie, and Ernest. All but two—Lily and William—bore the middle name McPherson.

SEE: Watson B. Duncan, *Twentieth Century Sketches of the South Carolina Conference, M. E. Church, South* (1901); William L. Sherrill, *A Brief History of Rev. Samuel Lander, Senior, and His Wife, Eliza Ann (Miller) Lander* (1918); *The Southern Methodist Handbook* (1908); John O. Wilson, "Sketch of the Late Rev. Samuel Lander, D.D." (clipping files, North Carolina Collection, University of North Carolina, Chapel Hill).

WILLIAM S. POWELL

Lander, William (*8 May 1817–8 Jan. 1868*), lawyer and Confederate congressman, was born in County Tipperary, Ireland, the oldest child of Samuel and Elizabeth (Eliza) Ann Miller Lander. The family immigrated to America in 1818, first landing in Boston and moving southwards in easy stages. The Landers reached Salisbury in 1824 and moved to Lincolnton in 1826. The father became a successful coach maker and also served as a lay Methodist minister. William attended Lincolnton Academy and Cokesbury College in South Carolina, then read law in Lincolnton under James R. Dodge. He was admitted to the bar in 1839. Lander's oratory and legal brilliance soon earned him a lucrative practice, and he later acquired and operated a small farm.

In 1852 Lander was elected to the House of Commons; in his one term, he directed most of his attention to clarifying the problems caused by the division of Lincoln and Gaston counties in 1846. He was elected county solicitor and served briefly before becoming district solicitor in 1853. He held the latter position until 1862 while continuing his law practice.

Lander made his political reputation during the secession crisis. At the Charleston Democratic Convention of 1860 he worked for party unity, but when the convention broke up and reconvened at Baltimore to nominate Stephen A. Douglas for president, Lander announced for his delegation "that a very large majority of our delegation is compelled to retire permanently from this convention on account . . . of the unjust course that has been pursued." He then joined the other Southern "bolters" to nominate the Breckinridge-Lane ticket. In October, in a highly publicized debate with Zebulon B. Vance, Lander admitted that the election of Abraham Lincoln would not itself be a cause of secession but warned that succeeding events might precipitate it. By early 1861 Lander was an active Secessionist, and as a member of the May convention he voted to leave the Union. In November, he won a seat in the Confederate House of Representatives over two other candidates.

In Richmond, Lander served on the committees of Patents and the Quartermaster's and Commissary departments. Generally he was a stalwart, though unassertive, Confederate nationalist, supporting most proposals giving the central government whatever controls it wished over individuals and the economy. For instance, during the debates on conscription his only concession to state interests was his support of an unsuccessful amendment requiring the president to make the first calls for conscripts on states that had furnished the least manpower. Only in his conviction that repudiating the old Treasury notes would constitute a violation of contract did Lander reflect the dissatisfaction of his state with Confederate legislation. In 1863 he lost his race for reelection as a peace candidate. After returning to private life, he practiced law until his death. He was buried in the Methodist church graveyard in Lincolnton.

Lander's contemporaries esteemed him as a constant student of the law and of classical literature, and they often commented on his phenomenal memory. His former law partner, Judge David Schenck, stated that he had "never heard one who was the equal of William Lander before a jury." From 1858 to 1867 Lander was a trustee of The University of North Carolina. On 8 May 1839, he married Sarah Connor of Cokesbury, S.C. They had six children—Samuel, Agnes, Ella, Frank, William, and Clara—though the last two died in childhood.

SEE: *Journal of the Congress of the Confederate States of America*, 7 vols. (1904–5); *Journal of the House of Commons of North Carolina, 1852–53*; Raleigh *North Carolina Standard*, 1861–63; William L. Sherrill, *Annals of Lincoln County, North Carolina* (1937 [portrait]); U.S. Census, 1850, 1860; Z. V. Walser Papers (Southern Historical Collection, University of North Carolina, Chapel Hill).

BUCK YEARNS

Lane, James Henry *(28 July 1833–21 Sept. 1907)*, Confederate soldier, educator, and engineer, was born in Matthews Court House, Va., the son of Colonel Walter Gardner and Mary Ann Henry Barkwell Lane. His great-grandfather, Ezekiel Lane, an early settler in Matthews County, was active in political and military affairs. His grandfather, William Lane, was a sergeant in the War of 1812, and his father was a colonel in the Matthews County militia while serving as a member of the state legislature during the Civil War. James Henry Lane was trained by tutors on his father's plantation and in private schools until 1851, when he entered Virginia Military Institute at Lexington and became a student of Thomas Jonathan Jackson. He was graduated on 4 July 1854, second in his class, and then attended the University of Virginia where he received a degree in science in 1857. After serving as engineer on a hydrographic survey of York River, he became assistant professor of mathematics and instructor in tactics at Virginia Military Institute. His next appointment was as commandant and professor of mathematics at the State Seminary of Florida at Tallahassee. When the Civil War began, he was professor of natural philosophy and instructor in tactics at the North Carolina Military Institute in Charlotte under D. H. Hill.

At the governor's call for troops, Lane volunteered, along with the other officers of the school, and became adjutant and instructor in tactics at a camp of instruction organized near Raleigh. D. H. Hill was commandant. With the creation of the First North Carolina Volunteers, Lane was elected its major. Being of only average height, he was called the "Little Major"; even after he became a general, he was the "Little General." His regiment went into Virginia at once, and, on 10 June 1861, he led an attack on a marauding party which the North Carolinians drove back. This brought on the action at Bethel and gave Lane's force the title, "Bethel Regiment." When Hill was promoted Lane became a lieutenant colonel, and with the reorganization of the North Carolina Troops, he was elected colonel for the Twenty-eighth Regiment. This regiment saw constant action under General Lawrence O'Brian Branch. After Branch was killed at Sharpsburg, Lane was placed in command of the brigade and promoted to brigadier general on 1 Nov. 1862. At twenty-nine, he was the youngest brigadier in the Confederate army. The members of his unit proudly presented their "Little General" with a sword, sash, bri-

dle, and saddle in honor of his promotion. Among the regiments that now came under his command was the "Bloody Eighteenth."

Lane was consistently placed in strategic positions. He covered the withdrawal from Sharpsburg just as he did later from Gettysburg. In the latter battle, his men were the last to leave the field although they had been fighting since 1 July. He lost 50 percent of his troops in the battle. When his brigade covered the break at the "Bloody Angle" at Spottsylvania, it turned the Union advantage into defeat. At Cold Harbor he received his third wound. Although it was considered to be mortal, he recovered and joined his troops before Appomattox. There he and his men surrendered. Lane was highly respected by both Generals Robert E. Lee and Thomas Jonathan Jackson. At Chancellorsville, after Jackson was fatally wounded, his last order was to Lane. Of Lane's brigade and its dauntless leader at Chancellorsville, Vice-President Hannibal Hamlin's brother, a colonel in the Union army, said: "the student who seeks to discover a higher degree of courage and hardihood among military organizations of either army will look over the records of war for a long time if not in vain."

When the war ended, Lane returned home to find his parents virtually destitute and in deep grief over the loss of two sons, both of whom served under their illustrious brother. He worked there for a while until he could borrow $150 to assist him in finding employment. Subsequently, he taught in private schools in Richmond, Va., and in Concord and Wilmington, N.C. In 1869 he married Charlotte Randolph Meade of Richmond, and they had four daughters. From 1872 to 1880, Lane was professor of natural philosophy and commandant at Virginia Agricultural and Mechanical College (later Virginia Polytechnic Institute). His next job was as superintendent of the Virginia Mining and Manufacturing Company. In 1881–82 Lane was back in teaching as professor of mathematics at the Missouri School of Mines and Metallurgy, and the following year he accepted a position as professor of civil engineering and commandant at the Alabama Agricultural and Mechanical College. Later he became professor of engineering and drawing at the same school, then called Alabama Polytechnic Institute (later Auburn University), where he taught for twenty-five years and became professor emeritus in June 1907. He died three months later and was buried at Auburn.

As a professor Lane was admired and respected just as he had been as a soldier. He received an honorary LL.D. degree from Trinity College (later Duke University) and a Ph.D. from the University of West Virginia in 1896. He was one of three guards of honor at the first interment of Jefferson Davis, who had said of him in 1886: "Endeared to me as he is by his service to the South, . . . I admit that I feel a warm interest in his success, not for himself alone, but also as a good example for the youth of the State I love so well." Lane was an Episcopalian.

SEE: Mrs. John Huske Anderson, "The Confederate Generals of the Old North State" (typescript, North Carolina Collection, University of North Carolina, Chapel Hill); Walter Clark, ed., *Histories of the Several Regiments and Battalions from North Carolina in the Great War, 1861–1865*, vols. 1–5 (1901); *Confederate Military History*, vol. 4 (1899); General William Ruffin Cox, "Address on the Life and Services of General James H. Lane, Army of Northern Virginia" (delivered before R. E. Lee Camp Confederate Veterans, No. 1, Richmond, Va., 4 Dec. 1908); *DAB*, vol. 5 (1932); *Nat. Cyc. Am. Biog.*, vol.

27 (1939); North Carolina Confederate Centennial Commission, *North Carolina at Gettysburg* (1963); Ezra J. Warner, *Generals in Gray: Lives of the Confederate Commanders* (1959); *Who Was Who in America, 1897–1942* (1943); Marcus J. Wright, *General Officers of the Confederate Army* (1911).

MAUD THOMAS SMITH

Lane, Joel (*ca. 1740–29 Mar. 1795*), legislator, Revolutionary Patriot, planter, and vendor to the state of the land on which the capital was established, was born presumably in Halifax (then Edgecombe) County, the son of Joseph and Patience McKinne Lane. His father is thought to have been a grandson of Richard Lane of Jamestown, Va., first of the name in America and, according to tradition, a kinsman of Ralph Lane, first governor of North Carolina. His mother was a daughter of Colonel Barnabas McKinne, provincial justice and colonial assemblyman.

In the early 1760s, Joel Lane was a justice of the peace for Halifax County. In April 1761 he was appointed sheriff by Governor Arthur Dobbs, who in July named him captain of a Halifax regiment of foot under Colonel Alexander McCulloch. Extant documents list him as a citizen of Halifax as late as July 1768. By August 1769, however, he had apparently settled near Walnut Creek in that portion of Johnston County that became Wake, where he acquired several thousand acres of land. In November he was commissioned a justice of the Johnston County Court.

As representative from Johnston to the 1770–71 General Assembly, Lane introduced the bill creating Wake County, effective 12 Mar. 1771. Named a commissioner to run the Wake boundaries, he also served on the commission to choose sites for and erect the new county courthouse, prison, and stocks. These were built near his home, still standing at 728 West Hargett Street, Raleigh, slightly southwest of its original site. Wake's first county court is thought to have convened at Lane's home on 4 June 1771. From that date until his death he was a member of that court, serving from time to time as presiding justice. During those years he was licensed to operate an ordinary at his home, apparently a well-known stopping place for travelers along main roads crossing in the vicinity. From 25 May 1772 until June 1777 he was register of Wake, evidently also serving for a year as Chatham County clerk of court. For most of the period 1778–79, he was entry taker for Wake. He represented Wake in the 1773 General Assembly, where he sat on the committee on public accounts.

On 19 Jan. 1771 Governor William Tryon appointed Lane lieutenant colonel of Wake militia under his father-in-law, Colonel John Hinton. The unit did not participate in the Battle of Alamance, rather being left at home, according to Tryon's journal, "to prevent the disaffected in [Wake] from forming into a Body and Joining the Regulators in the adjacent Counties." Theophilus Hunter succeeded him in the military post in about 1773. Lane was a Wake delegate to the Provincial Congress at Hillsborough in August 1775 and at Halifax in April 1776, although he apparently was not seated at Halifax. During the Revolution he was a commissioner for obtaining and distributing salt. The 1776 Council of Safety adjourned in late August to Lane's home, where the General Assembly also met from 23 June to 14 July 1781 in addition to using the Wake courthouse.

Lane was a senator from Wake County in eleven of the fourteen sessions of the General Assembly from 1782 through 1794. He was a member of the 1788 and 1789 constitutional conventions, the latter ratifying the U.S. Constitution and the former issuing the ordinance calling for a permanent state capital to be established within ten miles of Isaac Hunter's plantation in Wake. The commission on location appointed by the 1792 Assembly spent eight days in March at Lane's home while examining various tracts of land offered for sale. From these they selected Lane's tract of one thousand acres, on which they laid out the city of Raleigh the same year. Its western boundary was within a few hundred yards of his home and the Wake courthouse. During the last six years of his life, Lane served on the first board of trustees for The University of North Carolina and was one of those offering land for its site.

Lane was married twice, both times to daughters of Colonel John Hinton of Wake. Between their marriage on 9 Dec. 1762 and her death on 9 Sept. 1771, he and Martha Hinton Lane had three sons: Henry, James, and William. With her sister Mary, he had nine more children: Nancy, John, Martha, Elizabeth, Mary, Thomas, Dorothy, Joel Hinton, and Grizelle. Descendants include members of the Moses Mordecai family who gave that name to Raleigh's Mordecai House, the original portion of which was the home of Lane's son Henry and his wife Mary, granddaughter of Colonel Hinton. Governor and University of North Carolina President David Lowry Swain was Lane's grandnephew (grandson of Lane's brother Jesse), as was General Joseph Lane of Oregon, hero of the Mexican War and Oregon's first governor and U.S. senator. A nephew of Martha and Mary Hinton Lane, Hinton James, was the first student to enter The University of North Carolina, 12 Feb. 1795.

The deaths of Joel and Mary Lane occurred less than a week apart, Mary having survived her husband only five days when she died on 3 Apr. 1795. A small burial ground, believed to be the Lane family cemetery on South Boylan Avenue, Raleigh, was excavated in 1969, and those remains thought to be Joel Lane's were reinterred on 30 Mar. 1973 in Raleigh's City Cemetery. The Joel Lane House was acquired in 1927 by the Wake Committee of the National Society of the Colonial Dames of America in the State of North Carolina for preservation. Designated a Raleigh Historic Site, it is also listed in the National Register of Historic Places.

SEE: Chatham County Court Records, Johnston County Court Minutes, North Carolina Troop Returns of 8 May 1771, Report of Committee Establishing Capitol [*sic*], and Wake County Court Minutes (North Carolina State Archives, Raleigh); John L. Cheney, Jr., ed., *North Carolina Government, 1585–1974* (1974); Walter Clark, ed., *State Records of North Carolina*, vols. 19–21 (1901–3); R. D. W. Connor, *A Documentary History of the University of North Carolina, 1776–1799*, vol. 1 (1953); Marshall De Lancey Haywood, *Joel Lane: Pioneer and Patriot* (1900); *Journal of the House of Commons of North Carolina*, 17 Dec. 1770; *Laws of North Carolina, 1770*; George W. Mordecai Papers (Southern Historical Collection, University of North Carolina, Chapel Hill); William L. Saunders, ed., *Colonial Records of North Carolina*, vols. 8–9 (1890).

ELIZABETH DAVIS REID

Lane, John Randolph (*4 Jul. 1835–31 Dec. 1908*), Confederate soldier, was born in western Chatham County, the son of John Siler Lane (said to be a direct descendant of Joel Lane) and Kara Kidd Lane. Because of limited means, John R. Lane, according to a contemporary, "was reared with the advantages of self-denial." Although his formal education was apparently meager, his letters of later years reveal no lack of acquirements. Among the earliest volunteers for Confederate service,

Lane enlisted in May 1861 as a member of the "Chatham Boys," soon designated Company G of the Twenty-sixth North Carolina Regiment. He remained with this regiment, conspicuous among those of both sides for heroism and casualties, throughout the war.

Lane was made a corporal almost immediately and at the first vacancy was elected captain of the company over the heads of the commissioned officers. By that time he had taken part in the first Battle of New Bern. In the summer of 1862, when Zebulon B. Vance resigned and Henry K. Burgwyn became colonel, Lane was promoted to the rank of lieutenant colonel. His rapid rise owed nothing to political or social influence; rather, it rested entirely on native leadership ability. Succeeding the mortally wounded Burgwyn in command during one of the bloodiest assaults of the war—that on McPherson's Ridge on the first day of Gettysburg—Lane was himself shot through the neck by a retreating Federal soldier at the top of the ridge. The wound was thought to be mortal, and it was said that Lane was unable to take nourishment for nine days. While in this state, he avoided capture by abandoning his ambulance and escaping on horseback when the wagon train was attacked during the withdrawal from Pennsylvania.

In a few months Lane returned to duty as colonel, bringing new recruits and equipment with him. He participated in most of the major actions in Virginia for the rest of the war and was wounded four more times. The first three times he declined to leave the field or the regiment. The fifth wound, from a piece of shell in the chest at Ream's Station on 25 Aug. 1864, was again thought to be mortal, but Lane was back on duty by November and remained until the last few weeks of the war when he was hospitalized for exhaustion and complications. Except for the fact that he achieved higher rank than most, Lane exemplified the bravery of the soldiers in his regiment whom he praised in a postwar speech, men from "the great middle class that owned small farms in central and western North Carolina."

After the war, Lane resided on Little Brush Creek in Chatham County and became a prosperous landowner, merchant, and cotton gin and gristmill operator. His business interests were centered in Randolph County, two miles upstream from his home. In 1866 he married Mary Ellen Siler, daughter of Samuel Siler for whom Siler City was named. They had a son and a daughter. Lane was a member of Brush Creek Baptist Church, where he was buried, and is said to have been esteemed in the locality for kindness and generosity. He was active in veterans' affairs, although he never applied for a pension. In 1903 Lane delivered a speech on the Battle of Gettysburg at Gettysburg, Baltimore, and probably other places. During a reunion at Gettysburg, he met and became good friends with Charles McConnell, of Chicago, the Federal sergeant who had shot him down with the colors during the charge on McPherson's Ridge. A painting of the three colonels of the Twenty-sixth—Vance, Burgwyn, and Lane—is in the possession of the Museum of History, Raleigh.

SEE: Walter Clark, ed., *Histories of the Several Regiments and Battalions from North Carolina in the Great War, 1861–1865*, vol. 2 (1901); Clement A. Evans, ed., *Confederate Military History*, vol. 4 (1899); John R. Lane Papers (Southern Historical Collection, University of North Carolina, Chapel Hill); Raleigh *News and Observer*, 5 July 1903; Kathryn B. Rees (Siler City), personal contact.

CLYDE WILSON

Lane, Joseph *(14 Dec. 1801–19 Apr. 1881),* soldier, U.S. senator, governor of Oregon, and vice-presidential candidate, was born in a double log cabin on Beaverdam Creek, four miles north of Asheville. During the same year his cousin, David Lowry Swain, destined to become a North Carolina governor and president of The University of North Carolina, was born in the same cabin. Lane was a descendant of members of the noted Lane family, originally of Halifax County, who were pioneer settlers of Raleigh and Wake County. His grandfather was Jesse Lane; Jesse's brothers were Joseph and Joel, the latter of whom provided the land on which Raleigh was established. His father, John Lane, fought at the Battle of Kings Mountain and after the Revolution, in 1795, settled with his brother Charles in Buncombe County and established an ironworks. His mother was Elizabeth Street, daughter of an early sheriff of Buncombe County. Joseph was the second son of John and Elizabeth Lane.

In 1804 the family moved to Henderson County, Ky., where he attended common schools. In 1816 he moved to Warrick County, Ind., and clerked in a store. He married Mary (Polly) Pierre Hart in 1820 and settled on a riverbank farm in Vanderburgh County. Lane was a successful farmer and also bought produce and conducted a flatboat trade with New Orleans. He continued these operations for twenty-four years, becoming a prominent tradesman and community leader. In 1822 he held his first public office when he served in the Indiana legislature; he won reelection several times. During the Mexican War Lane received national attention after leading his brigade with distinction at Huamantla and in other battles. Entering as a private, he emerged as a hero with the rank of major general. At the close of the war in 1848, President James K. Polk named him governor of the new and virtually unexplored Territory of Oregon.

After a rigorous winter journey, Lane proclaimed the new government on 3 Mar. 1849. Many of his duties involved pacifying the region's Indian tribes, a task in which he was notably successful. He resigned the governorship on 18 June 1850 and was subsequently named a delegate to the U.S. Congress; he was reelected three times. When Oregon joined the Union on 14 Feb. 1859, he was chosen as its first U.S. senator, serving until 3 Mar. 1861.

In 1860 Lane was named vice-presidential nominee on the Democratic ticket headed by John C. Breckinridge. In this four-way campaign, one faction of the Democrats split in an effort to prevent the election of Stephen A. Douglas. It was thought that Lane—a native Southerner, considered prosecession, and popular in all parts of the country—in combination with Breckinridge could defeat both the Douglas forces and the strong Republican ticket of Abraham Lincoln and Hannibal Hamlin. But the Republicans won with 180 electoral votes; Breckinridge and Lane came in second with 72.

It was during this unsuccessful bid for the nation's second highest office that Lane returned to North Carolina, his first visit since childhood. He went to see his father's birthplace near Raleigh and the Joel Lane House, the city's oldest. He viewed the deed of conveyance by which Joel Lane in 1792 sold the state one thousand acres on which the capital city was founded. He also was reunited with his cousin, David Lowry Swain, then president of The University of North Carolina, with whom he had corresponded over the years. He learned much about the fortunes of the Lane family during the intervening years.

Oregon had become Republican in the 1860 election. Thus, after his Senate term expired, Lane retired from public life to his farm near Roseburg, Oreg., where he died. Lane and his wife were the parents of ten children who lived to maturity: Ratliffe B., Malissa, Joseph, Simon, John, Lafayette, Roseburg, Mary, Emily, and Winifred. In 1867 Lane, his wife, and three of their children (Simon, Lafayette, and Winifred) were baptized and confirmed into the Roman Catholic faith. At his own request, however, following his death nearly fifteen years later, Lane was buried in the Masonic Cemetery at Roseburg without religious ceremony.

He is recognized as one of Oregon's leading historical figures, and two thousand of his letters as well as several portraits and sketches of him are in the archives of the Oregon Historical Society. Lane County, site of the city of Eugene and the University of Oregon, is named for him.

SEE: *Asheville Citizen*, 30 Dec. 1951, 31 Oct. 1959; *Biog. Dir. Am. Cong.* (1971); *Biographical Directory of the Indiana General Assembly* (1980); *DAB*, vol. 5 (1932); James E. Hendrickson, *Joe Lane of Oregon* (1967); M. Margaret Jean Kelly, *The Career of Joseph Lane: Frontier Politician* (1942); Raleigh *News and Observer*, 6 Nov. 1960, 16 May 1965; John Savage, *Our Living Representative Men* (1860).

JAMES MEEHAN

Lane, Lunsford (*30 May 1803–ca. 1863*), slave, businessman, free black, and lecturer, was the only child of Edward and Clarissa Lane, slaves from Raleigh. His parents had assumed the surname of Lane from the white family that had originally owned them. At the time Lane was born, the family was owned by Sherwood Haywood.

Though Lane was a house slave and admittedly had an easier life than that of a field hand, he was troubled by the fact that he was a slave and he yearned to be free. His sale of a basket of peaches given him by his father was the beginning of Lane's business ventures. Trying to accumulate enough money to buy his freedom, he saved what he earned—mostly tips from guests of the Haywood family. Lane cut wood at night and during his spare time. With the help of his father, he made and sold pipes and special smoking tobacco, often to members of the state legislature. Lane bought supplies for the Haywood household, and he learned to buy in quantity when prices were low in order to save money. He began to buy goods for himself when he could buy at a bargain, store these items, and sell when prices rose. Lane was always careful not to appear prosperous lest his commercial undertakings be stopped.

In May 1828 Lane married Martha Curtis, who belonged to the Boylan family. She was soon bought by Benjamin B. Smith, a Raleigh merchant. When Sherwood Haywood died in 1829, his wife was forced to hire out her slaves in order to pay debts. This was fortunate for Lane, who bought his own time from Mrs. Haywood. He expanded his tobacco business under the name "Edward and Lunsford Lane" and had agents in Fayetteville, Salisbury, and Chapel Hill.

Lane's savings reached a thousand dollars, the price that Mrs. Haywood asked for his freedom. At the time, however, the North Carolina legislature would authorize manumission only for "meritorious service," which Lane could not prove. In 1835 he arranged for his wife's owner, Benjamin B. Smith, to "buy" him and take him to New York, where Lane received his manumission papers. Now a free man, he returned to his businesses in Raleigh in order to buy his wife and children, then valued at $2,500 by their owner. Lane arranged to buy them in installments. Smith allowed them to live with

Lane in a house that the industrious free black bought in Raleigh. In addition to his tobacco and firewood businesses, Lane also worked as a messenger and handyman in the office of Governor Edward B. Dudley.

But Lane's troubles were not over. In September 1840 he received notice that because he had been emancipated in New York, he was in violation of a state law prohibiting free blacks from other states from entering North Carolina. Lane had twenty days to leave. Although he received support from influential whites in his bid to stay in North Carolina, by May 1841 Lane was forced to go. Taking one of his children with him, he went to New York and Boston, where he raised money to buy other members of his family by lecturing at churches and abolitionist meetings.

In April 1842 Lane returned to Raleigh to purchase the rest of his family. Though he had received assurances of his safety from the governor's office and from Benjamin B. Smith, Lane was arrested, charged with delivering abolitionist lectures, and tried at a "call court." There was no proof of the charge against him, so Lane was released, only to be abducted by a mob, dragged towards the gallows, and finally tarred and feathered. His white friends sheltered him overnight and smuggled him, his wife and children, and his mother (a farewell gift from Mrs. Haywood) to a train bound for Philadelphia. About two years later they were joined by Lane's father, who was also freed by the Haywood family. The Lanes lived in Philadelphia, New York, Boston, Worcester, and Oberlin, Ohio. Lane continued to lecture. As late as 1863, the Worcester city directory listed him as steward at Wellington's Hospital. In 1865 he was no longer listed, though Lunsford Lane, Jr., was.

Lunsford and Martha Lane had seven children: Edward, William, Lunsford, Jr., Maria, Ellick, Lucy, and Laura. A lithograph of Lane is reproduced in the biography by the Reverend William G. Hawkins.

SEE: Richard Bardolph, *The Negro Vanguard* (1959); John Spencer Bassett, *Anti-Slavery Leaders of North Carolina* (1898); John Hope Franklin, *The Free Negro in North Carolina, 1790–1860* (1943); William G. Hawkins, *Lunsford Lane; or, Another Helper from North Carolina* (1864); Lunsford Lane, *The Narrative of Lunsford Lane, Formerly of Raleigh, North Carolina . . . .*, 2d ed. (1842).

ALICE R. COTTEN

Lane, Sir Ralph (*ca. 1530–October 1603*), first governor of "Virginia," was born in Lympstone, Devonshire, England, the son of Sir Ralph Lane (d. 1541) and his wife Maud Parr (daughter of William Lord Parr) of Northamptonshire. He is believed to have been a cousin of Edward Dyer, the poet. In 1563 he entered the service of Queen Elizabeth I as equerry and did a variety of court tasks, including searching Breton ships for illegal goods in 1571. In general, however, Lane was better suited as a soldier than as a courtier. After serving as sheriff of County Kerry, Ireland, from 1583 to 1585, he was invited by Sir Walter Raleigh to command an expedition to America. He sailed on 9 Apr. 1585 under Sir Richard Grenville, with whom he soon began to quarrel. Towards the end of June, they arrived at Wococon on the North Carolina Outer Banks and established a colony with Lane as governor.

After Grenville departed for England in August, the colony moved to Roanoke Island where it remained for the next eight months. As supplies became scarce, the colony was plagued with bickering and quarrels among its members and with the natives. Lane reportedly was not diplomatic in dealing with the Indians and often reacted violently to provocation. He quarreled with Wingina, an Indian chief, who was attempting to organize neighboring tribes to attack Lane's group. Lane solved this problem by killing Wingina on 10 June 1586 before the surrounding tribes convened and then managed to disperse the rest of the group. The next day, 11 June, Sir Francis Drake arrived and promised to leave men, supplies, and a ship. However, a hurricane blew the ship out to sea and plans were changed. Lane, discouraged, decided to return to England. In the frenzied rush to be gone, three colonists, exploring up-country, were left behind, and in an effort to lighten the ship's load, valuable records were destroyed or thrown overboard. Lane returned to England on 27 July 1586 and never again commanded a colonial expedition, probably to the benefit of everyone. Ironically, Grenville's relief squadron arrived shortly after Drake sailed for home, causing widespread criticism of Lane for leaving Virginia when he did. It has even been suggested that Lane's distrust of Grenville led to his abandoning the colony.

It is thought (without much proof) that Lane was the first to introduce tobacco to England. Following his return, Lane set down a "Discourse on the First Colony," which was sent to Sir Walter Raleigh and later printed in Richard Hakluyt's *Principall Navigations* (1589). Afterwards, Lane wrote another treatise on his experiences as a colonial commander and sent it to Lord Burghley on 7 Jan. 1592. In it he emphasized the need for strict discipline to avoid illness among the soldiers.

Among the colonists of this Virginia expedition were John White, an artist, and Thomas Harriot, a mathematician, who took meticulous notes and made remarkably accurate drawings of the wildlife, fauna, and natives of the New World. These efforts have been preserved in their book, *A briefe and true report of the new found land of Virginia*, published in 1588 and 1590. Lane wrote the foreword to this book.

After Lane's return to England, he performed a series of petty tasks for the court, including in 1588 the office of muster-master of the camp at West Tilbury in Essex and the next year as muster-master general of the army on the Spanish and Portuguese coast. In January 1592 he took the post of muster-master general and clerk of the check in Ireland. He remained in that country for the rest of his life.

Lane apparently never married but continued, as he had throughout his career, to beg favors from the well-placed for himself and his relatives. On 15 Oct. 1593 he was knighted by the lord deputy of Ireland, Sir William Fitzwilliam. In 1594 Lane was badly wounded in an Irish rebellion. He never regained his strength and his office was generally neglected during the last years of his life. Edward E. Hale summed up his career: "He seems to have been an eager courtier, a bold soldier, a good disciplinarian, an incompetent governor, a credulous adventurer, and on the whole, though not a worthless, an unsuccessful man."

SEE: *DAB*, vol. 5 (1932); *DNB*, vol. 11 (1967); Edward E. Hale, "Life of Sir Ralph Lane," *Transactions and Collections of the American Antiquarian Society*, vol. 4 (1860); David B. Quinn, ed., *The Roanoke Voyages, 1584–1590*, 2 vols. (1955).

JOHN W. SHIRLEY

Lang, John Albert, Jr. (15 Nov. 1910–27 June 1974), teacher, federal civil servant, and major general in the

U.S. Air Force Reserve, was born in Carthage, the son of John A., Sr., and Laura Kelly Lang. His father was a son of John Frederik Lang who changed his name from Jansson when he migrated in 1875 from Sodra Bro Gallesta, Sweden, to New Britain, Conn., where he was active in the cultural life of the Swedish community before moving to North Carolina. His mother was the great-granddaughter of Abel Alexander Kelly, a Presbyterian who left Ireland with his family sometime prior to 1825 and settled in Moore County, N.C., establishing a gristmill and subsequently serving two terms in the state legislature; he was a staunch Unionist with anti-slavery leanings.

Lang was graduated, Phi Beta Kappa, from The University of North Carolina in 1930, remaining for another year to earn a master of arts degree before accepting a position as head of the English Department and professor of government at Georgia Military Academy. The first significant step in his public or political life came in 1935, when for two years he served as president of the National Student Federation with offices in New York City. This led to his appointment as assistant to the director of Civilian Conservation Corps Camp Education in the U.S. Office of Education, a post he occupied until 1938, when he was appointed state administrator of the National Youth Administration in North Carolina. In 1942 he enlisted in the U.S. Army Air Corps, eventually serving in Alaska, North Africa, and Italy; he had advanced to the grade of major by the time he returned to private life in 1946. After a brief period with the Better Health Association in Raleigh, he was selected to be the administrative assistant of U.S. Representative Charles B. Deane, of North Carolina, whom he served for ten years until the congressman was defeated. During that time, Lang honed his political skills to a high polish and developed a wide circle of friends on Capitol Hill, becoming a valuable political asset in the process. As a consequence, after a brief stint with the House Committee on Government Operations, he was chosen to be the administrative assistant of U.S. Representative Robert E. Jones, of Alabama, whom he served from 1957 to 1961. In the latter year, he was appointed deputy for Reserve and ROTC Affairs in the Office of the Secretary of the Air Force.

Lang's move from Capitol Hill to the Pentagon marked a merger of his political career with his role as a member of the Air Force Reserve, in which he had been active since World War II. The assignment proved to be a happy one; Lang's expansive personality and willingness to work tirelessly in the interest of others made him nationally popular with reservists as well as with his superiors in the secretariat. Soon after taking office in 1961, he performed brilliantly in the mobilization of Air National Guardsmen and Air Force Reservists for the Berlin and Cuban crises. For his efforts in this period he was given the Exceptional Civilian Service award, an honor he subsequently received on two other occasions.

In 1964 the secretary of the Air Force appointed Lang administrative assistant, making him the senior career civil servant in the Air Force. As such, he was charged with the management and administration of the Office of the Secretary of the Air Force and, under the Presidential Transition Act of 1963, with the orderly transfer of power from one administration to the next. In 1968, while still serving in this capacity, he was promoted to major general in the Air Force Reserve with a mobilization assignment as assistant to the superintendent of the Air Force Academy. Probably the most impressive manifestation of the respect Lang had earned by his dedicated service on behalf of the Air Force came in 1969 when a Republican administration took over the government. Although a lifelong Democrat prominently identified with the party, he was retained as administrative assistant by the incoming Republican secretary whom he served loyally and efficiently, not only in his administrative role, but also as the secretary's personal representative on various boards and councils.

A big, broad-shouldered man standing well over six feet, Lang was ever concerned with keeping fit; during his years in the secretariat, he regularly used his lunch break to stride vigorously around the perimeter of the Pentagon. The principal qualities of personality that made him so effective were his expansive, outgoing nature, his generosity, and his genuine delight in serving others; his unspoken motto seemed to be: any friend of my friend is a friend to me. It was characteristic of him that despite the many public concerns that burdened him during his long residence in Washington, for nineteen years he found time to teach a Bible class in his church. His frequent references to the folk wisdom of rural sages from his beloved Moore County became something of a byword in the Pentagon and greatly endeared him to his colleagues. Lang was often called upon to present some message of concern to the Air Force before a large audience. With the reflexive response of a professional politician to crowds, he genuinely enjoyed these occasions; he was never happier than when the audience happened to be in North Carolina.

By the time he retired in 1971 after thirty-six years of federal service, Lang had received many marks of distinction, among them the Air Force Association Citation of Honor (1964) and on two occasions the U.S. Distinguished Service Citation of the Reserve Officers' Association (1964 and 1969), as well as military decorations including the Legion of Merit, the Meritorious Service Medal, the Army Commendation Medal, and the Air Force Commendation Medal.

Retirement from federal service did not end Lang's career. From Washington he moved to Greenville, where he was appointed vice-chancellor of East Carolina University. Scarcely had he embarked on this new career when Governor Robert Scott called him to Raleigh in March 1972 to accept a cabinet office as secretary of the newly formed Department of Military and Veterans' Affairs. In this position, he supervised the office of the North Carolina Adjutant General including the National Guard, Office of Civil Defense, Civil Air Patrol, Department of Veterans' Affairs, and Armory Commission. At the close of the Scott administration, Lang returned to his post as vice-chancellor of East Carolina University where he died unexpectedly at age sixty-four from an infection. He was buried in his hometown of Carthage.

Lang married Catherine Gibson of Gibson, N.C., on 20 Nov. 1947; they had four children: John A. III, Richard Gibson, Laura Catherine, and Martha Elizabeth.

SEE: John A. Lang Papers (Manuscript Collection, East Carolina University, Greenville); USAF Official Biography (1 Apr. 1971); *Who's Who in the South and Southwest* (1975–76); *Who Was Who in America*, vol. 5 (1973).

I. B. HOLLEY, JR.

Langley, Katherine Emeline Gudger *(14 Feb. 1888–15 Aug. 1948)*, member of Congress, was born near Marshall in Madison County, the daughter of James Madison, Jr., and Katie Hawkins Gudger. Her father was a congressman and a successful attorney. Katherine Gudger was educated in local schools and was graduated from the Woman's College in Richmond, Va. After attending the College of Oratory in Boston, she taught expression at the Virginia Institute in Bristol, Tenn.

In November 1904, in Washington, D.C., she married John Wesley Langley, whom she had first met in that city while her father was in Congress. She went with her husband to Pikeville, Ky., where she helped him campaign for a seat in the U.S. House of Representatives in 1906. He entered the House in 1907 as a congressman from Kentucky, and for the next twenty years Katherine Langley worked with her husband on campaigns, making speeches and serving as his secretary.

During World War I she was chairman of the Pike County Red Cross and from 1920 to 1922 she was vice-chairman of the Republican State Central Committee. In 1920 she also was chairman of the Kentucky Woman's Republican State Committee. She was an alternate delegate to the 1920 Republican National Convention and a delegate to the convention in 1924. From 1919 through 1925, she was clerk of the Committee on Public Buildings and Grounds.

After her husband retired from Congress in 1926 to return to his law practice, Katherine Langley ran for his vacated seat and was elected in the fall of 1926. She served in the Seventieth and the Seventy-first Congress from 1927 through 1931. Only the seventh woman to be elected to Congress, she was the first from Kentucky. She was unsuccessful in her bid for a third term and returned to Pikeville. Following her husband's death in 1932, Mrs. Langley remained active in civic and political affairs. She served as railroad commissioner for the Third Kentucky District from 1939 to 1942. She was a member of the Baptist church and of the Daughters of the American Revolution. Survived by three children, Katherine Bentley, John, and Susanna, she was buried in Johnson Memorial Cemetery, Pikeville.

SEE: *Asheville Citizen*, 16 Aug. 1948; *Biog. Dir. Am. Cong.* (1971); North Carolina Bar Association, *Proceedings*, vol. 22 (1920); *Who Was Who in America*, vol. 4 (1968).

JOE O'NEAL LONG

Langston, John Dallas *(22 Mar. 1881–29 July 1963)*, lawyer, army officer, and federal administrator, was born in Beaufort County about three miles from Aurora. His father, George Mifflin Dallas Langston, was a Methodist minister who ran unsuccessfully for Congress on the Prohibition ticket in 1888. His mother, Sarah Anne Gibbs Langston, was a teacher before her marriage. John, who was originally named Jonathon but changed his name, was the youngest of seven children. He was graduated from Trinity College in Durham in 1903. While teaching school for two years after his graduation, he studied law under the direction of attorneys. During the summer of 1904 he attended The University of North Carolina Law School and was admitted to the bar the following year. He practiced law in Mount Olive from 1905 to 1910, when he joined Matt H. Allen, an attorney in Goldsboro, to form the partnership of Langston and Allen. In 1914 W. Frank Taylor joined the firm and it became Langston, Allen and Taylor; in time, when Langston retired, he and his son formed the firm Langston and Langston but the elder partner practiced little.

During World War I, Langston was commissioned major in the infantry and he served as a special aide to the governor in administering selective service in the state. Later he was transferred to Washington, D.C., where he served on the staff of Major General Enoch H. Crowder and became chief of the Classification Division of the provost marshal general's office. Eventually, he was assigned to the judge advocate general's office as chief of the Clemency Division. In 1919 he was promoted to lieutenant colonel.

After the war Langston returned to his law firm but remained active in the U.S. Army Reserve. For several years he also was president and publisher of the *Goldsboro News*.

In the early stages of World War II, Langston was ordered to active duty as a colonel and in November 1940 was assigned to the national headquarters of the Selective Service System. Named chairman of the Planning Council, in 1943 he was appointed assistant director of the National Selective Service in charge of the Presidential Appeals and Advisory Division. After the war, he was appointed chairman of the Committee on Reorganization of the National Headquarters of Selective Service. Acclaimed the father of the National Selective Service System, his awards included the Distinguished Service Medal and the Distinguished Service Medal with the Oak Leaf Cluster for his service in World Wars I and II, respectively.

Langston was an active Methodist and a Democrat. A member of the American Legion, he also belonged to a number of fraternal and civic organizations. A volume of poems by him, *Life's Gleanings*, was published in 1959. He married Mary (Mollie) Williamson of Mount Olive in 1903, and they were the parents of two sons and three daughters: John Dallas, Jr., William Dortch, Dorothy, Mary, and Carolyn. He died in Goldsboro and was buried in Willow Dale Cemetery.

SEE: Daniel L. Grant, *Alumni History of the University of North Carolina, 1795–1924* (1924); *Heritage of Wayne County* (1982); Langston Manuscripts (Manuscript Department, Duke University Library, Durham); *North Carolina Biography*, vol. 5 (1941); *Trinity Alumni Register*, vols. 1–2, 5 (1915–17, 1919–20); *Who's Who in the South and Southwest* (1947).

MATTIE U. RUSSELL

Lanier, Edwin Sidney (*19 July 1901–5 Mar. 1983*), educator and government administrator, was born near Metter, Ga., in a rural section of the state, the son of Richard and Hassie Banks Lanier, farmers. He attended local schools and was graduated from State Normal Teachers School in Athens in 1921. From 1921 to 1924, he studied at The University of North Carolina in the School of Commerce. There he was president of the Philanthropic Society and won the Mary D. Wright Memorial Prize in debate and the Algernon Sidney Sullivan Award for humanitarian service. He was a member of the Order of the Grail and of the Order of the Golden Fleece, both distinctive honorary organizations.

In 1924 Lanier began teaching and coaching at the Baptist Orphanage high school in Thomasville, an experience that he regarded highly for the remainder of his life. In 1930 he returned to Chapel Hill to become a special student in the law school with a part-time position in the student aid office of the university. In 1934 he gave up his law studies to become director of student aid and in 1945 he also became director of Records and Registration, positions he held until 1961, when he resigned to accept an appointive post in state government.

While living in Chapel Hill, Lanier became deeply involved in educational and civic affairs. From 1945 to 1949 he was a member of the board of trustees of the Baptist Orphanage of North Carolina; he served on the Chapel Hill Board of Aldermen from 1949 to 1955 and was mayor of the town for three terms. Between 1954

and 1956 he served on the Orange County Board of Commissioners, and in 1957 he was elected to the state senate, a post he filled for a second term beginning in 1959. On leave from the university, he worked for increased pay for teachers and for funds to expand physical facilities of public schools. It was noted that as a state senator he lived off the meager income of that position and that he took a room in the local YMCA when the General Assembly was in session.

While he was director of student aid at The University of North Carolina, one of the students he helped was Terry Sanford. In 1961, when Sanford was governor of the state, he appointed Lanier state personnel director. The next year the governor named him commissioner of insurance following the death of the incumbent; Lanier was elected to the position in the fall and reelected in both 1964 and 1968. In this post, he was known as a great consumer advocate by keeping insurance rates low. He declined to seek a third term in 1972.

Lanier married Nancy Thelma Herden, of Durham, the daughter of a Baptist minister, and they were the parents of two children, Nancy and Edwin S., Jr.

SEE: *Asheville Citizen*, 17 July 1962; Chapel Hill *News Leader*, 16 Feb. 1956; *Chapel Hill Newspaper*, 3 Jan. 1973; *Chapel Hill Weekly*, 23 Oct. 1961; John L. Cheney, Jr., ed., *North Carolina Government, 1585–1979* (1981); *Daily Tar Heel*, 18 May 1946, 4 May 1949; *Durham Morning Herald*, 27 Sept. 1959, 20 Oct. 1961, 3 Dec. 1972; *North Carolina Manual* (1957–69); Raleigh *News and Observer*, 14 Jan. 1972; University of North Carolina, *Alumni Review*, (April 1941); *Who's Who in the South and Southwest* (1969).

JAMES D. GILLESPIE

Lanier, James Franklin Doughty (*22 Nov. 1800–27 Aug. 1881*), financier, was born in Washington, Beaufort County, the son of Alexander Chalmers and Drusilla Doughty Lanier. On his paternal side he was of Huguenot descent, shared a common ancestor with George Washington, and was distantly related to the poet Sidney Lanier. His grandfather, James Lanier, was a captain in the light cavalry regiment commanded by Colonel William Washington in the Revolution; later he served under General Anthony Wayne in the campaign against the Indians of the Northwest Territory.

In 1807, after living briefly in Bourbon County, Ky., the Lanier family moved to Eaton, Preble County, Ohio, where Alexander Lanier freed his only two slaves; during the War of 1812, he served as a major under General William Harrison. In 1817 the family moved to Madison, Ind., where the father operated a dry goods store. In declining health, he died in 1820 leaving debts that young James F. D. Lanier eventually paid.

While the family lived in Eaton, Lanier was a student at the village school. Beginning in 1815, he attended an academy for a year and a half at Newport, Ky. When the family moved to Madison in 1817, he was offered, but declined, an appointment to West Point; instead, he attended a private school in Madison for a year and a half. In 1819 Lanier began the study of law in the office of General Alexander Meek in Madison, completing his education in law in 1823 at Transylvania University. Lanier set up a law practice in Madison in 1824 and was appointed assistant clerk of the Indiana House of Representatives, becoming chief clerk in 1827. During this time, he made many influential friends and amassed a considerable fortune in real estate investments.

In 1833 he retired from his law practice to assume the presidency of the Madison branch of the State Bank of Indiana, in which he was the principal individual stockholder. As president, he served on the state bank's Board of Control with Hugh McCulloch, later secretary of the U.S. Treasury. When the Madison bank successfully weathered the panic of 1837, Secretary of the Treasury Levi Woodbury praised Lanier's management and appointed him as pension agent for part of the northwestern region.

After promoting railroad construction in Indiana, Lanier went to New York City in 1849; there he and Richard Winslow formed Winslow, Lanier and Company, a general banking business specializing in negotiating railroad securities. The firm prospered, and Lanier made extensive connections with prominent banking houses abroad. In 1865 and 1868, while abroad as an unofficial agent of the federal government, he used his connections to convince European banking houses of the financial stability of the government.

Lanier is best remembered for his financial support of Indiana during the Civil War. At the request of Republican Governor Oliver P. Morton, later a U.S. senator from Indiana, Lanier lent the state $400,000 to arm and equip troops and $640,000 to pay the interest on the state debt. The money was loaned without any security, but at the end of the war the legislature reimbursed Lanier the money plus interest.

In 1819, in Madison, Lanier married Elizabeth Gardner, by whom he had eight children. After her death in 1846, he married Mary McClure in 1848 and they had three children. His home in Madison, a sophisticated example of Greek Revival architecture designed by the noted architect Francis Costigan in 1844, is maintained as a museum by the state of Indiana. Lanier died in New York City and was buried in Greenwood Cemetery.

SEE: *DAB*, vol. 5 (1961); Talbot Hamlin, *Greek Revival Architecture in America* (1944); J. F. D. Lanier, *Sketch of the Life of J. F. D. Lanier* (1870); Albert Welles, *The Pedigree and History of the Washington Family* (1879).

J. MARSHALL BULLOCK

Lanier, Sidney Clopton (*3 Feb. 1842–7 Sept. 1881*), poet, musician, novelist, and author of books for boys, was born in Macon, Ga., the son of Robert Sampson and Mary Jane Anderson Lanier. Although the time he spent in North Carolina was brief, Sidney Lanier's name has, nevertheless, been associated with the state. Some of the family lived in Rockingham County before moving to Georgia. Lanier, himself, between August and November 1864, was in Wilmington serving as a signal officer on blockade-runners, and at the end of his life, suffering from tuberculosis, he went to live in the mountains of North Carolina. He died at his home at Lynn in Polk County.

Lanier was graduated at the head of his class from Oglethorpe University in 1860 and served on active duty as a Confederate soldier throughout the Civil War until taken prisoner in November 1864; during his incarceration he contracted a lung disease. Returning home in 1865, he taught school for a time before studying law and becoming a partner in a law firm. His first novel was published in 1867; he played the flute in a symphony orchestra, wrote and published poetry in leading magazines, gave public lectures, was a lecturer in English literature at Johns Hopkins University, and wrote (and adapted classic) books for boys. His poetry was widely read, particularly throughout the South, and has often appeared since in anthologies of American poetry.

Lanier married Mary Day in 1867, and they became the parents of four sons—Charles Day, Sidney, Jr.,

Henry Wysham, and Robert Sampson. He was buried in Greenmount Cemetery in Baltimore, the city where he had made his home for several years.

SEE: Kenneth Coleman and Charles S. Gurr, eds., *Dictionary of Georgia Biography*, vol. 2 (1983); *DAB*, vol. 5 (1961); Edwin Mims, *Sidney Lanier* (1905); *Southern Literary Messenger* 2 (January 1940).

WILLIAM S. POWELL

Lanneau, Sophie Stevens (*19 Aug. 1881–4 June 1963*), educational missionary, was born in Lexington, Mo., the daughter of John Francis and Louise Cox Lanneau. When she was eight, her family moved to Wake Forest, N.C., where her father joined the faculty of Wake Forest College. After attending Wake Forest Academy and Franklin (Virginia) Female Seminary, she entered the Baptist Female University (now Meredith College) where she was graduated in 1902.

While in college, Miss Lanneau decided to devote her life to foreign missions work for the Southern Baptist Convention but after graduation did not meet the minimum age requirement for an assignment. During the next five years she taught public school in Wake Forest, was an instructor of Latin and French at the Baptist Female University, and worked as a teacher in Puerto Rico. She also studied at the Training School in Louisville, Ky. (now part of the Southern Baptist Theological Seminary). On 3 July 1907, she received an appointment by the Foreign Missions Board of the Southern Baptist Convention and accepted assignment to China.

Sophie Lanneau arrived in China in November 1907 and was given responsibility for establishing and managing a small girls' school in Soochow (now Wuhsien). At her insistence, however, she concentrated on mastering the Chinese language first. In 1909 she assumed direction of the school's development. The process of purchasing the land for the facility, constructing the building, and planning for its operation took two years. By the time the school opened on 18 Feb. 1911, she had determined to name it "Wei Ling" (renaissance). She envisioned the school as a means of imparting a Christian view of life to the Chinese, educating Chinese girls, and upgrading the position of women in China. It operated on a small scale during the early years but gradually gained acceptance in Soochow; by 1922, 258 students were enrolled.

While on furlough in 1924, Miss Lanneau took some graduate courses in education at the University of Chicago. At the time, the issue of teaching evolution was raging in Protestant circles. She expressed her consternation at those who opposed teaching evolution, believing that, if successful, they would do a serious injustice to future generations. She returned to China in January 1925 to find an increasingly antiforeign climate in the Soochow area. Miss Lanneau, who was still the principal of Wei Ling School as well as an instructor, moved to replace all missionaries who were in administrative positions with Chinese. In 1926 a Chinese woman was made dean of students. Early in 1927 the fighting associated with the internal Chinese conflict intensified around Soochow and the missionaries sought refuge in nearby Shanghai for four months. During this period, the Chinese administrators operated the school.

By the time Miss Lanneau appointed a Chinese woman as principal in 1928, Wei Ling had an enrollment of 425 students. Sophie Stevens Lanneau, who was given the honorary title of "founder," served as dean of students and instructor until 1937. When the Japanese invaded China in the latter year, she was in Peiping (now Peking) studying at the College of Chinese Studies. Because of the Japanese occupation of Peiping, she was unable to leave for six months. Early in 1938 she was able to join the rest of the Soochow missionaries in Shanghai. They had sought refuge in the international sector of Shanghai when the Japanese hostilities made it impossible for them to remain in Soochow. Miss Lanneau taught in the University of Shanghai for some months while making plans to open Wei Ling on an interim basis in Shanghai in conjunction with three other mission schools. Wei Ling continued operations until December 1941. Enrollment had reached 1,050 when its administrative board closed the school rather than place the lives of the American missionaries in jeopardy following the U.S. declaration of war on Japan.

Miss Lanneau continued teaching at the University of Shanghai until February 1943, when the Japanese placed her in an internment camp. She was released in September when arrangements for a prisoner exchange between the United States and Japan were completed. After a three-month journey by ship, she arrived in the United States. She was met in Washington, D.C., by a representative of the U.S. Signal Corps who attempted to engage her in intelligence work, apparently because of her familiarity with the Chinese language. Then sixty-two, she was exhausted from her recent ordeal and declined to serve in such a capacity.

She returned to Soochow in May 1946. The main problems she experienced in reopening Wei Ling were financing building repairs, dealing with runaway inflation, providing facilities for the large number of students, and coping with the Communists. Her overall goal was to establish the school as a part of a self-sufficient Christian community in Soochow.

Beginning in 1948, the American consulate periodically urged the missionaries to withdraw because of the danger from the Communist forces. The Communists assumed control of Soochow in April 1949. Although Miss Lanneau did not feel that her personal safety was in jeopardy, she realized that hope of continuing missionary work was rapidly fading. By then, because of increasing government pressure, the school had become almost entirely secular. In June 1950, after the United States entered the Korean War, the restrictions on Americans and their activities became more stringent. She attempted to keep Wei Ling open but the presence of the Americans was placing their Chinese colleagues in serious danger. Her departure from China in August 1950 coincided with her scheduled retirement for that month. She had planned to stay for an extended period to study Chinese poetry, but the hostility of the Communists towards missionaries forced her immediate withdrawal from the country.

During her retirement, Sophie Lanneau maintained her interest in China and often expressed dismay about America's alienation from China during the crucial time when China was struggling to assert its dignity and might as a nation. She spent most of these years in Wake Forest, where she died.

SEE: Carolyn Howard Carter, "Sophie Stevens Lanneau: Southern Baptist Missionary to Soochow, China, 1907–1950" (M.A. thesis, Wake Forest University, 1974); Sophie Stevens Lanneau Papers (Baptist Historical Collection, Wake Forest University Library, Winston-Salem).

CAROLYN HOWARD CARTER

Lanning, John Tate (*13 Sept. 1902–15 Aug. 1976*), historian, was born in Linwood, Davidson County, the son of Baxter Franklin and Carrie Aletha Smith Lanning. After graduation from Trinity College (later Duke University) in 1924, he studied under the eminent Hispanic-American historian Herbert Bolton at the University of California at Berkeley, receiving an M.A. in 1925 and a Ph.D. in 1928. Returning to Duke University as an instructor in 1927, he rose to the rank of professor in 1942 and was named James B. Duke Professor of History in 1961, the highest award given by the university. He retired from teaching in 1972 but continued his research and writing until his death.

In 1932 Lanning married Elizabeth Baxter Williams, the daughter of Judge Wade H. Williams of Charlotte and a graduate of Duke in 1931. Prominent in many civic activities, Elizabeth Lanning became the first woman elected to political office in Durham when she served as a member (1951–57) and then chairman (1957–58) of the Durham County Board of Education. They had three children: John Tate, Jr., Lucy Hampton, and Thomas Pinckney.

Lanning's early work in southeastern colonial history, especially on Spanish influence in the area, was embodied in *The Spanish Missions of Georgia* (1935) and *The Diplomatic History of Georgia* (1936) as well as several later publications. This early interest soon grew into a broader concern with the entire field of colonial Hispanic-American cultural and social life, which formed the framework of a distinguished and productive career, including eleven books and numerous articles in major historical periodicals. From extensive research in the archives of Great Britain, Spain, and Latin America, Lanning laid the foundations of a revolution in the historiography of the intellectual history of the Spanish colonies, not only by exploring areas little touched by previous historians, but also by challenging the long-held view that Spanish colonial intellectual life had been hostile to learning during the Enlightenment of the seventeenth and eighteenth centuries. Besides his *Academic Culture in the Spanish Colonies* (1940), two articles written in the same period remain milestones in Hispanic-American historical studies: "Research Possibilities in the Cultural History of Spain in America" (*Hispanic American Historical Review*, 1936) and "The Reception of the Enlightenment in America" (A. P. Whitaker, ed., *Latin America and the Enlightenment*, 1942).

The summit of Lanning's scholarly work came with the publication of *The University in the Kingdom of Guatemala* (1955) and *The Eighteenth-Century Enlightenment in the University of San Carlos de Guatemala* (1956), which won, respectively, the Carnegie Revolving Fund Prize and the Herbert Bolton Memorial Prize of the American Historical Association. These two studies of an institution that granted 2,500 degrees between 1625 and 1821 analyzed virtually every facet of its academic and administrative life. More significantly, through a groundbreaking analysis of student theses, Lanning developed a tool for tracing the changes in thought and ideas in an academic institution. He thereby revealed the existence of an intellectual dynamism that kept the University of Guatemala in the forefront of Enlightenment ideas in philosophy, science, and medicine. The books were praised not only for their substantive content but also for their graceful style and lucidity. In 1974, two years after his retirement, he published *Pedro de la Torre: Doctor to Conquerors*, an offshoot of a large-scale study of the medical profession in the Spanish Empire (completed in draft form shortly before his death). In *Pedro de la Torre*, Lanning demonstrated once more a complete command of sources as well as interpretative and stylistic subtlety.

Lanning was concerned as much with the advancement of scholarship among his colleagues as with his own. His tenure as managing editor of the *Hispanic American Historical Review* from 1939 to 1945 (following upon four years as associate managing editor) saw an expansion of both format and scope as well as increased circulation among scholars in Latin America. He was also a member of the advisory editorial boards of *Americas* and the *Latin American Review*. A close interest in a broad range of research pursued by his colleagues at Duke is attested by his long membership on the Research Council (secretary, 1949–61; chairman, 1961–66). He was also active in the American Historical Association.

Lanning believed that a research library constituted the "irreplaceable heart," free of the coils of academic partisanship, of an institution of higher education. The fruit of this belief was the Hispanic Collection in the Duke University Library, which he, and like-minded colleagues from both his own and other fields, began to assemble in the 1920s. It later totaled over 225,000 volumes. His personal collection in Hispanic-American history (now at the University of Missouri in St. Louis) was also an important one: among more than 3,500 volumes were over 200 bound volumes of manuscript copies of original documents, mostly from the National Archives of Mexico and the Archives of the Indies in Seville.

The dedication Lanning brought to historical research and writing was reflected in his teaching. He demanded of the five thousand students whom he taught in his long career nothing less than the very best they could produce, and he was not inclined to be patient with those who did not do so. For his graduate students he felt a special sense of responsibility, and those who accepted his rigorous adherence to standards were the beneficiaries of his remarkable gift for combining scholarly training and guidance with patience, understanding, and, when needed, a timely push and admonition.

The list of honors earned by Lanning began in 1930 with one of the first Guggenheim Foundation Fellowships awarded, followed by grants from other distinguished agencies. Besides his election to various Latin American historical societies, he was offered and undertook numerous visiting lectureships in the United States and Latin America. Another mark of the esteem he enjoyed within the profession came in 1958, when he was given the prestigious Serra Award of the Americas by the Academy of American Franciscan History. In his acceptance speech, Lanning summed up his professional credo when he praised the work of the scholar who was able to "add an atom of clarity to the confusion of life or subtract a particle from the antagonism of peoples."

As these remarks indicate, Lanning pursued his discipline with a profound sense of mission, both in its practice and in the ultimate goals he intended his work to serve. Formal yet courteous in bearing, literate in the widest sense of the word, with an uncompromising devotion to high standards of accuracy, balance, and fairness, tempered by a wise (and at times humorously ironical) insight into humankind both past and present, Lanning was, above all, a "scholar's scholar."

One of the final tributes, and one closest to his heart, came in 1973, when his former students established an endowment fund in his name for the Duke University Library. Lanning was also one of three professors honored in similar fashion three years earlier by the P. H. Hanes Foundation.

Lanning was buried in Sandy Creek Cemetery in Davidson County. There are two portraits in the possession of his family.

SEE: George M. Addy, "John Tate Lanning (1902–1976)," *The Americas* 33 (1977); *Durham Morning Herald*, 16 Aug. 1976 and various issues; *Durham Sun*, various issues; John Tate Lanning, "The Hispanic Collection," *Gnomon* (1970); John Tate Lanning Papers (Duke University Archives, Durham); Arthur R. Steele, "John Tate Lanning (1902–1976)," *Hispanic Historical Review* 57 (1977); John TePaske, "Refreshing Reminder that Well Written History Can Be Remarkably Instructive," *Durham Morning Herald*, 10 Nov. 1974; *Who's Who in America* (1972–73).

GILBERT EDWIN SOUTHERN, JR.

LaPierre, John *(2 Feb. 1681–ca. 1755)*, French Huguenot, Anglican clergyman, and early educator, was born Jean de la Pierre in LaSalle, Cévenneu, France, the son of Charles de la Pierre and his first wife, Jeanne Roque. Following the revocation of the Edict of Nantes in 1685, his father, a "gentleman," emerged as a militant Huguenot leader as he assumed the duties of the Protestant clergy who had been imprisoned or executed. Facing similar persecution, Charles de la Pierre abandoned his homeland around 1700 and moved his family to England, where he became a minister at The Little Savoy in London.

On 8 Aug. 1701, John LaPierre enrolled as a pensioner at Trinity College, University of Dublin, Ireland, where on 5 Feb. 1706 he was awarded an A.B. and later, according to contemporary statements, an A.M. On 23 Feb. 1707, he was ordained as a Church of England priest by Henry Compton, the bishop of London, at Fulham Palace; and on 6 May of that year the vicar general to the archbishop of Dublin licensed him as a schoolmaster within the city of Dublin. On 1 Dec. 1707, he was made a deacon at St. Paul's Cathedral, London.

The next year LaPierre was sent by Bishop Compton, under the auspices of the Society for the Propagation of the Gospel in Foreign Parts, to South Carolina, where he became the friend and confidant of Governor Nathaniel Johnson. For twenty years he served the French parish of St. Denis at Orange Quarter and the Santee church "till the death of the old settlers who did not understand the English tongue." Meanwhile, he assisted at the English parish of St. Thomas at Charles Town, where in 1712–13 and again in 1728 he officiated at the French Protestant Church. He also conducted a school at Shrewberry.

In 1728 he moved to "Cape Fear, alias New Hanover," in North Carolina, as its first minister and helped found St. Philip's Church, Brunswick, and St. James's Church, Wilmington. From here his work as a missionary for the Society for the Propagation of the Gospel spread northwards, including, beginning in 1734, the New River Colony (later St. John's Parish) in the new county of Onslow.

Because the New Hanover colonists failed to pay him sufficiently, he was "forced to work in the field" at his plantation, Sandy Bay, a short distance upriver from Brunswick, next to Roger Moore's plantation. On 9 Oct. 1733 he wrote from Cape Fear to the bishop of London: "There is a certain Colony in this Province that requires my help upon promise of subscribing towards my maintenance with whom I will, with your Lordship's good will, comply upon any reasonable terms sooner than to see the country destitute of the light of the gospel."

Evidently obtaining the bishop's approval, he moved the following year (1734–35) to Craven Parish, which had been established by act of the Assembly in 1715 and which in 1741 was designated Christ Church Parish in Craven County. In 1740 he transferred his Cape Fear properties to John Fonveille, Jr., a fellow countryman of this parish, in exchange for 360 acres on the Neuse Road at Batchelder (now Bachelor) Creek, about ten miles west of New Bern. He also purchased from William Norwood a half-acre lot (number 357) on Jones Street in New Bern, where he reputedly had a home. Here until his death he lived "in great poverty" while ministering to a wide territory.

The Reverend George Whitefield (1714–70), eminent English evangelist, paid the first of his three visits to "Newborn Town" on Christmas Eve, 1739. On Christmas morning he took the "Holy Sacrament" from LaPierre at the courthouse and preached there during the afternoon. At New Bern Whitefield was "grieved" to learn that the minister had encouraged dancing and had "countenanced a dancing-master, by suffering his own son to be one of his learners." He wrote LaPierre a letter of protest in the conviction that "such a proceeding must be of dreadful consequence to *any*, especially a *new settled*, province."

LaPierre conducted services and provided educational instruction in New Bern and elsewhere throughout the area. At intervals the colonial Assembly appropriated compensation for sermons he preached to the legislators at New Bern, including £50 for his 1739 "claims" and £4 in 1749 for "several services."

Although not listed as a regular rector of Christ Episcopal Church, New Bern, perhaps because of incomplete records, he was heavily involved in its religious and educational affairs. Very likely because of his influence, sentiment was stimulated for the construction of a brick church, completed about 1750. Its foundations have been outlined in recent years at the corner of the site where the third brick church edifice now stands. Owing partly to his influence and partly to the vestrymen's request to English authorities that a new rector be assigned to the parish, in 1752 the church received from King George II a handsome gift of a huge 1717 Bible, a large 1752 *Book of Common Prayer*, and a five-piece silver communion service still in use.

Before the arrival in late 1753 of the Reverend James Reed, the first commissioned rector of Christ Church Parish, a number of chapels had been established in the region, eight of them within the extensive parish boundaries. Credited chiefly to LaPierre, they include a Palatine church or High German chapel on Trent River, which developed into Grace Episcopal Church at Trenton; a chapel at Jasper, later for some years St. Thomas's Church; a Bay River chapel; Maule's Run and Swift Creek Chapel, which became St. Paul's Church in Vanceboro; Grace Chapel, from which came St. John's Church near Grifton; and Atkins Bank Chapel, afterwards reorganized as St. Mary's Church at Kinston. Altogether, he was instrumental in organizing more than twenty churches.

When he visited the regional chapels, he was often away as long as three weeks at a time, preaching and conducting the services for marriages, baptisms, and last rites. It is likely that he also acted as a teacher to "the vast number . . . of children to be instructed" throughout the region. His grandfatherly figure must have been a familiar and welcome sight to the many— young and old—who were touched by his ministry, instruction, and example.

After forty-eight years of active service in the Carolinas, LaPierre grew infirm. Royal Governor Arthur Dobbs wrote that "by reason of his foreign Dialect and his age," he was of little aid to the people. Yet the *Virginia Gazette* reported in late 1752 that the septuagenarian missionary had recently attended counterfeiters in the New Bern jail and later on the gallows. The last mention of him in the Assembly minutes is in January 1755 when £20 was voted for him and £10 for Reed.

LaPierre and his wife, Susanna, who was blind, had at least five children, including a son and three daughters. Jeanne, a daughter, was born in February 1706 in St. James's Parish, before the LaPierres left England. Susannah, another daughter, married John Riggs, to whom she deeded sixteen acres at Batchelder Creek in 1745. Prior to 1740, Martha, a third daughter, married Benjamin Fordham, Sr., of Craven County, a planter, a colonial soldier, and from 1746 to 1755 an officer in the North Carolina Assembly. Many North Carolinians are descended from LaPierre through the Fordhams.

LaPierre was probably buried in Christ Church Cemetery or in the Fordham-Bryan Cemetery in the 1100 block of Queen Street in New Bern, where Benjamin and Martha Fordham were buried. In 1968 descendants erected a marker in the Fordham-Bryan Cemetery to memorialize the Fordhams and LaPierre. During the same year a state historical highway marker was dedicated to LaPierre at Brunswick; and in 1976 a plaque was placed in the Christ Church Parish House, New Bern, dedicating an area of the edifice to LaPierre. A tablet in the Huguenot Church, Charleston, memorializes his ministry there.

SEE: Raleigh *News and Observer*, 11 Nov. 1968; Lillian Fordham Wood, *The Reverend John LaPierre* (1943); Lillian Fordham Wood and Romulus Nunn, comp., *LaPierre-Fordham* (1944).

GERTRUDE S. CARRAWAY
W. KEATS SPARROW

Laprade, William Thomas (27 Dec. 1883–14 May 1975), educator, historian, and editor, was born in Franklin County, Va., the son of Mary Elizabeth Muse and George Washington Laprade. The family had long owned a mill on Snow Creek, near Penhook. His father subscribed to Watterson's *Weekly Courier-Journal*, which had a "Young Writer's Department" for the pseudonymous correspondence of young people. Using the pen name "Jebird," Laprade wrote letters and short stories and even tried his hand at poetry. Under the influence of local ministers and Sunday school, he became a Campbellite preacher and in 1904 entered Washington Christian College (no longer in existence), Washington, D.C. He was graduated in 1906 and then remained as associate professor of mathematics and Latin from 1906 to 1907. Concurrently, he was a teacher, a graduate student at Johns Hopkins University, and minister of the Antioch Christian Church near Vienna, Va. In June 1908 he made the first of many trips to England, and in 1909 he received a Ph.D. degree from Johns Hopkins with a dissertation on "England and the French Revolution, 1789–1797."

In the fall of 1909 Laprade landed at Trinity College (now Duke University), more by accident than choice, to become the first full-time professor of European history in North Carolina. Here he remained except for brief stints as a visiting professor at the University of Illinois (1916, 1930), the University of Pennsylvania (1925), and the University of Michigan (1929). For a few years he also occasionally preached. On 11 June 1913 he married Nancy Hamilton Calfee, a former student at Washington Christian College. Their only child was Nancy Elizabeth (Mrs. J. D. T. Hamilton).

Laprade was manager of the college "Book Room" from 1912 to 1926. He spent parts of 1926 and 1927 in England and acquired many important English books for the Duke Library. He was the first editor of the Trinity College Press (1922–26) and later acting director of the Duke University Press (1944–51), as well as managing editor of the *South Atlantic Quarterly* (1944–57). He was chairman of a growing history department from 1938 to 1953.

Active off the campus, Laprade was a "Minute Man" speaker during World War I, and he enjoyed lecturing on history and politics to business and professional men at the YMCA training school in Blue Ridge, N.C. (1918–19). He belonged to several civic clubs and was a charter member (president, 1926) of the Kiwanis Club. He was a member of the North Carolina Commission on Inter-racial Relations (1919–42), the North Carolina Literary and Historical Association (president, 1937), and the executive board of the Department of Archives and History (1941–60). Active in the American Historical Association and other professional organizations, he was initiated into Phi Beta Kappa (1909) and the Royal Historical Society of Great Britain (1926).

Undoubtedly his most important work—aside from editing, writing, and teaching—was with the American Association of University Professors. He was president from 1942 to 1943; from 1937 to 1942 and again from 1948 to 1953 he was chairman of Committee A, on Academic Freedom and Tenure, the most important committee of that organization at a time when repressive influences threatened the academic world. For the chairman, difficult and sometimes awkward problems involved a heavy correspondence, the appointment of committees of investigation, and final reports. Subsequently, Laprade wrote a special report on the work of Committee A from 1916 to 1953. Elsewhere he said that however elusive truth might be, its best hope was "unfettered, honest, intelligent inquiry." The "tyranny of an authoritarian government" was so "appalling" that "no sacrifice would be too great . . . to avert such a fate." Laprade was recognized as one who spoke with the voice of moderation and reason no matter how great the crisis. He had a reputation for both wisdom and practicality.

An effective teacher and something of an actor, Laprade (privately known to his students as "Lap") had the knack of connecting topics of current interest with historic events to show that the study of history was indeed relevant. It was "not the business of college professors to provide their students with opinions," he said; rather they would provide them with "the knowledge, and the training which will enable them to form and defend opinions of their own." His lectures to graduate students on his speciality, eighteenth-century England, were without formal notes and nearly always accompanied by brief illustrative readings from selected sources. He was at his best in the research seminar, which met at his home where his wife prepared refreshments. Students reported on assigned topics with fear and trembling, for they knew any weakness would be shrewdly dissected. They also knew they were learning a good deal about historical method. Laprade thought history more an art than a science, that it permitted a look at the past that could be had in no other way, and he was careful never to be dogmatic about the lessons of the past.

He thought of society as a complex whole with many interrelations that precluded an easy division into political, economic, and social phases. Thus he did not believe in economic determinism, but he learned that he who held the purse called the tune. A student of public opinion and especially the press in both olden and modern times, he concluded: "Newspapers are both monopolistic public utilities and dispensers of merchandise. . . . In the general interest they may require a measure of regulation as well as freedom." He had a skeptical view of the molders of opinion, whether organized groups, the media, or government.

In his later years, Laprade was slightly stooped, though he was above medium height. The grayness of his office pallor and scanty white hair was relieved by the mobile countenance and ready laughter. He was inclined to a lean physique, and his only known exercise was walking. Regularly he could be seen striding from his home near the East Campus to the city post office for the several newspapers he read, or to the grocery where he did most of the family shopping. He was remarkably healthy and was never a hospital patient until in his eighties. On campus he was never seen in anything heavier than a raincoat, though it was reported that he owned an overcoat. After retirement in 1953 he was allowed to keep his cluttered office in East Duke, where he continued to research and write and to hold forth on the topics of the day. In more than one emergency he went back to the classroom for a time. On the fiftieth convocation of the university, he was awarded in absentia the honorary degree of doctor of letters. A busy man but never in a hurry, he died at age ninety-one, quietly, almost willingly, as if he knew he had finished the course. He was buried in the New Maplewood Cemetery, Durham, beside his wife who died in 1968.

SEE: *Duke Alumni Review* (January 1954, Summer 1975, September–October 1977); *Durham Morning Herald*, 15 May 1975; *Durham Sun*, 14 May 1975; William B. Hamilton, *A Preliminary List of the Printed Writings of William Thomas Laprade* (1952); William Thomas Laprade Papers (Manuscript Department, Duke University Library, Durham); William T. Laprade, *Public Opinion and Politics in Eighteenth Century England to the Fall of Walpole* (1936) and *British History for American Students* (1926); William T. Laprade, ed., *Parliamentary Papers of John Robinson, 1774–1784* (1922); *Smithfield Herald*, 10 June 1975; Hersey E. Spence, "I Remember" Recollections . . . (1975); *Time*, 29 June 1953; *Who Was Who in America*, vol. 6 (1976).

ROBERT H. WOODY

Larkin, Thomas Oliver (16 Sept. 1802–27 Oct. 1858), businessman and diplomat, was born at Charlestown, Mass., the son of Captain Thomas Oliver and Ann Rogers Cooper Larkin. He was a descendant of Richard Warren, a passenger on the *Mayflower*, and his grandfather, Ebenezer Larkin, participated in the Battle of Bunker Hill.

On 8 Apr. 1808 Larkin's father died, and in 1813 Larkin's mother moved the family to Lynn, Mass. In 1817 Larkin was in Boston, where he had gone to learn the trade of making books. He had trouble with this work, however, because he could not tolerate being subjected to another's authority; he subsequently became dissatisfied with other jobs. On 20 Oct. 1821 he and his friend F. G. Thurston boarded the ship *Maria* and sailed for Wilmington, N.C., where they intended to "rise or fall together."

When the ship arrived in Wilmington, there were few

people there, for the town was in the midst of a yellow fever epidemic. The two friends decided to stay, and Larkin took a job as a store clerk. Later, he tried his hand at business, but the ventures did not succeed. At least one failure was due to unscrupulous partners, prompting Larkin to write that he "did not believe there was an honest man south of Phila. and that he would trust no one south of that place."

In the early summer of 1824, Larkin went to New York and visited several towns in the area. Later that year he returned to Wilmington with his brother William and in October opened a store. In March 1825 he took a trip to Charleston, S.C., probably for business and health (it is suspected that he suffered from asthma); on the return trip via Fayetteville, N.C., he entered in his diary that the people between Fayetteville and Wilmington were "the most horrible lot in the United States." On his return, he found that his former partner, F. G. Thurston, had undermined him financially by spreading the rumor that Larkin was "a Southerner in every sense of the word, a gambler" and that he was "not only ruined in business, but in both body and soul."

In August 1825 Larkin closed his store, probably because most residents left Wilmington in the summer to escape the poor climate. On 18 August he opened a new store at Rockfish in Duplin County. Here his brother William died on 4 September. Later that year Larkin was appointed justice of the peace, and on 28 Jan. 1826 he became justice of the Duplin County Court of Pleas and Quarter Sessions. On 26 Sept. 1826 he received from John McLean the commission of postmaster, and a post office was established in his store at Rockfish.

Little is known of Larkin's life during the period 1826–31, except for a letter written in 1831. He had continued to travel between Wilmington and Boston, and by the latter year he had become tired of North Carolina. He decided he could do one of three things: go to Boston, marry a cousin, and settle down; get an appointment in the Post Office Department; or go to Monterey, Calif. Larkin chose the latter.

In September 1831 he sailed on the *Newcastle*, captained by his half brother John B. R. Cooper, and arrived in Monterey in April 1833. There he worked as a clerk for Cooper, and in the same year, with a capital investment of five hundred dollars, he opened a store of his own, selling, among other items, dry goods and groceries. In 1834 he expanded by opening a flour mill. Larkin developed a successful business trading with the Sandwich Islands and Mexico, and in 1842 he opened a branch store in Santa Cruz under Josiah Belden. In this period, he also became renowned for establishing a precedent in land speculation in the area.

In 1833 Larkin married a widow, Mrs. Rachael Holmes, a fellow passenger on the *Newcastle*, whose husband had died before her arrival in Monterey. She was known as "the first American woman to live in California." Their son, Thomas, Jr., was the first child of U.S. parents born in California.

Larkin was appointed a U.S. consul at Monterey on 1 May 1843. In 1845, "he was commissioned secret and confidential agent [by Secretary James Buchanan] with instructions to create a favorable feeling toward the United States, to impress the advantages of a union with that country [California], to counteract English sympathies, and to keep his government fully informed of the affairs." The following year, he turned his business over to Talbot Green and spent his time trying to get California into the United States. About this time Larkin received a message from President James K. Polk asking him to stir up a revolt and to provoke the Americans

there into asking for annexation. After the War with Mexico, Larkin became the U.S. naval agent for California and a member of the California Constitutional Convention.

In 1850–53 Larkin and his family lived in New York, but he returned to California to attend to his property near San Francisco, which was developing after the Gold Rush. Here Larkin spent the last years of his life; he died from typhoid fever.

SEE: *DAB*, vol. 5 (1961); John D. Hart, *A Companion to California* (1978); Robert J. Parker, "A Yankee in North Carolina," *North Carolina Historical Review* (October 1937); Robert J. Parker and D. L. Corbitt, eds., "California's Larkin Settles Old Debts," *North Carolina Historical Review* 17 (October 1940); George Pete, ed., *The Larkin Papers* (1951).

JAMES D. GILLESPIE

Larkins, John Davis, Jr. *(8 June 1909–16 Feb. 1990),* judge, legislator, and political leader, was born in Morristown, Tenn., the son of Charles H. and Minnie Dorsett Larkins. His mother died of typhoid fever when he was just a few weeks old and his father died soon afterwards. He was adopted by an uncle, the Reverend John Davis Larkins, for whom he had already been named, and his wife, Emma Cooper Larkins. Young Larkins grew up in Cedartown and Hazelhurst, Ga., and Fayetteville, N.C., where his uncle, a Baptist minister, held pastorates.

Larkins entered school early and began in the second grade; he finished high school in Greensboro at age fifteen. Graduated from Wake Forest College in 1929, he entered law school in the fall but his money soon gave out. Nevertheless, with the assistance of the dean of the law school, he was granted permission to take the bar exam in January 1930; he passed but was obliged to wait until his twenty-first birthday the following June to be licensed. He took a job in a law office in Charlotte, learned more law, and met Pauline Murrill, of Jacksonville, a senior at Queens College, whom he married on 15 Mar. 1930. In August the newly licensed attorney and his bride went to Trenton in Jones County on vacation where a classmate persuaded him to open a law practice. There he remained until his death at age eighty.

Larkins served in the North Carolina Senate during the special sessions of 1936 and 1938 and for the regular terms of 1937, 1939, 1941 (when he was president pro tem), 1943, 1949, 1951, and 1953. In 1938 he was chairman of the State Constitutional Amendment Committee Campaign, and in 1945 during World War II he was a private in the army. In 1955–56 he was liaison officer and legislative counsel to Governor Luther H. Hodges. Long active in the Democratic party, Larkins was secretary and then chairman of the state Democratic executive committee and was a delegate to five national conventions between 1940 and 1960. On numerous occasions he was chairman of the Jackson Day Dinner, the annual Democratic fund-raising event. In 1960 he was an unsuccessful candidate for the party's nomination for governor.

In August 1961 Larkins was named U.S. judge of the Eastern District of North Carolina and in August 1975 was elevated to the position of chief judge for the district. In June 1979 he became senior judge, thereafter handling fewer cases. As a federal judge he presided over hundreds of criminal and civil cases; it was he who required the state to provide law libraries in the prison systems. Many of his decisions, especially in school desegregation cases, were unpopular, but a colleague pointed out that he did what he had to do rather than make a popular decision that would be overturned on appeal. Because of his many decisions concerning the environment, he came to be recognized as an authority on ecology.

Larkins and his wife were the parents of two daughters: Emma Sue and Pauline. A Baptist, he was buried in the Trenton cemetery.

SEE: Crockette W. Hewlett, *The United States Judges of North Carolina* (1978); *North Carolina Manual* (1953); Raleigh *News and Observer*, 12 Dec. 1954, 11 June 1979, 17 Feb. 1990; Cameron P. West, *A Democrat and Proud of It* (1950).

WILLIAM S. POWELL

Larkins, John Rodman *(24 Dec. 1913–21 Mar. 1980),* state government official, was born in Wilmington, the son of Maria McIver and John Larkins. He attended the public schools in Wilmington and was graduated from Williston High School in 1932. After working one year in New York City paving streets, Larkins returned to North Carolina to attend Shaw University under a National Youth Administration program. He received a B.A. in sociology in 1938. Moving back to New York after graduation, he worked for a year in the garment industry. In September 1939 he began graduate study at Atlanta University's School of Social Work, where he was influenced by the dean, W. E. B. DuBois. He received a master of social work degree in May 1941.

Larkins was a welfare worker in Warren County, N.C., for a year before joining the North Carolina Department of Public Welfare in 1942 as a consultant for work among blacks, a position he held until 1962. While working for the state, he continued his graduate studies at the University of Chicago (1947–48) and completed all the course work for a doctorate at the Columbia University School of Social Work (1953–54). He was also a special student at The University of North Carolina in 1951–52.

In 1962 Larkins became the coordinator for civil rights for the North Carolina Department of Welfare (later the Department of Human Resources). From 1968 to 1973 he was the associate director of the state Probation Commission, and in 1973–74 he was director of youth development in the Department of Corrections. Governor James B. Hunt in 1977 appointed Larkins a special assistant to the governor for minority affairs, the post he held at his death.

In addition to his jobs in state government, Larkins served on many state committees and commissions. Governor J. Melville Broughton named him to the executive committee of the Farm Labor Commission, Governor R. Gregg Cherry appointed him to the advisory committee of the state Recreation Commission, and Governor W. Kerr Scott designated him the state's delegate to the annual conference of the National Freedom Day Association. Larkins was a member of the board of trustees of North Carolina College at Durham (later North Carolina Central University) from 1961 to 1977 and served on the North Carolina Good Neighbor Council in the 1960s.

While working in state government, he wrote "The Negro Population in North Carolina, Social and Economic" (1944), "The Adjustment of Negro Boys Discharged from Morrison Training School" (1947), *The Employment of Negroes in Public Welfare in Eleven Southern States, 1936–1949* (1951), "The Contributions of Sociology to Social Work" (1951), "The Negro in North Carolina, 1945–1955" (1957), "Patterns of Leadership among Negroes in North Carolina" (1959), and *Alcohol and the Negro: Explosive Issues* (1965).

Larkins served in the 1960s as a public member of the U.S. State Department's Selection Board, which reviewed foreign service officers for promotion. He taught part-time at St. Augustine's College and Shaw University. Larkins was a member of the Southern Sociological Society, American Public Welfare Association, National Association of Social Workers, American Sociological Society, Alpha Kappa Delta (honorary sociological fraternity), and Omega Psi Phi fraternity. In 1973 he was elected the first black president of the North Carolina Conference for Social Service. He was a lifelong Democrat and belonged to the Davie Street United Presbyterian Church.

In addition to fellowships from the General Education Board and the National Mental Health Fellowship Act, Larkins received many awards and honors. Wilmington's Business and Professional Men's Club presented him a certificate of merit for public service in 1957, *Negro Progress* named him Man of the Year in 1958, and the state Generation of Negro Women's Clubs gave him a certificate for meritorious Christian and civic service in 1959. In 1965 a dormitory at the State Training School for Girls in Kinston was named for Larkins. The North Carolina Human Relations Council in 1977 honored him with a recognition banquet, and in 1978 the General Baptist Convention of the state presented him its public service award. Larkins received the state's Elk's Lem Long Humanitarian Award in 1979, and the state Young Democrats Club named him Democrat of the Year in 1980 shortly before his death. He was awarded the LL.D. twice: by North Carolina Agricultural and Technical College in 1958 and by North Carolina College in 1967.

In 1979 *We the People of North Carolina* commented: "It is quite possible that no other black man in North Carolina's history has been more influential over a longer period of time in changing majority attitudes in the state toward the rights and economic opportunities of black citizens." On Larkins's death, Governor Hunt said the state had "lost its greatest pioneer in the quest for equal opportunities for all its citizens," and the Raleigh *News and Observer* declared: "This gentle but determined man made his constructive influence felt in local and state race relations during the tense 1960s."

Larkins married Catherine V. Latimer on 29 May 1941. They had one daughter, Sandra. He died of cancer in Duke University Hospital and was buried in Carolina Biblical Gardens, Raleigh.

SEE: *Greensboro Daily News*, 22 Mar. 1980; Mrs. John R. Larkins, personal contact; Raleigh *News and Observer*, 24 Dec. 1958, 19 May 1959, 15 Aug. 1960, 22, 25 Mar. 1980; *We the People of North Carolina* (October 1979); *Who's Who among Black Americans*, 2d ed. (1977–78).

CHARLES W. EAGLES

Lash, Israel George *(18 Aug. 1810–17 Apr. 1878),* businessman, banker, and congressman, was a native of Bethania in Forsyth County. A Moravian by heritage and choice, he was the son of John Christian and Anna Lash. He was educated in the common schools and a local academy. At fifteen his formal schooling ended, and he returned to the family farm. When he was twenty,

Lash established a mercantile business to which he soon added an extensive cigar manufactory. Sagacious and diligent, he prospered. About 1845 he moved to Salem where he enjoyed continued business and financial success. His reputation for integrity and sound judgment having preceded him, in 1847 Lash became Salem's first banker as cashier of a branch of the Wilmington-based Bank of Cape Fear. The general financial crash occasioned by the Civil War ended this banking venture; but, undeterred, Lash founded the First National Bank of Salem in 1866 and served as its president until his death. Possessed of great financial acumen, he accumulated a fortune consisting of money, stocks, city property, and western lands. He was a kind man whose quiet generosity benefited the needy of all races as well as the Moravian church, the town of Salem, and other public charities.

Lash was a Union Whig who never abandoned his principles. He especially abhorred political demagoguery; and, although he owned many slaves, he was utterly opposed to secession. He considered secession the death knell of slavery and warned of devastation and ruin, despite the fanaticism that was rampant in the South in 1860–61. He did nothing to conceal his views during the Civil War, supported the peace movement, and advocated an early restoration of the Union. A cooperationist in the constitutional convention of 1865, Lash moved into the Republican party believing therein lay the easiest road to reunion. He was elected to the Fortieth Congress, defeating Conservative Livingston Brown by a substantial margin. He was easily reelected to the Forty-first Congress but subsequently declined nomination for another term because of poor health. His congressional service was honorable but undistinguished.

Before his death, Lash endured several years of painful physical affliction and long periods of confinement with great patience and fortitude. He was interred in the Moravian Cemetery at Bethania.

SEE: *Biog. Dir. Am. Cong.* (1961); *Congressional Globe* (1834–73); Adelaide L. Fries, *Forsyth: A County on the March* (1949); Israel George Lash, "Memoir" (Moravian Archives, Winston-Salem); Salem *Union Republican*, 18, 25 Apr. 1878; Max R. Williams, ed., *The Papers of William A. Graham*, vol. 6 (1976).

MAX R. WILLIAMS

Lash (or Loesch), Jacob (*13 June 1760–8 Oct. 1821*), craftsman, was born in Bethabara, the son of Johann Jacob and Anna Loesch. His father, who had moved from Pennsylvania to Wachovia from 1758 to 1768, was justice of the peace for Wachovia from 1758 to 1768, but was recalled to Pennsylvania in 1769 and apparently took his family with him. In 1781 young Lash returned to Wachovia to learn the trade of locksmith; he already was a gunsmith, but in his new home he was discouraged from engaging in the repair of guns for fear that too many soldiers would be drawn to the town, perhaps even quartered there. In the spring of 1783, however, at the end of the American Revolution, he was permitted to resume work as a gunsmith. A shooting range was authorized nearby, but instructions were issued that there should be no betting on shots. In 1794 Lash was a justice of the peace and at various times conducted a school, teaching English particularly. He repaired clocks and made the town clock for Bethania. He also played the flute and organ, sang for Moravian services, and taught singing to boys and girls. In addition,

he tuned organs and actually built several, one of which he sold to the Lutheran pastor Carl Storch near Salisbury in 1809. It was noted in 1804 that he smelted gold ore.

In the spring of 1816, with his wife and two children, Susanna Elisabeth and Joseph, Lash moved to Raleigh, bought a house, and announced his intention to live there, though in 1819 he expressed a wish to return to Salem. He was engaged to build a system to supply Raleigh with water from nearby springs. This water served the residents of the town and filled reservoirs, where it was held in reserve to fight fires. A reservoir survives under the sidewalk on Fayetteville Street in front of the Briggs Hardware building.

By the spring of 1820, Lash was again living in Bethabara and was asked to tune the organ in Salem. In the fall he was engaged in building waterworks in Fayetteville when he suddenly became ill and died. Hearing of his illness, his wife was on the way to join him when word reached her of his death. He was buried in Fayetteville. An obituary in the Raleigh *Register* described him as a musician of great skill who not only could play several instruments but also could make and repair them. Among his creations were "two or three pianos and other instruments."

On 28 Feb. 1790 Lash married Susannah Leinbach (1771–1832), and they became the parents of a son, Heinrich Jacob (who died shortly after returning home from having helped his father deliver the organ to Salisbury), as well as the daughter and son who moved with them to Raleigh.

SEE: Adelaide L. Fries, ed., *Records of the Moravians in North Carolina*, vols. 4–7 (1930–47); Raleigh *Register*, 10 Oct. 1821, 29 Mar. 1822.

WILLIAM S. POWELL

Lassiter, Rena Bingham (*10 Oct. 1886–17 Feb. 1960*), editor, columnist, and community leader, was born in Smithfield, the daughter of James Carroll and Isabelle Grantham Bingham. Her father and a brother, C. Elbert Bingham, served as mayor of Smithfield. An uncle, George K. Grantham, was a state legislator in the 1920s.

Rena Bingham was graduated in 1904 with the first class from Turlington Graded School (later Smithfield High School), which evolved from Turlington Institute, a leading college preparatory school in the eastern part of the state. She attended State Normal and Industrial College (now the University of North Carolina at Greensboro) for a year and continued her education through regular lifelong reading, including as a member of the early Chatauqua reading circles. After leaving the State Normal and Industrial College, she taught for a year near Benson and for two years in Smithfield. In 1908 she married Thomas James Lassiter, half owner and editor of the *Smithfield Herald*, a leading semiweekly. He too was a native of Johnston County. During World War I she taught school again for two years, but when her husband died suddenly in 1920, she entered journalism "to keep the paper for the boys." It was a momentous decision, for the *Herald*—with Rena Lassiter a vital member of the enterprise for forty years—thereby continued to be a significant voice in North Carolina journalism.

Thereafter, until the week of her death, Mrs. Lassiter was editor (senior editor beginning in 1932) of the *Herald* in its role of community voice, conscience, and bellwether. In 1932 she was joined by one of her sons,

Thomas J., Jr., who became junior editor following his graduation from Duke University. The paper became a wholly family enterprise beginning in 1934, when the young editor bought the outstanding half interest. In the early 1930s, her older son, William Carroll, a Duke University Law School graduate and Raleigh lawyer, joined the staff as legal counsel and business partner. Under Rena Lassiter's guidance the *Herald* maintained its reputation, acquired during her husband's twenty-four-year editorship, as one of the best nondaily newspapers in the state. Two years after she became editor, it won the Savory Loving Cup for "general excellence." Other awards through the years have been for "news coverage, editorial work, and community service." The "top flight" *Herald* exhibited "editorial courage" and "editorial responsibility," wrote fellow newspaperwoman Margaret Smethurst in 1947.

Rena Lassiter and her sons also continued the tradition established by T. J. Lassiter, Sr., of leadership in the North Carolina Press Association. (He had been its president in 1906.) She served as second vice-president and first vice-president during the twenties and remained an active member throughout her career. T. J. Lassiter, Jr., was president of the association in 1951–52, and William Lassiter was general counsel for well over forty years.

After more than a decade at the helm of the paper, Mrs. Lassiter assigned chief responsibility for editorial writing to the junior editor. She used her news space, her editorials, and her column to complement and underscore her innumerable endeavors to improve the community. For approximately thirty years her "Personal Slants" column appeared in every issue. Wide ranging in subjects and clearly and simply expressing her personality and views of life, it was always popular with readers. She described Smithfield as she was growing up, interesting people and interesting books, community projects, her grandchildren, and often people in need of community help.

In community work, nothing was closer to her heart than library development. A public library for the town and then for the county were projects she helped initiate and bring to reality. As early as 1914, the year of its formation, the Smithfield Woman's Club began sponsoring a public library as a club project. While Mrs. Lassiter was president, the library was provided a home in the new club building. She served as chairman of the first board of trustees when the town began to support the library in 1940. During her tenure, which lasted more than a decade, the board obtained a library building. In 1941 she presented plans for countywide library service to representatives of five other towns. The same year she chaired and spoke for the steering committee that asked for and received money from the county commissioners for support of a county library system. She also provided space in her paper for a weekly library column. In 1947, as spokeswoman for the board before the county commissioners, she requested money for Negro library service. In her annual report for 1950, she noted that in nine years of operation, circulation had increased from 5,329 to 146,717; book stock, from 6,406 to 26,688; and expenditures, from $4,298 to $29,653. She was the author of "The Development of Public Library Service in Johnston County," a typewritten account.

A charter member of the Smithfield Woman's Club and of the Business and Professional Women's Club, begun in 1924, she served in many offices of both, including the presidency. In 1924 the *Herald* issued a special edition featuring the work of the Smithfield Woman's Club in Johnston County. Then in its tenth year, the club boasted a membership of 117. Highlights of her presidency (1931–33) were constructing a new club facility (the only building erected in Smithfield during that depression year of 1932), sponsoring a new club for juniors, conducting a night school at the local cotton mill, and serving as the club's welfare council representative. At the state convention in 1938, she won first prize for the best piece of club reporting. In 1954, sponsored by her local club, she was named North Carolina Mother of the Year and accorded a parade welcome in her hometown when she returned.

Mrs. Lassiter was also active in other civic areas. During her earlier years as editor, she served on township, congressional district, and state executive committees of the Democratic party. For nine years she was a member of the Smithfield School Board, serving as secretary-treasurer. She helped organize the modern chamber of commerce in the 1930s and was a member of its board of directors. In addition, she was a charter member of the Johnston County Historical Society. She was one of the organizers of the Johnston County Tuberculosis Association in 1943 and was on its board of directors at the time of her death.

From her youth on, Rena Lassiter was a church leader. She joined Centenary Methodist Church when she was sixteen and for more than twenty-five years was active in Sunday school work as teacher and superintendent. She served as chairman of the Board of Stewards and as president of the Wesleyan Service Guild. She was the author of *Brief History of Centenary Methodist Church, 1939–1956*, a forty-two-page narrative.

Rena Lassiter died one week after suffering a heart attack and was buried in Riverside Cemetery, Smithfield. Her portrait hangs in the public library of Johnston County and Smithfield. The likeness was a gift from the Johnston County Home Demonstration Clubs, another beneficiary of her strong support.

SEE: Sara Storey Batten, "The History of the Johnston County Public Library System, 1941–1959" (M.A. thesis, University of North Carolina, Chapel Hill, 1960); Business and Professional Women's Club Yearbooks and Scrapbooks, 1939–57; Mrs. T. J. Lassiter, Sr., *Brief History of Centenary Methodist Church, 1839–1956* (n.d.); "Personal Slants" Folder (Public Library of Johnston County and Smithfield); Raleigh *News and Observer*, 2 Feb. 1947; *Smithfield Herald*, 19 Feb., 10 May 1960, Harvest Ed. (August 1967).

FRANCES P. WOODARD

Latham, Louis Charles (11 Sept. 1840–16 Oct. 1895), Confederate officer, congressman, and attorney, was born in Plymouth, the son of Charles and Ann Taylor Walker Latham. He was graduated with honors at age nineteen from The University of North Carolina, ranking second in his class. After reading law for a short while under Judge Asa Biggs, he studied law at Harvard during the year 1859–60. With the approach of the Civil War he returned home and on 20 May 1861, the day North Carolina seceded from the Union, he was named captain of a company in the First Regiment. Wounded at the Battle of Sharpsburg, he soon became major of the regiment and was regimental commander at Chancellorsville; wounded at the Wilderness on 5 May 1864, he returned home to recover and while there was elected to the North Carolina Senate. Before beginning his legislative duties, however, he returned to the army and was present when General Robert E. Lee surrendered at Appomattox. He then served in the legislative sessions between November 1865 and March 1866. Resuming his law studies, he was licensed to practice. In 1870–72 he again served in the state senate and for a time presided in the absence of the president. In 1875 he moved from Plymouth to Greenville.

Latham was an unsuccessful candidate for Congress in 1872, 1874, and 1878 but was nominated and elected in 1880. He served in the House of Representatives during the years 1881–83 but was defeated for reelection in 1882. Again a candidate, he was elected in 1886 and served a second term in 1887–89. Retiring from politics thereafter, he came to be recognized as one of the most able and eloquent lawyers in the state.

Married first to Annie Norcom of Plymouth, Latham was the father of a daughter, Camille. His second wife was Lavinia Emilia Monteiro of Richmond, Va., and they were the parents of Louise, Charles, Louis, and Andrew. A Democrat and a Methodist, Latham died in Baltimore, Md., following an operation and was buried in the Episcopal cemetery, Greenville.

SEE: John L. Cheney, Jr., ed., *North Carolina Government, 1585–1979* (1981); Jerome Dowd, *Sketches of Prominent Living North Carolinians* (1888); Henry T. King, *Sketches of Pitt County* (1911); William S. Powell, *The First State University: A Pictorial History of the University of North Carolina* (1979 [portraits]).

WILLIAM S. POWELL

Latham, Maude Moore (16 Dec. 1871–8 Apr. 1951), cultural leader and benefactor, was born in New Bern, the daughter of James Washington and Sarah Jane Gordon Moore. At Miss Corinne Harrison's School and the New Bern public schools she was an honor student and the recipient of gold medals for excellence in scholarship. While residing with her maternal grandparents in New York City, she continued her education in public schools and at Hunter College. For a short time she taught in a private school in her hometown.

In the First Presbyterian Church of New Bern, on 10 Aug. 1892, she married James Edwin Latham, a native of Wayne County. Twelve years later the couple, with their two children, Edward and May Gordon, moved to Greensboro where they became active in civic and business affairs.

For some time Maude Latham served on the City Planning and Zoning Board. As a member of the local Presbyterian church she was a trustee of the Presbyterian Home for the Aged, and to both she was a liberal contributor. The Latham Memorial Hospital at the Eastern Star and Masonic Home of Greensboro was begun by her gift of $30,000 in memory of her husband. Its reception room was attractively furnished as a memorial to her son, who died at Fort Thomas, Ky., in 1918 while in army service during World War I. Both the husband and the son were Thirty-second degree Masons.

A patron of the arts, long a musician and collector of fine paintings and antiques, Mrs. Latham traveled widely in America and Europe and studied art, music, and languages. She was vice-president and a life member of the North Carolina Art Society and belonged to the North Carolina Folklore Society, State Literary and Historical Association, Historical Book Club of North Carolina, Euterpe Club, and Woman's Club of Greensboro.

When an opportunity came for North Carolina to ac-quire the Carolina Charter issued by King Charles II of England to the Lords Proprietors, she was the first and largest donor towards its purchase.

The restoration of historic buildings especially appealed to her, and her aid in this movement was recognized by the North Carolina Society for the Preservation of Antiquities in 1948, when it awarded her one of its first Cannon Cups. She became a life member and served for a time as vice-president of the association. She also was a charter member of the National Council for Historic Sites and Buildings (now the National Trust for Historic Preservation) and was a member of its Ways and Means Committee. North Carolina Governor W. Kerr Scott appointed her to the Commission for the Restoration of the Governor Charles B. Aycock Birthplace. She also was a member of numerous other historical and patriotic organizations.

Her interest in gardens led to membership in many garden clubs, and she was a life member of the Garden Club of North Carolina and the National Council of State Garden Clubs. Her own garden was a noted showplace. Interested in sports, she enjoyed golf, tennis, bowling, and swimming and in her youth participated in fox hunts in Virginia.

After their marriage, James E. Latham began giving his wife gold dollars on special occasions. These she carefully put aside as she became interested in finance. After some years she surprised her husband by bringing out 125 gold dollars from their secret place and asking him to invest them for her. This formed the nucleus of a considerable fortune that she acquired with his advice and her own business acumen and sound judgment.

In 1939 she wrote an article for *Southern Life* in which she summarized her religious convictions: "When I look upon my little domain and realize that God has been so good to me, that He has enabled me to build this home and this lovely garden, I am most humble and most grateful." She often recalled accounts related to her by her father as they took walks around town of the role New Bern played in the history of colonial North Carolina. Sometimes they passed the surviving west wing of Tryon Palace, and she secretly harbored the hope that the whole palace might someday be restored.

As a step towards the attainment of her goal, Mrs. Latham helped finance the publication in 1939 of *Old Homes and Gardens of North Carolina* under the sponsorship of the Garden Club of North Carolina. Dr. Archibald Henderson, in the foreword, emphasized that "the Governor's Palace must be restored." For a period of time afterwards, interrupted by World War II, efforts were made to interest business firms and wealthy individuals in the restoration of Tryon Palace, which was also the first state capitol. These efforts were unsuccessful so in January 1944, with her husband's encouragement and financial assistance, she established the Maude Moore Latham Trust Fund of $100,000 toward the project. If the state would acquire the necessary land, she promised to restore what was called "the most beautiful building in the colonial Americas" when it was completed in 1770.

The General Assembly in 1945 appropriated $150,000 to acquire the site and authorized the appointment of a Tryon Palace Commission; Maude Latham was elected chairman and retained that position until her death. An additional $77,000 was appropriated for property after she added $150,000 more to the endowment in 1949. She also gave the state English antiques appraised at $125,000 towards furnishing the palace. After her death it was revealed that Mrs. Latham had bequeathed the remainder of her estate, amounting to $1,115,000, to the Tryon Palace Commission. Her daughter, May Gorden Latham Kellenberger, and her son-in-law, John A. Kellenberger, became chairman and treasurer, respectively, of the commission.

Through the capable management of the officers, the commission completed the restoration in 1959 and was able to purchase suitable antiques to furnish the palace as well as to acquire four fine old nearby homes for restoration and furnishing. All soon were opened to the public.

Maude Latham was buried in Green Hill Cemetery, Greensboro.

SEE: *Asheville Citizen*, 9 Apr. 1951; *Greensboro Daily News*, 28 June 1944; New Bern *Sun-Journal*, 4 Apr. 1959; Blackwell P. Robinson, *Three Decades of Devotion* (1978); Tryon Palace Restoration Records (New Bern).

GERTRUDE S. CARRAWAY

Lathrop, Virginia Terrell (3 Sept. 1902–1 Dec. 1974), author, journalist, and longtime member of the governing boards of The University of North Carolina, was born in Raleigh, the daughter of George Sumter and Lovie Park Terrell. She attended public schools in Raleigh, along with her brothers Benjamin Park and Franklin Sidney, and received her higher education at the North Carolina College for Women, from which she was graduated with a B.A. degree in 1923. President of the student body in her senior year, she returned in 1937 to establish the College News Bureau of which she was director until 1941. In 1966 she was chairman of the search committee to find a new chancellor for the institution and in the same year was awarded the honorary L.H.D. degree at commencement ceremonies.

During the 1920s Virginia Terrell pursued a career as a newspaperwoman, working as reporter and feature writer for the *Raleigh Times*, the Raleigh *News and Observer*, the London *Daily Express*, the Paris edition of the New York *Herald*, the New York *Evening Post*, and the *Asheville Citizen*. In 1928 she married Albert Henry Lathrop, a civil engineer, and they became the parents of a son, George Terrell Lathrop. She resumed her career for a brief time in 1944–45 as a program writer for radio station WISE in Asheville.

A resident of Asheville during the last decades of her life, she contributed her energy and talent to a wide range of community organizations and causes there. She served on the boards of the Asheville YWCA, the local chapters of the American Red Cross and the American Association of University Women, the Parent-Teacher Association, the Asheville Friends of the Library (president, 1941–50), Memorial Mission Hospital, and the Family Counseling Service. She was regional director for the Western North Carolina Division of Women's War Bond Committee (1942–44). In addition, she was a charter member of the North Carolina Presswomen's Association and a member of the Western North Carolina Historical Association, Delta Kappa Gamma, the Democratic party, and the Episcopal church.

The author of two books, *Educate a Woman* and *Bricks and People: A Walking Guide to the University at Greensboro*, she also wrote numerous magazine and newspaper articles, pamphlets, book reviews, and radio scripts.

Virginia Lathrop made her greatest contribution to the state in her long years of outstanding service as a member of the governing boards of The University of North Carolina. In 1949 she was appointed to the board of trustees of the Consolidated University of North Caro-

lina and was named to its executive committee in 1953, a position she held until the major reorganization of higher education in the state in 1972 brought all sixteen state colleges and universities into the University of North Carolina system under a single board of governors. She was an original member of the new board and continued to participate in its affairs until her death.

She was buried in Calvary churchyard, Fletcher.

SEE: *Asheville Citizen-Times*, 9 Feb. 1958, 3 Dec. 1974; Raleigh *News and Observer*, 3 Dec. 1974; University of North Carolina at Greensboro, *Alumni News* 63 (Winter 1975).

PHILIP A. WALKER

Latta, Edward Dilworth (4 May 1851–14 July 1925), industrialist, was born in the South Carolina summer resort village of Pendleton, the oldest of three sons of James T. and Angela Wetherell Lott Latta. He attended Pennington Seminary in New Jersey, his mother's native state, but was unable to continue his education at Princeton because of the death of his father. Latta began his business career as a salesman in a New York clothing store, but after a brief time he became a traveling salesman. In 1876 he moved to Charlotte and operated a clothing store, which he soon sold when he began purchasing real estate. On the outskirts of Charlotte, he bought a thousand acres and named the property Dilworth in memory of his grandmother. Latta bought a streetcar line, electrified it, and began selling lots at the end of the line in Dilworth. He organized the Charlotte Consolidated Construction Company in 1890 to develop his real estate and to operate the Charlotte Electric Railway, Light and Power Company. In 1911 he employed the noted landscape firm of Olmsted in Boston to design four hundred acres in his subdivision. This became Charlotte's first suburban expansion.

Latta also acquired considerable property on South Tryon Street about 1919 and with J. B. Duke, who had bought his street railway system, he built the Mercantile Building on First Street. He also erected the Latta Arcade and the Latonia Building on South Tryon. He gave the city over forty acres for use as a public park without restriction as to race.

In 1923 Latta moved to Asheville for health reasons and invested heavily in Asheville real estate. He died there from a paralyzing stroke. A member of the First Presbyterian Church in Charlotte, he was buried in that city's Elmwood Cemetery. His will created a continuing endowment estimated at more than a million dollars with the income going to Union Theological Seminary, Richmond, Va., and to the North Carolina Orthopedic Hospital and the Memorial Mission Hospital, both in Gastonia.

In 1877 Latta married Harriet Nisbet of Macon, Ga., and they became the parents of two sons, Marion Nisbet and E. D., Jr., and a daughter, Janet Acton (Mrs. William Haskell Porcher). Harriet Latta died in 1910, and in 1918 he married Jeannie Lea of Vicksburg, Miss.

SEE: J. B. Alexander, *Biographical Sketches of the Early Settlers of Hopewell Section* (1897); *Charlotte Observer*, 15 July 1925; C. G. Davidson, "Plantation House on the Catawba," *The State*, May 1978; Maurice A. Moore, *Reminiscences of York* (n.d.); Richard W. Simpson, *History of Old Pendleton District* (1913); Elizabeth Williams, Manuscript of Latta Family History and Latta Place (Plantation Files, Davidson College Archives, Davidson).

CHALMERS G. DAVIDSON

Laughinghouse, Charles O'Hagan (25 Feb. 1871–26 Aug. 1930), physician and state health officer, was born on the family plantation near Grimesland in Pitt County. He was the first of at least eight children of Joseph John and Eliza O'Hagan Laughinghouse. His father, a prominent farmer and Democrat, served in the North Carolina House of Representatives and as superintendent of the state prison in Raleigh. His maternal grandfather, Dr. Charles James O'Hagan, whose medical career in Greenville spanned the second half of the nineteenth century, achieved national recognition for his professional work. Charles O'Hagan Laughinghouse was educated at Trinity School in Chocowinity and at Horner School in Oxford. He attended The University of North Carolina in 1888–89 and received an M.D. degree in 1893 from the University of Pennsylvania. In 1896 he pursued postgraduate work at Johns Hopkins University.

After obtaining his degree, Laughinghouse joined his grandfather's practice in Greenville and quickly gained the respect of his colleagues for his professional activities and philanthropic endeavors. Noted for his powerful physique and physical endurance, he carried on an extensive medical practice for over thirty years while serving the people of Pitt County as county health officer, county coroner, and president of the Pitt County Medical Society. The students of East Carolina Teachers' Training School received medical attention from Laughinghouse, the school physician, between 1909 and 1926. Beginning about 1900 he labored to establish a community hospital for Pitt County. His efforts succeeded in April 1924 with the opening in Greenville of Pitt Community Hospital, a private institution established by Laughinghouse and three of his colleagues. As part of the hospital campaign, Laughinghouse in 1917 was instrumental in persuading the General Assembly to amend a 1913 act to allow towns and townships to establish and maintain public hospitals. He avidly supported the North Carolina School for the Feebleminded at Kinston, authorized by the General Assembly in 1911.

Active in state health affairs, Laughinghouse served the Medical Society of the State of North Carolina in many capacities beginning in 1895. In 1896 the society elected him chairman of the section on anatomy and surgery; the following year he served as orator, declaiming on "A Few Hints in Medico-Social Ethics." As chairman of the section on medical jurisprudence and state medicine in 1910, he successfully argued for increased state aid for public health. During 1916–17 Laughinghouse led the society as president. He was a member of the State Board of Medical Examiners from 1902 to 1908. As a member of the State Board of Health between 1911 and 1926, he assisted his colleagues on the board—notably Dr. Joseph Howell Way of Waynesville—and state health officer Watson Smith Rankin in establishing goals and priorities for health work in the state. On 1 Oct. 1926 Laughinghouse assumed the duties of state health officer and secretary of the Board of Health. During his brief tenure he worked to obtain improved quarters for the board, to strengthen several of the board's bureaus, to stimulate within and outside the medical profession interest in public health and greater cooperation among official health agencies, and to improve the quality of local health services. He also worked to foster interest in preventive medicine.

Laughinghouse's career involved him in medical affairs outside North Carolina. He was a member of the Southern Medical Association, president of the Seaboard Medical Society and of the Tri-State Medical Association of the Carolinas and Virginia, and a fellow in the American Medical Association. During 1917, as a member of the state committee of the Committee of American Physicians, he helped organize North Carolina's medical resources for the war effort. Following his appointment as a major in the Medical Reserve Corps of the U.S. Army, he received training at Fort Oglethorpe, Ga. In 1918 he served at Camp Forrest in Chattanooga, Tenn., and at Fort Sam Houston in San Antonio, Tex. Laughinghouse commanded Base Hospital No. 85 at Fort Sill, Okla., and in August 1918, after promotion to lieutenant colonel in the Medical Corps, he supervised the hospital's transfer to Paris. The hospital was moved to Angers, France, where Laughinghouse remained until March 1919.

Despite the demands of the medical profession, he raised a family and participated in a variety of organizations. On 10 June 1896 he married Carrie Virginia Dail, of Snow Hill, and they became the parents of three children: Helen (Mrs. Richard Stokes), Charles O'Hagan, and Haywood Dail. Laughinghouse was a member of the Methodist church, the Democratic party, the Knights of Pythias, and the Kiwanis Club. A Mason, he belonged to Greenville Lodge 284, A.F. and A.M. He was involved in several businesses, including the Greenville Banking and Trust Company and the National Bank Building. While satisfactorily recovering in High Point from phlebitis, Laughinghouse suddenly died of a heart blockage. He was buried near his grandfather's grave in Cherry Hill Cemetery, Greenville.

SEE: East Carolina Teachers' Training School, *Training School Quarterly* 3 (1916–17); Greenville *Daily Reflector*, 3 May, 2 Aug. 1902; Charles O'Hagan Laughinghouse Papers (Manuscript Collection, East Carolina University, Greenville); *North Carolina Biography*, vol. 3 (1928); North Carolina State Board of Health Records (North Carolina State Archives, Raleigh); Raleigh *News and Observer*, 27 Aug. 1930; *Transactions of the Medical Society of the State of North Carolina* (1896–1931); *Who's Who in America* (1928–29).

MAURY YORK

Law, Sallie Chapman Gordon (27 Aug. 1805–28 June 1894), humanitarian, was born in Wilkes County, the daughter of Chapman and Charity King Gordon. Her father was a native of Virginia and a soldier in the American Revolution who fought at the Battle of Kings Mountain and continued his military service under Generals Thomas Sumter and Francis Marion. Her mother was from South Carolina, and it has been inferred that the couple met during his days of military service. Nothing is known of Sallie Gordon's early schooling, but she often exhibited evidence that it was thorough. On 28 June 1825 she married Dr. John S. Law in Eatonton, Ga., and they made their home in Forsyth, Ga., where Law practiced medicine until 1834. In that year they moved to Columbia, Tenn., where he continued his practice until his death in 1843. They were the parents of seven children, one of whom was the Reverend John Gordon Law, a noted clergyman in South Carolina during the last half of the nineteenth century. After her husband's death, Sallie Law moved to Memphis because it offered better facilities for the education of her children.

The approaching Civil War stirred her to half a century of activity and service to humanity. Her sympathies were with the Confederacy, and she bemoaned the fact that she had "only one son [John Gordon] to lend to the Confederate Armies." Anticipating that there would be instances in which she might be of service, she began to seek out opportunities. Her first project was the establishment in April 1861 of the Southern Mothers' Hospital in Memphis for the treatment of the wounded without regard to their loyalty to either side. With constant expansion, the hospital proved to be of outstanding service following the Battle of Shiloh.

Mrs. Law made two early trips to field hospitals in Columbus, Ky., with food and clothing for the soldiers. When the hospital in Memphis was closed by invading Federal troops, its assets were invested in medical supplies, bedding, and clothing which she personally delivered to hospitals in many places including LaGrange, Ga. On those missions she attracted the attention of General Joseph E. Johnston, who was so impressed that he is said to have "ordered a review of thirty thousand troops in recognition of her services."

At the close of the war she was the leader in activating the Southern Mothers' Association. In May 1889 that group formed the nucleus of the Confederate Historical Association, which numbered Jefferson Davis among its early members. This pioneer memorial association "helped erect monuments, mark graves, and distribute historical data about the Southern cause and its conduct." Mrs. Law was the only president of this group during her lifetime. She wrote a sixteen-page pamphlet, *Reminiscences of the War of the Sixties between the North and the South*, published in 1892, setting forth her activities over a thirty-year period.

For all of these expansive and unselfish services, she was adored by soldiers during the war and by veterans afterwards. They knew something of how unswervingly she gave of herself without compensation or reimbursement of expenses. It was they who early referred to her as "the mother of the Confederacy," and that designation began to be repeated across the country.

Sallie Law was an active Presbyterian from her youth. She died at her home in Idlewild, a suburb of Memphis.

SEE: *DAB*, vol. 2 (1929); *Memphis Commercial*, 29 June 1894; *Nat. Cyc. Am. Biog.*, vol. 25 (1936); *Southern Historical Society Papers*, vol. 22 (1894); *Who Was Who in America*, vol. H (1963).

C. SYLVESTER GREEN

Lawler, Joab *(12 June 1796–8 May 1838)*, minister, educator, and politician, was born in Union County. Little is known about his parents except that his father was a small farmer who, shortly after the birth of his son, moved the family to Tennessee. From there the family went to the Mississippi Territory where Lawler attended public schools.

He settled in Alabama in 1815 and four years later established residence in Shelby County. Between 1821 and 1826 he was a circuit court judge and then county judge. While serving on the bench in Shelby, he studied theology; he received ordination as a Baptist minister in 1826 and began officiating as pastor of a local church. In the same year he was elected to the state senate. In 1827, however, Lawler resigned from the senate to accept an appointment as receiver of public moneys for the Coosa land district. To obtain the post, he was required to move to the town of Mardisville in Talladega County where the land office was situated. During his residence there he founded two churches and officiated in the town until 1835. He also became treasurer of the University of Alabama at Tuscaloosa in 1833 and held the position until 1836.

In 1835 Lawler was elected as a Whig to the Twenty-fourth Congress. Described as "a fluent orator . . . and a

pious man," he was one of a number of native North Carolinians to serve in the House of Representatives from Alabama during this period. He was elected to a second term in 1837 but died suddenly in Washington, D.C. The same day Congress resolved to wear "crape around the left arm for thirty days" in his memory and voted unanimously to attend the funeral, held on 9 May 1838.

Lawler married the sister of Robert A. Baker of Dallas, Tex.

SEE: *Appleton's Cyclopedia of American Biography*, vol. 3 (1900); *Biog. Dir. Am. Cong.* (1950); W. Brewer, *Alabama: Her History, Resources, War Record, and Public Men* (1872); Theodore Hensly Jack, *Sectionalism and Party Politics in Alabama, 1819–1842* (1919); Thomas M. Owen, *History of Alabama and Dictionary of Alabama Biography*, vol. 4 (1921); *United States Telegraph*, 8 May 1833; *Who Was Who in America*, vol. H (1963).

GEORGE DAVID TERRY

Lawrence, Joseph Joshua *(28 Jan. 1836–14 Mar. 1909)*, chemist, physician, editor, publisher, and philanthropist, was the son of Bennett Barrow and Martha Ann Frances Knight Lawrence and the grandson of Elder Joshua Lawrence. In 1838 his parents settled a short distance north of present-day Rocky Mount on a 359-acre plantation recently purchased by his paternal grandfather. His father appears to have been an impractical planter and businessman; he was rescued from financial catastrophe in the early 1850s by his wealthy father-in-law, Jesse C. Knight, who established a lifetime estate that would pass intact to his Lawrence grandchildren.

Lawrence was educated in a local private school but the dates and places of his "university and medical education" are unknown. The A.M. degree apparently was bestowed as an honor by Bethany College in western Virginia. He opened his first medical office in Wilson in March 1858. By January 1861 he had moved to Goldsboro to edit *The Daily Rough Notes*, which he and his brother-in-law, Richard H. Blount, had recently purchased. In August he enlisted in Company F, Fortieth North Carolina Regiment, and was soon elected captain, but bad health forced his resignation at the end of November. Returning to Wilson, he described himself as an editor when he reenlisted in April 1862; a month later, as a captain, he was in charge of a company of volunteers, the Wilson Partisan Rangers, sometimes denoted as a part of the Sixteenth Battalion of North Carolina Cavalry and sometimes as a part of the Seventh Cavalry. Resigning his commission in October, he returned to Wilson and may have been associated with the Wilson Confederate hospital. At some date before 28 Mar. 1863, he established a drug store. He served as county coroner in 1864 and 1865 and in 1866 resumed the practice of medicine.

The first major step destined to lead Lawrence in a new direction resulted from his preparation of "Lawrence's Compound Extract of Rosadalis," which appeared on the market by the end of August 1867. It was soon followed by "Dr. Lawrence's Celebrated Woman's Friend," then by "Koskoo" in 1869 and "Listerine" in 1879. Moving to Baltimore early in 1868, he established the Dr. Joseph J. Lawrence Chemical Laboratory at 244 West Baltimore Street prior to selling his Rosadalis trademark. In 1869 Lawrence was established in Norfolk, Va., as an "organic chemist" and was manufacturing his other nostrums, but success in this field eluded him and in 1870 he returned to Wilson. While practicing medicine and operating a drug store, he also began publication of *The Medical Brief* in July 1873. This monthly journal became extremely popular, attracted widespread advertising, and reputedly had "the largest circulation and is financially the most prosperous medical publication in the World."

Lawrence's financial record, nevertheless, was unstable. On 1 Jan. 1868 he borrowed $5,000 and signed a royalty contract with his wife's brother, Marcellus J. Edwards, followed by a promissory note on 28 September for half of the $35,000 realized from the sale of the Rosadalis formula. On 2 June 1869 Lawrence was declared a bankrupt in Virginia, having paid Edwards only $1,000. His second bankruptcy was adjudicated in North Carolina in April 1878. Edwards later settled in Raleigh and in October 1896 renewed his unsatisfied claims in the Wake County Superior Court. Although Lawrence's lawyers had the suit transferred to the U.S. Circuit Court, Edwards finally collected $7,500 in October 1897.

Lawrence left Wilson and moved to St. Louis, Mo., in 1875. There he seems to have become a partner in the firm of Battle and Company Chemists' Corporation, founded in St. Louis in 1882 by Jesse Mercer Battle with whom Lawrence had been associated while both resided in Wilson. As one of "the most able journalists in the city," Lawrence was "conspicuous in his efforts on behalf of almost every public work" and "generous [with] contributions of time and money." He prospered in everything he touched, including the successful efforts that resulted in the 1904 Louisiana Purchase Exposition in St. Louis.

After building a three-story, sixteen-room granite block residence and investing in other real estate in St. Louis, Lawrence also purchased a fine mansion on Fifth Avenue in New York City. He died in New York and was buried in the family mausoleum at the Bellefontaine Cemetery, St. Louis. He left an estate estimated at between $7 million and $11 million. Lawrence had married Josephine Edwards of Greene County, N.C. Their children, Frank and Minnie, both predeceased him, and in due course his only grandchild, Vera Siegrist, inherited the fortune.

SEE: William Hyde and H. L. Conrad, *Encyclopedia of the History of St. Louis*, vol. 3 (1899); *Nat. Cyc. Am. Biog.*, vol. 12 (1904).

HUGH BUCKNER JOHNSTON

Lawrence, Joshua *(10 Sept. 1778–23 Jan. 1843)*, Baptist minister, farmer, and pamphleteer, was born in Edgecombe County, one of several children of John and Absilla Bell Lawrence. His father died when he was about seventeen, leaving him a plantation on the west side of Fishing Creek about a mile and a half above its confluence with the Tar River. There he lived for the rest of his life; the shell of the house he built around 1810 was still standing in 1970.

Lawrence received little formal schooling and for several years after his father's death seems to have indulged a propensity for profligacy, though not to the extent of wasting his property; industry and frugality characterized his life, even as a tumultuous teenager. The precise nature of his alleged depravity is not known, but it must be remembered that card playing and dancing were in that day considered mortal sins by the fundamentalist sects. Whatever his transgressions, he repented after a few years and joined the Baptist church at Fishing Creek (later Lawrence's Meeting House), where he was baptized by Elder Nathan Gilbert. In 1801 he was ordained

to the ministry by Elders Lemuel Burkitt and Jesse Read and succeeded Gilbert as pastor of the Falls of Tar River Church.

His first efforts at preaching were awkward as he could scarcely read, but his natural gifts as an orator, combined with an application to self-education and a retentive memory, soon overcame that handicap. He became, according to contemporary accounts, a forceful and eloquent preacher, possessed of a pleasant voice, a great flow of words, and a commanding appearance. It was said that he could sing, pray, and preach sermons while asleep, without any knowledge of it himself. Within two years, over one hundred persons were baptized by him and added to his church.

In 1803 Lawrence was sent by his church as a delegate to the Kehukee Association, which in that year saw the first step within that association of churches toward the missionary cause. Dissension over that and other sectarian differences grew for the next twenty-four years, resulting finally in total disunion.

In 1817 Lawrence began to hold monthly meetings in Tarboro and in 1819, with the help of Elders Martin Ross, Thomas Billings, and Thomas Meredith, he succeeded in constituting the Tarboro Baptist Church, of which he was the first regular minister. He remained in that post until 1829, when the church was split, thereafter continuing as minister of the Old School or Primitive Baptist church until his death.

During the intervening years, as the controversy within the Kehukee Association grew more intense, Lawrence assumed the leadership of the opposition to the Missionary Baptists. He inveighed against them from the pulpit with all the considerable power of his oratory and, beginning in 1825, he attacked them in print. *The American Telescope* by "a Clodhopper of North Carolina," printed in Philadelphia in that year, was the first of the pamphlets that he produced intermittently throughout his career expressing forthrightly his religious and political opinions. He opposed the Missionary Baptists and, for that matter, all other churches, for what he called "craft," concluding in one of his sermons: "We shall next notice the established Christian religion, turned from its simplicity and virgin beauty into a craft." He believed that the ministry was God's calling and therefore not to be used for material gain. As a successful farmer Lawrence could afford to offer his ministry free of charge, but strict adherence to this principle worked a real hardship on less affluent ministers. A strong believer in religious and civil liberty, he also denounced all meddling in politics by any church. Among other pamphlets, he was the author of *The North Carolina Whig's Apology* (1830), *A Basket of Fragments for the Children* (1833), and *The Mouse Trying to Gnaw out of the Catholic Trap* (n.d.).

It was Lawrence who wrote the "Declaration of Principles" that the Kehukee Association submitted to the churches of the association in 1826 and considered during its session the next year. By this declaration, the association agreed to "Discard all Missionary Societies, Bible Societies and Theological Seminaries." It objected to seminaries not because it disapproved of the dissemination of knowledge but because "preaching would thereby become a lucrative employment like the law, physic, etc."

The vehemence with which Lawrence expressed his views evoked responses in kind, culminating in threats against his life. Whether there was real substance to these warnings is not known, but the fact that they were made indicates the depth of feeling engendered by the controversy. In 1829, on account of the threats, he withdrew from the pulpit for several months, during which time it was filled by Elder P. W. Dowd, who came out so strongly for the missionary cause that the church was divided into two hostile factions. When Lawrence was invited back by his supporters, Dowd seized the keys to the new meetinghouse. Lawrence then took the minute books and, followed by a majority of the congregation, went to the old meetinghouse, where they expelled from membership all who had remained with Dowd.

Lawrence was by far the most forceful and articulate apologist of the Primitive Baptists; without his leadership, they fell into decline and, except for a brief resurgence in the late nineteenth century, remained a minor sect. Despite failing health during the last several years of his life, Lawrence continued to preach at the old meetinghouse at Fishing Creek until a few months before his death. He died after a three months' illness and was buried on his home place. After his wife's death in 1851, identical stones were erected to mark their graves; on his, the year of his death was erroneously given as 1842. Moreover, the tombstone cutter had gratuitously added the title "Rev." before his name on both stones. Knowing how deeply Lawrence felt that such an appellation should be reserved for God and preempted by no man, his family chiseled those three letters from the stones. The controversial character of the man inspired the story that vandals had done it, but the neat, though amateurish, nature of the work belies that tale. These stones, the only ones in the family graveyard, were moved in 1970 to the Primitive Baptist Churchyard in Tarboro.

In about 1800 Lawrence married Mary Knight, daughter of Peter and Ann Bell Knight. They had thirteen children, seven of whom survived him: John, Josiah, M.D., Louisiana, Joshua L., Bennett B., Pherebe, and Thomas David. Of those who predeceased him, the name of only one, Lemuel, is known.

SEE: Joseph Biggs, *A Concise History of the Kehukee Baptist Association* (1834); Edgecombe County Wills, Estate Papers, and Guardians' Accounts (North Carolina State Archives, Raleigh); C. B. Hassell, *History of the Church of God* (1886); Minutes of the Kehukee Baptist Association (1843).

WILLIAM C. FIELDS

Laws, Romulus Don (*22 Aug. 1868–11 Nov. 1951*), newspaper publisher and editor, the son of Coffey and Amanda Robinson Laws, was born on his father's farm at Moravian Falls in Wilkes County. While largely self-taught, he did have eighteen months of schooling, including studies at Moravian Falls Academy. After teaching school in 1888, he worked on his father's farm until he was twenty-one.

Although he had never seen a printing press, young Laws at age thirteen made one and carved type for it from mountain laurel wood. While still in his teens, he acquired a small job press and a limited assortment of type. In June 1895 he began publishing *The Yellow Jacket*, a three-column, four-page monthly newspaper, at an annual subscription price of ten cents. Strongly Republican in orientation with fiery political expressions, it grew to as many as twelve pages with five columns, an annual subscription price of twenty-five cents, and a circulation of nearly half a million.

The newspaper was especially popular during the presidency of Woodrow Wilson, when Laws lambasted the Democratic administration. For many years thereafter, a regular column, "Stingers," contained short paragraphs in which the editor expressed his opinion on a wide range of subjects and attacked Democrats, Socialists, Nazis, "Liars and Leeches, Hypocrites and Humbugs and Demagogues and Dastards." One widely cited "Stinger" observed: "It is said that Adam named the animals and Seth named the stars. But that doesn't explain why a jackass is used to typify the New Deal Party."

In 1906 Laws developed waterpower on Moravian Creek near Moravian Falls when he erected an undershot waterwheel and installed a dynamo. Power from it provided light for his office and home and was used to operate his presses. Soon cornmeal and flour were produced at a mill he erected at the site. Laws eventually became the first publisher in the state to install a Hoe automatic, circular stereotype high-speed press.

The success of *The Yellow Jacket* made the community of Moravian Falls, which had a population of not over 250, a curious printing center. As many as eighteen publications, some of them amateur ventures, began there in the early twentieth century. North Carolina poet laureate James Larkin Pearson got his start in the printing business working for Laws, who was his brother-in-law. Other men, many of them related to Laws, began successful printing careers at *The Yellow Jacket*. Most of the young people in the community at one time or another worked for Laws, folding, addressing, printing, and doing other work to get out the newspaper.

In his later years Laws was a popular lecturer at schools in North Carolina and elsewhere where *The Yellow Jacket* was read. Much of his public speaking was centered on biblical and world history, and one of his most popular lectures was entitled "High Spots in History from Adam and Eve to Amos and Andy." Laws was also an organizer of the Deposit and Savings Bank in North Wilkesboro, while surveying and road construction were long-standing interests. In 1916 he was chairman of the Wilkes County Road Commission.

Laws continued to publish *The Yellow Jacket* until his death, but publication was interrupted for several months early in 1951, when one of his legs was amputated because of a blood clot. After he died, the *Journal-Patriot* in North Wilkesboro printed a few issues of *The Yellow Jacket* with Laws's daughter, Thelma, as editor.

Laws and his wife, Dora Carolina Wallace, had seven children: Barney Weaver, Shafter Robert, Thelma Margaret, Frances Amanda, Rose-Marie Jennings, Romulus Don, Jr., and Virginia Hairston. Laws was a lifelong supporter of the Moravian Falls Methodist Church, a member of the Republican party, and a Mason. He was buried in the Moravian Falls Cemetery.

SEE: John Crouch, *Historical Sketches of Wilkes County* (1902); R. Don Laws, Jr. (Moravian Falls), interview; James Larkin Pearson, "A History of Wilkes County Newspapers," in Johnson J. Hayes, *The Land of Wilkes* (1962); North Wilkesboro *Journal-Patriot*, 28 Oct. 1976, 22 Oct. 1987; *The Yellow Jacket*, October 1949.

JULE HUBBARD

Lawson, Hugh (*ca. 1697–1772*), pioneer settler of Rowan County and ancestor of statesmen and patriots, was the son of Roger Lawson of Cecil County, Md. Although the elder Lawson was living in Cecil County as early as 1712, neither the date nor the place of Hugh Lawson's birth are known. It may be inferred, however, that he was at least twenty-one by 1718, when he served as an agent or attorney in a Cecil County land transaction. Hugh Lawson, Gentleman, as he signed his name in later years, was typical of the settlers of more substantial means who moved southwards from Maryland and Pennsylvania to the Carolina Piedmont in the mid-eighteenth century. His descendants likewise were typical pioneers, for they continued the trek into the lower South, across the Appalachians, and as far west as Texas.

Lawson's progeny, however, was more distinguished than the average. A grandson, Jared Irwin (1750–1818), was twice governor of Georgia; another grandson, Hugh Lawson White (1773–1840), was a Tennessee jurist and a member of the U.S. Senate from that state for sixteen years; a great-grandson, James Pinckney Henderson (1808–58), was a diplomatic agent from the Republic of Texas to England and France, the first governor of Texas, a general in the Mexican War, and a U.S. senator from Texas. Another lineal descendant, Admiral James Harrison Oliver (1857–1928), was the first governor of the American Virgin Islands after they were acquired from Denmark in 1917. In addition to the impressive public service of these descendants, at least nine of Lawson's grandsons as well as his son Roger served as soldiers in the American Revolution.

If Hugh Lawson, the patriarch, could have foreseen the accomplishments of his breed, he might have even more confidently claimed the station of gentleman. But without such prescience, he could still survey his broad acres on the banks of Davidson Creek in 1764, the year when he made his will, and rejoice that he and his two sons and five daughters and their growing families were founding a new community. Moreover, he could recall that his father had first become a landowner in Cecil County not yet fifty years before and thereby laid the indispensable foundation for family position in colonial America.

It is not known when the Lawsons migrated to America and whether they came from Ulster. But in view of their settlement along the Maryland-Pennsylvania boundary in the midst of such staunch Presbyterian families as the Alexanders, Barrys, Brevards, and McDowells, all of whom would be neighbors or relatives of Hugh Lawson in North Carolina, it is almost certain that the Lawsons were Ulstermen, though Lawson is an English surname often associated with Yorkshire. The flood tide of Scotch-Irish emigration to America did not begin until the second decade of the eighteenth century, but a vanguard had reached Maryland and Virginia via the Chesapeake and the port of New Castle in Delaware by the late seventeenth century.

In this vanguard the name of Roger Lawson first appears in the records of Cecil County in 1712. Six years later in 1718, Charles Carroll deeded land in that county to Roger Lawson and other purchasers who apparently were already occupying land for which they had contracted several years earlier. In this 1718 transaction between Charles Carroll and Roger Lawson, the name of Hugh Lawson appears as Carroll's attorney or agent. Both Roger and Hugh Lawson were rising men by the 1720s. In 1724 Hugh Lawson was located at Milford Haven in Cecil County, and in 1740 he was a trooper in the Maryland militia. Roger Lawson in 1726 was an elder in the Upper Elk Presbyterian Church of the New Castle Presbytery. The Upper Elk Church (now known as the Rock Church) had been constituted in 1720 and was first located at the site of what is now the Stone Graveyard at Lewisville in Chester County, Pa., just across the boundary from Cecil County. In that original churchyard Elder Roger Lawson was buried in 1733. Neither the burial place nor the name of his wife, the mother of Hugh Lawson, are known.

In 1733 before his death, Roger Lawson deeded his lands in Cecil County to his three sons, Hugh, John, and George. Dower rights in Hugh's portion were held by his wife Margaret, who in 1749 agreed to the sale of the property. According to family tradition, Margaret Lawson was a Barry before her marriage. Hugh and Margaret Lawson remained until at least 1742 in Cecil County, where all of their children were probably born. Although he owned property in that county until 1749, Lawson in 1744 obtained a grant of 250 acres in Brunswick County, Va., and about that time moved south, probably over the Great Wagon Road through the Valley of Virginia, the road usually taken by emigrants to the backcountry.

The sturdy qualities of Hugh Lawson were soon recognized in Virginia, for when the new county of Lunenburg was formed from Brunswick in 1746, he became one of the first gentleman justices with a seat on the bench of the county court and served until 1756, which was about the time he moved to North Carolina. In colonial America as in England, the justice, who had important administrative and judicial responsibilities in local government, was generally a man of quality. In addition to Lawson's service as a justice, he was among those frequently designated to compile the lists of tithables for Lunenburg County, and in 1753 the Council of Virginia appointed him coroner for the county.

But despite his status as a Virginia justice, the ambitious Lawson looked beyond the Virginia Southside to the North Carolina Piedmont between the Catawba and Yadkin rivers, where old neighbors from Maryland, Pennsylvania, and Virginia, such as the Bakers, Brevards, Davidsons, McConnells, Osborns, and Whites, were settling in the 1740s and 1750s. Among these was the Reverend John Thomson, who went to that region of North Carolina as early as 1751. Thomson was a founder of the Buffalo settlement in Amelia County, Va., adjacent to Lunenburg County, and a pastor of the Buffalo Presbyterian Church as well as a former pastor of churches near Lawson's old home in Maryland. Moreover, Thomson's daughter Hannah married Roger Lawson, Hugh's older son, about 1752. While it was comforting to know that sound Presbyterian doctrine was being preached on the North Carolina frontier by his daughter-in-law's father, Hugh Lawson more likely was attracted to North Carolina by land and not by Presbyterianism or religious toleration, which in practice he had enjoyed both in Maryland and Virginia.

Sometime between 1749 and 1753, Lawson was granted 600 acres of land on the south side of Broad River in what was then a part of Anson County, N.C., but which became Rowan County in 1753. He began negotiations on 27 May 1756 for a second grant of land in North Carolina. This grant of 552 acres from Earl Granville was located on both sides of Davidson Creek a few miles from the Catawba River in that part of Rowan County that became Iredell County in 1788. Although this tract was not granted to Lawson until 22 Feb. 1759, he was apparently occupying the land by 1757, for in July of that year he witnessed a will in Rowan and in December he was named attorney or executor for his friend Samuel Baker of the same county. Lawson's son Roger preceded his father to Rowan County, where in 1753 he obtained land on Fourth Creek by the will of his father-in-law, the Reverend John Thomson. Roger's location on Fourth Creek probably caused Hugh Lawson not to settle on his Broad River lands, which lay much farther west, but to obtain land on Davidson Creek instead. He could have also been influenced by the fact that his son-in-law Thomas Irwin had been granted land in 1754 on Mc-

Dowells Creek in Rowan County not far from Roger Lawson's holding.

Whether Hugh Lawson's wife Margaret was still living when he settled in North Carolina is not known, but she was dead when he made his will in 1764. In addition to his son Roger, there was a younger son named Hugh who married Rebecca McConnell. There were also five daughters: Rebecca (m. Thomas Irwin), Catherine (m. George Ewing), Margaret (m. Hugh Barry), Violet (m. James Henderson), and Mary (m. James White).

Although he had served in Virginia as a justice, Lawson never held any office in North Carolina. Already approaching an advanced age for his time when he became a North Carolinian, he apparently directed most of his attention to increasing his worldly possessions, which his will indicates were considerable for that section of North Carolina. Token sums of five shillings were left to each of his four sons-in-law as well as to his son Roger, who by 1764 had moved to Georgia along with Hugh Lawson's daughter Rebecca and her husband Thomas Irwin. The token bequests suggest that he had already given portions to Roger and the married daughters. Provision was made in Lawson's will for his then unmarried daughter Mary, and the remainder of the estate was left to his younger son, Hugh, Jr. In 1767 Lawson was listed as having four slaves. While there is no record of his having been involved in the Regulator crisis, it is possible that as a man of considerable property whose neighbor, Colonel Alexander Osborn, opposed the Regulators in 1768, he frowned on the rioters in Rowan County.

As Hugh Lawson neared the end of his more than three score and ten years, he had witnessed the settling of the North Carolina frontier between the Yadkin and Catawba rivers for nearly two decades. Not only had he observed at first hand the migration of pioneers into a virgin territory, but also he had seen the growth of families and landholdings, both his and others. Some of the land would remain in the possession of his descendants for two centuries until it was covered by the waters of Lake Norman. Lawson had also seen in his immediate neighborhood the beginning in 1760 of a classical school, the Crowfield Academy, and the organization in 1765 of Centre Presbyterian Church. He died aware that a hardy pioneer stock had taken firm root in the North Carolina Piedmont. It is fitting that Lawson's dust found a final resting place in the churchyard of Centre after lying undisturbed for nearly two centuries in Baker's Graveyard, which was flooded by the Catawba River impounded at Cowan's Ford Dam. Nearby were buried the Reverend John Thomson and many other friends and relatives. A fragment of the slate marker on Lawson's original grave with the crudely joined letters "HL" has been carefully preserved at the base of a new gravestone to the memory of "Hugh Lawson, Gentleman and Ancestor of Patriots."

SEE: Landon C. Bell, *The Old Free State*, 2 vols. (1927); *Cecil County: A Reference Book of History, Business, and General Information* (1956); Deed Books of Cecil County, Md. (Cecil County Courthouse, Elkton); Deed Books, Inferior Court Minutes, and Will Books of Rowan County (Rowan County Courthouse, Salisbury); *Executive Journals, Council of Colonial Virginia, November 1, 1739– May 7, 1754*, vol. 5 (1945); J. H. Johns, *History of Rock Presbyterian Church* (1872); George Johnston, *History of Cecil County, Maryland* (1881); North Carolina Land Grant Records (North Carolina State Archives, Raleigh); Robert W. Ramsey, *Carolina Cradle: Settlement of the North West Carolina Frontier, 1747–1762* (1964); Jethro Rumple, *A History of Rowan County, North Carolina* (1881).

MALCOLM LESTER

Lawson, John (27 Dec. 1674–16 Sept. 1711), explorer, surveyor, and author of *A New Voyage to Carolina* (London, 1709), was apparently the only son of Dr. John Lawson (1632–ca. 1690) and his wife [Isabella] Love (ca. 1643–ca. 1680). The father was a member of St. Bennet's Church, Gracechurch Street, London, and his mother of St. Andrew's Church, Holborn. Dr. Lawson was a grandnephew of Vice-Admiral Sir John Lawson of Scarborough, Yorkshire. The family owned estates in the vicinity of Kingston-on-Hull, Yorkshire, where it is likely young Lawson first attended Anglican schools, followed by lectures at Gresham College near the family's London residence. At Gresham an endowment supported the teaching of astronomy, geometry, physics, law, divinity, and other subjects, while the natural sciences, mathematics, inventions, travel, and discoveries were subjects of special interest. It was also the usual meeting place of the Royal Society, dedicated to the pursuit and advancement of scientific methods of developing and verifying knowledge in the natural sciences. Membership in the society was elective, based on a demonstration of merit. Lawson apparently yearned to accomplish something so notable that he would be chosen for membership.

Lawson wrote that he met with a "gentleman" who had been abroad and who was familiar with much of the New World. When questioned, he suggested that Carolina was the best country for Lawson to visit, and it just happened that there was a ship about ready to sail there. Although Lawson did not name his informant, there is evidence that it was either Christopher Gale, a native of Yorkshire and an official in the northern part of Carolina, or James Moore, from Charles Town, then in London seeking the governorship. Moore was already a friend of Lawson, and he gave him free passage on the ship that he owned which was about to sail for Carolina. Moore also became Lawson's host and introduced him to the area after they arrived on 15 Aug. 1700.

A London botanist and apothecary, James Petiver, had recently published a notice seeking someone to collect American specimens for him, and Lawson volunteered to do this without charge. Thirty of the specimens that he sent still survive in the Sloane collection at the British Museum. Lawson proved to be an unusually keen naturalist. In South Carolina, James Moore had worked to improve relations with the Indians and had won the friendship and support of many of the tribes in the southern regions of Carolina. His experience, which he discussed with Lawson, was the source of useful information.

From Charles Town on 28 Dec. 1700, Lawson set off on a 57-day swing through the backcountry of what is now the two Carolinas. Accompanied by five other young Englishmen with Yorkshire backgrounds, three Indian men, and the wife of one the Indians, he continued his horseshoe-shaped trek of around 550 miles until arriving at the Pamlico River near Bath on 24 Feb. 1701. (On 8 February, however, some of his party left and went into Virginia.) After remaining briefly along the Pamlico, Lawson built a house on some high ground near a creek, still known as Lawson Creek, about half a mile from the Indian town of Chattoka at the site of modern New Bern. He shared the house, at least for a time, with William Kirk, apparently a nephew from Portsmouth, England. From here Lawson continued to travel, among other places, to Roanoke Island, where he observed the remains of the fort built by Sir Walter Raleigh's colonists in the 1580s. He also explored the uninhabited land up to "the Ledges of Mountains" and even visited Virginia, where he called on people with interests similar to his own. He probably also went as far as Philadelphia.

In January 1707 Lawson became clerk of the court and public register of the county; in the same year he and two other men (one of whom was his friend Christopher Gale) established a gristmill. Having worked privately as a surveyor, and after 1705 as a deputy surveyor, in 1708 he became the official surveyor for the Lords Proprietors and in 1709 published a map of Carolina.

After returning from his first expedition through the Piedmont region of the colony, Lawson acquired considerable land, some by purchase and some through a grant, so he was interested in the settlement of Carolina. On 8 Mar. 1706 (new style) the Assembly incorporated the town of Bath on the banks of the Pamlico River; it was on land owned by Lawson and two other men that this first town in the northern part of Carolina was established. As a surveyor Lawson laid it out, and by late September thirteen lots had been sold.

At this time there were some 13,000 foreign Protestant refugees in and around London, many of whom were French Huguenots. Recently a colony of Huguenots had been living along the Appomattox River in Virginia in a region that did not entirely please them and they were looking for a new location. About the same time, a Swiss land company headed by Baron Christoph von Graffenried, acquired title to a large tract of land near the mouth of the Neuse River. John Lawson and his friends undertook to encourage the settlement of these assorted people in their vicinity. The land company soon engaged Lawson's services to lay out another town and make preparations for the arrival of settlers.

During his exploration of the interior of Carolina in 1700 and 1701, Lawson kept a journal. Afterwards, in whatever leisure time he had, he began to prepare it for publication as well as to add further information based on his subsequent discoveries and observations. On 9 Feb. 1709 he and others, including some officials of the colony, went to Hampton, Va., from where they sailed for England. Lawson's purpose was to arrange for the printing of the book he had written as well as to discuss with the Lords Proprietors plans for the settlement of a group of refugees in North Carolina.

Perhaps the first business attended to was the publication of his manuscript. John Stevens, veteran of James II's army in Ireland and a renowned translator, scholar, and publisher (or perhaps editor is a better term), promptly accepted Lawson's work for an anthology that he was publishing serially, entitled *A New Collection of Voyages and Travels. With Historical Accounts of Discoveries and Conquest In all Parts of the World.* The April 1709 issue contained the first installment of Lawson's manuscript. Stevens apparently thought so highly of it that he interrupted another continued account to rush it into print. He explained to his readers that this was necessary because Lawson would soon be returning to America. There is evidence that Lawson edited the work as type was being set.

Extra copies of the printed parts were held by the printer, and when the series was completed they were issued with a title page as *A New Voyage to Carolina; Containing the Exact Description and Natural History of that Country: Together with the Present State therof. And A Journal of a Thousand miles travel'd thro' several Nations of Indi-*

ans. *Giving a particular Account of their Customs, Manners, &c.* In 1711 Lawson's work also appeared in the two-volume compilation of Stevens's *New Collection of Voyages and Travels.* The printer continued to hold unbound sets of pages, and as the need arose he printed new title pages with new dates (in 1714 and 1718) and the title was changed to *The History of Carolina.* He simply bound up as many copies as were needed. Editions in German were printed in Hamburg in 1709 and 1722.

This work has come to be regarded as a classic of early American literature, and the detailed information it recorded of native Americans and the natural history of the region is highly treasured. Among other interesting compilations, there is a lengthy list of words in different Indian dialects. The first part of the book contains Lawson's journal, followed by separate sections devoted to a description of North Carolina geography, produce, insects, animals, and fish, and of the Indians. While nearly everything that Lawson recorded was based on his own observation, a careful reading of some of the material in *The Discoveries of John Lederer* and in Richard Hakluyt's *Voyages* suggests that he relied on the writings of Lederer, Thomas Harriot, Giovanni da Verrazano, and other explorers who preceded him to the region.

Lawson arrived back in North Carolina on 27 Apr. 1710 accompanying some three hundred Palatines to be settled in the second town that he laid out, New Bern. Von Graffenried and additional settlers soon arrived; the town developed, and farmland was cleared in the surrounding countryside. Lawson continued to work as a surveyor and explored the surrounding region. In London, the Lords Proprietors named Lawson and Edward Moseley to a commission to serve with Virginia representatives in surveying the line between Virginia and North Carolina. Several meetings were held and Lawson made some observations as to where the line should be, but no agreement could be reached.

Relations with the Indians deteriorated. They resented whites' intrusion on their hunting grounds, as well as seeing their women and children kidnapped and enslaved, and being cheated by traders. In the late summer of 1711, Lawson and von Graffenried planned a trip up the Neuse River from New Bern to try to discover its source. They hoped that it might be a waterway that would provide a route for trade with Virginia. But their expedition was halted by a large group of Tuscarora Indians who took them prisoner and held them for a time before releasing von Graffenried, thinking he was the governor. Lawson, however, was put to death. A few days later the Tuscarora launched an attack on most of the white settlements and came very close to ending the occupation of their land.

Lawson had a spouse. His will, made in Bath County on 12 Aug. 1708, referred to her in strong terms of affection and provided her with a life interest in certain real estate and personal property. He also mentioned Isabella Lawson, his daughter by "my dearly beloved Hannah Smith," and "the child or children with which she is now pregnant by me." This will was written four days after Lawson and Louis Michel, one of the new settlers at New Bern, departed from the meeting at Manakin town in Virginia at which they completed plans to sail for London the following January. Isabella, born on or about 15 Apr. 1707, was further provided for by her father. On 4 July, in her name, he bought large tracts of land totaling about 520 acres, had the deeds made directly to her, and paid for the land the same day. The child or children expected when the will was made did not survive. Isabella married John Chilley in 1727, they had children and grandchildren, and she was still living in 1790.

After Lawson's death, William Kirk asserted the role of next of kin and heir at law. He sold Lawson's house in New Bern and also detained from Lawson's executrix the personal possessions of the deceased, including a "hair trunk" with Lawson's diary and other writings.

There is a pen-and-ink sketch of Lawson made by Michel in the Burgerbibliotek, Berne, Switzerland.

SEE: Geo. L. Armytage, ed., *Allegations for Marriage Licenses Issued by the Dean and Chapter of Westminster* (1886); Bath County Precinct Records, 1665–1729 (North Carolina State Archives, Raleigh); British Public Record Office, Records relating to Carolina and Virginia, 1607–1774 (microfilm, North Carolina State Archives, Raleigh); A. W. Hughes Clarke, ed., *Register of St. Dunstan's in the East* (1939); E. Bruce Kirkham, "The First English Editions of John Lawson's 'Voyage to Carolina': A Bibliographical Study," *Papers of the Bibliographical Society of America* 61 (3d quarter, 1967); Hugh T. Lefler, ed., *A New Voyage to Carolina by John Lawson* (1967); Charles B. Norcliffe, ed., *Visitations of Yorkshire* (1881); Dorothy Stimson, *Scientists and Amateurs: A History of the Royal Society* (1948); Vincent H. Todd, ed., *Christoph von Graffenried's Account of the Founding of New Bern* (1920); Louis B. Wright, ed., *The Prose Works of William Byrd* (1966).

CHARLES R. HOLLOMAN

Lay, George William (*26 Feb. 1860–12 Aug. 1932*), clergyman and educator, was born in Huntsville, Ala., the son of Bishop Henry Champlin and Eliza Withers Atkinson Lay. He received his early education at St. Paul's preparatory school, Concord, N.H., and was graduated from Yale University in 1882 and from the General Theological Seminary in 1886. The University of the South awarded him the D.C.L. degree in 1915. An Episcopalian, he was ordained to the diaconate in 1885 and to the priesthood in 1886.

Lay was rector of churches in Pennsylvania and New York until 1888, when he returned to St. Paul's in Concord as master, a position he held until 1907. He also served as secretary of the board of missions of the Diocese of New Hampshire from 1895 to 1907. In the latter year he became rector of St. Mary's School in Raleigh. Under his leadership, the school greatly enlarged its physical plant and raised its educational standards. Highly appreciated by the student body, he remained for eleven years. After a short period of service at Christ Church in Springfield, Mass., Lay became rector of St. Paul's Church in Beaufort, N.C. In 1928 he retired and moved to Chapel Hill.

He consistently attended diocesan conventions, even after his retirement, and for a time was chairman of the committee on canons. The improvement of public health was one of his concerns, and to this end he was the author of a small publication, *The Sanitary Privy*. He also wrote *Some Dangers in Specialization* and *Ye Are the Light of the World*. He was a member of the North Carolina Academy of Sciences and contributed to the *Elisha Mitchell Scientific Society Journal*.

In 1894 Lay married Anna Booth Balch of Baltimore. They were the parents of three sons, one of whom died young, and five daughters. He was buried in Chapel Hill, the home of his daughter Elizabeth (Mrs. Paul Green).

SEE: *Journal of the 48th Convention of the Episcopal Church, Diocese of East Carolina* (1931); *North Carolina Biography*, vol. 4 (1919); Thomas M. Owen, *History of Alabama and Dictionary of Alabama Biography*, vol. 4 (1921); Raleigh *News and Observer*, 13 Aug. 1932.

CHARLES S. POWELL

Lazarus, Rachel Mordecai (*1 July 1788–23 June 1838*), teacher and correspondent of author Maria Edgeworth, was born in Goochland County, Va., the daughter of Jacob and Judith Myers Mordecai. At age four, she moved with her parents to Warrenton, N.C., where her father was engaged in the mercantile business. After her mother's death in 1796, Rachel, along with some of her brothers and sisters, lived with her aunt in Richmond, Va., where she was educated. When her father opened a school at Warrenton in 1809, Rachel became one of the teachers as well as the general directress.

In preparing herself for teaching, Rachel Mordecai was greatly influenced by the works of Richard Lovell Edgeworth and his daughter Maria, in particular *The Parent's Assistant* (1796), *Practical Education* (1798), and *Early Lessons* (1801). At the time of their appearance, the ideas incorporated in these volumes were considered revolutionary, with their deemphasis of a classical, prescriptive education for children and their advocacy of encouraging the curiosity of children in natural and scientific phenomena. In one of her *Tales of Fashionable Life*, "The Absentee" (1812), Maria Edgeworth depicted a Jewish London coach maker in the clichéd characterization of Shylock; his name was Mordecai. On 7 Aug. 1815 Rachel Mordecai wrote the celebrated author a gentle letter of reproof, saying that happily her family had not experienced in either Virginia or North Carolina the prejudice against Jews evidenced in British literature. Richard Lovell Edgeworth immediately replied, commending the young teacher, and Maria Edgeworth attempted to make amends by writing *Harrington* (1817), a novel with a Jewish heroine. The result was a correspondence between Rachel Mordecai and Maria Edgeworth that grew into a remarkable commentary on literature, domestic customs, politics, and scientific inventions that lasted until Rachel's death. (Members of the two families continued to correspond until the mid twentieth century.) This literary friendship stimulated a wide range of interests in Rachel Mordecai, and while she led a relatively quiet life in Wilmington, N.C., she was undoubtedly one of the best educated women in the state during her time.

In 1821 she married Aaron Lazarus, a native of Charleston, S.C., but a resident of Wilmington, where he was engaged in the shingle and naval stores business. Lazarus was a widower with seven children, some of whom had attended the Mordecai School in Warrenton. Besides her household duties, Rachel Mordecai Lazarus concerned herself with the education of her stepchildren and her own four: Marx Edgeworth (b. 6 Feb. 1822), Ellen (b. 13 July 1825), Mary Catherine (b. 12 Sept. 1828), and Julia Judith (b. 9 Oct. 1830). Her son attended The University of North Carolina in 1838 and later studied medicine in Philadelphia. In later years, along with his sisters Ellen and Julia, he became involved in reform and social movements, and all three were considered eccentric by other members of their family.

As Rachel Mordecai Lazarus was traveling from Wilmington to Richmond to see her invalid father in 1838, she stopped in Petersburg to visit her brother Samuel. There she suddenly became ill and died. In her last moments she was converted to Christianity and was buried in Blandford Cemetery.

SEE: Caroline Cohen, *Records of the Myers, Hays and Mordecai Families from 1707 to 1913* (n.d.); Manuscript Collection (North Carolina State Archives, Raleigh); Lizzie Wilson Montgomery, *Sketches of Old Warrenton, North Carolina* (1924); Ellen Mordecai, *Gleanings from Long Ago* (1933); Gratz Mordecai, *Notice of Jacob Mordecai, Founder and Proprietor from 1809 to 1819 of the Warrenton Female Seminary* (1897).

EDGAR EDGEWORTH MACDONALD

Lea, Luke (*12 Apr. 1879–18 Nov. 1945*), newspaper editor and publisher, U.S. senator, financier, attorney, and World War I hero, was born at the family ancestral home in Nashville, Tenn., the son of Overton and Ella Cocke Lea. His paternal and maternal ancestors were of prominent North Carolina and Tennessee families. His great-grandfather, Luke Lea, served in the U.S. House of Representatives. Educated by private tutors in his home and at the University of the South at Sewanee, he received a bachelor of arts degree in 1899 and a master's degree in 1900. He was graduated from the law school at Columbia University and began to practice law in Nashville in 1903.

In 1907 Lea founded the *Nashville Tennessean*, of which he was editor and publisher. Becoming a dominant force in politics, he reached the peak of his influence in 1911, when the legislature became hopelessly deadlocked in the naming of a U.S. senator. Lea, a Democrat, was selected as an advocate of prohibition and elected, taking his seat on 4 Mar. 1911 at age thirty-three. Although involved in the political battles of his home state from the outset, he was unsuccessful in his bid for renomination in 1916. His senate term ended on 3 Mar. 1917. Lea was a vigorous foe of the E. H. Crump organization. He continued to be influential politically until the collapse of his publishing and financial empires in 1930.

After leaving the senate, Lea returned to Nashville and organized a volunteer military outfit which, on 6 Apr. 1917, became the First Tennessee Field Artillery. With the rank of lieutenant colonel, he was its commander until 18 October when he became colonel of this regiment of the Thirtieth Division in World War I. An imposing military figure, colorful and daring, Lea led the all-volunteer regiment in many battles. During the lull just after the armistice and the kaiser's abdication, he and a group of younger officers made a bold trip to Holland to capture the kaiser at his retreat. They got to the doorway of the retreat, but the coup attempt failed when the kaiser refused to turn himself over to Lea and his officers. The episode became an international incident, Holland protesting that its neutrality had been violated. Colonel Lea received the Distinguished Service Medal before his discharge on 12 Apr. 1919.

Returning to Nashville as a war hero, he resumed his newspaper interests, expanded his financial holdings, and continued his political organization. The financial panic of 1930 took its heavy toll, ending his publishing and financial empires and crumbling the political organization that had dominated Tennessee politics. Lea was charged with violating the banking laws of North Carolina for his involvement with the failed Central Bank and Trust Company in Asheville. In a dramatic trial in Buncombe County Superior Court in August 1931, he, along with several others, was sentenced to prison. The North Carolina Supreme Court subsequently denied a motion for appeal, and the U.S. Supreme Court refused to review the case. Lea was extradited to North Carolina and served a prison sentence in Raleigh from 10 May 1934 until 2 Apr. 1936, when he was paroled. A year

later he was given a full pardon. Many people felt that the crisis of the times had harshly singled out financial leaders, one of whom was Lea. On returning to Nashville, he was again given a hero's welcome: he was met by the mayor and driven into the city behind an escort of motorcycle policemen. While in Raleigh he was considered a model prisoner. He asked permission to sleep near the prison hospital ward so that he could attend to the sick inmates at night. The day of his discharge from prison, he was accompanied by several prominent North Carolinians who had known him during the war and during his trial.

Personal tragedy dogged him throughout life. While en route home from France he learned that his wife had died, and during his imprisonment his mother died and one of his sons was killed in an automobile accident. His first marriage was to Mary Louise Warner on 1 Nov. 1906. They had two sons: Luke, Jr., and Percy Warner. On 1 May 1920, he married Percie Warner, the sister of his first wife. They had three children: Mary Louise (m. Cromwell Tidwell), Laura (m. William N. Knox), and a son, Overton. Lea's second wife died on 7 May 1976 in Nashville. The Leas were members of the Episcopal church. In addition to their other accomplishments, they were known for their philanthropy.

After a brief period of declining health, Lea died at Vanderbilt Hospital. Burial was in Mount Olivet Cemetery, Nashville.

SEE: *Asheville Citizen*, scattered issues; *Asheville Citizen-Times*, 26 Aug. 1931, 29 Apr. 1934; John Berry, *Caldwell and Company: A Southern Financial Empire* (1969); *Biog. Dir. Am. Cong.* (1961); *Greensboro Daily News*, 15 Mar. 1933; *Nashville Banner*, 5 May 1950; *Nashville Tennessean*, 19 Nov. 1945 (portrait); *Tarheel Banker* 10, no. 4 (1931), 11, no. 7 (1933); *Who Was Who in America*, vol. 2 (1967).

T. HARRY GATTON

Lea, Solomon (*21 Nov. 1807–30 Apr. 1897*), Methodist minister and educator, was born in Leasburg, the son of William, a merchant and a county sheriff, and Sarah McNeil Lea. He was a descendant of James Lea, of King and Queen County, Va., a pioneer settler of Caswell County and a founder of Leasburg. Solomon's brothers, Lorenzo Dow and Addison, were also Methodist ministers. Lea was reared in Leasburg and attended The University of North Carolina, where he received an A.B. degree in 1833. He was awarded an A.M. degree in 1838.

Beginning in 1834, Lea taught for a year in the Warrenton Academy. There he met Sophia Ainger (1810–66), a native of England and a music teacher in the school, whom he married in 1837. Leaving Warrenton, he accepted a teaching position in the preparatory department of Randolph Macon College in Boydton, Va., where he remained until 1841, when he became president of Farmville Female School, also in Virginia.

On 1 Feb. 1846 Lea became the first president of Greensboro Female College in Greensboro, N.C. This new Methodist institution was the first chartered women's college in North Carolina and the second in the South. In addition to serving as president, he was professor of mathematics and ancient languages. Sophia Lea taught modern languages and was principal of the music department. Lea resigned from his position in December 1847 because of difficulties with a faculty member and lack of support from the trustees.

From Greensboro the Leas returned to Leasburg; here they resided for the rest of their lives except for two years when Solomon taught in Shelby, Tenn. In 1848 Lea opened the Somerville Female Institute, a preparatory school that gained a wide reputation for quality secondary education. His interest in astronomy led to naming the school for Miss Mary Somerville, a noted Scottish mathematician and astronomer. At its height, the institute employed four teachers and enrolled between fifty and seventy-five students from several states; Sophia Lea taught music until her death in 1866. Solomon operated the school for forty-four years, until declining health forced him to close it in 1892. In 1848 he had been licensed by the Methodist church to preach. Although he held no regular pastorates, he assisted on the Leasburg circuit for over fifty years and was in demand as a guest minister.

Solomon and Sophia Lea had six daughters and two sons, one of whom died in infancy. The surviving children were Annis Sophia, Lilyanne, Wilhelmina, Adeline, Eugenia, Henrietta, and Edward W. Wilhelmina studied music and taught for many years in the Somerville Female Institute and at Louisburg College.

SEE: Daniel L. Grant, *Alumni History of the University of North Carolina, 1795–1924* (1924); R. Irby, *History of Randolph-Macon College, Virginia* (1898); Lea Papers (Southern Historical Collection, University of North Carolina, Chapel Hill); N. C. Newbold, "Rev. Solomon Lea," *Trinity Archives* (February 1898); F. P. Otken, comp., "The Lea Family," Charles Lee Raper Scrapbook, and Frank L. Reid Papers (Manuscript Department, Duke University Library, Durham); William S. Powell, *When the Past Refused to Die: A History of Caswell County* (1977 [portrait]); Raleigh *Star*, 10 Jan. 1834; S. B. Turrentine, *A Romance of Education* (1946).

LINDLEY S. BUTLER

Leach, James Madison Brown (*17 Jan. 1815–1 June 1891*), lawyer, congressman, and advocate of education and internal improvements, was born at the family home, Lansdowne, in Randolph County, the son of William and Nancy Brown Leach. (He eventually dropped Brown as his third given name.) He attended the Caldwell Institute in Greensboro and entered the U.S. Military Academy in 1836 but resigned in 1838. Returning home, he studied law under his brother, Julian Elder.

Leach supported community efforts to establish a larger school to replace Brown's School House, built by his uncle John Brown. In 1839 he served on the committee that drew up a constitution for it, and he became secretary of the local educational society. Leach became a trustee of the new Union Institute Academy and delivered the address at the laying of the cornerstone of the building. He also spoke on education throughout the region to attract support for the school. In time, the institute became a normal school and still later Trinity College. The college was moved to Durham, and in 1924 Trinity became Duke University.

Leach was admitted to the bar in 1842 and established a practice in Lexington, where he remained for the rest of his life. His renown as a defense lawyer, particularly in murder cases, spread far and wide. Of his seventy-one murder cases, it is said that he lost only one—the first. Stories about his victories and unusual methods on behalf of his clients were widely related both during his lifetime and afterwards. The *Greensborough Patriot* included reports on the quickness of his rapierlike repartee to hecklers on the hustings. He was much in demand as a political speaker and as a maker of policies. In 1974 master raconteur Senator Sam Ervin, Jr., broadcast one of the stories about Leach over the radio.

Early in his career, Leach had important connections in the nation's capital; his oldest brother, Martin W. Leach, was the son-in-law of Senator Willie P. Mangum, for some years president of the Senate. The younger Leach made local arrangements for the senator to speak in North Carolina.

As a Whig, Leach served from 1848 until 1857 in the North Carolina House of Commons where he advocated the causes of education and internal improvements, the outstanding legislation being the Railroad Act of 1849. In 1856 he was a Fillmore elector for his district. Two years later he was unanimously nominated by his party to run in a Democratic district for the U.S. House of Representatives against the incumbent and was elected by a large majority. In Congress from 1859 to 1861, he opposed secession and both spoke and voted against it.

Leach happened to be in the mountains speaking against secession when he heard of Abraham Lincoln's call on North Carolina for troops. Returning home immediately, he raised a company of more than a hundred men to fight for the South. He was elected captain of the company, but on its organization he became lieutenant colonel of the Twenty-first Regiment, North Carolina Troops. He fought at the Battle of Manassas and elsewhere until he resigned on 23 Dec. 1861 (perhaps because of his age) and returned home. In 1864–65 he was a member of the Confederate Congress and introduced a joint resolution approving the appointment of General Robert E. Lee as general-in-chief and recommending that he be vested with the power to treat for peace. From 1865 to 1868, Leach served in the state senate and was chairman of the committee that reported the rejection of the Fourteenth Amendment to the U.S. Constitution.

As a Conservative Leach served in the Forty-second and the Forty-third Congress (1871–75) but declined to seek a third term. He was presidential elector for the state-at-large in 1876 on the Tilden-Hendricks ticket and in 1880 on the Hancock ticket, both times being president of the electoral college. During these campaigns he spoke in most of the counties of North Carolina as well as in at least ten in South Carolina, contributing to the return of the Conservatives to power in that state. Leach served a final term in the General Assembly when he was senator from Davidson County in 1879–80. This time he was chairman of the committee of the special session called in 1880 to consider the sale of the state-owned Western North Carolina Railroad to a New York syndicate.

Leach served in the state militia where he became a major general. He came to be routinely referred to as General Leach, and he never lost an election. In 1846 he married Elizabeth Lewis Montgomery, daughter of the pastor of the Presbyterian church in Lexington; they became the parents of three daughters and four sons, but all except James Madison, Jr., died young. This son joined his father in the practice of law. Leach died in Lexington and was buried in the Hopewell Church cemetery near the old family homestead.

SEE: *Biog. Dir. Am. Cong.* (1961); Nora Campbell Chaffin, *Trinity College, 1839–1892: The Beginnings of Duke University* (1950); John L. Cheney, Jr., ed., *North Carolina Government, 1585–1979* (1981); Deeds and other documents (Register of Deeds Office, Davidson County, Lexington); Jerome Dowd, *Prominent Living North Carolinians* (1888); Family records (possession of James Hoover, Thomasville); *Greensborough Patriot* (1839–79); *Journal* of the North Carolina House of Commons (1848–58); *Journal* of the North Carolina Senate (1865–68, 1879–80); Minutes of Davidson County Court of Pleas and Quarter Sessions, 1842–80 (North Carolina State Archives,

Raleigh); Raleigh *Christian Advocate*, June 1890; Henry T. Shanks, ed., *Papers of Willie Person Mangum*, 5 vols. (1950–56); Jessie Owen Shaw, *Johnsons and Their Kin of Randolph* (1955); M. Jewell Sink and Mary G. Matthews, *Pathfinders, Past and Present: A History of Davidson County, North Carolina* (1972); Stephen B. Weeks, "Biographical Sketch of James Madison Leach" (Van Noppen Papers, Manuscript Department, Duke University Library, Durham).

M. JEWELL SINK

Leach, James Thomas (*1805–28 Mar. 1883*), attorney, physician, and Confederate congressman, was born in the present-day Cleveland township of Johnston County. His grandfather, Dr. Thomas Leach, had lived in Bertie and Dobbs counties before the Revolution. After serving as a surgeon in that conflict, Thomas settled in Johnston County. In 1803 his son, John Thomas Leach, married Susannah Carter Parham of Mecklenburg County, Va. They established Leachburg Plantation near the Wake County line and with their slaves built a large log home. It was here that their son, James Thomas, was born, according to family tradition, "in a snowstorm."

Family tradition also maintains that Leach studied law in Europe and at Rutgers College, but no record of any such attendance has been found. Soon, however, his admiration for his grandfather persuaded him to study medicine and he entered the Jefferson Medical School in Philadelphia. In 1833 he married Elizabeth Willis Boddie Sanders, whose family had resided near Smithfield since before the Revolution. The young couple built a home on Leachburg Plantation, where for the remainder of his life Leach practiced both law and medicine. He also gradually bought all the remaining shares of Leachburg inherited by his brothers and sisters; according to the census of 1860, he owned forty-seven slaves and an estate valued at $53,200.

Leach was a community leader in other ways. Out of charity, he took into his sixteen-room home several orphaned boys and two destitute maiden ladies. For a while he maintained a school in his home, but later he built schoolhouses in the community for his and the neighborhood children. He also spent much time instructing his neighbors in better farming methods, urging them in particular to aim towards self-sufficiency.

An old-line Whig, Leach in 1858 was elected to one term in the state senate, where he served on the committee on claims and on the joint committee on finance. He was a candidate for the House of Commons in 1862 but this time was defeated. During the secession crisis, Leach was a confirmed Unionist and opposed secession even after Abraham Lincoln's call for volunteers in April 1861. In 1863 he campaigned fiercely against three Confederate enthusiasts for a place in the Confederate House of Representatives. He pledged to seek "a just, honorable and lasting peace" and won handily.

In the Confederate Congress, Leach served on the committees on post offices and post roads and on territories and public lands. On the floor his unbridled antagonism to "reckless legislation . . . endorsed by the President and the mighty strides toward a military despotism" (Raleigh *Weekly Standard*, 13 Jan. 1864) placed him among the extreme malcontents. He voted to override every veto, to impugn the competence of every cabinet member so charged, and to oppose every major administration war measure. When President Jefferson Davis refused to open peace negotiations, Leach urged separate state action on the best terms available.

Leach apparently avoided the loss of any property after the war, for Branson's *Business Directory* for 1872 lists

him as owning 2,900 acres of land. He was now an active prohibitionist and in 1875 resigned his place on the board of county commissioners rather than certify anyone as a "qualified" barroom operator. He also served as a director of the state asylum for a number of years.

Leach was a man of strong opinions and a fiery and sarcastic speaker. When Richmond newspaper editors criticized his opposition to the Davis administration, he publicly declared that he wanted the editors "Dead, dead, dead!" (Richmond *Daily Examiner*, 23 Nov. 1864). He was a long-standing Mason and Methodist. Leach and his wife had eight children: John Sanders, James Thomas, Jr., Elizabeth Mary, Nancy Temperance, Claudius Brock, Sarah Louenza, Cornelia Susan, and Delia Ida. He died at home and was buried in the family cemetery near Mount Zion Church.

SEE: Levi Branson, *North Carolina Business Directory* (1872); Mrs. J. C. Ferguson (Raleigh), personal contact; *Journal of the Congress of the Confederate States of America*, 7 vols. (1904–5); *Journal of the Senate . . . of North Carolina, 1858–59*; J. T. Leach Papers (Southern Historical Collection, University of North Carolina, Chapel Hill); "Proceedings of the Confederate Congress," *Southern Historical Society Papers* 51 (March 1959); Raleigh *North Carolina Standard*, 1863–65; Richmond *Daily Examiner*, 1864–65; U.S. Census, 1840–60.

BUCK YEARNS

Leake, Walter Francis (*26 Mar. 1799–28 Apr. 1879*), lawyer, politician, and textile manufacturer, was born in Richmond County, the son of Walter and Judith Leake. Growing up in the county, he attended local schools and was enrolled at The University of North Carolina in 1815–16; he was a trustee of the university from 1846 to 1868, and in 1847, when President James K. Polk was on campus, Leake participated in the oral examination of some of the students prior to their graduation. Returning home in 1816, he studied law and farmed. He was a delegate to the reform convention that met in Raleigh in November 1823 to discuss the needs of western North Carolina for constitutional reform. In 1831–32 he was a member of the North Carolina House of Commons, and in 1832–33 he served in the senate.

In 1840, as chairman of his Democratic district convention, Leake was directed to write President Martin Van Buren to determine his attitude as a presidential candidate towards slavery. Leake pointed out that "Southern Democrats . . . will not support any man for the Presidency, who does not give the South Satisfactory assurances, that he is opposed to the bold and mischievous movements of the Abolitionists." In 1844 he attended the Democratic National Convention in Baltimore that nominated his fellow North Carolinian and friend from college days, James K. Polk, for president. Leake was considered for appointment as ambassador to Cuba and to Brazil but withdrew his name from consideration for the former and the latter did not become available. In 1846 and again in 1857, he was a candidate for his party's nomination for governor but was defeated. In 1861, however, he represented Richmond County in the Secession Convention.

Leake is best known for laying the foundation for the textile growth of Richmond County. Perhaps his most notable accomplishment was the establishment of the Richmond Mill, the first cotton mill in Richmond County and the fifth in the state. It was chartered in 1833 with him as president. The mill was burned in 1865, when General William T. Sherman's troops invaded the state, but in 1869 a new mill, Great Falls

Manufacturing Company, began operation with Leake as president, a post he held until his death. As late as 1945, when the first textile mills were sold to outside interests, all but one of the eight textile mills in the county were being operated by Leake's descendants.

Leake's first wife was Mary Cole, and they were the parents of Anne Cole, Mary Cole, and Hannah Pickett. After Mary's death, he married Mrs. Harrison Lawyer. He was buried in the Leake cemetery in Rockingham.

SEE: *Charlotte Observer*, 29 Apr. 1879; John L. Cheney, Jr., ed., *North Carolina Government, 1585–1979* (1981); William Omer Foster, "The Career of Montfort Stokes in North Carolina," *North Carolina Historical Review* 16 (July 1939); James E. Huneycutt and Ida C. Huneycutt, *A History of Richmond County* (1976); James M. Ledbetter (Rockingham), interview; Elizabeth G. McPherson, ed., "Unpublished Letters from North Carolinians to Polk," *North Carolina Historical Review* 16 (July 1939); Elizabeth G. McPherson, ed., "Unpublished Letters from North Carolinians to Van Buren," *North Carolina Historical Review* 15 (April 1939).

WARREN L. BINGHAM

Leavitt, Sturgis Elleno *(24 Jan. 1888–3 Mar. 1976)*, teacher and scholar, was born in Newhall, Maine, the son of William Hooper and Mary Ellen Sturgis Leavitt, descendants of distinguished New England families whose ancestors arrived on the *Mayflower* in 1620. Sturgis Leavitt received his first schooling from his mother, followed by instruction in the public school of Gorham, Maine, where he studied Latin and Greek (1900–1904). At age sixteen he entered Bowdoin College and received a bachelor of arts degree in 1908. He remained an active alumnus of that institution throughout his life, serving in many capacities.

Leavitt began his career as a teacher of French in secondary schools, first in the Jackson Military Academy, Mo. (1908–9), then in Cushing Academy, Ashburnham, Mass. (1909–12). Convinced that he would be of greater service to more mature students, he entered the graduate school of Harvard University and was awarded a master of arts degree in 1913. The following year he joined the faculty of Northwestern University, then returned to Harvard where he received a doctorate in Romance languages in 1917. That fall he accepted a position as assistant professor of Spanish at The University of North Carolina, thus embarking on a long career of interpreting the literatures of Spain and Spanish America until his retirement in 1960. Even then he continued his research and worked in his office almost every day until a week before his death.

At the university, Leavitt rose to the rank of professor and in 1945 was named Kenan Professor. Over the years he served on almost every standing committee, many special committees, the board of governors of The University of North Carolina Press, the Fulbright Committee, and the Faculty Council. Two of his most valuable contributions were as director of the Institute of Latin American Studies (1941–58), which he founded, and as Adviser to Foreign Students. He was indeed friend, guide, and confessor to many foreigners in a strange land. In January 1941, 110 scholars from South American countries, sponsored by the U.S. Department of State, went to Chapel Hill for three months. These professors, physicians, lawyers, editors, and students were given permission to visit any department, school, or class in the university; they were also provided a fine course in basic English by I. A. Richards.

For more than half a century Sturgis Leavitt was associated with many linguistic, literary, historical, and professional organizations in the United States. He was a member of the American Association of Teachers of Spanish and Portuguese for fifty-seven years, serving two terms as president (1945–46) and publishing a history of the society in its journal, *Hispania* (vol. 50, 1967). From the day of its founding in 1928, Leavitt was an enthusiastic member of the South Atlantic Modern Language Association, served two terms as its president (1935–37), and was editor of its journal, the *South Atlantic Bulletin*, from 1935 to 1951. He was a representative of the Modern Language Association to the American Council of Learned Societies (1942–50), president of the Southern Humanities Council (1947–51), and associate editor of the *Revista Iberoamericana* (1936–51) and of the *Hispanic Review* (1937–69). In 1938 he represented the United States at the founding of the Instituto Internacional de Literatura Iberoamericana in Mexico and at the centennials of the births of José Toribio Medina in Santiago, Chile (1952), and José Martí in Havana (1953). Leavitt was a member of the Real Academia de Cádiz (1924), Hispanic Society of America (1937–68), Academia Mexicana (1974), Academia Nacional de la República de Colombia, Sociedad Chilena de Historia y Geografía, Fundación Nacional de Eloy Alfaro (Panama, 1953), and Order of the Golden Fleece of The University of North Carolina. He received honorary degrees from his alma mater, Bowdoin College (1943), Davidson College (1941), and The University of North Carolina (1965).

On receiving a doctorate in 1917, Leavitt was awarded a Sheldon Fellowship by Harvard University for study in Spain. World War I made such a project impossible, but in 1919 the fellowship was renewed and he and his wife set out for South America where they spent sixteen months visiting libraries and scholars in Argentina, Bolivia, Chile, Colombia, Peru, and Uruguay—the first of many journeys south of the border and to Europe. This trip saw the birth of one of Leavitt's main scholarly interests, Latin American literature. His second powerful interest was in the field of Spanish drama, especially the *comedia* of the *Siglo de Oro*. As one of the rewards of his investigation in this field, the city council of Zalamea de la Serena, in southern Spain, named him Honorary Perpetual Mayor (1965)—reflecting his enthusiasm for Pedro Calderon's play, *El alcalde de Zalamea*. In these two fields Leavitt produced innumerable articles, books, and reviews, as well as a dozen texts for American students studying Spanish.

In addition to his academic interests, Leavitt was an ardent, though not expert, golfer (for a time he served as president of the Chapel Hill Country Club) and a staunch Republican. A diligent member of the Mayflower Society, he was governor of the North Carolina chapter (1960–69) and editor of its *Newsletter*, in which he published a history of the North Carolina branch.

Leavitt could not have accomplished all this alone. On 29 June 1916, he married Alga Webber who came to be his guide, philosopher, confessor, secretary, and chauffeur. She also played a leading role in the social and professional life of Chapel Hill. She was active in the Carolina Playmakers, president of the Women's Club (1921–23), a vice-president of the North Carolina Society for the Eradication of Tuberculosis, and the first woman to serve on the board of directors of the Orange Savings and Loan Association. Alga Leavitt died on 22 Oct. 1964.

SEE: Sterling Stoudemire, "Sturgis E. Leavitt: Hispanista y alcalde perpetuo honorio de Zalamea de la Serena," *La*

Estafeta Literaria (Madrid), 1 June 1972; University of North Carolina Faculty Minutes (April 1976); *Who's Who in America* (1960–61).

STERLING STOUDEMIRE

Leazar, Augustus *(26 Mar. 1843–18 Feb. 1905),* farmer, educator, and public servant, was born on his father's plantation, Leazarwell, in Rowan County. Descended from French Huguenot, German, and Scotch-Irish stock, he was the son of John and Isabella Jamison Leazar. At age thirteen he enrolled at Davidson College and four years later, in 1860, was graduated with the first honors.

Although his father originally opposed secession, Augustus Leazar helped to organize Company G of the Forty-second Regiment, North Carolina Troops. On 16 Mar. 1862 he was commissioned first lieutenant. His regiment served in Robert F. Hoke's brigade and fought at or near New Bern, Richmond, Cold Harbor, Petersburg, Fort Fisher, Kinston, Bentonville, and other areas. He served until the Confederacy collapsed, and he was paroled on 2 May 1865.

The year the Civil War ended he married his childhood sweetheart, Cornelia Francis McCorkle, daughter of William Brandon and Mary Marshall McCorkle. The couple had two sons and one daughter, but only the daughter, Carry Augustus, reached maturity. Leazar's first wife died, and in 1888 he married Clara Fowler, daughter of William G. and Margaret Alexander Fowler. They had one son, Augustus, Jr.

Starting in 1866 Leazar taught classical schools at Prospect, Coddle Creek, and Mooresville in Iredell County. In Mooresville, where he established his permanent residence, he was coprincipal of a school with his brother-in-law, Stephen Frontis. Leazar also taught at a summer normal school established at The University of North Carolina in 1877 by President Kemp Plummer Battle to train common school teachers in educational methods. In 1870 Leazar received an honorary degree from Davidson College; when the college celebrated its fiftieth anniversary in 1887, Leazar delivered the address to the Alumni and Literary societies. For many years he served on the Davidson College Board of Trustees and was recognized as one of the leading educators in the state.

His political career began in 1882, when he was elected to the North Carolina House of Representatives from Iredell County. He served four consecutive terms (1883–91). According to Josephus Daniels, in the *Tar Heel Editor*, he was the most influential Democrat in the house during the 1887–89 session, and in 1889 he was elected speaker.

Leazar was a forward-looking and progressive legislator. He endorsed the objectives of the Watauga Club, formed in 1884 by a group of young Raleigh men under the leadership of William J. Peele and Walter Hines Page to make North Carolina a more dynamic state. Leazar's greatest legislative accomplishment grew out of the Watauga movement. He was coauthor with Charles William Dabney of a bill to establish the North Carolina Agricultural and Mechanic College in Raleigh. Leazar introduced and fought for passage of the bill that became law in 1887. When the college opened in 1889, Leazar was a member of its first board of trustees, and the Leazar Literary Society was named in his honor. Leazar also wrote and introduced a bill in 1885 to increase the appropriation for The University of North Carolina.

Leazar's fight to curb the power of railroads equaled his services in behalf of education. He publicized the fact that railroad property was woefully undertaxed.

Moreover, he pointed out to the General Assembly of 1889 that although railroad property in North Carolina was worth more than $50 million, the state collected less than $28,000 annually in taxes. As a result of his efforts, the railroads surrendered their privilege of exemption from taxation. He further sought to curtail the special privileges enjoyed by railroads when he opposed their lease of convict labor. By 1892 the practice had generally been abolished. He also favored the establishment of a railroad commission, an objective achieved by the farmer-controlled legislature in 1891.

In 1888 Leazar declined the nomination of lieutenant governor. If he had accepted, he would have succeeded to the governorship on the death of Governor Daniel G. Fowle. Refusal to run for lieutenant governor did not indicate any distaste for politics. Leazar owned a number of farms in Rowan County and during the 1880s became involved in the Farmers' Alliance movement. In 1890 and again in 1892, he ran for Congress as the farmers' candidate from the Seventh Congressional District but was defeated by the powerful conservative Democrat, John Steele Henderson. A brilliant orator, he served as Seventh Congressional District lecturer for the North Carolina State Farmers' Alliance. An allianceman of moderate views, he opposed the St. Louis platform of 1892, which demanded government ownership of railroads and ignored the protective tariff issue. He supported the nomination of conservative alliance leader, Elias Carr, for governor and campaigned vigorously for Carr's election.

Undoubtedly, Leazar's most distinguished position was as superintendent of the state penitentiary from 1893 to 1897 during the administration of Governor Carr. The penitentiary became self-supporting for the first time in its history in 1896. In fact, it yielded a surplus of $91,694 at the end of that year despite losses suffered on state farms as a result of floods. The practice of employing able-bodied prisoners on state farms and road construction was continued and expanded during Leazar's administration of the prison system. At the end of his tenure, he recommended separating the young prisoners from older and more hardened inmates and liberalizing the policy of commutation of prison sentences for good behavior. His treatment of prisoners was enlightened and humane. In 1895, before Leazar had completed his term, the Fusion legislature abolished his office and appointed a successor under a different title. Leazar refused to leave his post and won his case in the courts.

For many years Leazar served on the North Carolina Board of Agriculture and The University of North Carolina board of trustees. He was a director of the Bank of Mooresville and of the Home Insurance Company of Greensboro. Deeply religious, he joined the Presbyterian church at age fourteen and for forty years was an elder in the church.

Contemporaries like newspapermen Josephus Daniels and Samuel A'Court Ashe and politician Thomas J. Jarvis regarded him as a man of strong convictions who was unwilling to compromise his principles. Courageous and honest, he was an efficient executive both as speaker of the North Carolina House of Representatives and as superintendent of the state penitentiary. On leaving the latter position, he retired to private life because of ill health and died of diabetes. His funeral was held in the Presbyterian church in Mooresville.

SEE: Samuel A. Ashe, ed., *Biographical History of North Carolina*, vol. 4 (1906 [portrait]); Elias Carr Papers (Manuscript Collection, East Carolina University, Greenville); *Charlotte Observer*, 19 Feb. 1905; Charles William Dabney Papers and John Steele Henderson Papers (Southern Historical Collection, University of North Carolina, Chapel Hill); Governors' Papers and Letter-books of Elias Carr (North Carolina State Archives, Raleigh); *Greensboro Patriot*, 19 Feb. 1905; *Lenoir Topic*, 11 July, 3 Aug. 1892; Salisbury *Carolina Watchman*, 24 July, 7 Aug. 1890; Joseph Flake Steelman, "The Progressive Era in North Carolina, 1884–1917" (Ph.D. diss., University of North Carolina, 1955).

LALA CARR STEELMAN

Lederer, Johann (or John) *(fl. 1670–75)*, German physician and pioneer explorer of the Virginia Blue Ridge and Carolina Piedmont, was born about 1644, the son of Johann Lederer of Hamburg. He matriculated in the Hamburg Academic Gymnasium on 18 Apr. 1662. By 1670 Lederer was in Virginia. Governor William Berkeley, who with other contemporaries believed that the Pacific was not far beyond the "hills" west of the settlements, commissioned him to make explorations westward in the hope that Virginia might become the intermediary in carrying the wealth of the Indies to Europe.

On 19 Mar. 1670 Lederer reached the Blue Ridge northwest of present Charlottesville but found neither a pass nor the "South Sea." On his second "march," leaving Stegge's plantation (present-day Richmond) on 20 May 1670 with a Susquehanna Indian as guide, he reached Akenatzy (Occaneechi Islands near present-day Cartersville on the Staunton River) and continued southwest across the Yadkin ford near Spencer, N.C., through the Uwharrie Mountains to the Catawba River, probably near Rock Hill, S.C. Fearful of enslavement by Spaniards, he then returned by a more easterly route, reaching Appomattox (Abraham Wood's trading post) on 20 July 1670. This important, influential journey helped open the great Indian Trading Path (now roughly followed by Interstate 85) to the lucrative Virginia fur trade that flourished with the Catawba and Cherokee for several decades.

Lederer was a perceptive observer of the Indian settlements that he encountered; his comments on the location, customs, and beliefs of the Indian tribes are generally astute and ethnologically valuable. Unfortunately, his later published account with its accompanying map gives three geographic misconceptions: he describes the Piedmont as a savanna under water several months of the year, places a nonexistent lake in western Carolina, and says he crossed "a barren Sandy desert" on his return journey. The reasons for these errors are explicable: he followed the marshy river valleys leading up to the Virginia Blue Ridge during the spring freshets; the location and description of his "Lake Ushery," which he places beyond his actual route of travel, are similar to those found on most maps since Mercator's in 1606; and the "Arenosa Desert" resulted from his memory of crossing the Carolina pine barrens in July heat. These errors, soon incorporated in the first Lords Proprietors' map of Carolina (1672) by John Ogilby, the royal geographer, and followed by many later maps of the Southeast, have caused some historians to question unjustly Lederer's entire account and dismiss it as unimportant.

On 26 Aug. 1670 Lederer undertook a third "march" in northern Virginia in company with Colonel John Catlett and others, following a tributary of the Rappahannock and climbing a peak on the Blue Ridge. Discouraged by the endless vista of the Appalachian ranges westward instead of the hoped-for "Sea of China," they returned. Shortly afterwards, Lederer moved to Mary-

land where he gained the confidence and friendship of Sir William Talbot, then the powerful secretary of the province. By April 1761 the Assembly had granted him full citizenship. Talbot translated Lederer's account from Latin to English and took it with him to England, where it was published with a map as *The Discoveries of John Lederer In three several Marches from Virginia, To the West of Carolina* (London, 1672).

By 1674 or before, Lederer had moved again, this time to Connecticut where he was entertained by Governor John Winthrop, who sent him on medical missions and later corresponded with him. Lederer quickly developed a flourishing medical practice in Stratford and Stamford, but in early 1675 he decided to return via Barbados to Germany and disappeared from the American scene.

SEE: C. W. Alford and L. Bidgood, *The First Explorations of the Trans-Allegheny Region* (1912); W. P. Cumming, "Geographical Misconceptions of the Southeast in the Cartography of the Seventeenth and Eighteenth Centuries," *Journal of Southern History* 4 (1938); W. P. Cumming, ed., *The Discoveries of John Lederer* (1958); Dieter Cunz, *The Maryland Germans* (1948); *The Discoveries of John Lederer* (1670); Winthrop Papers (Massachusetts Historical Society, Boston).

W. P. CUMMING

Lee, Arthur Carl *(3 Sept. 1886–17 July 1974)*, engineer and construction company executive, was born in Anderson, S.C., the son of W. S. and Jennie Lind Williamson Lee. He completed his preparatory schooling at Anderson High School in 1904 and entered Clemson College in the fall. Following his graduation he enrolled in Cornell University, from which he received the degree of bachelor of civil engineering in 1910.

Lee began his professional career as an engineer with the Anderson Water, Light, and Power Company, where he worked for seventeen years on a wide range of construction and engineering projects for that and other subsidiaries of the Duke Power Company. In 1921 he became a registered engineer in North Carolina. The Piedmont and Northern Railway, an electrified line in the two Carolinas, and numerous hydroelectric and steam plants were built under his direction.

When James B. Duke and his family and associates were ready to build Duke University, they asked Lee to become the executive builder, responsible for all layout, planning, and construction of the vast educational and medical complex. He continued in that position through 1960.

In 1933 Lee created two private corporations: the Lee Engineering Corporation and the Lee Construction Company, both with headquarters in Charlotte. After retiring from the Duke University job, at age seventy-four, he devoted his remaining years to these two companies of which he was president and treasurer.

Lee was a member of the American Institute of Electrical Engineers and the American Society of Civil Engineers. By gubernatorial appointment, he was a member of the Board of Registration for Engineers and Land Surveyors from 1938 until 1956 and chairman for the last twelve years. For a number of years he also was a deacon in the Myers Park Presbyterian Church, Charlotte.

In 1913 Lee married Nellie Watkins of Anderson, S.C., and they were the parents of three children: Arthur C., Jr., Elizabeth (Mrs. E. Fred McPhail), and William Franke. He died in Charlotte and was buried there.

SEE: *Charlotte Observer*, 18 July 1974; Duke University, *Alumni Bulletin*, December 1974; William S. Powell, ed., *North Carolina Lives* (1962).

C. SYLVESTER GREEN

Lee, Charles Cochrane (*2 Feb. 1834–30 June 1862*), teacher and Confederate officer, was born in Charleston, S.C., the son of Stephen and Carolina (Lee) Lee. His father attended the U.S. Military Academy and was an instructor in the South Carolina Military Academy in Charleston until 1846, when he opened a boys' school in Asheville which he operated until his death in 1879. Young Charles undoubtedly was educated in his father's school before being appointed to the U.S. Military Academy in 1852. He was graduated fourth in his class in 1856 and commissioned second lieutenant of ordnance. Assigned to the Watervliet Arsenal, N.Y., he served until 31 July 1859 when he resigned.

At the urging of a number of prominent men in the state, Daniel Harvey Hill opened the North Carolina Military Institute in Charlotte with 40 students on 1 Oct. 1859. By the end of the year, enrollment had grown to 142. The first catalogue listed Lieutenant Charles C. Lee as professor of chemistry, instructor of infantry tactics, and commandant of cadets. Lee also taught mineralogy and geology, and in all of his classes, the catalogue noted, the standards of the U.S. Military Academy were to be maintained.

On 20 Dec. 1860 Lee's native state seceded from the Union, and on 8 Jan. 1861 the North Carolina General Assembly appropriated $300,000 for the purchase of arms and ammunition for use in case of need. Governor John W. Ellis designated Lieutenant Lee to arrange for this purchase by the state, and Lee departed for Richmond, Baltimore, Wilmington, Del., Philadelphia, New York, New Haven, Springfield, Hartford, and other places. He carried with him an extensive list of military supplies drawn up by D. H. Hill and C. W. Tew. Soon he was able to report to the governor that he had found what he sought and that suppliers were willing to sell to the state. Two, however, could not guarantee delivery if North Carolina seceded from the Union. In March, Lee served in the ordnance department at Charleston under General Pierre G. T. Beauregard preliminary to the capture of Fort Sumter on 13 April.

North Carolina seceded from the Union on 20 May. A Camp of Instruction had previously been established at the state fair grounds in Raleigh, and on the twenty-ninth the adjutant general of the state issued orders to D. H. Hill for the organization of the First Regiment of North Carolina Troops. Lee, accompanied by a corps of cadets from the North Carolina Military Institute, set out for Raleigh. There, on 11 May, Daniel H. Hill was elected colonel and Lee lieutenant colonel. Within a week the regiment was transferred to Virginia, where it erected fortifications at various places in the vicinity of Yorktown and Richmond; it also participated in the victory at Big Bethel on 10 June. Since the troops had been enlisted for just six months, they were returned to Raleigh and mustered out of state service on 12 November.

On 20 Nov. 1861 Lee was appointed colonel of the Thirty-seventh Regiment at the time of its organization near High Point. He was described as "a splendid officer—cool and courageous and [who] has the entire confidence of his regiment." His new command was soon transferred to Camp Mangum near Raleigh where it remained until it was moved to New Bern on 11 February. A Federal amphibious force landed below New Bern on 13 Mar. 1862 and quickly routed the Confederate de-

fenders. The Thirty-seventh regrouped at Kinston and in early May was sent to Virginia to help protect Richmond from Federal forces only seven miles away. It participated in the Battle of Hanover Court House as well as in other skirmishes. It was in the Seven Days' Battle where the Confederates suffered staggering losses. Colonel Lee was fatally wounded at Frayser's Farm (Battle of Glendale) on 30 June, but ultimately Federal forces withdrew and the Confederate capital was secure.

A few days before his death, Lee was commended by General L. O'B. Branch: "In the late brilliant operations below Richmond, you were the first brigade to cross the Chickahominy, you were the first to meet the enemy, the first to start him on that retreat in which the able combinations of our General-in-Chief allowed him to take no rest until he found shelter under the guns of his shipping." Lee's own men spoke of him as "an excellent man, and an accomplished officer," as "a brave experienced officer, and pure man," and as their "beloved colonel." According to D. H. Hill, he was "one of the finest officers of the South." He clearly was an officer of great promise and of undoubted devotion to the cause of Southern independence.

Soon after his graduation from the U.S. Military Academy, Lee married Anna Tripp, a native of South Carolina. Their first child, Anna C., was born while he was stationed in New York, but their other children, Eula, Charles, and Florence, were born in North Carolina. The 1860 census for Mecklenburg County indicates that Lee owned considerable real and personal property, and that Ann H. Tripp, forty-six, who was a member of his household, also owned a large personal estate. Presumably she was his mother-in-law. Lee died intestate. The trustees of his estate reported that he had $138 cash on his person and his horses, tools, and furniture realized only a modest sum. In 1911 his widow, now Annie P. Lee Moyle of Charlotte, applied for a Confederate widow's pension.

Lee's remains were returned to Asheville and buried in Riverside Cemetery.

SEE: *Catalogue of the Officers and Cadets of the North Carolina Military Institute* (1860); Walter Clark, ed., *Histories of the Several Regiments and Battalions from North Carolina in the Great War, 1861–1865*, vols. 1, 3, 5 (1901); Confederate Widows' Pension Applications (North Carolina State Archives, Raleigh); George W. Cullun, *Biographical Register of the Officers and Graduates of the U.S. Military Academy*, vol. 2 (1891); Ellsworth Eliot, Jr., *West Point in the Confederacy* (1941); J. G. de Roulhac Hamilton, ed., *The Papers of Thomas Ruffin*, vol. 3 (1920); Weymouth T. Jordan, comp., *North Carolina Troops, 1861–1865: A Roster*, vol. 4 (1983); Louis H. Manarin, comp., *North Carolina Troops, 1861–1865: A Roster*, vol. 3 (1971); Mecklenburg County Census, 1860, and Mecklenburg County Estate Records (North Carolina State Archives, Raleigh); North Carolina, *Senate Memorial No. 5*, Session 1860–61; Thomas Carpenter Read, *The Descendants of Thomas Lee of Charleston, South Carolina* (1964); N. J. Tolbert, ed., *The Papers of John Willis Ellis*, 2 vols. (1964).

WILLIAM S. POWELL

Lee, Jesse (*12 Mar. 1758–12 Sept. 1816*), a pioneer Methodist preacher in North Carolina and "the apostle of Methodism to New England," was born in Prince George County, Va., the son of Nathaniel and Elizabeth Lee, prosperous landowners and slaveholders and members of the Church of England who had been greatly influenced by the Reverend Devereux Jarratt, a minister of Bath Parish. After the introduction of Methodism into Virginia, the Lees, including Jesse and another son, were converted in 1774 by Robert Williams and joined the Methodist Society. Their home became a regular preaching place on the Brunswick Circuit (which extended into Halifax and Bute counties, N.C.), and Jesse attended the revivals.

Depressed by a youthful timidity and the limited schooling available nearby, he did not take an active part in the services until 1778 when, having moved to Halifax County, N.C., to care for a widowed relative, he became less shy and more zealously religious. He was appointed a class leader by William Glendenning and began to hold meetings in the neighborhood. According to Lee, he preached his first sermon on 17 Sept. 1779 "at a place called the Old Barn." To replace the Reverend John Dickens for a few weeks on the Roanoke Circuit, he began his first work as a traveling preacher. He kept a diary of his ministerial life, noting not only his public activities but also his daily Christian experience; although this record was destroyed by the fire that consumed the Methodist Book Concern in New York in 1836, the Reverend Minton Thrift of Petersburg, Va., had made copious extracts from it and published them in the *Memoir of the Rev. Jesse Lee* (1823).

Perhaps the first Methodist pacifist, Lee refused to bear arms in July 1780 when drafted into the militia. Encamped at Thomas Tavern near the present city of Raleigh and placed under guard, he sang and prayed and preached, happy to be suffering "for righteousness' sake." Having offered to perform other duties, he became a wagon driver and traveled with the army through sections of North Carolina. He was honorably discharged on 29 Oct. 1780 after three months' service.

When Lee visited Edenton in 1781, he was probably the first Methodist preacher to do so; he and Edward Dromgoole were well received there the following year. In 1783 Lee joined the Virginia Conference and was sent as junior preacher to the Caswell Circuit in North Carolina, "a moral wilderness." For the next six years he preached in North Carolina, Virginia, and Maryland.

Unable to attend the "Christmas Conference" held in Baltimore in 1784, when the Methodist Episcopal Church in the United States was organized, he worked on the Salisbury Circuit and in February 1785 went to Wilkes County to meet Bishop Francis Asbury at the home of Colonel Joseph Herndon. Lee was very much surprised to see Asbury in full canonicals—"black gown, cassock and band"—and objected to this dress, contending that it was an incentive to formalism and ill-suited to the simple form of worship of the times. The next year Asbury invited Lee to accompany him to Charleston, S.C. Lee had made a considerable reputation for himself as a preacher, and the two clergymen admired and enjoyed each other. Although they did not always agree, they remained close for many years.

Lee's next venture was to visit the newly formed Stamford Circuit in Connecticut, and on 11 July 1790 he preached his first sermon under the Old Elm on Boston Common. With his faith and zeal, he became the father of New England Methodism, planting in that unfriendly soil the germ of his ideals. A huge man, over six feet tall and weighing 250 pounds, he journeyed tirelessly through New England, sometimes using two horses, riding one and leading the other and changing mounts at intervals. His singing drew crowds that his forceful preaching held and convinced; he spoke with conviction, and under his preaching Methodist churches sprang up and new circuits were formed. Lee's keen wit and hearty good humor were proverbial. "I did not give them velvet-mouth preaching," he said of a sermon delivered in the meetinghouse at Newton, Conn.

At the General Conference in New York in October 1790, he was privately ordained a deacon by Bishop Asbury; in 1791 he was publicly ordained an elder. He continued to serve in New England for seven more years until called to assist Asbury. At the General Conference of 1800 Richard Whatcoat received four more votes than Lee, who was considered too jovial for the office of bishop. Moreover, Lee had always been aggressively independent in his attitudes towards ecclesiastical rules and authorities.

Returning to circuit work, Lee preached in Virginia for fourteen years. Having taken to heart the biblical injunction about storing up treasures on earth, he found in 1809, when trying to buy a small farm near his father's, that he had only two hundred dollars to put down towards its purchase after having devoted twenty-six years of his life to the church.

Jesse Lee was the author of *A Short Account of the Life and Death of the Rev. John Lee, a Methodist Minister in the United States of America* (1805), a memoir of his brother, and *A Short History of the Methodists in the United States of America* (1810), the first history of American Methodism. He also published some sermons.

In 1809, while in Baltimore arranging for the publication of his *History*, Lee was elected chaplain of the U.S. House of Representatives; he was reelected at the four succeeding sessions. In 1814 he was chosen chaplain of the Senate.

In 1815 he was transferred from Virginia to the Baltimore Conference but refused to go to Fredericksburg because he thought the transfer was a political move to keep him from being elected to the next General Conference. The next year he was appointed to Annapolis, Md. While attending a camp meeting near Hillsborough, N.C., in August, he became ill and died at age fifty-eight. He was buried in the old Methodist burying ground in Baltimore, but in 1873 his remains were moved to Mount Olivet Cemetery there.

Lee never married. In the extent and importance of his work for Methodism, he perhaps ranks next to Asbury.

SEE: L. S. Burkhead, *Centennial of Methodism in North Carolina* (1876); Elmer Talmage Clark, *Methodism in Western North Carolina* (1966); *DAB*, vol. 6 (1933); W. L. Grissom, *History of Methodism in North Carolina* (1905); M. H. Moore, *Sketches of the Pioneers of Methodism in North Carolina and Virginia* (1884).

JO WHITE LINN

Lee, Stephen (7 June 1801–2 Aug. 1879), teacher and Confederate officer, was born in Charleston, S.C., the son of Judge Thomas and Kezia Miles Lee. In 1819 he entered the U.S. Military Academy where he remained for two years, attaining rank as fifth in a class of eighty-six. It is not clear why he resigned or what he did between 1821 and 1826, when he entered the College of Charleston, but he was graduated from the latter in 1828. After studying law, he entered practice with his father. It is reported that he abandoned the profession after successfully defending a man accused of murder and in whose innocence he believed. After his acquittal, the accused confessed to Lee that he actually had committed the murder.

In 1835 Lee became professor of mathematics at the College of Charleston. Then, moving to Asheville, N.C., in 1846, he established a school for boys along the

Swannanoa River. This highly regarded school regularly drew large numbers of young men from various southern states, particularly those from distinguished South Carolina families. Except for a few brief interruptions, the school continued operations until Lee's death in 1879.

At the beginning of the Civil War, Lee, on 17 June 1861, was elected colonel of the Sixteenth Regiment, North Carolina Volunteers. With his regiment he saw service in western Virginia when Federal forces invaded that region; he afterwards served under General Robert E. Lee elsewhere in Virginia. He was present with his command or accounted for until 13 Feb. 1862, when ill health and advanced age forced his resignation. Returning to Asheville, he resumed his work as a teacher, recruited new troops, and organized both young boys and old men into a defense unit known as "Captain Lee's Company (Silver Greys)." These local defense troops participated in action against the marauding enemy near the end of the war. Reportedly, on 3 Apr. 1865 fewer than three hundred men under Lee repulsed over a thousand enemy troops when they marched over from eastern Tennessee intending to loot and burn Asheville.

About 1869 some of Lee's neighbors suggested that he clear some of his land to produce tobacco. Taking their advice, he began growing a new "bright yellow" leaf. Soon farmers in the area followed his lead, and the production of this tobacco became an important source of income in the county.

Lee married his first cousin, Caroline Lee, in 1824, and they became the parents of fifteen children: Julia Eliza, John Miles, Kezia Harriet, Emily Kezia, William Franklin, Charles C., Carolina, Thomas, Elizabeth Susan, Henry Buist, Mary Adeline, Stephen, Benjamin Markley, Joseph T., and James Hardy. In 1856, a year after the death of his first wife, Lee married Mrs. Sara Rosanne Patton Morrison, and they had a daughter, Carolina. Nine of the Lee sons fought for the Confederacy—four died, one lost an arm, and one was captured and imprisoned for a considerable time.

Lee was buried in Riverside Cemetery, Asheville.

SEE: Clement A. Evans, ed., *Confederate Military History*, vol. 4 (1899); Weymouth T. Jordan, comp., *North Carolina Troops, 1861–1865: A Roster*, vol. 6 (1977); *Official Register of the Officers and Cadets of the U.S. Military Academy* [for 1820 and 1821] (1884); Thomas Carpenter Read, *The Descendants of Thomas Lee of Charleston, South Carolina* (1964 [portrait]); F. A. Sondley, *A History of Buncombe County, North Carolina*, 2 vols. (1930); Doris Cline Ward, ed., *The Heritage of Buncombe County*, vol. 1 (1981).

WILLIAM S. POWELL

Lee, Thomas Bailey (10 Aug. 1873–1 Mar. 1948), lawyer and judge, was born in Mocksville, the son of the Reverend William Drayton, M.D., and Sarah Ann Bailey Lee. He attended the Bingham School in Mebane and was graduated with honors from The University of North Carolina in 1894. In Chapel Hill, he was a member of the Order of the Gimghoul and the Dialectic Society and was editor of the yearbook, *The Hellenian*, and of the student newspaper, *The Tar Heel*. From 1894 to 1898 he taught languages at the Bingham School, then located in Asheville.

In 1897 Lee was admitted to the bar, having studied law at The University of North Carolina between his teaching stints. The following year he moved to Butte, Mont., where he was admitted to the Montana bar and began practicing. He moved to Burley, Idaho, in 1904

and was prosecuting attorney for Cassia County from 1908 to 1912 and again from 1916 to 1920. Between 1912 and 1914 he served as municipal attorney for Burley. In 1920 Lee was elected district judge for Idaho's Eleventh District, a post he held until 1926, when he became an associate justice of the state supreme court. He served as chief justice in 1931–32 before losing his seat on the court in the election of 1932. In 1934 he was reelected to the judgeship of the Eleventh District.

A Republican, Lee was a member of the American Bar Association and the Idaho Bar Association. In 1895 he served as a captain in the North Carolina State Guard. He was also a Mason, an Elk, a Rotarian, and a member of the Sons of the American Revolution. On 4 Nov. 1907 he married Irene Teasdale of Pocatello, Idaho, and they became the parents of four children: Sarah Belle, Mary Katherine, Eleanor Jane, and Thomas Bailey, Jr.

SEE: Alumni Files (University of North Carolina, Chapel Hill); Daniel L. Grant, *Alumni History of the University of North Carolina, 1795–1924* (1924); John W. Leonard, *Who's Who in Jurisprudence: A Biographical Dictionary of Contemporary Lawyers and Jurists* (1925); *Who Was Who in America*, vol. 2 (1950).

ANASTATIA SIMS

Lee, William Carey (12 Mar. 1895–25 June 1948), army officer and "father of the Airborne," was born in Dunn, the son of Eldrege, a hardware merchant, and Emma Massengill Lee. He attended local public schools and studied at Wake Forest College from 1913 to 1915 and at North Carolina State College from 1915 to 1917, lettering in football and baseball. At twenty-two he entered the army as a second lieutenant of infantry. After seeing combat duty in France as a platoon leader and company commander, he received a regular army commission in 1920. Two years later he was graduated from the Company Officer's Course at Fort Benning, Ga., and then taught military science at North Carolina State College until 1926. Following that tour of duty he served in Panama for three years.

In 1930 Lee was graduated from Tank School and went to England and France in 1932 as an observer. He was graduated from the Infantry School's advanced course in 1933 and returned to France in 1935. There he was graduated from the French tank school and served for a year as an officer in a French armored unit. Now recognized as an expert on foreign armor, Lee was recalled to the United States and taught at the Army Tank and Infantry School for four years. Once again returning to the classroom as a student himself, he was graduated from North Carolina State College with a degree in education, and in 1938 he was graduated from the Command and General Staff School at Fort Leavenworth, Kans.

Lee was an executive officer of the Second Infantry Brigade, First Division, when he was ordered to the Office of the Chief of Infantry in Washington, D.C., in 1939. Here he became the leading member of a small group advocating the development of an American airborne force. Major Lee persuaded Major General George A. Lynch, chief of the infantry, that the vertical envelopment of troops was a practicality.

When the War Department ordered the formation of a test platoon of paratroopers, Lee, on 25 June 1940, was given responsibility for compiling information, coordinating various groups, and organizing the test platoon. Promoted to lieutenant colonel, he made several major contributions to the test platoon training program, the most important being the construction of four parachute towers to help recruits master the art of jumping. In March 1941, under the chief of infantry, the War Department created a Provisional Parachute Group headquartered at Fort Benning to direct the 501st Parachute Battalion. Lee opened this parachute school on 30 Apr. 1941.

Lee gradually convinced the chief of army ground forces, Lieutenant General Lesley J. McNair, of the value of airborne divisions as specially trained and separately developed fighting units. The need for unity of command for the newly created regimental organization was recognized on 21 Mar. 1942 with the creation of the U.S. Airborne Command under Lee, who was now a colonel. The Airborne Command was located at Fort Bragg, N.C., from 21 Mar. to 15 May 1942. Lee was promoted to brigadier general on 19 Apr. 1942.

The Airborne Command was the nation's first effort to train airborne units on a major scale. The parachute school was placed under the Airborne Command and the program continued to expand. For his leadership during this critical period of the Airborne's development, Lee received the Distinguished Service Medal.

In the summer of 1942 Lee went to England with Generals Dwight D. Eisenhower, Henry H. Arnold, and Brehon B. Somervell to coordinate with the British the invasion of Europe. Lee's suggestion that the American airborne forces be organized as divisions coincided with the British proposals. General Mark Clark and General McNair accepted Lee's recommendation, and on 30 July 1942 McNair ordered the activation of two airborne divisions to become effective 15 August.

Lee's leadership in the development of the concept of airborne divisions ensured his promotion to major general on 10 Aug. 1942. He assumed command of the newly created 101st Division at Fort Claiborne, La., and in September it moved to Fort Bragg for further training. By the following January, all types of training had been completed; exercises and maneuvers occupied the spring and summer of 1943. During this period, Lee successfully combined parachute and glider regiments of the 101st Division into a cohesive fighting unit. In March 1943 he went to England to participate in planning the Normandy invasion. His recommendation for an expanded role for airborne forces was accepted by President Franklin D. Roosevelt and Prime Minister Winston Churchill.

Lee returned to England on 23 Aug. 1943, and by January all of the 101st Division had arrived and was engaged in training and conditioning. Lee organized the airborne planning agency that began the detailed projection of the airborne phase of Operation Overlord. In the fall of 1943, he wrote the airborne doctrine and the tactical deployment procedures that were used in the Normandy invasion; in December and January, he participated in an almost constant series of conferences on the invasion with Generals Eisenhower and Omar Bradley. The selected drop zones fulfilled Lee's exact predictions of August 1942 to General Matthew Ridgeway, commander of the other original airborne division, the Eighty-second.

But fate played a cruel trick on the "father" of the American airborne forces. On 5 Feb. 1944 Lee suffered a heart attack and by 4 March it was confirmed that he could not return to active duty. Thus Lee was denied the opportunity to lead the 101st Division into Normandy personally. On 9 April he began the journey home, but his successor as commander of the 101st, General Maxwell Taylor, urged the men of the 101st to shout their founder's name as they jumped over Normandy. On the night of 5–6 June 1944, the name "Bill Lee" filled the sky behind Utah Beach. Major General Lee retired in December 1944.

Lee's first order to the 101st on 19 Aug. 1942 set the division's mission and was indeed prophetic. "The 101st," he wrote, "has no history, but it has a rendezvous with destiny . . . we have broken with the past and its traditions to establish our claim to the future. Due to the nature of our armaments and tactics . . . we shall be called upon to carry out operations of far-reaching military importance . . . we shall go into action when the need is immediate and extreme."

Lee spent his retirement in his native town, often writing and discussing airborne warfare and its future. A community and civic leader of Dunn and of Harnett County, he was a Rotarian, a Mason, and a member of St. Stephen's Church in nearby Erwin. He also was the first U.S. airborne adviser and consultant to the United Nations on the concept of an international airborne police force. In 1945, as the state's most distinguished leader of World War II, he was awarded the honorary doctor of military science degree by North Carolina State University.

On 5 June 1918 Lee married his childhood sweetheart, Dava Johnson. They had no children. Lee was buried in Greenwood Cemetery, Dunn.

SEE: Alexandria (La.) *Daily Town Talk*, 28 Aug. 1942; Dunn *Daily Record*, 4, 7 June 1976; *Fayetteville Observer*, 22 Jan. 1976; Kent R. Greenfield and others, *United States Army in World War II, the Army Ground Forces: The Organization of Ground Combat Troops* (1947); James A. Huston, *Out of the Blue: U.S. Army Airborne Operations in World War II* (1972); Mrs. Dava Johnson Lee (Dunn), personal contact; Charles MacDonald, *Airborne* (1970); Leonard Rapport and Arthur Northwood, Jr., *Rendezvous with Destiny: A History of the 101st Airborne Division* (1948); "Spearheading the Invasion: Vital Role of Airborne Troops," *United States News*, 26 May 1944.

W. LEE JOHNSTON

Leech, Joseph (*1720–1803*), businessman and soldier, was living in New Bern by 1758, when he was an executor of the will of his father-in-law, Frederick Jones. A wealthy landowner, he had rental property, a tannery, and other business interests. While a member of the colonial Assembly from 1761 to 1765, he served on numerous committees and introduced a number of bills. One of the latter, ratified on 6 Mar. 1764, established the New Bern Academy, a significant educational institution in North Carolina for many years taught by Thomas Thomlinson. Leech was one of its trustees.

During the Regulator troubles, Leech was a colonel of militia and his troops were called out to protect New Bern, the capital. When a spectator attempted to get his companions to throw eggs at an officer carrying out a court-martial sentence of 150 lashes for a militiaman charged with trying to breed mutiny, Leech put the bystander under guard and "Drawing his Sword, he declared he would punish with his own Hand any person that dared to insult the Fellow merely for executing a Duty he was put on by the Court Martial; which spirited Behaviour of the Colonel caused a profound Silence, and gave general Satisfaction to the numerous Company met on the Occasion, and must also reflect great Honour to his Conduct." Leech also saw active duty at the Battle of Alamance in the 1771 campaign of Governor William Tryon against the Regulators.

Leech was a delegate to the First, Second, and Third Provincial Congress (1774–75), as well as a member of the Council of State for four consecutive terms between 1776 and 1779 and again for three terms between 1784 and 1786. He was president of the council in 1778 and 1779. He also was a justice of the peace, a member of the Craven County–New Bern Committee of Safety, and a field officer of the Craven County minutemen with the rank of colonel. For some time he acted as treasurer and accounted for the commissary of prisoners. In 1783 he was named judge of the Admiralty Court, but he resigned that post on 25 Aug. 1787. During a part of the latter period, he was one of two custodians of the Palace Square in New Bern. In 1788 and 1789 he represented Craven County at the conventions held in Hillsborough and Fayetteville, respectively, to act on the new federal constitution. At the establishment of The University of North Carolina, Leech was an early and generous donor.

As a member of Christ Church, the Anglican parish in New Bern, Leech was an active churchman, and he was a delegate to the convention in 1790 that attempted to organize the Episcopal church in the state. He also was an active Mason and attended a Grand Lodge meeting in Hillsborough. As a Mason and mayor of New Bern, he read an address of welcome when President George Washington visited the town in April 1791. After attending a banquet and ball in his honor at Tryon Palace, Washington is said to have gone to a smaller party at Leech's home.

Leech's wife was the former Mary Jones, daughter of Frederick and Mary Vail Jones. After her death he married Mary Dorothy Mosley Vail, first cousin of his first wife. In 1788 Leech's daughter, Mary (Polly) Jones Leech, married Richard Dobbs Spaight, governor of North Carolina from 1792 to 1795. According to tradition, Polly Spaight led the first minuet with President Washington at the 1791 ball at Tryon Palace, and in 1795, as the wife of the governor, she was the first woman to attend a commencement program at The University of North Carolina.

Leech and a number of his relatives were buried in the Spaight burial plot across the Trent River from New Bern.

SEE: Alexander B. Andrews, *Richard Dobbs Spaight* (1924); Kemp P. Battle, *History of the University of North Carolina*, vol. 1 (1897); Gertrude S. Carraway, *Crown of Life* (1940) and *Years of Light* (1944); John L. Cheney, Jr., ed., *North Carolina Government, 1585–1979* (1981); Craven County Records (Craven County Courthouse, New Bern); Halifax *North Carolina Journal*, 20 June 1796; Archibald Henderson, *Washington's Southern Tour, 1791* (1923); William L. Saunders, ed., *Colonial Records of North Carolina*, vol. 6 (1888).

GERTRUDE S. CARRAWAY

Lefler, Hugh Talmage (8 Dec. 1901–21 Apr. 1981), historian and author, was born in Cooleemee, Davie County, the son of Charles Deems and Eva May Swicegood Lefler. After attending Weaver Junior College, he was graduated from Trinity College, Durham, in 1921 with honors in history and membership in Phi Beta Kappa. Receiving his master's degree at Trinity in 1922, he taught history in Greensboro High School for a year and then entered graduate school at the University of Pennsylvania where he received a doctoral degree in 1931. Lefler joined the faculty of North Carolina State College of Agriculture and Engineering in 1926 and remained there until 1935, when he became a professor of history at The University of North Carolina following the depar-

ture of Professor R. D. W. Connor to become archivist of the United States.

Although Lefler enjoyed his work in the history of colonial America and often said he preferred to be identified as a historian of colonial America, it was as a historian of North Carolina that he came to be widely known. Even before leaving Raleigh, he had prepared a sourcebook for North Carolina history and issued it in duplicated form. In 1934 it was published by The University of North Carolina Press as *North Carolina History Told by Contemporaries*, and it was revised and enlarged four times over a thirty-year period.

Proving to be a popular and effective teacher, he was named Kenan Professor in 1955. Prior to his retirement in 1972, he estimated that he had taught around 18,000 students in residence and many hundreds in extension courses. In the classroom he was both stimulating and entertaining, and although there might be as many as a hundred in attendance, each felt that Lefler was speaking directly to him. His sense of humor and his ability to recall appropriate stories to fit special occasions and to illustrate specific points were especially notable. In a variety of ways he served the university and the state well. He was a member of the board of governors of The University of North Carolina Press for nearly thirty years as well as of the administrative board of the School of Journalism and the advisory board of the Research Laboratories of Anthropology, and he served on numerous search committees for new faculty, hearing boards, and other faculty bodies. He was chairman of the editorial board of the *James Sprunt Studies in History and Political Science* and served as a member of the North Carolina Historical Commission, the Advisory Committee on Historical Markers, the editorial board of the *North Carolina Historical Review*, and the Historic Sites Commission. Editorial writers across the state relied on him for penetrating comments on events of the day, while feature writers found him a fount of knowledge concerning the state's history, geography, population, and problems in countless categories. When questions of fact or interpretation were raised, Lefler was called upon for the final and unquestioned answer.

During summer sessions, Lefler was visiting professor at Duke University, the Woman's College of the University of North Carolina, the College of William and Mary, Syracuse University, and the University of Pennsylvania. He felt strongly that good teachers "kept alive" by doing research and publishing significant findings. He took great satisfaction in the success of his students, both undergraduates and graduates. During his nearly forty-year-tenure at Chapel Hill, he directed fifty-two master's theses and twenty-six doctoral dissertations.

Publications by Lefler were numerous and varied. He contributed to the major encyclopedias as well as to the *Dictionary of American Biography*, the *Dictionary of American History*, and *Notable American Woman*. With Oscar T. Barck, Jr., he was the author of three textbooks: *Colonial America* (1958 and 1968), *A History of the United States*, 2 vols. (1968), and *The United States: A Survey of National Development*, 2 vols. (1952). With A. R. Newsome he was the author of *Growth of North Carolina* (1940 and 1947), *North Carolina: The History of a Southern State* (1954, 1963, 1973, and 1976), and *North Carolina: History, Geography, Government* (1959 and 1966). With Aubrey Lee Brooks he was editor of *The Papers of Walter Clark*, 2 vols. (1948–50), and with Louis R. Wilson he completed R. D. W. Connor's *Documentary History of the University of North Carolina, 1776–1799*, 2 vols. (1953). With Paul Wager he was editor of *Orange County, 1752–1952* (1953), and with William S. Powell he was author of *Colonial North Caro-*

lina (1973). He compiled a pioneer bibliography, *A Guide to the Study and Reading of North Carolina History* (1955, 1963, and 1969), and he contributed the history section to the *North Carolina Guide* (1939 and 1955). He also contributed to *Travels in the Old South: A Bibliography* (1956). With a thorough introduction and extensive annotations, he edited John Lawson's *New Voyage to Carolina* (1967). He was the editor of an early Federalist document, *A Plea for Federal Union* (1948), and the author of a study of a fellow native of Davie County, *Hinton Rowan Helper: Advocate of a "White America"* (1935). Lefler published a two-volume *History of North Carolina* in 1956 and a *History of the United States from the Age of Exploration* in 1960. He contributed biographical sketches of North Carolinians to *The Patriots: The American Revolution General of Genius* (1975) and to *Keepers of the Past* (1965). His articles and edited documents appear in a number of historical journals.

Noted as an excellent tennis player, a successful fisherman, and a generous gardener who shared his flowers and vegetables with neighbors, he was a Rotarian and a member of the Episcopal church. He contributed two chapters on the early history of the church to *The Episcopal Church in North Carolina, 1701–1959*, published in 1987. In 1931 he married Ida Eley Pinner of Suffolk, Va., and they were the parents of two sons, Hugh T., Jr., and Charles Deems. He was buried in the old Chapel Hill Cemetery.

SEE: University of North Carolina, *Alumni Review* 69 (June 1981); *Chapel Hill Newspaper*, 21, 22 Apr. 1981; *Chapel Hill Weekly*, 11 June 1959, 31 Oct. 1960, 22 Nov. 1964, 24 Sept. 1967, 4 Oct. 1970, 18 Nov. 1973; *Charlotte Observer*, 30 Nov. 1939; *Durham Morning Herald*, 31 July 1955, 22 May 1958, 24 July 1960; *Greensboro Daily News*, 22 July 1973; A. C. Howell, *The Kenan Professorships* (1956); William S. Powell, ed., *North Carolina Lives* (1962); Raleigh *News and Observer*, 9 Dec. 1951, 27 July 1954, 16 Jan. 1955, 21 Aug. 1960, 22 Apr. 1981.

WILLIAM S. POWELL

Legett, John *(1742–11 Dec. 1812),* captain in the Royal North Carolina Regiment, was a founder of the settlement of members of that corps, the South Carolina Royalists, and the King's Carolina Rangers at Country Harbour, Nova Scotia, and directed the community's affairs until his death. A native of North Carolina, he owned 2,200 acres along Rockfish and Drowning creeks, the Great Marsh, Raft Swamp, and the Cape Fear River in Bladen (largely present-day Robeson) County, most of it from grants in the early 1770s. He sold provisions and rum on Rockfish and managed a gristmill, sawmill, and blacksmith shop.

Legett raised and helped arm 120 men for the Moore's Creek Bridge campaign and after the battle was imprisoned twice, at Philadelphia and Boston, for a total of three years. Exchanged, and with his 1776 captain's commission in provincial service confirmed, he entered South Carolina with the British in 1780, raised a company for Lieutenant Colonel John Hamilton's North Carolina Volunteers (later Royal North Carolina Regiment), and commanded it for the remainder of the war. He accompanied Lord Charles Cornwallis through North Carolina but remained in Wilmington, where he occasionally commanded the post in the absence of Major James Craig. After returning to Charleston in the evacuation of Wilmington, the regiment went to St. Augustine and with two other southern provincial corps (the King's Carolina Rangers and the South Carolina Royalists) manned the garrison for a year.

Unlike many Loyalist exiles, Legett never tried to return to North Carolina. In 1786 he remarked that "being well acquainted in the country, and knowing the disposition of the Inhabitants, [he] was frequently employ'd in such Services as rendered him particularly obnoxious to the Rebels, and (as he conceives) makes it very unsafe for him to return to North Carolina." Legett was named in the 1779 and 1782 confiscation and banishment acts following the sale of his movable property by the revolutionaries. In 1780 General William Henry Harrington took most of Legett's land to compensate himself for indigo seized by the British. Legett's wife was in their home as late as 1777, but apparently she died during the war. He left two children with friends and seems never to have seen them again. They may have been Jeremiah who lived in Beaufort County and Wright who lived in Robeson County at the time of the 1790 census.

After Britain ceded East Florida to Spain, the provincials who were willing to go to Nova Scotia were discharged at Halifax in November 1783. The following June about 210 white men with their 25 wives and 20 children, 36 blacks, and 5 indentured servants moved to land allotted to the three corps at Country Harbour on the isolated and virtually unsettled eastern coast of Nova Scotia. Farming was possible on some of the inland lots and along the Country Harbour River, but most of the land was thinly soiled, steep, and extremely rocky, rendering agriculture grim and futile. Those who remained and survived the colds and scurvy quickly learned to fish and to exploit the untouched birch, beech, maple, pine, spruce, and hemlock trees. In 1787 only about one-half of the white male settlers were still living there.

The remaining twenty-eight years of Legett's life are inseparable from the fate of Country Harbour. Responsibility for the settlement rested with the ranking officers: five captains, of whom he was senior. Key leadership was taken by Legett, George Dawkins from South Carolina, and Joseph Marshall from Georgia. They laid out a town on the eastern side of the harbor and named it Stormont, probably at the suggestion of Marshall, whose family was from Northern Ireland.

Hope for Stormont's success lay in fishing, lumbering, and the development of the harbor, which was the largest inlet between Halifax and Canso. Ships could navigate to about ten miles inland, and the town site was six miles from the mouth, where the harbor still was more than one-half mile wide. By the end of 1784 Legett, Marshall, and Dawkins reported that roughly 3,000 salmon had been smoked and 800 quintals of cod taken. Early in 1786 seventeen officers headed by Legett obtained a grant of beach downstream from the town to be used by anyone in the settlement for staging and flaking their catch. The area was being used for the purpose already, and the grant ensured public access to it. Two schooners totaling 78 tons were built at Stormont in 1784, along with six boats from 23 to 30 feet in the keel and twelve small boats for inshore fishing. In addition, 50,000 feet of lumber had been sawed for shipping and 50,000 shingles and 30,000 clapboards produced. Nova Scotia was enjoying a brief expansion in shipbuilding, but both shipbuilding and fishing soon were hurt by the admittance into the British West Indies of fish in American vessels beginning in 1788.

"Legett's Landing" was the most prominent feature of the harbor, and traces of it remain at the water's edge. Legett's livelihood was in lumbering, fishing, and trade. In his store he sold provisions and spirits, as he had in North Carolina, and he consistently had the only license to retail spirits at Country Harbour. His two-story house stood between the homes of Dawkins and Marshall on a hillside overlooking the harbor. He called it "The Willows" and his nearest farm lot "The Wigwam."

Legett's partner was his well-educated and shrewd second wife, whom he married on 1 Nov. 1786, when they were aged forty-four and fifteen, respectively. Her father, the Reverend Bernard Michael Houseal, was pastor of the German church in Halifax under appointment from the Society for the Propagation of the Gospel in Foreign Parts. The German native had served as pastor of Lutheran churches in Maryland, Pennsylvania, and New York and had translated French and German for the British forces in New York. In marrying Legett, Eva Margaretta Houseal was the first of four sisters to marry officers at Country Harbour. Legett in effect made a connection that benefited his fellow officers; the Reverend and Mrs. Houseal were regarded as having "superior" education and culture, their sons were naval officers, and their remaining daughters married naval officers.

The Legetts' first child, Sibylla Eliza Amelia Maria Sophia, was born on 27 Aug. 1787. Thirteen more children were born at Country Harbour between 1789 and 1809: John George, Margaret Mary, Sophia Maria Salome Kelly, Charles Edward Dawkins, Bernard Houseal, Absalom Benjamin Charles, James Michael (lived six months), Frances Carolina, Ann Wilhelmina, Sophia (lived seventeen months), Amelia Dawkins, Arabella Sarah, and Luisa Kermiston (or Hamilton).

Legett was a justice of the peace and town official until his death. His supervision was still apparent in 1809, when he complained to the bishop's secretary that the schoolmaster at Stormont (employed by the Society for the Propagation of the Gospel) was frequently drunk and neglected his duties. The schoolmaster, who had been a quartermaster in the King's Carolina Rangers, was transferred but not replaced, and Margaretta Legett filled his function without appointment or salary.

In October 1811 Legett and much of what he had created since the Revolutionary War were destroyed by a tidal wave and hurricane force winds that hit eastern Nova Scotia. He was thirty miles away in Guysborough, the county town, when what his wife described as "a violent and sudden Tempest and Inundation" struck Country Harbour. In Guysborough the wind leveled buildings, including the sturdy parish church, but as the sixty-nine-year-old Legett picked his way home among the felled trees blocking the bridle path he saw the effect worsen. Weakened already by a fall from a cliff a year or two earlier, he never recovered from what he found at Stormont. Every structure he owned was flattened and its contents were laid waste. Legett was taken to his daughter's house a few miles away, where he lingered on for fourteen months. He was buried in Country Harbour in a family cemetery now unseen. The *Nova Scotia Royal Gazette* of 31 Dec. 1812 described him as "a good husband, a tender indulgent father; a pleasing sincere friend, and a general peace-maker amongst his neighbors." When his widow had their devastated property auctioned in 1818 to pay estate debts, the entire 2,860 acres brought only £122. She eventually moved to Liverpool, England, with the family of their son John George, who commanded a Cunard vessel, and died there in 1857.

One item that Margaretta Legett salvaged and kept for the rest of her life was the uniform coat that Legett had worn in the North Carolina Volunteers and the Royal North Carolina Regiment. In the Public Archives of Nova Scotia since 1941, a gift of great-great-grandchildren, the coat is the only extant uniform item of a North Carolina Loyalist unit known to this writer.

SEE: Audit Office Papers 12/35, 47, 65, 72, 109, 111 and 13/91, 138, John Legett Claim (quoted); Bladen County Grants (North Carolina Land Grant Office, Raleigh); Ward Chipman Papers, vols. 24, 26, Inglis Family Papers, ser. 1, 1809–10 (Public Archives of Canada); Walter Clark, ed., *State Records of North Carolina*, vols. 11, 15, 24 (1895–1905); Guysborough County, Nova Scotia, Land Books A–E; Margaretta and John Legett in Biography Card File, Sydney County Court of General Sessions, R.G. 34, vol. 5, Sydney County Militia List, 1787, R.G. 1, vol. 233, no. 155 (Public Archives of Nova Scotia); William L. Saunders, ed., *Colonial Records of North Carolina*, vol. 10 (1890); Stormont Town Book (possession of Ernest Cameron, Country Harbour, Nova Scotia); Margaretta Legett Pension Papers, War Office Papers 42/61, and Winslow Family Papers, 5, 105ff. (Harriet Irving Library, Fredericton, New Brunswick).

CAROLE WATTERSON TROXLER

Lehman, Emma Augusta (*28 Aug. 1841–6 Nov. 1922*), teacher and poet, was born at Bethania, the daughter of Eugene Christian and Amanda Sophia Butler Lehman. Her father was director of the village orchestra. She had two brothers, John Henry and Oliver J., and a sister, Sallie E. (Mrs. Kapp). Sent by her Moravian parents to Salem Academy at age thirteen, she was graduated in three years. At sixteen, she was put in charge of the school at Bethania, and she later taught at a school near Pilot Mountain. In 1864 she became a member of the faculty at Salem Academy, where she remained for fifty-two years. English literature was her specialty, but she also taught piano, art, astronomy, and botany. When she discovered a previously unknown plant, it was named *Monotropsis lehmani* in her honor.

Though a small, frail person, Emma Lehman was a strict disciplinarian who inspired her students. Her bright round eyes gleamed with intelligence and curiosity. Her *Sketches of European Travels* (1890) tells, in the fashion of the day, of England, France, Italy, and a brief Rhine journey. Among the forty-seven pages in her *Poems* (1904) are such titles as "Queen Flora's Opening Day," "At Easter-Tide," "Sunset on Pilot Mountain," "North Carolina's Heroes," "Our Graveyard Cedars," and "Sesqui-Centennial Ode: On the 150th Anniversary of the Arrival of the Moravian Settlers in Wachovia, N.C." Salem College awarded her an honorary M.S. degree in 1914 to celebrate her fiftieth year as a teacher there. Her name has been perpetuated in the endowed Emma Lehman Chair of Literature at the college.

SEE: E. C. Brooks, ed., *North Carolina Poems* (1912); Delta Kappa Gamma, comp., *Some Pioneer Women Teachers of North Carolina* (1955); Salem College, *Alumni Record* (November 1922); Sketches by Adelaide L. Fries (Drawer M, Moravian Archives, Winston-Salem).

RICHARD WALSER

Leigh, John (*ca. 1755–23 Dec. 1796*), physician and legislator, was born in Virginia, the oldest son of Francis and Elizabeth Roscow Leigh. He was an executor of his father's will dated 1780 and probated in Norfolk County, Va., in 1782. Later going abroad for his medical training, he was very likely a student at Edinburgh. He does not appear on the list of graduates but may not have taken a degree. In 1785 Leigh won the Harveian Prize at Edinburgh for his disputation, "An Experimental Inquiry into the Properties of Opium and Its Effects on Living Subjects." This paper, dated 5 May 1785 and dedicated to George Washington, was published as a pamphlet in

Edinburgh the following year. In his study Leigh carefully tested the composition of opium available in the pharmacies of London and Edinburgh and made detailed experiments of the effects of the drug on man and certain animals. Dr. Howard Kelly, the American medical historian, was impressed by this early research and commented later that while no discovery was made and no door to promise opened, "Leigh's work was the dawning of the critical experimental spirit destined to yield such a harvest in the next century."

On his return to America, Leigh married Mary Baker, the daughter of Benjamin Baker of South Quay, Southampton County, Va. He first appears in North Carolina records in June 1787, when he purchased a lot in Tarboro where he continued to reside until his death. His wife's sister was married to General Thomas Blount, the leading citizen of Tarboro, which perhaps had a bearing on his decision to locate there.

Leigh early began to take an active role in his new home. He represented Edgecombe County in the House of Commons from 1789 until his death, and for his last three terms he was speaker. He was a trustee of the Tarborough Academy in 1793 and the next year was one of the managers of the lottery for its benefit. Leigh also was a lay delegate to all four of the Tarboro conventions (1790–94) that made an abortive and premature attempt to establish the Episcopal church in North Carolina. He died in Raleigh while performing his legislative duties and was buried in the garden of the State Bank in Tarboro. In the medical field, Leigh did not live up to his early promise. He and his wife had no children. His three brothers also lived in Tarboro and died there.

SEE: [Joseph B. Cheshire], *Sketches of Church History in North Carolina* (1892); Edgecombe County Court Records (Edgecombe County Courthouse, Tarboro); Halifax *North Carolina Journal*, 11 Dec. 1795; Howard A. Kelly and Walter L. Burrage, eds., *Dictionary of American Medical Biography* (1972); Norfolk County Court Records (Norfolk County Courthouse, Portsmouth, Va.); New Bern *State Gazette of North Carolina*, 12 Jan. 1797.

CLAIBORNE T. SMITH, JR.

Leinbach, Traugott (7 July 1796–30 Apr. 1863), silversmith and watchmaker, was born in the Moravian community of Salem, the son of Johannes Ludwig and Anna Barbara Lauer Leinbach. The father, frequently called John or J. L. Leinbach in the Moravian records, was a man of good repute and the owner of considerable property, including an oil and flaxseed business, a sawmill, a cotton gin, and land. Later in life, however, he experienced business difficulties which also involved his sons Johann Heinrich and Traugott; an outcome of these financial entanglements was that Traugott, security for his father, agreed to a public sale of the latter's property, then bought his home for seven hundred dollars and sold it to "the Trustees."

In the 16 July 1811 minutes of the Aufseher Collegium is a notation that John Vogler had taken Traugott Leinbach into his silversmith and watch shop on a trial basis. Three months later it was reported that the boy had completed his probationary period and had been accepted as an apprentice to Vogler. This apprenticeship was concluded in the summer of 1819.

In February 1821 Leinbach and four others from the Salem congregation set out for Bethlehem, Pa., where on 15 March Traugott married the Single Sister Maria Theresia Lange, a member of the Bethlehem Moravian settlement. The young couple then returned to Salem,

where the silversmith had established his own shop in the older part of the Brothers' House. In 1823 the Aufseher Collegium approved Leinbach's plan for his new home, and a year later he relinquished his shop space in the Brothers' House. By that time his dwelling on "the building lot north of Thomas Wohlfahrt, near the corner lot opposite the tavern" had been completed. The Bethania Diary for 28 Jan. 1828 recorded the designation of Traugott Leinbach's house as the headquarters for the Salem branch of the Cape Fear Bank, since "the committee insisted that it [the bank headquarters] must be in a stone house" even though Leinbach's house was made of brick. The main objective was probably to provide storage space for a safe; Dr. F. H. Schumann was named agent of the Salem branch.

Among the few extant silver articles that Leinbach made are two cups and several spoons. Characterized by a simplicity of basic design and meticulous elegance in engraving and ornamentation, these pieces attest to his skill as a craftsman. In addition to being a silversmith, Leinbach was also a watchmaker and may have been a pioneer in the field of photography. This is suggested by the 22 Aug. 1834 entry of Heinrich Leinbach (Traugott's older brother and a master shoemaker) in his diary: "I saw my brother's [Traugott's] Galvanic battery in operation, he has also got a Daguerreotype Apparatus, all of which he bought of a gentleman who also instructed him how to operate [it]."

The silversmith's election to various positions of responsibility in Salem indicates that he was a respected and successful businessman. One apprentice who worked under him was Samuel Kitschelt, who had worked for the silversmith Miksch in Bethlehem before Kitschelt moved to Salem in 1826. According to the Aufseher minutes for 22 July 1833, another boy, Aug[ustine?] Reude, was "put on trial with Br. T. Leinbach, Sr." Leinbach's own son Nathaniel Augustine, who was born in Salem on 28 Aug. 1832, also learned the silversmith's trade from his father and worked for a while as a craftsman; he later studied medicine and moved to Bethlehem in 1861. To another son, William Felix, Leinbach in 1869 transferred his house in Salem before moving back to Bethlehem. Three years later the silversmith died in Bethlehem.

SEE: George B. Cutten and Mary Reynolds Peacock, *Silversmiths of North Carolina*, 2d ed. (1973); Adelaide L. Fries and others, eds., *Records of the Moravians in North Carolina*, vols. 7–9 (1922–69); Old Salem *Gleaner*, July 1973.

MARY REYNOLDS PEACOCK

Lemay, Thomas J. (1802–8 Sept. 1863), editor, publisher, and political and religious leader, was born in Granville County where a large number of people bearing his surname lived. The names of his parents have not been found nor has any record of his education, although a contemporary described him as a good English scholar. As a youth Lemay began to work as a printer for Thomas Henderson of the *North Carolina Star*, an unusually attractive, widely read weekly newspaper in Raleigh. Following a series of changes in ownership and partners, Lemay in 1826 purchased the interests of one of the partners and became co-owner of the paper with Alexander J. Lawrence. From a clearly expressed states' rights viewpoint, they supported a program of internal improvements by the state without assistance from the federal government. The *Star* also favored Andrew Jackson for president.

In September 1835 Lemay acquired control of the paper when Lawrence left North Carolina. He was joined by David Outlaw of Bertie County in producing the paper in 1836–37 and by Hugh McQueen of Chatham County in 1840; otherwise, Lemay remained the sole editor and publisher of this influential newspaper until 1853 when, because of failing health, he sold it to W. C. Doub. William Woods Holden, later renowned for a number of reasons and as editor of the *North Carolina Standard*, spent five years as an apprentice-employee under Lemay and lived at Lemay's house. Anxious to serve his readers well, Lemay telegraphed his friend, Secretary of the Navy William A. Graham, in November 1850, asking that his newspaper be included among those select papers named to receive the text of a significant presidential message by telegraph, a means of spreading the news just coming into use.

During Lemay's ownership of the *Star* there were several changes of name, the paper being known for a considerable time as *The Star and North Carolina Gazette*. Beginning in 1828 and continuing for at least ten years, Lemay and Alexander Lawrence annually issued the *North Carolina Almanac*. However, after Lawrence's departure it was published as *Lemay's North Carolina Almanac*. Lemay's enthusiasm for his native state was apparently boundless, and in 1843 he proposed to publish a periodical tentatively named the *North Carolina Literary Record*. But his enthusiasm exceeded that of his fellow North Carolinians and the scheme did not materialize.

Sensing the need for a farm journal in North Carolina, Lemay established the monthly *North Carolina Farmer* in August 1845 and continued it through the July 1850 issue, when ill health and a decline in subscriptions obliged him to cease publication. Yet in 1855 the State Agricultural Society prevailed upon Lemay to establish another periodical, the *Arator*, which it proposed to make the official journal of the organization. Although it never received this recognition, the *Arator* continued to appear through June 1857, when the same old reasons led to its demise. Both farm journals served a good purpose in the state by introducing new crops and methods of agriculture and discussing means of restoring fertility to exhausted soil; they also gave farmers an opportunity to express their hopes and concerns through its pages. Agricultural information of the antebellum period found in these journals has been of interest to later readers as well.

In 1837 Lemay joined editors Thomas Loring and Joseph Gales in calling a meeting in Raleigh at which thirteen out of the state's twenty-five newspapers were represented. The participants discussed a consistent financial policy and a code of ethics for their profession. Among the latter was a recommendation that "personal defamation" cease and the hope that all editors in the state would no longer discuss personalities and use "indecorous language." They also urged that the papers henceforth refuse to "insert an Advertisement of a husband against his wife." The time had not yet come for such a code, however, and a call in 1838 for compliance with these proposals was ignored by editors in remote parts of the state.

Lemay was a Freemason and in 1846 addressed the Hiram Lodge of Raleigh on the importance of charity and its practice by Masons. He also was an active member of the Methodist church and except for a period of two years served as superintendent of the church school from 1827 until 1850; there is some evidence as well that he preached from time to time. In politics he was a Whig and served as a member of the Whig Central Committee for the state. He was an officer of the Wake County In-ternal Improvements Association which supported railroad development, served as a delegate to a meeting concerning the building of the North Carolina Railroad, and was a marshal of the state fair, a project that received his enthusiastic endorsement.

In May 1828 Lemay married Eliza Ann Sledge of Franklin County. The census of 1850 records their children as Leonidas B., Eliza A. V., Thomas J., Voilus, Lucinda, and Julia. In addition, the household consisted of Aples P., age fifteen, and Sarah M. Sledge, age thirteen, natives of Mississippi and Tennessee, respectively, surely relatives of his wife. Lemay's will, dated from Johnston County, 27 Apr. 1863, mentions daughters Octavia, Fedelia, and Victoria [Eliza A. V.?] and notes that his son Leonidas (also referred to as Lidius) had recently died. Since the will contains no mention of his wife, she also probably was dead by that time.

When Lemay's son, Leonidas B. (1829–63), was nine, he began publishing his own small newspaper, the *Microcosm*, which he continued certainly until 1843 and perhaps until 1845, when the *North Carolina Farmer* required his assistance. It proclaimed its devotion to "the flowers of Literature, Science, Commerce, and Agriculture." In 1850 young Lemay also assisted with the *Star* during his father's illness. The cause of the son's death has not been discovered, but he apparently was not in Confederate service.

SEE: Richard Bardolph, "A North Carolina Farm Journal of the Middle 'Fifties," *North Carolina Historical Review* 25 (January 1948); J. G. de Roulhac Hamilton, ed., *Papers of William Alexander Graham*, vols. 2–3 (1959–60); W. W. Holden, *Address on the History of Journalism in North Carolina* (n.d.); Guion G. Johnson, *Ante-Bellum North Carolina: A Social History* (1937); H. G. Jones and Julius H. Avant, *Union List of North Carolina Newspapers, 1751–1900* (1963); Elizabeth Reid Murray, *Wake County: Capital County of North Carolina*, vol. 1 (1983); Raleigh *Register*, 20 May 1828; U.S. Census, 1850, Wake County (microfilm, North Carolina Collection, University of North Carolina, Chapel Hill); Wake County Wills (North Carolina State Archives, Raleigh); Wesley H. Wallace, "North Carolina's Agricultural Journals, 1838–1861: A Crusading Press," *North Carolina Historical Review* 36 (July 1959).

WILLIAM S. POWELL

Lemly, Samuel (*1 Mar. 1791–14 Jan. 1848*), builder and architect, was prominent in Rowan County from 1817 to 1841. Little is known about him and only three structures can be definitely attributed to his genius. He probably lived first in Craven County, whose records for 1816 list him as a house joiner. In 1817, according to county records, he purchased land in Rowan. The 1820 census of that county reveals that Lemly had a household of twelve, indicating that a number of apprentices lived in his home. The court records show that at one time or another he trained seven apprentices in the carpentry trade. But he is chiefly known as a builder, and during the time he spent in Salisbury he trained many young men in the trade. When Michael Davis, a man who built many fine homes in Salisbury, died in 1881, the editor of the local newspaper wrote that he had trained under Samuel Lemly, "at that time a master builder here."

Lemly's work in Salisbury drew attention from county officials, who in 1824 appointed him commissioner of public buildings. During the same year he was awarded a contract to erect a bridge over the South Yadkin River between Second Creek and the confluence of the South

Yadkin and the Yadkin at a place commonly called "The Point." In building the bridge, Lemly followed the design of Ithiel Town's "Patent Bridge." Covered with shingles and made from heart of pine, it has long since disappeared. Lemly was so fond of Town's work that he named a son after him.

In 1825 the newly organized Presbyterians selected Lemly to build their church. The cornerstone was laid in solemn ceremonies on 30 August, and the building was completed in 1826. The main entrance was on West Innes Street through a Greek revival portico supported by Ionic columns. Over the portico was a domed belfry and dark green shutters flanked the double-range windows. This building was replaced by a new church in 1892. Lemly, with Jacob Stirewalt, also designed and built the Cabarrus County Courthouse erected in 1824. This structure, of which no description remains, burned on 15 Feb. 1875.

While in Salisbury, Lemly distinguished himself in military and church affairs as well. He joined the local military company, becoming adjutant (1829) and then colonel (1831) of the Sixty-third Regiment, North Carolina Militia. A dedicated member of the First Presbyterian Church, he served as an elder from 1832 to 1841 and was an enthuiastic supporter of the Sunday school, the Rowan Bible Society, and the Temperance Society.

Lemly became associated with Charles Fisher, a leading statesman of Rowan County, in two enterprises. The first was a foundry at the falls of the South Yadkin River near the present site of Cooleemee. The second was a partnership in a plantation in Mississippi; under the terms of the partnership, which was to last for seven years, each would contribute an equal amount of land and slaves. Apparently the scheme succeeded, for in 1841 Lemly packed his family into two or three heavy wagons drawn by four horses each and moved to Mississippi. He died in Jackson, Miss., leaving a widow and eight children.

Samuel Lemly married Elizabeth Furr, the daughter of Tobias Furr, on 2 Jan. 1811. A daughter Mary Elizabeth married John I. Shaver, for many years mayor of Salisbury and the town's wealthiest citizen. One son, Samuel, Jr., married Emeline Steele of York District, S.C. Another son, Henry A., married Amanda, the daughter of Joseph Conrad of Stokes County; their son, William A. Lemly, became a prominent banker in Winston-Salem.

SEE: James S. Brawley, "Lemly, Master Builder . . .," *Salisbury Post*, 11 Apr. 1971; James H. Craig, *The Arts and Crafts in North Carolina, 1699–1840* (1965); Charles Fisher Papers (Southern Historical Collection, University of North Carolina, Chapel Hill); J. K. Rouse, *Historical Shadows of Cabarrus County* (1970); Rowan County Deed Book and Marriage Bonds (Rowan County Courthouse, Salisbury); Jethro Rumple, "In Memory of Mrs. John I. Shaver," *Charlotte Observer* (clipping in McCubbins File, Rowan Public Library); Salisbury *Carolina Watchman*, 23 Aug. 1834, 18 June, 24 Dec. 1836, 30 Aug., 11 Oct. 1839, 14 Dec. 1844, 3 Feb. 1848, 29 Jan. 1880, 10 Nov. 1881, 12 Oct. 1882; Salisbury *Western Carolinian*, 28 May 1822, 25 May, 3 Aug. 1824, 29 Sept. 1829, 4 May 1830, 18 Jan. 1831, 13 July 1833, 17 Jan. 1840.

JAMES S. BRAWLEY

Lenoir, Walter Waightstill (*13 Mar. 1823–26 June 1890*), lawyer, planter, Confederate officer, and patron of education, was born at Fort Defiance, the family home, in Wilkes (now Caldwell) County, the son of Colonel Thomas and Selina Louisa Avery Lenoir. Two North Carolina counties, Lenoir and Avery, were named in honor of his grandfathers, General William Lenoir and Waightstill Avery. After attending the Bingham School at Hillsborough, he was graduated from The University of North Carolina as valedictorian of the class of 1843. He read law for two years under Judge Frederick Nash of Hillsborough, studied privately another year, and was licensed to practice in the superior courts of North Carolina on 10 June 1846. Because the courts of Caldwell County, where he opened a law office, provided only a small amount of legal business, he gave much of his attention to farming, cattle raising, railroads, and manufacturing.

Before the Civil War, Lenoir strongly opposed slavery and secession and vigorously supported the efforts of Zebulon B. Vance to find a peaceful solution to the nation's problems. However, on 3 Jan. 1862 he enlisted as a private in Company F, Twenty-fifth Regiment, North Carolina Volunteers, then stationed in South Carolina. Early in May he returned to Caldwell County to help recruit a company for Vance's legion; he was elected a lieutenant of this unit, but in late July he became a captain in the Thirty-seventh Regiment and participated in General Thomas J. (Stonewall) Jackson's summer campaign. A severe wound on 1 Sept. 1862 resulted in the amputation of his right leg.

Lenoir engaged in farming and cattle raising in Haywood County from 1863 to 1876 and then moved to Watauga County, where he was elected to the North Carolina General Assembly for the 1883–84 term. He devoted much of his later life to the development of the town of Linville near Grandfather Mountain.

Appointed a trustee of The University of North Carolina in 1883, he served in that capacity until his death. In the 1850s he was a leader in the movement to establish Davenport Female College, a Methodist institution located at Lenoir. His name is perpetuated in the title of Lenoir Rhyne College, a Lutheran school at Hickory. As early as 1875 he offered to donate a tract of land on the outskirts of Hickory for school purposes, but it was not until shortly after his death that a Lutheran group accepted the offer and opened Lenoir College. Its name was changed to Lenoir Rhyne College in 1923 in recognition of the benefactions of Daniel Efird Rhyne. There is a portrait of Lenoir at the college.

Lenoir married Cornelia Isabella Christian (1827–59) of Augusta County, Va., on 10 June 1856. An only child, Annie Tate, died in infancy. He was baptized as a member of the Episcopal church on Easter Day, 1890, and his grave is in the Lenoir family cemetery at Fort Defiance.

SEE: Frank P. Cauble, "Walter Waightstill Lenoir" (1973, typescript, Lenoir Rhyne College Library); T. F. Hickerson, *Happy Valley History and Genealogy* (1940) and *Echoes of Happy Valley* (1962); Lenoir Family Papers (Southern Historical Collection, University of North Carolina, Chapel Hill); Thomas Lenoir Papers (Manuscript Department, Duke University Library, Durham).

FRANK P. CAUBLE

Lenoir, William (*8 May 1751–6 May 1839*), soldier, justice of the peace, state legislator, and planter-entrepreneur, was born in Brunswick County, Va. The youngest of ten children of Thomas and Mourning Crawley Lenoir, William was only eight when his father sold his Virginia plantation and moved the family to richer farmland in Edgecombe County, N.C. Before William received the education he desired his father died in 1765, leaving the fourteen-year-old to manage family affairs.

While many young men would have resigned themselves to remaining on the farm, Lenoir spent his leisure studying mathematics, enabling him in 1769 to open an elementary school in Brunswick County and in 1770 to establish a similar school in Halifax County.

In 1771 he married Ann Ballard of Halifax County and the following year their first child, Mary, was born. No longer able to support his family on the income of a teacher, Lenoir chose the more lucrative profession of surveying. In 1775, after mastering the new trade and deciding to seek opportunities in sparsely settled western North Carolina, he moved his small family to that part of Surry County that became Wilkes County in 1778.

Lenoir had barely established his new farm when the Revolutionary War erupted and he joined the Patriot cause by enrolling in the local militia. His ability to lead men caught the eye of his superiors, and in 1776 he received command of a ranger company that patrolled the Blue Ridge Mountains to defend white settlements against warring Indians. He also led troops in the Cherokee campaign of 1776 and four years later in the Battle of Kings Mountain, when he was wounded twice. In "Pyle's Massacre" of 1781 near the Haw River, Lenoir's horse was shot from under him and his sword was broken, but he escaped injury when the Patriot force overwhelmed an outnumbered Loyalist band. Throughout the war Captain Lenoir displayed a much-needed skill for assembling supplies and arms as well as recruiting soldiers.

Lenoir's affiliation with the state militia did not end with the Revolution. He encouraged regular musters to keep units of the Fifth North Carolina Division in readiness, especially during the early 1790s, when war between England and France threatened to involve America. Although Lenoir resigned from the military establishment in 1794 after being passed over for a division command in a statewide militia reorganization, he accepted in 1795 the commission of major general to take charge of the Fifth Division. Unwilling to rest on his laurels, he sought to strengthen the citizen army by pleading with state government officials for supplemental arms for his troops and for passage of stricter military regulations, and by encouraging better preparedness and self-discipline among his subordinates. In 1812 he mobilized over a thousand men to participate in America's second war with Great Britain, but his long military career ended with his resignation after he refused to serve under a despised political opponent.

Lenoir's leadership abilities during the Revolution gained him the necessary local support for an appointment in 1776 as a Wilkes County justice of the peace and in 1778 as the county's clerk of court. His dependability and fairness in exercising magistrate duties and his efficiency in performing court business impressed fellow justices and other county residents, who elected him to the North Carolina House of Commons in 1781. Lenoir served three terms in the house, won election to the state senate for the years 1784–85 and 1787–95, and was speaker of the senate during his last five terms. A delegate to the state ratifying conventions of 1788 and 1789, he voted against the U.S. Constitution because it did not contain a bill of rights. In 1789 he was designated a trustee of the newly chartered University of North Carolina and acted as president pro tem at the first meeting in 1790.

William Lenoir lost his senate seat in 1795 to James Wellborn, whose campaign criticizing Lenoir's activities in land speculation took Lenoir by surprise. Believing a candidate should "stand for office" rather than electioneer for it, Lenoir ensured his defeat by not presenting his own political views to the electorate. He stubbornly maintained this view later in unsuccessful races for the U.S. Senate (1789), North Carolina governorship (1792 and 1805), North Carolina Senate (1802), and U.S. House of Representatives (1803 and 1806). He was a Jeffersonian Republican and a Whig.

While continuing to serve as justice of the peace, Lenoir enjoyed considerable prosperity as a planter-entrepreneur. In addition to making money from the sale of crops grown on his plantation, Fort Defiance, he supplemented his income by operating a blacksmith shop, breeding horses, and lending money; he received revenue from idle acreage by leasing land to farmers whom he required to practice land conservation. Lenoir was successful in buying and selling his holdings of over 10,000 acres. But as a member of Rousseau and Company, he encountered difficulty during 1795–96 in managing the sale of over 100,000 acres of local land to Pennsylvania agents and received only a meager profit for the effort.

If Lenoir's land company endeavor was a financial fiasco and provided a political issue to help defeat him, his own acquisition of Moravian land in Wilkes County during the Revolutionary War was even more costly. Following the confiscation acts of 1777 and 1799 authorizing the expropriation of Loyalist property in North Carolina, he and county citizens claimed property held in trust for the Moravians of Forsyth (then Surry) County by a British citizen, Henry Cossart. In 1793 the Moravians entered a suit of ejectment against the Wilkes claimants, and the ensuing cases of *Marshall v. Loveless and Others* and *Benzien and Others v. Lenoir and Others* dragged through superior and state supreme courts for over thirty years. The tribunals ruled against the defendants, contending that Cossart's trust was valid and that as North Carolina citizens the Moravians were not subject to confiscation acts. As a result, Lenoir lost several thousand acres of land, over a thousand dollars in back rent, and a legal struggle that he considered to be a moral issue.

As a family man Lenoir was a loving father and a strict disciplinarian, enjoying obedience and respect from his nine children: Mary, William Ballard, Ann, Thomas, Elizabeth, Walter Raleigh, Eliza Mira, Martha, and Sarah Joyce. His wife Ann was considered by friends to be a woman of prudence, industry, and benevolence and lived with him almost "63 years in perfect tranquility" until her death in 1833. Surviving his wife by six years, the benevolent but impatient Lenoir faced death as he faced life—fighting. Even when the battle for his life appeared lost and the pain from terminal illness grew more intense, he remained composed and alert.

Lenoir was buried in the family cemetery at Fort Defiance. His contribution to North Carolina was recognized in the naming of a county, a town, a street in Raleigh, and a building at The University of North Carolina for him. His portrait hangs in South Building on the Chapel Hill campus. He was a Freemason.

SEE: Lenoir Family Papers (Southern Historical Collection, University of North Carolina, Chapel Hill); Richard A. Shrader, "William Lenoir, 1751–1839" (Ph.D. diss., University of North Carolina at Chapel Hill, 1978).

RICHARD A. SHRADER

Lente, Frederick Divoux (or Devereaux) *(23 Dec. 1823–17 Sept. 1883),* physician and surgeon, was born in

New Bern, the son of Maria Fredericka Devereaux and Christopher Lente, who was in East Indian trade. He was of Dutch descent on his father's side and of Huguenot descent on his mother's. Lente attended The University of North Carolina, receiving an A.B. degree in 1845 and an A.M. degree in 1848. Two undergraduate papers by him, "The Individual Influence of Studies in College" and "The Discovery of America and Its Influence upon the World," are preserved in the university archives at Chapel Hill. He received a medical degree from the University Medical College of New York in 1849. According to family tradition, he also studied in Paris.

Lente was house surgeon for the New York Hospital from 1848 to 1851, when he was appointed surgeon of the West Point Foundry at Cold Spring, N.Y. In 1870 he was named to the Chair of Gynecology and Diseases of Children at the University Medical College in New York City, where he was also consulting surgeon for the Women's Hospital, St. Mary's Hospital, and the Free Dispensary for Sick Children. Soon health considerations forced him to leave the city, and after 1875 he spent winters at Palatka, Fla., and summers at Saratoga Springs, N.Y.

Lente was a founder and first president of the American Academy of Medicine; a founder of the American Neurological Association; a vice-president of the New York Neurological Society; a member of the New York Medical Society, the American Public Health Association, and the New York Medico-Legal Society; and an honorary member of the North Carolina Medical Society. He contributed extensively to medical literature, including pioneer works on sunstroke, the danger of chloroform for anesthesia, the use of morphine to treat puerperal convulsions, and surgical procedures for broken bones. He invented several instruments for the use of gynecologists as well as an early method for blood transfusion.

Lente married Mary Kemble of New York City in 1852. He died of cerebro-spinal meningitis in Cold Spring, Putnam County, N.Y., and was buried there.

SEE: William B. Atkinson, ed., *Biographical Dictionary of Contemporary American Physicians and Surgeons* (1880); *Carolina Magazine* 3, no. 4 (January 1884); Gertrude Carraway, "Early Inventive Genius a Native of Craven City" (undated clipping from New Bern newspaper in possession of Gertrude Carraway); Daniel L. Grant, *Alumni History of the University of North Carolina, 1795–1924* (1924); *New York Times*, 12 Oct. 1883; Richard French Stone, ed., *Biography of Eminent American Physicians and Surgeons* (1894).

ROSAMOND PUTZEL

Lepper (or Leper), Thomas *(d. ca. July 1718)*, Council member, marshal, and justice of the County Court of Albemarle, County Court of Bath, and Perquimans Precinct Court, was in the North Carolina colony by August 1679, when he was marshal of the Palatine's court in the government recently established by the Lords Proprietors following the uprising called Culpeper's Rebellion. He may have come to the colony from Virginia, to which a Thomas Lepper had immigrated by October 1669.

Lepper sympathized with the losing faction in the Culpeper uprising, although he apparently had taken no active part in it. In 1680 he signed a petition to the king alleging that the "rebels" still controlled the government and seeking the king's aid in suppressing them. Like many other opponents of the rebels, Lepper belonged to the Quaker faith.

Insofar as surviving records show, Lepper's chief political activities began in the late 1680s. From February 1689 through April 1690 he was a justice of the Perquimans Precinct Court. In 1690 and 1691 he was a member of the Council of the colony. From July 1692 through February 1694 he was a justice of the County Court of Albemarle, which was then the highest court of law in the colony. In 1701 and 1702 he was a justice of the recently created court for Bath County.

In or about the fall of 1679, Lepper married Ann Kent, widow of Thomas Kent. He lived many years on Yeopim Creek, in Perquimans Precinct, where he held 470 acres of land, part of which had been patented by Thomas Kent and had come to Lepper through his marriage. In 1697 he sold his Perquimans plantation and moved to Bath County. Lepper appears to have had no children of his own, although he had several stepdaughters.

At the time of his death, Lepper was living in Craven Precinct, Bath County, where his will was proved on 22 July 1719. With the exception of bequests to two unidentified women, Ann and Catherine Nuss, he left his estate to his wife Ann.

SEE: Albemarle Book of Warrants and Surveys (1681–1706), Albemarle County Papers (1678–1714), Colonial Court Records, Council Minutes, Wills, and Inventories (1677–1701), Perquimans Births, Marriages, Deaths, and Flesh Marks (1688–93), Perquimans Precinct Court Minutes (1688–93), and Will of Thomas Lepper (North Carolina State Archives, Raleigh); J. Bryan Grimes, ed., *Abstract of North Carolina Wills* (1910); J. R. B. Hathaway, ed., *North Carolina Historical and Genealogical Register*, 3 vols. (1900–1903); Nell Marion Nugent, comp., *Cavaliers and Pioneers*, vol. 2 (1977); Mattie Erma E. Parker, ed., *North Carolina Higher-Court Records, 1670–1696* and *1697–1701* (1968, 1971); Records of Perquimans Monthly Meeting and Symons Creek Monthly Meeting (Quaker Collection, Guilford College Library, Greensboro); William L. Saunders, ed., *Colonial Records of North Carolina*, vol. 1 (1886); Ellen Goode Winslow, *History of Perquimans County* (1931).

MATTIE ERMA E. PARKER

Leslie, James *(ca. 1720–81)*, founder of the town of Halifax, was born in Northern Ireland. It may be significant that he first appeared in North Carolina not long after the arrival of Governor Arthur Dobbs, himself a native of Ulster. On 8 Feb. 1757 David Crawley sold to James Leslie, merchant, three hundred acres on Roanoke River near Quankey Creek in Edgecombe County. Later that year, the Assembly passed an act creating a town on one hundred acres of the land Leslie had so recently purchased. The commissioners of the new town, Thomas Barker, Alexander McCulloch, John Gibson, Richard Browning, and Robert Jones, the younger, were directed to lay off streets and alleys with a hundred lots of half an acre each. Four acres were to be reserved for a marketplace, and a public quay or landing was to be established on the Roanoke River. The act further provided that the ferry owned by James Leslie and already established by law over the river was to be the only ferry allowed at the new town. The proceeds from the sale of lots in the town were first to be applied to paying Leslie for the land and second towards building a bridge over Quankey Creek. The town a year later was named Halifax and became the seat of the new county of Halifax, created from the northern part of Edgecombe County in 1759.

There are few records pertaining to Leslie in his later

years. Throwing his lot with the Patriot cause, he was appointed a member of the Committee of Safety in the Halifax District in 1775. On 26 July 1776 he joined several other merchants in the town of Halifax in posting bond of £5,000 for a shipload of staves to be sent to some port in Spain or Portugal, there to be sold to procure a supply of salt and "war like stores" for the use of the state.

Leslie made his will on 23 Sept. 1781, and it was probated in Halifax the following November. He had no children by his wife Mary. Leslie bequeathed to his brother and sisters in Ireland lands in Colerain in the counties of Londonderry and Antrim in Ulster. He devised his New Hope property near Halifax to his nephew George, the son of his sister Elizabeth and her husband, John McClelland. New Hope later became the site of a well-known racetrack.

SEE: Walter Clark, ed., *State Records of North Carolina*, vols. 11, 23, 25 (1895, 1904, 1906); Halifax County Will Book (Halifax County Courthouse, Halifax); Margaret M. Hofmann, *Abstracts of Deeds, Edgecombe Precinct, Edgecombe County, North Carolina, 1732–1758* (1969).

CLAIBORNE T. SMITH, JR.

Leventhorpe, Collett (*15 May 1815–1 Dec. 1889*), physician and soldier, was born at Exmouth, Devonshire, England, where his parents were temporarily residing for reasons of sustaining his father's health. His family lineage went back to the ancient family of Leventhorpe Hall, of Yorkshire, which moved to Hertfordshire during the reign of Richard II in the fourteenth century. Later, the Leventhorpes were created baronets by James I and acquired prominent political and social connections. One member of the family was an executor of Henry V; another married Dorothy, sister of Jane Seymour, the third wife of Henry VIII. On his mother's side he was kin to a brother of the first lord of Sheffield and to John Colet, dean of St. Paul's and a noted reformer. It is from his mother, Mary Collett, that young Leventhorpe derived his forename.

The youngest of three children, he attended Winchester College until age fourteen, then studied for three more years under a private tutor. In 1832, at seventeen, he received a commission from William IV as ensign of the Fourteenth Foot Regiment, Royal British Army. For three years he served in Ireland and in 1835 was stationed in the British West Indies, where he spent several years before completing yet another year of duty in Canada. By now he had attained the rank of captain of grenadiers and had broadened his experience by utilizing his leaves of absence to travel throughout Great Britain and Europe.

In 1842 Leventhorpe resigned his commission in the army and returned to England to try his hand at civilian life. After studying medicine briefly, he sailed in 1843 to Charleston, S.C., on a business trip for a British firm. While thus engaged he went to Asheville, N.C., where he met the charming Louisa Bryan, second daughter of General Edmund and Urcilla Hampton Bryan of Rutherfordton, N.C., who was vacationing in the mountains. Their courtship ended with Leventhorpe declaring his affection for her, but before committing himself to marriage he, on the advice of her father, decided it best to prepare his financial situation in some way other than depending on his annual army pension of $1,200. Accordingly, he returned to Charleston where he entered the Charleston Medical College to finish the studies he had begun in England. On his graduation, he was awarded the college's silver cup, the highest honor given to a student. Leventhorpe immediately returned to Rutherfordton, married Louisa Bryan in April 1849, and settled in that town to practice medicine. In August he became a U.S. citizen, and for years afterwards he and his wife were prominent members of the community.

When North Carolina seceded from the Union at the outbreak of the Civil War, Leventhorpe offered his services to the state and was commissioned colonel of the newly formed Thirty-fourth North Carolina Regiment on 25 Oct. 1861. His experience in the British army had given him valuable insights into the problems of drilling and training raw recruits. Under his rigid discipline, the regiment soon became a very efficient and well-trained command. While in camp around Raleigh, Leventhorpe temporarily had charge of three regiments: his own, the Thirty-third, and the Thirty-seventh. In the spring of 1862 he and his regiment were stationed in the defenses on the Roanoke River at Hamilton to guard against the frequent incursions of Union gunboats on the river which threatened the security of the important Weldon Railroad bridge. On 2 Apr. 1862 he was elected colonel of the Eleventh, formerly the First, or "Bethel," Regiment and stationed at Wilmington. Here several unattached regiments were added to his command to form a brigade of about 3,500 men, serving in the area of Masonboro Sound and in the defenses of Wilmington.

Leventhorpe was in charge of the district of Wilmington until relieved in September by Brigadier General Thomas Clingman. Afterwards he was transferred with his regiment to the Department of Southeastern Virginia, where he commanded a defense line some twenty-six miles in length on the Blackwater River. Relieved of this duty in December by Brigadier General Roger Pryor, Leventhorpe returned to North Carolina with the Eleventh Regiment and served in a small force under Brigadier General B. H. Robertson. On 16 Dec. 1862 this force attempted to check the advance of powerful Union forces led by Major General John G. Foster on a raid inland from New Bern, at Whitehall, on the banks of the Neuse. This was to be Leventhorpe's first experience in battle. His regiment was at first held in reserve until another regiment under Robertson's command was forced to abandon its position on the river bank under a terrible fire of artillery and musketry from Foster's forces on the opposite bank. Ordered forward, Leventhorpe at once reoccupied the abandoned position with his regiment and held it throughout the day under the destructive and galling fire of the Union forces. By the same token, the Eleventh North Carolina responded in kind; one Union officer described it as "one of the severest musketry fires I have ever seen." General Robertson reported: "The conduct of this regiment reflects the greatest credit upon its accomplished and dauntless commander."

By the spring of 1863, Leventhorpe's regiment had become part of Brigadier General James J. Pettigrew's North Carolina brigade and at this time was reported as the best drilled in the service. So efficient was its discipline that in drilling contests among regiments, the Eleventh Regiment was barred. In April Leventhorpe participated with Pettigrew's brigade in the abortive siege of Washington, N.C., and on the ninth was involved in a small engagement near Blount's Mill. Afterwards Pettigrew's forces were transferred to Virginia and joined General Robert E. Lee's Army of Northern Virginia for the invasion of Pennsylvania. On 1 July 1863, the first day of the Battle of Gettysburg, Pettigrew's brigade made a bloody charge against Union forces on

McPherson's Ridge; during the charge Leventhorpe, while gallantly leading his regiment, was severely injured. After the ambulance in which he was riding was captured in the subsequent retreat of Lee's army, Union surgeons found his wound to be so serious that they cauterized it with nitric acid; Leventhorpe submitted to the procedure without anesthetics. He was hospitalized at Fort McHenry, near Baltimore, and in early 1864 was transferred to the prison at Point Lookout, Md. Friends in England deposited money for him in a New York bank, enabling him to obtain extra supplies for himself and some of his inmates. After being in Union hands almost nine months, he was exchanged and returned to Confederate service, although he did not resume command of the Eleventh North Carolina.

Leventhorpe was commissioned a colonel of one of North Carolina's two home guard brigades for a brief period before accepting a commission from Governor Zebulon Vance as brigadier general of state troops. He then commanded a large force of Confederate troops in eastern North Carolina and once more helped defend the Roanoke River and the Weldon Railroad. Recognizing his ability as a leader, General Lee commissioned him a brigadier general in Confederate service on 18 Feb. 1865 to rank from 3 February (confirmed 18 February) and ordered him to serve under General Braxton Bragg in North Carolina. For reasons not given, however, Leventhorpe declined this appointment on 6 Mar. 1865. Afterwards, Bragg placed him in command at Raleigh. Following the capture of that city by Sherman's Union troops, Leventhorpe accompanied the retreating Confederate forces towards Greensboro and was there when the surrender was signed at Durham.

Shortly after the war, he and his wife moved to New York and lived there for a number of years. He made several trips to England and worked for the restoration of citizenship rights of former Confederate leaders imprisoned by Federal authorities after the war. Eventually, the Leventhorpes returned to North Carolina and bought Holly Lodge in the Happy Valley region of Caldwell County, near Lenoir. In 1879, after the general's health had begun to fail, they went to live at Fountain, home of Louisa Leventhorpe's sister and husband in the Yadkin Valley, Wilkes County. Ten years later, Leventhorpe died quietly at Fountain.

Leventhorpe has been described as "a notably handsome man, nearly six and a half feet in height, erect and stately in bearing, and gentle as well as brave." Unfortunately, his Confederate service has largely escaped historical notice, chiefly because most of his duty involved the more administrative tasks of district and departmental commands rather than actually leading troops on the field of battle. Leventhorpe had no descendants, and he was buried at the Chapel of Rest Episcopal Cemetery in Happy Valley.

SEE: Walter Clark, ed., *Histories of the Several Regiments and Battalions from North Carolina in the Great War, 1861–1865* (1901); C. A. Evans, *Confederate Military History*, vol. 4 (1899); Leventhorpe Papers (Manuscript Department, Duke University Library, Durham); John Wheeler Moore, comp., *Roster of North Carolina Troops in the War Between the States*, 4 vols. (1882); *Nat. Cyc. Am. Biog.*, vol. 7 (1897); William S. Powell, "Here's a Little Known Confederate," Raleigh *News and Observer*, 4 Feb. 1951; *War of Rebellion: Official Records of Union and Confederate Armies* (1885–1900); Ezra Warner, *Generals in Gray* (1959); Marcus Wright, *General Officers of the Confederate Army* (1911).

PAUL BRANCH

Lewelling, John (*ca. 1715–94*), Tory partisan, was born in Norfolk County, Va., into a family of small landowners and boatwrights. He was the only son of William Lewelling, of the western branch of the Elizabeth River, whose Norfolk County will dated 28 Jan. 1751 was probated the following year. William devised his home plantation to his wife, Frances, for life with reversion to his son, John. Frances continued to appear on the tax lists of the western branch precinct from 1754 until 1767. After that date she and her daughters joined John Lewelling, who had moved to North Carolina some years earlier. The will of Frances Lewelling, now damaged and barely legible, was probated in Martin County, N.C., in January 1775. It mentions her five children: John, Amey [or Anneys?], Chloe, Lydia, and Abbey, and her grandchildren, William Manning and William and Fanny Culpepper. James Sherrod and Etheldred Andrews were appointed executors. Of the daughters, nothing is known of Amey and Abbey. Chloe married Thomas Grimes and Lydia married Robert Sherrod. The names Culpepper, Manning, and Sherrod later appear among those involved in John Lewelling's Tory plot.

After his father's death in 1752, John Lewelling bought additional property in Norfolk County. He was still residing in Virginia in 1759 when he sold land, but he seems to have moved to North Carolina early the next year, for on 19 Nov. 1760 John Lewelling, shipwright, and his wife Mary, of Tyrrell County, sold a lot in the town of Portsmouth. It is not known if Lewelling continued to ply his trade as a shipwright after moving to North Carolina. He settled on Conetoe Swamp, then in Tyrrell but after 1774 in Martin County. Here in 1765 he made his first purchase of land, buying from Thomas Staton 100 acres on the north side of Conetoe. On 21 Aug. 1772 Nathan Mayo and his wife Jillian of Halifax County and John Sherrod of Tyrrell, for five shillings, deeded John Lewelling of Tyrrell 399 acres on Conetoe. The small sum involved in the transaction suggests that the parties were related in some way either to John or to his wife. Her identity is not known. Thought not a large landowner, Lewelling attracted the attention of the colonial government and was appointed a justice of the peace for Tyrrell in 1772. He was confirmed in the position by the new state government in 1776.

In the summer of 1777 a Tory conspiracy came to light in eastern North Carolina. On 16 July Colonel Henry Irwin, then at Tarboro, wrote to Governor Richard Caswell about its existence and reported he had thwarted an attempt to take over the town. The Whig leaders did not immediately grasp that the ringleader of the plot was John Lewelling of Conetoe Swamp. It was first blamed on William Brimmage, an avowed Tory and former judge of the court of admiralty in the colony who had married into the West family of Bertie County and owned property there. Brimmage was incriminated by some of the conspirators who had been arrested. He was tried at Edenton but was exonerated when no evidence of his complicity was found. The affidavits for the later treason trial for the Lewelling conspiracy, held in Edenton in the fall of 1777, provide the main source of information about the plot. John and his cohorts planned to seize the powder magazine in Halifax, kill the governor and the leading Whigs in the surrounding counties, and incite an uprising among the slaves. In Lewelling's own words, the scheme was started in Virginia and forwarded to him on Conetoe, "from whence it extended into South Carolina, Haw River, and in short all the southern parts of the continent."

Lewelling appears to have been influenced by contacts in his native Norfolk County. John Wilson, county lieutenant of Norfolk, informed the Council of State for Virginia on 20 June 1777 of a conspiracy to form a dangerous insurrection in his county. On 6 September the council was again informed of unrest in the counties of Norfolk and Princess Anne. Although the Virginia records reveal no concern among the conspirators there over the Church of England, Lewelling at his trial ascribed his religious concern as the motive for his actions. He was dissatisfied with the constitution of North Carolina, which had been adopted the year before, feeling it would destroy the Church of England and, with French assistance, introduce popery into the state. He drew up a constitution of his own, apparently a quasi-religious document of which no copy survives, and termed his leading lieutenants "churchwardens," based on the parish officials of the former established church. Lewelling's attitude has led some to consider his conspiracy to be a manifestation of Anglican loyalty in North Carolina. Numerous affidavits of his fellow conspirators, however, show no such ecclesiastical concern. Rather, they reveal that Lewelling was the focus of discontented persons who for many diverse reasons, including resentment over the military draft, opposed the Revolutionary War.

The Lewelling plot was poorly planned, and the threat to the new state was soon over. On 6 Aug. 1777 General Allen Jones wrote to Thomas Burke that many of the conspirators were already in jail. They were first imprisoned in Halifax and then taken to Edenton under armed guard to stand trial in the superior court of the Edenton district. There is no record of the trial but affidavits taken for use therein have survived. The presiding judge was John B. Beasley and the prosecuting attorney was James Iredell. Lewelling was the only conspirator found guilty of treason, and he was sentenced to be hanged. The events that followed are of as much interest as the plot itself. Almost immediately many began to wonder if the death penalty was justified. Thomas H. Hall of Tarboro, later the able congressman from his district, wrote Governor Caswell on 23 Sept. 1777 that John Lewelling had been convicted at Edenton the previous Saturday of high treason. Hall requested a pardon, calling his actions his "first deviation from rectitude and virtue" and referring to the almost exemplary fairness of his former character. Other petitions followed, even including one from Judge Beasley. Tradition says that Lewelling's neighbor, Colonel Nathan Mayo, one of the Whig leaders he had planned to kill, escorted Lewelling's wife Mary to Hillsborough where she personally interceded with the governor for her husband's life. However, Governor Caswell was uncertain as to his powers of executive clemency as provided by the constitution. Nevertheless, on 15 Nov. 1777 he asked the court for a reprieve and two days later made the same request of both houses of the legislature, asking for a joint ballot in case they did not agree.

Meanwhile, in Edenton the execution date was set for 24 November. The House of Commons on 19 November sent a message to the senate saying that the sentence should be carried out and suggesting that Lewelling be kept under strong guard. The senate then sent a message to the governor reminding him of his powers under the constitution and commenting that the legislative, executive, and judicial powers of government should be forever separate. Caswell eventually granted the pardon, although the document, the first example of executive clemency in the state, has not survived.

The remainder of Lewelling's life was uneventful. On 11 Mar. 1778 he received a state grant for 619 acres on the north side of Conetoe along Tearful Branch. This was a confirmation of title for his land which had been forfeited during the conspiracy trial. His household at the time of the 1790 census included himself, two males under sixteen, three females, and twenty slaves. He is said to have lived to be eighty, dying in 1794. His wife Mary survived him until 1808. His will made in Martin County on 2 Oct. 1793 was probated in Edgecombe the following year. A recent change in the line between Martin and Edgecombe counties had placed Lewelling's Conetoe homestead in the latter county. Listed in the will were his wife's daughters Mary Bowers, Chloe Bowers (and her husband William), Clary Southerland (and her husband John), Charlotte Staton (and her husband Arthur), Grace Mooring (and her husband John), Anneys Moore (and her husband William), and Susannah Mooring (and her husband James); and his wife's son, John Lewelling, but afterwards also mentioned as his own son. A son William, active with his father in the 1777 plot, had died earlier without issue. Lewelling named his former enemy, Colonel Nathan Mayo, as one of his executors. Susannah Lewelling, after the death of her first husband, James Mooring, married successively Frederick Mayo and Nathan Mayo, Jr., sons of the colonel. John Lewelling's descendants and those of his sisters used the name Lewelling, spelled in the more conventional form Llewellyn, as a given and middle name for many generations, commemorating an ancestor the family tradition remembered as a stubborn Loyalist and devout Episcopalian who successfully defied the state.

SEE: "Affidavits Relating to Loyalists and Tories during the Revolution," *North Carolina Historical and Genealogical Register* 2 (April, July, October 1901); Walter Clark, ed., *State Records of North Carolina*, vols. 11–12 (1895); Jeffrey J. Crow, "Tory Plots and Anglican Loyalty: The Llewelyn Conspiracy of 1777," *North Carolina Historical Review* 55 (January 1978); Robert DeMond, *Loyalists in North Carolina during the American Revolution* (1940); Journals of the Council of State of Virginia, Wills and Deeds of Norfolk County (Virginia State Library, Richmond); Thomas C. Parramore, *Launching the Craft: The First Half Century of Freemasonry in North Carolina* (1975); Records of Bertie, Edgecombe, Halifax, Martin, and Tyrrell Counties (North Carolina State Archives, Raleigh); U.S. Census, North Carolina, 1790.

CLAIBORNE T. SMITH, JR.

Lewis, Exum Percival (*15 Sept. 1863–17 Nov. 1926*), physicist and educator, was born in Edgecombe County. His father, Henry Exum Lewis, grandson of Colonel Exum Lewis of the Edgecombe militia, practiced medicine in Edgecombe and Tyrrell counties. His mother, Emma T. Haughton, Dr. Lewis's second wife, died in 1873. After his father's death in 1875, young Lewis was left in difficult financial straits. Because of his own circumstances and the generally depressed conditions in rural parts of postwar eastern North Carolina, Lewis had no formal schooling. He had been encouraged to read and study by a country clergyman, who loaned him books. He improved his reading ability when as a very young man he left North Carolina and went to West Chester, Pa., where he served as a printer's apprentice. A few years later he found a position with the War Department in Washington, D.C., as a clerk. While serving in this capacity he attended night classes at Columbian University (now George Washington University), receiving a B.S. degree in 1888.

In 1891 Lewis enrolled as a graduate student in the physics department of Johns Hopkins University. There he became the student and follower of Professor H. A.

Rowland, a physicist noted for his work in spectroscopy. In 1895 Lewis received a Ph.D. degree from Johns Hopkins and went to the University of California as an instructor of physics. Within a year he was promoted to assistant professor. Because of his background in spectroscopy, he was well-suited to act as liaison between the physics department at the University of California and the Lick observatory at Mount Hamilton, Calif. During 1898–1900 he traveled to Europe to do research in physics as a Whiting Fellow at the Physical Institute of the University of Berlin. Returning to the University of California, he was made associate professor of physics in 1902. In 1908 he became full professor of physics, and in 1918 he was appointed chairman of the department, positions he held until his death.

Building on the knowledge he had gained from Professor Rowland, Lewis went on to study the nature of the spectra of gases when placed under different conditions of purity, excitation, and the like. In Berlin he experimented with hydrogen, oxygen, and nitrogen in combination with foreign elements and discovered that oxygen or water vapor caused an afterglow or fluorescence when allowed to come in contact with nitrogen discharged into a tube. This process was further developed and led to the discovery of "active nitrogen" by the British Nobel Prize winner, John William Strutt, Lord Rayleigh. At the University of California, Lewis was a member of astrophysical teams sent to observe solar eclipses in the South Seas in 1908 and at Goldendale, Wash., and Ensenada in Lower California in 1918. On these expeditions he concentrated his studies on solar flash and the coronal spectrum.

Lewis was a leader in the study of infrared and far ultraviolet spectroscopy. His lectures on these subjects were said to have been "models of clarity." It was this ability to break new ground and then to explain it so clearly that made Lewis such an asset to his profession. Although he published no books, he wrote a number of articles on various topics relating to spectroscopy and the ionization and conductivity of gases. He was editor of *The Effect of a Magnetic Field on Radiation* (1900) and contributed sections on "Wave Motion and Light" in Duff's *Textbook of Physics* (1908). His work appeared in the *Astrophysical Journal* and other scientific periodicals, and at the time of his death he was working on a textbook on spectroscopy.

Lewis also served on the Berkeley Board of Education from 1905 to 1909 (president, 1907–9). He was a member of the Phi Beta Kappa, Sigma Chi, and Alpha Tau Omega. Although raised as an Episcopalian, he never formally joined any church as an adult.

In 1901 he married Louise Sheppard of San Francisco. They lived in Berkeley and had two children, John Sheppard and Evelyn. He died in Oakland and was buried in the family plot in Sonoma, Calif.

Lewis has been described as a self-made man, a self-taught individual who rose in his profession to become a discoverer and teacher of uncommon ability. He was noted for his sense of honor and for his idealism and devotion to seeking scientific truth, qualities that led him to early support equal suffrage and political reform.

SEE: *Concise DAB* (1964); *DAB*, vol. 2 (1929); Edgecombe County Census Records (Edgecombe County Courthouse, Tarboro, 1870); Evelyn Lewis Stewart, personal contact, November 1979; Tyrrell County Census Records (Tyrrell County Courthouse, Columbia); *Who Was Who in America*, vol. 1 (1942); Ruth Williams and M. G. Griffin, *Bible Records of Early Edgecombe County* (1958) and *Tomb-*

stone and Census Records of Early Edgecombe, North Carolina: More Records (1959).

MEADE B. B. HORNE

Lewis, Helen Morris *(7 Dec. 1852–19 Aug. 1933)*, pioneer in the woman suffrage movement in the South and organizer of the first woman's rights association in North Carolina, was born in the Vander Horst mansion on Chapel Street in Charleston, S.C. The daughter of John Williams and Anna Raven Vander Horst Lewis, she was the third of ten children borne by her mother between 1850 and 1865. She was the great-great-granddaughter of Lewis Morris, of New York, a signer of the Declaration of Independence; great-granddaughter of Arnoldus Vander Horst, governor of South Carolina (1794–95); and granddaughter of Elias Vander Horst, a signer of the South Carolina Nullification Ordinance of 1832. She spent her childhood in privileged and affluent circumstances, dividing her time between her grandparents' home in Charleston and her father's rice plantation, Ravenwood, on the Ashepoo River.

The outbreak of the Civil War disrupted her mode of living. She remained in Charleston and vicinity until January 1865, when she fled to Columbia with her mother, grandmother, four sisters, a brother, and a faithful family servant. When General William T. Sherman's troops arrived in Columbia, she witnessed the burning of the city. Her mother, advanced in pregnancy, died there after giving birth to a son. The grandmother, Anne Elliott Morris Vander Horst, returned to Charleston to seek aid, leaving the children in the care of a black woman. Fearing to remain in Columbia, however, the woman took the children to Aiken where they had cousins. According to family tradition, they walked all of the way.

Some months later, the Lewis children returned to Charleston where their grandmother assumed responsibility for their upbringing. Helen received her education in the local schools and at St. Mary's Junior College in Raleigh, N.C. She often accompanied her grandmother on extended visits to relatives in New York and frequently vacationed in the mountains of western North Carolina.

During the 1890s Helen Morris Lewis and her younger sister, Raven (1862–1940), established residence in Asheville where they taught music and ran a boardinghouse. There, in 1894, she sponsored a public meeting on woman suffrage, the first ever held in the state. On 15 November a large audience of "ladies, businessmen, professional men, and people in every walk of life" heard speeches by Miss Lewis, Miss Floride Cunningham of South Carolina, and Asheville mayor Thomas W. Patton. On the twenty-second an equal suffrage association was organized with Helen Morris Lewis as president.

During the decade that followed, Miss Lewis was the motivating force in the woman suffrage movement in North Carolina. She traveled throughout the state, often addressing audiences that numbered in the hundreds. She brought to North Carolina such lecturers of prominence as Elizabeth Upham Yates of Maine, Laura Clay of Kentucky, Belle Kearney of Mississippi, and Frances Willard of the Woman's Christian Temperance Union.

In 1896 she was surprised to learn that she had received five votes for the office of representative in the U.S. Congress. Although she was not a candidate for that or any other post, five men, for reasons undisclosed, voted for her. Three years later, in 1899, she announced her candidacy for the position of superintendent of waterworks for the city of Asheville, and, thereby, became the first woman in North Carolina to seek an elective office. She did not expect to win the post and doubted that she, "a disfranchised creature," would have been allowed to fill it had she won. She ran against eight men and received a total of four votes.

Her crusading zeal sometimes took her to other states. In 1895 she was one of a group of women who toured South Carolina in behalf of "votes-for-women." During the same year, she attended the annual convention of the National American Woman Suffrage Association in Atlanta. In 1896 she represented North Carolina at that organization's convention in Washington, D.C. While there, on 28 January, she spoke at a hearing of the Senate Committee on Woman Suffrage. On this occasion she pointed out that many existing laws were "detrimental" to women and urged that they be given the ballot so that they could protect "their interests." Enfranchisement would contribute to the "betterment of the wives, mothers, and daughters" of the land. It would not make them less feminine, she said. Instead, it would stimulate their educational and personal growth and bring a "fresh dignity and respect to the home."

In spite of her efforts, the doctrine of votes-for-women won little acceptance in North Carolina. The suffrage association failed to gain new members, and, as old ones drifted away, its ranks became decimated. By 1899 the organization was showing signs of disintegration, and Miss Lewis expressed concern about its future. Early in the twentieth century it became inactive. The suffrage movement then entered a dormant phase which lasted more than a decade.

In 1906 the Lewis sisters gave up their home in Asheville and returned to Charleston. In 1912 they established the Squirrel Inn in nearby Summerville. This resort inn, which catered to winter visitors, became known for its hospitable atmosphere and distinctive cuisine.

In 1923 Helen Morris Lewis bought a house in Asheville where the sisters spent their summers during the next decade. She died in Asheville of cancer and her remains were taken to Charleston for burial in St. Lawrence Catholic Cemetery.

In appearance, Helen Morris Lewis was tall and stately. A contemporary described her as a woman of "queenly beauty and grace." She was an accomplished public speaker who often received standing ovations from her audiences. She was also a talented musician and a writer of some local reputation who often published articles in the Charleston *News and Courier*. She never married and left her entire estate to her sister and lifelong companion, Raven Lewis.

SEE: *Asheville Citizen-Times*, 20 Aug. 1933; *Asheville Daily Citizen*, 1894–1900; Sarah A. Russell, "North Carolina," in Susan B. Anthony and Ida H. Harpers, eds., *History of Woman Suffrage*, vol. 4 (1902); A. Elizabeth Taylor, "The Woman Suffrage Movement in North Carolina: Part I," *North Carolina Historical Review* 38 (January 1961); *Woman's Journal*, 1894–1900.

A. ELIZABETH TAYLOR

Lewis, Henry Wilkins (13 Mar. 1856–18 Oct. 1936), physician, was born at Spring Bank plantation in Brunswick County, Va., the son of Benjamin and Ellen Wilkins Lewis. After preparing at the Poyner Academy in Lawrenceville, Va., he entered the University of Virginia and began to study medicine. At the time, the ten-month medical course at Charlottesville was the longest in the nation. Lewis then transferred to the University of the City of New York from which he received a medical degree in 1877. After two years of practice in Lawrenceville, he moved to Jackson, Northampton County, N.C., sixty miles away. His connection with that area came through his mother, whose family had owned Roanoke River lands since 1803 and had lived at Belmont plantation in the upper part of the county since 1814.

As Lewis himself said fifty years later in an address before the Raleigh Academy of Medicine, he entered his chosen field as a young man of twenty-one at a time of great and momentous change. In the period of his active practice, the discoveries of science were to profoundly alter the course of medicine. The medical training Lewis had received was the equal of any then offered in the nation. Though a lone practitioner in a small community, he kept an inquiring mind and remained abreast of the medical advances that were then occurring in such rapid succession. Lewis was quick to apply this new knowledge to the benefit of his rural practice. His published papers on pneumonia and typhoid fever were well received in state medical circles.

As any form of postgraduate training was unknown at the time, when he had been a decade in Jackson, Lewis went to Baltimore to consult physicians there about problems he was facing in practice. His contact with Baltimore continued after the opening of the Johns Hopkins University Hospital in 1889. In November 1896 Lewis sent for Dr. William Osler, the noted Hopkins physician, as a consultant in the fatal illness of the son of Senator Matt Ransom. On the occasion of this visit to Jackson, Osler referred to Lewis as "the ideal family physician."

In the *North Carolina Medical Journal* of March 1899, Lewis published his most important paper: "Malarial Haemoglabinuria: Its Treatment by Injections of Normal Salt Solution." This condition, a severe complication of malaria known also as "yellow chills" and blackwater fever, was common in areas such as the lower Roanoke Valley where malaria was endemic. The treatment advocated by Lewis, resembling somewhat in effect the intravenous infusions developed later, combated the severe dehydration brought on by the disease. Dr. Osler quickly wrote his approval of the thesis, and this form of treatment attracted great attention at the time. Doubtless, as a result of the work done by Henry Lewis on malaria, Dr. William S. Thayer, Osler's assistant at Johns Hopkins and an authority on the disease, went to Jackson in the fall of 1899. The purpose of this visit was the collection of mosquitoes on the Roanoke to test the vector theory of the transmission of malaria, which was then being worked out by Sir Ronald Ross in England and other scientists.

The years of Lewis's active practice saw the rise of preventive medicine and in this area he made the most lasting contribution. Appointed in 1885 as the first public health officer in Northampton County, a position he held for thirty years, he led the fight against the unsanitary living conditions responsible for the spread of typhoid and malaria. His effective work against smallpox won statewide acclaim. From 1899 to 1907 Lewis served as a member of the State Board of Health, playing a major role in the support of quarantine laws. On his death, the chief of the U.S. Public Health Service paid tribute to his work in the field. Active in the North Carolina Medical Society, he was also an early member and onetime president of the Seaboard Medical Association of North

Carolina and Virginia. He died at his home in Jackson and was buried in the churchyard of the Church of the Savior.

In 1884, in Portsmouth, Va., Lewis married Sallie Ann Ridley, widow of Joseph John Long, Jr., of Halifax, N.C., and the daughter of Robert and Ann Eliza Blunt Ridley of Southampton County, Va. They were the parents of three children: Henry Stuart, Ellen Wilkins, and Edmund Wilkins.

SEE: *Jackson News*, 18 Oct. 1936; Henry W. Lewis, unpublished manuscript (Chapel Hill); John Burgwyn MacRae Diary, 9 vols. (Southern Historical Collection, University of North Carolina, Chapel Hill); *North Carolina Biography*, vol. 4 (1928); Benjamin E. Washburn, *As I Recall* (1960).

CLAIBORNE T. SMITH, JR.

Lewis, Kemp Plummer *(12 Sept. 1880–29 June 1952),* textile executive, was born in Raleigh, the son of Richard Henry Lewis, a noted physician, and Cornelia Viola Battle Lewis, daughter of Kemp Plummer Battle, president of The University of North Carolina. Also among his forebears was Joel Battle, of Rocky Mount, founder of one of the earliest cotton mills in the South.

Lewis attended the Raleigh Male Academy and was graduated from The University of North Carolina in 1900. A member of Phi Beta Kappa, he joined the baseball and tennis teams and sang in the choir of the Chapel of the Cross Episcopal Church. In October 1900 he was employed by the Erwin Cotton Mills and soon became secretary to founder William A. Erwin. After a short time he assumed the duties of purchasing agent, and in 1904, when a model mill town (named Duke— now Erwin—in honor of Benjamin N. Duke, then president of Erwin Mills) was established, Lewis was named manager of the new mill there. He continued to serve as purchasing agent for both mills. In 1919, when W. A. Erwin succeeded Duke as president of the company, Lewis was promoted to assistant secretary-treasurer. After Erwin died in 1932, Lewis became president and treasurer, positions he held until 1948, when he became chairman of the board, a post he recommended be created, and served until his death.

During his fifty-two years with the Erwin Mills, Lewis saw the company grow from a single mill operating 25,000 spindles to a complex of eight plants boasting nearly 200,000 spindles and producing a variety of cotton textiles. His reputation in the textile industry earned him the presidency of the Cotton Manufacturers Association of North Carolina (1931–32) and of the American Cotton Manufacturers Association (1939–40). He was president of Erwin Mills during the period when many mills in the state were racked by conflicts between union organizers and management. It is noteworthy that Erwin Mills weathered the transitional period with no unpleasantness, due to Lewis's familiarity with and concern for his employees as well as to his pragmatic view that unionization in the southern textile industry was inevitable.

A member of the Cotton Textile Institute, Inc., Lewis served as president of the Erwin Yarn Company of Philadelphia and as vice-president of the Oxford Cotton Mills. He sat on the board of directors of the Durham and Southern Railway Company and of the Fidelity Bank in Durham. He also was president of the Bank of Harnett in Erwin. An active member of St. Philip's Episcopal Church in Durham, he served for many years as a vestryman, including a number of terms as senior war-

den. He was appointed to the Executive Council of the Episcopal Diocese of North Carolina and was chairman of the finance committee of the diocese.

Lewis remained vitally interested in The University of North Carolina all his life and was a member of the board of trustees (1932–43). His community service included membership on the Durham Board of Education for twelve years. He belonged to the Durham Rotary Club (of which he was also president) and to the Durham Chamber of Commerce, which honored him with the City of Durham 1948 Civic Award.

In April 1912, in Belhaven, he married Lottie Hays Sharp, daughter of Carroll Sharp of Hertford County and niece of W. D. Pruden of Edenton. They became the parents of four daughters: Anne Foreman L. (Orgain), Margaret Pruden L. (Bridgers), Lottie Sharp L. (Woollen), and Martha Hoskins L. (Stanley). He was buried in Maplewood Cemetery, Durham. There are three portraits of Lewis: one as president of Erwin Mills owned by Mrs. Charles T. Woollen, Jr., Charlotte; a small one painted by a family friend, William Shelby Harney; and a larger one owned by the heirs of Mrs. E. S. Orgain, Sr., Durham.

SEE: Herbert B. Battle, *The Battle Book* (1930); *Durham Morning Herald*, 9 Jan. 1939, 4 Apr. 1948, 30 June, 1 July, 6 Sept. 1952, 10 Aug. 1958; *Durham Sun*, 30 June 1952; Daniel L. Grant, *Alumni History of the University of North Carolina, 1795–1924* (1924); *North Carolina Biography*, vol. 3 (1928).

B. W. C. ROBERTS
MEADE B. B. HORNE

Lewis, McDaniel *(24 Feb. 1894–13 Aug. 1978),* investment banker, civic leader, and supporter of various cultural and historical projects, was born in Asheville. Shortly after his birth, his parents, Elisha Betts and Dora McDaniel Lewis, moved to Kinston where he spent his childhood. Lewis was a direct descendant of two men who played significant roles in North Carolina's Revolutionary War effort—Exum Lewis, colonel of the Edgecombe County militia, and Elisha Battle, a representative in the Assembly and in the Provincial Congress during the 1770s and a delegate to the state's constitutional convention of 1788.

Lewis left Kinston in 1912 and enrolled at The University of North Carolina. As a student he participated in a wide range of activities including varsity baseball, the Philanthropic Society, publications (associate editor of the *Yackety-Yack* and *The Tar Heel*), and Alpha Tau Omega fraternity. An avid photographer, Lewis earned the nickname "Kodak Mac" and was seldom seen on campus without a camera.

After graduation in 1916, he taught and coached at the Raleigh High School for a year before moving to Greensboro where he began his career as an investment banker. In 1931 he founded the partnership of Lewis and Hall, and in 1941 he established the firm of McDaniel Lewis and Company, which specialized in municipal bonds. Near the end of his life, he served as a consultant to a Greensboro investment firm and was believed to be the oldest active investment banker in North Carolina.

From 1947 to 1965 Lewis was affiliated with the North Carolina Department of Archives and History. While serving for twelve years as executive board chairman, he helped to develop plans for the North Carolina Civil War Centennial (1961–65) and for the celebration of the Tercentenary of the Carolina Charter (1963).

Greensboro, Lewis's adopted hometown, was the beneficiary of many of his civic efforts. He was a charter member, secretary, and later president of the Greensboro Historical Museum. Lewis chaired the committee that developed the plans for the Greensboro Coliseum complex. As a result of his association with dozens of historical and patriotic societies in and around Greensboro, the Greensboro Chamber of Commerce presented him with the Dolley Madison Award in 1972 for outstanding contributions to historic preservation.

Lewis was outspoken on many issues and worked hard to sway public opinion to his side. He was the state's foremost advocate of a downtown Raleigh site for the North Carolina Museum of Art, but despite his objections the General Assembly decided on a location outside the city. He met with more success in his efforts to have the Guilford Courthouse Battleground park enlarged, to place the Greensboro Coliseum in an effective location, and to preserve the historical integrity of the area where David Caldwell's Log College once stood.

A lifelong Baptist and Democrat, Lewis was also a member of the American Legion, Masons, and Woodmen of the World. He served as a trustee of Chowan College (1957–61 and 1963–67) and was a charter member of the Educational Foundation at The University of North Carolina, remaining active in civic and business affairs until his death.

Lewis was survived by his wife, the former Lillian King Kimbrough of Greensboro, and two children from his first marriage to Lynwood Adams Cools of Danville, Va.: Margaret Betts Beard and Mary Lynn Johnson. He was buried in Forest Lawn Cemetery, Greensboro.

SEE: Herbert B. Battle, *The Battle Book* (1930); *Greensboro Business*, 19 May 1972; *Greensboro Daily News*, 14, 15 Aug. 1978; *Greensboro Record*, 6 June 1975; Raleigh *News and Observer*, 5 June 1966.

JOHN MERCER THORP, JR.

Lewis, Nell [Cornelia] Battle (*28 May 1893–26 Nov. 1956*), journalist, feminist, lawyer, and educator, was born in Raleigh, which remained her residence throughout her career. Her father, Richard Henry Lewis, was a well-known physician, educator, and public health pioneer in Raleigh; her mother, Mary Gordon of Charlottesville, Va., was Lewis's second wife and the mother of his only daughter. Nell was named for her father's first wife, Cornelia Battle. Among her distinguished ancestors were George Durant, an early landholder in the Carolina settlement; Winifred Wiggins, secretary of the Edenton Tea Party preceding the American Revolution; Judge Joseph John Daniel of the North Carolina Supreme Court; and Mary Long Gordon, one of the first thirteen students enrolled at St. Mary's College, Raleigh, in 1842.

Educated in Raleigh public schools and briefly at St. Mary's College (1910–11), Nell Lewis was graduated in 1917 from Smith College, Northampton, Mass., where she was elected to Phi Beta Kappa. In 1917–18 she was employed by the National City Bank of New York City, and in 1918–19 she worked with the YWCA's canteen service with the American Expeditionary Force in France. In 1920 she began her long career as a newspaperwoman on the staff of the Raleigh *News and Observer*, introducing her column, "Incidentally," in 1921. Except for a brief illness during the 1930s and for a period in 1948, when she was associate editor of the *Raleigh Times*, she worked continuously for the *News and Observer* until her death. A versatile writer, she served in various ca-

pacities including general and society reporter, literary editor, feature editor, and columnist.

Widely read despite its appearance on the society page, "Incidentally" contained keen analyses of topics ranging from rural poverty to poetry. The column, along with feature articles, provided Miss Lewis a forum for her concerns in the areas of human rights and social justice. Important focuses of her writing were women's political, legal, and educational rights and opportunities; working conditions of laborers, especially women and children; academic freedom and separation of church and state; antimaterialism; criminal justice and penal reform; and mental health. Her column, serious yet witty, made Tar Heels aware of social problems throughout the state.

Nell Lewis was a suffragist in her youth and later a feminist who interpreted the woman's movement as one for human rights. She was publicity director during the period 1922–24 for the Board of Charities and Public Welfare under the administration of Commissioner Kate Burr Johnson and in 1922 for the League of Women Voters, an organization in which she was persistently active, and the State Federation of Women's Clubs. After its formation in 1923 she became publicity director for the Legislative Council, a clearinghouse for seven major women's organizations that lobbied for the passage of various laws such as those restricting child labor and permitting a secret ballot. Concerned about eradicating the cultural images of women as inferior beings and as sex objects, she featured career women, female authors and politicians, and women's history in her articles and columns to encourage women to participate fully in society.

She used her position on the *News and Observer* to promote the higher education of women, to inform the public about the specifics of laws such as those pertaining to rape, marital consent age, and property rights; and to lobby for improvement. She addressed the general problems of working mothers and the high incidence of deaths relating to childbirth. Dismayed that homemakers were limited by discriminatory laws, she urged changes in the legal status of women. Appalled by the results of her own research on the conditions of women in industries in the state, Miss Lewis became attentive to the general plight of workers in North Carolina, particularly the textile laborers. Attempting to aid the Legislative Council in persuading state officials to finance a survey of women in industry and finding obstacles at every turn throughout the 1920s, she became increasingly critical of those in political and economic control of the state. Despite the fact that two of her half brothers were associated with the textile industry, she attacked textile manufacturers as materialists who selfishly opposed the improvement of working conditions. The churches were no better than the textile owners, she wrote in a scathing critique of the churches' defense of the status quo, and they encouraged the prevailing materialism of Tar Heels. Miss Lewis connected the rights of laborers with those of women, minorities, young people, and those out of power. Few institutions escaped her able and caustic pen as she tried to educate the citizenry and arouse its social consciousness. She believed that an educated populace, especially its female members, would lead the state towards social, economic, and political advancement.

General social concerns prompted her to expose the inadequate school system in North Carolina. She insisted that legislation should focus on reducing the high rate of illiteracy and reforming the compulsory school attendance laws. Again, she felt that textile manufacturers resisted such reforms for economic reasons. Miss Lewis fought adamantly against the antievolution bills that were introduced in the legislature during the 1920s. She also thought that education and a better way of life would reduce the number of youthful and female criminal offenders in the state.

The journalist noted that many problems of women stemmed from inadequate working and home conditions and the lack of educational opportunities. Most legislators, as well as the citizenry, were complacent, she wrote. Convinced that women would work more diligently to pass the laws that she and various women's organizations were advocating, Miss Lewis ran for the legislature in the Democratic primary of 1928. Her bid failed—in her opinion, because the textile manufacturers opposed her proposals to survey women in industry and to get the secret ballot for the state. But she thought that rural women also helped to defeat her because they could not accept a woman in a position of political power. She thought that the members of her sex were working against their own interests, that society encouraged them to remain in a position of inferiority. Yet defeat did not silence her typewriter. During the textile strikes of 1929 and 1930, she urged fair trials and presented the laborers' point of view to her readers. Better working conditions might have prevented the strikes and left-wing activity, she asserted.

As a believer in adult education and in legal justice, Nell Lewis offered herself as a role model. She read law under Assistant Attorney General Walter Siler and was admitted to the bar in 1929. Her brief practice of only a few years centered around legal action involving female inmates of the women's reformatory, Samarcand Manor, who were accused of arson. She contended that the accused were "mentally defective" and should have been separated from other inmates. The case influenced her to promote penal reform and the improvement of conditions for the mentally ill or retarded, the rehabilitation of prisoners, the establishment of juvenile homes and reformatories, and the investigation of conditions in women's prisons. She compiled the first full-scale study of capital punishment in the state and publicized deficiencies in the justice system. Also in the 1930s she developed a strong interest in the Mental Hygiene Society. From this period until her death, her writing reflected increased concern with mental health and with legal and penal reform.

From 1937 to 1944 and again in 1954, Miss Lewis taught English and Bible studies at St. Mary's College. A member of Christ Episcopal Church, she had long been interested in religion and in controversies such as that engendered by evolution during the 1920. A theological modernist, she compiled and annotated a manuscript of a textbook, "The Way: Studies in the Teachings of Jesus of Nazareth," for her classes at St. Mary's. Periodically, she worked on a novel, on biographies of Elizabeth Cady Stanton and Elizabeth Blackwell, on articles for publications such as the *Nation*, on plans for a biography of Dorothea Dix, on studies about psychic phenomena, and on a film production about Martin Luther. She also painted portraits. Still, she continued to publish much locally on the conditions of women in prisons and highly promoted and publicized a prison investigation in 1954. During the 1930s she had worked diligently on a program to finance a public library system for North Carolina; she used her talents thereafter to publicize many educational, historical, and literary needs in the state. Her concerns were exemplified by her association with such organizations as the North Carolina Historical Commission and the Folklore Society, as well as various other historical organizations and libraries. Textbooks for schools also became an interest in her later life. During the last fifteen years of her long career, she continued to write feature articles about women and to publicize the work of women's clubs.

Over time, Nell Lewis's political views became increasingly conservative. This was evident during the years immediately following World War II, when she renounced many of her earlier efforts for freedom of expression and thought, social justice, and reform. In her columns she raged against communism with a vengeance but often confused liberalism with communism. This impulse is especially noticeable in the editorials she wrote for the *Raleigh Times* in 1948. Obsessed with the notion that many social reformers were in reality Communists and fearful that Communists were infiltrating the state's institutions of higher learning, particularly The University of North Carolina, she launched an attack on many of her old "liberal" friends. A special target was Frank Porter Graham, former president of The University of North Carolina and a friend from earlier years. Active in political campaigns designed to discredit social reformers and civil rights advocates, she often wrote vindictive critiques that revived her former title, "Battling Nell," in a different context. Yet despite her susceptibility to the fears of the McCarthy era, Miss Lewis never quite undid all that she had done before that fear absorbed her energy. Somehow she never lost her delight in debunking the state's glorified self-image nor did she lose her interest in the improvement of conditions and opportunities for women. She also remained consistent in her advocacy of penal reform and in her concern for mental health.

Nell Lewis died suddenly of a heart attack and was buried in Oakwood Cemetery, Raleigh.

SEE: Mollie C. Davis Abernathy, "Southern Women, Social Reconstruction, and the Church in the 1920's," *Louisiana Studies* 13 (Winter 1974); Frank Porter Graham Papers and Kemp Plummer Lewis Papers (Southern Historical Collection, University of North Carolina, Chapel Hill); Linda Lou Green, "Nell Battle Lewis: Crusading Columnist, 1921–1938" (M.A. thesis, East Carolina University, 1969); Nell Battle Lewis Papers (North Carolina State Archives, Raleigh); Raleigh *News and Observer*, scattered issues, 1921–56; *Raleigh Times*, scattered issues, June–November 1948; Smith College Archives (Smith College, Northampton, Mass.).

MOLLIE C. DAVIS

Lewis, Richard Henry (21 Dec. 1832–15 May 1917), educator and physician, was born in Edgecombe County, the son of Dr. John Wesley and Catherine Battle Lewis. He received his early schooling in the Edgecombe Academy and Lovejoy Academy in Raleigh. Lewis was graduated from The University of North Carolina in 1852 and was granted the customary master's degree in 1855. Between 1852 and 1854 he taught in Person County at Mount Tirzah, in Fayetteville, and in Warren County. In 1856 he was graduated from the medical department of the University of Pennsylvania and began his practice in Halifax County, Va., and Edgecombe County, N.C. It was interrupted by brief service in the Civil War as captain of Company K, Fifteenth Regiment, North Carolina Troops. An illness that affected his sight resulted in his resignation from the army, after which he moved to Tarboro to resume the practice of medicine. A second attack affecting his sight more seriously turned him from medicine to education.

Lewis served as coprincipal of St. John's Female Academy at Oxford, directed the Mills River Academy near Hendersonville, and was president of Judson College in Hendersonville from 1889 to 1893. In 1877 he and C. W. Howard established and operated the Kinston Collegiate Institute. Lewis resigned from the institute in 1882 to open Kinston College. Returning to Kinston from Hendersonville in 1893, he and his wife conducted the Lewis School, a coeducational private school, in their home until 1902. Additionally, Lewis was on the faculty of the normal school conducted each summer at The University of North Carolina between 1880 and 1884.

Lewis's first wife, whom he married in 1857, was the former Virginia A. Cull of Washington, D.C. Following her death and that of their two sons, he married Eleanor Betts on 23 Dec. 1863. They became the parents of a daughter and three sons: Katherine, William Figures, Elisha Betts, and Frank Cox.

SEE: Kemp P. Battle, *History of the University of North Carolina*, vol. 2 (1912); Daniel L. Grant, *Alumni History of the University of North Carolina, 1795–1924* (1924); *Heritage of Lenoir County* (1981); Talmage C. Johnson and Charles R. Holoman, *The Story of Kinston and Lenoir County* (1954); *Kinston Daily Free Press*, 26 Mar. 1963; *North Carolina Teacher* 3 (February 1886 [portrait]); Ellen Ragan, "The Lewis School in Kinston," 1962 (typescript, North Carolina Collection, University of North Carolina, Chapel Hill); Stephen B. Weeks Scrapbook, vol. 2 (North Carolina Collection, University of North Carolina, Chapel Hill).

H. KENT STEPHENS

Lewis, Richard Henry (18 Feb. 1850–6 Aug. 1926), physician, teacher, and legislative counselor, the son of Richard Henry and Martha Elizabeth Hoskins Lewis, was born at Greenwreath near Greenville. He attended Owens School and the Tarboro Male Academy and entered The University of North Carolina in 1866. Until the university closed in 1868, he led his class in scholastic ability. In the fall of that year he entered the University of Virginia where his primary studies were philosophy and French, and in the fall of 1869 he began to study medicine. In 1870 he entered the School of Medicine at the University of Maryland, from which he was graduated on 1 Mar. 1871 with the M.D. degree. He remained in Baltimore for two years as resident and later as assistant physician in the University of Maryland Hospital. Returning to North Carolina, he engaged in general practice in Tarboro for a few months before determining to specialize in the treatment of eye and ear diseases. He began studies under Dr. Julian J. Chisholm in Baltimore and afterwards continued at the Royal Ophthalmic Hospital in London. In 1875 he began a practice in Savannah, Ga.

Finally settling in Raleigh, Lewis became a member of the North Carolina State Medical Society in 1877, the Board of Medical Examiners in 1880 (elected president, 1890), the North Carolina State Board of Health in 1885 (secretary, 1892–1909), and the American Public Health Association (president, 1908). For thirty-five years he served on the board of trustees of The University of North Carolina and for many years he was a member of the executive committee. For twenty-three years he was a trustee and a member of the executive committee of St. Mary's School, Raleigh, and for twenty-eight years he worked diligently for the education of blacks, serving as professor of the diseases of the eye and ear in Leon-

ard Medical School of Shaw University, Raleigh. For seven years he also was professor of the diseases of the eye and ear in the medical department of The University of North Carolina.

Lewis was influential in securing some of the earliest legislation for the improvement of rural roads, and while chairman of the street committee of the Raleigh Board of Aldermen he was responsible for the use of the first road machine in the city. For many years he was a member of the board of directors and, after 1916, second vice-president of the Citizens National Bank of Raleigh. At Christ Church he was an active member and senior warden.

His first wife was Cornelia Violet Battle, whom he married in 1877; she died in 1886 leaving four children: Richard Henry, Martha Battle, Kemp Plummer, and Ivey Foreman Lewis. In 1890 he married Mary Long Gordon, who died in 1895 leaving a daughter, Nell [Cornelia] Battle Lewis. His third wife, whom he married in 1897, was Mrs. Annie Blackwell Foreman; she died in 1917. Lewis was buried in Oakwood Cemetery, Raleigh.

SEE: *Charlotte Medical Journal* 88 (1926); Medical Society of the State of North Carolina, *Transactions* (1927); *North Carolina Biography*, vols. 5 (1919), 3 (1929); *North Carolina Medical Journal* 19 (1887); John H. Wheeler, ed., *Reminiscences and Memoirs of North Carolina and Eminent North Carolinians* (1884); *Who Was Who in America*, vol. 1 (1981).

JAMES FRANCIS HARPER

Lewis, William Gaston (3 Sept. 1835–7 Jan. 1901), Confederate soldier, civil engineer, farmer, and merchant, was born in Rocky Mount, the son of Dr. John Wesley and Catherine Anne Battle Lewis, and attended Lovejoy Academy in Raleigh. After the death of his father, Lewis's mother moved the family to Chapel Hill where he entered The University of North Carolina and was graduated in 1855 at age nineteen. He then taught in Chapel Hill (1855–56) and Jackson County, Fla. (1856–57). Appointed to the U.S. Survey Corps, Lewis worked in Minnesota in 1857–59 before returning to North Carolina to become assistant engineer on the Tarboro branch of the Wilmington and Weldon Railroad in 1859–61.

At the outbreak of the Civil War in 1861, he joined the Confederate Army and soon proved himself to be a highly efficient soldier; promotion came rapidly. Beginning his service as third lieutenant of Company A, First North Carolina ("Bethel") Regiment, he saw action in the Battle of Bethel on 10 June 1861. Commissioned major of the Thirty-third North Carolina Regiment on 17 Jan. 1862, he served in the Battle of New Bern in March. For his outstanding service here he was appointed lieutenant colonel of the Forty-third Regiment in April 1862. In June and July he took part in the Seven Days' campaign in Virginia and was under fire from Union batteries and gunboats during the Battle of Malvern Hill in July. During the remainder of the summer he participated in the defense of Richmond, was engaged in drilling the regiment, and supervised the digging of entrenchments for the defense of Drewry's Bluff.

In December 1862 his brigade returned to North Carolina to help turn back a raid on Goldsboro. Here Lewis supervised the rebuilding of the railroad bridge burned by the enemy as it retreated. In the spring of 1863 he was stationed at Kinston and took part in an unsuccessful attack on New Bern, then in enemy hands. Returning to Virginia with his unit, he fought at the Battle of Gettysburg, and when the regimental commander, Colonel Thomas Kenan, was wounded and captured,

Lewis assumed command of the Forty-third Regiment. His "bravery and coolness" in battle were mentioned in dispatches.

Lewis's regiment once again returned to North Carolina and saw action in the eastern part of the state, particularly around New Bern. On one occasion Lewis repaired a bridge while under fire, thus enabling the Confederates to drive Union forces back into New Bern. He participated in the successful attack on Plymouth when the brigade commander was killed. As senior officer, Lewis assumed command and went with the brigade to Virginia where he again won high praise for his skill in holding off the enemy until reserves could be brought up. In June 1864 Lewis was promoted to brigadier general, and his new command consisted of four North Carolina regiments and a battalion. He thereafter took part in the Battle of Cold Harbor, in pursuing Union forces in the Shenandoah Valley, and in a raid on Washington, D.C., in addition to other battles and skirmishes. Wounded in July 1864, General Lewis was out of action until September when he and his men served in the rear guard of General Robert E. Lee's army during the retreat to Appomattox. In an engagement outside Farmville, Va., on 7 Apr. 1865, Lewis was again severely wounded and captured while leading an assault. He was paroled at Farmville sometime between 11 and 21 April. His spotless war record shows him to have been a most capable commander, having participated in some thirty-seven battles and skirmishes.

After the war Lewis resumed his civil engineering practice, and for thirteen years served as state engineer. In 1865 he was road master for the Wilmington and Weldon Railroad; in 1866 he was assistant construction engineer for the Wilmington, Charlotte, and Rutherfordton Railroad; in 1867 he was general superintendent of the Raleigh and Gaston Railroad; and in 1868–69 he was chief engineer for the Williamston and Tarboro Railroad and the Edenton and Norfolk Railroad. From 1871 to 1878 Lewis was a hardware merchant in Tarboro, and from 1879 to 1884 he tried his hand at farming. He served as chief engineer for the North Carolina Phosphate and Swamp Land Surveys in 1885 and for the North Carolina State Guard in 1885–1901. On the State Board of Education he was also chief engineer for swamplands in 1886–92. In 1899 he was chief engineer for the Albany and Raleigh Railroad with residence at Goldsboro. Lewis died suddenly from pneumonia at his home. He was buried with military honors in Goldsboro.

On 15 Mar. 1864 he married Martha Lucinda Pender, daughter of Joseph John Pender of Edgecombe County. They had four daughters and three sons, one of whom died as an infant.

SEE: John G. Barrett, *The Civil War in North Carolina* (1963); Herbert B. Battle, *The Battle Book* (1930); Walter Clark, ed., *Histories of the Several Regiments and Battalions from North Carolina in the Great War, 1861–1865,* 5 vols. (1901); *DAB,* vol. 11 (1933); C. A. Evans, ed., *Confederate Military History,* vol. 4: *North Carolina,* by D. H. Hill, Jr. (1899); Douglas S. Freeman, *Lee's Lieutenants,* vol. 3 (1944); Daniel L. Grant, *Alumni History of the University of North Carolina, 1795–1924* (1924); Weymouth T. Jordan, comp., *North Carolina Troops, 1861–1865: A Roster,* vols. 4, 6, 9, 10 (1973, 1977, 1983, 1985); Louis H. Manarin, comp., *North Carolina Troops, 1861–1865: A Roster,* vol. 3 (1971).

PAUL BRANCH

Lichtenstein, Gaston *(17 Dec. 1879–16 Jan. 1954),* researcher, writer, and historian, was born in Tarboro, the son of David and Hannah Zander Lichtenstein. The oldest of seven children, he attended Tarboro Male Academy from September 1890 to February 1895. He was graduated from Hughes High School in Cincinnati, Ohio, in 1897. Afterwards, he studied at both the University of Cincinnati (1897–1900) and Hebrew Union College, Cincinnati, from which he received the degree of bachelor of Hebrew Letters in 1899. In 1903 Lichtenstein moved to Richmond, Va., with his parents, who had lived there before going to Tarboro. He remained in Richmond until his death.

Lichtenstein was fluent in seven languages and tutored Douglas Southall Freeman in Hebrew. His research at the Virginia State Library aided in the discovery of letters that Patrick Henry wrote while governor of Virginia. Lichtenstein was a frequent contributor of historical articles to *The Tarborough Southerner.* A Mason, he was a member of Beth Ahabah Temple in Richmond, the B'nai B'rith Lodge, the Sons of Confederate Veterans, the American Historical Association, and the Richmond Musicians' Association.

Among Lichtenstein's many publications are "Early History of Tarboro . . ." (1908), "Early Social Life in Edgecombe" (1904), "Edgecombe and the Revolution" (1912), "For Whom Was Edgecombe County Named?" (1918), *From Richmond to North Cape* (1922), "George Washington's Lost Birthday" (1924), "Louis D. Wilson . . ." (1911), "Recollections of My Teacher . . ." (1953), "Thomas Jefferson as War Governor . . ." (1925), "When Tarboro Was Incorporated . . ." (1910), "A Visit to Young's Pier . . ." (1908), and "The Virginia Lichtensteins" (1912). He compiled *Repatriation of Prisoners of War from Siberia . . .* (1924), and he was the coauthor of the *History of the Jews of Richmond* (1917).

Lichtenstein never married. He died in the hotel that was his home in Richmond and was buried in the Hebrew cemetery.

SEE: "Gaston Lichtenstein," *New York Times,* 18 Jan. 1954; "Gaston Lichtenstein, Historian, Dies Here," Richmond *Times-Dispatch,* 17 Jan. 1954; Gaston Lichtenstein, *The Virginia Lichtensteins: Amplified by Historical and Biographical Data* (1912); "Tar Heel Native Dies in Richmond," Raleigh *News and Observer,* 18 Jan. 1954; *Who's Who in American Jewry,* 2d ed. (1928).

ALICE R. COTTEN

Liddell, Anna Forbes *(6 Dec. 1891–30 Aug. 1979),* suffragist, organizing president of the first Equal Suffrage League in North Carolina, and university professor, was born at the family home on East Avenue (afterwards the site of the city hall) in Charlotte. She was the daughter of Walter Scott Liddell, president of Liddell Company, manufacturer of machinery, and Helen Sherman Ogden Liddell.

Anna Forbes Liddell, who preferred to be called Forbes, had early interests in creative writing and journalism. Between 1909 and 1920 she held a variety of jobs, attended college, and was a free-lance writer for several magazines and newspapers, including the New York *Evening Post.* She attended Presbyterian (now Queens) College in Charlotte from the primary department through the middle of her second year of college. She then began working with the advertising department of the *Charlotte Observer.* After attending summer school in 1908 at the University of Tennessee, she spent one semester at Columbia University in New York. For a time she wrote articles for magazines and prepared special articles for the Wildman Agency in New York City. Among her writings was a long serialized juvenile fairy story entitled "The Adventures of Arrabelle and Wigglewumps in the Enchanted Garden," published in *Holland's Magazine* (1919–20).

In the summer of 1913 there was renewed interest in the question of woman suffrage, a subject that had attracted little attention since the brief flurry of activity between 1895 and 1899. In November 1913, largely through the efforts of Forbes Liddell and Susanne Bynum of Asheville, the North Carolina Equal Suffrage League was organized in Charlotte. It played a very active role in bringing this issue before the state's citizenry. Miss Liddell also was one of the editors of a special suffrage edition of the *Charlotte Observer*. In a contest conducted by *Life* magazine for the best original article on "Feminism," her entry was one of eight selected and purchased from among the 3,000 submitted.

In 1915 Forbes Liddell left Charlotte to enter The University of North Carolina. After withdrawing for a year, she was graduated in 1918 with honors as an English major. At Chapel Hill, she was active in the Dramatic Club, was a member of *The Tar Heel* staff, and took courses under philosophy professor Horace Williams whom she admired very much. In January 1919 she once again moved to New York City to work in the circulation department of the publishing house of McGraw-Hill. Because of ill health, however, she soon returned to North Carolina and became principal of a two-teacher school in Mecklenburg County for a brief time and then taught English in the high school in Salisbury until 1921. In the latter year she entered Cornell University, where she received a master of arts degree in 1922 and was awarded the Sage Prize in philosophy in 1923. From Cornell, Miss Liddell transferred to The University of North Carolina and in 1924 became one of two women to receive a doctor of philosophy degree at the university—the first women to do so; her dissertation was written under the direction of Horace Williams. She later studied at the University of Heidelberg in Germany, as had Williams.

In the academic year 1925–26, Forbes Liddell was professor of social studies at Chowan College, Murfreesboro. In the fall of 1926 she joined the faculty of the Florida State College for Women (which became Florida State University in 1947), in Tallahassee, where she taught philosophy until her retirement in 1962; from 1932 to 1951, she was head of the Department of Philosophy and Religion. In 1959 she was elected Distinguished Professor of the Year.

She attended the International Congress of Philosophy at Oxford, England, in 1930 and the International Congress of Psychology at Copenhagen in 1932. At the Eighth International Congress of Philosophy in Prague in September 1934, as the first woman from the South to appear on a program, Miss Liddell read a paper entitled "Philosophy and Religion." She also read papers at the International Congress of Philosophers in Brussels in 1953 and in Venice in 1958. She was a member of many professional organizations in which she sometimes held office.

She was a Democrat and a member of the Baptist church until late in life when she became an Episcopalian. A lifelong advocate of woman's rights, in 1978 she rode in her wheelchair to a rally where she admonished state lawmakers for not ratifying the Equal Rights Amendment in Florida. She once said that all the argu-

ments the legislature used against ERA were exactly the same arguments she had heard used against women's right to vote.

Forbes Liddell never married. She died at age eighty-seven and was survived by a sister in Charlotte, a nephew, and three nieces.

SEE: Alumni Files (University of North Carolina, Chapel Hill); Daniel L. Grant, *Alumni History of the University of North Carolina, 1795–1924* (1924); William S. Powell, ed., *North Carolina Lives* (1962); A. Elizabeth Taylor, "The Woman Suffrage Movement in North Carolina," *North Carolina Historical Review* 38 (January 1961); *University Report* (December 1979); Mrs. J. A. Yarborough, "Interesting Carolina People," *Charlotte Observer*, 8 Sept. 1938.

BARBARA ELIZABETH LAMBERT

Lillington, Alexander (*1643–September 1697*), lawyer, planter, legislator, justice of the peace, and executive law officer, was one of the most distinguished citizens of seventeenth-century Albemarle County. Born in Great Britain, he migrated with two brothers to Massachusetts, then to Barbados, and eventually to the Albemarle Sound area before 1668. On 11 June 1668 he married Sarah James, by whom he had two sons, James and Alexander. On 13 June 1675 he was married a second time, to the widow Elizabeth Cooke; they had four daughters and a son, among whom were Elizabeth, Mary, Sarah, and John. A third marriage on 19 Mar. 1695 to the widow Ann Steward produced no issue.

Initially engaged in shipbuilding, Lillington quickly turned to planting and ultimately acquired several plantations, as noted in his will of 9 Sept. 1697. His main efforts, however, were devoted to law and public service. He participated in Culpeper's Rebellion during which George Durant and his associates opposed the collection of taxes on tobacco shipped to England. Elected a member of the "free parliament" of the period, he gave his full support to the rebels. Following the appointment of John Harvey as governor in 1679, Lillington was made a justice of the peace; in this position, he presided over the court of Perquimans Precinct for the remainder of his life.

During the 1680s and 1690s Lillington was involved in almost every aspect of public and legal service in Albemarle County. At various times he was a member of the Council; an assemblyman; sheriff of Albemarle County (an office provided for in the Fundamental Constitutions issued by the Lords Proprietors), by which he was executive officer of the courts held by the Council and tax collector of the county; and provost marshal of Perquimans Precinct. As a lawyer, he represented clients in numerous cases in the various courts of the colony.

It was in the role of chief judge of the County Court of Albemarle, which held four sessions in 1693 and 1694, that Lillington performed perhaps his greatest service. This court for all of Albemarle County, as the whole colony was then known, was also one provided for in the Fundamental Constitutions and was first organized in 1693. Lillington, Caleb Calloway, John Barrow, and Thomas Lepper, all from Perquimans, and Henry White from Pasquotank Precinct, composed the court. While most of the court's business pertained to residents of or land in Perquimans, a number of cases related to Chowan Precinct. The jurors came from all four precincts of Albemarle County.

The marriage of Lillington's daughters to such prominent leaders as Samuel Swann, Henderson Walker, John

Porter, and Edward Moseley, involved the family in the political and legal affairs of the colony for many years after his death. Following her husband's death, Mrs. Swann married Maurice Moore, principal promoter of the Cape Fear settlement and founder of Brunswick Town. Lillington's son, John, married into the distinguished Porter family. Descendants of Alexander Lillington played significant roles in North Carolina and the nation for more than three centuries. One was a justice of the U.S. Supreme Court and another was attorney general of the Confederacy.

SEE: Samuel A. Ashe, ed., *Biographical History of North Carolina*, vol. 1 (1905); James M. Clifton, "The Evolution of the Superior Court in North Carolina before 1868" (master's thesis, Duke University, 1957); J. Bryan Grimes, ed., *North Carolina Wills and Inventories* (1912); J. R. B. Hathaway, ed., *North Carolina Historical and Genealogical Register*, vols. 1–3 (1900–1903); Mattie Erma E. Parker, ed., *North Carolina Higher-Court Records*, vols. 2–3 (1968, 1971); William L. Saunders, ed., *Colonial Records of North Carolina*, vol. 1 (1886).

JAMES M. CLIFTON

Lillington, John Alexander *(1720s–April 1786)*, planter, politician, and soldier, was the son of John and Sarah Porter Lillington and the grandson of Alexander Lillington, who arrived in the Albemarle Sound area in the early Proprietary years, participated in Culpeper's Rebellion, and subsequently remained active in precinct and provincial government until his death in 1697. His father was one of four children of Alexander by the latter's second marriage. Born in Beaufort Precinct, John Alexander Lillington, the revolutionary, was orphaned and raised in the Cape Fear by Edward Moseley, his uncle and legal guardian.

Named John Alexander, but generally using only the middle name, Lillington was moderately active in local and provincial affairs. As a lieutenant in the New Topsail Company of militia, he helped to repel the Spanish invasion of Brunswick in 1748. He represented New Hanover County in the colonial Assembly in 1762, and in the county he served as a justice of the peace from 1764 to 1767 and from 1774 to 1775. The Assembly appointed him a commissioner of the roads in New Hanover in 1745 and 1773, a commissioner to lay off a town at Sand Hill in 1754, and a commissioner to survey the Duplin–New Hanover County boundary in 1766.

Best known for his military exploits in the Revolution, Lillington first evidenced publicly his incipient Whiggism in the Stamp Act crisis when he, John Ashe, and Thomas Lloyd, representing the inhabitants of the Cape Fear, indicated to Governor William Tryon their hope that the restrictions on commerce in the Cape Fear River would be lifted. Like many eastern politicos, Lillington subsequently supported the governor in the Regulator campaigns, serving as a lieutenant colonel and then colonel commandant of a company of light infantry on the 1768 expedition to Hillsborough. In 1771 he was assistant quartermaster general in the campaign that ended with the defeat of the Regulators in the Battle of Alamance.

As the Revolution approached, Lillington was elected to the New Hanover County Committee of Safety in 1775 and as one of the county's delegates to the Third Provincial Congress, which met at Hillsborough in August 1775. Appointed by the congress colonel of a battalion of minutemen in the Wilmington District, he played

a conspicuous, albeit debatable, role in the Patriot victory at Moore's Creek Bridge on 27 Feb. 1776. Lillington arrived first at the battlefield but was soon reinforced by Richard Caswell, who took command of the forces. Together they thwarted the advance of the Loyalists in a victory for which the ultimate credit probably belonged to General James Moore. Concerning the field of battle, however, the partisans of Lillington and Caswell wrangle over the merits of their respective heroes in a running debate that probably emanated from the observations of Joseph Seawell Jones, *A Defence of the Revolutionary History of North Carolina* (1834).

On 15 Apr. 1776 the Fourth Provincial Congress appointed Lillington colonel of the Sixth Regiment of North Carolina Continentals. He resigned on 31 Dec. 1776, ostensibly pleading advanced age but perhaps trying to avoid desperate supply conditions or attempting to open an avenue for political advancement. In 1777 he represented New Hanover County in the Assembly, and on 4 Feb. 1779 he was named brigadier general of the militia in the Wilmington District. As the British moved south to threaten Charles Town in 1780, North Carolina militiamen commanded by Lillington were sent to aid General Benjamin Lincoln. Since the term of enlistment for the mission expired before the fall of Charles Town, Lillington and at least half of his force returned to North Carolina; the remainder of the North Carolina militia surrendered with Lincoln on 12 May 1780.

From the capture of Wilmington in January 1781 to the departure of the British later in the year, Lillington remained busy fending against the forays of Major James H. Craig and the many Loyalists who appeared to support the king. Supply deficiencies and ammunition shortages caused Lillington to become increasingly distressed with the progress of the war. He castigated the Continental supply officers who heavy-handedly sequestered supplies and excoriated the rest of the state for failing to come to the aid of Wilmington and its environs.

At the end of the war Lillington reclaimed most of his estate that had been under British control. Lillington Hall, his impressive home, had been saved from the British torch (according to tradition, by Loyalists who retained great admiration and respect for Lillington), but many of his slaves, of which he had twenty-two according to a 1763 tax list, had been lost. Fortunately, his valuable library was preserved. At an unknown date the State Library of North Carolina acquired a portion of Lillington's books and in the 1950s the North Carolina Collection at Chapel Hill obtained those volumes as an "associational collection."

Lillington, reputedly a large man of exceptional strength, married Sarah Watters, daughter of Brunswick County planter William Watters. They had four children: John (d. 1785), George (1765–94), Sarah, and Mary. John served as a lieutenant in North Carolina's First Continental Regiment, justice of the peace in New Hanover County, and a trustee of Innes Academy. General John Alexander Lillington was buried according to Anglican rites in the family cemetery near Lillington Hall, now marked "Lillington Cemetery" and located in Pender County.

SEE: Samuel A. Ashe, ed., *Biographical History of North Carolina*, vols. 1, 3 (1905); John D. Bellamy, *General Alexander Lillington* (1905); Walter Clark, ed., *State Records of North Carolina*, vols. 11–25 (1895–1906); Minutes of the New Hanover County Court of Pleas and Quarter Sessions, 1739–86 (North Carolina State Archives, Raleigh);

New Hanover County Deeds and Wills (New Hanover County Courthouse, Wilmington); William L. Saunders, ed., *Colonial Records of North Carolina*, vols. 4–10 (1886–90).

ALAN D. WATSON

Lincoln, Nancy Hanks. *See* **Hanks, Nancy.**

Lindley, James (*22 Sept. 1735–April 1779*), Loyalist militia leader, was born in London Grove, Chester County, Pa., the son of Thomas (1706–81) and Ruth Hadley Lindley (1712–85). Of English origin, the Lindleys by the seventeenth century were in Ireland where they became members of the Society of Friends. James Lindley's grandfather, for whom he was named, emigrated from County Carlow in 1713, settled in Chester County, Pa., and was a founder of New Garden Monthly Meeting. Thomas Lindley moved his family to Orange County, N.C., acquiring grants on Cane Creek totaling 950 acres by 1759. He was received into Cane Creek Monthly Meeting on 6 Oct. 1753. On 10 Aug. 1755 he formed a partnership with Hugh Laughlin to construct Lindley's Mill, the first gristmill in the valley. This mill was the site of an important battle of the Revolution on 13 Sept. 1781, when a Whig militia force, seeking to release the captured Governor Thomas Burke, was defeated by Colonel David Fanning. As early as 1773 Thomas Lindley and neighboring Friends began a meeting for worship that became Spring Monthly Meeting in 1793.

James Lindley in 1754 married Mary Cox, the daughter of William Cox of Cox's Mill in present Randolph County. By 1761 Lindley had acquired 1,170 acres in Granville grants on Terrell Creek in Orange (now Chatham) County. The county court minutes of 1753–66 show that he was licensed to keep an ordinary in his home.

Early in 1768 James and Mary Lindley moved to South Carolina, settling on Reaburn's Creek near the junction of the Saluda and Reedy rivers in the Ninety-Six District. He acquired 200 acres that year and another 200 acres in 1773. On 2 Dec. 1768 he was commissioned a Crown justice of the peace for Granville County, and until the Revolution he held Crown commissions for Craven County, Ninety-Six District, and Cheraw District. The South Carolina General Assembly appointed him a justice for Ninety-Six District in 1776. Considering his Loyalist sympathies, it is unlikely that he served the Revolutionary government.

Lindley was a captain in the Upper Saluda Regiment of the provincial militia. In 1775 a majority of the South Carolina up-country settlers were loyal to the Crown and had to be forcibly subdued by the Revolutionary forces under Charles Town leadership. In mid-July 1775 the regiment was mustered by the commanding officer, Colonel Thomas Fletchall of Fair Forest, for the purpose of determining the loyalty of the militia. The regiment unanimously supported the Crown. At this time, David Fanning, who later became a noted Loyalist partisan commander, was a sergeant in Captain Lindley's company.

In November 1775 civil strife began between the Whigs and the Loyalists, and the Upper Saluda Regiment, now commanded by Major Joseph Robinson, successfully besieged a Whig force at Ninety-Six (19–21 November). With aid from the North Carolina Whig militia, a combined force in the "Snow Campaign" cornered the heavily outnumbered Loyalists under Patrick Cunning-

ham at the Great Cane Brake on 22 December. Lindley was among 130 Loyalist prisoners captured at this skirmish and sent to Charles Town where, in an effort at reconciliation, they were soon released.

By the summer of 1776 the British were encouraging the Cherokee to raid the frontier. On 15 July 1776 a Loyalist-Cherokee party attacked Lindley's Fort on Reaburn's Creek, presumably the home of James Lindley, but it is not known whether he participated in this battle. After two and one-half hours of inconclusive skirmishing, the Loyalists and Indians withdrew. Lindley remained an active Loyalist and probably resided at Reaburn's Creek or was occasionally "out lying" in the forest until 1779. Governor John Rutledge in a letter once referred to Lindley's participation in a raid, noting that he escaped capture.

Early in 1779 South Carolina Loyalists mustered under a Colonel Boyd and marched into the Georgia backcountry to cooperate with the British invasion. At Kettle Creek in Wilkes County on 14 Feb. 1779, the Loyalists were surprised and defeated by Whigs commanded by Colonels Andrew Pickens, John Dooley, and Elijah Clarke. Among the Loyalist prisoners taken to the Ninety-Six jail was James Lindley. He and four other Loyalist leaders were tried, convicted, and hanged for treason at Ninety-Six in late April 1779. His widow and their children returned to North Carolina, and in 1790 Mary Lindley was living in Orange County. The Lindleys had at least three sons: Jonathan, William, and Thomas.

William Lindley had moved back to North Carolina and settled in Chatham County by 1774. He was recruited with his father by Colonel Boyd in 1779 and was captured in the Battle of Kettle Creek. Although imprisoned at Ninety-Six and tried for treason, he was released shortly before the execution of his father. He returned to North Carolina and on 16 July 1781 Colonel David Fanning commissioned him a captain in the Chatham County Loyalist militia. In August he commanded a raid through Orange County, and in September he was in the Hillsborough raid and the Battle of Lindley's Mill. He became one of Fanning's most trusted officers. After the British evacuation of Wilmington and the overpowering of the Loyalists, William Lindley moved over the mountains to the Watauga settlement. He was murdered there by three Loyalist deserters in January 1782. Fanning reported that Lindley was "cut to pieces with their Swords," and Fanning personally avenged his death by tracking down and hanging two of the three assassins.

SEE: Lindley S. Butler, ed., *The Narrative of Col. David Fanning* (1981); E. W. Caruthers, *Revolutionary Incidents* (1854); Chatham County Deeds (Chatham County Courthouse, Pittsboro); Walter Clark, ed., *State Records of North Carolina*, vol. 22 (1907); Colonial Land Plats and Revolutionary Records (South Carolina State Archives, Columbia); R. W. Gibbes, ed., *Documentary History of the American Revolution*, vol. 2 (1855); W. W. Hinshaw, comp., *Encyclopedia of American Quaker Genealogy*, vol. 1 (1936); William Henry Hoyt, ed., *The Papers of Archibald D. Murphey*, vol. 2 (1914); Orange County Court Minutes and Deeds (North Carolina State Archives, Raleigh); *South Carolina Gazette*, 2 Feb. 1769, 23 Jan. 1775.

LINDLEY S. BUTLER

Lindley, John Van (*5 Nov. 1838–13 June 1918*), florist, nurseryman, and horticulturist, was born in Monrovia,

Ind. His father, Joshua Lindley, a fruit grower and native of North Carolina, had moved to Indiana to marry Judith Henley and returned to Chatham County, N.C., with his family in 1841. Judith Lindley died in 1846, and in 1851 Joshua moved his family to Guilford County and began operating the New Garden Nursery, near Greensboro, the first of its kind in North Carolina.

John Lindley's formal education was limited, although his practical experience working with his father was more than sufficient for his needs as a nurseryman. He attended community public schools and studied for a year at the New Garden Boarding School (now Guilford College).

In his early twenties, Lindley traveled west and was in Missouri at the outbreak of the Civil War. Although a Quaker, he joined the Union army and served for three years as a private. At the close of the war, Lindley returned home to find his father's business five thousand dollars in debt. With young Lindley's help, the New Garden Nursery was reestablished in 1866 as Joshua Lindley and Son. After ten years, with the debt paid and the business running in the black, the son became sole proprietor of the J. Van Lindley Nursery.

The business flourished and in 1889 Lindley built the first commercial greenhouses in the Greensboro area, located at Salem Junction (later Pomona). He experimented with strains of plants, shrubs, and trees to find the best possible varieties for different soils and climates. Becoming interested in the possibility of growing peaches in the Sandhills of North Carolina, in 1892 he planted fifty thousand peach trees in Moore County. His crop encountered difficulties until 1906, when sufficient pesticide sprays became available. By 1909 his peach yield was abundant; since then, peach growing has become one of the major sources of income for the Sandhills. The J. Van Lindley Nursery, which encompassed a vast amount of land in the Pomona area, was one of the largest in the state and sales reached into all of the South and into parts of the North.

Although the nursery was Lindley's main occupation, he was involved in many other business enterprises. In 1890 he bought the bankrupt clay-working industry, Pomona Terra-Cotta, from the founder and owner, A. M. Smith. Later, Lindley's associates, W. C. Boren and G. S. Boren, took over the operations and the company became one of the largest manufacturers of vitrified clay and sewer lines in the nation. In the early 1900s, Lindley was president of the Southern Mutual Fire Insurance Company and director of the Southern Loan and Trust Company. He helped establish and served as president of the Security Life and Annuity Company and supported its merger with the Jefferson Life Insurance Company in 1912; afterwards, he became vice-president.

Lindley was generous with his acquired wealth. From 1888 until his death, he served on the Guilford College Board of Trustees. He donated large sums of money to help relieve the college debt. Lindley contributed both money and land for the building of public schools throughout Guilford County. He started a school in the Pomona area, originally for his employees' children and his own. The Lindley Elementary School and the Lindley Junior High School in Greensboro were named for him. He also contributed large tracts of land in 1917 for the J. Van Lindley Park located between Pomona and Greensboro and for the Masonic lodge near Pomona. He was interested in internal improvements, especially roads, and was president of the Guilford County Road Association.

In 1870 Lindley married Mary W. Coffin of Guilford County. She died in 1871, and in 1875 he married Sandia Cook of Friendship, N.C. Early in 1918 Lindley suffered a paralytic stroke and died at his home in June. Sandia Lindley died in 1925. They had five children: Paul C., Eva J., Pearl, Cammie G., and Maie Lindley. Lindley was buried in the Guilford College Cemetery, Greensboro.

SEE: Ethel Stephens Arnett, *Greensboro, North Carolina* (1955); Samuel A. Ashe, ed., *Biographical History of North Carolina*, vol. 2 (1905); *Greensboro Daily News*, 14 June 1918, 18 Feb. 1960; *North Carolina Biography*, vol. 3 (1956); Raleigh *News and Observer*, 14 June 1918; A. D. Smith, *Western North Carolina: Historical and Biographical* (1890).

MARY A. BAKER

Lindley, Jonathan (15 June 1756–5 Apr. 1828), legislator and Quaker leader, was born in Orange County, the son of Thomas and Ruth Hadley Lindley and the grandson of James and Elinor Parke Lindley and Simon and Ruth Miller Kearns Hadley. These six of his forebears were all Irish-born Quakers who came to America around 1713. The Lindleys settled in Chester County, Pa., and the Hadleys only a few miles away in New Castle County, Del. Around 1751 Thomas Lindley moved his family to the Cane Creek Valley in what is now the southern part of Alamance County. They were among the founders of Spring Friends Meeting, and Thomas gave the land on which the meetinghouse and cemetery are located.

In 1775 Jonathan Lindley married Deborah Dicks, daughter of Zacharias and Ruth Hiatt Dicks, near neighbors of the Lindleys. Zacharias Dicks was one of the ablest and most widely known of the Quakers ministers in America, and his wife was also a minister.

Between 1786 and 1805, during the critical period of transition following the Revolutionary War, Lindley served five terms in the North Carolina House of Commons and one term in the senate. His continued appointment to committees that dealt with matters of finance leads to the conclusion that the General Assembly recognized his competence in this important field of public interest. While in the House of Commons, he introduced and pushed to a test vote a bill that would have prohibited further importation of slaves into North Carolina. The voters of Orange County elected him as one of the five delegates from that county to the convention that met in Hillsborough in 1788 to consider ratification of the Federal Constitution. He, with other members of the delegation from Orange County, voted against ratification with the view of waiting until a Bill of Rights could be added. A few months later, as a member of the House of Commons, he voted favorably on a resolution calling for a second convention to be convened to consider ratification of the Constitution. This convention met in Fayetteville in 1789 and voted for ratification.

In private life Lindley was a merchant and a surveyor. He had investments in lumber and the turpentine business, and he engaged in numerous land transactions. He is said to have accumulated considerable wealth and is reputed to have taken a large sum of money with him when he migrated to Indiana.

In 1811 he led a wagon train of emigrants from his section of Orange County to the Lick Creek watershed in the southern part of the Territory of Indiana. According to one Lindley tradition, two hundred people went to Indiana in this caravan. A Quaker history indicates that seventy-five of them were members of the Society of Friends. Quaker records further reveal that more than thirty of the emigrants were close relatives of Lindley and that eleven of them were his children, some married and with their own families. Jonathan Lindley's oldest son, Zacharias, had settled in Lick Creek Valley two years before the arrival of the great Lindley caravan. Two years before leaving North Carolina, Jonathan had made a prospecting trip to Indiana and had purchased a large tract of land where Terre Haute now stands, but Indian discontent in that region caused this large caravan of emigrants to stop in the southern part of the territory.

According to tradition, Lindley's unmarried daughters cut trees and hewed logs for the construction of their first home in Indiana. Jonathan was one of the founders of the Lick Creek Friends Meeting, the first in southern Indiana. He also constructed a gristmill along the upper waters of Lick Creek. He was the first judge of the circuit court of Washington County, which at the time covered a large part of southern Indiana. He took the lead in establishing Orange County, named for his native county in North Carolina. His son Zacharias was the first sheriff of the new county. When Indiana attained statehood, Jonathan Lindley was the first representative of his county in the General Assembly of the new state. He also introduced a bill that provided for the organization of a bank at Vincennes. The General Assembly named him to a board that established a State Seminary that later became the University of Indiana.

SEE: Arthur L. Dillard, comp., *Orange County Heritage* (1971); Jonathan Elliott, ed., *Debates, Resolutions and Proceedings on the Adoption of the Federal Constitution*, vol. 3 (1830); Hugh Lefler and Paul Wager, eds., *Orange County, 1751–1952* (1953); Minutes and Records of Spring Monthly Meeting of Friends (Quaker Collection, Guilford College Library, Greensboro); Nancy Lindley Oslund, *Jonathan Lindley: The Paoli Pioneer* (1947); John H. Wheeler, *Historical Sketches of North Carolina from 1584 to 1851* (1851).

ALGIE I. NEWLIN

Lindsay, Colin (1744–1 Dec. 1817), Presbyterian minister, was one of the first ministers in the Orange Presbytery and a bitter opponent of the Great Revival in the early 1800s. He was born in Scotland into a large, wealthy family. He received his commission to preach in Scotland before emigrating to North Carolina in 1792. He landed in Wilmington and was admitted into Orange Presbytery by October 1792.

The first position Lindsay held in North Carolina was as pastor at Black River Chapel, now in southern Sampson County. He held two services each Sunday, the first in English and the second in Gaelic, the latter for the older members of the congregation. His reputation for indulgence and outspoken independence began here when members of his congregation accused him of violating the Sabbath. Lindsay had bought a yoke of oxen on Saturday and had someone drive them home the next day, since there was no food for them at the place of purchase. This act divided his congregation so Lindsay decided to leave. From Black River, he moved farther into the Scottish settlement along the Upper Cape Fear. He held posts at Raft Swamp (now in Hoke County), Longstreet (now in Cumberland County), and

Bethel (now in Hoke County). Lindsay donated the land on which Bethel Church was built.

His first confrontation with the presbytery came in April 1796, when he was charged with "intoxication, profane swearing, and intention of dueling." He was found guilty and was suspended from the pulpit until he expressed sufficient "sorrow and reformation." He was restored to his position on 13 Nov. 1797. In March 1798 he was charged with "drunkenness and conduct unbecoming to an Elder" and was again suspended by the presbytery. The same thing happened in 1800, but in 1801 he repented and said that he had "acted contumaciously . . . and sinned as other men, from the depravity of nature . . . Truly Sorry." Again he was restored to the pulpit. On 1 June 1803 Lindsay was deposed from Orange Presbytery. Although these charges were a factor in his dismissal, his opposition to the Great Revival recently embraced by the Presbyterian church was the ultimate reason for his removal. A traditionalist in religious matters, Lindsay was unable to accept the emotional behavior of the evangelical movement. The Reverend Leonard Prather accused him of "calling the present Revival the work of the Devil," and Lindsay often referred to his opponents in the presbytery as "illiterate boys."

Lindsay continued to preach to a small band of followers in present Scotland County, claiming that he had received his commission to preach, not from Orange Presbytery, but from the "High Kirk" of Scotland. He declared that he would preach "in spite of presbyteries and their little devils." His will to preach was very strong; during his later years, he spoke from a sitting position when unable to stand.

He is perhaps best remembered for a story that he told about his mother. Very ill, she lapsed into a coma and was pronounced dead. Funeral services were held and she was buried. When mourners returned to the cemetery, they stumbled on a pair of thieves who had opened her grave to steal her valuables. When the thieves had tried to cut a ring from her finger, the shock apparently restored her circulation and she returned to consciousness. The thieves ran in terror, while the mourners rejoiced and took the woman home where she was nursed back to health. Colin Lindsay was born a few years later.

Lindsay spent the latter part of his life at Hill's Creek, below the Turnpike Bridge (now in Scotland County). He died childless, survived only by his wife, whose maiden name was Hamilton, and was buried in Old Stewartsville Cemetery in Scotland County.

SEE: "Born Several Years after His Mother's Death," *State Magazine*, 5 June 1948; "Early Presbyterian Divine and Turbulent Career," Raleigh *News and Observer*, 25 Dec. 1932; William Henry Foote, *Sketches of North Carolina* (1846); Neill McKay, *Centenary Sermon at Bluff Church* (1858); R. A. McLeod, *Historical Sketch of Long Street Presbyterian Church* (1923).

WALTER RICHARD BULLOCK, JR.

Lineberry, Gustavus Ernest (12 Jan. 1870–25 Dec. 1952), educator, was born in Chatham County, the youngest of five children of William Alson and Martha Kemley Duncan Lineberry. He was a descendant of Jacob and Elizabeth Lineberry, who emigrated from the Hartz Mountains in Germany and settled along the Randolph–Chatham County line around 1752. His maternal ancestors were Scottish.

Lineberry completed high school at Sanford under the tutelage of his older brother, Rufus Baxter Lineberry. He then enrolled at Wake Forest College, where he studied for two years (1891–93) before assuming a teaching position at Damascus, near Chapel Hill, for two years. He returned to Wake Forest in the fall of 1895 and received a B.A. degree in 1897.

After graduation Lineberry began a long and distinguished career as an educator and educational administrator, serving as principal of Ashpole Institute in Robeson County (1897–1901) and of Winterville High School (1901–9), educational secretary of the Baptist State Convention of North Carolina (1909–14), president of Chowan College (1914–18), and superintendent of the North Carolina State School for the Blind and the Deaf (1918–45).

Early in his career, Lineberry made significant contributions as chief administrator of Ashpole Institute and then Winterville High School, both denominationally sponsored schools, particularly with his emphasis on good instruction. As the first educational secretary for the Baptist State Convention, he launched that denomination on a course designed to eliminate the indebtedness accrued by many of its institutions, to improve their physical facilities, to increase endowments, and to "standardize" the college preparatory curricula offered by the several secondary schools. His tenure as president of Chowan College was characterized by improvements to both the curriculum and the physical plant, but at the expense of increased indebtedness since enrollment was not sufficient to generate the funds needed to operate the college adequately.

It was as superintendent of the State School for the Blind and the Deaf that Lineberry made his greatest contribution. When elected to this post in July 1918, he had already served for eleven years on the board of directors. Thus, he was acquainted with the needs of the school from the outset. His tenure of thirty-five years was marked by vast improvements to the 85-acre campus adjoining Pullen Park, with capital outlay totaling nearly a million dollars. The state legislature appropriated over a half-million dollars towards the development of the "Colored Department," located on a 346-acre tract about five miles southeast of Raleigh.

In addition to providing better physical facilities, Lineberry improved the educational standards of the school. He introduced a systematized course of study—covering kindergarten through twelfth grade—with grading and promotion comparable to that of the public school system. As a member and longtime chairman of the Publications Committee of the American Printing House for the Blind, Lineberry was instrumental in expanding the titles in Braille that were to become available to other institutions for the blind as well. While the teaching of vocational training and skills was a primary objective, he also championed academic studies as a necessary component of the total educational program for the blind and the deaf. Additional priorities during his administration were the health and the physical development of the students.

On 9 Aug. 1899 Lineberry married Ruth Estelle Fisher in Tolarsville. They had seven children: Ernest (died in infancy), Annie Ruth, Margaret Elizabeth (Mrs. Robert Harrison Owen), Martha Foy, John Alson, Doris Estelle (Mrs. Charles Glasgow Armstrong), and Paul Fisher. He was buried in Montlawn Cemetery, Raleigh.

SEE: "Centennial Exercise of the State School for the Blind and the Deaf" (1945); Grace Sanders Kimrey, *The Duncan-Johnson Family Tree* (n.d.); Ruth Lineberry (Ra-

leigh), Biographical sketch of Gustavus Ernest Lineberry (in possession of author); Minutes of the Board of Trustees, Chowan College, 1914–18.

R. HARGUS TAYLOR

Lingle, Walter Lee (3 Oct. 1868–19 Sept. 1956), Presbyterian clergyman and educator, was born in the Thyatira community of Rowan County, the son of Wilson Alexander and Martha Jane Lynch Lingle. He was graduated from Davidson College (A.B., 1892; M.A., 1893) and from Union Theological Seminary, then at Hampden-Sydney, Va., in 1896. At the seminary he was assistant instructor in Hebrew and Greek during his senior year and while pursuing graduate studies the following year. In the summer of 1896 he attended the University of Chicago.

Lingle was ordained by the Concord Presbytery in 1897. From 1898 to 1902 he served as pastor of the Presbyterian Church in Dalton, Ga.; while on leave from the church, he taught for six months at Union Seminary. His next position was at the First Presbyterian Church of Rock Hill, S.C., where he ministered from 1902 until 1907. From Rock Hill he went to the pastorate of First Presbyterian Church of Atlanta, Ga., serving until 1911.

Lingle was closely associated with four of the major institutions of the Presbyterian Church in the United States. In addition to his earlier teaching at Union Seminary, he was McCormick Professor of Hebrew in that school (1911–14) and occupied its chair of church history (1914–24). He served as president of the General Assembly's Training School (now the Presbyterian School of Christian Education) in Richmond from 1924 until 1929, when he became president of Davidson College. Here he remained until his retirement in 1941, at which time he was made president emeritus. He had previously officiated as president of the board of trustees of the college from 1906 until his assumption of the presidency. For fifteen years (1910–24), he was program chairman of the Montreat Summer Conference.

From 1913 to 1922 Lingle was editor in chief of the *Union Seminary Review*, and from 1923 to 1931 he was contributing editor of the *Presbyterian of the South*. In the latter year he began a series of popular articles for the *Christian Observer*, under the title of "Talks on Timely Topics," which ran for more than twenty-five years. He was the author of *Presbyterians: Their History and Beliefs*; *The Bible and Social Problems*, a volume incorporating the Sprunt Lectures that he had delivered at Union Seminary in 1929; *Thyatira Presbyterian Church*; and *Memories of Davidson College*.

The General Assembly of the Presbyterian Church in the United States elected Lingle moderator of its 1920 sessions. He received the honorary degree of D.D. from Davidson College (1906) and that of LL.D. from Southwestern Presbyterian University (1920), Duke University (1932), and The University of North Carolina (1933). The chapel of the Presbyterian church at Davidson College bears his name.

On 2 Jan. 1900 he married Alice Merle Dupuy of Davidson, and they became the parents of four children: Louise Denton, Nan Russell, Walter Lee, Jr., and Caroline Dudley. Lingle died at Mooresville and was buried in the town cemetery at Davidson. There are portraits of him at the Presbyterian School of Christian Education in Richmond and at Davidson College. His personal papers are in the Historical Foundation at Montreat.

SEE: *Christian Observer*, 10 Oct. 1956; William Crowe, Jr., *Life of Walter L. Lingle*; Walter L. Lingle, "Autobiography"

(Manuscripts in the Presbyterian Historical Foundation, Montreat) and *Memories of Davidson College* (1947); *Minutes of the Synod of North Carolina* (1957); *Who's Who in America* (1936–37).

THOMAS H. SPENCE, JR.

Linn, Stahle *(19 Aug. 1886–9 Mar. 1959)*, state senator, judge, and corporation lawyer, was born in Salisbury, the older son of Thomas Calvin and Annie Doll Stahle Linn. His mother was from Gettysburg, Pa., a descendant of Captain Jacob Stahle who commanded a fleet of boats at George Washington's crossing of the Delaware. The Linns settled in Rowan County, N.C., before 1753.

Linn was educated at Horner Military School and The University of North Carolina, where he received the LL.B. degree. He became an attorney for the Southern Railway as well as president of the Post Publishing Company (publisher of the *Salisbury Post*), chairman of the board of managers of the Wachovia Bank and Trust Company, a member of the Wachovia board of directors, and a director of the China Grove Cotton Mills. He was a member of the state senate during the 1917 session. He also served for ten years as a member of the Salisbury city school board and was a judge of the Rowan County Court. Linn was a trustee of the Consolidated University of North Carolina and a member of the John Motley Morehead Scholarship Foundation awards committee. Also a trustee of Catawba College, he was awarded a doctor of laws degree by that institution in 1943.

In 1925 he married Charlotte McNair Brown in Salisbury and they became the parents of Mary Anne (Mrs. James Leake Woodson) and Stahle, Jr. He was buried in Chestnut Hill Cemetery, Salisbury. Linn's portrait hangs in the superior courtroom in the Rowan County courthouse.

SEE: John L. Cheney, Jr., ed., *North Carolina Government, 1585–1979* (1981); Daniel L. Grant, *Alumni History of the University of North Carolina, 1795–1924* (1924); *North Carolina Biography*, vol. 5 (1919); *North Carolina Manual* (1917); *North Carolina Senate 1917: Character Sketches* (1917).

JO WHITE LINN

Linney, Romulus Zachariah *(26 Dec. 1841–15 Apr. 1910)*, lawyer and congressman, was born in Rutherford County, the son of William Cope and Martha Baxter Linney. His father was a well-to-do farmer; his mother was a sister of John Baxter, legislator, speaker of the House of Commons, and judge. Linney attended the local common schools and York Collegiate Institute. On 29 May 1861, at age nineteen, he enlisted in Company A, Seventh Regiment, North Carolina Troops, and served in the Civil War until he was seriously wounded at the Battle of Chancellorsville in May 1863. On 15 December he was discharged because of the permanent nature of his injury. Afterwards he read law under an attorney in Taylorsville, was licensed by the North Carolina Supreme Court in 1868, and opened a practice in Taylorsville to serve the surrounding area.

Linney quickly gained a reputation as a skilled orator and held audiences spellbound in the courtroom. He came to be recognized as a colorful character and was widely known throughout the state. Entering politics, he served as a Democrat in the North Carolina Senate for three terms (1870–72, 1874–75, and 1883). In a subsequent campaign he was defeated by William H. H. Cowles, a Republican. Linney felt that he had been double-crossed by the Democratic party and ran for Congress as an independent in the Eighth District. Switching his party affiliation, he finally won in 1894 and served three terms in the U.S. House of Representatives (1895–1901) as a Republican. Linney was a part of the Republican-Populist fusion as some of his opinions fell clearly into the Populist camp.

On several occasions his speeches created a sensation on the floor of the House. He lived up to his nickname, "Bull Moose" or "the Bull of the Brushies," from the Brushy Mountains in which his district lay. His bull-like domination of the courtroom and his antics on the floor of Congress were often commented on. He had a knack for illustrating his remarks with folksy, amusing stories that served to simplify the point he wished to make. He was a master at calling upon the great authors of the past for apt quotations and being able to draw suitable passages from his reading to clinch an argument.

Popular with his constituency, Linney supported local causes and on one occasion contributed five hundred dollars to the Appalachian Training School at Boone; a quotation from one of his addresses was carved in marble over the front door: "Learning, the Handmaid of Loyalty and Liberty. A Vote Governs Better than a Crown." He maintained his ties by traveling through his district in a buggy drawn by two matched black ponies and stopping from time to time to visit some old friend. In debate concerning the internal revenue system, he represented the views of his mountain supporters; these people often tried to supplement their limited income by distilling brandy and whiskey outside the law. They were hurt by the excise tax that the federal government placed on spirits, and throughout his career Linney tried to change this form of taxation.

Congressman Linney's views on the coinage of money were those of the Populists. He supported the free coinage of silver until the Republicans under President William McKinley announced in favor of the gold standard. Linney then switched his support to the gold standard. When questioned about this change, he answered in typical Linney style that the only two things that never changed an opinion were "a dead horse and a live ass."

In the field of foreign affairs he was inclined to vote with the majority. He supported the declaration of war against Spain in the Spanish-American War and the annexation of Hawaii. However, he did not favor the occupation of the Philippines because he feared that the people there were too different from Americans. Among other subjects, Linney spoke in favor of a protective tariff and against the crime of lynching.

With the conclusion of the Fifty-sixth Congress in 1901, Linney retired from public service and resumed his law practice in North Carolina.

In 1864 he married Dorcus A. Stephenson and they became the parents of a son, Frank Armfield. Linney suffered a fatal heart attack at age sixty-nine and was buried in Fairview Cemetery, Taylorsville.

SEE: Eric Anderson, *Race and Politics in North Carolina, 1872–1901* (1981); John Preston Arthur, *Western North Carolina: A History* (1914); *Biog. Dir. Am. Cong.* (1916); John L. Cheney, Jr., ed., *North Carolina Government, 1585–1979* (1981); Sanna R. Gaffney and others, ed., *The Heritage of Watauga County*, vol. 1 (1984); J. C. Tomlinson, *Assembly Sketch Book: Session 1883* (1883); *Trinity Alumni Register* 2 (1916); U.S. Census, 1860 (microfilm, North Carolina Collection, University of North Carolina, Chapel Hill).

SUSAN JORDAN

Little, Edward Herman (*10 Apr. 1881–12 July 1981*), industrialist and philanthropist, was born on a farm in Mecklenburg County, the fifth of twelve children of George W. and Ella Howie Little. His family was of respectable standing in the community but of meager means. "A boy," Little often said in later years, "is fortunate, as I was, to have good parents, and especially a good mother." As a boy, he worked on the farm, sold melons, and did what he could to assist his family. He attended the Mecklenburg County public schools and Grey's Academy in Huntersville, but there was no money for a college education. Since he was athletically inclined, he entered many of the riding and javelin contests then popular with country southern youths. The reward was "crowning the queen of the tournament." He remembered years later that being the youngest of the lancers, he was too shy to claim his reward. That shyness changed over time to modesty, which endeared him not only to family and friends but to his business associates as well.

At seventeen Little entered the business world as a cotton buyer for a firm in Charlotte. Four years later he became a soap and toilet article salesman for Colgate and Company, and in 1906 he was made district manager for Colgate in Memphis, Tenn. Here he met and won the hand of Suzanne Heyward Trezevant, but before the wedding could take place it was discovered that he had tuberculosis. The physicians ordered him to Denver, Colo., immediately. His fiancée went with him and they were married on 24 Nov. 1910 in Denver. For three years, according to his later recollection, his wife left his bedside only twice. Her parents were socially prominent in Memphis and of distinguished southern lineage. E. H. Little always said he married "up" and his gratitude for the loyalty of his wife in less prosperous times knew no bounds. They had no children.

In 1914 Little joined the B. J. Johnson Soap Company as a salesman. In 1918, a year after Johnson Soap became the Palmolive Company, he was district manager for Palmolive in Los Angeles; in 1919 he held the same position in New York. In 1928, when Palmolive merged with Colgate, he took charge of foreign sales. Over the years Little was instrumental in establishing forty-two Colgate-Palmolive international subsidiaries. He became vice-president in 1933, president in 1938, and chairman of the board in 1953. He was the chief architect and builder of the company's foreign business, which accounted for more than half the total sales and profits by the time he retired in 1960.

On his retirement the board of directors of Colgate-Palmolive passed a resolution containing the following statement: "Under his inspired leadership and direction, sales have increased from $100,000,000 in 1937 to the present $600,000,000 per annum; profits and dividends have multiplied; a strong financial position has been established; plants have been modernized and expanded; research has been greatly augmented; liberal benefits have been provided for employees and their families; management has been decentralized; and substantial progress has been made toward diversifying the Company's business."

On Colgate's 150th anniversary in 1956, Little was responsible for a gift of half a million dollars to be divided among selected colleges in the Northeast. After his retirement, he devoted his time to philanthropy, especially for the advancement of southern institutions and colleges. It was estimated that he gave away at least $5 million of his personal fortune before his death in 1981. Suzanne Little, who died on 18 Oct. 1964, left a sizable trust fund, 67 percent of which was to go to the University of the South at Sewanee, Tenn., on the death of her husband. In 1974 Little gave $1 million to construct the Trezevant Episcopal Retirement Home in Memphis, Tenn. He had, for many years, divided his time between New York and Naples, Fla. When Trezevant Manor was completed in Memphis, he spent his remaining years there.

His major benefactions went to Davidson College (ca. $2.5 million), where there is a dormitory named E. H. Little Hall as well as the E. H. Little Library; to the University of the South at Sewanee (ca. $1.5 million, including Mrs. Little's trust fund), where there is a dormitory called Trezevant Hall; to Queens College, Charlotte (over $500,000), where there is an E. H. Little Fine Arts Center; and to Southwestern at Memphis (ca. $500,000), where there is a dormitory named Suzanne Trezevant Hall. Major benefactions also went to Mary Baldwin College, Staunton, Va.; to Union Theological Seminary, Richmond, Va.; and to the Heinman Medical Research Center in Charlotte. Additional North Carolina institutions that benefited substantially from his generosity include Crossnore School; St. Andrews College, Laurinburg; Montreat College; Warren Wilson College, Swannanoa; Charlotte Country Day School; and the Presbyterian Retirement Home, Charlotte.

During his later years, Little was a liberal contributor to Republican presidential campaigns and counted General Dwight D. Eisenhower among his personal friends. He received an honorary doctor of laws degree from Davidson College in 1953 and an honorary doctor of humanities degree from Southwestern at Memphis in 1972.

Although a Presbyterian, Little frequently attended Grace St. Lukes Episcopal Church, Memphis, with his wife and made generous contributions to it. He was buried from that church a few days after his death in Memphis at the age of one hundred years, three months, and two days. Interment was in Elmwood Cemetery, Memphis.

SEE: Croswell Bowen, "Colgate-Palmolive's E. H. Little," *Madison Avenue* (April 1959); "Edward Little, 100, of Colgate Palmolive," *New York Times*, 14 July 1981; "Executive of the Week," *Salesweek*, 14 Nov. 1960; Barton Hickman, "Little of Colgate-Palmolive," *Television Magazine* (February 1958); L. M. Park, "Goodbye, E. H. Little," *Davidson College Update* (August 1981); Homer H. Shannon, "The Human Side of Soap," *Forbes*, 1 Sept. 1944; *Who's Who in America* (1960–61); "Will of E. H. Little," *Commercial Appeal*, 17 July 1981.

CHALMERS G. DAVIDSON

Little, George (*1731–28 Jan. 1800*), soldier, county official, and planter, was born in Chowan County, the son of Chief Justice William and Penelope Gale Little, daughter of Chief Justice Christopher and Sarah Laker Harvey Gale (the widow of Governor John Harvey). When Hertford County was formed in 1759, Little's home was in that part of Chowan that became a part of the new county. On 19 Apr. 1776 he was appointed to receive, procure, and purchase firearms for the use of troops, and on 2 Sept. 1777 he was appointed by the Council of State at New Bern to recruit men to fill up the regiments from the District of Hertford. He was a major of the Hertford County militia. On 3 Feb. 1781 he resigned his commission as colonel, the rank he apparently attained at some unknown date, and in 1782 he was a member of the Council of Safety. He also served for many years as a justice of the peace for Hertford County.

In 1760 Little married Mary Ann Person, of Surry County, Va., the sister of General Thomas Person. They became the parents of William Person and Penelope, who married Sharp Blount.

SEE: Samuel A. Ashe, ed., *Biographical History of North Carolina*, vol. 2 (1906); Walter Clark, ed., *State Records of North Carolina*, vols. 11, 14–15, 17, 22–23 (1895–1907); Estate Papers, Little-Mordecai Papers (North Carolina State Archives, Raleigh); William L. Saunders, ed., *Colonial Records of North Carolina*, vol. 10 (1890).

SUE DOSSETT SKINNER

Little, William *(27 Feb. 1691/2–1734)*, merchant, planter, and politician, was the son of Lieutenant Isaac and Bethiah Little. Born in Marshfield, Mass., he was graduated from Harvard in 1710, seventh in a class of thirteen. On 12 June 1712 he was admitted an inhabitant of Boston, and on 19 June he married Hannah Willard. Little was a merchant in Boston, but after the death of his wife on 29 Mar. 1715 he gradually relinquished his ties with that town and the Willard family.

Little traveled extensively, spending time in Ireland where he was converted to the Church of England and was baptized by the bishop of Cork. Afterwards he went to England to study at Cambridge. While in England he became acquainted with the Yorkshire family of Gale and through this connection met Christopher Gale, chief justice of North Carolina, who advised him to move to that colony. Influencing Little's decision may have been the death in Carolina of his brother, Nathaniel, who had left him some property.

Little arrived in North Carolina by 1720 and settled in Edenton by 1725. He began his political career in April 1724 by serving a brief term as attorney general of North Carolina at the appointment of Governor George Burrington. Little resigned in November, probably because he assisted Christopher Gale in efforts to remove Burrington from office, but returned to the post in July 1725 by appointment from the Lords Proprietors. In 1726 Governor Sir Richard Everard appointed him receiver general of the colony. Little held both offices until the Crown purchased the Carolinas in 1729. In 1728 Everard also named Little one of the commissioners to survey the boundary between Virginia and North Carolina. In his "secret history" of the survey, William Byrd referred to Little as "Puzzle Cause," who delayed the commissioners by stopping at every house that promised refreshment and who conducted himself as "a very wicked, but awkward, Rake."

During the last years of Proprietary rule, Little, as receiver general, became involved in the "blank patent" affair by which hundreds of thousands of acres of land were illegally engrossed. He also antagonized the lower house of the Assembly and alienated Everard. The Assembly accused Attorney General Little of instituting suits to harass individuals and then accepting bribes to dismiss the actions. The legislature described Little, Gale, and John Lovick, secretary of the province, as evil, avaricious men who were disturbers of the peace, and Everard declared in 1729 that he had been misled by the three men, "the only enemies to the Repose and quiet of the colony." Later the governor asserted that "three more flagrant Villains never came out of the Condemn'd Hole in New Gate for Execution at Tyburn."

Although Little had supported the dismissal of Burrington as Proprietary governor, he effected a reconciliation with him when Burrington in 1731 became the first royal governor of North Carolina. It was suggested but never proved that Little won Burrington's favor by gifts of land. In 1732 Burrington appointed Little chief justice of the colony and clerk of the General Court. Little held the former post until his death two years later, despite assertions of his manifold illegal, arbitrary actions in public and private capacities, his unfitness for office, and his disaffection for the House of Hanover. When he chose to reply to his detractors, particularly the Assembly, the legislature accused him of "Perversion of Justice, Oppression and Extortion" and ordered his arrest for contempt. Burrington released the chief justice and used the occasion once more to excoriate the Assembly.

Little's will, dated 25 June 1734, was probated on 5 Sept. 1734. He may have arrived in North Carolina intending to establish a mercantile trade but his will does not indicate his participation in that business. His income derived principally from his political offices and from land, slaves, and a half interest in a mill. Some of the property was mortgaged, and Burrington, asserting that Little had died in debt, felt that such circumstances exonerated the chief justice from charges of dishonesty. Little had married his second wife, Penelope Gale, daughter of Christopher Gale, in 1726, and by her had three children: Penelope (m. Robert Baker), William, and George.

SEE: Samuel A. Ashe, ed., *Biographical History of North Carolina*, vol. 2 (1905); J. Bryan Grimes, ed., *North Carolina Wills and Inventories* (1912); William L. Saunders, ed., *Colonial Records of North Carolina*, vols. 2–4 (1886); C. K. Shipton, ed., *Sibley's Harvard Graduates*, vol. 5 (1927).

ALAN D. WATSON

Little, William *(10 May 1775–30 Aug. 1848)*, cabinetmaker and planter, was born at Mallsgate, Stapleton Parish, Cumberland County, England, the son of John and Jane Phillips Little. His parents and their family were living at the time with John's brother George Little at his freehold messuage, Mallsgate (literally "gate to the Mall"), which he purchased in 1748. George listed himself, as did kin at "Mallsburn" (Mallsbrook) and "Mallshill," as a yeoman or farmer. Before his death in 1783, he willed the property to his wife and nephew George (son of John) jointly. Later this George helped his brother William to be apprenticed to a cabinetmaker named Graham; Graham's first name and location and the date of William's apprenticeship are unknown.

In 1798 "Brother George" helped William go to America where the latter worked with John Watson at Kingstrail, No. 12, in Charleston, S.C. About 1801 Little moved to Sneedsborough, N.C., a thriving, fashionable town where he bought a number of lots and built a home and a store. His known furniture is owned mostly by descendants and other relations. He made some pieces for Adam Lockhart and Robert Troy, of Wadesboro, both members of the state legislature (Troy was also solicitor general); Hugh McKenzie, postmaster and merchant of Sneedsborough; Judge Samuel Wild of Columbia, S.C.; and William Little's father-in-law, Robert Johnson Steele. Some of his furniture was of the Sheraton and Hepplewhite styles. A few pieces show Chippendale influence, and the latest were an Empire sideboard and bed. The woods were walnut, cherry, and mahogany, with local woods for secondary use.

In 1801 Little married Elizabeth Steele, and they became the parents of eleven children. Robert Johnson Steele, her father, who was from the vicinity of Carlisle, took out many land grants in Anson, Montgomery, and Richmond counties. He also acquired property in Kentucky. William went there in 1808 to see some of Steele's holdings, but no record shows that he bought any of it. Elizabeth's father gave land to her and sold some to them jointly. William, who had bought land of his own and, in the custom of the time, had control of his wife's, became a large landowner.

In 1815 Little built a home on Jones Creek near Wadesboro in Anson County. In his will he mentioned crops, not only from the Jones Creek plantation but also from "all my land on my Brown Creek plantation," and other property including a tannery in Wadesboro. He sent for one of his nephews in England to run the tannery. His will mentions 112 slaves and provisions for their welfare; one slave was named Cumberland. Little never returned to England, but there were occasional signs that he had not forgotten it.

Naturalization papers for William Little have not been found, nor is there any indication of his political views. Many of the English and Scots in Charleston did take out naturalization papers, but these documents were often lost to fires or burned with all the possessions of fever patients. According to a letter of 23 Dec. 1799 from a cousin, William had "the fever" that year. There were many indications that he was becoming a good American citizen, one of which was to follow the prevailing custom of naming his first son George Washington.

No picture of William has been discovered, although his brother Thomas had one painted of himself which is now owned by one of his descendants.

SEE: *Antiques Magazine* (June 1955); Original letters to William Little from his brother George and others in England (microfilm, North Carolina State Archives, Raleigh).

FLORENCE Q. STANBACK

Little, William Person (12 Nov. 1765–19 July 1829), state official, militia officer, and horse breeder, was born in Hertford County, the son of George and Mary Ann Person Little. Adopted by his uncle, General Thomas Person, from whom he inherited considerable money and land, he was educated at a school near Williamsboro in Granville County. As a planter he named his home in eastern Warren County Little Manor, from which the town of Littleton took its name. Mosby Avenue in the town was once the track where he raced his fine horses.

Little was a delegate from Hertford County to the Hillsborough Convention of 1788, which refused to ratify the U.S. Constitution. In 1791 he was elected a member of the Council of State but apparently declined to serve. He was a member of the state senate from Granville County from 1792 to 1798 and from Warren County from 1804 to 1806. For many years he was a justice of the peace in Warren County and a colonel in the militia. He founded a school in Littleton, where he also served as postmaster. On 27 Dec. 1787 Little took part in drawing up the Masonic "declaration of independence" from the British lodge.

In October 1798 he married Ann Hawkins of Pleasant Hill, Warren County, daughter of Philemon Hawkins, Jr., and sister of William Hawkins, governor of North Carolina from 1811 to 1814. They became the parents of George, Thomas Person, Susan, Lucy, Mary, Minerva, and William P., Jr. A portrait of Little hangs in the Mordecai House in Raleigh. He was buried at Little Manor, still owned by a descendant.

SEE: John L. Cheney, Jr., ed., *North Carolina Government, 1585–1974* (1974); Estate Papers, Little-Mordecai Papers (North Carolina State Archives, Raleigh); Manly Wade Wellman, *The County of Warren, North Carolina, 1586–1917* (1959).

SUE DOSSETT SKINNER

Little Carpenter. *See* **Attakullakulla**.

Littlefield, Milton Smith (19 July 1830–7 Mar. 1899), Union officer, dubbed "The Prince of Carpetbaggers," was born in Ellisburgh, Jefferson County, in northern New York, the son of James Pennell and Phoebe Smith Littlefield. His father was a miller and a licensed Baptist preacher; his mother was the daughter of a member of the New York Stock Exchange. Catherine Littlefield, wife of Revolutionary General Nathanael Greene, was his cousin. Littlefield grew up in adjacent Onondaga County near Syracuse, but nothing is known of his education. In 1851 he moved with his parents to Grand Rapids, Mich., where he taught school and served in the local militia.

In 1856, because (it has been suggested) of disappointment in love, Littlefield moved to the small, isolated town of Jerseyville, Ill. Here he began the practice of law, although there are no records to indicate that he was ever licensed. He became involved in the politics of the local Republican party, spoke frequently in public, wrote for the local press (sometimes as a reporter), and made a reputation for himself because of his careful dress and neat appearance. A handsome young man, he had a keen sense of humor and a good singing voice. He became acquainted with Abraham Lincoln and was deeply involved in campaigns on his behalf. Littlefield also was active in the local militia and rose to the rank of captain. With his unit he participated in numerous parades on the eve of Lincoln's election to the presidency and at the beginning of the Civil War.

On 9 May 1861 Littlefield and his troops went off to war. Acquainted with people in high places, particularly leaders of the Republican party, he became the personal emissary of a major general who was a personal friend of Lincoln. On one of his missions back to Illinois late in 1861, Littlefield married Anna Shull. Despite a critical report by his commanding officer, in 1862 Littlefield was promoted to lieutenant colonel in a different regiment and a month later he became deputy provost marshal of the forces around Springfield, Mo. At the Battle of Shiloh in Tennessee in April 1862, he was described as particularly brave in leading his troops. Soon, as the victorious Union army moved towards Mississippi, General William T. Sherman made him assistant provost marshal of Memphis, Tenn.

In Memphis, as Southern cotton became available for the mills of New England, traders with ready money appeared. Littlefield was in a position to deal with them for favors. Certificates of allegiance, much sought by Southerners who wanted to engage in trade, were available for a fee. Sudden fortunes acquired by the invaders were not unusual, and the pattern was set for much that took place a few years later during Reconstruction. Milton S. Littlefield was there to observe, to learn, and to participate. Nevertheless, before he moved on to his next assignment, there was a problem of some sort about both explaining and settling his accounts. He survived the investigation and was then made lieutenant colonel of a new cavalry unit assigned to Peoria, Ill., but he never served with it. Mustered out of service near the end of November 1862, Littlefield was soon in Washington, D.C., carrying out errands for Lincoln.

His first assignment took him to Hilton Head on the coast of South Carolina, occupied by Union forces since 1861 and a source of supplies for blockading ships. Large numbers of New England abolitionists were also there to serve recently freed slaves, and it was Littlefield's job to recruit black troops to join the Union army. Once again in uniform, this time as a colonel, he eventually was given the brevet rank of brigadier general. From a wealthy New England officer killed in an attack on Charleston, he inherited the command of some black troops from Massachusetts who were soon joined by local recruits from among the freed blacks who overran the coastal islands. The recruiting of blacks was promoted by Northerners as a means of reducing the need to draft whites, thus leaving them to be employed in mills and factories. Littlefield, thus encouraged, extended his work along the occupied coast even into Florida. He and his superiors also began to draft tentative plans for the "reconstruction" of the region as it fell under Federal control; some of their ideas later became a part of the radicals' plans adopted in Congress.

In time, Littlefield became general superintendent of the program to recruit black regiments throughout the South. It was he who paid bounties to new soldiers, and with his recruiting efforts he combined political activity for the reelection of Lincoln. He and his friends also engaged in a campaign to secure petitions from 10 percent of the prewar population of occupied states, thereby setting the stage for the creation of a "loyal" government. Following an invasion of Florida for these purposes, Union troops were repulsed with great losses especially among Littlefield's men, although he, himself, was not on the battlefield. The attempt to capture Florida and gain Republican support for Lincoln failed.

Littlefield returned to South Carolina where he recruited (or claimed to have recruited) more black troops, this time credited to the draft quota of his native county—in this way, making friends for himself in New York. Some of his cousins, friends, and associates were involved and, along with Littlefield, were suspected of profiteering in bounties. A total of nearly $200,000 was involved in payments to "paper recruits," but the war ended about the same time this was discovered and little was said of the matter. (Since the North spent about $300 million in bounties during the war, Littlefield's expenditures were not regarded as particularly significant.) It was also possible for someone in the North about to be drafted to "buy" a black substitute from South Carolina for around $500, although sometimes one might cost as much as $900 if the potential draftee were desperate to avoid service. Littlefield was as skilled in providing substitutes as he was in understanding the market.

As Sherman approached South Carolina, he arranged with Littlefield to take care of large numbers of blacks of all ages who had followed the invading army. This he was able to do. General Littlefield, a capable public speaker, was also put to work delivering messages to the public in newly occupied regions from Georgia through the Carolinas. He often spoke in condescending terms, stressing "Yankee" superiority and touching upon aspects of Lincoln's plans for Reconstruction. With the death of Lincoln, his hero, he displayed renewed contempt for the South, tinged with anger.

As Union troops returned home after the war, Littlefield's infantry was also disbanded and he went to Philadelphia where his wife and young son were living. There in the spring of 1866 he became a lumber mer-

chant, expecting to draw upon the splendid forests he had seen in the South for his stock-in-trade. After receiving payment for lumber for future delivery, he was unable to fill the orders when title to land he thought he had acquired in the South proved not to be valid. His scheme collapsed, and late in 1867 Littlefield moved to North Carolina. With several partners from New York, Maine, and elsewhere, he planned to buy depreciated prewar state bonds, use his position and political connections to persuade the state reconstruction convention to declare them valid, and sell them to his great benefit. A North Carolina banker, George W. Swepson, held most of the bonds that these men hoped to acquire; he had obtained them for practically nothing in exchange for postwar bonds.

Three of Littlefield's partners, carpetbaggers all, were elected to the convention. Gifts to representatives—sometimes as simple as a new hat and a pair of gloves—judicially presented, won votes at low cost. The bonds were recognized and the legislature was instructed to levy taxes to pay the interest on them beginning in 1869. The convention also adopted a new constitution destined to make significant changes in the state, and just before adjournment General Littlefield was called upon to address the body. According to an unsympathetic witness, his remarks were a "harangue." The stage was set for Littlefield, as "activator and orator," and his friends, some from the North and some native-born, to profit from their position and connections.

Littlefield acquired extensive land in the coal fields along Deep River, and he was interested in seeing work resumed on a railroad leading to it that had been begun during the war. As a skillful politician he worked diligently, particularly with the recently enfranchised blacks. He was frequently praised as the bearer of capital for investment in the state and as a man of vision. The new governor, newspaper editor William Woods Holden, appointed by President Andrew Johnson, was a strong supporter of Littlefield, and when his political and gubernatorial duties became pressing, Holden sold Littlefield his newspaper, the *North Carolina Standard*, for a very large figure. Littlefield, it was widely believed, had the backing of the owners of the New York *Tribune*. Before the year ended, the *Standard* became a daily instead of a semiweekly and an organ of support for the Republican party as well as for the nefarious activities of carpetbaggers.

Littlefield was involved in an unknown variety and number of schemes, usually with the collaboration of native-born George W. Swepson. They, together with others of their kind, were particularly active in swindling both the state and individuals of millions of dollars by carefully manipulating and bribing legislators and other officials in the acquisition of bonds. Littlefield and Swepson, working as officers and agents of the Western Branch of the Western North Carolina Railroad, acquired stock in their own names, in part by checks that were never presented for payment and through bribes paid members of the "carpetbag legislature." They employed many of the same scams in Florida. It was largely through the influence of friends in high position that they escaped punishment, although the North Carolina General Assembly afterwards appointed commissions to investigate the frauds. The state was unsuccessful in its attempts to have Littlefield returned to North Carolina for trial, and he spent his final years in New Jersey and New York in relative poverty. At one time he was jailed for failure to pay a hotel bill.

He was the father of two sons, Milton S., Jr., and Alfred Calvin. The former became a Presbyterian minister of some note in New York City. Littlefield joined his son's church shortly before his death. He was buried at Kensico, N.Y.

SEE: John P. Arthur, *Western North Carolina: A History* (1914); Cecil K. Brown, *A State Movement in Railroad Development* (1928); Jonathan Daniels, *Prince of Carpetbaggers* (1958); J. G. de Roulhac Hamilton, *Reconstruction in North Carolina* (1914); *New York Times*, 9 Mar. 1899; Charles L. Price, "The Railroad Schemes of George W. Swepson," in *East Carolina College Publications in History*, vol. 1 (1964); Raleigh *News and Observer*, 13 July 1947, 21 June 1953.

WILLIAM S. POWELL

Livermon, Carl Raby (*7 Nov. 1883–21 Mar. 1968*), inventor, was born at his parents' home in Roxobel, with his maternal great uncle, Dr. Preston C. Jenkins, in attendance. He was the son of Asa Thomas (1847–1929), a Roxobel merchant-planter, and Alberta Raby Livermon (1856–1947). He had one sister, Ruby, who married J. M. Jacobs, D.D.S. (1869–1954), in 1903. Livermon studied in Roxobel under a Mr. Kennedy, a teacher from Scotland whom the townspeople had hired. He attended boarding schools in Scotland Neck and Windsor, Va., before entering Wake Forest College.

After he left Wake Forest, his father set him up in a business that failed to prosper. One fall he persuaded his father to allow him to operate his peanut picker for hire. Although this project was financially successful, Livermon decided that there was too much time wasted on breakdowns. Consequently, he started studying the problems involved and thinking of ways to correct them. The internal chains seemed to be the major trouble, so he designed a machine that had only two chains.

In 1915, after nine years of thought and study in his spare time, while operating an automobile partnership with J. T. Cullifer, and three more years of testing, the P-Picker Company of Roxobel advertised The Samson. Munn and Company, patent attorneys of Washington, D.C., had filed the patent for this machine on 16 Feb. 1912, and the patent had been granted on 21 December. Other improvement patents were issued starting in 1915. Several years later, Livermon perfected a cylinder machine that was widely copied thereafter. This picker, the Livermon Peanut Machine, was manufactured for Livermon by the A. B. Farquhar Company of York, Pa., and was sold throughout the U.S. peanut belt (through dealerships set up in Alabama, Georgia, Florida, Louisiana, Tennessee, North Carolina, and Virginia) as well as in South Africa. Sales and distribution of the machine were handled in Roxobel under Livermon's direction from the Carl R. Livermon Company office, management of which he entrusted to his sister Ruby Livermon Jacobs.

On 2 Jan. 1937 Livermon married Annie Julia Norfleet, the daughter of Thomas S. Norfleet and the late Lelia Powell Norfleet of Roxobel. They returned from their honeymoon to his paternal home where he resided all his life.

Livermon did not let his inventive genius rest after creating his successful peanut machine. Later he invented and patented a self-feeder to increase the machine's efficiency. Other patents were issued to him for a target-throwing device, whose patent he sold in 1949; a ledger-holding device; wheel starters for aircraft landing wheels; and a three-wheel amphibious boat trailer that was rolled into the water and from which the boat was floated after the trailer had been anchored.

The name and goodwill of the Livermon Peanut Machine and self-feeder were purchased by the A. B. Farquhar Company in 1949. After this sale and before he decided to retire, Livermon maintained his Roxobel office for a few years in order to merchandise the L & J Boat Trailer. His other inventions, for which he did not seek patents, included a two-lever cart for hauling peanut stacks to the picker, a device that was widely copied in the industry; retractable wheels used under a rocking chair for moving infirm people from room to room without disturbing them; a central air-cooling device for his office in Roxobel; and a folding (to save space) wheelbarrow for carrying heavy luggage from the garage to his beach house in Nags Head.

After closing his office in 1951, Livermon devoted his time to his and his sister's farming interests and to his civic activities. Foremost among the latter was the operation of the Roanoke-Chowan Bank, where he served as a director from 16 Jan. 1918 to the day of his death—a period of fifty years. Livermon was buried in the Roxobel-Kelford Cemetery, Roxobel, in the plot with his father, mother, and paternal grandparents, Cader Monroe Raby (1827–92) and Mary Frances Jenkins Raby (1838–1924).

SEE: Laura Harrell, "Advice from an Inventor," *Bertie Ledger Advance*, 18 Nov. 1965; Roy F. Johnson, *The Peanut Story* (1964); Woodrow Price, "In the Open," Raleigh *News and Observer*, 13 Feb. 1949; Raleigh *News and Observer*, 28 Nov. 1965.

LOIS JACOBS PEELE

Llewellyn, John. See **Lewelling, John**.

Lloyd, Joseph Ross. See **Gregory, Mary Lloyd**.

Lloyd, Thomas (*d. August 1770*), physician and justice of the peace, was a native of Philadelphia who moved to Wilmington, N.C., prior to 1765 and became a leader in local affairs. In various records he is referred to as esquire, colonel, and doctor. He bought several large tracts of land on the North East River, all in the Welsh Tract, and at least one lot in Wilmington. This was part of Lot 31 on Princess Street and adjoined one belonging to the estate of Colonel John Ashe. An active patriot, Lloyd, with John Ashe and Alexander Lillington, signed the message presented to Governor William Tryon during the Stamp Act resistance at Brunswick in February 1766. This paper stated that the people were determined to obtain redress of their grievances from the commanders of the warships then in the river.

An Anglican, Lloyd was buried in St. James's churchyard, Wilmington. The following inscription appears on his stone: "Beneath this Stone [are] deposited the Remains of Colonel Thomas Lloyd of the Family of Lloyds in Philadelphia. He deceased in the Month of August MDCCLXX, age [illegible]."

Lloyd's wife Rebecca and daughter Margaret survived him, Margaret not yet of age. Archibald Maclaine and Alexander Hostler, prominent citizens of Wilmington, were appointed his executors and gave bond of £9,000. The amount of the bond indicates that he left a substantial estate. In 1772 Rebecca was living at Second and Market Streets. On her death in January 1786, Margaret was appointed administratrix of the estates of both her father and her mother. No other children of Thomas and Rebecca Lloyd have been identified.

About 1792 Margaret Lloyd married James Moore (b. 2 Apr. 1761), the son of George Moore and the grandson of "King" Roger Moore. James's mother was Mary Ashe, the daughter of John Baptista Ashe. Margaret Lloyd and James Moore had three children: Thomas Lloyd, Julia Rebecca, and Ann L.

SEE: Ida B. Kellam, *St. James Church, Wilmington, North Carolina: Historical Records, 1737–1852* (1965); Lawrence Lee, *Lower Cape Fear in Colonial Days* (1965); New Hanover County Deed and Will Books (New Hanover County Courthouse, Wilmington); Alexander M. Walker, *New Hanover County Court Minutes*, vols. 2–3 (1958); *The Wilmington Town Book, 1743–1778* (1973).

L. H. MCEACHERN

Lloyd (or Loyd, Loyde), Thomas *(ca. 1710–May? 1792)*, Loyalist planter and colonial official of Orange County, member of the colonial Assembly, an officer in the Orange County militia, and sometimes accounted the most influential citizen of Orange prior to the Revolution, has long been confused with Colonel Thomas Lloyd, of New Hanover County (died August 1770 and buried in St. James's churchyard, Wilmington), a politically active physician of the 1760s who was nominated by Governor William Tryon to the royal Council. References to the two Thomas Lloyds in William L. Saunders's *Colonial Records of North Carolina*, Walter Clark's *State Records of North Carolina*, and other pertinent sources were collected and identified about 1961–62 by the late Robert Bruce Cooke, of Durham, who concluded that existing brief biographies and notices of Thomas Lloyd of Orange County had mistakenly telescoped the lives and political activities of two different men, bearing the same name at the same time but pursuing different occupations and living in different, widely separated counties of the province of North Carolina.

Thomas Lloyd of Orange County, usually designated as Major Thomas Lloyd, was apparently of the third generation of Lloyds and also the third of his name in Prince George County, Va. (a part of which became a part of Brunswick County when it was formed in 1720). The first of the Lloyd family line in Prince George appears to have been Thomas Lloyd, a modest draper or cloth merchant who died before 11 Mar. 1717 and whose will was filed on that date by his widow Jane (or Jean) Mackmahon at a court held at Merchant's Hope Church, Va. The inventory of the Lloyd estate, officially appraised at £59.12.1½ on 5 Apr. 1718, lists a sizable number of ells and yards of nearly a dozen different kinds of fabrics—dowlas, "blew Linnen," osnaburg, Scotch cloth, duffel, crepe, and the like. Hu (or Hue) Mackmahon of Martin's Brandon Parish, evidently the father of Jane, died at nearly the same time, and his small estate, valued at only £6.18, was included with the appraisal of Thomas Lloyd's possessions since Jane Mackmahon Lloyd was the administratrix of both estates.

The second Thomas Lloyd, son of Thomas and Jane and the father of Thomas Lloyd of Orange County, was an acquisitive man who managed to collect various chattels, slaves, and plantations on the lower side of Sturgeon's Run in Brunswick County. He was able to deed plantations and slaves to two of his children, Elizabeth [Jackson] and John. The third Thomas appears to have secured a land patent of 2,000 acres for himself on 6 Aug. 1747 "including the Plantation he lives on."

This was the Thomas Lloyd (ca. 1710–92) who moved with his family to Orange County either late in 1752 or early in 1753. On 22 Dec. 1752 he sold 995 acres on Lloyd's Run, Reedy Creek, and Sturgeon's Run in Brunswick County to Edmund Tabb and others (deed registered on 26 Dec. 1752), the deed providing, however, that his father be allowed to remain on the property for his lifetime. (According to the evidence of a deed, the older Thomas Lloyd was still alive on 22 Feb. 1757.) Apparently at an early age the third Thomas Lloyd had married one Tabitha, and at least four of their seven children appear to have been born in Brunswick.

In Orange County, Thomas Lloyd promptly entered for two adjoining land grants on "Marks Creek the north side of the Piney Mountain," about three or four miles north of present-day Chapel Hill. The two grants, totaling 783 acres, were issued on 11 and 12 May 1757 and became the nucleus of Lloyd's well-known "Meadows" plantation home, marked "T. Loyde" on the Collet map of 1 May 1770 and "T. Loyd" on the Mouzon map of 1775. The first Orange County tax list of 1755 lists "Thomas Loyd" and two Negroes.

Lloyd appears to have been an aggressive, shrewd man of moderate education, great energy, considerable political sagacity, and attractive personality who rapidly became a powerful figure in Orange County politics. On 12 Mar. 1754 he was appointed a commissioner of roads in place of Mark Morgan (who did not appear in person to qualify) and was reappointed in 1756 and 1757. On 12 Apr. 1755 Lieutenant Colonel Josias Dickson recommended that Lloyd and John Patterson receive captain's commissions in the regiment of Orange County militia, again to replace Mark Morgan who had not appeared to qualify and whose company was found to be too large. In June 1757 Lloyd also qualified as a justice of the peace for the county; thereafter, he sat regularly, sometimes as chairman, on inferior courts, deciding and guiding the affairs of the vast new county.

As a justice, Lloyd took an interest in the two primitive county structures erected at the county seat (Corbinton, later renamed Childsburgh and then Hillsborough) and in June 1758 "viewed the Prison of this County" to put it in "good and sufficient repair." Later he served on a committee to build a new county jail. In September 1759 the court ordered Lloyd to "agree with some proper Person for four Barrells of Tar & [to] put it on the Courthouse to Preserve it from the Inclemency of the Weather."

On 31 Mar. 1761 he took his seat with surveyor William Churton as one of the two representatives of Orange County in the Provincial Assembly at New Bern, a position he occupied until 1768. It is clear that from 1761 onwards, Lloyd was one of the accepted inner circle of Orange officials sometimes called by the Regulators "the Courthouse Ring." The county court offered his name to the governor as a candidate for high sheriff no less than three times—in May 1761, May 1765, and May 1766. Lloyd is known to have been high sheriff in March 1775, and it is likely that he had served in the late 1760s (court records are missing for the period).

Apparently, Lloyd was also chairman of the vestry of the Parish of St. Matthew, then coterminous with Orange County; at least his name appears first in the list of seven vestrymen writing to the bishop of London on 29 Mar. 1769 to recommend the ordination of Edward Jones. (Lloyd had been a trusted member of the Parish of St. Andrews in Brunswick County, Va., appointed on 8 Nov. 1751 to "do procession"—that is, trace out the boundaries of the parish.)

Thus, in a relatively short time Thomas Lloyd had in Orange County acquired a half-dozen interlocking positions of administrative power in church, court, militia, and provincial government. In addition, two of his sons-

in-law, Colonel John Hogan of Orange and Adlai Osborne of Rowan, were among the most consequential
men of the backcountry and shed considerable luster on
the Lloyd family prestige.

Throughout these years, Lloyd and his oldest son Stephen built considerable estates both by land grant and
purchase. The second preserved Orange County tax list,
that of 1779, shows Thomas Lloyd's assessed worth in
that year to have been £10,871 and Stephen's, £7,065.8.

The Orange County court minutes and Saunders's *Colonial Records* steadily record Thomas Lloyd's faithful service to the local representatives of the royal government—going on personal bonds for Edmund Fanning
and Francis Nash and mustering out volunteers at Colonel John Gray's command to deal with Regulator disturbances. On 27 Apr. 1768 Governor William Tryon sent
personal compliments to Lloyd for his efforts.

On 10 Oct. 1766, however, Lloyd, like the other courthouse officials, failed to keep stated agreements and
promises to put in an appearance at a scheduled meeting of the Regulators at Maddock's Mill "where there is
no Liquor" and thereby roused distrust among the backcountry men. On 1 May 1768 he took an action that particularly angered Regulator leaders and incurred their
lasting hostility. After Secretary Isaac Edwards's conciliatory address intended to mollify a mob and save Hillsborough from a threat of fire, Lloyd as magistrate unexpectedly issued a warrant for the arrest of Herman
Husband under cover of night and on 2 May formally
made out papers committing him to the jail at New
Bern. Although Husband was finally released on bail,
the Regulators never forgave Lloyd for what they considered an act of duplicity.

On 22 Sept. 1768 Governor Tryon held a "Council of
War" in Hillsborough attended by both Major Thomas
Lloyd (Loyd) and a Major-General Thomas Lloyd, newly
promoted from the rank of colonel. It would appear
from all available data that Major Thomas Lloyd (Loyd)
was the Thomas Lloyd of Orange County, since he
signed his name "Major Thos. Lloyd, Esq." to the 29
Mar. 1769 letter sent by the vestry of St. Matthew's Parish to the bishop of London and since he is consistently
called Major Thomas Lloyd on subsequent Orange
County records until his death.

Specific formal complaints of the Regulators against
Lloyd began to mount—as to the way he and Justice
Tyree Harris had selected a jury and as to the way the
accounts of the vestry of St. Matthew's had been handled for the past ten years. In the September riots of
1770, Lloyd, Nash, and three other county officials had
to flee to the surrounding woods to escape the kind of
physical maltreatment inflicted on Edmund Fanning.
Nevertheless, Lloyd appears to have been appointed
coroner of Orange in the early summer of 1772 and high
sheriff in 1774–75.

Lloyd virtually vanished from public view after the
Revolution (in which he did not serve in any capacity).
His steadfast loyalty to the British monarchy and its local representatives had placed him in a difficult and
equivocal position even with his neighbors. It should be
noted that Lloyd was the only member of the Courthouse Ring who remained in the Hillsborough area
throughout the Revolution. It is also noteworthy that
Fanning did not attempt to make use of Lloyd's name as
a cover for the conveyance of his own deeds in 1775.

Orange County deed books reveal Lloyd's efforts to
stave off possible confiscation of his property. On 23
Oct. 1786 he conveyed to his son-in-law Daniel Hogan
for 5 shillings "current money," two Negroes, and all his
household and plantation furniture and livestock, all of

which Hogan leased back to him on the same day for an
annual rental of sixpence sterling. Lloyd made an identical arrangement with Colonel John Hogan relative to the
two Meadows plantations and five Negroes; the lease
agreement was dated 23 Oct. 1786 and again the yearly
rental was sixpence sterling. Lloyd's lands and property
were never confiscated.

No portrait of Lloyd is known to exist, but family tradition describes him as having had an impressive appearance, "athletic and strong." He died shortly after his
son Stephen was said to have been shot to death on his
own plantation by a slave named Isaac. Thomas Lloyd is
thought to have been buried with three other members
of his family approximately fifty yards east of his farmhouse. The graves, reportedly marked only by rough
fieldstones, have not been located.

On 6 Oct. 1937 the Thomas Lloyd Memorial Association erected an imposing memorial stone with bronze
plaque in Lloyd's honor on old Highway 86 north of
Chapel Hill near the Lloyd homesite. The memorial
plaque, however, also incorporated data from the life of
Thomas Lloyd of New Hanover County.

SEE: Brunswick County Deed Book 5 (Brunswick Coun-
ty Courthouse, Lawrenceville, Va.); Walter Clark, ed.,
State Records of North Carolina, vols. 19, 22 (1901, 1907);
Robert Bruce Cooke, *The Thomas Lloyds of North Carolina*
(1962); William Johnston Hogan, *Virginia Genealogical
Records of Major Thomas Lloyd of Orange County, North
Carolina* (Manuscript Collection, Keysville, Va.); Orange
County Deed Books, Will Books, Tax Lists, and Minutes
of the Inferior Court of Common Pleas and Quarter Ses-
sions (Orange County Courthouse, Hillsborough); "Pro-
gram of the Sixth Annual Convention of the Lloyd Clan
Unveiling a Marker in Memory of Thomas F. Lloyd," 22
Oct. 1941 (North Carolina Collection, University of
North Carolina, Chapel Hill); William L. Saunders, ed.,
Colonial Records of North Carolina, vols. 5–8 (1887–90); Eugene Sugg, *Sketches of Major General Thomas Lloyd of Orange County, North Carolina, and Some of His Descendants*
(1931).

MARY CLAIRE ENGSTROM

Lobb, Jacob (*d. April 1773*), English naval officer active
in the Lower Cape Fear region during the Stamp Act crisis, may have been from Devon or Cornwall in southwestern England, the home of several families of this
name. (One William Lobb in 1473 held Buckland Abbey.) In September 1732 it was reported that as master of
the *Love and Unity*, engaged in a long and stormy passage transporting Palatines from Rotterdam to New England, Jacob Lobb and the mate of his ship were seized
and confined without food for five days by some of the
passengers who insisted on being put ashore immediately. On 9 Jan. 1748 Lobb became a lieutenant, and in
1748 he served on the *Pansy*, presumably a tender in the
Mediterranean rather than a regular naval vessel. In
1756 he was sixth lieutenant of the *Invincible* and the
next year was first lieutenant of the *Royal George*.

Promoted to the rank of commander on 23 Dec. 1757,
in 1759 he was master and commander of the *Swan*
sloop which sailed out of Sheerness, Kent, in January
1763. Before the end of the year, however, as a captain
he was commander of the sloop *Viper* stationed off the
coast of North Carolina "for the protection of our
Trade." Among his concerns was the threat of pirates
along the isolated Outer Banks, so one of his first acts
was to prepare a pen-and-ink drawing of a good harbor
along the coast from which passing ships might be ob-

served. It was sent to the Lords of Admiralty, but the original is now in the Library of Congress. On the drawing Lobb wrote: "A Plan of the Harbour of Cape lookout Surveyed by His Majesty's Sloop Viper Captain Lobb in Sepr 1764 this Harbour is the best on the Coast of North Carolina being Landlock'd and sheltered from all Winds, and the going in attended with on [no?] difficulty in the Day or Night having no bar it Flows 7 hours full and change and the tide was observed to rise 5 feet and when the wind blows hard from the Eastward it will rise 7 feet. That Strangers may know this Harbour there is a Flag-staff erected by Captain Lobb about 50 feet high on a Sorel Hill near Davis's House and on Landlock Point a Port Which small Vessells may Moor too, they bear NE b[y] E from each other—Cape lookout is in the Lattd 34°-40″ Variation 2°-40″ East."

Lobb obviously lost no time in becoming familiar with his new station and reporting to his superiors at home. The Assembly of North Carolina recognized his usefulness to the colony shortly after his arrival, when it named him one of the commissioners of pilotage of the Cape Fear River. When William Tryon arrived with his family at the mouth of the Cape Fear River in North Carolina in October 1764 to assume his duties as lieutenant governor, he boarded the Viper's barge for the trip upriver from Brunswick to Wilmington. Accompanied by Lobb, he was greeted by a seventeen-gun salute.

Lobb purchased a house in the town of Brunswick and his wife, Phillis, and their children apparently lived there. In June 1766 the house was acquired by Governor Tryon, and since Lobb's wife was privately examined concerning its sale and relinquished her dower right, it undoubtedly had been bought with her money.

An unfortunate incident occurred near the end of March 1765 between two members of Lobb's crew. Alexander Simpson, apparently a midshipman, challenged Lieutenant Thomas Whitehurst to a duel, reportedly over the affections of a woman. Each with a pair of pistols met in the woods not far from St. Philip's Church where shots were heard. On investigation, it was found that both men were struggling on the ground and Simpson was beating Whitehurst on the head with the butt of his pistol. Whitehurst's thigh already had been broken by a pistol shot. He lingered for six days and on 22 March, the day before his death, drew up his will by which he left some land in Stafford, England, to his sister and £50 to "William Grenfell Lobb," the youngest son of Captain Lobb. Simpson fled to Smith Island where he was concealed for a time by friends, but he later returned to Brunswick and was tried and convicted of manslaughter.

The most significant role Lobb played in North Carolina had its origin in the Stamp Act, passed by Parliament in March 1765 and scheduled to become effective on 1 November. The validity of this act to tax the colonies without their representation—a substantial contributor to the unifying of the colonies and the coming of the American Revolution—was widely discussed in all of the colonies. In North Carolina it was anticipated that stamped paper, which was to be used in printing certain documents, would arrive in Brunswick where Captain Lobb and the Viper were stationed. The people of the region forced the stamp agent to resign and prepared to resist the collection of the new tax. When the Diligence arrived on 28 November with stamped paper, men of the Lower Cape Fear refused to let it be taken ashore. In mid-January two ships, the Dobbs from Philadelphia and the Patience from St. Christopher, arrived in the Cape Fear River without the required stamped clearance papers from their previous ports. Lobb seized both of

these ships as well as the Ruby, which arrived a few days later. In retaliation, the merchants and residents of the town of Wilmington, a source of supplies a few miles up the river, refused to sell anything to sailors from the Viper sent there for supplies. An armed party of local men set out in search of Lobb and approached Governor Tryon, who had succeeded the late governor in that post. Tryon refused to say whether Lobb was in the governor's protective custody, but it soon was learned that the captain was aboard his ship.

Following a confrontation with them, Lobb wisely agreed that they were justified in seeking the release of the seized ships since there had been no stamped paper available when they sailed for North Carolina. Commenting on this action, the Virginia Gazette reported the remarks of Robin Jones, Jr., a North Carolina attorney: "Reason does not require the performance of impossibilities." Furthermore, Lobb permitted the seized ships to depart with their old papers even though stamped paper had arrived in North Carolina aboard the Diligence on 28 November. None of the stamped paper was ever landed in North Carolina and the small quantity that had arrived was returned to England after the repeal of the act in mid-March.

Correspondence between Lobb and Admiralty officials in London reveals that he remained on station in North Carolina for a time but also was elsewhere along the Atlantic coast as far as Halifax, Nova Scotia, where facilities existed for the repair of ships. On one occasion, after a hurricane along the North Carolina coast, he went to Halifax for this reason. In 1772 he was commander of the twenty-four-gun Fowey, which at various times served in North Carolina and Virginia waters; under a different commander it removed Lord Dunmore, the last royal governor of Virginia.

Lobb was the father of at least two sons. One, William Granville Lobb, became a lieutenant in the Royal Navy in 1777 and a captain in 1795. The May 1773 issue of the Gentleman's Magazine, published in London, reported the death of Captain Jacob Lobb "of his Majesty's sloop King Fisher, North Carolina." Mrs. Lobb in 1784 was living in Kentish Town, London.

SEE: ADM 1/2051 and 2/725 (Public Record Office, London; copies, North Carolina State Archives, Raleigh); Walter Clark, ed., State Records of North Carolina, vol. 22 (1904); William P. Cumming, The Southeast in Early Maps (1958); Gentleman's Magazine, September 1732; J. Bryan Grimes, ed., Abstract of North Carolina Wills (1910) and North Carolina Wills and Inventories (1912); E. Lawrence Lee, "Days of Defiance: Resistance to the Stamp Act in the Lower Cape Fear," North Carolina Historical Review 43 (April 1966); North-Carolina Magazine; or, Universal Intelligence, 28 Sept. 1764; William S. Powell, ed., The Correspondence of William Tryon and Other Selected Papers, 2 vols. (1980–81); S. M. Riley, National Maritime Museum, Greenwich, England, to William S. Powell, 7 June 1988.

WILLIAM S. POWELL

Locke, Francis *(1722–96)*, Revolutionary soldier, farmer, trader, and carpenter, was born in Northern Ireland, the son of John and Elizabeth Locke who moved to Lancaster County, Pa., when Francis and his brother, Matthew, were young. Francis was still living in Lancaster County in 1738. The older Locke died in 1744, his widow married John Brandon, and about 1752 the family moved to Anson (now Rowan, formed from Anson in 1753) County, N.C. In 1753 Francis purchased 640 acres from his stepfather and established his home four miles west of Salisbury on the Lincolnton road. He and Matthew began dealing in skins and operated a fleet of wagons from the frontier of the colony to Salisbury, Salem, and Charles Town, S.C., in a profitable trade that netted them a comfortable living.

Whether Locke had previous military training in Pennsylvania is not known, but in 1759 Governor Arthur Dobbs commissioned him an ensign under Captain Griffith Rutherford in the Rowan regiment commanded by Colonel Adlai Osborn. By 1764 he was interested in politics, and the best way to attain office in those times was to become a tavern owner. In that year he was licensed to operate an ordinary at his dwelling house; there he could meet and entertain his countrymen and become a familiar figure. Although it was unlawful for a tavern owner to be appointed sheriff, the highest local office in the colony, Locke was recommended to Governor Dobbs by the county court as the best candidate for that office. He was appointed and served a year and a half (1765–66).

Locke's term as sheriff fell during the Regulators' rising against abuse in government and improper taxes. It was the worst possible time to be sheriff, for it was his duty to collect taxes while also keeping the peace. In this undertaking Locke was not successful. He was able to collect taxes from only about 1,000 of the 3,043 taxables and had to explain to the satisfaction of the county court why this was so. He pointed out that he had done his utmost to collect taxes but had been violently opposed. In one instance, he explained, when he seized a certain sorrel gelding from James Dunlap in lieu of taxes, fifteen of Dunlap's friends came to his aid and rescued the gelding from Locke.

Between his political and military service, Locke worked as a carpenter and as a planter. Tax returns for 1768 reveal that he owned four slaves. Unsullied by his experience as sheriff, Locke held the confidence of the next royal governor who appointed him coroner in 1773. The county court also relied on Locke to lay out roads, build bridges, and keep the jail in repair.

With the coming of the Revolution, Francis Locke came to the attention of the Provincial Congress. On 9 Sept. 1775 he was appointed lieutenant colonel of the minutemen of Rowan County under Colonel Griffith Rutherford. Assuming his new duties, Locke was almost immediately involved in the "Snow Campaign" in up-country South Carolina when North Carolina helped to quell an uprising there. In April 1776 the Provincial Congress promoted him to colonel in the First Regiment of the Rowan militia. That spring, when the Cherokee took up arms against the back settlers, Locke and his men accompanied Rutherford on an expedition against them. The campaign succeeded in laying waste the Indians' towns and suppressing any further threat from them.

During 1777 and 1778 Locke was busy keeping an eye on the Tories in the state, as there was little other activity in the South at that time. In 1779, however, he was under the command of General John Ashe when they were sent to Georgia to fight the British, who had recently taken Savannah. Against the remonstrances of Ashe, General Benjamin Lincoln pushed forward his troops at Briar Creek, where they were surprised and defeated by General Augustine Prevost. After the battle Colonel Locke was a member of the court-martial to examine that disastrous affair.

Locke and his Rowan militia moved towards Charles Town and scouted for the American army, but they did not participate directly in the Battle of Charles Town which resulted in the city's capitulation. Next, Locke was called upon to disperse a gathering of Tories in Lincoln County under Colonel John Moore in 1780. With 400 militiamen from Rowan, Mecklenburg, and Lincoln counties assembled at Mountain Creek, Locke marched on the night of 19 June some eighteen miles towards Ramsour's Mill. The next morning he made a sudden attack on the enemy and after a fierce engagement routed the Tories in a battle that lasted about an hour and a half. Each side lost about 150 men, and only about 300 of Moore's soldiers were able to join the British in South Carolina. This significant victory threw the Tories in western North Carolina into confusion. The Loyalist Samuel Bryan collected 800 men in the forks of the Yadkin and made his move. He led them down the Yadkin River into South Carolina with Locke and General Rutherford close on their heels.

In Lord Charles Cornwallis's first invasion of North Carolina in 1780, Locke served as the eyes for the American army, keeping between Cornwallis and Colonel Patrick Ferguson who was then in Burke County. Locke's troops served as a "force in being" held in readiness to attack Ferguson should he move towards Charlotte. Ferguson was decisively defeated at Kings Mountain, and Cornwallis retreated back into South Carolina.

Locke was not called upon again until the second British invasion of the state early in 1781. In the retreat of General Nathanael Greene and his American army across the state, Locke was instrumental in helping to delay the advance of Cornwallis. After leaving Salisbury, Cornwallis, unable to cross the Yadkin River at Trading Ford nearby, chose a northern route to the upper fords of the Yadkin. On his advance, Locke and his one hundred Rowan militiamen had stationed themselves at a bridge across Grants Creek (some historians say Second Creek) near Salisbury. The van of Cornwallis's army, seeing Locke's troops engaged in destroying the bridge, attacked but were repelled. Colonel Banastre Tarleton dispatched his soldiers up and down the stream and came in behind Locke. The Americans fled but only one man in Locke's force was wounded. Following this skirmish Locke was placed under the command of General Andrew Pickens, who dogged Cornwallis's march through the state and hampered his movements until the Battle of Guilford Court House in March 1781. Locke did not participate in that engagement but remained as a bulwark to the backcountry in the event the British moved in that direction. Cornwallis chose instead to march to Wilmington and then to Yorktown, where the war ended. Locke remained in the army until 8 Nov. 1784, when he resigned his commission.

As an officer Locke earned the confidence of the people he served. Even the harassed Moravians spoke of him as being friendly when he requisitioned stores from their dwindling supplies in 1781. After his resignation from the army he retired to his plantation. In 1794 the Rowan court appointed Locke to succeed William Sharpe as attorney for the state. He died two years later and was buried in Thyatira Presbyterian Church cemetery, where his grave is marked by a simple stone bearing his name.

Locke married Ann Brandon, and they were the parents of four sons and three daughters. One son, John, was an officer in the Revolution; a daughter, Margaret, married George Gibson and after his death married Richard Armstrong. Another son, Matthew, married Nancy Brandon, while another, Francis, became a superior court judge from 1803 to 1813 and afterwards was elected to Congress. The other children were Ann, Mary Locke, and William. William married Elizabeth Marshal and moved to Kentucky.

SEE: Steven Belk, "The Locke Family," 1977 (manuscript, Rowan Public Library, Salisbury,); Walter Clark, ed., *State Records of North Carolina*, vols. 14–15, 19, 23 (1896, 1898, 1901, 1904); Adelaide L. Fries, ed., *Records of the Moravians in North Carolina*, vols. 2–3 (1925–26); William Henry Hoyt, ed., *The Papers of Archibald D. Murphey*, 2 vols. (1914); Mary Elinor Lazenby, *Catawba Frontier, 1775–1781: Memories of Pensioners* (1950); George McCorkle, "Col. Francis Locke," *North Carolina Booklet* (July 1910); William S. Powell and others, eds., *The Regulators in North Carolina* (1971); Robert W. Ramsey, *Carolina Cradle: Settlement of the Northwest Carolina Frontier, 1747–1762* (1964); Hugh F. Rankin, *The North Carolina Continentals* (1971); Rowan County Court Minutes, 1754–95, and Deed Book 1 (Rowan County Courthouse, Salisbury); Jethro Rumple, *History of Rowan County* (1881); *Salisbury Post*, 22 June 1930, 5, 12, 19 Dec. 1976; William L. Saunders, ed., *Colonial Records of North Carolina*, vol. 10 (1890).

JAMES S. BRAWLEY

Locke, Matthew *(1730–7 Sept. 1801)*, colonial and Revolutionary leader and member of Congress, was born in Northern Ireland, the son of John and Elizabeth Locke. His parents moved to Lancaster County, Pa., where his father died in 1744; his widowed mother married John Brandon and moved to Anson County, N.C., probably in 1752, when John Brandon acquired 640 acres on Grants Creek in present-day Rowan County. Matthew, of course, was grown by this time, and on 25 Mar. 1752 he purchased 200 acres adjoining Brandon's farm. Acquiring still more land, he built his home on the road to Charlotte. His chief occupation at this time was trading skins from the backcountry in Charles Town, S.C., for needed articles, some of which he sold in the North Carolina Moravian settlements. He also delivered to Charles Town goods produced by the Moravians. Matthew and his brother, Francis, became wealthy through this trade.

Matthew Locke's first public responsibility came during the Regulator uprising in the backcountry. On 7 Mar. 1771 the officers of Rowan County appointed him and three other men to meet with some Regulators to iron out difficulties that existed between them. Locke and his companions agreed to repay any unlawful fees to those from whom they were illegally extracted. This action mollified the Regulators gathered near Salisbury and they dispersed. Moving into politics, Locke was elected to the colonial Assembly in 1771 and served until 1775.

As the break with England became more apparent, Locke moved decidedly towards the Patriot cause. By this time he was middle-aged and had more to lose than most men of his stature if the cause were lost. In September 1774 he was named to Rowan County's first Committee of Safety, and the next year he became a delegate to the Third Provincial Congress at Hillsborough. Here he served on the committees to persuade the disaffected to be friends of liberty, to finance the colony, and to make arrangements for minutemen throughout the colony. He saw further service on a committee charged with making arrangements for governing the colony in the absence of royal authority when Governor Josiah Martin departed. Governor Richard

Caswell afterwards commended Locke for the performance of these duties. In April 1776 he was a delegate to the Fourth Provincial Congress at Halifax. There the members adopted the Halifax Resolves instructing North Carolina's representatives in the Continental Congress in Philadelphia to concur with other delegates in voting for independence, making North Carolina the first colony to take such action.

Later in 1776 he was a member of the Rowan committee on secrecy and intelligence, which probed the activities of those not in sympathy with liberty. In this capacity he was probably responsible for the arrest of John Dunn, a founder of Salisbury, and Benjamin Booth, both of whom were suspected of treason. It was to Locke's home on the Charlotte road that these two men were taken after their arrest. They had signed a document that was later found to support royal authority. Locke also was paymaster of the troops in the Salisbury District, the largest in the state, comprising the six frontier counties.

While a member of the Halifax congress, Locke was chairman of the committee to settle and allow military accounts. As a member of the final (Fifth) Provincial Congress at Halifax in November 1776, he participated in drawing up the state's first constitution. Between 1771 and 1780, as a member of the House of Commons, Locke was generally occupied with procuring supplies for the Continental army as well as the state militia. His experience as a trader enabled him to purchase in 1778 a great quantity of skins which he sent to Pennsylvania to be made into shoes for troops. In the same year John Moore, a Tory, gathered about two thousand troops in Tryon County. To meet this threat, a force of equal number was called out and directed to assemble at Salisbury. Because General Griffith Rutherford was absent in South Carolina at the time, Matthew Locke was appointed brigadier general pro tempore of the Salisbury District to command the force. He had no chance to engage the enemy, however, as the Tories dispersed on orders of Lord Charles Cornwallis, the British commander.

Locke served in the North Carolina House of Commons (1777–80, 1783–84, 1785, and 1789–93) and the state senate (1782 and 1784–85). At the national level, he was a member of the last Continental Congress, sitting from 3 Nov. 1788 to 2 Mar. 1789. On many social and political questions of the day, Locke took a resolute and conspicuous stand in the state legislature. He favored giving ministers of all denominations the right to perform marriages, and he advocated the abolition of property qualifications for suffrage and officeholding, championing the cause of universal manhood suffrage. In so doing he anticipated this reform by almost a century. In education, he supported the bill for founding and endowing Queen's Museum at Charlotte and promoted a bill to establish a state university.

As a delegate to the Hillsborough Convention of 1788 to consider the new U.S. Constitution, Locke spoke for the poor, radical, and democratic farmers who were apprehensive that the new government would be expensive and oppressive. The opponents by a vote of 184 to 84 adopted a resolution neither rejecting nor ratifying the Constitution, but declaring that a declaration of rights ought to be laid before the Congress to be incorporated into the new Constitution. In the second convention, which met in Fayetteville in November 1789, Federalists overwhelmed the opponents and North Carolina adopted the Constitution. Locke, however, still opposed, voted with the minority.

The Federalists, riding a wave of popularity, elected

John Steele of Salisbury as the congressman from their district. He was reelected, but the policies of his party, which he advocated, proved to be unpopular, and in 1793 Matthew Locke, "the honest farmer," replaced Steele. In Congress, Locke became a charter member of Jeffersonian democracy in North Carolina. He consistently followed the lead taken by North Carolinian Nathaniel Macon, a Jeffersonian who was Speaker of the House.

Locke was seldom given to oratory and rarely spoke on the floor of Congress. However, he broke the rule when he made a forceful speech in December 1796 against a bill calling for the payment of state debts. Locke denounced the "unfairness and privacy of the settlement," as North Carolina owed the federal government half a million dollars when it had assumed that it would be a creditor.

Although an elderly man, Locke was reelected in 1796 and in 1798 to serve four more years in the House of Representatives. In the election of 1800 the "honest farmer" lost to Archibald Henderson, the "professional gentleman" who was a Federalist, and so ended Locke's public career. Basil Gaither of Salisbury defended Locke in his last bid for office by stating that he trusted farmers more than lawyers (Henderson was a lawyer) "who jump out of the cradle into college, and out of college into government, such men not having a feeling sense of the necessities of the great mass of mankind whom they represented."

Following Locke's death, an obituary in the Raleigh *Register* edited by Joseph Gales, a staunch Jeffersonian, bemoaned the passing and called him a "friend and fixed Republican" who had "served his state admirably in Congress." He was buried in Thyatira Presbyterian Church cemetery in Rowan County.

Locke was married first to Mary, a daughter of Richard Brandon, and had at one time four sons in the Revolution. One of them, Lieutenant George Locke, was killed at Kennedy's farm near Charlotte in a skirmish with the British. Francis Locke's household in 1790 consisted of three males over age sixteen, including himself, two males under sixteen, two females, including his wife, and twenty-seven slaves. Mary Locke died on 31 July 1790. While in Congress Locke courted and in 1798 married Elizabeth Gostelowe, widow of a Philadelphia cabinetmaker.

SEE: Steven Belk, "The Locke Family," 1977 (manuscript, Rowan Public Library, Salisbury); James S. Brawley, *The Rowan Story* (1953); John L. Cheney, Jr., *North Carolina Government, 1585–1979* (1981); Walter Clark, ed., *State Records of North Carolina*, vols. 11–22 (1895–1907); R. D. W. Connor, ed., *A Documentary History of the University of North Carolina*, vol. 1 (1953); Adelaide L. Fries, ed., *Records of the Moravians in North Carolina*, vols. 2–3 (1925–26); William S. Powell and others, eds., *The Regulators in North Carolina* (1971); Raleigh *Register*, 13 Oct. 1801; Rowan County Deed Book 1 (Rowan County Courthouse, Salisbury); Jethro Rumple, *History of Rowan County* (1881); H. M. Wagstaff, ed., *Papers of John Steele*, vol. 1 (1924); Winston-Salem *Journal-Sentinel*, 26 May 1935.

JAMES S. BRAWLEY

Lockhart, James Alexander (2 *June 1850–24 Dec. 1905*), congressman and lawyer, was born and spent his entire life in Wadesboro. He was the son of Adam Lockhart, a successful farmer, and Ann McDiermid Lockhart, daughter of Martin and Mary McDiermid who came

from Scotland in 1820 and settled in the Cape Fear section. Mary McDiermid was a descendant of Colonel Patrick Ferguson, the British commander killed during the Battle of Kings Mountain. Young Lockhart attended the common schools of Anson County and was only in about the equivalent of the fifth grade when the Civil War interrupted his education for a time. In 1869 he entered Trinity College, from which he was graduated in 1873. Reading law under the guidance of Clement Dowd, he was admitted to the bar in 1874 and established a practice in Wadesboro.

Soon gaining recognition for his honesty and trustworthiness, Lockhart was elected mayor of Wadesboro in 1875. In 1878 he won election to the North Carolina House of Representatives and in 1880, to the state senate. After serving in both houses of the General Assembly, he resumed his legal practice in Wadesboro until 2 Dec. 1895 when he took his seat as a Democrat in the U.S. House of Representatives. On 5 June 1876, however, he was obliged to step down when his election to that post was successfully challenged by Charles H. Martin, a Populist. Lockhart then returned to his law office in Wadesboro.

While he was a member of the General Assembly, Lockhart married, on 6 Feb. 1878, Caroline Ashe, daughter of North Carolina Supreme Court Justice Thomas Ashe and granddaughter of Governor Samuel Ashe. They were the parents of five children, one of whom, James, Jr., also served in both houses of the General Assembly. Mrs. Lockhart died on 28 Dec. 1904, a few days less than a year before her husband. He was buried in Eastview Cemetery, Wadesboro.

SEE: *Biog. Dir. Am. Cong.* (1961); John L. Cheney, Jr., ed., *North Carolina Government, 1585–1979* (1981); *Cyclopedia of Eminent and Representative Men of the Carolinas*, vol. 2 (1892); *North Carolina Biography*, vol. 4 (1928).

BLAKE A. MARTIN

Loesch, Jacob (22 *Nov. 1722–8 Nov. 1782*), one of the Moravian settlers of Wachovia and the first *Vorsteher* (manager) of Bethabara (now Old Town), was born near Schoharie, N.Y., the son of George and Anna Loesch. At age twenty-two, fully trained as a cabinetmaker, Loesch went to Bethlehem, Pa., and was accepted into the Moravian congregation. He was assigned to the position of Vorsteher for the outlying farming community of Christiansbrunn. Loesch must have proved himself a good business manager and organizer because in 1752 he, together with fourteen other single men, was chosen to settle the Wachovia tract in North Carolina that had been purchased by the Moravians from Earl Granville of England. The town the men carved out of the wilderness was called Bethabara, the first Moravian town to be established in the colony.

On arriving in North Carolina, Loesch familiarized himself with the laws of the province so that he could guide the Brethren accordingly. As Vorsteher of the town, Loesch was responsible for their legal and business affairs. He filled many required legal positions for the colony while he was also the primary representative of the Moravian people. To appease the authorities in regard to the religious requirements of each county, Loesch served as "Church Warden" from his area. This title was merely a formality for the Moravian congregation in a government organized under the Anglican church.

In Bethabara from 1753 to 1768, Loesch performed a host of duties including surveying, road planning, farming, mediating disputes, representing the town in business and legal matters, and helping to establish the town of Salem a few miles away. He also traveled throughout the South establishing trade relationships with various communities and occasionally conducted religious services in Bethabara.

As the town became established, the obligations of every individual increased. Loesch was designated Farm Vorsteher in 1756. The next year, during the French and Indian uprisings, he was commissioned captain of an independent company of militia for the inhabitants of Dobbs Parish in Rowan County. This was a strictly defensive force to protect the nearby settlers from the sporadic Indian attacks. In 1758 Loesch qualified as a justice of the peace under North Carolina law. By 1759 Bethabara was a thriving town and the job of managing it was too big for one person alone. This prompted the Brethren to organize a Committee of Outward Affairs, allowing Loesch to travel more frequently as the town's representative. In the same year, while attending the Assembly in Wilmington, he impressed the governor and other representatives with his descriptions of the Moravian community system. In 1767 Loesch had the honor of hosting Governor William Tryon in Bethabara.

Late in 1768 the Moravian Oeconomie Conference in Pennsylvania recalled Loesch to serve as Vorsteher and justice of the peace in Nazareth, Pa. Reluctantly, but dutifully, he and his family left North Carolina in April 1769; he had contributed fifteen years of energy and enthusiasm to the establishment of both Bethabara and Salem. Loesch's sensible and skillful leadership was a major factor in the success of the Moravian venture in North Carolina.

Loesch died after falling from his horse while traveling to Hope, N.J. He was survived by his wife, Anna Blum, whom he had married in 1757, and five children, Jacob (who adopted the spelling Lash for his surname), Johann Christian, Anna Philippina, Abraham, and Susanna Catharina Elizabeth, most of whom eventually returned to North Carolina to serve its Moravian congregation.

SEE: Adelaide L. Fries, ed., *Records of the Moravians in North Carolina*, vol. 1 (1922).

ROSAMOND C. SMITH

Loesch, Jacob. *See* **Lash (or Loesch), Jacob**.

Logan, George Washington *(22 Feb. 1815–18 Oct. 1889)*, Confederate congressman, superior court judge, Unionist, and Republican leader during Reconstruction, was born in Rutherford County, the son of John and Martha Harton Logan. For a time his father kept a hotel in Rutherfordton. George W. Logan read law, was admitted to the bar, and practiced in Rutherfordton. Early in life he held a succession of judicial offices in the county, serving as clerk and master in equity (1838–39), clerk of the county court (1841–49), and county solicitor (1855–56). Before the Civil War he rose to brigadier general of militia. Sometime after 1858, Logan edited the *Rutherfordton Enquirer*. He also farmed and speculated in real estate; in 1860 he was listed as the owner of eleven slaves.

A Whig in politics, Logan was a staunch Unionist during the secession crisis. He adhered to this position during the Civil War and it determined the remainder of his political career. Opponents identified him, probably correctly, as a leader of the pro-Union Red String order,

which was widespread in western North Carolina during the latter part of the war. He was elected to the Confederate Congress in 1863 as an avowed peace candidate and an opponent of the Davis administration. Although Logan took no leading part in congressional deliberations, his voting record in 1864–65 bore out his antiwar and anti-Confederate stance.

After the war Logan was elected to the constitutional convention of 1865 and to the legislature of 1866–67. He affiliated with the Republican party, apparently at its inception in the state, and was regarded as an outspoken partisan, first against the slaveholding aristocracy before 1865 and later against the Conservative or Democratic party and even in some measure the eastern wing of his own party headed by Governor William Woods Holden. His political mouthpiece after 1866 was the *Rutherford Star*, edited by J. B. Carpenter.

Although occasionally mentioned as a gubernatorial candidate, Logan attained his highest postwar office when he was elected a superior court judge in 1868. On the bench he gained fame as an uncompromising foe of the Ku Klux Klan, which infested Cleveland, Rutherford, and other counties of his circuit in 1871. An oft-threatened target of the Klan, Logan in his vigor to root it out helped to inspire charges by opponents of judicial incompetence. The Democratic legislature of 1871–72 considered impeaching him on this ground but ultimately declined to do so. One of his enemies and an erstwhile Klansman, David Schenck, defeated Logan for reelection in 1874, after which he retired to private life. He bought the Chimney Rock property in Rutherford County and there spent his last years.

Logan was married twice, in 1841 to Dovey Amelia Wilson (1817–51) and in 1854 to Mary Elizabeth Cabiness, each of whom bore him six children: John Amelia, George, Robert Wilson, Georgiana, Alice Dovey, and Margaret by the first marriage, and Mary Hannah, George W., Laogan, Felix B., Frank L., and James Andrew by the second. He was buried in St. Francis's Episcopal Cemetery, Rutherfordton.

A portrait of Logan was hung in the Rutherford County Courthouse in 1926.

SEE: Thomas Alexander and Richard E. Beringer, *The Anatomy of The Confederate Congress* (1972); *Asheville Democrat*, 24 Oct. 1889; Katherine Logan Conley, *The Genealogy of Major Francis Logan* (1970); Mrs. J. B. Eaves to Zebulon Vance Walser, 23 Mar. 1925, Walser Papers (Southern Historical Collection, University of North Carolina, Chapel Hill); Clarence W. Griffin, *History of Old Tryon and Rutherford Counties, 1730–1936* (1937); J. G. de Roulhac Hamilton, ed., *The Shotwell Papers*, vols. 1–3 (1929–36); Ezra J. Warner and W. Buck Yearns, *Biographical Register of the Confederate Congress* (1975).

ALLEN W. TRELEASE

London, Arthur Hill, Sr. *(9 July 1874–8 Dec. 1969)*, textile executive and banker, was born in Pittsboro of English ancestry, the son of William Lord London who became a captain in the Civil War at age twenty-four and later was inspector general and adjutant of his brigade. His mother was Caroline Haughton London, the daughter of John H. Haughton, a Pittsboro lawyer and legislator. London attended school in Pittsboro and the Horner Military School in Oxford before entering The University of North Carolina. In 1894 he joined his father in the operation of a Pittsboro mercantile firm with which he remained associated until it was dissolved in 1923. After his father's death in 1916, London became secretary-treasurer of the J. M. Odell Manufacturing Company, a post he filled until 1962, when named chairman of the board. He also was president of the Bank of Pittsboro from 1917 to 1964.

A member of the Episcopal church, London held offices at both the parish and diocesan levels, serving for about thirty-five years as senior warden and attending every diocesan convention from 1916 to 1949. He served on the Executive Council of the diocese and was a lay deputy to the General Convention of the church in 1928, 1931, and 1934. In 1937 he became the first chairman of the Chatham County Board of Public Welfare, and he was chairman of the Pittsboro school board for forty years. From 1935 to 1959 he was a member of the board of trustees of The University of North Carolina. Except for time away at school, London spent his entire life of ninety-five years in the house where he was born.

In 1900 he married Elizabeth Foushee, and they became the parents of seven children: William Lord, Arthur Hill, Jr., Frank Marsden, Lawrence Foushee, John Haughton, Elizabeth, and Fred Williams. He was buried in the churchyard of St. Bartholomew's Church, Pittsboro. A portrait is owned by his grandson, Dr. William L. London of Durham.

SEE: *Durham Morning Herald*, 6 Dec. 1969; Daniel L. Grant, *Alumni History of the University of North Carolina, 1795–1924* (1924); Wade Hadley and others, eds., *Chatham County, 1771–1971* (1971); Pittsboro *Chatham Record*, 20 Sept. 1962.

B. W. C. ROBERTS

London, Arthur Hill, Jr. *(5 July 1903–24 Apr. 1976)*, pediatrician and medical educator, was born in Pittsboro, the son of Arthur Hill, Sr., and Elizabeth Foushee London. He was graduated from The University of North Carolina in 1925 with a bachelor of science degree in medicine and immediately enrolled in the University of Pennsylvania School of Medicine, from which he was graduated in 1927. Following a year of general internship at the Methodist Hospital, Philadelphia, he served one year as assistant resident in pediatrics at the Children's Hospital, Cincinnati, and another year as chief resident in pediatrics at the University of Pennsylvania postgraduate school.

Returning to North Carolina in the summer of 1930, London entered private practice in Durham. During the first year he began a forty-five-year affiliation with the Pediatrics Department in the Duke University School of Medicine, and in 1933 he began a similar association with the School of Medicine of The University of North Carolina. He held the rank of assistant professor of pediatrics at Duke and that of clinical professor of pediatrics at Chapel Hill, continuing both appointments until his death at age seventy-two. For thirty-five years (1933–68) he was chief of pediatric services at Watts Hospital, Durham, and served as an instructor in pediatrics in the Watts Hospital School of Nursing. Also for thirty-five years he was a member of the Durham County Board of Health and chairman for five years.

In 1958 The University of North Carolina School of Medicine gave him its Distinguished Service Award, and in 1972 in elaborate ceremonies the North Carolina Memorial Hospital in Chapel Hill dedicated the Arthur Hill London Pediatric Clinic Library in his honor.

London held membership in many professional organizations, including the American Medical Association, Southern Medical Association (councillor), North Carolina State Medical Society (district councillor), North Carolina Pediatric Society (president), and American Academy of Pediatrics (district chairman), as well as local groups such as the Durham-Orange Medical Society. Throughout his long career, he conducted numerous research projects and wrote many articles on his findings for professional journals in this country and abroad. London was ranked among the leading pediatricians not only in North Carolina but also throughout the nation.

A member of St. Philip's Episcopal Church from the time of his arrival in Durham, he served as vestryman, senior warden, and leader in many of the church's internal organizations. In addition, he was a member of the board of trustees of the North Carolina Episcopal Foundation. London was a registered Democrat.

In 1930 he married Jeannette Brinson of Savannah, Ga., and they were the parents of two children: Arthur Hill III and Jeanne Elizabeth. Although stricken with a terminal illness early in 1976, he continued his practice until a few days before his death. He was buried in the cemetery at St. Bartholomew's Church, Pittsboro. After he died, the *Durham Sun* related: "As a boy, when he graduated at the top of his high school class, he was awarded a scholarship providing tuition at the state university free of charge. But, he gave it to a less financially able friend and classmate who he thought needed it more than he did. This is the kind of man he turned out to be."

SEE: *Durham Morning Herald*, 25 Apr. 1976; *Durham Sun*, 25, 28 Apr. 1976; News Release, School of Medicine, University of North Carolina, 2 June 1971; William S. Powell, ed., *North Carolina Lives* (1962); Raleigh *News and Observer*, 25 Apr. 1976.

C. SYLVESTER GREEN

London, Frank Marsden *(18 Apr. 1876–10 Mar. 1945)*, artist, was born in Pittsboro, the son of William Lord and Caroline Haughton London. He attended The University of North Carolina between 1893 and 1895 and afterwards studied art in New York with Arthur Dow and William M. Chase. Early in his career he designed stained glass and is represented by windows in the Belmont Chapel of the Cathedral of St. John the Divine in New York, the Church of the Good Shepherd in Raleigh, and St. Bartholomew's Church in Pittsboro, as well as in churches elsewhere in the United States.

In the 1920s London turned entirely to painting, specializing in still life described as being in the style of the romantic old Dutch painters. Moving to Paris in 1926, he remained for two years before returning to New York where he spent the rest of his life except for extended stays in England, Italy, and Spain. While in France he was awarded the Diplôme d'Honneur at the International Exposition of Beaux Arts at Bordeaux. His work was exhibited in Paris, New York, Chapel Hill, Raleigh, and elsewhere, and he was associated with several galleries, notably the Montross Galleries. He was a member of the Woodstock Art Association and the Whitney Studio Club and belonged to the Federation of Modern Painters and Sculptors.

London married Augusta Johnson and they were the parents of Caroline Haughton, who died young, and F. Marsden, Jr.

SEE: Chapel Hill *Daily Tar Heel*, 30 Nov. 1948; Ola Maie Foushee, *Art in North Carolina* (1972); *Frank London* (catalogue of a 1967 exhibition at The Contemporaries, a New York gallery); *Frank London: A Retrospective Showing of His Paintings* (1948); *New York Journal and American*, 8

Jan. 1939; *New York Post* and *New York World-Telegram*, 7 Jan. 1939; *New York Times*, 11 Mar. 1945; North Carolina Museum of Art, *Calendar of North Carolina Art Events* 1 (December 1957); Raleigh *News and Observer*, 1 Dec. 1948, 17 Jan. 1949, 29 Jan. 1967.

WILLIAM S. POWELL

London, Fritz Wolfgang (*7 Mar. 1900–30 Mar. 1954*), physicist and theoretical chemist, was born in Breslau, Germany (now Wroclaw, Poland), the son of Franz and Luise Hamburger London. In 1904 his father, a professor of mathematics, accepted a position at the University of Bonn, where Fritz London spent his formative years. After a classical secondary education, he studied physics, mathematics, and philosophy at the universities of Bonn, Frankfurt, and Munich. In 1921 London submitted a treatise to his philosophy professor for his information and criticism. Unexpectedly, this work became the dissertation for his Ph.D. in philosophy from the University of Munich. But London's scholarly interests soon changed from philosophy to theoretical science. In 1927, with Walter Heitler, he formulated a seminal study in quantum chemistry concerning homoeopolar bonding which came to be known as the Heitler-London Theory. In 1937 he received a Ph.D. in physics from the University of Paris.

Of Jewish background, London left Nazi Germany in 1933 and moved to Oxford, England. There, in collaboration with his equally gifted brother, Heinz, the London equations of superconductivity were established in 1935. This led to a lifelong investigation of the peculiar phenomena, associated with extremely low temperatures, known as superconductivity and superfluidity. Fritz London held appointments at Oxford University and the Institut Henri Poincaré (University of Paris) before accepting in 1939 a position as professor of theoretical chemistry at Duke University in Durham.

At Duke London continued his investigation of the effects of low temperature, concentrating on the existence of strong diamagnetism and the behavior of liquid helium. This work culminated in the publication of *Superfluids* in two volumes: *Mascroscopic Theory of Superconductivity* (1950) and *Macroscopic Theory of Superfluid Helium* (1954). These studies are landmarks in modern low-temperature physics.

In 1953 London was named James B. Duke Professor of Chemical Physics at Duke. The same year the Royal Dutch Academy of Sciences awarded him the prestigious Lorentz Medal in recognition of his scientific achievements; he was the first American citizen, and the first person serving an American institution, to be so honored. At the time of his premature death, he was considered to be a leading candidate for a Nobel Prize. He is memorialized by the annual Fritz London Memorial Lecture at Duke University and by the biannual international Fritz London Award in low-temperature physics.

In 1929, in Berlin, London married Edith Caspary, an artist; they had two children: Francis Michael and Rose Louise. Following his death from a heart ailment, London was buried in Maplewood Cemetery, Durham.

SEE: *Dictionary of Scientific Biography* (1973); Fritz London, *Superfluids*, 2d ed. (1961); Fritz London Papers (Duke University Archives, Durham).

MARK C. STAUTER

London, Henry Adolphus (*9 Apr. 1808–27 Nov. 1882*), merchant, was born in Wilmington, the son of John and Ann Mauger London. He obtained his early education in the schools of Brooklyn, N.Y., where his mother had moved following the death of her husband in 1816. After attending The University of North Carolina in 1825, London entered the American Literary, Scientific and Military Academy in Middletown, Conn. (later Norwich University). On his graduation in 1828, he returned to his native state and went into the mercantile business in Wilmington. In 1836 he moved to Pittsboro to become a member of the firm of Evans, Horn and Company. When this company dissolved, he operated a mercantile business of his own until a few years before his death. In 1853 London became treasurer of the Cape Fear and Deep River Navigation Company, which had been organized to open a water route on the Cape Fear River between Fayetteville and Gulf in Chatham County. He served in that capacity until the company disbanded in 1868.

Active in the public and religious life of Pittsboro, London was chairman of the Court of Pleas and Quarter Sessions for thirty years. In 1870 he was elected to a two-year term as treasurer of Chatham County. For more than forty years he was a vestryman and senior warden of St. Bartholemew's Parish. From 1839 until his death, he attended almost every annual convention of the Episcopal Diocese of North Carolina. London died in Pittsboro and was buried in St. Bartholemew's churchyard.

On 29 Feb. 1832 he married Sally Margaret Lord, the daughter of William Campbell and Eliza Hill Lord of Wilmington, and they had ten children: John Rutherford, Ann Mauger (m. Lawrence J. Haughton), William Lord, Eliza Catherine (m. Dr. P. G. Snowden), Rufus Marsden, Henry Armand, Mary Cowan (m. Joshua T. James), Fanny Thurston (m. John W. Taylor), Frederick Hill, and Frank Olmstead. After the death of his first wife, London married Catherine S. Moore of Pittsboro in 1860. There were no children from his second marriage.

SEE: Kemp P. Battle, *History of the University of North Carolina*, vol. 1 (1907); William A. Ellis, *Norwich University, 1819–1911: Her History, Her Graduates, Her Roll of Honor*, vol. 2 (1911); Henry A. London Papers (Southern Historical Collection, University of North Carolina, Chapel Hill); Pittsboro *Chatham Record*, 30 Nov. 1882, 20 Sept. 1962.

CLAIBORNE T. SMITH, JR.

London, Henry Armand (*1 Mar. 1846–20 Jan. 1918*), journalist and lawyer, was born in Pittsboro, the son of Henry Adolphus and Sally Lord London. He attended the Pittsboro Academy before entering the sophomore class at The University of North Carolina in July 1862. London kept an interesting diary of his student days at Chapel Hill during two years of war. It was popular in its day and widely read for many years afterwards. He left the university in the first session of his senior year to join the Confederate army in November 1864. Serving as a courier in Company I of the Thirty-second North Carolina Regiment, he participated in one of the last actions of the Civil War in carrying the message to General William R. Cox to cease firing because General Robert E. Lee had just surrendered. On the return of peace, President David L. Swain of the university offered to grant a B.A. diploma to all the members of the class of 1865 who had gone to war, if they returned to the campus and gave an oration. London was one of the three young veterans to do so, speaking on "The Crusades."

Following graduation London returned to Pittsboro to read law under Dr. John Manning, receiving his license to practice in January 1867. He was a lifelong Democrat and served for forty years as a member of the Democratic state executive committee. From 1870 to 1872 he was reading clerk of the North Carolina Senate, and in the campaign of 1872 he was a presidential elector for the Fourth Congressional District. London represented Chatham County in the state senate in 1901 and 1903, serving in the latter year as president pro tem. During his first term, he successfully introduced the London Libel Law. This law, one of the first of its kind enacted by any state legislature, was effective in maintaining a free press in North Carolina. The law remains on the statute books but was amended in 1943 to include radio and television stations.

Active in local affairs in Pittsboro, London founded in 1878 a successful weekly newspaper, the *Chatham Record*, which he edited and published until his death. From 1883 to 1884 he served as president of the North Carolina Press Association and for several years was a member of the executive committee of the National Editors Association. At a convention of newspaper editors held in Buffalo, N.Y., in 1901, London made a speech on the reconciliation of Civil War differences that was enthusiastically received. As a businessman, he was a director of the Bank of Pittsboro, director of the Commercial National Bank of Raleigh, and for a short time president of the Pittsboro Railroad Company, which built in 1886 the railroad linking Pittsboro to a main line of the Seaboard at Moncure. A member of St. Bartholomew's Church, London served the parish as vestryman, treasurer, lay reader, and delegate to diocesan conventions. He also was adjutant general and chief of staff in the North Carolina division of the United Confederate Veterans.

Interested in history, London delivered an address on the Revolutionary history of Chatham County at the centennial celebration in Pittsboro on 4 July 1876. He was the author of a memorial on the life and services of General Bryan Grimes, published in 1886; "The Last at Appomattox," appearing in *Literary and Historical Activities in North Carolina, 1900–1905*; and the "Thirty-Second Regiment," published in Walter Clark, ed., *Histories of the Several Regiments and Battalions from North Carolina*. In 1916 he was president of the State Literary and Historical Association. An enthusiastic alumnus of The University of North Carolina, London served as a trustee from 1901 to 1917. In 1911 the university awarded him an honorary M.A. degree.

In 1875 London married Bettie Louise Jackson (1853–1930), the daughter of Joseph John and Lucy Worth Jackson, daughter of Governor Jonathan Worth. The Londons had eight children: Henry Mauger, Lucy Worth (Mrs. John H. Anderson), Sallie Lord (Mrs. Henry Fell), Captain John Jackson, Bettie Jackson (Mrs. James H. Cordon), Worth, Isaac Spencer, and Camelia Rutherford (Mrs. Fred Jerome). Henry Armand London was buried in the churchyard of St. Bartholomew's, Pittsboro. Judge Walter Clark, a classmate at Chapel Hill, observed that he was "as gallant a soldier as ever wore the gray, and since the war, a leading lawyer and editor and one of the most prominent men in the state."

SEE: Kemp P. Battle, *History of the University of North Carolina*, vols. 1–2 (1907); Wade Hadley and others, eds., *Chatham County, 1771–1971* (1971); Henry A. London Diary (Southern Historical Collection, University of North Carolina, Chapel Hill); Pittsboro *Chatham Record*, 20 Sept. 1962; Raleigh *News and Observer*, 21 Jan. 1918; Royal G. Shannonhouse, ed., *History of St. Bartholomew's Parish, Pittsboro, North Carolina* (1933).

CLAIBORNE T. SMITH, JR.

London, Henry Mauger (*11 Apr. 1879–30 Dec. 1939*), state legislative reference librarian, was born in Pittsboro, the oldest son and second of eight children of Henry Armand and Bettie Louise Jackson London. Both of his parents were from old and influential families in the town, but the Londons had lived in Wilmington before moving to Pittsboro around 1836.

London received his early education at Pittsboro Academy. In 1896 he entered The University of North Carolina, the alma mater of his father and both of his grandfathers. At Chapel Hill he was an active member of the Dialectic Literary Society and editor of the student newspaper, *The Tar Heel*. Graduated with honors in 1899, London worked as a clerk in the U.S. census office, in Washington, D.C., from 1900 until 1902 and at the same time began a law course at George Washington University, then known as Columbian University. In the fall of 1902 he returned to Chapel Hill, completed his study of law, and was admitted to the North Carolina bar in 1903.

For the next ten years, London resided in Pittsboro and practiced law with his father while also assisting in the editing of the *Chatham Record*. He served as mayor of Pittsboro from 1903 to 1905 and represented Chatham County in the lower house of the General Assembly in 1907–8 and in the state senate in 1911. In 1913 he was a Democratic presidential elector.

In 1913 London moved to Raleigh to become chief deputy collector of internal revenue for the state of North Carolina, a post he retained until 1919, when he became legislative reference librarian. In this position he directed the drafting of bills to be introduced in the General Assembly, and in the following twenty years he assisted in the drafting of around five thousand bills. Biennially from 1931 until 1939, it was also his responsibility as librarian to edit the *North Carolina Manual*.

In 1918, at the death of his father, London assumed the editorship of the *Chatham Record* but sold the newspaper after two years. In other aspects of his life, however, he continued to reflect his father's concerns—state and local history, Democratic-conservative politics, the Episcopal church, The University of North Carolina, and a variety of Confederate memorial associations. His brother, Isaac, continued the family's newspaper interests by establishing and for many years editing the Rockingham *Post-Dispatch*.

In February 1921 London was elected to the board of trustees of The University of North Carolina and in June he became secretary of the trustees, a position he held for the remainder of his life. From 1919 onwards he was treasurer of the Episcopal Diocese of North Carolina. He also served as secretary-treasurer of the North Carolina Bar Association and secretary (1933–38) of the State Bar, Inc., a state agency and therefore an entirely different organization. At various times London was president of the North Carolina Society of Sons of the American Revolution, state commander of the Sons of Confederate Veterans, president and secretary of the Raleigh Rotary Club, director of the Raleigh Building and Loan Association and of the Raleigh Travelers Aid Association, and secretary-treasurer of the Capital Construction Company.

On 25 Nov. 1908 he married Mary (Mamie) Elliot, the

daughter of George and Nelia McNeill Elliot of Cumberland and Harnett counties. They had two children: Henry Mauger, Jr., and George Elliot. London died in Raleigh and was buried at St. Bartholomew's Church, Pittsboro.

SEE: John L. Cheney, Jr., ed., *North Carolina Government, 1585–1974* (1974); *Durham Morning Herald* and *Durham Sun*, 31 Dec. 1939; Frank Porter Graham Papers, Henry Mauger London Papers, and London Family Papers (Southern Historical Collection, University of North Carolina, Chapel Hill); *North Carolina Manual* (1919–39); Minutes of the Board of Trustees of the University of North Carolina, 1916–32 (University Archives, Chapel Hill); Raleigh *News and Observer*, 6 Aug. 1933; Chapel Hill *Daily Tar Heel*, 26 Mar. 1932.

SUSAN C. BALLINGER

London, John (23 Oct. 1747–1 March 1816), colonial official, merchant, and banker, was born in Holborn, London, the son of John and Mary Wollaston London and the great-grandson of Sir Robert London who was knighted by Charles II in 1664 for services rendered his father, Charles I. According to a memorandum made by London, he came to North Carolina in the spring of 1764. Sometime between then and November 1764 he was appointed a deputy auditor by Governor Arthur Dobbs. This fact is attested to by a land grant registered in the "office of the Aud. Gen. at Wilmington the 20th of November 1764," which London signed as "D. Aud." On 21 Dec. 1765 he took the oath as "one of the Clerks of the Secretary's office," and in 1768 he was promoted to the position of deputy secretary of the colony. Following the death of Benjamin Heron, secretary of the province, Governor William Tryon, in October 1770, appointed London "Secretary and Clerk of the Crown." He held this office for only two months, resigning in December. London was also clerk of the New Hanover court from 1769 until the fall of 1775, when he was granted a twelve-month leave to settle his personal affairs in England. As he had been a Crown officer, he was not ready at that time to cast his lot with the American Patriots.

On 20 Jan. 1776 he sailed from Wilmington to England, where he remained for about twenty months. According to a fragmentary diary London kept during his stay, he visited Bristol, Bromsgrove, Stourport, Loughborough, and Glasgow but did not mention the nature of his business in these places. While in Glasgow he was granted on 3 Oct. 1776 a "Burges Ticket," a handsomely illuminated document, which made him a "Burges and gild Brother" of the city. The Burges Ticket entitled him to become a member of the Merchants' House of Glasgow. London evidently made this arrangement so that he could carry on business with the Glasgow merchants at some future time. This proved to be the case, because a few years later he became a member of the mercantile firm of Burgwin, Jewkes and London of Wilmington.

He returned to America on 25 Sept. 1777, landing in New York. Two months later he and Samuel Cornell, a fellow Loyalist from North Carolina, arrived at New Bern in the brig *Edwards*. They requested permission from Governor Richard Caswell to come ashore to settle their private business under a flag of truce secured from General Henry Clinton for this purpose. Permission to land was granted, but they were instructed not to "proceed further into the Town, than Mr. Cornell's dwelling House." Caswell ordered them to return to New York on the *Edwards* by 29 December, stipulating that "Mr. London is permitted to take with him his two servants." London did not go to New York but went to Wilmington instead, having received permission from the governor who placed him under parole and limited his movements to the bounds of New Hanover County. London assured Caswell that he would not in any way concern himself "with any measure whatever inimical to the liberty of America."

In September 1778 London applied to the justices of the peace to be allowed to take the oath of allegiance to the state. They turned down his application on the grounds that they doubted its legality since London was in Wilmington on parole under the Confiscation Act. These doubts appear to have been removed, for on 25 Jan. 1779 he was admitted to citizenship. Further evidence of London's return to favor in his community came a year later when Charles Jewkes, commissary to General Alexander Lillington, wrote Governor Caswell requesting £6,000 for provisions to be sent to John London. Jewkes said that London "manages . . . in my absence" and would "do everything that will be wanting for your service." Notwithstanding this show of confidence, London seems to have felt secure in his position, for when the British troops left Wilmington in November 1781, he went with them to Charles Town. He had already been placed under parole not to take up arms against the king when the British occupied Wilmington in January 1781. Remaining in Charles Town until 1783, he took the oath of allegiance and citizenship before the governor of South Carolina. But his citizenship was not recognized in North Carolina, as he soon learned when he returned to Wilmington on 24 July 1783. He was placed under bond to answer any charges made against him under the confiscation acts, as were other citizens who had left the state during the Revolution.

Writing to a friend concerning London's loyalty, Archibald Maclaine remarked that although he and London differed in politics, he preferred having him and others like him "among us . . . than many that shall be nameless." London remained under bond until 1785, when he was formally discharged and was once again in the good graces of his fellow citizens. Summing up his losses of personal property during the Revolution, he estimated them to be £5,795 sterling. In making this estimate he was realistic enough to state that he did not expect to recover his losses, which he never did.

Nevertheless, London was able to purchase property in 1785 on the south side of Market Street in Wilmington where he made his home. In 1796 he was appointed "Treasurer for the Public Buildings" by the New Hanover court and elected one of the Wardens for the Poor. He served for many years as magistrate of police for the town of Wilmington. It was in this capacity that on 1 July 1812 he issued a call for the citizens of Wilmington to meet in the courthouse for the purpose of considering what measures should be adopted "for the security of this Town and its vicinity at this alarming crisis." This is an interesting turn of events, a former Loyalist now providing for the protection of his town against the British.

In December 1804 the General Assembly chartered the Bank of Cape Fear, to be located in Wilmington. In the act of incorporation, London was named one of the seven commissioners to solicit the sale of stock in the bank. By August 1805 the required number of shares— one thousand—had been sold. On 19 September the stockholders met at Dick's Hotel in Wilmington to elect eleven directors, one of whom was London. He was reelected a director each year until his death. The *Wilmington Gazette* for 29 Oct. 1805 carried a notice stating that the Bank of Cape Fear would open for business on 4

November. The notice was signed "Geo. Hooper, President." Hooper held this office until January 1806, when Joshua Grainger Wright was elected president. Wright served until his death on 10 June 1811. London succeeded Wright as president of the bank in 1811 and continued in that office until 1816.

London married first a widow, Peggy Marsden Chivers (1748–86), on 12 July 1785 and by her had one child, John Rutherford (1786–1832). He married second Anne Thorney Mauger (1774–1858) of Charleston, S.C. She was born in St. John's Parish, Isle of Jersey, the daughter of John and Anne Thorney Mauger. In 1783 Anne and her father, then a widower, left Jersey to make their home in Charleston. John London and Anne were married on 12 June 1796 at The Hermitage, a plantation a few miles outside of Wilmington belonging to John Burgwin, an old friend of London. They had ten children, five of whom died in childhood. Those who survived were Henry Adolphus, Mauger, Frances Maria (m. Lallerstedt Mallett), Mary Ashe (m. Thomas Cowan), and Margaret (unmarried).

At the death of his first wife, Peggy Chivers, a rich widow, London inherited the income from her estate for his lifetime. At his death the estate went to their only child, John Rutherford. This inheritance partly explains how London was able to leave his business and take a five-month trip to New York and New England. In a diary London kept of this trip, he stated that he, his wife, and son John left Wilmington on 5 June 1800. Shortly after arriving in New York, he entered John in an academy in Newark, N.J., which was under the direction of the Reverend Uzal Ogden, rector of Trinity Church, Newark. In his diary London made interesting comments on the people he met, the towns visited, the public buildings of the area, particularly churches, and the agriculture of the region. Returning to Wilmington on 6 November, he remarked that the trip had been "one of the most agreeable I ever took" and that it had quite restored his and his wife's health.

No record has been found as to what school, if any, London attended in England before coming to North Carolina. Judging from the style of his letters and the sort of books in his library, he was a man of some intellectual ability. Among his extant collection are eight volumes of Shakespeare's works, Middleton's life of Cicero, the maxims of La Rochefoucauld, the essays of Montaigne, *The Iliad* and *Odyssey*, and the poetical and prose works of Pope, Addison, and Goldsmith. All of these volumes were published in London or Edinburgh in the second half of the eighteenth century.

London was a member of the Anglican church. In 1770 he purchased a pew in the newly completed St. James's Church, Wilmington. Following his death, the *Wilmington Gazette* asserted: "ardent in his attachments, sincere in his friendship, devout in religious exercises, temperate in his habits, and distinguished for method, precision and industry in business, his character presents a fit model for imitation." The officers of the Bank of Cape Fear marched in his funeral procession, and during the day the ships in the harbor flew their colors at half mast. London was buried in Oakdale Cemetery, Wilmington.

SEE: Burges Ticket (possession of George E. London, Raleigh); Walter Clark, ed., *State Records of North Carolina*, vols. 11–13, 15–16 (1895–99); Robert O. DeMond, *The Loyalists in North Carolina during the Revolution* (1940); Family Bible and manuscripts (possession of Jack London, Uniontown, Ala.); Don Higginbotham, ed., *Papers of James Iredell*, vol. 2 (1976); Donald R. Lennon and Ida

Brooks Kellam, eds., *Wilmington Town Book, 1743–78* (1973); Henry Adolphus London Papers (Southern Historical Collection, University of North Carolina, Chapel Hill); John London Diary, 1800 (North Carolina State Archives, Raleigh); "London Family," in *American Families: Genealogical and Heraldic*, pp. 279–89 (ca. 1928); London Family Papers (Southern Historical Collection, University of North Carolina, Chapel Hill); William L. Saunders, ed., *Colonial Records of North Carolina*, vols. 7–9 (1890); Henry McG. Wagstaff, ed., *Papers of John Steele*, vol. 2 (1924); Alexander McD. Walker, ed., *New Hanover County Court Minutes, 1738–1800* (1958); *Wilmington Gazette*, 24 Sept., 25 Oct. 1805, 7 Jan. 1806, 6 Jan. 1807, 3 Jan. 1809, 2 Jan. 1810, 13 Jan., 9 Mar. 1816.

LAWRENCE F. LONDON

London, William Lord (3 Apr. 1838–30 Nov. 1916), merchant, banker, and manufacturer, was born in Pittsboro, the son of Henry Adolphus and Sally Lord London. On completing his education in the local schools, he entered his father's mercantile business where he worked until the outbreak of the Civil War.

London enlisted in the Chatham Rifles on 15 Apr. 1861 and remained on active duty until the surrender of General Robert E. Lee. In June 1861 he was promoted to the rank of first lieutenant and a year later was made captain of Company I, Thirty-second Regiment, North Carolina Troops. On 1 July 1862 he was wounded while leading a charge on Malvern Hill. He was wounded again while commanding the sharpshooters of General Junius Daniel's brigade at Gettysburg and received a third injury in the Battle of Winchester. Following the Battle of Gettysburg, Colonel E. C. Brabble of the Thirty-second Regiment reported: "Where all behaved so well it is difficult to discriminate, yet justice requires that I should mention Captain William L. London. To his skill and gallantry is greatly due whatever of service the regiment may have rendered in the battle." In recognition of his services at Gettysburg, London was promoted in July 1863 to inspector general of General Daniel's brigade and a few months later was made adjutant general of the brigade.

On returning home after the war, London reentered his father's business. In 1901, when he and other citizens of Pittsboro organized the Bank of Pittsboro, he was elected president, an office he held until his death. His business activities were further expanded in 1902, when he became secretary-treasurer of the J. M. Odell Manufacturing Company, whose textile mill was located at Bynum with offices in Pittsboro.

For more than thirty years London served as senior warden of St. Bartholomew's Church. His parish sent him to almost every convention of the Episcopal Diocese of North Carolina from 1875 to 1916, and he was elected a lay deputy from the diocese to the triennial meetings of the denomination's General Convention during 1898–1907 and 1913. London was a trustee of the University of the South in Sewanee, Tenn., from 1892 to 1910 and for several years was a trustee of St. Augustine's College in Raleigh.

Taking an active role in the organization of the United Confederate Veterans in 1895, London was elected brigadier general of the Second Brigade, North Carolina Division. He contributed the chapter, "The Daniel-Grimes Brigade," to Walter Clark's *Regiments and Battalions from North Carolina*. He died in Pittsboro and was buried in St. Bartholomew's churchyard. On 21 Oct. 1917, in St. Bartholomew's Church, Bishop Joseph B. Cheshire dedicated a stained-glass window in memory of Captain London which was designed by his son, Frank M. London. In his dedicatory address, the bishop said: "I saw in him whom we now remember that faith, patience, goodness, and helpfulness, which St. Paul saw in those whom he commended, and because his life and character, like theirs, was the strength and power of the Church." He stood "fast in the integrity of a high and honorable character."

On 14 Nov. 1864 London married Maria Caroline Haughton (1839–1923), the daughter of John Hooker and Eliza Alice Hill Haughton of Pittsboro. They had seven children: Alice Hill, Henry Adolphus, John Haughton, William Lord, Arthur Hill, Frank Marsden, and Caroline Haughton.

SEE: Walter Clark, ed., *Histories of the Several Regiments and Battalions from North Carolina in the Great War, 1861–1865*, vols. 2, 4 (1901); Clement Evans, ed., *Confederate Military History*, vol. 4 (1899); *Journals of the Diocese of North Carolina*, 1882–1916; Henry Adolphus London Papers (Southern Historical Collection, University of North Carolina, Chapel Hill); Pittsboro *Chatham Record*, 6 Dec. 1916, 20 Sept. 1962.

CLAIBORNE T. SMITH, JR.

Long, Andrew Theodore (*6 Apr. 1866–21 May 1946*), naval officer, was one of ten children in the family of Thomas Simpson Long, an Iredell County planter, and Rosanna Camilla Neill Long. In 1881 he enrolled in a military school conducted by Captain W. T. R. Bell at Kings Mountain, N.C. Two years later he entered the U.S. Naval Academy, where he was president of his class for four years and was graduated in 1887. Beginning as an ensign on 1 July 1889, he progressed up the scale until reaching the rank of rear admiral on 15 Sept. 1918.

Long had a distinguished naval career that stretched for forty-seven years. He served on board the battleship *Minnesota* during the Spanish-American War, and he was with American naval forces in China during the Boxer Rebellion of 1900. In 1901 and 1902 he was navigator of the cruiser *Vicksburg*, which transported U.S. troops commanded by General Frederick Funston to the Philippines for a campaign against native insurrectionists led by Emilio Aguinaldo. While commanding the presidential yacht *Mayflower* in 1906 and 1907, Long became a close friend of President Theodore Roosevelt and his family. As executive officer of the USS *Illinois*, he was with the Great White Fleet when it sailed around the world in 1907 and 1908. For three years (1909–12), the North Carolina native was naval attaché at the U.S. embassies in Rome and Vienna. After commanding the cruiser *Des Moines* for a year, he was supervisor of naval auxiliaries from 1914 to 1916.

During World War I, Long commanded two battleships: the *Connecticut* and the *Nevada*. Before the conflict ended, he was appointed liaison officer for the Supreme War Council. For his service during the war, Long was awarded the Distinguished Service Medal. Afterwards, as naval attaché in Paris, he helped draft the Treaty of Versailles. Between January and September 1920 Long commanded Battleship Division Four, Atlantic Fleet. He then served briefly as director for Naval Intelligence in Washington, D.C. In 1921 he became chief of staff for Admiral Hilary P. Jones, commander in chief of the Atlantic Fleet. In 1922 Long assumed command of U.S. naval forces in European waters, and in 1923 he was appointed chief of the Bureau of Navigation in the Navy Department. The following year he became a member of

the navy's General Board, a position he held for six years.

In addition to his duties on the General Board, Long performed a number of other valuable services for his government. He was aide to the king and queen of Belgium on their visit to the United States in 1924 and served in the same capacity during the visit of Queen Marie of Rumania in 1928. Between 1926 and 1928 he was naval adviser to the head of the American delegation to the Preparatory Commission for the Disarmament Conference at Geneva, Switzerland. He was also adviser to the American delegates to the Three-Power Naval Conference in 1927. After his retirement from the navy in 1930, Long served for seven years as director of the International Hydrographic Bureau at Monte Carlo, Monaco.

On 3 Mar. 1928, in New York City, Long married Mrs. Viola Vetter Fife, the daughter of Carl Ernest Vetter and the former wife of George Buchanan Fife. The couple had no children. Long was a Methodist and a Democrat. He died in St. Augustine, Fla., and was buried in Arlington National Cemetery. His personal papers, which contain numerous photographs, are in the Southern Historical Collection of the University of North Carolina, Chapel Hill.

SEE: *Greensboro Daily News*, 23 May 1946; Andrew T. Long, "Around the World in Sixty Years" (autobiography, Southern Historical Collection, University of North Carolina, Chapel Hill); *Nat. Cyc. Am. Biog.*, vol. 38 (1953); *Who Was Who in America*, vol. 2 (1950).

CHARLES H. MCARVER, JR.

Long, Benjamin Franklin (*19 Mar. 1852–14 Mar. 1925*), superior court judge, was born in Alamance County, near Graham, at the home place settled by his great-grandfather, Conrad Long (Lange), who had emigrated from Germany to Pennsylvania and then to North Carolina about 1760. Benjamin was the youngest son of Jacob and Jane Stuart Stockard Long. He received his early education at Graham Institute under the guidance of his older brother, the Reverend William Samuel Long, D.D., at that time head of the institute but later founder and first president of Elon College. After finishing school at Graham, Benjamin entered Trinity College in Randolph County. An excellent student, he was graduated in 1874 as valedictorian of his class. He then taught Latin and history at Graham High School for two years before entering the University of Virginia Law School, where he completed the two-year course in one year, was awarded the Orator's Medal, and was selected to deliver the commencement address as a representative of the Washington Society.

On returning home, he was offered the Democratic nomination for state senator but decided to move to Statesville to become the law partner of William McKendree Robbins, who was at that time a congressman with a good practice in Statesville. Long was an industrious worker and in 1879, in addition to his legal duties, he edited the *Law Lectures* of Judge Richmond Pearson from notes taken during the time he had been a student before entering the University of Virginia.

Long served as solicitor of the Iredell County court for three terms, as attorney for the city of Statesville, and as receiver for the western division of the Western North Carolina Railroad from 1880 to 1885. For two years he was mayor of Statesville, resigning to become solicitor of the Eighth Judicial District; he subsequently was reelected to that post. First nominated in 1894 as the Democratic candidate for judge in the Tenth Judicial District of the North Carolina Superior Court, he was defeated by the Republican-Populist coalition. In 1902 he again received his party's endorsement for the judgeship and was elected by a large majority; continuing to win reelection, he held this position until his death.

In 1901 Long was the author of the bill that created the graded schools of Statesville, and with two other persons he organized the Statesville Cotton Mill, the first in the town. During the same year, he served as defense counsel at the impeachment trial of Chief Justice David M. Furches and Associate Justice Robert M. Douglas. Long's speech on 25 March was considered a masterpiece. The Republican justices were acquitted by the senate, which was composed largely of Democrats; Long, also a Democrat, conducted the defense because he was convinced that acquittal was just.

Two famous cases over which he presided were the Lyerly lynching case in Salisbury and the Southern Railway rate case in Raleigh. On 6 Aug. 1906 several blacks were in the Salisbury jail awaiting trial for the murder of a white family. The local authorities had taken every precaution to ensure their safety, including alerting a military unit. Judge Long himself, with the sheriff, had spoken to some of the presumed leaders of a mob that had assembled in the area. Later that night the mob, composed of many from outside Salisbury, battered down the door of the jail and killed three of the six prisoners. The next morning, Long opened court, called the grand jury, and began his charge to the jurors as follows: "God Almighty reigns and the Law is still supreme. This court will not adjourn until this matter is investigated." Proof was difficult, every effort being made to protect the mob, but one person, George Hall, was convicted and sentenced to fifteen years; Hall was the first white man in the state to be convicted in a lynching case. Through all appeals, Long's ruling was upheld. Newspapers, both state and national, approved his decision.

The rate case, tried in Raleigh in July 1907, had grown out of legislation passed during the previous February fixing the railroad passenger rate at 2¼ cents a mile. Two days before the new rate went into effect, the railroad companies obtained an injunction from federal circuit judge Jeter Pritchard, prompting the Southern Railway to sell tickets at a higher rate than the new law permitted. In question was the authority of the state courts to prosecute violators of state law. In the opening day of court, Long directed the grand jury to decide whether Southern Railway was violating North Carolina law by using the higher rate. As a result, ticket agent Thomas F. Green was indicted and arrested. Feelings had been running high over the passage of the rate law, and Judge Pritchard announced that officers and agents of the railway company would be protected under his order. He then went to Raleigh, reportedly for the purpose of obtaining a habeas corpus for Green's release. Long ordered the sheriff to deliver up the prisoner, Green, to the court and confined him temporarily in his own hotel room. Green was not required to stay in his presence, however, except when court was in session. Pritchard, recognizing the delicacy of the situation, returned to Asheville. Long ruled that a federal court could not suspend the criminal laws of a state nor protect a citizen who was violating state law. On Green's promise to obey the North Carolina law, he was fined $5 and freed. Southern Railway, which would not accept the rate ceiling, was fined $30,000. On appeal, the North Carolina Supreme Court held that the law only applied to the person selling the tickets, although it sustained the lower court on all other questions. Eight days later, the

Southern Railway suggested to the governor that it would abide by Long's ruling and compromises were worked out.

In 1912 Long was urged to be a candidate for associate justice on the North Carolina Supreme Court but declined to run. Two years later Senators Lee S. Overman and Furnifold M. Simmons recommended him to President Woodrow Wilson for appointment to the U.S. Supreme Court, but he was not selected.

Raised in a religious and close-knit family, Long maintained strong family ties all of his life. Both of his parents had a longtime interest in the orphanage at Oxford and were active in their church. He joined the First Presbyterian Church in Statesville after his marriage on 23 Dec. 1879 to Mary Alice Robbins, the daughter of his law partner Major William McKendree and Mary Montgomery Robbins. The Longs had three sons and two daughters. The oldest son died in infancy. The second son, Benjamin F., Jr., when a freshman at The University of North Carolina in 1899, was critically injured in a train accident at University Station, Chapel Hill, while waiting to meet his father; he died the same day. The other children were Lois (Mrs. Franklin Riker), a concert soprano; Marie (Mrs. Edward Mayo Land), president of the North Carolina Federation of Women's Clubs; and the youngest son, McKendree Robbins, an artist and a minister.

Long was a Mason and an Elk. He was buried in the family plot in Oakwood Cemetery, Statesville. A portrait, painted by his son McKendree, hangs in the Iredell County Hall of Justice.

SEE: Samuel A. Ashe, ed., *Biographical History of North Carolina*, vol. 8 (1917); *Baltimore Sun*, 5 Dec. 1907; *Indianapolis Star*, 12 Aug. 1906; Benjamin Franklin Long, *Published Opinions on Two Important Cases: State vs. Southern Railway Co. and State vs. George Hall* ([1912] copy in North Carolina Collection, University of North Carolina, Chapel Hill); *New York World*, 23 July 1907; Raleigh *News and Observer*, 6 Jan. 1912; *Salisbury Post*, 7 Jan. 1912.

CAROLINE LONG AVERY

Long, Daniel Albright (*22 May 1844–26 Oct. 1933*), clergyman and educator, was born in Graham, the son of Jacob and Jane Stuart Stockard Long. He had a sister, Bettie, and five brothers: John, William Samuel, Jacob A., George W., and Benjamin F. After attending Graham Institute, Long, then sixteen, began teaching school in Alamance County but interrupted his career to serve in the Confederate army. After the war, he attended The University of North Carolina from 1866 until 1868 and was ordained a minister in the North Carolina and Virginia Conference of the Christian church, South, in 1867. For several years he both served churches and taught school in Rockingham County, Va., while continuing his studies at Yale University, the University of Virginia, and the University of Pennsylvania.

In 1874 Long returned to his native Graham and purchased the Graham Institute property from his brother, William Samuel Long. On 3 Mar. 1875 the Graham High School was incorporated with Daniel Albright Long as principal; in 1881, by another charter, the name of the institution was changed to Graham Normal College, with Long as president. One of its students was the English-born David F. Jones, who expressed a desire to become a Christian minister and enter the foreign mission field. It was largely due to Long's efforts on his behalf that Jones and his wife sailed for Japan in 1887, becoming the first missionaries in the Orient dispatched by the American Christian church.

In 1883 Long accepted the presidency of Antioch College, an institution founded by the northern Christian church at Yellow Springs, Ohio. Reportedly, he was the only Confederate veteran ever elected to the presidency of a college above the Mason-Dixon Line. He turned the operation of Graham College over to his brother, William Samuel Long, and moved to Ohio. Antioch had opened with insufficient funds and suffered financial privations throughout its existence. The president labored valiantly but was unable to raise the necessary funds from the Christian church to place the college on a sound financial basis. He resigned in 1899, and the school eventually became the property of the Unitarian church; it is still in operation today.

From 1877 to 1887 Long served as a trustee of The University of North Carolina, which awarded him an honorary M.A. degree in 1882 and an honorary D.D. degree in 1887. In the latter year he received an LL.D. degree from Union Christian College, and in 1893 he was made a fellow of Columbia University. From 1886 to 1894 Long served as president of the U.S. Christian Conference, which was the governing body of the Christian church in the North and the West. During his tenure, he was influential in effecting a reconciliation between the conference and the southern Christian church, which had severed relations in the 1850s as a result of a disagreement over the slavery issue. This led to the formation of one denomination in 1922 known as the Christian church. (Due to mergers, this church became the Congregational Christian church and, later, the United Church of Christ.)

In 1890 Antioch College began publishing *Spirit and Life: A Christian Magazine*. Long edited the second volume of the paper, after which its publication was suspended. He also edited the *Yellow Springs Review*. In 1893 he became president of the reorganized Christian Publishing Association, at Dayton, Ohio, and served for eight years.

Long was pastor of the Hillsboro Street Christian Church in Raleigh, N.C., before accepting the presidency of Union Christian College, at Merom, Ind., in 1911. After serving in this capacity for a number of years, he returned to North Carolina and assisted in the operation of Franklinton Christian College. This institution constituted the initial effort of the Christian church to educate the blacks in the state, and it was maintained largely through the support of Long and other clergymen. Long held numerous other minor offices in his denomination until advanced age forced his retirement. He was the author of *Legal History of Antioch College* (1890) and *Jefferson Davis: An Address Delivered at Concord, N.C., June 3, 1921* (1923). One of his sermons was published in *Gospel Sermons of Christian Ministers* (1890), edited by Asa W. Coan.

Long's first wife was Ava R. Waters, who died in 1874. His second wife, and the mother of his five children, was Carrie Eugenia Bell. After her death in 1893, he married Mrs. A. B. Beech (Sadie S.), who died in 1907. His fourth wife was Mrs. Robert Easley (Lula Price), who survived him. His children were Margaret (Mrs. D. K. Wolfe), Carrie (Mrs. Charles H. Belvin), Lillian (Mrs. George Albert Kernodle), Joseph C., and Daniel Albright, Jr.

Long was a Mason, a member of the Sons of the American Revolution, and a recipient of the Southern Cross of Honor. He died in Graham and was buried in Linwood Cemetery. Numerous photographs, taken at various times during his life, appear in various issues of the *Christian Sun*.

SEE: Alumni Files (University of North Carolina, Chapel Hill); *American Men of Science*, 9th ed. (1955); *Christian Sun*, 1890–1935; *Laws and Resolutions of the State of North Carolina Passed by the General Assembly at Its Session of 1881*; Milo True Morrill, *History of the Christian Denomination in America* (1912); *Proceedings of the Southern Christian Convention*, published in *The Christian Annual* (1890–1936).

DURWARD T. STOKES

Long, Jacob Alson (*6 Apr. 1846–4 Oct. 1923*), attorney and Ku Klux Klan leader, was born at the old Long home place near Graham, the son of Jacob and Jane Stuart Stockard Long. His grandfather, John Stockard, served in the War of 1812 and represented Orange County in the General Assembly almost continuously from 1826 to 1846. Young Long attended Alexander Wilson's school near Graham and an academy at Hyco, Va., but left school in 1864 to join the Army of Northern Virginia; he served as a gunner until General Robert E. Lee's surrender at Appomattox. After the war he spent four years on the family farm and in school before studying law in Hillsborough under William K. Ruffin, son of Chief Justice Thomas Ruffin.

Licensed to practice in 1870, Long established himself as an attorney in Graham for two years. Afterwards he was a railroad conductor for a year and taught school for another year before moving to Yanceyville, where he practiced law for a decade. For three years he was an attorney in Durham but then returned to Graham, where he remained for the rest of his life. For a time he was in partnership with his son, J. Elmer Long, who was lieutenant governor from 1925 to 1929.

In 1868, when the Ku Klux Klan was introduced into Alamance County from Guilford County, Long was named chief of Camp Number One. He soon organized ten camps to which the leading citizens of Alamance and Caswell counties belonged. Their stated objective was to keep law and order; reportedly, Long's only order as chief was to get armed blacks off the streets of Graham. Eventually, federal authorities learned about the Klan's activities through James E. Boyd, a former member. As a result, Long left Graham and went to Arkansas. After six months, however, he returned and resumed his law practice. Within a short time, he was arrested and charged with being an accessory to the murder of Wyatt Outlaw, a black, who had been hanged near the courthouse in Graham on 26 Feb. 1870. While appearing as attorney in another case, Long was required to post a daily bond of ten thousand dollars. When told that he would be exonerated of all charges if he would reveal the names of others involved with the Klan, he refused. On 20 Dec. 1871, while under arrest but free on bond, Long married Esta Teague. Two days later all charges against him were dismissed.

In 1886 Long was nominated by the Democratic party for solicitor of the Fifth District, but he was defeated by the Republican candidate. In 1893 he was his party's candidate for the General Assembly and was elected, serving a single term.

The Longs were the parents of six children: Julia Stuart (m. Seth E. Everatt), Jenny Patterson (m. John C. Halliday), Jacob Elmer (m. Lessie E. Peay), Pearl M. (m. Robert J. Mebane), Anna Claudia (m. Hershey Woodward, Jr.), Ralph (m. Cornelia Taylor), and Rebekah Kathleen (m. A. H. Graham, lieutenant governor, 1933–37). Among Long's brothers were William S., president of Elon College; Daniel A., president of Antioch College; George W., a member of the State Board of Medical Examiners; and Benjamin F., a superior court judge.

Long was an elder in the Presbyterian church and a Sunday school superintendent.

SEE: Samuel A. Ashe, ed., *Biographical History of North Carolina*, vol. 8 (1917 [portrait]); Personal papers of Ben F. Long (possession of Caroline Long Avery, Statesville); W. F. Tomlinson, *State Officers and General Assembly of North Carolina* (1893); Allen W. Trelease, *White Terror: The Ku Klux Klan Conspiracy and Southern Reconstruction* (1971); *Western North Carolina: Historical and Biographical* (1890).

CAROLINE LONG AVERY

Long, Jacob Elmer (*31 July 1880–29 Apr. 1955*), lieutenant governor, legislator, and attorney, was born in Yanceyville, the son of Jacob A. and Esta Teague Long. He received his early schooling at Graham College (1888–90) and Elon College (1891–95) and his secondary education at Horner Military School (1896–98). Long attended The University of North Carolina between 1900 and 1903, studying law in 1902–3. As a student in Chapel Hill, he was active in social and professional organizations and served as president of the Order of the Sphinx.

Long established his law practice in Durham but had an office in Alamance County as well. During the years 1912–16 he was private secretary to Congressman Charles M. Stedman. From 1912 to 1917 he was chairman of the Democratic executive committee for his district and represented Alamance County in the General Assembly in the sessions of 1911 and 1913. He served in the state senate in 1917 and 1921 and was lieutenant governor from 1925 to 1929. During the administration of Governor W. Kerr Scott, he was legislative counselor, serving as liaison officer between the governor and the legislature.

In 1909 Long married Lessie Ermine Peay. They had no children. A Methodist, he was buried in Maplewood Cemetery, Durham.

SEE: *Durham Morning Herald*, 28, 30 Apr. 1955; *North Carolina Biography*, vol. 4 (1956); *North Carolina Manual* (1925); *Who's Who in the South* (1927).

GEOFFREY A. DEROHAN

Long, John, Jr. (*26 Feb. 1785–11 Aug. 1857*), congressman, legislator, and farmer, was born in Loudoun County, Va., and moved with his parents to the northeastern corner of Randolph County. The family settled at what later became Long's Mill, where a post office was established, and engaged in agricultural pursuits, including a gristmill, flour mill, and tannery. John Long, Jr., attended private and subscription schools.

He served in the legislature in 1811 and 1812 and in the state senate in 1814 and 1815. In 1820 he was elected as a Whig to the Seventeenth Congress. Reelected three times, he occupied a seat in the House for eight years (1821–29). An unsuccessful candidate for reelection in 1828, he returned home to Long's Mill. After his defeat, he received a federal contract for a mail route from Hillsborough by Rock Creek to Asheboro.

A prolific letter writer, Long exhibited some of his political savvy and doctrine in his correspondence. In 1832 he wrote to Senator Willie P. Mangum advocating a high protective tariff on "any product not made or produced in this country." "Tax them well," he declared. In 1841 he again wrote to Mangum in an effort to get a post office established at the home of Squire Eli Cobb and to

appoint Cobb postmaster. In the same letter he added: "If Congress don't adjourn soon, do more and do it better I candidly believe the honest position of the Whigs will soon begin to despair." Long himself had been a National Republican before becoming a Whig.

Long was reared a Quaker, but he was turned out of the meeting for marrying Sabra Ramsay who was not a Quaker. The Friends later offered to take him back if he would say he was sorry. To this, Long retorted: "I am not sorry and I won't say so." It was a very happy marriage. Long was buried in the graveyard at Richland Lutheran Church, less than a mile from his home.

The congressman had an illustrious family. Four of his sons were graduates of The University of North Carolina: James, an attorney as well as editor of the *Greensboro Patriot*; William J., also an attorney, who lived in a house which is still standing about one-half mile from his father's home; John Wesley, a physician, whose son of the same name is honored by the Long Hospital in Greensboro; and Osmond Long, a merchant. A fifth son, Edwin, was graduated from West Point.

A granddaughter was Mary Alves Long, who wrote *High Time to Tell It*, a family chronicle. In it, she says that her grandparents "maintained a home where there was freehanded hospitality for all who came and charity for the poor. How many people they fed, only the recording angel knows. It was so easy to write an order to the miller calling for a bushel of cornmeal or flour. No wonder they were respected and even loved by the whole community."

SEE: *Biog. Dir. Am. Cong.* (1989); John L. Cheney, Jr., ed., *North Carolina Government, 1585–1974* (1974); J. G. de Roulhac Hamilton, ed., *Correspondence of Jonathan Worth*, 2 vols. (1909); Mary Alves Long, *High Time to Tell It* (1950); Henry T. Shanks, ed., *Papers of Willie Person Mangum*, vols. 1–4 (1950–55).

L. BARRON MILLS, JR.

Long, John Wesley (*10 Jan. 1859–1 Aug. 1926*), physician and surgeon, was born at Long's Mill in Randolph County. He was the son of Dr. Wesley, a general practitioner, and Margaret Troy Long. His father died when John Wesley was only a few years old, and he had to work his way through school. He began his medical education under a preceptor, Dr. John F. Miller of Goldsboro, before attending Vanderbilt University Medical School where he was graduated in 1883. Long also spent a year at the University of Nashville, receiving a diploma in 1884. In 1888 he studied for a time at the New York Polyclinic Medical School.

After practicing briefly at Aurora, Long moved to Randleman, in his home county. Ten years later he went to Richmond, where he taught pediatrics and gynecology at the Medical College of Virginia for four years. He then returned to North Carolina, working first in High Point and then in Salisbury, where he helped Dr. John Whitehead establish the Whitehead-Long Sanatorium.

Because he was interested in surgery, Long moved in 1903 to Greensboro, where he helped establish the Greene Street Hospital. After St. Leo's Hospital was organized in 1906, he practiced surgery there for eleven years. In 1917 he opened the Wesley Long Hospital, a small private institution which was being enlarged and modernized at the time of his death. Long's work in Greensboro was interrupted by military service in World War I. During the conflict, he organized Base Hospital No. 65, which was first located at Fort McPherson, Ga., and later moved to France. After the armistice he returned to the United States to take charge of reconstructive surgery at Camp Gordon, Ga.

In spite of his demanding practice, Long found time for other professional activities, including much writing. Most of his papers were on surgical techniques. One of them, "Enterostomy—A Perfected Technique," he read before the Southern Surgical Society in 1916 and used as his thesis at the University of Manitoba, which conferred on him the M.C. (master of chirurgery [surgery]) degree. He also wrote several historical papers, including one on the early history of the state medical society, of which he was an active member and once president. Long was one of the founders of the Southern Surgical and Gynecological Society, of which he was president in 1914. He was also a founder of the American College of Surgeons and probably originated its practice of holding clinical meetings in various places, as he had done with the North Carolina Surgical Club. Dr. H. H. Ogburn, in an obituary of Long, wrote that one surgical procedure he devised became a standard operation at the Mayo Clinic, where Long had conducted some clinical sessions. Long is said to have been personally interested in each of his patients and to have found time for constant study.

During his early practice in Randleman, Long married Mary Eliza Woollen, the daughter of Dr. W. A. Woollen. They had four children, three of whom—Wyeth W. and Mrs. C. D. Benbow of Greensboro, and Mrs. August Klipstein of New York—survived him. Long was buried at the Green Hill Cemetery, Greensboro.

SEE: C. W. Banner, "Dr. John Wesley Long of Greensboro, North Carolina," *Medical Society of North Carolina, Transactions* 74 (1927 [portrait]); *Greensboro Daily News*, 2 Aug. 1926; H. H. Ogburn, "John Wesley Long, M.D.," *Southern Medicine and Surgery* 88 (1926).

DOROTHY LONG

Long, Nicholas (*ca. 1726–97*), deputy quartermaster general under General George Washington, militia colonel, and Revolutionary statesman, also represented Halifax County for several terms in both houses of the state legislature. He was the son of Gabriel Long and moved to North Carolina about 1750 from eastern Virginia. A wealthy planter, Long was a literate man, but existing records cast no light on how or where he was educated.

A member of the Halifax County Committee of Safety in 1774, Long was one of two representatives from his county elected as delegates to the First Provincial Congress in New Bern, 25–27 August. He was one of three men sent from Halifax to the Second Provincial Congress in New Bern, 3–7 Apr. 1775, and one of five sent to the Third Provincial Congress at Hillsborough, 20 Aug.–10 Sept. 1775. On 9 September the Hillsborough congress appointed Long as colonel to command the 500 men of the Halifax battalion, one of six militia units to be raised in the province. When deposed royal governor Lord Dunmore of Virginia was leading raids against the Patriot forces, Colonel Robert Howe, commander of the Second North Carolina Continental Regiment, offered to send troops under his command to assist the Virginians. The Virginia Convention accepted the offer, and 150 volunteer militiamen from the Halifax District under Nicholas Long arrived in time to participate in the American victory of 9 Dec. 1775 at Great Bridge, Va. This is the only combat where it can be said for certain that Long led any troops. His Halifax battalion of 500 took part in the mopping-up action after the surrender at

Black Mingo Creek in February 1776 of the retreating Loyalist army of Highlanders led by General Donald MacDonald.

On 17 Apr. 1776 the Provincial Congress named Long acting quartermaster for North Carolina and requested the Continental Congress to appoint him "Quarter Master General to the Southern Department, to rank as Colonel." A month later Joseph Hewes, a North Carolina delegate in the Continental Congress, communicated home the news that Long had been appointed deputy quartermaster general. He served in that capacity throughout the war and was heavily involved in the acquisition, transportation, and dispersal of materials. Workshops were set up on his property to manufacture military clothing and implements. The First North Carolina Continental Regiment, commanded by Colonel Francis Nash, sent to protect the meeting of the Provincial Congress in October 1776 in Halifax, camped for three days along the Roanoke River in one of Long's old fields. At one point there was an investigation into Long's alleged misuse of funds. Not only was he found innocent of any wrongdoing, but the Continental Congress discovered that Long had been using his personal fortune to pay for quartermaster goods and reimbursed him several dollars. Long returned to the state legislature in Hillsborough as a Halifax representative in the House of Commons during 19 Apr.–3 June 1784. He served two terms, in the New Bern Assembly of 1784–85 and Tarborough Assembly of 1787, as a senator from Halifax.

Except for his nearby neighbor, Willie Jones, Long was the largest slaveholder in Halifax County. He owned ninety-three slaves when he was enumerated on 24 Dec. 1785 in the state census. His holdings had diminished slightly, to eighty-nine slaves, by the first federal census in 1790.

Long was married twice. His first wife was Mary Reynolds (1736–58), of Virginia, whom he wed in 1752; they had two children: Gabriel (b. 1754), who married Sarah Ann Richmond, daughter of William Richmond, who was the brother-in-law of Sir Peyton Skipwith; and Anne, who married William Martin of Halifax. On 24 Aug. 1761 Long married Mary McKinne. They had eight children: Nicholas, Jr. (m. Rebecca Hill; d. 22 Aug. 1819), Mary (m. Bassett Stith of Virginia), Richard H. (m. Betsy Pasture), Lunsford (m. first Rebecca Edwards and second Mary Copeland), Martha (m. General William Gregory), George Washington (m. Sarah C. Jones), John Joseph (m. Frances Quintard), and Lemuel McKinne (m. Mary Amis). The second Mrs. Long was active in supporting the work of her husband. When the army of British commander Lord Cornwallis quartered in Halifax on its way to Yorktown, Va., an officer of the staff of Colonel Banastre Tarlton appropriated her riding horse. The lady, according to a family story, approached Tarlton and demanded, in no uncertain terms, the return of her mount. Apparently, she impressed the old soldier, who granted her request. Surviving for many years after her husband's death, she died at home on 21 Nov. 1821. Long and both his wives were buried at their plantation, Quanky, in Halifax County.

Perhaps because of the repeated use of the Christian name Nicholas in the Long family over a number of generations, there have been some errors in statements regarding the activities and dates of the first Nicholas Long. Carrie L. Broughton's *Marriages and Death Notices* (1966) erroneously cites 21 Nov. 1821 as the death date of "Col. Nicholas Long," when the person who actually died on that date was his widow, Mary. Jasper L. Long's *Long Family Records* (1965) confuses and combines the military records of Colonel Nicholas Long the elder, who fought only in the Revolution and died in 1797, and Colonel Nicholas Long, Jr., who fought in both the Revolution and the War of 1812 and died in 1819. In that volume, both records are mistakenly credited to the elder Long.

SEE: Carrie L. Broughton, *Marriages and Death Notices from Raleigh Register and North Carolina Gazette, 1799–1825* (1966); John L. Cheney, Jr., ed., *North Carolina Government, 1584–1974* (1974); *First Census of the U.S. 1790* (1908); Cadwallader Jones, *A Genealogical History of the Jones Family of Virginia and the Carolinas* (1900); Jasper L. Long, *Long Family Records* (1965); Raleigh *Register*, 7 Dec. 1821; Hugh F. Rankin, *The North Carolina Continentals* (1971); William L. Saunders, ed., *Colonial Records of North Carolina*, vols. 9–10 (1888–90); *State Census of North Carolina, 1784–1787*.

E. T. MALONE, JR.

Long, Sylvester Clark. *See* **Long Lance, Buffalo Child**.

Long, Thomas Williams Mason *(14 Jan. 1886–3 Feb. 1941)*, physician, legislator, and administrator, was born at Longview, Northampton County, the son of Lemuel McKinne and Betty Gray Mason Long. He spent his childhood at Longview, the residence of his grandfather, Judge Thomas Williams Mason. Here, with his brothers and sister, he was taught by tutors until his early teens, when he attended Petersburg Academy in Petersburg, Va., and Virginia Polytechnic Institute for one year. In 1903 he entered the Medical School of The University of North Carolina, from which he transferred in 1905 to the University College of Medicine in Richmond, Va. Due to a lengthy illness resulting from typhoid fever, he was out of college for a year and received his degree in 1908. In the same year he was licensed to practice in North Carolina.

Long served his internship at Petersburg State Hospital and returned to Northampton County to practice briefly in Garysburg. In 1910 he began a lifelong practice in Roanoke Rapids in adjoining Halifax County. On 7 Dec. 1910 he married Maria Greenough Burgwyn, also from Northampton County. They were the parents of five children: Betty Gray, Maria Greenough Burgwyn, Margaret Ridley, Thomas Williams Mason, Jr., and Nicholas.

When Long went to Roanoke Rapids, on the banks of the Roanoke River, it was a cotton mill village plagued by malaria and called by many people a death trap; the eradication of this dreaded malady challenged the doctor's learning and skill. With the help of the U.S. Public Health Service and the cooperation of public officials, he successfully campaigned for mosquito control and transformed Roanoke Rapids into the healthiest town on the Roanoke River.

At the time of his arrival in Roanoke Rapids, there was no hospital in Halifax County and the income of mill workers was low. To bring adequate medical service and to lighten their burden, he and two other physicians, H. C. Irwin and E. H. Adkins, founded the Roanoke Rapids Hospital in 1912. Long was president of the institution's board of directors from 1912 to 1931 and a director until his death. He also devised a plan whereby a small deduction was made from the pay of each employee for medicine and hospitalization. Immediately successful, the plan resulted in the formation of the

Hospital Savings Association with the cooperation of the Medical Society of the State of North Carolina, and that evolved into the Blue Cross–Blue Shield plan.

Long was chairman of the board of directors of the North Carolina Sanatorium (1922–31), a member of the State Board of Medical Examiners (1926–32), and director of the State Hospital in Raleigh (1918–20). He was secretary-treasurer of the Medical Society of North Carolina from 1937 until his death. In business, he became successively director, vice-president, and president of the First National Bank, Roanoke Rapids; a director of the Roanoke Mills Company and of the Rosemary Bank and Trust Company; and president of the Roanoke Pharmacy Corporation. In public life, he was chairman of the Roanoke Rapids Board of Commissioners (1915–22), mayor (1922–39), and a trustee of the graded school district (1915–30). During the period, he was a dominant political force in Halifax County.

At the state level, Long served in the house of representatives during part of the 1931 session and in the senate in the sessions of 1933, 1937, and 1939. Death cut short another senate term in 1941. He successfully guided the legislature in enacting outstanding health laws: premarital health tests, blood tests for syphilis for expectant mothers, and diphtheria immunization for all children. Through his efforts, the legislature approved an appropriation for the establishment of the tubercular sanatorium in eastern North Carolina. He died in Raleigh following a meeting of the Senate Finance Committee.

SEE: Wilbert Davidson, "Birth of the Blue Cross," *Roanoke Rapids Herald*, 24 Jan. 1965; R. Hunt Parker, "Thomas Williams Mason Long: A Memoir," *North Carolina Medical Journal* 4 (1943).

BETTY GRAY LONG ZOUCK

Long, Westray Battle *(10 Aug. 1901–31 Jan. 1972)*, second director of the Women's Army Corps, was born in Rocky Mount, the daughter of Jacob, Jr., and Mattie Nash Wright Battle. The Battle family had immigrated from England to Virginia in 1654 and had settled in Edgecombe County in 1747. Westray attended the Women's College of the University of North Carolina at Greensboro (1918–19), where she was president of her class, and Pell's Law School in Raleigh (1921–22).

From 1919 to 1924 she worked in local and general insurance agencies and in the home office of an insurance company in Raleigh, and from 1929 to 1934 she worked with her first husband in the Boyce Insurance Agency in Gastonia. Entering civilian service of the federal government in Washington, D.C., in March 1934, she served with the National Recovery Administration as administrative director of the Litigation Division (1934–35); with the Rural Electrification Administration, first as administrative assistant to the general counsel and later as chief of the insurance section (1936–40); and with the Federal Works Agency as assistant chief of the insurance section (1941–42). In 1938 she was the principal speaker at the convention of the Mutual Alliance, an organization of mutual casualty insurance companies, and at the convention of the International Society of Casualty and Surety Companies, which was composed of the country's leading stock casualty insurance companies.

In August 1942 Westray Battle Boyce, her name during these years, entered military service as an officer candidate in the Women's Army Auxiliary Corps, transferring to the Women's Army Corps in September 1943, when the WAAC became the WAC. Commissioned third officer (equivalent to second lieutenant) on 12 Sept. 1942, she was appointed WAAC staff director at Headquarters Fourth Service Command, Atlanta, Ga., the following October. She was promoted to the grade of first officer (captain) on 23 Dec. 1942.

In August 1943 she was transferred to the North African theater of operations as WAAC staff director under General Dwight D. Eisenhower and promoted to the grade of major. In that capacity, she was responsible for the reenlistment of WAACs assigned to North Africa in the Women's Army Corps effective 1 Sept. 1943 and for the health and welfare of all WACs in the North African theater and later the Mediterranean theater. Over two thousand women, assigned to approximately twenty different locations throughout North Africa and Italy, were under her command. Promoted to the grade of lieutenant colonel on 8 Feb. 1944, she received the European-African ribbon with battle star and the Legion of Merit for her work during the latter assignment. This was the first Legion of Merit to be awarded to a woman.

In August 1944 she was transferred to the War Department General Staff, Washington, D.C., and assigned as military personnel staff officer of Personnel Division, G 1. She represented her division on the team engaged in extensive study of psychoneurosis in the army. This study, which lasted approximately eight months, involved consideration of army standards for the induction, training, and assignment of all personnel, and for the treatment and possible discharge of those psychiatrically ill.

In May 1945 she was named deputy director of the Women's Army Corps. The following July she was appointed to succeed Colonel Oveta Culp Hobby as director of the corps and promoted to the grade of colonel. As director, she was responsible for the health and welfare of all WACs as well as for recommendations to the chief of staff concerning the reduction of the strength of the corps. In September 1945 she made a flight around the world to arrange for the orderly return to the United States of WACs eligible for discharge and subsequently was awarded the Pacific theater ribbon. In November 1946, on an inspection tour, she visited installations in the European theater. Westray served as director of the Women's Air Corps until March 1947, when she was hospitalized; she was retired for physical disability effective 7 May 1947.

In January 1946 Colonel Boyce was awarded an Oak Leaf Cluster to the Legion of Merit for her work concerning the problems of psychoneurosis in the army and for her service as director of the WAC. In November 1946 she was the first woman to receive the Cross of Military Service, conferred by the United Daughters of the Confederacy.

Westray Battle Long was married three times: on 11 Nov. 1924 to James Stacy Boyce, of Gastonia, from whom she was divorced in 1941; on 30 July 1948 to William Leslie, of New York, who died in November 1962; and on 22 Dec. 1964 to Willie Jones Long of Garysburg, N.C. From her first marriage she had a daughter, Westray, who married James Roy Nicholas of New York. An Episcopalian and a Democrat, Westray Battle Long died in Walter Reed Hospital in Washington, D.C., and was buried in the old Battle family burial ground near Cool Spring Plantation in Edgecombe County. A portrait of her in uniform is in the Archives Building in Raleigh. Her wartime papers are at the Truman Memorial Library in Independence, Mo.

SEE: Herbert B. Battle, *The Battle Book* (1930); *New York Times*, 3 Feb. 1972; *Washington Post*, 4 Feb. 1972; *Washington Star*, 3 Feb. 1972; *Who's Who in America* (1948–49).

WESTRAY B. NICHOLAS

Long, William Lunsford (*5 Feb. 1890–24 Jan. 1964*), business executive and legislator, was born at Longview, his maternal grandmother's plantation near Garysburg, Northampton County, the fourth child of Bettie Gray Mason and Lemuel McKinne Long. Among his ancestors were Colonel Nicholas Long, Willie Jones of The Grove, and Governor Hutchins G. Burton. Long studied under private tutors and, with his three brothers, enjoyed a vigorous boyhood of farming, fishing, and hunting at Longview as well as at Occoneechee Neck. There also were summer visits to his maternal grandfather's plantation in nearby Brunswick County, Va. He was graduated from The University of North Carolina in 1909, as a member of Phi Beta Kappa, Sigma Alpha Epsilon, the Philanthropic Society, and the Order of the Gimghoul. Throughout his life, Long was devoted to the members of the class of 1909, especially Kemp Davis Battle, Frank Porter Graham, Charles W. Tillett, Jr., and Francis E. Winslow. Between 1909 and 1911 Long studied law at The University of North Carolina; he also taught Greek. In 1911, on his twenty-first birthday, he was admitted to the bar and began to practice in Jackson with the firm of his grandfather, Judge Thomas W. Mason. After Mason's death in 1921, Long established the firm of Long and Crew at Roanoke Rapids.

Beginning in 1916 Long became active in business, serving as vice-president and general counsel of Roanoke Mills at Roanoke Rapids and later as president (1926–28). He also was vice-president and general counsel (1919–26) and later president (1926–28) of the Rosemary Manufacturing Company. After moving to Raleigh in February 1934, Long was president of the Boylan-Pearce Company (1934–41) and vice-president of the Carolina Apartment Hotel Company. Interested in mining operations early in his career, he served as vice-president and general counsel (1936–55) and then as president (1955–57) of Haile Mines, Inc. He was also general counsel and vice-president of the Tungsten Mining Corporation (1949–55) and president of Manganese, Inc. (1955–57); both of these firms had their headquarters in New York City. Although he retired from the business world in April 1958, Long continued as a consultant to the Tungsten Mining Corporation and Manganese, Inc., until his death; in 1955 he organized the Tungsten Institute and served as its president until 1958.

Long was elected to the North Carolina House of Representatives in 1914 and to the state senate in 1916. He served in the senate until 1924 and again in 1927–28. A strong leader of the Democratic party and a powerful speaker, he exercised considerable influence. He was long remembered for a speech advocating the outlawing of the Ku Klux Klan in the state, a measure defeated at the time but afterwards approved. Long played a significant role in securing passage of the state's first child labor law, and he helped to overcome strong opposition to a bill for the state's first bond issue for constructing public highways. He contributed significantly towards the creation of the State Board of Public Welfare. A member of the state Democratic executive committee from 1918 until 1928, he no longer held public office after 1928 but was a delegate to the Democratic National Convention in 1932 and 1960 as well as an alternate in 1948. After Long's death, the Raleigh *News and Observer* commented that he was one of a few men to exercise so much influence on legislation in North Carolina in the 1920s.

In other public service, Long was a trustee of The University of North Carolina (1917–31) and of Elizabeth City State Teachers College (1956–64). He was a vestryman and warden of Emmanuel Episcopal Church, Warrenton; an honorary life member of Rotary International; and president of the Warren County Historical Society. In the latter position he was instrumental in having a history of the county written and published. During his later life, Long lived in Warrenton. He collected art, enjoyed historical and literary study, and engaged in boating, hunting, fishing, and swimming. A noted host, he entertained a wide circle of friends and acquaintances. He was also a supporter of the North Carolina Museum of Art and of the Ackland Art Center at The University of North Carolina at Chapel Hill and presented several works of art to both facilities.

On 12 Jan. 1914, at Petersburg, Va., Long married his distant cousin, Rosa Arrington Heath, the daughter of Tarlton Fleming and Rosa Gilmour Arrington Heath; she attended the Southern Female Seminary in Petersburg and St. Mary's School in Raleigh. They became the parents of three children: Rosa Arrington Heath (Mrs. James Payne Beckwith), Ruth Mason (Mrs. Peter Pescud Williams), and Dr. William Lunsford Long, who married Rebecca Davis Williams, sister of Peter P. Williams. Long died at his home in Warrenton and was buried in Fairview Cemetery. A portrait of him is owned by a grandson.

SEE: Archibald Henderson, *North Carolina: The Old North State and the New*, vol. 2 (1941); *North Carolina Senate, 1917: Character Sketches* (1917); William S. Powell, ed., *North Carolina Lives* (1962); Raleigh *News and Observer*, 25 Jan. 1964; *Raleigh Times*, 24 Jan. 1964; *Warren Record*, 31 Jan. 1964.

MANLY WADE WELLMAN

Long, William Samuel *(22 Oct. 1839–3 Aug. 1924),* clergyman and educator, was born in Graham, the son of Jacob and Jane Stuart Stockard Long and the great-grandson of Conrad Long, who immigrated to America from Germany. He had a sister, Bettie, and five brothers: John, Jacob A., George W., Benjamin F., and Daniel Albright. William Samuel Long was ordained into the ministry of the southern Christian church shortly before the Civil War. From 1861 to 1865, he engaged in ministerial work and taught school in Halifax County, Va.

Returning to Graham in 1865, Long purchased the property of the old Graham Institute and opened a school. In 1874 his brother, Daniel Albright Long, bought the property from him and incorporated the school as Graham High School in 1875 and then as Graham Normal College in 1881. The school had a large enrollment; one student was Julius Foust, who later became president of the State Normal and Industrial School (now the University of North Carolina at Greensboro). The faculty was enlarged to include, besides the two Long brothers, C. W. Smedes, J. L. Scott, J. L. Foster, William Wesley Staley, John Urquhart Newman, Henry Jerome Stockard, Silas A. Holleman, and Mrs. James A. Graham. Stockard later became president of Peace Female Institute in Raleigh, Staley became president of Elon College, and both Newman and Holleman served for many years on Elon's faculty. In 1883 William Samuel Long took complete charge of the college when his brother Daniel went to Ohio to become president of Antioch College.

In 1887 the General Convention of the Christian church, South, leased Graham Normal College and Long accepted the denomination's challenging offer to build a new college for the church and become its first president. After considerable negotiations, a site along the railroad a few miles west of Burlington and Graham was selected and work began on Elon College, so named because it was located in an oak grove and Elon is the Hebrew word for oaks. Due to the indefatigable efforts of the president and his family, for Long often did the carpentry himself and used his own property to raise necessary funds, the college opened on 2 Sept. 1890. Just at this time the buildings of the college in Graham burned and the church abandoned its plans to operate the former college as a high school, but Elon College continued to grow and thrive. Long was a firm believer in coeducation, a policy of the college throughout its existence.

At the end of the academic year 1894, Long resigned the presidency of Elon to become superintendent of schools for Alamance County, serving until 1904. Remaining active in the affairs of his church, he was elected in 1879 to its higher office: president of the Southern Christian Convention. In addition, he held many minor offices in the denomination. In 1887 he was influential in the founding of a church, named Long's Chapel, several miles north of Haw River. From 1898 through 1905 Long served on a Southern Christian Convention committee that raised the money for and constructed the Christian Orphanage at Elon College, and for several years he served as a trustee of the orphanage.

Long received an M.A. degree from Trinity College in 1871 and a D.D. degree from Union Christian College in 1889. For a number of years he was a trustee of The University of North Carolina.

Long married first Elizabeth Faucette, and the couple had four children: Elizabeth Jane, William Samuel, Jr., Edgar, and Benjamin F. After Elizabeth's death in 1902, he married Mary Virginia Gaskins Ames. There were no children of the second marriage. During his later years, Long often served as a visiting minister and church official. He died as the result of an automobile accident and was buried in Linwood Cemetery, Graham. In 1966 the William S. Long Student Center at Elon College was erected in his honor; in the lobby is an excellent portrait of the college's first president.

SEE: Alamance County Deed Book 4 (Alamance County Courthouse, Graham); *Christian Sun*, 1890–1924; *Minutes of the Faculty Meetings of Elon College*; Milo True Morrill, *History of the Christian Denomination in America* (1912); *Proceedings of the Southern Christian Convention*, published in *The Christian Annual* (1890–1926).

DURWARD T. STOKES

Long Lance, Buffalo Child *(1 Dec. 1890–20 Mar. 1932),* author and actor, was one of the best-known North American Indians of the late 1920s. In 1928 he vividly described his boyhood among his people, the Blackfoot Indians of the Western Plains, in his autobiography, *Long Lance*. The book, complete with his memories of the last buffalo hunts and the final intertribal skirmishes, received very favorable reviews and enjoyed considerable commercial success. Immediately after the book appeared, Long Lance was asked to star in *The Silent Enemy*, a motion picture about the Indians of northern Canada before the arrival of white people. When Paramount released it in 1930, the critics praised Long

Lance for his interpretation of the role of Baluk, the Ojibwa brave who successfully guides his starving tribe to a caribou herd. Impressed by the book and the film, the B. F. Goodrich Rubber Company asked Long Lance to design a running shoe for the firm based on his moccasins.

It was at this time—at the height of his fame—that the inexplicable happened. On 20 Mar. 1932 Chief Buffalo Child Long Lance was found dead in a friend's mansion near Los Angeles. The coroner's inquest ruled that his death was a suicide but failed to establish the motive. Only recently has the reason become clear. In reality, Long Lance was not a Blackfoot Indian at all, but rather a black man from Winston-Salem, N.C. His story is that of a person trapped within three cultures—Indian, black, and white, a man so torn that he took his own life.

Nearly half a century after his death, Long Lance's real identity came to light. His name was actually Sylvester Clark Long, and he was raised in a black enclave in West Winston, a predominantly white residential area. His father, Joe Long, worked as the janitor of the white West End School. Born a slave, Joe Long believed, and told his children, that he was half white and half Indian. But he had no legal proof of his ancestry. His wife, Sallie Long, was apparently seven-eighths white and one-eighth Croatan Indian. Because Winston authorities classified the family as "colored," Sylvester could not attend the neighboring West End School; instead, he had to enroll at the Depot Street Graded School for Negroes.

From a very early age Sylvester fantasized about the West and about Indians. In 1904 the thirteen-year-old joined a Wild West show. Having inherited high cheekbones and straight black hair from his distant Indian ancestors, he discovered that away from Winston he "passed" as an Indian. While traveling with the show, he began to learn Cherokee from one of the Indian performers. As an "Indian" he could escape being treated as a "colored." On returning to Winston in 1909, he resolved to gain entrance to the famous Carlisle Indian School in Pennsylvania. As luck would have it, his application, stating that his father was half Cherokee and his mother was half Croatan, was not properly checked. After appearing at the school and proving that he could speak some Cherokee, he was admitted.

Carlisle completely changed Long's life. Accepted as a Cherokee following graduation in 1912, he Indianized his name to Sylvester Long Lance. Having achieved an excellent academic and athletic record at the Indian School, he was admitted to Conway Hall, the preparatory school of Dickinson College in Carlisle. After a year's study there, he won a scholarship to St. John's Military School in Manlius, N.Y., where he remained for three years.

On leaving St. John's in 1916, Sylvester moved north to Canada. The war was on in Europe—the United States had not yet entered the conflict—and he wanted to fight. Enlisting in the Canadian army, he fought in France until severely wounded in the summer of 1917. On his release from the army in 1919, he asked to be discharged in Calgary, Alberta, where he spent the next three years working as a reporter for the *Calgary Herald*. When anyone in Calgary inquired where he was from, he would say that he was a "Cherokee from Oklahoma," separating himself from his true origins by nearly one thousand miles.

Leaving the *Herald* in 1922, Long Lance began to write for western Canadian newspapers in Vancouver, Regina, and Winnipeg. By the mid-1920s his articles on the Indians of western Canada also appeared in major

American magazines like *McClures, Cosmopolitan*, and *Good Housekeeping*. After his adoption in 1922 by the Blood Indians of southern Alberta (members of the Blackfoot Confederacy), he began to use the name they gave him, Buffalo Child, in his byline and to present himself as a Blackfoot.

In 1927 Long Lance moved to New York City and a year later published his "autobiography," in which he brazenly described his "Blackfoot boyhood." Success followed success until early January 1931, when his world began to fall apart. On Monday, the fifth, he met his brother Walter after twenty-two years. The meeting took place because their father, Joe Long, was extremely ill and the family could not pay his hospital bills. Immediately Long Lance began to send money home, but he could not return home himself. Unable to resolve his inner conflict of being a black man masquerading as an Indian in a white man's world, he ended his life. He died as he wished, as Buffalo Child Long Lance, a Blackfoot Indian.

His life is a tragic example of the horrors of racism and of the distortions that it can cause in an individual's life. One is left wondering what this remarkable man might have achieved had he been able to apply all of his creativeness to writing, rather than to "passing" and trying to escape the southern color bar.

SEE: Ronald Jordan, "Famed 'Indian Chief' Really Winston Man," *Winston-Salem Journal*, 29 Aug. 1976; Buffalo Child Long Lance, *Long Lance* (1928); *New York Times*, 21 Mar. 1932; Donald B. Smith, "The Legend of Chief Buffalo Child Long Lance," *The Canadian*, 7, 14 Feb. 1976.

DONALD B. SMITH

Loretz, Andrew (14 Apr. 1762–31 Mar. 1812), German Reformed clergyman, was born in Chur (Coire) in the canton of Graubünden (Grisons), Switzerland, the only son of the Reverend Andrew Loretz. He received a formal education in Kaufbeuren in the kingdom of Bavaria until May 1779.

In 1784, his father, the Reverend Barnard Willy, and the Reverend Peter Pernisus were sent to Pennsylvania. Acknowledging the need of ministers there, the Reverend John Jacob Kessler, deputy in the classis of Amsterdam, solicited and even sent a letter of recommendation for the younger Loretz. In 1786 Andrew arrived in Baltimore with a passport signed by the burgomaster of Chur. At this time, he married a widow, a Mrs. Schaeffer, formerly of Hagerstown, Md., and probably was ordained. His father left for Switzerland in the same year.

In the fall of 1787 or 1788 Loretz went to Lincoln County, N.C., where in 1789 he entered his first land grant for twenty-two acres. Then, from Jacob Shuford he bought land adjoining the Schoolhouse Church where the Lutheran and German Reformed congregations met. On the Shuford land, he built a two-story brick house measuring twenty-six feet by thirty-six feet. The dark red bricks on the east wall of the existing house form "A. L. 1793," the initials and date of the builder. Down the center of the east wall, the dark red bricks form two hearts and a cross. The original log kitchen is gone. The house stands one-half mile from the site of the Schoolhouse Church, where Daniel's Reformed and Lutheran churches later were established.

Due to the scarcity of German Reformed ministers, Loretz's charge extended from the Haw River of North Carolina to the Saluda River of South Carolina. Between 1788 and 1812 he was the pastor of the Schoolhouse Church, which began as a small log building; a frame church was built during his pastorate. Concurrently (1789–95), he was counted on as the pastor of Lower Stone (Grace) Church in Rowan County. In the year of George Washington's death, Loretz gave a funeral sermon for the former president. He laid the cornerstone of Lower Stone Church in 1795, but, due to the lack of money, he did not perform the dedication ceremonies until November 1811. In 1802 he ordained George Boger at Savitz Church in Rowan County.

At the time of his death, Loretz owned six horses which he had used for his travels. For example, he visited Guilford County four times a year, particularly the Stoner Church. His wide range of activities indicates that he worked hard to bring the church to the frontier.

Throughout his lifetime, he had a genial disposition and enjoyed people. He was fluent in German, French, and Latin, although his services were only in German. *Jefferson's Manual* was in his library, which consisted mainly of theological books. With over nine hundred acres, cattle, sheep, hogs, four slaves, and a large household, Loretz was wealthy for his time. After a Sunday-evening ride from St. Paul's in Catawba County, he died suddenly without a will and was buried in Daniel's graveyard. His five children had guardians who helped settle the estate.

SEE: Bernard W. Cruse and others, *Foundations of Lutheranism in North Carolina* (1973); Junius B. Fox, "Centennial of the Loretz-Fox Residence," 1893 (clipping files, North Carolina Collection, University of North Carolina, Chapel Hill); Ronald Vern Jackson and G. Ronald Teeples, *North Carolina 1800 Census* (1974); Jacob Calvin Leonard, *The Southern Synod of the Evangelical and Reformed Church* (1940); Lincoln County Estate Records, 1779–1925 (North Carolina State Archives, Raleigh); Alfred Nixon, *History of Daniel's Evangelical Lutheran and Reformed Churches* (1898); William L. Saunders, ed., *Colonial Records of North Carolina*, vol. 8 (1890); Banks D. Shepherd, *New Gilead Church: A History of the German Reformed People on Coldwater* (1966); William L. Sherrill, *Annals of Lincoln County, North Carolina* (1972); *Two Hundredth Anniversary Booklet, 1774–1974* (Daniel's Lutheran Church, Lincolnton).

MICHAEL EDGAR GOINS

Loring, William Wing (*4 Dec. 1818–20 Dec. 1886*), a soldier of many wars under several flags, was born in Wilmington, the son of Reuben and Hannah Kenan Loring. He grew up in Florida, where at age fourteen he first saw action with the Second Florida Volunteers against the Seminoles. During his teens, he participated in the encounters of Wahoo Swamp, Withlacoochee, and Alaqua. On 16 June 1837, when only nineteen, he earned his second lieutenant's commission. Loring received his education at Georgetown College, studied law under Senator David L. Yulee, and was admitted to the Florida bar in 1842. He became a member of the first legislature of Florida, serving three years. In May 1846 he was appointed senior captain, Mounted Rifles, U.S. Army, and in February 1847 he became a major. During the Mexican War he played an active role in General Winfield Scott's campaign from the landing at Vera Cruz to the capture of Mexico City, serving as regimental commander at Contreras. In the storming of Chapultepec, he lost his left arm. For his actions he was brevetted lieutenant-colonel in August 1847 and colonel a month later; he also received a sword from the citizens of Florida.

Loring decided to remain in the regular army and in March 1848 was given the permanent rank of lieutenant colonel. In 1849 he led his regiment with a train of six hundred mule teams 2,500 miles across the continent from Fort Leavenworth to the mouth of the Columbia River, "undergoing great hardships and not losing a man." This feat won him widespread recognition. From 1849 to 1851 Loring commanded the Department of Oregon, and from 1851 to 1858 he fought numerous engagements with the Indians in Texas and New Mexico. According to one source, "His Indian experience on the great plains . . . is probably unsurpassed. He battled . . . all the warlike tribes except the Sioux." His Indian exploits led to his promotion to colonel in December 1856, "the youngest line colonel in the old army." In 1858–59 Loring and his regiment participated in the Mormon war in Utah. A leave of absence in 1859–60 provided him with the opportunity to study military tactics and armaments in Egypt and Europe. On his return, he commanded the Department of New Mexico until his resignation from the army in May 1861.

The Confederacy promptly recognized Loring's military record by commissioning him brigadier general one week after he resigned from the U.S. Army. Six weeks later, he assumed command of the remnants of Robert S. Garnett's shattered brigade in western Virginia. Controversy whirled about him for six months until his promotion to major general in February 1862. The controversy involved an encounter with Robert E. Lee in August and a vicious disagreement with Thomas J. (Stonewall) Jackson during the Romney campaign. Loring's promotion and transfer to southwestern Virginia were more of a rebuke of Jackson and Joseph Johnston than the result of Loring's achievement. Assigned to the Army of Mississippi late in 1862, Loring fought as a division commander under John C. Pemberton. His force escaped capture at Vicksburg, and Loring earned the nickname "Old Blizzards" at the Battle of Fort Pemberton atop a parapet cheering his men on with, "Give them blizzards, boys! Give them blizzards!"

Loring accompanied Leonidas Polk to join the Army of Tennessee in Dalton, Ga., in early 1864. In the subsequent campaign he handled his division ably, assuming command of Polk's corps on 14 June, when the latter was killed at Pine Mountain. Loring directed the corps for a difficult month of constant fighting until relieved by A. P. Steward. On 28 July he was severely wounded at Ezra Church. Nevertheless, he returned to the field, serving as a division commander under John Bell Hood, and was present at the surrender in North Carolina in April 1865.

After trying his hand at banking in New York, Loring entered the service of the khedive of Egypt as brigadier general. Immediately given important commands, he succeeded in earning further promotions, "the Dignity of a Pasha," and the orders of the Osmanli and of the Medjidie. By 1875, during the Abyssinian war, Loring commanded the Egyptian army.

In 1879 he left the Egyptian service and returned to the United States where he devoted himself "to literary pursuits, and became a gentleman of leisure," dividing his time between Florida, Chicago, and New York. In 1884 he published a narrative of his most recent military career, *A Confederate Soldier in Egypt*, but died before he could complete his autobiography, "Fifty Years a Soldier."

Short, heavy-set, and unmarried, "Old Blizzards," or "Fereck Pasha," "was not only a very charming companion, he was altogether a remarkable man. A braver man never lived." He died at the St. Dennis Hotel in New York City and was buried in St. Augustine, Fla.

SEE: Douglas S. Freeman, *Lee's Lieutenants*, vol. 1 (1942); F. V. Greene, *The Mississippi* (1882); F. B. Heitman, *Historical Register and Dictionary of the United States Army* (1903); S. Herbert, "A Life Long Soldier," *At Home Abroad* 3 (July 1882); Quintard Loring Papers (Duke University Library, Durham); William Wing Loring, *A Confederate Soldier in Egypt* (1884); *New York Times*, 31 Dec. 1886; Arthur H. Noll, *Doctor Quintard: Chaplain, C.S.A.*; Charles H. Pope and K. P. Loring, *Loring Genealogy* (1917).

N. C. HUGHES, JR.

Love, James Spencer (6 July 1896–20 Jan. 1962), textile manufacturer and founder, president, and chairman of the board of Burlington Industries, was born in Cambridge, Mass., the son of James Lee and June Spencer Love. His father, a native of Gastonia, N.C., was assistant professor of mathematics, secretary of the Lawrence School of Science, and director of the summer school at Harvard University before he joined his son in business. His mother's family had strong ties with The University of North Carolina; his maternal grandfather was Professor James Munroe Spencer, and his maternal grandmother was Cornelia Phillips Spencer.

Love was graduated from the Cambridge Latin School, received a B.A. at Harvard in three years, and studied for a year at the Harvard Business School. Joining the U.S. Army in 1917, he rose to the rank of major and served in the adjutant general's office of his division before leaving the service in 1919. He sought employment in Boston but, deciding opportunities would be greater elsewhere, moved to Gastonia, where his paternal grandfather, Robert Calvin Grier Love, and an uncle had pioneered in the textile industry. Love borrowed money to purchase the Gastonia Cotton Manufacturing Company in 1919. Three years later, he sold the land and the building and took the machinery to Burlington. There, supported by a $250,000 loan underwritten by the Burlington Chamber of Commerce, he opened a mill that originally employed two hundred people. Shortly afterwards, he decided to gamble on a new product, rayon. Throughout his business career, Love continued to be bold, expanding frequently and seeking new products even in the hard times of the 1930s.

Burlington Mills eventually became Burlington Industries, the largest textile manufacturing company in the world; in 1961 *Fortune* listed it as the forty-eighth largest corporation in the United States in sales ($913 million). The company then had assets of nearly $607 million and plants in eighteen states and seven foreign countries, processing more than thirty-four man-made and natural fibers and employing 62,000 people.

Love, a Democrat, engaged in a wide range of business, political, and community activities. He was the director of the Textile Clothing and Leather Board of the War Production Board during World War II. He also was a director of the Carolina Cotton Manufacturers Association, Economic Club of New York, North Carolina Textile Foundation, National Safety Council, North Carolina Research Triangle Foundation, North Carolina National Bank, American Cotton Manufacturing Institute, and North Carolina Symphony Society, Inc. In addition, he was a member of the Anglo-American Productivity Council, Business Advisory Council of the U.S. Department of Commerce, Advisory Committee on Labor-Management Policy, Federal City Council of Washington, Ad Hoc Textile Research Committee of the National Academy of Sciences, National Research Council, and Visiting Committee of the Harvard Graduate School of Business Administration. He was a trustee of the Palmer

Memorial Institute of Greensboro, the New York Trust Company, The University of North Carolina, and the Committee on Economic Development. He was president of the National Rayon Weavers Association, chairman of the Davidson College Development Commission, and North Carolina state chairman of the Christmas Seal sale in 1956.

Although known for his opposition to labor unions, Love persistently supported the federal minimum wage, which upset other textile manufacturers. He also asked Governor Terry Sanford to grant clemency to one of those convicted of conspiracy in connection with a textile strike in Henderson.

Love received honorary degrees from The University of North Carolina, Elon College, the Philadelphia College of Textiles and Science, and the Agricultural and Technical College of North Carolina. He was a member of the First Presbyterian Church in Greensboro and maintained residences in Greensboro, New York, and Palm Springs, Calif.

James S., Jr., Robert Lee, Richard, and Julian were the children of Love's first marriage, to Sara Elizabeth Love on 22 Jan. 1922; they were divorced in 1940. Charles Eskridge, Martin Eskridge, Cornelia Spencer, and Lela Porter Love were the children of his second marriage, to Martha Eskridge on 23 July 1944. Love created the Burlington Industries Foundation and helped start the James Lee Love Educational Loan Fund. At his death, one-third of his estate went to the Martha and Spencer Love Foundation, a general philanthropic institution. He was buried in Forest Lawn Cemetery, Greensboro.

SEE: [Burlington Industries, Inc.], *The Spencer Love Story* (1962); *Charlotte Observer*, 21 Sept. 1941; *Durham Morning Herald*, 7 May 1950; *Fortune*, July 1968; *Greensboro Daily News*, 8 May 1946, 5 Dec. 1954, 27 Sept. 1956, 1 Oct. 1961, 21, 23, 25 Jan. 1962; *History of North Carolina*, vol. 3 (1956); *Nat. Cyc. Am. Biog.*, vol. G (1946); Newspaper Clipping Files (North Carolina Collection, University of North Carolina, Chapel Hill); Raleigh *News and Observer*, 22 Jan. 1962; Rockingham *Post-Dispatch*, 25 Jan. 1962; *Time*, 14 Mar. 1949; *Who's Who in America*, vol. 29 (1957); *Who Was Who in America*, vol. 4 (1968).

THOMAS E. TERRILL

Love, Robert Calvin Grier (15 Dec. 1840–23 Jan. 1907), Gaston County textile pioneer, was born at or near Crowder's Creek (now Crowders, Gaston County), the fifth son and sixth of eight children of Andrew and Mary Wilson Love. His parents were members of the Associate Reformed Presbyterian Church and named their son for Robert Calvin Grier, their onetime pastor who later became president of Erskine College. His father was a member of the commission that established the boundary between Lincoln and Gaston counties and was the surveyor of that boundary; he was also the presiding justice at the first court in Gaston County.

Little is known about Love's early life other than that he completed whatever formal education he might have had by the time he was sixteen, when his father died and left him Fairview, a farm two miles west of the site on which the Gastonia railroad depot later was built. Love moved there in the late 1850s, built a house on the property, and began cultivating corn, cotton, and other crops and raising livestock. He also did a small amount of surveying with instruments inherited from his father. On 29 Mar. 1860 he married Susan Elizabeth Rhyne (5 Oct. 1839–8 Jan. 1916), the daughter of Moses H. and Elizabeth Hoffman Rhyne. Love was a captain in the

Home Guard in Gaston County during most of the Civil War, serving briefly in eastern North Carolina towards the end of the war.

In the winter of 1870–71 he bought the dry goods store of his brother-in-law, Abel P. Rhyne, in Woodlawn (now Mount Holly), Gaston County, and moved his family there; about 1874 he added a cotton gin to his business, trading for cotton that he sold in Charlotte. He trained as clerks in his store several of the future business leaders of Gaston County (among them, David Rhyne and Alonzo Abernethy). Love also made loans at interest to his neighbors, served for some years as postmaster, built in 1873 the first framed schoolhouse in Gaston County, and was an elder in the Goshen Presbyterian Church. Seven of his eight children had been born by the end of his ten-year stay at Woodlawn.

As his children began to enter their teens, Love decided to move to Kings Mountain so they could more easily attend W. T. R. Bell's high school. In the summer of 1880 he built a steam-powered cotton gin in Kings Mountain and moved there the next spring. Love also operated a gristmill and traded in cotton and other farm products before problems at the high school and opportunities in Gastonia led him to move to the latter town in the fall of 1883.

Love's first enterprise in Gastonia was a general store which he operated with I. Q. Holland and S. M. Wilson as Holland, Love and Company. In 1887 Love left merchandising for the textile business. In that year, with George A. Gray and others, he founded Gastonia's first textile mill and the first steam-driven mill in Gaston County, the Gastonia Cotton Manufacturing Company. Love was the president and manager of the company from its beginning and remained so for the rest of his life. Under his direction, the company paid for itself in three years and thereafter consistently yielded impressive profits. The mill, which opened with one hundred employees, produced cotton yarns and eventually cotton cloths for curtains, flags, and other items. Both the number of employees and the physical plant grew through the years, and the enterprise, popularly known as the "Old Mill," was the forerunner of a sustained textile boom in the Gastonia area.

Among Love's other interests, he became president of Love Trust Company, a pioneer bank in Gastonia, which later became the Citizens National Bank. He was active in the development of public schools, donating the building that served as the first public high school in Gaston County. A dedicated opponent of the liquor industry, he once expressed a wish that every distillery in the county be replaced with a cotton mill and lived to see that happen. Love helped establish the First Presbyterian Church of Gastonia where he became an elder; he also was an elder of Olney Presbyterian Church. While maintaining his membership in the Presbyterian church, towards the end of his life he frequently attended services at the local Associate Reformed Presbyterian Church.

Love was instrumental in the establishment of other cotton mills in Gaston and Lincoln counties, including the Avon Mill in Gastonia and the Daniel Mills in Lincolnton. Three of his sons were involved in the management of area mills; these undertakings were successful except for a disastrous situation at the Loray Mills, the salvaging of which involved Love in a great deal of emotional strain and financial sacrifice in his last years. In 1924 Love's son James Lee (for many years a mathematics professor at Harvard University) and his grandson James Spencer Love moved the Gastonia Cotton Manufacturing Company equipment to Burlington, laying the foundations for what was to become Burlington Industries. James Lee Love's first wife was Julia James (June) Spencer, the daughter of James M. and Cornelia Phillips Spencer. Love's other children were Margaret Elmira, John Franklin, Edgar, William Abel, Mary, Robert Andrew, and Susan.

R. C. G. Love was known as a self-effacing, shrewd, thrifty, and dutiful man who was impatient with behavior less energetic and determined than his own. His native shyness and resolute support of causes he considered worthwhile limited his popularity, but Love was highly respected by much of the Gastonia area business and community leadership. He died of an apparent heart attack at the home of one of his daughters in Brunswick, Ga.

Two memorials to Love have been established since his death. The seventeen-acre Love Park was given to the town of Gastonia by James Lee Love and his wife in 1941. In 1956 Burlington Industries Flint No. 1 Plant in East Gastonia was renamed the R. C. G. Love Mill.

SEE: *Announcing a New Plant Name: The R. C. G. Love Mill* (1956); *Charlotte Observer*, 24 Jan. 1907; James Lee Love, *R. C. G. Love: A Builder of the New South* (1949); James Lee Love Papers (Southern Historical Collection, University of North Carolina, Chapel Hill); *North Carolina Biography*, vol. 5 (1919); Robert A. Ragan, *The Pioneer Cotton Mills of Gaston County: The First Thirty Years* (1973?).

WALTER CARR WEST III

Love, William Carter (*1784–3 Dec. 1824*), lawyer and congressman, was born near Norfolk, Va., the son of Samuel and Jean Love. He moved with his family to Chapel Hill where his father was steward of The University of North Carolina in 1799. Love was tutored at home, then studied law at the university from 1802 to 1804. He was admitted to the bar and began to practice in Salisbury in 1806. From 1815 to 1817 he served as a Democrat in the Fourteenth Congress. After his term in the House, Love resumed his law practice in Salisbury. He lived on a plantation seven miles east of Salisbury on the Yadkin River.

Love first married Elizabeth Macay, daughter of Judge Spruce and Fanny Henderson Macay. They had one child, Robert E., who later moved to Mobile, Ala. His second wife was Sally Yarboro, daughter of Captain Edward Yarboro and granddaughter of Alexander Long. They had two sons, William and Julius.

Love and his second wife were buried in the Yarboro family graveyard in Salisbury on the east side of the first block of North Main Street. By 1880 a hotel covered the burying ground. His obituary in the *Western Carolinian* reads in part: "Died at his seat near Salisbury William C. Love attorney, age 40. He had a mind and talents of the first order and he was no less distinguished for forensic eloquence at the bar than for the urbanity of his deportment in the private and social circle. He had already represented this district in Congress and promised to attain higher honors for himself and become more useful to his country."

SEE: *Biog. Dir. Am. Cong.* (1961); James S. Brawley, personal contact, April 1978; Daniel L. Grant, *Alumni History of the University of North Carolina, 1795–1924* (1924); Orange County Deed Book 31 and Will Book D (Orange County Courthouse, Hillsborough); Rowan County Deed Book 10 (Rowan County Courthouse, Salisbury);

Jethro Rumple, *History of Rowan County* (1881); Salisbury *Western Carolinian*, 9 Nov., 7 Dec. 1824; John H. Wheeler, *Historical Sketches of North Carolina from 1584 to 1851* (1851); *Who Was Who in America*, historical vol. (1963).

RALPH HOUSTON GROGAN

Lovejoy, Jefferson Marshall [Madison?] (5 June 1814–26 June 1877), educator, was born in Sharon, Vt., the youngest son of the Reverend Daniel and Elizabeth Pattee Lovejoy. His older brothers were Elijah Parrish and Owen. Jefferson Lovejoy studied at Middlebury College for three years (1832–35). When he journeyed south to take charge of the Pittsborough Academy in 1838, he was described as "a first-rate mathematician and linguist." He reserved his enthusiasm for Greek and Latin.

In January 1842 Lovejoy "opened a classical and English school, on Burke Square" (later the site of the Executive Mansion) in Raleigh, known as the Raleigh Male Academy or simply the Lovejoy Academy, where he lived on the second floor of a Spartan two-story house with classrooms on the ground level. His technique was to hear "lessons out of a book with corrections of wrong answers," and he punished recalcitrant students by striking the palms of their hands with a short stick. "Old Jeff" knew his textbooks so well that he rarely used them during recitations. In spite of his sternness, his students never knew him to be unfair and were proud to call themselves "Lovejoy Boys."

In 1848 he was nominated for a professorship in Latin at The University of North Carolina but was not offered the position. He wrote poems from time to time, and Mary Bayard Clarke's *Wood-Notes* (1854) includes his twenty-five-page reminiscence, "A Day on the Hills," and two shorter selections. His uncollected verses are scattered throughout the issues of the Raleigh *North Carolina Standard*, notable among them "The Fair" (28 Oct. 1854), an eighty-line panegyric on the glories of North Carolina.

In 1861 Lovejoy became a loyal Secessionist and in April wrote his son George S., then at West Point, to come home. He added military instruction to the curriculum of his school and joined the local Home Guard. Two of his sons were killed in the war.

Lovejoy married Virginia Steptoe, the daughter of Dr. William N. Steptoe of Pitt County. Though fourteen years younger than he, she did not survive him; nor did four of his eleven children: George S., Charles C., Henry (Harry), Ann, Ross W., Kate (Mrs. Godwin Cotten), Maud, Guy Mannering, Helen, Queen, and Jefferson. At his school, Lovejoy was assisted by, among others, his son Ross, who taught art, and Silas Bigelow. Some of his students were Thomas Badger, Kemp P. Battle, Henry Ravenscroft Bryan, F. J. Haywood, Jr., Howard Haywood, Theophilus Hunter Hill, Charles McKimmon, John Nichols, Leonidas Polk (son of Colonel William Polk), Edward T. Pescud, W. I. Royster, and George V. Strong, Jr.

On 22 June 1877 Lovejoy was stricken with apoplexy. His funeral at Christ Church, Raleigh, was "largely attended, and all classes of our citizens," wrote a newspaper editor, "were represented in the line of march to the cemetery. His boys, as he always called them, the pupils of his school formed a line of procession to themselves, and at the conclusion of the burial service performed the honors of covering up the remains."

SEE: Kemp P. Battle, *History of the University of North Carolina*, vol. 1 (1907) and *Memories of an Old-Time Tar Heel* (1945); Willis Briggs, "Lovejoy Academy . . . ," Raleigh *News and Observer*, 10 Jan. 1937; Census of 1860 (North Carolina State Archives, Raleigh); Charles L. Coon, *North Carolina Schools and Academies, 1790–1840* (1915); *Raleigh: Capital of North Carolina* (1942); Raleigh *Observer*, 24, 27–28 June 1877; *Raleigh Times*, 6, 24 June 1961, 25 Oct. 1972; Raleigh *Register*, 20 Apr., 22 May 1861.

RICHARD WALSER

Lovick, John (d. 2 Nov. 1733), colonial official, entered North Carolina early in 1713 in the company of Governor Edward Hyde. William Byrd, in his *Secret History of the Dividing Line*, noted that Lovick had been Hyde's valet. Byrd described Lovick as a merry, good humored man and probably was referring to his profession when he called him "Shoebrush" in the *Secret History*.

Whatever his origins, Lovick made a sizable place for himself in North Carolina politics and society. At some time around 1720, Governor Charles Eden appointed him to the Proprietary Council, where he also served broken terms during the administrations of George Burrington and Sir Richard Everard (1723–25). Lovick was a delegate in the lower house of the General Assembly in 1731 and secretary of the province in 1719, 1721–23, and 1729. During the latter year he estimated his annual income from the office to be £582. Among other appointments he held in the Proprietary years were those of vice-admiralty court judge (1722) and boundary commissioner with the Virginia survey (1728).

By far the most interesting facet of Lovick's career revolved around his relationship with George Burrington while the latter was royal governor. As late as August 1729, Burrington numbered Lovick among his enemies. However, because of Lovick's own efforts as well as Sir Richard Everard's complaints about his former secretary, Burrington began to change his opinion. On 26 July 1731, he named Lovick to the royal Council as part of his strategy to expel Edmund Porter from that body. Lovick soon became the governor's closest ally and consistently voted as Burrington desired. Burrington later justified his appointment of Lovick to the Council by praising his services as a legislator and his extensive knowledge of Indian affairs.

In 1732 Lovick became embroiled in a series of events growing out of attempts by certain officials to blunt Burrington's power. For a brief period that year the governor made his ally both chief justice and surveyor general of the colony. The former appointment particularly nettled Burrington's opponents, who argued that Lovick was unskilled in the law. By early 1733 the governor was openly praising Lovick as his best councillor and the only person who could effectively convey executive concerns to the lower house.

When Lovick died, Burrington's already deteriorating relations with the General Assembly worsened. Lovick had written a will in 1727 naming Richard Everard as one of his beneficiaries. On his deathbed, however, he declared his wish that all of his property pass to his wife, the former Penelope Galland. Although Lovick had listed two plantations in Chowan County and several slaves in his 1727 will, Burrington stated in 1734 that he had died heavily in debt. Lovick had no children, but his brother Thomas continued a long service in the colonial government.

SEE: William S. Price, Jr., "A Strange Incident in George Burrington's Royal Governorship," *North Carolina Historical Review* 51 (Spring 1974); William L. Saunders, ed., *Colonial Records of North Carolina*, vols. 2–3 (1886); Will of John Lovick (North Carolina State Archives, Raleigh).

WILLIAM S. PRICE, JR.

Lovick, Thomas (*1680–4 Apr. 1759*), assemblyman, member of the General Court, and militia colonel, held a variety of governmental posts in eastern North Carolina. The older brother of John Lovick, he was born in Chowan County but little is known about the first half of his life. Lovick became active in colonial government when the Council appointed him a justice of the peace for his home county in 1724. The next year he was given a similar position in Bertie County and was named to the General Court at Edenton. Lovick served as a grand jury member from 1724 to 1731 and in the latter year became assistant justice of the General Court, a position that he reportedly obtained through the scandalous dealings of Governor George Burrington.

According to a petition sent by three members of the Assembly to the Duke of Newcastle in England, Lovick's appointment as assistant justice was only part of a scheme by Burrington to gain control of the court. Apparently the current chief justice of the General Court, William Smith, resigned early in June 1731, but instead of appointing a new justice immediately, the governor waited nearly seven weeks. He then declared that a state of emergency existed which would allow him to appoint two new members to the court. Burrington named Christopher Gale chief justice and Lovick assistant justice, even though their appointments raised the total number of justices to eight instead of seven—the maximum number set by law. Governor Burrington took this action, according to the Assembly members, to ensure that there would be men on the court who were sympathetic to his point of view.

Lovick's position allowed him better access to colonial authorities, and he managed to prosper through a series of political appointments. In 1733 he moved to Beaufort and in 1734 was appointed justice of the peace for Carteret County, a post he held for the next twenty-one years. He was elected to the Assembly in 1734 and served on a number of committees, mainly dealing with monetary and fiscal matters. In 1739 Lovick was appointed powder receiver for Old Topsail Inlet, a position he used as a stepping-stone to obtain the post of port receiver for Core Sound in 1746. As port receiver, he was responsible for collecting the duties on all liquor and rice shipped from the sound. His performance in this post led the Assembly to appoint him tax collector for Carteret County, a position he held from 1746 until his death. In 1748 Governor Gabriel Johnston recommended him for the Council but he was not appointed.

Lovick also played a significant role at the local level. For example, from 1745 until his death he was the commissioner of roads for the northeastern part of Carteret County. He was responsible for the construction of Fort Dobbs on Old Topsail Inlet, begun in 1748 and completed by 1753. Lovick was also appointed commissioner for public building at New Bern in 1749. As a colonel in the militia, he commanded a regiment of two companies with 195 men.

Thomas Lovick died and was buried in Beaufort. Named as beneficiaries of his estate were his wife, Sarah; son, George Pheny; son-in-law, James Parkinson; grandson, Thomas Lovick; and granddaughter, Sara Jones.

SEE: J. R. B. Hathaway, ed., *North Carolina Historical and Genealogical Register*, vol. 1 (1900); William L. Saunders, ed., *Colonial Records of North Carolina*, vols. 1–5 (1886–87).

NEIL C. PENNYWITT

Lovill, Edward Francis (*10 Feb. 1842–3 Jan. 1925*), Confederate officer, attorney, legislator, and Indian agent, was born near Siloam, Surry County, the son of William R. and Eliza J. Reeves Lovill. His great-grandfather, Edward, who used the spelling Lovell, came to North Carolina from Cornwall, England, and was a pioneer in the iron industry in the Surry County region.

Educated locally and at an academy at East Bend, Yadkin County, young Lovill—then nineteen—enlisted as a private in Company A, Twenty-eighth Regiment, North Carolina Troops, on 4 May 1861 and was elected second lieutenant on 4 October. Soon after his promotion to captain on 9 Apr. 1862, he was given command of the company. In the absence of the colonel at the Battle of Chancellorsville, Lovill commanded the regiment; as senior officer, he also commanded on other occasions. In March 1865 he was recommended for promotion to colonel, but the war ended before this appointment was approved. In combat Lovill was wounded on three occasions, most seriously at Gettysburg in July 1863 and near Petersburg in September 1864, returning to duty after periods of recuperation. He was present when General Robert E. Lee surrendered at Appomattox Court House on 9 Apr. 1865.

After recovering at home from his wartime injuries, Lovill married Josephine L. Marion and moved to Warrensburg, Mo. From this base he farmed for a time and briefly worked as a cowboy in Texas. In 1874 Lovill returned to North Carolina and settled in Boone, where he established a mercantile business, began a career of public service, and studied law. Elected to the General Assembly, he served in the senate in 1883 and in the house in 1885. In the latter year, he was admitted to the bar and soon developed a distinguished practice in Boone. It was during the 1885 session as well that Lovill secured the passage of a bill that led to the creation of what is now Appalachian State University. He was again elected to the house in 1893 and to the senate for terms in 1907–8 and 1919–20. During his final term he had the distinction of being the last Confederate veteran to serve in the North Carolina General Assembly, and it has often been observed that he was among the minority of legislators who supported woman suffrage.

Among Lovill's other public services he was for a time director of the Masonic Orphanage at Oxford by appointment of Governor Charles B. Aycock. As commissioner to the Chippewa Indians (1893–97), by appointment of President Grover Cleveland, he was involved in classifying lands ceded by the Indians to the U.S. government. For many years Lovill was chairman of the board of trustees of the Appalachian Training School, where a building on the campus now bears his name. As a community leader, he was responsible for the establishment of a tobacco warehouse in Boone.

A Methodist and a Mason, Lovill was the father of four children, including a son, William R., who practiced law with him.

SEE: *Assembly Sketch Book, Session 1885* (1885); John L. Cheney, Jr., ed., *North Carolina Government, 1585–1979* (1981); *Heritage of Watauga County, North Carolina*, vol. 1 (1984 [portrait]); Weymouth T. Jordan, Jr., comp., *North Carolina Troops, 1861–1865: A Roster*, vol. 8 (1981); *North*

Carolina Biography, vol. 6 (1919); *North Carolina Manual* (1919); W. F. Tomlinson, *State Officers and General Assembly of North Carolina* (1893 [portrait]).

RICHARD DAVIS HOWE

Lowdermilk, Walter Clay *(1 July 1888–6 May 1974)*, soil conservationist, was born in Liberty, Randolph County, the son of Henry Clay and Helen Vashti Lawrence Lowdermilk. In his youth the family moved to Missouri, then to Oklahoma, where he spent much of his childhood, and eventually to Arizona. He attended Park College Academy in Missouri and the University of Arizona (1910–12). Awarded a Rhodes Scholarship, he spent three years at Oxford University from which he received B.A. (1914) and M.A. (1915) degrees. In the summers he studied forestry in Germany and also served in Europe on Herbert Hoover's Belgian Relief Commission.

Returning home in 1915, Lowdermilk became a ranger for the U.S. Forest Service in the Southwest where he developed an interest in erosion on the livestock ranges. Following service during World War I as the timber acquisitions officer, he returned to the Forest Service as the regional research officer in Montana. His budding career as a forester was changed in 1922 with his marriage to Inez Marks, from Arizona, with whom he had corresponded while abroad. A devout Methodist, she was a graduate of the University of Southern California and had served as a missionary in China from 1916 to 1921. After their marriage they went to China, where Lowdermilk taught and engaged in research in forestry and famine prevention at the American Union University, Nanking. Visiting various sections of China, he focused on the problems of erosion and drainage. He and his Chinese associates compared runoff and erosion on the bared hillsides to the ancient, and protected, temple forests. At this time, his scientific articles on his experiments and resulting recommendations for soil conservation began to bring him international recognition.

Escaping the Communist uprising of 24 Mar. 1927, the Lowdermilks returned to the United States, and he again entered the Forest Service, continuing his study of erosion and streamflow in California. In 1929 he completed his Ph.D. at the University of California School of Forestry, with minors in soil science and geology. Following the funding of a federal program in 1930 to establish erosion experimental stations, Lowdermilk designed and supervised a station in California to study forest hydrology. In 1933 he became assistant chief of the Soil Erosion Service, a temporary agency. When the Soil Conservation Service was created in 1935, Lowdermilk was appointed its assistant chief. In 1938 and 1939 he was in Europe studying soil conservation practices. The results of some of his research appeared in abbreviated form in a U.S. Department of Agriculture pamphlet, *Conquest of the Land through 7,000 Years*, of which over a million copies were distributed in the department's educational efforts.

Lowdermilk also toured the Middle East and wrote *Palestine: Land of Promise*, in which he advocated sound conservation measures to enable the land once again to support a large population. In time he also worked in the new state of Israel. During 1942–43, at the request of the Chinese government, Lowdermilk and a staff of eight Chinese specialists traveled nearly 7,000 miles to the Yellow River drainage basin in northwestern China. There they looked for indigenous soil conserving methods of farming, meanwhile setting up demonstrations of simple conservation practices based on American experience.

After his retirement from the Soil Conservation Service in 1947, Lowdermilk was often called upon for advice on soil and water conservation projects abroad. He went to Morocco and Algeria in 1948, and to British colonies in Africa in 1949–50. In 1951 he worked for the Natural Resources Division of the Supreme Allied Command in Japan, and in 1951–54 he assisted the United Nations in New York in organizing a Soil Conservation Service. In 1955–57 he was a visiting professor at the Technion University at Haifa, Israel. Also in 1957 Lowdermilk was involved in formulating a river basin development plan for the Cetina River in Yugoslavia. From 1960 to 1969 he was a consultant for the Save the Redwoods League in California.

Lowdermilk received numerous awards for his work, including the Stephen S. Wise Award for Service to Mankind. His professional honors included election as a fellow of the American Geophysical Union and of the Society of American Foresters; he also was president of the American Geophysical Union (1941–44). In addition to awarding him an honorary doctorate, the Technion University at Haifa named its Lowdermilk School of Agricultural Engineering in his honor. The Israelis, in appreciation of his contributions, dedicated a grove of trees in Galilee to his memory.

The Lowdermilks had two children, William Francis and Winifred Esther. Walter Lowdermilk was buried in Altadena, Calif.

SEE: J. Douglas Helms, "Walter Lowdermilk's Journey: Forester to Land Conservationist," *Environmental Review* 8 (Summer 1984); Inez Marks Lowdermilk, *All in a Lifetime: An Autobiography* (1983); Oral history interview (Bancroft Library, University of California, Berkeley); Randall E. Stross, *The Stubborn Earth: American Agriculturists on Chinese Soil, 1898–1937* (1986).

J. DOUGLAS HELMS

Lowe, Thomas G. *(10 Aug. 1815–13 Feb. 1869)*, Methodist minister of Halifax, was known as "a forest born Demosthenes," "one of the best equipped preachers of the Methodist denomination," and the "Foremost Natural Orator of North Carolina." He was born between the towns of Halifax and Enfield near the historic Hayward's Chapel Methodist Episcopal Church.

Lowe received his early education in the old field schools of his day and became a local minister in the Methodist Episcopal church before he was twenty-one. Although he never entered the Annual Conference of the church, he preached and held stated appointments in many areas of eastern North Carolina and Virginia. He was frequently called upon "to deliver funeral discourses and Masonic addresses, in both of which he very greatly excelled." According to tradition, his sermons always attracted large audiences. "Men of intelligence would ride twenty or thirty miles to listen to this sweet and fascinating orator." In a eulogy to Lowe, presented in 1882, Theodore B. Kingsbury observed that Lowe's name "should be added to that roll of illustrious American preachers who were eminent for a rich, glowing, and inspiring eloquence."

Lowe never wrote out his sermons, made an outline, or even used notes, feeling that he lost all inspiration and fervor when he resorted to a pen. Instead, he mentally organized his sermons, which usually lasted thirty to forty minutes, while working or fishing and then memorized the language he wished to use. His "finest oratory," however, was generally extemporaneous with no previous preparation.

Lowe spoke with a clear, musical voice and always used pure, correct English. He had "a splendid imagination but under the control of reason and taste and allied to wisdom and discretion. He was a very sound piece of American timber." He "spoke fine poetry, although presented in the garb of prose." Once, after delivering a sermon at the St. John's Street Methodist Church in New York City, he was invited to preach there for the then unheard-of salary of $12,000 a year. But he chose not to leave his home and work in North Carolina.

Lowe married Maria J. Wade of New Bern in August 1842, and they had two daughters. He was apparently buried in an unmarked grave near his home in Halifax County.

SEE: W. C. Allen, *History of Halifax County* (1918); Nolan B. Harmon, ed., *Encyclopedia of World Methodism* (1974); Theodore B. Kingsbury, *An Oration on the Life and Character of the Late Rev. Thomas G. Lowe, Delivered at Hayward's Church, Halifax County, on June 24th, 1882* (1882).

RALPH HARDEE RIVES

Lowry, Henry Berry (*ca. 1846–72?*), outlaw and Robin Hood-like bandit, was born near present-day Pembroke, of native American and Scottish ancestry, one of fourteen children of Allen and Mary Cumbo Lowry and the youngest of their ten sons. The family was Methodist and had lived in the community for more than a century. Lowry's great-grandfather and grandfather had been large landholders, but, for reasons that are not entirely clear, the family became involved in a series of lawsuits, or land suits, which resulted in the loss of most of their holdings. According to one source, this was because they had supported the Whigs during the American Revolution and for more than a generation afterwards were subjected to a bitter vendetta by their predominantly Tory neighbors. It appears more likely, however, that they were caught up in the general ruination of Indian and mixed Indian families during the age of Andrew Jackson. As the racial attitudes of whites hardened, those Indians who escaped removal to the West found themselves faced with a gradual loss of civil rights and diminishing educational opportunities. It is probable that the position of native Americans in eastern North Carolina was never more difficult than it was during the Civil War generation into which Henry Berry Lowry was born.

Following the outbreak of the war, the Confederate government made extensive use of compulsory Indian labor for the construction of a system of forts around the mouth of the Cape Fear River. This was because a yellow fever epidemic in the area had sent free labor in a headlong flight for higher and healthier ground, and planters vehemently protested the government's policy of commandeering their slaves for this deadly work.

Lowry joined a band of Indian bushwackers who were hiding out in the swamps to stay out of reach of Confederate conscription officers. These men were led by his older brother, William, and were already known as "the Lowry band." During the closing months of the war, they were reinforced by Federal soldiers and officers who had escaped from the Confederate prison camp near Florence, S.C., and they engaged in guerrilla warfare with the Confederate Home Guard. Though one of the youngest members of the band, Henry Berry Lowry attracted attention to himself by assassinating a Confederate postmaster who was serving as a scout for the Home Guard as well as a conscription officer who had recently killed three of his first cousins. After William and his father were captured and executed by the Home Guard in March 1865, young Henry Berry came to be regarded as the new leader of the Lowry band.

With the collapse of the Confederacy, as Union army regulars returned to their homes in the North and local bushwacker veterans to their peacetime occupations, it appeared for a time that the Lowry band also had ceased to exist. On 7 Dec. 1865, Lowry married Rhoda Strong. But immediately after the ceremony, and in the presence of several hundred wedding guests, the young groom was arrested by former members of the Home Guard (now reconstituted as the county militia) and charged with murder for the wartime killing of James Barnes, who had been serving as a Home Guard scout. Lowry never stood trial on this charge, however. Friends smuggled a file to him in the jail at Whiteville, where he was being held, and he escaped. The Conservative governor, Jonathan Worth, declared him an outlaw and offered a three-hundred-dollar reward for his capture, dead or alive. But protected by a band of wartime companions and other sympathizers, he remained at large for the next three years despite efforts of the sheriff and the militia to recapture him.

With the Republican victories of 1866–67 and the establishment of a radical administration in North Carolina the following year, it appeared that what had come to be called the "Lowry War" might at last be settled. In many ways the Republican leaders spoke the same language as the Lowry sympathizers. To many Indians, however, the Republicans in power seemed to be less radical than the Republicans seeking power. Now that they were in control, the Republican leaders did not renew their earlier efforts to prosecute members of the Home Guard who had executed Indians without proper trial. Also they were strangely silent on the question of whether the Conservative governor's proclamation of outlawry against Lowry still had the force of law. The only concession that they would make to his sympathizers was an agreement that if Lowry surrendered, he would be subjected to no personal indignity and would receive a fair trial in courts that were now purged of Confederate influence.

Lowry agreed to these terms and in December 1868 surrendered and was jailed in Lumberton. But again he did not come to trial. A rumor spread among his supporters that a group of Conservatives was plotting a lynching attempt and that the Republican authorities were not providing him adequate protection. After another spectacular jail break, Lowry was at large for a second time.

Once their agreement with him had collapsed, the Republican leaders adopted a policy of suppression that in some respects was more zealous than that of their Conservative predecessors. The legislature reaffirmed the proclamation of outlawry and raised the reward for Lowry's capture several times until it eventually reached $11,000. Moreover, they outlawed a half dozen of his chief followers and offered a total of more than $25,000 in rewards for their capture, dead or alive. These were among the highest rewards that had ever been offered in the history of American manhunts.

When the local county regiments were unable to suppress the Lowry band, Governor William Woods Holden was able to obtain the aid of a battery of federal artillery which was brought to Lumberton in the summer of 1871. Still the hit-and-run conflict dragged on until 1874. By that time, Lowry's chief lieutenants had been either assassinated or driven from the area.

It has never been definitely determined what happened to Lowry, who disappeared in February 1872 amid conflicting reports of his death and of his escape. No one ever located his remains or collected the reward offered for them, nor could the subsequent reports of his appearances in Atlanta, New York, California, and elsewhere be verified. Members of the Lowry family generally insisted that he survived. The one exception would appear to be the Reverend Patrick Lowry who, as a delegate to the Republican state convention in 1872, announced tersely that his brother (Henry Berry) and Boss Strong, Henry Berry's bodyguard and closest friend, were both dead. Indeed, he had visited their graves. Henry Berry's wife, Rhoda, though she remarried a few years after his disappearance, insisted until her death in 1909 that he had made good his escape. The Lowrys had three children: Sally Ann (b. 1867), Henry Delany (b. 1869), and Nealy-ann (b. 1870).

Although Lowry's band was composed mostly of Indians, among his chief lieutenants was the white youth, Zachariah McLaughlin, and the black man, George Applewhite. During their decade of activity, Lowry and his followers conducted many robberies. Yet they reputedly showed their prey certain considerations. Victims were treated courteously; they were not robbed if they could demonstrate that they could not afford it; and, if robbed, only a portion of their possessions were taken. Sometimes the Lowry band gave their victims a receipt for the stolen property, exempting them from further robberies for a specific time, and returned to the owners such items as horses and wagons when the band no longer needed them. Furthermore, the outlaws occasionally used their booty for a public rather than a private purpose, such as distributing stolen corn to the poor. Perhaps on balance their conduct could stand comparison to that of the business and government leaders of the Gilded Age. There is evidence that the Lowry band enjoyed considerable support among the Indians, the blacks, and the white poor.

SEE: W. McKee Evans, *To Die Game: The Story of the Lowry Band, Indian Guerrillas of Reconstruction* (1971); Mary C. Norment, *The Lowrie History. . . .* (1875); George Alfred Townsend, comp., *The Swamp Outlaws* (1872).

WILLIAM MCKEE EVANS

Ludlow, Jacob Lott (20 Dec. 1862–18 Aug. 1930), engineer, was born in Spring Lake, N.J., the son of Samuel and Nancy Johnson Ludlow. He completed his education at Lafayette College in Easton, Pa., where he received a degree in civil engineering in 1885 and an honorary master of science degree in 1890.

Soon after graduation Ludlow moved to Winston, N.C., and began his pioneering work in municipal engineering and public health. In 1888 he installed the first municipal sewerage system in North Carolina at Raleigh. Subsequently, he served as a construction engineer on water and sewerage projects in numerous southern cities. Between 1890 and 1920 he was a member and consulting engineer of the North Carolina State Board of Health, and many of the state's laws dealing with water treatment and protection resulted from his recommendations.

From 1908 to 1916 Ludlow was a colonel and chief of engineers in the North Carolina National Guard, and on the eve of World War I he became chairman of a board of engineers appointed to survey potential facilities for manufacturing munitions in North Carolina. During the war, he directed the construction of the cantonments at Camp Greene in Charlotte and served as supervising sanitary engineer for the thirty shipyards of the U.S. Shipping Board for the South Atlantic and Gulf States. In 1924 and 1925 Ludlow was a member of the Engineering Board of Review of the Sanitary District of Chicago, an organization that wrestled with the controversies existing between Chicago and other communities and states over the use of water in the Great Lakes.

Jacob Ludlow's "abundant faith in civic patriotism" was reflected in the time and energy he dedicated to the growth, development, and betterment of Winston-Salem. As its first city engineer, he led the movement to establish its first comprehensive sewerage system. His advocacy of paved streets induced the city to initiate an impressive program of street improvement. As president of the local board of trade from 1910 to 1918, he became a leading proponent for the consolidation of Winston and Salem into one municipality and under his guidance the city revised its charter to obtain more efficient government, improved housing, and expanded educational, park, and recreational facilities. In 1912 he became the first president of the Winston-Salem branch of the National Citizens' League for the Promotion of Sound Banking, and in the following year he ran unsuccessfully in the Democratic primary for mayor.

In the meantime Ludlow was active in the Anti-Tuberculosis Committee of One-Hundred, which worked diligently and effectively to improve the public health conditions in Winston-Salem and its suburbs. He also was a member of the Red Cross Seal Campaign Committee. An active Mason and Shriner, he belonged to such civic and social organizations as the Rotary, Twin-City, and Cosmos clubs. After 1920 Ludlow devoted less time to public affairs and gave more attention to the management of Ludlow Engineers, Incorporated.

As a nationally prominent engineer, Ludlow belonged to a wide variety of professional and quasi-public organizations. He was a member of the American Society of Civil Engineers and the American Institute of Consulting Engineers. He was also chairman of the Sanitary Engineering Section of the American Public Health Association, director of the American Association for the Study and Prevention of Tuberculosis, president of the North Carolina Section of the American Water Works Association, a national councillor of the Chamber of Commerce of the United States, and the first lay member of the North Carolina State Medical Society.

Ludlow married Myra Margarette Hunt in Easton, Pa., on 5 Jan. 1887. They had three daughters: Annie, Louise, and Margarette. He died in Winston-Salem. Funeral services were held in the Presbyterian church and he was interred in the family plot in Salem Cemetery. His life was a testimonial to the concept of community service, which he considered a "sacred public duty."

SEE: "Jacob Lott Ludlow," in American Historical Society, Inc., *North Carolina* (1927); J. L. Ludlow Scrapbooks (Southern Historical Collection, University of North Carolina, Chapel Hill); *North Carolina Biography*, vol. 3 (1929 [portrait]); *Who Was Who in America*, vol. 1 (1943); Winston-Salem *Twin City Sentinel*, 18 Aug. 1930.

CHARLES H. MCARVER, JR.

Ludwell, Philip (1638?–1723?), governor of North Carolina, governor of South Carolina, and Council member, secretary of state, and speaker of the House of Burgesses in Virginia, was the son of Thomas and Jane

Cottington Ludwell of Bruton Parish, Somersetshire, England. About 1660 he emigrated to Virginia, where his older brother, Thomas, was a member of the Council and another native of Bruton, Sir William Berkeley, was governor. The Ludwell brothers, who are believed to have been cousins of Berkeley, were members of the governor's small circle of close friends and were among his leading political supporters.

In the spring of 1675 Philip Ludwell was appointed to the Council and became deputy secretary of state under his brother, who held the office of secretary but was leaving for England on official business. Philip was deputy secretary until the summer of 1677. He later served briefly as secretary in his own right.

Philip was one of Berkeley's chief aides during Bacon's Rebellion, which occurred while Thomas was in England. As a colonel in the militia he commanded troops that captured prominent leaders in the uprising, and as a Council member he participated in most of the trials of the rebels. He ardently defended the governor's handling of the rebellion, even after Berkeley's recall to England and his death there in 1677.

Ludwell quarreled with Berkeley's successor, Herbert Jeffreys, who removed him from the Council because of his bitter language. In 1681 Ludwell was reappointed by Lord Thomas Culpeper, who was then serving as governor, but he was removed again in 1687 because of his opposition to the current governor, Francis Howard, Lord Effingham. Ludwell had aroused Effingham's anger by opposing the governor's efforts to increase his own power at the expense of the Assembly.

Ludwell's opposition to Effingham won him popularity with the colonists, and in 1688 he was elected to the House of Burgesses. He was not allowed to take his seat, however, because of his status as a suspended Council member. The following year he went to London as agent for the House of Burgesses in presenting charges that the Burgesses brought against Effingham. He obtained decisions favorable to the colonists.

While Ludwell was in England, the Lords Proprietors of Carolina appointed him governor of their northern colony, issuing their commission on 5 Dec. 1689. The Proprietors had been associated with Ludwell previously, for Ludwell's wife, who was the widow of Sir William Berkeley, had inherited Berkeley's proprietorship in Carolina. By 1689, however, Ludwell had sold his wife's interest to some of the other Proprietors. His arrival in London coincided with a crisis in North Carolina, where the colonists had revolted against Governor Seth Sothel and banished him. In appointing him governor, the Proprietors gave Ludwell the task of bringing order out of the confusion resulting from several years of misrule by Sothel.

Ludwell organized his government in North Carolina in the spring of 1690. His right to office was challenged immediately by one John Gibbs, a Virginian who had gone to North Carolina, acquired land, and proclaimed himself governor about the time of Sothel's expulsion. Gibbs claimed that Ludwell's appointment was invalid, apparently basing his claim on the Fundamental Constitutions of Carolina, which restricted the governorship of the Carolina colonies to resident Proprietors, heirs apparent of Proprietors, and members of the Carolina nobility (in which the ranks were landgrave and cacique). Gibbs, a relative of one of the Proprietors, had been made a cacique of Carolina in 1682, but he had settled in Virginia instead of Carolina. On the departure of Sothel, a Proprietor, there was no one in North Carolina qualified for the governorship under the Fundamental Constitutions, which no doubt prompted Gibbs's move to that colony. As Ludwell had sold his wife's proprietor-

ship, he had no claim to the governorship other than his commission from the Proprietors, who either did not know of Gibbs's action or chose to ignore it.

In the fall of 1690, after several months of agitation and at least one episode of violence, both Gibbs and Ludwell went to London and laid the controversy before the Proprietors. Gibbs's claim was disallowed, and he returned to Virginia. The following year the Proprietors suspended the Fundamental Constitutions, directed significant changes in the government of their colonies, and appointed Ludwell governor of the entire province of Carolina. Under his new commission and instructions, issued in November 1691, Ludwell was to make his headquarters at Charles Town and appoint a deputy governor for North Carolina.

Suspension of the Fundamental Constitutions not only removed the legal basis for Gibbs's claim but also provided a solution to a problem in South Carolina, where Seth Sothel had assumed the governorship after his expulsion from North Carolina. Sothel, like Gibbs, had based his action on the Fundamental Constitutions. Thus Ludwell, as governor of the entire province under a new governmental system, had the assignment of ousting Sothel from office in South Carolina, cleaning up after him in both colonies, and reorganizing the government in both.

Ludwell arrived in Charles Town in April 1692 and published his commission and other papers from the Proprietors. Sothel challenged the validity of Ludwell's appointment, but he soon left the colony after his supporters, who had become disillusioned, withdrew their support. Despite Sothel's departure, Ludwell faced an impossible task. South Carolina had long been plagued by serious problems and bitter factional rivalries. Conditions had worsened under Sothel, who had aggravated the problems and exacerbated the animosities. Moreover, the Proprietors took adamant positions on troublesome issues, which made it extremely difficult for Ludwell to work out compromises between the local parties. Instead of bringing harmony, he found himself in the middle of a three-sided battle on practically all issues. Although he made progress in some areas, particularly in relations with the Indians, he failed to solve other problems, such as the illicit trade with pirates and the colonists' refusal to pay rent because of their dissatisfaction with land policies.

About the middle of May 1693, Ludwell left Charles Town, having informed the Council a few days earlier that he intended to go to Virginia and North Carolina to attend to governmental matters in the latter colony. He left the South Carolina government in the hands of an early settler, Thomas Smith. Although he expressed his intention to return in four months, he did not return. In November 1693 the Proprietors issued a commission appointing Smith governor of Carolina, thus formally terminating Ludwell's tenure.

Differing explanations have been offered for the sudden ending of Ludwell's administration in Charles Town. Some writers indicate that he quit in disgust; others say that the Proprietors dismissed him. The available records do not show clearly what occurred. It is noteworthy, however, that they indicate that Ludwell questioned the validity of his appointment, apparently doubting the legality of the Proprietors' suspension of the Fundamental Constitutions. The records also reveal serious differences between Ludwell and the Proprietors respecting policies appropriate for the colony and Ludwell's powers as governor. Whoever initiated the action, ending his administration probably was agreeable to both Ludwell and the Proprietors.

That the Proprietors were not entirely dissatisfied

with Ludwell is evidenced by his continuing as chief executive of North Carolina for two years after he left Charles Town. Apparently the deputy governor of North Carolina, Thomas Jarvis, had become too ill to officiate, or perhaps had died, before Ludwell left South Carolina. In fact, the vacancy probably prompted, or at least precipitated, Ludwell's departure from the southern colony. By fall Ludwell had taken charge of the North Carolina government, which he presided over until the summer of 1695. As in his earlier period of governing the colony, Ludwell resided in Virginia, presiding intermittently over the North Carolina government in person and governing through a deputy in the intervals between visits.

Ludwell solved a serious problem in North Carolina, namely, discontent with land policies and refusal to pay rents. The colonists were resentful because the Proprietors had rescinded concessions they had made in 1668 and had promulgated more stringent policies than those to which they had agreed. The colonists maintained that the 1668 concessions were irrevocable and the later policies invalid. Ludwell agreed with the colonists, and on 28 Nov. 1693 he announced that he would grant land under the terms specified in 1668, which he did. Although the Proprietors appear not to have been consulted on the matter, some years later, on the recommendation of Governor John Archdale, they accepted Ludwell's view.

Ludwell also supervised the reorganizing of the government to conform to the instructions the Proprietors had issued in 1691. By the summer of 1695, when his role in North Carolina ended, the colony had a stable government as well as acceptable land policies. For the first time in its history, North Carolina was experiencing a period of relative calm and prosperity.

By 1695 Ludwell's public career was nearing its close. That year he was speaker of the Virginia House of Burgesses, and he continued as a member through 1698. About 1700, however, he retired to England, where he spent his remaining years in relative obscurity.

Ludwell was married twice. In or before 1667 he married Lucy Higginson Bernard, the daughter of Robert and Joanne Tokesay Higginson and the widow of William Bernard. Before her marriage to Bernard, Lucy had been the widow of Major Lewis Burwell. She died in 1675. By October 1680 Ludwell had married Frances, Lady Berkeley, the widow of Sir William Berkeley and previously the widow of Samuel Stephens, the second governor of North Carolina. Frances was the daughter of Thomas and Katherine Culpeper of Feckenham Parish, Worcestershire, England, who had emigrated to Virginia with their family in 1650. She died about 1691.

Ludwell had two children who lived to maturity, a son, Philip, and a daughter, Jane. Both were born of his first marriage. Philip, Jr., like his father, was prominent in governmental affairs, serving as a member of the Virginia Council, as colonel in the militia, and in other capacities. He married Hannah Harrison, the daughter of Benjamin Harrison, and he had a son and two daughters who lived to maturity. He died in January 1726/27. Jane Ludwell married Daniel Parke, the son of Colonel Daniel Parke. She and her husband lived for a time in England and later in the Leeward Islands, where Parke was governor. She had two daughters.

During his first marriage, Ludwell lived at Fairfield plantation, also called Carter's Creek, in Gloucester County. He later moved to his brother's plantation, Rich Neck, near Williamsburg, which he inherited at Thomas's death in 1678. On his second marriage he moved to nearby Green Spring, the estate of Governor Berkeley, which had been bequeathed to Lady Berkeley.

Little is known of Ludwell's life after he retired to England. Not even the date of his death is known, although a letter dated 4 Jan. 1723/24, written to Philip, Jr., by a cousin in England, indicates that Ludwell had died recently. Ludwell was buried in the family vault in Bow Churchyard, near Stratford, in Middlesex.

SEE: Fairfax Harrison, *The Proprietors of the Northern Neck: Chapters of Culpeper Genealogy* (1926) and *Virginia Land Grants: A Study of Conveyancing in Relation to Colonial Politics* (1925); William Waller Hening, ed., *Laws of Virginia. . . .* (1823); Edmund Jennings Lee, *Lee of Virginia, 1642–1892* (1974); E. R. McIlwaine, ed., *Minutes of the Virginia Council and General Court* (1924); *New England Historical and Genealogical Register*, vols. 33, 47; Nell Marion Nugent, comp., *Cavaliers and Pioneers*, vol. 1 (1934); William P. Palmer, ed., *Calendar of Virginia State Papers. . . .* (1875); Mattie Erma E. Parker, ed., *North Carolina Higher-Court Records, 1670–1696* and *1697–1701* (1968, 1971); W. Noel Sainsbury, ed., *Calendar of State Papers, Colonial Series, America and West Indies*, vols. for 1675–1701 (1880); Alexander S. Salley, Jr., "Abstracts from the Records of the Court of Ordinary . . . 1692–1700," *South Carolina Historical and Genealogical Magazine* 8 (1907); Alexander S. Salley, Jr., ed., *Commissions and Instructions to Public Officials of South Carolina. . . .* (1916); William L. Saunders, ed., *Colonial Records of North Carolina*, vol. 1 (1886).

MATTIE ERMA E. PARKER

Luelling, Henderson (23 Apr. 1809–28 Dec. 1878), nurseryman and agricultural entrepreneur, was born in Randolph County, the son of Mesheck Luelling, a physician and nurseryman of Welsh descent and a member of the Back Creek Monthly Quaker Meeting. His mother's maiden name was Brookshire. Young Luelling studied under his father and developed an interest in the nursery business. In 1825 the family moved to Greensboro, Ind., where, on 30 Dec. 1830, Henderson Luelling married Elizabeth Presnell, a childhood neighbor in North Carolina.

In 1837 Henderson and his brother John began a nursery in Salem, Iowa, which they operated for ten years. During that time Henderson made many trips around the country seeking newer and hardier strains of fruit trees. As settlers moved farther west Luelling began to think of joining them, and on 17 Apr. 1847, with his wife and eight children (the youngest named Oregon Columbia), he left Salem. A friend, William Meek, joined the expedition. Using a wagon pulled by four oxen, the Luellings transported nearly a thousand trees and shrubs to their new home. This strange caravan is said to have astounded bands of marauding Indians as they watched living trees rolling across the prairie. Having lost about half of its nursery stock, the expedition reached Fort Vancouver and Henderson found a suitable site for his unusual cargo near the modern site of Milwaukie, Oreg. Among the fruits that he introduced to settlers in the region were grapes, apples, cherries, plums, pears, quinces, and various types of berries. His available stock sold quickly and his business flourished. By 1850 Luelling was sufficiently prosperous that he invited his brother Seth to move west and join in the operation.

In 1854, following the death of his wife, Henderson Luelling moved to California. There the climate and the demand for vines and fruit trees soon made him a rich man. Anxious for even wider markets, by 1859 he decided to move again. He purchased a ship and sailed for Honduras with two of his sons and their families. This proved to be a disastrous venture and they all returned to California. By that time, however, the boom days of the frontier were past and Luelling never enjoyed the success he had known before. As the head of a large family, many of his offspring having also become nurserymen, he remained in California for the rest of his life. He died in San José and was buried in Mountain View Cemetery, Oakland.

SEE: *DAB*, vol. 11 (1958); William W. Hinshaw, *Encyclopedia of American Quaker Genealogy*, vol. 1 (1936); *Who Was Who in America*, historical vol. (1963).

PAUL B. THOMPSON

Luis, Don de Velasco (*fl. 1561–71*), Indian chieftain, was the brother of the cacique of Ajacan, located inside Chesapeake Bay between the thirty-seventh and thirty-eighth parallels. As a boy, he was picked up by Spaniards, probably Dominicans who had been in Florida with Villafañe in 1561, and taken to Mexico City. There he was baptized and given the name of his godfather, the viceroy Don Luis de Velasco. In 1566, having driven the French out of Florida and wishing to gain a foothold in the Baya de Santa Maria region (Chesapeake-North Carolina sounds), Pedro Menéndez de Avilés decided to send Don Luis back to his native land with an escort of two Dominicans, three officials, and fifteen soldiers.

The expedition sailed from San Mateo on 2 August aboard the patache *Trinidad*, commanded by Domingo Fernández. By 14 August they sighted land at 37°30′ north latitude, outside Chesapeake Bay, but could not disembark because of bad weather. Driven south, they again struck land on 24 August at 36° north latitude and entered a "river," which must have been Albemarle Sound or Currituck Sound. The military commander of the expedition, Captain Pedro de Coronas, christened the river San Bartolomé and solemnly took possession of it in the name of the king of Spain, but Don Luis did not recognize it as Ajacan, the land of his forefathers. During the next two days the party explored one bank and then the other, but still Don Luis failed to find any familiar landmarks. On the twenty-seventh, realizing that the Rio de San Bartolomé was not Ajacan, the explorers agreed to return to their first landfall (37°30′ north latitude) but were again prevented from landing when a hurricane blew them out to sea. The storm raged for several days, and, giving up their mission, they sailed across the Atlantic and reached Cádiz, Spain, on 23 Oct. 1566. Don Luis was taken to the court by the two Dominicans.

Four years later, Pedro Menéndez took Don Luis back to Florida and once more sent him to search for his homeland with nine Jesuit missionaries but without a military escort. This time the young Indian chieftain successfully reached Ajacan, situated inside Chesapeake Bay between the James and the York rivers, on 10 Sept. 1570. A few days later, however, Don Luis deserted the missionaries and went to live with his kinsfolk, adopting their customs and even practicing polygamy. Apparently angered by the criticism of the Jesuits, he killed three of them on 4 Feb. 1571. The others were murdered a few days later and the mission was destroyed.

SEE: Clifford M. Lewis and Albert J. Loomie, *The Spanish Jesuit Mission in Virginia, 1570–1572* (1953); Records of Diego de Camargo, Secretary of the 1566 Expedition (Archiva General de Indias, Seville); L. A. Vigneras, "A

Spanish Discovery of North Carolina in 1566," *North Carolina Historical Review* 46 (1969).

L. A. VIGNERAS

Lunsford, Bascom Lamar (*21 Mar. 1882–4 Sept. 1973*), performer and collector of folk music and organizer of folk festivals, was born in Mars Hill, Madison County. He was the son of James Bassett and Luarta Leah Buckner Lunsford and the great-grandson of Thomas Shepard Deaver, a founder of Mars Hill College. Having grown up in a rural area where folk songs, ballads, and instrumental tunes provided entertainment in homes, at square dances, and at other social functions, Lunsford developed an early appreciation for this music. He and his brother Blackwell were accomplished fiddlers by their teens, and they often performed for neighbors and at school entertainments. Even as a young man Lunsford sought songs and tunes from family, friends, and acquaintances, learning to sing and play them in order to collect and preserve them.

Following graduation from Camp Hill Academy in Leicester (Buncombe County), he enrolled in Rutherford College in 1901. A year later he accepted a teaching position in Madison County. After leaving that post Lunsford worked for two years for the East Tennessee Nursery Company, traveling on horseback to sell fruit trees throughout western North Carolina and adjacent states. This job enabled him to contact families in remote areas and collect even more songs and tunes. He returned to Rutherford College from 1906 to 1909, then taught school in McDowell County. In 1912, having studied law on his own, he entered Trinity College (now Duke University) as a second-year student where he studied under Samuel Fox Mordecai. He received his law degree and license to practice in 1913. Returning to western North Carolina, he pursued a number of occupations during the next decade. These included practicing law, newspaper publishing, and investigating draft evaders for the U.S. Department of Justice in New York.

On 2 June 1906, Lunsford married Nellie Sara Triplett (22 June 1881–4 May 1960). The couple had seven children: Sara Kern, Blackwell Lamar, Ellen Chapman, Lynn Huntington, Nellie Triplett, Merton Bacum, and Josepha Belle. After the death of his first wife, Lunsford married Mrs. Freda Metcalf English on 25 Aug. 1960.

Lunsford's interest in collecting folk songs brought him to the attention of the growing number of folklorists following the British collector Cecil Sharp, who toured the southern mountains between 1916 and 1918. Although Lunsford never met Sharp, he did make the acquaintance of his assistant, Maud Karpeles. Lunsford contributed innumerable items to Frank C. Brown of Duke University for the North Carolina Folklore collection. In 1925 he accompanied Dr. Robert W. Gordon, the first head of the Library of Congress Archive of Folksong, on a search for ballads and songs in western North Carolina and South Carolina. Gordon encouraged Lunsford to continue collecting and preserving the songs and to be thorough and systematic in his approach. Dr. Dorothy Scarborough, from Columbia University, also toured the mountains with Lunsford in 1930. As a result of these contacts, in March 1935 Lunsford received an invitation to go to New York to record his "personal memory collection" for Columbia; the collection included 315 items. In 1949, in a two-week marathon session, Lunsford recorded 330 items for the Library of Congress. Up to that time his was the largest repertory that a single informant had contributed to the Archive of Folksong.

In addition to collecting traditional songs, Lunsford composed several new ones, including "Good Old Mountain Dew" in 1920. In 1929 he and composer Lamar Stringfield collaborated on *30 and 1 Folk Songs from the Southern Mountains*, a volume of songs arranged with musical accompaniment.

Lunsford's major contribution to the perpetuation of folk music was the formation and promotion of folk festivals. In 1927 he advised the Asheville Chamber of Commerce to add a program of dancing and singing to its Rhododendron Festival. The program was so successful that the Mountain Dance and Folk Festival was established the next year. Lunsford organized or helped to found numerous festivals throughout his life, including the first National Folk Festival in St. Louis in 1934.

A high point in his career as a performer and promoter occurred in 1939, when he and his Soco Gap dance team performed at the White House for President and Mrs. Franklin D. Roosevelt and King George VI and Queen Elizabeth of Great Britain. In 1949 Lunsford represented the United States at the first International Folk Festival in Venice, Italy. He spent his later years at home in South Turkey Creek, near Leicester, where he continued to receive and entertain visitors and to participate in local festivals until his death at age ninety-one. He was buried in the Old Brick Church Cemetery, Leicester.

SEE: Anne W. Beard, "The Personal Folksong Collection of Bascom Lamar Lunsford" (M.A. thesis, Miami University, Ohio, 1959); Pete Gilpin and George Stephens, *Bascom Lamar Lunsford: Minstrel of the Appalachians* (1966); *JEMF Quarterly* 9 (Spring 1973); Loyal Jones, "Bascom Lamar Lunsford" (typescript, Appalachian Center, Berea College, Berea, Ky.); Bascom Lamar Lunsford Collection (Appalachian Room, Mars Hill College, Mars Hill); John A. McLeod, "Minstrel of the Appalachians: An Interpretive Biography of Bascom Lamar Lunsford" (typescript, Appalachian Room, Mars Hill College, Mars Hill); *North Carolina Folklore Journal* 25 (May 1977); *Saturday Evening Post*, 22 May 1948; Irwin Stambler and Grelun Landon, *Encyclopedia of Folk, Country, and Western Music* (1969).

LAUREL MCKAY HORTON

Luten (or Leuten, Luton, Lutten), Thomas *(d. ca. March 1731),* justice of the General Court and Chowan Precinct Court, Assembly member, and provost marshal, was in the North Carolina colony by October 1684. He became justice of Chowan Precinct Court before April 1694 and remained on the court at least through October 1695. Luten sat as justice at a special term of the General Court in the spring of 1698 and was appointed provost marshal that April. He continued as provost marshal through June 1702 or longer. In February 1711/12 he was a member of the Assembly, and from May 1727 through April 1730 he was a justice of the General Court. Throughout most of his career he held military titles, first captain and later major.

From time to time Luten served in other capacities. In May 1701 he was appointed to investigate an alleged assault by Indians, and in the early 1700s he was deputy surveyor for Chowan Precinct. In 1712 he and three others were appointed by the Court of Chancery to hear and determine an appeal from the Court of Admiralty. He was on the vestry of St. Paul's Parish from 1701 until his death.

Luten married Mary Currer, widow of John Currer, in 1684. He lived in Chowan Precinct, where he had extensive landholdings. He was survived by his wife, Mary; four sons—Thomas, William, Constance (or Constant), and Henderson; and five daughters—Christian Luten, Rachel Farlow, Ann Brinn, Sarah Standing, and Mary Haughton. Luten's daughter Mary was married to Jonathan Evans, and had children by him, before her marriage to Haughton. Little more is known of the lives of his daughters.

Thomas Luten, Jr., shared his father's interest in public affairs. He was justice of Chowan Precinct Court from 1717 to 1719 and again in the 1730s and represented Chowan in the Assembly in 1733, 1735, and 1739. He also served on the vestry of St. Paul's Parish. He died about 1766, survived by his wife, Hannah, a daughter, Elizabeth Mathias, and three sons—William, John, and Thomas.

Henderson Luten also represented Chowan in the Assembly in 1735, but little more is known of his life or of the lives of Constance and William. All four brothers appear to have lived in Chowan. Constance died before 12 Feb. 1742/43, Henderson died before 2 July 1740, and William died sometime after October 1745.

SEE: Administrators' Bonds, boxes 4, 11, Albemarle Book of Warrants and Surveys, 1681–1706, Albemarle County Papers, 1678–1739, Chowan Precinct Court Minutes, 1715–19, General Court Minutes, 1727–30, Wills of John Curren and Esther Pollack (North Carolina State Archives, Raleigh); John L. Cheney, Jr., ed., *North Carolina Government, 1585–1974* (1974); J. Bryan Grimes, ed., *Abstract of North Carolina Wills* (1910); J. R. B. Hathaway, ed., *North Carolina Historical and Genealogical Register*, 3 vols. (1900–1903); Mattie Erma E. Parker, ed., *North Carolina Higher-Court Records, 1702–1708* and *1709–1723* (1974, 1977); William L. Saunders, ed., *Colonial Records of North Carolina*, vols. 1–4 (1886).

MATTIE ERMA E. PARKER

Lutterloh, Thomas S. *(16 July 1816–15 July 1900),* commission merchant, steamboat owner, turpentine distiller, and political leader, was born in Chatham County. Little is known about his family or education except that as a youth he moved to Fayetteville and lived for several years with James Kyle, a merchant. Subsequently he clerked in the store of Charles T. Haigh until he entered the mercantile business for himself about 1840. In the two decades before the Civil War, Fayetteville, at the head of navigation on the Cape Fear River, and with a network of plank roads radiating from it, increased in importance as a trading center. Goods brought upriver from Wilmington by steamboat were forwarded in covered wagons to merchants in the Piedmont and western regions of the state. Lutterloh operated a local store and a commission and forwarding business specializing in heavy commodities, such as Swedish iron, salt, brown sugar, and molasses.

He soon entered the river transportation phase of the business and was reputed to have been the first man in Fayetteville to become sole owner of a steamboat. In 1847 he was one of the organizers and chief promoters of the Merchants Steamboat Company. In about 1850, when the naval stores industry began to develop in the upper Cape Fear region, Lutterloh built and operated the first turpentine distillery in Fayetteville. By 1853 his interests included a store and forwarding agency, distillery, cooper's shop, drayage service, and major steamboat line on the river. With a total of four boats, he inaugurated daily service between Fayetteville and Wilmington. Two years later he participated in the organization of the Bank of Clarendon. With fifty-nine slaves, he was the largest slaveholder in Fayetteville in 1860. The Civil War brought the destruction of his steamboat line and the end of slavery. Unable to recoup these losses, he adjusted his business interests to changing times and became one of the largest cotton merchants in the area.

Lutterloh also played a role in local and state politics. He was appointed a town commissioner in the 1840s, and when the office became elective in 1847, he was elected from Ward 6. Originally a member of the Whig party, he was elected mayor on the American, or Know-Nothing, party ticket, serving from 1855 to 1857. By 1860 he was prominent in the movement to organize a "Southern Rights" party for the defense of the South. During the Civil War Lutterloh served on various committees concerned with the welfare of Fayetteville and its people. In the postwar period he became a leader in the Republican party and served in the House of Commons in 1866–67, 1872–74, and 1879–1880.

Contemporaries regarded Lutterloh as an eminently successful businessman, "honest, fearless, . . . very quiet in all his ways, but determined in all his acts." In his later years he was addressed with the honorary title of "Colonel." An Episcopalian, Lutterloh married Mary Frances Buxton, daughter of the Reverend Jarvis B. Buxton, rector of St. John's Episcopal Church (1831–51), and they had nine children: Jarvis B., Harriet Ann, Thomas C., Ralph B., Frances, Edward, Elizabeth, Anna, and Herbert. He died from the infirmities of advanced years and was buried in Cross Creek Cemetery.

SEE: Levi Branson, ed., *North Carolina Business Directory* (1878, 1884); *Eighth Census of the United States, 1860*, Population Schedules, Cumberland County; *Fayetteville Observer*, 19 July 1900; John A. Oates, *The Story of Fayetteville* (1972).

PERCIVAL PERRY

Lyerly, Jacob Martin Luther (*18 Nov. 1862–17 Mar. 1923*), clergyman, teacher, and newspaper editor, was born near Salisbury, the son of Martin and Camilla Fisher Lyerly. He was educated in local schools and in 1889 was a member of the first graduating class of Catawba College. He received a master's degree in 1892 and later was awarded a Ph.D. from Hopedale College in Ohio. Soon after leaving Catawba, he was ordained by the Reformed church and assigned a charge in central Rowan County. Three years later he began to serve churches in Lincoln and Catawba counties and thereafter ministered to congregations in Guilford, Davidson, and Forsyth counties. In addition to his clerical duties, he supervised his family farm of some one hundred acres. He was an instructor at Catawba College in 1909–10 and at various times also taught in the public schools.

In 1896, at his home in southern Rowan County, Lyerly established the Crescent Academy and Business College for the benefit of his own children as well as the sons and daughters of poor families who had no other means of education. Attended in some years by as many as 250 students, the academy over a period of years educated around 2,000 students. Lyerly remembered with satisfaction that 23 of his graduates entered the ministry. Fond of children, he sometimes took orphans into his home and was the founder of the Nazareth Orphan Home, serving as chairman of its board of managers until his death.

Between 1912 and 1917 Lyerly was owner, editor, and publisher of a newspaper that moved from one town to another—the *Concord Chronicle* and then the *Albemarle Chronicle*. Since only incomplete files have survived, it is not possible to determine the exact dates of each. He also was editor of the *Reformed Church Standard*, published in Hickory.

In 1889 Lyerly married Mary Eugenia Peeler of Rockwell, and they became the parents of eleven children: Maye, Sudie Gray, Jacob N., Carl H., Ray Palmer, Vergil, Maud, Ruth, Ethel, Bernice, and Jean. He died in Winston-Salem and was buried at Crescent.

SEE: *Nat. Cyc. Am. Biog.*, vol. 20 (1929 [portrait]); *Winston-Salem Journal*, 18, 19 Mar. 1923.

WILLIAM S. POWELL

Lyman, Theodore Benedict (*27 Nov. 1815–13 Dec. 1893*), Episcopal bishop of North Carolina, was born at Brighton, Mass., the son of Asa Lyman (1777–1836), Congregational clergyman, educator, and bookseller, and Mary Benedict Lyman; both were of distinguished New England families. His brother was a priest in the Roman Catholic church. After graduation in 1837 from Hamilton College in New York, Lyman entered the General Theological Seminary in New York City to prepare for the ministry. He was graduated in 1840, and on 20 September of that year, at Christ Church, Baltimore, he was ordained a deacon by the Right Reverend William Rollinson Whittingham. On 19 Dec. 1841 he was ordained to the priesthood by Bishop Whittingham.

From 1841 to 1850 Lyman was rector at St. John's Church in Hagerstown, Md., where he assisted in founding the College of St. James. From 1850 to 1860 he was rector at Trinity Church in Pittsburgh, Pa. For a decade he and his family lived in Europe, where he established a church outside the Vatican; he traveled extensively in Europe and the Orient. In 1870 he accepted a call, arranged in part by tourists in Rome, to the rectorship of Trinity Church in San Francisco.

On 30 May 1873 at the diocesan convention in Fayetteville, N.C., Lyman was elected assistant bishop of the Diocese of North Carolina; on 11 Dec. 1873 consecration services were held at Christ Church, Raleigh, the first such ceremony in the diocese. Following the selection of Raleigh as his official residence, he built a house at North and Wilmington streets, where he housed his collection of art works. His summer home, Buena Vista, was in Hillsborough. The family became members of the Church of the Good Shepherd on Hillsborough Street, Raleigh, which had been founded in 1874 and to which he left a legacy in his will for the construction of a new sanctuary. At the death of Bishop Thomas Atkinson on 4 Jan. 1881, Lyman succeeded to the bishopric of North Carolina (fourth of North Carolina and one hundred and third in succession of the American episcopacy). In 1883 the Diocese of East Carolina was formed from the Diocese of North Carolina, with Alfred Augustin Watson, whom Lyman had consecrated, elected first bishop.

Lyman attended several Lambeth conferences in England and traveled in Europe. In 1886 he was selected as successor to the Right Reverend Abram Newkirk Littlejohn to supervise American Episcopal churches on the Continent. He was the recipient of honorary degrees from Hamilton College (D.C.L.), the College of Saint James (D.D.), and The University of North Carolina (LL.D.).

Bishop Lyman was married twice. On 24 June 1845 he married Anna Margaret Albert, and they had six children: Albert Benedict, M.D., Frances Augusta, William Whittingham, Theodore Benedict, Augustus Julian, and Anna Cornelia Roma. Anna Lyman died on 13 Apr. 1889. On 6 Feb. 1893 he married Susan Boone Robertson. After his death at age seventy-eight, he was interred in Oakwood Cemetery, Raleigh; in 1914 he was reinterred in the sanctuary of the Church of the Good Shepherd, and a stone marks the location. On display in the Parish House of Christ Church, Raleigh, are portraits of all the Episcopal bishops of North Carolina. Lyman was succeeded by Joseph Blount Cheshire (1850–1932), whom he consecrated.

SEE: *Durham Morning Herald*, 3 July 1927; Marshall De Lancey Haywood, *Lives of the Bishops of North Carolina* (1910); William Whittingham Lyman (St. Helena, Calif.), personal contact; Raleigh Sesquicentennial Commission, *Raleigh: Capital of North Carolina* (1942); *Raleigh Times*, 3 Mar. 1973; LaRene R. Ward, *Therefore with Angels and Archangels: The Church of the Good Shepherd, 1874–1974* (1974).

GRADY L. E. CARROLL

Lynch, Lemuel (5 Apr. 1808–19 Sept. 1893), silversmith and watchmaker, was born at Back Creek, the son of Moses and Susan Dickey Lynch. He was trained as a craftsman in the Hillsborough shop of William Huntington, one of the best known silversmiths of his day and son of the prominent Roswell Huntington. In the *Hillsborough Recorder* of 30 July 1828, William Huntington recommended Lynch to the public and announced that he had sold his materials and rented his tools to Lynch. Two years later Lynch advertised in the *Greensboro Patriot* that he had a shop in that city and was prepared to do all kinds of work in silver. In 1832 he stated in the *Western Carolinian* that he was operating a business in Concord. However, by 18 Mar. 1834 the silversmith was back in Hillsborough where he remained for the rest of his life. Other than during a two-year partnership with William Huntington from 1834 to 1836, Lynch operated his shop alone except, perhaps, with the assistance of his sons or apprentices.

Although there is nothing to indicate any exceptional interest in politics, Lynch was a successful businessman and a civic-minded individual. An account book preserved in the Duke University Library reveals that many distinguished residents of Hillsborough were among Lynch's regular customers. In 1841 he was appointed a justice of the peace and thereafter held court in the town. It was he who repaired the famous cupola clock when the courthouse was built in 1844 and who regulated the clock thereafter.

An open letter to William A. Graham, published in the Raleigh *Sentinel* on 21 Sept. 1865, was signed by Lemuel Lynch and nine other "neighbors and friends." This letter, preserved in the Graham Papers, the Southern Historical Collection, at the University of North Carolina, Chapel Hill, expressed confidence in Graham and the hope that he would be pardoned so he could be elected as a delegate to the state convention. This, of course, referred to the fact that Graham, as a Confederate sympathizer, had to obtain a pardon before he could enjoy the rights of a citizen after the Civil War.

On 25 Sept. 1828 Lynch married Margaret W. Palmer, of Hillsborough, a niece of Mrs. Roswell Huntington. There were three sons who learned the art of silversmithing from their father: Thomas M. (1829–81) of Oxford; Seaborn J., who inherited his father's silver-smithing tools and worked intermittently as a craftsman; and L. George, who worked with his father.

Lemuel Lynch died in Hillsborough. The extant pieces of silver known to have been made by him are expertly crafted and are obviously the work of a skilled artist.

SEE: George B. Cutten and Mary Reynolds Peacock, *Silversmiths of North Carolina, 1696–1850* (1973); *Greensboro Patriot*, 30 June, 29 Sept. 1830; *Hillsborough Recorder*, 30 July 1828, 4 June, 4 Oct. 1834; Orange County Marriage Records (North Carolina State Archives, Raleigh); Salisbury *Western Carolinian*, 23 Apr. 1832.

MARY REYNOLDS PEACOCK

Lyon, Francis Strother (25 Feb. 1800–31 Dec. 1882), lawyer, congressman, and bank commissioner, was born in Stokes County. His father was James Lyon, a Virginian who had moved to North Carolina and become a prosperous tobacco planter; his mother was Behethel-and Gaines Lyon, the daughter of Revolutionary soldier James Gaines of Moore County. After attending the local schools, Francis, at age seventeen, went to live with his uncle, who was an Indian agent in St. Stephens, Ala. His excellent penmanship gained him work as a bank clerk, then as clerk of court; at night he studied law. He was admitted to the bar in 1821 and began a practice in Demopolis.

From 1822 to 1830 Lyon was secretary of the state senate. In 1833 he was elected to the senate, and in 1835 he won a seat in Congress as a Whig. After two terms Lyon returned to his law practice and soon became one of Alabama's foremost attorneys, noted for his skill in cross-examination. By 1860 he had also become one of the wealthiest planters in his district. In 1846 he was appointed sole commissioner to liquidate the state bank. Years of mismanagement had hopelessly muddled its affairs, and Lyon's efforts won him a wide reputation in public finance.

By 1860 Lyon was a Democrat. He was chairman of the state party in 1860 and a delegate to the Charleston convention, where he supported the radical Southern position. On Abraham Lincoln's election, Lyon demanded immediate secession. He served briefly as a state senator in 1861 but in December was elected to the Confederate House of Representatives. In 1863 he won reelection without opposition.

Lyon's wealth and experience won him a place on the House Committee on Ways and Means, and in the Second Congress he was its chairman. Besides his routine committee duties, he proposed to double all taxes, repudiate all old Treasury notes and replace them with new issues of paper money, and permit the Confederate government to seize any railroad equipment it needed. He was just as much a Confederate nationalist on all other administration programs, making him one of President Jefferson Davis's most stalwart supporters.

Lyon had subscribed so heavily to the Confederate cotton loan that the end of the war found him almost bankrupt. His postwar years, therefore, were largely devoted to recouping his fortune through his law practice. In 1875 he was a member of the constitutional convention that returned Alabama to conservative white control, and in 1876 he was elected to the state senate for one term. He died at Demopolis and was buried in the Old Glover Vault.

A contemporary described Lyon as a handsome and cultivated individual who worked long but unhurried hours at practical pursuits, "a gentleman of the Old

School with the energy of the New." On 4 Mar. 1824 Lyon married Sarah Serena Glover, the daughter of Allen and Sarah Glover of Demopolis. They had seven children: Mary Amanda, Sarah Norwood, Helen Gaines, Amelia, Eugenia, Ida, and Frank Glover.

SEE: Joseph G. Baldwin, *The Flush Times of Alabama and Mississippi* (1853); *Biog. Dir. Am. Cong.* (1928); *DAB*, vol. 11 (1937); *Journal of the Congress of the Confederate States of America*, vols. 2–7 (1904–5); Mobile (Ala.) *Daily Register*, 2 Jan. 1883; Thomas M. Owen, *History of Alabama and Dictionary of Alabama Biography*, vol. 4 (1921).

BUCK YEARNS

Lyon, George Leonidas (3 Feb. 1881–11 Jan. 1916), sportsman and world champion trapshooter, was born in Durham, the second son of Robert E. and Mary Duke Lyon. His paternal grandfather was Zachariah Inge Lyon, pioneer tobacco manufacturer; his maternal grandfather was Washington Duke, tobacco manufacturer and philanthropist. After receiving his early education at Horner School (Oxford), Bingham Military Academy (Mebane), and Guilford College, he matriculated in 1897 for two years at Trinity College (now Duke University).

Beginning in 1901, Lyon developed unusual skills in the use of guns which later led to his employment as field representative and demonstrator for the Union Metallic Cartridge, Remington Arms, and Du Pont Powder companies. He once wrote: "I have been more closely identified with the Remington pump gun than with any other shooter on account of my having won two Handicaps with the same in one year (1908), the first year of its manufacture." A special trapshooting cartridge, the George Lyon Load, was named for him.

Lyon's championship status in trapshooting began in 1904, when he won the North Carolina–Virginia combined meet, the first of three such victories, and progressed year by year for four state wins in North Carolina, the Grand American Preliminary in Chicago, the Southern at Birmingham, and the Great Eastern in Boston, all as an amateur. For two years he shot as a professional representing the manufacturers, and in 1911 and again in 1912 he won the cup that was "emblematic of world's championship marksmanship at inanimate objects." During this period as a professional, he was unable to qualify for amateur status for participation on the U.S. Olympic trapshooting team in Stockholm in 1912. However, as coach and adviser for the twenty selected shooters, he led the group to team and individual victories for first place, and with the team he himself performed brilliantly in post-Olympic invitational meets all over Europe.

In 1913, competing as an amateur, Lyon won the Grand American Handicap at Dayton, Ohio, which made him a national champion with a new world's record of ninety-four out of one hundred double targets. The 1914 and 1915 annual championships of the Long Island Sound Clubs brought him national recognition again and the popular title of "Chief Bull Durham," which had previously been given him in the trapshooting social organization, the Okoboji Indian Chiefs.

Lyon's last important shoot was on 11 May 1915 at the Southern Handicap in Memphis, with a high of 147 out of 150 despite his rapidly declining health. He died of tuberculosis eight months later in Albuquerque, N.Mex., where he had gone at Thanksgiving in an effort to recover. At the time of his death he was said by the *New York Sun* to have belonged to more than seventy-

four sports, social, and benevolent organizations; during the last weeks of his life, he was initiated as a Thirty-third degree Mason in Albuquerque in recognition of his service to Masonry over the years. He was a member and stockholder of the New York Athletic Club, which established the thousand-dollar George L. Lyon Memorial Cup annual award in 1916 following his death. In August 1976 he was inducted posthumously into the Trapshooting Hall of Fame at Vandalia, Ohio, at the time of the Seventy-seventh Grand American Tournament.

His wife, also a victim of tuberculosis, had died in 1914 after the birth of their third child; she was Annie Snowden Carr Lyon, the daughter of L. A. and Clara Watts Carr of Durham and a niece of George W. Watts, the Durham philanthropist. Married on 6 Nov. 1900, they were the parents of Clara A. (Mrs. Roland McClamroch), George L., Jr., and Mary Duke (Mrs. Elliott Newcombe).

Lyon, a Presbyterian, was a man of wealth and a stockholder in several Durham businesses at the time of his death; he was survived by his three young children, his brother, Edward Buchanan Lyon, and a sister, Mary Washington Lyon (Mrs. J. E. Stagg). He was buried in Maplewood Cemetery in the mausoleum of his grandfather, Washington Duke, near Lyon's Park, in Durham, a city park named for him and the site of many of his trap shoots.

SEE: Samuel A. Ashe, ed., *Biographical History of North Carolina*, vol. 8 (1917 [portrait]); "Chief Bull Durham Lyon," *National Cash Register Weekly*, 26 June 1913; *Durham Morning Herald*, 10 Nov. 1946 (portrait), 4 Mar. 1969 (portraits); "Hall of Fame Inductees," *Trap and Field*, May 1976; Clara E. Lyon McClamroch, interview, 15 Mar. 1978; Stoney McLinn, "The End of the Most Popular Trapshot," *American Shooter*, 1 Feb. 1916 (portraits); *Trinity Alumni Register* 2 (April 1916).

CLARA HAMLETT ROBERTSON FLANNAGAN

Lyon, Homer Legrand (1 Mar. 1879–31 May 1956), congressman, lawyer, and solicitor, was born in Elizabethtown of English ancestry. His great-great-grandfather, James Lyon, settled in Bladen County in 1735 and helped in its early organization and administration as one of the county's first public magistrates. His great-grandfather, Robert Lyon, was a leading slaveholder and planter who served in the state legislature as a representative from Bladen County. Lyon's ancestors also figured prominently in the Civil War. His grandfather, Joseph Lyon, an agriculturalist-slaveholder, was a colonel in the state militia. Joseph's brother, Captain Robert Henry Lyon, was a member of the famed "Immortal 600"; another brother, Captain Cassius Wade Lyon, who also distinguished himself in the war, became sheriff of Bladen County and later chairman of the Board of County Commissioners. Homer Lyon's father was Chatham Calhoun Lyon, a lawyer, legislator, solicitor (1901–6), and for sixteen years superior court justice in North Carolina. Chatham married Margaret Richardson, also of Elizabethtown, and they had two other sons of note: Joseph Alden Lyon, a lawyer and mayor of Elizabethtown, and Terry A. Lyon, a lawyer in a prominent firm in Fayetteville.

As a judge's son, Homer L. Lyon was reared with a vigor for the law and politics. After receiving an education at the Davis Military School in Winston, N.C., he went on to earn a law degree from The University of North Carolina. In 1900 he was admitted to the bar, and the following year he set up a practice in Whiteville. He attended the North Carolina Democratic Convention from 1901 through 1921 and the Democratic National Convention in 1901 and 1940. In 1913 he became solicitor of the Eighth Judicial District of North Carolina, serving until 1920. In the latter year he ran for Congress from the Sixth District, which included Harnett, Cumberland, Robeson, Bladen, Columbus, and Brunswick counties.

Lyon began his illustrious congressional career at a time when Washington, D.C., was not the fashionable place it was to become. In fact, very few members of that day found the city exciting. Taking his seat in the Sixty-seventh Congress, he was assigned to the Rivers and Harbors Committee (now defunct). Although this committee received little national attention, Lyon served prominently. He was a sponsor and cosponsor of many bills directed at midsize cities and towns like those in his own district. His legislative activity contributed to the prosperity of the state and showed his firm commitment to his personal constituency as well as to what was good for the country as a whole. This prompted others to refer to him as "liberal-minded, whole-soled, and clear-minded" and made him very popular back home. Described by colleagues on Capitol Hill as "fair-minded," Lyon demonstrated broad legal and statesmanlike abilities throughout his years of service.

Among his most admirable crusades were those for internal improvements and for the separation of church and state. His work on the Rivers and Harbors Committee made him an architect of much of the internal improvements legislation. He also vigorously supported anti–blue law legislation, arguing that the statute violated the First Amendment concerning the separation of church and state. When Congressman Lyon left office in 1929, Representative Robert L. Doughton was among those who expressed regret at his decision not to run for reelection. He returned to the practice of law until his retirement in 1950 due to failing health.

Lyon married Kate Burkhead in Elizabethtown. He died in Whiteville at age seventy-seven after a long illness. Funeral services were held at the Whiteville Methodist Church where he served as a layman and member of the board of trustees, and he was buried in Memorial Cemetery. In addition to his wife, he was survived by two daughters, Mrs. Vance Brand of Urbana, Ohio, and Mrs. John Sharp May of Burlington, N.C.; a sister, Mrs. Mattie Lyon Clark of Elizabethtown; a brother, Colonel Terry A. Lyon of Fayetteville; and eleven grandchildren.

SEE: *Biog. Dir. Am. Cong.* (1961); *Congressional Record*, 70th Cong., 2d sess. (1929); Daniel L. Grant, *Alumni History of the University of North Carolina, 1795–1924* (1924); *Nat. Cyc. Am. Biog.*, vol. 48 (1965 [portrait]); *North Carolina Biography*, vol. 4 (1919); *North Carolina Manual* (1921–29); Raleigh *News and Observer*, 1 June 1956; *Whiteville Reporter*, 1 June 1956; *Who's Who in the South* (1927).

J. RONALD JONES, JR.

Lyon, John (*1765?–14 Sept. 1814*), botanist and plant collector, was born in Gillogie in Forfarshire, a center of flax production in Scotland. Little is known about his early life or the circumstances that brought him to America. In 1796 he was working as a gardener in Philadelphia, where he met William Hamilton, a wealthy landed gentleman and art collector. Hamilton hired Lyon to manage the three-hundred-acre garden on his Woodlands estate on the Schuylkill River just outside Philadelphia. Under Lyon's care, the garden soon contained over ten thousand native and exotic plants, re-

portedly "the finest collection in America in variety and beauty."

In 1799 Lyon went on a plant-collecting trip to the Allegheny Mountains of western Pennsylvania, the first of ten such trips he made throughout the Southeast over the next fifteen years. Though these excursions took him as far south as Florida and as far west as Nashville, Tenn., most of his traveling was centered in the southern Appalachians. Seven of his ten trips included exploration in western North Carolina, where he followed in the footsteps of earlier botanical explorers André Michaux and John Bartram. A journal he kept of his travels indicates that he collected plants on Roan, Grandfather, and Pilot mountains, among others, and that he stayed on several occasions with acquaintances in Asheville, Morganton, Lincolnton, and Salem. Lyon's journal is preserved in the library of the American Philosophical Society in Philadelphia; it was published in the society's journal, *Transactions*, in 1963. The only published works of Lyon himself were two catalogues circulated during trips he made to England in 1806 and 1812 which listed the American plants he brought with him to sell through both private transactions and public auctions.

A fellow botanist described Lyon as "a gentleman through whose industry and skill more new and rare American plants have lately been introduced into Europe than through any other channel whatever." He introduced thirty-one new varieties of plant life into horticulture, including one genus and at least three species that bear his name.

Late in the summer of 1814, Lyon contracted a "bilious fever" en route from Tennessee into North Carolina. He traveled as far as Asheville, where he spent his last weeks in bed at the Eagle Hotel under the care of a young friend, Silas McDowell, later a prominent Macon County leader who wrote a moving account of Lyon's death. He was buried in Asheville, though the site of his grave was disputed until the early 1960s, when it was found in the Riverside Cemetery. His gravestone, thought to be the oldest inscribed gravestone in western North Carolina, was sent from friends in Scotland. Now growing around his grave are plants named for or discovered by Lyon.

SEE: Joseph Ewan and Nesta Ewan, "John Lyon, Nurseryman and Plant Hunter, and His Journal, 1799–1814," *Transactions of the American Philosophical Society* (May 1963); Francis Harper, "The Grave of John Lyon," *North Carolina Wildflower Preservation Society Newsletter* (October 1964); Silas McDowell Papers (Southern Historical Collection, University of North Carolina, Chapel Hill); F. A. Sondley, *A History of Buncombe County, North Carolina*, vol. 2 (1930).

JOHN INSCOE

Lyon, Zachariah Inge (*1 June 1815–7 Aug. 1887*), one of the founders of Durham and a pioneer smoking tobacco manufacturer, was born in Granville County, the son of Zachariah T. and Nancy Lanier Lyon. He was the grandson of John, a Revolutionary soldier, and Lydda Billinsly Lyon; the grandson of Robert Lanier, also of Granville; and the great-grandson of Henry and Anna (or Anne) Lyon of Calverton Manor, Charles County, Md., where Henry's will, made on 19 May 1778, is recorded. John Lyon settled in Granville County after the Revolution and bought several tracts of land, including some in the Ledge of Rocks Creek area where his grandson Zachariah Inge Lyon later lived.

About 1852 Lyon moved to what is now the city of Durham to supervise railroad grading, first for the North Carolina Railroad and then for the Western North Carolina and Chatham Railroad. This work, and his continued operation of his home farm, exempted him from service in the Confederate army.

Like many other farm owners, he produced a smoking tobacco for home use. Among the Lyon family papers is a letter written in 1886 from a Northern veteran who recalled how Union soldiers would swap sugar and coffee with the Confederate soldiers for some of their fine tobacco. Thus, Zachariah and J. Edwin, his oldest son, had been encouraged after the war to produce a small quantity of smoking tobacco for sale, using three or four laborers on their farm to prepare the granulated mixture for distribution in small sacks. They expanded their operations and coined the brand name, Pride of Durham. In Durham they built a two-and-one-half story wooden building, thirty-two by seventy feet, equipped it with steam power, and hired enough labor to process over 200,000 pounds of Pride of Durham smoking tobacco annually, selling it across the nation.

J. Edwin left the business briefly for that of John R. Green in the manufacture of the Durham Bull brand but returned to remain his father's partner until 1886, when they sold the entire business including the brand name to Captain E. J. Parrish. Parrish continued the operation until a disastrous fire led him to sell the business as well as the Pride of Durham name to the American Tobacco Company.

Lyon was married twice. On 12 Oct. 1837 he married Nancy B. Walker of Orange County, and they had eleven children: J. Edwin, Annie B., Cadmus H., John C., Robert E., Sarah E., Zachariah F., Nancy V. C., William G. who died in infancy, Andrew J., and Thomas F. After her death in 1873, he married on 24 July 1874 Mary P. McMannen, the widow of the Reverend John A. McMannen, a popular minister in the Methodist churches of the area. Lyon died about a year after selling his business and retiring. He was survived by his second wife and all ten of his children who had lived to adulthood. An active supporter of the Methodist church, he was buried in the graveyard of Trinity Church, Durham.

SEE: Samuel A. Ashe, ed., *Biographical History of North Carolina*, vol. 8 (1917 [portrait]); Benjamin Guy Childs, *Centennial History of Trinity Methodist, Durham, North Carolina* (1961); Granville County Court Records: Marriages, Deeds, and Wills (Hays Scrapbook, Oxford Public Library, Oxford); Hiram V. Paul, *History of the Town of Durham* (1884); Raleigh *Christian Advocate*, 28 Sept. 1887; Raleigh *News and Observer*, 8 Aug. 1887; A. Davis Smith, *Western North Carolina: Historical and Biographical* (1890 [portrait]); Nannie May Tilley, *The Bright Tobacco Industry, 1860–1929* (1948).

CLARA HAMLETT ROBERTSON FLANNAGAN

Lytch, James (*24 July 1814–30 Oct. 1890*), inventor, was the son of Archibald and Flora McEachin Lytch. His mother was the daughter of John McEachin (b. 1740) and his wife Mary Currie (b. 1750). John McEachin emigrated from Scotland at a young age and settled in the Highland Scot community on the Upper Cape Fear River, near present-day Fayetteville.

Lytch was raised and educated in the tradition of his Scottish Presbyterian family, but his mechanical ingenuity appears to have been a natural gift. His first patent was issued in 1870 for a cotton planter, which he called the Eclipse Lytch Cotton Planter. It was his most successful invention and was widely used throughout the South; some planters were sold as far away as California. The Cape Fear Agricultural Association awarded Lytch a medal for his planter at its 1872 fair in Wilmington. Other inventions for which Lytch received patents were a cotton scraper (1870), a cider mill (1870), and an improved fertilizer distributor (1873).

The Lytch planter was manufactured in shops Lytch built near his home at X-Way in Richmond (now Scotland) County. He also built and operated a gristmill at the site. As of 1980 this mill was still in operation, producing cornmeal and whole wheat flour under the X-Way brand. The Lytch home and grounds are included on the National Register of Historic Places. In 1957 the state of North Carolina erected a historical marker near the Lytch home on State Road 1108 to honor James Lytch and his accomplishments.

On 16 Mar. 1837 Lytch married Sarah James Shaw (9 Sept. 1813–20 Apr. 1878), and they had eight children: John Archibald, Hector McNeill, Mary Jane, Flora Ann, James Martine, Milton, Daniel Calder, and Sarah Shaw. Lytch left his shops to Daniel, the most mechanically inclined of his children, who continued to produce planters after his father's death.

Lytch was a faithful member of Gum Swamp Presbyterian Church (now Laurel Hill). In his later years, he would travel on Saturday from his home to that of his son Milton, who lived near Laurel Hill, and spend the night, attending church the next day. He was buried in the Lytch family cemetery near his home.

SEE: James Lytch File (Highway Marker Program, North Carolina State Archives, Raleigh); Will of James Lytch (North Carolina State Archives, Raleigh).

WALTER RICHARD BULLOCK, JR.

Lytle, Archibald (*1730–20 June 1790*), Revolutionary officer, was born in Argyllshire, Scotland, and died in Robeson County, N.C., although most of his life in North Carolina was spent in Hillsborough. Lytle began his military career on 16 Apr. 1776 as a captain in the Sixth North Carolina Continental Regiment. By 26 Jan. 1777 he had been promoted to lieutenant colonel and that summer he joined General Francis Nash's brigade at Morristown, N.J. Lytle was with the North Carolina brigade in the campaign in defense of Philadelphia. Held in reserve at the Battle of Brandywine, the brigade was in the defeat at Germantown where General Nash was killed.

By 1778 the Sixth Regiment was recalled to North Carolina as part of a move to reinforce the Southern Department. The British invaded Georgia in December and by February 1779 Lytle and the available North Carolina Continentals were on the north side of the Savannah River, posted at Briar Creek with militia under the command of General John Ashe. Lytle had command of the Continentals, who were organized as light infantry. At the Battle of Briar Creek on 3 March, Ashe's force was routed by a British surprise attack but Lytle's light infantry maintained discipline and covered the retreat. During the campaign and siege of Charles Town, S.C. in 1779–80, Lytle was wounded in the Battle of Stono Ferry on 20 June 1779. In the siege of Charles Town he commanded militia and was captured when the city surrendered on 12 May 1780. He was exchanged on 9 Feb. 1782 and on his return to North Carolina was given command of the Fourth Regiment of the reorganized Continental line. On 30 Sept. 1783 he was promoted to the rank of colonel.

After the war Lytle remained in public service. He was a commissioner of the town of Hillsborough in 1784 and a commissioner for confiscated estates for the Hillsborough District in 1785. He was elected to two terms in the House of Commons in 1784 and 1785, representing the town of Hillsborough. In the General Assembly, he was appointed to a number of joint committees—among them, the committees on disabled Continental veterans, state currency, and the Richard Henderson Company. Lytle was a delegate to the Society of the Cincinnati meeting at Philadelphia in May 1784.

Entitled to 7,200 acres of land for his wartime service, Lytle received 985 acres in present-day Rockingham County in state grants. These grants included the Speedwell Furnace Ironworks on Troublesome Creek, and in partnership with Peter and Constantine Perkins he attempted to revive the forge and furnace. In 1786 he sold his interest in the venture to his partners.

In 1756 Lytle married Margaret Johnson (1736–79), and they had a son, William (1757–1804), who was a captain in the Continental line.

SEE: Lindley S. Butler, "Speedwell Furnace: The Ironworks on Troublesome Creek" (1973); Walter Clark, ed., *State Records of North Carolina*, vols. 17, 19 (1899, 1901); Guilford County Deeds (Guilford County Courthouse, Greensboro); Hugh F. Rankin, *North Carolina Continentals* (1971); Rockingham County Deeds (Rockingham County Courthouse, Wentworth); *Sons of the American Revolution Lineage Book* (1951); U.S. Census, 1790 (1908).

LINDLEY S. BUTLER

Mabley, Jackie (Moms) *(1898–23 May 1975)*, comedienne and actress, was born Loretta Mary Aiken in Brevard, the daughter of "Uncle" Jim and Mary Aiken. Known as an "overbearing, dogmatic, infuriating and sweet" black comedienne, she entertained American audiences from the 1920s into the 1970s. At age fourteen, on the advice of her great-grandmother Harriet Smith (who was part Cherokee Indian and reportedly lived to be 118), Loretta Aiken left Brevard after being raped and becoming pregnant. She went to Cleveland, Ohio, where her mother lived, to find the "big world out there," and Bonnie Bell Drew offered her a job with a vaudeville group. Since Loretta was boarding with a clergyman and his wife, she felt that she could not tell them that she was going into show business, so she threw her bag over the back fence where Bonnie Drew was waiting with her car. After arriving in Pittsburgh, Pa., Loretta Aiken made her debut in the play, *The Rich Aunt from Utah*. She was very successful in her role—she "didn't make a mistake or nothing"—and continued her career after the birth of her child.

Loretta Aiken soon changed her name because her brother thought that a female in the theater would disgrace the Aiken family name. She chose Jackie Mabley in honor of Jack Mabley, a young Canadian to whom she was then engaged. However, he would not live in the United States and she would not live in Canada, so they never married. Apparently she was so "unselfish with her time and sympathy for fellow performers who need a great deal of mothering that she was nicknamed 'Moms.' " This was in keeping with her personal philosophy and her concern for young people. "I'm just a Mom," she once said. "A child is born, and it ain't no good, no where, no how without a Mom. I'm that Mom."

Moms became associated with the Theatre Owners Booking Association or TOBA—which was sometimes said to also stand for "Tough on Black Actors." This agency booked performances from New York to Florida and from Chicago to New Orleans. Her weekly starting pay was twelve dollars, and her later recollections were none too pleasant as she realized how she and her friends were treated.

The black comedy team of Butterbeans and Suzie saw her act and told her she was too good to be working for such low pay. They persuaded her to join another acting association, and by 1923 Moms was playing in Harlem's best playhouses such as Connie's Inn and the Cotton Club. Her comedy routines quickly became a hit on the black concert circuit, and on one occasion she noted that every comedian except Jack Benny came to see her perform and to steal her material. In the 1960s she came to be accepted by white audiences and made club concert and television appearances on the programs of such celebrities as the Smothers Brothers, Bill Cosby, Mike Douglas, and Flip Wilson. It was Harry Belafonte who first put Moms on television in 1967, when he aired an all-black comedy show.

During her career Moms had several small parts in movies, including *Boarding House Blues* and *Emperor Jones*. She appeared on Broadway as well in *Swinging the Dream* and *Blackbirds*. She also recorded two comedy albums, *Moms Mabley at the U.N.* and *Moms Mabley at the Geneva Convention*. In 1975 she had the lead in the film *Amazing Grace*, her first starring role in the cinema. While making the film she suffered a heart attack, and the filming had to be postponed until she had a pacemaker implanted. She said she wanted to make another movie based on a true story "that I saw live," but within a few months she died at age seventy-eight.

In the latter part of her life, Moms Mabley lived in Westchester County, north of New York City, and it was reported that she was survived by three children as well as others whom she had "adopted." She also was deeply involved in politics, especially as a member of the NAACP. She was a guest at the White House Conference to Fulfill These Rights (1966), and she used politics as a major component of her comedy routine.

Moms always remained close to North Carolina, frequently visiting family and friends in the Brevard area. She often commented: "I love North Carolina. I love the people." Once when she returned to Brevard, she tearfully observed: "Lord, what a wonderful place God picked out for me to be born in."

SEE: *Asheville Citizen*, 21 Mar., 22 Oct. 1971, 3 Mar. 1975; *New York Times*, 25 May 1975; *Plain Dealer Sunday Magazine*, 23 June 1968; Raleigh *News and Observer*, 7 Nov. 1967; *Transylvania Times*, 28 Oct. 1971.

JAMES D. GILLESPIE

McAden, Hugh *(ca. 1720–20 Jan. 1781)*, Presbyterian minister, was born in Pennsylvania to "poor but pious parents" of Ulster Scots ancestry. He was graduated from the College of New Jersey (now Princeton University) in 1753 and was awarded a master's degree in 1756. McAden studied theology with John Blair at Fagg's Manor in Chester County, Pa., and was licensed in 1755 by the New Castle Presbytery, which was affiliated with the "new side" or "new light" Synod of New York. In June 1755 the presbytery sent him to the Carolinas as a missionary.

The young licentiate kept a journal of his eleven-month mission. Although the original manuscript has been lost, lengthy excerpts appear in William Henry Foote's *Sketches of North Carolina*. It is one of the few primary accounts of the early Presbyterian congregations in North Carolina. McAden spent nearly two months preaching to Presbyterian congregations in Virginia before he entered North Carolina near the site of modern Milton in Caswell County. During the nine months he spent in the colony, he visited the nucleus of nearly all of the early Presbyterian congregations. After a month in the area now comprised of Caswell and Person counties, he visited churches in Orange, Granville, and present-day Guilford before moving on to the Ulster Scots settlements in Rowan and what later became Mecklenburg County. Following a visit of nearly two months to South Carolina he returned to preach in Anson County, in the Highland Scots settlements on the Cape Fear River, and in Wilmington. While in the Ulster Scots settlements along the Northeast Cape Fear River, he received calls from what became the Rockfish and Grove churches in Duplin County. McAden continued itinerant preaching as he traveled through Edgecombe County and revisited some of the churches in Granville and Orange counties before leaving the colony.

After his ordination in 1757 by the New Castle Presbytery, McAden returned to North Carolina to accept the calls from the Duplin County congregations. His pastorate covered most of present-day Duplin, Pender, and New Hanover counties. He bought land and built a house near Grove Church in the vicinity of present-day Kenansville. When he returned to Pennsylvania, McAden persuaded James Campbell, a Gaelic-speaking minister, to settle among the North Carolina Highlanders. McAden and Campbell, who also came in 1757, were the only settled Presbyterian ministers in the colony until 1765.

In 1759 McAden joined the Hanover Presbytery in Virginia and was frequently assigned to preach at churches in North Carolina. His continued association with congregations in northern Orange where he often was assigned to preach, as well as the conviction that the coastal climate was bad for his health, prompted him to accept a call from the Hyco, Dan River, and Country Line Creek churches in 1768. When McAden moved to Orange County, he made his home at the Middle Hyco Church (later Red House) in present-day Semora. He also served various churches in Caswell and Person counties and in Virginia. At the time of his death he was preaching at Middle Hyco, Griers (Upper Hyco), and a church in Pittsylvania County, Va. McAden was one of the seven original members of the Orange Presbytery, created in May 1770 to serve the congregations in the Carolinas.

During the Regulator movement McAden and the other three Presbyterian ministers in the Piedmont supported the colonial government. In a letter to the governor they expressed their "abhorence" of the Regulator's "turbulent and disorderly spirit." The ministers counseled their brethren who had signed the Regulator oath to repent and warned that "greater guilt" would "lie upon them" if they kept it.

In 1762 McAden married Catherine Scott of Lunenburg County, Va. He was buried at Red House Church in Caswell County, survived by his wife and seven children. Two weeks after his death, a detachment of Lord Cornwallis's army occupied the church building and burned his library and papers.

SEE: William Henry Foote, *Sketches of North Carolina, Historical and Biographical: Illustrative of the Principles of a Portion of Her Early Settlers* (1846); Hanover Presbytery, "Records of the Proceedings of the Hanover Presbytery from the Year 1755 to the Year 1786" (typescript, Presby-

terian Historical Foundation Library, Montreat, N.C.); James McLachlan, *Princetonians, 1748–1768* (1976); *Nat. Cyc. Am. Biog.*, vol. 9 (1899); William L. Saunders, ed., *Colonial Records of North Carolina*, vol. 5 (1887); George Wesley Troxler, "The Establishment of Presbyterianism in North Carolina" (master's thesis, University of North Carolina, 1966).

GEORGE W. TROXLER

McAden, Rufus Yancey (*4 Mar. 1833–29 Jan. 1889*), legislator and financier, was born in Caswell County, a member of a distinguished North Carolina family of Scottish ancestry. His great-grandfather, the Reverend Hugh McAden, was a Presbyterian minister who came from Philadelphia to North Carolina a few years before the American Revolution to preach and do missionary work. His grandfather, Dr. John McAden, a prominent physician in Caswell County, married Betsy Murphey, the sister of Archibald D. Murphey, an eminent North Carolina judge and legislator. Dr. Henry McAden, Rufus's father, was also a successful doctor in Caswell County; he married Frances Yancey, the daughter of Bartlett Yancey of North Carolina.

Rufus was raised by his grandmother, Mrs. Bartlett Yancey, after both his parents died when he was young. He received his primary education in Caswell County schools and then attended Wake Forest College. After graduating in 1853, he read law with Judges Frederick Nash and John L. Bailey in Hillsborough. In 1858 he married Mary F. Terry, the daughter of Dr. B. F. Terry of Prince Edward County, Va., moved to Graham in Alamance County, and established a law practice.

McAden entered politics in 1860 as a Whig candidate for the state legislature but was defeated by thirteen votes. In 1861 he was elected as a Union candidate to the state constitutional convention, which did not meet because North Carolinians rejected this early attempt at secession. From 1862 to 1865 he served in the House of Commons as a member of the Conservative faction. As a peace advocate, he introduced, in May 1864, the first peace resolution to pass the General Assembly. He continued to represent Alamance County in the house until the beginning of congressional Reconstruction in 1867; in 1866 he served as speaker.

In 1867 McAden embarked on a new career when he was chosen president of the First National Bank of Charlotte. He built a fortune through this and other business activities. In 1868 he became a railroad promoter and, along with A. S. Buford, constructed the Atlantic and Charlotte Airline Railroad, of which he was vice-president. He also organized and built the Spartanburg and Asheville Rail Road. In 1881 he entered into cotton manufacturing, establishing a large cotton mill in McAdenville, Gaston County, that employed almost five hundred people.

While McAden was extremely successful as a financier, he encountered several problems along the way. During the Civil War, Calvin Wiley, the first superintendent of the common schools in North Carolina, accused McAden of cheating him in a land deal. This caused a delay in McAden's pardon from President Andrew Johnson after the war when the provisional governor, William Woods Holden, a friend of Wiley's, recommended that McAden's request for pardon be "suspended" because of Wiley's complaints. During Reconstruction, McAden was involved in a minor way in a major scandal over fraudulent railroad bonds. The chief figures were George W. Swepson, a native North Carolinian, who was president of the western division of the

Western North Carolina Railroad and McAden's nephew, and Milton S. Littlefield, a northern speculator. Together they sold approximately four million dollars worth of bonds and appropriated the proceeds for their own use. McAden either handed over some bonds for blackmail or for "services rendered." However, he was never tried or convicted for these actions.

In 1885 McAden clashed with Richmond Pearson. Pearson had been elected to the state legislature on a platform promising "to bend every energy to force the completion of the Spartanburg and Asheville railroad." To carry out this pledge, Pearson traveled to New York City to obtain information about the railroad. This, according to Pearson, "provoked the violent displeasure" of McAden, who was president of the line. In fact, McAden severely criticized Pearson in a letter to a Charlotte newspaper. Pearson declared on the floor of the house, in response to a question from Lieutenant Governor James L. Robinson, that he had not replied to McAden's article because he felt it was "unworthy" of his notice. About a half hour later, McAden assaulted Pearson on the streets of Raleigh. A year later, after another controversy, Pearson challenged McAden to a duel, which McAden declined because, he argued, duelling was illegal.

McAden was a handsome, distinguished-looking man of medium height with blue eyes. He died at his home in Charlotte. At the time of his death, he was president of the First National Bank of Charlotte, the Spartanburg, Union and Columbia Rail Road, the Spartanburg and Asheville Rail Road, the Falls of Neuse Manufacturing Company, and the McAden Cotton Mills. He left an estate valued at $850,000, not including $110,000 in life insurance, which was the largest estate recorded in Mecklenburg County to that date. He was survived by his wife and five children: Benjamin T., George S., Virginia Y., Giles M., and Mary T.

SEE: J. P. Arthur, *Western North Carolina: A History* (1914); Samuel A. Ashe, *Biographical History of North Carolina*, vol. 5 (1905 [portrait]); *Cyclopedia of Eminent and Representative Men of the Carolinas of the Nineteenth Century*, vol. 2 (1892 [portrait]); Jerome Dowd, *Sketches of Prominent Living North Carolinians* (1888); Richmond Pearson Papers and Calvin Wiley Papers (Southern Historical Collection, University of North Carolina, Chapel Hill); Stephen B. Weeks Scrapbook, vols. 2–3 (North Carolina Collection, University of North Carolina, Chapel Hill); John H. Wheeler, ed., *Reminiscences and Memoirs of North Carolina and Eminent North Carolinians* (1884).

ROBERTA SUE ALEXANDER

McAlister, Alexander Worth (21 Mar. 1862–20 Nov. 1946), insurance executive and longtime member of the state welfare board, was born in Asheboro, the son of Alexander Carey and Adelaide Worth McAlister. On his father's side, he was a descendant of Scottish settlers; his grandfather, Colonel Alexander McAlister, had served in the American Revolution. On his maternal side, the Worths were Quakers who had descended from John Havland, a Nantucket whaler; his great-grandfather was the brother of Governor Jonathan Worth.

McAlister attended local schools in Asheboro, Bingham Military School in Mebane, and The University of North Carolina where he obtained a bachelor's degree in 1882. He then taught for four years at Bingham School before returning to Chapel Hill to study law for one year. Although he was licensed to practice in 1887, he entered the lumber business in Asheboro with his father rather than pursue a career in law. He soon consolidated the lumber firm with one in Greensboro and moved to that city.

In 1890 he became associated with his uncle, Thomas C. Worth, and with Edward P. Wharton in a new firm, the Worth Wharton Real Estate and Investment Company. The charter for that company became the building block for the later Pilot Life Insurance Company. Following his uncle's death in 1891, McAlister became a partner in the firm and in 1895 he and Edward Wharton established the Southern Stock Mutual Fire Insurance Company of Greensboro. This was the first insurance company established in Greensboro after the Civil War. McAlister brought to the venture his experience as an agent for other insurance companies in the Worth-Wharton company. Because sufficient capital could not be raised, the company began without capital; instead, it had guarantees of $5,000 each from twenty prominent men. Every year the firm's profits were set aside to establish the original capital that had been guaranteed. When sufficient capital had been accumulated, the name of the company was changed in 1899 to the Pilot Fire Insurance Company. Meanwhile, McAlister was instrumental in the founding of three other fire insurance companies in Greensboro: Greensboro Fire Insurance Company, George Washington Fire Insurance Company, and McAlister Underwriters; these, together with Pilot, were often referred to as the McAlister companies. Through these firms he attempted to provide lower rates and better service than out-of-state companies had offered.

In 1903 the Pilot company entered the life insurance field as the Pilot Life Insurance Company. In the meantime, given the success of McAlister and Worth's ventures, other insurance companies moved to Greensboro or were established there, making the city an insurance center for the state and the region. Among these firms were the Dixie Fire Insurance Company and the Jefferson Standard Insurance Company, which moved from Raleigh and eventually subsumed Pilot and many others.

McAlister, who had been vice-president of the Pilot company, became president of Pilot Life in 1908 and remained so until 1931, when he became chairman of the board. He served in the latter position until his death.

The real estate functions of the parent company were assigned to the Southern Real Estate Company in 1904. Under McAlister's direction, that company developed Irving Park in North Greensboro and Sedgefield between Greensboro and High Point. In 1903 McAlister had directed the construction of the tallest skyscraper in North Carolina, the five-story Southern Trust Building in Greensboro. Later, with the development of Sedgefield, he pioneered in creating a suburban home office of Pilot Life in Sedgefield. Modeled after the Tryon Palace in New Bern, this facility offered beautiful grounds and many recreational facilities for employees whose activities were paternalistically overseen by McAlister.

Jefferson Standard purchased a controlling interest in Pilot Life while McAlister was still president. Although that interest was briefly repurchased, Jefferson Standard gained permanent control of the company after McAlister's death and eventually brought it and other companies under the Jefferson-Pilot holding company.

McAlister learned to play golf in 1908 and became such a devotee of the game that he helped establish the Greensboro Country Club and the Sedgefield Country

Club, serving as first president of both. In 1910 he published *Eternal Verities of Golf*.

While his business leadership was highly important, McAlister is as well known for his service to welfare administration in North Carolina. In 1915–16 he was president of the state's Social Service Conference, and in December 1916 he succeeded his father as a member of the State Board of Charities, which in 1917 was renamed the North Carolina State Board of Charities and Public Welfare. By 1919 he had pioneered on the board the concept of the county-unit plan whereby each of the state's one hundred counties had a separate welfare board. He showed constant and detailed interest in the activities of the state board, where he repeatedly served as vice-chairman under William A. Blair. He especially opposed the action in 1931 of transferring supervision of county jails from the welfare board to the State Highway Commission. Often referred to as the "father of the county welfare system," McAlister was forced by ill health to retire from the state board in 1944. His memory was honored by a portrait presented to the board in 1946 by the North Carolina Association of County Welfare Superintendents.

During World War I McAlister served for one year as fuel administrator for the state. He was active in religious affairs and, while nominally a Presbyterian, preferred to ignore denominational distinctions. He organized the Church-by-the-Side-of-the-Road, Greensboro, which eventually became the nondenominational Community Church known for its community service programs. He also organized and was first president of the Greensboro Council of Catholics, Jews, and Protestants. Constantly attentive to many civic affairs, McAlister was forthright and articulate in his defense of causes in which he believed.

On 11 Apr. 1894 he married Sarah Reid Little, the daughter of Colonel Frank Little of Richmond County. They had six children: Frank Little, who died in 1945; James Worth, who became involved in a general insurance agency in Greensboro; Lacy Little, who became secretary of Pilot Life; Jean Colvin, who became a prominent pediatrician in Greensboro; Alexander Worth, Jr., who entered the oil business in Rockingham; and Flax Reid, who lived with her mother in Greensboro.

Although in declining health, McAlister died unexpectedly while he was designing his 1946 Christmas cards, an annual custom prior to each holiday season. He was buried in Green Hill Cemetery after a funeral at the family home.

SEE: American Historical Society, *North Carolina* (1927); R. D. W. Connor, *North Carolina: Rebuilding an Ancient Commonwealth*, vol. 2 (1929); *Daily Industrial News*, 20 May 1908; Andrew Dobelstein, "The Effects of the Reform Movement on Relief Administration in North Carolina: The Contributions of Alexander Worth McAlister," *South Atlantic Quarterly* 75 (Spring 1976); *Greensboro Daily News*, 15 Aug. 1926, 22 Oct. 1939, 21 Nov. 1946, 13 Aug. 1956; *Greensboro Daily Record*, 7 Mar. 1930, 16 Nov. 1940; Thomas S. Morgan, "A Step toward Altruism" (Ph.D. diss., University of North Carolina, 1969); North Carolina Association of Superintendents of Public Welfare, *Leaders in North Carolina's Public Welfare Program* (1949); *North Carolina Biography*, vols. 4 (1941), 3 (1956); Pilot Life Insurance Company, 75th Anniversary Tribute, 1978; R. C. Price, "Life Insurance in Greensboro," 1921 (typescript, Greensboro Public Library); Raleigh *News*

and Observer, 21 Nov. 1946, 19 Apr., 7 June 1953; *The State*, 12, 19 Dec. 1953.

THOMAS S. MORGAN

McArthur, Neil *(fl. 1764–84)*, Loyalist leader during the American Revolution, moved from his native Scotland to Cross Creek in 1764 and opened a store. When the war began he was a prosperous merchant and planter, owning two plantations and six uncultivated tracts in Cumberland and Bladen counties and wagons and boats for hire. He supplied provisions, camp equipment, and boats to the Loyalists at Moore's Creek Bridge and fought there as a captain. He was imprisoned with other Loyalist leaders for almost three years afterwards. In April 1779, on his way from New York to Georgia, he was captured off the coast of Virginia and confined at Boston for four months. Freed again, he rejoined the British at New York and accompanied Sir Henry Clinton to Charles Town in 1780.

Under Lord Charles Cornwallis's commission McArthur raised the reactivated North Carolina Highlanders, and in 1782 he joined that corps to John Hamilton's Royal North Carolina Regiment. McArthur accompanied the regiment to East Florida in 1782 and to Nova Scotia in 1783. When he moved to Nova Scotia, there were six people in his household. He received one thousand acres at the regimental settlement near Country Harbour and seven hundred acres on Swan Creek in Kings County. McArthur and his family left Nova Scotia in March 1784 to present his compensation claim in London. There he was allowed £2,345 of his £4,056.18 claim.

SEE: British Headquarters Papers, no. 4211, Lawrence Collection, Chipman Papers, and Muster Rolls of North Carolina Highlanders and Royal North Carolina Regiment (Public Archives of Canada); Marion Gilroy, comp., *Loyalists and Land Settlement in Nova Scotia* (1937); Public Record Office, London, AO 12:71, 101, 109, 13:121–22, 130:1259, FO 4:1; Royal North Carolina Regiment Warrant to Survey (Public Archives of Nova Scotia); William L. Saunders, ed., *Colonial Records of North Carolina*, vol. 10 (1890).

CAROLE WATTERSON TROXLER

McAuslan, Alexander *(d. 1793)*, merchant and Loyalist, was a native of Scotland who settled in New Bern several years before the American Revolution. He left for a time in 1775 as tensions mounted. In 1777 the Georgia Revolutionaries confiscated a sloop of which he was half owner because it was carrying provisions to the British garrison at St. Augustine, Fla. McAuslan went to New York in 1777 but returned with the British success in the South. From September 1780 to February 1781, he was inspector of North Carolina refugees under Lord Charles Cornwallis. He was named in the North Carolina Confiscation Act of 1779.

By 1784 McAuslan was in New York. From there he went to New Bern (via Newfoundland and the West Indies) to try to collect some of his debts; however, he was mobbed and did not remain long ashore. He settled at Shelburne, Nova Scotia, in 1785 but took no land. In 1787 he petitioned for five hundred acres on the nearby Tusket River where he intended to build a herring fishery. Although the petition was approved, McAuslan did not remain to take the grant. He returned to North Carolina and resumed trading, largely in cloth. The 1790 census shows that he owned three slaves; the female listed probably was his wife but no children are indicated. He died in Chatham County.

SEE: Chatham County Estates and Alexander McAuslin [sic] Estate Papers (North Carolina State Archives, Raleigh); Walter Clark, ed., State Records of North Carolina, vol. 24 (1905); Petition of Alexander McAuslan, 1787 (Public Archives of Nova Scotia); Public Record Office, London, AO 12:37, 13:80.

CAROLE WATTERSON TROXLER

Macay, Spruce (ca. 1755–29 Feb. 1808), lawyer, judge, and law tutor of Andrew Jackson, was born in the Jersey Settlement on the banks of the Yadkin River in Rowan (now Davidson) County, the son of James Macay, a large landowner and sheriff of Rowan County from 1774 to 1778. His mother's name is not known. After preparing for college at David Caldwell's school in Guilford County, forty miles from Macay's home, he was graduated from the College of New Jersey (now Princeton University) in 1775. Afterwards, he began the study of law in Salisbury, probably under Waightstill Avery whom he had known at Princeton. He was licensed to practice in the several courts of the state in 1778.

Macay's rise to prominence was rapid. In 1779 he was appointed state's attorney, a position he held until 1786. In 1781 he was named one of two commissioners in Rowan County to settle confiscated property; this property formerly belonged to Loyalists and was sold to the highest bidder. In 1783 Macay became attorney and solicitor for Rowan County, and from 1784 to 1785 he served as Salisbury's representative to the House of Commons. In 1782 he was elected judge of the court of oyer and terminer for the Western District, which comprised western North Carolina and the present part of eastern Tennessee. In 1790, when a fourth position was created on the superior court, the state legislature selected Macay to fill it. At that time the superior court was the supreme court of North Carolina. He remained on the bench until his death.

In 1800 the people chose Macay to be one of the Federalist electors. At the electors' meeting in Raleigh to cast their votes for president, Macay was elected chairman.

Possessing large tracts on both sides of the Yadkin River as well as in Tennessee, Macay was one of Rowan's largest landowners. In 1783 he purchased lots 17 and 27 in the western square of Salisbury where the Rowan Public Library now stands. In the purchase he acquired a small law office and a home that belonged to Adlai Osborn, former clerk of the Rowan court and of the Committee of Safety. It was in this little office that Macay taught Andrew Jackson law during 1784 and 1785; it has been claimed that he also taught William R. Davie law here. He sold this property in 1796 to Archibald Henderson, a lawyer and his brother-in-law. Henderson found the law office too small for his needs and erected a larger one on the corner of Church and Fisher streets which still stands. Macay's office was sold by A. H. Boyden, Henderson's grandson, to an entrepreneur who dismantled it and shipped it to Philadelphia for display in the exposition of 1876. It was never seen again.

After selling his town property, Macay probably moved to the plantation he had acquired from Thomas Frohock in 1794. It included 20 slaves and two thousand acres on both sides of Grants Creek near Salisbury; later, Macay owned 111 slaves. The saw- and gristmill that Frohock operated had fallen into decay by the time of the purchase. It was an old mill, having been the site of a muster ground during the Revolution. Macay rebuilt the dam, millpond, and mill which stood until the early twentieth century. The millpond, known for its mosquitoes and ice skating, was drained in 1872 as a health measure.

Macay, who was interested in education, was one of thirty-two trustees appointed for the Salisbury Academy. In the 1784 bill that created the academy, which Macay helped draw up, there was a provision for the establishment of a school for higher learning in North Carolina. That provision of the bill failed to pass but was revived ten years later by William R. Davie and was enacted, thus creating The University of North Carolina.

As mayor of the borough of Salisbury, Macay headed the delegation that welcomed President George Washington on his arrival on 30 May 1791. The original address of welcome read by Macay and the president's response are on display in the Rowan Public Library.

Macay was married twice, the first time to Frances Henderson, daughter of Richard Henderson and sister of Judge Leonard Henderson and of Archibald Henderson; they had one child, Elizabeth, who married William C. Love, a congressman. His second wife was Elizabeth Haynes, of Halifax, by whom he had a daughter and two sons, William and Alfred. Macay was buried with his kin in the old Jersey Meeting House burial ground along the banks of the Yadkin River. There is no marker at his grave.

SEE: John L. Cheney, Jr., ed., North Carolina Government, 1585–1974 (1974); Walter Clark, ed., State Records of North Carolina, vols. 16–24 (1889–1905); Richard A. Harrison, Princetonians, 1769–1775 (1980); Archibald Henderson, "Spruce Macay," Raleigh News and Observer, 15 May 1927; Rowan County Court Minutes, 1771–1808, Deed Books 4, 12–15, 23, and Will Books E, G (Rowan County Courthouse, Salisbury); Jethro Rumple, History of Rowan County (1881); William L. Saunders, ed., Colonial Records of North Carolina, vol. 5 (1887).

JAMES S. BRAWLEY

McBee, Silas (14 Nov. 1853–3 Sept. 1924), editor, architect, and educator, was born in Lincolnton of Scottish ancestry. His father was Vardry Alexander McBee, three times clerk of the Lincoln County Superior Court and an investor in railroads and cotton mills; his mother was Mary Elizabeth Sumner McBee. Silas was educated at Lincolnton Academy and the University of the South at Sewanee, Tenn., where he received a degree in 1876. He later served on the university's board of trustees (1878–86 and 1887–1907). In recognition of his service as an Episcopal layman, editor, and architect of church buildings, the University of the South awarded him an honorary doctor of civil laws degree in 1919.

Before entering the field of religious journalism, McBee devoted himself to educational work in the South. Interested in raising the level of funding for his alma mater, he served as the university's commissioner of endowment from 1891 to 1893. For a time, beginning in 1883, he taught and served as principal of the Fairmount School for girls at Monteagle, Tenn. McBee also traveled in Europe during the 1880s to study cathedral architecture. Returning to the United States, he designed and supervised the building of churches in Houston, Tex., Nashville, Tenn., Lincolnton, N.C., and Florence, S.C. He also designed Walsh Memorial Hall at the University of the South, assisted in planning the bronze of Zebulon Baird Vance for Statuary Hall in the U.S. capitol, and acted as consulting architect with Ralph Adams Cram in planning a cathedral at Manila. He lectured widely on church architecture and contributed to the idea of constructing the Cathedral of St. John in New York and the National Cathedral in Washington, D.C. McBee was associated with the firm of Nixon and McBee of Atlanta, Ga.

In 1896 McBee became editor of *The Churchman*, a leading religious periodical. He held this position until 1912 but still maintained an interest in architecture. In 1913 he founded and became editor of *The Constructive Quarterly*, an interdenominational journal concerned with the discussion of Christian philosophy; he continued as editor until 1923.

In his theology McBee was ecumenical. In 1911 the continuation committee of the Edinburgh Conference sent him on a tour of Europe, Africa, and the Middle East in the interest of Christian unity. McBee's account of his journey, *An Eirenic Itinerary*, relates his travels and interviews with leaders of the Anglican, Greek Orthodox, Roman Catholic, Coptic, Jewish, and Moslem faiths. Through his devotion to the ecumenical movement, he developed many intimate friendships with Anglican and Roman Catholic prelates. McBee served as vice-president of the Brotherhood of St. Andrew and of the Laymen's Missionary Movement. On three occasions he was a delegate to the Quadrennial General Convention of the Episcopal church.

McBee was also interested in foreign missions and the propagation of the social gospel in American politics and international affairs. His correspondents included Albert T. Mahan, Jacob Riis, William Howard Taft, and Theodore Roosevelt. If not a registered Republican, McBee was entirely sympathetic with the Republican party of Roosevelt and Taft and encouraged Roosevelt to broaden the party's base of support in the South.

In his later years, declining health prompted McBee to move from New York to Charleston, S.C., where his daughters Emma Estelle and Mary Virginia Vardrine operated Ashley Hall, a school for girls. He died in Charleston but was buried at University Cemetery, Monteagle, Tenn. McBee was married twice: in 1877 to Mary Estelle Sutton (d. 1891) of Mississippi and, after her death, to Louise J. Post of Great Neck, N.Y.

SEE: "Address Delivered by the Rev. William Haskell DuBose, D.D., at the Memorial Service for the Late Silas McBee. . . ." (manuscript, University of the South Archives, Sewanee, Tenn.); Silas McBee, *An Eirenic Itinerary* (1911); Charleston *News and Courier*, 4 Sept. 1924; Silas McBee Papers (Southern Historical Collection, University of North Carolina, Chapel Hill); *New York Times*, 4 Sept. 1924; *Sewanee Alumni Directory* (1913); William L. Sherrill, *Annals of Lincoln County, North Carolina* (1937); *Who Was Who in America*, vol. 1 (1897–1942).

ALLEN H. STOKES, JR.

McBee, Vardry (19 June 1775–23 Jan. 1864), merchant, farmer, and clerk of county court, was born in Spartanburg District, S.C., the son of Quakers who had moved to the area from Virginia. His father, also named Vardry, was captain of a militia company in the American Revolution though he was a Quaker. McBee left school when he was twelve and worked for six years, then moved to Lincolnton to learn to be a saddler under Joseph Morris, his brother-in-law. He went to Kentucky for a short time with his parents, then to Tennessee, before returning to Lincolnton as co-owner of a store.

About 1805 he sold his interest in the store and bought a farm.

McBee was clerk of the Lincoln County Court from 1812 to 1833. A strong supporter of schools, he helped found and support the Pleasant Retreat Academy for boys and the Lincolnton Female Academy, both in Lincolnton, and served as a trustee. He also was a delegate from Lincoln County to the state Internal Improvement Convention in Raleigh in 1833.

About 1815 McBee bought several thousand acres of land around Greenville, S.C., where he eventually built several flour mills, a paper mill, a cotton factory, and a wool factory. In 1836 he moved to Greenville to be nearer his large holdings of land and mills and to farm. He was active in agricultural organizations and won several prizes for the quality of his farm. In South Carolina McBee owned stock in a number of railroads and was president of the Louisville and Cincinnati Railroad. He continued to support education and religious institutions.

In 1804 McBee married Jane Alexander, the daughter of Colonel Elias Alexander of Rutherford County. They had nine children: Joseph Gallishaw, Malinda Penelope, Silas Leroy, Luther Martin, Hannah Echols, Martha (Patsy) Adeline, Vardry Alexander, William Pinkney, and Alexander. McBee, his wife, and five of their children were buried in the churchyard of Christ Church, Greenville, S.C.

SEE: Alfred Nixon, *In Memoriam: Vardry Alexander McBee, 1818–1904* (1904); William L. Sherrill, *Annals of Lincoln County, North Carolina* (1937).

ALICE R. COTTEN

McBee, Vardry Alexander (17 Apr. 1818–17 Feb. 1904), lawyer, superior court clerk, and promoter of public improvements, was born in Lincolnton of Scottish ancestry. His father was Vardry McBee (1775–1864), a merchant, clerk of the Lincoln County Court, promoter of manufactures, and railroad promoter and president; his mother was Jane Alexander. McBee received his early education at Lincolnton's Pleasant Retreat Academy, of which his father was a founder. He also attended the school of Peter S. Ney. Entering The University of North Carolina in 1837, he was graduated in 1841 with an A.B. degree. Afterwards he studied law and was licensed but he never practiced.

McBee's career followed closely that of his father, although he did not begin as a saddler. For one term he represented Lincoln County in the state legislature. On three occasions, for a total of fourteen years, he served as clerk of the Lincoln County Superior Court. Appointed in 1847, he was elected to a full term in 1849. He was appointed again in 1860 but resigned to run for the legislative seat of John F. Hoke, who was serving in the army. He received his third appointment in 1882 and in the same year was elected to a full term without opposition.

McBee invested in several public improvement projects. He was a principal stockholder of the Western North Carolina plank road from Charlotte to Lincolnton, and he helped to promote the Wilmington, Charlotte and Rutherford Railroad, which he also served as treasurer and master of transportation. He assumed a prominent role in the organization, location, and construction of the Chester and Lenoir Narrow Gauge Railroad and was a director for many years. He was also a stockholder of the Camperdown [Cotton] Mills in Greenville, S.C. In addition, he was a trustee of the male and female academies in Lincolnton that his father had promoted. McBee owned a large plantation near Lincolnton where he bred blooded stock, including cattle, horses, and hogs.

On 16 Dec. 1847 he married Mary Elizabeth Sumner (b. 1829), the daughter of Professor Benjamin Sumner, who was principal of both Lincolnton academies. The McBees had ten children. McBee was buried in the family plot at St. Luke's Episcopal Church, Lincolnton.

SEE: Alfred Nixon, *In Memoriam: Vardry Alexander McBee, 1818–1904* (1904); William L. Sherrill, *Annals of Lincoln County, North Carolina* (1937); James Thomas Williams, Sr., Papers (South Caroliniana Library, University of South Carolina).

ALLEN H. STOKES, JR.

McBrayer, Louis Burgin (*27 Dec. 1868–1 Apr. 1938*), physician, medical administrator, and pioneer in the fight against tuberculosis, was born near Wolf Top Mountain in Buncombe County, the only child of Adolphus and Lou A. Case McBrayer. He attended Venable School (later Montford School) and Newton Academy, both in Asheville, and Judson College in Hendersonville. In 1889 he received an M.D. degree from Louisville Medical College (now the University of Louisville).

Returning to North Carolina, McBrayer was in general practice in Asheville until 1914. During this period he was elected coroner of Buncombe County for three terms (1901–7) and health officer of Asheville (1910–14). Under his leadership, Asheville set up a model Health Department with a laboratory to curb typhoid. McBrayer was also a surgeon at Asheville's Mission Hospital (1904–14) as well as a surgeon for the Southern Railway (1910–14). From 1908 to 1914 he served as president of the State Board of Medical Examiners.

On 2 Apr. 1914 McBrayer moved to Sanatorium (now McCain) to become superintendent of North Carolina's Sanatorium for the Treatment of Tuberculosis and chief of the Bureau of Tuberculosis of the State Board of Health. He held both positions until 1924, when he moved to Southern Pines. In 1915 he organized the North Carolina Tuberculosis Association and was managing director from 1915 to 1937. He was president of the North Carolina State Medical Society in 1915 and of the Southern Conference on Tuberculosis in 1924–25. In 1921 he became secretary of the Medical Society and served until 1937. McBrayer edited the society's annual *Transactions* from 1918 to 1937 as well as the section on North Carolina in *Southern Medicine and Surgery* (1920). He was one of the incorporators of the Hospital Savings Association as a Blue Cross plan in 1935.

McBrayer married Lillian Cordelia (Cordie) Deaver (1867–1921) on 20 July 1890, and they had three children: Reuben Adolphus, Sarah Louise (Sadie Lou) (Mrs. Paul Pressly McCain), and Louis Burgin II. He was a Democrat, a Baptist, and a member of Kiwanis. Also active in the Independent Order of Odd Fellows, he served as chairman of the board of trustees of its home for orphans in Goldsboro and was grand marshal of the Sovereign Lodge in 1933–34. McBrayer was buried in the Bethesda Cemetery, Aberdeen.

SEE: Dorothy Long, ed., *Medicine in North Carolina*, vols. 1–2 (1972); *The Sanatorium Sun*, May 1938; Mrs. Charles R. Whitaker and L. B. McBrayer, *McBrayer Genealogy* (1926); *Who Was Who in America*, vol. 1 (1943).

PAUL M. MCCAIN

McBryde, Archibald (*28 Sept. 1766–15 Feb. 1837*), congressman and state senator, was born in Wigtown, Scotland, the son of James, a farmer, and Janet McMiken McBryde. Because of "the high rent of land," his parents left Scotland in 1775 with their three children, including Archibald, aboard the ship *Jackie* (formerly the *Stanraer*) bound for North Carolina via the port of New York. The family ultimately settled with other Scots in Cumberland County, and young Archibald was working on local roads in Moore County by 1787. The death of his father sometime before 1790 shifted the responsibility for taking care of his mother and three sisters to Archibald's shoulders and probably motivated him to reach out for a better life.

In 1790 McBryde was appointed deputy clerk of Moore County, and two years later he became a justice of the peace and county clerk (1792–1808) by "unanimous choice." His attainment of these positions by the time he was twenty-six indicates that he must have had excellent educational qualifications for the period, despite the almost complete absence of formal schooling in the region. It is probable that he acquired a basic education through disciplined self-study and private tutors and picked up legal training through association with the educated men who frequented the county courthouse in Carthage.

McBryde early became acquainted with the eminent and respected Ramsey family of adjacent Chatham County. On 10 Nov. 1796 he married Lydia Ramsey, the daughter of John and Sarah Birdsong Drake Ramsey, widow of Matthew Drake. John Ramsey, who was then county clerk of Chatham County, had performed invaluable intelligence services for Governor Thomas Burke of North Carolina during the American Revolution. Young Archibald's association with the Ramseys helped to widen his circle of friends and gain political support from the leading men of the area. Two years after his marriage, he joined Aaron Tyson and Murdock McKenzie in a business partnership selling dry goods under the name of its major stockholder, Aaron Tyson and Company. The firm was highly interested in the development of cheap transportation to expand inland markets from the deep water ports along the coast and invested in the Deep and Haw River Navigation Company and the Cape Fear River Navigation Company to achieve these ends. Periodic lotteries were held to gain public support and capital for these developments but with only limited success. After Tyson's death in 1805, the firm operated under the name of Murdock McKenzie and Company until 1811, when Aaron's son, William Tyson, joined the partnership and it became McKenzie, Tyson and Company. Over time, the business prospered and acquired considerable real estate from debtors who were unable to settle their accounts in any other way. In turn, this land was leased out to others for farming, and the firm began to expand into agriculture.

Despite his business interests, McBryde's primary love was the law, and he developed a successful practice as a lawyer. In 1806 the North Carolina Assembly voted him one of the six state solicitors in the judicial system. This position required considerable travel within the state and increased McBryde's opportunities for making new friends and sampling popular opinion. The political scene of the day had crystallized into two factions—Republicans and Federalists—and in the Fayetteville Congressional District, of which Chatham and Moore counties were a part, the sentiment was almost solidly Federalist. McBryde found common cause with these people, who were mostly small farmers and merchants, a large number of them being Presbyterian Scots whose background and life-style were staunchly conservative. Many of these Scots remembered well their Tory heritage during the American Revolution and, in their eyes, the prominent Republicans of the day were the same anti-Tory radicals who had opposed them in earlier and more bitter days. The Republicans were identified with support for France and the republicanism, liberty, and democracy of the French Revolution. The Federalists, including these Scots, saw this support as the beginning of anarchy, atheism, and poverty and concluded that Great Britain was the only power that could save the United States from the radical ideas of the French Republic. The conservative bent of the Fayetteville District was incompatible with the new Jeffersonian philosophy of equality, and aversion to Jefferson's Embargo Act of 1807 hurried Federalists into Congress.

In 1808 and again in 1810, McBryde was elected from the Fayetteville District on the Federalist ticket and took his seat in the U.S. House of Representatives. For four years (1809–13), he joined other North Carolinians in Congress to vote against President James Madison's restrictive foreign trade policies and took steps to obstruct efforts of those who were rushing the country into war. On 4 June 1812, when the formal war declaration against Great Britain passed the House, Archibald McBryde was one of a small minority to vote against it. Even after the war began, he voted against measures to continue the conflict.

During North Carolina's political campaign of 1812, McBryde espoused the platform of the "Peace party," which promised no tax increases and an immediate end to the war. The movement was not overwhelmingly popular at the time, but it did bring about the election of a few candidates in the Federalist strongholds, including McBryde, who won a seat from Moore County in the state senate (1813–14). He continued to oppose the war in this capacity until 1814 and the coming of peace. From this time, the Federalists became a defunct political organization.

After leaving the senate, McBryde resumed his law practice. In 1818 he was nominated to fill the vacancy left by Thomas Ruffin on the North Carolina Superior Court; however, he withdrew his name from consideration on learning that his longtime friend, Archibald D. Murphey, had also been nominated for the post.

When McBryde's mercantile partner, Murdock McKenzie, died in 1823, no effort was made to continue the business, which by now had amassed considerable real estate in both Moore and Chatham counties. Over the next few years, McBryde continued to work in the legal profession and became involved in several drawn-out cases involving both the private affairs of his clients and estate entanglements stemming from his business partnerships. Many of these remained in litigation for several years after his death.

McBryde was a Presbyterian and though ardently proud of his Scottish ancestry, he was devoted to his adopted country. One of his favorite pastimes involved the collection of historical material about the Scots in North Carolina during the American Revolution. In 1822 he made an effort to obtain the diary of David Fanning, a Tory leader in Chatham and Randolph counties during 1780–82, but was curtly rebuffed in this attempt by Fanning himself, who escaped and went to East Florida in 1782. McBryde intended to publish his collections but died at his home, The Grange, near Carbonton before he could complete the task. (Information relating to the date of his death is contradictory. The tombstone inscription of Archibald McBryde in the Farrar Cemetery in Lee County gives 15 Feb. 1836; however, several

documents in the North Carolina Supreme Court records indicate that he was alive as late as September 1836. A statement by his wife, written in June 1841, notes that her husband died in the "month of February 1837.") In 1844 his widow moved to Madison County, Tenn., and settled on land that had been willed to her by her father.

Archibald and Lydia McBryde had eleven children who lived beyond infancy: Jannet (m. William L. Hays), Ann (m. first the Reverend Kenneth McIver and second Green Womack), Mary (m. first Benjamin W. Williams, son of Governor Benjamin Williams of North Carolina, and second Dr. Charles Chalmers), James (unmarried), Eliza W. (m. first Dr. Archibald L. McQueen and second James T. DeJarnett), Frances (m. William P. DeJarnett), John R. (unmarried), Sarah T. (m. James Alston), William M. (m. Sarah Grigsby), Archibald, and Sarah T.

SEE: Eli W. Caruthers, *Revolutionary Incidents and Sketches of Character Chiefly in the "Old North State"* (1854); Walter Clark, ed., *State Records of North Carolina*, vols. 14–15, 19, 22 (1896–1907); Deed Books, 1794–1849, Estate Records on Archibald McBryde, Inferior Court Minutes of May 1837 Session, and Wills of Archibald McBryde and John Ramsey (Chatham County Courthouse, Pittsboro); Letters from Archibald McBryde to Archibald D. Murphey in the Archibald D. Murphey Papers and North Carolina Supreme Court Cases 1720, 3193, 3908, 3999, 7605 (North Carolina State Archives, Raleigh); Raleigh *Register*, 25 Aug. 1808, 23 Aug. 1810; William L. Saunders, ed., *Colonial Records of North Carolina*, vol. 9 (1890); Francis C. Symonds, *Descendants of Four Members of the First Colony of Virginia* (1964).

BENJAMIN RANSOM MCBRIDE

McCain, Hugh White (27 Feb. 1882–3 Oct. 1922), physician and surgeon, was born in Waxhaw, the fifth son of William Johnson and Mary Jane Walker McCain. He received his early education in the Waxhaw public schools and studied for a year at Presbyterian College in Clinton, S.C. Transferring to The University of North Carolina, he received a B.A. degree in 1906 and then attended the university's two-year medical school. He completed his medical training at Jefferson Medical College in Philadelphia and was awarded an M.D. degree in 1909. For eighteen months following graduation, McCain was a resident physician in Philadelphia's Polyclinic Hospital.

In 1911 McCain moved to High Point to become an associate of Dr. J. R. Reitzel in the practice of medicine. After Reitzel's death in 1914, he formed a partnership with Dr. J. T. Burrus; together they established the High Point Hospital, which by 1922 had become known by the name of the two owners, Burrus-McCain, and had grown to a capacity of sixty beds. McCain was considered to be an able physician and a skilled surgeon. Beyond that, he was soon recognized as a man of fine character and a citizen who was committed to the welfare of his fellowmen and his community.

During the war years, McCain was a member of the medical examining board for his district. Professionally, he belonged to the Guilford County Medical Society, North Carolina State Medical Society, Tri-State Medical Association, Southern Medical Association, and American Medical Association. He also was a member of the Guilford County Board of Health. In civic and church affairs, McCain was active in the High Point Kiwanis Club and served on the Board of Stewards of the Wesley Memorial Methodist Episcopal Church.

McCain died from a streptococcal infection. The funeral services were conducted by his pastor, the Reverend W. A. Lambeth, and the Reverend Charles P. Coble of High Point's First Presbyterian Church. Interment was in Oakwood Cemetery. He was survived by his wife, Alma Cunningham McCain, whom he had married in 1912, and their young daughter, Alma Virginia. Tributes subsequently published in the newspaper and in medical society journals attest to his contributions to North Carolina and to his adopted city. The memorial resolution of the state Medical Society notes that as a physician and surgeon, he had few equals.

SEE: J. J. Farris, ed., *High Point, North Carolina, in Word and Picture* (1916 [portrait]); *High Point Enterprise*, 4 Oct. 1922 (portrait); Madeline McCain, telephone interview, 1 Sept. 1979; Holt McPherson, correspondence, 23 July, 1 Aug. 1979; *Southern Medicine and Surgery* 84 (1922); *Transactions of the North Carolina Medical Society*, 70th sess. (1923).

J. ISAAC COPELAND

McCain, Paul Pressly (26 June 1884–25 Nov. 1946), physician and leader in the fight against tuberculosis, was born and educated in Due West, S.C., the son of John Irenaeus and Lula Todd McCain. He received an A.B. degree from Erskine College in 1906 and an honorary LL.D. degree from The University of North Carolina in 1936.

In the hope of becoming a medical missionary, McCain taught school for a year after graduation but found that he could not save enough to pay the costs of his medical education. Instead, he borrowed funds and received an M.D. degree at the University of Maryland in 1911. During his internship at Baltimore's Bay View Hospital, he contracted tuberculosis but was able to finish his appointment. After a second flare-up of the disease, he entered Gaylor Farm Sanatorium in Connecticut in 1912 and later took a position on its staff.

In 1914 McCain accepted an appointment as chief of medical service and assistant superintendent of the North Carolina Sanatorium. In 1924 he became superintendent and medical director of the sanatorium and director of its extension service. As the leader of North Carolina's fight against tuberculosis, he was also in charge of the Western Sanatorium when it opened in 1936 and the Eastern Sanatorium in 1941. In addition, McCain was one of the incorporators of the Hospital Savings Association as a Blue Cross plan in 1935, as well as a leader in the effort to expand The University of North Carolina's School of Medicine to a four-year program.

Professionally, he was a Fellow of the American College of Physicians, Diplomat of the American Board of Internal Medicine, and member of the Subcommittee on Tuberculosis of the National Research Council. In 1935 he was elected president of the North Carolina Medical Society. He served as president of the Southern Tuberculosis Conference and held various offices in the National Tuberculosis Association, becoming president for the period 1940–41.

On 17 Oct. 1917 McCain married Sarah Louis (Sadie Lou) McBrayer. They were greatly beloved by people throughout the state because of their personal consideration of patients in the sanatorium. Mrs. McCain herself was a leader. In 1923 she helped organize the Auxiliary to the North Carolina Medical Society and served as its first president. The McCains had five children: Sarah Louise (Mrs. N. H. McCollum, Jr.), Paul Pressly, Jr., Lillian Irene (Mrs. Dan McFarland), John Lewis, and Jane Todd (Mrs. John Reagan).

McCain was a Democrat, an elder in the Presbyterian church, a Mason, and a member of Kiwanis and Sigma Xi; he served as a trustee of Flora MacDonald College. He was buried in the Bethesda Cemetery, Aberdeen. After his death, the town of Sanatorium was renamed McCain in his honor.

SEE: Dorothy Long, ed., *Medicine in North Carolina*, vols. 1–2 (1972); *North Carolina Medical Journal* (December 1946, November 1947, January 1949); *Sanatorium Sun* (Sanatorium, N.C.), January 1949; *Who Was Who in America*, vol. 2 (1950).

PAUL M. MCCAIN

McCall, Adeline Denham (11 Nov. 1901–15 Feb. 1989), music teacher, was born in Denver, Colo., the daughter of Frank S. and Helene Hanigan Denham. She spent part of her youth in California and in England. When Adeline was twelve, her mother, a professional singer, died, and she went to Grand Forks, N.D., to live with her aunt, Jean Hanigan Koch, and uncle, Professor Frederick Koch. In 1918 they all moved to Chapel Hill when Koch joined the faculty of The University of North Carolina. Adeline attended the University of Denver in 1918–19 and was graduated with honors from The University of North Carolina in 1922. She went to Baltimore to study piano at the Peabody Institute, then returned to Chapel Hill and worked for a time with the Extension Division.

Giving up her ambition to become a concert pianist, Adeline chose instead to teach music and to compose for the symphony. She continued her education at the Seymour School in New York, the Juilliard School of Music, and L'École Normale in Paris; she also was a student of Johanna Gjerulff in Dalcroze eurythmics and improvisation. She was music supervisor in the public schools of Chapel Hill and Carrboro for thirty years and was on the faculty of Duke University for seventeen years; at Duke she taught music education and music history. She also held music workshops throughout the United States and pioneered in creative techniques for music education. While working with day-care centers and kindergartens in Connecticut and New York, she produced children's radio programs for the WJZ Blue network.

Mrs. McCall was one of the founders of the North Carolina Symphony in the early 1930s and helped establish the symphony's education program. For many years she also played the timpani in the University Symphony Orchestra. In 1949 she received an M.A. degree in musicology from The University of North Carolina. She was the author of an extensive series of booklets used by teachers to prepare children for the arrival of the symphony in their towns. Her *Symphony Stories* (1945–49) were eagerly used by young people across the state as they learned the instruments and to appreciate and enjoy good music. Mrs. McCall composed some of the music for Paul Green's outdoor dramas, notably *The Lost Colony* (1938) and *The Common Glory* (1951). Among her other published works were *Adventures with Music and Musicians* (1935), *Adventures with the Opera* (1940), and *Music in America* (1944).

In 1980 Adeline McCall received the North Carolina Distinguished Service Award for Women from the Chi Omega sorority and in 1981 she was the recipient of the North Carolina Award in Fine Arts; she also received other tokens of appreciation from the people of the state. She was married to Frederick B. McCall, professor of law at The University of North Carolina; they had no children.

SEE: *Chapel Hill Weekly,* 17 Nov. 1963; Friends of the North Carolina Symphony, *Crescendo* (Summer 1989); Daniel L. Grant, *Alumni History of the University of North Carolina, 1795–1924* (1924); Fred Koch, Jr., and William J. Koch to William S. Powell, [May 1989]; *The North Carolina Award* (1981).

WILLIAM S. POWELL

McCall, Frederick Bays *(7 Oct. 1893–8 Apr. 1973),* professor of law, was born in Charlotte, the son of Johnston Davis and Sallie Lee Nooe McCall. His father was a leading member of the Mecklenburg County bar for a half century and at one time served as mayor of Charlotte. Young McCall entered The University of North Carolina in 1911 and received an A.B. degree in the classics in 1914. Following graduation he taught Latin and mathematics in the Charlotte High School. In 1918 he resigned his teaching position to become assistant secretary of the Charlotte Chamber of Commerce. Some months later, he was elected principal of the Charlotte High School; he served in that post for two years before returning to Chapel Hill to study law.

After one year of formal study, McCall passed the bar examination and began to practice law with his father in Charlotte. In a few months, he accepted a position at the university teaching Latin. While on campus, he also attended classes in the law school. At the end of the year, he returned to Charlotte to resume the practice of law with his father. In 1926, when the dean of the law school became ill, The University of North Carolina asked McCall to pinch-hit for him. Dean Lucius Mc-Gehee died shortly thereafter and McCall was chosen to replace him on the faculty.

In 1927–28 he took a leave of absence to attend Yale Law School, where he completed his work for the J.D. degree in 1928. This was a vintage year in the life of Fred McCall. Returning to Chapel Hill, he married Adeline Denham, the niece of Professor Frederick H. Koch, who founded the Carolina Playmakers. Thus he began his thirty-eight-year career as a permanent member of the law school faculty and his forty-five-year marriage to a talented teacher of music.

At the law school, McCall first taught courses in common-law pleading, torts, damages, sales, domestic relations, equity, corporations, and civil procedure. Later he specialized in the field of property, including real property, personal property, titles, wills and administration, and future interests.

A crowning achievement in his career was the enactment of a new Intestate Succession Act in 1959 by the North Carolina General Assembly. The impetus for this legislation began in 1933 when changes were recommended by McCall and Allen Langston, a former student, in an article published in the *North Carolina Law Review.* This led to the authorization of a study commission by the General Assembly in 1935 on which McCall served at the appointment of Governor J. C. B. Ehringhaus. The commission, which was chaired by Senator Carl L. Bailey, produced far-ranging proposals to reform the law of intestate succession, administration of estates, wills, and guardianships. A 195-page bill passed the senate but failed enactment by a single vote in the house of representatives. Rather than returning to the drafting board, McCall went back to the classroom to teach more students about the need for law reform. In

1957 the General Assembly appropriated funds to enable the General Statutes Commission to recommend changes in the laws relating to intestate succession. The commission appointed McCall, Professor Norman A. Wiggins of the Wake Forest Law School, and Professor W. Bryan Bolich of the Duke University Law School as a special committee to prepare new legislation. The work of the committee was approved by the General Statutes Commission and submitted to the General Assembly. This time the legislature was prepared to adopt a modern law of intestate succession, which included equal inheritance rights for women among its many salient features, and the bill passed without difficulty.

In 1961 the General Statutes Commission again called upon McCall, Wiggins, and Bolich to produce proposals for a new law on the estates of missing persons. Based on the recommendations of the special committee and the General Statutes Commission, a new law was enacted in 1965. In the latter year, the special committee turned its attention to the complex task of revising the law on the administration of estates. McCall was the only member of the original committee to serve until this work was completed. In 1974 the General Assembly, with minor exceptions, approved the proposed legislation of more than one hundred pages.

McCall was a careful thinker and wrote with clarity, precision, and accuracy. His articles for the *North Carolina Law Review,* beginning with volume 1 in 1922 and concluding with volume 44 in 1966, were solid and substantial contributions to legal scholarship. These included "Appellate Practice and Procedure in North Carolina" (vol. 7, 1928), "The Family Automobile" (vol. 8, 1930), "The Torrens System—After Thirty-five Years" (vol. 10, 1932), "A New Intestate Succession Statute for North Carolina (with Allen Langston; vol. 11, 1933), "The Destructibility of Contingent Remainders in North Carolina" (vol. 16, 1937), "Estates on Condition and on Special Limitation in North Carolina" (vol. 19, 1941), "Some Problems in Administration of Estates" (vol. 35, 1957), "North Carolina's New Intestate Succession Act" (vol. 39, 1960), and "Estates of Missing Persons in North Carolina" (vol. 44, 1966).

Through unwavering interest and devotion, and a sustained and painstaking approach, McCall was for many years the premier authority on North Carolina law in the fields of real property, wills, and decedents' estates. He was a member of the Order of the Coif, Phi Delta Phi, Sigma Chi, and Phi Mu Alpha. In 1971 four hundred attorneys in the state awarded him the Silver Urn in recognition of his achievements in teaching, research, and public service relating to the law of real property.

Fred McCall had a great capacity for loyal friendships. A gentle man, he could be firm in expressing his thoughts on controversial matters but always sought ways to avoid giving personal offense. He was a talented musician, and his performance as a timpanist graced many a symphonic concert. Love of music was a bond he shared with his wife, Adeline. He was buried in Chapel Hill where he worked and lived for fifty-two of his seventy-nine years.

SEE: Jacques Cattell, ed., *Directory of American Scholars,* vol. 4 (1963); Records, Alumni Office and Office of the Secretary of the Faculty (University of North Carolina, Chapel Hill).

WILLIAM B. AYCOCK

McCallum, James *(2 Oct. 1806–16 Sept. 1889),* public official, lawyer, and farmer, was born in Robeson County, the son of Daniel and Sarah Smith McCallum. The extent of his education is unknown. On 14 Feb. 1829 he married Elizabeth Brown, and they became the parents of eleven children: an infant son unnamed, Daniel Jerome, Katherine, Mary Elizabeth, James Joseph, Sarah Anne, William Hugh, John Neill, George Burder, another infant who died, and Neill Brown. By the 1820s the McCallum family was living in Pulaski, Tenn., as in 1828 he was recorded as a Master Mason in the lodge there. The 1860 census listed him as the owner of twenty-five slaves and property valued at $46,000.

McCallum practiced law in Pulaski from 1842 to 1861, and for a time he was also clerk and master of Chancery. Originally a Whig and a Unionist, he became a Secessionist at the time of Tennessee's secession from the Union. In 1861 he was elected to represent Giles County in the General Assembly, and in 1863 he was elected to the Confederate Congress where he served on the committees on Accounts, the Medical Department, and Post Offices and Post Roads. McCallum introduced resolutions advocating government seizure of all vital railroads, the impressment of all gold and silver plate, and the reduction of currency to be followed by a new issue of treasury notes. His voting record suggests that he wanted the Confederacy to use every possible resource in the prosecution of the war.

At the end of the Civil War, McCallum returned to Pulaski. In 1870 he became a director of the Pulaski Savings Bank. He was also a ruling elder of the Presbyterian church, a Sunday school teacher, and superintendent of the Sunday school. His *Brief Sketch of the Settlement and Early History of Giles County* was published in 1876. He was buried in Maplewood Cemetery, Pulaski.

SEE: Thomas B. Alexander and Richard E. Beringer, *The Anatomy of the Confederate Congress: A Study of the Influences of Member Characteristics on Legislative Voting Behavior, 1861–1865* (1972); *Biographical Directory of the Tennessee General Assembly, 1796–1967* (1968); *Journal of the Congress of the Confederate States of America,* vol. 7 (1905); *Pulaski Citizen,* 19 Sept. 1889; Ezra J. Warner and W. Buck Yearns, *Biographical Register of the Confederate Congress* (1975).

RICHARD W. PARRIS

McClammy, Charles Washington *(29 May 1839–26 Feb. 1896),* Confederate officer, congressman, legislator, and farmer, was born at Scotts Hill, a farming community on the New Hanover–Pender County line, the son of Luke S. and Anna Chadwick McClammy. His father and grandfather were planters who held land granted in the eighteenth century. After attending Scotts Hill Academy, McClammy was graduated from The University of North Carolina in 1859. He taught at and became principal of the Black River school in Pender County. In 1860 he married Margaret Fennell, whose father was sheriff and a political leader of New Hanover County.

With the coming of the Civil War, McClammy helped organize a Confederate unit which became Company A of the Third North Carolina Cavalry. He was a captain from September 1863 and a major after December 1864. He served in eastern North Carolina, particularly around New Bern, until May 1864, when his unit was sent to join the Army of Northern Virginia. Following engagements there, his troops disbanded on the road to Appomattox Courthouse in the spring of 1865.

As a Democrat, McClammy represented New Han-

over County in the North Carolina General Assembly between December 1866 and March 1867 and was a member of the state senate in the session of 1870–72 which impeached Governor William Woods Holden. He was elected by large majorities to the Fiftieth and Fifty-first Congress, serving from 1887 to 1891, but was defeated for reelection in 1890 by Benjamin F. Grady of Duplin County, a classmate at The University of North Carolina. McClammy returned to the family farm and was killed a few years later when a steam boiler exploded. He was buried in the local family cemetery near Scotts Hill.

SEE: *Biog. Dir. Am. Cong.* (1971); John L. Cheney, ed., *North Carolina Government, 1585–1974* (1974); *Nat. Cyc. Am. Biog.,* vol. 9 (1907 [portrait]).

ROY PARKER, JR.

McClure, Albert Bonner *(16 June 1905–28 Oct. 1972),* Presbyterian minister, youth worker, and orphanage superintendent, was born in Toccoa, Ga., the son of William and Kate Heidt Bonner McClure. At the time of his birth, his father was county sheriff, but he soon began sawmilling in northern Georgia and the family moved from place to place. By the time Albert was twelve, his parents had separated and his mother took the younger children to Sautee, Ga., so they could attend a Presbyterian church school. At her death Albert and two siblings were entered in the boarding department of the Nacoochee Institute by the superintendent, Dr. John Knox Coit. Albert was graduated in 1927 and in the fall entered Davidson College. There he joined the college Presbyterian church and became a candidate for the ministry. In his junior year he became student pastor of the Davidson Chapel, where he organized young people's groups and began to build a church. As a student he was a member of several fraternal and scholastic organizations and held various class offices. At his graduation in 1931, he was elected by the faculty to receive the Algernon Sidney Sullivan Award for his selfless service to the community.

McClure entered Union Theological Seminary in Virginia in the fall of 1931, served as assistant pastor at churches in Petersburg and Rapidan, and was graduated in 1934. Returning to Davidson College, he became YMCA secretary and in 1935 married Mary McGehee of Atlanta. In the summers of 1935 and 1936 he worked with youths at camps in the mountains of North Carolina. He was ordained at Davidson in the spring of 1936 and the following year became pastor of the Presbyterian church in Lincolnton where he served both the church and the community in many capacities, particularly with young people. In 1945 he became pastor of the Presbyterian church at Valdese, continuing much the same kind of work as before. Here he also became interested in the history of the Waldensian community and named a committee to collect, arrange, and preserve records, artifacts, and other sources of local history. A building for this purpose was constructed near the church.

In 1950 McClure became superintendent of the Barium Springs Home for Children, a position he filled effectively for over sixteen years. During this period he introduced new concepts of child care and expanded the physical facilities. Under his guidance, the children and young people at the home were integrated into the life of the community; they attended local public schools and participated in a wide range of activities. On leaving Barium Springs, McClure became pastor of a church in nearby Statesville and served until his retirement. Continuing to live in Statesville, he was a hospital chaplain, organized the ministry, worked on committees, and participated in other activities where he could be useful. Although a registered Democrat, he prided himself on voting for candidates and issues rather than by party. In 1965 Davidson College awarded him a doctor of divinity degree.

McClure and his wife Mary had four children: Mary Emma, Albert B., Jr., Beverly Kate, and Emily Sue. He was buried in Oakwood Cemetery, Statesville.

SEE: Doris Brown, Historian, Davidson Chapel, personal contact; Frank C. Brown to Albert B. McClure (14 Oct. 1936), Ben R. Lacy to Albert B. McClure (27 Oct. 1936), and Taliaferro Thompson to Albert B. McClure (26 Oct. 1936) (possession of Mary McClure, Statesville); Lincolnton *Lincoln Times*, July 1945; Statesville High School *Blue and Gray* [monthly newspaper], 21 Nov. 1972; Frank C. Wilkinson, Pastor, Calvary Church (1937), personal contact.

MARY MCCLURE
NEILL R. MCGEACHY

McClure, Alexander Doak (9 July 1850–6 Apr. 1920), Presbyterian clergyman, was born at Lewisburg, Tenn., the son of Robert Green and Mary Elizabeth Ewing McClure. He attended the College of New Jersey (now Princeton University), receiving a B.A. in 1874 and an M.A. in 1877, and later enrolled at Princeton Theological Seminary where he was graduated in 1879.

During the school year of 1874–75, McClure acted as principal of Jones Academy in Maury County, Tenn. North Mississippi Presbytery ordained him to the work of the gospel ministry on 15 Apr. 1878. He was stated supply of the Presbyterian church at Oxford, Miss., from 1877 to 1880 and then served successively as pastor of the Bardstown, Ky., Church (1880–82), the Highland Church of Louisville, Ky. (1882–88), and the Maryland Avenue Church of Baltimore, Md. (1888–91). In the latter year McClure accepted a call to St. Andrew's Presbyterian Church in Wilmington, N.C., where he remained until his death twenty-nine years later.

In Wilmington his ministry reached beyond the bounds of his congregation, though he served it devotedly. McClure was known and beloved for his calls on the town's businesses which he made every Monday, his teaching at the YMCA, his contacts as chaplain of the Seaman's Bethel, his work at the James Walker Memorial Hospital, his visits to area prison camps, and his preaching at various points throughout the surrounding region. The community's wide affection for him was evident at the time of his funeral, when thousands of people, unable to gain entrance into the church, stood outside in the street during the service. Moreover, twelve trucks were required to carry the floral arrangements from the church to the cemetery where he was buried.

McClure was a delegate to the meeting of the Alliance of Reformed Churches held in Belfast, Ireland, in 1884 and moderator of the Synod of North Carolina in 1896. He received an honorary D.D. degree from Davidson College in 1901. In addition to various contributions to the religious press, he was the author of *Another Comforter*, a devotional volume published in 1897 by Fleming H. Revell Company.

On 31 Dec. 1878 he married Louise Bergman Miller of Oxford, Miss. They had three children: Eunice, Alexander Miller, and Ewing Girham; the first and third child died in infancy. His wife died in 1886. On 27 Mar. 1888 he married Frances Roberta Callaway of New Castle, Ky., and they became the parents of a son, Robert Edwin, and a daughter, Elizabeth Lyle (Mrs. D. P. McGeachy, Jr.). McClure died at Mount Olive and was buried in Oakdale Cemetery, Wilmington. His portrait is in St. Andrew's–Covenant Presbyterian Church of Wilmington.

SEE: Joseph Akerman and others, *In Memoriam: Alexander Doak McClure, D.D.* (n.d.); *Minutes of the Synod of North Carolina*, 1920; Multivolume journal of Alexander Doak McClure (Archives of the Presbyterian and Reformed Churches, Montreat); Princeton Theological Seminary, *Bulletin: Necrological Record*, August 1921; Princeton University, Class of 1874, *Semi-Centennial Record*.

THOMAS H. SPENCE, JR.

McClure, James Gore King, Jr. (28 Oct. 1884–17 June 1956), Presbyterian minister and president of the Farmers Federation Cooperative, was born in Lake Forest, Ill. His ancestors came to the United States in 1801 from County Armagh, Ireland, where they had earlier fled to avoid persecution in Scotland. His father, James Gore King McClure, served for twenty-five years as pastor of the Lake Forest Presbyterian Church and intermittently as president of Lake Forest College; from 1905 to 1929 he served as the first president of McCormick Theological Seminary in Chicago.

Young McClure was educated at Lake Forest Academy, graduating at age fifteen. Believing he was too young to enter college, his father arranged for him to spend a year on the XIT Ranch in the Texas Panhandle, where he established a reputation as an expert bronc buster. He subsequently returned east and entered Yale University, where he was graduated in 1906. Afterwards he studied theology for a year at New College in Edinburgh, Scotland, before earning a divinity degree from McCormick Seminary. He then served for a year as pastor of a small church in Iron River, Mich. After leaving that position for further study abroad, McClure became seriously ill and for the next three years limited his activities to traveling and working on an orange grove in Arizona.

In his study of theology, McClure had been greatly influenced by the social gospel movement. Leaders of the movement, such as Walter Rauschenbusch, sought to convince young clergymen that they should seek solutions to pressing social problems rather than strictly ministering to the "spiritual needs" of their parishioners. The social gospel movement inculcated a focus on the material difficulties faced by the poor, the oppressed, and the disadvantaged. It was characterized by a belief that only when steps were taken to alleviate those difficulties would the people oppressed by them be able to benefit fully from the spiritual aspect of Christian ministry.

In 1916 McClure married Elizabeth Skinner Cramer of Lake Forest, and they became the parents of James Gore King III and Elizabeth (Mrs. James Clarke). On their wedding trip, the couple went to Asheville, N.C. Attracted by the beauty and the healthful climate of western North Carolina, the McClures purchased the former Sherrill's Stagecoach Inn, located in Fairview Township, Buncombe County.

As they began to restore the house and operate the farm, McClure soon became aware of the harsh life and almost insurmountable obstacles faced by the farm families of the region. The largely underdeveloped transportation system, the minimal availability of mechanized equipment, the severe erosion problems created by years of improper methods of cultivation, the unavailability of markets for farm produce, and other conditions combined to make life on the mountain farm exceedingly difficult. Out of McClure's firsthand experience with these conditions grew a lifelong career dedicated to their alleviation.

In 1920 McClure and several neighboring farmers formed the Federation of Farmers of Fairview, with McClure as president. After constructing a warehouse at the nearest railroad siding, the federation began to purchase supplies in bulk and to seek better markets for its members' produce and livestock. The cooperative's rapid success attracted the attention of farmers in other sections of the county, and within the next two years, warehouses were constructed in two other communities, the name of the organization was changed to the Farmers Federation Cooperative, and a marketing department was opened in Asheville. In 1925, with a gift of $25,000 from Dr. E. W. Grove, a wealthy real estate investor in Asheville, and a matching amount raised by Asheville merchants, the federation constructed a larger marketing and storage facility in Asheville with space for its expanding central office. By that year the federation was doing more than a half-million dollars worth of business annually and had expanded to five locations. A disastrous fire in 1925 destroyed the new facility, but through the perseverance of its officers, the federation was able to replace it and to extend its operations into Rutherford and Polk counties.

Despite the enormous initial success of the federation, McClure soon realized that, given the limited financial resources of its members, the progress to be achieved through cooperative efforts alone would be limited as well. The willingness of Dr. Grove and the citizens of Asheville to support the federation's activities led him to seek other sources of outside financial assistance. In 1927, with a gift from George Vanderbilt's widow, McClure created the Farmers Federation Educational and Development Fund. Much of the fund's support came from local sources, but McClure soon took his appeal annually to cities like New York, Pittsburgh, and Detroit. There he was able to attract the backing of prominent industrial and financial leaders such as Thomas K. Watson of the International Business Machines Corporation and Henry Ford.

Drawing on the contributions to the fund, McClure embarked on an ambitious program to expand the federation's activities. An experimental sweet potato curing house was constructed in Polk County, and a poultry improvement program was initiated and carried on for many years. The federation also hired a poultry specialist to work with its members and to build both a hatchery and a poultry dressing plant. In 1930 the fund sponsored a drive to raise the capital to construct the first burley tobacco warehouse in Asheville. At the same time, the federation encouraged its members to produce burley tobacco, making available information on the cultivation and curing process and the supplies necessary for its production. Those early efforts helped lay the foundation for what became a flourishing sector of the region's agricultural economy.

During the depression, the resources of the fund enabled the federation to weather the financial crisis and, remarkably enough, to expand with warehouses and new members in Burke, Haywood, Jackson, Macon, McDowell, Cherokee, Transylvania, Caldwell, Swain, and Yancey counties. Also during the thirties, the federation established a Religious Department to develop programs for the support of the rural church. One of its most enduring programs was the Lord's Acre Plan, whereby the members of a participating church dedicated a portion of the proceeds of a particular crop to the church or joined together in raising a crop for the same purpose. Over time, this enabled thousands of small churches to strengthen both their financial and their cooperative foundations. Beginning with 6 churches, the plan expanded to more than 1,000 by 1940; by 1954 the director estimated that it was being used by over 15,000 churches, many of them in foreign countries.

With the aid of the fund, the federation also established during the 1930s a Forest Products Department to market timber for its members and to encourage members to adopt sound forestry practices. Another project resulted in the erection of a vegetable cannery in Henderson County that helped lay the base for a flourishing vegetable industry in the region.

McClure saw education of its membership as one of the primary goals of the federation. Thus, early on the federation began to publish and distribute to members a monthly newspaper, the *Farmers Federation News*. The paper was filled with articles about programs initiated by the fund and the federation and also contained general articles on agricultural subjects. Beginning in 1935, the federation sponsored an annual picnic in each county where it operated. These picnics were daylong affairs, regularly attracting large crowds. Music and other entertainment, provided primarily by local people, were interspersed with educational programs designed to acquaint members with the federation's activities and to impart information about progressive farming methods.

Drawing on the fund's resources and a gift from E. Parmalee Prentice of Williamstown, Mass., McClure established during the 1940s a dairy herd improvement program that helped create the base for a thriving dairy industry in the region. Dairy specialists were hired to work with the members of the cooperative, and a breeding program was developed with federation's purchase of several quality bulls. The federation also spearheaded the development in the Southeast of artificial breeding of dairy cows, operating the Southeastern Artificial Breeding Service, which served all of North Carolina and parts of other southern states. A cooperative dairy processing plant was built in the late forties to market members' production.

During the 1950s western North Carolina, like much of the rest of the nation, witnessed a rapid decline in its farm population. As more and more small farms were consolidated or abandoned, the federation's base of local support began to erode. Those who carried on McClure's work after his death in 1956 arranged to merge the federation with a larger statewide cooperative in order to adjust to the situation. A dissident group prevented this and operated the business until 1960, when it was forced into bankruptcy. The fund, which had been organized separately from the federation, was renamed the James G. K. McClure Educational and Development Fund and with a substantial endowment continued to operate, awarding scholarships to young people from the region and carrying on elements of the Lord's Acre Plan.

McClure's contributions to the region extended beyond the agricultural sector. For many years he served as chairman of the Western North Carolina Committee to support the North Carolina Symphony. He organized and served as chairman of the Buncombe County Citizens Committee for Better Schools, which initiated an ambitious program of school construction and spearheaded the consolidation of county high schools. He was chairman of the committee formed in 1949 to promote Governor W. Kerr Scott's state bond issue for improved rural roads and schools. Further, he organized separate cooperatives for the marketing of items such as hooked rugs and hand-knit sweaters that could be produced in the homes of families in the region. He also exerted every effort to attract private industry to western North Carolina as a means of diversifying its economy.

McClure's abilities were recognized outside the region as well. He served for several years on the National Citizens Committee for Better Schools. He also served as president of the North Carolina Forestry Association. In 1937 McClure became president of the American Forestry Association, the first North Carolinian to serve in that position. In recognition of his many contributions to the development of western North Carolina, he was awarded honorary degrees by Berea College (1929), Yale University (1939), Harvard University (1941), and The University of North Carolina (1942).

SEE: *Asheville Citizen*, 18 June 1956, 20, 26 Feb. 1957; *Asheville Citizen-Times*, 27 July 1941; Dumont Clarke IV, "The Farmers Federation Cooperative: A Study of a Cooperative Movement" (thesis, North Carolina Collection, University of North Carolina, Chapel Hill, 1974); *Congressional Record*, 19 Feb. 1957; *Farmers Federation News*, December 1956; James G. K. McClure, *Help Yourself* (1945); *North Carolina Biography*, vol. 4 (1956); Harry C. Rickard, "A Study of the Lord's Acre Movement" (Divinity School thesis, Duke University, Durham, 1938); Ina W. Van Noppen and John J. Van Noppen, *Western North Carolina since the Civil War* (1973); *Who's Who in the South* (1956); *Who Was Who in America*, vol. 3 (1960).

DUMONT CLARKE IV

McConnell, James Rogers (*14 Mar. 1887–19 Mar. 1917*), World War I aviator and author of *Flying for France*, was born in Chicago, Ill., the son of Judge Samuel Parsons McConnell and his wife. The family moved to New York City following the judge's resignation from the bench and then to Carthage, N.C. James was educated in private schools in Chicago, Morristown, N.J., and Haverford, Pa. In 1908 he entered the University of Virginia, spending two years in the academic department and one in the law school. While there he founded an "aero club," indicating his early interest in aviation. He engaged in numerous collegiate pranks, was elected "King of Hot-Foot" (later painting a red foot on the side of his plane in France), was assistant cheerleader, and joined Beta Theta Pi and Theta Nu Epsilon. In 1910 McConnell left law school and went to live with his family in Carthage, where he was employed as the land and industrial agent of the Seaboard Air Line Railway and secretary of the Carthage Board of Trade. He also wrote promotional pamphlets for the Sandhills area of North Carolina. He never married.

Only a few months after the outbreak of war in Europe in 1914, McConnell joined the American Ambulance Corps and went to France. In a letter to a friend in 1915, he wrote: "Tomorrow I am going to the front with our squad and twelve ambulances. . . . I am having a glorious experience." His rescue of a wounded French soldier while under fire was one of many similar acts that won him the Croix de Guerre for conspicuous bravery.

Dissatisfied with his field of service and believing that America needed to do more in the war against Germany, McConnell resigned from the Ambulance Corps and entered the aviation training program along with many other young Americans including Kiffin Yates Rockwell of Asheville. On completion of this training, thirty-eight pilots formed the famous Lafayette Escadrille, or squadron. Flying Nieuport biplanes that traveled at 110 miles per hour, the pilots were the darlings of the army. McConnell's group consisted of six pilots and seventy ground personnel. Operating from Luxeuil Field in eastern France, they customarily lifted off each day at daylight, clad in fur-lined outfits, to patrol for two hours. Armed with a machine gun, the pilot fired it with one hand while maneuvering the plane with the other hand and his feet. Following the Battle of Verdun, McConnell was given a new plane on which the 500-round Vickers machine gun was synchronized with the propeller. This was the era of dogfights high above the battlefields, of "aces" who shot down five enemy planes, of hot pursuit, of the last resort of individualism in the midst of mechanized warfare. In letters home and in *Flying for France*, McConnell wrote of the sun on the fog, of silver bullets, of red flames from the artillery below looking like a Doré painting of Dante's hell.

After being wounded once and narrowly escaping death several times, McConnell was flying in the vicinity of St.-Quentin when two German planes cornered him and shot him down on 19 Mar. 1917. The plane and his body were found by the French, and he was buried on the spot at the edge of the village of Jussy. According to one obituary, his death came "far above the smoke and filth and grime in the clear, clean air of heaven, attended by the stern joy of combat."

A monument erected to McConnell in Carthage bears an inscription reading in part, "He fought for Humanity, Liberty and Democracy, lighted the way for his countrymen and showed all men how to dare nobly and to die gloriously." A statue by Gutzon Borglum adorns the grounds of the University of Virginia, with these words at the base: "Soaring like an eagle into new heavens of valor and devotion."

SEE: P. A. Bruce, *History of the University of Virginia, 1819–1919*, vol. 5 (1922); Sarah McCulloh Lemmon, *North Carolina's Role in the First World War* (1966); James R. McConnell, *Flying for France with the American Escadrille at Verdun* (1917); "James Rogers McConnell," in Charles L. Van Noppen Manuscripts (Manuscript Department, Duke University Library, Durham).

SARAH MCCULLOH LEMMON

McCorkle, Lutie Andrews. *See* **McCorkle, Sarah Tallulah Andrews**.

McCorkle, Samuel Eusebius (*23 Aug. 1746–21 Jan. 1811*), Presbyterian minister and educator, was born in Lancaster County, Pa., near Harris's Ferry (now Harrisburg), the son of Alexander and Nancy Agnes Montgomery McCorkle. Both of his parents were born in Northern Ireland and migrated with their families to Pennsylvania about 1730. Reared among the Scotch-Irish settlers, Samuel attended a grammar school from age four to ten; there he learned the basic five "Rs"—reading, writing, arithmetic, self-restraint, and religion. The oldest of ten children, Samuel knew his lessons by 1756, when the McCorkles departed for the new lands in western North Carolina. The family settled on a 300-acre farm about fifteen miles from Salisbury, and they became regulars at a meetinghouse later named Thyatira Church.

There being no teacher in the neighborhood, young McCorkle taught his brothers, sisters, and neighbors for two years until he began classical studies under the Reverend Joseph Alexander at Crowfield Academy. He then completed further work with the Reverend David Caldwell. Deeply influenced by these Presbyterian teachers and by a religious revival, McCorkle left in 1768 to study for the ministry at the College of New Jersey. At Princeton he studied under a third Presbyterian minister, John Witherspoon. The youth absorbed the lessons in the classics, geography, history, languages, and science in addition to those in piety, love of learning, and religion. Witherspoon was decisive in disseminating moderate Calvinism (as opposed to the New Divinity and Edwardeanism) and instilling in McCorkle a confidence in reason and learning. He also taught him Scottish commonsense philosophy. The Witherspoon training guided McCorkle especially in education, where his emphasis, too, became to "Train up a child in the way he should go, and when he is old he will not depart from it."

McCorkle was graduated in the fall of 1772, having "grown in grace." Afterwards he taught school, studied for the ministry with an uncle who was a pastor in New Castle, Del., and in 1774 began itinerating as a Presbyterian probationer in western Virginia. In 1776 McCorkle answered a call to the pulpit of Thyatira Church in Rowan County, N.C., after having turned down a similar call in Virginia and suffering from a case of unrequited love. He was ordained on 2 Aug. 1777.

McCorkle's pastoral charge extended from his pulpit to the classroom and to the university. His personal creed endorsed the sovereignty of God and the depravity of man, and he urged the members of his flock to be reborn so they might discern the pattern in the universe, the natural laws that God had established. He served as a trustee of Liberty Hall Academy in Charlotte, and after the Revolutionary War shut it down, he helped move the school to Salisbury, where in 1784 it was chartered as Salisbury Academy. McCorkle served as president and teacher for a few years until it closed in 1791. Meanwhile, in 1784 he drafted, in accordance with the provisions of the 1776 constitution of North Carolina, the first proposal to found a university in the state. For political reasons, the legislature rejected this proposal, and The University of North Carolina was not chartered until 1789. Nevertheless, believing that learning promoted diligence, happiness, and piety as it prevented ignorance, and that it would advance government, agriculture, and manufacturing, McCorkle steadily supported education. When the Salisbury Academy closed and there were no funds for a public school, he and his congregation founded Zion-Parnassus Academy in 1794. It continued until about 1798, when the second Salisbury Academy opened.

As he trained boys for the university, McCorkle repeated the lessons that his Presbyterian mentors had taught him. For those who were not going to college, he taught an early normal (teacher training) course so they might themselves become schoolmasters and further promote piety and learning in the frontier society while supporting their families. He included the five "Rs" in his curriculum as well as classical languages, geography, and natural philosophy (science).

McCorkle was one of twenty-three graduates of the College of New Jersey trained under John Witherspoon who went to North Carolina as Presbyterian ministers and educational leaders. Five of them became trustees of The University of North Carolina, two (McCorkle and William R. Davie) were principal founders, and two served as the first presidents. McCorkle had first suggested a university; he chaired the committee that planned the course of instruction; he wrote regulations concerning its curriculum (but they were rejected in favor of Davie's), the daily schedule, discipline, and attendance at religious services, duplicating the system at the College of New Jersey; and he delivered the address of the day in 1793 at the laying of the cornerstone of the first building. Yet he was denied a position as the university's acting president when Davie objected to the choice. After December 1799 McCorkle refused to continue in the service of the university because he believed its leaders were governed by the philosophical principles of French deism.

Like other Presbyterian ministers, McCorkle supported the American Revolution, education, revivals in congregations, and outreach of ministries, and he opposed the rising French "infidelity" (deism). McCorkle even preached in support of the Revolution, and he published sermons on a variety of topics. Most advertised were *A Charity Sermon* (1795), in which he encouraged support of the new university, and *Four Discourses on the General First Principles of Deism and Revelation Contrasted: Discourse I* (1797), which challenged what McCorkle felt was false thinking. If reason was sufficient to assure human progress, as the deists maintained, why was evil continuing? Or could not reason distinguish between virtue and vice? He then demonstrated his belief that the ability to tell right from wrong came through revelation from God and not through mere human reason. Yet McCorkle viewed the revival of 1802 with ambivalence, wanting it to refresh his people but fearing the bodily exercises that made it a spectacle.

In a third of a century of active pulpit leadership at Thyatira, McCorkle continually spoke out for education, trained forty-five young men for the ministry, published more sermons for his people than other Presbyterian ministers in the state, and led in synod and presbytery meetings. Desiring to diffuse knowledge as the cure for ignorance, the cause of most human difficulties, he geared his normal course to further both piety and learning. This goal was suggested by his choice of the name for his academy, Zion-Parnassus—two hills, one noted for religion and the other for learning. McCorkle received an honorary doctorate from Dickinson College, Carlisle, Pa., in 1792 and thereafter was referred to as Dr. McCorkle.

On 29 June 1776 he married Margaret Gillespie, the daughter of Elizabeth Maxwell Gillespie Steele and the half sister of John Steele, a congressman and comptroller of the U.S. Treasury. Of the McCorkles' ten children, six survived—a boy and five girls. Alexander (Sandy), the son, was graduated from the University of Pennsylvania and became a small planter in the Rowan area. (Alexander apparently was sent to Pennsylvania because of McCorkle's dispute with the trustees in Chapel Hill.) There is no portrait of McCorkle, but he was described as six feet one inch tall with light hair and blue eyes, looking much like Thomas Jefferson, and as cheerful, mild, and dignified. (They supposedly once were introduced to each other in Philadelphia because of their marked resemblance.)

McCorkle was infirm by 1801, although he lived another ten years, and was too frail for the pulpit by 1806. He died at Westfield, his 300-acre farm, at age sixty-four; after his funeral at Thyatira Church he was buried in the churchyard. His grave is still marked by a large stone slab with a somewhat cryptic epitaph: "The tall, the wise, the reverend head must lie as low as ours." Eli

Caruthers, who had been a member of McCorkle's church as a boy, relates that McCorkle left detailed instructions for his funeral and interment and, in fact, selected the epitaph.

SEE: Kemp P. Battle, *History of the University of North Carolina*, vol. 1 (1907); Eli W. Caruthers, "Samuel Eusebius McCorkle, D.D., 1774–1811," in *Annals of the American Pulpit*, ed. William B. Sprague (1859); R. D. W. Connor, *A Documentary History of the University of North Carolina*, 2 vols. (1953); William R. Enger, "Samuel Eusebius McCorkle: North Carolina Educator" (Ed.D. diss., Oklahoma State University, 1973); William Henry Foote, *Sketches of North Carolina, Historical and Biographical: Illustrative of the Principles of a Portion of Her Early Settlers* (1846); James Hall, *A Narrative of a Most Extraordinary Work of Religion in North Carolina* (1802); Richard A. Harrison, *Princetonians, 1769–1775: A Biographical Dictionary* (1980); James F. Hurley and Julia G. Eagen, *The Prophet of Zion-Parnassus: Samuel Eusebius McCorkle* (1934); Samuel E. McCorkle Manuscripts (Manuscript Department, Duke University Library, Durham, Southern Historical Collection, University of North Carolina, Chapel Hill, and Archives of the Presbyterian and Reformed Churches, Montreat [McCorkle's Journal]); Rowan and Iredell County Records (North Carolina State Archives, Raleigh); Thomas T. Taylor, "Essays on the Career and Thoughts of Samuel Eusebius McCorkle" (master's thesis, University of North Carolina at Greensboro, 1978) and "Samuel E. McCorkle and a Christian Republic, 1792–1802," *American Presbyterians: Journal of Presbyterian History* 63 (1985); H. M. Wagstaff, ed., *The Papers of John Steele*, 2 vols. (1924).

WILLIAM RANDOLPH ENGER
THOMAS T. TAYLOR

McCorkle, Sarah Tallulah (Lutie) Andrews *(1858–20 Apr. 1939)*, writer, was born in Charlotte, the fourth child and second daughter of Ezra Harnwood and Sarah Ann Bolton Andrews. She was the sister of Edgar Murchison, Francis (Frank) Harnwood, Oleona M., Thomas W. G., and Mary. Her father, a native of England, was a dentist. She was educated at the Charlotte Female Institute (later Queens College). In 1865 her father died after being released from a Federal prison, where, on his return from a visit to England, he had been confined as a suspected Confederate spy.

On 30 Dec. 1879 Lutie, as she was called, married William Parsons McCorkle, a Methodist clergyman; he became a Presbyterian pastor in 1888. They lived in El Paso, Tex., High Point, Lexington, Shelby, and Graham, N.C., Savannah, Ga., Martinsville, Va., and Burlington, N.C., where he served churches. Following her husband's death in Burlington in 1933, Mrs. McCorkle returned to Charlotte to live with her brother Frank. She was buried in Elmwood Cemetery. There were no children.

Lutie McCorkle's interest in North Carolina history prompted her to write *Old Time Stories of the Old North State* (1903; reprint, 1921), a series of narratives related with imagined conversation to hold the attention of young readers. It was used as a textbook in the lower grades of the state's schools for many years. The stories are about such figures as Virginia Dare and William Gaston and such events as the Edenton Tea Party. "Was Alamance the First Battle of the Revolution?" published in the November 1903 issue of the *North Carolina Booklet*, is representative of her other historical writing.

SEE: Census of 1860 and 1870; *Charlotte Observer*, 2 Feb. 1913, 8 Mar. 1933, 15 May 1937, 22 Apr. 1939; McCorkle Papers (Southern Historical Collection, University of North Carolina, Chapel Hill); *North Carolina Authors* (1952).

RICHARD WALSER

McCorkle, William Parsons *(2 Apr. 1855–7 Mar. 1933)*, clergyman and religious writer, was born in Talladega, Ala., the second son and third child of Alexander B. and Lucila Agnes Cambol McCorkle. Alexander (1806–86) was a native of Rockbridge County, Va., and a descendant of the McCorkle and Glasgow families of that state. A Presbyterian minister, he preached widely in Virginia, Georgia, and Alabama and later helped to found a synodical college for women in Talladega (later the Presbyterian Collegiate Institute and Isbell College). Lucila Cambol McCorkle was the daughter of an Alabama minister.

William McCorkle received his early education in private schools in Alabama, and in 1870 he entered Washington and Lee University. Although referred to as "Dr. McCorkle" later in life, he was never graduated from Washington and Lee, nor did he ever receive a D.D. degree. Rather, according to a eulogizer, "this degree was conferred upon him by those who knew him and his work."

After leaving Washington and Lee, McCorkle taught briefly at private schools in Staunton, Va., and Lenoir, N.C. In 1876 he was licensed to preach by the Virginia Conference of the Methodist Episcopal Church, South, and five years later was ordained. On 30 Dec. 1879 he married Sarah Tallulah (Lutie) Andrews, a Charlotte writer. From 1881 to 1884 he served as pastor to churches in Beaufort, LaGrange, and Elkin; he then was called to serve in El Paso, Tex. On his return to North Carolina in 1888, he became a minister of the Presbyterian church and remained so until his death. After a brief pastorate in a rural church near Charlotte (1888–89), McCorkle served churches in High Point, Jamestown, and Lexington (1889–91), Shelby (1891–96), Graham (1896–1901), Savannah, Ga. (1901–7), Martinsville, Va. (1908–19), and Burlington, N.C. (1920–21). From 1921 until his death, he served several churches of the Orange Presbytery in the Burlington area, and in 1927 he became pastor-at-large for the presbytery.

Although McCorkle was well known among Presbyterians for his preaching and pastoring, he became best known to the public through his many writings. His interest in the relationship of Christianity to science and the modern world led him to publish one book, *Christian Science; or, The False Christ of 1866*, and a host of articles in church publications such as the *Presbyterian Standard*, *Southern Presbyterian Review*, *Biblical Recorder*, and *Union Seminary Review*. Particularly during 1925 and 1926, he became a leader of ministerial opposition to the sociologist Howard W. Odum and the *Journal of Social Forces* at The University of North Carolina. McCorkle wrote frequent articles expressing his views in newspapers in Charlotte, Greensboro, and other Piedmont cities, and he produced a controversial pamphlet attacking Odum and modern science, entitled *Anti-Christian Sociology as Taught in the Journal of Social Forces*. . . . During this time, he also was active in mustering the support of Presbyterians for the Poole bill, introduced by Representative D. Scott Poole in 1926 to prohibit the teaching of evolution in the state's schools.

McCorkle continued to preach until his death, becoming involved near the end of his life in efforts to oppose the national unification of Presbyterian, Reformed, and other Calvinist churches. He died and was buried in Burlington. He was survived by his wife, but no record exists of any children.

SEE: Burlington-Alamance County Chamber of Commerce, *Histories of Presbyterian Churches in Burlington and Alamance County, North Carolina* (1963); William P. McCorkle, *Anti-Christian Sociology as Taught in the Journal of Social Forces. . . .* (1925), *Christian Science; or, The False Christ of 1866* (1899), and *Popular Errors as to Inspiration* (1931); *Minutes of the One Hundred and Twentieth Annual Sessions of the Synod of North Carolina* (1933); *Minutes of Orange Presbytery*, vol. 8 (1933); Howard Washington Odum Manuscripts (Southern Historical Collection, University of North Carolina, Chapel Hill); Rev. Eugene Scott, *Ministerial Directory of the Presbyterian Church, U.S., 1861–1941* (1942); Robert Hamlin Stone, *A History of Orange Presbytery, 1770–1970* (1970).

NEVIN C. BROWN

McCoy, Millie-Christine *(11 July 1851–8–9 Oct. 1912)*, Siamese twins, were born in Welches Creek Township near Whiteville, the daughters of Jacob and Monemia, slaves of Jabez McCoy, a local farmer. Their potential show value was recognized early, and between 8 May 1852 and 1860 they passed through several hands. Their first real promoter was W. J. L. Millar, a professor turned showman, who picked them up in Boston when they were four and took them to Canada, Great Britain, and the Continent. Their last manager and legal owner was Joseph Pearson Smith, and sometimes the twins were known as Millie and Christine Smith. Smith reportedly paid $30,000 for them. The twins were abducted twice before they were ten, once by some men described as "a group of prizefighters sent for the purpose." During this period, Smith's father and Monemia searched for them for three years, the trail leading from New Orleans to Scotland and England.

Having regained possession of them, the elder Smith brought them back to America about 1860 and later hid them in the countryside near Spartanburg, S.C., to prevent their being taken by Union troops during the Civil War. Freed after the war, the twins embarked on their major tours and were seen by "the crowned heads" of Europe. Queen Victoria presented them with matching brooches. Millie and Christine appeared in forty-six of the American states and traveled widely around the world, often in conjunction with P. T. Barnum's circus.

They were presented primarily as medical curiosities and were frequently examined by local physicians. While still infants they were examined in Edinburgh by Dr. James Simpson, the discoverer of chloroform. Millie and Christine together weighed seventeen pounds at birth and were joined by a short ligament about five inches in diameter. According to a medical report, "Millie-Christine was united at the lateral, posterior portion of the pelvis, the sacrum and the coccyx joined, the lower part of the spinal cord united."

Although so handicapped, in their childhood they tumbled about playfully, two bodies acting as one and being able to walk on two or four legs. In conversation the twins referred to themselves as "I." Their native intelligence, cheerful nature, and vocal talents presented the more human side of their personalities. They often were billed as the "Carolina Nightingale," with Christine singing soprano and Millie alto. As children they re-

ceived private tuition and in their travels picked up two or three languages.

Prosperity enabled Millie and Christine to buy the original McCoy property and on it they built a ten-room house where they lived between tours. After 1900, they left it only occasionally to appear at county fairs. The house burned down in 1909, destroying treasures from the far corners of the world. Three years later Millie succumbed to tuberculosis, and Christine died the next day.

The twins were buried in a double coffin. The grave marker is inscribed: "A soul with two thoughts. Two hearts that beat as one." In 1969 the Columbus County Historical Society moved the grave from an overgrown, almost forgotten plot to the nearby Welches Creek community cemetery.

SEE: Leslie Fiedler, *Freaks* (1978); *Godey's Magazine* 82 (February 1896); *The Greatest Wonder of the World: Millie Christine, the Two-Headed Lady* (n.d. [portrait]); *History and Medical Description of the Two-Headed Girl* (1869; reprint, 1976); *The Millie-Christine Concert and Exhibition Co.* (n.d., copy in North Carolina Collection, University of North Carolina, Chapel Hill); Miscellaneous papers in the African Twin Collection (North Carolina State Archives, Raleigh).

JOHN MACFIE

McCrary, Doctor Bulla *(11 Apr. 1875–28 Oct. 1946)*, merchant, manufacturer, philanthropist, and chairman of the North Carolina State Highway Commission, was born on a farm near Asheboro, the son of William Franklin and Frances Briles McCrary. Known throughout his life as "D. B.," he was educated at Oak Ridge Academy and at Trinity College before its removal from Randolph County to Durham. His earliest business experience was as a dealer in timber products. In 1898 he established residence in Asheboro where he opened a hardware and farm implement store in partnership with Thomas Henry Redding, who became his brother-in-law. In 1908 the two acquired Acme Hosiery Mills, a small plant in Asheboro making women's cotton stockings. In 1916 they purchased Sapona Cotton Mills, which had been operating as a cotton yarn mill in nearby Cedar Falls for about eighty years. Sapona was a source of yarn for the hosiery plant until cotton was superseded by silk and synthetic fibers.

McCrary Hosiery Mills was established in 1927 to produce ladies' full-fashioned silk stockings to complement the circular knit product made in Acme. In 1936 the cotton mill became the Sapona Manufacturing Company, converting to silk processing at the time and later to the production of nylon and other synthetic textured yarns. With the acquisition of Marlowe Manufacturing Company of Florence, S.C., after McCrary's death, the textile complex that he had founded became Acme-McCrary Corporation, one of the largest of its kind. In the 1980s it was still a closely held corporation—its stock never having "gone public."

When his two sons, Charles Walker and James Franklin, proved to be able executives early in their business careers, McCrary was able to devote much of his time to the building of a hospital for the people of Randolph County. With his generous contributions plus funds raised by public subscription and substantial help from the Duke Endowment, Randolph Hospital was constructed and opened to receive patients during the early depression years. His continued support and a large bequest at his death enabled the hospital to maintain a steady growth and to expand its facilities many times. The D. B. McCrary Wing was added to house the administrative offices and two additional floors for patient care. His portrait hangs in the reception area at the entrance.

McCrary's innate integrity and reliability made him a natural leader of his community; he served two terms as mayor, was a founder of the first building and loan association of Asheboro, and served as president of the Bank of Randolph (later merged with Wachovia Bank and Trust Company). He was a charter member of the chamber of commerce and the Rotary Club. For many years he was chairman of the administrative board of the First Methodist Church and a principal benefactor, holding at various times a number of posts in the Western North Carolina Conference of the Methodist church.

In 1937 McCrary was appointed a district commissioner of the North Carolina State Highway Commission by Governor Clyde R. Hoey; he was reappointed by Governor J. Melville Broughton. During the terms of these governors, when it became necessary to appoint an interim chairman of the commission, McCrary was named on each occasion. He declined to accept the chairman's salary during the many months he headed the state system, receiving only the district commissioner's per diem stipend. He was intensely interested in construction projects of every sort, and his knowledge of the state's roads and highways was extensive.

In 1901 McCrary married Allie Walker of Asheboro. She died in 1944.

SEE: *North Carolina Manual* (1943); Raleigh *News and Observer*, 4 Dec. 1942, 29 Oct. 1946; James R. Young, *Textile Leaders of the South* (1963).

WILLIAM UNDERWOOD, JR.

McCulloch, Alexander (*d. 1798*), provincial official, was the son of James McCulloch of Great Britain. He was residing in North Carolina as early as 1745 and serving as deputy auditor of the province in Edenton. As the nephew of Henry McCulloh (Alexander's branch of the family retained the third *c* in the surname, although his contemporaries often dropped it when writing his name), he was early involved in his uncle's heavy land speculations in North Carolina and served as his attorney for land transactions in 1756 and afterwards. Alexander's loyalty to Henry McCulloh led to the nephew's participation in the Enfield Riot of early 1759, when Earl Granville's land agents were forcibly taken to the Edgecombe County seat and compelled to assure reformation of Granville District land administration.

McCulloch held a number of provincial offices. He was appointed auditor in November 1757 but replaced two years later, reverting to his previous position as deputy auditor. Despite the fact that he usually resided at his plantation, Elk Marsh in Halifax County, McCulloch was an officer in the Orange County militia, a post he resigned in 1754 because of his distance from the county. In 1760 he became colonel of the Edgecombe County militia and accompanied Governor William Tryon on the initial Regulator expedition to Hillsborough in 1768. McCulloch held the lucrative position of clerk of court in Bute County in 1772.

Elected to the lower house of the Assembly from Halifax County in 1760, he served one full year. In 1762 he began active service on the royal Council, where he was an irregular attendant until its disbandment in 1775. As a councillor he advised Governor Josiah Martin to pre-

vent the meeting of the Provincial Congress at Halifax in April 1775. However, he was later reported to have expressed sentiments in favor of liberty and sat out the Revolution at Elk Marsh unmolested. Indeed, he named Patriots John Baptist Ashe and Willie Jones as executors of his estate. During the Revolution his cousin, James Iredell, frequently visited him while riding the court circuit.

The father of Benjamin, Elizabeth, and Mary, McCulloch was also father-in-law of William Frohock. The Frohocks served as agents in Rowan County for Henry McCulloh's speculations. At his death, Alexander McCulloch owned more than seventy slaves and had plantations in Warren and Halifax counties.

SEE: Walter Clark, ed., *State Records of North Carolina*, vols. 15, 17 (1898–99); Halifax County Wills (North Carolina State Archives, Raleigh); Don Higginbotham, ed., *The Papers of James Iredell*, 2 vols. (1976); William S. Powell, ed., *The Correspondence of William Tryon and Other Selected Papers*, 2 vols. (1980–81).

WILLIAM S. PRICE, JR.

McCulloch, Henry (*d. 27 Oct. 1755*), was a British placeman who resided briefly in North Carolina. Little is known of his early life or ancestry, except that he was probably a cousin of Henry McCulloh, the enterprising land speculator, from whom he acquired over six thousand acres in North Carolina.

From 1746 to 1748 McCulloch was a naval officer at Cape Breton while it was under English control. He spent the next six years in England trying to secure another office from the powerful Duke of Newcastle. Appointed secretary of North Carolina, judge of the vice-admiralty court, and a member of the Provincial Council in 1754, McCulloch served in these posts until his death. He left a wife, Mary, and four daughters.

SEE: John Cannon, "Henry McCulloch and Henry McCulloh," *William and Mary Quarterly*, ser. 3, 15 (1958); Land Grants (North Carolina State Archives, Raleigh); William L. Saunders, ed., *Colonial Records of North Carolina*, vol. 5 (1887); Will Book 7, 1755-58, Secretary of State Papers (North Carolina State Archives, Raleigh).

A. ROGER EKIRCH

McCulloch, Joseph Flavius (*24 June 1856–1 Oct. 1934*), professor, college president, minister, and editor, was born in Guilford County, the son of Joseph D. and Sara Julian McCulloch. He studied at Adrian College in Michigan and at Johns Hopkins and Clark universities. He taught at the University of Michigan and at Adrian College, of which he became president. He also was pastor of Methodist Protestant churches in Piedmont North Carolina.

McCulloch's compelling goal was to have a Methodist Protestant college established in North Carolina, and for forty years he directed his energies towards that end. To further his efforts and with the approval of his church's conference, he founded a periodical, *Our Church Record*, in 1894; in 1910 it became the *Methodist Protestant Herald*. He was editor, printer, and publisher of this sole conference periodical of the Methodist Protestant church.

Over a number of years individuals and institutions contributed to a fund to establish a new college to supplant the struggling Yadkin College, which had had a checkered career, sometimes serving merely as a high school. A special attempt was made to obtain support in

Burlington, Greensboro, and High Point. Finally, in 1924, the combined efforts of many people resulted in the closing of Yadkin College and its consolidation with the new High Point College, which opened in September. McCulloch had served on the board of education during the planning and fund-raising period, and when High Point College opened he sat on the board of trustees.

In September 1883 he married Mary Elizabeth Barrow, and they became the parents of three children. He died and was buried in Greensboro.

SEE: J. Elwood Carroll, *History of the North Carolina Annual Conference of the Methodist Protestant Church* (1939); *Journal of the Annual Conference of the Methodist Protestant Church* (1934); J. E. Pritchard, *A Brief History of the First Twenty-Five Years of High Point College* (1957).

RALPH HARDEE RIVES

McCulloh, Henry (ca. 1700–17 June 1779), London merchant, land speculator in North Carolina, colonial official, and author of a stamp tax scheme for the American colonies, was the son of James McCulloh (or McCulloch) of Grogan, Scotland. Frequently he has been confused with Henry McCulloch, who was secretary of North Carolina, and may have been his cousin.

Although McCulloh spent only about seven years in North Carolina, he was the largest landholder, after Lord Granville, in the history of the colony or the state. He was a prosperous merchant in London and had already acquired his vast landholdings in North Carolina when, in 1739, he was appointed "Commissioner for Supervising, Inspecting, and Comptrolling our Revenues and Grants of Land in South and North Carolina." In his efforts to receive the appointment, he had sent a memorial to the Privy Council about the defective land and quitrent system in the Carolinas and how it could be remedied. It has been said that after he went to America late in 1740, he had little success in South Carolina and in North Carolina used his position to wage an unsuccessful vendetta against Governor Gabriel Johnston, a former protégé, and his chief American competitors. These competitors were a group of speculators in the Cape Fear region who had become the dominant political force in the colony.

As a former benefactor of Governor Johnston, McCulloh had profited handsomely. He received two grants of 60,000 and 72,000 acres, while a third grant of 1.2 million acres to James Huey, Murray Crymble, and their associates actually went to McCulloh since Huey and Crymble were acting as his trustees. The latter grant was awarded on the condition that six thousand Protestants be settled on the land and quitrents be paid, but the contract did not have to be complied with for ten years. McCulloh's two earlier grants had also been conditioned on his paying quitrents and installing Protestant settlers on the land to produce raw materials needed in England. He fell far short of meeting both of these obligations and was charged not only with failing to pay the rents but also with conniving with purchasers of his lands to do likewise. It is little wonder that he did not collect sufficient rents to cover his salary, which he was also committed to do.

In fact, by the time the patents for the 1.2 million acres were issued in 1746, McCulloh received only about two-thirds of the grant. His failure to live up to his contract led to his losing that holding in 1765. At its greatest extent, his land lay along the Cape Fear, Deep, Uwharrie, Tar, Flat, Eno, Yadkin, and Catawba rivers. He be-

came involved in numerous disputes and lawsuits over land matters, and he seems to have spent most of his time in America looking after his own interests.

McCulloh's involvement in provincial politics led to his taking sides with the Albemarle counties against Governor Johnston and the counties of the Cape Fear region during the Great Schism that developed in 1746 over representation in the North Carolina General Assembly. Even after he returned to England in 1747, he continued to fish in these troubled waters. He still had important connections within the home government, and when Johnston died in 1752, he was succeeded as governor by McCulloh's fellow speculator, Arthur Dobbs. Dobbs's successor, William Tryon, was also friendly to the interests of McCulloh.

McCulloh agreed to surrender extensive acreage within the tract established as the Granville District to satisfy Lord Granville's claim. By the time his son, Henry Eustace McCulloh, arrived in 1761 as his agent, the elder McCulloh had disposed of a large percentage of his land other than the tract he was to lose in 1765. The land he retained devolved to Henry Eustace, and all of it was confiscated during the American Revolution despite the efforts of his great-nephew, James Iredell, to save it. Although it is not known whether McCulloh realized much money from his speculative ventures, it has been assumed that they were quite valuable.

After McCulloh returned to England, he wrote pamphlets and memorials about the American colonies in an attempt to receive another appointment. Two of them, each containing just over 130 pages, were published in 1755. One was entitled *A miscellaneous essay concerning the courses pursued by Great Britain in the affairs of her colonies: With some observations on the great importance of our settlements in America, and the trade thereof.* Another was *The wisdom and policy of the French in the construction of their great offices so as best to answer the purposes of extending their trade and commerce and enlarging their foreign settlements: With some observations in relation to the disputes now subsisting between the English and French colonies in America.*

From his pen in 1757 came a report raising the idea of a stamp tax. This was not original with him but he developed it into a plan that he presented to the Earl of Halifax. In 1761 he prepared still another version that remained in manuscript form until about 1905, when it was printed for the first time; it was entitled "Miscellaneous representations relative to our concerns in America, submitted to the Earl of Bute." Soon the idea was adopted by the government of Lord Granville, and McCulloh was employed to draft a stamp tax bill. His draft, however, was rejected for a more moderate version that became the Stamp Act of 1765.

At the time of his death McCulloh was residing in Chiswick, Middlesex County, near London, to which he had moved from nearby Turnham. He was buried at St. Nicholas Church, Chiswick.

SEE: Fanning-McCulloh Papers (Southern Historical Collection, University of North Carolina, Chapel Hill); Don Higginbotham, ed., *The Papers of James Iredell*, 2 vols. (1976); Henry McCulloh Papers (Manuscript Department, Duke University Library, Durham); Griffith J. McRee, ed., *Life and Correspondence of James Iredell*, vol. 1 (1857); William L. Saunders, ed., *Colonial Records of North Carolina*, vols. 6–7 (1888–90); *William and Mary Quarterly*, 3d ser., 8 (1951), 10 (1953), 15 (1958).

MATTIE U. RUSSELL

McCulloh, Henry Eustace *(ca. 1737–ca. 1810)*, was the only son of Henry McCulloh of Turnham Green, Middlesex, England, the largest land speculator in colonial North Carolina. Henry Eustace entered North Carolina as an infant in 1740 but returned to England in 1747 to be educated. Entering Middle Temple, one of the inns of court, in 1757, he was called to the bar in 1760. He returned to North Carolina the following year with an appointment as collector of the port of Beaufort. In April 1762 he assumed a seat on the royal Council.

McCulloh served as his father's chief agent and attorney in North Carolina and surveyed many of the tracts in the 1.2-million-acre Huey-Crymble grant, which was in fact controlled by his father. In 1764 Henry Eustace was residing in Orange County and serving as a justice of the peace. There he established a close friendship with Edmund Fanning, the target of so much of the Regulators' hatred. By 1766 he had become collector of the port of Roanoke and was living in Edenton. The following year he returned to England and in 1769 began three years of service as the provincial agent for North Carolina. Henry Eustace resigned his seat on the Council in 1770 because he would not soon be returning to the colony. However, he did come back in 1772 and left the next year never to return. In 1774 he stood for election to Parliament for the borough of Cricklade, Wiltshire, but lost.

With the outbreak of the American Revolution, McCulloh tried to maintain friends on both sides of the Atlantic. To the Loyalist Claims Commission in England he professed his allegiance to the mother country, while in North Carolina (as his son claimed in 1792) he paid and maintained a substitute in the Continental line. Throughout the war and after, Henry Eustace corresponded regularly with such Whigs as James Iredell (his cousin), Cornelius Harnett, and Willie Jones.

McCulloh journeyed to New York in 1778 in the ultimate hope of arguing for his North Carolina holdings but never traveled south. James Iredell pleaded with the General Assembly not to confiscate McCulloh's lands because of his service as provincial agent. Nevertheless, the property was confiscated in 1779. Back in England in 1779, Henry Eustace became attorney for North Carolina Loyalists submitting claims to the Crown. He continued to press his own claims for compensation even more strongly after his father's death that June.

McCulloh's dealings with the Loyalist Claims Commission were frustrating to him. In 1783 he asserted that he held deeds on over 800,000 acres in North Carolina (primarily in Anson, Guilford, and Rowan counties) and had lost over £1,000 in annual revenues from the various provincial offices he had held. The commission eventually compensated him to a total of £12,047, but he had claimed losses nearly five times that figure. McCulloh, greatly dissatisfied with the settlement, continued to try to get more money from the commission but to no avail. Finally his wife, Udell, wrote to the Claims Commission in September 1807 that her husband had become deranged earlier that year and had been confined to an asylum at Clapton. She had had to sell their house at Lincoln Inn Fields to meet expenses.

Henry Eustace's illegitimate son George, a native North Carolinian, had pressed his father's claims in the state almost as avidly as Henry Eustace had done in England. In a petition to the legislature in 1792, he asked that all of his father's lands still unsold be turned over to him based on his nine-month confinement as a prisoner of the British during the war. The General Assembly rejected his request.

Henry Eustace was an urbane man with a taste for high living. His library in North Carolina contained books by Pope, Swift, and Homer. Set against this erudition was his reputation as a notorious womanizer. McCulloh's political duplicity was manifested in his efforts to maintain control of a landed empire in North Carolina (ranging in size at various times from 400,000 to 1.5 million acres) by playing one faction against another. If it had not been for the American Revolution, he might have succeeded. Undoubtedly, that event, which by its sheer enormity voided his manipulative skills, contributed to McCulloh's dying a lonely, broken man in a madhouse.

SEE: Robert O. DeMond, *The Loyalists in North Carolina during the Revolution* (1940); Fanning-McCulloh Papers (Southern Historical Collection, University of North Carolina, Chapel Hill); Don Higginbotham, ed., *The Papers of James Iredell*, 2 vols. (1976); William L. Saunders, ed., *Colonial Records of North Carolina*, vols. 6–7 (1888–90).

WILLIAM S. PRICE, JR.

McDaniel, James *(22 Dec. 1803–25 Dec. 1869)*, Baptist leader, was born in Cumberland County, the son of John and Rebecca Cade McDaniel. He received his education at Redia Marsh Academy and at Wake Forest Institute, which he helped establish in 1834. In 1851 he was granted a master's degree and in 1869 an honorary doctor of divinity degree by Wake Forest College. As a young man he joined the Cape Fear Baptist Church and was ordained soon afterwards; in the fall of 1827 he was made clerk of the Cape Fear Baptist Association, a post he held for fourteen years.

After serving as pastor of several rural churches, McDaniel was persuaded to establish a Baptist church in Fayetteville despite the fact that there were no members of that denomination in the town. Riding horseback across the state to visit Baptist congregations, he succeeded in collecting funds to build the first Baptist church in Fayetteville; the building was completed and the church was "established" on 25 Nov. 1837. With the exception of eight years when he was pastor of the First Baptist Church in Wilmington (1844–52), McDaniel served the Fayetteville congregation until his death. In 1849, while in Wilmington, he established a periodical, *Religious and General Intelligence*; with McDaniel as its editor, it continued into the following year.

McDaniel was one of fourteen men who met in Greenville in 1830 to organize the Baptist State Convention, and he was the convention's secretary for nineteen years and president for eighteen years. He also was elected a delegate to the organizing session of the Southern Baptist Convention in 1845 but was unable to attend; nevertheless, he was present the next year. He also was an active member of the Masonic order and held various offices in the lodges to which he belonged.

In 1830 McDaniel married Ann Elizabeth Smith, the daughter of John and Elizabeth Clark Smith of Craven County. They were the parents of Amanda (Mrs. R. P. Jones), Lillias Margaret (Mrs. W. W. Vass), Sophia (Mrs. H. E. Colton), Cornelia, Lida, and Adolphus Meredith Wait. His wife died in 1855, and in 1858 he married Mrs. Mary Taylor Strong.

SEE: *American Baptist Register* (1852); *Biblical Recorder*, 21 Mar. 1846, 28 July, 4 Aug. 1869, 5 Jan. 1870, 11 Feb. 1874, 9 June 1973; *Cape Fear Baptist Association Minutes* (1870); *Fayetteville Observer*, 29 Jan. 1934, 15 Nov. 1939, 12 Apr. 1954, 24 Sept. 1960, 16 Aug. 1969, 23 July 1971, 18

May, 3 June 1973; First Baptist Church, Fayetteville, Minutes, 1848–70; M. A. Huggins, *A History of North Carolina Baptists* (1967); John A. Oates, *The Story of Fayetteville and the Upper Cape Fear* (1950); George W. Paschal, *History of North Carolina Baptists*, vol. 1 (1930), and *History of Wake Forest College*, 3 vols. (1943); *Southern Baptist Convention Annual* (1945).

LOU ROGERS WEHLITZ

MacDonald, Allan (d. 1792?), of Kingsborough, Scotland, was one of the most important Scottish Highlanders to serve the king's cause in North Carolina and elsewhere during the American Revolution. The husband of the famed Flora MacDonald (heroine of the escape of Charles Edward Stuart, Bonnie Prince Charlie, the Young Pretender, to France following the Battle of Culloden), he had suffered with many others of his homeland the breaking up of the vast clan holdings and the enforced loyalty to the House of Hanover. In 1774 Allan and Flora arrived in North Carolina, where he bought two plantations in Anson County.

With the approaching Revolution, MacDonald was one of the first to come to the aid of Governor Josiah Martin in his clashes with the Assembly and the local Patriots. As early as 3 July 1775 he journeyed to Fort Johnston (at the mouth of the Cape Fear), to which Martin had fled from the capitol at New Bern, and proposed to the governor that he raise a battalion of "the good and faithful Highlanders" from among those who had recently come to the Upper Cape Fear. Later in the month, Allan's brother Donald and his son-in-law, Donald McLeod, arrived in the colony from Massachusetts, sent by General Thomas Gage to recruit men for a battalion of the Royal Highland Emigrant Regiment. Over the next several months these three enlisted Highlanders and Regulators from the backcountry in a force that eventually numbered about 1,600 for a march to Brunswick to join an expedition heading south led by Sir Peter Parker and Sir Henry Clinton. Joined together, these forces were intended to crush the rebellion in North Carolina.

Highlanders willingly joined the cause (300 in the battalion being formed for the Highland Emigrant Regiment, the rest in the governor's militia), encouraged by Martin's generous land grants of two hundred acres, remission of arrears in quitrents, and twenty years of tax exemption. Also, those in the militia were to receive the same pay as regular soldiers and liberal compensations for the use of any equipment such as horses or wagons, and they would not have to fight outside the colony. Moreover, most had entered the colony too recently (some as late as 1775) to feel any commitment to the rebel cause. Regulators embraced the king's cause more slowly; in the end only 130 joined the expedition. The Loyalist force, commanded by Donald MacDonald as brigadier general with Donald McLeod as major and second in command and Allan MacDonald as captain, finally assembled on 18 Feb. 1776 a few miles below Cross Creek (now Fayetteville), actually three days later than Martin's planned rendezvous at Brunswick, for its march to the sea to join the larger force from the North. However, the Patriots in the area became aware of the Loyalist activities and raised their own forces in retaliation, commanded by James Moore, colonel of the First North Carolina Regiment from the Wilmington District. By 18 February Moore had 1,100 men at Rockfish Creek (a few miles to the south of MacDonald's camp), with more on the way from the New Bern District commanded by Richard Caswell.

What followed was a series of small-scale movements, complicated by the necessity of crossing several streams, with the Loyalists trying to get through to the coast (Donald MacDonald's main concern was to deliver his Highland battalion to Clinton) and the Patriots trying to stop them. At Moore's Creek Bridge (the last stream before Wilmington), the deciding action of the campaign took place. The Patriots (Richard Caswell's forces of 800 from New Bern plus Alexander Lillington's 150 minutemen from the Wilmington District dispatched there by Moore) removed the planks from the bridge, leaving only the log stringers, and entrenched themselves on the east bank. Arriving at the scene and observing the difficulty of the situation, the Loyalists (in a council of war, led on by the younger officers and over the opposition of Donald MacDonald) nevertheless chose to attack. This they did on the dawn of 27 February to their own decimation. McLeod, John Campbell, and a few others leading the attack actually got across the bridge, to be killed later; a number were killed before they got that far. Within three minutes the Loyalists were routed. The Patriots left their entrenchments, quickly relaid the bridge, and gave chase to the main Loyalist force, capturing both Allan and Donald MacDonald (who had been too ill to direct the attack), several other officers, and about 850 soldiers, plus 13 wagons, £15,000 in gold, and about 800 rifles and muskets and 150 swords and dirks. In the fight about fifty of the Loyalists had been killed or wounded; only two Patriots were wounded (one of whom died four days later).

The regular soldiers, on their capture, were paroled and allowed to return to their homes on their oaths not to take up arms against the Patriot cause in the future. However, the officers were not treated so generously. Allan, his brother Donald, and the others were transported first to New Bern and then to the Halifax jail as prisoners of war. From there Allan MacDonald and at least twenty-five other prisoners, including his son Alexander, were sent to Philadelphia. Here he soon was released, on account of "his candor and low state of health," on parole, with liberty to live at Reading, Berks County. In 1777 he raised at New York a company of eighty-six North Carolinians and Virginians which he led for about a year. In October 1778 he rejoined the Royal Highland Emigrant Regiment in Nova Scotia, where he remained for the rest of the war.

When the war ended, the regiment was reduced in size, and MacDonald, his wife Flora, and their daughter settled on regimental land along the Kennetcook River in Hants County, Nova Scotia. In October 1784 he left for London to present a claim for compensation, telling the commissioners that he intended to return to Nova Scotia. Ironically, on the way home, the ship on which he and Flora were traveling was attacked by a French man-of-war. During the clash Flora, ever the heroine, remained on deck spurring on the sailors and was thrown down, breaking her arm. She said later that she "had now perilled her life in behalf of both the house of Stuart and that of Brunswick, and got very little for her pains." Flora died in 1790 and was buried in a shroud made from the sheet on which Prince Charles had slept and which she had preserved for that purpose through all her adventures and migrations of almost a half century. Allan survived Flora by a few years and died on the half-pay list of the British army.

Allan and Flora were survived by three sons and a daughter; their other son, Alexander, had been killed during the war. All four sons—John (ultimately to achieve the rank of colonel in the British army and become a writer on military subjects), James (a lieutenant of infantry in the British Legion by 1782), and Charles (by 1782 a captain in the British Legion), as well as Alexander—served the British cause during the Revolution. John died in Exeter, England, in 1821 at age seventy-two. The only surviving daughter, the widow of Major McLeod, died at Steine, Isle of Skye, in 1835.

SEE: Robert M. Calhoon, *The Loyalists in Revolutionary America, 1760–1781* (1973); Walter Clark, ed., *State Records of North Carolina*, vol. 11 (1895); Robert O. De-Mond, *The Loyalists in North Carolina during the Revolution* (1940); English records: American Loyalist Claims, 1775–89, Colonial Office, 1773–76, and Foreign Office, 1783–94 (North Carolina State Archives, Raleigh); John Fortescue, ed., *The Correspondence of King George the Third from 1760 to December 1783*, vol. 3 (1928); Laura P. Frech, "The Wilmington Committee of Public Safety and the Loyalist Rising of February, 1776," *North Carolina Historical Review* 41 (1964); Hugh F. Rankin, "The Moore's Creek Bridge Campaign, 1776," *North Carolina Historical Review* 30 (1953); Lorenzo Sabine, *Biographical Sketches of Loyalists in the American Revolution*, vols. 1–2 (1864), and *The American Loyalists* (1847); William L. Saunders, ed., *Colonial Records of North Carolina*, vol. 10 (1890); Carole W. Troxler, "The Migration of Carolina and Georgia Loyalists to Nova Scotia and New Brunswick" (Ph.D. diss., University of North Carolina, Chapel Hill, 1974).

JAMES M. CLIFTON

McDonald, Angus Morris (Monk) *(21 Feb. 1901–2 Sept. 1977)*, college athlete and physician, was born and raised in Charlotte, the son of Angus Morris, Sr., and Ann Howard McDonald. His father was founder of the Southern Real Estate Company and chairman of the Mecklenburg County Board of Commissioners. Young Angus attended Charlotte High School and the Fishburne Military School.

After high school McDonald enrolled at The University of North Carolina, where he became a three-sport star. Only five feet, seven inches tall, he made up for his lack of size with superior quickness and athletic ability. In football he was an all-star quarterback. In 1922 he led North Carolina to a nine-win, one-loss season, including victories over arch rival Virginia and in-state foes North Carolina State, Trinity, Wake Forest, and Davidson. North Carolina's only loss that year was a controversial 18–0 defeat at Yale. McDonald's contributions that season included a 95-yard kickoff return for a touchdown that propelled the university to a 14–9 victory over North Carolina State. McDonald continued to excel in 1923, although North Carolina slipped slightly to a record of five wins, three losses, and one tie.

In basketball McDonald was a clever playmaking guard. He made the Southern Conference all-star team in 1922 and 1924 and was captain of the university team in 1923. In those three years he led North Carolina to successive win-loss records of 14–3, 15–1, and 26–0. The 1922 and 1924 teams won the Southern Conference tournament championship. The undefeated 1924 team was voted mythical national champion by the Helms Foundation. McDonald was also a standout baseball shortstop and leadoff hitter. A career .300-hitter, he was considered a professional prospect had he chosen that option. He led the 1922 team to a 19–2 record. McDonald received four university letters each in football, basketball, and baseball.

McDonald was in medical school at The University of North Carolina in the 1924–25 academic year when bas-

ketball coach Norman Shepard abruptly resigned shortly before the beginning of the season. McDonald was asked to fill the void and coached the team to an 18–5 record while carrying a full academic load. The university won another Southern Conference tournament that year, although McDonald's studies forced him to miss the post-season event.

In 1926 he transferred to the University of Pennsylvania Medical School, where he received an M.D. degree in 1928. A urologist and surgeon, McDonald served his internship at the Protestant Episcopal Hospital in Philadelphia. In 1930 he began a two-year fellowship in surgery at the prestigious Mayo Clinic in Rochester, Minn. After its completion he worked for two years at New York's Presbyterian Hospital, where he assisted noted urologist Dr. J. Bentley Squier. He also worked for a brief period at the Vanderbilt Clinic in New York.

In 1935 McDonald moved back to North Carolina to join the Greensboro practice of Dr. Fred Patterson. He remained there until June 1939, when he returned to Charlotte to help establish the Crowell Clinic. In September 1942 he became a lieutenant commander in the U.S. Navy Medical Corps. Originally stationed at Chapel Hill's Navy Pre-Flight School, he was transferred to the U.S. Naval Hospital in San Francisco in 1944. He was discharged from the navy following the end of hostilities.

After the war he resumed his urology practice in Charlotte and remained associated with the Crowell Clinic until his retirement in June 1969. He was also associated with Charlotte's Mercy Hospital. McDonald was a member of the American Urological Association, the North Carolina Medical Society, and the Charlotte Chamber of Commerce. He was inducted into the North Carolina Sports Hall of Fame in 1977.

McDonald married Mary Letitia Mebane of Greensboro in 1939. They had three children: Letitia, Ann, and Angus. All three were graduated from The University of North Carolina. McDonald continued to live in Charlotte after his retirement. He was buried at Elmwood Cemetery.

SEE: Alumni Files (University of North Carolina, Chapel Hill); Smith Barrier, *On Tobacco Road: Basketball in North Carolina* (1983); *Charlotte Observer*, scattered issues; Bob Quincy, *They Made the Bell Tower Chime* (1973); Ken Rappoport, *Tar Heel: North Carolina Football* (1976).

JIM L. SUMNER

MacDonald, Donald *(1712–post-1784)*, veteran of the battles of Culloden and Bunker Hill, was the most significant Scottish Highlander to serve the king's cause in North Carolina during the Revolutionary War. Early in the war he went to Massachusetts, where as a lieutenant colonel he fought in (and was wounded at) the Battle of Bunker Hill. Soon afterwards he was sent to North Carolina by General Thomas Gage (then in overall command of the British troops in America) to recruit troops for a Royal Highland Emigrant Regiment. MacDonald, accompanied by his nephew by marriage, Captain Donald McLeod, arrived at New Bern in July 1775 and was able to convince the town's Committee of Public Safety that the two had come to recover from wounds suffered at Bunker Hill and to visit relatives.

Immediately, MacDonald was authorized by Governor Josiah Martin to enlist troops from among the Scottish Highlanders of the Upper Cape Fear. These recent immigrants (some as late as 1775)—their vast clan holdings having been broken up back in Scotland following the Battle of Culloden, thus encouraging a number of them to migrate to America—had received rather generous land grants from Martin and in turn readily renewed their oaths of allegiance to the Crown. Consequently, the governor was counting heavily on their support to reestablish his power over the rebellious planters along the coast. Prior to MacDonald's arrival, agents of General Gage had succeeded in enlisting 800 of the Highlanders (mainly from among the most recent immigrants) in the king's cause; however, the local Patriots had been able to prevent the agents from carrying out their orders. While MacDonald (now appointed by Martin brigadier general of militia "for the time being") was enlisting the services of the Scottish Highlanders around Cross Creek (now Fayetteville), McLeod (now commissioned lieutenant colonel and second in command) journeyed into the backcountry to arouse the former Regulators to the royal colors. McLeod met with little success—only 130 men joined the cause. But MacDonald's task proved to be much easier. The thrifty Scots, most of whom were too new in the country to feel any attachment to the rebel cause, were quick to take full advantage of the British inducements for enlistment—two hundred acres of land, the same pay as regular troops with liberal compensation for the use of their equipment such as horses and wagons, and the assurance that they would not have to fight outside the colony.

Martin's plans called for the Highlanders and the Regulators to march to Brunswick for a rendezvous on 15 February with an expedition under Sir Henry Clinton and Sir Peter Parker then on its way south. Together, these forces would crush the rebels in the colony. However, such a grandiose plan was not to be. MacDonald was unable to bring together all his forces at Cross Creek until after the specified time for the rendezvous. Finally, on 18 February he assembled about 1,500 Scots and Regulators four miles below Cross Creek. In the meantime, the Patriots had become aware of the danger developing at Cross Creek. Accordingly, the Committees of Public Safety at both Wilmington and New Bern ordered out their militia and minutemen. By mid-February James Moore, colonel of the First North Carolina Regiment from the Wilmington District, had set up camp at Rockfish, seven miles below Cross Creek, which by the eighteenth (with recent additions) numbered about 1,100. An odd exchange of communications ensued from the two camps. MacDonald sent Moore a copy of Martin's proclamation of 10 Jan. 1776 commanding "all His Majesty's faithful subjects" to rally to the king's cause and condemning those who would not do so, inviting the Patriots "to join the royal standard." Moore countered with a copy of the Patriots' Test Oath which, if MacDonald's men would sign it, would entitle them to join the Continental army. Neither side would concede.

What followed was a series of small-scale movements, complicated by the necessity of crossing several streams, with the Loyalists trying to get through to the coast and the Patriots trying to stop them. Moore decided to make an all-out effort to stop MacDonald's forces at Moore's Creek, the last stream before Wilmington. Accordingly, he dispatched Alexander Lillington and the Wilmington battalion of 150 minutemen to join Richard Caswell from New Bern with about 800 men. Caswell and Lillington decided to remove the planks from the bridge across the creek (leaving only the log stringers) and to construct breastworks a short distance from the east bank of the creek. This time the Loyalists decided not to bypass

their opponents but to meet them head-on. But this was not the position of MacDonald. An elderly man and near collapse from exhaustion, he was in no position to direct the attack; besides, as a regular officer in the British army, he was more interested in delivering the troops to Clinton than he was in subduing the rebels for the immediate moment. Also, he felt he was outnumbered and half of his group was without firearms. However, in the council of war that was held, the younger Scottish officers prevailed, and the attack was set for dawn on 27 February.

MacDonald, now quite ill, assigned the command to McLeod. Arriving at Moore's Creek from their camp some distance from the west bank and finding the bridge almost impassable, the Loyalists nevertheless attacked. A picked company of 80 Scots under John Campbell led the van, to be followed by McLeod and the main force. Campbell, McLeod, and some others actually got across the bridge, to be killed later; many were killed before they got that far. With the Loyalists in retreat, the Patriots left the entrenchments and ran to the creek, where they quickly relaid the planks and chased the Loyalists, capturing Donald MacDonald, his brother Allan, several other officers, and about 850 soldiers, along with the spoils of the wagon train—about 800 rifles and muskets and 150 swords. In the battle at the bridge, which lasted only a few minutes, only two Patriots were wounded, one of whom, John Grady of Duplin County, died four days later.

As to its import, the Battle of Moore's Creek Bridge would inspire the Halifax Resolves on 12 Apr. 1776 (the first declaration of independence in any colony) and be a major factor in the Declaration of Independence on 4 July in Philadelphia. Also Moore's Creek, joined with the British defeat in June at Charles Town, would forestall a British offensive in the South for two and one-half years.

MacDonald, on his capture, was taken to the Patriot camp where he tendered his sword to Colonel Moore (who had arrived at Moore's Creek after the battle to assume overall command), his way of insisting on a formal surrender. Moore returned the sword (according to the custom of the day), assuring MacDonald that he would be well treated as a prisoner. MacDonald and the other Loyalist officers—the regular soldiers captured were paroled and allowed to return to their homes on the oaths not to take up arms against the Patriot cause in the future—were conveyed to Halifax jail via New Bern. From there he was moved to Philadelphia, where he was kept in close confinement for several months. Finally, in the fall of 1776, he was exchanged along with General Richard Prescott for the American generals John Sullivan and Lord Stirling, William Alexander. Apparently, MacDonald remained in North America with the British forces in the United States or in Nova Scotia for the remainder of the Revolution. In 1784 he was in London.

SEE: Robert M. Calhoon, *The Loyalists in Revolutionary America, 1760–1781* (1973); Walter Clark, ed., *State Records of North Carolina*, vols. 11, 15 (1895, 1898); Robert C. DeMond, *The Loyalists in North Carolina during the Revolution* (1940); English records: Colonial Office, 1773–75, and Foreign Office, 1783–94 (North Carolina State Archives, Raleigh); John Fortescue, ed., *The Correspondence of King George the Third from 1760 to December 1783*, vol. 3 (1928); Laura P. Frech, "The Wilmington Committee of Public Safety and the Loyalist Rising of February, 1776," *North Carolina Historical Review* 41 (1964); Donald MacDonald Paper (North Carolina State Archives, Raleigh); J. P. MacLean, *Scotch Highlanders in America* (1900); Hugh F. Rankin, "The Moore's Creek Bridge Campaign, 1776," *North Carolina Historical Review* 30 (1953); Lorenzo Sabine, *Biographical Sketches of Loyalists in the American Revolution*, vols. 1–2 (1864), and *The American Loyalists* (1847); William L. Saunders, ed., *Colonial Records of North Carolina*, vol. 10 (1890).

JAMES M. CLIFTON

MacDonald, Flora (*1722–5 Mar. 1790*), Tory and befriender of the Young Pretender, was the daughter of Ranald and Marion MacDonald, who lived on the Isle of Uist in the Hebrides. Her father died when she was a small child. When her mother married Hugh McDonald, Flora was left with relatives who were responsible for her education. For several years she lived with Lady Clanranald, of her father's family, who hired a governess for Flora. In 1739 Lady Margaret, the wife of Sir Alexander McDonald, invited her to Monkstadt, their home on the Isle of Skye. She went with them to Edinburgh to complete her education but returned to Skye in 1745, an accomplished young lady.

Meanwhile, Charles Edward, the Stuart pretender to the Crown of England, decided to challenge the Hanoverian right to the Crown. When he landed in Scotland, he did not have the support of all its people. Many followed him out of loyalty to the Stuart family, not because they considered it good politics. However, a fair-sized army flocked to his support, but its threat was crushed at the Battle of Culloden on 16 Apr. 1746 by the Duke of Cumberland of the royal family. This man, who became known in Scotland as "the Butcher" and "the Bloody Duke," was determined to capture Charles Edward and prevent any future uprisings by the Scots in his support.

Many Scots died for the Young Pretender, and many helped him escape, but the one who received the most attention was Flora MacDonald. The prince reached Skye, but there it seemed that he would be taken, for the island was virtually covered and surrounded by the king's men, many of whom were Scots. Through Lady Clanranald, Flora became a part of the plot to help him escape. The young woman attained from her stepfather, an officer of the king, passports for herself and Betty Burke, an Irish spinning maid who was the fugitive in disguise. After much difficulty she reached Lady Margaret's home, where officers of the king were dining. Flora was so self-contained and so charming that no one suspected that anything was amiss. The next day she and the prince traveled some distance to a boat that took him back to France.

Shortly afterwards the prince's escape became known, and Flora was arrested. For a time she was imprisoned in Scotland, then taken to London and imprisoned in the Tower. She was released under the Act of Indemnity in 1747. All London knew who she was, and many paid homage to her. After accomplishing the release of those arrested with her, Flora returned to Scotland early in 1750. On 6 November of that year she married Allan MacDonald, who was heir to the home in which Charles Edward Stuart, as Betty Burke, had spent the night. Flora became mistress of the home, where she delighted in honoring such guests as Dr. Samuel Johnson by allowing them to sleep on the same bed—even on the same sheets—that had been a refuge for the Stuart prince.

After Culloden many Scots moved to the New World, more for economic reasons than any other. Of these, one-fourth settled in North Carolina after signing the "bloody oath" by which they promised loyalty to the House of Hanover. It was for economic reasons that Allan and Flora MacDonald finally settled in North Carolina in 1774. Wilmington gave a ball in Flora's honor, and she was an overwhelming success socially. When the family reached Cross Creek (now Fayetteville), the people gave her a welcome that far outdid Wilmington. The MacDonalds lived for a while at Cross Creek, then at Cameron Hill, after which Allan bought a tract of land in Anson County. On this property they built a home and named it "Killiegray."

Flora had chosen a bad time to immigrate because the American Revolution was virtually inevitable. She had two sons with the British forces, two sons and a daughter who had come to America with their parents, and a young son and daughter who had been left with relatives in Scotland to go to school. When the king's standard was raised among the Scots in the Cumberland County area, Flora went among the people encouraging them to volunteer.

Allan MacDonald received a commission and joined General Donald MacDonald's forces. The plan for this army was to march to Wilmington, where they would join with British forces to keep North Carolina loyal. General MacDonald was clever, but so were his antagonists: James Moore, Richard Caswell, and Alexander Lillington. At Moore's Creek Bridge on 27 Feb. 1776, the Scots ran into Caswell and Lillington. Among the eight hundred prisoners taken by the Whig forces were Allan MacDonald and one of his sons. Allan was imprisoned at Halifax for a time, then transferred to Pennsylvania. He prevailed upon his wife to return to Scotland, which she was finally able to do in 1779. Since her house had been burned and most of her possessions destroyed, Flora MacDonald sold the silver tea service and other gifts given to her during her imprisonment in London. With this money she was able to secure passage for herself and her daughter on a British man-of-war. On the trip home the British vessel was attacked by the French, and during the skirmish Flora was injured. After the French were driven off she reportedly said, "I have hazarded my life for the House of Stuart and for the House of Hanover and I do not see that I am a great gainer by either." According to some stories, the Scottish heroine had two small children who died and were buried in North Carolina, but there is no proof of this.

Flora MacDonald lived with her brother in Scotland until her husband was released in a prisoner exchange. They returned to Kingsburg (or Kingsborough), their ancestral home in the Highlands. When Flora died, the sheets on which the Stuart prince had slept became her shroud. They had been with her on all of her travels. One of her sons had a marble slab placed on her grave, but over the years it was totally chipped away by souvenir seekers.

For a time an outstanding women's college at Red Springs in Robeson County bore her name, but it is now a part of St. Andrews Presbyterian College in Laurinburg.

SEE: Samuel A. Ashe, ed., *Biographical History of North Carolina*, vol. 7 (1908); Elizabeth F. Ellett, *The Women of the American Revolution* (1900); William Henry Foote, *Sketches of North Carolina, Historical and Biographical: Illustrative of the Principles of a Portion of Her Early Settlers* (1846); Ian Charles Cargil Graham, *Colonists from Scotland: Emigration to North Carolina, 1707–1783* (1956); *Greensboro Daily News*, 1 Feb. 1962; C. H. Hamlin, *Ninety Bits of North Carolina Biography* (1946); J. P. MacLean, *An Historical Account of the Settlement of Scotch Highlanders in*

America prior to the Peace of 1783 (1968); Duane Meyer, *The Highland Scots of North Carolina* (1963); *North Carolina Historical Review* 18 (July 1941); *The* (Lumberton) *Robesonian*, 26 Feb. 1951; *We the People* (June 1943); Stephen B. Weeks Scrapbook, vol. 1 (North Carolina Collection, University of North Carolina, Chapel Hill); John H. Wheeler, *Historical Sketches of North Carolina from 1584 to 1851* (1851).

MAUD THOMAS SMITH

McDonald, Ralph Waldo (*19 Mar. 1903–21 Jan. 1977*), educator, legislator, gubernatorial candidate, and president of Bowling Green State University, was born near Shawneetown in Gallatin County, Ill., the son of G. L. and Lillie Sanders McDonald. Reared in Illinois and Arkansas, McDonald was graduated from the public high school in Paragould, Ark., in 1919. After working a year to pay his way through college, he attended Hendrix College in Conway, Ark., where in 1923 he received an A.B. degree with majors in economics, English, and mathematics. Immediately after graduation, he taught high school mathematics in Fort Smith, Ark., then moved to North Carolina as principal of the Sunnyside Consolidated Schools in Fayetteville from 1924 to 1927. From 1928 to 1934 he was head of the Department of Psychology and Education at Salem College in Winston-Salem, while also serving as business adviser to the college president and leading Salem's extension work.

While at Salem McDonald began graduate work in educational psychology at Duke University, where he obtained an M.A. degree in 1927 and a Ph.D. in 1933. His master's thesis on public school revenue in North Carolina pointed to an abiding interest in improving public school finances in the state. This interest led him to obtain a seat in the North Carolina House of Representatives from Forsyth County in 1934. In the 1935 legislature he quickly became an important force in leading the opposition to the sales tax that Governor J. C. B. Ehringhaus had succeeded in getting through the General Assembly in the previous session. McDonald filled an important void that had been created by the death of Dennis G. Brummit in January 1935. In effect, he replaced Brummit as the antiestablishment candidate for governor against Clyde R. Hoey in the Democratic primary of 1936. Despite the presence of a third candidate, McDonald came within 4,468 votes of leading Hoey in the first primary and garnered over 214,000 votes to Hoey's 266,354 in the second primary. The depth of opposition to the sales tax and McDonald's emphasis on the so-called Gardner machine gave him a strong popular following at the time.

McDonald showed his loyalty to the Democratic party when he campaigned for Hoey in the general election. Rather than return to teaching, he planned to further his political career by entering law school at The University of North Carolina in September 1936 and to set up a practice in Winston-Salem. His plans were aborted when he developed tuberculosis in 1937 and was forced to spend two years recovering in sanitariums. Emerging cured in late February 1939, he soon accepted a position in Chapel Hill as associate director of extension; at the same time he was appointed professor of education in the graduate school and head of the radio department. The latter post became a major vehicle for McDonald to create a unique educational radio network that used commercial stations in North Carolina and South Carolina to broadcast at least twenty hours of programming each week.

Meanwhile, in politics he supported J. Melville Broughton's successful bid for governor in 1940, then re-signed his positions at The University of North Carolina in 1943 to begin his long campaign for governor in 1944. While he was able to resurrect many of his supporters from 1936, issues like the sales tax and the "machine" were no longer enough to stimulate the same enthusiasm for his candidacy. He was defeated by R. Gregg Cherry.

In August 1944 McDonald reentered the education arena as director of conferences for the National Education Association but maintained his residence in Winston-Salem for a year to serve out his term as president of the North Carolina Education Association. After he moved to Washington, D.C., his duties expanded to executive secretary of the National Commission on Teacher Education and Professional Standards (1946–51) and executive secretary of the National Education Association's Department of Higher Education. In the latter role he became responsible for the National Conference on Higher Education, predecessor to the American Association for Higher Education. He also had time for noneducational issues such as serving as president of the National Committee on Atomic Information (1945–51).

In 1951 McDonald accepted an offer to become the fourth president of Bowling Green State University in Ohio. For ten years he presided over that institution's growth from 3,200 to over 7,000 students. His abrupt resignation in September 1961 came at a time of increasing dissatisfaction on the campus.

From Bowling Green McDonald moved to Florida to study that state's higher education system, then settled into semiretirement in Fort Lauderdale as an educational consultant. In later years he made frequent trips to Charlotte as adviser to the city's teachers' association. He eventually retired to Russellville, Ark., where he died and was buried in Plummerville Cemetery.

McDonald married Athleen Taylor of Arkansas on 12 June 1923. The couple had one daughter, Athalea, who married John M. Haygood and moved to California. As president emeritus of Bowling Green, McDonald was honored by having a quadrangle on the campus named for him.

SEE: *Charlotte Observer*, 3 Nov. 1935; John L. Cheney, Jr., ed., *North Carolina Government, 1585–1979* (1981); *Durham Morning Herald*, 12 Oct. 1945, 18 Dec. 1960; *Greensboro Daily News*, 3 Dec. 1936, 28 May, 6, 18 Sept., 11 Oct. 1942, 24 June 1961; Joseph L. Morrison, *Governor O. Max Gardner* (1971); Press releases from Bowling Green State University, 6 June 1951, 17 Aug. 1964 (Duke University Alumni Office, Durham); Elmer L. Puryear, *Democratic Party Dissension in North Carolina, 1928–36* (1962); Raleigh *News and Observer*, scattered issues.

THOMAS S. MORGAN

McDougald, Archibald (*fl. 1767–96*), Loyalist militia leader, moved from Scotland to Cumberland County, N.C., in 1767. When the American Revolution began, he owned 640 acres. In 1779 he tried to reach the British in Georgia but was captured and confined in a prison ship at Charles Town for ten months. He escaped to Savannah and joined John Hamilton's Royal North Carolina Regiment, serving until Lord Charles Cornwallis passed through Wilmington. At that time Major James Craig, commanding at Wilmington, made McDougald commander of the Cumberland County militia. Archibald led his men in three skirmishes with the rebels and was a leader in the capture of Governor Thomas Burke. Left in the country by the evacuation of Wilmington, McDougald was captured, paroled to Charles Town, and exchanged. He rejoined the Royal North Carolina Regiment and went with the corps to East Florida in 1782 and to Nova Scotia in 1783.

McDougald took 550 acres at the regimental settlement near Country Harbour, Nova Scotia, and an additional 600 acres in Kings County; the latter grant was escheated in 1796. He lived at Country Harbour until late 1787, when he went to London because the Loyalists' claims commissioners at Halifax had refused his claim on account of lateness. In spite of his strenuous efforts, red tape kept him in London until March 1790, when the commissioners gave him thirty pounds with which to return to Nova Scotia. McDougald resettled in North Carolina, however, apparently in Anson County.

SEE: Anson County Deed Book Z (North Carolina State Archives, Raleigh); Lindley S. Butler, ed., *The Narrative of Col. David Fanning* (1981); Marion Gilroy, comp., *Loyalists and Land Settlement in Nova Scotia* (1937); A. W. Savary, ed., *Col. David Fanning's Narrative of His Exploits and Adventures as a Loyalist of North Carolina in the American Revolution* (1908).

CAROLE WATTERSON TROXLER

McDougald, Samuel *(fl. 1782–94)*, clerical impostor, appeared on the tax lists of Northampton County in 1782 along with his brother James. Their antecedents are unknown, and both were unmarried. It is probable that they were schoolteachers. The existing records suggest an association between the McDougalds and General Allen Jones of Mount Gallant in Northampton County. From his first appearance in North Carolina, Samuel presented himself as a clergyman of the Church of England. This deception was plausible at the time due to the dual role of many of the eighteenth-century clergy as minister and schoolmaster.

By 1786 Samuel McDougald had moved across the Roanoke River to Halifax County. In that year he was enrolled as a member of the Royal White Hart Masonic Lodge in the town of Halifax. Soon afterwards he began serving the lodge as chaplain, an office that had not been filled since the death of the Reverend Charles Edward Taylor late in 1784. According to the lodge minutes, McDougald also became active as a clergyman in the neighborhood. He must have made a good impression in the lodge, for late in 1787 he was one of its representatives to the meeting of the Grand Lodge held in Tarboro. Earlier in the same year General Allen Jones had proposed a bill in the North Carolina legislature, then meeting in Tarboro, that the Reverend Mr. McDougald be made chaplain of the Assembly. The measure was defeated. In the same year McDougald is said to have officiated as a clergyman in St. Mary's Parish, Edgecombe County.

Less is known about James McDougald. In 1789 a Reverend James McDougald advertised in the Edenton *State Gazette* that he planned to open an academy seventeen miles above the town of Halifax on 1 November of that year where he would teach English, Latin, Greek, and French as well as writing, arithmetic, bookkeeping, and geography. Nothing further is known about the academy. As there is no other reference to James McDougald as a clergyman, the advertisement may have been an error and Samuel intended instead of James. It is possible, of course, that both brothers posed as clergymen. The only property that Samuel McDougald owned in Halifax County was a tract of twenty-five acres located in the area where the proposed academy was to be established. It was not far from Quankey Chapel of the old colonial establishment, but it is not known if McDoug-

ald held services there. He sold this land to Edward Good in 1791.

James McDougald died late in 1793. He and Samuel may not have been on good terms at the end, as James devised his whole estate to his nephew in his will, probated in Halifax in February 1794. It is of interest that Allen Jones, his wife Mary, and their son-in-law, John Sitgreaves, were the witnesses for this document. Samuel McDougald tried to substitute a will naming himself as beneficiary, but the forgery was detected. For this crime, described by his fellow Masons as disgraceful to humanity and derogatory to his character as a Mason, he was brought before the lodge and, after being given a chance to defend himself, was found guilty and expelled from the membership. His clerical deception undoubtedly came to light at this time. McDougald left Halifax in disgrace and nothing further is known of him.

On 9 Nov. 1789 the Reverend Charles Pettigrew had written to McDougald to enlist his support for and participation in the Tarboro convention of the Episcopal church planned for the following year. There was no reply to the letter and McDougald took no part in any of the Tarboro meetings. From his later history, it is clear why he did not. In 1830 the Reverend Robert J. Miller, then about eighty years old, wrote a letter to the historian and clergyman Francis L. Hawks on the state of the Episcopal church in North Carolina during the post-Revolutionary period. He mentioned that Samuel McDougald was then living in Halifax and had charge of the congregations that had formerly been under the care of the Reverend Thomas Burges and the Reverend Charles E. Taylor. He went on to say that McDougald had proved to be an impostor, which had a pernicious influence on the Episcopal church in that part of the state.

SEE: Halifax and Northhampton County Records (North Carolina State Archives, Raleigh); Thomas C. Parramore, *Launching the Craft* (1975); Claiborne T. Smith, Jr., and Stuart H. Smith, *The History of Trinity Church* (1955); *State Gazette*, 1 Oct. 1789.

CLAIBORNE T. SMITH, JR.

McDougall, William *(22 June 1871–28 Nov. 1938)*, psychologist, was born in Lancashire, England, the son of Rebekah Smalley and Isaac Shimwell McDougall. He was a precocious child, and his Scots father enrolled him at fifteen in the newly established University of Manchester, where he studied science—particularly biology and paleontology. McDougall was graduated with first-class honors in 1889 but, dissatisfied with a merely provincial training, he won a scholarship to St. John's College, Cambridge, in 1890. The next four years were decisive for his development. He took a medical degree, specializing in physiology, and received a double First in the natural science Tripos. The result was to nurture a tendency towards what he himself came to see as a characteristic intellectual arrogance. In 1894 he went up to St. Thomas's Hospital, London, for the final three years of study for the M.B. and did research with C. S. Sherrington; at the same time, he encountered William James's *Principles of Psychology*, which convinced him that a full understanding of human nature would have to proceed from psychology and anthropology fused with physiology. A year's service on an expedition to the Torres Strait and Borneo convinced McDougall that "field" anthropology was "too easy" for him, and he turned to psychology. In 1899 he married Annie Aurelia Hickmore.

The years from 1900 to 1914 were perhaps McDougall's most productive. After spending a year in Göttingen with G. E. Müller (at work on the psychophysics of color vision), he returned to England to give a course in laboratory methods in psychology at University College, London. His own research developed along two lines: his basic empiricism led to further psychophysical research, and his Jamesian tendencies led to more speculative papers on the general functioning of the brain. In 1904, in search of an audience, he applied for and was appointed to the post of reader of moral philosophy at Oxford; his lectures ranged over the whole of psychology, broadly conceived. The position involved no experimental work, but he found space in the physiology laboratory where he could pursue his private research. In these years McDougall helped literally to create psychology as a professional discipline in Britain: he was one of the principal organizers of the British Psychological Society in 1901 and an associate editor of the society's *Journal* from its establishment in 1910. The small group of students who clustered around him at Oxford became the first generation of professional psychologists in Britain, including J. C. Flugel, William Brown, Cyril Burt, and others.

At this point his first books appeared, two of which deserve particular mention for their originality and for the light they throw on McDougall's mind. Coupled with his "intellectual arrogance" he exhibited a nearly habitual skepticism of established doctrine. In his second book, *Introduction to Social Psychology* (1908), McDougall first proposed his hormic theory of psychology, emphasizing the purposive aspect of behavior and insisting on the presence of innate dispositions or instincts within animals; for much of his life this hormic theory was a major competitor to associationist and behaviorist psychology. *Body and Mind* (1911), subtitled *A History and Defense of Animism*, remains perhaps the strongest case for the existence of mind and its role in human development.

When the war broke out in 1914, McDougall was made an officer in the Royal Army Medical Corps and had to leave moral philosophy for the treatment of shell-shocked patients. But when he returned to Oxford in 1919, he was still among the most eminent British psychologists.

In 1920 McDougall accepted the chair of psychology at Harvard—attracted by the prestige of the position that had been James's and Hugo Münsterberg's, and by the promise of equipment and students. Yet it was a profoundly tragic decision. McDougall found the students at Harvard to be thoroughgoing mechanists in psychology, unsympathetic to his own ideas. Cambridge he disliked, as a "noisy, Irish city," and Harvard itself did not provide for its faculty as he thought proper. Finally, the arrogance and iconoclasm that had been acceptable in England were looked on with suspicion in America. His various unorthodoxies—eugenics, psychical research, animism, his book *The Group Mind* (1920)—and the antimaterialist tenor of his thought caused him to be regarded by many of his colleagues as the defender of reactionary viewpoints in both the social and scientific realms. (The most ambitious of his unorthodox projects was a long-term experiment to test the Lamarckian theory by seeing whether the effects of training could be inherited from one generation of rats to the next. Begun in 1921, the experiment was studying the fiftieth generation at McDougall's death.) His importance as a psychologist went largely unquestioned to the end of his life, but his actual influence on the development of psychology, so decisive in England, was much less obvious in his American years.

When President William P. Few of Duke University

wrote McDougall in 1926 asking for the names of psychologists who might be approached to head the new psychology department at the school, McDougall suggested his own. By the fall of 1927 he was in North Carolina. Here he was more nearly content. As one of the most eminent scientists at Duke, he was widely courted by the university community. McDougall took pains to build up around him a department of younger men who shared his commitment to a purposive psychology—scholars like Helge Lundholm, Karl Zener, and Donald Adams. He carefully arranged for them a light teaching load of the courses they wanted in order to leave them free for research; in turn, they revered him. His own stream of publications did not slacken. Now much of his energy was given over to writing books that systematized or developed his earlier ideas; his only experimental work of note was the continuing Lamarckian experiment. In 1928 McDougall hired a young botanist, J. B. Rhine, to help him with the Lamarckian project. Rhine had gone to Duke hoping to begin a career in psychical research, and the next year McDougall found him a teaching position in the department. Rhine had already begun a program of parapsychological investigation, with McDougall's approval, and when Rhine's first book, *Extra-Sensory Perception*, appeared in 1934, McDougall wrote an enthusiastic preface.

Beginning in 1932, McDougall spent half the academic year in England, but he continued to play an active role at Duke for the other half. He refused to let his increasing deafness prevent the intellectual exchanges to which he was committed. The cancer that caused him great suffering in his last year did not stop him from teaching—or from working on his last book, *The Riddle of Life*—until shortly before his death, and he was careful to record a series of observations on his pain.

McDougall was survived by four children: Lesley, Duncan, Angus, and Kenneth. Another daughter, Janet, died young.

SEE: William McDougall Letters and Papers (Manuscript Department, Duke University Library, Durham); Carl Murchison, ed., *A History of Psychology in Autobiography*, vol. 1 (1930); R. C. Oldfield, "Psychology in Oxford—1898–1949," *Bulletin of British Psychological Society* 2 (1950); Anthony Lewin Robinson, *William McDougall, M.B., D.Sc., F.R.S.: A Bibliography* (1943); Benjamin B. Wolman, ed., *Historical Roots of Contemporary Psychology* (1968).

MICHAEL R. MCVAUGH
SEYMOUR H. MAUSKOPF

McDowell, Archibald (*10 Apr. 1818–27 May 1881*), educator and clergyman, was born in Kershaw District, S.C., the ninth of twelve children of the Reverend Archibald and Mary Drakeford McDowell. His parents are believed to have emigrated from Scotland around 1800.

After spending several years working on his father's farm and in a mill, McDowell enrolled at Wake Forest College in 1842, receiving a B.A. degree in 1847; Wake Forest subsequently awarded him a D.D. degree in 1867. After graduation he was named principal of the Wake Forest Female School. This institution—adjacent to the college campus—had been in operation since 1844 under the supervision of William Hayes Owen, professor of ancient languages at Wake Forest, his mother (Mrs. John Owen), and his sisters (Mary and Sallie). McDowell also served as a tutor for the college during the academic year 1847–48.

In the late summer of 1848, McDowell was elected principal—or president—of the newly established Chowan Female Institute, in Murfreesboro, which opened on 11 Oct. 1848. He remained in the post until late April or early May 1849, when driven away by a smallpox epidemic that threatened the town and the vicinity. Subsequently, he served as principal of Milton Female Academy (1849–53) and of Metropolitan Female Seminary in Raleigh (1854–55).

The autumn of 1855 found McDowell returning to the Chowan Female Institute as professor of mathematics and natural sciences. He became president of the institution in 1862 and served until his death. In addition, he was pastor of the Murfreesboro Baptist Church from 1855 to 1872 and from 1876 to 1879.

Although McDowell advocated educational advantages and opportunities for women beyond "ornamental" and "domestic" studies, his concept of their proper role in society caused him to stop short of any suggestion that men and women should pursue identical courses of study. In offering degree programs for women, he would eliminate the study of mathematics—beyond plane trigonometry—and much of metaphysics. On the other hand, he proposed to expose women to a broader knowledge of Latin and more extensive study of English and of belle lettres.

McDowell viewed the objectives of all education as the promotion of happiness and the increase of efficiency in the business pursuits of life. Its chief purposes, he believed, were to enlighten, to liberalize, to cultivate, and to refine. His philosophy was summarized in the *Biblical Recorder* of 26 Feb. 1873—in an article that he represented as the outgrowth of more than twenty years of work and reflection. He noted: "Woman is to be the presiding genius of the social and domestic circles, and by her intelligence, her refinement, her purity and affection to charm away every evil and to make every home, however humble, a sanctuary dearer to its inmates than the haunts of pleasure or the abodes (of) wealth. She is also to be the nurse and teacher of children. . . . Hence, to fill her position well and to discharge her duties successfully, she needs an intellectual culture not less varied and complete than that needed by the other sex."

McDowell married Mary Hayes Owen in Wake Forest on 15 June 1847. They became the parents of seven children: Fannie (d. in childhood), Mary Henderson (d. in infancy), William Owen, Sallie (m. John B. Neal), Ruth Rebecca (m. David Alexander Day, Sr.), Eunice, and Archibald.

A portrait of McDowell hangs in the foyer of the administration building—named McDowell Columns in his memory—on the Chowan College campus. He was buried in the town cemetery at Wake Forest.

SEE: *Biblical Recorder* (obituary), 8 June 1881; Memory Aldridge Lester, *Old Southern Bible Records* (1974); Archibald McDowell, "What Should Be the Extent of the Course of Study in Female Schools?" *Biblical Recorder*, 26 Feb. 1873; Edgar V. McKnight and Oscar Creech, *A History of Chowan College* (1964); George W. Paschal, *History of Wake Forest College*, vol. 1 (1935).

R. HARGUS TAYLOR

McDowell, Charles (1743–31 Mar. 1815), Revolutionary War officer, was born in Winchester, Va., the son of Joseph McDowell, who settled at Quaker Meadows, west of present-day Morganton in Burke County, N.C., and his wife Margaret O'Neil McDowell. He was a brother of Joseph McDowell. At the beginning of the

American Revolution Charles McDowell became a captain of militia (in what was then Rowan County), but in April 1776 he was promoted to lieutenant colonel. He was occupied in quieting Indian raids and in preventing the activity of scattered Loyalists in the backcountry. He also participated in the expedition of 1776 led by Brigadier General Griffith Rutherford against the Cherokee Indians.

When Loyalists led by British Major Patrick Ferguson invaded the Carolinas in 1780, McDowell called for assistance from the "Overmountain Men" in the counties that had been created by North Carolina west of the mountains (in what is now Tennessee). Together they engaged in guerrilla warfare, harassing the enemy on every occasion and preventing other Loyalists from joining Ferguson. As the summer advanced the British and Loyalists became a more serious threat, and McDowell called for reinforcements from across the mountains. Although McDowell was not actually present, it was the Overmountain Men who won the important Battle of Kings Mountain (7 Oct. 1780) that started the enemy on the road to surrender at Yorktown a year later. The North Carolina General Assembly commissioned McDowell brigadier general, and he was placed in command of troops once more sent against the Cherokee Indians.

McDowell served in the state senate in 1777 and 1778 and for nine additional consecutive terms between 1782 and 1789. In 1784 he was one of three commissioners named to lay off the county seat town of Morganton in Burke County. At various times he also served as a county justice of the peace, sponsored a school, and was county entry taker. He served in the Hillsborough and Fayetteville conventions (1788 and 1789), where he favored ratification of the federal constitution.

Near the end of the Revolution McDowell married Grace Greenlee Bowman, the widow of Captain John Bowman. They had several children, including Charles and Sarah Grace.

SEE: John L. Cheney, Jr., ed., *North Carolina Government, 1585–1979* (1981); *DAB*, vol. 12 (1933); Cyrus L. Hunter, *Sketches of Western North Carolina* (1877); Edward W. Phifer, Jr., *Burke: The History of a North Carolina County* (1982).

WILLIAM S. POWELL

MacDowell, John (1717–63), Anglican missionary, was licensed on 8 Aug. 1753 by the bishop of London to serve in the colony of North Carolina and to receive the king's bounty of twenty pounds for travel expenses. In January 1754 MacDowell became rector of St. James's Parish, Wilmington, where he served until May 1757. For the next year he had charge of both St. James's and St. Philip's Parish in Brunswick. In addition to his work in these parishes, he held occasional services at St. John's, Onslow; St. Gabriel's, Duplin; and St. Martin's, Bladen. Traveling on horseback through swamps and wilderness to minister to these scattered missions, he underwent many hardships for which he was poorly compensated. On 5 June 1758 he resigned his work in Wilmington to be rector of St. Philip's, Brunswick, but continued to hold occasional services in the neighboring counties.

In April 1760 the members of St. Philip's vestry wrote to the Society for the Propagation of the Gospel in Foreign Parts requesting that MacDowell be appointed to their parish as a missionary of the society. They noted that since coming to St. Philip's, he had "always behaved himself as became a worthy Minister of Jesus Christ." Further, MacDowell had been "very well liked by all the Vestries of every Parish, where he hath officiated." Governor Arthur Dobbs also urged the society to make MacDowell one of its missionaries, as St. Philip's parish was unable to support a minister on its own. He went on to say that the parish had gone to great expense to erect a church that, when completed, would be the largest in the province. The king had given St. Philip's its communion silver, a Bible, and prayer books. Dobbs proposed to make it "his majesty's chapel in this government."

Less than a year later MacDowell complained that he was overworked and underpaid by his vestry. Following the death of his wife in November 1760, the vestry had reduced his salary on the grounds that his expenses were less. In July 1761 he wrote the Society for the Propagation of the Gospel that he had been forced to sell three of his slaves "for the discharge of debts contracted by last years sickness Death & misfortunes in my family." At this time he was so despondent about his health that he petitioned the society to care for his infant son in the event of his death in North Carolina. Six months later he wrote to the Moravians at Wachovia asking them to do the same if the society rejected his request. One of his problems was solved in June 1762, when he received an official appointment as a missionary of the society, but his health steadily declined.

In hopes of improving his health, MacDowell went to Wachovia in the summer of 1763 to place himself under the care of a Moravian doctor. MacDowell remarked that "among the Gentry of this land it is the fashion to visit the Moravian towns." During his two-month stay he preached once in the Moravian church and baptized 150 children of English parents in the area. In spite of the kind attention of the Moravian doctor, MacDowell's condition did not improve. When he left Wachovia he was "too weak to ride, so was borne in a two-horse litter, led by his negro." Several weeks after returning to Brunswick he died of "chronic diarrhoea." He was buried in the churchyard of St. Philip's Parish beside his wife.

MacDowell married Sarah Grange of the Lower Cape Fear section. They had one child, John Baptist.

SEE: Gerald Fothergill, *A List of Emigrant Ministers to America, 1690–1811* (1904); Adelaide L. Fries, ed., *Records of the Moravians in North Carolina*, vol. 1 (1922); Lawrence Lee, *The Lower Cape Fear in Colonial Days* (1965); William L. Saunders, ed., *Colonial Records of North Carolina*, vol. 6 (1888); Alfred M. Waddell, *A History of New Hanover County* (1909).

LAWRENCE F. LONDON

McDowell, Joseph (15 Feb. 1756–11 July 1801), Revolutionary War officer and U.S. congressman, was born in Winchester, Va., the son of Joseph McDowell, who settled at Quaker Meadows, west of present-day Morganton in Burke County, N.C., and his wife, Margaret O'Neil. Because of the several contemporary men of the same name, the subject of this sketch was sometimes designated as "of Quaker Meadows," as "Quaker Meadows Joe," or simply as Q.M. He was the brother of Charles McDowell and the second cousin and brother-in-law of Joseph McDowell "of Pleasant Gardens" or P.G. He was also a cousin of "Hunting" John McDowell. They all moved with their families to western North Carolina. Joseph of Quaker Meadows was sent back to Winchester for his early education and then attended

Washington College (later Washington and Lee) in Lexington, Va.

With the outbreak of the American Revolution, McDowell served with his cousin Joseph in the Burke County militia, commanded by his older brother Charles. The regiment was involved in incursions against the Cherokee Indians under General Griffith Rutherford and in suppressing Tory uprisings in its own area. Early in 1780 it participated in the Battle of Ramsour's Mill. Joseph and his brother are credited with initiating the plan to organize a force to challenge the Tory troops under British Colonel Patrick Ferguson, and it was under the "Council Oak" on their Quaker Meadows estate that their regiment joined the "Overmountain Men" of Isaac Shelby and John Sevier and proceeded towards Kings Mountain. Just prior to the battle there, Charles left his troops and turned the command over to his brother Joseph, though some believe that it was his cousin Joseph (of Pleasant Gardens) who took charge. The Burke County regiment played a decisive role in the victory over Ferguson, after which Colonel McDowell led his troops home. However, they were soon active again and in January 1781 fought in the front ranks of General Daniel Morgan's force at the Battle of Cowpens. In 1782 McDowell led a final expedition against the Cherokee.

After the war, he, like his brother, was noted for his tolerance towards the former Tories. On several occasions he offered protection to persecuted Loyalists and ordered those formerly under his command to cease their maltreatment of them. He practiced law in Burke County and served with his brother and cousin in the state legislature; he was in the House of Commons for consecutive terms between 1780 and 1789 and then moved to the state senate, where he served from 1790 to 1795. In 1786 he held a seat in the Council of State, and in 1787 he was elected to the Continental Congress although there is no record of his attendance.

All three McDowells, Charles and the two Josephs, were delegates to the North Carolina conventions for the ratification of the federal constitution in 1788 and 1789. Of the three, only Joseph of Quaker Meadows, a strong anti-Federalist, voted against it, stating that he still had reservations as long as the proposed Bill of Rights was not approved by the requisite number of states. In 1789 he was named a member of the first board of trustees of The University of North Carolina. He served as a representative in the Third and the Fifth Congress (1794–95 and 1797–99). During his first term he was identified as a Federalist, but in the second he was a Republican and worked against various Federalist policies such as the Alien and Sedition Acts. He chose not to run for reelection in 1798.

In 1797 McDowell served on the commission to survey the boundary line between Kentucky and Tennessee. Impressed with the land he traveled through, he moved to Kentucky in 1800. In 1801, however, he returned to Burke County and died soon afterwards of apoplexy at his brother's home at Quaker Meadows. He was survived by his wife, Margaret Moffitt McDowell, and two sons and six daughters.

SEE: Samuel A. Ashe, ed., *Biographical History of North Carolina*, vol. 7 (1908); J. D. Bailey, *Commanders at Kings Mountain* (1926); *Biog. Dir. Am. Cong.* (1971); Burke County Wills and Estate Records (North Carolina State Archives, Raleigh); John Hugh McDowell, *The McDowells, Erwins, Irwins, and Connections* (1918); E. W. Phifer, Jr., *Burke: The History of a North Carolina County* (1977); Raleigh *Register*, 18 Aug. 1801; "Sketches of Burke

County Pioneers," in Thomas G. Walton Papers (Southern Historical Collection, University of North Carolina, Chapel Hill); *Western North Carolina: Historical and Biographical* (1890).

JOHN INSCOE

McDowell, Joseph (25 Feb. 1758–18 May 1795), Revolutionary War officer, the son of "Hunting" John McDowell, was born at his father's newly acquired Pleasant Gardens home in what is now McDowell County. To distinguish him from his second cousin and brother-in-law of the same name who lived at Quaker Meadows, he was usually referred to as "Pleasant Gardens Joe," Joseph McDowell, Jr., or P. G. Young McDowell was sent to Winchester, Va., his father's former home, to attend school. At age eighteen he enlisted, along which his cousin Joseph, in a Burke County regiment commanded by another cousin, Charles McDowell. He served with the regiment in various encounters with Tories and Cherokee Indians and during its most effective action at the Battle of Kings Mountain. There is some uncertainty among descendants as to which Joseph commanded the regiment in that battle, though the best evidence indicates that "Pleasant Gardens Joe," then a major at age twenty-two, served under "Quaker Meadows Joe," then a colonel. Soon after the war Major McDowell was made an honorary militia general and continued to be referred to as General McDowell for the remainder of his life.

With his military career behind him, McDowell resumed his education, studying both medicine and law. He was admitted to the bar in 1791 and seems to have limited himself to a legal practice in Burke, Rowan, and Rutherford counties. From 1787 to 1793 McDowell represented Burke County in the House of Commons. He was also a delegate to the constitutional conventions of 1788 and 1789 from Burke County, as was his cousin of Quaker Meadows. From 1790 to 1794 he served on the board of trustees of The University of North Carolina.

McDowell married Mary Moffitt, who survived him as did three children; Ann, James, and John. His widow married Colonel John Carson and became the mother of Samuel P. Carson, congressman and secretary of state of Texas.

When McDowell County was formed in 1842, it was named for Joseph McDowell of Pleasant Gardens, which fell within the bounds of the new county.

SEE: Samuel A. Ashe, ed., *Biographical History of North Carolina*, vol. 7 (1908); *Biog. Dir. Am. Cong.* (1971); Burke County Wills and Estate Records (North Carolina State Archives, Raleigh); John L. Cheney, Jr., ed., *North Carolina Government, 1585–1979* (1981); Mildred B. Fossett, *History of McDowell County* (1976); Halifax *North Carolina Journal*, 29 June 1795; John Hugh McDowell, *The McDowells, Erwins, Irwins, and Connections* (1981); "Sketches of Burke County Pioneers," in Thomas G. Walton Papers (Southern Historical Collection, University of North Carolina, Chapel Hill).

JOHN INSCOE

McDowell, Joseph Jefferson (13 Nov. 1800–17 Jan. 1877), congressman, was born in Burke (now McDowell) County, the son of Joseph McDowell (of Quaker Meadows)—a native of Winchester, Va., who moved to North Carolina in 1758, served in the American Revolution, and held a number of elective positions—and Margaret Moffitt McDowell. Following her husband's death in July 1801, Mrs. McDowell moved first to Virginia and then,

when her son was five, to Kentucky. In 1817 they returned to Virginia and lived in Augusta County. During these years young McDowell received some education and engaged in farming. In 1824 he moved to Highland County, Ohio, where he farmed until 1829, then became a merchant.

McDowell was elected to the Ohio House of Representatives in 1832 and to the state senate the following year. In 1834 he was appointed brigadier general in the state militia. After studying law, he was admitted to the bar in 1835 and began practicing in Hillsboro, the seat of Highland County. He was an unsuccessful candidate for Congress in 1840 but was thereafter elected as a Democrat to the Twenty-eighth and Twenty-ninth Congress, serving from 4 Mar. 1843 to 3 Mar. 1847. Returning to his law practice and farming, he resided in Ohio for the remainder of his life. He was buried in Hillsboro Cemetery.

SEE: *Biog. Dir. Am. Cong.* (1971); *Cyclopaedia of American Biography*, vol. 4 (1888); John H. Wheeler, *Historical Sketches of North Carolina from 1584 to 1851* (1851); *Who Was Who in America, 1607–1896*, historical vol. (1967).

BRADFORD M. SHELBY

McDowell, Silas (16 May 1795–14 July 1879), tailor, farmer, court clerk, scientific observer, and writer, was born in York District, S.C., the natural son of Elizabeth McDowell. He was raised by his mother and her father, William ("Pacolet William") McDowell, a cousin of General Charles McDowell and a distant relative of Major Joseph ("Pleasant Gardens") McDowell. From about 1805 to 1812 Silas lived with his grandfather in Rutherford County, and in 1812 he went to Asheville and completed his formal education at Newton Academy. He was an apprentice tailor in Charleston, S.C., from 1814 to 1816, after which he practiced his trade in Morganton, N.C., for ten years. In 1826 he moved to Asheville, married two years later, and in 1830 took his wife and child to a farm in Macon County that he had purchased in 1820. From about 1830 to 1846 he served as clerk of the superior court of Macon County while continuing his trade as tailor and building up a large apple orchard.

McDowell served as a guide to several botanists in western North Carolina, which was becoming recognized as an area of great botanical richness. He went on several collecting trips with John Lyon between 1812 and 1814 and was present at Lyon's death in the latter year. In 1839 he served as a guide to Moses Ashley Curtis on an extended jaunt, and Curtis named a new sunflower, *Helianthus dowellianus*, after him. McDowell was then gaining fame because, as a storyteller, he had been the source of much of Senator Robert Strange's *Eoneguski*, "the first North Carolina novel," which had just appeared (1839). Called "the outstanding apple producer in the state" in the 1850s, McDowell sold apples, apple tree graftings, and rhododendrons to individuals and nurseries in North Carolina and Georgia and apparently traveled as far as Asheville to graft trees. After a disastrous freeze in April 1858, he turned to viticulture and to writing about the phenomenon of "thermal belts" in western North Carolina.

After the Civil War, in the face of advancing age and declining fortunes, McDowell gave up his lands and businesses and devoted his remaining years to writing historical and autobiographical pieces, romances based on events of his youth, and sketches and poems illustrating the local landscape. He had a wide circle of friends and correspondents, among whom were Zebulon Vance, Hinton Rowan Helper, David Lowry Swain, Moses Ashley Curtis, Thomas Clingman, Asa Gray, and Lyman Draper. There is a collection of McDowell's materials in the Southern Historical Collection at The University of North Carolina.

On 15 May 1828 McDowell married Elizabeth Erwin (1806–48), whose mother, Patience Lowry, was a half sister of David Lowry Swain. They had eight children, six of whom lived to maturity. McDowell died on his farm near Franklin, N.C., and was buried in Franklin.

SEE: *Appleton's Cyclopedia of American Biography*, vol. 4 (1888); J. P. Arthur, *Western North Carolina: A History* (1914); J. W. Davidson, *The Living Writers of the South* (1869); T. F. Davidson, *First Annual Transactions of the Pen and Plate Club of Asheville* (1905); G. S. Dunbar, "Silas McDowell and the Early Botanical Exploration of Western North Carolina," *North Carolina Historical Review* 41 (1964), and "Thermal Belts in North Carolina," *Geographical Review* (1966 [portrait]).

G. S. DUNBAR

McDowell, Thomas David Smith (4 Jan. 1823–1 May 1898), planter, legislator, and Confederate congressman, was born on his parent's plantation in Bladen County. His father, Dr. Alexander McDowell, was born in Ballydavy, County Down, Ireland, on 1 Nov. 1775. He was graduated from Edinburgh College and the medical school of the University of Glasgow, Scotland, but he became so deeply involved in the Irish struggle for independence that eventually the deteriorating fortunes of that movement forced him to immigrate. He reached the Cape Fear region in 1812, began practicing medicine in Elizabethtown, and married the widow Mary Jane Smith Purdie.

Thomas McDowell studied at the Donaldson Academy and then entered The University of North Carolina, where he was graduated in 1843; he later served as a university trustee from 1858 to 1860 and from 1874 to 1881. Both his parents died within the decade and for the rest of his life McDowell managed the Purdie plantation on which he had been reared. In 1860 it contained 320 acres and 57 slaves and was valued at $65,000.

A lifelong Democrat, McDowell served in the state House of Commons from 1846 to 1850 and in the senate from 1852 to 1855 and from 1858 to 1860. He was a longtime member of the Senate Committee on Education and the Literary Fund, but he sponsored no particular program; his bills ranged from the incorporation of the Cape Fear Division of the Sons of Temperance to the banning of the emancipation of slaves by the owner's will after his death. McDowell's strong Unionism is indicated by a resolution he introduced in 1851 that the states "may well yield somewhat in the conflict of opinion and policy" and that the legislature should endorse the Compromise of 1850. He opposed secession until President Abraham Lincoln's call for troops following the firing on Fort Sumter, but then as a member of the secession convention he voted for disunion. He won a close contest in the convention for a seat in the Confederate Provisional Congress, and in October 1861 he was elected to the First Congress without opposition.

McDowell's chief interest as a congressman was the defense of the North Carolina coast, his only other proposal being that Negroes captured from Union armies should be sold and the proceeds distributed among the troops capturing them. At first he consented to legislation granting the administration of Confederate president Jefferson Davis the necessary war powers, but after

1861 he resisted most efforts to amplify or extend them. When the administration requested new and even more extreme measures, such as suspending the writ of habeas corpus or repudiating the inflated currency, McDowell opposed them adamantly. He did not run for reelection in 1863.

After the war McDowell took no further role in public affairs. By 1885 he had turned over to his sons most of the operation of his plantation. He died there and was buried in the family cemetery outside of Elizabethtown.

In his *Reminiscences*, John H. Wheeler wrote that McDowell was "one of the purest men in public and private life that I ever knew." McDowell married Mary Elizabeth Davis, the daughter of Dr. Goodwin Davis of Richmond County. They had two sons, Alexander and John. The McDowell family was Presbyterian.

SEE: Wanda S. Campbell, Clerk of Superior Court, Bladen County, personal contact; *Journal of the Congress of the Confederate States of America*, vols. 1–2, 5–6 (1904–5); *Journal of the Convention of . . . 1861; Journal of the House of Commons of North Carolina* (1846–50); *Journal of the Senate . . . of North Carolina* (1852–60); John G. McCormick, "Personnel of the Convention of 1861," in *James Sprunt Historical Monographs*, vol. 1 (1900); Thomas D. McDowell Papers (Manuscript Department, Duke University Library, Durham, and Southern Historical Collection, University of North Carolina, Chapel Hill); U.S. Census, 1840–60; John H. Wheeler, ed., *Reminiscences and Memoirs of North Carolina and Eminent North Carolinians* (1884).

BUCK YEARNS

McDowell, William Wallis (13 Feb. 1823–22 June 1893), merchant, Confederate soldier, and banker, was born at Pleasant Gardens in present-day McDowell County, the grandson of Revolutionary War hero Major Joseph McDowell and the son of James (ca. 1791–1854) and Margaret Erwin McDowell (1801–31). He moved to Asheville in 1845 and on 21 July 1846 married Sarah Lucinda Smith, the fifth daughter of James McConnell Smith (1787–1856), a wealthy Asheville merchant and hotelkeeper who is said to have been the first white person born in North Carolina west of the Blue Ridge Mountains, and his wife Mary (Polly) Patton (ca. 1793–1853).

McDowell soon entered into a mercantile partnership with his father-in-law; the firm, known as Smith and McDowell, maintained a store directly across from the well-known Buck Hotel (which was owned by Smith) on Asheville's main street (now Patton Avenue). In addition, he served as an officer in the Asheville Branch of the Bank of Cape Fear. In 1858 McDowell purchased a brick house that had been built by James M. Smith for his son, John Patton Smith. The latter had died unmarried and intestate in 1857. The Smith-McDowell House, said to be Asheville's oldest surviving structure, was restored as the headquarters of the Western North Carolina Heritage Center.

On 20 Nov. 1860 Governor John W. Ellis named McDowell captain of the Buncombe Riflemen, organized on 20 Dec. 1859 in response to John Brown's raid at Harpers Ferry. In February 1861 this county regiment of militia was reorganized as one of North Carolina's first volunteer companies, and McDowell, along with three other men, was named in the act passed by the General Assembly incorporating the company. He formally enlisted on 24 Apr. 1861 at age thirty-eight and was appointed captain of the volunteers. Following the fall of

Fort Sumter the Buncombe Riflemen became Company E of the First North Carolina Volunteers or the "Bethel Regiment." In the early summer of 1862 the First Regiment was made a part of the newly created Sixtieth Regiment, which had been organized by McDowell's brother, Dr. Joseph A. McDowell of Madison County. William Wallis McDowell was named captain, and later major, of this regiment.

Poor health compelled him to return to Asheville before the end of the Civil War. He and his wife continued to reside in the house built by his father-in-law, and he apparently resumed his banking career. Early in 1866 he declined the offer of a friend in Texas to become an officer of a bank there. He noted that his family was too large and that he was then unable to raise enough money to move to Texas without selling his real estate.

McDowell was the father of nine children. Although he was long associated with the mercantile business and with banking, the censuses of 1860 and 1870 declare him to have been a farmer, and the 1880 census lists his occupation as builder. Census data suggest that McDowell was a large slaveholder—he owned forty slaves in 1860 —and a man of considerable wealth. The McDowells disposed of the Smith-McDowell House in April 1881 but apparently continued to reside in Asheville. Mrs. McDowell died there about 1905.

SEE: *Asheville Citizen-Times*, 30 Apr. 1961; Walter Clark, ed., *Histories of the Several Regiments and Battalions from North Carolina in the Great War, 1861–1865*, vols. 1, 3 (1901); John Hugh McDowell, *The McDowells, Erwins, Irwins, and Connections* (1918); William Wallis McDowell Papers (Southern Historical Collection, University of North Carolina, Chapel Hill); Louis H. Manarin, comp., *North Carolina Troops, 1861–1865: A Roster*, vol. 3 (1971); *Morganton Herald*, 29 June 1893; *Private Laws of North Carolina, 1860–1861*, chap. 99; F. A. Sondley, *A History of Buncombe County, North Carolina*, 2 vols. (1930); U.S. Works Progress Administration, Pre-1914 Graves Index (North Carolina State Archives, Raleigh); Wilmington *North Carolina Presbyterian* (obituary), 6 July 1893.

ROBERT M. TOPKINS

McElwee, John Harvey (*7 Oct. 1834–4 Feb. 1926*), industrialist and father of the Statesville tobacco industry, was born in York County, S.C., the son of Jonathan Newman and Martha Orr McElwee. He attended the rural schools of York County and later the military academy at York. At the beginning of the Civil War he was engaged in a mercantile business in Columbia, S.C., that later was burned by General William T. Sherman's army. He joined the Confederate army from Columbia and was given the task of collecting supplies for the armies in Virginia.

McElwee's work brought him to Statesville, N.C., where he met and married, on 8 Sept. 1862, Marian Victoria Alexander. Victoria was born and educated in Mississippi, but her mother was part of the pioneer Simonton clan of Iredell County, and in 1862 she and her mother had moved back to the old William Simonton home place just east of Statesville.

After the war, perhaps as early as 1865, McElwee formed a partnership with T. A. Burke for the manufacture of tobacco at Elmwood on the Western North Carolina Railroad, producing a brand of smoking tobacco known as Yellow Rose, which took premiums at several fairs. In 1870 he moved into Statesville and began manufacturing tobacco there. Soon he was advertising a brand he labeled as "Ante-Bellum Durham Tobacco, genuine Durham tobacco, manufactured in Statesville,"

using the Durham "bull" as a trademark. According to family tradition, he had been influenced to go into the tobacco business by J. R. Green, who was then manufacturing a smoking tobacco known as Durham's at a little crossroads on the North Carolina Railroad between Hillsborough and Raleigh. While Green and McElwee were discussing the possibilities of the tobacco culture, the McElwee story goes, the bellowing of a nearby bull suggested to them a name for their tobacco and they subsequently agreed to use the bull as a trademark. Green's venture had a stroke of rare luck. General Joseph Johnston surrendered his Confederate army to General Sherman a few miles from Green's, and soldiers of both sides broke into the factory and appropriated tobacco bearing the bull trademark. As a result, such tobacco came to be in great demand, and orders for more of it poured in from all over the country.

Green's successor in Durham, W. T. Blackwell and Company, objected to McElwee's use of the bull as a trademark and the name Durham, leading to lawsuit after lawsuit and countersuits over a twelve-year period and in half a dozen counties. Finally, in 1888, McElwee was compelled to give them up, but not before he had forced Blackwell to make the bull more decent by putting a fence in front of him.

John H. McElwee was the first of many small tobacco manufacturers in Statesville and was in the lead in establishing tobacco markets there. Just before World War I his "Planter's Warehouse," opposite his home on Water Street, was very active. In addition to the Yellow Rose and Antebellum smoking tobaccos, he manufactured a third brand, Indian Girl, more popular and better known than the others, whose trademark was a picture of a well-known Indian princess of the day. He also produced several brands of chewing tobacco.

The McElwees had three daughters and four sons. One daughter, Mamie, was prominent in the work of the Presbyterian church; another married S. S. Thomas, and the third became the wife of W. E. Selby. His oldest son, William Henry, was a lumberman; the youngest, Ross, was a longtime physician in Iredell County. The other two sons, Thomas N. and John N., carried on the tobacco business. During the 1920s they attempted to manufacture cigarettes but were unable to compete with the established companies. By the time of the depression, the tobacco industry in Statesville had disappeared. The McElwees were also involved in the manufacture of furniture, establishing the Carolina Parlor Furniture Company in 1919 and after World War II the Ross Furniture Company, named for Dr. Ross McElwee.

On 4 July 1920, John Harvey McElwee became paralyzed; after nearly six years, he died at his home on Water Street in Statesville and was buried in Oakwood Cemetery.

SEE: Homer M. Keever, *Iredell: Piedmont County* (1976); Statesville *Landmark*, 1874–1926.

HOMER M. KEEVER

McFarland (or McFarlane, McFarlan), Duncan (*d. 7 Sept. 1816*), promoter, contractor, merchant, and politician, was born sometime before the American Revolution in the Laurel Hill community of Anson (later Richmond and now Scotland) County. Little is known about his early life. The 1790 census lists two Duncan McFarlands in Richmond, and the one who was probably the subject of this sketch had a household of nine males, six females, and six slaves.

Duncan apparently had unlimited energy. He constructed roads and bridges in both Carolinas. He surveyed and helped build, partly at his own expense, a road from Fayetteville to Camden, S.C., where the 1798 Assembly allowed him to charge a toll for crossing a bridge. In 1810 he helped promote a lottery to improve navigation on the Lumber River. A land speculator, he once developed plans for a town in the Laurel Hill area that included a section for free blacks. The city never became a reality but the Old Scotch Fair, located at the same place, did attract traders to a thriving market for several years.

McFarland was a contentious man. Hardly a session of the superior court was held without some case against him on the docket. Hog stealing, forgery, interference with the mails, perjury, and witchcraft were among the alleged offenses. He was once extradited to South Carolina on a charge of murder. Witnesses for the prosecution were hard to find, and juries were reluctant to rule against him, except once for rape. He always claimed that the prosecution was political. In his will he testified that he had never injured anyone except in retaliation for harm done to him. His will also provided that his slaves be freed and given three acres of land each when they reached fifty, stipulations that probably were never fulfilled.

One of North Carolina's first Populists, McFarland was constantly agitating the poor against the propertied. Called "the Stormy Petrel" of North Carolina politics, he found his political base among the Highland Scots of the Cape Fear Valley whom he enjoyed addressing in Gaelic. The Fayetteville Congressional District, created in 1791, was usually dominated by Federalists before 1816. McFarland was one of the most vocal and active leaders of the opposition. He represented Richmond County in the House of Commons in 1792 and in the state senate in 1793, 1795, 1800, and 1807–9.

He first ran for Congress in 1796 against Federalist William Barry Grove, who defeated him 2,950–1,068. McFarland was so disliked in Anson County that only one vote was cast for him in that election. Seven years later, when Grove announced his retirement, Duncan and two other Republicans opposed Samuel Purviance, a Federalist, for the empty seat. Grove hated the Stormy Petrel so much that he threatened to leave the district if the feisty Scotsman was elected his successor. When Purviance was elected, McFarland tried unsuccessfully to have the results invalidated. After one term Purviance decided to return home and McFarland again declared his candidacy. Federalist William Martin and anti-Jefferson Republican Joseph Pickett divided the opposition vote and allowed McFarland to win by a plurality of less than 300 votes ahead of Pickett. Two years later the Federalists confronted the new congressman with John Culpepper, a popular Baptist preacher. Two other candidates divided the Republican vote, and McFarland lost by less than 100 votes behind Culpepper. McFarland contested the results, and in January 1808 the U.S. House of Representatives ordered a special election in which Culpepper was victorious.

Richmond returned its Republican leader to the state senate three more times, and in 1812 McFarland announced that he would be a candidate for the Thirteenth Congress. His old enemy, Culpepper, also ran as did John A. Cameron, a man with important political connections across the state. McFarland had lost much of his spirit and energy, and the returns showed his tally a poor third. Now he finally retired from public life. The former congressman died several years later and was buried in the yard at Laurel Hill church. The gravestone does not record his birth date.

SEE: *Biog. Dir. Am. Cong.* (1971); D. H. Gilpatrick, *Jeffersonian Democracy in North Carolina, 1789–1816* (1931); Leonard L. Richards, "John Adams and the Moderate Federalists: The Cape Fear Valley as a Test Case," *North Carolina Historical Review* 43 (1966); Bill Sharpe, *A New Geography of North Carolina*, vol. 4 (1965); Harry L. Watson, *Jacksonian Politics and Community Conflict* (1981).

DANIEL M. MCFARLAND

McGeachy, Neill Roderick (2 Apr. 1909–17 Dec. 1979), clergyman, church historian, and author, was born in Lenoir, the son of the Reverend Daniel Patrick and Lila Peck English McGeachy. Educated at Greenbrier Military School in Lewisburg, W.Va., and the public schools of Decatur, Ga., he was graduated from Davidson College in 1930 and served as headmaster of the American Mission School in Omdurman, the Sudan, from 1930 to 1932. In 1935 he received a bachelor of divinity degree from Union Theological Seminary, in Richmond, Va., which also awarded him a master of theology degree in 1954. Ordained in 1935, he was pastor of Presbyterian churches in Selma (1935–37), Spencer (1937–41), Charlotte (Sugaw Creek) (1941–45), and Statesville (1945–70).

Long interested in history, McGeachy led the Mecklenburg Presbytery in 1943 in celebrating the three hundredth anniversary of the Westminster Assembly. In 1952 he preached at the centennial observance of the Presbyterian church in Lenoir, and the following year in Statesville he celebrated the two hundredth anniversary of the founding of Fourth Creek Congregation. He participated in pageants depicting the history of the Presbyterian church and played the part of the Reverend Alexander Craighead at anniversaries in both North Carolina (1943) and Pennsylvania (1952). McGeachy served on a committee that planned the centennial of the Presbyterian church in the United States in 1960, and in 1962 he was elected chairman of the synod's committee on historical matters. In 1963 he was instrumental in having a film made depicting the history of the Synod of North Carolina.

In connection with the bicentennial of his former church in Charlotte, McGeachy was the author of *A History of Sugaw Creek Presbyterian Church* (1954), and he was invited back to preach at the anniversary observance. In 1964 he published *A History of Old Fourth Creek Congregation*. In 1970 he was named chairman of the special committee for the celebration of the 175th anniversary of the Concord Presbytery, and he was commissioned to write its history. This work was completed in 1979 and published in 1985 as *Confronted by Challenge: A History of the Presbytery of Concord, 1795–1973*. When several presbyteries in Piedmont North Carolina were making plans to unite, McGeachy in 1971 prepared a paper, "1741 vs. 1971," that was widely circulated and used by those responsible for making the decision about the union. He also was a contributor to the *Dictionary of North Carolina Biography*.

He was active in a number of historical organizations including the National Historical Society, the Presbyterian Historical Society of Philadelphia, and the North Carolina Presbyterian Historical Society. As a churchman he was moderator of two presbyteries in which he served, a member of the board of regents of the Presbyterian Home for Children, a trustee of Mitchell College when it was owned and operated by the Concord Presbytery, a trustee of Davidson College, and often a member of committees on Christian education, on ministers, and others.

In 1935 McGeachy married Frances Roberts Hamilton

of Oxford, and they were the parents of four children: Lila Frances (Mrs. Richard A. Ray), Margaret Ann (Mrs. William C. Roberson), Neill R., Jr., and Elizabeth Gooch (Mrs. William A. Mills). He was buried in Oakwood Cemetery, Statesville.

SEE: Family papers furnished by Mrs. Neill R. McGeachy; *Presbyterian News*, September 1984; *Statesville Record and Landmark*, 20 Feb. 1965, 27 Jan. 1985.

WILLIAM S. POWELL

McGehee, Lucius Polk *(14 May 1868–11 Oct. 1923)*, lawyer and educator, was born at Woodburn, his father's plantation in Person County. He was the youngest of four sons of Montford (1822–95) and Sally Polk Badger McGehee (1833–1903), the daughter of George Edmund Badger, a U.S. senator and secretary of the navy. McGehee received his early education at Morson's School in Raleigh and was graduated from The University of North Carolina with highest honors in 1887. He then worked briefly as a railway surveyor and on the canal at Weldon. He taught in the Episcopal High School at Asheville, at a school in Enfield, and at the Bingham School near Mebane. Returning to Chapel Hill, he completed the law course in 1891 and was admitted to the bar. Afterwards McGehee moved to New York, where he was a contributing editor and later associate editor (1895–1904) of the *American and English Encyclopaedia of Law*.

In 1904 he returned to The University of North Carolina as professor of law and in 1910 was named dean of the law school, a position he held until his death. He was the author of a legal text, *Due Process of Law under the Federal Constitution* (1906), and was one of the commissioners who revised the public laws of North Carolina in 1917. Under his administration, the university law school made rapid strides in prestige and added greatly to the size of its student body and faculty. He spent the final year of his life facilitating the construction of a new law building, but a sudden and fatal paralysis prevented him from seeing it completed. Louis Graves, Chapel Hill newspaper editor and a family friend, said of McGehee that "deeply interested as he was in building up the department of the university that was under his charge, probably there was never anybody who talked less about himself, what he had done, and what he planned to do. In an age of automobiles and jazz and all the furor of progress, he somehow seemed to carry over with him the flavor of tranquil days gone by."

On 28 Jan. 1903 he married Julia Leslie Tilley Covert, of Digby, Nova Scotia, who died the following August. McGehee was a Democrat and an Episcopalian; he and his wife were buried in Oakwood Cemetery, Raleigh.

SEE: Kemp P. Battle, *History of the University of North Carolina*, vol. 2 (1912); *Greensboro Daily News*, 12 Oct. 1903; North Carolina Bar Association, *Proceedings* 26 (1924); *North Carolina Law Review* 2 (1923); Raleigh *News and Observer*, 12–13 Oct. 1923; *Who Was Who in America*, vol. 1 (1943); L. R. Wilson, *The University of North Carolina, 1900–1930* (1957 [portrait]).

WILLIAM POLK CHESHIRE

McGehee, Montford *(4 Dec. 1822–31 Mar. 1895)*, lawyer, planter, legislator, and public official, was born at Woodburn, his father's plantation in Person County, the youngest child of Thomas (1784–1867) and Elizabeth M.

Jeffreys McGehee (1795–1825). He was graduated from The University of North Carolina in 1841 and received a master of arts degree in 1844. From 1841 to 1842 he attended the Harvard Law School and returned to read law under Judge W. H. Battle. He was licensed by the North Carolina Supreme Court in 1844.

Except for a European tour in 1849, during which he is said to have studied briefly at universities in Paris and London, McGehee practiced law in Milton until his father's death in 1867. He was a member of the General Assembly from Caswell County in 1864 and from Person County in 1872, 1876, and 1879, as well as a delegate to the constitutional convention of 1865. McGehee, a Democrat, and his brother-in-law, Richard C. Badger, a Republican, are credited with the legislation transferring the authority to appoint University of North Carolina trustees from the State Board of Education to the General Assembly, thus making it possible for the university to reopen in 1875 after being closed for four years.

In 1867 McGehee moved to Woodburn and managed the plantation until 1879 when, in the general financial collapse following the Civil War, it was sold, along with McGehee's considerable library, the many volumes of which were tied up with string and disposed of at ten cents a bundle. The family holdings gone, McGehee moved to Raleigh where he was commissioner of agriculture from 1880 to 1887.

McGehee was appointed by the bench and bar to deliver the memorial oration on the death of Governor William A. Graham in 1876. Governor Thomas Jarvis in 1879 appointed him to be one of three commissioners assigned to negotiate a satisfactory funding arrangement with bondholders of the North Carolina Railroad, in danger of passing beyond control of the state. He was a member of the board of trustees of The University of North Carolina from 1864 to 1868, when the trustees were replaced by a Reconstruction board, and again from 1877 to 1893. He also was among the founders of the Alumni Association in 1843.

In Christ Church, Raleigh, on 25 Sept. 1854, he married Sally Polk Badger (1833–1903), the daughter of George Edmund Badger, a U.S. senator and secretary of the navy. They were the parents of four sons, the youngest of whom was Lucius Polk McGehee, dean of the law school at The University of North Carolina from 1910 until his death in 1923. McGehee was a Presbyterian and a Whig until after the Civil War, when he became a Democrat.

SEE: John L. Cheney, Jr., ed., *North Carolina Government, 1585–1979* (1981); *Handbook of North Carolina* (1879); Thomas Jordan Jarvis Papers (North Carolina State Archives, Raleigh); Montford McGehee Papers (Southern Historical Collection, University of North Carolina, Chapel Hill); William S. Powell, *The First State University* (1972); John H. Wheeler, *Historical Sketches of North Carolina from 1584 to 1851* (1851).

WILLIAM POLK CHESHIRE

McGilvary, Daniel *(16 May 1828–22 Aug. 1911)*, missionary to Siam, was of Highland Scottish ancestry. The son of Malcolm and Catharine McIver McGilvary, he was born in Moore County. Following his father's death, Daniel, at age thirteen, moved to Pittsboro to learn the tailor's trade. At the same time he attended a local academy. He later enrolled in the Bingham School, then at The Oaks, where he completed his studies in May 1849. After teaching for four years in Pittsboro, he entered Princeton Theological Seminary, graduating in

1856. On 14 June of that year the Orange Presbytery licensed him as a ministerial candidate. McGilvary supplied the Carthage and Union Presbyterian churches for a period during 1856–57. On 13 Dec. 1857 the Orange Presbytery ordained him to the ministry "as an Evangelist with a view to his entering upon the work of a missionary to Siam."

After a passage of "only one hundred days," McGilvary landed at Bangkok on Sunday, 20 June 1858. His ministry in Siam revolved around three centers. From 1858 to June 1861, he lived and worked in Bangkok. Pechaburi was the scene of his activities from the latter date until January 1867. From April 1867 until his death, his base of operations was at Chiengmai in the northerly province of Laos.

After coming in contact with some of the people from Laos at Pechaburi, he made an exploratory tour to Chiengmai, then moved there, reaching the city on 3 Apr. 1867. McGilvary readily accommodated himself to the travel facilities of his adopted homeland. The Mission Board in New York considered his suggestion that an elephant be purchased for such purposes a great joke, but he later acquired two of these animals which were his means of transportation to Presbytery meetings and in making extended exploratory tours throughout Laos.

With no physician within hundreds of miles, he undertook to provide certain basic remedies for the sick. He incurred the animosity of the prince when his grandson died from the effects of McGilvary's vaccination. The acceptance of Christianity by a number of leaders in the region accentuated this opposition, and two Christian converts were clubbed to death on the prince's orders. Although in dire danger, McGilvary and his family remained at their post, and he boldly confronted the prince with his actions before a commissioner from Bangkok who had been sent to investigate the matter. In the role of missionary-statesman, McGilvary succeeded in obtaining a decree of religious toleration from the king of Siam as a climax to a controversy involving efforts to eliminate a pagan practice from the marriage ceremony of two Christians.

McGilvary demonstrated his competence as a scholar by translating the Books of Ezekiel and Jonah from the Hebrew into Siamese and, assisted by his wife, the three Epistles of John and the Epistle of Jude from the original Greek into Siamese, as well as the Gospel of Matthew from Greek into the language of the Lao. He received an honorary D.D. degree from The University of North Carolina in 1880 and an LL.D. from Davidson College in 1906. The McGilvary Theological Training School at Chiengmai was established to memorialize his work.

On 6 Dec. 1860, in Bangkok, he married Sophia Royce Bradley, the daughter of Dr. D. B. Bradley, a veteran missionary to Siam. They became the parents of two sons and three daughters. McGilvary died and was buried at Chiengmai. His autobiography, *A Half Century among the Siamese and the Lāo*, was published a year after his death. This volume has an excellent photograph of its author.

SEE: Arthur Judson Brown, *One Hundred Years: A History of the Foreign Missionary Work of the Presbyterian Church in the U.S.A.* (1936); Lillian Johnson Curtis, *The Laos of North Siam* (1903); *DAB*, vol. 6 (1933); Daniel McGilvary, *A Half Century among the Siamese and the Lāo* (1912); *Missionary of the World* (October 1912); *Princeton Theological Seminary Bulletin* (August 1912).

THOMAS H. SPENCE, JR.

McGirt, James Ephraim *(1874–13 June 1930)*, black poet, editor, and publisher, was born in Robeson County near the town of Lumberton. The son of Madison and Ellen Townsend McGirt, he grew up on the family farm and was sent to a private school near Lumberton. Later the family lived on a farm near Rowland before finally moving to Greensboro. There James attended public school, worked at odd jobs, and began to write verse. In 1892 he enrolled in Bennett College, a Methodist-affiliated institution then just outside Greensboro. What he did immediately afterwards is not known, but in the preface to his first book, *Avenging the Maine, a Drunken A.B., and Other Poems* (1899), he blamed exhausting manual labor and a lack of leisure time for the slimness of the volume and the feebleness of the verse. Whatever his employment, it did not prevent him from revising and enlarging the first edition of this work in 1900, as well as issuing in the next year a new collection of poems entitled *Some Simple Songs and a Few More Ambitious Attempts.*

The publication in 1901 of a third revised and enlarged edition of *Avenging the Maine* by a Philadelphia printer rather than the Raleigh firm that had prepared the first two editions indicates the direction in which McGirt's ambitions would take him in 1903. After briefly residing in Hampton, Va., he established himself in Philadelphia where, in September 1903, he issued the first number of *McGirt's Magazine*, an illustrated monthly dealing with the activities of black Americans in art, literature, science, and general affairs. Although his duties as editor and publisher of the magazine consumed most of his time and all of his savings, McGirt continued to write music and poetry while living in Philadelphia. *For Your Sweet Sake: Poems* (1906), his third book of verse, testified to his abiding wish to win recognition for himself as a poet. In 1907 he published his last book, a volume of short stories entitled *The Triumph of Ephraim.*

In 1909 *McGirt's Magazine*, reflecting its declining sales, changed from a monthly to a quarterly. A year later it ceased publication, as McGirt decided to return to Greensboro to join his sister in managing the Star Hair Grower Manufacturing Company. After accumulating a considerable amount of property in and around Greensboro, he became a realtor. At his death he was remembered as "one of the best-known Negro citizens of Greensboro." He was buried in Maple Cemetery.

McGirt's contribution to literature was small. His first book of verse is, as he recognized, amateurish and undistinguished. His technical skill increased with each volume that he published, but he was never a sure metrist or a skilled rhymer. McGirt's understanding of the art of the short story was equally uncertain. The stories in *The Triumph of Ephraim* usually deal with problems of romantic love encountered by youthful and largely unindividualized black heroes and heroines. A few of his stories are set in North Carolina, but little particularity is given to these settings in McGirt's fiction. Unlike his poems, which, despite their lack of polish, often give evidence of deep personal feelings, McGirt's short stories reveal both the lack of experience and the uncertainty of purpose that together account for the author's brief and unsuccessful literary career.

Neither McGirt nor any of his three siblings ever married.

SEE: James W. Parker, "James Ephraim McGirt: Poet of Hope Deferred," *North Carolina Historical Review* 31 (July 1954); Margaret F. Peterson, "Suspended Animation: Race Relations in the Literature of Charles Waddell Chesnutt, David Bryant Fulton, and James Ephraim

McGirt" (M.A. thesis, University of North Carolina, 1972).

WILLIAM L. ANDREWS

McGready, James (1763–February 1817), clergyman and evangelist, born in Guilford County, was the son of James and Jean McGready, who had immigrated to America from Ireland. He had one sister, Hannah, and six brothers: Samuel Rutherford, Judah, Aaron, Moses, David, and Israel. The respect of the parents for the Scriptures is indicated in the names of the children, who were reared in the strict Calvinist tradition as members of the Buffalo Presbyterian Church. As a child, James displayed an unusually pious attitude towards religion, and this increased as he grew older. This trait so impressed a visiting uncle that he took the youth to his Pennsylvania home to be educated for the ministry. In that state, McGready first enrolled in a school conducted by Joseph Smith, a Presbyterian minister. Later he attended an institution directed by another Presbyterian clergyman, John McMillan, which eventually became Cannonsburg College. On 13 Aug. 1788 McGready was licensed by the Redstone Presbytery and began his ministerial career. En route to North Carolina the following year, he visited Hampden-Sydney College where he was impressed by the pietistic evangelism of the Reverend John Blair Smith and determined to conduct his ministry along similar lines.

In 1793 McGready was ordained by the Orange Presbytery and assigned to the pastorates of the Stony Creek and Haw River Presbyterian churches. The following year he married Nancy Thompson, whom he had met in Pennsylvania, and settled near High Rock, N.C. The minister then applied himself zealously to the emphasis of Christian piety among his congregations. On one occasion he created a sensation when he refused to ask the blessing of a meal after a funeral because of the excessive amount of whiskey that was being consumed. In 1796 his pulpit was removed from the Stony Creek church and burned, and a message written in blood was sent to him threatening physical violence unless he changed his preaching emphasis.

In the same year, discouraged by a sense of failure, McGready decided his ministry would be more useful on the frontier. Moving to Logan County, Ky., he took charge of the congregations at Muddy River, Red River, and Gasper River. He was followed west by William Hodge, Barton Warren Stone, John Rankin, and John and William McGee. The evangelistic fervor of these zealots led to the introduction of camp meetings, which provided the opportunity for a series of services. The zeal of the church meetings was intensified by the outbreak of strange physical demonstrations on the part of individuals in the congregations. These phenomena became known as "Exercises," or sometimes as "the jerks," and as they accelerated, the entire southwestern frontier came under the influence of the Great Revival of 1800. Within a year, the revival spread into North Carolina and other southern states. This event is credited with having set the religious pattern for the South and the Southwest during the nineteenth and part of the twentieth centuries.

To supply the demand for clerical leadership caused by the rapidly increasing number of converts made during the revival, McGready and his associates in the Transylvania Presbytery licensed as exhorters young men who had acquired only a small amount of educational training. The Synod of Kentucky disapproved of this action and, after considerable debate, suspended Mc-

Gready, Hodge, Stone, and others from the Presbyterian ministry in 1806 and 1807. The result was the formation of the Cumberland Presbytery, which eventually became the keystone of the Cumberland Presbyterian Church. In 1809, the dissension having subsided somewhat, Hodge was restored to the fellowship of the Transylvania organization and McGready was reinstated the following year. Stone, however, did not return but founded a church that eventually became the Disciples of Christ. Shortly after this event, McGready moved to Henderson County, Ky., undertaking occasional missionary tours through Ohio and Indiana until his death. His burial place is unknown.

McGready was known for his fiery and emotional sermons, which depicted in detail the glories of heaven and the furies of hell. His personality as a "Son of Thunder" was dynamic and he was responsible for the decisions of both Barton Warren Stone and William Hodge to enter the Christian ministry. His interest was Christian piety and evangelism rather than denominational creeds and theology. A number of his homilies were preserved by W. W. Worsley, a publisher in Louisville, Ky., in *The Posthumous Works of the Reverend and Pious James M'Gready* (2 vols., 1831–33), edited by the Reverend James Smith. This work also contains an account of the Great Revival penned by McGready during his lifetime.

No portrait has been found, but McGready was described by Barton Warren Stone as follows: "His person was not prepossessing, nor his appearance interesting, except his remarkable gravity, and small piercing eyes. His coarse tremulous voice excited in me the idea of something unearthly. His gestures were *sui generis*, the perfect reversion of elegance. Everything appeared by him forgotten, but the salvation of souls. Such earnestness—such zeal—such powerful persuasion, enforced by the joys of heaven and miseries of hell, I had never witnessed before."

SEE: William Henry Foote, *Sketches of North Carolina, Historical and Biographical: Illustrative of the Principles of a Portion of Her Early Settlers* (1846); Elder John Rogers, ed., *The Biography of Elder Barton Warren Stone, Written by Himself, with Additions and Reflections* (1847); James Smith, *History of the Presbyterian Church from Its Origin to the Present Time, including a History of the Cumberland Presbyterian Church* (1835); William Buell Sprague, *Annals of the American Pulpit*, vol. 3 (1858); Durward T. Stokes, "North Carolina and the Great Revival of 1800," *North Carolina Historical Review* (October 1966); Will of James McGready, Guilford County Court Records for November 1800 (North Carolina State Archives, Raleigh).

DURWARD T. STOKES

McGuire (or McGwire), Thomas (fl. 1754–1802), colonial official, the youngest son of William M. McGuire of Dublin, completed his studies in law at Gray's Inn, London, in 1754. By early 1760 he was in North Carolina serving as a judge of the vice-admiralty court. In 1763 he married Rebecca Dry, the daughter of William Dry, a prominent figure in the Lower Cape Fear. She died a few years later, and McGuire apparently never remarried.

McGuire progressed steadily in North Carolina. In March 1764 he was named justice of the peace for Brunswick County and also represented the county in the Assembly in the session of 1764–65. In October 1767, by royal appointment, he became attorney general of the colony. In that post he urged strong measures against the Regulators during Governor William Tryon's administration. In 1773 Governor Josiah Martin nominated McGuire to a vacancy on the royal Council, but he was not sworn in until April 1775. McGuire supported resolutions against the Provincial Congresses, but Patriot leaders seem not to have condemned him for it. Indeed, Governor Richard Caswell offered him the attorney generalship of the state in 1779 and the legislature approved, although McGuire refused it. He remained on his plantation in Bladen County throughout the war and never took any oath contrary to his allegiance to the Crown.

In July 1785 McGuire returned to England after selling his North Carolina holdings for a total of £3,500. In England he claimed a loss of £645 per year for his attorney generalship and received an annual compensation from the Loyalist Claims Commission until 1802, when he probably died.

SEE: Audit Office, Loyalist Claims, English Records (North Carolina State Archives, Raleigh); John L. Cheney, Jr., ed., *North Carolina Government, 1585–1979* (1981); Robert O. DeMond, *The Loyalists in North Carolina during the Revolution* (1940); Joseph Foster, *Register of Admissions to Gray's Inn, 1521–1889* (1889); William S. Powell, ed., *The Correspondence of William Tryon and Other Selected Papers*, 2 vols. (1980–81); William L. Saunders, ed., *Colonial Records of North Carolina*, vol. 6 (1888); *Virginia Gazette*, 27 Aug. 1767.

WILLIAM S. PRICE, JR.

McInnes, Miles (*d. 1818*), Loyalist militiaman, moved from his native Scotland to Anson County in 1774 and bought a farm. He escaped after fighting at Moore's Creek Bridge. In 1780, with the British success in the South, he joined the Anson County Loyalist militia as a lieutenant and accompanied the British forces on their evacuation from Wilmington to Charles Town.

In 1783 McInnes went to London and then to Nova Scotia, where he settled on two hundred acres on the Musquodoboit River in Halifax County and became a justice of the peace. He died there, survived by his wife Christiana, whom he had married in Nova Scotia.

SEE: English Records, box 17, North Carolina names from T 50:8–28 (North Carolina State Archives, Raleigh); Marion Gilroy, comp., *Loyalists and Land Settlement in Nova Scotia* (1937); Public Archives of Nova Scotia, vol. 214; Public Record Office, London, AO 12:100, 13:121, T 50:1.

CAROLE WATTERSON TROXLER

McIver, Alexander (*7 Feb. 1822–19 Aug. 1902*), college professor, superintendent of public instruction, and farmer, was born in Sanford, then in Moore County, to Daniel and Margaret McLeod McIver. In 1853 he was a first-honor graduate of The University of North Carolina, where he remained for a few months as tutor of mathematics before becoming principal of an academy in Wadesboro. In 1859 he became professor of mathematics at Davidson College.

A Republican, McIver was elected to represent Mecklenburg County at the two sessions of the constitutional convention of 1865–66. In 1869 he became professor of mathematics at The University of North Carolina. Governor Tod R. Caldwell in 1871 appointed him state superintendent of public instruction, and McIver made reports to the General Assembly for the four years between 1871 and 1874. In the latter year he was defeated for the office by Stephen D. Pool. In 1875 he applied for but did not receive a professorship at the university; instead, he became principal of the Greensboro graded schools where he also taught for five or six years.

McIver then turned to farming and assumed a role in battling the problems facing farmers. As a delegate to the two farmers' conventions held in Raleigh on 18 and 26 Jan. 1887, he was elected a member of the legislative and executive committees. In August 1887, by appointment of Governor Alfred M. Scales, he was North Carolina's delegate to the Inter-State Farmers' Congress in Atlanta; at the congress, he was elected one of the vice-presidents. McIver also attended meetings in 1888 at Raleigh and in 1889 at Montgomery, Ala. In 1890 he was a candidate for Congress on the Republican ticket to represent the Fourth District but was defeated by B. H. Bunn, the Democratic incumbent.

McIver married Mary Ann Wilcox on 14 Jan. 1858, and they became the parents of six children: George Wilcox, Margaret Rockwell, Herman Martin, Alexander, Elizabeth Nash, and Mary. His wife died on 7 June 1878 in Greensboro, and in 1884 McIver married Catherine Laird Gilmour, by whom he had two sons: Mathew Gilmour and Robert Russell. He died in Sanford and was buried in the Buffalo Presbyterian churchyard.

SEE: Kemp P. Battle, *History of the University of North Carolina*, 2 vols. (1907, 1912); Daniel L. Grant, *Alumni History of the University of North Carolina, 1795–1924* (1924); Kenneth L. Kelly, *McIver Family of North Carolina* (1964); *North Carolina Public School Bulletin*, December 1946; S. D. Pool, ed., *Our Living and Our Dead*, vol. 1 (1874–75); Raleigh *News and Observer*, 4 Sept., 7 Nov. 1890.

LEE BOUGHMAN

McIver, Charles Duncan (*7 Sept. 1860–17 Sept. 1906*), founder and first president of the State Normal and Industrial School for Girls (now the University of North Carolina at Greensboro), was born in a part of Moore County that became Lee in 1907. His family soon moved to the home in which he lived as a child; it still stands on Highway 421 north of Sanford. He was the son of Matthew Henry and Sarah Harrington McIver. One grandfather, Evander McIver, owned six thousand acres and a hundred slaves; his other grandfather, William D. Harrington, also owned a large plantation in Moore County. McIver's father had a farm, a gristmill, a lumber mill, and part interest in a store in Sanford. The first school he attended was built by Henry McIver and some neighbors. He later prepared for college at a school operated by John E. Kelly. Entering The University of North Carolina in 1877, he was graduated in 1881. Other future educators who studied with him were Charles Brantley Aycock, James Y. Joyner, and Edwin A. Alderman. His alma mater subsequently awarded him two honorary degrees: a doctor of literature in 1893 and a doctor of laws in 1904.

After graduation McIver became assistant headmaster of the Presbyterian Male Academy, a small private school in Durham. Shortly after the term began, the headmaster took another job and left him the school. At that time the graded-school movement was growing in North Carolina, and though many people considered this a threat to private schools, the first vote McIver ever cast was to establish such a school in Durham. There he served as teacher, principal of the high school, and acting superintendent from 1882 to 1884. He then became principal of the high school in Winston. While in Winston he married Lula Verlinda Martin, who bore him four children: Annie Martin in 1886 (Mrs. James R. Young), Charles D., Jr., in 1887, Verlinda Millie in 1895, and Lula Martin in 1899 (Mrs. John Dickinson).

McIver's interest in the education of teachers led him to offer a normal course at the Winston Graded School. In the spring of 1886 he was elected vice-president of the North Carolina Teachers' Assembly. The following summer he made the first of many speeches advocating improved education for women. At that time the state provided a university for white men and normal schools for black men and women, but there was no such provision for white women.

In 1886 McIver accepted a position as head of the literary department at Peace Institute in Raleigh, where he established the first normal course in a private institution in North Carolina. The following summer the Teachers' Assembly made him chairman of the committee to introduce a bill to the General Assembly providing for a teacher training school. Undaunted by its failure, he went to Yadkinville to teach a normal school for Yadkin County. On the last Sunday there he conducted a "Sunday School Normal" because he believed Sunday schools also needed improvement. In 1888 McIver taught the state normals at Wilson and at Sparta. Again the Teachers' Assembly appointed him to petition the legislature for a normal school for white girls. In 1889 a school for Indians was established, but after passing the senate, the bill that McIver advocated to train white women teachers failed the house by sixteen votes.

The same legislative session abolished the eight summer normal schools then in operation and in their place set up county institutes that were to both educate teachers and inform the public about the need to improve education. On 1 July 1889 McIver and Edwin Alderman began a three-year stint as conductors of these institutes. Dr. Jabez Lamar Monroe Curry provided additional money from the Peabody Fund to employ J. Y. Joyner, M. C. S. Noble, and Edward P. Moses to offer additional institutes during the summer. These men promoted the cause of education in all the counties of the state and brought about an increased respect for the teaching profession.

The legislature of 1891, prodded by the Farmers' Alliance, the King's Daughters, and the Teachers' Assembly, as well as McIver, Alderman, and State Superintendent Sidney M. Finger, finally approved the establishment of the State Normal and Industrial School for Girls. Its purpose was to prepare young women to earn a livelihood in teaching or in business. Major Finger announced the selection of Greensboro as the site, adding his hope that one day the institution might be for both sexes. This hope was realized in 1964. Both McIver and Alderman received support for the post of first president and each expressed a willingness to serve the other should he be chosen. McIver was the ultimate choice at a salary of $2,250.

On 5 Oct. 1892 he was at the railroad station to greet the 176 students when they arrived to attend the new college. They enrolled in three departments: normal, business, and domestic science. In 1893 McIver established a "practice and observation school" to provide training for teachers, and it survived until 1970. The school prospered despite the activities of some detractors, a typhoid epidemic that cost fifteen lives and closed the school in 1899, and a fire that destroyed the major dormitory in 1904.

In addition to his duties at the college, McIver held offices in many professional organizations. He was presi-

dent of the Southern Education Association and of the Normal School Department of the National Education Association, a trustee and member of the executive committee of the board of trustees of The University of North Carolina, and secretary and district director of the Southern Education Board. He also was considered as a candidate for governor of North Carolina and for president of The University of North Carolina but refused to allow his name to be submitted, choosing to remain at his post in Greensboro.

On 17 Sept. 1906 McIver went to Raleigh to board the campaign train of William Jennings Bryan but suffered a stroke and died before the train reached Hillsborough. Children in schools across the state donated pennies to erect a statue of him on the capitol grounds; a copy of that statue was also placed in front of the library on the campus of the University of North Carolina at Greensboro.

SEE: Elisabeth A. Bowles, *A Good Beginning* (1967); Rose Howell Holder, *McIver of North Carolina* (1957); Charles Duncan McIver Papers (Archives, University of North Carolina at Greensboro).

ELISABETH BOWLES

McIver, Colin (*9 Mar. 1784–18 Jan. 1850*), minister and teacher, was born on Stornoway, Isle of Lewis, in the Hebrides. In 1808 he was a student at Hampden-Sydney College in Virginia and a member of the Union Society. In 1809 he went to Fayetteville, N.C., to teach in the Fayetteville Academy, where in 1811 he was listed as second assistant to the principal.

In April 1811 McIver was licensed to preach by the Orange Presbytery. He was ordained by the Harmony Presbytery in South Carolina on 9 Apr. 1812. As required, he preached a year at Saltcatcher (Saltkehatchee) Church and then was assigned to Chesterfield and Darlington churches after being formally admitted to the presbytery. He was transferred to the Fayetteville Presbytery in 1814 and remained in it for the rest of his life.

McIver's connection with the Presbyterian Church of Fayetteville (First Presbyterian) was significant. He was never pastor, but on 31 July 1815 he was elected stated clerk of the session and was asked to prepare a sketch of the history of the church. This sketch, along with the minutes he recorded until 1849, are among the records of the church. He was stated clerk of the Fayetteville Presbytery and the Synod of North Carolina from 1818 to 1835.

In 1819 McIver was appointed as agent to solicit funds for the Presbyterian church then under construction. From his "Northern excursion" he collected $293. Among his contributors were President James Monroe, $25; George Washington Campbell, U.S. ambassador to Russia, $10; and John Quincy Adams, secretary of state, $10. From his "Southern excursion" he collected $55.

Through McIver's efforts, Sardis Presbyterian Church was organized in 1813. During the five years he served as pastor, he preached one sermon in Gaelic and one in English at each worship service. Churches throughout the area requested his services.

During his ministry he represented his presbytery as commissioner to the General Assembly of the Presbyterian Church of the United States more than any other minister. The Moravians in Salem said that when McIver visited on 1 Oct. 1826, "He preached an edifying sermon here." He was active on committees in formulating rules and in attending to the business of the assembly. McIver was also an original trustee of Donaldson Academy, which received its charter in 1833. The name came from Robert Donaldson, a benefactor of New York and a former citizen of Fayetteville. The academy was closed when graded schools were established in Fayetteville.

McIver was the author of the *North Carolina Register and United States Calendar* (1823); *Evangelical Museum* and *Virginia–North Carolina Presbyterian Preacher*, both monthly pamphlets (1828); *The American Preacher*, a monthly magazine (1829); and *The Southern Preacher*, a book. In 1842 he wrote *An Essay concerning the Unlawfulness of a Man's Marriage with His Sister by Affinity*. A member of the Order of Ancient, Free, and Accepted Masons (Phoenix Lodge AF and AM), McIver served as chaplain for many years. At his request he was buried in his bands and Geneva Gown. His epitaph in Old Cross Creek Cemetery, Fayetteville, reads: "He was a consistent Christian, a sound Divine, a laborious and faithful servant of the church. He fulfilled the duties of the Gospel Ministry for a period of more than forty years."

He married Sarah Barge, the daughter of Lewis Barge, a signer of the Liberty Point Resolves of Cumberland County in 1775. The couple had no children of their own but adopted two daughters of Sarah's brother, Carolina and Sarah Barge.

A photograph of McIver is among the memorabilia in the Historical Room of the First Presbyterian Church of Fayetteville.

SEE: Robert S. Arrowood, "The Reverend Colin McIver," *Presbyterian News* (October 1970); Cumberland County Deeds and Wills (Cumberland County Courthouse, Fayetteville); A. J. Morrison, *College of Hampden-Sidney: Dictionary of Biography, 1776–1825* (1921); Harriet Sutton Rankin, *History of the First Presbyterian Church, Fayetteville, N.C.* (1928); Session Minutes of First Presbyterian Church, Fayetteville.

LUCILE MILLER JOHNSON

McIver, George Willcox (*22 Dec. 1858–9 May 1947*), military officer, was born in Carthage, the son of Alexander and Mary Ann Wilcox McIver. Both his father and his cousin, Charles Duncan McIver, were distinguished North Carolina educators. He received his early education at the Mebane school established by Major Robert Bingham. In 1877, as a result of a tie in examination scores with his competitor, he won a draw of straws and entered the U.S. Military Academy at West Point.

After completing his military education in 1882, McIver began a twenty-two-year career with the Seventh U.S. Infantry, which he joined at Fort Pembina, Dakota Territory. He subsequently served at various western garrisons, including Fort Bridger, Fort Fred Steele, and Fort Logan. While on duty in the West, he suppressed civil riots between white and Chinese miners in Rock Springs, Wyo., and fought in the Sioux campaign of 1890–91. This conflict, according to McIver, was "one of the most tragic and unfortunate clashes that ever took place between Indians and soldiers."

Following a tour of duty as West Point tactical officer, he served as an instructor for the California National Guard and participated in the control of violent railroad-labor strikes. During the Spanish-American War, he commanded a company of the Seventh Infantry and in the Santiago campaign led these troops in the Battle of El Caney. After serving briefly at the Leech Lake, Minn., Indian agency (1900), McIver was transferred to Nome, Alaska, where he enforced federal law during the famous gold rush era. He served a short tour in the Philippines, then commanded troops at the Alcatraz military prison in San Francisco. When the destructive San Francisco earthquake and fire left 250,000 residents homeless, McIver was involved in the military effort to facilitate relief work and restore order. In 1907 he became commandant of the army's musketry school in Monterey, Calif., the forerunner of the modern-day Fort Benning infantry school. As commandant of the school, he instituted the study of weaponry and revised the *Army Small Arms Firing Manual*.

After a second tour of duty in the Philippines (1911–15) and office duty in the Militia Bureau of the War Department (1917), McIver accepted a temporary wartime commission as brigadier general. He was assigned to command the 161st Brigade, 81st Division, later known as the "Wildcat Division." In 1918, having completed a period of training in South Carolina and New York, the 161st embarked for duty with the American Expeditionary Force in France. Initially assigned to the Saint-Dié sector of the Vosges Mountains, McIver's troops moved to Verdun and subsequently joined the November 1918 Meuse-Argonne offensive.

Returned to the rank of colonel after the war, McIver served at Fort Slocum until his retirement in 1922. Subsequently he wrote "North Carolinians at West Point before the Civil War," which was published in the *North Carolina Historical Review*. In addition, he was the author of "The Musketry School at Monterey."

McIver married Helen Smedberg on 28 June 1893. They had five children: Francis (1896), Renwick Smedberg (1901), Alexander (1907), Cora Louise (1912), and George Willcox (1897).

SEE: George Willcox McIver Papers (Manuscript Collection, East Carolina University, Greenville); *Who Was Who in America*, vol. 3 (1960).

DENNIS R. LAWSON

McIver, Lula Verlinda Martin (*8 June 1864–22 Dec. 1944*), educator and wife of the founder of the University of North Carolina at Greensboro, was born in Salem, the daughter of Dr. Samuel Martin, a physician and dentist whose office was a block from Salem Academy. Her mother, Verlinda Miller Martin, was an honor graduate of Edgeworth Seminary in Greensboro. The family moved to Missouri when she was two and she received her early education at home. Feeling deprived, however, at age eight—at her request—she entered public school and was placed in the fourth grade. She returned to North Carolina in 1875 and was graduated from Salem Academy in 1881. She then conducted her own one-room school, worked at the Oxford Orphanage, and taught at the Winston Graded School.

At the Winston school she met Charles Duncan McIver in 1884. In the same year they both attended the summer normal school at The University of North Carolina. They were married in 1885. Considering a wedding ring a badge of slavery, she refused ever to wear one.

Having been thwarted in her desire to study medicine because of her sex, Lula McIver joined her husband in his crusade to provide higher education for women. When Charles McIver and Edwin A. Alderman were appointed to direct the teachers' institutes, she stayed in Raleigh to teach at Peace Institute. When she was free, however, she often accompanied Charles as he traveled around the state. She cleaned up the courthouses in which classes were held and frequently assisted him with the teaching.

On leaving Peace Institute, Mrs. McIver became "lady principal" of Charlotte Female Institute. While in Charlotte, she studied medicine with Dr. Annie Laurie Alexander, the state's first practicing woman physician.

The McIvers moved to Greensboro in 1892, when he became the first president of the State Normal and Industrial School. Mrs. McIver entertained visitors to the campus and participated in civic organizations. She served on the board of directors of the YMCA and with her husband founded the Woman's Association for the Betterment of Public School Houses. The purpose of the latter group was to improve the appearance of classrooms and grounds and to campaign for regular and compulsory school medical examinations.

After her husband's death in 1906, Mrs. McIver continued to live in their residence on the Greensboro campus until her death. The McIvers were the parents of four children: Annie Martin, Charles D., Jr., Verlinda Millie, and Lula Martin.

SEE: Elisabeth A. Bowles, *A Good Beginning* (1967); Rose Howell Holder, *McIver of North Carolina* (1957); Charles Duncan McIver Papers (Archives, University of North Carolina at Greensboro).

ELISABETH BOWLES

McKay, James Iver (*17 July 1792–15 Sept. 1853*), attorney and congressman, was born in Bladen County near Elizabethtown, the son of James and Mary Salter McKay. His mother was the daughter of William Salter. Some sources list his middle initial as "J" and his birth date as 1793. After attending the Raleigh Academy and The University of North Carolina, he became a lawyer. In 1817 he was appointed U.S. district attorney for North Carolina.

McKay represented Bladen in the state senate from 1815 to 1818 and in 1822, 1826, and 1829–30. In December 1830 he was a strong contender for governor in the Assembly, but after nine ballots Montfort Stokes was selected instead. In 1831 McKay ran without opposition, as a Jackson man, for the congressional seat of the Wilmington District, beginning a career in Washington, D.C., that stretched over eighteen years. Dr. Lewis Dishongh opposed him in 1833 and 1835, but after that his congressional seat was relatively safe. When in 1847 the Whigs combined his district with that of another Democrat, his colleague, James C. Dobbin, stepped aside to allow him to run for reelection. McKay easily defeated Robert K. Bryan, an independent Democrat, and William R. Hall, a Whig. In 1846 Democrats in the Assembly supported him first for the U.S. Senate and then for governor, but Whigs won both contests. At the Democrats' Baltimore convention in 1848, the North Carolina delegation supported him on the first two ballots as a candidate for vice-president of the United States; subsequently, the convention nominated William Butler of Kentucky.

During his first years in Congress, McKay served on the Committee on Expenditures in the State Department, the Commerce Committee, and the Military Affairs Committee. By the Twenty-fifth Congress, in 1837, he had become chairman of the latter committee. In the Twenty-sixth Congress he was chairman of the Committee on the Post Office and Post Roads. For his last two terms he served as chairman of Ways and Means, where his conservative management of affairs gave him the reputation of "Watch-dog of the Treasury."

In 1837 former president John Quincy Adams described McKay as "a very sensible, well-meaning, timid man, forever struggling between an anxious desire to correct abuses and a shivering terror of being cast off by his party." In 1840 Adams, a Whig, called McKay "a political Mrs. Candour, smooth as oil in outward form, and fetid as a polecat in inward savor." By 1841 Adams felt that "McKay fancies himself a great financier, affects great moderation, and covers an insidious and invidious spirit under a mask of candor. . . . He is a plain, mean-looking man, with a blacksmith air, and as careless of dress as myself; mild, gentle, wary in discourse and conduct, and priding himself upon occasionally voting against his party." In February 1849, a few days before he retired from Congress, McKay stormed out of a meeting with James K. Polk. The president commented in his diary for 4 February, "I knew he was a man of peculiar temperament and manner."

McKay was active in militia affairs before he went to Congress and was frequently addressed as "general." He married Ann Eliza Harvey, and they had one son who died in infancy. Four and a half years after retiring from Congress, McKay died in Goldsboro. His will instructed that his slaves be freed and sent to Liberia and that his home, Belfont, be given to Bladen County as an experimental farm and orphanage.

SEE: J. Q. Adams, *Memoirs of John Quincy Adams*, vols. 9–10 (1970); Samuel A. Ashe, ed., *Biographical History of North Carolina*, vol. 4 (1906); *Biog. Dir. Am. Cong.* (1971); J. G. de Roulhac Hamilton, *Party Politics in North Carolina, 1835–1860* (1916); James Sprunt, *Chronicles of the Cape Fear River, 1660–1916* (1916).

DANIEL M. MCFARLAND

McKay, Neill (*11 Feb. 1816–27 Feb. 1893*), Presbyterian minister, was born at Flint Hill on the Upper Cape Fear River in Cumberland (now Harnett) County. His mother, Flora McNeill (1785–1868), was the great-granddaughter of Neill McNeill (called "Black Neill" to distinguish him from the redheaded Neill), who from Argyllshire, Scotland, led 350 highlanders to Wilmington, landing in September 1739 and going up the Cape Fear to Cross Creek, Bluff, and Little River. Neill McKay's maternal ancestors also included John Smith, who lived in the Cape Fear section by 1736 with his celebrated daughter Jennet (Jennie Bahn); Archibald McNeill, an early leader of the Fayetteville Presbytery; and Colonel Alexander McAlister, a church leader and Patriot. Neill's father, Neill McKay (1776–1830), was one of the founders and first two elders of Tirza Presbyterian Church (1811–12); his paternal great-grandfather was Alexander McKay who came from Scotland in the 1730s and from whose home Longstreet Church on the Yadkin Road in Cumberland County was founded in 1758. The Reverend Neill McKay was one of ten children, most living to adulthood; one sibling, Dr. John Wilson McKay, was a South Carolina physician and a business partner of Neill in the successful turpentine and naval stores industries.

Following the Scottish tradition of rigorous education for its ministers, Neill McKay was educated at Donaldson Academy (chartered in 1833), in Fayetteville, where he was tutored by Dr. Simeon Colton, an outstanding educator and minister from Massachusetts. From Donaldson, McKay entered the sophomore class at Princeton in 1835, joined the Whig Society, and during his junior year was "suspended for fighting" with another student over the issue of slavery. On 7 Mar. 1837 he was "restored to College" but withdrew and entered the senior class at Union College in Schenectady, N.Y., graduating in 1838. He enrolled in Columbia Seminary, S.C., that fall and was graduated in 1841. Licensed to preach on 27 Mar. 1841, he was ordained by the Fayetteville Presbytery on 13 November.

Described after his death as "a staunch Calvinist, a theologian of the old school type," McKay was associated with some of the historic churches in the Cape Fear Valley. He was the sixth minister of Buffalo (1845–70), the eighth minister of the Longstreet Church (until 1856), the first minister of Flat Branch (founded 1873), and the first minister of Dunn Presbyterian Church (founded 1889). He also served the churches of Salem, Mount Pisgah, Sardis, and Sandy Grove; he was intermittently the minister of the Summerville Church after its reestablishment in 1848 (formerly Tirza), especially during the late 1870s and 1880s. Throughout his half-century ministry, he was a leader in the synod and especially in the Fayetteville Presbytery as moderator and preacher. Of his extant sermons, *A Centenary Sermon*, delivered at Bluff Church on 18 Oct. 1858, was published by the Fayetteville Presbytery (1858). Eleven other sermons in manuscript include "Slavery and the Obligation of Masters," "Depravity," and "The Errors, Absurdities and Impositions of the Romish Church." He was one of the founders of the *North Carolina Presbyterian* (established in 1858), first edited by the Reverend George McNeill and Bartholomew Fuller. This periodical became the *Presbyterian Standard*.

Again following the Scottish Presbyterian tradition, Neill McKay was committed to Christian education. Largely through his efforts the Cumberland Academy (later the Summerville Academy for Boys) was organized in the early 1840s with the Reverend James Johnson as the first principal. From 1848 to 1853 the second principal, Dr. Simeon Colton, McKay's old tutor at Donaldson, brought it into prominence. The Reverend J. C. McNair, the third principal, added a strong science department to the curriculum. The Summerville Academy was the site of the selection of the first Harnett County officials, and court was often held there.

McKay's interest in education was not limited to parochial schools. In 1862 he was elected to the board of trustees of The University of North Carolina, serving until 1868; under the constitution of 1868, he was one of the five members from the old board elected to the new. In 1869, during some of its darkest days, the university conferred on this "prominent and influential Presbyterian minister of Harnett County" a doctor of divinity degree. In 1870 he was made an honorary member of the North Carolina Historical Society and elected a member of the executive committee of the university board of trustees, being one of two members reelected to the board that year. According to Kemp Battle, McKay was active in seeking the university's restoration during the four years after it closed in February 1871. In July 1873 at the State Educational Convention (convened at the request of the State Board of Education), he introduced a resolution stating that the "revival of the University at the earliest practicable moment is essential to the thorough improvement of the education of the people." At that convention, he was appointed to the Committee on the University; in 1874 he was elected a member of the board of trustees, and in 1875 he became a member of the Visiting Committee to evaluate teaching and curriculum. According to one contemporary source, he was considered for the presidency of the university but declined in favor of his calling as a minister. He served on the board of trustees until his death.

McKay was married three times. On 22 Dec. 1841 he married Sarah Adaline James (18 Apr. 1822–8 June 1861), the daughter of the Reverend Robert W. James of Sumter, S.C.; two of their three daughters survived

childhood: Mary Louise McKay Salmon and Cornelia McKay McLauchlin. On 14 May 1863 he married Ann Blount Shepard Pettigrew (30 June 1830–13 Jan. 1864), the daughter of the Honorable Ebenezer Pettigrew of Tyrrell County. She died in childbirth along with twins. On 10 Dec. 1873 he married Maggie Murchison (30 Jan. 1835–9 Dec. 1924), the daughter of Duncan Murchison of Manchester, N.C. They had one daughter, Frances Reid (4 Apr. 1880–9 Dec. 1977), who married Charles Ross (10 Mar. 1878–11 Dec. 1951) of Asheboro. Many of Neill McKay's descendants lived in Lillington, including four grandchildren.

In 1845 McKay built a home called Summer Villa in the village where he was an extensive landowner and, by the 1860 census, the largest slaveholder in the county. He was a life member of the American Colonization Society (1851); at the time of the Civil War, he gave land or equivalent sums of money to his former slaves. Most remained nearby, and he helped them build churches and often preached there when they were without ministers. When Harnett County was formed in 1855, Neill and his brother John built a courthouse at Toomer (now Summerville), hoping to assure that location as the county seat, but by vote in 1859, Lillington was chosen.

Neill McKay died in his home in Summerville after a two-year illness and was buried in the Summerville Church cemetery. The chronicles of the Whig Society at Princeton described him as "unmistakably Scotch-Irish in every fibre of his body; genial, bright, companionable, attractive, muscular; of clear and strong opinions, held tenaciously, which he was always ready to argue for or even to fight for." In articles published in the *North Carolina Presbyterian* after his death, he was remembered as a man of decided convictions, magnetic personality, excellent health, vivacious disposition, and warm hospitality; he was called "an intense North Carolinian."

SEE: Samuel A. Ashe, *History of North Carolina*, vols. 1–2 (1925); James Banks, "A Centennial Historical Address. . . .," Fayetteville, 1858; Kemp P. Battle, *History of the University of North Carolina*, vols. 1–2 (1907, 1912); William Henry Foote, *Sketches of North Carolina, Historical and Biographical: Illustrative of the Principles of a Portion of Her Early Settlers* (1846); Lawrence Lee, *The Lower Cape Fear in Colonial Days* (1965); James D. MacKenzie, *Colorful Heritage* (1969); R. A. McLeod, *Historical Sketch of Long Street Presbyterian Church, 1756–1923* (1924); *North Carolina Biography*, vol. 5 (1919); *North Carolina Presbyterian*, 9, 30 Mar., 6 Apr. 1893; John A. Oates, *The Story of Fayetteville and the Upper Cape Fear* (1950); William E. Schenck, *Biography of the Class of 1838 of the College of New Jersey at Princeton, N.J.* (1889); James Sprunt, *Chronicles of the Cape Fear River, 1660–1916* (1916).

SUE FIELDS ROSS

McKee, Gertrude Dills (8 June 1885–27 Nov. 1948), homemaker, clubwoman, and state legislator, was the first woman to serve in the North Carolina Senate. She was the second of three daughters of William Allen and Alice M. Enloe Dills. Her father, a businessman and politician, founded the town of Dillsboro on a portion of his farm that overlooked the Tuckasegee River in Jackson County; in 1889 he represented Jackson County in the state house of representatives.

After attending the local public school, Gertrude Dills was graduated from Peace Institute in Raleigh in 1905 as president of her class. Later she was awarded an honorary doctor of laws degree by the Woman's College of The

University of North Carolina. On 13 Aug. 1913 she married Ernest Lyndon McKee, a widower of Sylva and the father of a son. They became the parents of two sons, William Dills and Ernest Lyndon, Jr. The elder McKee, a businessman, was president of the Sylva Tanning Company and the Dillsboro and Sylva Electric Company; he also was a director of a building supply and lumber company and vice-president of a bank. In 1922 the McKees purchased High Hampton Inn, a leading resort hotel in western North Carolina.

Mrs. McKee was active in many organizations, clubs, and committees and through these became familiar with the operation of state government. During World War I she helped direct Liberty Loan and Salvation Army drives and was director of the War Savings Stamps drive. From 1925 to 1927 she was president of the North Carolina Federation of Women's Clubs, and from 1928 to 1930 she was president of the North Carolina Division of the United Daughters of the Confederacy. In 1925, as president of the North Carolina Federation, she persuaded Governor Angus McLean to authorize a survey of working conditions for women in industry, a survey that he previously had refused to sponsor. Unfortunately, conflict over the administration of the survey resulted in its cancellation. In 1926, however, Governor McLean appointed Mrs. McKee to the North Carolina Educational Commission, where she worked for a state-wide eight-month school term.

Between 1926 and 1928 she was president of the Southern Council of Federated Club Women, and between 1927 and 1929 she served a term on the County Government Commission. During the latter period she also was president of the Southeastern Council of Federated Club Women, composed of thousands of members from eight southeastern states. In 1931 she became a member of the Commission for Consolidation of The University of North Carolina. Between 1933 and 1935 Gertrude McKee was chairman of the Jackson County Board of Education, for a time was a member of the State Board of Public Welfare, and at different times was a trustee of Western Carolina Teachers College, Peace College, The University of North Carolina, and Brevard College. Active though she was in these areas, Mrs. McKee was involved in the Sylva Methodist Church, where she played the piano and sang in the choir. She also was noted locally for her skill as a housekeeper and as the baker of excellent cakes.

In 1930 the Democratic party nominated Gertrude McKee for the state senate. After campaigning through the three counties of the district, she was elected by the largest majority of any candidate on the ticket. She not only served this first term (1931–33) but also was elected to two other terms (1937–39 and 1943–45). She resigned on 8 Apr. 1943 following the end of that year's session. She was reelected in 1948 but died a few days after the election.

In the legislature Mrs. McKee sat on a number of committees, including Appropriations; Education; Election Laws; Finance; Internal Improvements; Manufacturing, Labor, and Commerce; Institutions for the Deaf; Mental Institutions; Pensions and Soldiers' Home; Public Health; Conservation and Development; Library; and Printing. As chairman of the Public Welfare Committee during each of her three terms, she pioneered welfare programs that served as models for other states. As a vocal proponent of education, she constantly fought to equalize educational opportunities for children throughout North Carolina. Outspoken in her belief that all pupils should complete school at least through the sixth grade, she secured passage of a bill towards that end de-

spite opposition from several of her male colleagues. She was buried in the Keener Cemetery, Jackson County.

SEE: *Asheville Citizen-Times*, 18 Mar. 1973; Biographical Directory of the General Assembly of North Carolina (typescript, North Carolina State Archives, Raleigh); W. E. Bird, "Some Highlights of the History of Jackson County" (a paper read at a meeting of the Town-College Club, 26 Oct. 1970); John L. Cheney, Jr., ed., *North Carolina Government, 1585–1979* (1981); Raleigh *News and Observer*, 15 June, 7 Dec. 1930, 11 Feb. 1931.

TERESA KAY BECK

McKee, James (5 Jan. 1844–10 Jan. 1912), physician, educator, and Confederate officer, was born in Raleigh, one of four children of William Henry and Susan E. Battle McKee. His father was a prominent medical doctor in Raleigh; his mother, who died when he was eight, was the sister of Judge William H. Battle. James McKee attended the Lovejoy Academy in Raleigh until 1859, then entered The University of North Carolina. He left the university to join the Confederate army and never returned to study there, although the trustees awarded him a B.A. degree in 1911.

In 1861 McKee enlisted as a private in Company D, First Regiment of North Carolina Volunteers, and was mustered out in October. After reenlisting as a lieutenant and serving as a drill master in Confederate instructional camps at Raleigh and Morganton until December 1862, he entered active service and participated in the Battle of Kinston. He then joined the Seventh North Carolina Regiment and remained with it until the end of the Civil War.

Returning to Raleigh after the war, McKee was employed as a special messenger for the National Express and Transportation Company for about a year before he began the study of medicine in his father's office. He entered Bellevue Hospital Medical College in New York in October 1867 and was graduated with an M.D. degree in March 1869. At first McKee practiced in Raleigh with his father but soon established a successful practice of his own. Thereafter he earned the admiration and respect of his acquaintances, both personal and professional.

McKee contributed to the improvement of health care in his community as a member and for a time as president of the Raleigh Medical Academy, as president of the Raleigh Board of Health, as an organizer of the Wake County Medical Society, and as the first superintendent of the Wake County Board of Health. He was secretary of the Medical Society of the State of North Carolina for six years and a delegate to the American Medical Association. In addition, he was an alderman of the city of Raleigh, a surgeon for the Southern Railway Company, and a trustee of Rex Hospital. One of the directors of the state Hospital for the Insane (now Dorothea Dix Hospital) from 1896 to 1901, McKee was in the latter year unanimously elected superintendent of that institution. Under his leadership the hospital's facilities greatly improved, and he remained dedicated to his work there until the end of his life.

His chief contribution to education was as a pioneer in providing instructional programs in medical science for blacks. This he did as professor of obstetrics and gynecology and dean of the faculty at the state's first four-year medical school, the Leonard Medical School of Shaw University, until failing health forced his retirement; he was emeritus dean of the faculty at the time of his death. McKee was also professor of nervous and mental diseases in the medical department of The University of North Carolina.

An oil portrait of McKee, now privately owned, originally hung in Raleigh's Capital Club, of which he was a founder and president for twenty years. A Democrat, an Odd Fellow, and a member of Christ Episcopal Church, he married, on 30 Sept. 1873, Mildred Sasser, the daughter of John W. and Lucinda Haywood Sasser of Wayne County. The couple had six sons: William Henry, John Sasser, James Battle, Edwin Borden, Lewis Middleton, and Philip Sasser. McKee died in Raleigh and was buried in Oakwood Cemetery.

SEE: *Cyclopedia of Eminent and Representative Men of the Carolinas of the Nineteenth Century*, vol. 2 (1892 [engraving]); *North Carolina Biography*, vol. 5 (1919); Raleigh *News and Observer*, 11 Jan. 1912; *Transactions of the Medical Society of the State of North Carolina* 59 (1912).

JAMES BATTLE MCKEE

McKee, William Henry (7 Sept. 1814–24 Apr. 1875), physician, was born in Raleigh, the son of James and Priscilla Macon McKee. His mother was the niece of Nathaniel Macon, a longtime congressman from North Carolina. James McKee died in 1819, leaving his widow and four young children, of whom William was the only son. At about age fifteen William became a clerk in C. D. Lehman's Raleigh apothecary shop, where he developed into a skilled pharmacist. When Lehman retired, McKee found employment with the firm of Williams and Haywood, Raleigh druggists, and he soon became a partner. Meanwhile, he studied medicine with a preceptor and in 1837 entered the medical school of the University of Pennsylvania, from which he received an M.D. degree in 1839. During the summer of 1838 he was an intern at Philadelphia's Blockley Hospital for the indigent. In the academic year of 1838–39, while still a medical student, he was promoted, after examination, to the position of resident physician of the hospital.

In 1840 McKee returned to Raleigh and established a practice that he continued until a few weeks before his death. He was also active in civic affairs. He was a longtime member of the board of city commissioners and served for many years as president of the board of directors of the North Carolina State School for the Deaf and the Blind, where he was also the attending physician. After holding almost every office in a Subordinate Lodge, he was elected Grand Master of the Grand Lodge of Odd Fellows in North Carolina.

Deeply interested in raising the standards of the medical profession in the state, McKee was a founder of the North Carolina Medical Society and served as secretary (1849–51) and president for two terms (1858 and 1859). He was frequently a member of the society's executive committee as well as its delegate to the American Medical Association. In 1859 he was appointed to North Carolina's first State Medical Examining Board, the first such agency in the United States. In 1873 he was named a member of the Board of Censors, created that year by the Medical Society to police the practice of medicine in the state and to adjudicate disputes arising out of the professional activities of the society's members. In addition, he was a member of the Raleigh Academy of Medicine.

On 8 Mar. 1842 McKee married Susan Esther Battle, the daughter of Joel Battle, of Edgecombe County, a planter and an industrialist, and the sister of North Carolina Superior (later Supreme) Court Judge William

Horn Battle. The McKees had one daughter, Laura, and three sons, James, Lewis, and William. James (b. 5 Jan. 1844) became a practicing physician in Raleigh, where he was the first professor and the first dean of the Leonard Medical School of Shaw University, North Carolina's first four-year medical school; from 1901 until his death on 10 Jan. 1912, he served as superintendent of what is now Dorothea Dix Hospital. McKee's first wife died in 1852, and in November 1854 he married Eliza O. Nixon, of Wilmington, whom he survived. They had one child, Eliza N., who became the wife of Kemp P. Battle, Jr., M.D., a Raleigh ophthalmologist and the son of President Kemp P. Battle of The University of North Carolina.

McKee died at his home in Raleigh of "heart disease, attended with effusion into the Pericardium and an oedematous condition of the lungs and lower extremities." He was buried in Raleigh's Oakwood Cemetery. In a memoir written shortly after his death and read before the North Carolina Medical Society on 19 May 1875, S. S. Satchwell described McKee as an able physician who was ready "at all times to go, as ever he went, to the calls of the poor and down-trodden, as well as to the calls of the affluent and prosperous." Although he was not a party man, his political and economic views were apparently those of the Henry Clay Whigs. He attended the Episcopal church as his medical practice allowed but never became a member of any church. A photograph of McKee is in the Michaux-Randolph Papers, North Carolina State Archives, Raleigh.

SEE: Battle Family Papers (Southern Historical Collection, University of North Carolina, Chapel Hill); Kemp P. Battle, *Memories of an Old-Time Tar Heel* (1945); *Cyclopedia of Eminent and Representative Men of the Carolinas of the Nineteenth Century*, vol. 1 (1892); Guion G. Johnson, *Ante-Bellum North Carolina: A Social History* (1937); Dorothy Long, ed., *Medicine in North Carolina*, 2 vols. (1972); *North Carolina Biography*, vol. 5 (1919); *North Carolina Medical Journal* 1 (January 1878); S. S. Satchwell and William G. Hill, *Memoir of Dr. W. H. McKee, a Member of the North Carolina Medical Society and Fellow of the Raleigh Academy of Medicine* (1875); *Transactions of the Twenty-second Annual Meeting of the Medical Society of the State of North Carolina* (1875).

W. CONARD GASS

McKelway, Alexander Jeffrey (6 Oct. 1866–16 Apr. 1918), clergyman, social reformer, and journalist, was born in Salisburyville, Pa., the son of John Ryan and Catherine Scott Comfort McKelway. His father, a Presbyterian minister in Albemarle County, Va., was sympathetic towards the South during the Civil War but was persuaded by his fiancée not to enlist because his father was in the Union army. John R. McKelway died when his son was four, and his mother took Alexander and his brother to Charlotte County, Va., where they grew up in the home of their grandfather, David Comfort. Catherine McKelway taught school and was largely responsible for Alexander's early education.

Graduated from Hampden-Sydney College in 1886, McKelway taught for a time in Virginia and Georgia before entering Union Theological Seminary. Following his graduation in 1891 he was ordained by the Albemarle Presbytery in North Carolina. In the summer of that year he married Lavinia Rutherford Smith, the daughter of one of the seminary professors. He began his ministry in home mission work in Smithfield, N.C., where he organized a church, but the next year, when he was just twenty-six, he accepted a call to the large First Presbyterian Church in Fayetteville. Here his assignment in home missions introduced him to cotton mills and their workers, and he became concerned about conditions that came to his attention. One of these was the abuse of alcohol. McKelway took the lead, with the assistance of other Fayetteville ministers, in distributing blank petitions in support of liquor regulation in the county. Thousands of voters signed, and the petitions won the approval of the General Assembly.

In part because of his feelings for the welfare of the working class, McKelway became superintendent of home missions in the Synod of North Carolina. A series of articles on church history that he wrote in 1896 for the *North Carolina Presbyterian* (later the *Presbyterian Standard*) brought him to the attention of denominational leaders. Two years later he was named editor of the journal, the state organ of the church, and he moved his family to Charlotte where it was published.

From this base and through this organ McKelway became a lifelong "advocate of every reform." He was described as "the friend of education and of temperance and of social purity." His particular concern, however, was "the tender care of the little ones." He began a random series of editorials opposing the labor of young children in mills for long workdays and under unhealthy conditions. For his work in this area Davidson College awarded him an honorary doctor of divinity degree in 1900. In 1902 he also began to agitate for and support others who favored legislative protection for working children.

In 1903 an opportunity came to expand his influence when he became editor of the *Charlotte News*, and he broadened his field of concern to include the whole South. In that year the North Carolina General Assembly passed a weak law, with no enforcement provisions, prohibiting the employment of children under twelve and establishing a maximum sixty-six-hour week for children under eighteen. In 1904 a National Child Labor Committee was formed and McKelway became the southern secretary. The following year he resigned as editor of the *Presbyterian Standard* to devote the remainder of his life to the protection of working children. He lived in Atlanta from 1907 to 1911 and thereafter in Washington, D.C.

With the support of Raleigh newspaper editor Josephus Daniels and former governor Charles B. Aycock, McKelway began a vigorous campaign that eventually resulted in an effective law raising the age limit for employing young people in mills, limiting the hours of work, and requiring school attendance as a condition for working. Far from ideal, of course, these provisions were superior to earlier ones and were built upon by subsequent advocates. In 1919, the year after McKelway's death, the General Assembly created a Child Labor Commission.

McKelway was the author of many pamphlets and tracts. While living in Charlotte he also was one of three ghostwriters of Daniel A. Tompkins's *History of Mecklenburg County*, published in two volumes in 1903. Survived by his wife and five children, he was buried in Charlottesville, Va.

SEE: Betty Jane Brandon, "Alexander Jeffrey McKelway: Statesman of the New Order" (doctoral dissertation, University of North Carolina, 1969); *Charlotte Observer*, 18 Apr. 1918; *Minutes of the One Hundred and Sixth Annual Session of the Synod of North Carolina* (1919); Eugene C. Scott, comp., *Ministerial Directory of the Presbyterian Church, U.S., 1861–1941* (1942).

WILLIAM S. POWELL

McKelway, Benjamin Mosby *(2 Oct. 1895–30 Aug. 1976)*, newspaperman, was born in Fayetteville of Scottish ancestry. His father was Alexander Jeffrey McKelway, Presbyterian minister, journalist, and child labor reformer; his mother was Lavinia Rutherford (Ruth) Smith, the daughter of the Reverend Benjamin Mosby Smith, a professor at Union Theological Seminary in Virginia. Journalism and the ministry drew numerous members of McKelway's family. His great-uncle, St. Clair McKelway, was editor of the Brooklyn *Daily Eagle*, his brother St. Clair was a staff writer for *The New Yorker*, and his brother Alexander Jeffrey was a Presbyterian minister and navy chaplain during World War II. Successive generations inherited not only one another's names but also dominant character traits, especially determination and optimism.

At the time of McKelway's birth, his father was pastor of the Fayetteville Presbyterian Church. In 1898, when Alexander McKelway assumed the editorship of the *Presbyterian Standard*, the state organ of the church, the family moved to Charlotte. The senior McKelway's affiliation with the National Child Labor Committee in 1904 prompted moves to Atlanta in 1906 and permanently to Washington, D.C., in 1909, when he became the organization's chief congressional lobbyist. Although the McKelways lived modestly, they retained a Scottish housekeeper and, as an intimate family, frequently entertained relatives.

Vacations at eastern seashores, football, and hunting highlighted Benjamin's upbringing. Nicknamed "Bo," he possessed a "winning and forceful personality" which enchanted his younger brothers and sister who emulated his example as the oldest male. McKelway attended Western High School in the District of Columbia and entered Virginia Polytechnic Institute with ambitions to be a "scientific farmer." Service in World War I in 1917 and 1918 as a first lieutenant in the U.S. Army Infantry interrupted his education. A newspaper career apparently attracted him first in 1916, when he was briefly a reporter for the *Washington Times*, which employed his father as an editorial writer in 1917. Although McKelway studied at George Washington University and the University of Virginia, he was never graduated from college; instead, he began a practical apprenticeship as news editor and editorial writer with the New Britain (Conn.) *Herald* in 1919 and 1920. In 1921 he initiated his distinguished fifty-five-year association with the *Washington Star*. From 1921 to 1946 he rose through the paper's ranks as reporter, city editor, news editor, managing editor, and associate editor. Selected as the first nonfamily editor in 1946, he retained that position until 1963, when he assumed the title of editorial chairman, which he held for the remainder of his life.

His colleagues honored him by electing him president of the Associated Press (1958–63), president of the Gridiron Club (1958), and president of the American Society of Newspaper Editors (1949–50). A resolution of tribute by the board of directors of the Associated Press in 1963 emphasized McKelway's devotion to freedom of the press, the shibboleth of his career. The theme of his 1964 Pulitzer Memorial Lecture at the Columbia University Graduate School of Journalism was resistance to any form of press censorship.

His role in the inspection of German concentration camps and his advocacy of the Nazi war crimes trials demonstrated that he had acquired his father's commitment to public service and social justice. Although McKelway identified with no political party, as a concerned citizen of the District of Columbia he campaigned for presidential suffrage for District residents and promoted civil rights before the cause was popular.

As a trustee of the District of Columbia Public Library, the Rockefeller Foundation, George Washington University, the National Geographic Society, and the Washington National Monument Society, McKelway supported education and philanthropy. He served as president of the Washington Board of Trade in 1945 and 1946. Social memberships in the National Press, Gridiron, Alibi, Cosmos, Chevy Chase, and Metropolitan clubs reflected his gregariousness. A member of Delta Tau Delta, he was an adviser to the Pulitzer Prize Committee and was honorary president of Sigma Delta Chi. He continued his family's affiliation with the Presbyterian church.

In 1920 he married Margaret Joanna Prentiss, who died in 1974. He was the father of three sons: Benjamin Mosby, Dr. William Prentiss, and John MacGregor. John maintained tradition as a reporter for the *Washington Star*. McKelway succumbed to kidney failure at Sibley Memorial Hospital and was buried in Rock Creek Cemetery, Washington, D.C. A portrait of him on a sailboat in Maine hangs in his son John's home.

SEE: McKelway's own works in the *Washington Star*; St. Clair McKelway, various articles in *The New Yorker* (1952–57, 1961, 1963); *New York Times*, 1 Sept. 1976; *Who Was Who in America*, vol. 7 (1981).

BETTY J. BRANDON

McKenna, Richard Milton (*9 May 1913–1 Nov. 1964*), novelist and free-lance writer, was born in Mountain Home, Idaho, the oldest of four sons of Milton Lewis and Lucy Ertz McKenna. After graduating from high school and attending the College of Idaho, he was forced by the depression to join the U.S. Navy. He served from 1931 to 1953, retiring as a chief machinist's mate. While serving aboard a variety of ships at home and abroad, McKenna began to read widely, collecting books and observing the naval life—especially in China and Japan—which later became the material for his fiction. At thirty-six he discovered that he wanted to be a writer, and his remaining years were forged into an enduring American success story.

Leaving the navy after twenty-two years, McKenna enrolled at The University of North Carolina with the idea of becoming a writer. Taking a variety of courses, he was elected to Phi Beta Kappa and was graduated in three years. He received a B.A. in English in 1956. The day after graduation he married Eva Mae Grice, a librarian at the university.

The story of his apprenticeship as a writer is recorded in *New Eyes for Old* (1972), a posthumous collection of essays and speeches. He was forty-four when he published his first story, a fantasy entitled "Casey Agonistes." There followed other stories that appeared in popular magazines, most of them collected in *Casey Agonistes and Other Science Fiction and Fantasy Stories* (1973), which earned the Nebula Award. When he was forty-nine he published *The Sand Pebbles* (1962), the dramatic story of a gunboat in China in the 1920s. This novel won him the Harper's Prize and a national reputation as a novelist. *The Sand Pebbles* was a Book-of-the-Month Club selection and later was made into an award-winning movie. When McKenna died in Chapel Hill, he left a second novel of naval life unfinished. It was published as *Sons of Martha and Other Stories* (1966).

SEE: Book-of-the-Month *Club News* (1962); *Contemporary Authors*, vols. 5–6 (1963); *National Observer*, 11 Mar. 1963; *New York Times*, 10 Sept. 1962; Raleigh *News and Observer*, 14 Oct. 1962; *Time*, 16 Nov. 1962.

GUY OWEN

McKethan, Alfred Augustus (*8 July 1809–5 Jan. 1890*), carriage manufacturer, railroad promoter, and political and civic leader, was born in Cumberland County of Scottish Highland forebears who had settled the region prior to the American Revolution. He was the son of Christian McKethan, the daughter of John and Grisella McAllister McKethan. The name of his father is unknown. Little is known of McKethan's early life and education. In 1832 he began the manufacture of carriages, an enterprise that later made him a prominent figure in the economic and political life of the Cape Fear region.

Antebellum Fayetteville was the center of a large wagon trade in goods brought from Wilmington by steamboat and dispatched overland throughout the Piedmont and mountain regions. Originally, the firm of McKethan and Gardner made wagons and carriages; eventually, McKethan became sole owner and concentrated on carriages. By 1853 he was reputed to be the largest carriage manufacturer in the South, producing a variety of vehicles, including sulkies, gigs, rockaways, buggies, and the more elaborate barouches; orders came from as far away as Kentucky and Texas. In 1866 his sons joined the business, which grew to six buildings, including two smith shops with several forges. The postwar demand for carriages was large from people who had lost every vestige of transportation after General William T. Sherman's march through the Carolinas, and production averaged twelve to fifteen carriages per month.

McKethan played a significant role in promoting other improvements in transportation. During the plank road movement of the 1850s he became a stockholder and director of the first plank road company, the Fayetteville and Western (to Salem), and a promoter of the Fayetteville and Warsaw to connect Fayetteville with the Wilmington and Weldon Railroad. Realizing the primacy of railroads over plank roads, he became a major stockholder and indefatigable supporter of the Fayetteville and Western (Coal Fields) Railroad, which was expanded into the Cape Fear and Yadkin Valley Railroad after the war. As president of the Fayetteville and Florence (S.C.) Railroad, he pushed surveying and grading to the South Carolina line, later incorporating it into the Yadkin Valley Railroad. He was a large stockholder in Carolina City, a rival of Morehead City, as the terminus for the North Carolina Central Railroad and a projected Fayetteville-Beaufort Railroad that was never constructed.

In addition to maintaining his extensive business interests, McKethan was a perennial leader in local political affairs. In 1847, when the office of town commissioner became elective, he was elected to the board from Ward 5. Continuing to hold this post, he received ninety-four of the ninety-five votes cast in 1860, and he was mayor in 1876–77. During the Civil War he served on important committees concerned with the safety, defense, and relief of the city and people of Fayetteville. In the postwar period he led the effort to redeem local elective government from Reconstruction appointees. In 1870 McKethan and his ticket were elected as the Board of County Commissioners and he became chairman, a position he held for the next decade. Originally a Whig, he had joined the American or Know-Nothing party in the 1850s, but by the time of the Civil War he was a leader in organizing a "Southern Rights" party for the defense of the South. Reconstruction adversities made him a confirmed Democrat.

Contemporaries characterized McKethan as a man of industry, integrity, candor, and perseverance. He was "impulsive by disposition, fiery by temperament . . . an active, zealous, whole souled man—in the front rank when any danger was to be met or any responsibility borne." At the same time, "His charity was open, and he gave willing ear and helping hand to tales of woe." His Scottish ancestry made him a staunch Presbyterian.

McKethan died after a brief illness, following a fall resulting in a broken leg, advanced in years and held in high esteem by his fellow citizens. He was buried in Cross Creek Cemetery (No. 2). By proclamation of the mayor, a town meeting was held to pay tribute to him and his contributions to Fayetteville.

On 21 Dec. 1833 McKethan married his half first cousin, Loveday Campbell McAllister, and they had three sons: Hector McAllister, Edwin Turner, and Alfred Augustus, Jr.

SEE: Jack Crane Collection (Cumberland County Public Library, Fayetteville); *Fayetteville Observer*, 2, 9 Jan. 1890; D. S. McAllister, *Genealogical Record of the Descendants of Col. Alexander McAllister* (1900); Alfred Augustus McKethan Manuscripts (Manuscript Department, Duke University Library, Durham); John A. Oates, *The Story of Fayetteville* (1972).

PERCIVAL PERRY

McKevlin, Anthony John (7 May 1902–23 Dec. 1946), newspaper writer and editor, was born in Charleston, S.C., the son of Thomas Joseph and Mary Cecilia Scharlock McKevlin. He was educated in Charleston, where he was graduated from the Cathedral of St. John the Baptist Parochial School in 1914 and the Bishop England High School in 1918 before attending the College of Charleston in the period 1918–20.

Having trained himself to be an exceptionally rapid typist, he became the private secretary to Mayor John Patrick Grace of Charleston. A frequent public speaker, Grace called upon his young secretary to accompany him and record his extemporaneous speeches. Often McKevlin did that directly on the typewriter without the intermediate step of shorthand. The mayor sometimes asked him to record other speeches as they were delivered. Once he was assigned to record the speech of a notable visiting from Ireland who surprised McKevlin by delivering his opening remarks in Gaelic. The speaker was Eamon De Valera, who later served Ireland as president and as prime minister.

In 1922 Mayor Grace, who was editor and publisher of the *Charleston American*, prevailed upon his secretary to join his news staff as a reporter—thus beginning a lifelong and distinguished career in journalism. McKevlin was a reporter for the Florence (S.C.) *News Review* in 1923–24 and a reporter and sports editor of the Rocky Mount (N.C.) *Evening Telegram* in 1924–26. He moved to Raleigh in 1926 to report city news and sports for the *News and Observer*. A year later he became the newspaper's first full-time sports editor. During the fourteen years he served in that position, McKevlin introduced innovations in sports reporting and standards of accuracy and excellence that established a model for sports sections of newspapers throughout the South and stimulated circulation and newspaper revenue. His efforts also added to the stature and strength of collegiate and high school athletic programs.

His exceptional speed as a typist enabled him to record football games play-by-play on his portable typewriter, and slower reporters who missed plays often peered over his shoulder to read what his blazing typewriter had recorded before their own eyes could catch it. Regarded as an authority on sports, particularly football

and baseball, he served as official scorer for Raleigh's professional baseball team in the old Piedmont League and worked closely with Judge W. H. Bramham, of Durham, then head of the minor league. To honor McKevlin's memory, the Southern Conference Sports Writers Association established the annual Anthony J. McKevlin Award for the conference's outstanding athlete. In March 1950 the first award was presented by his young daughter, Johanna, to Whitt Cobb of Davidson College. Since a conference reorganization, the McKevlin Award has been given by the Atlantic Coast Conference Sports Writers Association.

On 12 Oct. 1941 McKevlin was appointed managing editor of the Raleigh *News and Observer*, succeeding the late Frank Smethurst, who had held the post for seventeen years. Tony, as his friends called him, assumed the job just as World War II began draining his staff of manpower, and he worked overtime to recruit and train female replacements (a rarity then). During those lean years, he served in the dual capacity of both managing editor and city editor. His discipline demanded accuracy, objectivity, and clarity of style and transformed many a cub reporter into a true journalist. Women reporters who carried his training to higher positions included Marjorie Hunter, who later was a highly respected Washington correspondent for the *New York Times*.

One unmistakable casualty of the war was Tony McKevlin himself. Personal adversity, which dogged most of his life, cost him an eye, and robbed him of close kin, finally brought a terminal illness during the demanding months near the war's end. Neglecting much needed medical attention, he continued the complex task of publishing a daily newspaper even by telephone from his bed at Rex Hospital, where he died.

On 11 June 1933 McKevlin married Elizabeth Webster Forrest, of Raleigh, the daughter of Mortimer Elliott and Stella Gleaves Brightwell Forrest; they had one child, Johanna Forrest McKevlin Grimes, born on 22 July 1939. Mrs. McKevlin predeceased him on 23 June 1941.

McKevlin, a member of the Sacred Heart Cathedral of Raleigh, was buried in Oakwood Cemetery.

SEE: Raleigh *News and Observer*, 12 June 1933, 23 July 1939, 24 June, 13 Oct. 1941, 24–25 Dec. 1949.

JACK RILEY

McKimmon, Jane Simpson (13 Nov. 1867–1 Dec. 1957), agricultural educator and civic leader, was a director of women's institutes (1908–11), state home demonstration agent (1911–37), and assistant director of Agricultural Extension in North Carolina (1924–36). She was born in Raleigh of Scottish ancestry, the oldest of nine children. Her father, William Simpson, was born on 21 May 1839 in New York City, where his parents had settled after their arrival from Scotland; his family moved to Richmond, Va., and later to Warrenton, N.C. Her mother, Anne Cannon Shanks Simpson, had moved with her family to Virginia from Glasgow, Scotland, when she was eight; after their marriage in 1860, her parents moved to Raleigh.

Jane Simpson grew up in a cultivated atmosphere where her mother strongly upheld Christian ideals. Her father had musical talent and, as a retail druggist in Raleigh for thirty-eight years, was known nationally as an outstanding pharmacist and as a leader in the formation of the North Carolina Pharmaceutical Association. He conducted one of the first schools of pharmacy in North Carolina and in 1894 became president of the National

Pharmaceutical Association. Her uncle, Dr. John A. Simpson, served for fifty-seven years as a music teacher at the North Carolina School for the Blind. Jane also exhibited these musical and organizational talents and in later years became a living example of similar cultural and religious ideals.

After attending the public schools for four years, she spent five years at Peace Institute, in Raleigh, devoting one year to the study of art. She was graduated at age sixteen, at the time the youngest ever to graduate from Peace. In her mid-fifties she went back to school to earn a degree in conjunction with her work as state home demonstration agent. On receiving a bachelor of science degree in 1927, at age fifty-nine, she was the first woman to graduate from North Carolina State College. Under the pressures of a heavy work load and severe eyestrain, she completed the requirements for a master of science degree in 1929. The University of North Carolina awarded her an honorary doctor of laws degree in 1934.

Dr. McKimmon characterized the home "demonstration" method she developed as "one of the world's great movements in adult education." After teaching school at age eighteen, she spent the next twenty-two years establishing a home and teaching her own children. In 1908 she began working as a lecturer in the women's division of the Farmers' Institute, and in 1910 she became director of the division. When I. O. Schaub, director of the North Carolina Agricultural Extension Service and her next door neighbor on Blount Street in Raleigh, decided to organize girls' clubs in North Carolina, he encouraged Mrs. McKimmon to accept the leadership. She was appointed state home demonstration agent in 1911.

Beginning with a small group of girls who formed a tomato club, she organized fourteen counties the first year, and under her supervision the organization grew to a statewide system of supervisors, trained specialists, and county home agents. As the work expanded throughout the state, systematic instruction was given in nutrition, clothing, child care, home furnishing, labor-saving devices, landscaping, marketing, and any other area that might contribute to the "uplift" of the rural woman. These clubs provided a valuable service through the conservation and distribution of food during two world wars, an influenza epidemic, and the Great Depression. The educational program stressed leadership qualities, and Extension Service statistics revealed the progressive ideas and methods of the leaders and the people with whom they worked. Mrs. McKimmon extended her efforts not only to the "forgotten" white families but also to the black families as well. She traveled miles to their homes, trained their leaders, and gave demonstrations at their meetings. She became known internationally as her teaching methods and home ideals came to be used as models in other states and foreign countries.

Jane McKimmon was a gifted administrator, leader, and speaker who could "capture an audience with her personality." She covered thousands of miles on foot, with horse and buggy, by rail, and eventually by automobile, speaking at club meetings, conferences, and universities throughout the nation. She contributed articles regularly to leading newspapers and farm magazines, and her radio broadcasts provided information on such topics as clothing, canning, and gardening. As a trustee for Raleigh's Olivia Rainey Library, she worked to secure needed appropriations to improve facilities and to supply books to rural areas. In 1917 Governor Thomas W. Bickett appointed her director of home economics to help administer the food conservation program during World War I. Governor J. C. B. Ehringhaus

in 1935 named her to the first state Rural Electrification Authority, on which she served as vice-chairman. She served on the board of directors of the Farmers Cooperative Exchange under governors Clyde R. Hoey and J. Melville Broughton. Both made her a member of the State Council for National Defense during World War II. Governor Broughton also appointed her to the Committee on Hospital and Medical Care for Rural People.

Mrs. McKimmon was one of the founders of the National Home Economics Association and for a time served as president. She was a member of the North Carolina Literary and Historical Association, the Fortnightly Book Club, and the Raleigh Woman's Club, contributing regularly to the programs of the latter two organizations. She played an important role in the North Carolina and National Granges. For many years she was a soloist in the choir of Christ Episcopal Church, Raleigh, where she was a member. She attended political conventions and was an active supporter of the Democratic party.

An alert, practical, far-sighted organizer, Mrs. McKimmon remained an intensely human personality throughout her years of service. For her service to humanity, she received recognition throughout the world. She was elected to the National Honor Society of Phi Kappa Phi in 1927 and was presented the Distinguished Service Ruby in 1936 by Epsilon Sigma Phi, the national honorary society of the Agricultural Extension Service. In 1927 the home demonstration agents established the Jane S. McKimmon Loan Fund in her honor. For her "distinguished service to agriculture" she received an award from the North Carolina Grange in 1940. In the same year the *Progressive Farmer* named her Woman of the Year in agriculture, and in 1942 she was presented the bronze medallion at the Southern Agricultural Conference in Memphis.

Resigning her position as state home demonstration agent in 1937, she devoted her time to writing a history of her work, *When We're Green We Grow*, published in 1945. The next year, then nearing eighty, she went into full retirement. She died at age ninety in the Wake Forest Rest Home. After services at Christ Episcopal Church, she was buried in Oakwood Cemetery, Raleigh.

On 10 Nov. 1886 she married Charles McKimmon, a prominent Raleigh merchant. They had four children: Charles, Anne (Mrs. Robert W. Winston), William Simpson, and Hugh.

SEE: Jane S. McKimmon's own works; Jane S. McKimmon Papers (portraits) and Nell Battle Lewis Papers (North Carolina State Archives, Raleigh).

MARIE A. MCBRIDE

McKinne, Barnabas (*ca. 1673–ca. 1740*), planter, justice of the General Court, assemblyman for Edgecombe County, justice for Bertie County, and militia officer, was born in Isle of Wight County, Va., the son of a McKinnon clansman, Michael Mackenny, who emigrated from Scotland to Virginia, and his wife, Elizabeth. There is no record of the year of his birth, although an agreement exists by which his brother, John McKinne, held custody of his brother Barnabas's land after their father's death in 1686 because Barnabas was not of age. John granted Barnabas full custody of his land on 13 Jan. 1694, presumably at the time he attained his majority.

In 1702 Barnabas McKinne, who seems to have initiated this spelling of the family name, petitioned the Virginia Assembly for permission to build a gristmill on his Black Creek plantation in Isle of Wight (now Southampton County, Va.). Although North Carolina records show him as a petitioner for a land patent in Chowan County in 1713, it was probably in 1721 that he actually moved to that part of Chowan precinct in Albemarle County that in 1722 became Bertie Precinct; his land later fell in the new Edgecombe County proposed by the Assembly in 1735 (but not laid out until 1741) and in Halifax County after 1758. Located near Caledonia Woods on the Morattuck (now Roanoke) River, in an area already settled by Scots, McKinne in time owned several thousand acres of land and a large number of slaves.

In July 1722 McKinne was appointed a justice of the General Court, which usually met in Edenton, the home of Chief Justice Christopher Gale. He served at least until 1730 during a period of recurring controversy between the chief justice and governors George Burrington and Sir Richard Everard. As Gale asserted the prerogatives of his office, there was much debate over whether the General Court justices were equals of the chief justice as associates or were subordinates as assistants. Reappointed from time to time, McKinne served at least intermittently until 1730 or later. He also represented Bertie County in the Assembly of 1723 and Edgecombe County in 1734–35. He was appointed commissioner of the peace for Bertie Precinct and in 1727 was a vestryman of North West Parish in Bertie. He also came to be referred to as Major McKinne and later as Colonel, indicating his rank in the local militia.

McKinne was married twice. His first wife was named Mary in the deed of sale of his father's plantation in Isle of Wight County, Va., in 1703, but she is not further identified. His second wife was twice-widowed Mary Exum, the daughter of Judge Jeremiah Exum by his wife, Ann Lawrence. Her first marriage was to Jacob Ricks, by whom she had two children, Jacob and Martha. After Ricks's death in 1703 or 1704 she married William Murfrey (who died early in 1715), by whom she had a daughter, Ann. In 1719 she married McKinne.

McKinne's will was drawn in 1737 and a codicil added in 1739. He died soon afterwards. He named the following children either in his will or in deeds: Barnabas, Jr. (m. Mary Brown), William (wife's name unknown), John (m. Mary Parrish), Ann (m. William Murfrey), Mourning (m. John Pope), Christian (m. William Hurst), Mary Jane (m. John Brown), Patience (m. Joseph Lane), Richard (m. Mary Kitchen), Robert (m. Martha [family name unknown]), and Sara (m. Isaac Ricks). It is not known which or how many of his children were by the first marriage, but there were at least five, one of whom probably was Sara. At the July 1727 meeting of the General Court a grand jury presentment against John Brown, identified as the husband of McKinne's daughter, charged him with bigamy, which he admitted.

In addition to his children, McKinne reared his second wife's two children by Jacob Ricks as well as three sons of his deceased nephew, William McKinne, who were his wards. William McKinne was the son of John McKinne and had owned land in Nansemond County, Va., before moving with his wife, Mary, and their sons, Michael, Matthew, and William, to North Carolina where they settled near Barnabas McKinne. Of these great-nephews, William eventually settled in what became Wayne County where he was a militia officer and political leader.

Among the grandchildren of Barnabas McKinne were Joel Lane, of Wake County, whose land was purchased as a site for the state capital; and Mary McKinne, who married Nicholas Long of Halifax County.

SEE: John Bennett Boddie, *Seventeenth-Century Isle of Wight County, Virginia* (1938) and *Southside Virginia Families*, vol. 2 (1956); Robert J. Cain, ed., *North Carolina Higher-Court Minutes, 1724–1730* (1981); John L. Cheney, Jr., ed., *North Carolina Government, 1585–1979* (1981); Walter Clark, ed., *State Records of North Carolina*, vols. 22, 25 (1907, 1906); Stuart Hall Hill, "The Hill Family of Bertie, Martin, and Halifax Counties, North Carolina," vol. 8 (typescript, North Carolina Collection, University of North Carolina, Chapel Hill); William S. Price, Jr., ed., *North Carolina Higher-Court Minutes, 1709–1723* (1977); William L. Saunders, ed., *Colonial Records of North Carolina*, vols. 2, 4–6 (1886–88); Lillian F. Wood, "Michaill Mackquiny of Virginia, His Sons John and Barnabas McKinne," 1946 (typescript, North Carolina State Archives, Raleigh).

JAMES P. BECKWITH, JR.
JOHN BAXTON FLOWERS III

McKinne, Richard *(1752–27 Jan. 1800)*, militia general and politician, was born on one of his father's plantations in Johnston (now Wayne) County, the son of Colonel William McKinne and his wife Anne Grimes, the daughter of John Grimes of Dobbs County. His father was a distinguished planter, politician, member of the first vestry of Christ Church Parish in New Bern, and Revolutionary soldier. The McKinne family descended from Michael Mackenny, a Scottish immigrant who settled in Isle of Wight County, Va., in the seventeenth century. Colonel Barnabas McKinne, Michael's son, was the first to bring the family name to North Carolina, where he settled in 1702 in present-day Edgecombe and Halifax counties.

Little is known of Richard McKinne's early life. Sustained family tradition states that he received some formal instruction from Thomas Thomlinson at the New Bern School (later the New Bern Academy). This school was opened in January 1764 under the patronage of the Reverend James Reed, rector of Christ Church. McKinne was at that time twelve years old, and doubtless his father's place on the vestry of the parish influenced his attendance at the new school. What remains of McKinne's library attests to an interest in good literature and a cultivated mind.

For a time during the American Revolution young McKinne was a soldier in the Whig forces, and in the years that followed he rose in the militia; eventually, the General Assembly appointed him a brigadier general. In public life he was a justice of the county court, a commissioner for Wayne County (1782), and a justice of the peace. When the first court convened in the new courthouse at Waynesborough on 9 July 1787, he was one of the justices attending. For a long period he was an influential member of the General Assembly, serving in the House of Commons in 1782–83, 1786–87, and 1790. He was a member of the senate in 1788–89 and 1791–99.

McKinne was a delegate from Wayne County to the constitutional convention held at Hillsborough on 21 July 1788 to ratify the U.S. Constitution. There he supported the Anti-Federalist faction led by his father's old friend, Willie Jones of Halifax. McKinne voted for the resolution calling for enactment of a bill of rights asserting civil and religious liberty before ratification of the federal Constitution. At the second convention, which met the next year in Fayetteville, McKinne again represented Wayne County and on 21 Nov. 1789 voted for ratification of the Constitution. Since he represented both agricultural and commercial interests, he was doubtless persuaded by the Federalist economic argument that these interests would suffer unless the state joined the Union. He remained firm in his Anti-Federalist outlook, as evidenced by his refusal to take the oath of allegiance to the Constitution after the federal government passed the Judiciary Act of 1789 giving the Supreme Court authority over state courts.

In 1773 McKinne married Sarah Fellows, the daughter of Robert Fellows, a wealthy planter of Johnston (now Wayne) County who in 1759 was authorized to operate a tobacco inspection warehouse at Fellows Ferry on the Neuse River. The Fellows family had come to North Carolina from Surry County, Va., in the first half of the eighteenth century. Richard and Sarah Fellows McKinne had eight children: Anne (m. Joseph Everett), Richard, Jr. (m. Julia Sasser), John (m. Olive Fellows, his cousin), Barnabas (m. Chellie McKinne, his cousin), Matthew, Robert (m. Zilphia Smith), Sarah, and Mary.

The Price-Strother map of North Carolina places "Gen. McKinney" on the south side of the Neuse River at the "Roundabout." Jonathan Price surveyed for the map about 1795, though it was not published until 1808, eight years after McKinne's death. His wife, Sarah, survived until 1837. It is said that General and Mrs. McKinne were buried on their estate at the Roundabout on the Neuse River, but their graves are no longer in evidence.

SEE: John L. Cheney, Jr., ed., *North Carolina Government, 1585–1974* (1974); Frank Daniels, *History of Wayne County* (1916); North Carolina Adjutant General's Reports, 1784–99, Revolutionary Militia Returns for Wayne County, and Wayne County Records (North Carolina State Archives, Raleigh); Lillian F. Wood, "Michaill Mackquiny of Virginia, His Sons John and Barnabas McKinne," 1946 (typescript, North Carolina State Archives, Raleigh).

JOHN BAXTON FLOWERS III

MacKinney, Loren Carey (*16 Dec. 1891–27 Oct. 1963*), university professor, was born in Lake Crystal, Minn., the son of Everson Rider and Jennie May (Amy) MacKinney. He received his early education in the public schools of Minneapolis–St. Paul and of Appleton, Wis. Continuing his studies in Wisconsin, he was awarded an A.B. degree from Lawrence College, in Appleton, in 1913 and a master's degree from the University of Wisconsin in 1916. Further graduate work earned him a certificate from the University of Grenoble, France, in 1919 and a Ph.D. degree in medieval history from the University of Chicago in 1925.

MacKinney taught at North High School in Milwaukee from 1914 to 1918, then served in the U.S. Army during World War I (1918–19). He began his college teaching career with professorships at William Jewell College, in Liberty, Mo. (1919–22), Knox College, in Galesburg, Ill. (1923–25), Louisiana State University (1925–29), and Ohio State University (1929–30). In 1930 he moved to Chapel Hill as professor of medieval history at The University of North Carolina, remaining in the post until his death. He was named Kenan Professor of History in 1955 and held visiting appointments at the universities of Chicago and Illinois, Stanford University, the University of Virginia, the University of California at Los Angeles, and elsewhere.

MacKinney's research interests and publications were in three major areas: early medieval culture, early medieval medicine, and the humanities in the United States. He was the author of *Early Medieval Medicine* (1937), *The Medieval World* (1938), *Bishop Fulbert and Education at the*

School of Chartres (1957), *Medical Illustrations in Medieval Manuscripts* (1965), and more than fifty articles. A world renowned collector of medieval medical miniatures, he lectured at numerous universities and conferences in this country and in Europe. In 1936 he delivered the Noguchi Lectures on the history of medicine at Johns Hopkins.

He was a member of the American Historical Association, the Mediaeval Academy of America, the American Association of the History of Medicine, the Southern Historical Association, the History of Science Society, and many other professional organizations. He also served on the editorial boards of the *American Historical Review* (1952–57) and *Manuscripta*, the journal of the Vatican Microfilm Collection at St. Louis University.

Professor MacKinney's keen mind, optimistic spirit, and enthusiasm for his subject were reflected in his teaching, which he enlivened with illustrative material such as slides and musical recordings. He emphasized the progressive and humanistic aspects of medieval culture and vigorously denied the undeserved reputation of the Middle Ages as a "dark age," even as he deplored the frequently exaggerated reputation of the Renaissance as the dawn of the modern era. His dynamic personality attracted to him a large number of friends and admirers. His encouragement of scholarship among his students and his unfailing interest in their academic work bore fruit in the productivity and scholarly achievements of a number of his graduate students.

MacKinney was survived by his wife, the former Abigail Elizabeth Greenwood, whom he married on 30 June 1917, and a son, Dr. Loren G. MacKinney.

SEE: *Chapel Hill Weekly*, 30 Oct. 1963; *Directory of American Scholars*, vol. 1 (1963); *Greensboro Daily News*, 28 Oct. 1963; A. C. Howell, *The Kenan Professorships* (1956); *Who's Who in America*, vol. 32 (1963).

J. CARLYLE SITTERSON

McKnight, Colbert Augustus (Pete) (*19 Aug. 1916–16 Aug. 1986*), newspaper editor, was born in Shelby, one of three sons of John Samuel, a wholesale grocer, and Norva Proctor McKnight. On graduation from Shelby High School in 1933, McKnight originally intended to teach Spanish at the college level. Although he had been accepted for admission to Davidson College, he decided to delay his enrollment and spend a year studying Spanish in Havana, Cuba, where his brother John was the Associated Press bureau chief. That summer he wrote his first news story—an eyewitness account of mob murders during the coup that deposed President Geraldo Machado. When a hurricane destroyed the school he was to attend, McKnight returned to Shelby and worked for nine months as a cub reporter on the Cleveland *Star* (now the Shelby *Daily Star*). He then entered Davidson College but continued to work on the newspaper during the summers. By 1938, when he was graduated summa cum laude with a major in Spanish and a minor in economics, McKnight had given up the idea of teaching in favor of journalism.

In 1939 McKnight joined the *Charlotte News*, the city's afternoon newspaper, as a general reporter, covering most of the city beats and editing the radio, book, and cultural pages. He left the *News* in 1943 to become managing editor of the San Juan (Puerto Rico) *World-Journal*, an English-language daily distributed mainly to American military bases throughout the Caribbean. Subsequently named editor and then executive editor, with responsibility for supervising all operations of the paper, he also served as a part-time Associated Press war correspondent and as a special correspondent for the *Baltimore Sun* and *Business Week*. In October 1944 McKnight returned to the *Charlotte News* as news editor. He was appointed managing editor in 1947 and editor in 1949.

As early as his senior year in high school, McKnight had spoken out publicly against racial prejudice, and in his *News* editorials he frequently reflected on the problems of segregation and the need for change. In "Handwriting on the Wall," written in June 1950, he discussed three Supreme Court decisions that seemed to presage the end of governmentally sanctioned segregation. Warning that the impact of these decisions would soon be felt in North Carolina, McKnight declared: "We have said it before. We say it again today. Segregation as an abstract moral principle cannot be defended by any intellectually or spiritually honest person." At the same time, however, he felt that the system would have to "be worn down, bit by bit" and worried that the Supreme Court or Congress might force change too rapidly for Southerners to accommodate.

Anticipating the Supreme Court's decision declaring segregation in public schools unconstitutional, McKnight and several southern members of the American Society of Newspaper Editors met with representatives of the Fund for the Advancement of Education in April 1954 to plan the establishment of a news service to provide "objective, accurate, and authoritative" reporting on developments arising from the Court's action, which occurred in May. By June, McKnight had been named the first executive director of the Southern Education Reporting Service and he moved to Nashville, Tenn., to open the headquarters. From the District of Columbia and the seventeen states where segregation in the public schools was then required by law, he recruited correspondents to provide reports for publication in the *Southern School News*, a monthly sixteen-page tabloid that he edited. In the first issue, dated 3 Sept. 1954, McKnight denied allegations by critics that the Southern Education Reporting Service had been established either to promote integration or to preserve segregation. It would "not be an advocate for or against anything" but would "adhere scrupulously to the accurate and objective reporting of facts as it finds them." By the time he resigned in July 1955, the organization's newspaper was being distributed free to 30,000 government officials, school administrators and school board members, libraries, newspapers, radio and television stations, federal agencies, and interested citizens.

McKnight resigned from the Southern Education Reporting Service because Knight Newspapers, Inc., had picked him to be editor of the *Charlotte Observer*, which it had recently acquired. Although the *Observer* surpassed its afternoon rival, the *Charlotte News*, in advertising revenue and circulation, the *News* was the livelier of the two papers. The *Observer* tended to be an uncritical booster of business and to avoid controversy. With full responsibility for the news and editorial functions of the paper, McKnight had greater authority than any *Observer* editor since 1909, and he undertook to implement the new owner's plan to rebuild the paper from top to bottom. He soon opened bureaus in Raleigh and Columbia, S.C., added a dozen new correspondents throughout the Carolinas, encouraged his staff to do investigative reporting, and began to endorse political candidates.

The *Observer*'s new editor was not timid in supporting causes he believed in, and under his direction the paper spoke out forcefully on such issues as urban renewal,

city-county school consolidation, better race relations, the arts, and the conversion of Charlotte College into the fourth campus of The University of North Carolina. He further assisted these and other causes by serving on the boards of directors of numerous civic and arts organizations and on the advisory boards of several educational institutions. From 1963 to 1965 he was president of the North Carolina Fund, a statewide demonstration project to test antipoverty plans.

Although most of his contemporaries regarded McKnight as a liberal, a recent assessment by Frye Gaillard has pointed out the conservative motivation behind the editor's beliefs and actions. He wanted to preserve the tranquility and prosperity of his community, but he knew that to do so required change. In 1963, for example, he told Charlotte's mayor that if the city were to avoid the open racial strife occurring elsewhere, the civic leadership had to begin to stimulate and direct that change. As a member of the executive committee of the Charlotte Chamber of Commerce, he was the primary author of the resolution passed by the chamber in support of voluntary desegregation of hotels, restaurants, theaters, and public swimming pools. The school busing controversy of the late 1960s and early 1970s was a much more divisive issue, however, and the McKnight-led *Observer* was one of the few local institutions to support, from the beginning, the federal court orders requiring busing to desegregate the Charlotte-Mecklenburg schools.

During the busing controversy, McKnight faced his own personal crisis when an inflammation in his one good eye left him nearly blind for a year and a half. (A childhood injury had cost him the sight of one eye.) As a result of this battle, the constant daily work pressures, and an assortment of other ailments, he became increasingly isolated from the paper's day-to-day operations. In September 1976 he was replaced as editor and named associate publisher.

McKnight was a founder of the North Carolina Conference of Editorial Writers and served as president of the North Carolina Press Association and of the American Society of Newspaper Editors. In the latter role, he testified in 1971 before the U.S. Senate Judiciary Subcommittee on Constitutional Rights concerning the application of First Amendment principles to the press and the relationship between the press and the government. In 1977 the society named him director of its Newspaper Readership Project to research and report on the needs and desires of newspaper readers. McKnight retired as associate publisher of the *Observer* in 1978, but he continued as director of the readership project until a heavy schedule and recurrent health problems forced him to resign in August 1981.

Colby College conferred on McKnight its Elijah Parish Lovejoy Award and an honorary doctor of laws degree in 1965, and Davidson College gave him an honorary doctor of letters degree in 1977. His friends endowed a scholarship in his name at the School of Journalism at the University of North Carolina at Chapel Hill, where he was also one of the first five inductees in the North Carolina Journalism Hall of Fame. At the University of North Carolina at Charlotte, a lecture hall in the Cone University Center bears his name.

McKnight married Margaret Henderson in 1941, and they had three children: John Peter, Margaret Carson, and David Proctor. After his first marriage ended in divorce, McKnight married Gail Oliver Ehle in 1968. They had one child, Colby Augustus. McKnight died in Charlotte and his body was cremated.

SEE: *Charlotte Observer*, 30 June 1978, 29 Oct. 1983, 17, 18 Aug. 1986; Jack Claiborne, *The Charlotte Observer: Its Time and Place, 1869–1986* (1986); Frye Gaillard, *The Dream Long Deferred* (1988); C. A. McKnight, "The 'Unique Experiment' Is Done," *Southern Education Report* 4 (June 1969); Colbert Augustus McKnight Papers (Atkins Library, University of North Carolina at Charlotte); *Southern School News*, 3 Sept. 1954.

ROBIN BRABHAM

Macknight, Thomas *(fl. 1757–87)*, Loyalist planter and public officeholder, was a native of Scotland. Little is known about him except for the years he spent in North Carolina, where he settled in 1757. A landowner in both the Albemarle and Upper Cape Fear regions, he was also involved in shipbuilding and the export trade in Norfolk, Va. He served in the North Carolina Assembly in 1762, 1771, 1773 (both terms), and 1775 and in the latter year was nominated to the Council. Governor Josiah Martin described him as a "gentleman of character . . . of greatest weight and abilities."

At the New Bern Provincial Congress of 1775, where Macknight represented Currituck County as a Loyalist, he was the only member who refused to sign the Association approving the Continental Congress at Philadelphia. In an explanation published in the *North Carolina Gazette* on 14 Apr. 1775, Macknight said that, although he could comply with the nonconsumption and nonimportation agreements and give passive support to the nonexporting section, he could not repudiate debts to British merchants and asked for time to settle his obligations. Radical members refused to allow a delay, and the house, declaring that his intentions were "inimical to the cause of liberty," recommended that all persons "withdraw from all connection with him as an object of contempt." Macknight and other members for Currituck and Pasquotank then withdrew from the convention.

After he received threats, an attempt was made to assassinate him, and his house, crops, and slaves were plundered, he fled to Governor Dunmore of Virginia at the end of 1775. At his own expense, he paid £150 to build a wall around Norfolk to help in its defense. In February 1776 he was with Governor Martin, in July and August he was in the Cape Fear region, and later in the year he fled to England, where he was given £500 on his arrival. Subsequently, he made claims for the loss of land, ships, slaves, and merchandise in both North Carolina and Virginia valued at over £30,000. Macknight was last noted giving evidence on 19 Mar. 1787 with regard to the claim of another Loyalist. His later career is unknown, and his name does not appear in the 1790 census of North Carolina.

SEE: Evangeline Walker Andrews, ed., *Journal of a Lady of Quality* (1921); Walter Clark, ed., *State Records of North Carolina*, vol. 12 (1895); *North Carolina Historical Review* 2 (1925); Lorenzo Sabine, *Biographical Sketches of Loyalists in the American Revolution*, vol. 2 (1864); William L. Saunders, ed., *Colonial Records of North Carolina*, vol. 9 (1890); John H. Wheeler, *Historical Sketches of North Carolina from 1584 to 1851* (1851).

JOHN D. NEVILLE

McKoy, Allmand Alexander *(11 Oct. 1825–11 Nov. 1885)*, politician and superior court judge, was born in Clinton, the son of Dr. William and Ann Hall McKoy. He was the grandson of Allmand Hall, a Wilmington printer and newspaperman. McKoy attended The University of North Carolina during the years 1846–47 and afterwards probably read law for a time. At any rate, he opened a law office in Clinton, but until he built up a practice he also taught school. The legislature voted him a seat on the Council of State for the period 1856–57, and he was elected a member of the state senate for the session of 1858–59. In 1864 he was commissioned colonel of the Seventy-third Regiment of Infantry, Senior Reserve, but did not see active service. As a Democrat he was elected a delegate to the constitutional convention of 1865–66.

McKoy was a candidate for Congress in 1868 but was defeated by Oliver H. Dockery, a Republican. In the general election of 1874 McKoy won a seat on the superior court bench. Reelected in 1882, he served until his death. It was noted in 1885 that he had had the fewest reversed decisions of any judge then serving.

His wife was the former Lydia Anciaux Howard of Atlanta; married in 1851, they were the parents of five children: Thomas Hall and Susan Howard, who lived to adulthood; and Ann, Carrie, and John, who died young. The McKoys were members of the Episcopal church.

SEE: Kemp P. Battle, *History of the University of North Carolina*, vol. 2 (1912); John L. Cheney, Jr., ed., *North Carolina Government, 1585–1979* (1981); Daniel L. Grant, *Alumni History of the University of North Carolina, 1795–1924* (1924); J. G. de Roulhac Hamilton, *Reconstruction in North Carolina* (1914); Henry Bacon McKoy, *The McKoy Family of North Carolina* (1955); Stephen B. Weeks Scrapbook, vol. 4 (North Carolina Collection, University of North Carolina, Chapel Hill).

H. KENNETH STEPHENS

McKoy, William Berry *(24 Dec. 1852–16 Nov. 1928)*, attorney, historian, and botanist, was born in Wilmington, the son of William Henry (11 Aug. 1827–28 July 1858) and Francenia Eliza Berry McKoy (24 Dec. 1833–24 Apr. 1889). William Henry, the son of Dr. William McKoy of Clinton, moved to Wilmington and became a merchant; Francenia was the daughter of Dr. William Augustus and Ann Eliza Usher Berry and a descendant of James Hasell, chief justice of the colony and acting governor at the departure of Governor William Tryon.

William Berry McKoy attended private schools in Wilmington, including the school of the Reverend Daniel Morrelle and the Cape Fear Academy. He entered Princeton University in 1872 and was graduated in 1876. He then went to Raleigh, where he read law with George V. Strong and was admitted to the North Carolina bar in June 1879. Returning to Wilmington, he specialized in title law and practiced his profession until his death.

A Democrat, McKoy was a member of the executive committee of his party for twenty years and served as chairman in 1898. He was the New Hanover County attorney from 1896 to 1899 and court attorney for several years. When still a young man he made a set of abstracts of titles for the county.

On 23 Oct. 1876 McKoy organized the Historic and Scientific Society of Wilmington, and in 1897 he organized and was the first president of a fencing club. He was a member of the Wilmington Light Infantry and Grand Master of the Masonic order in North Carolina in 1912.

Intensely interested in the history of the Lower Cape Fear, he devoted much of his time to historical research and writing. Among his articles are a sketch of Governor Benjamin Smith who was an aide-de-camp to General George Washington, a history of Masonboro and Hilton Plantation, an account of Indian pottery found near Wilmington, and a biographical sketch of Captain Johnston Blakeley.

McKoy and Katherine Bacon were married on 15 Dec. 1886. She was the daughter of Henry and Elizabeth Kelton Bacon and the sister of Henry Bacon, who designed the Lincoln Memorial in Washington, D.C. The McKoys had five children: Elizabeth Francenia, William Ancrum, Henry Bacon, Francis Kelton, and James Hasell. McKoy was an Episcopalian. His funeral was conducted from St. James's Church, and he was buried in Oakdale Cemetery, Wilmington, with Masonic rites.

SEE: Elizabeth Francenia McKoy, personal contact; Henry Bacon McKoy, *The McKoy Family of North Carolina* (1955); *North Carolina Biography*, vol. 5 (1919); Wilmington *Star*, 17 Nov. 1928.

LEORA HIATT MCEACHERN

Maclaine, Archibald (9 Dec. 1728–20 Dec. 1790), attorney and Patriot legislator, was born in Banbridge, Ireland, where his father, the Reverend Archibald Maclaine (b. 1695), was a Presbyterian minister. The Reverend Mr. Maclaine had immigrated to Ireland from Lochbuie, Scotland. In April 1750, after serving a mercantile apprenticeship, young Archibald departed Ireland for America, arriving in Philadelphia on 24 June. In July 1752 he left Philadelphia bound for Charleston, S.C., and Cape Fear, N.C.

Maclaine settled in Wilmington, N.C., where, on 6 Nov. 1752, he married Elizabeth (Polly) Rowan (b. 8 May 1731), the daughter of the late Jerome Rowan and the stepdaughter of Matthew Rowan, president of the Council and acting governor (1753–54). The couple had six children, but only their first son, Jerome (27 Sept. 1753–1777), and their first daughter, Catherine (Kitty) (b. 24 Sept. 1755), lived beyond infancy. Kitty married George Hooper, one of the Tory brothers of William Hooper. Maclaine's grandchildren were the writer Archibald (Archy) Maclaine Hooper (7 Dec. 1775–25 Sept. 1853), Spence Hooper (b. 10 Jan. 1779; lived only a few months), and Mary Hooper (b. 15 July 1780).

In Wilmington Maclaine put his former mercantile apprenticeship to good account by becoming a merchant, but the business failed after his partner John Maclaine died. Although he was said to have had only a rudimentary education, Maclaine turned to the study of law and subsequently became one of the preeminent attorneys of the colony and of the state. In 1759 he was appointed a clerk of the supreme court and was reprimanded at least once (in 1764) while in office. Although sympathetic to the old order (he greatly admired Matthew Rowan), he early identified himself with the Patriot cause, standing against the government during the Stamp Act crisis. Maclaine was a member of the Committee of Safety for the Wilmington District from 1774 to 1776. In the summer of 1774 he served on the committee appointed to issue the call for a Provincial Congress by the inhabitants of Wilmington; he was elected to the congress in 1775 and 1776.

In 1776 Maclaine was a member of the committee appointed to draft the Bill of Rights and the Constitution, as well as one of the commissioners elected to revise the statutes and acts for North Carolina. In 1777 he was one of the senators who drafted the law for the court system. He was also chairman of the committee appointed to inquire into the internal security of the state. In 1779

he was nominated to be a judge of the superior court, but he declined to be a candidate. In 1780 and 1781 he was a member of the General Assembly, where he twice refused nomination for election to the Continental Congress. He again served in the General Assembly from 1783 to 1787.

An able legislator and an active committee worker, Maclaine exerted considerable influence among his colleagues. He might have accomplished even more than he did in the political arena if he had not spent so much time looking after the interests of his Tory stepson, George Hooper, and other Loyalists. Indeed, he became so identified with Tory interests that he was assaulted during the fall term of 1782, when Captain Robert Raiford of the Continental line incited a riot by breaking into the Bladen County court with thirty armed men and attacking Maclaine with a sword. Maclaine was one of the prime movers among the lawyers who attempted to write the judges off the bench in 1787. His acrimonious feelings towards Samuel Ashe and other justices related to their differences over the settlement of Tory claims in 1782.

Despite his Revolutionary politics, Maclaine was essentially a conservative, firmly committed to the concept of law and order. In 1783 he wrote Hooper that he preferred the men of the old order and would be dealing with them in the legislature "if the late British ministry had had common sense"; only a few months later he claimed that he was a strong supporter of Alexander Martin because of who the governor's opponents were. He supported the state's decision to take part in the constitutional convention. In 1788 he was a delegate to the Hillsborough convention, voting with the minority for adoption. He wrote in support of the Constitution under the pen name, "Publicola," and more than once referred to the opponents of the Constitution "as a set of fools and knaves." Even though he was not a delegate, he influenced the vote for adoption at the Fayetteville convention. Maclaine provided a model for those who would advance the theory of conservative and radical continuity in early American politics. In that tradition, he was one of the original trustees of The University of North Carolina.

According to Stephen B. Weeks, Maclaine was a handsome man with an athletic figure in his youth. He was an individual of righteous character and, like many conservatives, was willing to stand in the minority for his principles. He died at his home in Wilmington, leaving his considerable estate to George and Catherine Hooper, with a bequest for his wife.

SEE: Walter Clark, ed., *State Records of North Carolina*, vols. 11, 13, 16 (1895–99); George Hooper Papers (Southern Historical Collection, University of North Carolina, Chapel Hill); Hugh T. Lefler and Albert R. Newsome, *North Carolina: The History of a Southern State* (1963); Archibald Maclaine, *An Address to the People of North Carolina with the charges against the Judges in the last Assembly: The Protests in both Houses and other Papers relative to that Business* (1787); Archibald Maclaine Book (Southern Historical Collection, University of North Carolina, Chapel Hill); *North Carolina University Magazine* 4 (1855); Charles Van Noppen Papers (Manuscript Department, Duke University, Durham).

D. A. YANCHISIN

McLane, James Woods (22 May 1801–26 Feb. 1864), teacher, clergyman, and church official, was born in Charlotte, probably the son of George McLane, the only one of the name recorded under the various spellings of the surname in the 1800 census for Mecklenburg County. The family moved to Illinois when he was quite young, and after local schooling McLane entered Phillips Academy in Andover, Mass. It has been said that he rode horseback for the thousand-mile journey from his home. Following his graduation from Yale College in 1829, he taught school for several years in New London, Conn., before returning to Andover to study theology. While at the seminary, from which he was graduated in 1835, he served as a tutor.

In 1836 McLane became pastor of the newly organized Madison Street Presbyterian Church, in New York, where he remained until 1844, when he was called to the First Presbyterian Church in Williamsburgh, Long Island, N.Y. The latter church had recently suffered two splits—one over abolitionism, when seven members left, and another when twenty-three transferred to the Old School Presbytery. Under McLane's leadership, however, the breach was healed, and within a few years the congregation erected a large new brick church. He served there until 1863, when ill health forced his retirement.

McLane was a delegate to the General Assembly of his church and devoted many years of service to ecclesiastical and benevolent institutions. He also was the director and recorder of the Union Theological Seminary and secretary of the Presbyterian Church Erection Fund. The American Bible Society's Committee on Versions engaged him to collate various editions of the English Bible in order to prepare a standard copy for adoption by the managers of the society in 1851. This work, it was reported, "he performed with great fidelity, pains-taking and accuracy." Under the pseudonym "Coneroy," he contributed articles on biblical revision to the *New York Observer* and sometimes sent pieces to the *Quarterly Review* as well. In recognition of his scholarly contributions, New York University awarded him an honorary doctor of divinity degree in 1852.

In 1833 McLane married Ann Huntington Richards of New London, Conn., and they had six children, one of whom, James Woods, Jr., became a noted surgeon and president of the College of Physicians and Surgeons.

SEE: American Bible Society, *Bible Society Record* (1865); Eugene L. Armbruster, *Brooklyn's Eastern District* (1942); *Obituary Record of Graduates of Yale College from July, 1859, to July, 1870* (1870).

WILLIAM S. POWELL

MacLean, Angus Dhu (12 July 1877–1 Sept. 1937), lawyer and legislator, the son of John Allan and Mary Virginia Brown MacLean, was born in Maxton in Robeson County, the heart of the Scottish settlement in North Carolina. He attended Miss Hattie McBryde's school in Maxton and the academy of Professor W. G. Quackenbush in Laurinburg. In 1894 he entered The University of North Carolina, and shortly after his graduation in 1898 he was licensed by the North Carolina Supreme Court to practice law.

MacLean practiced briefly with G. B. Patterson in Maxton, but through the influence of Judge George H. Brown, a maternal uncle, he moved to Washington, Beaufort County, where he became the law partner of John H. Small, a congressman from the First Congressional District. During his career he was associated with various other partners in Beaufort County, including judges Stephen C. Bragaw and William B. Rodman, Jr., Harry McMullan, and John C. Rodman, Jr.

As a young lawyer MacLean was responsible for many important cases handled by the firm while Small was in Congress. The first quarter of the twentieth century saw northern capital coming into heavily timbered areas of eastern North Carolina. As the representative for several lumber companies, MacLean had the mammoth task of securing railroad rights-of-way as well as abstracting titles to the lands in question. In 1912 the "Second Civil War" broke out for Camden, Chowan, Currituck, Gates, Hyde, Pasquotank, and Perquimans counties when litigation developed between the Roper Lumber Company and the Richmond Cedar Works over titles in these counties. MacLean did much of the work in this conflict, both in preparing and trying cases.

However, the case that brought him most attention locally was that of the Peterson will. The wealthy E. R. Peterson had willed all of his property to his wife. MacLean represented relatives who alleged "undue influence." He won locally but lost when the case was appealed to the supreme court. His argument was that since no other relative was mentioned in the will, this alone was "evidence of lack of testamentary capacity and undue influence." As it happened, he argued the case before a court in which each judge had made his own wife sole heir to his property.

In 1927 MacLean was persuaded to accept nomination to the state legislature. His area needed a strong representative because of the dire economic situation. Agriculture had gone into a depression shortly after World War I and stayed there. Moreover, a land boom after the war resulted in the revaluation of land, and taxes, spent primarily for schools and roads, soared. During the period of readjustment more problems presaged public bankruptcy. From the moment MacLean entered the legislature, he became the champion of state-supported schools. In 1927, 1929, and 1931 he was able to get some legislation passed. In 1933 he returned to Raleigh as a senator from the Second District (Beaufort, Dare, Hyde, Martin, Pamlico, Tyrrell, and Washington counties) and was successful in convincing the legislature to vote for eight-month, state-supported schools. Since the country was in the depths of the Great Depression at the time, this legislation was considered to be a significant accomplishment.

In August 1933 MacLean accepted a post with the federal government as assistant solicitor general. In this position he became one of the major defenders of New Deal policies. The most important case he handled concerned the "Gold Clause" by which the federal government could be called on to pay off securities, bonds, and notes in gold. MacLean defended the government's right to pay them off in currency other than gold, won the case, and prevented the total depletion of the country's gold reserves.

In August 1935 he became assistant attorney general but resigned on 30 October to return to Raleigh. He was a senior member in the law firm of MacLean, Pou, and Emanuel until his death two years later. There were many tributes to MacLean by leaders of both state and nation, but Judge William B. Rodman, Jr., who knew him well, summed it up by saying that he "was blessed with a sharp sense of humor, a keen, analytical mind, a high sense of duty and a deep sympathy for the unfortunate."

MacLean married Annetta Everett of Laurinburg on 24 Oct. 1900. Their only son, Angus, died young. Their four daughters were Mary Virginia, Martha Lawrence, Annetta Everett, and Jane Duart.

In Washington, D.C., MacLean was a member of the Brewster and MacLean law firm. He served as president and counsel of the Washington and Vandemere Railroad, attorney for the Atlantic Coast Line, counsel for the Norfolk Southern, and counsel for several large development companies, several banks, and some other business organizations in eastern North Carolina. He was a member of the North Carolina Bar and American Bar associations, the Knights of Pythias, the Benevolent and Protective Order of Elks, the Presbyterian church, and the Democratic party.

SEE: Daniel. L. Grant, *Alumni History of the University of North Carolina, 1795–1924* (1924); Robert C. Lawrence, *The State of Robeson* (1939); *North Carolina Bar Association Fortieth Annual Session* (1938); *North Carolina Biography*, vols. 3 (1941), 5 (1919); *North Carolina Manual* (1927, 1929, 1931, 1933); Raleigh *News and Observer*, 7 Apr. 1933, 2 Sept. 1937; *Who Was Who in America*, vol. 1 (1942).

MAUD THOMAS SMITH

McLean, Angus Wilton (20 Apr. 1870–21 June 1935), lawyer, businessman, and governor, was born on a farm in Robeson County, the son of Archibald Alexander and Caroline Amanda Purcell McLean and a descendant of a proud line of hardy Scots who settled in the Upper Cape Fear Valley. Angus Wilton was the first of seven children. Born in the tradition of education and the stern culture of Scottish Presbyterianism, he received the best education available in the North Carolina of his day. After his early training in the local schools of Richmond (now Scotland) County, he attended the Laurinburg Academy. In the fall of 1890 he entered The University of North Carolina, where for two years he studied law under the direction of Dr. John Manning, Dr. Kemp P. Battle, Associate Justice James E. Shepherd, and Professor George T. Winston.

In 1892 McLean was admitted to the bar and began practicing in Lumberton as the associate of a kinsman, Thomas A. McNeill. Their firm handled much of the legal business of the town and for many years served as counsel for the Atlantic Coast Line Railroad. When McNeill left the office to accept a position on the state superior court bench, the firm was expanded and reorganized and in time was called McLean, Varser, and McLean. In 1917 McLean was elected president of the North Carolina Bar Association.

On 16 Apr. 1904 he married Margaret Jane French, and to them were born two sons and a daughter: Angus Wilton, Jr., Hector, and Margaret French.

In the meantime, McLean became one of the leading businessmen in Lumberton. In 1897 he joined a number of interested persons to establish the Bank of Lumberton, the first bank in town. Between 1895 and 1909 he helped to establish three textile mills in Lumberton, and in 1906 he played a significant role in building the Virginia and Carolina Railroad from Lumberton to St. Pauls, where it tapped the Atlantic Coast Line. This road provided the transportation needed for industrial and agricultural expansion in Robeson County.

In addition to his activities as lawyer and businessman, McLean was deeply interested in politics. Although his only experience in public office during his early years in Lumberton was as a member of the town board of commissioners for two terms, he was recognized as a leader in the Democratic party. For sixteen years he was a member of the state executive committee of his party and in 1912, and again in 1916, he served as chairman of the finance committee in North Carolina to raise funds for the Woodrow Wilson campaign. He assumed his first important political office when President Wilson appointed him to the War Finance Corporation in 1918, and his second when he was named assistant secretary of the Treasury in 1920.

McLean had been contemplating the governorship of North Carolina for a number of years and while in Washington, D.C. (1918–22), he watched his record in view of the contest in 1924. After returning home in the spring of 1922, he set up an efficient statewide organization, and early in 1924 he opened his campaign with a series of speeches in major towns across the state. His opponent in the primary was Josiah W. Bailey, a lawyer and former editor of the *Biblical Recorder*.

During the campaign McLean was no match for Bailey on the speaker's platform, but uncertain economic conditions in the state and rumors of a deficit in state funds led people to support the practical Scotsman, who promised to achieve efficiency and economy in state government. In the primary McLean carried eighty-three of the one hundred counties, and in November he carried the state against his Republican opponent by a wide margin.

In keeping with his campaign pledges, Governor McLean presented to the legislature when it met in January 1925 a recommendation calling for the establishment of an executive budget system. On 26 February an act to provide such a system became law. The act made the governor ex officio director of the budget and head of a bureau whose duty it was to prepare the biennial budget. All monies were to be appropriated and all funds disbursed from the state treasury according to the budget that had been approved and adopted by the General Assembly. The Appropriations Act of that year placed all institutions, departments, and agencies on a biennial appropriation basis. The Daily Deposit Act required that all agencies receiving or collecting funds deposit their collections daily to the credit of the state in some officially designated bank. This practice not only eliminated the borrowing of money in anticipation of revenues from taxes but also provided added income from interest on deposits. By the second year the efficiency of the new system began to be evident in a treasury surplus. When McLean's term ended in 1928, he left $2.5 million for the next administration. Governor O. Max Gardner later acknowledged that this surplus kept North Carolina from going into bankruptcy when the Great Depression hit.

In addition to his fiscal reforms, McLean initiated a much-needed overhauling of the whole executive branch of state government. Among the steps taken were (1) the classification of all state employees and the establishment of a uniform salary and wage schedule for comparable work in all public offices, (2) the consolidation of all revenue-collecting forces into the Revenue Department, (3) the allocation of all responsibility for supervision and regulation of business, financial, and industrial organizations to the Corporation Commission, (4) the centralization of all legal activities of state agencies under one head, the attorney general, thus eliminating the employment of additional lawyers in the several departments, and (5) the consolidation of all agencies dealing with natural resources into a new State Department of Conservation and Development.

Even more than state government, county government in North Carolina was in need of reform and in 1927 McLean undertook that task. He had served on a commission appointed by Governor Cameron Morrison in 1922 to make a study and recommend changes in laws relating to county government. Building on that experience, McLean encouraged the General Assembly to pass five significant measures. An Act to Provide Improved Methods of County Government established procedures for changing the structure of county government without a special act of legislation and clearly defined responsibilities of the boards of commissioners in all counties. The Act to Provide for the Administration of the Fiscal Affairs of Counties placed all counties on a budget system and provided the machinery for making periodic appropriations of revenue and the annual tax levies. The third measure, the County Finance Act, regulated the borrowing and repayment of money. The fourth, An Act to Provide for the Collection of Taxes, required that taxes be collected and settlement completed within the same fiscal year in which the levy was passed. This made it possible for counties to go on a budget system. The fifth act amended the Consolidated Statutes relating to tax deeds and foreclosures.

Second only to his interest in efficiency in government was McLean's interest in good public education for all children in the state. He recognized that schools must furnish leaders for the new industrial development that was rapidly placing North Carolina in the forefront among southern states. He also saw in the rural schools the state's best chance for building a better agricultural community. In 1927, with McLean's encouragement, the General Assembly approved a bill increasing the Equalization Fund to $3.25 million, the largest appropriation made to this date for public education in North Carolina. Expenditures per child enrolled in public schools were increased from $25.97 to $32.67, and the foundations were laid for a statewide eight-month school term. In addition to the increased appropriation for public schools, the McLean administration completed the six-year, $20 million program of appropriation for the institutions of higher learning, a plan initiated by his predecessor in 1921, and in 1927 secured increased funds for expanding teacher-training programs at state-supported colleges and normal schools. Through these several efforts state aid to education was doubled, appropriations reaching a figure that represented 52.18 percent of the state's income from taxes, a percentage surpassed by only four states in the Union.

Although Governor McLean is best known for his fiscal reforms and reorganization of the administrative machinery of state and county government, he made significant contributions to the economic development of the state. His promotion of improved methods of marketing and diversification in agriculture and industry laid a foundation for more prosperous years in the decades to follow. A farm-supported campaign launched late in 1926 led to a 13 percent reduction in cotton plantings and a marked expansion of other crops. The establishment of the State Department of Conservation and Development was a major contribution towards diversification of industry and utilization of all natural resources. Surveys made by this agency pointed the way to the development of building stone and clay products industries, as well as woodworking industries, and to further development of fisheries along the coast. A major publicity campaign began to attract outside capital and new industries for North Carolina.

McLean's continuation of the Good Roads campaign initiated by Governor Cameron Morrison contributed, in like manner, to the state's economic development. In 1925 he asked the legislature for $20 million in bonds for the Highway Department, and in 1927 he supported a bond issue of $30 million to complete the major highway system and to take over at least 10 percent of the six thousand miles of county roads for maintenance and improvements.

McLean's work in fiscal and administrative reform

placed him among the progressive governors of the nation, but his stand on matters of social and political reform was always that of a conservative. He withheld his support for efforts to secure workmen's compensation, and bills to provide such assistance were killed in 1925 and again in 1927. Efforts to improve the state's child labor laws suffered the same fate. He refused to raise a voice in support of a bill providing for the secret ballot in North Carolina or for other reforms of the election laws. His intervention, however, did save the state's primary law from repeal.

When McLean left the governor's office in January 1929, he returned to his law firm and business interests in Lumberton. Later he also opened a law office in Washington, D.C. He still had one political ambition, that of becoming a U.S. senator, but he gave that up out of respect for his friend, Senator Furnifold M. Simmons. In 1932 he was considered for a position in the U.S. Treasury Department, but he declined the offer.

On 19 Apr. 1935, while on route from Washington to Atlantic City, McLean suffered a thrombosis from which he never recovered. He died two months later, and his remains were returned to Lumberton for burial. For most of his life he had been a member of the Presbyterian church and a staunch supporter of its programs. A number of portraits and a good many of his papers and personal effects are in the Angus Wilton McLean Library in Lumberton.

SEE: David Leroy Corbitt, ed., *Public Papers and Letters of Angus Wilton McLean* (1931); Angus Wilton McLean and others, *Lumber River Scots and Their Descendants* (1942); Gary E. Trawick and Paul B. Wyche, *One Hundred Years, One Hundred Men, 1871–1971* (1971); Mary Evelyn Underwood, "Angus Wilton McLean: Governor of North Carolina" (Ph.D. diss., University of North Carolina, Chapel Hill).

EVELYN UNDERWOOD

McLean, David Alexander *(13 May 1918–16 July 1980)*, minister, missionary, and college teacher, was born on the family farm near Eagle Springs, Moore County, the third of six children of Robert C. and Rose E. Cochran McLean; he had four brothers and one sister. He entered Davidson College in 1935 and was graduated in 1940 with a degree in English. He studied at the Université de Poitiers, France, in 1939 and began studies at Union Theological Seminary in Richmond, Va., in the fall of 1940. McLean received a D.D. degree in May 1943 and was ordained in the Norfolk Presbytery at the end of the month. He served as pastor of the Suffolk Presbyterian Church in Suffolk, Va., from 1943 to 1945.

In 1945 McLean went to Lubandai, the area of the Belgian Congo that became Zaire, where he directed schools, taught industrial arts courses in carpentry and masonry, and studied local culture, especially the medicine cults. He established a number of churches in the surrounding areas. When the civil war of 1961 forced many missionaries to leave, McLean remained to serve as a pilot and an interpreter for the Red Cross. He was awarded the Australian Red Cross Medal of Honor for his services. During this period McLean was imprisoned several times and underwent physical hardships, including one crippling beating—the result of mistaken identity—that forced him to return to Winston-Salem for surgery.

At various times between 1957 and 1969 McLean studied at the University of Witwatersrand in Johannesburg, receiving M.A. and Ph.D. degrees in anthropology. Returning to the United States, he was professor of anthropology and archaeology at St. Andrews Presbyterian College, Laurinburg, from 1963 to 1980. During this time he led a number of archaeological expeditions and digs to study the civilization of Meso-America. In 1971 he helped found and build the Indian Museum of the Carolinas in Laurinburg in order to emphasize the role of the American Indian in the development of the region and the state. He served as the first director of the museum. He was a member of the American Anthropological Association, the Society of Applied Anthropology, the North Carolina Archaeological Association (president, 1971–72), and a Fellow in the African Studies Association. He was also elected to membership in the Society of Professional Archaeologists.

On 1 Dec. 1944 McLean married Anne Taylor Wilds, the daughter of Samuel Hugh and Lucille Keller Wilds, Luebo, Congo. They had six children: Nancy Anne (Mrs. Baxter Lee), David Alexander, Jr., Lucille Ellen (Mrs. Sam Mitchener), Judith Kennedy (Mrs. Michael McCall), Carolyn Rose Britt, and Helen Paige.

He was a Presbyterian and a Mason. Among his publications were *The Sons of Muntu: An Ethnological Study of the Bena Lulua Tribe in South Central Congo* (1962), his master's thesis at the University of Witwatersrand, and *The Role of Fire in Northern Circumpolar Ecosystems* (1983).

SEE: Alumni Records, Davidson College and Union Theological Seminary; Dick Brown, "David McLean: Man of Many Talents," *Fayetteville Observer*, 25 July 1980; *The* (Southern Pines) *Pilot*, 23 July 1980; *Presbyterian News*, July 1980; Raleigh *News and Observer*, 11 Mar. 1979; E. C. Scott, comp., *Ministerial Directory of the Presbyterian Church* (1950).

PATTIE B. MCINTYRE

McLean, Hector (*18 Aug. 1807–3 July 1889*), Presbyterian minister, teacher, and farmer, was born in Randlesville, Robeson County, the son of John and Effie McLean. He attended Union Theological Seminary in Virginia (1829–32), was licensed at Clinton, S.C., on 6 Nov. 1832, and served as stated supply for Bethel, Pee Dee, and Bennettsville. On 13 Dec. 1833 he was ordained in the Fayetteville Presbytery and called to Antioch Church in Robeson County, which he served until his death fifty-six years later. After receiving a call in November 1844, he also ministered at Philadelphus Church, Robeson County, until his death.

McLean was active in the early beginnings of the Temperance Society in Robeson in the 1830s. The county had large fruit crops, and he often preached to his congregation about the distilling that was done among his flock. But there were other activities of which he approved. The Antioch Bible Society, organized during his second year, was important in the work of the church and received an annual collection from the congregation. Antioch also had a Sabbath school that flourished under the pastor's influence and a Female Foreign Missionary Association, both of which began in the 1830s. "Father McLean," as he came to be known throughout the county, established a Sabbath school among the Indians of Robeson County, visited with them, and periodically taught them the Bible.

Many of the ministers of the nineteenth century were also teachers, and Hector McLean was no exception. In 1838 he established a school in Antioch. In 1844–45, his first year in the pastorate at Philadelphus, he established one there as well. He taught in both schools for

many years. Although he was in ill health much of his life, he still had a full and productive career. Ministers and teachers were paid such small salaries that it required both for the McLeans just to get by. During the Civil War everyone sacrificed, but after Union General William T. Sherman came through, life was extremely difficult; McLean became a farmer in order to feed his family. In 1871, for the first time in several years, he did not refer to the poverty within his congregation.

His coworkers said of him that he was "practical rather than philosophical," conscientious, gentle, sympathetic, and sensitive to the feelings of others. This did not prevent him from preaching what he considered the pure gospel or from sessioning members who broke the rules of the church. His simplicity, consistency, and impartiality combined with his gentleness won respect and love from all denominations.

McLean married Susannah Brown, but they had no children. They lived at Melrose, which was within commuting distance of his two churches. He was buried in Melrose.

SEE: Diary of the Reverend Hector McLean, 1832–79 (possession of Hector McLean, Lumberton); *Minutes of . . . the Fayetteville Presbytery* (1844–88); *Minutes of the Synod of North Carolina* (1889); *The* (Lumberton) *Robesonian*, 29 Nov. 1937, 26 Feb. 1951.

MAUD THOMAS SMITH

McLean, Hector (*14 May 1818–1 Dec. 1877*), physician, surgeon, and medical educator, was born in Hoke County, the son of John and Christian McLean. His grandparents, Hector and Jennet Murphy McLean, came to America from Scotland and settled in the Antioch–Red Springs area of North Carolina around 1770. Little is known of McLean's early life, education, or medical training. He was reported to have received a doctor of medicine degree about 1840 from the University of Louisville, but there are no extant records to document the claim.

During the two decades prior to the Civil War, McLean developed an extensive medical and surgical practice and became widely respected for his skills and knowledge. About 1850 he began clearing land near Raeford for his plantation and home site of Edenborough, a large estate that eventually had approximately five hundred acres under cultivation. Sometime during this period, probably as early as 1850, McLean began training medical students under the preceptor system. At least some of his students went on to receive medical degrees from accredited institutions, such as the New York University. It is likely that McLean made the transition from a preceptor system for individual students to a formal medical school curriculum during or just after the Civil War, since the building used as the medical school may have been constructed in the early 1860s.

After the war McLean petitioned the North Carolina General Assembly for a charter to incorporate the medical school. This was granted by an act of the legislature in February 1867, and McLean began formally operating the Edenborough Medical College, the first chartered school of medicine in North Carolina. Although most of the details of its history were lost, McLean signed all the diplomas and was probably the only faculty member. The medical school building located on McLean's estate was a two-story frame structure, with the upper floor for the lodging of students and the lower floor divided into four rooms for lectures, dissections, and clinical instruction. McLean used his extensive rural practice as the basis for all clinical training of students, who numbered a maximum of eight per year.

The Edenborough Medical College continued under McLean's directorship until 1876, when the Medical Society of the State of North Carolina appointed a committee to investigate certain "irregularities" in the operation of the school. In May 1877 the committee voted to recommend that the General Assembly rescind the 1867 charter. Apparently the inquiry never progressed to the point of revoking the charter, since McLean's death effectively ended the school's existence in late 1877. Although the Medical Society had expressed grave concerns over the quality of the graduating students, McLean's pioneering efforts in medical education clearly produced a number of skilled practitioners in North Carolina. Formal medical education resumed in the state only two years after his death, when The University of North Carolina opened its medical school in 1879 with Dr. Thomas W. Harris as dean.

McLean married Flora McNair (1829–1910). They had one son, Angus Murphy (1855–88), who trained under his father and practiced medicine until sometime before his death. McLean and his family were buried in the family cemetery at Edenborough.

SEE: *Fayetteville Observer*, 26 Oct. 1967; William W. McLendon, "Edenborough Medical College: North Carolina's First Chartered School of Medicine," in Dorothy Long, ed., *Medicine in North Carolina*, vol. 2 (1972); *North Carolina Medical Journal* 1 (1978); J. Howell Way and L. B. McBrayer, "Medical Colleges in North Carolina," *Transactions of the Medical Society of North Carolina* 75 (1928).

MARCUS B. SIMPSON, JR.

McLean, James Augustus (2 May 1904–29 Mar. 1989), artist and teacher, was born in Lincolnton, the son of James Thomas and Lilly Haynes McLean. After attending The University of North Carolina for the session of 1922–23, he was admitted to the Pennsylvania Academy of Fine Arts where he remained for five years. During four of those years he was an assistant in charge of the academy's summer school held at Chester Springs. He also won a competition for a summer of study abroad and visited Italy, France, the Netherlands, and Germany.

After graduation young McLean was offered a teaching position at the Academy of Fine Arts, but he chose instead to accept an opportunity to return to North Carolina. With the encouragement of the new North Carolina State Art Society, he founded the Southern School of Creative Arts in Raleigh in the fall of 1929. McLean was trained in both painting and drawing and used oil, watercolor, tempera, charcoal, pencil, and crayon; he was also a sculptor. Interest in the arts began to develop and enrollment in the school increased. McLean convinced the city schools in Raleigh to start art classes, and he talked with administrators at North Carolina State College and at The University of North Carolina about adding art courses to their curriculum. At State College he taught art in night classes for two years prior to the establishment of the School of Design, and he taught on the Chapel Hill campus on a free-lance basis for a similar period.

At his own school he was soon joined by Carrie Ann Simpson, a dancer, and the young enterprise seemed destined to become a well-rounded school of the arts. To earn money in the early lean times, McLean painted sce-

nery for school auditoriums. As his reputation grew, he became one of the founding members of the North Carolina Association of Professional Artists. Six of his paintings were used in movie sets in Hollywood. Although enrollment at his school declined during the depression, he continued to teach for more than twenty years. His broad interest in all of the arts was reflected in his role in establishing the Raleigh Little Theater in the 1930s and in his effective service as its first president. McLean's studio was the Little Theater's first headquarters.

Because of the depression the federal government began to sponsor numerous new programs intended to occupy people otherwise unemployed, as well as to provide them an income. When he heard that a program in the arts was under consideration, McLean drew up plans that were readily accepted by the government and evolved into the Federal Art Project. Before long, artists across the nation were busily creating works of art for post offices, schools, and public buildings. As well as painting murals himself, for a time he also administered this program in North Carolina.

For six years McLean was one of the directors of the North Carolina State Art Society; he also was responsible for the North Carolina State Fair art exhibit. After the state's educational television station, WUNC-TV, opened, he was its staff artist for twelve years. His work has been exhibited at Rockefeller Center, the Pennsylvania Academy of Fine Arts, annual exhibitions of the North Carolina State Art Society, and various exhibitions in Washington, D.C., and in states as far removed as Maine and Mississippi. His series of four large murals (on agriculture, architecture, engineering, and science) painted for the North Carolina State College Library in the 1930s were removed in 1941 because their style was no longer appreciated on the campus; three were lost, but the mural on engineering was discovered in 1958. Restored by the artist, it was hung in the student center at North Carolina State University where it came to be much admired. Other murals are in Concord, Greensboro, and elsewhere. A new appreciation of his work was demonstrated in September and October 1983, when a retrospective exhibit was mounted on the North Carolina State campus.

McLean married Carrie Ann Simpson soon after she began teaching in his school, and they became the parents of four children. He was buried in Oakwood Cemetery, Raleigh.

SEE: Charlotte Vestal Brown, *James McLean Retrospective* (1983); Richard Cooper, *James Augustus McLean: A Life of Art* (1985); Ola Maie Foushee, *Art in North Carolina: Episodes and Developments, 1585–1970* (1972); S. Parker, *James Augustus McLean* (n.d.); Raleigh *News and Observer*, 22 Mar. 1941, 31 Mar. 1989.

WILLIAM S. POWELL

McLean, James Robert (21 Sept. 1823–15 Apr. 1870), lawyer and Confederate congressman, was born in Enfield of Scottish descent, the son of Levi H. McLean, an educator who was a native of Guilford County, and his wife, Rebecca Hilliard Judge. Though James was orphaned early, his relatives provided him with a good education at the Bingham School in Mebane and the Caldwell Institute in Greensboro. He then read law under John A. Gilmer and was licensed in 1844 to practice in the county courts and in 1846 in the superior court.

For a brief time McLean practiced in and around Greensboro before moving to Rockford, then the county seat of Surry. During the session of 1850–51 he represented Surry as a Democrat in the House of Commons. He served on the Committee on Propositions and Grievances but took little part in the house deliberations. He soon returned to Greensboro and entered a law partnership with Cyrus P. Mendenhall and W. S. Hill. By 1860 he had a good practice and owned a small plantation and twenty-five slaves.

McLean was an early and active Secessionist, and as the Confederacy was popular in North Carolina during 1861, he won a seat in the Confederate House of Representatives over two men who had become Secessionists only after Abraham Lincoln's call for volunteers to quell the Southern rebellion. During his two years in Congress McLean served on the committees of Claims and Foreign Affairs, but he generally let others initiate legislation. For the most part he approved any reasonable delegation of war-making powers to the Davis administration and differed with it significantly only on financial matters. McLean preferred to curb inflation by heavier taxes rather than by repudiating part of the paper currency already in circulation. He also believed that the government should pay market prices for army supplies rather than impress them at a lower and therefore unfair price. In August 1863 he was forced to announce that poor health would prevent his seeking reelection.

In November 1864 McLean was elected major of the Alamance County Senior Reserve, the Seventy-seventh North Carolina Regiment, which had been formed in July. In December President Jefferson Davis nominated him to be commandant of a camp of instruction for the training of new recruits, but the senate rejected the nomination. On 7 December the Seventy-seventh left for Savannah and on the ninth took part in the engagement at Coosawhatchie, S.C. It then fought around Savannah until that city fell to General William T. Sherman's army, then retreated northwards. After the Battle of Bentonville it retreated to Smithfield, then to Raleigh, where it finally surrendered.

The war left McLean almost penniless, and he spent the next few years trying to recoup his fortune. He had just about recovered financially when he died in Greensboro. He was buried in the old First Presbyterian Church Cemetery.

Though physically frail, McLean seems to have been a man of wit and good humor. One of his contemporaries considered him "a man of strong mind and brilliant intellect" who prepared his cases thoroughly. McLean married Narcissa Jane Unthank, the daughter of W. R. Unthank of Guilford College. Their children were William, Robert, Edward R., Thomas L., Rufus H., Cora, and Charles E.; the first two died in childhood.

SEE: Walter Clark, ed., *Histories of the Several Regiments and Battalions from North Carolina in the Great War, 1861–1865*, vol. 4 (1901); *Journal of the Congress of the Confederate States of America*, 7 vols. (1904–5); *Journal of the House of Commons of North Carolina* (1850–51); *North Carolina Biography*, vol. 4 (1919); Raleigh *North Carolina Standard*, 1861–64; Ezra J. Warner and W. Buck Yearns, *Biographical Register of the Confederate Congress* (1975).

BUCK YEARNS

McLean, John (*4 Feb. 1791–14 Oct. 1830*), lawyer, congressman, and U.S. senator from Illinois, was born near Guilford Courthouse (now Greensboro) and four years later moved with his parents to Logan County, Ky. In 1815 he moved across the Ohio River to the Shawneetown district of the Illinois Territory, where he established a law practice.

McLean was a member of a group of young men, largely from the South, who were influential in organizing Illinois as a state. A Democrat, he was elected as the first congressman from Illinois in 1818, the year of statehood. For the next twelve years he served either as a congressman (two other terms—in 1820 and 1822); as a member of the state house of representatives (1820, 1826, and 1828), where he was speaker; or in the U.S. Senate, to which he was named in March 1825 to fill a vacancy for a few months and then elected in 1828. He died two years later and was buried in Westwood Cemetery near Shawneetown.

SEE: *Biog. Dir. Am. Cong.* (1950); Robert Howard, *A History of a Prairie State* (1972).

ROY PARKER, JR.

Maclean, William (*2 Apr. 1757–25 Oct. 1828*), physician, was born in Rowan County, the son of Alexander, an emigrant from Northern Ireland, and Elizabeth Ratchford McLean. Alexander lived first in Pennsylvania, working to pay for his passage over, then moved to Rowan County and settled in the Dobbin neighborhood, eight miles from Salisbury, where his sons John and William were born (three daughters were born in Pennsylvania). He then purchased land near the junction of the South Fork and the main Catawba River in Tryon (now Gaston) County. This became his permanent home and the birth place of his three youngest sons. Both Alexander and his wife were members of the Presbyterian church, lived to a "good old age," and were buried near their farm.

William attended Queens College (later Liberty Hall Academy), in Charlotte, from about 1776 to 1778. His older brother John joined the Revolutionary army and was later killed in the Battle of Buford's Bridge in South Carolina. William was studying to become a physician when the war moved inland. He was offered a commission as surgeon's mate by Dr. Joseph Blythe. Near the end of his life, in his application for bounty land due him as a Revolutionary soldier, he gave the following account of his military service: "I William Maclean [,] now in the seventieth year of my age, Do upon oath testify and declare that in the latter part of 1781 or early in the year 1782, I joined the Continental Southern Army, as Surgeon's Mate under Doctr. Joseph Blythe, and served in the first North Carolina Regiment commanded by Col. Archibald Lytle and continued in service as aforesaid until the close of the War in 1783 when the Regiment was regularly discharged from public service in Charleston So Carolina by the aforesaid Col. Archibald Lyttle."

Dr. C. L. Hunter, in his *Sketches of Western North Carolina*, elaborates on Maclean's services and places them prior to the end of 1781 or in early 1782. Young Maclean may have served irregularly with the state militia before joining the Continental army as surgeon's mate, but no contemporary evidence of this has been discovered.

In 1783, at the close of the war, Maclean joined the North Carolina Society of the Cincinnati as an original member. The membership was composed of the surviving officers of the Continental army, and its purpose was to provide assistance to the widows and orphans of deceased officers and to maintain the bonds of friendship forged during the war. General George Washington was the society's first national president.

In 1786 Maclean went to Philadelphia to pursue his medical studies at the medical college of the University of Pennsylvania, then considered the best school of medicine in the country. According to university records, he left in 1787 without a degree but with a certificate of membership in the American Medical Society signed by William Shippen, M.D., president. The certificate states, in Latin, that membership was granted "because of his true medical knowledge, in which on examination, he has shown himself brilliant, all the honors and privileges of this institution."

Maclean represented Lincoln County in the House of Commons in the sessions of 1788, 1789, 1790, and 1791. In 1814 the county sent him to the state senate. As a legislator he was conscientious in attending all sessions, served on several financial committees, was opposed to a permanent site for the state capital in the east, and apparently supported the state university at Chapel Hill.

More important was his service as a delegate from Lincoln to the constitutional conventions at Hillsborough (1788) and Fayetteville (1789), which considered the ratification of the proposed Constitution of the United States. A Federalist, Maclean voted for ratification in both conventions, unlike many other delegates from the western counties.

On 19 June 1792, at age thirty-five, Maclean married Mary (Polly) Davidson, the third daughter of Major John Davidson, a wealthy ironmaster. The wedding took place in the new brick mansion on Major Davidson's plantation, Rural Hill, on the Catawba River, considered the finest in Mecklenburg County. The Reverend James McRee, the county's most fashionable Presbyterian minister (too fashionable for many of his plainer session members at Steele Creek), performed the service. It was a long-remembered social event and the bride, ten years younger than her husband, wore a "green silk and silver Paris gown," pieces of which were preserved by her descendants for several generations.

The record further notes that the bride had been religiously reared at Hopewell Church, liked to read and read well, and was of a happy disposition. Of the groom it was later said that he was "a polished and elegant gentleman," was "fine looking and dressed always with great care; wore a queue and knee britches and frills, the very graceful style of the period." Shortly after his marriage, Maclean built a homestead, known as Willow Plain, on his plantation in Lincoln (now Gaston) County. The house is no longer standing, but what is believed to have been his doctor's office, built earlier on his father's place, is located on the "Button" McLean farm. William and Polly Maclean were the parents of ten children who reached maturity.

For his Revolutionary services as "Surgeon's Mate to the First Battalion in the Line," the state of North Carolina awarded Maclean 2,560 acres "in our country of Tennessee on the waters of the Red River." He made a survey of this grant in 1797 and again fourteen years later, when he found trees that he had marked with his initials on the earlier journey. The journal he kept of the latter trip from Lincolnton to Nashville, Tenn., during May–June 1811 was edited, with biographical notes, by Alice B. Keith for the *North Carolina Historical Review* (October 1938).

Maclean served his local community as a justice of the peace and as an officer in the militia. He and his wife supported the Presbyterian church. His medical practice was extensive and often charitable, for he "treated slave and neighbor alike." He soon became wealthy, and many regarded him as the leading layman of the area.

It was important to Maclean to preserve the history of the American War of Independence and the men who had sacrificed their lives and fortunes for its achievement. He was distressed that no monument had been erected to the heroes of the Battle of Kings Mountain, not far from his home. Chiefly at his instigation and ex-

pense, a slate monument, three feet high, was placed on the mountain commemorating American heroes on one side and mentioning the death of the British Colonel Patrick Ferguson on the other. On 4 July 1814 Maclean delivered his Kings Mountain address celebrating the victory and the first monument erected to it. A considerable part of this speech is preserved in the Robert L. Adams Collection in the North Carolina State Archives. In the same collection are several letters from the doctor to his wife that show the writer to have been a gentleman of some literary accomplishment and considerable humor.

The Raleigh *Register* of 25 Nov. 1828 carried the following brief obituary: "Died—at his residence in Lincoln county on the 25th inst. after a protracted and painful illness, Doct. William McClean [sic], sen., in the 72nd year of his age. Skilful and assiduous in his profession, he acquired an enviable reputation within the circle of his acquaintance; ardently devoted to his country in her eventful struggle for national existence, he was famed among the worthies of the Revolution, as a brave and determined Whig, and the dread of both foreign and domestic enemies. As a public man, Dr. McClean was extensively useful and much respected; in private life, he was loved by his relatives, and highly esteemed by his acquaintances."

Concerning his appearance, his wife's nephew, Alexander Caldwell, said that his "Uncle McLean [sic] was the handsomest man he ever saw, six feet tall, straight as an arrow, and of the most polished manners. He also said he often heard old men refer to the fact that his Uncle McLean had been several times taken for General Washington when he was in the Army."

Polly Davidson Maclean outlived her husband by nearly thirty-four years, dying at age ninety-five; her father, John Davidson, lived to be ninety-six. Of her later days, her great-nephew Dr. John Brevard Alexander wrote: "She was known far and near as 'Aunt Polly McLean.' She was a woman of great talent, read much and digested what she read, was a close student of the Bible and a good influence in her neighborhood."

Maclean and his wife were buried under handsome gravestones in Bethel Presbyterian churchyard in York County, S.C. Their ten children in order of birth were: Richard Dobbs Speight, Alexander Augustus, John Davidson (M.D.), Elizabeth Jackson (Campbell), Violet Wilson (Lindsay) (Hart), William Bain (M.D.), Thomas Brevard, Rebecca Isabella (Wilson), Mary Margaret (Erwin), and Robert Hamilton Graham.

SEE: Robert L. Adams Collection (North Carolina State Archives, Raleigh); C. L. Hunter, *Sketches of Western North Carolina* (1877); Alice B. Keith, "William Maclean's Travel Journal," *North Carolina Historical Review* 15 (October 1938); A. A. McLean, "Life and History of Dr. William McLean," 1971 (typescript, Davidson College Library, Davidson).

CHALMERS G. DAVIDSON

McLendon, Lennox Polk (12 Feb. 1890–7 Aug. 1968), attorney, was born in Wadesboro, the son of Dr. Walter Jones and Sarah Josephine Polk McLendon. He was a nephew of Colonel Leonidas Polk, also of Anson County, who was the founder of the *Progressive Farmer* magazine, the organizer of the Farmers' Alliance, and the leader of the Populist party. McLendon received a bachelor of science degree in agriculture from the North Carolina College of Agriculture and Mechanic Arts in 1910 and a bachelor of laws degree from The University of North Carolina in 1912. He reportedly was the only man to be manager of the football teams at both of those institutions, and the only graduate of either to receive an honorary degree from both. He also received an honorary degree from the University of North Carolina at Greensboro.

He served as mayor of Chapel Hill in the year 1913–14 and was graduate manager of athletics at the university. He organized the University Athletic Association, based on the requirement that each student must be a member and pay an annual fee and be privileged to attend all athletic contests—a system that was rapidly adopted by colleges and universities throughout the country.

McLendon practiced law in Durham from 1914 to 1933, first alone and after 1916 as senior partner in the firm of McLendon and Hedrick. His early legal career had several interruptions. First, as a member of the National Guard he was called to active duty in 1916 to serve as a first lieutenant on the Mexican border under General John J. Pershing in an expedition that failed to capture the notorious Mexican leader, Pancho Villa. Second, in 1917 he represented Durham County in the state house of representatives. And third, as a captain in the U.S. Army, he recruited Battery C, 113th Field Artillery, and was sent to France with the Advanced School Detachment, 30th Division, in May 1918, rejoining the 113th Field Artillery in August 1918. He participated in the Battle of St.-Mihiel and the Argonne Forest offensive, then served with the Army of Occupation; he was discharged as a major in March 1919. From that time on, he was known to friends and the public generally as "Major McLendon" or "Mac."

Back home from World War I, he resumed his law practice in Durham and served as solicitor of the Tenth Judicial District in the early 1920s. In 1931, as a special prosecutor for the state, he helped convict Colonel Luke Lea (banker, newspaper publisher, and former U.S. senator from Tennessee) of violating the North Carolina banking laws, and Lea was sent to prison. In 1932 McLendon managed the successful campaign of J. C. B. Ehringhaus of Elizabeth City for the governorship, then later turned down Ehringhaus's offer of appointment to the North Carolina Supreme Court.

From 1933 until his death, Major McLendon practiced law in Greensboro as a partner in a firm that had various titles over the years but was generally known as Brooks, McLendon, Brim and Holderness. Considered one of the ablest trial lawyers in the South, he served as president of the North Carolina Bar in 1941. He represented many large corporations and participated in a number of noted court cases in the early 1940s. In one of his few defeats, he defended the R. J. Reynolds Tobacco Company, which was charged, along with other tobacco companies, with violating the federal antitrust laws. His fame spread nationwide, thanks to extensive television and newspaper coverage, when he served as general counsel for the U.S. Senate Rules Committee in the Bobby Baker investigation of 1963–66. During these hearings Senator Carl Curtis of Nebraska and McLendon got into a shouting match. Curtis later said that McLendon was the "most impertinent" employee in Senate history, which accusation induced only amusement in McLendon. "Fine, fine, I enjoyed it," he said. Republicans attempted to turn the hearings to political advantage and Democrats wanted the hearings ended, but McLendon refused to take seriously the political aspects of the investigation. He said later that he carried out his orders, trying to run down all the rumors and the involved business dealings of the former Senate Democratic secretary. Based on the facts brought out in the hearings, McLendon took it upon himself to submit a suggested stringent code of ethics for the Senate, which, if adopted, might have enhanced the reputation of that body.

Despite a full schedule of legal duties, McLendon managed to devote many hours to public service, particularly in the upbuilding of public education, a cause dear to the heart of his father-in-law, Governor Charles B. Aycock. McLendon's interest in public education was of long standing. His uncle, Colonel Leonidas Polk, was one of those instrumental in the organization of the North Carolina College of Agriculture and Mechanic Arts. McLendon was a member of the board of trustees of North Carolina State College when it and the trustees of The University of North Carolina voted to approve Governor O. Max Gardner's plan for consolidating the institutions. He continued to serve for many years as a member of the Consolidated Board and its executive committee. He devoted much time to his work as chairman of the Committee on Escheats, whose funds grew from a few thousand dollars to almost two million dollars. He served as vice-chairman (1955–59) and chairman (1959–63) of the State Board of Higher Education. As a member of Governor Terry Sanford's Committee on Higher Education, known as the Carlyle Commission, McLendon was the first person to present to the commission a plan to give university status to State College at Raleigh and Woman's College at Greensboro. For several years he served as a trustee of North Carolina Agricultural and Technical College in Greensboro and at the time of his death was chairman of the executive committee of the Oak Ridge Military Institute Foundation.

The son of a country doctor, McLendon was greatly interested in the field of health. He served as a trustee of the North Carolina Baptist Hospital in Winston-Salem, as the first president of the Medical Foundation of North Carolina, Inc., as a member of the board of trustees of the Moses Cone Hospital in Greensboro for thirty years, and as chairman of the Medical School Committee and Health Affairs Committee of the Greater University Board of Trustees.

In other areas of public service he was chairman of the State Board of Elections (1932–36) and of the Commission on a State Department of Justice for North Carolina (1937–38)—such a department was established during that era. From 1939 to 1954 he was a member of the North Carolina Probation Commission.

On 27 June 1917 McLendon married Mary Lily Aycock. He was survived by her and by their five children: Mary Louise (Mrs. Berry Wall), Lennox Polk, Jr., Charles Aycock, William Woodard, and John Aycock. McLendon was a Democrat and a Baptist.

SEE: *Greensboro Daily News*, 8 Aug. 1968; L. P. McLendon Papers (Southern Historical Collection, University of North Carolina, Chapel Hill); Rosalind McLendon Redfearn, *The McLendons of Anson County, 1696–1957* (privately printed, n.d.); *Who Was Who in America*, vol. 5 (1973).

CHARLES AYCOCK POE

McMillan, Alexander *(1785–13 Nov. 1817)*, lawyer and legislator, was born in Richmond (now Scotland) County. Because there are no known records of his birth and there were numerous families with the same given and surnames, it is not possible to determine the names of his parents. A Federalist, he represented Richmond County in the state senate during the sessions of 1810, 1811, and 1812. In his first political campaign he defeated Republican Duncan McFarland for the seat, but

McFarland insisted that the election inspectors had "acted contrary to law." Although he charged that "sundry false and calumnious reports had been raised by McMillan and friends prior to the election," he did not claim that McMillan was unqualified. McMillan declined an opportunity to respond to McFarland's charges.

Identified as an attorney as early as 1809, he represented clients in the Richmond County court in 1815, and the next year he represented The University of North Carolina in registering a deed. In 1814–15 he purchased two lots in the town of Rockingham in Richmond County. In the election held in March 1817 McMillan was elected to the U.S. Congress from the Seventh Congressional District, but he died in Fayetteville in some unfortunate way, apparently a duel, before taking his seat. He apparently left no will, nor has any positive record been found of a family, although one Alexander McMillan married Sarah Martha Gilchrist and they were the parents of Angus Augustine and Daniel.

SEE: *Biog. Dir. Am. Cong.* (1961); John L. Cheney, Jr., ed., *North Carolina Government, 1585–1979* (1981); Information from local sources provided by Mrs. Joyce Gibson (Laurel Hill), 20 Feb. 1981; Angus W. McLean, *Lumber River Scots and Their Descendants* (1942); Raleigh *Minerva*, 28 Nov. 1817; Raleigh *Register*, 6, 27 Dec. 1809; Washington, D.C., *National Intelligencer*, 25 Nov. 1817.

ROY PARKER, JR.

McMillan, Hamilton (*29 Aug. 1837–27 Feb. 1916*), lawyer and author, described as "a full-blooded Scotchman," was born in Cumberland County near Fayetteville, the only child of William and Ann Patterson McMillan. His earliest schooling was at local schools and under the guidance of the Reverend George Benton, but in 1853 he attended Trinity College in Hartford, Conn. The next year he entered The University of North Carolina and was graduated in 1857. Moving to Red Springs, he taught school until the beginning of the Civil War. On 17 Apr. 1861, even before North Carolina seceded from the Union, twenty-three-year-old McMillan enlisted as a private in Company F, First Regiment of North Carolina Infantry, for six months. He was mustered out in November at the end of his enlistment, having participated in the Battle of Bethel. The company's records indicate that he then enlisted in Company G, Sixth Regiment, but the records of that regiment contain no information as to his further service.

In 1868 McMillan was licensed and began to practice law in Wadesboro. He soon returned to Red Springs, however, and resumed teaching as well as practicing law. Here he became interested in the historical background of the Indians of Robeson County. His inclination towards research led him to undertake an investigation of their past, and he came to believe that they were descendants of Sir Walter Raleigh's "Lost Colony" of 1587. In 1885, the three hundredth anniversary year of the departure of the Ralph Lane colony from Roanoke Island, McMillan published a pamphlet on the Lost Colony that presented his personal conclusions linking the Croatan Indians and the English colonies to the Robeson County Indians. His conclusion was based on what he considered to be evidence of old English pronunciations used by these Indians and the occurrence of some family names of Roanoke colonists among them. In 1888 and 1907 he repeated his theory in editions of *Sir Walter Raleigh's Lost Colony*. Continuing his crusade, he wrote *The Lost Colony Found*, which was printed about

1898. In 1911 *The North Carolina Booklet* (vol. 10) published his article, "The Croatans."

In 1885 the voters of Robeson County sent McMillan to the General Assembly, where he was responsible for enacting legislation to officially recognize these people as "Croatan Indians" and to establish a separate school system under their control. Returning to the house in 1887, he supported the passage of another act that established the Indian Normal School in Pembroke. His efforts on behalf of the Indians in his county greatly improved their lot and brought them increased respect—not only among themselves but from others as well.

McMillan married Elizabeth Gillespie Robeson of Bladen County on 17 Feb. 1863. They became the parents of seven children: Mary Eliza, Janie Robeson (Mrs. B. W. Townsend), John Robeson, Cornelia Spencer, David Gillespie, William Graham, and one who died as an infant. William Graham died soon after his graduation from the U.S. Naval Academy. McMillan died in Red Springs.

SEE: Daniel L. Grant, *Alumni History of the University of North Carolina, 1795–1924* (1924); Weymouth T. Jordan, comp., *North Carolina Troops, 1861–1865: A Roster*, vol. 4 (1973); Hamilton McMillan to Stephen B. Weeks, 11 Dec. 1890, bound in Weeks's copy of *The Lost Colony* (North Carolina Collection, University of North Carolina, Chapel Hill); Louis H. Manarin, comp., *North Carolina Troops, 1861–1865: A Roster*, vol. 3 (1971); *North Carolina Bar Association Report* (1916); *Tar Heel Sketch-Book* (1885).

ROBIN PURSER STACY

McMillan, John Archibald (*28 Sept. 1879–6 Jan. 1949*), Baptist minister and editor, was born in Marlboro County, S.C., the son of Archibald Alexander and Mary Amanda Johnson McMillan, both of Scottish ancestry. Within a few weeks after his birth the family moved to Riverton, Richmond (now Scotland) County, N.C., which McMillan always considered his home. The youth received most of his early education from his father, an 1862 graduate of The University of North Carolina who was both a teacher and a farmer. His brothers were Henry Hudson, a missionary to China, and Robert Leroy, a Raleigh attorney who was vice-commander of the American Legion of the United States; his sisters were Frances, Kate, Netah, Eupha, and Mamie. Other close relatives included editors Archibald, Gerald W., and Livingston Johnson and physician-editor Wingate M. Johnson, as well as the poet John Charles McNeill.

After graduation from Spring Hill Academy at Wagram, McMillan entered Wake Forest College. He was enrolled from 1898 to 1900 and in 1901–2, receiving a B.A. degree in 1902 after three years of study. He pitched for the baseball team and in 1901–2 was coeditor of the *Wake Forest Student*, a literary magazine. During 1902–3 he was president of the first Wake Forest College medical class. The class historian chided him in the college annual "for studying too hard and for not visiting enough," but another entry listed him as the "Highcockalorum" of the "'02 Club," a fun organization.

After practicing medicine for a year McMillan returned to the family farm so that his younger brothers could go to college. Subsequently he felt a call to the ministry and in January 1908 enrolled at the Southern Baptist Theological Seminary in Louisville, Ky. He completed one semester, then accepted the pastorate of the Baptist church at Burnsville, N.C., serving until September 1910, when he returned to the seminary for a year.

From 1911 to 1914 he was pastor of the Asheboro church and also of the nearby Pleasant Grove and Worthville churches. In 1914 he became minister of the church at McColl, S.C., twenty miles from Riverton. Except for the eight months in 1918–19 when he was a YMCA secretary with the American Expeditionary Force overseas, he remained at McColl until 1922.

In that year McMillan became alumni secretary of Wake Forest College, with duties that included counseling students, representing the college at meetings, fund-raising, and recruiting athletes. His last move came in 1929, when he went to Thomasville in the dual position of pastor of the Mills Home church, which he served until 1933, and assistant (later associate) editor of *Charity and Children*, the orphanage's newspaper. Under the editorship of Archibald Johnson, this weekly had gained an interdenominational, statewide, and national reputation for being in the forefront among those journals espousing worthy causes and moral issues. On Johnson's death (26 Dec. 1934), McMillan immediately became acting editor, serving in this position until 16 May 1935, when the Mills Home trustees elected him editor. From then until his death fourteen years later, he carried on the tradition Johnson had established for the publication. The circulation increased, reaching forty thousand, and his editorials treated an unusually wide range of topics. The *Charlotte Observer* said of McMillan at the time of his death: "His weekly front page editorials, dealing with state, national and world affairs, were sound and among the most interesting to be found in North Carolina newspapers." Like his speaking, which was straightforward and appealing, his writing was characterized by sincerity, emotional warmth, and imagination, as well as a homely philosophy and humor. John Arch McMillan, as his name appeared on the masthead of *Charity and Children*, was assisted as editor by his oldest daughter, Louise, whose column "Patchwork" was perhaps as widely read and quoted as were many of his own editorials.

McMillan served as a trustee of Wake Forest College from 1933 to 1943. He was also a trustee of North Carolina College in Durham and a member of the Thomasville School Board and Rotary Club. On 27 Dec. 1906, in Campobello, S.C., he married Louise Culpepper Fant, of Edgefield County, S.C., who had recently gone to Riverton to teach school. They had four children: Elbert Alexander, M.D., and Louise Fant, who were residents of Winston-Salem at the time of their deaths; Betty Brown (Mrs. Allen Greene) of West Point, Va.; and Mary Johnson (Mrs. Richard W. Goldsmith) of Litchfield, Conn.

McMillan was a Democrat; his hobbies were hunting and fishing. He died in Winston-Salem and was buried in the old Spring Hill Cemetery at Wagram.

SEE: Baptist State Convention of North Carolina, *Annual* (1949 [portrait]); Mary Johnson McMillan Goldsmith to Henry S. Stroupe, 19 Mar. 1980; Liberty Baptist Association, *Minutes* (1929–49); Jasper Livingston Memory to Henry S. Stroupe, 15 May 1980; Thomasville *Charity and Children*, 10 Jan. 1935–20 Jan. 1949 (portrait); *Wake Forest Howler* (1903, 1922–29); *Wake Forest Student* (1901–2).

HENRY S. STROUPE

McMullan, Thomas Shelton (*29 Nov. 1868–4 Apr. 1954*), physician and author, was born in Hertford, Perquimans County, the son of William Thomas, a merchant, farmer, and mayor of Hertford, and Sally Wood McMullan. His first known ancestor in America, John McMullan, was an officer in the Virginia line during the American Revolution. Thomas was graduated from the Hertford Academy and Randolph Macon College, where he received an A.B. degree in 1886. By borrowing money to pay for his expenses, he attended medical lectures at the University of Virginia (1888) and the University of New York (1889).

He began to practice medicine in Edenton, N.C., in 1889 and became a medical examiner for various life insurance companies in eastern North Carolina. He later returned to Hertford, where he practiced for twenty-five years before entering military service as a captain in the Medical Corps in World War I. After the war he moved to Elizabeth City, where he continued to practice and serve as city physician until his death. McMullan was chairman of the North Carolina State Board of Health and president of the North Carolina Medical Society. He was also a member of the U.S. Army Reserve and the American Legion.

McMullan was the author of *The Southron's Burden; A Human Drama* (1904), an eighty-eight-page pamphlet dedicated to the "White Men of Dixie" and written in verse. He also published a number of short topical poems in the newspapers of North Carolina.

On 18 Dec. 1890 he married Lydia A. Pailin, of Elizabeth City, the daughter of William and Elizabeth Pailin. McMullan and his wife had six children. He died in Albemarle Hospital in Elizabeth City.

SEE: Raleigh *News and Observer*, 5 Apr. 1954; Charles L. Van Noppen, "Biographical Sketch of Thomas Shelton McMullan" (Manuscript Department, Duke University Library, Durham).

E. THOMAS SIMS

McMullen, Harry, Sr. (*23 July 1884–24 June 1955*), attorney general of North Carolina, was born in Edenton, the son of Dr. James Henry and Carolina Tucker McMullen. He attended Edenton Academy and at age seventeen entered The University of North Carolina, from which he was graduated in 1905. In Chapel Hill he was active in numerous campus organizations, especially a debating society, and was editor of the yearbook. Admitted to the bar in the year of his graduation, he began a practice in Plymouth but in 1907 joined the firm of Small and McLean in Washington, N.C. In 1913 he opened his own law office and practiced alone for the remainder of his life.

During World War I McMullen was chairman of the Beaufort County Draft Board, and from 1926 to 1933 he was county attorney. In 1929 he was elected to the state senate, where he came to the attention of Governor O. Max Gardner; in 1933, at the end of his term in the General Assembly, McMullen was tapped by the governor to become director of the Collections and Assessments Division of the state Department of Revenue. The following year he was chosen by Governor J. C. B. Ehringhaus as chairman of the North Carolina Industrial Commission, and after two years in that post he was named assistant attorney general of the state. In 1938 Governor Clyde R. Hoey elevated McMullen to the position of attorney general following the promotion of the incumbent to the state supreme court bench. Thereafter he was regularly elected to the post, serving a total of seventeen years. As attorney general McMullen was ex officio member of the State Board of Education, the Municipal Board of Control, the State Board of Assessment, the State Banking Commission, the Eugenics Board, and other agencies, to each of which he rendered useful service. As a member of the State Art Commission, he was especially active in the movement that resulted in the multimillion-dollar North Carolina Museum of Art.

He held office in many professional organizations serving tax administrators, attorneys general, and the legal profession. An ardent Democrat, he held posts in the party organization from the precinct level to national ranks, the latter especially during the administration of President Harry S Truman. McMullen is credited with one of the many stories told about the president, much to Truman's delight. Greeting the president on one of his visits to North Carolina, McMullen earned a good laugh when he told Truman: "One of us has been slandered. Several people have told me today that you and I look alike."

A provocative and popular speaker, McMullen shared his thoughts with state civic and professional groups and was an especially welcome speaker on college campuses. He often spoke on matters pertaining to business, government, and law. The University of North Carolina granted him an honorary doctor of laws degree. He was cited by the North Carolina Society for the Preservation of Antiquities for his support of historic preservation in the state and by the Tryon Palace Restoration Commission for his support of its work. The Ackland Art Center in Chapel Hill also expressed appreciation to McMullen for his role in securing significant bequests.

On 4 Oct. 1911 he married Pattie Mary Baugham of Washington, N.C., and they became the parents of four children: Pattie Mary (Mrs. W. T. Old, Jr.), Mildred Louise (Mrs. Henry Blount Rumley, Jr.), Harry, Jr., and James Baugham. McMullen was an active Episcopal layman. He was buried in Washington, N.C.

SEE: *Greensboro Daily News*, 24 June 1955; McMullen Family Papers (possession of Mrs. Henry Blount, Washington, N.C.); Raleigh *News and Observer*, 24 June 1955; *Who's Who in America*, supplement (June–August 1955).

C. SYLVESTER GREEN

McNair, Evander (15 Apr. 1820–13 Nov. 1902), Confederate general, was born near Laurel Hill in Richmond County, the son of John E. and Nancy Fletcher McNair, natives of Argyllshire, Scotland. Soon after his birth, his parents moved to Mississippi, settling finally in Simpson County. There McNair received an informal education, taught school, and farmed with his father. In 1843 he formed McNair and Company, a mercantile enterprise, in Jacksonville, Miss. He left the firm three years later to join Jefferson Davis's First Mississippi Rifles. During the Mexican War campaigns, he rose in rank from private to orderly sergeant. After the war McNair reentered the mercantile business in Brandon, Miss. In 1856 he moved to Washington, Ark., where he met and married, on 11 Aug. 1859, Hannah Merrill, of Oxford, N.Y., a teacher in the local school for girls.

Although a Whig prior to 1861, McNair enthusiastically entered the Confederate service, raising a battalion of seven infantry companies that became the Fourth Arkansas Infantry. On 17 August he was elected colonel. He and his men fought with Ben McCullough in the fiercely contested Battle of Wilson's Creek in southwestern Missouri in August 1861 and again at Elkhorn Tavern in March 1862. In the latter engagement, Colonel McNair commanded the brigade after McCullough's death on the field. He then crossed the Mississippi River with Sterling Price and joined Kirby Smith's successful campaign in eastern Kentucky. At the Battle of Rich-

mond, in August 1862, McNair performed with distinction and shortly afterwards was commissioned brigadier general. His brigade (consisting of the First and Second Arkansas Dismounted Rifles, the Fourth and Thirteenth Arkansas Infantry regiments, the Fourth Arkansas Infantry Battalion, and Humphrey's battery) contributed significantly to the success of General William J. Hardee's flank attack at Murfreesboro on 31 Dec. 1862. In May 1863 McNair's brigade left the Army of Tennessee and assisted Joseph Johnston in his futile attempts to save General John C. Pemberton in Vicksburg. Recalled to the Army of Tennessee in September, McNair arrived in time for Chickamauga.

One of the two leading brigades in Bushrod Johnson's successful attack against the center of the Union army, McNair's force won the label of "the Star Brigade at Chickamauga." The brigade executed its movements splendidly, although McNair himself fell wounded during the assault. Following Chickamauga, McNair's brigade was shifted back to Mississippi and then to the Trans-Mississippi Department. In a closing campaign, McNair fought under Sterling Price in his "Missouri Raid." In light of his extraordinary competence at Richmond, Murfreesboro, and Chickamauga, Evander McNair's lack of recognition by the Confederate War Department remains a mystery.

After the war McNair returned to Washington, Ark., and then entered the wholesale grocery business in New Orleans. He moved to Magnolia, Miss., before finally settling in Hattiesburg, Miss., where he died. He was buried in Magnolia.

SEE: *Confederate Veteran*, vol. 11 (1903); N. C. Hughes, Jr., "William Joseph Hardee, C.S.A., 1861–1865" (Ph.D. diss., University of North Carolina, 1959); Jacksonville, Miss., *Daily Clarion-Ledger*, 9 Feb. 1903; Joseph E. Johnston, *Narrative of Military Operations* (1874); James B. McNair, *McNair, McNear, and McNeir Genealogies* (1923); Glenn Tucker, *Chickamauga: Bloody Battle in the West* (1961).

N. C. HUGHES, JR.

McNair, John Calvin (22 Feb. 1823–19 Jan. 1858), teacher and minister, was born near St. Pauls, the son of Malcolm and Margaret Dalrymple McNair. His maternal grandfather, Archibald Dalrymple of Moore County, served in the House of Commons in 1801 and the senate in 1807. His paternal grandparents were Duncan and Katherine McCallum McNair, who emigrated from Scotland in 1786.

McNair obtained B.A. (1849) and M.A. (1852) degrees from The University of North Carolina. Afterwards he taught at various schools and became principle of the Summerville Academy near Lillington. During his formative years and probably also in college, McNair developed "a passionate devotion to natural science" and on many occasions during his teaching period he gave public lectures at schoolhouses "to the very great delight of the community."

In the fall of 1856 he entered the Theological Seminary of Columbia, S.C., where a leader of the faculty "was not at all hostile toward the allegorical interpretation of the [Garden of] Eden narrative," and in April 1857 he was licensed to preach by the Fayetteville Presbytery. Early that summer McNair sailed for Scotland to attend the New College of the Free Church and the University of Edinburgh. There he studied church history, belles lettres, and natural science.

Early in January 1858, while touring the western coast

of Scotland with a small excursion party, he was "seized with a low fever," probably pneumonia, and died in Edinburgh a few days later. He was buried in the old Grange cemetery there. At the base of the monument erected by his mother was inscribed a quotation from Gen. 23.4: "I am a stranger and a sojourner with you; give me a possession of a burying place with you." McNair was survived by his mother, who lived to be ninety-seven, and two sisters, Catherine and Mary Ann.

McNair left his estate to The University of North Carolina on condition that it establish a lecture series to demonstrate the mutual relation of science and theology to each other and to prove, as far as possible, the existence of God from nature; moreover, the speakers should have both an evangelical background and a grounding in science. No doubt McNair envisioned that the lectures would display equal regard for each viewpoint. In practice, this proved to be difficult. Nevertheless, the wide range of subjects and the selection of speakers indicate that McNair's objectives have been largely realized.

The first lecture was given in 1908 by Francis H. Smith, professor emeritus of the University of Virginia, who spoke on *Nature: A Witness for the Unity, the Power, and the Goodness of God*. Other speakers included Henry Van Dyke, on "Poetry," in 1911; William L. Poteat, on *Can a Man Be a Christian Today?* in 1925; Robert A. Millikan, on *Time, Matter, and Values*, in 1932; J. Robert Oppenheimer, on "Some Reflections on Science and Culture," in 1959; and Loren Eiseley, on "The Search for Man," in 1971.

SEE: *Alumni Review* 16 (1927–28 [portrait]); *Charlotte Observer*, 15 Jan. 1928; John L. Cheney, Jr., ed., *North Carolina Government, 1585–1979* (1981); Daniel L. Grant, *Alumni History of the University of North Carolina, 1795–1924* (1924); Malcolm Fowler, *They Passed This Way* (1955); S. C. Linder, "William L. Poteat," *North Carolina Historical Review* 40 (Spring 1963); James B. McNair, *McNair, McNear, and McNeir Genealogies* (1923).

JOHN MACFIE

MacNair, Ralph (*16 Feb. 1742–October 1784*), merchant, legislator, and Tory, was born in Glasgow, Scotland. His father is said to have been killed on the battlefield of Culloden in the ranks of the Duke of Cumberland when he defeated Prince Charles Edward Stuart in 1746. While a young man MacNair, with his brothers, Ebenezer and John, settled near Hillsborough, N.C., where he became a merchant. He named his new home Blanton Farm.

During the trouble with the Regulators in Orange County, Ralph MacNair became identified with the local officials and wrote a long letter to Herman Husband, the rebel leader, setting forth his thoughts on the matter. Governor William Tryon, on his expedition to subdue the Regulators, bought supplies from MacNair's Hillsborough store, including such unusual items as Delft bowls and gilt tin cups. Elected to represent Orange County in the Assembly in December 1771, MacNair served until late 1775. With the onset of the American Revolution, he became a Tory and had to leave North Carolina. Alexander Telfair, the Scottish merchant and Tory of Halifax, who had married Pauline Hall, the sister of MacNair's wife, bought a brig to help evacuate the North Carolina Loyalists. It appears that the MacNair family sailed on this ship, which landed first at New York before proceeding to England. Ralph MacNair remained on Long Island for the duration of the war. His North Carolina holdings were confiscated by the state in 1779.

With the advent of peace he made an unsuccessful attempt to return to his North Carolina home. On 21 Jan. 1784 Governor Alexander Martin, in response to a request from MacNair to have his citizenship restored, wrote that he would send his petition on to the legislature, noting that the letter enclosed from General Nathanael Greene on MacNair's behalf and the services MacNair had rendered the American prisoners on Long Island would carry weight. The governor could not resist lecturing the petitioner, remarking that, while on a personal level he would always be his friend, "You have deserted the country in which you say you wish to spend your days. What satisfaction can you have in returning to her in her triumphant prosperity, when your late principal desire is frustrated which was to subjugate her to British despotism." MacNair's petition was rejected by the legislature.

On 9 Aug. 1784 he took the oath of allegiance in Philadelphia before William Rush, later the well-known American sculptor, and became a citizen of that commonwealth. He died in exile in Richmond, Va. In 1785 his brother-in-law, Edward Hall of Tarboro, as executor of the deceased's estate, successfully petitioned the legislature for the return of his property to the three orphans of MacNair and his wife.

MacNair married Dorothy Hall, the daughter of Thomas Hall, a native of Prince George County, Va., who settled in Tarboro, N.C. Her brother, Edward Hall, a Tarboro merchant, was clerk of the court of Edgecombe County (1772–1818). Her nephew, Thomas H. Hall, was a member of Congress. Mrs. MacNair died at sea en route from New York to Charleston, S.C., on 9 Oct. 1782. She was buried at sea, latitude 25°40', longitude 75°50'. Ralph MacNair and his wife had two sons who reached maturity, Thomas Ebenezer and Edmund Duncan.

SEE: Walter Clark, ed., *State Records of North Carolina*, vols. 17, 19–20, 24 (1899–1905); James B. MacNair, *McNair, McNear, and McNeir Genealogies* (1923); Thomas C. Parramore, *Launching the Craft: The First Half Century of Free Masonry in North Carolina* (1975); Personal papers of Ralph MacNair (possession of Mrs. Thomas H. Battle); William L. Saunders, ed., *Colonial Records of North Carolina*, vol. 9 (1890).

CLAIBORNE T. SMITH, JR.

McNairy, John (*30 Mar. 1762–10 Nov. 1837*), noted as the man who gave Andrew Jackson the opportunity that led to the presidency, was born on Horsepen Creek, near what in 1771 became the Guilford County seat at Martinsville, a town now extinct. He was the first of nine children of Francis and Mary Boyd McNairy, who moved to North Carolina immediately after their marriage in Lancaster County, Pa., on 27 Apr. 1761. The couple purchased from Herman Husband a tract on Horsepen Creek, later famous as part of the scene of the Battle of Guilford Court House (15 Mar. 1781) during the American Revolution. North Carolina *State Records* show payment to one John McNairy for services rendered, but no details of his war service remain. The McNairy house was used as a hospital after the battle.

McNairy received a liberal education for that day at the school of the Presbyterian minister, David Caldwell, to whose church the family belonged. He also read law, probably under the direction of his neighbor, Governor Alexander Martin, and in 1783 received a license to practice, thus becoming the first native-born lawyer in Guilford County. In 1784 he moved to Salisbury for two years, studying further under Judge Spruce Macay. Here began a lifelong intimacy with a fellow student, Andrew Jackson. The two spent the winter of 1787–88 in the McNairy home, riding circuit with the court and gaining experience in legal affairs. In December 1787 the state of North Carolina appointed McNairy as judge of the newly planned Mero District in Davidson County (now in Tennessee). With Jackson and another friend, Thomas Searcy, he began the journey to Nashville early in 1788, joining at Morganton a party that included the family of General William Lee Davidson for the Indian-haunted overmountain trip.

There being no court organization in Davidson County, on first declaring the Superior Court of Law and Equity in session, on 4 Nov. 1788, Judge McNairy appointed Andrew Jackson attorney general, an appointment ratified by the North Carolina legislature in June 1789. That year the Mero District was ceded to the federal government, and President George Washington named McNairy as one of the three federal judges who, with Governor William Blount, ruled it from Nashville, where McNairy had settled. In 1796, when the district became the state of Tennessee, McNairy, with Jackson, was a delegate to the constitutional convention. In 1797 he was reaffirmed by the new state as superior court judge. In less than a year, he received a second appointment from President Washington as federal judge of Tennessee.

A rift began in 1788 between McNairy and Jackson that lasted many years. McNairy's judicial temperament and Jackson's impulsiveness caused a number of differences of opinion in the business of organizing the new state, as well as in personal affairs, and the close friendship ceased, though they continued public service together in developing the state. During the slanderous campaign of 1828, McNairy rallied to Jackson's support and served on what was known as the Whitewashing Committee. He wrote: "You and myself began life together and time rolls on apace. We shall soon cease to act. Until then and after, may you be happy." Jackson answered that they should forget their differences, remembering only their youthful friendship. The judge resigned his long-held office on 29 May 1833, and the president accepted the resignation of his old friend.

While most of his life was spent in his judicial capacity, McNairy exerted a great influence over the early growth of Tennessee. A large landowner, businessman, and respected citizen, he was active in the social, cultural, and educational development of the state, and in the expansion of its natural resources. McNairy County was named for him. He was president of the State Bank of Tennessee and a trustee of the Nashville Bible Society, of which Jackson was vice-president. He was a trustee of Davidson Academy and of the school resulting from its merger with the Federal Seminary. Throughout his life, he gave much time and thought to the development of educational facilities. Childless, he educated several nieces and nephews. About 1790 all of his family moved to Tennessee, with the exception of James, who remained a lawyer in Guilford County. Margaret married Thomas Hamilton, Catherine married Jason Thompson, and Mary married Elisha Nicholson. Robert settled in Giles County. Nathaniel and Andrew were lawyers. Boyd, a noted physician, is remembered as host of Lafayette on his visit to Nashville in 1825.

Either in 1788 or 1789, Judge McNairy married Mary Bell Hunt Robertson (Mrs. Mark Robertson), twice widowed by Indian raids. His funeral was attended by members of the General Assembly of Tennessee and many other prominent citizens. His remains were placed in an impressive family vault in Nashville City Cemetery which bears this inscription: "John McNairy,

appointed first Judge of the Mero District of N.C. (Nashville) in 1787. Later Judge of Tennessee Supreme Court and U.S. District and Circuit Courts. Schoolmate and friend of Andrew Jackson."

SEE: *Greensboro Daily News*, 4 Aug. 1929, 26 June 1938; Guilford and Rowan County Court Records (North Carolina State Archives, Raleigh); Marquis James, *Andrew Jackson: The Border Captain* (1933); Stephen S. Lowrance, "Life and Times of John McNairy" (thesis, possession of Mary Katherine Hoskins, College Grove, Tenn.); James Parton, *Life of Andrew Jackson* (1860).

MARY KATHERINE HOSKINS

McNeill, Archibald (ca. 1796–1849), congressman and militia colonel, was born in Moore County. He represented Moore in the House of Commons in 1808 and 1809 and in the senate in 1811 and 1815. In 1821 he ran for Congress as a Republican against the incumbent, John Culpepper, a Federalist. McNeill was elected and served in the Seventeenth Congress (1821–23), where he made one speech against the tariff. Culpepper opposed McNeill for reelection in 1823. During that campaign, both candidates refused to declare a preference on the upcoming presidential election of 1824, but McNeill rejected the principle of a caucus nomination. McNeill also accused his opponent of insufficient support for the War of 1812 while a member of the General Assembly, but Culpepper won the election. Running against Culpepper again in 1825, McNeill was elected and served in the Nineteenth Congress (1825–27).

The 1830 census for North Carolina records Archibald McNeill as a resident of Robeson County, living alone in his household (presumably, therefore, unmarried) but owning a female slave between the ages of forty and fifty who was deaf and dumb.

McNeill moved to Texas in 1836. In 1849 he organized and led a group of about a hundred men on an expedition to the newly discovered gold fields of California. A sandstorm struck the party while it was crossing the Arizona desert. McNeill and most of the others perished, and his body was never found.

SEE: *Annals of Congress* (1823); *Biog. Dir. Am. Cong.* (1961); *Carolina Observer*, 24 July, 7 Aug. 1823.

HARRY L. WATSON

MacNeill, Ben Dixon (21 Nov. 1889–26 May 1960), author and journalist, was born on a farm four miles from Laurinburg, the third child of Scottish parents. His father, Angus Benjamin MacNeill, cultivated a small farm but was more interested in singing and fiddling than in agriculture. Known as "Ben MacNeill the Singing Master," he traveled in several southern states, frequently conducting singing schools. His mother, Flora McKinnon MacNeill, exercised an especially strong influence on young Ben, sharing with him an interest in flowers, birds, animals, and even snakes, and encouraging his inquisitiveness. Recognizing his natural affinity for words and their usage, she bought him a blue-back speller, his first book, and followed that later with a copy of *Webster's Dictionary*.

The family moved to Laurinburg, where Ben attended a classical academy conducted by Professor W. G. Quakenbush and worked in the summer in the Dickson Cotton Mills. Even then, at age eleven, he had a reputation for telling tall tales, and with encouragement from Mrs. Walter McEachin, his Sunday school teacher in the Presbyterian church attended by the family, he became an avid reader of classical literature and poetry. Later he was to describe his acquaintance as a teenager with John Charles McNeill, the poet, who at the time was a columnist for the *Charlotte Observer*: "He was vaguely my cousin. I doubt that he was really. He was a magnificent figure—godlike. And he treated me like a contemporary. I would look dumbly at him and know that, somehow, I'd be a writer, too."

In 1905 MacNeill was sent to Bingham Military Academy, near Mebane, and later attended Davidson College for a brief period. His first full-time job was as a teacher at the Troutman School in Iredell County, followed by another stint as a teacher in the Marvin School in Grays Creek, to which his family had moved from Laurinburg. His students remembered him more for his storytelling than for his teaching ability.

The urge to write was still strong, and he gave up teaching for a job as a reporter with the Wilmington *Morning Star*, an association that was interrupted during World War I by three years of service in the army, in which he became a machine-gun instructor. Returning to the *Morning Star*, he was promoted to city editor, though his interests were more in writing than in editing. In 1920 he left Wilmington to become a reporter for the Raleigh *News and Observer*, covering state government and the General Assembly among other assignments. His flair for words and his ability to write interesting stories about otherwise mundane happenings attracted the attention of the paper's editor, Josephus Daniels, whom the reporter once described as "a daddy to me," and Ben Dixon was given a special roving assignment, traveling throughout the state and writing about anything that interested him. His column, "Cellar and Garret," became one of the most popular in the South.

Following the death of his father in 1931, he returned to Grays Creek and for a brief period managed the family's gristmill, but it was not long before he was writing special features for the *People's Advocate* in Fayetteville.

In 1937 MacNeill went to Manteo to become publicity director for Paul Green's symphonic drama, *The Lost Colony*, the focal point of the celebration on Roanoke Island of the 350th anniversary of the first attempt at English colonization in the New World. His articles on this innovative experiment with drama were published throughout the country and were a contributing factor to the success of the Green play, which became the longest running outdoor drama in America; it is still shown annually in Waterside Theatre at Fort Raleigh. When *The Lost Colony* was forced to close during World War II, MacNeill reenlisted in the army, this time as a major, and subsequently became public relations officer at Fort Knox, Ky. After three years of service he was discharged for physical disability with the rank of lieutenant colonel.

He resumed his duties as publicity director for *The Lost Colony* when it reopened in the summer of 1946, but failing health and a desire to do some serious writing resulted in his retiring to the village of Buxton, at Cape Hatteras, where he lived until his death in a small cottage on a knoll close by the Cape Hatteras Lighthouse. It was here that he wrote, and put aside, his first and only novel, *Sand Roots*, which was published after his death, and his highly successful personalized account of the people who lived on the Outer Banks, *The Hatterasman*, winner of the Mayflower Cup award in 1958.

In his declining years he frequently "held court," seated in a special chair in the small living room of the cottage at "Buxton on Cape Hatteras" when visitors came to call, recounting his experiences and telling fascinating stories for hours on end. To one such visitor, in late May 1960, he said: "I am in the place in this world where I most want to be." Death came to him a week later while he was seated in his favorite chair.

SEE: *The Coastland Times*, 3 June 1960; *Fayetteville Observer*, 6 Nov. 1966; "The Hatterasman: Ben Dixon MacNeill," Manteo *Coastlander*, September 1974; Raleigh *News and Observer*, 13 Aug. 1967; Richard Walser, *Young Readers' Picturebook of Tar Heel Authors* (1966).

DAVID STICK

McNeill, Daniel (1752–5 May 1818), Loyalist partisan fighter, was born near the Lower Little River in Cumberland County, the son of Archibald and Janet McNeill. When the American Revolution began, he owned over one thousand acres near the Cape Fear River and lived about twelve miles from Cross Creek. McNeill refused the state oath of allegiance twice in 1777 and was ordered to leave North Carolina. He hid near the Virginia border until the autumn of 1778, when he heard that British troops were moving south. Traveling overland, he joined them at Savannah in January 1779. Later he raised a company of about one hundred men for John Hamilton's Royal North Carolina Regiment.

McNeill was a guide and a fierce commander of small raiding parties in the Carolinas. He evacuated from Wilmington to Charles Town and then to East Florida and Nova Scotia with the Royal North Carolina Regiment. He took three relatives and eight servants or slaves with him and received 1,250 acres at the regimental settlement near Country Harbour, Nova Scotia. He married Mary Nutting and settled at Loyal Hill near Windsor.

McNeill returned at least twice to North Carolina. In 1786–87 he barely escaped being mobbed in New Bern as he obtained proof of the sale of his confiscated land, which he then took to the Loyalists' Claims Commissioners in Quebec. In 1811 he was unable to take possession of land bequeathed to him by his father in Chatham and Cumberland counties. Instead, he took slaves from his father's estate to Nova Scotia, where most of them escaped.

SEE: Lindley S. Butler, ed., *The Narrative of Col. David Fanning* (1981); Cumberland County Court Minutes, October 1778 (North Carolina State Archives, Raleigh); Marion Gilroy, comp., *Loyalists and Land Settlements in Nova Scotia* (1937); Lawrence Collection, Chipman Papers, and Muster Rolls of the Royal North Carolina Regiment (Public Archives of Canada); Public Record Office, London, AO 12:35, 65, 13:91, 138, WO 65:65, T 64:23; Royal North Carolina Regiment Warrant to Survey (Public Archives of Nova Scotia); A. W. Savary, ed., *Col. David Fanning's Narrative of his Exploits and Adventures as a Loyalist of North Carolina in the American Revolution* (1908).

CAROLE WATTERSON TROXLER

McNeill, James Hipkins (23 May 1825–31 Mar. 1865), Presbyterian clergyman and Confederate officer, was born in Fayetteville, the son of George McNeill. His mother's name is unknown. He attended The University of North Carolina, Yale, and Delaware College (between 1840 and 1844), Union Theological Seminary in New York (1845–47), and the Presbyterian Theological Seminary (1847–48). Licensed by the Fayetteville Presbytery in June 1848, he was ordained in May 1849.

McNeill served the Presbyterian church in Pittsboro

from 1848 until 1853, when he became secretary of the American Bible Society and moved to Elizabeth, N.J. At the beginning of the Civil War he returned to North Carolina and from 24 Aug. 1861 to 8 Mar. 1865 was editor of the *North Carolina Presbyterian*, which his brother George, a graduate of Princeton, had established in 1858 with offices in Fayetteville. In June 1862 he was commissioned captain in Company A, Sixty-third Regiment (Fifth Regiment of Cavalry), but in November he was promoted to major and transferred to the Field and Staff of the regiment. He was wounded in action at Middleburg, Va., in June 1863 and was promoted to colonel to rank from 24 Nov. 1864.

Even though he was on active duty, McNeill, with the help of local ministers, continued to issue the *North Carolina Presbyterian*. He was killed in action at Chamberlain Run, Va., nineteen days after General William T. Sherman's men demolished the office, broke the press, and melted the type of the North Carolina Presbyterian Publishing Company in Fayetteville.

In October 1848 McNeill married Kate Chamberlain of Newark, Del. He was survived by at least one son, George Palmer, and there are numerous McNeill descendants.

SEE: Louis R. Manarin, comp., *North Carolina Troops, 1861–1865: A Roster*, vol. 2 (1968); Eugene C. Scott, *Ministerial Directory of the Presbyterian Church in the U.S., 1861–1942* (1942); Henry S. Stroupe, "The Beginnings of Religious Journalism in North Carolina, 1823–1864," *North Carolina Historical Review* 30 (January 1953).

WILLIAM S. POWELL

MacNeill, Janet Smith (Jennie Bahn) (1720–91), subject of North Carolina legend, was born in Scotland, the daughter of John, a lowland Scot, and Margaret Gilchrist Smith. The Smiths migrated to the colonies about 1739 and settled in the region that became Harnett County, N.C. Margaret Gilchrist died on the voyage to America and John Smith died sometime before 1754.

A contemporary of Flora MacDonald, Janet Smith was well known to her Scottish neighbors as a spirited, attractive young woman. Traditionally, she is said to have been small, redheaded, and fair complected. Her neighbors nicknamed her "Jennie Bahn," meaning Jennie the Fair.

Jennie Bahn and her husband, Archibald MacNeill, were said to be the largest cattle raisers in America before the Revolution. One of the earliest and most famous legends surrounding Jennie Bahn has her regularly driving 3,000 head of cattle from Cross Creek to Philadelphia. Because it was impossible to take enough feed for a herd this size, much less buy it during the long journey to Philadelphia, this legend has been refuted. It is known, however, that she would occasionally help drive a herd of around 1,500 to Petersburg, Va. According to one story, on one trip she tried to buy feed from a Virginia farmer but he refused to sell it to her. Not to be outdone, she let her cattle inside his fences to graze. It is also known that Jennie Bahn did visit Philadelphia, where she met Benjamin Franklin. She was so impressed by Franklin that there has been a Benjamin Franklin in the MacNeill family and collateral families since that trip.

Another legend concerns her original, though inaccurate, surveying techniques. She would take a slave to a tract of land and send him walking until he heard her bell. At the clang, he would change direction. Her neighbors did not like her methods of surveying and ac-

cused her of infringing on their land. She was never taken to court for these infringements, however, because she wisely patented the tracts under the names of her husband and children. Her name never appears on the records at the land grant office in Raleigh or on the records of the Fayetteville courts.

As the driving force in her family, Jennie Bahn is said, at the start of the Revolution, to have divided her six sons so half would serve the king and the other half would serve the cause for independence. She remained neutral in order to sell cattle to both sides. This way the MacNeill family could brag about its sons no matter which way the war was going and make money at the same time. Actually, five of her six sons served with Loyalist forces. Of these five, "Nova Scotia" Daniel and "Leather Eye" Hector were known as outstanding Tory leaders, and "Cunning" John led his troops in the onslaught at the Massacre of Piney Bottom. As for Jennie Bahn, it is said that she regarded the British troops stopping by her home with the utmost distaste.

Jennie Bahn married "Scorblin'" (scrubbling) Archibald MacNeill sometime before 1748. They had seven sons and two daughters. After the war Jennie Bahn and Archie MacNeill moved to their home in Cumberland County on the lower Little River in the Sandhills. They were buried together in the nearby MacNeill cemetery. The final legend surrounding Jennie Bahn comes after her death. Her tombstone is said to have been so heavy that it was 125 years before it was taken from Fayetteville and placed on her grave.

SEE: Malcolm Fowler, *They Passed This Way* (1976); Ben Dixon MacNeill, "Highland Family Comes Home to Celebrate" (clippings, North Carolina Collection, University of North Carolina, Chapel Hill); John Oates, *Story of Fayetteville* (1972).

NANCY V. SMITH

McNeill, John Charles (24 July 1874–17 Oct. 1907), poet, journalist, and lawyer, was born at Ellerslie, his father's farm near Wagram in Richmond (later Scotland) County. His two grandfathers had emigrated from Argyllshire, Scotland. Daniel White, his mother's grandfather, was a Baptist minister who had been converted from Presbyterianism. John Charles, as he was always called, was the youngest child of Captain Duncan and Euphenia Livingston McNeill, both industrious, thrifty, and educated. Captain McNeill, a graduate of old Trinity College in Randolph County, had been a newspaper editor and poet. One of his last efforts was a eulogy to his son (*Charlotte Observer*, 18 Jan. 1908). John Charles had three sisters and a brother: Mary Catherine (Mrs. Jasper Lutterbok Memory), Ella (Mrs. Daniel A. Watson), Wayne Leland, and Donna. In and around Wagram lived his many cousins and kinfolk, the Johnsons and the McMillans.

Young McNeill's boyhood was an unusually happy one. He worked on the farm alongside the white and black laborers; he roamed the woods and swamps beside the Lumber River; he went swimming and hunting and fishing. He attended Richmond (later Spring Hill) Academy, a one-teacher old-field school three miles from his home, where he won most of the prizes offered. Adjoining the academy was the unique Hexagonal House, in times past the meeting place of the local Temperance Society. When he was twelve, the family moved to neighboring Riverton, a community of McNeills and Johnsons and McMillans. His preparatory schooling nearing an end, he was sent for a year to the

Whiteville Academy, where he lived with his sister, Mary Memory, and paid for his board by working in a store and doing other odd jobs. The year following, at eighteen, he taught in a rural school not far from Statesboro, Ga., where he lived with his second sister, Ella Watson. Like John Charles, his sister Donna never married.

Predictable it was, perhaps, that sooner or later he would go to Wake Forest College. McNeill was past his twentieth birthday when he enrolled there as a freshman in 1894. Almost immediately he attracted the attention of his English teacher, Benjamin F. Sledd—"Old Slick" to the students—who, because he was impressed with the maturity of McNeill's first composition, signed him up as his theme reader. McNeill's first printed poem seems to be one included in the December 1894 issue of the *Wake Forest Student*, a campus journal of which he later became editor. His years as an undergraduate were busy ones. He excelled in all his subjects, particularly the courses in English, French, and German. He read carefully prepared papers before the college Historical Society. During his junior year he studied law and in the summer of 1897 passed an oral bar examination. He was graduated with an A.B. in 1898 *summa cum laude*, the valedictorian of his class, and returned to Wake Forest as an instructor in English, receiving an M.A. in 1899. Then he went to Mercer University in Georgia and taught English for a year while a professor was on leave.

At this time, McNeill was tall and angular, with gray eyes and black hair, and rather poetically careless of his appearance. Many writers who knew him have remarked on his "melodious voice." He was twenty-six, and, with the notion that he ought to settle down, he opened a law office in Lumberton. His interests lay in people and writing, not in abstract law, which bored him. Only when a case presented the personalities and capricious actions of his clients was he avidly involved. For the most part he lazed about his office, where he kept a pet possum, or fished in the Lumber River. He purchased an interest in the weekly *Argus* of Lumberton and, it is said, wrote poems and editorials for it. (No copies of 1900–1902 are extant.) When requested to do so, he happily wrote a brief county history to be included in the *Dictionary of Robeson County* (1900).

In 1904 McNeill sold his interest in the *Argus* and moved to Laurinburg to practice law among his home folks. He entered politics and in 1903 was elected to the state house of representatives. Among the many local bills he introduced was one to prohibit the sale of liquor in Scotland County and another to "prohibit the sale of fire-crackers more than three inches long." Meanwhile, he was pursuing his love of poetry. "Barefooted" appeared on 6 June 1901 in the *Youth's Companion*, one of the nation's most popular periodicals. Between January 1902 and December 1905 the prestigious *Century Magazine* used eighteen of McNeill's poems, both lyrics and dialect verses. On 6 Sept. 1903 the *Charlotte Observer* printed two selections he had sent in. In this way McNeill's reputation as a poet began to grow.

In Charlotte, editor Joseph P. Caldwell of the *Observer*, a man of humor and ability, was searching for a feature-story writer to succeed Isaac Ervin Avery, recently deceased. When in the summer of 1904 H. E. C. (Red Buck) Bryant, a traveling representative of the *Observer*, called on McNeill in Laurinburg, McNeill admitted he was ready to leave the law profession; and after an interview in Charlotte, Caldwell hired him. Immediately McNeill started sending in copy to the *Observer*, though he did not officially join the staff until 1 Sept. 1904. Caldwell specified no definite duties. McNeill was to write whatever and whenever he wished; if he turned in no copy, Caldwell would understand. For the next three years, the editor's faith in McNeill was amply rewarded. True, his columns came out irregularly, often on successive days, then nothing appeared for weeks. Perhaps McNeill was off to a courthouse town reporting a murder trial, or perhaps he simply lacked inspiration. His columns had various titles: among them, "From Street and Lobby," "Little Essays," "Sunday Observations," and "Unclassified Stunts." A popular column of poetry began—before he settled in Charlotte—with "Coonalities" on 10 August. He first used the heading "Songs Merry and Sad" on 2 October.

Besides the columns, he wrote news stories on weddings and fires and funerals, reviews of current periodicals, and criticisms of music and dramatic performances in Charlotte. A series of fables delighted *Observer* subscribers. Often he left town as a roving reporter, covering the Baptist State Convention, the dedication of the agriculture building at State College, the inauguration of President Theodore Roosevelt, commencement at Chapel Hill, and political speeches anywhere and everywhere. His comments on books were alive and unconventional. Of the popular but turbulent Reconstruction novels of his friend Thomas Dixon, Jr., he wrote: "No one of enough reading to form a comparative judgment would accuse our own Tom Dixon . . . of writing literature." Yet McNeill could himself transform violence into poetry, as he did in his much admired "To Melvin Gardiner: Suicide," about the death of an itinerate alcoholic journalist. His reports on the famous Dargan murder case in South Carolina read more like the installments of a mystery novel than like press dispatches. Though an unashamed and proud man of his region, McNeill relished a visit to New York, where he attended the theater and called on publishers; and almost the event of his life was a railroad trip through New England with Governor R. B. Glenn's party in September 1905.

On 19 October the Patterson Cup, the first literary trophy in North Carolina, was awarded McNeill for a manuscript of poems published later as *Songs Merry and Sad* (1906). President Theodore Roosevelt, in Raleigh at the time, presented the cup to McNeill during ceremonies conducted in the senate chamber at the state capitol. McNeill was now in demand. He was reluctant to accept an invitation to read his own poems to the Round Dozen Book Club in Hickory on 2 Jan. 1906, but accounts of the event prove how thoroughly he charmed the ladies. Archibald Henderson recalled an occasion when McNeill mesmerized his listeners with "a running fire of dialect verse, humorous commentary, negro anecdotes, and folk-lore tales."

His popularity merely stimulated his productivity. He wrote his poems on a rough tablet, sought criticism from his well-disposed colleagues, then finally located a typewriter, using his two index fingers, to prepare smooth copy for the compositor. But often no typewriter was available in the "Mule Pen," the city office at the *Observer*. An irregular member of the staff, McNeill was simply not assigned one. Sometimes he retreated to the Manufacturers Club, where he resided in a room on the upstairs floor, or went up to the roof garden and gazed down at the traffic in the street and on the sidewalks. To the rural McNeill, Charlotte seemed like a metropolis, and he was always delighted with the throngs coming and going. Yet his mind was never far away from Riverton, and when he occasionally disappeared, even during a busy time at the *Observer*, everyone knew he had gone for a while to walk the banks of the Lumber River.

In the summer of 1907 he became ill and went to Wrightsville Beach in hopes of regaining his strength. When his condition worsened, he left his work and retreated to Riverton. There in "Thunder Castle," his large room on the second floor of his parents' home, he died of what was diagnosed as pernicious anemia. He was buried in the family plot at Spring Hill Cemetery. On the tombstone were engraved lines from his "Sundown" and the designation "Poet Laureate of North Carolina," an unofficial title tendered him after he received the Patterson Cup.

McNeill's contemporaries described him as a gentle man of an even disposition, joyous, considerate, companionable. About his poetry, McNeill declared: "The little loves and sorrows are my song." He wrote nature poems, love poems, and religious poems. He phrased scores of his verses in the dialect of his people, exhibiting their humor and their folklore. *Songs Merry and Sad*, primarily a selection of lyric poems, contains "When I Go Home," "Sunburnt Boys," "Sundown," "The Bride," and fifty-five other poems. At the time of his death, McNeill was making selections for a second book, perhaps to be titled "Possums and Persimmons." The manuscript, prepared for the press by others and published as *Lyrics from Cottonland* in December 1907, included "The August Meeting," "Legion," "A Few Days Off," "Punishment," "The Crown of Power," "Holding Off the Calf," "Autumn," "To Sleep," and sixty-nine others, mainly in dialect. There are hundreds of uncollected poems.

McNeill was a Democrat and a Baptist. A bronze bust (1913) of him by the Chicago sculptor, Mable Landrum, is in the Public Library of Charlotte and Mecklenburg County, and a posthumous portrait by William C. Fields hangs in the restored McNeill Birthplace near Wagram.

SEE: Agatha Boyd Adams, *John Charles McNeill: A Biographical Sketch* (1949); Samuel A. Ashe, ed., *Biographical History of North Carolina*, vol. 7 (1908); *Charlotte Observer*, various issues, 1904–7; Jasper L. Memory, Jr., ed., *Select Prose of John Charles McNeill* (1936); Alice Morella Polk, "John Charles McNeill: A Poet of North Carolina" (M.A. thesis, Duke University, 1941).

RICHARD WALSER

McNeill, William Gibbs (3 Oct. 1801–16 Feb. 1853), civil engineer and army officer, was born in Wilmington of Scottish ancestry; his great-grandfather was a member of a Highland clan that immigrated to North America in 1746. His father, Charles Donald McNeill, after serving in the British army in the West Indies, established the family's permanent residence in Wilmington, N.C. Young McNeill received his early education in Long Island, N.Y. Initially planning on becoming a minister, he became interested in pursuing a career in the military after a visit to West Point. He received an appointment to the U.S. Military Academy and was graduated as a third lieutenant of artillery in 1817. Among his classmates at the academy was George W. Whistler, who married his sister, Anna, and with whom he remained closely associated in several engineering projects during his career. McNeill married Maria Matilda Cammen of New York, and they had seven children.

In 1819 he served in the Florida campaign as an aide-de-camp to Andrew Jackson and later worked with the U.S. Coast Survey in the South under the Corps of Engineers. Early in 1823 he was transferred to the Corps of Topographical Engineers, where he worked on surveys related to a feasibility study for constructing the Chesa-

peake and Ohio Canal across the Allegheny Mountains. McNeill also worked on surveys for the James River and Kanawha canals, and in 1827 the government loaned him to the Baltimore and Ohio Railroad Company to locate a satisfactory route to the Ohio River. The following year he was appointed to the Board of Engineers and traveled to Europe to study various public works including railroads, which he believed had the most potential as a mode of transportation.

After returning from Europe, he and his brother-in-law, George Whistler, became joint engineers on a large number of new railroads in the East. Besides the Baltimore and Ohio, they worked on such lines as the Baltimore and Susquehanna, the Paterson and Hudson River, the Boston and Providence, the Taunton and New Bedford, the Long Island, the Boston and Albany, and the Charleston, Louisville, and Cincinnati. Becoming the most prominent civil engineers in the nation, they "exercised an influence throughout the country for many years much greater than any others. Indeed there were few works of importance undertaken at that time in connection with which their names do not appear." Their influence was increased by the fact that during this period they directed the early work of the next generation of engineers.

In 1834 McNeill was promoted to brevet major of engineers. However, he resigned from the army in 1817 to become engineer for the state of Georgia, where he was employed primarily on a survey for a railroad from Cincinnati to Charleston. In 1842 he was appointed a major general in the militia of Rhode Island in an effort to quell the Dorr Rebellion in that state, serving until 1845. President John Tyler appointed him the chief engineer of the Brooklyn Naval Yard, for which he prepared the plans for the large dry dock and directed its initial construction before his removal by President James K. Polk following the election. His dismissal was attributed to his involvement in the Dorr Rebellion, as was his failure at the outbreak of the Mexican War to obtain a commission as a brigadier general.

Between 1851 and 1853 he took trips to Europe in efforts to improve his health. While in England, he supported the interests of several large American mining companies and became the first American to be elected to the Institution of Civil Engineers of Great Britain. On a visit to Russia, McNeill was asked to direct the construction of a railroad from St. Petersburg to Moscow but declined. A few days after returning to the United States, he died suddenly in Brooklyn, N.Y.

SEE: G. W. Cullum, *Biographical Register of the Officers and Graduates of the U.S. Military Academy*, vol. 1 (1890); *DAB*, vol. 6 (1933); George M. McIver, "North Carolinians at West Point before the Civil War," *North Carolina Historical Review* 7 (1930); *The Memoirs of General Joseph Gardner Swift* (1890); Arthur May Mowry, *The Dorr War or the Constitutional Struggle in Rhode Island* (1901); New York *Herald*, 17 Feb. 1853; *Who Was Who in America*, historical vol. (1967).

GEORGE DAVID TERRY

MacNider, William de Berniere (25 June 1881–31 May 1951), physician, pharmacologist, and medical educator, was born in Chapel Hill, the son of Virginius St. Clair and Sophia Beatty Mallett MacNider. Both his father and his grandfather were physicians. In 1898 MacNider enrolled in The University of North Carolina, where he was graduated in the first class of the medical school with a doctor of medicine degree in 1903. Returning from special medical studies at the University of Chicago and Case Western Reserve, he resumed his life-long association with the university in Chapel Hill, where he had served as assistant in biology (1899–1900), assistant in anatomy (1900–1902), and assistant in clinical diagnosis (1902–5).

In 1905 MacNider organized the university's first Department of Pharmacology, where he served as professor from 1905 to 1918, Kenan Professor in 1918, and Kenan Research Professor from 1919 until his appointment as dean of the School of Medicine in 1937, following the retirement of Charles Staples Mangum. Desiring to devote his energies to research, MacNider resigned the deanship in 1940. He served as chairman of the Pharmacology Department until 1943 and as Kenan Research Professor until his retirement as professor emeritus in 1950.

As MacNider rose to national prominence in medical research and education, his influence and activities extended well beyond the Chapel Hill campus. In addition to his work at the university, he was physician-in-chief pro tem at Peter Bent Brigham Hospital in Boston (1925), Smith-Reed-Russell Lecturer at the George Washington University School of Medicine (1938), Brown-Sequart Lecturer at the Medical College of Virginia (1938), Mayo Foundation Lecturer (1939), Harvey Society Lecturer (1928–29), special lecturer in pharmacology at Duke University Medical School, and Chandler Memorial Lecturer at Columbia University.

As a specialist in pharmacology, toxicology, and gerontology, MacNider contributed extensively to the study of human renal and hepatic diseases, both in original research publications and as associate editor of the *Proceedings of the Society for Experimental Biology and Medicine*, the *Quarterly Journal of Alcohol Study*, and the *Journal of Pharmacology and Experimental Therapeutics*. In recognition of his contributions to medical research, he received the Gibbs Prize for Medical Research for 1930–31 from the New York Academy of Medicine, the Research Medal of the Southern Medical Association in 1933, and the Kober Medal of the Association of American Physicians in 1941. He was awarded an honorary doctor of science degree by the Medical College of Virginia in 1933 and an honorary doctor of letters degree by Davidson College in 1934.

MacNider was also widely recognized for his leadership and management abilities. He served as chairman of the Division of Pharmacology and Therapeutics of the American Medical Association in 1929 and as chairman of the Council of the Gerontology Society. He was elected president of the Elisha Mitchell Scientific Society, Medical Society of North Carolina (1925–26), the American Society for Pharmacology and Experimental Therapeutics (1932–34), the International Anesthesia Research Society (1934–35), and the Society for Experimental Biology and Medicine (1941–42). MacNider served as consultant on gerontology to the National Institutes of Health, committee chairman of the National Board of Medical Examiners, and chairman of the American division of the International Club for Research on Ageing. He was an active member of the National Red Cross committee on nutritional aspects of aging, the Executive and Cellular Physiology committees of the National Research Council, and the research committee of the National Anesthesia Research Society.

In addition to his leadership roles, MacNider was active in the American Physiological Society, American Association of Pathologists and Bacteriologists, American Association of Biological Chemists, American Association of University Professors, American Society of Experimental Pathology, Association of American Physicians, American Association of Anesthetists, American Association of the History of Medicine, North Carolina Academy of Science, National Academy of Science, New York Academy of Science, American Society of Naturalists, American Philosophical Society, Harvard Society, British Physiological Society, Pathological Society of Great Britain, Phi Chi, Sigma Nu, Phi Beta Kappa, and Alpha Omega Alpha. In recognition of his work in the biomedical sciences, MacNider was elected a Fellow of the American Association for the Advancement of Science, the American Academy of Arts and Sciences, and the American College of Physicians.

An active member of the Episcopal church and a Democrat, he belonged to the Cosmos Club of Washington, D.C., and the Masonic order. His hobbies included hiking, natural history, gardening, and the collecting of bronze statuary, silver, and scientific and religious books. On 23 Jan. 1918 he married Sarah Jane Foard of Davie County. They had one daughter, Sarah Foard. MacNider died in Durham and was buried in the Chapel Hill Cemetery. MacNider Hall in The University of North Carolina School of Medicine was named for him.

SEE: W. Reece Berryhill, William B. Blythe, and Isaac H. Manning, eds., *Medical Education at Chapel Hill: The First Hundred Years* (1979); W. C. George, in *Science* 115 (1952); W. W. McLendon and S. G. Cochrane, eds., *The Good Doctor* (1953); *Nat. Cyc. Am. Biog.*, vol. 40 (1955); *North Carolina Medical Journal* 13 (1952); *Who Was Who in America*, vol. 3 (1960).

MARCUS B. SIMPSON, JR.

McNinch, Frank Ramsay (27 Apr. 1873–20 Apr. 1950), attorney and government official, was born in Charlotte, the son of Franklin A. and Sarah Virginia Ramsay McNinch. At age seventeen, after a period of study at Barriers Military Academy in Charlotte, he became a salesman for a local grocery firm; this was followed by further employment as a salesman for a Richmond mercantile business and then for a New York company. Altogether, McNinch spent four years as a traveling salesman. After studying law on his own, he enrolled in the law course at The University of North Carolina in 1898 and was licensed to practice in January 1899.

After opening an office in Charlotte, his practice slowly grew. In 1904 he was elected to the General Assembly and during the 1905 session led the Prohibition forces in a highly successful temperance program; he was also responsible for making the divorce laws of the state much stricter. Fascinated by politics, he thereafter took an active part in numerous campaigns even though he was not a candidate for office himself. He did, however, serve as mayor of Charlotte from 1917 to 1921. In the latter year he resigned as mayor to become the regional director of the National Recreation Association of America.

McNinch seems to have been a particularly able orator at a time when political speaking was very important. Although he was a Democrat, during the presidential campaign of 1928 he played a leading role among members of his party who supported the Republican candidate, Herbert C. Hoover, against Alfred E. Smith. Smith's position as a "wet" and his Catholicism, many North Carolinians concluded, made him unacceptable, and McNinch encouraged defection from the Democratic party standard.

President Hoover, a Republican, was required by law to name one member of the opposite party to the Federal Power Commission and he chose McNinch. Appointed in 1930, the North Carolinian proved to be a very capable member and President Franklin D. Roosevelt, a Democrat, reappointed him. There were objections by leaders of the Democratic party in North Carolina to the initial appointment because of McNinch's failure to support the party in 1928. McNinch became chairman of the commission in 1933, however, and served until 1937. In that position he was a strong supporter of the president's program to provide cheap power to all the people. In 1935 he was the U.S. representative to the World Power Conference at The Hague, the Netherlands. As chairman of the Federal Communications Commission from 1937 to 1939, he steadfastly opposed any form of censorship of radio. He also supported the granting of equal prime time for the airing of opposing points of view. In an address in Chapel Hill on 26 Jan. 1939, he said: "A broadcaster's duty is to see that his station is never used by persons or groups especially interested in some public question in such a way that his station's listeners are left without sufficient information to make their own independent judgments on questions they should help to decide." From 1939 until 1946, when he retired, he was special assistant to the attorney general.

In 1905 McNinch married Mary Groome of Greensboro, and they became the parents of Frank R., Mary Groome, and Ariel. Following his wife's death he married Huldah Groome, and they were the parents of Huldah and Robert Groome. A Democrat and a Presbyterian, McNinch was a Mason and belonged to a number of other fraternal organizations. He was buried in Charlotte.

SEE: *Asheville Citizen*, 21–22 Apr. 1950; Daniel L. Grant, *Alumni History of the University of North Carolina, 1795–1924* (1924); *Prominent People of North Carolina* (1906); Raleigh *News and Observer*, 22 July 1933, 4, 23 June 1934, 3 Jan. 1935, 20 Aug. 1937, 27 Jan. 1939, 22 Apr. 1950; *Who Was Who in America*, vol. 3 (1960).

WILLIAM S. POWELL

Macon, Nathaniel (*17 Dec. 1758–29 June 1837*), "Old Republican" statesman, the foremost public man of North Carolina in the early nineteenth century, was the sixth child of Gideon and Priscilla Jones Macon; he was born at his father's plantation on Shocco Creek in what later became Warren County. The Macons were French Huguenots in origin, the Joneses English or Welsh. Both families had entered Virginia in the seventeenth century and were of the gentry when they moved to lands south of the Roanoke River in the 1730s. Macon's early life is known only in outline. Although he attended school under Charles Pettigrew and was enrolled in the College of New Jersey (now Princeton) when the American Revolution began, he was apparently, like George Washington, largely self-taught. Certainly his reading was wide and his mind neither provincial nor narrow as some have suggested. His speeches indicate an astute knowledge of foreign lands and public finance, and in a fairly typical letter Macon could casually mention David Hume, Gustavus Adolphus, and the Apocrypha.

Macon took to the field with the New Jersey militia in 1776. When his college closed, he returned home to Warren County to read law (which he never practiced) and English history. The interruption in his military service was not unusual since the Revolutionary War was fought by fits and starts and gentlemen served at will. (A similar hiatus occurred in the service of James Monroe and John Marshall.) Macon reentered the army in 1780 in a company raised and commanded by his brother. Typically, he refused a commission and the enlistment bounty. He was probably present with the American forces during the disastrous Camden campaign. In 1781, as a twenty-year-old private encamped on the Yadkin River, Macon received word of his election to the North Carolina Senate, which he reluctantly entered and to which he was reelected until 1786. He was immediately recognized as a leading member.

After the Revolution, Macon served for a time in the House of Commons and was identified with Willie Jones and the predominant anti-Federalist sentiment in North Carolina. He declined to serve in the Continental Congress in 1786, and his brother John voted against the federal Constitution in both North Carolina ratifying conventions. However, Macon accepted election to the federal House of Representatives and entered the Second Congress in 1791. He served in the House for the next twenty-four years, then took a seat in the Senate, where he remained for thirteen years, thus representing North Carolina in Congress from age thirty-three until his voluntary retirement at seventy.

In the House from 1791 to 1815, he was Speaker (1801–7), a candidate for Speaker (1799 and 1809), and chairman of the Foreign Relations Committee (1809–10). In the Senate from 1815 to 1828, he was chairman of the Foreign Relations Committee (1818–26) and president pro tempore (1826–28). In both houses he served on the main financial committees and was chairman of numerous select committees. During his congressional service he declined cabinet appointments at least twice, and he served long periods as a trustee of The University of North Carolina and as a militia officer and justice of the peace in Warren County. For the first third of the nineteenth century he was the dominant personality of the predominant Democratic-Republican party and the most respected citizen of North Carolina both within and outside the state.

It was Macon's pride that he never campaigned for an office or asked any man for a vote. His legislative and political skills were neither rhetorical nor managerial. His strength and influence lay in personal force, exemplary integrity, shrewdness, a contented (or static) public, and undeviating adherence to fundamental principles. These principles, forged in the Revolution, did not change in a political career of half a century. They included individual freedom, strict economy and accountability in government expenditures, frequent elections, limited discretion in officials, avoidance of debt and paper money, and Republican simplicity in forms. Macon was the purest possible example of one type of "Republican" produced by the American Revolution. He was satisfied with a society of landowners who managed their own affairs and wanted neither benefits nor burdens from government. He wanted a government conducted with honesty, simplicity, and the maximum liberty for the individual, community, and state. He believed that North Carolina approached this ideal, and he fought a losing battle to hold the federal government to it. To Macon, the success of a democracy depended not on the progressiveness and vision of leaders but on the willing consent of the people. Because he opposed most appropriations and innovations, even when he stood nearly alone, he has often been described as a "negative radical." True to the spirit of "esse quam videri," Macon practiced what he preached. He was in his seat faithfully when public business was being conducted, drew from the Treasury only his actual travel expenses rather than the maximum allowance (as was the practice), and lived simply in Washington, often sharing a bed with a visiting constituent.

Ideological purity did not detract from Macon's political shrewdness (he advised Jefferson against the abortive Chase impeachment, for instance,) or prevent him from being chivalric towards opponents in personal relations. Despite his firmness, Macon was often pragmatic in matters of political tactics and knew when to compromise and yield to his party on smaller issues. His judgment was always well balanced, his dealings moderate. His speeches were businesslike and to the point, his first congressional speech reportedly being one sentence. With one pithy question in debate, he burst many grand congressional bubbles. "Be not led astray by grand notions or magnificent opinions," Macon told a young follower. "Remember you belong to a meek state and just people, who want nothing but to enjoy the fruits of their labor honestly and to lay out their profits in their own way." With this philosophy he dominated the state for decades. In only one brief period (1801–5) was he a dispenser of federal patronage, and then he refused to use it politically.

Macon's political career had three phases: Jeffersonian Republican leader, 1791–1807; "Tertium Quid," 1807–ca. 1815; and elder statesman thereafter. When he entered the House of Representatives in 1791, he was immediately identified with the group opposed to the emerging Federalists and took a leading role in the parliamentary battles of the 1790s in which the Jeffersonian coalition was forged. These services led to the speakership, a post that, Macon said, he entered without seeking and left without regret. Losing the chair in a disagreement with the administration wing of the party, which he felt had compromised with Federalist principles and had used rather than eliminated the federal patronage, he was thereafter identified with the "Old Republican" group. He opposed taxes, the protective tariff, internal improvements (at federal expense), all expenditures not necessary to the honest fulfillment of the most essential functions of the government, a national bank, executive patronage and discretion, and any compromise with northern antislavery agitation. The principles that John Taylor expounded and John Randolph dramatized, Macon personified. Remaining independent, never attending the party caucus, and opposing the election of both James Madison and James Monroe, he supported the incumbent administration when he could and never engaged in opposition for opposition's sake. He reluctantly voted for the Embargo. During the War of 1812 he was willing to raise and support troops but opposed a navy, national conscription, and executive discretion.

By the time he entered the Senate in 1815, Macon was already a venerable figure, a stature that increased as survivors of the Revolution and exponents of pure Republican principles became rarer. Although he was evidently displeased with the increasingly dynamic politics of the postwar period and felt that true Republican virtue was being lost, Macon undoubtedly had a considerable impact on the next generation as a prophet of both "Jacksonian democracy" and southern separatism. Towns and counties across the South were named for him. He was widely discussed for the vice-presidency in 1824 and received the electoral votes of Virginia for that office. In 1828 he was wooed unsuccessfully by John Quincy Adams as a running mate. He was lukewarm to Andrew Jackson but gave the Jacksonian coalition his support as a lesser evil from 1828, and he served as a Van Buren elector in 1836. He evidently regarded the emergent Democratic party as the nearest available approach to a coalition of southern planters and northern republicans against antislavery agitation and economic exploitation. Opposing nullification and considering secession the proper remedy, he also chastised Jackson for his responding proclamation, which he found to be as contrary "to what was the Constitution" as nullification. In 1835 Macon was unanimously elected presiding officer of the state constitutional convention, although in the end he opposed the revisions that were adopted, especially the change from annual to biennial elections.

Macon's private life was the source of his public principles. Indeed, his classical Republicanism postulated that leaders should possess virtue independent of office and should reflect and defend their social fabric rather than attempt to mold it to their own design. His father died when he was five, leaving him land and slaves; both increased under his mother's management and his own. Above average in height, of impressive presence, dignified yet simple in manners, treating all classes with courtesy and attention, a pillar of his neighborhood, colloquial in private conversation, devoted to agriculture, horses, hunting, and an outdoor life, laboring in his own tobacco fields, sipping whiskey before meals and keeping fine wine only for guests, Macon was an exemplary patriarchal southern planter. He never joined a church but attended services accompanied by his slaves and, not surprisingly, is said to have found the Baptist most to his taste. A lifelong resident of the most slaveholding county of the state, he is said to have owned two thousand acres and seventy slaves and to have divided his estate equally with his two daughters, Betsy and Seignora, on their marriages. His home, Buck Spring, about twelve miles northeast of Warrenton, was built in the most isolated portion of his holdings and was modest for so wealthy and eminent a statesman. The plantation has in recent years been the subject of a restoration project. Macon married Hannah Plummer on 9 Oct. 1783. She died in 1790, leaving the two daughters and a son who died in 1792 at age six.

Macon is said to have destroyed his own accumulated papers, probably out of the same "republican" distaste for pomp and idolatry that led him to oppose expenditures for a tomb for George Washington and to forbid the erection of a monument over his own grave at Buck Spring. This fact has discouraged biographers, although a large number of Macon's letters survive in scattered depositories and publications. He has figured in many articles, addresses, and theses concerning him specifically or Jeffersonian and Jacksonian politics. William E. Dodd's *Life of Nathaniel Macon* (1903) could be amplified and corrected in many details but remains a substantially accurate and usable work. Perhaps more valuable and practicable than a new biography would be a reliable and complete edition of Macon's speeches and letters, a project that probably could be encompassed in one volume.

Likenesses of Macon are rare. Neither the state nor The University of North Carolina owns a portrait. The massive American Library Association index to nineteenth-century engravings does not even contain an entry for Macon. Perhaps the most readily available likeness is the unidentified portrait published in William Henry Smith's *Speakers of the House of Representatives*. . . . (1928).

Macon was a Plutarchian figure who helped to mold the character of his era and his state. "Mr. Macon was one of those patriots who fill a vast space in the nation's eye," eulogized the Richmond *Enquirer*, chief organ of the Democratic party, on his death. To Thomas Jefferson he was "the last of the Romans." John Randolph, in making his will, alluded to the Virginian he had named as his executor as "the wisest man I ever knew—except for Mr. Macon." Later generations preferred a different style of democracy and tended to agree with progress-minded John Quincy Adams, who found in Macon "a narrowness of mind which education cannot enlarge, and covered by an encrustation of prejudices which experience cannot remove." Hugh T. Lefler's *History of North Carolina* (1956) was typical of later evaluations in observing that North Carolina remained "the Rip Van Winkle" of the states until it "repudiated the spirit of Macon." Even a sympathetic writer, J. G. de Roulhac Hamilton, found him "not a constructive force," although a detailed reexamination of Macon's career might well reveal that he was more of a "progressive" on the state and local level than has been believed, that it was remote federal power in the hands of a hostile northern majority eager to tamper with the southern social fabric and exploit the southern economy that he wished to negate.

At any rate, Macon's republicanism was one of deliberate choice, not of inertia. As William E. Dodd commented with a sense of marvel, *"He actually believed in democracy,"* in allowing the people to govern themselves. He was of a generation, class, and region that "knew the difference between the demands of popular institutions and special interests" and that deliberately chose a limited government as the accurate reflection of its social fabric. Certainly it would seem that the "spirit of Macon" was long the spirit of North Carolina, a spirit that, however foreign to the modern temper, lies at the heart of the origins of American democracy. Perhaps no one ever served the state more unselfishly or better displayed its traditional modest virtues.

SEE: *DAB*, vol. 7 (1933); William E. Dodd, *The Life of Nathaniel Macon* (1903); Warren County Historical Society, *Buck Spring Plantation: Home of Nathaniel Macon* (1974). The card catalogue of the North Carolina Collection of the University of North Carolina, Chapel Hill, contains citations to Macon's published letters and the most complete guide to Macon periodical and thesis literature.

CLYDE WILSON

McPheeters, Samuel Brown (*18 Sept. 1819–9 Mar. 1870*), Presbyterian clergyman, was the fifth child of William, a prominent Presbyterian clergyman and educator in Raleigh and Fayetteville, and Margaret Ann Curry McPheeters. Born in Raleigh and educated at the Caldwell Institute near Greensboro (1836–38) and The University of North Carolina (graduated 1841), McPheeters studied law in Raleigh and later theology at the Princeton Theological Seminary. Licensed as a clergyman by the Orange Presbytery in 1846, he performed his first pastoral charge as a missionary to slaves in Amelia and Nottaway counties, Va. In 1848 he began a three-year pastorate at the church in Amelia Courthouse, Va. He then moved to St. Louis, Mo., where he served a twelve-year tenure as pastor of the Westminster or Pine Street Church. As the distinguished pastor of the city's largest Presbyterian church, he was awarded a D.D. degree by Westminster College.

When his health failed in early 1860, McPheeters took an extended leave of absence to reside in New Mexico, where he served as chaplain at Fort Union. After severing his ties with Westminster Church, he moved to Shelbyville, Ky., and served as minister to Mulberry Church from 1865 until his death five years later. In 1851 he had married Eliza Cassandra Shank of Fincastle, Va.

McPheeters's chief claim to national prominence resulted from the notoriety he achieved as a border state minister during the Civil War. Because he derived from a Southern family, it was assumed at the outset that his sympathies lay with the Confederacy and with slavery. Although he was on leave in New Mexico when the war began, many of his parishioners wished him to state his position with regard to the Union publicly. On his return to St. Louis in late 1861, he refused to do so. In June 1862 his refusal to support the Union became a matter of controversy when he chose not to answer a public demand to announce "in a plain and candid manner, whether you are in favor of the Government of the United States . . . or whether you are in favor of the rebellion, and wish the success of those who seek to dismember the Union, and to establish a 'Southern Confederacy.' " McPheeters's persistent refusal to respond despite wide public pressure throughout the border states fed presumptions that he privately supported the Confederacy and aided its cause. Despite an eloquent defense of his right to maintain his views privately in a publication entitled *A Correspondence between Some of the Members of the Pine Street Presbyterian Church and Its Pastor* (1862), the pastor and congregation parted company in 1863.

SEE: Samuel Brown McPheeters, *A Correspondence between Some of the Members of the Pine Street Presbyterian Church and Its Pastor* (1862); Alfred Nevin, *Encyclopedia of the Presbyterian Church in the United States of America* (1884); Eugene C. Scott, *Ministerial Directory of the Presbyterian Church in the U.S., 1861–1941* (1942).

LARRY E. TISE

McPheeters, William (*28 Sept. 1778–7 Nov. 1842*), Presbyterian minister and educator, was born in Bethel (Augusta County), Va., of Irish and Scottish ancestry. He was the son of William, a magistrate in Virginia, and Rachel Moore McPheeters, who traced her family back to the illustrious Rutherfords of Scotland. McPheeters began a classical course in Staunton, Va., and completed his education at Liberty Hall Academy (later became Washington College; now Washington and Lee University) under the Reverend William Graham. In 1797 he went to Kentucky to study medicine with his brother James. Two years later he returned to Virginia, was received under the care of the Lexington Presbytery, and studied theology under the guidance of Samuel Brown of New Providence. On 19 Apr. 1802 he was licensed and in 1803 assumed responsibility for a church in Danville, Ky. Since the church provided a scant income, he had to teach school to support himself.

In 1804 McPheeters and his bride, the former Elizabeth McDowell, returned to Bethel, Va., and in December 1805 he was ordained to the Christian ministry. While serving his home church, Bethel, his first wife died in December 1806, and in 1809 he married Lavinia Moore, by whom he had a daughter, Lavinia. Shortly after the death of his second wife in 1810, he was called to Raleigh to serve as principal of the Raleigh Academy and as "Pastor to the City."

In 1816 he organized what is now the First Presbyterian Church of Raleigh. As the church grew, McPheeters, believing his primary duty to be to the academy, resigned as pastor in 1824 but served as a stated supply pastor for several years afterwards. The congregation was not in a hurry to call another pastor while McPheeters was available. In 1826 he severed his relationship with the Raleigh Academy but continued to work for the betterment of the city and the church for ten years. During this period he and two other men organized the North Carolina Institution for the Instruction of the Deaf and Dumb.

From February 1836 to July 1837 McPheeters served as administrator and teacher of a female school in Fayetteville. He resigned that position to become a representative for the Board of Domestic Missions of the General Assembly of the Presbyterian Church, serving until the spring of 1839. Because of his knowledge, integrity, amiable personality, and compassion, he was an accepted and admired leader in the courts of the church. For many years he was a trustee of The University of North Carolina. In 1840 he was offered the presidency of Davidson College but declined the appointment for reasons of poor health.

McPheeters was a man of learning and personal magnetism. As a teacher he was a severe disciplinarian but was greatly admired. In recognition of his abilities and contributions, The University of North Carolina awarded him an honorary doctor of divinity degree in 1819. He enjoyed great physical strength—although short and rather plump, he was very muscular. His influence on the social and religious life of Raleigh was substantial, and he took much pride in the city's progress.

In 1812 McPheeters married, for a third time, Margaret Ann Curry McDaniel of Washington, N.C. They had twelve children, many of whom distinguished themselves in various professions. After several years of poor health, he died at his home in Raleigh at age sixty-five and was buried in the City Cemetery. A portrait hangs in the First Presbyterian Church, Raleigh.

SEE: First Presbyterian Church, Raleigh, *One Hundred Twenty-fifth Anniversary* (1941); William Henry Foote, *Sketches of Virginia, Historical and Biographical* (1855); Alfred Nevin, *Encyclopedia of the Presbyterian Church in the United States of America* (1884); North Carolina Museum of Art, *Jacob Marling Retrospective Exhibition* (1964 [portrait]); Raleigh *News and Observer*, 24 Apr. 1966; Raleigh *Register*, 8 Nov. 1842.

ALBERT S. EDWARDS

McQueen, Hugh (*ca. 1800–1 Apr. 1855*), orator and politician, was the oldest son of Murdo (Murdoch) McQueen of Chatham County. His father had come to North Carolina from Scotland in 1795, bringing with him a colony of Scots. In the same year Murdo purchased a thousand acres in lower Chatham County between the Deep River and the Brooks and Petty creeks, where young Hugh was born and raised. He had a number of brothers and sisters, but the name of their mother is unknown.

McQueen received his early education at home, achieving enough academic proficiency to enter The University of North Carolina in 1818. During his single year at the university, he became a member of the Philanthropic Society and achieved recognition as an orator. He was present at the commencement of 1822 but did not receive a degree. In 1829 he entered the North Carolina House of Commons as a representative from Chatham County; he also served in 1831 and 1832. In 1834 he won a seat in the state senate, serving in 1834 and 1835. He was a trustee of The University of North Carolina from 1833 to 1845.

At the 1835 constitutional convention in North Carolina, McQueen was a challenging figure. His brilliant oratory stressed the need for education and for constitutional provisions that would result in the economic stability necessary for the growth of schools. The educa-

tional reforms he proposed were gradually adopted in future years.

McQueen moved to Chapel Hill from Chatham County in 1835 and in 1836 published his first newspaper, the *Columbian Repository*. It survived only a few weeks, but this did not discourage McQueen, who later became the editor of the Chapel Hill *Emerald* and of the Raleigh *Star* for brief periods. While editor of the *Star* in 1839, he moved to Wake County and remained there until he left the state.

Between 1839 and 1842, McQueen reached his peak of achievement in North Carolina. In Chapel Hill the Philanthropic Society called upon him to deliver the alumni address at the commencement of 1839. Recently there had been unrest in the Dialectic Society, and in his remarks McQueen urged the students to stand by the university as well as the Dialectic and Philanthropic societies. This speech, presented in Gerrard Hall on 26 June 1839, the evening preceding graduation, was so well received by alumni and the graduating class that it was printed in August 1839 by the Raleigh *Register* at the request of the Philanthropic Society.

In 1840 McQueen became the attorney general of North Carolina. He held this position until, for unknown reasons, he resigned and moved to Texas in 1842. Later, he earned distinction with the publication of his book, *The Orator's Touchstone*, by Harper Brothers of New York in 1854.

According to the *LaGrange* (Tex.) *Paper*, for 7 Apr. 1855, Hugh McQueen had died a few days earlier. He was buried in the public graveyard in LaGrange. The paper noted that McQueen had been a member of the Galveston and LaGrange bar associations. The myths about his heroism in the Texas rebellion and his death under Sam Houston are all unfounded. He was never known to marry, and no descendants can be found.

SEE: Daniel L. Grant, *Alumni History of the University of North Carolina, 1795–1924* (1924); *LaGrange* (Tex.) *Paper*, 7 Apr. 1855; Hugh McQueen, *The Orator's Touchstone* (1854); John H. Wheeler, *Historical Sketches of North Carolina from 1584 to 1851* (1851).

CLAUDE II. SNOW, JR.

McQueen, John (*9 Feb. 1804–30 Aug. 1867*), congressman, Confederate official, lawyer, and planter, was born in Queensdale, near the town of Maxton, Robeson County. Educated by private tutors, he was graduated from The University of North Carolina. In 1827 he moved across the state line to Bennettsville, the most prominent town in Marlboro District, S.C., where he read law and was admitted to practice in 1828. McQueen's early career is rather obscure. He apparently did not become a political candidate until he unsuccessfully sought the congressional seat of Alexander Dromgole Sims in 1844.

During the 1830s McQueen established himself as a successful lawyer and prominent member of the community. He served in the state militia from 1833 to 1837. It is not known what rank he attained, but a county history refers to him as General McQueen. On 12 Dec. 1830 an Academical Society was organized at Bennettsville, and McQueen's name appears along with those of other influential citizens as a signer of its constitution. McQueen, John McCollum, C. W. Dudley, Nathan B. Thomas, and E. W. Jones comprised the board of trustees. McQueen was also active in promoting industry. Marlboro District's first cotton factory, built in 1836, was organized by a joint stock company consisting of John

Williams of Society Hill, John Taylor of Cheraw, and William T. Ellerbe and John McQueen of Bennettsville. Between 1830 and 1840, McQueen's financial situation improved markedly. Unmarried in 1830, he owned a single slave. By 1840 he was married and had one son; he owned seventy-two slaves, twenty-eight of whom were employed in agriculture and fifteen in industry. Some of them may have worked at the cotton factory, which employed slave labor.

In 1848 Alexander D. Sims died shortly after his reelection to Congress, and McQueen was elected to fill the vacancy. He served in the House of Representatives until his retirement on 21 Dec. 1860, the day after the South Carolina convention passed the Ordinance of Secession. In the House McQueen did not often appear as an orator. During the various political crises of the 1850s, he voted as a states' rights Democrat and advocated resistance by the South on the issues of the tariff and the admission of California as a state, the subject of his initial speech in Congress. He thought that secession was inevitable and that the South should risk the consequences rather than abandon what he considered to be Southern rights and liberties. In South Carolina's first election after secession, McQueen won a seat in the Confederate Congress.

After the war he retired from public life and settled in Society Hill near Darlington, S.C. He was buried in the Episcopal cemetery at Society Hill. There is a photograph of McQueen in the Manuscripts Division of the South Caroliniana Library; it was probably taken for Charles Lanman's first edition of the *Biographical Directory of the American Congress.*

SEE: *Biog. Dir. Am. Cong.* (1950); *Charleston Daily Courier,* 2 Sept. 1867; *Charleston Mercury,* 2 Sept. 1867; J. A. W. Thomas, *A History of Marlboro County,* 2d ed. (1971); U.S. Census, 1830, 1840, Marlboro District.

A. H. STOKES, JR.

McRae, Colin John (*22 Oct. 1812–February 1877*), businessman and Confederate official, was one of eleven children of Elizabeth Mary and John M. McRae, a merchant of Sneedsboro (now McFarlan) in Anson County. Colin moved with his family in 1818 to Winchester, Miss., where his father quickly established a successful trading and commission merchant business that operated its own barges to ply local rivers and ocean-going schooners to carry cotton to domestic ports. In 1827 the family moved to the mouth of the Pascagoula River in Jackson County. McRae and his brothers boarded with a French family at Pascagoula and attended Frederick's School, operated by one of Napoleon's former officers. After receiving additional tutoring, he attended a small Jesuit college in Biloxi for a year. McRae took over his father's business when he died on 11 Mar. 1835 and remained devoted to his family for the rest of his life. He never married. His brother, John Jones, became governor and senator of Mississippi in the 1850s.

In 1837 McRae helped to organize the Mississippi City Company, which established the town of Mississippi City on the Gulf coast west of Pascagoula. He served one term in the Mississippi legislature in 1838 but did not stand for reelection. In 1840 he moved his successful cotton factorage and commission merchant business to Mobile, Ala., and in 1842 formed a partnership with his brother-in-law, Burwell Boykin. With his brother John, he bought stock in and promoted the Mobile and Ohio and the Mobile and New Orleans railroad companies and speculated in land.

With the advent of secession, McRae served the Confederacy in various capacities. Always a strong states' rights Democrat, he supported the secession of Alabama. In January 1861 he was elected to the Provisional Confederate Congress, which inaugurated the Confederate government. His major concerns were the defense of Mobile, the preparation of war, and making provision for privateering. At McRae's urging, the Confederate government in 1862 purchased the Selma Manufacturing Company for the manufacture of ordnance, armor plate, and munitions and appointed him as agent to supervise its establishment and operation.

McRae's major contribution to the Confederacy was as chief financial agent in Europe from May 1863 to the end of the war. When he arrived in Europe, the Erlanger loan agreement had been concluded and his duty was to manage the sale of bonds and disburse the proceeds. In September 1863 all Confederate financial transactions of the War and Navy departments were centralized under McRae's authority. At his suggestion, the Confederate government assumed control of all blockade-running in 1864 in order to improve credit in Europe and secure essential supplies for the Confederacy. The major sources of McRae's funds were loans and cotton credits, and he never had enough money. In 1864 he was engaged in an unsuccessful attempt to recruit Polish exiles in Europe for the Confederate service. The capture of Fort Fisher in January 1865 closed the Confederacy's last blockade-running port and virtually ended his duties. English creditors and the United States sued McRae for Confederate assets, but by the time the court of equity ruled that U.S. claims took precedence, he had no assets. Although he was in personal financial straits, McRae remained in England to arrange a legal defense fund for Jefferson Davis. Believing that he would not be pardoned if he returned home, he moved to Puerto Cortés, British Honduras, in October 1867, where he acquired a plantation and a store.

McRae, about six feet tall, was of medium build and had light brown hair and blue eyes. A shrewd business manager, he was energetic, impatient, and scrupulous in keeping commitments. He died in Puerto Cortés.

SEE: Charles S. Davis, *Colin J. McRae: Confederate Financial Agent* (1961 [portrait]); Frank L. Owsley, *King Cotton Diplomacy* (1931); Dunbar Rowland, ed., *Jefferson Davis: Constitutionalist* (1923); U.S. War Department, *The War of the Rebellion,* ser. 1, vols. 6, 15, 34, 41, 52–53, and ser. 4, vols. 1–3 (1882–1900); Ezra J. Warner and W. Buck Yearns, *Biographical Register of the Confederate Congress* (1975).

JOHN L. BELL, JR.

McRae, Duncan Kirkland (*16 Aug. 1820–12 Feb. 1888*), lawyer, diplomat, and Confederate officer, was born in Fayetteville, the son of John (1793–1880), a local editor and postmaster, and Margaret S. Kirkland McRae (1797–1820). He attended local schools before entering The University of North Carolina in 1835. In 1837 he transferred to the College of William and Mary, where he was graduated with high honors. After studying law with Judge Robert Strange, he was admitted to the bar in 1841. Setting up a practice in Oxford, McRae quickly gained prominence as an outstanding criminal lawyer and speaker. His reputation for oratory perhaps was the basis for the legend that on the visit of the Marquis de Lafayette in 1825, five-year-old Duncan gave an eloquent speech of welcome at a public reception for the general. After just a few months in Oxford, McRae left to serve the State Department as a courier of dispatches to Mexico City.

His political beliefs did not follow party lines; he had strong Whig sympathies on many issues, having been schooled in the Calhoun brand of states' rights democracy. Joining the Democratic party, he sought his first elective office in 1842, when he was chosen to represent his native county in the state House of Commons.

After this single term in the legislature, McRae decided that he preferred practicing law and he opened an office in Raleigh. During his seven years there he became an expert in criminal law and, according to the North Carolina Bar Association (*Proceedings*, 1920), the "greatest criminal lawyer the State has produced." In 1851 he moved to Wilmington to take up a banking venture while also continuing his practice. It was during this period that he participated in the case for which he is most renowned, defending his childhood sweetheart, Ann Simpson, who was charged with murdering her husband. She was acquitted, but later McRae said that he knew her to be guilty.

In 1853 he ran for Congress from the Cape Fear District against William S. Ashe, a favorite of the Pierce administration. As a result, largely through the efforts of a colleague of Ashe, North Carolina-born Secretary of the Navy James C. Dobbin, McRae was offered the post of consul to Paris in return for his withdrawal from the race. McRae later claimed that he was drugged into capitulation. As a consul he served as secretary to the Council of American Foreign Ministers and was appointed to be bearer of the Ostend Manifesto from London to Washington, D.C. In 1857 he resigned because of poor health and once again returned to the practice of law, this time in New Bern.

The 1858 state Democratic convention was badly split over whether the proceeds from the sale of public land should be used for internal improvements. Those in favor of the proposal bolted the party and, with the support of the remnants of the American or Know-Nothing Whigs, nominated McRae for governor. Aside from the public land issue, McRae ran on a platform calling for the stimulation of diverse economic development in North Carolina and removal of what he felt was undue emphasis on the slavery issue. The party regulars nominated the ultimate victor—John W. Ellis.

At the outbreak of the Civil War, Ellis appointed McRae a colonel, assigned to duty on 15 July 1861 with the Fifth North Carolina Regiment, which was formed at Halifax that month. Within days the regiment was at Manassas Junction, Va., in General James Longstreet's brigade. It saw its initial action at the first Battle of Manassas on 21 July.

After fighting several small skirmishes while in winter quarters in northern Virginia, the Fifth Regiment, as part of General Jubal Early's brigade, was one of the first to arrive on the peninsula to stop General George G. McClellan's advance on Richmond. At Williamsburg on 5 May 1862, McRae led a gallant charge against a strong Union position commanded by General Winfield S. Hancock, who later stated that the Fifth North Carolina "should have 'immortality' inscribed on their banner." Following the wounding of Early, McRae was given command of the brigade, but he became seriously ill from a minor injury received at Williamsburg and could not assume the post, which then passed to Colonel Samuel Garland.

McRae was able to return as the commander of the Fifth North Carolina for the Battle of Boonsboro (or South Mountain) on 13 Sept. 1862. On the death of Garland early in the battle, he assumed command of the bri-

gade, holding the far right of the Confederate line against heavy frontal assaults until heavy casualties forced him to withdraw. Four days later, at the Battle of Sharpsburg (Antietam), with McRae still in command, the brigade fought in the infamous Corn Field, suffering the loss of the majority of the brigade, including McRae, who was badly wounded. Passed over for promotion, McRae resigned effective 13 Nov. 1862.

On his recovery in 1863, Governor Zebulon B. Vance appointed him as special envoy to southern Europe to find a market for North Carolina cotton and to buy very badly needed supplies. On the successful completion of this mission, he returned to run for a seat in the Confederate Congress but was defeated. He then founded a newspaper, *The Confederate*, at Raleigh, which was an organ for the Davis and Vance administrations. McRae stayed in Raleigh to publish the paper until General William T. Sherman's troops arrived.

After the war, because he felt that the Reconstruction government would not provide an atmosphere in which he could work comfortably, he moved to Memphis, Tenn., to practice law in the firm of McRae and Sneed. He eventually returned to North Carolina in 1880 and practiced in Wilmington.

McRae married Louise Virginia Henry, the daughter of Judge Louis D. Henry of Raleigh, on 8 Oct. 1845. They had three daughters: Margaret Kirkland, Virginia Henry, and Marie. McRae was always rather frail, and his wounds worsened his condition. He spent his last years in rapidly declining health. Seeking special medical attention, he went to Chicago in 1879 and to New York City in the summer of 1887. He died in Brooklyn as a final result of his war injuries and was buried in Woodlawn Cemetery, New York City.

SEE: Walter Clark, ed., *Histories of the Several Regiments and Battalions from North Carolina in the Great War*, vols. 1, 5 (1901); *DAB*, vol. 7 (1934); Clement A. Evans, ed., *Confederate Military History*, vol. 4 (1899); Weymouth T. Jordan, comp., *North Carolina Troops, 1861–1865: A Roster*, vol. 4 (1973); North Carolina Bar Association, *Proceedings* 22, 27 (1920, 1925); Raleigh *News and Observer*, 15 Feb. 1888; *Who Was Who in America*, historical vol. (1967); Wilmington *Morning Star*, 14–15 Feb. 1888.

MARTIN REIDINGER

MacRae, Elizabeth Ann (*13 Nov. 1825–8 Apr. 1907*), missionary and teacher, was born in Marion County, S.C., the daughter of Daniel S. and Harriet Brown Harlee. In 1842 she married Dr. Neill McNair and became the mistress of Argyle, the McNair home in Alma, near Maxton, in Robeson County. They attended Centre Presbyterian Church in Maxton.

Dr. McNair died in 1863, and their only child, David Harlee, was killed at Fort Caswell in July 1864. During the post–Civil War period, Mrs. McNair suffered much at the hands of the Henry Berry Lowry gang. Shortly afterwards she married Alexander MacRae, of Wilmington, who died in 1881. Already reputed as capable of training the young, Mrs. MacRae had been responsible for teaching many of her young relatives and neighbors.

After the death of her second husband, her teaching and missionary work spread throughout the region. A Presbyterian, she began a campaign to organize missionary societies for the women of the Fayetteville Presbytery. Her own minister, Dr. D. H. Hill, encouraged her in her work, but this was not true of a majority of his fellow ministers. Mrs. MacRae faced opposition from the men and a lack of interest among the women. She refused to be deterred, however. At her own expense she visited all the churches of the presbytery scattered over eight large, sparsely populated counties. Since railroads were not always available, she traveled most often by horse and buggy. If no one came to a meeting, she scheduled another one for a later time. Gradually she wore down resistance, and the Missionary Union grew. When she was seventy she traveled eight hundred miles to visit fifty-three communities, and by the end of 1896 she had traveled a total of nearly six thousand miles, generally in an open buggy regardless of the weather.

Meanwhile, Mrs. MacRae continued her teaching. Most of the year she taught in her home community, but she spent her summers teaching in the mountains. Once the success of her missionary societies was assured, she went out in search of a new career. In Banner Elk she established a school for poor mountain girls in a building that cost twenty-five dollars. She had no salary and no source of income. She had to battle suspicion as well as ignorance. She had no equipment or supplies, but she had faith. Mrs. MacRae taught academic subjects during the week and the Bible on Sunday. Her work attracted the attention of Mrs. S. P. Lees, who gave generously in support of the school. From it was established the present-day Lees-MacRae College.

During a five-year terminal illness Mrs. MacRae lived with her stepdaughter, Mrs. J. F. Payne of Wilmington. At her own request, she was buried at Centre Church Cemetery, Maxton.

SEE: Robert C. Lawrence, *The State of Robeson* (1939); Lumberton *Robesonian*, 26 Feb. 1951; John A. Oates, *The Story of Fayetteville and the Upper Cape Fear* (1950).

MAUD THOMAS SMITH

MacRae, Hugh (30 Mar. 1865–20 Oct. 1951), mining engineer, developer, and industrialist, was born in Carbonton, Chatham County, of Scottish and English descent. He was the son of Julia Norton and Donald MacRae, who served as British vice-consul in Wilmington. His grandfather, General Alexander MacRae, was a railroad president. His great-great-grandfather, Ruari Doun (Brown Roderick) MacRae, landed in Wilmington from Scotland in 1770. The MacRaes produced three generations of entrepreneurs whose business enterprises stretched from the mountains to the seacoast of North Carolina and beyond.

Hugh was born in Carbonton, the family's "up-country" summer place, because it was considered safer for his expectant mother than the McRae residence in Wilmington during the fierce fighting for strategic Fort Fisher near the end of the Civil War. When the Federal occupation of Wilmington ended, his family returned home. There and at Bingham School in Asheville he was prepared for college. He entered the Massachusetts Institute of Technology at age sixteen and was graduated in 1885.

Returning to his native state, MacRae worked mica, feldspar, and kaolin deposits as a mining engineer at Bailey Mountain, between Spruce Pine and Burnsville, until 1889. Becoming interested in land development, he acquired 16,000 acres and organized the Linville Company, of which he was president and later chairman of the board of directors. His company developed the mountain resort town of Linville in Avery County and purchased Grandfather Mountain, which, under the management of his grandson, Hugh MacRae Morton, became a major scenic attraction of western North Carolina. The firm also built Yonahlossee Road between Linville and Blowing Rock in Watauga County, using simple tools to carve a highway traversing the highest, most rugged terrain in the eastern United States. In the east, MacRae developed the seacoast resort of Wrightsville Beach.

In 1895 Hugh MacRae became president of the Wilmington Cotton Mills Company. In 1900 he became head of the Wilmington Gas Light Company, which later was merged with the Wilmington Street Railway and the Seacoast Railway to become the Consolidated Railways, Light and Power Company. He continued until 1929 as president of this concern and its successor, the Tide Water Power Company, which became a part of the Carolina Power and Light Company in 1952.

Tide Water drew some of its power from as far away as Blewett Falls, a hydroelectric project of the Great Pee Dee Electric and Power Company, which MacRae persuaded the legislature to charter in 1905. It was authorized to build or develop and operate mills, power companies, transmission lines, railways, turnpikes, telephone and telegraph lines, real estate, and other properties. In 1906 the name was changed to Rockingham Power Company and its authorized capitalization tripled. Blewett Falls and its transmission lines were regarded as pioneers of an infant electric industry.

Along Tide Water's electric trolley route to the beach, MacRae developed the suburban areas of Winter Park, Audubon, and Oleander. The line was extended to Carolina Place, Sunset Park, and Carolina Heights. To develop Wrightsville Beach, he erected a pavilion in 1905–6 and named it Lumina, which was to become legendary for seaside fun and frolic. The picturesque beach trolley made its last run on 26 Apr. 1940, yielding to the horseless carriage.

One of MacRae's beliefs became an agricultural watchword: "The South will come into its own when its fields are green in winter." On his farm, Invershiel, near Rocky Point in Pender County, he experimented for thirty years with a grazing program that supported a Black Angus herd year-round. After little luck in inducing midwestern Americans to exploit his more fertile region, he offered free transportation and a chance to buy farmland to Europeans who would settle in his planned communities. In time MacRae colonized six rural communities in Pender, New Hanover, and Columbus counties—Italians at St. Helena, Hollanders at Castle Hayne and Van Eden, Greeks at Marathon, Poles at Artesia, and Germans and Hungarians at New Berlin. Due to anti-German sentiment during World War I, New Berlin was renamed Delco. Although successful for more than a half century, as were Castle Hayne and St. Helena, the Marathon colony lost its identity as a place name.

His agricultural efforts won MacRae mention as a potential secretary of agriculture during the administration of both Woodrow Wilson and Herbert Hoover. His farm colonization intrigued the New Deal and led to the federal government's Penderlea resettlement project under Rexford G. Tugwell. His "continuous grazing" pastures for inexpensive winter feeding were ascribed value "beyond estimate" for the South. And his influence brought dairies, nurseries, and bulb-growing, blueberry, and truck farms in southeastern North Carolina, where many family names trace back to his settlers from Europe.

MacRae's broad interests included investment banking, and his personal investment left to his heirs large acreages of Appalachian coal resources that were to add enormous value in a future plagued by energy shortages. He was a patron of the arts, a member of St. James's Episcopal Church of Wilmington, a Democrat, and a member of many professional and fraternal groups.

On 4 Feb. 1891 he married Rena Nelson, the daughter of Benjamin Franklin Nelson, and they had three children: Dorothy, Nelson, and Agnes. He was buried in Oakdale Cemetery, Wilmington.

SEE: John Faris Corey, "The Colonization and Contributions of Emmigrants Brought to Southeastern North Carolina by Hugh MacRae" (M.A. thesis, University of North Carolina, 1957); Jack Riley, *Carolina Power and Light Company, 1908–1958* (1958); William Sharpe, *A New Geography of North Carolina*, vol. 1 (1964); James Sprunt, *Chronicles of the Cape Fear River, 1660–1916* (1916); Gary E. Trawick and Paul B. Wyche, *One Hundred Years, One Hundred Men, 1871–1971* (1971); Ina W. Van Noppen and John J. Van Noppen, *Western North Carolina since the Civil War* (1973).

JACK RILEY

MacRae, James Cameron (*6 Oct. 1838–17 Oct. 1909*), jurist, legislator, and educator, was born in Fayetteville, the son of John, the mayor and postmaster of Fayetteville, and Mary Shackleford MacRae, a native of Marion, S.C. He was the brother of Duncan, Thomas Ruffin, Robert Strange, Johanna Carolina, and Alexander.

MacRae received his basic education at Donaldson Academy in Fayetteville, where he was graduated in 1854. He planned to attend The University of North Carolina, but when financial problems prevented this, he secured a position teaching school in Cumberland and Brunswick counties and in Horry County, S.C. Meanwhile, against the advice of his brother Duncan, who wanted James to become a civil engineer, he taught himself the law. By 1859 he was proficient enough to receive his license to practice in county court and a year later in superior court. He entered a practice in Fayetteville with C. W. Broadfoot.

When war came, MacRae enlisted on 17 Apr. 1861 and served as a private in Company H, First North Carolina Regiment, known as the Fayetteville Independent Light Infantry, a military unit in continuous existence since 1793. In May 1861 the company moved to Raleigh and from there into southern Virginia, where on 10 June it encountered Union troops at the Battle of Big Bethel. In August 1861 MacRae was commissioned second lieutenant and transferred to Company D, Fifth Regiment, a part of the defense of Yorktown. This company also saw action at the Battle of Williamsburg.

By 30 May 1862 MacRae was promoted again and ordered to report to the Conscript Bureau in North Carolina. In September 1863 he was assigned under Colonel Peter Mallett as a major of battalion in the North Carolina cavalry. The battalion, later known as MacRae's Battalion, was headquartered in Morganton and Asheville. Its chief purpose was to search out and arrest conscripts and deserters in the western part of the state. When the battalion was disbanded in June 1864, MacRae was ordered back east as the assistant adjutant under General Laurence Baker. In this capacity, MacRae, on 20 Apr. 1865, issued General Order No. 25 which disbanded Baker's troops in compliance with the terms agreed to by General William T. Sherman. MacRae then left the military, returned to Fayetteville, and renewed his law practice.

On 31 Oct. 1867 he married Frances Hinsdale, whose father was a Fayetteville druggist. Because she was Episcopalian, they were married in St. John's Episcopal Church. Though reared a Presbyterian, MacRae now joined his wife's church. The couple had nine children:

James Christopher, Samuel Hinsdale, Cameron Farquhar, Duncan, Theodore, John, Mary Shackleford, Elizabeth, and Frances.

Besides teaching a Bible class in the Episcopal church, MacRae joined the Fayetteville Phoenix Lodge of the Masonic order in April 1867. In politics he was a lifelong Democrat. In 1874 he was elected a Cumberland County representative to the General Assembly. He served on the internal improvements committee and supported a movement to reopen The University of North Carolina, which had closed in 1868.

In April 1881 MacRae presided over the Temperance Convention in Raleigh, even though many people felt that his position favoring prohibition would endanger his nomination to a superior court judgeship. But on 8 July 1882, Governor Thomas J. Jarvis appointed MacRae to take the place of Judge Risden Bennett. In November MacRae was elected to a full term, and he served on the court until 1890. In 1883 The University of North Carolina awarded him an honorary doctor of laws degree.

Prior to the 1890 election, the Fourth and Seventh Judicial districts were combined so that Judge MacRae was pitted against Judge James McIver of Moore County in the contest for superior court judge in that district. On 16 July 1890 at the Democratic nominating convention in Laurinburg, MacRae was defeated by a vote of 163 to 157.

On 24 Aug. 1892 Governor Thomas M. Holt appointed MacRae to take the place of Joseph Davis as associate justice of the North Carolina Supreme Court. In November he was elected to complete the term, serving until 1894, when he was defeated by David Furches. MacRae remained in private practice in Raleigh and was the attorney for the Seaboard Air Line Railway.

In 1899 he moved to Chapel Hill when he was appointed professor and dean of the law school. Under his leadership, the law school expanded in many directions. The curriculum was enlarged to include a combination of two years in liberal arts and two years in law. The practice of inviting members of the bar to be guest lecturers was increased. The moot court was divided into civil and criminal divisions. The number of books in the law library doubled from 1,500 in 1903 to 3,000 in 1909, and a librarian was added to the staff. At the beginning of MacRae's tenure, the law school's physical facilities consisted of two small dormitory rooms. By the end of his term, the school was housed in two large rooms in South Building, and MacRae had begun to advocate a separate building for the law school. Finally, enrollment grew from thirty-eight in 1899 to eighty-two in 1909.

In addition to his teaching and administrative duties, MacRae, at the request of the Bar Association, established and edited the *North Carolina Law Journal*. It was published monthly until 1905, when it was discontinued because a publisher could not be found.

MacRae died in Chapel Hill. After a funeral service at the Chapel of the Cross, his remains were taken by train to Fayetteville, where he was buried in Cross Creek Cemetery.

SEE: Kemp P. Battle, *History of the University of North Carolina*, vol. 2 (1912); Aubrey Brooks and Hugh Lefler, *The Papers of Walter Clark*, vol. 1 (1948); John L. Cheney, Jr., ed., *North Carolina Government, 1585–1974* (1974); Jerome Dowd, *Sketches of Prominent Living North Carolinians* (1888); Clement Evans, ed., *Confederate Military History*, vol. 4 (1899); Duncan MacRae, *The Descendants of James Cameron MacRae and Frances Broadfoot MacRae* (1966); Raleigh *News and Observer*, 28 Apr. 1881, 18 Oct. 1909; *Who Was Who in America*, vol. 1 (1942).

LINDA MYLAN

MacRae, John (*fl. 1774–80*), Loyalist poet and song-writer, born in Kintain, Scotland, was a recognized Gaelic poet and singer before sailing for North Carolina in 1774 and settling on McLendons Creek (now in Moore County). In Gaelic, his name was Iain mac Mhurchaidh 'ic Fhearchair. MacRae was among the Highland Scots defeated in February 1776 by the Patriots at Moore's Creek Bridge, where his son Murdock was fatally wounded. During the American Revolution his Loyalist sentiments kept him in trouble, his taxes were increased, and finally, if legend can be trusted, he was captured and put to death in retaliation for the fierce devotion to George III expressed in his songs.

His patriotic and autobiographical poems, his lyrics, and his much admired lullaby, "Duanag Altrium," were all written in Gaelic. Most of them were composed during his North Carolina sojourn and, it is said, are still sung and recited in Nova Scotia and Scotland. MacRae's songs and poems are included in *Gaelic Bards from 1715 to 1765* (1892) and *Mactalla nan Tur* (1901), collections compiled by A. Maclean Sinclair.

SEE: Charles W. Dunn, "A North Carolina Gaelic Bard," *North Carolina Historical Review* 36 (October 1959); James MacKenzie, "The Odyssey of John MacRae," *State* magazine (Raleigh), 1 Dec. 1971.

RICHARD WALSER

McRae, John Jones (*10 Jan. 1815–31 May 1868*), editor, governor of Mississippi, U.S. senator, and Confederate congressman, was born in McFarlan, Anson County, the son of Elizabeth Mary and John H. McRae. In 1818 his family moved to Mississippi and settled at Winchester. His father's success as a trader and commission merchant, with his own fleet of barges and schooners, made it desirable for the McRaes to move to the mouth of the Pascagoula River in Jackson County in 1827. John Jones was educated at Frederick's School in Pascagoula, by private tutors, and at Miami University, in Ohio, from which he was graduated in 1834. After studying law at Pearlington in Hancock County, he was admitted to the bar in 1835.

After practicing law, McRae edited the *Eastern Clarion* at Paulding in the 1840s. During the depression of 1840 he suffered financial losses that he never regained. His first venture into politics resulted in his election as a Democrat to the lower house of the legislature in 1848 and as speaker in 1850. He served in the U.S. Senate from 19 Dec. 1851 to 17 Mar. 1852, filling out the unexpired term of Jefferson Davis until a successor could be elected.

McRae's major political contribution was as governor of Mississippi for two full terms (January 1854–January 1858). His achievements included the establishment of an institution for the deaf and dumb, completion of the hospital for the insane, the state investment of $1.5 million in railroads, and the adoption of a code of laws. McRae and his brother especially pushed the development of the Mobile and Ohio Railroad. Elected to fill the unexpired term of Congressman John A. Quitman, McRae was elected to another full term, serving from December 1858 until January 1861, when he withdrew in support of the secession of his state.

He was most noted for his advocacy of reopening the African slave trade and seceding if Abraham Lincoln won the presidency. When Lincoln was elected, McRae counseled secession. As an elected member of the lower house of the Confederate Congress from 1862 to 1864, he was committed to the program of the Davis administration. Disaffected by the conduct of the war in Missis-

sippi, his constituents did not return him to Congress. When the war ended, McRae was in ill health and "utter despair." In May 1868 he departed for Belize, British Honduras, to visit his brother Colin and died a few days after his arrival.

In 1835 McRae married a Mrs. McGuire, a widow. In personal appearance he was of slight build, and in temperament he was high-strung and excitable. In deportment he was genial, generous, frank, and courteous to all persons.

SEE: *Appleton's Cyclopedia of American Biography*, vol. 4 (1888); *Biog. Dir. Am. Cong.* (1961); *Congressional Globe* (1851–52, 1858–61); Charles S. Davis, *Colin J. McRae: Confederate Financial Agent* (1961); Reuben Davis, *Recollection of Mississippi and Mississippians* (1889); Clement Eaton, *Jefferson Davis* (1977); Robert Lowry and William H. McCardle, *A History of Mississippi* (1891); *Nat. Cyc. Am. Biog.*, vol. 13 (1906 [portrait]); *New York Times*, 12 June 1868; Percy L. Rainwater, *Mississippi: Storm Center of Secession, 1856–1861* (1938); Dunbar Rowland, *History of Mississippi*, 4 vols. (1925); Jon L. Wakelyn, ed., *Biographical Dictionary of the Confederacy* (1977).

JOHN L. BELL, JR.

MacRae, William (*9 Sept. 1834–11 Feb. 1882*), railroad manager, civil engineer, and Confederate general, was born in Wilmington. His family was descended from the clan MacRae from Rosshire on the seacoast of the western Highlands of Scotland, and its members participated with great valor in wars from the Crusades to Waterloo. MacRae's father, General Alexander MacRae, was an officer in the War of 1812 and was destined to lead a battalion of infantry in the Civil War though nearly seventy years of age; he was also a civil engineer and president of the Wilmington and Weldon Railroad. MacRae's mother was the daughter of Zilpah McClammy. All of MacRae's eight brothers served in the army or navy, one of them remaining with the Union during the Civil War and fighting against his brothers and father.

William MacRae was raised in affluence and given the benefits of private education. At an early age he developed a fascination for railroads and did much study in this area. At age sixteen he left home and took a job with I. P. Morris and Company of Philadelphia, where he learned the trades of locomotive builder and skilled machinist. In this capacity he served as an apprentice until he was twenty-one, then returned to North Carolina to work in the machine shops of the Wilmington and Weldon Railroad. Here he became a locomotive engineer and track boss. Afterwards MacRae took up the study of civil engineering under his brother, John C., as well as under his father and worked with them in North Carolina, South Carolina, and Florida.

The outbreak of the Civil War found MacRae working as assistant engineer of the Carolina Central Railroad at Monroe. He enlisted in the Confederate army as a private in a company known as the Monroe Light Infantry. This company soon became Company B of the Fifteenth North Carolina Regiment, of which MacRae was elected captain on 1 May 1861. The regiment was ordered to Virginia but was soon hurried back to North Carolina to reinforce General L. O'B. Branch at Goldsboro after the Battle of New Bern. Once again transferred to Virginia, the regiment became part of the brigade of General Howell Cobb of John B. Magruder's (later Lafayette McLaws's) command and saw service in the Peninsular and Seven Days' campaigns. On 2 May 1862 Captain MacRae was promoted to lieutenant colonel of the regiment. On 1 July the regiment participated in the Battle of Malvern Hill, the closing engagement of the Seven Days' campaign, where 164 out of 600 men were killed or wounded. In the Maryland campaign, the regiment took part in the fighting at Crampton's Gap during the Battle of South Mountain, on 14 Sept. 1862, where another 186 men were either killed, wounded, or captured. In the bloody Battle of Sharpsburg three days later, Lieutenant Colonel MacRae succeeded to the command of the brigade in the absence of General Thomas R. R. Cobb and, the brigade reduced to 250 men, repelled three attacks of the enemy, falling back with only 50 men remaining and ammunition exhausted.

In the autumn of 1862 MacRae and the Fifteenth North Carolina were transferred to the all–North Carolina brigade of General John R. Cooke and on 13 December participated in the Battle of Fredericksburg. Stationed on Marye's Heights, the Fifteenth North Carolina suffered a terrible loss of 274 out of 563 men killed and wounded. In early 1863 Cooke's brigade was transferred to South Carolina, and the Fifteenth North Carolina was stationed to guard the Charleston and Savannah Railroad, where it was engaged in heavy skirmishing. On 27 February MacRae was commissioned colonel of the Fifteenth North Carolina. In April Cooke's brigade was ordered back to Virginia and, in passing through North Carolina, took part in the Battle of Bachelor's Creek outside New Bern. Arriving at Richmond, the brigade remained there through the summer of 1863. In October Cooke's brigade joined General Henry Heth's division of General Robert E. Lee's army in the Bristoe Station campaign. In the Battle of Bristoe Station MacRae was complimented by General Lee for his valor.

In the spring of 1864 he participated with Cooke's brigade on the right flank at the Battle of the Wilderness (5–6 May), at Spotsylvania Court House (8–21 May), and at Cold Harbor (June). On 23 June MacRae was promoted to the rank of temporary brigadier general, to rank from 22 June, and was assigned to the command of the brigade of General William W. Kirkland, who had been wounded at Cold Harbor. This force consisted of the Eleventh, Twenty-sixth, Forty-fourth, Forty-seventh, and Fifty-second North Carolina regiments. One of MacRae's officers said that "he [MacRae] could place his command in position quicker and infuse more of his fighting qualities into his men than any other officer I ever saw . . . [he] changed the physical expression of the whole command in less than two weeks, and gave the men an infinite faith in him and in themselves which was never lost, not even when they grounded arms at Appomattox." MacRae's brigade served in the siege of Petersburg and on 25 Aug. 1864, with the North Carolina brigades of James Lane and John Cooke, took part in the Battle of Reams's Station on the old Weldon Railroad. These brigades attacked and drove the Union II Corps from its entrenchments, capturing flags, nine pieces of artillery, and over two thousand prisoners. The success of the attack was due to General MacRae's selecting the right moment to attack without orders, and he was again complimented by General Lee.

Later MacRae was given a separate command on the extreme right of the Confederate line near Poplar Spring Church. He commanded his own brigade, Archer's Infantry, a battalion of artillery, and General James Dearing's cavalry brigade. When Union forces attacked Fort Harrison near Richmond, MacRae was ordered to take part of his command and help reinforce Richmond on 30 Sept. 1864. During his absence, Union soldiers attacked and captured the position he had been holding. MacRae returned at 5:00 P.M. on the thirtieth, however, and recaptured part of the lost ground. In the first Battle

of Hatcher's Run, or Burgess's Mill, on 27 October, MacRae attacked the Union lines and broke through, capturing a battery. Holding the position until that night, he received no support and, nearly surrounded, had to fall back. He had carried 1,050 men into the action and lost all but 525. On 5 Nov. 1864 MacRae was made a permanent brigadier general, in accordance with a special congressional law of October 1862, to rank from 4 November.

MacRae was not present at the second Battle of Hatcher's Run, during 5–7 Feb. 1865, where some of the Confederate units were badly battered. Of the battle MacRae's corps commander, General A. P. Hill, said: "Had William MacRae been here, the result would have been different." MacRae's brigade participated in the retreat to Appomattox in April 1865 and was the last brigade to stack arms at the surrender. MacRae had been wounded only once in the war, when he was shot through the jaw, but his sword was shot in half on two occasions and his hat and clothing were pierced by bullets and shell fragments many times.

After the war he returned to North Carolina penniless and in January 1866 was appointed general superintendent of the Wilmington and Manchester Railroad. The war had left this organization in severe disarray, but within a short time MacRae was able to get it functioning properly. He later managed the Macon and Brunswick Railroad, making it such a profitable organization that northern capitalists were vying for its control and ownership.

In 1873 MacRae became general superintendent of the Western and Atlantic (State) Railroad of Georgia. Eventually his health began to deteriorate as a result of overwork and exposure. Finally, he resigned his position and went to Florida, hoping to gain relief and some rest in the warm climate. The lung disease that was gripping him was too far advanced, however, and he set out for Wilmington where he wished to spend his last days. While stopping over at a hotel in Augusta, Ga., he was seized with a congestive chill and died. Tragically, he was only forty-seven. His remains were returned to Wilmington for burial in Oakdale Cemetery.

General MacRae was a brilliant and energetic man, recognized as one of the best railroad managers in the country and certainly one of the finest brigade commanders in Lee's army. It was generally understood that if the war had continued, he would have been made a major general. He never married.

SEE: Lucy Anderson, "Confederate Generals from the Old North State" (typescript, North Carolina Collection, University of North Carolina, Chapel Hill); *At Home and Abroad* 6, no. 6 (1882); Walter Clark, ed., *Histories of the Several Regiments and Battalions from North Carolina in the Great War, 1861–1865*, 5 vols. (1901); Clement A. Evans, ed., *Confederate Military History*, vol. 4 (1899); John Moore, *Roster of North Carolina Troops* (1881); James Sprunt, *Chronicles of the Cape Fear River, 1660–1916* (1916); Charles Manly Stedman, *Memorial Address on the Life and Character of Gen. William MacRae, with an Account of the Battle of Reams' Station* [1890]; Ezra J. Warner, *Generals in Gray* (1959); *Wilmington Daily Review*, 13 Feb. 1882; *Wilmington Weekly Star*, 17 Feb. 1882; Marcus J. Wright, comp., *General Officers of the Confederate Army* (1911).

PAUL BRANCH

McRee, Griffith John (20 Sept. 1819–28 Apr. 1872), author of the *Life and Correspondence of James Iredell*, an associate justice of the U.S. Supreme Court, was born in

New Hanover County, the older son of Dr. James Fergus, of Scottish and Scotch-Irish descent, and Mary Ashe Hill McRee, the daughter of William H. Hill and the granddaughter of John Ashe. He was the nephew of colonels William and Samuel McRee and Joseph Alston Hill. Young McRee was educated at academies in Pittsboro and Raleigh and at Princeton, from which he was graduated in 1838 in the same class with Lawrence O'B. Branch. In 1842 he married Penelope Johnston Iredell, the daughter of Governor James Iredell and the granddaughter of Judge James Iredell, Revolutionary leader and U.S. Supreme Court justice.

McRee practiced law in Wilmington, operated a rice plantation at Schawfields north of the city, and was an unsuccessful Whig candidate for the General Assembly in 1844. His avocation, however, was writing. His known antebellum productions, other than his major work on Iredell, include poetry that appeared in the Wilmington press; some still-interesting humorous sketches satirizing local foibles, published in a pamphlet entitled *Squibs* (n.d.); a sketch of Cornelius Harnett (Raleigh *Register*, 3 Aug. 1844); an account of colonial Wilmington (Wilmington *Chronicle*, 2 and 16 Sept. 1846); *A Memoir of Major Griffith J. McRee of the Continental Line of North Carolina* (n.d.), about his grandfather; "An Exposition of Major McRee's Differences with General Greene," unpublished; a memoir of John Alexander Lillington (ca. 1854), unpublished until it appeared in the *University of North Carolina Magazine* (new ser., 8 [1888]); *A Memoir of General John Ashe, of the Revolution* (1854), in collaboration with Archibald MacLaine Hooper; and a memoir of Hooper (*U.N.C. Magazine* 4 [February 1855]). His public lectures on Timothy Bloodworth (1855) and on the ratification of the U.S. Constitution in North Carolina (1857) are lost, but a manuscript of a lecture on the Regulators, given in 1860, has survived.

McRee's interest in the history of North Carolina was first aroused by family papers and by numerous associations of local places and families with events of the Revolution. The interest was further stimulated by exchanges with David L. Swain and Eli W. Caruthers. In his *Life and Correspondence of James Iredell*, McRee hoped to substantiate the contributions of North Carolina to the Revolution, which he thought had been slighted, as well as to redeem the low intellectual reputation of the state. The two-volume work on Iredell, published in New York by D. Appleton and Company (1857–58), was paid for out of his own pocket. It earned what was for the author disappointingly small recognition in North Carolina. However, it brought McRee invitations to membership in the New England, New York, and Wisconsin historical societies in his own day, and it has remained a useful work. Combining Iredell's letters, diary, and public papers of the colonial, Revolutionary, and early national eras with McRee's own research and interpretations, it certainly made public much otherwise unknown material, and it was possibly the most significant historical work produced in antebellum North Carolina. In his skill and integrity as an editor of documents, McRee equaled or surpassed the standards of the time. A graceful style free from the excessive ornamentation of the period, a critical and at times even ironical spirit, and the relative moderation in the expression of his family, state, and sectional feelings made McRee, as a historian, a match for a number of his better-known contemporaries.

Despite the strong Federalist-Whig tradition of his family, McRee viewed secession optimistically. He entered the Confederate army but, chronically in bad health, served as a clerk. His only known postbellum

writings are some unidentified contributions to Francis S. Drake's *Dictionary of American Biography Containing Nearly Ten Thousand Notices* (1872). At age fifty-two he died of "consumption." An Episcopalian, he was survived by six children. No likeness has been found, but McRee was described in youth as short and thickset, good-natured and humorous. He was buried in a vault at Hilton, his father's and once Cornelius Harnett's plantation. About 1904 the remains were moved to an unmarked grave in Oakdale Cemetery, Wilmington.

SEE: Griffith John McRee Papers (Southern Historical Collection, University of North Carolina, Chapel Hill); Griffith John McRee's own works; Clyde Wilson, "Griffith John McRee: An Unromantic Historian of the Old South," *North Carolina Historical Review* 47 (January 1970).

CLYDE WILSON

McRee, James Fergus (*18 Nov. 1794–9 Aug. 1869*), physician, was born at Lilliput plantation, Brunswick County, the son of Major Griffith John and Ann Fergus McRee and the brother of Colonel William McRee. He received a medical degree from the Medical College of New York in 1814 and established a practice in Wilmington about 1819. McRee also studied botany under Dr. Nathaniel Hill in Wilmington, specializing in medical botany. He is credited with having introduced to North Carolina such food plants as tapioca, rhubarb, cantaloupe, and artichokes, and he collaborated with Moses Ashley Curtis and Hardy Bryan Croom in botanical investigations.

Participating in local affairs, McRee supported the building of the Wilmington and Weldon Railroad and was one of the organizers of the New Hanover County Medical Society, of which he was also president. He received high praise for his work among victims of a yellow fever epidemic that struck Wilmington in 1821. McRee retired first in 1834 or 1835 and settled at Rocky Point as a planter and a student of botany. He resumed his practice in 1837, however, until a second retirement in 1846.

McRee married Mary Ashe Hill on 14 Nov. 1816. She was the daughter of William Henry Hill, one of President John Adams's "midnight judges" and a brother of Dr. Nathaniel Hill, under whom McRee studied botany. They were the parents of two sons: Griffith John, the historian, and James F., a physician and surgeon in the Confederate army. McRee was a vestryman of St. James's Church, Wilmington. He died suddenly in Wilmington at age seventy-five.

SEE: William Carter Mebane, Jr., medical history in *Wilmington Daily Journal*, 10 Aug. 1869; *New England Historical and Genealogical Register* 28 (1874); New Hanover County Medical Auxiliary, *The Lonely Road: A History of the Physics and Physicians of the Lower Cape Fear, 1735–1976* (1978); Clyde Wilson, "Griffith John McRee: An Unromantic Historian of the Old South," *North Carolina Historical Review* 47 (January 1970); Thomas F. Wood, "James Fergus McRee, M.D.: A Biographical Sketch with Portrait," *North Carolina Medical Journal* 29 (January 1892).

JEAN POOLE

McRee, William (*13 Dec. 1787–15 May 1833*), career army officer, was born in Wilmington, the oldest son of ten children of Major Griffith J. McRee, of the North Carolina Continental Line, and his wife, Ann Fergus.

Two of his brothers, Griffith John and James Fergus, became physicians; another brother, Samuel, entered the army and rose to the rank of major during the Mexican War; and a sister, Margaret Ann, married one Dr. Morrison who was a naval surgeon.

McRee attended Bingham's Academy at Pittsboro and in 1803, after his father's death, received an appointment to the U.S. Military Academy at West Point. After his graduation he was commissioned second lieutenant of engineers on 1 July 1805. Various promotions and assignments followed, including first lieutenant (1806), commander of the Engineer Department at Charleston, S.C. (1807), captain (1808), and major (31 July 1812).

At the outbreak of war with Great Britain in 1812, McRee was given charge of completing the fortifications of Fort Jackson at Savannah and of rebuilding Fort Wayne. From there he was sent to Charleston to construct a military hospital. Consulted by General Thomas Pinckney as to the ordnance necessary to seize St. Augustine and blockade the harbor, the "principal Engineer in this Department," as McRee was called, gave a critical estimate that persuaded Pinckney not to be hasty. He was highly regarded by the general, who praised his "talents and experience" when McRee was transferred to the northern front.

Appointed chief engineer and chief of artillery for Major General Wade Hampton in 1813, McRee took part in the abortive attacks along the Châteauguay River near Montreal. In the campaigns of the following year under the command of Major General Jacob Brown, he distinguished himself in the Battle of Niagara, for which he was brevetted lieutenant colonel, and in the defense of Fort Erie, for which he was brevetted colonel. In addition to serving as a staff officer and adviser to his commanding general, McRee constructed a bridge across the Chippawa River prior to the battle of that name, planned the capture of British artillery on the heights of Niagara, occasionally manned a piece of artillery during battle, and supervised the construction of American fortifications at Fort Erie. On 23 Aug. 1814 Brigadier General Edmund P. Gaines wrote: "To Major McRea [sic], chief engineer, the greatest credit is due for the excellent arrangement and skilful execution of his plans for fortifying and defending the right, and for his correct and seasonable suggestions in regaining the bastion." Brown spoke of his "high military talents" and regarded him as "worthy of the highest trust and confidence." General Winfield Scott, reminiscing in 1843, said of McRee, with whom he had served, "In my opinion and perhaps in that of the whole Army he combined more genius and military science with high courage than any other officer who participated in the War of 1812."

With the treaty of peace came a reduction of the army and thereby little opportunity for advancement. In a postwar assignment, McRee was sent to Europe in 1815 to examine foreign military schools and fortifications and to purchase books for the West Point Library. In 1816 the United States invited the French general, Simon Bernard, to give the government advice on American fortifications; McRee was a member of the committee assigned to assist him, but he considered himself to be more qualified for the work than Bernard. He did not receive a lineal commission as lieutenant colonel until 12 Nov. 1818, while he was a member of the Board of Engineers for projecting a system of Atlantic coastal defense as a part of this program. It was perhaps largely because of his lingering unhappiness about the naming of a French officer over him that McRee, on 31 Mar. 1819, resigned his commission.

As a civilian McRee held the post of surveyor general of the United States for the Illinois, Missouri, and Arkansas territories. He also served as U.S. commissioner for locating the "National Road" west of the Ohio River. His letters written from the West are filled with interesting and descriptive detail.

McRee never married, lived frugally, assisted his friends, and bought and read a great many books. He admired the military careers of Julius Caesar, Napoleon, and Frederick the Great; he also venerated the law and, perhaps oddly, was fond of the poetry of Lord Byron. Described as being "below the ordinary stature," pale, with a high forehead, gray-blue eyes, and a "prominent, straight and handsome nose," his dress was "remarkably plain." He was reportedly modest and shy, of no political persuasion, grave and dignified. He died of Asiatic cholera at St. Louis, Mo., on the eve of his appointment to survey the boundary between the United States and Mexico. He was buried in St. Louis. There is a silhouette of him in Benson J. Lossing's *Pictorial Field Book of the War of 1812* (1868).

SEE: *Biographical Register of the Officers and Graduates of the U.S. Military Academy*, vol. 1 (1891); Francis Heitman, *Historical Register and Dictionary of the United States Army*, vol. 1 (1916); Sarah M. Lemmon, *Frustrated Patriots: North Carolina and the War of 1812* (1973); Griffith J. McRee, *A Memoir of Major Griffith J. McRee of the Continental Line of North Carolina* (n.d.); *Memoir of Colonel William McRee* (1833?) (copy in the North Carolina Collection, University of North Carolina, Chapel Hill); *Niles' Register*, 29 June 1833; *North Carolina Medical Journal* 29 (January 1892); *North Carolina University Magazine* 1 (June 1844); John H. Wheeler, ed., *Reminiscences and Memoirs of North Carolina and Eminent North Carolinians* (1884).

SARAH MCCULLOH LEMMON

McVea, Emilie Watts (17 Feb. 1867–26 July 1928), nationally recognized educator, was born in Clinton, La., the daughter of Judge Charles and Emilie Rose Watts McVea. Her ancestry was Scottish and French. After Judge McVea's death, Mrs. McVea moved with her young daughters to Raleigh to be near her sister, Mrs. John Esten Cooke Smedes, wife of the second president of St. Augustine's College. Young Emilie was educated at St. Mary's School in Raleigh (1877–84), where her record was outstanding. She remained active in St. Mary's alumnae affairs and in the Episcopal church throughout her life.

In 1886 she returned to St. Mary's to teach and in 1898 became lady principal. She worked with the Reverend Dr. Bennett Smedes, second rector of the school, to enrich the curriculum. She was, according to her students, an inspiring teacher who made her classes in literature and history "an unforgettable experience . . . an introduction to life." Scholarly and deeply religious, she was also forthright and tough-minded. Perceptive, friendly, and witty, she was so quick to sympathize that her young students loved as well as respected "Emmie Mac." A large and energetic woman, she gave the impression of vitality, always accomplishing incredible amounts of work. In reality, she endured chronic poor health that eventually forced her into early retirement.

After the death of Dr. Smedes in February 1899, Miss McVea supervised the school until the new rector, the Reverend Theodore DuBose Bratton, was established. She then began long-planned advanced studies at George Washington University, where she received an A.B. degree in 1902 and an A.M. degree the next year.

She taught English literature briefly at the University of Tennessee, where she was active in extension work with public school teachers. When Dr. Charles W. Dabney, formerly director of the North Carolina Agricultural Experiment Station and then president of the University of Tennessee, was named president of the University of Cincinnati, he recommended Miss McVea for the position of assistant professor of English literature at the latter institution. In 1909 she was elected dean of the Women's Departments.

Emilie McVea's career at the University of Cincinnati was distinguished and her contributions to the life of the city were considerable. When she left Ohio in 1916, she was honored at a civic reception by tributes from the leaders of almost every reform movement of the time. She worked and lectured on behalf of many liberal causes—child labor laws, better secondary schools, more competent teachers in women's colleges, an open university forum, the parity of men and women in university posts, and, above all, the right of women to equal education, equal job opportunities, and suffrage. She also gave lectures in support of the YWCA, and in 1903–4 she served as secretary-treasurer of the Southern Association of College Women. Among the administrators at Cincinnati, she was the indisputably equal colleague whose firmly held convictions came to be "the solidifying force" of the institution, while, according to one of her fellow professors, the home she shared with her mother was "the social heart of the university."

Sweet Briar, a small, nonsectarian academy and college for women near Lynchburg, Va., was barely ten years old when Dr. McVea became its second president. By 1925 Sweet Briar was a fully accredited and respected college with a scholarly faculty and a strong liberal arts curriculum. The endowment had been increased and a number of buildings added. Dr. McVea believed that the times demanded rigorous training of women and that women should attack the root causes of social and economic problems. She continued her interest in local and national affairs, lecturing widely on education and, during World War I, for the Federal Food Administration. In recognition of her contributions, she received the honorary Litt.D. degree from the University of Cincinnati in 1916 and an honorary LL.D. degree from The University of North Carolina in 1921. In 1922 she was appointed to a four-year term on the board of visitors of the University of Virginia; she was the first woman member of that body.

When she retired in May 1925, Dr. McVea was made president emerita of Sweet Briar College. By then she was nationally recognized for over forty years of service to the cause of women's education. From 1926 to 1928 she lectured on English literature at Rollins College. She died while on a visit to Cincinnati and was buried in Oakwood Cemetery, Raleigh.

SEE: Raleigh *News and Observer*, 24 Nov. 1904, 26 June 1916, 28, 29 July 1928; *St. Mary's Muse*, April 1906, February 1909; *St. Mary's School Bulletin*, April 1910; Katherine Batts Salley, *Life at Saint Mary's* (1942); *Sweet Briar College Bulletin*, April 1928.

MARTHA S. STOOPS

MacWhorter, Alexander (15 July 1734–20 July 1807), Presbyterian clergyman and Revolutionary chaplain, was born in New Castle County, Del., the son of Hugh and Jane MacWhorter, both of Scottish descent but born in Northern Ireland. His parents settled in Delaware about 1730. In 1748, following the death of her husband, Mrs. MacWhorter moved with young Alexander to the western limits of Bladen County, N.C., in the area that in time became Mecklenburg County, where three of her children had already settled. The family property in Delaware was left in the care of a guardian. Young Alexander was exposed to impressive religious services of the Presbyterians, which "overwhelmed him with anxiety and distress." He left for West Nottingham, Pa., to attend school and resolved his religious concerns by joining a local Presbyterian church. At age twenty-two he entered the junior class at the College of New Jersey (then at Newark but moved to Princeton the following year) and was graduated in 1757.

About to return to North Carolina, MacWhorter learned of his mother's recent death and changed his plans. He remained in New Jersey to study theology and was licensed by the New Brunswick Presbytery in 1758. It was intended that he should return to North Carolina as a missionary in the region where he had friends and family, but a congregation in Newark requested that he become their pastor. He was installed in the summer of 1759 at age twenty-five.

Finally, in 1764 his appointment as a missionary in North Carolina was renewed, and he undertook an extensive tour of the colony. MacWhorter helped organize congregations along the Eno River as well as eight in the region around Sugar Creek Church in the newly created county of Mecklenburg. Several churches tried to persuade him to become their permanent pastor, but he declined. While in the colony he became ill from some malady that plagued him for two years, but a stay in Boston in 1766 served to improve his health. Declining further calls, including one to remain in Boston, he returned to Newark, where he found that his congregation had experienced several religious "revivals."

The Continental Congress on 20 Dec. 1775 assigned MacWhorter and Elihu Spencer the task of going to North Carolina to do whatever they could to persuade the residents with Tory sympathies to look with favor on the American cause. From Philadelphia on 4 Jan. 1776 William Hooper, Joseph Hewes, and John Penn, delegates to the Continental Congress and afterwards signers of the Declaration of Independence, wrote to Richard Bennehan in Orange County, expressing their respect for MacWhorter and his missionary colleague, Spencer, "as clergymen-gentlemen & Patriots," and asking for his "Civilities" on their behalf. In this undertaking, however, they seem to have met with little or no success.

In 1776 the Corporation of Yale College awarded MacWhorter an honorary doctor of divinity degree. During the winter of 1776–77 he joined General George Washington's army on the Pennsylvania side of the Delaware River and participated in the drawing up of plans to defend New Jersey. He was also present when Washington crossed the Delaware and surprised the Hessians. The following year he became chaplain to General Henry Knox's brigade, and Washington was often among those who attended MacWhorter's sermons. Later in the year, after his wife was struck by lightning and considerably weakened by the experience, he resigned his duties as chaplain to attend to his family.

It must have been very late in 1778 that the trustees of Liberty Hall Academy in Charlotte persuaded MacWhorter to become president of their school as well as pastor of the local Presbyterian church. The family had hardly become settled when the British invaded Charlotte in September 1780 and the MacWhorters were forced to flee, leaving behind nearly all of their possessions. MacWhorter eventually returned to Newark, where he was pastor until his death.

As a churchman MacWhorter contributed significantly to settling the confession of faith and in preparing the constitution of the Presbyterian Church of the United States. He was a charter member of the board of trustees of the church until infirmity forced him to retire four years before his death. Named a trustee of the College of New Jersey in 1772, he served during the remainder of his life, and after the school burned in 1802 he journeyed to New England to solicit contributions to assist with the rebuilding. His *Collection of Essays, on a Variety of Subjects, in Prose and Verse* appeared in 1797, while several of his sermons were published as pamphlets, including one in 1800 in memory of George Washington. Two volumes of his collected sermons appeared in 1803. Another sermon, published in 1807, included a history of his Newark congregation.

SEE: *DAB*, vol. 6 (1933); Joel T. Headley, *The Chaplains and Clergy of the Revolution* (1864); *Journal of the Continental Congress, 1774–1789*, vol. 3 (1905); Alfred Nevin, ed., *Encyclopaedia of the Presbyterian Church in the U.S. of A.* (1884 [portrait]); William L. Saunders, ed., *Colonial Records of North Carolina*, vols. 5–6 (1887, 1890); William B. Sprague, *Annals of the American Pulpit*, vol. 3 (1858); Herbert S. Turner, *Church in the Old Fields* (1952).

WILLIAM S. POWELL

Maddock, Joseph *(1722–96),* pioneer Quaker leader in colonial Orange County, N.C., and Columbia County, Ga., founder of Wrightsborough, Ga., miller, and horticulturist, was born in the Newcastle, Del., area, the son of tailor Nathan Maddock. His father was the grandson of English linendraper Abel Maddock (b. 1668) of Cheshire, England, who had settled on Brandywine Creek, Del., and a descendant of Thomas Maddock (1615–90) of the city of Chester, England.

In 1739 Joseph Maddock married Rachel Dennis (b. 1718), the daughter of Samuel (b. 1680) and Ruth Tindall Dennis of the Haddonfield, N.J., Monthly Meeting of Friends. The Maddocks lived for about fifteen years in Chester County, Pa., where they joined the Newark, Pa., Monthly Meeting and where Joseph operated a mill and for a time served as magistrate. They had eight children.

In August 1754 they migrated southwards to the Eno River Valley in Orange County, N.C., bringing with them Joseph's apprentice, John Frasier. All three certificates of dismissal from the Newark Monthly Meeting are dated 3 Aug. 1754, and all three certificates of acceptance by the Cane Creek, N.C., Monthly Meeting are dated 2 Nov. 1754. The Maddocks joined a sizable colony of Irish and English Friends already settled along the Eno River, a number of whom were their relatives by marriage.

Maddock immediately entered for a land grant of 507 acres on both banks of the Eno River a short distance west of the new county seat of Corbinton; in 1758 he purchased an additional 360 acres. He and Frasier dammed the river a short distance below the mouth of McGowan's Creek and were operating a water gristmill on the west bank of the Eno by August 1755. Maddock's Mill, which became a historic landmark during the Regulator disturbance, was one of the earliest mills in the region and the nearest gristmill to the county seat until 1768, when Francis Nash's mill began operating in Hillsborough.

Maddock, still in his mid-thirties, also built the first prison for Orange County before 1757 on a 25' × 25' plot at the northwestern corner of Lot 6 in Corbinton (Hillsborough), and he probably assisted in building the first primitive courthouse on Lot 1. In 1756 he was appointed one of the twenty-four commissioners of roads, possibly because he had the year before, by permission, cleared and opened a new road westward to his mill.

Both Maddock and his wife Rachel were of prominent Quaker ancestry, and Maddock quickly assumed a position of leadership among both the Eno Valley Quakers and those of Cane Creek. In 1759 he was made a trustee of a five-acre plot of land northeast of Corbinton to be used as a Quaker burying ground and on which a meetinghouse (in use by 1761 and probably before) and a schoolhouse were built. (The old burying ground, surrounded by a rough stone wall, today survives intact on Highway 57.) In 1760 Maddock was a representative at the Yearly Meeting of North Carolina Friends at Old Neck in Perquimans County, and by 1762 he had successfully petitioned the Cane Creek Friends to establish a preparative meeting at Eno for the Eno Valley Friends. Maddock and the miller John Embree were appointed overseers of the new meeting.

Maddock, however, unfortunately became embroiled in what came to be known as "the Cane Creek Commotion," an internal disagreement among the Cane Creek Friends that united in protest Herman Husband, Joseph Maddock, and a number of like-minded Quakers, all of whom were disowned for their activities. All except Husband were eventually reinstated at Cane Creek, but the affair resulted in a deep-rooted disaffection that may have persuaded some Quakers to assist the Regulators and driven others to migrate to Georgia.

In 1766 Husband announced in an open court session in Hillsborough that Maddock's Mill, "where there is no Liquor," had been selected as a gathering place for Regulators to discuss their grievances on 10 October with county officials. Although no county officials ever appeared (except the former clerk of court, James Watson, who merely acted as a messenger) and no joint meeting was ever held, the essential damage was done so far as Maddock was concerned. He had been publicly linked with the firebrand Herman Husband not once but twice. (According to Maddock family tradition, Joseph Maddock was not actually consulted about the choice of his mill as a meeting place and afterwards constantly feared confiscation of his mill and mill property by Governor William Tryon.)

Maddock quickly made contact with a Georgia land agent, Leroy Hammond, and on 1 Sept. 1767 a vanguard of Orange County Quakers, led by Joseph Stubbs, Maddock's son-in-law, petitioned the royal governor of Georgia, Sir Joseph Wright, to reserve 12,000 acres for them on Sweetwater Creek, St. Paul's Parish, in Columbia County. Later, the reserve was enlarged to 40,000 acres. Maddock himself sold his mill and 20 acres of surrounding "Mill Lands" to Colonel Thomas Hart in November 1767. The twelve-year-old gristmill was thereafter known as "Hart's Mill" and became the nucleus of the sprawling Hartford Plantation. On 1 July 1768 Maddock returned from Georgia and formally deeded 434 acres of his former plantation to Governor William Tryon, with Edmund Fanning as the subscribing witness.

At least 132 families, and possibly more, followed Maddock to take up residence on the reserved lands in eastern Georgia. There, new homes, mills, and cowpens were built, and a new town, Wrightsborough, was laid out on Town Creek, similar to Hillsborough but rather more spacious in conception. Once again, as in the Eno

River Valley, Joseph Maddock occupied the position of leader—as justice of the peace, trustee of the cowpens, clerk of the Wrightsborough Monthly Meeting, governor's deputy, head of the land grant office, and representative to the colonial Assembly of Georgia. A notable event in the early days of the Georgia colony was a visit in 1773 by naturalist William Bartram, who much admired Maddock's skill in propagating apples and grapes.

The migrant Quakers, however, had failed to take the Creek Indians into account, and continued Indian attacks on their settlement and crushing losses of their cattle and horses as well as violent guerrilla raids finally forced them to abandon Wrightsborough and their great reserve and to search for peaceable homes in Indiana. Maddock himself, who had apparently married Mary Watson as a second wife in 1784 or 1785, remained in Georgia and died in 1796, according to the Augusta (Ga.) *Chronicle & Gazette*. The site of his grave is unknown.

In the 1970s the Wrightsboro Restoration Foundation began assembling records of the Wrightsborough Quakers, originally the Orange County Quakers. The Eno Meeting of Friends, weakened by disownment and migration, was, after ninety-three years, officially "laid down" in November 1847. A Stubbs-Maddock family museum has been assembled in Long Lake, Minn., by the family genealogist, Roger Avery Stubbs.

SEE: *Augusta* (Ga.) *Chronicle and Gazette*, 10 Dec. 1796; Pearl Baker, "Joseph Maddock: Quaker Leader" (typescript) and *The Story of Wrightsboro, 1768–1964* (1965) (Wrightsboro Restoration Foundation, Thomson, Ga.); Allen D. Candler, ed., *Colonial Records of the State of Georgia*, vols. 10–11 (1907); Minutes of the Western (N.C.) Quarterly Meeting and of the Wrightsborough (Ga.) Monthly Meeting (Quaker Room Vault, Guilford College Library, Greensboro); Orange County Records (North Carolina State Archives, Raleigh); William L. Saunders, ed., *Colonial Records of North Carolina*, vol. 7 (1890).

MARY CLAIRE ENGSTROM

Maddry, Charles Edward (*10 Apr. 1876–17 Sept. 1962*), Baptist minister, executive secretary of the Foreign Mission Board of the Southern Baptist Convention (1933–44), and secretary emeritus (1945–62), was born near Chapel Hill, the son of William Alexander and Julia Sugg Maddry. His great-grandfather, Josiah Maddry, had moved to Orange County from Virginia about 1801. Maddry's grandfather, Abel, was a farmer and a deacon in the Baptist church. Maddry attended the Canada School in Chapel Hill and The University of North Carolina, where he was awarded a Ph.B. degree in 1903. He later studied at the Southern Baptist Theological Seminary in Louisville, Ky., and the University of Texas and received honorary degrees from The University of North Carolina, Baylor University, Wake Forest College, and Stetson University.

After graduation Maddry served several small churches and was ordained at Chapel Hill (now University) Baptist Church on 4 June 1902 by the Reverend J. William Jones and the Reverend Thomas Hume. From 1901 to 1904 he also was superintendent of the Orange County schools. He served as pastor of Hillsborough First Baptist Church (1902–4); College Park, Greensboro (1906–9); First Baptist Church, Statesville (1909–11); and Tabernacle Baptist Church, Raleigh (1911–16). Maddry was then called to the pastorate of University Baptist

Church in Austin, Tex., serving from 1916 to 1921. During those years he also was moderator of the Austin Baptist Association.

In 1921 Maddry was recalled to his native state to become executive secretary of the Baptist State Convention of North Carolina. After serving for eleven years, he was appointed as the sixth executive secretary of the Foreign Mission Board of the Southern Baptist Convention. When he took this position, the board was more than a million dollars in debt and without credit.

By 1944, for the first time since its formation in 1845, the Foreign Mission Board was completely out of debt. Maddry led the board through most of the difficult days of World War II and laid the foundation for postwar growth. At the time of his retirement, the board had 504 missionaries under appointment.

Other accomplishments during his administration included the establishment of a pension plan for missionaries (1933); publication of *The Commission*, a missionary journal begun in 1938, which he edited for five years; election of regional secretaries to direct overseas work; establishment of the department for missionary personnel (1943) and tightening of requirements for missionary appointment; distribution of more than one million dollars of relief funds in famine-stricken areas of the world; and initiation of mission work in Hawaii and Colombia.

Maddry was the author of *Day Dawn in Yoruba Land* (1939), *Christian Ownership* (1940), *Christ's Expendables* (1949), *History of the First Baptist Church of Hillsboro, North Carolina* (1953), *Charles E. Maddry: An Autobiography* (1955), an unpublished history of the Foreign Mission Board, and many articles for the religious press.

On 2 May 1906 he married Emma Parker of Hillsborough. They had one daughter, Catherine (Mrs. R. W. Severance of Montgomery, Ala.).

Dr. Maddry returned to Hillsborough, where he served his final pastorate from 1951 to 1954. He continued to live in Hillsborough until his death at Memorial Hospital in Chapel Hill following a heart attack. Funeral services were held at the First Baptist Church of Hillsborough and at the Foreign Mission Board in Richmond, Va. He was buried in Hollywood Cemetery, Richmond.

SEE: Biography File (Baptist Historical Collection, Wake Forest University, Winston-Salem); Baker J. Cauthen, "Charles Edward Maddry," *Southern Baptist Encyclopedia*, vol. 3, supp. A–Z (1961); Hugh T. Lefler and Paul Wagner, eds., *Orange County, 1752–1952* (1953); Maddry's own works; *North Carolina Baptist State Convention Annual* (1962 [portrait]); Raleigh *Biblical Recorder*, 22 Sept. 1962.

JOHN R. WOODARD

Madison, Dolley Payne Todd (*20 May 1768–12 July 1849*), First Lady, social arbiter, and heroine of the War of 1812, was born in the New Garden settlement of Rowan County (now Guilford College in the bounds of Greensboro). Her Quaker parents, merchant John Payne and his wife Mary Coles, had moved there from Hanover County, Va., in 1765. In keeping with Quaker custom, her name was entered in the records of the New Garden Monthly Meeting under her parents' names: "Dolley their daughter was born ye 20 of ye 5 mo 1768." All of her life, when writing her name, she always spelled it Dolley.

When Dolley was just eleven months old, her family returned to Hanover County, where she spent her childhood and attended an old-field school and later a Quaker school in the local Cedar Creek meetinghouse to which the Paynes belonged. Opposed to slavery, John Payne in 1782 freed his slaves and the following year moved his family to Philadelphia, the national capital. Here Dolley was witness to governmental as well as social activities. She married a promising young Quaker lawyer, John Todd, Jr., and they became the parents of two sons, John Payne (1792) and William Temple (1793). In the summer of 1793 a yellow fever epidemic struck the city, and both Dolley's husband and her younger son fell victim on the same day.

With her first son, John Payne, she continued to live in the house that she and her husband had bought in 1791. She had many admirers, among whom was Congressman James Madison, of Virginia, often referred to as "The Father of the United States Constitution." She met Madison in May 1794 and they were married in September. Her public life began in 1801, when President Thomas Jefferson named Madison secretary of state. Since both the president and the vice-president, Aaron Burr, were widowers, Mrs. Madison became Jefferson's acting hostess and she soon set high standards for the social life of the new national capital, Washington, D.C. She opened her own new home to congressmen, to representatives from other countries, and even to visitors to the city. At these gatherings topics of wide-ranging importance were discussed, and occasionally Dolley was criticized for her role in some of them. Nevertheless, she received guests without regard to party politics and attempted to make everyone feel welcome. One of her friends, Mrs. Samuel Harrison Smith, in her later biography of Dolley Madison, stated: "The kindly feelings thus cultivated, triumphed over animosity of party spirit, and won a popularity for her husband, which his lofty reserve and old manners would have failed in ineffecting."

She presided at the president's house on 4 July 1803 at a great reception announcing the Louisiana Purchase. Jefferson and the Madisons were congenial, and during Jefferson's administrations she was his hostess when ladies were invited or when he needed advice concerning his family. It was observed that Jefferson loved Madison as if he were a son, and he endorsed the secretary of state as his successor as chief executive.

In 1809, when Madison was inaugurated as the fourth president of the United States, his wife became First Lady in name as well as deed. Although she did not dance, she approved of closing the inaugural celebrations with a grand ball. By that time she was so popular that she was almost pressed to death by those seeking a close glimpse of her. Mrs. Smith wrote: "It would be *absolutely impossible* for anyone to behave with more perfect propriety than she did. Unassuming, dignity, sweetness, grace."

The presidential mansion had never been adequately furnished; Thomas Jefferson had used furnishings from his own home during his two terms in office. Before Madison's inauguration, however, a congressional grant of five thousand dollars had been made for the decoration of the interior of the house, and it was Dolley who undertook the assignment. With the assistance of architect Benjamin Latrobe, the president's home was decorated and furnished in a highly acceptable manner. It won consistent praise. Mrs. Madison conducted weekly dinners for thirty invited guests, and on a regular basis the drawing rooms were opened to the public. She often was present to greet casual visitors and to discuss the progress and development of the country; she frequently shared with President Madison her sense of the concerns of the people.

Dolley Madison is credited with softening some of the verbal attacks leveled against her husband, particularly with reference to the War of 1812; even in the face of national divisions, he was reelected to a second term. In spite of the war, she continued her weekly dinners and drawing-room receptions, which provided her an opportunity to gain an understanding of the issues confronting the nation as well as to give heart to the people away from Washington. She also served refreshments to passing groups of soldiers, wrote letters to family and friends, and pledged herself to do everything she could for the good of the country.

When it was known that the British had landed along the Chesapeake and were headed towards Washington, she packed the Cabinet papers and other valuable records for transport, directed that Gilbert Stuart's portrait of George Washington be removed from its heavy frame and taken to safety, and loaded conveyances with various items of value and sent them off for safekeeping. A letter that she hastily wrote to her sister, Mrs. Lucy Washington, is perhaps the most valuable surviving source concerning the British capture and burning of Washington. The presidential mansion was gutted, and afterwards the blackened walls were painted white to help conceal the damage; it was henceforth known as the White House.

As the British entered the city, Dolley Madison drove off in a carriage to take refuge in the Virginia countryside. Returning to the ruined capital a few days later, the Madisons rented a house and Dolley resumed her efforts to reassure the people that conditions were returning to normal. Once again, she invited guests into the president's home regardless of their political beliefs. At the end of Madison's second term in 1817, it was said that Dolley Madison was the most popular person in the United States.

At their home, Montpelier, in Virginia, Mrs. Madison worked on her husband's papers and entertained a constant flow of visitors from at home and abroad. After Madison's death in 1836, she returned to Washington, where she was almost as popular as she had been as First Lady. She was invited to be at the forefront of all important occasions. Nevertheless, she faced difficult financial responsibilities. The Madison estate in Virginia was sold, as were some of Madison's papers; she mortgaged her home in Washington and even was reduced to borrowing from understanding friends. Relief came on her eightieth birthday when Congress purchased the remainder of Madison's papers and placed them in the Library of Congress.

On one occasion Henry Clay remarked to her, "Everybody loves Mrs. Madison." She instantly replied, "That's because Mrs. Madison loves everybody." She promoted music, drama, art, the Library of Congress, an orphan's asylum, inventions, sports, the George Washington Monument, and—according to legend—the writing of "The Star Spangled Banner," as well as keeping the nation's capital in Washington after the War of 1812.

Dolley Madison knew personally the first eleven presidents of the United States. In February 1849, as a special guest at the President's Ball, she strolled through the White House with another North Carolina native, President James K. Polk. In July of that year she died at age eighty-one and was buried in the Madison family cemetery at Montpelier.

SEE: Ethel Stephens Arnett, *Mrs. James Madison: The Incomparable Dolley* (1972); Irving Brant, *James Madison*, vol. 3 (1953); Allen C. Clark, *The Life and Letters of Dolly Madison* (1914); J. Madison Cutts, Jr., "Dolley Madison,"

Records of the Columbia Historical Society 3 (1900); Elizabeth L. Dean, *Dolly Madison: The Nation's Hostess* (1928); Maude W. Goodwin, *Dolly Madison* (1900); James Herring and J. B. Longacre, *The National Portrait Galley of Distinguished Americans* (1835); Charles J. Ingersoll, *Historical Sketch of the Second War between the United States of America and Great Britain* (1849).

ETHEL STEPHENS ARNETT

Madison, Robert Lee *(17 Feb. 1867–2 Oct. 1954)*, educator, legislator, and founder of Cullowhee High School, which became Western Carolina University, was born in Staunton, Va., the son of Robert Lewis and Helen Banister Madison and a descendant of President James Madison. His father was a staff physician at Virginia Military Institute, Lexington, and the physician of General Robert E. Lee. Because of the friendship that developed from the relationship, the senior Madison named his younger son Robert Lee.

In his youth Robert Lee had expected to become a doctor like his father, two uncles, and four cousins, yet his interests changed. In 1885 he received a Ph.B. degree from the University of Chattanooga, from which he later earned an A.M. degree in 1890. In taking a break from the rigors of preparing for medical school and to oblige his older brother Monroe, Robert Lee moved to North Carolina. For a time he taught at Qualla, near the Cherokee Indian reservation, but left in 1888 to take a teaching position in Sylva. Here, at age twenty-one, he also served as editor of the *Tuckaseigee Democrat*, the county newspaper. He was exact and precise in both activities, often working all day and late into the night to achieve his goals.

When the Cullowhee Academy offered him a post in 1889, Madison came to the realization that he wanted to stay in North Carolina. "So I resolved, God willing, to remain in this region and to do my best to begin supplying the very real educational needs of the mountain boys and girls," he wrote.

With the backing of the community, a semiprivate school was opened with eighteen pupils. By the end of the first year enrollment had reached one hundred. After the school had been running successfully for two years, the General Assembly in 1891 gave it a charter and officially named it Cullowhee High School. In 1893 Madison worked to obtain state support for the school; until this time Cullowhee's residents had provided all the funding. As a result of his efforts, the legislature appropriated $1,500 for the establishment of a "normal department." With this modest sum the school began to train teachers.

From this point the mountain school began to grow. In 1905 its name was changed to Cullowhee Normal and Industrial School. Successively, the school became Western Carolina Teachers College, Western Carolina College, and finally Western Carolina University. Madison served as president from 1889 to 1912 and from 1920 to 1923, after which he was named president emeritus. In 1912 he had been asked to resign because of the decline in the number of women enrolling and because the board of directors had the notion that he was too complacent about how the school was being run. Nevertheless, Madison served another term as president (1920–23) and continued as a professor of languages until his final retirement in 1937.

In 1925 he served a term in the state legislature, where he sat on seven committees and introduced the first recorded sales tax bill. In addition, he was a member of the Jackson County Board of Education for seventeen years.

Madison married Ella Virginia Richards of Elizabeth, N.J.; she had gone to Cullowhee as a music and art teacher. They were the parents of six children: Robert Edward, Jane Ambrose, Annie Louise, Monroe Bolling, William Haight, and John Banister.

SEE: *Asheville Citizen-Times*, 24 Apr. 1938, 16 Feb. 1950, 3 Oct. 1954; William Ernest Bird, *The History of Western Carolina College* (1963); Raleigh *News and Observer*, 14 Apr. 1934.

ROBERT O. CONWAY

Maffitt, John Newland *(22 Feb. 1819–15 May 1886)*, Confederate navy captain and blockade-runner, was born at sea, the son of Ann Carnic and the Reverend John Newland Maffitt. His father was graduated from Trinity College in Ireland and became a Methodist missionary and preacher. His sermons drew large crowds and as a result of his popularity, he was elected chaplain to the U.S. House of Representatives in 1841.

Young Maffitt lived in Connecticut until, at age five, he was adopted by his uncle, Dr. William Maffitt of Ellerslie near Fayetteville, N.C. At an early age he demonstrated leadership in sports. After attending school in Fayetteville, the nine-year-old continued his education in White Plains, N.Y. Three days after his thirteenth birthday he was commissioned a midshipman in the U.S. Navy. Following a cruise on the sloop-of-war *St. Louis*, he spent three years in the Mediterranean aboard the *Constitution*, a frigate, about which he later wrote a novel, *Nautilus; or, Cruising under Canvas* (1871). In 1838, after a thorough oral examination, he was promoted to passed midshipman, and three years later he became acting master of the frigate *Macedonian*.

In 1842 Lieutenant Maffitt was ordered to the U.S. Coast Survey. He spent more than fourteen years in hydrographic operations—mapping, graphing, charting, making soundings to determine water depths, plotting the location of shoals, determining the set or direction and velocity of currents, recording tidal observations, taking bottom and water specimens, and recommending the placement of buoys, lights, and lighthouses. The superintendent of the Coast Survey, Professor A. D. Bache, reported that Maffitt "as a surveying officer has not been excelled by any one with whom I have come in contact."

Unexpectedly, in 1857 Maffitt was called for a hearing by the navy "Retiring Board" concerning his professional fitness. Prior to the inquiry he received an apologetic and complimentary letter from Secretary of the Navy J. C. Dobbin, and during the proceedings a number of naval officers acknowledged his professional ability. After the hearing Maffitt was restored to active duty and placed in command of the brig *Dolphin*. Ordered to capture pirates and slaves, he became the first American officer to capture a slaver with its cargo.

In 1861 Maffitt resigned from the navy in order to join the Confederacy, thereby sacrificing property he owned in the North. President Jefferson Davis appointed him a lieutenant in the Confederate navy, where he enjoyed temporary duty as a naval aide to General Robert E. Lee while preparations for the defense of Savannah were in progress. In early 1862 Maffitt was ordered to the steamer *Cecile* to run the blockade with supplies for the Confederacy. Because privately owned blockade-runners were not dependable in supplying munitions for the

Confederacy, the Davis administration employed Maffitt as the first of several naval officers to obtain vital supplies.

For a short period he commanded the *Nassau* (formerly the *Gordon*) and later the iron-screw steam cruiser, the *Florida*, which had been built in Liverpool. The crew of the *Florida* experienced an epidemic of yellow fever in which Maffitt's stepson, John Laurens Read, died. In order to rebuild his sickly crew and refit the cruiser (by this time her guns were inoperable), Captain Maffitt entered the port of Mobile by running the blockade in daylight. The bombardment from the blockaders was severe. According to Maffitt, "We had about 1,400 shrapnel shot to our hull, and our masts were pitted like a case of smallpox." The damage was so great that he did not return to sea for over three months. To prevent his escape, the Federal navy increased the blockading force near Mobile. Maffitt waited for a violent storm before setting out and used trickery to lose six pursuing blockaders. For his ingenuity, he received a letter of approbation from S. R. Mallory, secretary of the Confederate navy. Yankee Admiral David Dixon Porter, author of *The Naval History of the Civil War*, stated: "During the whole war there was not a more exciting adventure than this escape of the *Florida* into Mobile Bay."

Early in 1863 Maffitt was promoted to the rank of commander in the Confederate navy "for gallant and meritorious conduct in command of the steam sloop *Florida*." Due to impaired health as a result of yellow fever, he requested detachment from the vessel in September 1863. After several months' recuperation, he returned to active duty as commander of the *Lilian*.

During his service to the Confederacy, Maffitt repeatedly ran the blockade to carry needed supplies and captured and destroyed more than seventy prizes worth an estimated $10 million to $15 million. In 1863 the *Royal Gazette* of Hamilton, Bermuda, reported that "the ship *Benj. Hoxie*, of Mystic, Conn., about 1300 tons burthen . . . laden with logwood, hides, 30 tons of silver ore and about $500,000 in bars of silver and $7000 to $8000 in gold became a prize of the *Florida*."

In the summer of 1864 Maffitt was commander of the gunboat *Albemarle* at Plymouth. After southern ports were captured, he refused to surrender his ship to the United States; instead, he followed his orders and returned his steamer, the *Owl*, to agents in Britain. He chose to remain in England, and after passing the British naval examination, he served for approximately two years in command of the British merchant steamer *Widgeon* running between Liverpool and South America. Then returning to America, he settled on a farm near Wilmington by 1868.

Maffitt was married three times. On 17 Nov. 1840, at age twenty-one, he married Mary Florence Murrell in Mobile, Ala. Their children included Mary Florence (Florie) Maffitt Wright and Eugene Anderson. The cause of the end of this marriage is undetermined. On 3 Aug. 1852, at St. Paul's Church in Charleston, S.C., he married Mrs. Caroline Laurens Read, a widow with three children. They became the parents of John Laurens and Colden Rhind, who was named for a longtime navy friend. His second wife died in 1859. The third marriage was to Emma Martin and took place in the bride's home in Wilmington, N.C., on 23 Nov. 1870. They lived on his farm, The Moorings, located on the sound at Wrightsville Beach, and together worked on *Nautilus; or, Cruising under Canvas* and some magazine articles. There were three children by this marriage: Mary Read Maffitt Borden, Clarence Dudley, and Robert Strange.

Maffitt died of Bright's disease and was buried in Oakdale Cemetery, Wilmington. He had been the only officer of the grossly outnumbered Confederate navy who had successfully engaged in both commerce raiding and blockade-running.

SEE: Charles C. Beamun, Jr., *The National and Private "Alabama Claims" and Their "Final and Amicable Settlement"* (1871); Edward Boykin, *Sea Devil of the Confederacy: The Story of the Florida and Her Captain, John Newland Maffitt* (1959); Robert Carse, *Blockade: The Civil War at Sea* (1958); *The Chase of the Rebel Steamer of War Oreto, Commander J. N. Maffitt, C.S.N., into the Bay of Mobile by the United States Steam Sloop Oneida, Commander Geo. Henry Preble, U.S.N., September 4, 1862* (1862); Moses Elsemore, *An Impartial Account of the Life of the Rev. John N. Maffitt* (1848); Virgil Carrington Jones, *The Civil War at Sea* (1960); Emma Martin Maffitt, *The Life and Services of John Newland Maffitt* (1906); John N. Maffitt, "Blockade Running," *United Service* 6–7 (1882), *Nautilus; or, Cruising under Canvas* (1871), and "Reminiscences of the Confederate Navy," *United Service* 3 (1880); John N. Maffitt, defendant, *The Case of Lieut. J. N. Maffitt, U.S.N., before Naval Court of Inquiry*, no. 1, Baltimore; John Newland Maffitt Papers (Southern Historical Collection, University of North Carolina, Chapel Hill); David Dixon Porter, *The Naval History of the Civil War* (1886); Raleigh *News and Observer*, 19 May 1906; Duncan Rose, *The Romantic Career of a Naval Officer, Federal and Confederate: Captain Maffitt of the C.S.S. Florida* (1935); James R. Soley, *The Blockade and the Cruisers* (1901); James Sprunt, *Chronicles of the Cape Fear River* (1916), *Derelicts: An Account of the Lost at Sea. . . .* (1920), *Tales of the Cape Fear Blockade* (1902), and *Tales and Traditions of the Lower Cape Fear, 1661–1896* (1896).

B. W. C. ROBERTS

Magness, Sallie Stockard. *See* **Stockard, Sallie Walker.**

Mahan, Frank Hoyt (17 Oct. 1867–11 Feb. 1905), YMCA official who gave the name *basketball* to that game, was born in Griggsville, Ill., the son of George and Sarah Hoyt Mahan who very soon after his birth moved to Memphis, Tenn. Both parents died when he was small, and he was raised by an uncle, George Mahan. He spent his youth in Memphis and in Pine Bluff, Ark., and after a brief stint working in a furniture factory he determined to prepare himself to become a Christian worker. In 1893 he was graduated from the secretarial department of the International YMCA Training School, in Springfield, Mass., where he proved to be one of the best athletes in the student body and was captain of several teams.

One December day in 1891—perhaps the twenty-first—after several days of rain had kept the young men indoors at the YMCA Training School, a Canadian physical education student, James Naismith, decided to try to devise a new game to entertain the gym class with which his teacher had assigned him to work for two weeks. Naismith hung a peach basket from a railing at opposite ends of the gymnasium. In order to give the young men adequate exercise and at the same time hold their interest, he drew up a set of thirteen rules that are now in the Basketball Hall of Fame in Springfield. Mahan, noted for his physical vigor and strength, scoffed at the new game, but he soon realized that it was a hit with others. The game with no name was played for about a month—both before the students left for the

Christmas holidays and after they returned. In January 1892 the student newspaper printed the rules of the game, calling it simply "A New Game." Afterwards, when Mahan asked Naismith what he intended to call the game, Naismith said he had not thought about it. When Mahan suggested "Naismith ball," he was told that such a name would immediately kill it. To this, Mahan responded: "Why not call it basketball? We have a basket and a ball, and it seems to me that would be a good name for it." The name he suggested stuck.

On leaving Springfield Mahan accepted a position at the YMCA in Charlotte, N.C., where he may also have lived before going to Springfield—Naismith's biographer in 1973 described Mahan, at the time the game was named, as "a troublemaker from North Carolina." During six years of service in Charlotte Mahan was responsible for numerous improvements: the building was remodeled, a library of 2,500 volumes was added, night classes were begun, and strong religious classes were established. The track and football teams that he organized were considered to be the best in the South. On leave of absence during the Spanish-American War, Mahan, based in Tampa, Fla., was in charge of YMCA work in army camps. His skill as an organizer attracted wide attention, and he was regarded as one of the best YMCA secretaries in the nation. While in Florida he came to the attention of officials from Lynn, Mass., and in October 1899, after his wartime service, he was named secretary there. Rejecting offers of more rewarding positions elsewhere, he remained in Lynn to direct the building of new facilities and enlargement of the program.

At Pine Bluff, Ark., on 5 July 1893, Mahan married Maud McEwen Henderson. They became the parents of four children: William Henry, Hoyt Henderson, Louise, and Maude. He died of pneumonia in Springfield, Mass., and was buried in Pine Grove Cemetery, Lynn.

SEE: Anonymous memorial booklet published in Lynn, Mass. (with a portrait), at the time of Mahan's death (original in possession of his granddaughter, Mrs. A. T. Prentiss, Springfield, Va., Xerox copy in possession of William S. Powell, Chapel Hill); *Charlotte City Directory,* 1897–1900; Lynn, Mass., *Daily Evening Item Centennial,* 23 Sept. 1977; James Naismith, *Basketball: Its Origins and Development* (1941); Recollections of Mrs. Fritz F. (Maude Mahan) Nelson, Swampscott, Mass., Mahan's daughter (correspondence in possession of William S. Powell); Bernice L. Webb, *The Basketball Man* (1973).

H. LEE BOUGHMAN, JR.

Mahler, [Gerhard] Henry (11 May 1832–19 Nov. 1895), silversmith and founder of a jewelry store in Raleigh, was born in Osnabrück, Kingdom of Prussia. His father was a merchant and his grandfather was a Lutheran minister. Young Mahler emigrated from Germany to the United States in the early 1850s, the move probably prompted by the earlier emigration of his older brothers, Frederick and Christian; two other brothers remained in Germany. Henry stopped briefly in New York before moving to Raleigh, where Frederick was operating a general store "next to Pomeroy's." Frederick was willing to let his younger brother have a silversmith's shop in the store. Henry Mahler—he dropped his first name, Gerhard—had served his apprenticeship as a silversmith and an engraver in Hanover, Germany, so he readily found employment as a craftsman in Raleigh, possibly working at first with John Palmer, an established silversmith. At any rate, by 15 Nov. 1854 Mahler was advertising his trade in the *North Carolina Standard.*

He announced that he made and sold all kinds of jewelry, hollowware, and flatware, placing special emphasis on his skill as an engraver. In 1857 he was operating independently in a small frame building near the Negro deaf and dumb asylum.

During the Civil War Mahler supported the Confederacy by making belt buckles, buttons, sword butts, and other necessary metal accoutrements in partnership with A. W. Fraps, Phillip Theim, and other German citizens. After the war he concentrated on his jewelry business in the capital city, building it into one of the largest in eastern North Carolina. In 1876 he built a brick building on Fayetteville Street and bought a residence on the corner of Fayetteville and Cabarrus streets. A large quantity of handsome silver, much of it made and engraved by Mahler himself, has been preserved.

Although Henry Mahler was not especially interested in politics, he was active in civic affairs. One of his first responsibilities was as a commissioner appointed by the state's provisional governor, William Woods Holden. Later he served as an alderman and was instrumental in effecting such city improvements as better street lights and a well-regulated market. In 1872 the Democratic county convention named him as a candidate for the head of the Wake County Board of Commissioners, but he declined to run for office. Records of legislative proceedings and state officers' reports include frequent references to Mahler as the maker of county seals and presses.

Mahler had the reputation of being an exceptionally well-read man who was particularly knowledgeable about the works of Shakespeare, Goethe, and Schiller. He was also an avid horticulturist and in 1869 planted two large vineyards known as the "Thomasburg" and "Mikelbo," which he enjoyed sharing with fellow townsmen. He was a member of the Lutheran church and belonged to the Hiram Lodge, a Masonic organization.

On 7 Sept. 1866 Mahler married Mrs. Fanny Kramer, a widow with four children. Mrs. Mahler (1834–1914), like her husband, was German-born. Her first husband was Nathan N. Kramer of New York, but after his death the widow moved to Raleigh. The children of Mrs. Mahler by her first husband were Albert, Clara Blake, Samuel, and Henrietta. Henry and Fanny Kramer Mahler had four children: Ludwig August, Frederick Wilbelur, Julius Henry, and Frances. Louis and Frederick eventually became affiliated with their father's jewelry store and on the death of their father changed the name of the firm to H. Mahler's Sons.

Henry Mahler's funeral was held in Christ Church, Raleigh, with the last rites being conducted by the Masons. Interment was in Oakwood Cemetery.

SEE: Mrs. Mary Frances Mahler and Mr. and Mrs. John C. Mahler to Mary Reynolds Peacock; Raleigh *News and Observer,* 19–20 Nov. 1895; Wake County Marriage Bonds and North Carolina Wills (North Carolina State Archives, Raleigh).

MARY REYNOLDS PEACOCK

Mainer, James Emmitt (20 July 1898–12 June 1971), country musician, was born in Weaverville, the son of Joseph and Polly Arwood Mainer. When he was five the family moved to Glendale, S.C., and he soon began to work in the cotton mill with the rest of the family. At age thirteen Mainer wrote "Hard Times in a Cotton Mill," a song that later became a popular recording. At fifteen the lad hopped a freight train and went to Knoxville, Tenn. There he worked for two years in a mill until he and his brother, Wade, moved to Concord, N.C. Both young men were musically talented, Emmitt having begun to play the banjo at the age of nine. Although the brothers both worked in a cotton mill, they began to spend their evenings with others who were interested in music. Soon a group was formed and known as J. E. Mainer and His Mountaineers. The nucleus of this group, and others with which he was later associated, consisted of the fiddle, banjo, and guitar. The Mountaineers began to travel around the state to play.

Beginning in 1932 Mainer's Mountaineers played on a noontime radio program broadcast over station WBT in Charlotte. Sponsored by the Crazy Water Crystal Company, the show continued for four years; in the summer at noon, when doors and windows were open in the heat, the Mountaineers could be heard from house to house by anyone walking along the city sidewalk in central North Carolina.

In 1935 Mainer produced his first recording for the RCA Victor Recording Company; he eventually recorded over two hundred numbers for RCA Victor. Mainer's Mountaineers later had a radio show on station WPTF in Raleigh and for a brief time also were on WWL in New Orleans. In 1941 they were invited to the White House to play and have refreshments with President and Mrs. Franklin D. Roosevelt. Enjoying a national reputation, they made guest appearances on nearly two hundred radio stations, broadcasting in both Carolinas, Virginia, Georgia, Alabama, Louisiana, Texas, Illinois, Tennessee, Kentucky, Ohio, and Mexico. They also played at the University of California at Berkeley in 1963.

Mainer, who was named to the Country Music Hall of Fame in 1969, was sometimes referred to as the "number-one fiddler in the nation." He was recognized for such hit songs as "Maple on the Hill," "Hard Times in a Cotton Mill," and "Mother's Not Dead, She's Only Sleeping."

Mainer married Sadie McDaniel. He died of a heart attack at his home in Concord just before leaving for a country music show in Virginia. A member of Poplar Grove Baptist Church, he was buried in Carolina Memorial Park, Concord. He was survived by his wife and eight children: Carolyn Wilson, Mrs. May Jarvis, Mrs. Irene Teassner, J. E., Jr., Charles, Earl, Glenn, and Earl Wayne—the latter an adopted son.

SEE: Clippings on J. E. Mainer (North Carolina Collection, University of North Carolina, Chapel Hill); *Concord Tribune*, 13 June 1971; *Sing Out* 20 (1971); *Variety*, 16 June 1971.

WARREN L. BINGHAM

Mallett, Charles Beatty (*18 June 1816–7 July 1872*), merchant, was born just outside Fayetteville in Eutaw, the son of Charles Peter, a merchant of Fayetteville, and Sophia Sarah Beatty Mallett. He was the grandson of Colonel Peter Mallett, commissary general of North Carolina during the Revolutionary War. Charles studied under private tutors until he entered Kenyon College, in Gambier, Ohio, where he was trained in science and engineering. He later joined his father in the textile business in Fayetteville and was owner of the Mallett Cotton Mill, burned by General William T. Sherman's troops and never rebuilt. He owned a controlling interest in several other spinning and weaving mills in and around Fayetteville.

Mallett's interest and participation in railroading brought him statewide prominence, especially for his actions during the Civil War. Between 1855 and 1870 he was president of the Western and Fayetteville Railroad, which reached from the first navigable part of the Cape Fear River (Fayetteville) to Egypt Station in Chatham County, the coal-mining region of the state. During the war, Mallett, in partnership with James Browne of Charleston, S.C., contracted with the Confederate States of America to mine and transport coal and other freight by rail out of Egypt, and by steamer and barge down the Cape Fear to Wilmington. He also engaged in the production of kerosene and railroad wheels as by-products of the coal industry.

Sherman destroyed Fayetteville on 11 Mar. 1865 and with it all of Mallett's mills, freighters, and barges, as well as his home and furnishings. Troops burned and pillaged many homes in Fayetteville; they were especially interested in finding food and valuables. According to tradition, when the Federals came to the Mallett home, they found only "rancid" beef in the kitchen. Mrs. Mallett had sewed all the family jewels into the hems of the children's clothes and spilled flour on the meat to make it appear spoiled.

With all of his capital left in worthless Confederate notes, Mallett attempted several business ventures after the war but failed at them all. He moved his family to a farm, Woodside, in the country outside of Fayetteville and lived in a deserted slave cabin until his death.

Prior to the war Mallett was a Conservative Whig and against secession, but when the Southern states made their decision he fully supported it. Two of his sons and three brothers fought for the cause. He never served because of a physical disability. He was a member of the Committee of Council in Fayetteville and died as a senior warden of St. John's Episcopal Church.

Mallett was married twice: to Margaret Winslow Wright, of Fayetteville, who died in 1859, and to Marion Winslow, whom he married in 1861. He had four sons and three daughters, all by his first marriage: John Wright (a captain in the Confederate army), Charles Peter (a lieutenant), Caroline Green, Margaret Anderson, Charles Beatty, Mercer Wright, and Alice Hazelton.

SEE: Joseph Caldwell Huske, "In Memoriam," a sermon preached at Mallett's funeral, 14 July 1872, St. John's Church, Fayetteville; Charles Beatty Mallett Papers (Southern Historical Collection, University of North Carolina, Chapel Hill); John A. Oates, *The Story of Fayetteville and the Upper Cape Fear* (1950); James R. Young, ed., *Textile Leaders of the South* (1963).

AGNES R. BURHOE

Mallett, Charles Peter (*14 Feb. 1792–23 Aug. 1873*), planter and merchant, was born in Fayetteville, the son of Colonel Peter Mallett, commissary general of North Carolina during the Revolutionary War, and his wife, Sarah Mumford (1744–1836). Thirteen years later his father died and left him the ward of two Fayetteville friends, through whom he acquired a private education as a "genteel and relatively affluent birthright" should have afforded him. He was later instructed in mercantile management.

As a merchant in Fayetteville, Mallett had many business ventures, including an extensive stagecoach line and several textile mills. In 1836 he took over the Merchant Mills on Blount's Creek, near Fayetteville, where his father's old mill stood, and converted it into a cotton spinning mill. He was the first successful producer of spun cotton in Cumberland County. In 1837 Mallett and several partners chartered the Rockfish Manufacturing Company, which was authorized to establish factories for the manufacture of cotton, wool, flax, hemp, and other products on Rockfish Creek. During the Civil War these mills provided cloth for the South, but all of them were burned by General William T. Sherman in 1865. The Rockfish Manufacturing Company was reestablished after the war under that name by a Northern officer from Sherman's troops who recognized its potential. It eventually became Hope Mills, the largest textile mill in North Carolina at the time.

Mallett opened a third mill, the Phoenix Company, in 1839 for the spinning and weaving of cotton. He was also a major stockholder of the Union (Cotton) Manufacturing Company and president of the Fayetteville branch of the Bank of North Carolina. In 1853 he left the state to attempt a business venture in New York. When it failed three years later, he returned to North Carolina to open a textbook store in Chapel Hill. He was in Chapel Hill when Union troops were there and left a diary of the Union occupation. After the war he left the state to help his sons reestablish themselves financially on a farm in Bastrop, La., where he died.

He had six children by his first wife, Sophia Sarah Beatty (1796–1829): Caroline Eliza, Charles Beatty, William Peter, Alexander Fridge, Peter, and Edward. By his second wife, Sarah Green, he had three sons and a daughter: Richardson (who died at Gettysburg), Cecil, Herbert, and Margaret (Meta) Wright. William Peter became a physician in Chapel Hill and was the grandfather of the late dean of the medical school at The University of North Carolina, Dr. William de Berniere MacNider.

Mallett was a prominent member of Fayetteville society. He was one of the first communicants of St. John's Episcopal Church, sat on its first vestry, and served often as a delegate to the diocesan convention.

SEE: Charles Mallett Papers and Peter Mallett Papers (Southern Historical Collection, University of North Carolina, Chapel Hill); John A. Oates, *The Story of Fayetteville and the Upper Cape Fear* (1950); James Richard Young, ed., *Textile Leaders of the South* (1963).

AGNES R. BURHOE

Mallett, Peter, Jr. (*14 Nov. 1744–3 Feb. 1805*), merchant and Revolutionary commissary officer, was born in Connecticut of French Huguenot ancestry. His father, Peter Mallett, Sr., the youngest of five children of David Mallett II and his second wife, Johannah Lyon, served as a commissary officer for the British forces in America during the French and Indian War. Peter Mallett, Jr., assisted his father in the purchase of cattle, horses, and provisions. After his father's death in 1761, he continued to supply the British forces on his own account. As executor of his father's estate he was unable to collect debts owed his father, and when the estate proved insolvent, he became liable for the debts, having failed to take proper legal precautions.

Because of his strained financial condition, in 1765 Mallett assumed command of a merchant ship in which he owned part interest. In an autobiographical sketch prepared for his children, he recounted his adventures as a merchant captain. Mallett visited the major European ports; he also purchased slaves on the Guinea coast and sold them in the West Indies. After his first ship was lost in the treacherous waters off Cape Hatteras, he found his way to New Bern and then to Charles Town, S.C., where he assumed command of a second vessel. His adventures were not over. While trading illegally at Campeche, Mexico, his ship was attacked by the Spanish *guarda costa*. Despite damages incurred in the ensuing battle, he sailed to New Orleans, where he received permission to sell his trade goods to French settlers on the Mississippi.

When Mallett finally returned to the English colonies, he retired from the sea. With the profits of his last voyage and the insurance claims from the ship lost at Hatteras, he secured credit and established himself as a commission merchant at Edenton. There he met Maurice Moore, who encouraged him to move to Wilmington. In 1769 he settled in Wilmington and within five years his mercantile and shipping business was among the most successful in the Cape Fear area.

In January 1775 the Wilmington Committee of Safety ordered Mallett to reship Negro slaves imported in violation of the Continental Association, but he apparently cooperated with the trade boycott. He was elected to the Committee of Safety in July and appointed to the seven-member "Committee of Secrecy and Correspondence" in October. His participation in the Revolutionary movement is elsewhere evident by his appointment the following May as commissioner to inventory Tory estates and by his election in 1778 to the House of Commons.

Mallett's service in the French and Indian War and his business experience made him a logical choice to supply the state's military forces. On 23 Apr. 1776 the Provincial Congress appointed him commissary to the Fifth North Carolina Regiment. As the war continued, Mallett was given increased responsibilities for provisioning state militia and Continental troops. He supplied General Francis Nash's Continentals who were on their way to join George Washington in the spring of 1777, and in December 1778 he was appointed to supply the North Carolina troops sent to join General Benjamin Lincoln at Charles Town.

Mallett often complained of slow payment and fussed over draft exemption for his employees, but the inflation of state and Continental currency and the failure of public credit posed the greatest threat to his business. Commissaries received a 5 or 6 percent commission on all purchases and expenses. Slow payment and depreciation wiped out profits and created staggering losses. Mallett claimed to have lost over $80,000 in the three months following the British victory at Camden. Unable to purchase goods on public credit, he had assumed personal liability for purchases that were taken by the state forces for worthless paper currency. His personal losses forced his resignation from the army in September 1780, but he agreed to continue purchasing goods with public funds. Suspected of being a Tory because of his resignation from the army, Mallett established a guard at his plantation, Council Hill, near Campbellton (present-day Fayetteville). It was attacked by both Whig mobs and Tory partisans.

Following Lord Charles Cornwallis's invasion of the state in early 1781, the British confiscated large quantities of supplies that Mallett had gathered for the Whig forces. When he applied to the state for payment for these captured stores, he was refused because the supplies had not been formally turned over to the army. Some persons even accused him of gathering the provisions in the line of British advance. With documented evidence from the state declaring the goods private property, Mallett applied to the British forces for compensation. Cornwallis paid Mallett for the provisions. Many of the British officers were old acquaintances with whom Mallett had served in the French and Indian War, and he moved freely behind British lines. He claimed that Cornwallis had offered him an appointment as commissary officer to the British forces but that he refused because of his sympathy for the American cause.

In January 1782 Mallett returned to North Carolina from Charles Town under a British flag of truce and voluntarily surrendered to state officials. In May the General Assembly ordered that he be prosecuted for treason. When the legislators passed the Act of Pardon and Oblivion the following April, they specifically excluded Mallett from pardon, along with the notorious Tory partisans David Fanning and Samuel Andrews. Tried and acquitted in June 1783, Mallett returned to his plantation and resumed his Wilmington mercantile business. Soon he was outfitting ships for London and was involved in trade with John Gray Blount of Edenton. Public resentment of his action during the British occupation did not die easily, however. Nor was he ever satisfied with the settlement of his public accounts. In 1797 he petitioned the state treasurer to reexamine his Revolutionary accounts, claiming that he had suffered heavy financial losses due to depreciation and British confiscation of goods for which he had not been paid following Horatio Gates's defeat at Camden.

Mallett was married twice: first to Eunice Curtis, who died in 1776, and afterwards to Sarah Mumford. By his first wife he had two children, one of whom died in infancy; by his second wife he had fifteen children, three of whom died in infancy. Mallett died at Fayetteville and was buried in the family cemetery near Mallett's Pond. The land is now owned by the state and is used as the district highway headquarters.

SEE: Walter Clark, ed., *State Records of North Carolina*, vols. 11–16, 22 (1895–1907); Ernest Haywood Collection, John De Berniere Hooper Collection, and Peter Mallett Papers (Southern Historical Collection, University of North Carolina, Chapel Hill); New Hanover County Court Minutes and Wilmington District Superior Court Minutes, 1782–83 (North Carolina State Archives, Raleigh); Raleigh *Register*, 18 Feb. 1805; William L. Saunders, ed., *Colonial Records of North Carolina*, vols. 9–10 (1890).

GEORGE W. TROXLER

Mallett, William Peter (*19 Jan. 1819–16 Oct. 1889*), physician, pioneer surgeon, and benefactor of The University of North Carolina, was born in Fayetteville, the second son of Charles Mallett, who, along with his three Huguenot brothers, had fled France following the revocation of the Edict of Nantes. William received some schooling in Fayetteville, then studied for several years at Trinity College in Hartford, Conn. He eventually entered the Medical College of Charleston, S.C., where he received a doctor of medicine degree in 1841. After graduation he began a practice in Tuscaloosa, Ala. Two years later he returned to Fayetteville, where he practiced for the next fifteen years.

While in Fayetteville, William Mallett earned a place in the annals of American medical history. On the night of 26 Mar. 1852, Mallett, assisted by Dr. H. A. McSwain of Fayetteville, performed one of the first cesarean sections in the South in which the patient survived. The patient, called "Mrs. Taylor" in Mallett's journals, was seventeen years old and in labor with her first child. In the process of giving birth, "the (umbilical) cord prolapsed and a fully developed child's head was locked in the pubes in the transverse presentation." Dr. Mallett informed Mrs. Taylor that her only chance for survival was a cesarean section, to which she consented. It is interesting to note that he operated without chloroform or ether, both of which were available. The patient, for religious reasons, had refused an anesthetic. However, she was given opium to relieve the pain of the operation. The child was delivered dead, and the wound was closed with four or five needles transfixing and uniting the sides of the wound by twisted sutures. The woman recovered fully, did not develop any infection, and later gave birth to several more children.

In 1855 Mallett was forced to retire because of a heart condition. After two years of farm life, he felt ready to resume his practice. Influenced by the educational advantages his children could derive at The University of North Carolina, Mallett in 1857 moved to Chapel Hill where he served the general community as well as the university. He was also instrumental in the establishment of the first university infirmary in a three-room cottage (the present site of Spencer Dormitory). Mallett stood by the university as a loyal friend and benefactor and played a prominent role in its reestablishment in 1875 following the ravages of Reconstruction.

During the Civil War, he volunteered his services to the Confederate army and for a time served in the field. Once again his health broke under strain, and he was reassigned to the Confederate General Hospital in Richmond, Va., as a surgeon. He was honorably discharged from the Confederate service in 1864 after a severe attack of typhoid fever, returning to Chapel Hill to recover his health and reenter general practice.

Mallett, who served the Chapel Hill area for more than thirty years, was believed to possess all the qualities necessary of a good physician. He relied mainly on a more natural form of medicine (*vis medicatrix naturae*) and was reluctant to use drugs unless they were absolutely necessary. It was also his habit to make long and careful studies of special cases and to compare his findings and diagnosis with similar cases treated by other physicians and recorded in medical literature.

Although troubled by continued heart disease, Mallett remained active in his medical practice. He died at his home in the presence of family and friends and was buried in the Chapel Hill Cemetery. He was survived by his wife, Caroline De Berniere, whom he had married in 1841 following his graduation from medical school, and several children.

SEE: *State Chronicle*, 1 Nov. 1889; *Transactions of the Medical Society of the State of North Carolina* (1935).

CLAUDE H. SNOW, JR.

Maltravers, Lord. *See* **Howard, Henry Frederick.**

Maney, Thomas (*1795?–15 Apr. 1864*), legislator and judge, was the son of James and Mary Roberts Maney of Hertford County. His own was the fourth generation of Maneys, originally Huguenot refugees of New York, who had lived in the Maney's Neck section of the county since James Maney's settlement there around 1725. James Maney III, the father of Thomas, represented the county in the General Assembly for two terms in the late eighteenth century.

Thomas Maney, after studying law with William Hardy Murfree of Murfreesboro, won election in 1817 to the state House of Commons. Following one term in office, he served briefly as secretary to Governor Jesse Franklin before settling in Murfreesboro and practicing law. In 1821 he married Mrs. Rebecca Southall Boon, a young widow. They had two daughters, Betty and Annie; a third child died in infancy in 1825.

Maney was active in the civic affairs of Murfreesboro as trustee of the boy's academy, militia officer, and town commissioner. In February 1825 his fellow townsmen appointed him to the committee on arrangements for entertaining the Marquis de Lafayette during his southern tour. Maney also delivered the welcoming address when the general arrived in Murfreesboro, his first stop in North Carolina.

By the close of 1825, when the legislature appointed him to the Council of State, Maney had already decided to leave North Carolina and may not have been confirmed in office. He moved with his family in 1826 to Franklin, Tenn. In 1839 he was elected to a judgeship on the state's superior court, soon moving to Nashville in order to be at the center of his judicial district. An outstanding lawyer and capable jurist, Maney retired after serving as circuit judge for the better part of two decades. He died in Nashville late in the Civil War.

SEE: Annie Campbell, comp., "Rutherford County (Tenn.) Bible and Family Records, Tombstone Records, Miscellaneous Records," 1938 (typescript); John L. Cheney, Jr., ed., *North Carolina Government, 1585–1974* (1974); John H. Wheeler, ed., *Reminiscences and Memoirs of North Carolina and Eminent North Carolinians* (1884); B. B. Winborne, *Colonial and State Political History of Hertford County, North Carolina* (1906).

T. C. PARRAMORE

Mangum, Adolphus Williamson *(1 Apr. 1834–12 May 1890),* Methodist minister and educator, was the youngest of eight children of Ellison Goodloe and Elizabeth Harris Mangum. He was born at Locust Grove, the family home on the Flat River near Rougemont in Orange (now Durham) County. His father was the cousin of Willie Person Mangum, congressman and later U.S. senator. Mangum attended South Lowell Academy and Randolph-Macon College, then in Boydton, Va., where he was graduated with highest honors in 1854. His college letters to his parents amply illustrate that he was a pious and serious student with a strong inclination for the ministry.

In 1856 Mangum became a junior preacher in the Hillsborough Circuit and during 1858–59 was pastor of the Methodist church in Chapel Hill. Ordained by Bishop Robert Paine of the Methodist Episcopal Church, South, on 8 Dec. 1860, Mangum was appointed pastor of the Roanoke Circuit and after one year was transferred to Salisbury. Late in 1861 he joined the Sixth North Carolina Regiment, which he served as chaplain. After seeing action at the Battle of First Manassas, Mangum brought home the body of his cousin, William Preston Mangum, and did not return to the battlefield.

Settled once again in Salisbury, Mangum ministered to the Union soldiers in the Confederate prison and was appalled at conditions there. His account of his experiences, though never published, provides an excellent picture of life at Salisbury Prison.

From 1863 to 1865 Mangum was pastor of the Methodist church in Goldsboro, and during 1866 he was a circuit rider in Orange County. In 1867 he journeyed north as a fund-raiser for the Greensboro Female College but returned to Orange County in 1868 to nurse his father through his last illness. During 1870 and 1871 Mangum served churches in Greensboro and Charlotte, and from 1872 to 1875 he was pastor of the Edenton Street Methodist Church in Raleigh. He received a doctor of divinity degree in 1879.

When The University of North Carolina reopened in 1875, Mangum was appointed to the faculty as professor of mental and moral science, history, and English language and literature. He also preached occasionally in the local churches. President Kemp Plummer Battle, a contemporary of Mangum, characterized him as a "man of warm and generous emotions, exceedingly kind to his students."

On 24 Feb. 1864 Mangum married Laura Jane Overman, of Salisbury, the sister of U.S. Senator Lee Slater Overman. Between 1865 and 1876 they had five children: Ernest Preston, Mary Elizabeth (Mrs. N. H. D. Wilson), Juliet LeRoy, Charles Staples, and Adolphus Williamson, Jr. Charles S. Mangum became a professor in The University of North Carolina School of Medicine and was a founder of the School of Public Health.

Mangum was the author of two volumes of poetry, *Myrtle Leaves or Tokens at the Tomb* (1858) and *Safety Lamp* (1866). One of his sermons, "Hindrances of the Gospel," was included in a compilation of Southern Methodist sermons, and a short essay, "Boys," appeared in an 1887 anthology of recitations and declamations entitled *The North Carolina Speaker.* He also wrote *The Introduction of Methodism into Raleigh, N.C.* (1876), *Sermon* (1881), and *Your Life Work* (1884).

While attending a church conference in New Bern in the summer of 1889, Mangum suffered a stroke. He returned to Chapel Hill to teach in August, but poor health forced him to retire shortly afterwards. He lapsed into a coma on 10 May 1890 and died two days later. A memorial address was given at the university by Josephus Daniels, who in his youth had been a frequent guest in the Mangum home on Rosemary Street in Chapel Hill (now known as the Betty Smith House). Mangum was buried in the old Chapel Hill Cemetery, where his marker was inscribed: "In all thy ways acknowledge Him, and He will direct thy paths."

SEE: Kemp P. Battle, *History of the University of North Carolina,* vol. 2 (1912); Mangum Family Papers (Southern Historical Collection, University of North Carolina, Chapel Hill); Raleigh *News and Observer,* 14 May 1890.

BRENDA MARKS EAGLES

Mangum, Priestley Hinton, Jr. *(21 Aug. 1829–26 Feb. 1907),* farmer and agricultural promoter, was born in Wake County, the son of Priestley Hinton and Rebecca Hilliard Sutherland Mangum. He was the brother of Willie P. Mangum, Jr., and the nephew of Willie Person Mangum. Priestley Hinton, Jr., attended the Bingham School in Orange County and was graduated from Wake Forest College in 1851. For the remainder of his life he was a farmer in northern Wake County.

As a farmer Mangum was a student and an advocate of progressive agricultural techniques. In particular, he found success in the practice of and fame in the promotion of terracing as a form of erosion control. In 1885, on his farm two miles west of Wake Forest, Mangum constructed the first examples of what became known as the "Mangum terrace." Two factors had pushed him to this development. The first was the wasted land necessary for the ditches then used in the southern Piedmont to control water runoff from farmlands. The second was the advent of farm machinery that could not be used efficiently on ditched land. Consequently, Mangum constructed his "terraces" as broad ridges with a gentle slope that would break the flow of water yet permit the growth of crops and be accessible to machinery.

Initially, the news of Mangum's method of erosion control spread by word of mouth. Within a decade, however, his terraces were being publicized by the Agricultural Experiment Station of the North Carolina College of Agriculture and Mechanic Arts. By 1912 the Mangum terrace had gained the support of the U.S. Department of Agriculture. Thereafter it was so widely used that both the second and third editions of *Webster's International Dictionary* (1934 and 1961) carried "Mangum terrace" as an entry.

In 1856 Mangum married Mary Thomas Price, and they became the parents of six children. In his politics Mangum was a Whig before the Civil War and a Democrat afterwards. He was a member of the Episcopal church. On his death he was buried in the family cemetery on his farm. This cemetery is now located on the Horsecreek Golf Course on U.S. Highway 1 west of Wake Forest.

SEE: Samuel A. Ashe, ed., *Biographical History of North Carolina*, vol. 5 (1906); F. R. Baker, "The Prevention and Control of Erosion in North Carolina with Special Reference to Terracing," North Carolina Agricultural Experiment Station, *Bulletin 236* (1916); J. S. Cates, "The Mangum Terrace in Its Relation to Efficient Farm Management," U.S. Department of Agriculture, Bureau of Plant Industry, *Circular 94* (1912); J. R. Chamberlain, "Report of the Agriculturist," North Carolina Agricultural Experiment Station, *Annual Report, 1889* (1890); F. E. Emery, "Hillside Terraces or Ditches," North Carolina Agricultural Experiment Station, *Bulletin 121* (1895); Arthur R. Hall, "Terracing in the Southern Piedmont," *Agricultural History* 23 (1949); A. T. Holman, "Terracing Farm Lands," North Carolina Agricultural Extension Service, *Circular 173* (1935); P. H. Mangum, "My Father Invented It," *Country Gentleman* 107 (1937); Raleigh *News and Observer*, 3 Mar. 1907; W. Turner Ray (Wake Forest), interview, 11 Apr. 1981.

H. THOMAS KEARNEY, JR.

Mangum, Willie Person (*10 May 1792–7 Sept. 1861*), lawyer, judge, congressman, and U.S. senator, was born at Red Mountain in a part of northeastern Orange County that became Durham County in 1881. The son of William Person and Catharine Davis Mangum, he received his earliest education at academies in Hillsborough, Fayetteville, and Raleigh. Graduated from The University of North Carolina in 1815, he became a tutor in the family of Judge Duncan Cameron at the same time he was studying law under the judge. In 1817 he began the practice of law. The University of North Carolina granted him the customary master of arts degree in 1818 and awarded him an honorary LL.D. degree in 1845. He was a trustee of the university from 1818 to 1859.

In 1818 and 1819 Mangum began a long career of public service when he represented Orange County in the General Assembly for two terms. As an advocate of constitutional reform, he won many friends in the western part of the state. He was elected a superior court judge in 1819 but resigned the next year because of financial needs. Between 1823 and 1826, as a member of the Republican party (which evolved into the later Democratic party), he served most of two terms in Congress but resigned for political reasons before completing the second; he was then reappointed to the court by the governor to fill an unexpired term but was not reelected by the legislature. In 1828 Mangum was a Jackson elector as well as a candidate for the U.S. Senate, but he withdrew his candidacy before the election. Instead, he was elected a judge of the superior court but once more resigned after a year.

Apparently still seeking a satisfactory place in public life, he was elected by the General Assembly, as was then the practice, to the U.S. Senate and served from 4 Mar. 1831 until he resigned on 26 Nov. 1836. In 1837 he received the electoral votes of South Carolina for president of the United States, perhaps as a reward for his sympathetic attitude towards that state's stand in the Nullification controversy even though he himself was opposed to nullification. Nevertheless, Mangum on occasion expressed clear states' rights sentiments.

Political issues were splitting the old Republican party, and among them was the question of the authority of state legislatures to *instruct* senators as to how they should vote. This and other questions led Mangum to resign from the Senate, and he soon joined the new Whig party. In 1840, in the interim between service in Washington, D.C., Mangum was a member of the state senate. As chairman of the committee on education, he played an important role in preparing legislation that established the public school system of North Carolina. In the same year he was named to succeed his adversary and fellow senator, Bedford Brown; thereafter, he was regularly returned to Washington, serving in the Senate from 1840 to 1853. He was an active member of many important committees including Finance, Foreign Relations, and Judiciary, and he was chairman of the committee on naval affairs. Following the death of President William Henry Harrison and the advancement of John Tyler to the presidency, Mangum was president pro tempore of the Senate from 31 May 1842 to 4 Mar. 1845. On a number of occasions his name was mentioned as a candidate for president or vice-president, and in 1852, because of the political climate in North Carolina, he declined the Whig nomination for vice-president.

Declining health led Mangum to retire to his home, Walnut Hall, at Red Mountain, but he continued to practice law as long as he was able. Many of his business affairs during his years of public service had been ably managed by his wife and one of his daughters.

In 1819 Mangum married Charity Alston Cain, and they became the parents of five children: Sallie Alston, Martha Person, Catharine Davis (who died in infancy), Mary Sutherland, and William Preston. The latter, a lieutenant with North Carolina troops, died on 28 July 1861 at age twenty-four from wounds received at the first Battle of Manassas. The loss of his son so distressed the elder Mangum that his health worsened and he died soon afterwards. He was buried in the family cemetery at Walnut Hall.

SEE: Samuel A. Ashe, ed., *Biographical History of North Carolina*, vol. 5 (1906); *Biog. Dir. Am. Cong.* (1971); *Cyclopedia of Eminent and Representative Men of the Carolinas of the Nineteenth Century*, vol. 2 (1892); *DAB*, vol. 12 (1933); Daniel L. Grant, *Alumni History of the University of North Carolina, 1795–1924* (1924); Henry T. Shanks, ed., *The Papers of Willie P. Mangum*, 5 vols. (1950–56).

WILLIAM S. POWELL

Mangum, Willie Person, Jr. (*7 May 1827–11 Feb. 1881*), diplomat and foreign service officer, was born in Wake County, the son of Priestley Hinton and Rebecca Hilliard Sutherland Mangum. He was the brother of Priestley Hinton Mangum, Jr., and the nephew of his namesake, Willie Person Mangum. He was educated at the Bingham School in Orange County, Wake Forest College, and The University of North Carolina, where he was graduated in 1848. Afterwards he was a tutor at Wake Forest for one year before reading law with his father. After his father's death in 1850, he took a position with the Federal Census office in Washington, D.C. Three years later he returned to North Carolina and resumed his law studies, this time under the tutelage of George Badger. Mangum continued to read law with E. W. Stoughton, a prominent judge and attorney in New York City, and ultimately was admitted to the bar in New York and the District of Columbia, where he began practicing in 1855. He was also licensed to practice before the U.S. Supreme Court.

Mangum practiced law until 1861, when he was commissioned, on 27 March, as consul to Ning-po, China. There he rendered valuable service during the disorders of the Taiping rebellion. In 1864 he was transferred to Chinkiang but in the same year was forced to return to the United States because of poor health.

In 1865, having recovered his health, Mangum was appointed consul to Nagasaki, Japan. He held this post until 1880, through the momentous years of the opening of Japan to the West. In 1867 he returned briefly to China where, as acting consul at Shanghai, he established the first American mail service in China. In 1874–75 he was chosen by the representatives of England, Holland, and Japan to arbitrate the Takashima mines dispute. In 1880, for reasons of health, Mangum was transferred to Tientsin, in northern China, where he died the next year.

During his tours of duty, Mangum was highly regarded by the consular corps in both China and Japan. He was among the first Caucasians to visit parts of Japan after its opening to the West. He was elected a nonresident member of the North China branch of the Royal Asiatic Society.

In 1855, shortly after he began practicing law in Washington, D.C., Mangum married Fannie Vaulx Ladd. They had no children. During her travels with her husband in the Far East, Mrs. Mangum became something of an authority on Chinese and Japanese coins and ceramics. After his death, Mangum's remains were interred briefly in China but subsequently were brought back to the United States and reinterred in the congressional cemetery in Washington.

SEE: Mrs. Willie P. (Fannie L.) Mangum, "Willie Person Mangum, Jr.," *North Carolina University Magazine* 9 (1890); Willie P. Mangum Papers, 2d ser. (Library of Congress); Willie P. Mangum Papers (North Carolina State Archives, Raleigh); Henry T. Shanks, ed., *The Papers of Willie P. Mangum*, vol. 5 (1956); Payson J. Treat, *Diplomatic Relations between the United States and Japan, 1853–1895*, 2 vols. (1932); Stephen B. Weeks, "Willie Person Mangum, Jr.," in Samuel A. Ashe, ed., *Biographical History of North Carolina*, vol. 5 (1906).

H. THOMAS KEARNEY, JR.

Manly, Alex (fl. 1895–98), black newspaper editor and Republican party leader in Wilmington, published the Wilmington *Daily Record*, which described itself as "the only negro daily in the world." The *Record* covered local as well as national news and championed the interests of the black community.

Manly is usually remembered for an editorial he published during the violent "white supremacy campaign" of 1898. The article was in response to a speech by a white supremacist, Rebecca Felton, who charged that black males were raping white women and needed to be suppressed. Manly countered that the whole black race should not be blamed for the folly of a few. He also argued that in many cases of so-called rape, the white women were willing participants until the liaison was revealed. In conclusion, he pointed out the hypocrisy of

white supremacists who railed against black "rapists" while overlooking the many whites who were debauching black women.

Under headings such as "An Insult to the White Women of North Carolina," Democratic newspapers republished Manly's editorial to convince white voters that blacks condoned rape and favored miscegenation. In Wilmington itself, well-armed whites gathered on the day after the election to denounce "black Republican rule" and issue an ultimatum to the black community that Manly must leave the city. By this time Manly was already gone, but the white posse, receiving no reply to its demand, sacked and burned the office of the *Daily Record*. In the ensuing riot several people (mostly blacks) were shot, the Republican city council was replaced by a Democratic one, and many prominent blacks were forced into permanent exile. Manly appealed to President William McKinley to reverse this coup d'état, but neither the president nor North Carolina's Republican governor, Daniel L. Russell, would take action. Manly moved to Philadelphia, where his later career remains obscure.

SEE: J. H. W. and Mary Bonitz Papers (portrait), Thomas W. Clawson Collection, and A. M. Waddell Papers (Southern Historical Collection, University of North Carolina, Chapel Hill); Helen G. Edmunds, *The Negro in Fusion Politics* (1951); Harry Hayden, *The Story of the Wilmington Rebellion* (1935); Wilmington *Daily Record*, 18 Aug. 1898; Wilmington *Messenger*, 8–11 Nov. 1898.

DANIEL R. MILLER

Manly, Basil (28 Jan. 1798–21 Dec. 1868), Baptist minister and educator, was born near Pittsboro, the second of six children of Basil and Elizabeth Maultsby Manly, who had moved to Chatham County from Bladen. His father, originally from St. Marys County, Md., became a captain of militia during the American Revolution. Members of his mother's family were among the early Quaker settlers of Bladen; her paternal grandmother, Ann Carver Maultsby, was the daughter of James Carver, the namesake of Carvers Creek and the Quaker meetinghouse of the same name and a benefactor of the latter. Elizabeth Maultsby, however, had become a Baptist in young womanhood, while Captain Manly was a Roman Catholic. This disparate doctrinal heritage was reflected in the denominational divisions among their three oldest children: Charles, who later was governor of the state, was an Episcopalian; Basil was a Baptist; and Matthias Evans, later a distinguished jurist, was a Catholic. The two oldest children were legitimated by an act of the General Assembly in 1799.

Basil received his early education at the Bingham School in Orange County. Soon after his baptism on 26 Aug. 1816, he announced his desire to study for the Baptist ministry. Despite his father's opposition and refusal to assist him, he obtained the necessary instruction and was licensed to preach by the Rocky Spring Church, Chatham County, on 26 Apr. 1818. Shortly afterwards, his natural gifts impressed the Reverend W. T. Brantly, who was visiting the area. Brantly persuaded him to enter the small college in Beaufort, S.C., of which Brantly was president, where Manly could secure financial assistance.

In December 1819, after eighteen months of study at Beaufort, he entered the junior class of South Carolina College, from which he was graduated on 3 Dec. 1821 as valedictorian and honor man of his class. Encouraged by Jonathan Maxcy, president of the college, he began to preach in nearby churches, where his abilities were recognized and his services were much in demand. In January 1822 he moved to Edgefield, S.C., becoming pastor there and at Stevens Creek, a neighboring country church. He joined the latter church, where he was ordained on 10 Mar. 1822 by John Landrum and Enoch Breazeale.

Soon afterwards Manly was elected secretary of the Baptist State Convention and in 1823 was named to the five-man committee charged with selecting a site and completing all necessary arrangements connected with the founding of Furman Academy and Theological Institution, the forerunner of Furman University.

In February 1826 he accepted a call to the First Baptist Church of Charleston, S.C., the oldest and, at that time, the wealthiest church of his denomination in the South. After nearly twelve happy and prosperous years there, having meanwhile declined the presidency of South Carolina College in 1835, he accepted in September 1837 the presidency of the University of Alabama, where he served until 1855. Manly played a leading role in founding the Alabama Historical Society and Judson, Howard, and Central colleges, and he was a promoter of the Insane Hospital at Tuscaloosa. In 1853 he declined the presidency of Furman College, but two years later he returned to South Carolina as pastor of the Wentworth Street Church, Charleston. As an ardent promoter of the Southern Baptist Theological Seminary, he was president of the three conventions (1856, 1857, and 1858) that established it. In 1859 he returned to Alabama as state evangelist, then became pastor in Montgomery.

Manly supported the secession movement wholeheartedly. In 1844 he was the author of the resolutions that led to formation of the Southern Baptist Convention at Augusta, Ga., in 1845, a denominational cleavage occurring fifteen years before the political rupture. On 22 Feb. 1861 he was chaplain at Jefferson Davis's inauguration as president of the Confederacy, riding with the presidential party and delivering the prayer.

In 1863 Manly returned to South Carolina, where he became partially paralyzed in 1864 and died four years later at the home of his son, Basil, Jr., in Greenville. He was buried in the town's Greenwood Cemetery. A portrait of Manly hangs in the Amelia Gayle Gorgas Library at the University of Alabama, and another belongs to his great-grandson, Dr. Basil Manly IV of Greenville.

On 23 Dec. 1824 Manly married Sarah Murray Rudulph, of Edgefield, S.C., by whom he had eight children: Basil (also a distinguished Baptist minister), Zebulon Rudulph, John Waldo, Sarah Rudulph, Charles (also a Baptist minister), Abby Murray, James Syng, and Richard Fuller.

SEE: Bladen County Wills (North Carolina State Archives, Raleigh); *DAB*, vol. 12 (1933); *Encyclopedia of Southern Baptists*, vol. 2 (1958); Joyce Lamont to William C. Fields, 20 Oct. 1978; Dr. Basil Manly IV to William C. Fields, 24 Oct. 1978, 6 Jan. 1979; Louise Manly, *The Manly Family* (1930).

WILLIAM C. FIELDS

Manly, Charles (13 May 1795–1 May 1871), lawyer, governor, and treasurer of The University of North Carolina, was born in Chatham County. His father was Basil Manly, a native Marylander of Scottish ancestry who served in the Revolutionary War, rising to the rank of captain; following the war he settled in Chatham County, where he died in 1824. His mother was Elizabeth Maultsby. Charles and his brother Basil, who became president of the University of Alabama and was a founder of the Southern Baptist Theological Seminary,

were legitimated by Chapter 64, the *Laws of North Carolina of 1799*. Though their father was a devout Roman Catholic and their mother a staunch Baptist, the parents evidently married; various legal documents refer to Elizabeth Maultsby as the widow of Captain Basil Manly. Another brother, Matthias Evans Manly, was a justice of the North Carolina Supreme Court. Charles was an Episcopalian, Basil was a Baptist minister, and Matthias was a Roman Catholic.

Charles studied under the Reverend William Bingham at Chatham Academy in Pittsboro prior to entering The University of North Carolina, where he received an A.B. degree in 1814 and later an A.M. degree. After graduation he tutored the sons of John Haywood of Raleigh to earn money for the study of law under Robert Williams. He was admitted to the bar in 1816 and licensed to practice in superior courts.

In 1823 Manly was appointed clerk to the commission for the settlement of claims under the Treaty of Ghent, in Washington, D.C., but after a year he returned to his legal practice in Raleigh. He was clerk assistant of the House of Commons from 1824 until 1830, when he was elected principal clerk. Except for one session (1842–43) when he was defeated, he held the position until the end of the 1846–47 session. Though previously a Republican, Manly joined the Whig party when it was formed. He served as a presidential elector in 1840.

Twice nominated for governor by the Whigs, he was elected on 3 Aug. 1848, defeating David S. Reid. Manly took the oath of office on 1 Jan. 1849, with Thomas Ruffin presiding. His two-year administration is remembered for his support of public education, his interest in internal improvements, his recommendation that a geological survey be undertaken, and his promotion of efforts to obtain documents on the colonial history of North Carolina from London. His defeat by Democrat Reid in the 1850 election was attributed to his overconfidence and to the inactivity of the Whig party. During the campaign Manly had pressed the issue of free suffrage in the election of state senators.

From 1821 to 1849 Manly served as secretary and treasurer of the board of trustees of The University of North Carolina. During his tenure as governor he was ex officio president of the board. On leaving office in 1851, he again served as secretary-treasurer until 1868, when the university was temporarily closed. In a letter of 4 Aug. 1868, he lamented the "death" of the university and expressed his fear that "the glory of our beloved *Alma Mater* is gone forever." Manly did not live to see the university reopen.

Prior to the Civil War he urged legislators to keep North Carolina in the Union. When war actually came, however, he supported the South. Three of his sons served in the war and two sons-in-law were killed in battle.

During his long stay in Raleigh, Manly accumulated a considerable amount of property. His large home at the foot of Salisbury Street was ultimately acquired by the trustees of Rex Hospital and became the site of that facility. He owned a plantation, Ingleside, east of Raleigh, which contained 1,060 acres when he bought it. His father-in-law gave him additional acreage so that Manly could vote in senatorial elections. After the war, his son, Major Basil C. Manly, operated the plantation. In 1853 Charles Manly owned as many as forty slaves.

In 1817 he married Charity Hare Haywood, the daughter of William Henry Haywood, Sr., of Raleigh; she was the sister of U.S. Senator William Henry Haywood, Jr., and of the wife of Governor Edward B. Dudley. The Manlys had six daughters and five sons.

Following a long illness, which resulted in the loss of

his eyesight, Manly died at his residence in Raleigh. According to the *Raleigh Daily Telegram* of 2 May, "Charles Manly was a great and good man; and it has been long since North Carolina mourned the loss of a nobler son, or a people mournfully announced, one to another, the death of a more honored or loved fellow-citizen." The funeral was held at Christ Episcopal Church, of which Manly had been a member, with interment in Raleigh's City Cemetery.

SEE: Samuel A. Ashe, ed., *Biographical History of North Carolina*, vol. 7 (1908 [portrait]); Daniel L. Grant, *Alumni History of the University of North Carolina, 1795–1924* (1924); Journals of the North Carolina House of Commons and Wake County legal records pertaining to Manly (North Carolina State Archives, Raleigh); Manly's message to the General Assembly, in *Executive Documents* (1850–51); *Raleigh Daily Telegram*, 2 May 1871.

MEMORY F. MITCHELL

Manly, Matthias Evans (*12 Apr. 1801–9 July 1881*), lawyer and jurist, was born near Pittsboro, the third of six children of Basil and Elizabeth Maultsby Manly, who had moved to Chatham County from Bladen. His father, originally from St. Marys County, Md., and a Roman Catholic, became a captain of militia during the American Revolution. His mother was of the fourth generation of Quaker settlers of Bladen, but Matthias, unlike his older brothers Charles and Basil, adhered to the religious affiliation of his father.

He received his early education at the Bingham School in Orange County and was graduated with honors from The University of North Carolina in 1824. Five years later he received an M.A. degree, and in 1862 the university awarded him the honorary degree of LL.D. For a while after graduation Manly tutored mathematics at the university, then studied law under his brother Charles. He later settled in New Bern and became a successful lawyer.

In 1834 and 1835 Manly served in the legislature, and in 1840 the governor appointed him a superior court judge to complete the term of Judge R. M. Saunders, who had resigned. When the legislature met the following year, he was elected to that position, which he held for the next nineteen years.

In December 1859 he was appointed to the North Carolina Supreme Court and served for six years. As a judge Manly had always been known for his impartiality and, of his first four opinions as a supreme court justice, which were on appeals in cases he had tried as a superior court judge, he reversed himself in two. During the Civil War there was not much litigation so he had no great opportunities to express himself as a writer of judicial opinions. When the habeas corpus cases were before the court in 1863, he was absent on account of illness and did not participate in those decisions, but in 1864 he was present for the cases involving the power of the Confederate government. He held that the government, in its struggle for independence, had a right to the services of all its citizens, an opinion that often put him in the position of dissenter on the court, differing as he did with those who sought to limit that power.

In the turbulent political atmosphere that prevailed after the war, when Secessionists were denounced as traitors, he was one of the few former supporters of the Confederacy to be elected to the constitutional convention of 1865. At that convention an ordinance was introduced declaring that the ordinance of 1789, by which the state had become a member of the Union, had always been in force, notwithstanding the "supposed or-

dinance of 1861," that of secession. Manly supported a substitute that annulled and repealed the 1861 ordinance. His view, which was not supported by the majority of the convention, was that it was "uncandid in us now to say that we were . . . put into a position of hostility to the Government of the United States without our privity or consent." He insisted that the action of the 1861 convention was not a nullity but had failed because it had been overthrown by force of arms, and that decency and candor therefore required that it be repealed rather than declared a nullity.

A correspondent of the Boston *Advertiser*, Sidney Andrews, who attended the convention, characterized Manly as "perhaps the leading Calhoun man of the State, as he is certainly the only member of the convention who has courage and frankness enough to openly avow his belief in the doctrine of State rights." Andrews also gave a graphic description of his physical appearance at that time: "Mr. Manly is a tall, spare man . . . with a noticeably long, thin face, much cut up with fine wrinkles. He has a firm mouth, thin Roman nose, and square forehead, almost covered with reddish-gray hair, which falls from above and is combed up from the sides. . . . Having seen him even but once, you could never forget his eyes—small, steelly, restless, incisive, half closed, set far back under jutting frontals—eyes that at first glance seem to see nothing, but that unquestionably do see everything."

The convention declared all state offices vacant and the General Assembly of 1865 elected a new supreme court, which did not include Manly. In 1866, however, he was elected to represent Craven County in the state senate, of which he was voted president. At that session he was elected by the General Assembly to the U.S. Senate, winning by a large majority over the incumbent, John H. Pool. But when the state was denied representation in Congress, he was not permitted to take his seat in the Senate.

Afterwards Manly resumed his law practice in New Bern and served as presiding justice of Craven County until the county court system was abolished in 1868. He also became mayor of New Bern and represented the state as its proxy in the Atlantic and North Carolina Railroad.

In June 1881 he fell at his residence; a month later he suffered a fatal stroke of paralysis and was buried in Cedar Grove Cemetery, New Bern. A portrait of Judge Manly hangs in the supreme court building in Raleigh.

In 1832 Manly married Hannah Gaston, the daughter of Judge William Gaston, by whom he had two daughters: Jane and Hannah. After her death he married, in 1844, Sarah Louisa Simpson, the daughter of Samuel Simpson, of New Bern, and they had nine children: Matthias Evans, Jr., Maria, Elizabeth, Gaston, Basil, Clement, Mary, William, and Sarah Simpson.

SEE: Samuel A. Ashe, ed., *Biographical History of North Carolina*, vol. 6 (1905); Cedar Grove Cemetery Records (City Hall, New Bern); Craven County Marriage Bonds (North Carolina State Archives, Raleigh); Louise Manly, *The Manly Family* (1930).

WILLIAM C. FIELDS

Mann, Thomas Nicholson (*29 Dec. 1797–17 July 1824*), lawyer, legislator, and U.S. agent to Guatemala–designate, was born in Nash County, the son of Allen Mann, a wealthy planter, and his wife, Elizabeth Nicholson. Named for his maternal grandfather, he entered The University of North Carolina in 1815 but was suspended following an episode of rowdy behavior by a group of students on 18 Sept. 1816 in support of one of their group who was reprimanded by President Joseph Caldwell. Where Mann continued his education is not known, but he became a practicing attorney and occasionally accepted a young man to train in the law. One of his outstanding pupils was Bartholomew F. Moore. Mann represented Nash County in the House of Commons in the sessions of 1822 and 1823–24 and was a member of the committee on education during both terms. On the death of his father, he inherited all of his father's land on the north side of Swift Creek, together with a number of slaves. His brother, James N., inherited the land on the south side with a portion of the slaves.

At the recommendation of senators Nathaniel Macon and John Branch, President James Monroe directed Secretary of State John Quincy Adams to invite Mann to accept appointment as an informal agent to the region between Colombia, Mexico, and Peru which "appears to have established the separate government of Guatemala." A letter of 21 Apr. 1824 from Adams explained that he was to consider this appointment confidential but that it would involve observing and reporting on conditions in the region so that it could be determined whether the United States should support the new government. At his own initiative Mann discovered something about the dangers he might face including the hazards of travel, the lack of conveniences, and the threat of robbers, yet he agreed to accept the assignment. He was already in Norfolk, Va., prepared to sail as instructed by the secretary of state, when the terms of his employment were agreed upon on 4 July 1824. Mann requested that a young relative be permitted to accompany him and serve as his secretary; this apparently was Samuel L. Arrington, his half brother. On 17 July, aboard the U.S. ship *Hornet* off Old Point Comfort, Mann died suddenly of pulmonary consumption, as tuberculosis was then called.

Meeting later in the month, members of the Nash County bar, of which B. F. Moore was secretary, adopted resolutions in Mann's honor, mentioning his "unwearied industry, indefatigable research, distinguished talents and correct and honorable deportment." These qualities, it was noted, "acquired for him an early and elevated standing in his profession." Young Mann drew up a will shortly before he left Nash County as he was "about to take a sea-voyage and reside in foreign parts." The land inherited from his family he left to his brother James. Other property was willed to his half brothers Samuel L. and Archibald Arrington and to his half sister Elizabeth A. N. Arrington. For many generations members of the Arrington family used Thomas Mann as given names for their sons.

Mann's successor as U.S. agent to Guatemala, former governor William Miller of Warren County, also died in transit before taking up his post.

SEE: Archibald Hunter Arrington Papers (Southern Historical Collection, University of North Carolina, Chapel Hill); Kemp P. Battle, *History of the University of North Carolina*, vol. 1 (1907); John B. Boddie, *Southside Virginia Families*, vol. 2 (1956); Charles L. Coon, *The Beginnings of Public Education in North Carolina: A Documentary History, 1790–1849*, vol. 1 (1908); Daniel L. Grant, *Alumni History of the University of North Carolina, 1795–1924* (1924); Nash County Wills (North Carolina State Archives, Raleigh); Raleigh *Register*, 23 July, 20 Aug. 1824; Joseph W. Watson, *Estate Records in the Deed Books of Nash County, North Carolina, 1781–1897* (1982).

WILLIAM S. POWELL

Manning, Isaac Hall *(14 Sept. 1866–12 Feb. 1946)*, physician and educator, was born in Pittsboro, the son of John and Louisa Jones Hall Manning. In 1881 the family moved to Chapel Hill, where John Manning became the first professor of law at The University of North Carolina and later served as dean of the law school.

Young Manning enrolled at the university in the fall of 1883, was graduated in 1887, and worked as a chemist with the Navasso Company of Wilmington until 1893, when he entered medical school at Long Island College in New York. After receiving a doctor of medicine degree with honors in 1897, he served as surgeon for the hospital of the Atlantic Coast Line Railroad in 1899 and 1900. In 1901 he pursued graduate medical training at the University of Chicago and was appointed professor of physiology at The University of North Carolina School of Medicine. Manning attended Harvard University for additional graduate work in 1902 and 1906 and began teaching courses in bacteriology at The University of North Carolina in 1902.

Following the departure of Dr. Richard H. Whitehead (1865–1916) to the University of Virginia, Manning was appointed dean of The University of North Carolina School of Medicine in 1905. His energy and leadership were critical in transforming the young school into one of the nation's leading medical education centers. Manning guided the School of Medicine through several difficult periods, particularly the turmoil surrounding the forced closing of many medical schools in the aftermath of Dr. Abraham Flexner's survey of American medical education. Additional upheaval occurred with the efforts to expand the curriculum to a four-year program and the attempt to merge the school with Trinity College in Durham. Manning served as dean until September 1933, when he resigned following a disagreement with Dr. Frank Porter Graham. He continued his active role in education as Kenan professor and chairman of the Department of Physiology until his retirement from the university in 1939, thereafter holding the title of Kenan professor emeritus.

In addition to his work in medical education and research, Manning was involved with one of the nation's first successful movements to provide equal access to quality medical care for all citizens. In the summer of 1935 he spent two months studying European medical care and financing systems in France and England. Largely as the result of this trip, Manning organized the Hospital Savings Association of North Carolina in an attempt to control the cost of hospitalization. Among the progressive concepts he promulgated through the association were those of cost sharing among a broad-based constituency, provision of equal access to medical care for the poor and the disadvantaged, and establishment of quality control standards for performance by hospitals. The Hospital Savings Association, sponsored by the Medical Society of the State of North Carolina, was the first hospital insurance plan administered by a state medical organization. In February 1942 Manning was elected chairman of the board and medical director of the association, a position that he held until his death. In the 1960s the organization merged with the Hospital Care Association to become Blue Cross and Blue Shield of North Carolina.

On 26 Apr. 1908 Manning married Martha Battle Lewis, who died the following year. On 6 June 1911 he married Mary Best Jones, and they became the parents of three sons: Isaac, Jr., John Taylor, and Howard Edwards. Dr. Manning served as president (1933–34) and secretary (1942) of the Medical Society of the State of North Carolina. He was an active member of the American Medical Association, Phi Kappa Sigma, the American College of Surgeons, and Alpha Kappa Kappa. He was a Fellow of the American College of Physicians and an active member of the Episcopal church in Chapel Hill.

SEE: Walter Reece Berryhill, William B. Blythe, and Isaac H. Manning, *Medical Education at Chapel Hill: The First One Hundred Years* (1979); Daniel L. Grant, *Alumni History of the University of North Carolina, 1795–1924* (1924); *North Carolina Medical Journal* 8 (May 1947).

MARCUS B. SIMPSON, JR.

Manning, James Smith (1 June 1859–28 July 1938), judge, was born in Pittsboro, the son of John and Louise Hall Manning and the grandson of Commander John Manning, U.S. Navy. His father was a distinguished professor of law at The University of North Carolina; his mother was the granddaughter of Judge John Hall of the North Carolina Supreme Court. He was educated at Pittsboro Female Academy (Dr. Sutton) and A. H. Merritt's School, then entered The University of North Carolina, graduating in 1879 and receiving the Phi Beta Kappa key years later. After teaching school in Pittsboro for a year or two, he reentered the university to study law and earned an LL.B. degree in 1882. Subsequently he obtained his license to practice and established himself in Durham in 1883. Manning was attorney for the city of Durham during the period 1886–87. On 12 Dec. 1888 he married Julia Tate Cain, of Hillsborough, the daughter of Dr. James F. and Julia Tate Cain.

In 1906 Manning, a Democrat, was elected to the legislature from Durham County and served as chairman of the Committee on Public Service Corporations. In 1908 he won a seat in the state senate and became chairman of the Judiciary Committee. In 1909 Governor W. W. Kitchin appointed him to fill an unexpired term as justice of the North Carolina Supreme Court, where he served until January 1911. In 1912 Manning moved to Raleigh with his wife and family and joined a partnership with former Governor Kitchin in the firm of Manning and Kitchin. In 1916 he was elected attorney general of North Carolina, a position he held for eight years. He served as a trustee of The University of North Carolina from 1899 to 1931 and for a time was president of the North Carolina Bar Association.

An Episcopalian, Manning took a leading part in various efforts to enhance the well-being of his community and state, despite his pressing legal activities. He was esteemed throughout North Carolina as a lawyer of exceptional ability and integrity. Judge and Mrs. Manning had four sons and two daughters: John Hall, James S., Jr., Frederick C., Sterling, Julia Cain, and Anna Louise. He was buried in Raleigh. His portrait hangs in the North Carolina Supreme Court building.

SEE: Adolph O. Goodwin, *Who's Who in Raleigh* (1916); Daniel L. Grant, *Alumni History of the University of North Carolina, 1795–1924* (1924); *North Carolina Biography*, vol. 4 (1941); *North Carolina Manual* (1909, 1917, 1919, 1923); *Sketch of Class of '79*, University of North Carolina; *Who Was Who in America*, vol. 1 (1943).

ELIZABETH W. MANNING

Manning, John (23 Dec. 1803–13 Aug. 1872), naval commander, was born in Edenton, the son of Joseph and Sarah Pell Manning. His father was a captain of a volunteer company in the War of 1812. John Manning was appointed a midshipman in the U.S. Navy on 10

May 1820, serving four years in the West India Station and Gulf of Mexico, three years on the Pacific west coast of South America, and one year in the naval school at New York. Promoted to lieutenant on 17 May 1828, he served in that rank for twenty-three years.

After commanding the brig *Bainbridge* for about one year, Manning was promoted to commander on 13 Oct. 1851. He remained with the *Bainbridge* on the west coast of Africa until relieved of his command at New York about 1 Sept. 1853. In January 1854 Commander Manning was given command of the receiving ship *Pennsylvania* at Norfolk, Va. In September 1855 he was relieved of that command by James C. Dobbin, secretary of the navy. He was not informed as to why he was relieved, but knowing there were no charges against him he assumed it was because of a serious bronchial affliction he had developed from so many years at sea. Secretary Dobbin's letter to Manning praised him highly for his command of the *Bainbridge*, as did Commander William L. Hudson's report to the commandant of the New York Navy Yard, Captain Charles Boarman, following inspection of the *Bainbridge* when she returned to New York after three years at sea.

Manning had been on the U.S. Naval Reserve list for almost six years when he resigned his commission on 18 May 1861. On 1 June he was appointed chief of bureau, ordnance, clothing, and provisions at New Bern. He was discharged from this post after only two months in compliance with an Ordinance of the Convention of North Carolina, transferring the navy of North Carolina to the Confederate government. He was then activated as a commander of the Confederate navy. He died at the home of his son, John, Jr., and was buried in Pittsboro. Manning and his wife, Tamar Haughton Leary, also had another son, Joseph Alonzo.

SEE: Jerome Dowd, *Sketches of Prominent Living North Carolinians* (1888); Commander John Manning, "Robert R. Heath Letters, 1860–1863" (Manuscript Department, Duke University Library, Durham).

ELIZABETH W. MANNING

Manning, John, Jr. (30 July 1830–12 Feb. 1899), lawyer, congressman, and teacher, was born at Edenton. His grandfather, Joseph Manning, was the first of the family to settle in North Carolina; in 1803 Joseph left the plantation known as Manning Manor near Norfolk, Va., moving first to Currituck County and then to Edenton, where he became a merchant. John's father was a commander in the U.S. Navy before holding that rank in the Confederate navy at the beginning of the Civil War. In 1829 John, Sr., married Tamar Haughton Leary, a member of one of Chowan County's oldest families. In addition to John, Jr., they had a son, Dr. Joseph Alonzo, who died at age twenty-six.

John Manning, Jr., attended Edenton Academy. Later his parents moved to Norfolk and he entered Norfolk Military Academy, where he was promoted to captain of the cadets in his senior year. Entering the sophomore class of The University of North Carolina, he was graduated near the top of his class after only two years. He then sailed with his father to South America. On his return he read law in the office of his cousin, John H. Haughton, in Pittsboro. In 1852 he obtained his license and after the statutory period of twelve months was permitted to appear in the superior and supreme courts. He then formed a partnership with Haughton. The young, overworked lawyer, an "old-line Whig" in politics, was often solicited to be a candidate for a seat in the General Assembly, which he firmly declined, believing his first duty was to his clients. He likewise declined appointment to the offices of secretary of state and judge of the superior court.

When the Civil War began, Manning enlisted in the Chatham Rifles, soon becoming first lieutenant and then adjutant of his regiment, the Fifteenth Volunteers. While his regiment was at Yorktown, he was appointed as receiver under the sequestration acts. He held this very responsible office throughout the war. On 17 May 1861 he was a delegate to the Secession Convention in Raleigh. There he pledged himself to the policy of meeting force with force, although deploring the haste with which the convention adopted the constitutions of the provisional government and the Confederate States of America.

When the war ended, Manning returned to the practice of law until November 1870, when he was elected a member of the Forty-first Congress. On the expiration of this short term, he won reelection and continued to hold his seat until he was elected a delegate to the constitutional convention of 1875, which was called to change features in the Constitution adopted in 1868 that were not suitable to conditions in North Carolina. His work there extended his reputation as a prudent statesman and lawyer.

In 1874, when the election of trustees of The University of North Carolina was taken from the Board of Education and given to the General Assembly, Manning was chosen as a trustee. He remained in that post for twenty years, participating in all the measures leading to the university's revival in 1875. While a member of the General Assembly in 1881, he took part in securing the university's first annual appropriation from the state. At the same session Manning, William T. Dortch, and John S. Henderson were appointed commissioners to revise and consolidate the public laws of the state. Such was their diligence that on 2 Mar. 1883 *The Code of North Carolina* was ratified as law.

In 1881, without his knowledge, the university board of trustees unanimously elected Manning professor of law to fill the vacancy created by the death of William H. Battle. This required him to move his large family to Chapel Hill, with no salary promised; he could rely only on fees from his students and emoluments from his profession, which necessarily were diminished by the incessant demands of his new duties. Beginning with a class of seven, he built enrollment to eighty-seven students by 1897–98. In 1883 he received the honorary degree of LL.D., which was conferred, as President Kemp P. Battle observed, not only as a tribute to his learning but also in recognition of his valuable services in behalf of his alma mater. It was Dr. Manning's purpose to prepare a series of works that would adapt Blackstone's *Commentaries on English Common Law* to modern needs. His *Commentaries on the First Book of Blackstone*, published after his death, gave evidence of the high quality of the work he was fitted to do.

Manning was an active member of the Episcopal church and held all its offices open to laymen, including a seat in the General Convention. He often was a lay reader supplying the minister's place.

On 5 June 1856 he married Louisa J. Hall, of Pittsboro, the daughter of Dr. Isaac Hall, a noted physician, and the granddaughter of John Hall, one of the first three justices of the North Carolina Supreme Court. They raised eight children: John Moore, a Durham physician and mayor for many years; James Smith, a Durham lawyer, who became attorney general and then a supreme court justice of North Carolina; Isaac Hall, dean of The University of North Carolina School of Medicine; Mary

Southerland; Sally Charleton, wife of Dr. F. P. Venable, president of The University of North Carolina; Eliza H., wife of William Weldon Huske of Fayetteville; Tamar H., wife of the Reverend Gaston Battle of Edgecombe County; and Louise H., wife of Professor William R. Webb of Webb School, Bellbuckle, Tenn.

John Manning was buried in Pittsboro. Manning Hall, The University of North Carolina's law school building, was named for him. A portrait hangs in the present law school building; another portrait was owned by his grandson, John T. Manning, an attorney of Chapel Hill.

SEE: William J. Adams, *North Carolina Supreme Court Justice*, reprinted from *North Carolina Law Review* 2, no. 4 (December 1924); Jerome Dowd, *Sketches of Prominent Living North Carolinians* (1888); Wade Hadley and others, eds., *Chatham County, 1771–1971* (1971); *The Life and Influence of John Manning* (n.d.); *North Carolina University Magazine* (March 1899); Raleigh *News and Observer*, 17 Feb. 1899; University of North Carolina, *The Hellenian '96* (1896).

ELIZABETH W. MANNING

Manning, John Hall (27 Sept. 1889–21 July 1963), lawyer and government official, was born in Durham County, the son of Julia Tate Cain and James Smith Manning, who served as attorney general of North Carolina and later as a justice of the state supreme court. Young Manning attended the Durham public schools and received A.B. (1909) and LL.B. (1913) degrees from The University of North Carolina. He taught school in Oxford (1909–10) and Durham (1910–11) before becoming a football coach at Stetson University in De Land, Fla. (1911–12). In 1913 he joined an infantry unit of the North Carolina National Guard as a private but was soon made a first lieutenant. He served along the Mexican border at the time of the raids into U.S. territory conducted by Mexican insurgent Pancho Villa. In World War I he was an intelligence and operations officer of a unit that broke through the Hindenburg Line. Near the end of the war he commanded the Third Battalion of the 119th Infantry. After the war he was made a lieutenant colonel and became the executive officer of the First Infantry unit of the North Carolina National Guard. In 1937 he was promoted to colonel and placed in command of the unit.

When the National Guard was activated in 1940, Manning was placed in command and remained in that position for two years. During World War II he served in the European theater, receiving the Legion of Merit for his performance as commander of a replacement depot in Italy. In 1946 Governor R. Gregg Cherry called upon Manning to assist in reorganizing the North Carolina National Guard. Cherry later appointed Manning commander of the Thirtieth Infantry Division with the rank of major general. In 1951 Governor W. Kerr Scott named Manning adjutant general of North Carolina, a post that he held until replaced by Capus Waynick on 7 July 1957. Manning retired with the rank of lieutenant general.

Following his admission to the bar in 1913, Manning practiced law in Selma, Kinston, and Raleigh. He served as assistant U.S. attorney from 1934 to 1946, when he became U.S. attorney for eastern North Carolina. From 1921 to 1931 he was a trustee of The University of North Carolina. For his services to the state he was awarded the North Carolina Distinguished Service Medal.

On 23 Nov. 1920 Manning married Jane Stillman, and they became the parents of two children: Richard de Yarman and Jane Stillman (Mrs. Charles A. McKenney, Jr.). Manning died at his home in Raleigh following a heart attack. A memorial service was held at St. Michael's Episcopal Church, Raleigh, and burial was in the National Cemetery, Raleigh. Manning was an Episcopalian, a Mason, and a Democrat.

SEE: D. L. Corbitt, ed., *Public Addresses, Letters, and Papers of William Bradley Umstead, Governor of North Carolina, 1953–1954* (1957); James W. Patton, ed., *Addresses and Papers of Luther Hartwell Hodges, Governor of North Carolina, 1954–1961*, vol. 2 (1962); Raleigh *News and Observer*, 22–23 July 1963; *Who's Who in America*, vol. 31 (1961).

W. CONARD GASS

Manning, Thomas Courtland (*14 Sept. 1825–11 Oct. 1887*), minister to Mexico, lawyer, and chief justice of Louisiana, was born in Edenton, the son of Joseph and Sarah Haughton Manning. In the 1840s he attended The University of North Carolina for a time before reading law and obtaining his license. He practiced in Edenton until 1855, when he moved to Alexandria, La., and opened a law firm in Rapides Parish.

A highly respected attorney, Manning was elected to the state Secession Convention in 1861 and appointed as aide-de-camp to Governor Thomas O. Moore, a fellow North Carolinian; he served until the governor's term expired in 1863, when Manning was made a brigadier general. He became an associate justice of the Louisiana Supreme Court in 1864 and served until the end of the war, when he returned to the private practice of law. In 1872 he was a delegate to the conventions of the Reform and Liberal parties. In the same year he was a presidential elector for the state at large to the Democratic National Convention in St. Louis.

In 1877 Governor Francis R. T. Nichols took office and appointed Manning chief justice of the state supreme court. It so happened that at the time there was a chief justice as well as a full bench of associate justices appointed by the previous governor. When the old justices refused to give way, a dispute arose between the two factions. President Rutherford B. Hayes appointed a commission that attempted to resolve the dispute, but without results. The court crier refused to open court for the old justices; the sheriff of the parish, however, demanded that they vacate the court. When they refused, a sheriff's posse was formed to oust the old justices; it marched along with the Nichols-appointed court, led by Manning, to the court building and took possession. The former justices vacated the courtroom just before the arrival of the posse. Manning served as chief justice until 1886, when President Grover Cleveland appointed him U.S. minister to Mexico.

On 6 June 1883 Manning addressed the literary societies of The University of North Carolina on "The Performance of Political Duties: The Great Need of the Present Day." It was published later in the year and widely read. In 1887 the university awarded him an honorary LL.D. degree.

On 18 Jan. 1848, at Athol in Edenton, Manning married Mary L. Blair, the only daughter of George Blair. They became the parents of eight children: Elizabeth, Mary Cortelia, Winnifred Whitmell, Alston, Nina, Sarah, Maud, and Thomas Cathcart. He died in New York City while attending a meeting of the trustees of the Peabody Fund, of which he was a member. He was buried in New Orleans.

Thomas C. Manning was the uncle of John Manning, Jr., who served as professor of law and dean of the law school at The University of North Carolina from 1881 to 1899. There was a difference of only five years in their ages. John Manning, Jr., was awarded the same honorary degree.

SEE: Family records (possession of John T. Manning, Chapel Hill); Percy Roberts, *Sketch of the Hon. Thomas Courtland Manning* (1880); *North Carolina University Magazine* 6 (November 1886 [portrait]).

JOHN T. MANNING

Manning, Vannoy Hartrog (*26 July 1839–3 Nov. 1892*), congressman from Mississippi, was born near Raleigh but moved with his parents to Mississippi in 1841. He attended Horn Lake Male Academy in De Soto County, Miss., and the University of Nashville, Tenn. In 1860 he moved to Arkansas, where he studied law, was admitted to the bar in 1861, and began a practice in Hamburg. During the Civil War Manning served in the Confederate army as a captain and subsequently as a colonel in the Third Arkansas Infantry and the Second Arkansas Battalion. Captured at the Battle of the Wilderness, he was held as a prisoner of war until August 1865. After the war he practiced law in Holly Springs, Miss.

A Democrat, Manning was elected to the Forty-fifth, Forty-sixth, and Forty-seventh Congresses, serving from 4 Mar. 1877 to 3 Mar. 1883. He presented his credentials as a member-elect to the Forty-eighth Congress but did not qualify, and on 25 June 1884 the seat was awarded to James R. Chalmers, who had contested Manning's election. In 1883 Manning returned to the practice of law in Washington, D.C. He died in Branchville, Prince Georges County, Md., and was buried in Glenwood Cemetery, Washington, D.C.

SEE: *Biog. Dir. Am. Cong.* (1971); Leonidas Polk, *Handbook of North Carolina* (1879); *Who Was Who in America*, historical vol. (1967).

ELIZABETH W. MANNING

Manson, Otis Frederick (*10 Oct. 1822–25 Jan. 1888*), physician and educator, was born in Richmond, Va., the son of Otis and Sarah Dews Ferrill Manson, who were married in Richmond on 1 Feb. 1818. Otis Frederick, the second surviving child of his parents, was the brother of Sarah Anna (b. 4 July 1820; m. Eli H. Richards of Richmond), George W. (b. 8 June 1825), Eliza Sanger (b. 7 Dec. 1827; m. Cornelius J. Eaton of Richmond), Charles Henry (b. 14 Jan. 1830), and Mary Ann (b. 27 Mar. 1832; m. Joseph Littlejohn of Oxford, N.C.). His mother was from Petersburg, Va., and the records of his maternal grandparents, William and Sarah Dews Ferrill, are located in Halifax and Pittsylvania counties. His father was the son of Frederick and Anna Hemmenway Manson, of Framingham, Mass., both of whom were buried in Shockoe Cemetery, Richmond.

The elder Otis Manson was established in Richmond by 1822; in December he advertised his readiness to supply drawings of plans and elevations of town and country houses. Records and appraisals of his work are in the Valentine Museum, Richmond, and in Scott's *Old Richmond Neighborhoods*. His son, Otis Frederick, was probably born in the family residence at the southwestern corner of Nineteenth and Franklin streets. He may have spent all of his childhood at that location since his father, although residing in 1850 at the corner of Ten and Main streets, probably did not move before 1840. The boy completed his early schooling at the Richmond

Academy. Adopting the profession of his paternal great-grandfather, Dr. Ebenezer Hemmenway, he studied medicine at Hampden-Sydney College (afterwards the Medical College of Virginia of Virginia Commonwealth University) and was graduated at an early age.

By 1841 Manson had settled in Granville County, N.C. The 1850 census lists him as a physician in the Nutbush District and the father of four children. He gave twenty years of service to the people of his adopted state and for a time was a member of its Board of Medical Examiners, a position he later held in Virginia. In 1862 Manson was commissioned a surgeon in the Confederate army and placed in charge of a hospital in Virginia for the care and rehabilitation of North Carolina troops. For his devotion to duty he received the personal commendation of Governor Zebulon Vance. The community of Cheatamville in Warren County changed its name to Manson in his honor.

After the war Manson returned to his native Richmond, where he devoted the remainder of his life to the practice of medicine and to teaching. From 1869 to 1882 he was professor of pathology and physiology at the Medical College of Virginia; subsequently its board elected him professor emeritus. His career was especially noteworthy for his work on the pathology and treatment of various fevers, a subject on which he published several works. The extent of his medical as well as his general knowledge may be judged from the catalogue of his extensive personal library. In addition, he served as a member of the Richmond City Council from 1874 to 1882.

Manson was married twice. His first wife was Mary Ann Spotswood Burwell, the daughter of Spotswood Burwell of Granville County and the great-granddaughter of Colonel Alexander Spotswood, a governor of colonial Virginia. Their children included Sallie Spotswood (m. A. L. Huntt), Otis, Eliza Sanger (m. T. L. Alfriend), William Frederick, Mary Anna (the second wife of A. L. Huntt), and Lewis Burwell. Manson's second wife was Mrs. Helen Gray Wattson, whom he married on 25 Oct. 1881. He died in Richmond and was buried in Hollywood Cemetery.

SEE: Architects of Nineteenth-century Richmond (Valentine Museum, Richmond); Robert Alanzo Brock, *Professor Otis Frederick Manson, M.D.* (n.d.); Otis Frederick Manson, *Catalogue of the Medical Library of the Late Professor Otis Frederick Manson* (1889); Myron A. Munson, *The Portsmouth Race of Monson-Munson-Manson* (1910); *Richmond Compiler*, 12 Dec. 1822; *Richmond Dispatch*, 26 Jan. 1888; *Richmond Enquirer*, 10 Feb. 1888; *Richmond Times-Dispatch*, 27 Mar. 1892, 9 July 1909, 2 Jan. 1910; Mary Wingfield Scott, *Old Richmond Neighborhoods* (1950); U.S. Census, Granville County (North Carolina State Archives, Raleigh); U.S. Census, Richmond, Va. (1830 Madison Ward, 1840 Jefferson Ward).

RICHARD W. SLATTEN

Manteo *(fl. 1584–87),* leading Carolina Algonquian Indian, was a member of the ruling family of the Croatoan subtribe of the coastal Algonquian group. His mother (or adopted mother) appears to have been the chieftainess of the subtribe that acknowledged some dependence on the Indians of Roanoke Island. Manteo encountered the English visitors in 1584 and agreed to go with them to England, as did another Indian, Wanchese. It was possibly on this voyage that Thomas Harriot began to teach him to speak English and he to teach Harriot Algonquian. By mid-October he was at Queen Elizabeth's court, wearing English brown taffeta clothing but unwilling to speak the new language. By mid-December, however, the two Indians, possibly with Harriot's aid, had proved capable of describing the geography and resources of their region in some detail with, we suspect, Manteo taking the lead.

He sailed with Sir Richard Grenville and Ralph Lane to the Carolina Outer Banks in 1585, probably taking part in the exploration of the banks in July and almost certainly playing a significant role as interpreter and negotiator during August and September, when the English settlement was established close to the village of high chief Wingina (Pemisapan) on Roanoke Island. From then to June 1586 he is likely to have divided his time between Croatoan (three Indian sites at or south of Buxton may represent the center of his subtribe's territory) and guiding English parties through the rivers and sounds.

In June 1586 Manteo was at Roanoke Island, possibly having brought some of his men to assist Lane, who had broken with and killed the high chief. When Lane decided to abandon the colony, Manteo, of his own accord, accompanied him to England. We know nothing of his experiences there, except that he was exposed to Anglican teachings and had responded to them. He probably also advised Governor John White in his preparations for a permanent colony to be established in 1587 on Chesapeake Bay. The expedition that reached Roanoke Island in late July was not carried on to Chesapeake Bay by the recalcitrant sailors. Manteo accompanied Edward Stafford to Croatoan, whose men were prepared to fight until Manteo revealed himself to them. At a later stage White's party mistakenly attacked some Croatoan Indians who were plundering Dasemunkepeuc, where the remnant of Pemisapan's men were living, but the incident was glossed over with Manteo's aid.

It was intended that the colonists should make their own way to Chesapeake Bay, leaving a party at Roanoke Island to await John White's return from England with further supplies in 1588. They were placed under the protection of Manteo, who, by Sir Walter Raleigh's appointment, was, on 13 Aug. 1587, "christened in Roanoak, and called Lord thereof, and of Dasmongueponke, in reward of his faithful service." This honor indicates how highly he was regarded in England. The majority of the colonists appear to have soon departed for their Chesapeake abode and reached there safely. A group of men was left to await John White. But White did not come in 1588, and sometime between 1588 and the latter part of 1589 the party moved down to live with Manteo, leaving as a sign the clear carving of CROATOAN, without any suggestion they were in distress, to show White where he would find them. White arrived only in August 1590 to find the remains of his own possessions strewn about, a new defensive enclosure, and indications that he would find his party with Manteo. Bad weather and the loss of a boat's crew led impatient seamen to prevent White from making his way to Croatoan. Plans made to find a place for the winter and return in the spring of 1591 came to nothing, and White returned to England in October 1590, leaving his colonists to their own devices.

Nothing further is known of Manteo or of the Englishmen he had sheltered. Some may have rejoined their comrades on Chesapeake Bay; some or all may have stayed with Manteo, joined his tribal group, and become assimilated. Rumors in the early seventeenth century seemed to suggest that some white men were still living in this southern area, but no trace of them was found by parties searching from Jamestown.

Manteo was evidently a man of some distinction and

intellect. He favored the English intruders (and was favored by them) as against the traditional leader of his tribe. Raleigh's respect for him, his own loyalty to John White, his desire for assimilation rather than conflict, and his baptism and acceptance of the lordship of his tribe's territories at English hands are evidence of his role. Nevertheless, had the colonists established themselves in strength close to his domain, his inclinations might well have been put to a more severe test. As it was, he passes out of history merely as one of the first eastern American Indians to be glimpsed as an independent personality.

SEE: Richard Hakluyt, *The Principall Navigations*. . . . (1589) and *The Principal Navigations*. . . . , vol. 3 (1600); David B. Quinn, *England and the Discovery of America* (1974); David B. Quinn, ed., *The Roanoke Voyages*, 2 vols. (1955).

DAVID B. QUINN

Marchant, Frederick (Frank) (*ca. 1872–6 Feb. 1942*), photographer, was born in Pennsylvania, one of three children of William J. and Henrietta (Hattie) S. Makeley Marchant. His father (b. ca. 1835) and his paternal grandparents were natives of Massachusetts. His mother, also born in Massachusetts, was the daughter of Irish immigrants.

The family was living in Pennsylvania by 1872 and in Philadelphia in 1880. Educated in the schools of Philadelphia, Marchant studied civil engineering at some unknown institution. His father probably was dead by 1900, when his mother was employed at a Methodist home for the aged in Philadelphia. Census records for 1900 do not show Frank Marchant residing in either Pennsylvania or North Carolina. By the early 1900s, however, he was living in Hamlet, N.C., and was employed as a civil engineer by the Seaboard Air Line Railway. About 1907 he opened a photography studio in Hamlet in rented space on the second floor of O. T. Goodwin's wholesale grocery on Raleigh Street; apparently, he also served for a number of years as the official photographer for the Seaboard Railway. A bachelor, he was living with his elderly mother in a rented house on the corner of Raleigh and Charlotte streets by 1910. The majority of Marchant's photographs were taken on location rather than in a studio, and few portraits have been found.

Most of his work was done in and around Hamlet and Rockingham and consists largely of trains and train wrecks, parades, snow scenes, hotels, town scenes, and people. In addition, he occasionally photographed unusual and newsworthy events and subjects that he believed would appeal to the public. He did other work in Anson and Union counties, while he photographed some train wrecks in Richmond, Moore, and Lee counties and as far west as Rutherford County and east to the railway terminus in Wilmington. Some of his photographs were registered with the copyright office in Washington, D.C. In 1911 he photographed the infamous murder trial of Lewis West and his gang of desperadoes in Wilson County. His camera also documented the construction of Blewett Falls Dam and powerhouse on the Pee Dee River at the Richmond-Anson County border in 1911–12. Leading newspapers throughout the nation carried a few of his photographs to illustrate their stories.

As a part of his photographic enterprise, Marchant produced some of his best photographs as picture postcards. These souvenir cards actually were three-by-five-inch prints developed on emulsified cards designed for mailing and sold at depots, hotels, and drugstores. His work was successful into the 1920s, when it apparently began to decline following the death of his mother from pneumonia on 20 Jan. 1922. Over the years he had been drinking, and an apparent addiction to alcohol worsened after her death. By the 1930s he had ceased to work as a photographer but did continue to develop film for a living.

As his health declined in the 1930s, Marchant became increasingly reclusive. There is nothing to suggest that he was ever a member of any church or fraternal organization in Hamlet. At the time of his death he was living in an old tin-roofed shack on Vance Street. He was buried in the Mary Love Cemetery, Hamlet. Unfortunately, his glass plate negatives and prints were destroyed after his death, but an assortment of his postcards and prints and between seventy-five and one hundred of his negatives are at the State Archives in Raleigh.

SEE: *Charlotte Observer*, 11 Feb. 1942; *Hamlet News-Messenger*, 12 Feb. 1942; James E. Honeycutt and Ida Honeycutt, *A History of Richmond County* (1976); Interviews: J. R. Barbour (4 Mar. 1989), Dan Bennett (12 Feb. 1989), Joe Blalock (4 Mar. 1989), Durwood Brown (4 Mar. 1989), Mrs. Murphy McDonald (22 Apr. 1989), and staff of the National Railroad Museum (12 Feb., 4 Mar. 1989), all of Hamlet, Dick Brown (Laurinburg, 30 Jan. 1989), C. J. Jones (Garner, 13 Feb. 1989), and Joe M. McLaurin (Rockingham, 30 Jan. 1989); North Carolina State Board of Health, Bureau of Vital Statistics, Death Certificate of Hattie S. Marchant (North Carolina State Archives, Raleigh); U.S. Census, North Carolina (1910) and Pennsylvania (1880).

STEPHEN E. MASSENGILL

Mare, John (*1739–17 Feb. 1803*), painter, merchant, and politician, was born in New York City, the oldest child of John and Mary Bes Mare. His father was from Devonshire, England, and his mother was presumably of Dutch origin. His sister Mary married the English painter, William Williams, who may have given young Mare encouragement and assistance, though nothing is known of the boy's education or training. In 1759 Mare and his wife Anne Morris moved to Albany, N.Y., where their son John was baptized in 1760. Apparently she and the child died before Mare returned to New York in 1761.

The earliest portraits attributed to Mare are those of the brothers Henry and Robert G. Livingston. Henry's is signed and dated 1760; Robert's is unsigned and undated. Both are believed to be copies by Mare of earlier portraits by John Wollaston. The first official record of Mare as an artist is his admittance to the freedom of the city of New York as a "limner" in 1765. In 1766 the city council paid him for a portrait of King George III, which probably did not survive the American Revolution. His best-known portraits, both done in 1767, are those of Jeremiah Platt (owned by the Metropolitan Museum of Art) and John Keteltas (owned by the New-York Historical Society). The latter is famous for a fly on Keteltas's wristband, "the first, widely known *trompe l'oeil* in American art history [and] the only case . . . where an insect was put into a portrait." In the same year he copied a Wollaston portrait for Dr. James Lloyd of Boston. In 1768 he painted John Torrey of Boston and probably Torrey's brother William, whose strikingly similar portrait is now known only from a photograph. A 1769 portrait of Gerard Beekman (at the Philipse Castle Restoration near Peekskill, N.Y.) and an undated portrait of a member of the Werden-Wilcocks family (at Old Deerfield, Mass.) are attributed to Mare.

Returning to Albany in 1772, he painted a portrait (now owned by the state of New York) of Sir John Johnson, who became one of the chief Tories of the Revolutionary period. In 1774, back in New York, Mare did portraits of Dr. Benjamin Youngs Prime and John Covenhoven (the latter his only known pastel, owned by the Shelburne Museum, Shelburne, Vt.). A recently discovered portrait of an unknown man, unsigned and undated, is attributed to Mare partly because of its display of Masonic emblems.

Masonry remained an important interest in Mare's life even after he stopped painting. It may have provided his contact with Sir John Johnson, who was provincial grand master. In Albany Mare joined Master's Lodge No. 2, and he and Johnson were visiting brothers of St. Patrick's Lodge, Johnstown, N.Y., in the winter of 1772–73. On his return to New York he transferred to St. John's Lodge No. 2, of which he was senior warden when he made his first visits to Unanimity Lodge, Edenton, N.C., in 1776 and 1777. In 1778 he became a member of Unanimity Lodge, in 1779 its master, and for the next twenty years its mainspring. He is believed to have helped draft the constitution of the Grand Lodge of North Carolina, and in 1787 he presided at the Masonic convention that revived it.

Why Mare moved from New York to North Carolina is unknown, as is why he stopped painting. His nephew, the younger William (Joseph) Williams, was living in his household and painting portraits in 1785, but Mare had dropped art and gone into business as a merchant. For about fifteen years he was very successful, trading with the West Indies and acquiring much land in several counties, as well as property in Edenton. His last years, however, were fraught with financial difficulties and apparently a disabling illness, and he died in almost desperate circumstances.

From his earliest years in North Carolina, Mare aligned himself with the Revolutionary leaders of Chowan County. In 1780 he suffered the loss of a ship he owned with other merchants when it was captured by the British. He provided supplies for North Carolina troops. When British row galleys got into Albemarle Sound, he contributed £1,000 to the expedition to drive them out.

Mare's public career began with three years as postmaster (1783–86), followed by two years as county coroner (1786–88). In 1786 he became treasurer of the town of Edenton and in 1789 a town commissioner, serving for years in both capacities. From 1787 to 1799 he was a notably conscientious justice of the peace, frequently serving as auditor of legal accounts. The height of his political career was his appointment to the Council of State in 1787, when his friend Samuel Johnston became governor. He was renominated in 1789 when Johnston was reelected, but he was not reappointed, because Johnston became senator without taking office as governor. In the same year Mare represented the borough of Edenton at the convention that ratified the U.S. Constitution and voted for ratification.

John Mare's second wife, Marion Boyd Wells (daughter of William Boyd of Chowan County and widow of Dr. George Wells), died long before him. His only survivors were two young daughters, Mary and Elizabeth Ann. A member of St. Paul's Church, Edenton, he may have been buried in its churchyard.

SEE: Chowan County Court Records, September Term, 1808 (North Carolina State Archives, Raleigh); Edith Gaines, ed., "Collectors' Notes," *Antiques* 98 (1970); Helen Burr Smith, "John Mare (1739–c. 1795): New York Portrait Painter," *New-York Historical Society Quarterly* 35 (October 1951), and "A Portrait by John Mare Identified: 'Uncle Jeremiah,'" *Antiques* 103 (1973); Helen Burr Smith and Elizabeth Vann Moore, "John Mare: A Composite Portrait," *North Carolina Historical Review* 44 (January 1967).

ELIZABETH VANN MOORE

Marks, Sallie Belle (21 May 1891–11 Nov. 1968), first woman professor at The University of North Carolina, was born in Albemarle, the daughter of Whitson A. and Arana Hall Marks. She attended Meridian Female College, Meridian, Miss., in 1908 and was graduated from Southwestern Teachers College in 1923. Her professional career began when she taught in junior high school in Oklahoma in 1916–17, followed by service as principal of an elementary school in Fort Smith, Ark., and as assistant superintendent of schools in La Crosse, Wis. She received a master of arts degree from Columbia University in 1926. Having also begun courses at George Washington University towards a Ph.D., she taught at the University of Arkansas from 1924 to 1927, finishing her doctorate at Columbia some years later.

For the term 1927–28 Miss Marks was supervising principal of the elementary grades of the training school at The University of North Carolina with the rank of assistant professor of education, thus becoming the first female professor on the faculty at Chapel Hill. Her title soon became assistant professor of elementary education, a position she held until 1934. She was cocontributor of "The Geography of North Carolina" to a textbook, *Geography: Southern Lands*, published in 1933.

From 1934 to 1936 she was professor of education and psychology at Salem College, and from 1936 to 1938 she taught at Meredith College, Raleigh. For the six years between 1938 to 1944 she held a professorship at the University of Chicago. In the latter year she became an educational specialist in the Institute of Inter-American Affairs in Washington, D.C., working in a number of foreign countries until 1954. Miss Marks was decorated by the government of Peru for her contribution to that nation's reading program. She was a member of the American Education Team in Korea in 1954–55, holding the rank of lieutenant colonel with the army. She was coauthor of *Building Our Hemisphere*, published by Scribner's in 1957.

Following her retirement Sallie Marks spent part of each year in Black Mountain while continuing to maintain her home in Washington, where she was active in the World Organization for Early Childhood Education, the Society of Women Geographers, the Children's Book Guild, and other organizations. She was buried in the Albemarle cemetery.

SEE: *Charlotte Observer*, 13 Nov. 1968; *Greensboro Daily News*, 26 Apr. 1931; William S. Powell, ed., *North Carolina Lives* (1962); Stanly County Historic Properties Commission Files, Albemarle; *Stanly News and Press*, 15 Nov. 1968; Harriette H. Walker, *Busy North Carolina Woman* (1931).

WILLIAM S. POWELL

Marling, Jacob (1774–18 Dec. 1833), painter, decorator, and teacher, lived in Warrenton, where he taught at the academy and executed scenes for the Thespian Society at the Warrenton Theatre. Taking up residence in Raleigh, he became director of the North Carolina Museum in 1813, the year of its founding. The North Carolina Museum, which was a general museum, had a reading room where most of the principal newspapers, reviews of literary works, and so forth, were filed, as well as natural and artificial curios, sketches, maps, drawings and paintings, rare coins, and books. Jacob Marling may well be called North Carolina's first serious collector of works of art: at his death, his entire collection, containing fine oil paintings and prints, was put up for sale, and his collection of natural artifacts was transferred to The University of North Carolina in Chapel Hill.

About 1825 Marling did his best known painting, that of the North Carolina statehouse after its restoration. In the landscape he also shows a small fireproof building, erected by Edmund Lane in 1819, as a one-story house; its door is evidently located a few feet north of the present bronze statue of George Washington just south of the Fayetteville Street entrance to the statehouse.

Although Marling's oil paintings are not signed, his works can be easily identified through stylistic means. The crispness of his line and color is his trademark. He seldom used the brownish tones usually associated with his period of art. His portraits of men and women, his landscapes, and his miniatures (usually watercolor on paper) all have a uniqueness that is easily identifiable. More and more of his works are being found in local collections, and they all attest to the genius of the artist. His portraits of statesmen and other well-known early nineteenth-century persons form a valuable historical document of the time. The portrait listing includes John Gray Blount, William A. Blount, James Clark, William Donnell Cobb, Joseph John Daniel, John Robert Donnell, Edward Graham, Dr. Fabius Julius Haywood, the Reverend William McPheeters, William Miller, John Owen, Thomas Gilchrist Polk, John Mushro Roberts, and Montford Stokes. Many other portraits listed in the inventory of his estate have not been located.

Louisa Marling survived her husband by thirty years. In her later life she ran a millinery business in Raleigh, and it is recorded that she provided lamp shades for the new statehouse in the 1850s.

SEE: Marshall De Lancey Haywood, *Builders of the Old North State* (1968); Raleigh *Register*, 24 Dec. 1833; Ben F. Williams, "Jacob Marling: Early Raleigh Painter, 1774–1833," in *Jacob Marling: Early North Carolina Artist* (North Carolina Museum of Art, 1964 exhibition catalogue).

BENJAMIN F. WILLIAMS

Marsden, Richard (ca. 1675–1742), Anglican clergyman, had an extraordinary and versatile career which involved crossing the Atlantic a dozen times. A native of Hornsea in Yorkshire, England, he immigrated to Maryland. In May 1700 Marsden was listed as lay reader of St. Michael's Parish in Talbot County; five months later he went to England for ordination. Returning as rector of the parish, he remained until 1706. In that year, he moved to South Carolina. While awaiting ship in North Carolina, destined to be his final home, he performed the Holy Eucharist and baptized forty-five persons on Trinity Sunday. William Glover, governor of North Carolina, later wrote the bishop of London that this was the first time the communion service had ever been held in the colony.

Arriving in Charles Town, S.C., Marsden stated that he had been appointed rector of St. Philip's but that the necessary credentials had been blown overboard while he was at sea. He became so popular with the parishioners that when the Reverend Gideon Johnston arrived in

1708 with a commission as rector from London, they wanted to retain Marsden in his place. The South Carolina authorities, however, supported the legitimate claimant, and Richard Marsden was appointed to Christ Church Parish in Berkeley. In 1709 he left South Carolina for England, where he met the Reverend Samuel Beresford, rector of St. Michael's in Barbados, who was on a visit home to regain his health. Marsden persuaded Beresford to let him supply the parish in his absence. It is not known how long he remained in Barbados. Returning to England, he in some way obtained a living in Leicestershire and two small cures in Warwickshire.

The year 1714 found Marsden teaching school in Chester, Pa., where he complained that most of his pupils were Quakers. After two years he went to England, where he managed to become domestic chaplain to William Henry Bentinck, duke of Portland, and for a time he was steward of the manor of Thwing, an estate owned by the duke in County York. When Portland became governor of Jamaica in 1721, his chaplain accompanied him there. On 2 July 1723 Marsden wrote the bishop of London that he was unwilling to accept a presentation in Jamaica for fear of losing his living in England. During his stay in Jamaica, in addition to his duties in Portland's household, he was locum tenens in St. John's Parish. Unfortunately, his patron died of the fever in Jamaica in 1726 and Marsden had to leave. Facing bankruptcy proceedings in England, he went to New England for a while and then appeared in Virginia without a license. Commissary James Blair wrote to London in 1727 that Marsden seemed to be a "man of figure" and good sense. Late in the same year Governor William Gooch reported that the clergyman had been sent to Lynnhaven Parish in Princess Anne County. This county, on the border of North Carolina, was visited by William Byrd and the other commissioners when the line was being surveyed between the two colonies in 1728. In March of that year Byrd commented that the party had attended church, where Marsden delivered an edifying sermon. Elsewhere he referred to the priest, incorrectly, as "the parson of the parish, a painful apostle from the Society."

By 1729 Marsden had again mismanaged his business affairs and had fled Virginia, four hundred pounds in debt. Arriving in the Cape Fear section of North Carolina, which had only recently been open to settlement, he claimed to have a commission as a roving missionary and an inspector of clergy. Marsden made a business trip to Lisbon before settling down and, in the words of a contemporary, began to traffic as a merchant and offered his services free of charge. This upset the Reverend Jean La Pierre, who had already been assigned to the area by the Society for the Propagation of the Gospel in Foreign Parts. On 10 Mar. 1732 Governor George Burrington, who seems to have liked him, said that Marsden was holding services at a place called Onslow, forty miles from his residence.

All of colonial America was considered the see of the bishop of London, and no clergyman was legally permitted to settle in any colony without a license from that prelate. Edmund Gibson, bishop of London, took a dim view of Marsden's appearance in Virginia, and later in North Carolina, without his license. In 1736 the principal inhabitants of the parish of St. James in Cape Fear River petitioned the church authorities in London that their "worthy pastor" be officially assigned to them. Commissary Alexander Garden in Charles Town, no admirer of Marsden, was not impressed by the petition, saying the Cape Fear men would support any person for any cause for a single bowl of punch. As a result of the intercession of many people, including the archbishop of Canterbury, the Society for the Propagation of the Gospel held a hearing to consider the petition from St. James's Parish. Testimonials were examined and Marsden, who had gone to England himself, was asked to preach a sermon on a specific text. Trying to mend fences with the bishop, Marsden called on him in London, but Gibson refused to see him. The clergyman then wrote his superior to profess his repentance, saying: "I do with great sincerity and sorrow, confess that I have given your lordship great cause to be offended." He begged the bishop to at least accept a map of North Carolina he had brought with him.

On 19 May 1738 the Society for the Propagation of the Gospel acted in favor of Marsden, appointing him missionary for that part of North Carolina south of the Neuse and authorizing him to reside at his plantation, the Hermitage, on Prince George Creek. However, Marsden, remaining in England until some decision was reached, wrote in 1739 from Peckenham, near Alcester in Warwickshire, that the bishop had not given him the necessary license. Acting on the negative report from Commissary Alexander Garden, Bishop Gibson asked the society to revoke Marsden's appointment. He returned to North Carolina and apparently never regained the bishop's favor. Marsden is generally considered to have been the first rector of St. James's Parish.

No portrait of Marsden is known. However, he was described as a full-bodied man, six feet tall, and stoop-shouldered, with a swarthy complexion marked with smallpox. James Murray of North Carolina said he was the best preacher he had heard in America. Marsden's career is best summed up by the words of the Reverend Francis Le Jau, who was with him in South Carolina: "I believe that the itching for trading which he does not understand has been the cause of his misfortunes, for in the main he is a sober man and has an art of pleasing the common people."

Less is known about Marsden's private life. In 1709 his wife died in South Carolina and the children were placed among the neighbors. He is said to have remarried in England and again in Jamaica. A son Thomas left a will probated in New Hanover County, N.C., in 1739. He had no issue but mentioned his father, his brother William, and his mother Elizabeth Marsden "of Halifax, in ye County of York in England." William Marsden, the brother mentioned in the will, apparently did not settle in North Carolina. The only child of the Reverend Mr. Marsden who left descendants in North Carolina was his daughter Margaret, who married Roger Haynes of Castle Haynes. Margaret Marsden Haynes had a daughter who married General Hugh Waddell and a daughter Margaret who, by her marriage to John Burgwyn, carried the Hermitage property into that family.

SEE: J. Bryan Grimes, ed., *Abstract of North Carolina Wills* (1910); Fleming H. James, "Richard Marsden: Wayward Clergyman," *William and Mary Quarterly*, 3d ser. (1954); Frank W. Klingberg, ed., "The Carolina Journal of Dr. Francis Le Jau," *University of California Publications in History* 53 (1956); Lawrence Lee, *The Lower Cape Fear in Colonial Days* (1965); Louis B. Wright, *The Prose Works of William Byrd of Westover* (1966).

CLAIBORNE T. SMITH, JR.

Marsden, Rufus (*1695–1750*), merchant and legislator, was born in the Chorley-Liverpool section of Lancashire, England. He settled in the Cape Fear region of North Carolina in 1736. The next year he was granted 1,040 acres in New Hanover County, and over the next five years he continued to receive additional grants. In 1743 the freeholders of Wilmington elected Marsden one of five commissioners for the town and reelected him each year thereafter until his death. He also served for several years as one of the justices of the peace for New Hanover County.

Marsden was elected a member of the House of Burgesses from New Hanover for the session that met in New Bern on 12 June 1746. This Assembly was shortly prorogued by Governor Gabriel Johnston to meet at Wilmington the following November. It marked the beginning of the controversy between the northern and southern counties concerning representation in the House of Burgesses. Until then the Albemarle counties had five representatives each in the house, while the other counties had only two each. On 22 Nov. 1746 Marsden introduced a bill in the house providing for "establishing a more equal Representation of all his Majesty's subjects in the House of Burgesses." Three days later it was passed by both houses of the Assembly.

While continuing to represent New Hanover in the house through 1749, Marsden served on several important committees. One of his most significant pieces of legislation was a bill calling "for the Encouragement of James Davis to set up and carry on his Business of a printer in this province, and for other purposes therein mentioned." He introduced the bill on 6 Apr. 1749; four days later it was passed by both houses. In June James Davis established his printing business in New Bern.

By the time of his death Marsden had acquired considerable properties. He owned a plantation, Lotham, on Smiths Creek; a brigantine, *John and William*; and several lots and houses in Wilmington. On 7 July 1732 he married Alice Rigby, and they had three children: Hannah (1735–56; m. Arthur Mabson), Alice (1746–1813; m. Benjamin Heron), and Peggy (1748–86; m. first Edward Chivers and second John London).

SEE: Mrs. Gilmer Brenizer Papers (Southern Historical Collection, University of North Carolina, Chapel Hill); J. Bryan Grimes, ed., *Abstract of North Carolina Wills* (1910); Donald R. Lennon and Ida Brooks Kellam, eds., *Wilmington Town Book, 1743–1778* (1973); William L. Saunders, ed., *Colonial Records of North Carolina*, vol. 4 (1886).

LAWRENCE F. LONDON

Marsh, Robert Henry (*8 Nov. 1837–6 Oct. 1924*), Baptist minister and president of the Baptist State Convention of North Carolina, was born in Chatham County, the son of Robert and Lucy Marsh. His grandfather, William Marsh, moved to Chatham County from Virginia as a young man, served in the American Revolution, and obtained land grants from the state of North Carolina. Young Marsh received a B.A. degree from The University of North Carolina in 1858 and was appointed tutor in languages at Wake Forest College in 1859. After attending the Southern Baptist Theological Seminary, Greenville, S.C., in 1860–61, he was awarded the M.A. degree at Chapel Hill in 1861. In 1886 he received an honorary D.D. degree from Wake Forest College.

Marsh was baptized on 2 Oct. 1856 and was licensed to preach by the Chapel Hill (now University) Baptist Church on 5 Mar. 1859. He was ordained on 1 Sept. 1861 at the First Baptist Church, Raleigh. A few hours after ordination, he was on the march as chaplain of the Twenty-sixth Regiment, North Carolina Infantry. He served with this regiment until superseded by a Confederate army chaplain. In the spring of 1862 Marsh became a professor in the Oxford Female Seminary, where he taught until 1864.

The Reverend Mr. Marsh served as pastor in the Flat

River Baptist Association for fifty years, including Grassy Creek (1863–65 and 1887–97), Tally Ho (1863–65 and 1874–93), Hester (1869–1916), Oxford (1869–72), Enon (1875–86 and 1897–1916), Henderson (1877–80), State Line (1894–1901), Bullock (1905–16), and Dexter (1906–12). He was deeply interested in everything that affected the people to whom he ministered, and they sought his advice about their business affairs as well as their spiritual welfare.

The work of Robert H. Marsh lay far beyond the borders of the Flat River Association. He was president of the Baptist State Convention of North Carolina for fourteen years (1891–1905), a trustee (1870–1916) and president of the board of trustees (1890) of Wake Forest College, a trustee of the Southern Baptist Theological Seminary (1896–1913), and vice-president of the Southern Baptist Convention (1897 and 1912).

On 22 June 1863 he married Lizzie Hayes (24 Sept. 1842–19 Sept. 1917), the daughter of Henry C. and Ann E. Hayes, of Mecklenburg County, Va. They had one daughter, Mrs. C. D. Ray. Marsh died, according to his physicians, of "advanced age." The funeral services were held in the Oxford First Baptist Church, with burial in Oxford.

SEE: John Thomas Alderman Papers and Robert Henry Marsh Papers (Baptist Historical Collection, Wake Forest University, Winston-Salem); *Flat River Baptist Association Minutes, 1924* (portrait); *North Carolina Baptist State Convention Annual, 1924* (portrait); John R. Sampey, *Southern Baptist Theological Seminary: The First Thirty Years, 1859–1889* (1890).

JOHN R. WOODARD

Marshall, Frederic William (5 Feb. 1721–11 Feb. 1802), senior civilis of the Moravian church, oeconomus (chief administrator) of the Wachovia settlement, town planner, and architect, guided the development of Salem from a wilderness to a thriving community by the end of the eighteenth century. His given name was Friedrich Wilhelm von Marschall, but he liked using the English language and often wrote his name with the English spelling, which frequently appears in the Moravian records. Called the "Father of Salem," Marshall supervised the temporal affairs of the community for the first period of its existence.

Born in Stolpen, Upper Lusatia, Germany, Marshall was the son of Georg Rudolph von Marschall, an army officer, and his wife Louisa Marciana von Loka. Marshall considered his education excellent preparation for his duties as administrator in North Carolina. First tutored at home, he learned money management by taking charge of the family's cash and household accounts a week at a time. He excelled in his academic studies and in oratory, attending universities in Leipzig and Herrnhaag. In 1739, with his father's consent, Frederic Marshall joined the Unity of Brethren (Moravian church) and began to travel to Holland and England in the service of the church.

In England Marshall first dealt with matters relating to North Carolina. He assisted in negotiations with Parliament, culminating in the Act of 1749 which encouraged Moravians to settle in the American colonies. This act granted them freedom of conscience and religion, abstention from military duty, and permission to affirm rather than to swear an oath. In 1753 the Unity of Brethren decided to colonize in North Carolina. In 1761 Marshall was appointed senior civilis, an office conferred on select Moravians excelling in administration, finance, and the ministry. That year Marshall and his family first

traveled to America, where he supervised financial affairs in Moravian settlements in Pennsylvania.

In July 1763 the Directorial Conference of the Unity of Brethren in Europe appointed Marshall agent for the Unity in North Carolina and oeconomus of Wachovia, the 100,000-acre tract of land in North Carolina belonging to the Moravians. Delayed from visiting Wachovia by the French and Indian War, Marshall finally arrived late in 1764 to choose the site for a new central town. That first duty in North Carolina accomplished, he began to plan the town of Salem.

Marshall advocated a planned community, believing that an indefinite town plan would be the source of great confusion. The plan for Salem reflected the life that his religious community fostered. The Moravian church had designated Salem to be the trade center of Wachovia. The church supervised both the secular and the spiritual lives of Salem's citizens. Therefore, Marshall conceived a central square as the focus for the vital activities of the community: religious, commercial, and educational. A church, workshops, and schools surrounded the square. Marshall designated narrow but deep lots for single-family dwellings to allow space for a garden and recreation, and to permit residents to attend religious functions regularly. This plan also prevented town sprawl. Marshall's design satisfied not only community requirements but also aesthetic principles; he did not sacrifice appearance for practicality.

Carving a commercial center out of the wilderness was no easy task. Construction began in January 1766, and by 1772 Salem had established itself as a community. Marshall's expertise in town planning produced a functional congregation town and trade center. The quality of Salem's planning was noteworthy in Piedmont North Carolina in the eighteenth century.

Marshall exercised dual roles, both as oeconomus of Salem and as administrator of Unity property in Wachovia. Equipped with naturalization papers from Pennsylvania and a power of attorney from Wachovia's British trustee, he established regulations for the sale and lease of lands in newly reorganized plots. Marshall preferred the leasing of land in order to preserve title to the property for the Unity of Brethren. In this way the Unity could exclude undesirable settlers from the congregation's community. To retain some control over lands sold, Marshall contracted for the Moravians to be granted first refusal to buy property sold within Wachovia. In the early 1770s there was no great demand to buy tracts in Wachovia; however, there was a threat to confiscate parcels of that land.

The Regulators in 1771 charged individual Moravians with unfairly settling on land belonging to others. Marshall, acting as intermediary, heard these charges and referred them to the individuals concerned. The Regulators pursued their claims no further. Because they did not document their charges, Marshall surmised that they were testing the Moravians to see how easily they would give up their lands.

During the American Revolution the Moravians suffered difficulties due to their neutrality, the influx of paper money, and the attempted confiscation of lands by the General Assembly. The Moravians did not renounce Great Britain, fearing such an act would jeopardize fellow Brethren in England and the British West Indies. Too, the British Parliamentary Act of 1749 exempted the Moravians from swearing oaths and military service. Having lived in America, however, they did not want to offend the new government. In 1775 Marshall, who had remained in close communication with the Unity of Brethren in Europe, was called to a General Synod of the Moravian church in Germany. There he remained for four years, detained in Europe by the Revolutionary War. In North Carolina the problems of the Moravians, without benefit of their administrator's guidance, were compounded.

The most serious threat to the Moravians was the Confiscation Act of 1777, allowing state seizure of property belonging to individuals not living in America and not citizens of the state. North Carolinians wanted to seize Wachovia because the trustee of the lands was a British subject living in Great Britain. Marshall received title to the land as its trustee in 1778; he returned to Salem in 1779. For the remainder of the war Marshall professed continual apprehension about the Moravians' property. After the surrender at Yorktown, he approached the General Assembly to request recognition of Wachovia ownership. By April 1783 an act of the Assembly recognized him as trustee for all Moravian lands in North Carolina and as authorized agent for the Unity of Brethren. Marshall had successfully safeguarded the property in Wachovia for the Moravians.

Marshall continued to represent Salem in political and legal matters, traveling frequently to the General Assembly to defend Moravian titles to land. He also supervised the church's business enterprises in Salem, retaining inventory controls, overseeing profits, and compensating for currency fluctuations. He sought pietistic and productive individuals to settle in the community. In the established Wachovia settlements of the late eighteenth century, Marshall continued his commitment to progress by designing several new buildings. As his earlier interest in town planning increased, he drew plans for the community store, the second tavern, the boys' school, and the Bethabara church. He capped his service to the community with a plan for the Home Moravian Church in Salem. Marshall's adaptation of well-designed buildings to the materials and environment of Wachovia left a permanent statement of his ability and his era.

Marshall himself was pleased with what had been accomplished in Wachovia under his guidance. A devout Moravian, he saw God's direction in his life, especially in North Carolina, where, due to isolation, human counsel was slow to arrive. He exhibited superior ability in business. Moravians and non-Moravians alike considered him one of the leading religious figures of his era. On his death in Salem, he was called the father of the community, for through his leadership Salem had become a thriving town on the North Carolina frontier. Frederic William Marshall was buried in God's Acre at Salem on 5 Feb. 1802, thirty-eight years after his arrival as Salem's administrator.

Marshall married Hedwig Elizabeth von Schweinitz on 30 June 1750. They had three children: Maria Theresia (23 Feb. 1752), Anna Dorothea (12 Aug. 1754), and Christian Frederic (19 Sept. 1762). A pencil sketch of Marshall in profile exists at the Moravian Church Archives of the Southern Province in Winston-Salem.

SEE: Walter Clark, ed., *State Records of North Carolina*, vols. 13–15 (1896–98); Adelaide L. Fries, ed., *Records of the Moravians in North Carolina*, vols. 1–6 (1922–43); F. W. Marshall to J. Ettwein, 22 Sept. 1765; F. W. Marshall to Unity Elders Conference, July 1786; Memoir (Moravian Church Archives of the Southern Province, Winston-Salem).

CYNTHIA GRANT ARMSTRONG

Marshall, Matthias Murray (13 Aug. 1841–22 Oct. 1912), Episcopal clergyman and Confederate chaplain, was born in Pittsboro, the son of Abel and Delana Gun-

ter Marshall. His father was a cabinetmaker and local official; his mother was the daughter of Abner Gunter, clerk of court of Chatham County for over forty years. Educated first in local schools in Pittsboro and Graham, he attended Trinity College in Hartford, Conn., from December 1858 until May 1861, when he was obliged to leave because of the outbreak of the Civil War. He enlisted in the Confederate army and was commissioned a lieutenant, but frail health—a constant throughout life—forced him to resign after a brief service. Resuming his education, this time at The University of North Carolina, he was graduated in June 1863 and received the M.A. degree in 1866. The College of William and Mary later awarded him a D.D. degree.

Early in December 1863 Marshall was ordained a deacon in the Episcopal church and was named chaplain of the Seventh Regiment, attached to the Army of Northern Virginia. He went at once to join the regiment near Orange Court House, Va., but soon became ill from exposure and never returned to camp. Instead, he was made chaplain at the army hospital at Kittrell Springs, where he served until the end of the war. He also was in charge of St. James's Church, which had been recently established there. Fifty-two soldiers died at the hospital during Marshall's tenure, and each was given burial according to the ritual prescribed by the soldier's professed faith.

Ordained to the priesthood in September 1865, Marshall officiated at Christ Church, Elizabeth City, from 1865 to 1867. Here, in 1866, he married Margaret Susan Wingfield, the only daughter of the Reverend John H. Wingfield of Portsmouth, Va. They had eight children, six of whom survived infancy.

From 1867 to 1874 Marshall was rector of Emmanuel Church, Warrenton. He then served as rector of Christ Church, Raleigh, until his retirement in 1907 because of failing health. For many years he was president of the diocesan convention and president of the standing committee that shared authority with the bishop of the diocese.

Marshall died in Morganton and was buried in Oakwood Cemetery, Raleigh.

SEE: Joseph Blount Cheshire, ed., *Sketches of Church History in North Carolina* (1892); *Cyclopedia of Eminent and Representative Men of the Carolinas*, vol. 2 (1892); Daniel L. Grant, *Alumni History of the University of North Carolina, 1795–1924* (1924); Matthias Murray Marshall, *Ministers and Members of Christ* (1872); Samuel Thomas Peace, *Zeb's Black Baby* (1955); *Raleigh Times*, 23 Oct. 1912.

GEORGE T. BLACKBURN II

Martin, Alexander (1738–2 Nov. 1807), merchant, lawyer, legislator, governor, and senator, was born at Lebanon, Amwell Township, Hunterdon County, N.J., the oldest son of Hugh and Jane Hunter Martin. Hugh Martin was born near Inniskilling, County Tyrone, Ireland, about 1700; Jane Hunter Martin was born in County Antrim, Ireland, about 1720. The two families migrated within a few years of each other in the late 1720s, landing at New Castle, Del., but settling soon afterwards in New Jersey, where Hugh and Jane first met and were married.

Little is known of Alexander Martin's childhood except for a comment of his brother that he did not speak a word until he was four. His father became a moderately prosperous farmer, served as a justice of the peace, and for a period conducted an English school. Alexander attended Francis Alison's academy at New London,

Conn., and then Newark College, which, while he was a student, was moved, under the direction of President Aaron Burr, to Princeton, N.J. Martin received A.B. (29 Sept. 1756) and A.M. (1759) degrees from Princeton. After graduation he moved to Cumberland, Va., where, for just over a year, he served as a tutor to the son of N. Davies and conducted a school. He returned briefly to New Jersey, apparently on family business, before making a permanent move south to seek his fortune.

Martin settled in Salisbury, N.C., about 1760, and became a merchant. In 1761 he received a 436-acre grant on the Dan River (in present-day Rockingham County), where eventually he established his home. That year, on learning of the death of his father, he again returned to New Jersey—this time to help settle his father's estate and to arrange for the education of his younger brothers. In 1765 he bought a lot and a storehouse in Salisbury and was appointed a justice of the peace by Governor William Tryon. The next year he was made king's attorney for Rowan County.

In 1767 his brother Thomas, an Anglican minister and a 1764 graduate of Princeton, moved to Orange County, Va., to become the rector of the Brick Church and the tutor for the family of James Madison, Sr., at Montpelier. On several occasions on his way to and from New Jersey, Alexander Martin visited his brother. It was probably during such a visit in the summer of 1769 that the two brothers convinced the elder Madison to send young James to Princeton College instead of the College of William and Mary. James Madison and the Martin brothers proceeded to New Jersey, where Madison was enrolled in the college. It was, of course, Princeton that did much to shape the political philosophy of James Madison. So close had the Madisons and Martins become that Alexander's mother and younger brothers went to live at Montpelier. Soon after the Reverend Thomas Martin's death in 1770, however, Alexander situated his mother and family on his own land on the Dan River.

Meanwhile, the Regulator movement had gathered momentum in the upper Piedmont. Much of the discontent focused on the administration of county government, which was frequently capricious if not downright dishonest. In September 1770, during a meeting of the court at Hillsborough, a Regulator mob assaulted several lawyers, including Alexander Martin. When a similar crowd in March 1771 threatened the court of Salisbury, Martin, Alexander Frohock, and a few others rode out to the Regulator camp, negotiated with the rebels, and signed an agreement by which they would refund any excess fees they had received and adjust any differences. Martin and the others were rebuked by Governor Tryon for their interference, and two months later the governor routed the Regulators at the Battle of Alamance.

In settling his family on his Dan River land, Martin became more oriented to that locale. In 1773 he established his residence on this property, located in the newly created county of Guilford, and soon named his home Danbury. He retained most of his holdings at Salisbury and moved easily between the two areas.

Elected to the state Assembly from Guilford, Martin rose quickly to prominence. He introduced bills to pardon the Regulators and to attach property of Englishmen who owned land in North Carolina and did not pay just debts. Before long he became embroiled in the growing administrative conflict between the Assembly and Governor Josiah Martin. In 1774 he accepted the judgeship of the court of oyer and terminer in Salisbury. Guilford County did not send delegates to the

First Provincial Congress, but when the Second Provincial Congress met at New Bern on 3 Apr. 1775, Alexander Martin represented that county. By this time he was recognized as an active Patriot and late that year attended the Third Provincial Congress as a delegate from Guilford.

The third congress formed two regiments of line troops and appointed Alexander Martin as lieutenant colonel in the Second North Carolina Continental Regiment. The regiment was first involved in the "Snow Campaign" against the Scovellites, a band of Tories, in western South Carolina, then fought the Loyalist Scots at Moore's Creek Bridge in February 1776. In June Martin, who had been promoted to colonel, led his troops in the defense of Charles Town. In April 1777 he marched his men north to join General George Washington's army. The regiment saw active duty at Chad's Ford and Germantown. During the latter battle on 4 October, the fog was so thick that the Continentals confused their own men for the British. Colonel Martin was accused of cowardice in the wake of the charge and recrimination that followed the fighting. Although cleared by a court-martial, Martin, fatigued and still hounded by the accusation, resigned from the army and returned home.

In 1778 Guilford County sent Martin to the state senate, where he served in consecutive sessions until 1782. With the fall of Charles Town in 1780, the state lost its entire Continental line and much of the militia had gone home when enlistments expired. It was described as North Carolina's darkest time. To assist Governor Abner Nash in dealing with the internal and external pressures, the legislature created a Board of War, but instead of helping him, the board soon, in effect, superseded him. Five members had been appointed but only three ever served, and of those Alexander Martin was the most active and became its president. The board pushed for the recruitment of troops, corresponded with the generals, and urged that supplies be assembled. Responding to Nash's objections, the Assembly abolished the Board of War and replaced it with a Council Extraordinary, to which Martin was also named. The council continued the general functions of its predecessor board but on a limited basis until it too was abolished.

Beginning in 1780, Martin was speaker of the senate in three sessions of the Assembly. He was serving in that post in September 1781, when Governor Thomas Burke was captured by a band of Tories under David Fanning and became a prisoner of the British. As speaker of the senate, Martin became acting governor for four months, serving until Burke escaped his captors at Charles Town and resumed office.

Martin's actions in these years of crisis had gained him much popularity, and although he represented the underrepresented western section of the state, he was elected governor on 20 Apr. 1782. Martin pledged to work for commercial control, public credit, support of the army, proper use of the state's soil and climate, and the education of youth. However, he had difficulty in executing the business of the state because of the utter confusion that prevailed. The Assembly failed to meet in October 1782 and again in January 1783; General Nathanael Greene was pressing Governor Martin for supplies; the Continental Congress was requisitioning troops for the Continental line while the state militia was undermanned; and the British were threatening another campaign.

In spite of these difficulties, Martin sought reelection. It was his support of Fayetteville as the temporary seat of government that garnered for Martin, the westerner, enough eastern votes to be reelected then and a year later, when he won a third term. He supported federal control of commerce and in 1785 issued his manifesto against the state of Franklin.

As hostilities ended, one of the major considerations of the Assembly was the confiscation of Tory and Loyalist property. Martin was conciliatory, favoring the return of all property except that of the most offending Tories. He himself had acquired some of David Fanning's land in Guilford County. In 1785 he founded the town of Martinville on land adjoining Guilford Courthouse and built his home there, expecting to profit from the development of the town. The following year Guilford was divided and the opportunity was lost.

After his term as governor, Martin was a delegate to the Assembly and became speaker of the senate each year until 1788, with the exception of 1786, when he was not in the Assembly. In December 1786 he was elected a delegate to Congress but resigned without attending. In 1787 the legislature named him as one of the five North Carolina delegates to the Philadelphia convention to consider the revision of the Articles of Confederation. Martin was not active in debate, but as William Pierce of Georgia observed, he was "a Man of Sense, and undoubtedly a . . . good politician." He left the convention in August and thus was not a signer of the Constitution. He was not elected to the state ratifying convention that failed to ratify the Constitution.

In 1787 Martin was again elected governor; he also served three consecutive terms from 1789 to 1792. Although he campaigned as a Federalist, his views were those of a moderate. The state's spirit of accord with the central government waned, and not even the staunchest Federalists in North Carolina supported the extreme national program of Alexander Hamilton. President Washington's visit in 1791 helped restore some support; on that occasion, Martin entertained the president at his home in Martinville.

Throughout his public career Martin had advocated the establishment of a system of higher education for the state. This led to the creation in 1789, under his governorship, of The University of North Carolina. Soon after the university received its charter, he was elected a trustee, and he served on the board until his death. From 1791 to 1793 Martin was the first president of the board of trustees. Also while he was in office the permanent seat of government was located in Wake County and called Raleigh.

At the end of his final term as governor, Martin was elected to the U.S. Senate over incumbent Samuel Johnston. He entered that chamber with strong approval at home for his increasingly anti-Federalist actions. He attacked the secret sessions of the Senate and in 1794 guided the passage of the resolution that threw open its doors to the public. He voted regularly for economy, was generally pro-French, and opposed the administration's foreign policy, voting against the Jay treaty. By 1797 actions taken by France, such as rejecting Charles C. Pinckney as minister and the insult represented in the XYZ affair, caused Martin's sentiments to shift. He voted to establish a Navy Department, to arm the navy heavily, and to raise an army, but he hesitated for a time before voting for the Alien and Sedition Act.

Anti-Federalist feeling in North Carolina weakened, and although Martin sought bipartisan support from the Federalists, he failed to win reelection to the Senate in 1799. He retired to his home, Danbury, on the banks of the Dan River and spent a quiet five years with his elderly mother, enjoying the life of respect that fame had earned him. In 1804 his neighbors elected him to the state senate, and the next year he again became speaker. This single term was his last. He died at Danbury.

Throughout his life Martin aspired to write poetry, and several of his funeral odes survive. While a U.S. senator he wrote a patriotic play, *A New Scene*, dedicated to George Washington. Elected to the American Philosophical Society in 1797, he also was a member of the Society of the Cincinnati and a Mason.

Although Martin never married he had a natural son, Alexander Strong Martin, whom he always acknowledged during his lifetime as well as publicly stating the relationship in his will.

A portrait of Martin, which is believed to have been executed in 1793 in Philadelphia, is owned by the state of North Carolina.

SEE: Irving Brant, *James Madison: The Virginia Revolutionist, 1751–1780*, vol. 4 (1941); Adelaide L. Fries, ed., *Records of the Moravians in North Carolina*, vols. 2–4 (1925–30); James McLachlan, *Princetonians, 1748–1768: A Biographical Dictionary* (1976); James Martin, "A History of the Martin Families as Received by Tradition from One Generation to Another" (typescript, possession of Mrs. W. T. Lauten, Madison); Rockingham County Wills (North Carolina State Archives, Raleigh); Elizabeth Winston Yates, "The Public Career of Alexander Martin" (M.A. thesis, University of North Carolina, 1943).

CHARLES D. RODENBOUGH

Martin, Charles Henry (28 Aug. 1848–19 Apr. 1931), congressman and Baptist clergyman, was born near Youngsville, Franklin County, the son of William K. and Lucy Temperance Jones Martin. He was the great-grandson of Nathaniel Macon. After his graduation from Wake Forest College in 1872, he taught Latin at the college for two years and then at the Chowan Baptist Female Institute in Murfreesboro. For a time he was principal of Yadkin Mineral Springs Academy at Palmerville in Stanly County. Martin studied law at the University of Virginia, was admitted to the North Carolina bar in 1879, and practiced first in Louisburg and later in Raleigh. Ordained to the ministry in the Baptist church in Rolesville in 1886, he undertook a course of study at the Southern Baptist Theological Seminary in Louisville, Ky. With no initiative on his part, he received the Populist nomination for Congress in 1895. Following a contested election, he was declared the winner and served two terms from 1896 until 1899, his opponent already having served a part of the first term.

Martin was pastor of churches in Richmond, Stanly, and Anson counties. In Anson, he was pastor of the Polkton Baptist church for many years. A poet and a contributor to numerous periodicals, he had the manuscript of a book, "The Theory of Evolution," ready for publication at the time of his death. Its purpose was to refute Darwin's theory of evolution.

Martin married Mary Lemuel Williams in 1889, and they were the parents of Isaac W., Lucie, Annabel, and Mildred. He was buried in the Williams cemetery at Polkton.

SEE: *Biblical Recorder*, 29 Apr. 1931; *Biog. Dir. Am. Cong.* (1961); *Central Baptist Association Minutes* (1887); Mary L. Medley, *History of Anson County, 1750–1976* (1976); Bessie Hursey Nash, *From a Mustard Seed: A History of the First Baptist Church, Hamlet, N.C.* (1973); George W. Paschal, *History of Wake Forest College*, vol. 2 (1943); Charles E. Taylor, *General Catalogue of Wake Forest College, 1834/35–1891–92* (1892); Wadesboro *Messenger and Intelligencer*, 20 Apr. 1931.

WILLIAM S. POWELL

Martin, François-Xavier *(17 Mar. 1762–10 Dec. 1846)*, editor, author, attorney, and jurist, was born in Marseilles, France. Little is known of his parentage and childhood, for while yet a teenager he sailed for the island of Martinique, where he worked for his uncle, a businessman. Near the end of the American Revolution, he appeared in New Bern, N.C., where he taught French, carried the mail, and worked in the print shop of James Davis. He then started a newspaper, titled the *Noth-Carolina Gazette; or, New-Bern Advertiser*, the earliest extant issue of which was dated 3 Nov. 1785. By 11 July 1787 the title had been changed to *Martin's North-Carolina Gazette*, and Martin appears to have owned the press. Within three years his name was dropped from the title, but he continued publishing the paper until at least 24 Feb. 1798.

Meanwhile, Martin prepared and published a variety of almanacs, pamphlets, books, and acts of the Assembly, and he edited and published several volumes of laws. Perhaps the best known of his early works was his revised edition in 1791 of *The Office and Authority of a Justice of the Peace, and of Sheriffs, Coroners, &c. . . .* His most valuable works, however, were published early in the new century, including *The Public Acts of the General Assembly of North-Carolina* (1804), containing laws passed from 1715 to 1803. Martin also translated and published several French novels, including three by Mme. Marie-Jeanne de Riccoboni. Both his newspaper and his books contained many errors, some attributable to his incomplete mastery of the English language, others to carelessness and poor proofreading.

After reading law, Martin was admitted to practice in 1789, and while not a good speaker, he became a skilled interpreter of the law. His research into the statutes impressed upon him the need for a history of the state, and as early as 1791 he began collecting documentary materials. In 1806, while representing New Bern in the House of Commons, he gained access not only to the state records in Raleigh but also to important private documents which he copied.

Martin's work in collecting and publishing the laws of North Carolina came to the attention of President James Madison, who in 1809 appointed him to a judgeship in the Mississippi Territory and the following year transferred him to the superior court in the Orleans Territory. In New Orleans, the native of France made a noteworthy contribution by synthesizing the tangled jurisprudence of three successive administrations—Spanish, French, and American. When Louisiana became a state in 1812, Martin was appointed its first attorney general, and three years later he took a seat on that state's supreme court. Joining the court at age fifty-three, he served for thirty-one years; during the last eleven years, he was presiding justice.

A bachelor and a prodigious worker, Judge Martin was not content just to hear and decide cases. For twenty-one years he carried on the arduous task of editing twenty-three volumes of cases heard by the superior court of the Orleans Territory and the supreme court of Louisiana. In the interim, he published a two-volume history each of Louisiana (1827) and North Carolina (1829).

The History of North-Carolina, from the Earliest Period would probably have been the first history of the state except for the interruption caused by the author's move to Mississippi and then Louisiana. The twenty-one-year delay in its completion enabled Hugh Williamson to earn the distinction of publishing the first history of North Carolina (1812). Martin, however, had carried his materials with him, and despite their damage aboard ship and subsequent attacks by "mice, worms, and the

variety of insects of a humid and warm climate," they provided him with the sources necessary to complete his two-volume work in 1829. Martin's *History* had the strength of incorporating texts of documents not then in print but the weakness of careless copying as well as the absence of specific citations. His chapter on the Regulators, for instance, cited only "Records—Magazines—Gazettes."

The prolificity of his publications and his notoriety as a shrewd jurist made Martin one of the best-known judges in the country. He was elected to associate membership in the Academy of Marseilles in 1817 and received an honorary doctor of laws degree from Harvard College in 1841. Legends concerning his methods of interrogation abound; there are also numerous stories about his peculiar personal habits. Always a frugal man, he became more eccentric with age, grasping every dollar in sight and spending as little as a miser. He was even accused of refusing to pay the twenty-dollar cost of burying his body servant, who died on one of his circuit travels; he denied the obligation to pay the debt inasmuch as he did not live in the district of the burial, but he did offer one dollar, which he considered generous for the burial of a black servant.

Martin, whose eyesight was never good, became increasingly blind in the 1830s, and with the affliction, he was a pitiful figure. He lived in squalid quarters and dressed little better than a beggar. As he felt his way along the streets of New Orleans, his eyes closed, he was often taunted by mischievous children. He refused to give up his seat on the supreme court, however, and at age eighty-two traveled to his native Marseilles in hopes of having an operation on his eyes. He returned disappointed and retained his seat until the new state constitution was adopted in 1846. Married to his work throughout life, he died a few months later and was buried in St. Louis Cemetery. The old man amassed an estate of $396,000—a fortune in 1846—which in a holograph will dated two years earlier was left to a younger brother. The state contested the will, but the supreme court, on which he had sat for more than three decades, ruled that it was entirely within the realm of possibility that the aged man had used guides that enabled him to write the almost undecipherable one-page document.

François-Xavier Martin's influence on North Carolina was through the newspaper that he published for more than a decade, the books and pamphlets of laws that he compiled and published, and a history which, though poor by later standards, was the most objective study of the colonial period published to that time.

SEE: *DAB*, vol. 6 (1933); Charles Gayarre, *Fernando de Lemos, Truth and Fiction: A Novel* (1872); William Wirt Howe, "Memoir of François-Xavier Martin," in *François-Xavier Martin, The History of Louisiana. . . .* (1882); H. G. Jones, *For History's Sake* (1966); Edward Laroque Tinker, "Jurist and Japer: François-Xavier Martin and Jean LeClerc," *Bulletin of the New York Public Library* 39 (1935); W. B. Yearns, "François X. Martin and His *History of North Carolina*," *North Carolina Historical Review* 36 (1959).

H. G. JONES

Martin, James *(21 May 1742 (o.s.)–30 Oct. 1834)*, merchant, soldier, and legislator, was born in Lebanon Township, Hunterdon County, N.J., the second son of Hugh and Jane Hunter Martin. His father conducted an English school for a time, and all the Martin children were well educated. His brothers Alexander and Thomas were graduated from Princeton, where James may also have studied. In 1761, when Hugh Martin died, Alexander was already located in North Carolina; he returned to New Jersey to help settle the estate and see that his mother and his family were adequately situated.

James married his cousin, Ruth Rodgers, in 1763 and probably lived with his mother to help with the care of the younger members of the family. Through his brothers, James became a friend of James Madison, who visited in the Martin home during the years he was a student at Princeton. In 1769 Mrs. Martin and her youngest children went to live with the Madison family at Montpelier, but James remained in New Jersey. In May 1774 he moved his immediate family to Guilford County, N.C., where by now his brother Alexander had located Mrs. Martin and all the other brothers and sisters. James settled on the Haw River near the center of the county (part of present-day Rockingham County).

On 22 Apr. 1774 Martin was appointed colonel-commandant of the Guilford militia, an assignment that may have encouraged his move to North Carolina. In late 1775 his brother Alexander, now colonel of the Second North Carolina Continental Regiment, ordered James to raise the militia and move against the Scottish Tories near Fayetteville. In February 1776 the Guilford troops arrived at Moore's Creek after the battle and were involved only in rounding up prisoners. Later in the same year James raised a militia force of four thousand men, which joined General Griffith Rutherford in maneuvers against the Cherokee towns. During the next four years Martin was called on several times to assemble militia forces to contend with scattered Tory forces.

In December 1780 the main focus of the war moved into the Guilford area. Martin had difficulty in raising a significant militia force and joined General Nathanael Greene in the maneuvering along the Dan River. His troops did not play a major part in the Battle of Guilford Court House. Although Greene had a low regard for the performance of the local militia, he does seem to have valued the service of James Martin.

During the war Martin began acquiring significant acreage in Surry County, much of it centered around Snow Creek, a tributary of the Dan River. He obtained an entry grant from Marshall Duncan for a tract on which Duncan was already burning lime for the early settlers. On 4 July 1778 Martin himself entered two claims to this tract, which he characterized as "his Lime Kiln Plantation." It was to this tract, eighteen miles from his Haw River home, that Martin moved his family in 1781. His lime kiln became a center of commerce and was much relied on by the Moravians.

In his new residence, Martin became involved in politics and in 1783, 1784, 1785, and 1786 was elected to the House of Commons from Surry County. In 1789, when Surry was divided and the eastern portion became Stokes, he was appointed one of the original justices of the peace for the new county. Subsequently, his residence became the center of one of the militia districts. In 1792 and 1793 he represented Stokes County in the house; in the latter year he lost his bid for a seat in the U.S. Congress to his neighbor and fellow Patriot, Joseph Winston. Apparently, Martin was a Federalist and remained so most of his life.

Near the Martin home in Hunterdon County, N.J., there had been an early ironworks, known as Union Forge, where Martin may have worked as a young man. By 1786 he had established on his Snow Creek lands an ironworks and a forge, which he named the Union Iron Works. With transplanted Virginians, Peter Hairston and Colonel Peter Perkins, Martin became heavily involved in the exploitation of the mineral wealth of the area. In 1788 North Carolina passed a bounty act that encouraged the building of forges. According to the

terms of this act, Martin entered bounty claims on 3,000–5,000 acres in the county. The ironworks and lime kiln made him a wealthy man.

In 1792 he was appointed to the commission to locate a permanent capital for the state. As a member of that commission, he is reputed to have been the first to propose the name Raleigh for the site chosen.

His first wife had died and his children were mostly grown and married when Martin, on 12 Mar. 1800, married Martha Loftin Jones, the widow of Hamilton Jones, Sr. By this second marriage he had five children.

In 1808 he was defeated by Meshack Franklin for a seat in the U.S. Congress. He appears to have represented Stokes in the North Carolina House of Commons in 1811 and 1813, although by this time his son James had become active in politics and the references are confusing. His portrait, owned by a descendant, was painted in old age and shows a crusty old gentleman with white hair. At age ninety he rode on horseback to the courthouse at Germantown to apply for a veteran's pension and described vividly his service during the Revolutionary War. Two years later he died at his home on Snow Creek and was buried on the plantation.

SEE: Irving Brant, *James Madison: The Virginia Revolutionist, 1751–1780*, vol. 4 (1941); John L. Cheney, Jr., ed., *North Carolina Government, 1585–1974* (1974); Walter Clark, ed., *State Records of North Carolina*, vol. 22 (1907); *Early Families of the North Carolina Counties of Rockingham and Stokes with Revolutionary Service* (1977); James Martin, "A History of the Martin Families as Received by Tradition from One Generation to Another" (typescript, possession of Mrs. W. T. Lauten, Madison); James Martin Pension Application (General Services Administration, Washington, D.C.).

CHARLES D. RODENBOUGH

Martin, James Green (*14 Feb. 1819–4 Oct. 1878*), Confederate officer and lawyer, was born at Elizabeth City, the oldest son of William and Sophia Scott Daugé Martin. His father, a prominent planter and shipbuilder, had served in the North Carolina General Assembly. Martin himself was named after his grandfather, James Green Martin, a Methodist minister of Norfolk, Va. His mother was the daughter of General Peter Daugé of Camden County. Young Martin received his early education at St. Mary's in Raleigh and then at a boys' school. Entering the U.S. Military Academy at West Point in 1836, he was graduated in 1840 fourteenth in his class, ranking behind two other prominent Civil War officers: Richard S. Ewell and George H. Thomas.

Commissioned as second lieutenant of artillery in the U.S. Army, Martin served on the northern coast, chiefly in Maine, and participated in the coast survey. While in New England, he met and married Marian Murray Read, the great-granddaughter of George Read, a signer of the Declaration of Independence for the state of Delaware. Two years later, in 1846, Martin served with distinction in the War with Mexico as a battery commander, participating in the fighting around Monterey and Vera Cruz. His leadership abilities quickly earned him promotions on 16 Feb. 1847 to first lieutenant and on 5 August to captain. In the advance of the American army on Mexico City, Captain Martin participated in the battles of Cerro Gordo, Contreras, and bloody Churubusco. In the latter engagement his right arm was shattered by grapeshot and had to be amputated. On 20 August, for his gallantry and meritorious conduct, he was brevetted with the rank of major.

After recovering from his wound, he saw action at

Fort Monroe, Va., at Schuylkill Arsenal, Pa., and on the midwestern frontier at Nebraska City. At the latter place his wife died, leaving him with their four young children, but Martin was fortunate enough to meet Hetty King, the daughter of Charles King, president of Columbia College. They were married in 1858. Afterwards Martin accompanied Albert Sidney Johnston as quartermaster on Johnston's Utah expedition of that year. His last service in the "Old Army" was at Fort Riley, Kans., on staff duty.

On the outbreak of the Civil War and the secession of North Carolina from the Union, Martin resigned his commission (14 June 1861) and hurried to Raleigh to offer his services to the state. Initially, he received a commission as captain of cavalry in the Confederate Provisional Army. On 20 Sept. 1861 he was appointed adjutant general of North Carolina Troops, a force of ten regiments being raised to serve for three years or the duration of the war. In this capacity Martin was responsible for organizing, training, and equipping the ten state regiments, a task for which his natural energy and previous military training were well suited. Eight days later, when state Adjutant General John F. Hoke resigned to take command of an infantry regiment, Martin was appointed as his successor with the rank of major general of militia. This post gave him command of all of the state's military forces and defenses, subject to the orders of the governor, and charged him with organizing, arming, training, feeding, and clothing the troops as well as overseeing the defense of North Carolina, particularly the vulnerable coastal sections.

Martin tackled this enormous responsibility with his characteristic energy; in fact, it was for his accomplishments in this role that he received his greatest recognition. Through his efforts, volunteers were raised, regimented, armed, and trained. By January 1862 Martin had forty-one regiments ready for Confederate service, representing about 12,000 men above the quota that had been established for the state. At his suggestion militia laws were revised and updated, and the state purchased a number of fast, sleek steam vessels to act as blockade-runners for the purpose of bringing supplies and war material from Europe. The scarcity of quartermaster stores was met by sending purchasing agents throughout the new Confederacy to procure them for the state. Martin also contracted with individuals and firms to manufacture arms and ammunition in various towns and cities in North Carolina.

To enable his newly organized regiments to meet that first winter of 1861–62, Martin established or contracted with cloth factories to manufacture uniforms, blankets, and other articles. In addition, purchasing agents bought spare cloth and articles of clothing from the general populace and went to other Confederate states to buy cloth. It is to Martin's credit that the state's soldiers on the whole endured the winter comfortably and that North Carolina was the only Confederate state to clothe its own troops in the field. Only in the area of coastal defense did his energy and skill fail to make a significant impression. Here, through no fault of his own, sufficient heavy cannon and naval forces were simply not available in time to stop the overwhelming onslaught of the Burnside expedition.

After establishing the state's offensive and defensive capabilities at an operational level, Martin applied for a field command. This he received with his appointment as brigadier general in the Confederate army on 17 May 1862, to rank from 15 May. On 2 June he was assigned to command the District of North Carolina, with headquarters at Kinston. However, on the night of 30 June General Robert E. Lee ordered Martin to move at once to

Virginia to reinforce Lee's Army of Northern Virginia, then engaged in the fierce Seven Days' Battle around Richmond with General George B. McClellan's Union army. Leading a brigade of North Carolina regiments then under his command, Martin arrived too late to participate in the fighting and was ordered back to North Carolina. There he assumed the double duty of adjutant general and commander of all the state's forces. For reasons not disclosed in the records, he resigned his commission on 25 July but was reappointed to brigadier general on 11 August (confirmed 30 September). On 18 August he was formally assigned to command the District of North Carolina, comprising all the territory from the Roanoke River to the South Carolina line. He continued in this capacity until the fall of 1863, when he was instructed to organize a brigade of troops from the regiments under his command.

Martin formed a brigade consisting of the Seventeenth, Forty-second, Fiftieth, and Sixty-sixth North Carolina regiments and encamped at Wilmington. The brigadier general was a strict disciplinarian, a quality that was usually unpopular with the rank and file, but he made these regiments a well-drilled and efficient military unit. In February 1864 he led his brigade up the coast to attack Morehead City and Fort Macon as a diversionary operation while Confederate General George Pickett attacked New Bern. Martin had pushed his way as far as Newport when he received word that Pickett's attack had failed, whereupon he returned to Wilmington. On the opening of the spring offensive of the Union forces in Virginia in May 1864, Martin's brigade was ordered to reinforce the defenses of Richmond. Arriving on 14 May, his brigade took part in the "bottling" of General B. F. Butler's Union army in the Battle of Drewry's Bluff two days later and on 20 May, as a part of D. H. Hill's division, participated in an attack resulting in the capture of part of Butler's advanced entrenchments near Howlett's House. Martin's conspicuous role in this attack won him the admiration and enthusiasm of his men, who hoisted him on their shoulders and jubilantly carried him about, shouting "Three cheers for Old One Wing!" Afterwards Old One Wing became his nickname to the troops, coined because of the loss of his right arm in Mexico, and they regarded him with warm affection.

His brigade became a part of Major General Robert F. Hoke's division and joined Lee's army in its desperate struggle against Ulysses S. Grant's Union army outside Richmond. In the battles around Cold Harbor on 1–3 June, the division occupied a critical sector on the right center of Lee's battle line, which was held against Grant's famous grand attack on the morning of the third. Afterwards Hoke's division was shifted to Petersburg and enabled General P. G. T. Beauregard's thin Confederate line to hold out against Grant's attacks on the city until the rest of Lee's army arrived to protect it. Martin's brigade played a prominent role here and in Grant's subsequent siege around Petersburg. During this engagement, Martin's health failed due to the constant strain and exposure in the stagnant trench lines. This compelled him to relinquish his field command and accept a quieter assignment as commander of the District of Western North Carolina, with headquarters in Asheville, where he remained until the end of the war. His last service for the Confederacy was to resist George Stoneman's Union cavalry raid through western North Carolina. Some of the forces under Martin's command were among the last Confederate units to surrender, and he himself was paroled at Asheville on 3 May 1865.

Martin's war record had been brilliant and untarnished. He had won the respect and admiration of his men and superiors alike—among them General Robert E. Lee, who said: "General Martin is one to whom North Carolina owes a debt she can never repay." After the war, dispossessed of much of his former holdings, Martin took up the study of law and practiced successfully in Asheville from 1866 until his death twelve years later. He also devoted some of his time to the Episcopal church as a layman and a delegate to the diocesan and general conventions. He was buried in Asheville.

SEE: John G. Barrett, *The Civil War in North Carolina* (1963); Walter Clark, *Memorial Address upon the Life of General James Green Martin*, delivered in Raleigh, 1916; Walter Clark, ed., *Histories of the Several Regiments and Battalions from North Carolina in the Great War, 1861–1865*, 5 vols. (1901); *DAB*, vol. 6 (1961); C. A. Evans, *Confederate Military History*, vol. 4 (1899); F. B. Heitman, *Historical Register and Dictionary of the United States Army* (1903); George W. McIver, "North Carolinians at West Point before the Civil War," *North Carolina Historical Review* 7 (January 1930); Ezra Warner, *Generals in Gray* (1959); Marcus J. Wright, *General Officers of the Confederate Army* (1911).

PAUL BRANCH

Martin, John Sanford (*30 May 1886–14 Apr. 1957*), newspaper editor, better known under the pen name Santford Martin, was one of nine children of Asbury Jackson and Victoria Brown Martin. His father was a teacher and later superintendent of public schools in Yadkin County. His younger brother, LeRoy Brown Martin, was an officer of Wachovia Bank and Trust Company in Raleigh, executive secretary of the State Board of Equalization (1927–35), and secretary of the state Democratic executive committee (1944–48).

Born in Hamptonville, Martin attended the Yadkinville Normal School and Wake Forest College, where he was graduated in 1909 and completed the law course the following year. Though admitted to the North Carolina bar, Martin accepted employment in 1910 as a reporter for the *Winston-Salem Journal*. In 1912 he was made editor of the paper, and in 1927 he also became editor of the *Twin-City Sentinel*. Martin considered himself a liberal Democrat and at least through the mid-1930s used his editorial influence in support of the liberal wing of the Democratic party both in North Carolina and nationally. When Owen Moon sold the Winston-Salem papers to the more conservative Gray family in 1937, Martin, contrary to his expectations, was retained as editor. Thereafter he became less active politically. His interests turned increasingly to education and the need for improvement in the state's public school system. Martin remained editor of both papers until 1952, and from 1952 until his retirement in 1954 he was editor of the Sunday *Journal-Sentinel* editorial page.

During his career as an editor, Martin held a number of appointive positions in state government. He served as private secretary to Governor Thomas W. Bickett from 1917 to 1921 and afterwards compiled Bickett's public papers and letters for publication. From 1917 to 1918 he was North Carolina state director of the Four-Minute Men, a volunteer organization of men prepared, at a moment's notice, to give a four-minute speech on the necessity of buying war bonds during World War I. In 1921 he was appointed by Governor Cameron Morrison to the North Carolina Fisheries Commission and in 1926 by Governor A. W. McLean to the State Board of Conservation and Development. He served as a member of the latter board until 1943 and as its chairman from 1941

to 1943. In 1943 Martin was appointed to the State Board of Education, and in 1955 he was also named to the newly established State Board of Higher Education. Ill health caused him to resign both positions in 1956.

In 1910 Martin married Ava Michael Poole. They had two children: Edwina Martin Crowther and Santford, Jr. Martin was a member of Brown Memorial Baptist Church, Winston-Salem, where he taught a men's Sunday school class for more than twenty-five years. He served on the board of directors of the *Biblical Recorder* and as a trustee of the North Carolina Baptist Hospital and Campbell College. He was a Mason and a member of the Winston-Salem Kiwanis Club, the International Press Institute, and the American Society of Newspaper Editors. In 1918 Martin served as president of the North Carolina Press Association. In 1942 he received the association's annual award for the best editorial written in the state. He was granted honorary degrees from Western Carolina College in 1954 and Wake Forest College in 1956.

Martin died in Winston-Salem and was buried at Forsyth Memorial Park.

SEE: John Sanford Martin Papers (Manuscript Department, Duke University Library, Durham); *North Carolina Biography*, vol. 5 (1941); *Who's Who in the South and Southwest* (1950); *Winston-Salem Journal*, 15 Apr. 1957 (portrait).

ROBERT L. BYRD

Martin, Joseph (*1740–18 Dec. 1808*), soldier, pioneer, and Indian agent, was born near Charlottesville in Albemarle County, Va., the son of Joseph, a farmer, and Susannah Childs Martin. Instead of pursuing an education as his father wished, young Martin chose to hunt and roam the woods near his hillside home. In such an environment, he developed a strong, athletic frame, standing over six feet and weighing about two hundred pounds.

In 1756 Martin's father insisted that he serve an apprenticeship in carpentry, but the youth became dissatisfied with this trade and ran away to join the British army at Fort Pitt. How long he remained at the fort and what part he played in the French and Indian War is not known. When the elder Martin died in 1760, Joseph was present to receive a small inheritance, using it to purchase a farm in Orange County, Va.

Martin became restless with farm life and in 1763 decided to make a living as a "long hunter," staying for long periods of time in the remote areas of western North Carolina (present-day eastern Tennessee). His hunting career ended in 1768, when he accepted an offer by Dr. Thomas Walker of Virginia to establish a supply station in Powell's Valley about twenty miles east of the Cumberland Gap. However, in the late summer of 1769, before the first harvest could be gathered, Indians destroyed the small settlement and its inhabitants returned to Virginia. Martin made other attempts to settle Powell's Valley—in the summer of 1775, the spring of 1783, and the fall of 1783. His final effort proved successful. By 1788, when he sold his interest in the valley settlement, it was a thriving supply station; subsequently, it became the nucleus from which several permanent towns developed.

When Lord Dunmore's War erupted in 1774, Martin enlisted as a captain in the militia of Pittsylvania County (his new residence), Va., but commanded a separate unit of scouts for the duration of the conflict. The following year, after British-inspired Indians attacked

American settlements along the Appalachian frontier, he again accepted a captain's commission in the Pittsylvania County militia, which in June 1776 marched into western North Carolina for a successful six-month campaign against the Cherokee Indians. He remained in this area until the Treaty of Long Island was concluded in July 1777.

The fall of 1777 marked a turning point in Martin's career as he began to serve the Patriot cause in another capacity. In November Governor Patrick Henry of Virginia appointed him the state's agent to the Cherokee; Martin established his headquarters at Long Island on the Holston River. During the fall of 1780, when British forces under Captain Patrick Ferguson began to move towards North Carolina, Martin kept a large segment of the Cherokee peaceful, allowing the frontiersmen of western North Carolina to participate in the Patriot victory at Kings Mountain.

In the spring of 1783 Martin won a seat in the North Carolina Assembly from Sullivan County, a newly formed county that included Long Island. While attending the May session of the Assembly, he was commissioned North Carolina's agent to the Cherokee and Chickamauga Indians. Before the end of the year he represented both North Carolina and Virginia in treaties with the Chickamauga and Chickasaw Indians. By 1785 Martin had gained the respect of Congress, which appointed him one of four commissioners to hold the Treaty of Hopewell with the Cherokee. The November treaty served to lessen hostilities between the Indians and frontiersmen for one year.

In 1787 Martin was again elected to represent Sullivan County in the Assembly. Because of his loyalty to the state and his leadership experience, the legislature appointed him brigadier general of the North Carolina militia in the Western or Washington District of the state. In the summer of 1788, after the Chickamauga attacked several frontier settlements in western North Carolina, Martin led an army of eight hundred frontiersmen against the Chickamauga stronghold near present-day Chattanooga, Tenn. Due to strategic deployment of the Chickamauga along mountain perches and timely reinforcements, the Indians quickly defeated Martin's army. Absolved of any blame for the military disaster, Martin was granted full pay for his service by the 1789 Assembly.

Also in 1789 the Assembly ceded its western counties to the United States and repealed its law establishing an agent to the Indians. After being relieved of his appointment, Martin returned to Henry (formerly Pittsylvania) County, Va., and, at age forty-nine, became a private citizen for the first time since 1774.

Martin was married twice: in 1762 to Sarah Lucas, who died in 1782, and in 1784 to Susannah Graves; he had seven children by his first wife and eleven by his second. During the time he served as Indian agent, he also maintained an Indian "wife" named Betsy Ward, the daughter of the highly regarded Cherokee councilwoman, Nancy Ward. Neither of his legal wives seem to have objected to their husband's Indian "marriage," which actually increased his influence with the Cherokee and on a number of occasions saved his life.

Though leaving an eventful frontier life, Martin remained active until his death. He served in the Virginia legislature from 1791 to 1799, was commissioned brigadier general of the Twelfth Brigade of Virginia militia during the Whiskey Rebellion of 1793–94, and was appointed a commissioner to survey the Kentucky-Virginia boundary in 1795 and the Tennessee-Virginia boundary in 1802. He died at age sixty-eight and was buried near Martinsville, Va., named in his honor in 1791. A portrait of Martin hangs in the local high school.

In serving his contemporaries through public office, Martin never hesitated to sacrifice his popularity for the causes he felt to be just. As with individuals who seek moderation in the midst of conflict, he was not always popular. But as history reveals, no nation can survive long without such people.

SEE: G. Aronhime, "Gen. Joseph Martin: A Forgotten Pioneer," *Historical Sketches of Southwest Virginia*, no. 2 (1966); Samuel A. Ashe, ed., *Biographical History of North Carolina*, vol. 2 (1905); R. A. Shrader, "Joseph Martin: Indian Agent" (M.A. thesis, University of North Carolina, 1973); Stephen B. Weeks, "Gen. Joseph Martin and the Rev. in the West," in American Historical Association, *Annual Report for 1893* (1894).

RICHARD A. SHRADER

Martin, Joseph John (*21 Nov. 1833–18 Dec. 1900*), lawyer and congressman, was born in Williamston, the son of Wheeler and Caroline Watts Martin. Educated at Williamston Academy, he made his first public move in 1856, when he and a friend, Augustus Moore, bought a Williamston newspaper, the *Young American*. They changed its name to the *Democratic Banner*, the first issue appearing on 7 Aug. 1856. The paper was plagued with problems and publication was suspended during the latter part of 1859. In the same year Martin, having studied law under Judge Richmond Pearson, was admitted to the bar and began his practice. The 1860 census records his occupation as lawyer. He made a good impression locally and was appointed prosecuting attorney for Martin County.

There is some question as to whether he was the Joseph J. Martin of Martin County who enlisted as a private in Company G, Seventeenth Regiment, on 10 May 1861. One of this name was captured at Fort Hatteras in August and confined in prison at Fort Columbus, New York Harbor, and at Fort Warren, Boston Harbor, but paroled in late January 1862. Returning to his company, he served until 20 Mar. 1862, when the company was disbanded. In October he joined Company E of the same regiment and served until October 1864. (The question arises because in the latter position he once was described as aged forty-one; if the age were thirty-one, there would be no question.)

In 1868, when he was registered as a Republican, Martin was elected solicitor for the Second Judicial District. Reelected in 1874, he represented North Carolina in the Republican National Convention at Cincinnati in 1876. Resigning his position as solicitor in 1878, he ran for Congress. He was closely associated with the post–Civil War federal and military authorities, and this is said to have been significant in his election despite suspicions of corrupt vote gathering and tallying by local officials. He served in the Forty-sixth Congress from 4 May 1879 to 29 Jan. 1881, when his election was successfully contested by Jesse J. Yeates.

Congressional records suggest that Martin spent much of his time in the House of Representatives arguing the validity of his election. At the beginning of his term, however, he was appointed to the Select Committee to Inquire into the Causes of the Present Depression of Labor. His accomplishments were limited primarily to presenting legislation for pensions and relief for selected individuals who had been adversely affected by the Civil War. In addition, Martin introduced legislation to establish a national mail steamship service but had to step down before the measure received final action.

Returning to North Carolina, Martin moved from Williamston to Tarboro, where he resumed his law practice. He served as an active trustee of Williamston Academy during the period 1881–82. In 1897 he was appointed postmaster for Tarboro and served until his death three years later. He was survived by his wife, the former Victoria Fagan; four sons, Wheeler, Joseph John, Jr., John W., and John F.; and a daughter, Fannie. He was buried in the Williamston cemetery.

SEE: *Biog. Dir. Am. Cong.* (1950); W. H. Booker and Francis Manning, *Religion and Education in Martin County* (1974) and *Martin County History* (1977); John L. Cheney, Jr., ed., *North Carolina Government, 1585–1979* (1981); *Congressional Reports*, 46th Cong.; Shelby J. N. Hughes, ed., *Martin County Heritage* (1977); Weymouth T. Jordan, comp., *North Carolina Troops, 1861–1865: A Roster*, vol. 6 (1977); Raleigh *News and Observer*, 19 Dec. 1900; *Tarborough Southerner*, 20 Dec. 1900; John H. Wheeler, ed., *Reminiscences and Memoirs of North Carolina and Eminent North Carolinians* (1884); Williamston Academy Board of Trustees Minutes, May 1881–82 (Southern Historical Collection, University of North Carolina, Chapel Hill).

MICHAEL WESLEY HICKMAN

Martin, Josiah (*April 1737–April 1786*), last royal governor of North Carolina, was born in Dublin, Ireland, the son of Colonel Samuel and Sarah Wyke Irish Martin of Greencastle, Antigua, West Indies. He was a scion of the eminent Anglo-Irish branch of the Martin family that was forced to flee Cromwell's wrath when he conquered Ireland. The Martins belonged to the country gentry class that had helped staff British imperial and provincial agencies since the sixteenth century. Through marriage alliances and careful investment, the family acquired estates and plantations in the British Isles, the islands of the Caribbean, and North America. Josiah and his six brothers received their training through tutors, preparatory schools, universities, and the inns of court. They were members of the Church of England.

Young Josiah was molded by his astute and loving father and his older half brother, Samuel, Jr., MP, sometime secretary of the Treasury, treasurer to the dowager princess of Wales (the mother of George III), and friend of Lord Bute and Hogarth. Samuel was a great expediter of his younger brothers' careers.

Overcoming his father's objections, Josiah Martin entered the army as an ensign in the Fourth Foot Regiment in 1756 and rose to the rank of lieutenant colonel in the Twenty-second Regiment of Foot, afterwards called Gage's Regiment. Because of financial and health problems, he sold his commission in 1769. In January 1761 he married his cousin, Elizabeth, the daughter of Josiah Martin at whose estate, Rockhall, on Long Island, the young couple resided at various times.

After failing to advance himself in the army, Martin enlisted the aid of both his father and his brother Samuel in seeking a position in one of the imperial or provincial agencies. Samuel's efforts to secure a prestigious position for his younger brother began to bear fruit in 1770, when the governors of New York and Virginia died. Lord Hillsborough, the secretary of the colonies and a close friend of Samuel, reshuffled the governorships of the thirteen colonies. Hillsborough transferred William Tryon to New York and appointed Josiah Martin governor of North Carolina. Delayed by ill health and a series of operations, Martin conferred with Tryon in

New York and in July 1771 sailed for New Bern, N.C., where he took the oath of office before the Council on 12 August.

The young governor was an amiable, personable, intelligent, and hardworking man. Favorable reports to some of the North Carolina leaders preceded his arrival in New Bern. Tryon's legacy to Martin involved five major problems: the fiscal and psychological effects of the War of the Regulation; the unsettled and expensive dispute between the Carolinas about their mutual boundary line; the struggle over the court law bills and the judiciary, especially the attachment of the property of debtors who had never been in the province; "the old quorum trouble" in the house, which caused a conflict between the house and the governor; and the dispute over the selection of the chief personnel of the provincial government by the Crown rather than through the Assembly.

The conflict between the Assembly and the royal prerogative as exercised by the governor lay at the root of North Carolina's difficulties. This controversy reappeared in 1771, when the Assembly discontinued the sinking-fund tax. Martin disallowed the bill as illegal. The house then instructed the sheriffs regarding noncollection of the poll taxes for the fund. Martin issued a proclamation reminding the sheriffs that the bonds they had posted (or at least signed for) when they took office would have to be forfeited to cover the amount they did not collect. The governor won his first skirmish with the Assembly, but the legislature continued the controversy over the collection of taxes throughout his administration.

The experience with the Debenture Bill of 1771 to finance the Regulator war was a more satisfying one for both the governor and the Assembly. The county oligarchs, including many of the assemblymen, were paid for their military service in crushing the Regulators.

The remaining four problems were never satisfactorily resolved, because the house insisted on establishing control over its internal proceedings and usurping the royal prerogative. Of the four problems, the most fateful one for Martin as well as the radical leaders was the foreign attachment law issue, which deprived North Carolina of its courts and left the province defenseless. The Assembly, dominated by a coalition of eastern merchants and planters with western Presbyterian leaders, would pass no new court law without the foreign attachment clause. The Crown's ministers instructed Martin not to give his assent to a law containing the clause. When the old court law expired in 1773, the judicial system in the colony collapsed. Martin created criminal courts through his commission as governor, but the Assembly in December refused to appropriate funds for their operation.

The 1773 attachment crisis revived the old court quarrel between the governor and the Assembly and swept on to become one of the major reasons for the revolution in North Carolina. Once the radicals saw that they could manipulate the rest of the colonists through the propaganda that the king and the governor were intent upon bending them to their will, the radicals embarked on a program for revolution. The speaker of the house, John Harvey, defied the governor when he convened at New Bern in August 1774 a revolutionary Provincial Congress that elected delegates to the first Continental Congress and began a system of county committees of safety, which gradually usurped the royal government as the source of authority.

With his authority and influence dissipated, Martin sent his wife and children by ship to his uncle's estate,

Rockhall, on Long Island, for safety. On the evening of 29 May 1775 Martin and his friend Archibald Neilson rode in the governor's coach through open country to Cross Creek and then down the Cape Fear River to Fort Johnston near Wilmington. They arrived on 2 June.

Using the fort as his headquarters, Martin summoned the royal Council to meet with him and assess the situation. The Wilmington Committee of Safety kept close watch on Martin's activities and began to draw an intelligence net around the fort, screening his visitors and mail. At the fort, he formulated a plan for subjugating the southern colonies which was approved by the British government. Martin ordered the artillery of the fort to be dismantled and placed along the shore under the protection of the *Cruizer*'s guns. With the disarming of the fort and the transfer of his headquarters to the *Cruizer*, Martin foiled the plans of the radicals to capture the fort and himself. He watched the radicals burn the fort, but he refused to give the order to discharge the *Cruizer*'s guns because he did not wish to fire on the colonists.

Martin had interviewed and corresponded with various Highland Scots in North Carolina who were loyal to the Crown. They were receptive to the governor's plan to regain control of the province. The plan was that the Highlanders would raise the king's standard at Cross Creek and march to Wilmington, where British troops and the navy would meet them. However, the troops and the navy were delayed by red tape and storms. When the Highlanders marched towards Wilmington, they were defeated by a Patriot army at Moore's Creek Bridge on 27 Feb. 1776.

In May Martin departed with the British for an attack on Charles Town; that summer he returned to Rockhall to care for his family. In 1779 he accepted Sir Henry Clinton's invitation to join him in the expedition against South Carolina, where he served with Lord Charles Cornwallis, who praised him for his advice and bravery as a volunteer. In April 1781 Martin accompanied Cornwallis to Wilmington and from there sailed for New York to receive medical attention and to care for his motherless family; his wife Elizabeth had died in October 1778.

Seeking expert medical attention, Martin took his family to London, where he resigned his governorship and devoted his time to his children and to arguing cases for the North Carolina Loyalists before the American Loyalist Claims Commission. He was granted partial compensation for his confiscated North Carolina property and received a pension for his loyal services. He died ten days before his forty-ninth birthday and was buried in the cemetery of his parish church, St. George's in Hanover Square. Martin died faithful to the Crown but frustrated because he could not return to North Carolina and govern the people whom he had come to know and like.

SEE: Josiah Martin Papers (Add. MSS., British Museum, London); Charles Ross, ed., *Correspondence of Charles, First Marquis Cornwallis* (1859); William L. Saunders, ed., *Colonial Records of North Carolina*, vols. 8–9 (1890); Vernon O. Stumpf, "Governor Josiah Martin: The Road to the Cape Fear," Lower Cape Fear Historical Society, Inc., *Bulletin* 19 (1976), "Josiah Martin and His Search for Success: The Road to North Carolina," *North Carolina Historical Review* 52 (1975), and *Josiah Martin: The Last Royal Governor of North Carolina* (1986).

VERNON O. STUMPF

Martin, Robert, Jr. *(12 Apr. 1784–25 May 1848)*, state legislator and planter, was the son of Robert and Martha Drennen Martin of Rockingham County. He was the nephew of Alexander Martin, an early governor of North Carolina and a U.S. senator. In 1825 Martin married Mary Settle (1798–1860), who was the sister of Thomas Settle, Sr., founder of a noted North Carolina political dynasty, and the aunt of Governor David S. Reid. Martin owned extensive plantations on the Dan River in Rockingham County and on the Pearl River in Lawrence County, Miss. In Mississippi alone he had nearly 150 slaves, and in Rockingham County in 1840 he had 33 slaves. In addition to his plantations, he owned a gristmill near Wentworth.

In a predominantly Democratic county, Martin, a Whig, won seats in the House of Commons (1822–26) and the state senate (1829–35). He was very active in the legislature, serving on several standing and select committees. In both the lower house and the senate he sat on the Claims Committee, and for two sessions of the senate he was chairman. His chief legislative interest was banking, and during most of his terms in the General Assembly he introduced bills to establish a state bank. When the Bank of the State of North Carolina was finally chartered, Martin became a stockholder.

Robert and Mary Martin had two daughters, Lucinda Settle (d. 15 Sept. 1846) and Martha Drennen (b. 1828), both of whom were educated in a Philadelphia finishing school. On a family visit to Washington, D.C., Martha was introduced by her cousin, Congressman David Reid, to one of his close friends, Stephen A. Douglas, of Illinois, who became a prominent Democratic senator and a presidential candidate in 1860. Martha Martin and Stephen Douglas were married in Rockingham County on 7 Apr. 1847; they had two sons, Robert Martin and Stephen Arnold, Jr., and a daughter who died shortly after the death of her mother on 19 Jan. 1853. The Martins were members of the Hogan's Creek Baptist Church, located east of Reidsville. Robert Martin died in Rockingham County and was buried in the Settle family cemetery.

SEE: Stephen A. Douglas Papers (Library, University of Chicago); Robert W. Johannsen, *Stephen A. Douglas* (1973); *Journals of the Senate and the House of Commons of the General Assembly of the State of North Carolina* (1829–35); William R. Reece, *The Settle-Suttle Family* (1974); Rockingham County Deeds and Wills (North Carolina State Archives, Raleigh); Settle Family Cemetery, near Reidsville; U.S. Census, 1840.

LINDLEY S. BUTLER

Martin, William Joseph *(11 Dec. 1830–23 Mar. 1896)*, educator and Confederate officer, was born in Richmond, Va., the son of Edward Fitzgerald and Frances Anne Foster Martin. His father, a native of County Cork, Ireland, immigrated to the United States in 1803; he apparently was a teacher and a physician until his death in 1860.

After graduation from the University of Virginia in 1854, Martin became professor of natural science at Washington College in Pennsylvania. While there he married Susan A. McCoy of Warrenton, Va. In 1857 he joined the faculty of The University of North Carolina as professor of chemistry, mineralogy, and geology; his wife died the following year. Also in 1858 Columbian College in the District of Columbia awarded him an honorary A.M. degree. Martin soon earned a reputation as an able chemist, and in 1861 he classified the collection of rock specimens of Ebenezer Emmons, state geologist. During the school terms of 1860 and 1861, as drillmaster, he instructed students in the military arts. Nevertheless, he was giving serious thought to entering Union Theological Seminary in 1861, when the Civil War began.

Granted a leave of absence from the university, Martin became captain of Company G, composed of Orange County men, Twenty-eighth Regiment of North Carolina Troops, on 2 Sept. 1861. In April 1862 he was promoted to the rank of major and in May was transferred to the Eleventh Regiment as a lieutenant colonel. He saw extensive duty in Virginia (sometimes in command of the brigade), was seriously wounded four times, and was promoted to colonel in April 1864. In 1865 paperwork was under way to make him a brigadier general, but the war ended and he was paroled at Appomattox Court House on 9 Apr. 1865.

In the fall Martin returned to Chapel Hill to resume his position on the faculty. Because of the university's lack of support during Reconstruction, he resigned in 1867 and moved to Columbia, Tenn. There he founded Columbia High School and remained at its head until 1870, when he returned to North Carolina and became chairman of chemistry, geology, and natural history at Davidson College. In 1875, when The University of North Carolina reopened (it had closed four years earlier), efforts were made to entice Martin to return to Chapel Hill, but he felt his services were more important to Davidson. In 1887, after having declined numerous other offers, he accepted the chair of chemistry at Davidson, a post he occupied for the remainder of his life. For a time he also served as bursar of the college, and in 1884 he became vice-president. He served as acting president during the period 1886–88 but declined an appointment as president because of his age and ill health.

Martin received honorary LL.D. degrees from Hampden-Sydney in 1887 and The University of North Carolina in 1889.

In 1863, five years after the death of his first wife, he married Letitia Coddington Costin of Wilmington, N.C. They became the parents of ten children, but only Miles Costin, William Joseph, Jr., Mary (the noted Dr. Mary Martin Sloop who, with her husband, founded and maintained the mountain school at Crossnore), and Lucy Battle lived to maturity. Martin was buried in the Davidson College cemetery.

SEE: Maurice M. Bursey, *Carolina Chemists: Sketches from Chapel Hill* (1982 [portrait]); *Charlotte Observer*, 24 Mar. 1896; Walter Clark, ed., *Histories of the Several Regiments and Battalions from North Carolina in the Great War, 1861–1865*, vols. 1 (portrait), 2, 4 (1901); Clement A. Evans, *Confederate Military History*, vol. 4 (1899); Weymouth T. Jordan, comp., *North Carolina Troops, 1861–1865: A Roster*, vols. 5, 8 (1975, 1981); Cornelia A. Shaw, *Davidson College: Intimate Facts* (1923); Stephen B. Weeks Scrapbook, vol. 1 (North Carolina Collection, University of North Carolina, Chapel Hill).

LUCY MARTIN CURRIE JOHNSTON
DEBORAH BUNDY WILSON

Martin, William Joseph, Jr. *(10 Feb. 1868–7 Sept. 1943)*, college president and churchman, was born in Columbia, Tenn., the son of Colonel William Joseph Martin of Richmond, Va., and his wife, Letitia Coddington Costin of Wilmington, N.C. When he was four, his parents moved to Davidson, N.C., where his father

held the chair of chemistry at Davidson College until his death in 1896 and for a time served as vice-president and then acting president.

After attending local schools, young Martin entered the Reidsville Academy for Boys in South Carolina. He was graduated from Davidson College in 1888 and received a master's degree the following year. He then earned M.D. and Ph.D. degrees from the University of Virginia, where he also was an instructor in chemistry. He pursued further graduate study at Johns Hopkins and at the Polyclinic and Manhattan Eye and Ear Hospital in New York. In 1888 and 1889 he taught briefly at Presbyterian College in Clinton, S.C., and during the illness of his father he filled in for him at Davidson by teaching chemistry.

These stints at Clinton and Davidson convinced Martin that he preferred teaching to the practice of the sciences. At the death of his father in 1896, he became Chambers Professor of Chemistry at Davidson; from time to time he also served as bursar and proctor. In 1912 he was elected president of the college and served "with notable skill and commensurate success" until his retirement in 1929. During his term as president—the longest in Davidson's history—the institution survived two crises and experienced a windfall. World War I drained the campus of many of its students until Martin secured a Student Army Training Corps program. In 1921 the Chambers Building, the largest on campus, burned to the ground, but he secured funds to replace it with a bigger and better building. Finally, in 1925, at the time of the magnificent James B. Duke endowment, he laid plans for its wise use in the future.

Following his retirement Martin accepted the presidency of the Assembly's Training School of the Presbyterian Church of the United States, in Richmond, Va., where he served until 1933. Six years later he returned to Davidson and began taking courses in chemistry and political science.

Martin's first wife, Eloise Vernam Coite of Washington, D.C., died shortly after their marriage in 1894. In 1897 he married Mrs. Jennie D. Vardell Rumple of Charleston, S.C.; they became the parents of four children: William Joseph III, Eloise Vernam (Mrs. A. L. Currie), Jean Vardell (Mrs. Martin Foil), and Mary Katherine (Mrs. K. P. Maddox). Also a part of his household was J. Malcomson Rumple, Mrs. Martin's son by her first marriage.

The recipient of numerous honors, Martin was a member of Phi Beta Kappa and was active in the Mecklenburg County and North Carolina medical societies. He received honorary degrees from Wake Forest College, Central University of Kentucky, and Davidson College. He demonstrated a lifelong devotion to the Presbyterian church and served on many important committees of the presbytery and General Assembly. In 1914 he was moderator of the General Assembly of the Presbyterian Church of the United States.

Martin and his second wife were buried in the Davidson College cemetery.

SEE: *Charlotte Observer*, 19 May 1929; Davidson College Archives; *Nat. Cyc. Am. Biog.*, vol. 44 (1962); Raleigh *News and Observer*, 8 Sept. 1943; Stephen B. Weeks Scrapbook, vol. 1 (North Carolina Collection, University of North Carolina, Chapel Hill).

LUCY MARTIN CURRIE JOHNSTON

Masa, George *(1882?–21 June 1933)*, Japanese photographer and cartographer, for whom the Great Smoky

Mountains were an adopted home, was born Masahara Iisuka (or Iizuka—spellings vary). He was a reticent and somewhat reclusive man, after the fashion of his acknowledged mentor, Horace Kephart. Barbara Thorne, who frequently hiked with Masa in his later years, gives a telling glimpse into his personality in her recollection of a long day on the trail with him. Gently trying, in the course of conversation during a trailside rest break, to learn more about him, she was rebuked for her efforts with an abrupt "more walk, less talk." The statement was typical of this wiry, enigmatic figure who adopted the Smokies and Blue Ridge as his home and cherished them as a region of singular beauty.

Masa came to the United States shortly after the turn of the century (probably in 1906). He had been a graduate student in mining engineering at Meiji University in Tokyo and intended to continue his studies in this country. The unexpected death of his father changed these plans, and the young man abandoned his work towards a career as an engineer.

Apparently, he never returned to his native Japan. Deeply troubled by his father's death, Masa undertook a lengthy period of vagabondage and spent time in— among other locales—Colorado, New Orleans, and St. Louis. In 1915 he went to Asheville with a group of touring Japanese students. Immediately fascinated by the mountains, he left his companions and spent the remaining eighteen years of his life in western North Carolina. It was at this juncture that he adopted the first name George and the shortened form of his last name.

Shortly after his arrival in Asheville, Masa was befriended by a prominent local businessman, Fred L. Seely, and through Seely's influence he procured employment as a valet at the fabled Grove Park Inn. Within a few months he turned to photography for his livelihood. Masa was adept with cameras and first did some part-time work for guests at the inn. Subsequently, he established the Photo-Craft Shop (later renamed the Asheville Photo Service) and in time gained prominence in the region through his work.

Sometime during this period, Masa made the acquaintance of Horace Kephart, who had recently published his widely acclaimed regional study, *Our Southern Highlanders*. The two men were kindred spirits—reclusive, great lovers of nature's solitude, and more than a little eccentric. Through Kephart, Masa developed an abiding affection for the mountains and their remote, rhododendron-laden ridges, and they would henceforth feature prominently in his life. "Kep," as Masa affectionately styled his companion and teacher, became his idol, and the two worked closely on a number of projects designed to draw national attention to the region.

Masa's photographic enterprise was soon a thriving one. He was especially talented in taking "views" of scenic areas in the Smokies, which were reproduced as postcards. He also did considerable work on brochures as well as supplying photographs to the Asheville Chamber of Commerce, newspapers, and national magazines. Like Kephart, though, he cared little for material things and was happiest when hiking, carrying his camera on his back, on some remote mountain path. He frequently traveled by bicycle, a bright red bandana wrapped around his brow as he negotiated trails seemingly impassable except on foot. More than once he startled mountain folks, who had never seen a bicycle, by appearing on wheels in the most unlikely places.

His interest in hiking and the paucity of suitably detailed maps of the Smokies and Blue Ridge led to his becoming an excellent amateur cartographer. Masa's maps were models of accuracy, always based on firsthand knowledge of the region being covered, and he played a key role in laying out southern portions of the Appalachian Trail. Masa was also an enthusiastic advocate of the proposed Great Smoky Mountains National Park, and he assisted Kephart, mostly working behind the scenes, in efforts to make the park a reality. He was an original member of the Nomenclature Committee, which supplied names for the peaks, streams, and other geographic features of the park once it had been created. In keeping with these interests, Masa was also an active charter member of the Carolina Mountain Club, and he served on its council and in other official capacities.

While Masa never fully mastered English, as his extant letters readily indicate, he was the coauthor, with George W. McCoy, of *A Guide to the Great Smoky Mountains National Park*. In his later years he became a widely known and well-liked "character," and although retiring, he enlivened hiking groups with quips like "off your seats and on your feets."

Shortly after Kephart was killed in a 1931 automobile accident, Masa began to develop health problems. Although the cause of his death was listed as "influenza and complications," it seems likely that he had contracted tuberculosis. He died at the Buncombe County sanitarium and was buried in Asheville's Riverside Cemetery; there was considerable talk, both at the time of his death and later, regarding eventual reinterment within the Great Smoky Mountains National Park. In 1961, after many years of effort by those who fondly remembered the man and his abiding affection for the mountains, an unnamed peak on the main ridge of the Smokies between Mount Kephart and Charlie's Bunion was designated Masa Knob by the U.S. Geodetic Survey.

SEE: *Asheville Citizen*, various dates; Michael Frome, *Strangers in High Places* (revised ed., 1980); Horace Kephart Papers (Western Carolina University, Cullowhee); North Carolina Collection (Pack Library, Asheville); John Parris, "Great Smokies Were a Temple to George Masa," *Asheville Citizen*, 27 Aug. 1959; Private correspondence with individuals who knew Masa.

JIM CASADA

Mason, Mary Ann Bryan (6 Sept. 1802–31 Aug. 1881), writer, was born in New Bern, the daughter of John Council and Mary Ann Fulford Bryan. The Bryan family had been prominent in North Carolina for many generations. Mary Ann was educated in New Bern. On 10 June 1823 she married Richard Sharpe Mason, a native of Barbados in the West Indies; at that time, he was rector of Christ Church, New Bern. Between 1828 and 1840 Mason served Episcopal parishes and taught in colleges in New York State and Delaware. From 1840 until his death in 1874, he was rector of Christ Church, Raleigh. There were six children: William S., Martha Ann, Richard Henry, Mary G. (Mrs. S. G. Ryan), Rebecca E. (Mrs. William S. Mitchell), and Annie (Mrs. Ben Brokenbough). A niece and adopted daughter, Mary A. Kinsey, married William Montfort Boylan in 1846.

Mrs. Mason, whose many talents were praised by Samuel A. Ashe, was a painter, sculptor, and musician as well as a writer. Her cameos were singularly prized. She is best remembered for *A Wreath from the Woods of Carolina* (1859), the first book written exclusively for children by a North Carolinian. It is a group of religious moral stories, each illustrated by Mrs. Mason with a colored engraving of a native wildflower. *Her Church and Her Mother: A Story of Filial Piety* (1860) is an anonymous short novel with its setting in Raleigh. *Spring-Time for Sowing*, no copy of which has been cited, preceded *The Young Housewife's Counsellor and Friend, Containing Directions in Every Department of Housekeeping, Including the Duties of Wife and Mother* (1871), which was reprinted in 1875 with the cover title, *Mrs. Mason's New Cookery*. Mary Ann Mason was buried in Oakwood Cemetery, Raleigh.

SEE: *North Carolina Authors* (1952); Mary T. Tardy, *The Living Female Writers of the South* (1872); Richard Walser, *Young Readers' Picturebook of Tar Heel Authors* (1966).

RICHARD WALSER

Mason, Richard Sharpe (29 Dec. 1795–21 Feb. 1874), Episcopal clergyman and educator, was born on the island of Barbados in the West Indies and came to the United States with his parents when he was quite young. In 1812, at age seventeen, he was graduated from the University of Pennsylvania, and on 21 Sept. 1817 in Philadelphia he was ordained deacon in the Episcopal church. In the spring of 1818 he became rector of Christ Church, New Bern, N.C., where he remained for ten years. However, it was not until 30 Apr. 1820 that he was advanced to the priesthood by the Right Reverend Richard Channing Moore of Virginia in St. Paul's Church, Edenton. While he was in New Bern, the parish built its second brick church to replace the smaller colonial edifice. It was consecrated on 1 Feb. 1824 by the Right Reverend John Stark Ravenscroft, first bishop of the Diocese of North Carolina.

On 10 June 1823, at the church in New Bern, Mason married Mary Ann Bryan, the daughter of John Council and Mary Ann Fulford Bryan of Edenton. They became the parents of six children: William S., Martha Ann, Richard Henry, Mary G., Rebecca, and Annie.

As an earnest pastor, Mason worked to win religious converts. Among them was Jarvis B. Buxton, who gave up his business, was ordained deacon and priest, and served as rector of St. John's Church, Fayetteville. At the 1826 diocesan convention Mason reported that he was giving instruction in catechism and lectures on the scriptures to "colored" residents. Numerous infants he baptized were named for him. He kept neat, meticulous records of all his official acts.

Although comparatively young, Mason is said to have been quite absentminded. Once in planting vegetables in his garden, he put the peas in his pocket and his spectacles in the ground.

His transfer to the Diocese of Pennsylvania was reported in 1828. Later the same year he became rector of St. Matthew's Church, Geneva, N.Y., and the next year he was appointed acting president of Geneva (now Hobart) College. Also in 1829 the University of Pennsylvania awarded Mason a doctor of divinity degree. Still president of Geneva College in 1835, he declined a call to return to New Bern but did accept the presidency of Newark College in Delaware. In 1840, however, he returned to North Carolina as rector of Christ Church, Raleigh, where he remained until his death. The Episcopal church was relatively weak in North Carolina, and in both New Bern and Raleigh Mason engaged in extensive missionary work, thereby enlarging church membership and support.

When the Reverend Mr. Mason was at Christ Church, New Bern, the congregation gave him the large *Book of Common Prayer* presented to the parish by King George II in 1752, the year in which it was published. As Mason had requested, it was returned to the parish by his widow after his death.

While Mason was in North Carolina, there was considerable controversy in the state over the Episcopal practice of infant baptism. In support of the rite, Mason wrote a pamphlet published by his son in the year of Mason's death. He also was the author of *A Letter to the Bishop of North Carolina on the Subject of His Late Pastoral*, published in New York in 1850.

SEE: *Appleton's Cyclopedia of American Biography*, vol. 4 (1888); Gertrude S. Carraway, *Crown of Life* (1940); Craven County Records (North Carolina State Archives, Raleigh); *Nat. Cyc. Am. Biog.*, vol. 12 (1904).

GERTRUDE S. CARRAWAY

Mason, Thomas Williams (3 Jan. 1839–15 Apr. 1921), planter, judge, railroad commissioner, and orator, was born at Brunswick plantation in Brunswick County, Va. He was the youngest child of Dr. Nathaniel, Jr., and Temperance Arrington Mason, the daughter of Mourning Ricks and Joseph Arrington, sheriff of Nash County, N.C. Thomas Williams Mason was the grandson of Judith Stewart and Captain Nathaniel Mason of the Fourth Virginia Regiment of the Continental line. He was the great-grandson of Mary Eppes and Colonel David Mason, of Shell Bank in Sussex County, Va., who was a member of the Virginia House of Burgesses and of the Virginia Revolutionary Convention (1775–76) and colonel of the Fifteenth Virginia Regiment of the Continental line.

Young Mason was named for his first cousin, Nathaniel Thomas Williams, of Bloomfield plantation in Southampton County, Va., who, it is said, was visiting Brunswick at the time. Out of pleasure at the name, Williams gave his namesake Huon, a cotton plantation on the Mississippi River in Madison Parish, La. In the fall of 1851, at age twelve, after being taught by private tutors in Brunswick, Mason was sent to boarding school in Ridgeway, Warren County, N.C., where he spent his first night away from home. In 1854 he entered The University of North Carolina. At Chapel Hill he became a charter member of Delta Kappa Epsilon and a member of the Philanthropic Society.

In the spring of 1858 Mason was graduated from the university and gave the salutatory address. By then he had decided to study law at the University of Virginia and to pay court to Elizabeth Marshall Gray, the daughter of William Henry Gray of Longview plantation near Garysburg in Northampton County. In 1860 Mason was graduated from law school, and, with war approaching, he and Betty Gray were married at Longview on 25 September.

With the outbreak of the Civil War, Mason, who had gone to Louisiana on business, returned from Huon and was soon commissioned lieutenant and aide-de-camp on the staff of Brigadier General Robert Ransom. In June 1862 Ransom's brigade was ordered to Virginia, and in September Mason fought at Sharpsburg in what became the bloodiest battle of the war. Mason's letters paint a vivid picture of the carnage and its enormous impact on him. In 1863 he returned to North Carolina with Ransom's brigade to protect the Wilmington and Weldon Railroad. After the engagement at Boone's Mill near Jackson in late July 1863, Mason did not return to Virginia until the brigade joined General Robert E. Lee's forces near Petersburg in May 1864. From then until May 1865, the brigade held the line from the Appomattox River to the Crater. Following the surrender at Appomattox, Mason, by then a captain, returned to Northampton County.

Making his home at Longview with his wife's parents,

he began to oversee his farming operations in Virginia and Louisiana. During these years Mason often spent the winter at his Louisiana plantation. In 1876 he was admitted to the bar of Northampton County and in 1877 was chosen presiding judge of the inferior court for Northampton County, an office he held until 1885. In the fall of 1884 he was elected to the North Carolina Senate for one term; he served again in the senate in 1905 and in the house in 1915. From 1891 to 1894 he was a member of the North Carolina Railroad Commission. A noted orator and classicist, Mason gave a number of memorable speeches, including addresses at the celebration of The University of North Carolina's centennial and at the laying of the cornerstone of the Confederate monument on the west front of Capitol Square in Raleigh in May 1895.

In 1894 Mason was the nominee of the Democratic caucus for U.S. senator but lost to Marion Butler. In 1896 he ran unsuccessfully as the Democratic nominee for lieutenant governor, carrying the burden of the entire campaign because of the illness of the gubernatorial candidate, Cyrus Watson. He was a member of the board of trustees of The University of North Carolina from 1885 to 1909.

Mason and his wife were the parents of four children: Sally Williams (3 Nov. 1861), who, on 20 Dec. 1884, married William Williams Long of Union Hill plantation in Warren County; Betty Gray (22 Aug. 1863), who, on 20 Dec. 1883, became the wife of Lemuel McKinne Long, a first cousin once removed of William Williams Long; Ruth (21 Nov. 1864), who lost her sight in childhood and never married; and Nathaniel Thomas Williams (17 Sept. 1866–16 Sept. 1869).

A lifelong Methodist, Mason was a member of the Garysburg Methodist Church and an active layman whose family had, since the early nineteenth century, helped build the Methodist church from its earliest circuits in the Roanoke Valley. He died at Longview and was buried in the Garysburg Methodist churchyard. On 9 Nov. 1959 a portrait of Mason was unveiled at the Northampton County Courthouse in Jackson. Other portraits hang at Longview and at the residence of a great-granddaughter.

SEE: Josephus Daniels, *Editor in Politics* (1950) and *Tar Heel Editor* (1939); Gray Family Bible (possession of William Gray Long, Garysburg); W. W. Hall, "The New Railroad Commissioners: Brief Sketches of Their Lives Together, with Likenesses of Each of the Gentlemen," in Stephen B. Weeks Scrapbook, vol. 7 (North Carolina Collection, University of North Carolina, Chapel Hill); Royal Eason Ingersoll, *The Masons of South Side Virginia* (1958); Sally Long Jarman Papers and John Burgwyn MacRae Papers (Southern Historical Collection, University of North Carolina, Chapel Hill); Henry W. Lewis, *The Doctor and Mrs. Lewis* (1980); Mason Family Bible (possession of Nicholas Long, Roanoke Rapids, N.C.); Northampton County Court Records, 9 Nov. 1959 (North Carolina State Archives, Raleigh); Raleigh *News and Observer*, 15 Apr. 1921.

JAMES P. BECKWITH, JR.

Massey, Wilbur Fisk (30 Sept. 1839–30 Mar. 1923), horticulturist, educator, and agricultural journalist, was born in Onancock, Accomac County, Va., the son of James A. and Anne Parker Massey. After spending much of his childhood in Philadelphia, he attended Washington College in Chestertown, Md., and Dickinson College in Carlisle, Pa. In the late 1850s Massey went west and worked on a number of railroads. At the

outbreak of the Civil War, he returned to Virginia and served for a time in the Confederate army.

After the war Massey was an administrator in the Kent County, Md., school system and at the same time developed a nursery and florist business. From his experiences in the West and through his own horticultural enterprises, he formulated ideas about the sensible use of land and determined to promulgate them as an educator. Consequently, in 1884 he took a position as professor of horticulture at the Miller School near Charlottesville, Va. Through his teaching of practical agriculture, he became known to land grant college educators in both Virginia and North Carolina. Massey twice declined offers of a professorship at Virginia Polytechnic Institute before accepting a position on the original faculty at the North Carolina College of Agriculture and Mechanic Arts (now North Carolina State University) in Raleigh. He served as professor of horticulture from 1889 to 1901 and as horticulturist of the North Carolina Agricultural Experiment Station from 1889 to 1905.

While at the Experiment Station, Massey wrote numerous Station bulletins on horticultural topics, including farming and gardening in North Carolina. Of special interest is his *Agricultural Suggestions to the Waldensians*, published as a special bilingual (English-French) bulletin of the Experiment Station in 1895 to aid the Waldensian colonists in Burke County.

In 1905, after leaving North Carolina, Massey was editor of the *Practical Farmer*, published in Philadelphia, for about three years. For the remainder of his active career he was an agricultural journalist and an associate editor of a number of periodicals, including the *Southern Planter, Southern Farm Gazette, Market Growers' Journal, Southern Agriculturist*, and *Progressive Farmer*. In the pages of these journals he crusaded for more progressive agricultural practices, especially those that contributed to soil improvement. He sought to interest farmers in planting legumes, especially the cowpea, for their nitrogen-enriching capabilities. So dedicated was Massey to this task that he became known as "the father of the cowpea." He also published *Practical Farming for the American Farmer* (1907) and *Massey's Garden Book for the South* (1910). For his efforts North Carolina State College of Agriculture and Engineering awarded him an honorary doctor of science degree in 1917.

Massey continued writing for agricultural periodicals until shortly before his death at age eighty-three. He summed up his career with this statement: "My morning prayer for forty years has been that I might that day help someone to a better use of God's soil."

On 4 May 1861 he married Sarah E. M. Phoebus of Somerset County, Md. After her death he married her sister, Aurilla James Phoebus, on 4 Apr. 1876. These two marriages produced nine children, one of whom was Arthur Ballard Massey, who became a noted botanist at Virginia Polytechnic Institute. Massey died in Salisbury, Md.

SEE: *Progressive Farmer*, 7 Apr. (portrait), 14 Apr. 1923; Raleigh *News and Observer*, 31 Mar. 1923; Dr. J. R. Troyer, interview, 23 July 1981; *Who Was Who in America*, vol. 1 (1942).

H. THOMAS KEARNEY, JR.

Massey, Zachary David (14 Nov. 1864–13 July 1923), educator, physician, and Tennessee legislator and congressman, was born at Big Pine, Madison County, the son of Robert Hardee and Rena Brown Massey. He spent the first twenty-two years of his life in North Carolina, where he attended public school in Marshall. From 1882 to 1886 he taught in the Madison County schools. In 1886 he enrolled in Louisville Medical College, Louisville, Ky., and after graduation in 1888 began a practice in Wear's Valley, Sevier County, Tenn. During 1889 Dr. Massey sometimes had a captive clientele, for he served as physician and surgeon to the Tennessee State Penitentiary. In the same year he became a captain and surgeon in the local Sixth U.S. Volunteer Infantry, and during the Spanish-American War (1898) he saw brief service as an assistant surgeon in the army.

From 1899 to 1904 Massey served as postmaster in Sevierville in Sevier County. A Republican, he became involved in East Tennessee politics and was elected in 1904 and 1906 to the state senate, where he represented the counties of Blount, Cocke, Hamblen, Jefferson, and Sevier. In November 1910, after the death of Congressman Walter P. Brownlow, Massey was elected to complete his unexpired term from 5 Dec. 1910 to 3 Mar. 1911. While in Congress he was appointed to the committee on weights, measures, and pensions and to the committee on pensions for retired veterans.

After completing Brownlow's term, Massey resumed his medical practice in Sevier County. During this time he became a member of the board of managers of the National Soldiers Home in eastern Tennessee. In 1922 he was again elected to the state senate but served in only one session prior to his death. He also was involved in real estate and was a member of the Baptist church and a Mason.

On 25 Nov. 1886 Massey married Sallie Mullendore, and they became the parents of five children: Roy, Wanita, Mrs. Charles C. Pack, Mrs. T. A. Wood, and Mrs. W. H. Wilson. He was buried in Shiloh Cemetery, Sevierville.

SEE: *Biog. Dir. Am. Cong.* (1971); *Biographical Directory of the Tennessee General Assembly,* vol. 3 (1975); *Congressional Record,* 61st Cong., vol. 3 (10 Jan. 1911); *New York Times,* 9 Nov. 1910; *Senate Journal of the Sixty-third General Assembly of the State of Tennessee,* vol. 1 (1923).

R. A. MASSEY, JR.

Maule, William *(1690–1726),* planter, politician, and military leader, belonged to a noted Scots family, though little is known of his youth. After being captured twice by the French in the War of Spanish Succession, he arrived about 1709 in Virginia, where countryman Thomas Pollock was in self-imposed exile due to the ascendancy of his political adversaries in North Carolina led by Thomas Cary. Pollock recommended young Maule to Surveyor General John Lawson, who apparently took no sides in the political struggles, and the next year Maule was involved as Lawson's deputy in the first attempt to lay out the northern boundary. The Virginia and North Carolina commissioners immediately disagreed over the use of instruments, which the latter asserted were faulty, a judgment that was vindicated in 1729. This was a propitious event for the career of a newcomer, as were political developments occurring at the same time.

In 1711 the arrival of Governor Edward Hyde in North Carolina precipitated the abortive Cary's Rebellion and the return of Thomas Pollock and ascendancy of the Albemarle "party" over the Bath men. Maule was closely identified with the Albemarle group and Hyde. The Tuscarora war (1711–13) followed hard on Cary's Rebellion and offered a man of military experience a new opportunity. From 1712 to 1713 Maule led the North Carolina Volunteers effectively at the height of military operations. Thereafter he was known as "Col. William Maule

of Chowan, Gentleman." During this time he had remained deputy surveyor, and in 1714 he became surveyor general of the colony, a post he held until 1723. After the war Maule, with the exception of his surveyorship and an appointment to the vestry of the Southwest Parish of Chowan, was not politically active, concentrating instead on building his fortune.

As surveyor general Maule was well placed to expand his landholdings, and during the years he served he laid claim to over 16,000 acres—all located in Chowan Precinct, principally in the western portion, which became Bertie Precinct in 1722. Although these were the normal benefits of office during the eighteenth century, it has been argued that a large number of irregularities occurred during Maule's tenure and the situation improved only with the succession of Edward Moseley. There were complaints against him in the Council, and Maule, unlike John Lawson, was not the least bit concerned about the rights of the Indians. As deputy surveyor he had attempted through sharp dealing to deprive the Wyanoke Indians of lands; he later continued the pressure on the Meherrin Indians begun by Thomas Pollock, taking land for himself and allowing encroachment by settlers. He was also dilatory in laying out the lands of the Tuscarora, and in this matter complaints were heard in the Council as late as 1722.

In addition to lands he acquired through patent and purchase, Maule's marriage to Penelope Golland, the stepdaughter of Governor Charles Eden, brought him the governor's land and Eden House in 1722. While the income from his surveyorship was lucrative—Eden charged that he had withheld fees that were rightfully the governor's—Maule was also an active planter. Moreover, he dealt in the coastal trade, shipping naval stores and North Carolina's more important export at the time, cattle. On occasion he traded in slaves and indentured servants and supplemented his income by mercantile activities and ferry keeping on the Chowan.

By the early 1720s Maule, a more mature and experienced man, had entered the political arena. Ultimately, he served in the Council (1724–25), as a judge of the vice-admiralty court (1724–25), as a justice of the peace in Bertie Precinct (1724–25), and in the Assembly (1725–26). The politics of this period has long been defined in terms of the conflict between the established Albemarle group led by Thomas Pollock and the rising planters, eventually known as "The Family," led by Edward Moseley. Maule's career, like that of Frederick Jones, the chief justice, illustrates how difficult it is to maintain these categories when one examines closely the marital and social ties of the men involved. Maule was associated with Thomas Pollock and governors Hyde and Eden. Yet, like Jones, he maintained close contacts with the opposition through his business dealings and friendship with Edward Moseley. He was apparently on good terms with John Porter and his brother Edmund, both of whom were key figures in the opposition to Hyde in Cary's Rebellion. Perhaps Maule was gradually drawn into the circle of the opposition due to the fact that his interests, like the opposition's, were essentially in frontier expansion and because his younger brother, Dr. Patrick Maule, had become prominent in Bath County. It may also be that the death of his old benefactor, Thomas Pollock, in 1722 forced him to take new political directions.

As a member of the Moseley faction, Maule was closely allied with Governor George Burrington during the latter's first administration (1724–25). Burrington counted him among the most influential leaders of the time. Burrington actively supported frontier expansion, especially in the South, and by remaining in the colony after his dismissal from office, defined the alignment of factions in his successor's term. Within less than two years, the Albemarle party was able to engineer the removal of Burrington and the appointment of Sir Richard Everard as governor. Maule's tenure on the Council came to an abrupt end.

The Assembly had been the focus of the opposition led by Moseley since 1715, and when it convened for its first session in 1725, William Maule was one of the burgesses for Bertie. He quickly became one of the leaders in the Assembly's battle with Everard over the governor's right to prorogue the lower house. In April 1726 he was again present when the new Assembly convened. Maule must have been ill during this time, for he made his will. By late 1726 his promising political career was cut short by his untimely death. It is speculative, but likely that Maule—whose experience, wealth, and connections were equal to those of the other leaders of the rising Cape Fear group—would have enjoyed the same eminence as Edward Moseley had he lived as long.

Maule divided his estate, notably the plantations of Mount Gallant, Calledonia, and Scotts Hall, between his wife Penelope and his daughter of the same name. The administration of his estate and the guardianship of his daughter he assigned to his brother, Dr. Patrick Maule, of Beaufort and Hyde. Maule's daughter Penelope married Dr. William Cathcart but apparently had no children. His wife married first John Lovick and, after his death, Governor Gabriel Johnston, and into this line passed the greatest portion of Maule's estate.

SEE: Samuel A. Ashe, "William Maule" (Charles L. Van Noppen Papers, Manuscript Department, Duke University Library, Durham); Estates, Land Patent Books, Miscellaneous Land Grants, Patents, and Indentures, and John Devereaux Papers, 1712–1867 (North Carolina State Archives, Raleigh); J. Bryan Grimes, ed., *North Carolina Wills and Inventories* (1912); J. R. B. Hathaway, ed., *North Carolina Historical and Genealogical Register*, 3 vols. (1900–1903); Hayes Collection (Southern Historical Collection, University of North Carolina, Chapel Hill); Margaret M. Hoffman, *Chowan Precinct, North Carolina, 1696–1723: Genealogical Abstracts of Deed Books* (1972); Land Grant Record Books (North Carolina State Archives, Raleigh); Herbert Paschal, "Proprietary North Carolina: A Study in Colonial Government" (Ph.D. diss., University of North Carolina, 1961); William S. Price, Jr., and Robert J. Cain, eds., *The Colonial Records of North Carolina*, 2d ser., vols. 5–8 (1974–88); William L. Saunders, ed., *Colonial Records of North Carolina*, vols. 1–2 (1886); Jacquelyn H. Wolf, "The Proud and the Poor: The Social Organization of Leadership in Proprietary North Carolina, 1663–1729" (Ph.D. diss., University of Pennsylvania, 1977).

CHARLES B. LOWRY

Maxwell, Allen Jay (24 Jan. 1873–9 Dec. 1946), editor, politician, and state official, was born in Duplin County, the son of Hugh Gillespie and Nancy S. Maready Maxwell. He was a descendant of James Maxwell, Revolutionary War soldier, lawyer, and judge of Duplin County. Allen Jay attended the Goldsboro Public School but was largely self-educated. He began work at age twelve as a printer's devil for the *Goldsboro Argus* and three years later moved to the *Wilmington Messenger*. At eighteen, Maxwell became editor of the *Columbus County News*, which he bought three years later. As editor of this newspaper, and as a young mayor of Whiteville, he

waged a strident local fight for white supremacy in Columbus County.

In 1899 Maxwell became clerk for the legislature's *Senate Journal* and simultaneously assumed editorship of the Rockingham County *Rocket and Republic*, whose name he changed to the *Anglo-Saxon*. His editorial policy continued the fight for white supremacy by advocating the suffrage disfranchisement amendment to the state constitution.

Maxwell and his four brothers established a lumber business in Craven County in 1903, but after seven years the business floundered and failed. In 1910 he became a clerk in the Corporation Commission, of which he was appointed a commissioner in 1918. As a commissioner until 1929, and as an administrator in other offices, Maxwell suggested taxation reforms that were instituted by Governor Locke Craig. He also was instrumental in establishing the Local Government Commission; worked for taxes other than property taxes; proposed the state income tax amendment to the state constitution, which went into effect in 1921; worked for the establishment of the Department of Revenue; and fought for fair railroad freight rates for North Carolinians.

A public official for forty-seven years, Maxwell served in numerous agencies and commissions. He was securities commissioner ex officio (1925–29), president of the National Association of Securities Commissioners (1927), chairman of the State Tax Commission (1927–32), commissioner of revenue (1929–42), member of the Constitution Commission (1931–32) and of the Local Government Commission (1931–42), chairman of the Classification Amendment Commission (1937–38); president of the National Tax Association (1940–41), and director of the North Carolina Department of Tax Research (1942–46).

Also a prominent member of the Democratic party, Maxwell was a key figure in the administration of Governor O. Max Gardner. Maxwell and other Democratic stalwarts wrote Gardner's 1930 platform even before the party's platform committee met in convention. In addition, he drew up the Gardner administration budget bill, which recommended the enactment of a small gross-receipts tax on a selected group of commodities. It was, according to a historian of the period, a luxury tax set at a low rate, which was expected to add about $3 million to the state coffers. Maxwell, an ardent opponent of the sales tax, advocated the raising of state revenues by increased income, franchise, and license taxes.

In July 1931, believing that he had the support of Governor Gardner, Maxwell announced his candidacy for the upcoming gubernatorial primary. Running against him were Lieutenant Governor Richard T. Fountain and John C. B. Ehringhaus. Too blunt to be a politician, Maxwell campaigned on a straightforward platform of retrenchment and readjustment of state revenues. According to him, state spending, the salaries of both legislators and state employees, the cost of higher education, public school "extravagance," property taxes, and governmental "mismanagement" must all be reduced if the state were to survive the burdens imposed by economic depression. Considered to be the candidate of the conservatives, Maxwell lost the primary to both Ehringhaus and Fountain as a result of his positions on the issue of economy.

In 1940 he again ran for the executive office, this time against Democrats J. Melville Broughton and Lieutenant Governor Wilkins P. Horton. Generally regarded as a strong contender in the 1940 race, Maxwell suffered a debilitating stroke shortly before the primary vote.

Overcoming the paralysis after the election, he was reappointed commissioner of revenue in 1941. In 1942 Governor Broughton named him director of tax research, a position he filled until his death.

Maxwell married Della Ward on 20 Apr. 1892, and they had five children: Justin, Raymond, Hazel, Allen Jay, Jr., and Harold. After the death of his wife in 1933, Maxwell married Minnie Bradshaw.

SEE: Hugh Talmadge Lefler, *North Carolina History Told by Contemporaries* (1956); Allen Jay Maxwell Papers (Manuscript Collection, East Carolina University, Greenville); Raymond C. Maxwell, *Life and Works of Allen Jay Maxwell, 1873–1946* (1949 [portrait]); Elmer L. Puryear, *Democratic Party Dissention in North Carolina, 1928–1936* (1963).

DENNIS R. LAWSON

May, Benjamin (17 Mar. 1736–8 Aug. 1808), Revolutionary War officer, landowner, farmer, and saddler, was born in Scotland. Around 1750 he moved to North Carolina and settled on the south side of Contentnea Creek, two miles west of what is now the Pitt County town of Farmville. Pitt County deeds show that, beginning in 1763, May purchased thousands of acres of land and a large number of slaves. He was a farmer, and several property deeds identify him as a saddler.

By 1773 May was serving as a captain in the Pitt County militia. In 1774 the colonial Assembly appointed him one of five commissioners responsible for the transfer of the county courthouse, prison, and stocks from a private citizen's land to the newly established town of Martinsborough. In the same year, May was elected by his fellow freeholders to the Pitt County Committee of Safety. Active in that committee throughout 1775, he joined eighty-seven other citizens in signing a committee resolution that acknowledged the sovereignty of England's King George III but deplored the repressive acts of the British government and supported the Continental Congress. At the July meeting where this resolution was approved, companies of patrollers were organized and authorized to disarm and punish Negro slaves found off their masters' premises without permission. May was assigned to the Fifteenth Company of patrollers and soon became one of its captains.

May continued to serve on the Committee of Safety during 1776. In May he and James Gorham were directed by the Provincial Congress at Halifax to acquire arms for Pitt County troops. On 19 Nov. 1776 May took his seat at Halifax as one of five Pitt County delegates to the Provincial Congress. This session of the congress wrote the constitution by which the fledgling state of North Carolina was to be governed.

In 1779 May was made a field officer with the rank of first major in the Pitt County militia. He may have been among the Pitt County soldiers who fought in the Battle of Guilford Court House in March 1781. In 1782 he was serving as a justice of the peace, a post he resigned in late 1784. Two years later he was among thirteen prominent North Carolinians named trustees of Pitt Academy, established by the state legislature in an act that also changed the name of Martinsborough, the site of the academy, to Greenesville (now Greenville). In 1804 May won a seat in the North Carolina House of Commons, where he represented Pitt County until his death.

May married Mary Tyson in 1765. They had at least ten children: Benjamin, Jr., Fannie, Patsey, Sallie, Elizabeth, Delitha, Mary (Polly), Clara, James, and William. Another son, John, is mentioned in May's will, but

nothing more is known of this eleventh child. Mary Tyson May died in 1800, and by 1805 May had married a woman named Anna. After her death, he contemplated marriage to a woman with property and children of her own and proposed an agreement whereby each spouse would independently control his or her property. However, the agreement's complicated language excited the lady's mistrust, and the wedding was canceled.

May was buried in the family cemetery near Farmville. Not far from the cemetery is a monument that was erected in 1925 under the auspices of the Daughters of the American Revolution to commemorate the major's Revolutionary War service. The DAR also designated its Farmville branch the Major Benjamin May Chapter.

SEE: Walter Clark, ed., *State Records of North Carolina*, vols. 14, 16, 19, 23–24, 26 (1896–1905); Tabitha DeVisconti, interview, 23 Jan. 1979; Judith DuPree Ellison, *Index and Abstracts of Deeds of Record of Pitt County, North Carolina*, vols. 1–3 (1968); Henry T. King, *Sketches of Pitt County, 1704–1910* (1976); Laura Foster Renard, *The May, Lang, Joyner, Williams Families of North Carolina (Pitt County Area)* (1974); Jeannette Cox St. Amand, *Pitt County Gravestone Records*, vol. 1 (1960); William L. Saunders, ed., *Colonial Records of North Carolina*, vols. 9–10 (1886).

MEREDITH S. FOLTZ

Means, Alexander (6 Feb. 1801–5 June 1883), Methodist clergyman, physician, scientist, and teacher, was born in Statesville, the son of Alexander (1767–1845), a tailor from County Tyrone, Ireland, and Sarah McClelland White Means, the widow of James White and a native of Pennsylvania. Initially educated in the Statesville Academy taught by the Reverend John Mushat, young Means became a teacher himself at an early age, conducting a school apparently at Mock's Old Field in Rowan County, the site of the future Mocksville in Davie County. His own poor health and the death of his mother in 1821 led him to move to Georgia, where friends assisted him in finding a school in Greensboro. After a year in the schoolroom, he went to Madison to teach and study medicine. In 1825 he left Madison to study medicine at Transylvania College in Lexington, Ky. Following a single session there he began a practice in Hearnville, Putnam County, Ga., and soon afterwards at Covington.

In the same year that he went to Kentucky, Means joined the Methodist Episcopal church; three years later he was licensed to preach. As opportunity offered, in the face of his other commitments, Means continued to preach for the rest of his life. As a clergyman he took part in a great revival in Atlanta in 1847; in 1850 he was invited to deliver a memorial sermon in Philadelphia on the death of President Zachary Taylor; and, as a close friend, he preached a funeral sermon in 1874 memorializing President Millard Fillmore.

While a physician in Covington, Ga., Means began to study chemistry, and when the Methodists established the Georgia Conference Manual Labor School there in 1834, he became its head. He left after four years to join the faculty of Emory College in Oxford, Ga., when it opened in 1838. To prepare himself for his new duties as professor of natural science, he undertook special study during the winter of 1838–39 at Pennsylvania College and at Jefferson Medical College in Philadelphia. During his eighteen years at Emory, Means also served as professor of chemistry at the Medical College in Augusta, where he taught during the winter for nineteen years.

For reasons of health as well as to conduct some scientific research, Means was in England in 1851. There he met the natural philosopher, Sir Michael Faraday, discoverer of magneto-electricity as well as other features of electricity, and the geologist, Sir Charles Lyell. When Lyell visited America, Means had occasion to act as his host. Perhaps inspired by his contact with Faraday, Means returned home to begin his own experiments with electricity; he has been credited with anticipating the phonograph, the electric motor, and electric lights. In 1857, in Atlanta, he told an audience that he believed it was through the use of electricity that Moses parted the Red Sea. Some of the apparatus that he used in his experiments is preserved at Oxford College.

In 1853, while continuing to teach at Emory and Augusta, Means became president of the Masonic Female College in Covington, but after one year he resigned to become president of Emory College. Retaining that position for only a year, he concluded that he did not care for administrative work and returned to the classroom as professor of natural science; he also taught geology and biblical literature. Still conducting his classes at Emory and Augusta, he became professor of chemistry at the recently established Atlanta Medical College, where he taught in the summer from 1854 to 1868.

Although holding strong Southern points of view, Dr. Means rejected secession as a solution to sectional differences until the very last. As a member of the Georgia Secession Convention, however, he voted to leave the Union. Ending his affiliation with both Emory and Augusta, he was an inspector of munitions during the Civil War. In 1868 he also resigned his post at Atlanta Medical College to become examining chemist for the state, a position he filled until 1877.

Means was the author of numerous published sermons, tracts, and pamphlets on a variety of subjects. A "gentleman poet," he also wrote *A Cluster of Poems: For the Home and the Heart* (1878). He received honorary degrees from the University of Middletown in Connecticut, the Medical College of Georgia, and Emory College. There are portraits of him at Emory University and at Oxford College.

On 27 Dec. 1827 Means married Sarah Ann Eliza Winston, and they became the parents of eleven children: Thomas Alexander, Leonidas Summerfield, Olin Samford, Mary Elizabeth Payne, Victoria Ann, George Winston, Susan Cade, Francis McClelland, Henry Gaither, Hendree Winston, and Sarah Leonora. He died at age eighty-two and was buried in the cemetery at Oxford.

SEE: Edwin A. Alderman, ed., *Library of Southern Literature*, vol. 15 (1910); *Dictionary of Georgia Biography*, vol. 2 (1983); William L. Northern, ed., *Men of Mark in Georgia*, vol. 2 (1910); Notes by W. N. Watt (Taylorsville) culled from wills, deeds, and other records in the Iredell County Courthouse, Statesville (in possession of William S. Powell).

WILLIAM S. POWELL

Means, Gaston Bullock *(11 July 1879–12 Dec. 1938),* detective, scoundrel, and swindler, was born on his family's plantation, Blackwelder's Spring, near Concord in Cabarrus County, the son of William Gaston Means, a lawyer and longtime mayor of Concord. His grandfather, W. C. Means, known as "the General," was a wealthy antebellum planter with ties to the Barringer family. The family fortune was considerably reduced after the Civil War, and the general's fifth son, William Gaston, "the Colonel," went to Memphis, Tenn., and

practiced law with T. B. Chambers from 1872 to 1874. Before returning to the plantation in North Carolina, he married Corallie Bulloch of a prominent northern Mississippi family. After a short residence at Blackwelder's Spring, where his oldest son Gaston was born, William Gaston Means began practicing law in Concord, moving his family into a large three-story Victorian house on North Union Street. In time there were three more sons and three daughters.

Although they could be charming, the Means boys were described by more than one Concord resident as being "meaner than hell." Gaston, who apparently inherited the bad disposition of his father and grandfather, claimed that his first memorably satisfying experience was achieved not only by stealing money from his mother's purse but also in seeing the maid discharged for the theft. Yet the home in Concord was his haven, where throughout his life he returned for refuge and from which he attended All Saints Episcopal Church.

Gaston Means was a pathological liar; his activities thrived on complication, implication, and innuendo. His stories were unreliable even in the face of concurring testimony, which he always managed to taint in some manner. He maintained that he became interested in investigative work in emulation of his Uncle George Means, who had worked for the U.S. Secret Service, but his first practical experience as a detective was in trailing and occasionally suborning jurors for his father. In 1898 he entered The University of North Carolina, where he took a pre-law curriculum. While he was sociable and in his second year won election to the Dialectic Society, he was not intended for the classroom. He did not complete his third year at the university, though many a biographer has repeated his claim that he was graduated. Although he had the capability to play football and turned out for the team, he was lackadaisical and was never more than a scrub. At that time he was nearly six feet tall, weighing about two hundred pounds. Heavyset, his normal weight in maturity was about two hundred and thirty pounds.

In 1900 Means became superintendent of the graded schools in Albemarle, where he remained for two years. Meanwhile, his father had become an attorney for James W. Cannon, the textile entrepreneur. During his college summers Bud, as Gaston B. Means was known, had worked in the Cannon Mills, and in 1902 he joined the firm as a salesman. While he initially traveled a good deal for the firm, he ultimately settled in New York City. In 1909 he apparently requested a transfer to Chicago because of a breach-of-promise suit brought against him by a former New York City girlfriend, Edith Catherine Pool. But Means did not like Chicago and he went back to New York as often as possible. On one of his trips between the two cities, he was rendered senseless when he fell from a defective Pullman berth. A university classmate, Louis Graves, claimed the fall altered Means's personality. If that was so, then the change was immediate because Means tried to sue the Pullman Company in 1911 but failed in the attempt.

On 14 Oct. 1913 he married Julie Patterson, a twenty-three-year-old debutante from Oak Park, Ill. In 1914 Means quit his post with the Cannon Mills before he was dismissed and went to work for the New York detective agency of William J. Burns, formerly chief of the U.S. Secret Service. In 1915 Captain Karl Boy-Ed, a German naval attaché and the sub-rosa head of German espionage in the United States, became interested in Means because of his textile news reports in the New York *Journal of Commerce*. At the same time Means supposedly attempted to make a connection with the Germans for the Burns agency and enlisted in their service as "Agent E-13." In a typical act of Means flamboyance, Gaston used German money to rent an entire floor of a swank Manhattan hotel for himself. At that time Julie Means was recovering from the stillborn birth of her first baby.

In April 1915 Means first attracted the attention of the national press when his scheme to produce a propaganda scoop for the Germans, by showing that American captains were providing German sailing dates to British warships, failed. Means rationalized his work for the Germans by claiming that it was carried on before the United States entered the war; later he attempted to extort money from the Germans and, on the other side, more than once offered to trade his knowledge of German espionage activities in order to escape federal prosecution.

While he worked for the Germans, Means was in the midst of another swindle, which culminated in the death of his victim, Maude King, the widow of a wealthy Chicago lumberman, James C. King. Acting for the Burns agency, Means had rescued Mrs. King from a group of English confidence men who were robbing her. Means knew a dupe when he saw one, and through the family connections of his wife and with the assistance of his father-in-law, W. R. Patterson, and his brother, Afton, he gradually wrested control of Maude King's fortune. In 1917 Means was forced to bring forward a bogus will that was supposed to establish Maude King's right to the entire fortune of her dead husband. Finally, in need of money and faced with the possibility of losing his detective's license, he committed a desperate act. In August he persuaded Mrs. King to visit Concord, and on the twenty-seventh he purchased a gun. On 29 August Maude King was shot in the company of Means. A coroner's jury ruled that her death was an accident, but the news coverage given the event led to the development of suspicions against Means. The Northern Trust Company of Chicago revealed the bogus will, and officials in Illinois and New York began to investigate. Soon afterwards the dead woman's body was exhumed, while officials in New York City arrested Afton Means and searched Gaston's apartment. In September Gaston was arrested in Concord, N.C. He mounted a remarkable defense, claiming—among other things—that Maude King committed suicide and that the case against him had been engineered by German espionage agents. He was acquitted only because of local hostility towards the Illinois and New York attorneys and a rigged jury.

For a short time after his acquittal Means gave the appearance of settling into the life of a rural squire, but he quickly tired of the countryside near Concord, moving first to Chicago and then to New York City. He attempted to expose his former German employers to U.S. Military Intelligence, but his story did not sit well with that agency. When Means appeared before the Senate committee of Lee S. Overman, the committee denied his evidence. He also lost his last chance to collect from the King estate. In 1916 Means and his wife had their first live baby, a daughter called "Sister," and in 1917 they had a son, Billy, who was born in Charlotte. In the spring of 1921 Sister died and Gaston was nearly inconsolable. As in previous crises, he returned to his home in North Carolina. While in Concord he attempted to defraud the Southeastern Express Company of $57,000, which he claimed was sent in a package to Chicago but when opened contained only a block of wood.

In 1921 Means saw an opportunity that must have made his larcenous heart swell when his former employer, William J. Burns, became head of the Justice De-

partment's Federal Bureau of Investigation. Burns hired his former employee as a special investigator starting in November. Means seems to have been particularly well suited to what became known during the Harding administration as "the Department of Easy Virtue." He immediately hired a "paper" informer, pocketing the salary, and started to accept bribes from bootleggers. By January 1922 Means was broadcasting to the criminal world that he could fix federal prosecutions, but he had a setback and was placed on suspension. While on suspension from the Justice Department, he acted as a customs agent for the Treasury Department. Nevertheless, he continued to occupy his office at the Justice Department, which incensed honest officials including J. Edgar Hoover, who later succeeded Burns as head of the FBI. To avoid a confrontation, Burns sent Means to New York City in the spring of 1922, when Means began commuting between New York City and Washington, D.C. According to Julie Means, by October 1922 her husband had collected $50,000 in bribes. In Washington, he moved his family from lodgings on Newton Street to a Georgetown mansion with three servants and a chauffeur-driven limousine.

At this juncture in his career, Means made some serious errors. Elmer Jarnecke, who handled his payoff monies, signed a receipt for Charles Johnson. Until then Means's criminal clients' only protection was to communicate indications of his untrustworthiness to one another, but in February 1923 Johnson took his evidence against Means to Justice Department officials. At the same time Means was employing the services of Thomas B. Feldon, an attorney in the King case, to negotiate bribes. The two men also conspired in "The Glass Casket Case," in which they fraudulently sold glass coffins through the mails. By May Burns was no longer able to protect Means from investigations by the Justice Department and the press. Finally, Attorney General Harry M. Daugherty hired Hiram C. Todd as a special counsel to prosecute Means. Indictments were brought against Feldon and Means in October 1923, but the two men were able to forestall prosecution for the rest of the year. Means thought he saw a way out of his troubles through the announced enmity of Senator Burton K. Wheeler towards Daugherty. While Todd fumed over the delay, Means appeared before the select committee of the Senate to investigate the attorney general. He even had the temerity to offer Daugherty a deal for his testimony, which was promptly refused. By June 1924 he was short of cash, despite the enormous sums he had pocketed. In his last attempt to evade prosecution, he tried to implicate not only his old friend, Jess Smith, but also President Warren G. Harding, Attorney General Daugherty, and Secretary of the Treasury Andrew W. Mellon. His bid failed, and for the first time Means was found guilty in a court of law. He received a two-year prison sentence and a $10,000 fine.

While Means was free on appeal, Todd was preparing other cases against him, and his former confederate, Elmer Jarnecke, who eventually was pardoned and became a Justice Department informer, agreed to testify for the government. Means took refuge in Concord and claimed he was too ill to travel, but in January 1925 he was arrested and taken to New York City. There he was again found guilty and given another two years in prison and an additional $10,000 fine. Claiming to know something about the motives of Senator Wheeler, Means asked to see Attorney General Daugherty but settled for talking with investigators from the Justice Department. He stated that Wheeler intended to make Senator Robert La Follette president by attacking

Daugherty, and without blinking an eye he made the outrageous claim that both senators were Communists. His final ploy to stay out of prison failed to convince the investigators, and on 20 May 1925 he was sent to the federal penitentiary in Atlanta, Ga. His sisters, Kate and Belle, got Julie a teaching position in Concord, whereby she managed to care for herself and her son Billy. Meanwhile, Gaston Means fared well in prison, where he became the warden's spy. Released a number of times to testify in Justice Department cases, he even spent a month at the beginning of 1926 in a Park Avenue apartment in New York City. In 1927 other cases pending against him were dropped because of pleas from his family. On 19 July 1928 he was released from prison and returned to Concord.

While in prison, Means had become acquainted with Mrs. May Dixon Thacker, a free-lance writer and the wife of a prominent evangelist, who developed an interest in his story and agreed to write it for him. In the spring of 1930 the scurrilous *Strange Death of President Harding* was published and immediately became a bestseller. Mrs. Thacker repudiated the book in November 1931, but Means, who was then engaged in one of his most rewarding swindles, was unaffected by her denial.

After his release from prison, Means had convinced Ralph M. Easley of the National Civic Federation that he was just the man to investigate and expose Communists, which he accomplished with periodic reports made from reading the newspapers. In February 1930, while taking his family on a jaunt around the country at the federation's expense, apparently for no other reason than to keep in practice, Means smuggled $4,000 in gold out of Mexico into the United States. Altogether, he defrauded the National Civic Federation of $200,000, and by the fall of 1931 he had deposited over $100,000 in his bank account. Despite his wealth and apparent well-being, he began to suffer from bouts of acute depression. His wife had to call the police more than once for protection, and on one occasion he struck an officer who was attempting to restrain him.

Brooding in his Georgetown mansion, Means began to consider how he might profit from the kidnapping of the Lindbergh baby. Through Julie's connections he managed to meet Mrs. Evalyn Walsh McLean, the estranged wife of the publisher of the *Washington Post* and a friend of the Lindberghs, and Captain Emory Land, a naval officer and a Lindbergh cousin. Means persuaded Mrs. McLean and Land that he could recover the child. In a fantastic scheme carried on throughout the country, Means extorted $104,000 from Evalyn McLean. When he informed her that another $35,000 was needed, her lawyers became aware of the hoax and informed the FBI. It was with much satisfaction that his longtime foe in the bureau, J. Edgar Hoover, arranged for Means's arrest. In June 1932 he was found guilty of "larceny after trust" and sentenced to fifteen years in prison; in April 1933 another two years were added to his sentence.

The federal authorities decided that neither the federal reformatory at Lorton, Va., from where he might be able to recover the McLean money, nor the prison at Atlanta, Ga., where he knew too many people, would be suitable for his incarceration, so they sent him to the Northeastern Penitentiary in Lewisburg, Pa. He was unpopular there, and in September 1934 he was transferred to the federal facility at Leavenworth, Kans. Although he continued his scheming, he seemed to lack vitality. In the summer of 1936 his application for parole was denied. By 1938 Means was in extremely poor health: he had suffered a number of gallstone attacks and had lost over forty pounds. In the middle of the year he was transferred to the U.S. Hospital for Defective Delinquents in Springfield, Mo. His condition was sufficiently serious in November 1938 for hospital doctors to operate without his permission. On 7 December his gall bladder was removed, but his heart began to fail and he died a few days later. Julie Means, who was working as a department store clerk to support herself and her son, visited Means before his death. She returned his remains to Concord for burial in the family plot at Oakwood Cemetery.

Photographs of Means abound in the nation's newspapers and magazines and in biographical accounts of the Harding administration. There is an unusually true likeness of him as he appeared before the Wheeler committee in the frontispiece of his book. While his numerous crimes attracted a number of journalists before and after his death, the definitive biography of Means was written by Edwin P. Hoyt in 1963. No one stated the inordinately difficult problems he posed for his biographers better than Means in his book, *The Strange Death of President Harding*, where he admitted to being a "consummate liar" but observed that "it is difficult for the lay mind to distinguish between trained dissimulation and lying."

SEE: Baltimore *Evening Sun*, 16 Dec. 1938; *Charlotte Observer*, 10 May 1936; *Christian Century*, 28 Dec. 1938; *Colliers*, 19 Apr. 1924; *DAB*, suppl. 2 (1958); Harry M. Daugherty with Thomas Dixon, *The Inside Story of the Harding Tragedy* (1932); *Greensboro Daily News*, 6 May 1956; J. Edgar Hoover with Courtney Ryley Cooper, "The Amazing Mr. Means," *American Magazine*, December 1936, condensed in *The Reader's Digest*, March 1937; Edwin P. Hoyt, *Spectacular Rogue: Gaston B. Means* (1963); *Liberty* (7 Nov. 1931, 17 Apr. 1937); *Literary Digest* 81 (12 Apr. 1924), 122 (22 Aug. 1936); *Newsweek*, 20 May 1933; *New York Times Index*, 1915–38; Raleigh *News and Observer*, 29 Oct., 21 Nov. 1931, 17 June, 5 Aug. 1932, 10 Sept. 1939, 4 Oct. 1964, 4 May 1972; Francis Russell, *The Shadow of Blooming Grove: Warren G. Harding in His Times* (1968); *Time*, 19 Dec. 1938; *United States Senate Select Committee on Investigation of Harry M. Daugherty, Formerly Attorney General, Hearing pursuant to Senate Resolution 157* (1924); Don Whitehead, *The FBI Story: A Report to the People* (1956).

D. A. YANCHISIN

Means, Paul Barringer (7 Apr. 1845–19 Apr. 1910), lawyer, legislator, and university trustee, was born near Concord, the son of Catherine Jane Barringer and General William C. Means, a progressive farmer in Cabarrus County. His father was among the first to implement the newest inventions in farm machinery such as the grain mower and reaper.

Means attended private school in Concord and then Dr. Alexander Wilson's School at Melville in Alamance County. In 1862 he entered The University of North Carolina but interrupted his studies to join the Confederate army. During the Civil War he served as a member of the Sixty-third Regiment, North Carolina Cavalry, and as a special courier to General Rufus C. Barringer. Returning to the university, he was graduated with honors in 1868. With his father's encouragement, he studied law under Chief Justice R. M. Pearson and entered practice in Concord in 1879. During his legal career, he was counsel for the Southern and Old Richmond and Danville railway companies.

An avid Democrat, Means served several terms as state senator from Cabarrus County. In the legislature he drafted the "No Fence Law," supported internal improvements, and rallied support for university funding.

As an alumnus of The University of North Carolina, Means became a trustee in 1873 and served for over thirty-two years. He was persistent in his efforts to upgrade the level of funding for the university. Means was the author of a history of the Sixty-third Regiment, North Carolina Cavalry, and published several articles on the issue of free silver.

In 1894 he married Mrs. Moselle Partee Foard of Concord, and the couple had one daughter. Means died at age sixty-five and was buried in the cemetery of Saint James's Lutheran Church, Concord.

SEE: Samuel A. Ashe, ed., *Biographical History of North Carolina*, vol. 1 (1905); *Assembly Sketch Book, Session 1885* (1885); *Concord Tribune*, 22 Mar. 1967; D. H. Hill, Jr., *Confederate Military History: North Carolina*, vol. 4 (1899); *North Carolina Manual* (1909).

SUZANNE CONNER

Meares, Oliver Pendleton *(24 Feb. 1818–21 Nov. 1906)*, jurist, lawyer, secession leader, political activist, and Confederate officer, was born in Wilmington, the sixth son of William Belvidere and Catherine Grady Davis Meares. Like his brothers, he attended Bingham School at Hillsborough, then went on to graduate from The University of North Carolina in 1848. Afterwards he studied law under Judge William H. Battle in the university law school and in 1850 began his legal career in Wilmington.

An old-line Whig and a recognized political leader in the state, Meares was a significant figure in the campaign of 1852. In 1856 he was a presidential elector on the Millard Fillmore ticket, and four years later he gained further prominence in the campaign of 1860.

Meares played an important role in the duel between Dr. W. C. Wilkings and J. H. Flanner in which the former was killed. Wilkings had challenged Flanner over remarks made during a political debate in Wilmington during the campaign of 1856, and Meares acted as Flanner's second. The dueling party went to South Carolina, where dueling was legal, and after the customary ceremonies, the duel with pistols began. After two exchanges of fire, neither man was down, and settlement negotiations were initiated by Wilkings's seconds and friends. However, when Meares demanded a full apology in accordance with the *code duello*, the negotiations collapsed. The duel resumed and on the third exchange of fire, Flanner killed Wilkings. This is believed to have been the last political duel fought between North Carolinians.

Following Abraham Lincoln's election as president, Meares became one of North Carolina's most outspoken Secessionists. The Cape Fear historian James Sprunt records that at a public meeting in Wilmington in 1861, Meares delivered a ringing call for the state's immediate secession from the Union. Describing the occasion, Sprunt wrote that Meares "was an ardent secessionist and a fiery speaker, and the younger element were carried away by his eloquence." When the break with the Union finally came, Oliver P. Meares was immediately commissioned a captain of the Wilmington Rifle Guards, which occupied Fort Caswell on 16 Apr. 1861. Just the day before he had been elected captain of a company in the Eighteenth Regiment, and on 20 July he was elected lieutenant colonel of the regiment. Defeated for reelection on 24 Apr. 1862, when the regiment was reorganized, he later became assistant quartermaster (captain)

of the Sixth Regiment. In 1863 he was a candidate for a seat in the Confederate Congress but was defeated by Thomas C. Fuller.

After the war Meares resumed his law practice in Wilmington and became politically active. In January 1867 he was elevated to the bench in New Hanover County, a post he held until the adoption of the new state constitution in 1868. Returning to his law practice, he played a role in the campaigns of 1868, 1870, 1872, and 1876. In 1877 he was reappointed to the bench by the General Assembly and had a long and distinguished career as judge of the criminal circuit for New Hanover and Mecklenburg counties.

Meares married Ann Elizabeth Wright, the daughter of Dr. Thomas H. Wright of Wilmington.

SEE: Samuel A. Ashe, ed., *Cyclopedia of Eminent and Representative Men of the Carolinas of the Nineteenth Century*, vol. 2 (1892); Kemp P. Battle, *History of the University of North Carolina*, vol. 1 (1907); John L. Cheney, Jr., ed., *North Carolina Government, 1585–1979* (1981); Wymouth T. Jordan, comp., *North Carolina Troops, 1861–1865: A Roster*, vol. 6 (1977); James Sprunt, *Chronicles of the Cape Fear River* (1914).

JOHN R. JORDAN, JR.

Meares, William Belvidere *(8 Dec. 1787–11 Oct. 1841)*, lawyer, planter, and politician, was born in Spring Garden, New Hanover County, to Jane Meares, a spinster. His father was Henry Hyrne Watters, a prominent planter who acknowledged his paternity, helping raise young Meares and giving him a large plantation when he was twenty-one. Meares attended the Reverend William Bingham's school at Hillsborough and The University of North Carolina, where he gave an oration at the 1804 commencement; he was a member of the class of 1806. Kemp Battle (1907) called him a "non-graduating contemporaneous matriculate," but according to the 1954 *Alumni Directory*, he received an A.B. degree. In any case, Meares read law with William Gaston and became something of a protégé of the prominent lawyer (he named his second son William Gaston; his first was named after Henry Watters).

In 1818 Meares was elected to represent Wilmington in the state legislature, and the following year he was among the civic leaders toasting President James Monroe during Monroe's visit to Wilmington. In 1822, by then a fairly prominent lawyer himself, Meares was a director of the Bank of Cape Fear. He was a member of the North Carolina Senate in 1829–30 and again in 1833–34, when he received all·sixty-eight votes cast in Wilmington. In 1835 he was a delegate from Sampson County to the state constitutional convention, where he served on the rules committee. An Episcopalian, Meares voted for a resolution offered by William Gaston, a Roman Catholic, changing the religious requirement for state officeholders from "Protestant" to "Christian."

At the first meeting of the new Wilmington and Weldon Railroad on 14 Mar. 1836, Meares was elected a director of the company that owned what was to be, for a while, the world's longest single line of railroad track (161½ miles). Just three years earlier, on 13 Mar. 1833, he had been appointed a director and chairman of a group of subscribers wishing to erect a "free bridge between this place [Wilmington] and Hilton."

Sometime between 1835 and 1840, Meares quit politics and the practice of law and devoted himself to running his big rice plantation at Meares Bluff on the Cape Fear River. He reportedly "adopted and improved . . . scientific methods of farming [with] great success." A trustee of The University of North Carolina from 1835 to 1840, he was an "ardent advocate and supporter of the state university as well as of an efficient system of public schools throughout the state." Meares also took an interest in amateur theater as a member of the Thalian Association. Like other observers, James Green Burr, in a pamphlet on the association (1871), described Meares as outspoken and perhaps rather stubborn once his mind ("more solid than brilliant—more practical than imaginative") was made up. He had strong principles and was "a devout lover of truth," and he capped all that by being handsome and "possessed of elegant manners."

On 11 Nov. 1811 Meares married Susan Mary Pendleton at St. James's Church; she died two years later, at age eighteen, after giving birth to a daughter. In 1816 he married Catherine Grady Davis, the daughter of General Thomas Davis of Fayetteville; they had eight sons. Meares died suddenly while visiting friends in Warren County. He was buried at Magnolia Cemetery in Auburn, Brunswick County; the grave has since been lost. There is a portrait in the possession of Henry Jay MacMillan, 118 South Fourth Street, Wilmington.

SEE: Samuel A. Ashe, ed., *Cyclopedia of Eminent and Representative Men of the Carolinas of the Nineteenth Century*, vol. 2 (1892); Kemp P. Battle, *History of the University of North Carolina*, vol. 1 (1907); J. G. Burr, *The Thalian Association of Wilmington* (1871); Daniel L. Grant, *Alumni History of the University of North Carolina, 1795–1924* (1924); *Journal of the [Constitutional] Convention* (1835); Ida B. Kellam and Elizabeth F. McKoy, *St. James Church Historical Records, 1737–1852* (1965); *The Peoples Press* (Wilmington), 13 Mar., 4 Dec. 1833; *Reports of the Wilmington and Raleigh Railroad* (1836); James Sprunt, *Chronicles of the Cape Fear River* (1914).

EUGENIE W. CARR

Meares, William Belvidere, II (22 Jan. 1826–7 Apr. 1896), physician, planter, and Confederate officer, was the fifth son of William Belvidere and Catherine Grady Davis Meares. He followed in the footsteps of his father in many ways, particularly in agricultural and educational pursuits. Young Meares attended the Bingham School at Hillsborough and was graduated from The University of North Carolina in 1846. After receiving a medical degree from Jefferson College in Philadelphia, he returned to Wilmington and joined in the management of the family lands as he continued to carry out agricultural improvements devised by his father. On 20 May 1850 he married Mary Thomas Exum of Verona, the Exum plantation in Northampton County. Mary's sister, Martha (Pattie), married Matthew W. Ransom, and their husbands became close friends, their lives and careers touching each other's from that time.

With the outbreak of the Civil War, Dr. Meares volunteered for service and was commissioned in June 1861 as assistant surgeon of the Twentieth Regiment. Although initially assigned to Fort Caswell, his brother-in-law, Matt Ransom, was now in the field as a general of the Confederate army and called for his services. Meares was then transferred to Ransom's staff and served throughout the war as the general's aide-de-camp (lieutenant).

In May 1862, while the naval war was raging along the North Carolina coast, Meares took the precaution of moving his family from Wilmington to Davidson County, where he purchased the Ellis plantation (formerly the home of Governor John W. Ellis). When the war ended,

the family chose to remain there rather than return to Wilmington. Meares resumed the farming activities for which he had already demonstrated great skill. For the remainder of his life he was also a loyal supporter of Matt Ransom, whose career had taken him to the U.S. Senate. Ransom continued to rely on Meares as one of his closest advisers until his retirement from the Senate in 1895.

In his seventy-first year Meares became seriously ill and was rushed to New York City for treatment by specialists, but his life could not be saved. His remains were returned to North Carolina, where they were received by Senator Ransom and interred in the Ellis family cemetery in Davidson County. Ransom outlived his old comrade by seven years.

SEE: Kemp P. Battle, *History of the University of North Carolina*, vol. 1 (1907); William Belvidere Meares Papers (Southern Historical Collection, University of North Carolina, Chapel Hill); John Wheeler Moore, comp., *Roster of North Carolina Troops in the War between the States*, vol. 2 (1882); Noble J. Tolbert, ed., *The Papers of John W. Ellis* (1964).

JOHN R. JORDAN, JR.

Mearns, William Skipwith (6 July 1745–1805), eccentric, was the son of William Mearns, clerk of court for Chowan County (1748–50) and Currituck County (1757–58), and his wife Dorothy Skipwith, the daughter of Sir William Skipwith of Middlesex County, Va. She is mentioned as a sister in the will of Sir William Skipwith of Greencroft, Prince George County, Va., in 1764. While clerk of court for Chowan, the elder Mearns also served as clerk of the vestry for St. Paul's Parish. Taking advantage of this position in 1748, he recorded in the vestry minutes the birth of his only son, William, three years earlier. He stated that his son had been born at Millikins on the Roanoke River in the county of Edgecombe. This location, downriver from the town of Halifax, fell in the county of the same name when it was created in 1759. The will of William Mearns of Currituck, dated 15 Apr. 1769, was probated in Chowan County. He devised his estate to his wife Dorothy and son William Skipwith and appointed Neill Snodgrass, a merchant of Norfolk, as executor.

William S. Mearns eventually moved to the Hilliardston section of present-day Nash County and settled on Swift Creek. He was preceded to that section by his first cousin, Skipwith Richmond, who, according to the court minutes of Edgecombe, was operating a store there in 1761 on the old Indian trading route known as "the green path." In Richmond's will, probated in Edgecombe County in 1774, mention is made of his aunt Dorothy Mearns and his cousin William S. Mearns, who received the bulk of his estate. After the American Revolution, Mearns represented Nash County in the constitutional conventions of 1788 and 1789. He voted Anti-Federalist at the former and Federalist at the latter. He is said to have been an attorney.

On 13 July 1793 Hardy Griffin, for five silver dollars, sold to Arthur Arrington, Edmund Drake, Hardy Griffin, William Drake, William S. Mearns, Joseph Arrington, James Hilliard, John Arrington, James Battle, and John Green, commissioners of Nash County, one and three-fourths acres on which to build a meetinghouse called Mearns Chapel, where preachers and people of every denomination could conduct the religious rites and ceremonies of their respective churches.

Mearns was the first registrar of deeds for Nash

County after its creation in 1779. But in at least one instance he was remiss in his duties: the court minutes for 1809 refer to an order that the attorney for the state be requested to inquire whether any law would authorize a suit against the representatives of William S. Mearns for his not having registered the deeds.

After Mearns's death, his property went to members of the Skipwith family in Virginia. Writing to another family member on 12 May 1806 about the inheritance, George B. Skipwith, of Hickory Hill, Cumberland County, Va., commented on the deceased: "I will give you a slight introduction to this eccentric genius. His talents were universal. He was the amanuensis of the neighborhood, drew up all the agreements, deeds, wills and etc. for those who were too ignorant to do it for themselves. He was a legislator, having served some sessions in the assembly of his state. He was something of a practical botanist and physician, as he would procure plants from the woods and administer them to those who needed his aid and performed some cures which made him be deemed a second Aesculapius, and lastly, being of a religious cast, he would sometimes supply the want of a parson in the parish by holding forth most learnedly on subjects of religion. He died a batchelor at the age of sixty or seventy years and so poor did he live that I am told his little dwelling had more the appearance of the cave of a hermit than the house of a person who had it in his power to live comfortably."

SEE: John L. Cheney, Jr., ed., *North Carolina Government, 1585–1979* (1981); Raymond P. Fouts, *Vestry Minutes of St. Pauls Parish* (1983); William Short Papers (Manuscript Division, Library of Congress, Washington, D.C.); Wills, Deeds, and Court Minutes of Chowan, Edgecombe, and Nash Counties (North Carolina State Archives, Raleigh).

CLAIBORNE T. SMITH, JR.

Mebane, Alexander (*26 Nov. 1744–5 July 1795*), statesman, was born at Hawfields, Orange County (near present-day Mebane, Alamance County), the son of Scotch-Irish settlers, Alexander and Mary Tinnin Mebane. After attending the county's common schools, Mebane remained in Orange County and in time became a prosperous farmer. He married Mary Armstrong of Orange County on 25 Feb. 1767.

Mebane began a long career of public service in December 1776, when, as the result of a special election, he was chosen one of Orange County's delegates to the Provincial Congress meeting at Halifax. In the same year he served as justice of the peace of Orange County. In 1777 Mebane became the first sheriff of Orange County under statehood, serving through 1780.

During the American Revolution, he served in the Orange County militia, probably with the rank of colonel. He is known to have been present at the capture of Governor Thomas Burke by a group of Tories under David Fanning at Hillsborough on 12 Sept. 1781. Mebane escaped and made his way on foot to Hawfields, warning the citizenry that the raiders were nearby. The next day the marauders were ambushed by a hastily assembled Patriot force, resulting in the Battle of Lindley's Mill. Continuing his militia ties after the war, Mebane was commissioned in 1788 as colonel of horse for the Hillsborough District and in 1789 as brigadier general of the district.

The last two decades of his life were Mebane's most active politically. In 1783 and 1784 he was both a member of the House of Commons and auditor of the Hillsborough Convention of 1788, which met to consider the ratification of the U.S. Constitution. Aligning himself with the Anti-Federalist faction, he voted with the majority in refusing to ratify the Constitution as presented, without a bill of rights. At the behest of Mebane and others a second convention was called at Fayetteville in 1789. There Mebane supported an unsuccessful effort to place five proposed amendments before the U.S. Congress. Defeat of this plan led him to oppose ratification a second time. On 19 Nov. 1789, however, a majority vote of the convention was returned in favor of ratification.

Also in 1789 Mebane was named one of the original trustees of the newly established University of North Carolina. In that capacity, he was a member of the committee that in early November 1792 selected New Hope Chapel hill as the site for the university. On 8 Dec. 1792 Mebane was named one of the commissioners to erect the university buildings and to lay out the town of Chapel Hill. Fittingly, he was present for the laying of the cornerstone of the first building on 12 Oct. 1793.

Mebane attained his highest public office in 1793, when he was elected to the Third Congress of the United States, sitting from March 1793 to 3 Mar. 1795. In the first year of his term, he married Anne Claypoole of Philadelphia; his first wife, Mary, had died on 2 Sept. 1792.

At the adjournment of the Third Congress, Mebane returned to Hawfields, where he remained until his death. He was survived by six daughters and four sons: Jennet (or Jeanette, who married Richard Stanford), Mary Hodge, Fanney, Susannah, Elizabeth, Nancey, James, William, Robert, and John Alexander.

SEE: *Biog. Dir. Am. Cong.* (1961); E. W. Caruthers, *Revolutionary Incidents and Sketches of Character, Chiefly of the "Old North State"* (1854); Walter Clark, ed., *State Records of North Carolina*, vols. 12–13, 15, 19–23, 25 (1895–1906); *Debates and Proceedings of the Congress of the United States: Third Congress* (1849); Halifax *North Carolina Journal*, 16 Jan., 13, 20 Mar., 18 Dec. 1793, 9 Apr. 1794; Orange County Superior Court Records (1795); William L. Saunders, ed., *Colonial Records of North Carolina*, vols. 7, 10 (1890).

THOMAS E. BAKER

Mebane, Benjamin Franklin (*28 May 1823–9 Sept. 1884*), physician and manufacturer of a widely used patent medicine, was born at Mason Hall in the part of Orange County that became Alamance County in 1849, the son of George Allen and Otelia Yancey Mebane. Young Mebane obtained his earliest education at Caldwell Institute under Alexander Wilson. In 1847 he was graduated from The University of North Carolina, where his senior graduating paper, written in 1846, was entitled "The Effects of Climate on the Physical and Intellectual Constitution of Man." He received the M.D. degree from the University of Pennsylvania in 1850.

Mebane established a medical practice at Mason Hall, where he was born, and soon enjoyed the confidence of people throughout the region. It was observed that he demonstrated sincere concern for the ill, that "he never forgot to advise the sick about their eternal interests," and that he prayed at the bedside of those who were dying. His practice continued without interruption during the Civil War.

He patented a medicine that was produced by a company he formed in nearby Mebansville, where he moved his office. The Taraxacum Company sold its "Taraxacum Compound" throughout the nation; it was particularly successful in such distant states as Michigan, Iowa, Kansas, and Missouri. The compound was also in demand on the East Coast between New York and North Carolina and perhaps elsewhere. Describing the remedy as a "vegetable tonic," Mebane advertised that it "Cures and prevents Indigestion and Dyspepsia" as well as asthma; in addition, he claimed that it prevented colic and cramps and was "a good apetizer." Although it was prepared from a secret formula, the name suggests that at least one of its ingredients was the dried rhizomes and roots of dandelions. Mebane's family continued to produce the compound after his death.

A Democrat, Mebane represented Alamance County in the General Assembly in 1879–80. By a very close vote in 1881, he was elected to one term in the state senate, where he represented the district composed of Alamance and Guilford counties.

Married to Frances (Fannie) Lavinia Kerr of Caswell County in 1857, Mebane was the father of five children: Benjamin F., Jr. (m. Lily Connally Morehead), George Allen (m. Mary Holt), James Kerr (m. Carrie Banks Holt), Mary Belle (m. James Edwin Scott), and Fannie Kerr (m. H. William Bason).

SEE: John L. Cheney, Jr., ed., *North Carolina Government, 1585–1979* (1981); Graham *Alamance Gleaner*, 18 Sept. 1884; Daniel L. Grant, *Alumni History of the University of North Carolina, 1795–1924* (1924); Mebane Family Papers (Southern Historical Collection, University of North Carolina, Chapel Hill); Durward T. Stokes, *Company Shops: The Town Built by a Railroad* (1981).

WILLIAM S. POWELL

Mebane, Benjamin Franklin, Jr. *(4 Feb. 1865–15 June 1926),* textile industrialist, was born in Mebansville, the son of Dr. Benjamin Franklin, of patent medicine fame, and Frances Lavinia Kerr Mebane. He was educated at the Bingham Military School in Mebane and became self-employed at age seventeen.

On 8 Feb. 1893 Mebane married Lily Connally Morehead, the granddaughter of Governor John Motley Morehead, founder of Leaksville Cotton Mill, the first textile mill in Leaksville. Governor Morehead's son, James Turner Morehead, greatly expanded the family's landholdings and textile interests and in 1892 consolidated them into two companies, the Leaksville Cotton and Woolen Mill Company and the Spray Water Power and Land Company. B. Frank Mebane was made president of both of these companies by his father-in-law and founded six textile mills and one warehouse company in his own right: Nantucket Mill (1898), American Warehouse (1899), Lily Mill (1900), Spray Woolen Mill and Morehead Mills (1902), Rhode Island Mill (1903), and, with William F. Draper, the German-American Stock Company Mill in Draper (1906).

By 1912 Mebane had overextended his investments, and the Marshall Field Corporation of Chicago, which held partial interest in the mills, assumed control of all but Morehead Mills and the Leaksville mill. The mills that Mebane founded were purchased from Marshall Field by Fieldcrest, Incorporated, in 1953.

Mebane also was president of the Imperial Bank and Trust Company, as well as the founder and director of the Spray Institute of Technology. A Republican, he was a prominent political figure in Rockingham County for many years. He was a member of the Presbyterian church. The *Greensboro Daily News* characterized Mebane as a millionaire and "one of the largest landowners in North Carolina." He died suddenly in New York City,

where he was awaiting the sailing of the *Aquitania* for England.

SEE: Lindley S. Butler, *Our Proud Heritage: Rockingham County, N.C.* (1971); Bettie Sue Gardner, *History of Rockingham County, N.C.* (1964); *Greensboro Daily News*, 17 June 1926; Mebane Family Papers (Southern Historical Collection, University of North Carolina, Chapel Hill); *Who Was Who in America*, vol. 4 (1968).

BRENDA MARKS EAGLES

Mebane, Charles Harden *(27 Oct. 1862–16 Dec. 1926),* lawyer and educator, was born in Guilford County, the son of William Milton and Margaret Jane Harden Mebane. Educated in the common schools of Guilford County, he taught school for six years to earn money to attend college. In 1892 he was graduated from Catawba College at Newton, then joined the faculty. A Republican, he ran on the Fusion ticket in 1896 for the office of superintendent of public instruction and was elected. The first experienced schoolteacher to hold the post, he served from 1897 to 1901 but was defeated for reelection in 1900.

Putting aside party politics and with wide newspaper support, Superintendent Mebane undertook to improve educational facilities in the state. Under his leadership, the General Assembly passed a law to encourage local taxation for schools and made an appropriation for those counties that provided for such taxation. He further suggested that railroads should be taxed as a means of raising a substantial amount of money to support education. Mebane also advocated strict qualifications for both teachers and members of local school committees. He proposed higher standards for the education of prospective black teachers and the adoption of textbooks by a board of examiners rather than by local committees. Compulsory school attendance, he stressed, should become a state policy. Finally, in numerous ways he attempted to remove the question of public education from partisan politics.

Mebane also published two biennial reports containing information on current work, plans for the future, and historical information, some prepared by Professor Kemp P. Battle of The University of North Carolina. In some respects he laid the foundations on which his successor, Charles F. Toon, under the leadership of Governor Charles B. Aycock, would build. At the end of his term of office, Mebane became president of Catawba College, remaining in that post until 1904, when he became superintendent of the Catawba County schools. As this was not a position that occupied him full time, during the term 1904–5 he studied law at The University of North Carolina. He was licensed to practice in 1906. With this training, he served as judge of the Catawba County Recorder's Court in 1914 and 1915.

Clearly a man of diverse talents, Mebane purchased the *Catawba County News* in 1903 and soon became its editor. Later consolidated with the Newton *Enterprise*, the paper became the *News-Enterprise*, which Mebane edited until shortly before his death. In 1917 he was one of the directors of the Anti-saloon League in North Carolina and state director of the prohibition drive. For the last thirty years of his life, he served as a trustee of the North Carolina College for Women.

In 1894 Mebane married Minnie Cochrane of Newton. He was survived by his wife and six children: Charles H., Jr., William, Mrs. G. W. Mann, Mrs. C. W. Rothrock, Elizabeth, and Evelyn. While a student at Catawba College, Mebane became an admirer of Dr. J. C. Clapp, president of the college and active in the German Reformed church, of which Mebane became a member.

SEE: David K. Eliades, "The Educational Services and Contributions of Charles H. Mebane, Superintendent of Public Instruction, 1897–1901" (M.A. thesis, East Carolina University, 1963); Daniel L. Grant, *Alumni History of the University of North Carolina, 1795–1924* (1924); Newton *News-Enterprise*, 17 Dec. 1926; Oliver H. Orr, Jr., *Charles Brantley Aycock* (1961); *State School Facts*, vol. 19 (April 1947).

WILLIAM S. POWELL

Mebane, George Allen (b. 4 July 1850), black educator, legislator, editor, businessman, and writer, was born at the Hermitage in Bertie County of slave parents. His father was Allen Mebane. Nothing is known of his early life except that his parents were refugees to McKean County, Pa., in the latter part of 1864. Young Mebane served in the Civil War as a mess boy in Company A, Eighty-fifth New York Regiment of Volunteers. While living in McKean County in the towns of Prentissvale and Eldred, he attended the common schools for fifteen months.

Returning to Bertie County in 1871, Mebane for a time was a schoolteacher, probably in Windsor, and held a first-class teachers' certificate. Over the course of his life he taught for at least fifteen years in three counties.

Twice he was elected as a Republican to represent the Third District (Bertie and Northampton counties) in the state senate (1876–77 and 1883). He won his first campaign by 2,161 votes and the second by 1,200. Senator Mebane served on the committees of education and corporations and claimed credit for introducing a Sunday prohibition law. In reaction to laws sponsored by white legislators to restrict relationships between black men and white women, Mebane proposed a bill to prohibit white men and black women from cohabitating. The bill was killed in committee. Around this time Mebane also was an editor of the black-owned newspaper, *Carolina Enterprise*, along with E. E. Smith and John H. Williamson. Soon after leaving the senate, he was elected register of deeds of Bertie County and operated a provisions store in Windsor.

In 1885 Mebane proposed writing a book entitled "The Prominent Colored Men of North Carolina." Covering the period from 1860 to 1885, the study would include biographical sketches of over two hundred prominent black businessmen and politicians, as well as a description and history of those institutions in the state aiding blacks. He even went so far as to send out a detailed questionnaire to the prospective subjects of the sketches to obtain information on whether their parents had been freedmen or slaves before the war, the extent of their schooling, their occupations, and the amount of property they owned. Although there is no evidence that this book ever was completed, Mebane did publish two other works in 1900. His article, "Have We an American Race Question? 1. The Negro Vindicated," which appeared in *The Arena*, a national publication, used data from the 1890 federal census and other statistical material to document the progress blacks had made in education and to refute the claim that they committed a disproportionate number of crimes. Mebane also edited a pamphlet, *"The Negro Problem" as Seen and Discussed by Southern White Men in Conference at Montgomery, Alabama, with Criticisms by the Northern Press*, which analyzed the issues raised at the Montgomery race conference.

In May 1888 he challenged Henry P. Cheatham for the Republican nomination for the Second Congressional District. The district convention resulted in a split nomination for the two black candidates, which might have ensured the election of the incumbent white Democrat, Furnifold Simmons. Although perhaps for political reasons, a prominent Democratic newspaper praised Mebane and his candidacy. Mebane decided to drop out of the race in late September. According to some accounts, the Democrats offered him money to stay in the campaign, while others say the Republicans paid him to leave. Whichever version is correct, and both may be true, Mebane's withdrawal enabled Cheatham to win a narrow victory; thereafter the Republicans won a majority of the campaigns in the district through the end of the century.

In 1893, his political career behind him, Mebane was an incorporator of the Elizabeth City Colored Normal and Industrial Institute. After moving to Elizabeth City sometime during the mid-1890s, he served as the school's financial agent and general superintendent.

On 11 Feb. 1877 Mebane married Jennie Mills Sanderlin, the daughter of Robert Sanderlin. They had at least three children.

SEE: Eric Anderson, *Race and Politics in North Carolina, 1872–1901: The Black Second* (1981); Frenise Logan, *The Negro in North Carolina, 1876–1894* (1964); George Allen Mebane, "Have We an American Race Question? 1. The Negro Vindicated," *The Arena* 24 (November 1900), and *"The Negro Problem" as Seen and Discussed by Southern White Men in Conference at Montgomery, Alabama, with Criticisms by the Northern Press* (1900); "The Prominent Colored Men in North Carolina," an undated questionnaire, and George A. Mebane to Charles N. Hunter, 20 Feb., 6 Apr. 1885 (Charles N. Hunter Papers, Manuscript Department, Duke University Library, Durham); R. A. Shotwell and Natt Atkinson, eds., *Legislative Record* (1877); J. S. Tomlinson, ed., *Assembly Sketch Book, Session 1883* (1883).

ROBERT C. KENZER

Mebane, Giles (25 Jan. 1809–3 June 1899), lawyer, farmer, and legislator, was born in Orange (now Alamance) County, near the present town of Mebane, which was named for his family. He was the son of James Mebane, and the grandson of Alexander Mebane, a veteran of the American Revolution. Both of these men served numerous terms in the state legislature, and the latter was a member of the U.S. Congress for a term.

Young Giles attended the Bingham School in his native county and was graduated from The University of North Carolina in 1831. He remained in Chapel Hill for several years as a tutor before beginning the practice of law. Mebane then followed in the footsteps of his forebears by embarking on a political career. From 1844 to 1849 he represented Orange County in the House of Commons. On 1 Jan. 1849 he introduced a bill to create a new county from a section of Orange. The bill passed, and he named the new political unit Alamance; at his wife's suggestion, its county seat was called Graham in honor of Governor William A. Graham. The new county paid tribute to its virtual founder by electing him to the legislature from 1854 to 1860 and to the state senate from 1861 to 1865; in the senate he served for a time as speaker. Among his friends and associates in public office were William A. Graham, Thomas Ruffin, and George E. Badger.

While a legislator, Mebane was a staunch supporter of the bill to create the North Carolina Railroad. Successful in this endeavor, he contracted to build a section of the road and served for eighteen years on its board of directors, which recognized his interest by naming one of its engines the "Giles Mebane."

On 8 Mar. 1827 Mebane married Mary C. Yancey, the daughter of Bartlett Yancey of Caswell County and the sister of Mrs. George W. Swepson. They had six daughters and one son: Mary Catherine (Mrs. L. Banks Holt), Emma (Mrs. E. C. Mebane), Fanny Y. (Mrs. W. H. Smith), Betsy Ann (Mrs. C. P. Mebane), Virginia (Mrs. J. E. Robertson), Sue, who never married, and DeBurnia Y.

A staunch Whig as long as that party existed, Mebane was one of a group that entertained Henry Clay in 1844 on his historic visit to Raleigh. At the same time, the young lawyer's diplomacy and affability enabled him, on occasion, to work in harmony with the Democrats. This accounted to some extent for his accomplishments as a legislator and for his election to the Secession Convention (1861), constitutional conventions of 1861 and 1865, and Council of State (1866).

In 1855 Mebane was named a commissioner of the Alamance and Caswell Plank Road Company, and in 1861 he was an incorporator of the Caswell Railroad Company. After the Civil War, he moved to a plantation in Caswell County and in 1868 was elected vice-president of the newly organized Country Line Agricultural Society of Caswell County. In 1877 he was an incorporator of the Milton and Sutherlin Narrow-Gauge Railroad, and in 1879 he was one of the founders of the Farmer's Bank of Milton. In the latter year Mebane was elected to the state senate from the district composed of Caswell and Orange counties. During this term, he served on the important Committee of State Debt, where "he took a very decided part devising and maturing plans to compromise and settle the State debt." In 1885 he aided in the futile attempt to revive the Caswell Railroad Company. He also served for many years as chairman of the county courts.

In his old age, Mebane moved to Graham. He was a Presbyterian, and his funeral was conducted in the local church of that denomination. He was buried in Linwood Cemetery, Graham.

SEE: *Alamance Gleaner*, 8 June 1899; Hugh T. Lefler and Paul Wager, *Orange County, 1752–1952* (1953); William S. Powell, *When the Past Refused to Die: A History of Caswell County, 1777–1977* (1977); Sallie W. Stockard, *The History of Alamance County* (1900); Walter Whitaker, *The Centennial History of Alamance County, 1848–1949* (1949); Wills of Alamance County (North Carolina State Archives, Raleigh).

DURWARD T. STOKES

Mebane, James (5 Sept. 1774–12 Dec. 1857), legislator, was probably born at Hawfields, Orange County, one of four sons of Alexander, Jr., and Mary Armstrong Mebane. His father and uncles William, James, John, and Robert were active in the American Revolution, most of them serving as colonels in the North Carolina militia.

Nothing is known of Mebane's early education, though it is likely that he studied under the Reverend Henry Patillo. In 1795 he was one of the first students to enter The University of North Carolina, where he served as the first president of the Dialectic Literary Society; for over a century the society displayed his portrait in a prominent location in its hall. However, he left the university in 1797 without a diploma.

Mebane married Elizabeth Kinchen (1778/79–7 Aug. 1832), and the couple had five sons, including Giles Mebane, and one daughter.

His political career began with his election to the House of Commons in 1798; he was reelected in 1801, 1803, 1818, 1820, 1822, 1823, and 1831. During the 1820–21 term he was speaker. In addition, he served in the state senate from 1808 to 1811 and in 1828. In the senate Mebane sponsored the Electoral Act of 1811, which would have given the choice of presidential electors to the state legislature.

Mebane served on the board of trustees of The University of North Carolina from 1811 until his death. He was buried beside his wife in the second graveyard of Hawfields Presbyterian Church in Alamance County.

SEE: *An Alphabetical List of Those Identifiable Graves in the Second Hawfields Burying Ground, 1783–1975* (1975); Kemp P. Battle, *History of the University of North Carolina*, vol. 1 (1907); Ruth Blackwelder, *The Age of Orange* (1961); Daniel L. Grant, *Alumni History of the University of North Carolina, 1795–1924* (1924); Hugh T. Lefler and Paul Wager, *Orange County, 1752–1952* (1953); *North Carolina Biography*, vol. 5 (1941); Herbert S. Turner, comp., *The Scott Family of Hawfields* (1971); Stephen B. Weeks Scrapbook: History and Biography of North Carolina, vol. 10 (North Carolina Collection, University of North Carolina, Chapel Hill); John H. Wheeler, ed., *Reminiscences and Memoirs of North Carolina and Eminent North Carolinians* (1884).

ROGER N. KIRKMAN

Medici, Cosimo de (fl. May 1767–December 1789), Revolutionary War officer, was probably born in Italy; however, little is known about him either before he came to North Carolina or after he left. Letters for him arrived in Norfolk, Va., in May 1767 and in February 1768. On 16 Apr. 1776 he was commissioned a lieutenant in the Third Company of Light Horse in the North Carolina Continental Line, and in January 1777 he was made captain of an Independent Company of Light Horse.

His career, however, was checkered with irregularities. In 1777 he enlisted men but had no supplies; since the men were not attached to a corps, they were of little use to the state and were discharged. Also there was some question about the delay in his delivery of $650,000 in Loan Office certificates to Governor Richard Caswell, although in time they were delivered. When sent to North Carolina to purchase horses, he remained over eighteen months without finding any. At a court-martial convened to inquire into his behavior, colleagues and men he commanded testified that de Medici was "haughty, imperious, and neglectful of duty." He was also accused of withholding the pay of his soldiers, of being in debt to some of them, of lending or hiring out horses belonging to the company, of being addicted to gaming, of "sporting away £100 belonging to the public," of rarely attending to any public duty, and of treating his soldiers "with great indifference and inhumanity."

By 6 June 1779 de Medici had resigned from his corps, which was then disbanded. Yet in November 1789, the North Carolina General Assembly noted that he should be paid for a debt of £6 2s. 8d. he had personally incurred in 1776 to Colonel Joel Lane of Wake County to support himself and his troops in service to the United States. In December 1789, on the other hand, his petition for interest on a claim for a boat burned at Halifax was rejected. According to one tradition, he went with Count Axel DeFersen in a futile attempt to save Queen Marie Antoinette of France.

A Mason, de Medici was a member of Unanimity Lodge in Edenton, St. John's Lodge in New Bern, and Washington Lodge No. 15 in Beaufort County.

SEE: Thomas Burke Papers and William R. Davie Papers (Southern Historical Collection, University of North Carolina, Chapel Hill); Walter Clark, ed., *State Records of North Carolina*, vols. 11, 13, 21 (1895–1903); Curtis C. Davis, *Revolution's Godchild* (1976); Ernest M. Green to R. B. Downs, 13 Aug. 1934 (clipping files, North Carolina Collection, University of North Carolina, Chapel Hill); William L. Saunders, ed., *Colonial Records of North Carolina*, vol. 10 (1890); Frederick G. Speidel, *North Carolina Masons in the American Revolution* (1975); *Virginia Gazette*, 28 May 1767, 18 Feb. 1768.

JOHN D. NEVILLE

Meekins, Daniel Victor *(19 July 1897–8 Jan. 1964),* newspaper editor and publisher, sheriff, postmaster, and county official, was born at Sunnyside on the northern end of Roanoke Island, the son of Daniel and Rowena Homer Meekins. His father was a farmer and a fisherman; both parents were natives of Roanoke Island, as had been their ancestors since the colonial period. Educated in the public schools on Roanoke Island, young Meekins moved in 1916 to Norfolk, Va., where he attended Norfolk Business School and worked in a shipyard before entering the U.S. Army. Discharged from military service at the end of World War I, he returned to the Norfolk area. There he gained his first experience as a newspaperman, first in advertising and then as a reporter.

In 1922 he was hired by W. O. Saunders, editor and publisher of the Elizabeth City *Independent*, where he remained until 1927, serving during the later years as associate editor of the newspaper. Like so many other natives of the Outer Banks region, Meekins harbored both a desire and a sense of obligation to return to his homeland once he had received an education and professional experience elsewhere. He made the move in 1927, just in time to reestablish his identity and residency and to submit his name to the electorate as a candidate for sheriff of Dare County. Elected in his first bid for public office, he served as sheriff from 1928 until 1946.

Meekins met Catherine Deaton, a talented musician, music teacher, and daughter of a Mooresville newspaper publisher, on her first visit to Roanoke Island in the summer of 1929 and proposed to her the next day. They were married that winter, and throughout their married life they continued to live at his family homestead on the western shore of Roanoke Island overlooking Croatan Sound.

Dare County was without a newspaper, and in 1935 Meekins decided to provide the people of his home area with a paper of their own, founding a weekly publication he called the *Dare County Times*. At the same time he set up a small job-printing shop in rented office space in Manteo, but the equipment was inadequate to handle the larger-format newspaper, and for years it was printed in Elizabeth City. He later acquired a used press large enough to print the paper, built a shop to house both the printing business and the newspaper office, and expanded the publishing venture to include weekly newspapers in nearby counties: the *Tyrrell County Tribune* in Columbia, the *Hyde County Herald* in Swanquarter, the *Pilot* in Belhaven, and for a brief period the *Seashore News* in Nags Head. Acute shortages of newsprint brought on by World War II, as well as increasing difficulty in putting out newspapers with a shortage of available help over a relatively wide geographic area, resulted in consolidation of the papers in 1949 as the *Coastland Times*.

With his service as sheriff terminated in 1946, Meekins waited less than two years before getting back into local government. He was elected to the Dare County Board of Commissioners and served as chairman from 1948 to 1950 and again from 1958 to 1960.

His writing style, reflected in both the editorial and news columns of his papers, was straightforward and earthy, most often with short words rather than long ones, simple sentences rather than complicated ones. His penchant for using words and phrases common in spoken English but seldom seen in print served to enrage those who considered some of his writings "filth" while titillating others. His papers were seldom overburdened with formal editorials, but his editorial views were often made clear in his news stories. When he championed a project or an idea he did so wholeheartedly, and when he disapproved he was never reluctant to attack with vigor.

For nearly thirty years Meekins devoted a considerable part of his time to developing closer ties among the small counties on the southern side of Albemarle Sound, and he was a prime mover in the formation of the Southern Albemarle Association in 1935. He served as secretary of the association for several years and later as vice-president and president (1949–50). He was probably as responsible as any individual for the network of modern bridges that connect the Outer Banks and Roanoke Island, an area he liked to call "The Walter Raleigh Coastland," with the interior.

Meekins was a Thirty-second-degree Mason, a Shriner, an Oddfellow, a Rotarian, and a Ruritan. He served as secretary of the North Carolina Cape Hatteras Seashore Commission (1941–44), was an organizer and for many years secretary of the Fessenden National Memorial Association, and was active in the Kill Devil Hills Memorial Society, serving as both secretary and vice-president.

In addition to his newspaper publishing and job-printing activities, he was engaged in a number of business ventures, ranging from insurance and real estate to billboard advertising and the sale of office equipment and supplies. For many years he wrote a column for his papers, "The Old Sea Captain and the Drummer," which attracted a wide following. In 1950 he assembled the most popular of the columns and published them in book form with the subtitle, "Salty Dialogue from the Land of Wind and Water."

Throughout his adult life Meekins was active in the Democratic party. He was an organizer of the first Young Democrats Club in Dare County and was a delegate to the 1956 Democratic National Convention in Chicago. In 1962 he was appointed postmaster of Manteo, and two years later, at the time of his death, he was president of the Association of Eastern North Carolina Postmasters.

His wife worked closely with him in the publishing and printing business, helping with both the writing and office management. They had two sons, Roger P. and Francis W.; and a daughter, Mrs. Boyce W. Harwell.

SEE: *Coastland Times*, 10, 17 Jan. 1964; William S. Powell, ed., *North Carolina Lives* (1962); *Who's Who in the South and Southwest* (1963).

DAVID STICK

Meekins, Isaac Melson (13 Feb. 1875–21 Nov. 1946), mayor, postmaster, general counsel for Alien Property Custodian, general counsel and manager of Enemy Insurance Companies, and U.S. district court judge, was born at Gum Neck, near Columbia in Tyrrell County. The son of Jeremiah Charles and Mahalah Melson Meekins, he was a member of the First Baptist Church, Elizabeth City. His father was a merchant, farmer, and banker in Tyrrell County.

In 1896 he was graduated from Wake Forest College with an A.B. degree. Before completing his degree, he had begun to read law, and in the year of his graduation he was admitted to the North Carolina bar and began a practice in Elizabeth City. He received an honorary doctor of laws degree from Wake Forest College in 1932.

Meekins entered the political scene at an early age, serving as mayor of Elizabeth City in 1897 and as city attorney in 1898. He was appointed postmaster in 1903. From 1910 to 1914 he was the assistant U.S. attorney of the Eastern District. A member of the Republican state committee from 1900 to 1918, he was the Republican candidate for governor in 1924. In 1936 the Republican state committee endorsed his nomination for president of the United States.

On 23 Nov. 1924 Meekins was appointed district judge of the U.S. Court for the Eastern District of North Carolina by President Calvin Coolidge and served until 13 Feb. 1945. He was a special U.S. district judge in New York, Illinois, and other states by order of Chief Justice William Howard Taft. Judge Meekins traveled with Taft as a speaker after the latter became president.

Meekins married Lena Allen of Wake Forest on 4 June 1896. They had five children: William Charles (d. 1967; buried at Calvary Episcopal Church, Fletcher), Mahalah Melson (d. 1925; buried at Old Hollywood Cemetery, Elizabeth City), Jeremiah Charles (drowned in 1912; buried at Old Hollywood Cemetery, Elizabeth City); Isabella James (m. Dr. Joseph J. Combs, Raleigh), and Mary Purefoy (m. Oliver F. Gilbert, Elizabeth City). Meekins and his wife were buried at Old Hollywood Cemetery, Elizabeth City.

SEE: R. D. W. Connor, *North Carolina: Rebuilding an Ancient Commonwealth*, vols. 2–3 (1929); David E. Davis, *History of Tyrrell County* (1963); Thomas Dixon, *A Day in Court: History of North Carolina*, vol. 5 (1919); *The Independent*, 22 Nov. 1935; *North Carolina Bar* 22 (1975); *North Carolina Biography*, vol. 5 (1919 [portrait]; 1941); Keith Saunders, *The Independent Man* (1962); *Who's Who in America*, vol. 19 (1937); John Elliott Wood, ed., Pasquotank Historical Society *Year Book*, vol. 1 (1954–55).

WILLIAM C. MEEKINS, JR.

Melbourn, Julius, said to have been born on 4 July 1790 in Wake County, was apparently a fictitious character invented to perpetrate a literary hoax. In 1847 the firm of Hall and Dickson in Syracuse, N.Y., published the purported autobiography of a former slave, entitled *Life and Opinions of Julius Melbourn*. Advertised as having been edited by "a late member of Congress," the narrative was said to have been written by a blue-eyed mulatto whose master had been a Major Johnson, owner of a Wake County plantation about ten miles from Raleigh. At age five the slave was purchased by the wealthy widow of an English naval lieutenant, a Mrs. Melbourn, who for some reason had moved to Raleigh, even though it was then a village less than three years old. The narrative states that she emancipated Julius, gave him her name, educated him in her late husband's ex-

tensive library, and left him a sizable inheritance at her death in 1809.

After an incredible series of dramatic intrigues involving a wife and son, separation and eventual reunion, the hero was said to have lived in New Orleans and New England before finally moving to England to escape racial prejudice, termed by the writer "greater in the Northern, particularly in the New England free states, than in the Southern slaveholding states." The "autobiographical" section of the book comprises approximately one-fourth of its pages, the remaining three-quarters consisting of his "opinions" on a variety of social and political subjects, including the American Colonization Society and his "reminiscences" of conversations with such persons as John Marshall, John Quincy Adams, and Thomas Jefferson, at least one such encounter having taken place at Monticello.

Soon after the book's appearance and review in northern newspapers, the Raleigh *Register* engaged in a lively exchange with the Albany (N.Y.) *Journal*, the Washington *Era*, and the Richmond *Whig* concerning its authenticity. The narrator had mentioned a Mr. Gale [*sic*], whom, if intended to represent the founder of the *Register*, Joseph Gales, he had mistakenly placed in Raleigh four years before the actual Joseph Gales arrived. His son Weston R. Gales, editor of the *Register* in 1847, expressed the absolute conviction that Melbourn never existed—at least not in the Raleigh area. After consulting "the oldest inhabitant" and numerous other Wake County citizens, Gales stated emphatically that the book was "sheer fabrication from beginning to end, unless fictitious names have been resorted to, in place of real ones." These names included the Major Johnson who was Melbourn's master but "whose Christian name [he was] unable to give"; Johnson's son George, who speculated in Negroes; the narrator's benefactor, Mrs. Melbourn, whose given name he never listed; her son Edward; the slave Maria whom the hero married and tried to purchase; their son J———; a slave broker named Return Jonathan Fairport who went to Raleigh from Lynn, Mass.; a Colonel Boyd and his daughter Laura, who married one Alexander St. John from Norfolk, Va.; a Methodist minister from Virginia called Mr. Smith; and a Raleigh lawyer named Mr. Grip.

In 1928 Professor Vernon Loggins of Columbia University, doubting the genuineness of the book, wrote to Vitruvius Royster, clerk of Wake County Superior Court, seeking emancipation documents or any other information that might verify details given as biographical facts. Neither the county records at that time nor subsequent research by the writer of the present sketch supports authenticity of any one of the names or facts in the book, with the possible exception of "Mr. Gale." Apparently unaware of the searches made in 1847 and in 1928 for proof, at least two twentieth-century historians have mentioned Melbourn as though he actually existed.

SEE: John Hope Franklin, *The Free Negro in North Carolina, 1790–1860* (1943); Guion Griffis Johnson, *Ante-Bellum North Carolina: A Social History* (1937); Julius Melbourn (pseud.?), *Life and Opinions of Julius Melbourn* (1847); Raleigh *News and Observer*, 13 July 1928; Raleigh *Register*, 18, 28 Aug. 1847; Wake County Census Records, Death Notices, Estates Papers, Marriage Bonds, Tax Lists, and Wills (North Carolina State Archives, Raleigh).

ELIZABETH DAVIS REID MURRAY

Mellyne, Robert (*ca. 1666–ca. 1708/9*), silversmith, was living in North Carolina for some years prior to 1702 and may well have been the colony's earliest silversmith. His name, with all its variations of spelling (Moline, Mellyn, Morlines, Meline, Mulline, Mullines, Mollyn, Moliones, Moloines), appears numerous times in the *Colonial Records*, the *North Carolina Higher-Court Records, 1670–1696*, and the Beaufort County Deeds (vol. 1). In the wills of David Makee and Edward Wood, which Mellyne signed as a witness, his name is spelled "Mellyne."

The earliest extant reference to Mellyne occurs in the county court records for November 1693, when "Robert Mulline" was called to serve on the grand jury. Subsequent documents reveal that both Mellyne and his wife Ellinor were involved in several cases brought before the courts. In one such case, *Crown v. Fewox*, tried in the Council Court of Albemarle during November–December 1696, the witness Peter Middleton testified that tools "Mr. Fewox Fech out of Virginia" were "Fewoxis Tooles" and that "Mollines was allonge with them to Doe itt that is to be said to quoine money."

A deed of land dated 1 July 1702 indicates that Mellyne purchased from John Lawson (through Lawson's legal representative) Narrows, a tract of land containing 640 acres along the "north dividing creek in Pamtico River." In the same deed book is a document dated 12 June 1703 giving rights of entry to this property to Philip Howard. The owner is identified as "Robert Mellyne of Bath County, Silversmith." Another such document in which Mellyne sold rights of entry to William Price also designates him as a silversmith.

Mellyne made his will on 29 Dec. 1708, and he had died by 4 Jan. 1708/9, when the will was probated. Since there were no children, he willed his property to his sisters still living in Ireland and to their heirs on the death of Ellinor Mellyne, wife of the craftsman. Edward Mackswine, a nephew, claimed the property in 1720.

The appearance in his will of the words "still living in Ireland" suggests that Mellyne was of Irish extraction. No silver made by him has been found, and nothing is known about him except through court records and deed books. One document contains a reference to a suit brought against him by Jonathan Bateman in 1697 for failing "to fix the lock of a gunn for the plaintiff," so Mellyne may also have been a gunsmith of sorts. At any rate, his designation as "Robert Mellyne, Silversmith" supports the suggestion that he may have been the first such craftsman to live in North Carolina.

SEE: Beaufort County Deed Books (North Carolina State Archives, Raleigh); George B. Cutten and Mary Reynolds Peacock, *Silversmiths of North Carolina*, 2d ed. (1973); Mattie Erma E. Parker, ed., *North Carolina Higher-Court Records, 1670–1696*, vol. 2 (1968) and *1697–1701*, vol. 3 (1971); Secretary of State Records and North Carolina Wills (North Carolina State Archives, Raleigh).

MARY REYNOLDS PEACOCK

Memminger, Christopher Gustavus (*9 Jan. 1803–7 Mar. 1888*), lawyer, statesman, and secretary of the Confederate Treasury, was born in Nayinghen in the Dukedom of Württemberg, Germany, the only child of Christopher Godfrey and Ebarhardina Elisabeth Kohler Memminger. Christopher was an infant when his father, an officer in the Prince-Elector's Battalion of Foot Jaegers, was killed in the line of duty. He immigrated with his mother and her parents to Charleston, S.C., to escape Napoleon's continuing wars, but there his mother

died and four-year-old Christopher was placed in the Orphan's House of Charleston. At age eleven he was adopted by Thomas Bennett, later governor of South Carolina, and was reared in an atmosphere of refinement and opportunity.

Before his thirteenth birthday Memminger entered the South Carolina College in Columbia, the forerunner of the University of South Carolina. Although the youngest in his class, he was singled out for academic excellence and exemplary conduct. After graduation he returned to Charleston and prepared for a career in law.

In time he was elected to the South Carolina House of Representatives, where, as chairman of the Committee on Education, he reformed the entire public school system of the state and implemented a program of graded schools in Charleston that was considered second to none in the United States. As chairman of a committee on finance for the state, he established a reputation as a sound financier. For thirty-two years he was a trustee of his former college.

Prior to South Carolina's secession from the Union, Memminger played a leading role in the Union States Rights party. He opposed nullification and presented his arguments against it in *The Book of Nullification*, a widely read satire that he wrote in biblical style. Following John Brown's raid at Harpers Ferry, Governor William H. Gist of South Carolina assigned him the task of expressing to Virginians the desire of South Carolinians to unite with them in measures of defense. By his address Memminger appealed to thinking men and prepared their minds for the events that would soon plunge the country into war. Before the year ended, he was won over to secession, becoming an active member of the Secession Convention of South Carolina and heading a committee to draft a statement justifying the state's actions.

At the beginning of the war President Jefferson Davis appointed Memminger secretary of the Confederate Treasury. When he assumed his duties, there was neither money in the Treasury nor paper on which to print it. The Northern blockade prevented the exportation of cotton, the South's only resource that could demand cash. Memminger developed Treasury policies that proved ineffective against the problems of the Southern states during a four-year war, and when he resorted to levying taxes to raise funds, it was too late. The Confederacy collapsed, but responsibility for it lay with the government, not with Memminger, who had frequently been compelled to carry out policies of which he did not approve. Realizing that his job was hopeless, he resigned from office in June 1864.

Memminger sought refuge with his family in Flat Rock, N.C., where Rock Hill, his summer home for twenty-five years, had become a wartime haven for friends and relatives. Earlier he had urged President Davis to move the Confederate capital from Richmond to Rock Hill, believing it could be more easily defended against invasion by Northern troops. But Glassy Rock Mountain, rising behind Rock Hill, harbored renegades at a time when no civil or military law existed to protect the community. The steps of the house were pulled down, portholes were cut in doors, windows and doors were barricaded with sandbags, and slits were cut in the walls so the renegades could be fired on by unseen defenders.

In 1867 Memminger was fully pardoned by President Andrew Johnson, and all of his privileges of citizenship were restored. He returned to Charleston and to the legislature of South Carolina, where, as chairman of Ways and Means, he endeavored to recover the lost credit of the state. He resumed efforts as well on behalf of the

South Carolina public school systems for both races. In addition, Memminger had long been among those who advocated a railroad connecting the southern seaboard with the navigable waters of the western Carolinas. With the resumption of construction interrupted by the war, he accepted the presidency of the railroad company for the time necessary to complete the vital link between Spartanburg, S.C., and Asheville, N.C. Then he bowed out of public life.

Memminger was married for forty-three years to Mary Wilkinson, the daughter of Dr. Willis and Leonora Withers Wilkinson. Of their seventeen children, eight survived childhood: Robert Withers, Ellen, Lucy (Mrs. Charles Coatesworth Pinckney), Edward Read, Sarah Virginia (Mrs. Ralph Izard Middleton), Mary (Mrs. Robert Francis Louie Dincotte), Willis Wilkinson, and Allard. After Mary's death, Memminger married her sister Sarah Ann, who survived him.

Memminger died in Charleston at age eighty-five. In accordance with his request, he was buried in Flat Rock beside the grave of his wife Mary in the cemetery of St. John-in-the-Wilderness Episcopal Church, of which he had been a member for fifty years.

SEE: Louise Howe Bailey, *From "Rock Hill" to "Connemara"* (1980); Henry D. Capers, *The Life and Times of C. G. Memminger* (1895); Frank L. Fitzsimons, *From the Banks of the Oklawaha*, vol. 1 (1976); Edward Read Memminger, *An Historical Sketch of Flat Rock* (1922).

LOUISE HOWE BAILEY

Menatonon (*fl. 1580s*), king of the Chowanoc Indians, was old and infirm in his limbs when Governor Ralph Lane explored the Chowan River in the spring of 1586. Both the English and the Indians regarded him as the wisest and most influential ruler among the Algonquian-speaking natives from the Neuse River in present-day North Carolina to the Chesapeake Bay and Powhatan Confederacy. His age cannot be accurately determined, but it may be observed that his son, Skiko, had attained manhood. Menatonon was able to give the English information about places nearby as well as those at a great distance. His name may have meant "he listens carefully to someone (something) which he sees."

Unmistakably, Thomas Harriot had in mind Menatonon and the Chowanoc Confederacy when he said that the "greatest wiroans or chief lord" had eighteen towns in his government, whereas in some parts there were chief men who ruled only one. Moreover, the English already had explored the coastal region and found the towns to be small and scattered. They had but little corn which, together with vegetables, was necessary to sustain a large and stable population.

Harriot explained that the greatest ruler could put only seven or eight hundred fighting men in the field. His estimate was more conservative than that of Lane, who said that the town of Chowanoc itself could field seven hundred warriors. (Archaeological excavations in the 1980s suggest that the town of Chowanoc was around one thousand years old at that time.) Various scholars have estimated the combined population of the town and province to be between 1,500 and 2,500. Both Arthur Barlowe and Ralph Lane indicated that Menatonon's town of residence was on the upper Chowan River. Barlowe referred to one Pooneno as being ruler of Chowanoc on a river called Nomopana, but when Lane had a personal look he made no mention of him. Thus Pooneno may be regarded as one of many subchiefs.

The explorers found that as they moved inland, the country became as good as the coastal Indians had represented it to be. Harriot said that farther in the interior "we found the soil to be fatter, the trees greater and to grow thiner, the ground more firm and deeper mould, more and larger champions [potatoes?], finer grass . . . more inhabited with people, and of greater policy and larger dominions, with greater towns and houses."

Lane indicated that the Chowanoc Confederacy commenced near the mouth of the Chowan River; the map of John White and Theodor De Bry shows it extending to the north of the confluence of the Chowan and Meherrin rivers. The northern bounds were confirmed by John Smith and William Strachey of the Jamestown colony. The Virginia Indians told Smith that the "Chawwonocke" lived "one daies journey" from the Nansemond tribe on the Nansemond River, and both Smith and Strachey mentioned the "Chowanokes" or "Chawonocks" as one of the nations that bordered the Powhatan territories on the south.

Inasmuch as the English named only seven Indian towns on the Chowan River, it is likely that some of the eighteen mentioned by Harriot were situated on the stream's larger tributaries such as Bennetts Creek and the Wiccacon and Meherrin rivers. Numerous Indian town sites of the Late Woodland period have been located on these streams.

Lane referred to the Chowanocs as being friendly, but he took no chances. That he and his men might not fall victim to some sort of treachery, he held Menatonon "prisoner with me" during the two days they spent at the chief's town. He then took the king's son, Skiko, to Roanoke as a hostage. Lane found Menatonon to be "a very grave and wise man, and of a very singular good discourse in matters concerning the state, not only of his own country, and the disposition of his own men, but also of his neighbors round about him, as well far as near, and of the commodities that each country yielded." When Menatonon and the other chief men of the Moratocs learned that the English were interested in precious metals and pearls, they told them the kind of tales they wished to hear. A great king and his men harvested huge quantities of pearls from waters of the Northeast, and this king had visited Menatonon two years earlier.

More alluring still was the fable of Chaunis Temoatan, which Menatonon related to Lane. It was a place "notorious to all the country." A mine supplied this country with "a marvelous and most strange mineral." The Indians called the mineral *wassador* (probably copper), and it was a valuable trade item among them. But the English had learned that the Indians called all metals by this name, and that they had no particular names for gold or silver; moreover, this Chaunis Temoatan metal was soft and pale red like gold. An aborted journey up the Roanoke River left the strange metal still a mystery. It would fascinate the English for more than a century.

SEE: David B. Quinn, *Roanoke Voyages*, 2 vols. (1955), and *Set Fair for Roanoke: Voyages and Colonies, 1584–1606* (1985); Douglas L. Rights, *The American Indian in North Carolina* (1947).

F. ROY JOHNSON

Mendelsohn, Charles Jastrow (*8 Dec. 1880–27 Sept. 1939*), cryptographer, was born in Wilmington, the son of Rabbi Samuel and Esther Jastrow Mendelsohn. He was graduated from the Episcopal Academy, Philadelphia, Pa., in 1896 and received an A.B. degree in 1900 and a Ph.D. degree in 1904 from the University of Pennsylvania, where he was a Harrison Scholar and a member of Phi Beta Kappa. Joining the faculty of the College of the City of New York as a tutor in Greek in 1905, he became an instructor in 1907. On leave from his teaching position during World War I, he served in the censorship division (foreign language, postal, and newspaper censorship) of the Post Office Department in 1917. In 1918–19 he was a captain in the Military Intelligence Division of the War Department General Staff. Here he worked on the solution of codes used by the German Foreign Office.

Returning to City College in 1920, he never abandoned his interest in cryptography. He prepared a number of papers on code-word structure, the theory and construction of cable codes, and allied subjects, particularly the mathematics of code-word structure. His continued research on codes led to the preparation of studies in diplomatic codes for the U.S. government.

Mendelsohn also became interested in the history of cryptography and began collecting books on the subject. At the time of his death, he owned what has been described as "probably the most important cryptographic library in America, if not in the world." This collection was bequeathed to the University of Pennsylvania. Shortly before his death he completed what is considered to have been his most important work, "The Earliest Solution of a Multiple Alphabet Cipher Written with a Key," published in 1939 in the *Signal Corps Bulletin*. He was also the author of *Studies in the Word-Play in Plautus . . .: I. The Name-Play and II. The Use of Single Words in a Double Meaning* (1907), the first portion being his doctoral dissertation, and the coauthor of *The Zimmerman Telegram of January 16, 1917, and Its Cryptographic Background*. He contributed to many scholarly journals including the *Proceedings of the American Philosophical Society* and *Scripta Mathematica*, as well as to government publications.

In the fall of 1939, in connection with the war in Europe, Mendelsohn was recalled to active duty, but in the midst of preparations to leave New York he became ill and died of meningitis. Burial followed in the Hebrew Cemetery at Oakdale Cemetery, Wilmington. Never married, he was survived by his mother.

SEE: *New York Times*, 28 Sept. 1939 (portrait); *Signal Corps Bulletin*, no. 106 (October–December 1939); Wilmington *Morning Star*, 28 Sept. 1939.

WILLIAM S. POWELL

Mendelsohn, Samuel (*31 Mar. 1850–30 Sept. 1922*), rabbi and scholar, was born in Russia, the son of S. Feiwel and Jetta M. Mendelsohn. He studied in Vilna, Russia, and Berlin before coming to the United States in 1868. In 1870 Mendelsohn began two years of study at America's first Jewish theological seminary, Maimonides College of Philadelphia. In 1873 he became the rabbi of Congregation Beth El of Norfolk, Va., and in 1876 he was appointed rabbi to North Carolina's first permanent Jewish congregation, Temple of Israel in Wilmington. The only previous attempt to start a synagogue in the state was in Wilmington in 1867, but the group had folded within five years.

In Philadelphia Mendelsohn studied with the renowned American Jewish scholars, the Reverend Isaac Leeser and the Reverend Sabato Morais, although his favorite was Dr. Marcus Jastrow. After two years Mendelsohn and fellow student, David Levy, began publishing a weekly Jewish religious, political, and community journal, *The Jewish Index*, in an attempt to fill the void

created by the discontinuance in 1869 of the noted Philadelphia-based Jewish periodical, *The Occident*. This ambitious project lasted only a few months, with Mendelsohn leaving for Norfolk and his first pulpit. Three years later, in February 1876, he was appointed rabbi of the Wilmington congregation, and on 12 May he officiated at the dedication of North Carolina's first synagogue. In 1879 Mendelsohn married Esther Jastrow, the niece of his former teacher, and in 1880 their only child, Charles, was born.

Rabbi Mendelsohn's career in Wilmington was highlighted by examples of scholarship, community participation, and involvement in state and national fraternal organizations. His book, *Criminal Jurisprudence of the Ancient Hebrews* (1891), compiled material from Talmudic and other rabbinical writings and compared the ancient Hebrew system of laws and justice to that of ancient Rome and to England prior to 1800. The work described Israel's Talmudic laws as mild, fair, and highly humanitarian in contrast to the other systems discussed. Mendelsohn stressed the rarity of capital punishment and the early abolition of the "eye for an eye" ethic. In 1915 he contributed an article, "The Arterial Function and the Circulation in Ancient Rabinnical Literature," to the *Charlotte Medical Journal*, in which he pointed out that early Jews were aware of the function of the arteries fourteen centuries before William Harvey's "discovery." Mendelsohn also was responsible for the translation of the Book of Haggai for the Jewish Publications Society in America. He compiled the index of biblical citations for the *Jastrow Talmudic Dictionary* and wrote numerous articles for the *Jewish Encyclopedia* (1901–6), *Revue des Etudes Juives*, published in Paris, and the American Jewish secular press.

Mendelsohn held office in such organizations as the Fraternal Mystic Circle, the Masonic group Royal Arcanum, the Odd Fellows, and the Independent B'nai B'rith. He was grand ruler of Jurisdiction No. 9 and supreme representative-at-large of the Fraternal Mystic Circle; secretary for thirty-five years of the Cornelius Harnett Lodge of the Royal Arcanum as well as grand chaplain for North Carolina, statewide recruiter, and lodge regent; president of the North State Lodge of B'nai B'rith; and supreme president of the U.S. Benevolent Fraternity. Mendelsohn was active in the community as the director of the Associated Charities of Wilmington, and he often preached in local Christian churches, including those composed of black members. In 1883 he received an honorary doctor of laws degree from The University of North Carolina. He served as the rabbi of the Temple of Israel until his death.

SEE: James Sprunt, *Chronicles of the Cape Fear River* (1916); *Who Was Who in America*, vol. 1 (1943); Wilmington *Morning Star*, 1 Oct. 1922.

DAVID J. GOLDBERG

Mendenhall, Nereus (*14 Aug. 1819–29 Nov. 1893*), educator, physician, civil engineer, and legislator, was born at Jamestown, the son of Richard and Mary Pegg Mendenhall. Jamestown was named for his grandfather, James Mendenhall, who had come to North Carolina from Chester County, Pa. James was the son of John Mendenhall, one of three Mendenhall brothers who immigrated to Pennsylvania from the Manor of Mildenhall in Wiltshire, England. Nereus's mother was the daughter of Valentine and Mary Cook Pegg. Both sides of his family were of Quaker stock.

Young Mendenhall was a delicate and sensitive child

who early manifested a love of reading and study. He was educated in the village schools of Jamestown, one of which was conducted by his father and was also open to slave children. To help meet expenses for his college education, he worked in a printing office in Greensboro while continuing his studies. He entered Haverford College in Pennsylvania as a freshman in 1837 and finished the four-year requirements with honors in two years. Mendenhall returned to North Carolina in 1839 to become the principal teacher of New Garden Boarding School. A distinguished Latin and Greek scholar, he was also widely read in philosophy. As busy as he was with his many duties at the boarding school, he still found time to "read" medicine and prepare for entrance into Jefferson Medical College, Philadelphia, from which he was graduated in 1845. Although he established a successful medical practice in his home community, Jamestown, his sensitive nature made him overanxious for his patients and his health suffered to such a degree that he abandoned medicine. Believing that time spent outdoors would be beneficial, he accepted a position as civil engineer with the North Carolina Central Railroad. At intervals throughout his life, he alternated this work with service in various capacities at the New Garden Boarding School. He finally left the school for good in 1867, having served for a total of twelve years.

In 1851 Mendenhall married Oriana Wilson, a native of Mississippi though of Nantucket, Mass., Quaker stock. They had met while he was teaching at New Garden and she was a student. Following the outbreak of the Civil War, Nereus came under serious suspicion for his Quaker attitudes on slavery and for his hostility to war itself. On one occasion, he narrowly avoided being caught in possession of incendiary literature against slavery.

Mendenhall's natural inclination was to teach, and he said many times that when he was doing other things—enjoyable perhaps in themselves—he was wasting his time. The fundamental thing was to instill in young people's minds a love of truth, and he challenged students to think for themselves. He firmly believed that true education was the great lever to lift men to higher and nobler views of life. From time to time he was involved with other Quaker schools. At Haverford College he was a member of the faculty and superintendent for two years; he also taught for two years at Penn Charter School in Philadelphia. Mendenhall was deeply committed to coeducational education, which New Garden Boarding School adopted as a matter of principle at its founding in 1838. This principle found application in the education of his own five daughters. One was a graduate of Wellesley College and taught mathematics at the Woman's College at Greensboro for many years. Another, Mary, was a graduate of the Howland's School on Lake Cayuga, N.Y., and wrote extensively in the area of public affairs; she married L. L. Hobbs, the first president of Guilford College after its transition from New Garden Boarding School in 1888. Also concerned about public education in North Carolina, Mendenhall served as chairman of the Board of Examiners of Public School Teachers for more than forty years.

Twice he was elected to represent Guilford County in the state legislature. Appointed to the board of directors for the State Hospital for the Insane at Morganton, he was instrumental in having it called a hospital rather than an asylum and assisted with planning and construction. An active and highly concerned Quaker, Mendenhall participated in numerous Quaker missions, including one to Jefferson Davis, president of the Confederacy, to speak on behalf of the cruel treatment of conscientious objectors. He served the North Carolina Yearly Meeting as assistant clerk from 1845 to 1849 and as clerk from 1860 until 1872. He was also a member of the Meeting for Sufferings.

SEE: Samuel A. Ashe, ed., *Biographical History of North Carolina*, vol. 4 (1906); Deep River Monthly Meeting of Friends, "Memorial of Nereus Mendenhall," 2 Feb. 1894 (typescript, Quaker Collection, Guilford College Library, Greensboro); Mary Mendenhall Hobbs, "Dr. Nereus Mendenhall, 1819–1893," *Greensboro Daily News*, 10 Jan. 1926; "Nereus Mendenhall," *Quaker Biographies*, ser. 2, vol. 5 (n.d. [portrait]); Mendenhall-Hobbs Papers (Quaker Collection, Guilford College Library, Greensboro).

GRIMSLEY T. HOBBS
TREVA W. MATHIS

Mercer, George (23 June 1733–Apr. 1784), Virginia officer and lieutenant governor of North Carolina, was born at Marlborough, the family home near Mount Vernon in Virginia, the son of John, a native of Dublin, and Catherine Mason Mercer. He was educated at the College of William and Mary and studied law. Mercer was named aide-de-camp to George Washington in 1755, served as an officer in the French and Indian War, and was elected to the House of Burgesses in 1761 at the same time as Washington. In 1763 he was in England as an agent of the Ohio Company, in which Governor Arthur Dobbs of North Carolina also was interested. Mercer returned to Virginia intending to distribute stamped paper for Maryland, Virginia, and North Carolina under the Stamp Act but was prevailed upon to resign. He was again in England in 1767, when he married Mary Neville of Lincoln.

On 14 Sept. 1768 a commission was issued naming him lieutenant governor of North Carolina. In July 1769 Henry Eustace McCulloh, then in London, wrote to John Harvey that "Col. Mercer of Virginia has been for sometime appointed your Lieut Govr & I do believe has thoughts of succeeding: when Mr Tryon leaves America." This did not materialize, however, but Mercer was named a member of the North Carolina Council in 1771 in the commission of Governor Josiah Martin, who was Tryon's successor. There is no clear evidence that Mercer ever was in the colony, although the *Virginia Gazette* of 23 Mar. 1769 reported that "the Honorable George Mercer, Esq; Lieutenant Governor of North-Carolina is arrived at Newbern at that province." Mercer, as a matter of fact, was in London for long periods representing the Ohio Company. In November 1771 Martin referred to a report that Mercer was about to become governor of a new colony on the Ohio, but again this never occurred.

A Loyalist in sympathy, Mercer went to England sometime before the American Revolution. There a series of misfortunes and disappointments culminated in his physical impairment and insanity. He was in France for his health in 1777, when he was informed that his commission as lieutenant governor of North Carolina was still in effect. In 1783 his wife asked the Lords Commissioners of the Treasury to continue his allowance and sought reimbursement for losses he had sustained as stamp distributor. He died in England.

SEE: John C. Fitzpatrick, ed., *The Writings of George Washington*, vol. 1 (1931); *Gentlemen's Magazine*, August 1767, September 1768; Lawrence Henry Gipson, *The Triumphant Empire: The Rumbling of the Coming Storm, 1766–1770* (1965) and *The Triumphant Empire: Thunder-Clouds Gather in the West, 1763–1766* (1961); Donald Jackson, ed., *The Diaries of George Washington*, vol. 1 (1976 [portrait]); Alfred Procter James, *George Mercer of the Ohio Company* (1963); Helen H. Miller, *George Mason: Gentleman Revolutionary* (1975); Richard L. Morton, *Colonial Virginia*, vol. 2 (1960); Lois Mulkearn, ed., *George Mercer Papers Relating to the Ohio Company of Virginia* (1954); William S. Powell, ed., *The Correspondence of William Tryon*, vol. 2 (1980); Robert A. Rutland, ed., *The Papers of George Mason*, vol. 1 (1970); William L. Saunders, ed., *Colonial Records of North Carolina*, vols. 8–9 (1890); *Virginia Gazette*, 24 Nov. 1768, 23 Mar. 1769, 7 Feb. 1771, 23 Sept. 1772.

WILLIAM S. POWELL

Mercer, Jesse (*16 Dec. 1769–6 Sept. 1841*), Baptist minister and patron of missions and education, was born in Halifax County, the oldest of eight children of Silas Mercer, an able pioneer preacher in Georgia. His brother Daniel became a distinguished Latin and Greek scholar. Mercer's opportunities of education were limited, though he received instruction from John Springer, a Presbyterian minister and graduate of Princeton, for two years and studied for a year in Salem Academy, a school maintained by his father. On 31 Jan. 1788 Mercer married Sabrina Chivers. Two daughters died in childhood, but the marriage was a happy one, lasting thirty-eight years until Sabrina's death in 1826.

Mercer was ordained to the ministry by his father and Sanders Walker on 7 Nov. 1789. His first pastorate was at Hutton's Fork (now Sardis). Following the death of his father in 1796, he became principal of Salem Academy and added to his ministry three of his father's churches, Phillips' Mill, Wheatley's Mill (later Bethesda), and Powelton, which he served for thirty-nine, thirty-two, and twenty-eight years respectively. Powelton became the center for the early activities of Georgia Baptists. A conference there in 1801 laid the foundation for missionary undertakings among the Creek Indians, and conferences in 1802 and 1803 established the general committee of Georgia Baptists for itinerant preaching and missionary work. In 1822 the Georgia Baptist Convention was organized in the Powelton Church, where it met seven times during the first eleven years of its existence. Mercer was president of the convention from its founding until his death.

As leader of the Georgia Baptists, Mercer played the principal role in the founding of Mercer University and in the purchase of the *Christian Index*, which he published for seven years. He also published *Cluster of Spiritual Songs*; revised several times, this work has been regarded as "a worthy contribution to American hymnology." Mercer was the author of *A History of the Georgia Baptist Association [Convention]* (1838).

In 1827 he moved to Washington, Ga., where he founded the First Baptist Church, which he served for the rest of his life. In December 1827 he married Mrs. Nancy Simons, of Wilkes County, the widow of Captain Abraham Simons, who had left her a large estate. Mercer outlived his wife by four months and carried out their mutual decision to leave everything to religious causes, with Mercer University as the principal beneficiary. He died in Butts County, Ga., and was buried at Penfield, the first location of Mercer University.

SEE: Jesse H. Campbell, *Georgia Baptists: Historical and Biographical* (1847); *Encyclopedia of Southern Baptists*, vol. 2 (1958); C. D. Mallary, *Memoirs of Elder Jesse Mercer* (1844).

LOULIE LATIMER OWENS

Mercer, William Parker (*16 Mar. 1855–28 May 1919*), physician and state senator, was born on his father's plantation in the Town Creek section of Edgecombe County. He was the only son of John Routh and Susan M. Vick Mercer, who were also the parents of seven daughters. The elder Mercer farmed and practiced medicine in the area.

Like his father, William chose medicine as a career. He left the family farm for Trinity College in 1873 and was graduated in 1877 with an A.B. degree. He attended medical school at the University of Virginia in 1878 and finished his medical education at Bellevue Hospital in New York. Returning home in 1879, Mercer began to practice medicine with his father. Late in 1880 he married Mary Speed Jones, of Warren County, who later achieved fame as an author and composer. The couple had one son and four daughters.

Although active in local Democratic politics, Mercer was surprised when he was nominated for the North Carolina Senate by his fellow citizens without his knowledge or consent. He reluctantly accepted the nomination and won the election in a close race. Mercer went on to win a second term in the senate, where he served on the education and agriculture committees.

A devout Methodist, he was a lifelong member and benefactor of the Temperance Hall Church near his home (his grandfather, John Mercer, had donated the land and the building for the church). His service to Methodism included involvement with Trinity College as an active supporter and trustee.

Mercer also participated in local affairs in Edgecombe County. The first telephone line in the county ran from Tarboro to his home—an improvement that increased the speed with which he could deliver medical care to the countryside. Near the end of his life, he was chairman of the Edgecombe County Exemptions Board for the draft in World War I. A decline in his health forced his retirement and resulted in his death at age sixty-four. Mercer was buried in a family cemetery in Edgecombe County within sight of his home.

SEE: Raleigh *News and Observer*, 30 May 1919; R. H. Routh, *The Routh Family in America* (1976); W. F. Tomlinson, *Biography of the State Officers and Members of the General Assembly* (1893); J. K. Turner and J. S. Bridgers, *History of Edgecombe County, North Carolina* (1920).

JOHN MERCER THORP, JR.

Merchant (or Marchant), Christopher (*d. ca. November 1698*), Council member, clerk of Council, customs collector, clerk of precinct court, and deputy escheator, was in the North Carolina colony by November 1679. In November 1681 he was clerk of the Council, and in March 1694/95 he was a Council member. Nothing more is known of his service in those capacities, which no doubt was longer than surviving records show. In the 1690s he was customs collector for the Currituck port, a position that he held from 1696 or earlier until his death. In April 1694, and probably as early as 1690, he was clerk of court for Currituck Precinct. He held that office through July 1697. In 1695 and presumably other years he was deputy escheator for Currituck.

Merchant's plantation, consisting of 908 acres, lay in northern Currituck, an area then claimed by Virginia as well as North Carolina. In 1696, when he was customs collector for Currituck under commission from London officials, the Virginia Council ordered his arrest on a charge that he was collecting customs in Virginia without presenting authorization to officials of that colony.

The incident seems to have been settled without a trial. When the boundary between the colonies was surveyed in 1728, the Merchant plantation, then owned by Christopher's grandson, was found to lie in North Carolina.

Merchant died between 6 Nov. 1698, when he made his will, and 1 Mar. 1698/99, when the will was probated. He left bequests to his wife, Abiah; his son, Willoughby; his daughter, Abiah; and his daughter's husband, Thomas Tooley.

Although Merchant was survived by only two children, he had at least thirteen grandchildren. Abiah and Thomas Tooley had five daughters: Jane, Elizabeth, Mary, and two whose names are unknown, although records show that they became the wives of Edward Old and William Leary. Willoughby and his wife, Elizabeth, had at least eight children. Willoughby died about February 1726/27, survived by his wife; by sons Christopher, Caleb, Keader, Willoughby, Haberaniah, and Gideon; and by daughters Jane and Elizabeth. The Christopher Merchant who was appointed justice of Currituck Precinct Court in 1728 no doubt was Willoughby's son.

SEE: William K. Boyd, ed., *William Byrd's Histories of the Dividing Line between Virginia and North Carolina* (1929); British Records, Council Minutes, Wills, Inventories, Council Order for the Arrest of William Wilkinson and Wife, 7 Mar. 1694, in Colonial Court Records, and Wills of Dorothy Harvey, Christopher and Willoughby Merchant, Thomas Tooley, and Thomas Vandermullen (North Carolina State Archives, Raleigh); J. R. B. Hathaway, ed., *North Carolina Historical and Genealogical Register*, vol. 1 (1900); Mattie Erma E. Parker, ed., *North Carolina Higher-Court Records, 1670–1696* and *1697–1701* (1968–71); William L. Saunders, ed., *Colonial Records of North Carolina*, vol. 2 (1886).

MATTIE ERMA E. PARKER

Meredith, Hugh (ca. 1697–ca. 1749), printer and pioneer visitor to the Lower Cape Fear, was of Welsh descent, born in the country near Philadelphia and "bred a farmer." He was the son of Simon Meredith. When he was thirty, Hugh went to Philadelphia and entered an apprenticeship to learn the trade of printing. He and Benjamin Franklin were employed in the shop of printer Samuel Keimer. In the autumn of 1727 Franklin organized the Junto, "a debating society or club for mutual improvement," of which Meredith was a member. About 1728 Meredith and Franklin formed a partnership, with Simon Meredith providing half of the necessary money. In 1729 the two men bought Keimer's newspaper, *Universal Instructor in All Arts and Sciences: Pennsylvania Gazette*, and entered into a printing partnership. The following year Franklin undertook to buy Meredith's interest in the venture. He commented that his partner was seldom sober. By May 1732 Franklin had completed the financial transactions necessary to acquire Meredith's share in his own name.

About the time the partnership was dissolved, Meredith noted that many Welsh people had left Pennsylvania to settle in North Carolina, where they could easily acquire land. Others went from Delaware. He expressed an inclination to join them "and follow my old employment." Whether he meant farming or printing he did not say, but probably the former since there was no printer in North Carolina until 1749. Franklin noted that Meredith left Philadelphia soon after they agreed to end the partnership—undoubtedly in the summer of 1730. Preparing to leave, and as a part of the settlement of ex-

penses, Meredith asked Franklin for a new saddle, suggesting that he rode horseback.

The next year, after reaching the Lower Cape Fear region of North Carolina where other Welsh had settled, Meredith wrote Franklin two very long letters informing him of conditions in the Welsh Tract where he was living. Franklin printed them in the *Pennsylvania Gazette* of 29 Apr. and 6 May 1731; they contain information on the countryside, weather, wildlife, water transportation, Indians, farming, and settlers, including Welshmen David Evans and Thomas James. Although the record seems to be silent as to Hugh Meredith's subsequent life, he most likely returned to Pennsylvania as it has been documented that Franklin lent him a modest sum of money in 1739.

SEE: Joseph E. Illick, *Colonial Pennsylvania* (1976); Charles P. Keith, *Chronicles of Pennsylvania*, vol. 2 (1917); Leonard W. Labaree, ed., *The Papers of Benjamin Franklin*, vol. 1 (1959); *Pennsylvania Magazine of History and Biography* 54 (July 1930), 61 (October 1937); Earl G. Swem, ed., *An Account of the Cape Fear Country, 1731, by Hugh Meredith* (1922).

WILLIAM S. POWELL

Meredith, Solomon (29 May 1810–21 Oct. 1875), Civil War general, sheriff, legislator, U.S. marshal, surveyor general, and livestock breeder, was born in Guilford County. The youngest of twelve children and a six-foot, six-inch giant in his time, he left North Carolina in 1829 at age nineteen and walked to Wayne County, Ind. In Indiana his occupations expanded quickly in number. Starting out as a woodchopper, he later became a store clerk and then in 1834 and 1836 was elected sheriff of Wayne County. In 1838 he began a mercantile business in Milton, Ind., continuing it in Cambridge City from 1839 to 1843.

During the years 1846–48 and 1854–56 he served in the state legislature. As a delegate to the Whig National Convention in 1840, he was an ardent supporter of William Henry Harrison for the presidency. He was appointed U.S. marshal for the Indiana District in 1849 by President Zachary Taylor and held this position until 1853, when he was removed by President Franklin Pierce, a Democrat. As a Whig, Meredith had worked hard for the election of General Winfield Scott to the presidency in 1852. One of the first to join the new Republican party, he was a delegate to the convention in 1856.

Meredith was active in improving the educational system in Indiana, as well as in making public improvements. He was director and financial agent for the Indiana Central Railroad, going to England to hire many workers. Later he was president of the Cincinnati and Chicago Railroad Company. From 1859 to 1861 he was clerk of the courts in Wayne County.

On 29 July 1861 Meredith became colonel of the Nineteenth Indiana Infantry; he first saw action at Gainesville, Va., where he was wounded. He commanded his regiment at Antietam and was promoted to brigadier general of volunteers on 6 Oct. 1862. He commanded the "Iron Brigade," which consisted of one Michigan, two Indiana, and three Wisconsin regiments, at Fredericksburg, Chancellorsville, and Gettysburg, where he was severely wounded. Early in 1864 he was put in command of the military post at Cairo, Ill., and later that year he became commander of the District of Western Kentucky at Paducah, serving in the latter position until the end of the war. On 14 Aug. 1865 he was brevetted major general of volunteers.

After the war Meredith became U.S. assessor of internal revenue for his district (1866–67) and surveyor general of the Montana Territory (1867–69). He then retired to his farm, Oakland Place, near Cambridge City, Ind., where he became active in the breeding of improved livestock, especially shorthorn cattle and Southdown sheep. He imported animals from England and was a prominent exhibitor at the leading agricultural fairs.

Meredith is mentioned in the Quaker records of North Carolina. Although born into that sect, he became associated with the Methodist Episcopal church, where his children were baptized. In addition to having been a member of the Society of Friends, he held fraternal membership in the Masonic order and the Independent Order of Odd Fellows.

In 1836 he married Anna Hannah, the daughter of Samuel C. Hannah, who was born in Pennsylvania in 1812 and moved to Wayne County. They had four children. Samuel Hannah, the oldest, died in 1864 as a result of injuries received in the Civil War. David Macy, a captain in the war who was brevetted for courage at Chickamauga, died in Mobile, Ala., on 4 Apr. 1867. Henry Clay (17 July 1843–5 July 1882) established the *Cambridge City Tribune* before becoming a partner with his father in raising pedigreed livestock; he married Virginia Claypool, the daughter of Austin B. and Hannah A. Petty Claypool, and they had no children. Mary, the only daughter and the fourth child, died in infancy.

Meredith was buried in Riverside Cemetery, Cambridge City.

SEE: *Appleton's Cyclopedia of American Biography*, vol. 4 (1900); *Biographical Directory of the Indiana General Assembly* (1980); *Biographical and Genealogical History of Wayne, Fayette, Union, and Franklin Counties, Indiana*, vol. 1 (1899); *Chicago Tribune*, 22 Oct. 1875; Jacob Piatt Dunn, *Indiana and Indianans*, vol. 2 (1919 [portrait]); Henry Clay Fox, *Memoirs of Wayne County and the City of Richmond, Indiana* (1912); Francis B. Heitman, *Historical Register and Dictionary of the United States Army*, vol. 1 (1903); William W. Hinshaw, *Encyclopedia of American Quaker Genealogy*, vol. 1 (1936); *History of Wayne County*, vol. 2 (1884); *Indianapolis Journal*, 22 Oct. 1875; *Nat. Cyc. Am. Biog.*, vol. 5 (1894 [portrait]); *New York Times*, 22 Oct. 1875; Richmond (Ind.) *Evening Item*, 10 Mar. 1882; *Richmond Palladium*, 27 Oct. 1875, 21 Dec. 1953; *Richmond Palladium and Sun Telegram*, 17 May 1911; *Richmond Telegram*, 22, 29 Oct. 1875; *Richmond Weekly Telegram*, 2, 9 Dec. 1865; Ezra Warner, *Generals in Blue* (1964 [portrait]).

DAVID K. BOWDEN

Meredith, Thomas (7 July 1795–13 Nov. 1850), minister and editor, was born in Warwick Township, Bucks County, Pa., the son of John, a prosperous farmer, and Charlotte Hough Meredith. John Meredith's great-grandfather, Simon Meredith, emigrated from Montgomeryshire, Wales, to Chester County, Pa. in 1708. Charlotte Meredith's great-grandfather, Richard Hough, a friend of William Penn, emigrated from Cheshire, England, in 1683.

Young Thomas attended Doylestown Academy, a famous classical school in its day, where his master, the Reverend Uriah Dubois, called him "a vigorous and successful student." He was graduated from the University of Pennsylvania on 4 Jan. 1816, valedictorian of a class of nine. He had gone to the university intending to be a lawyer, but before graduation he decided to enter the

Christian ministry, a decision due largely to the influence of his mother, a devout Quaker. An earnest study of the New Testament led him to the Baptist faith, and in 1817, after a year of theological training, he went to eastern North Carolina as a missionary. There he was befriended by Martin Ross, a tower of strength in the early Baptist work in North Carolina. Driving together in a buggy, Ross, fifty-five years old, and Meredith, twenty-two, made many evangelistic trips in the eastern part of the state. A deep friendship developed between the two, a relationship that several have compared to that of Paul and Timothy, his "own son in the faith."

Between 1819 and 1837 Meredith was pastor successively of churches in New Bern, Savannah, Ga., Edenton, and, again, New Bern. During these years he became an important denominational leader in the state. One of the fourteen founders of the North Carolina Baptist State Convention organized in 1830, he drew up its constitution and wrote—at the convention's request—a letter to North Carolina Baptists explaining the necessity of the new enterprise and its vast possibilities. George W. Paschal, in his *History of North Carolina Baptists*, compares this document with the Declaration of Independence. It has the same clear statements and interpretation of pertinent facts, the same lucid reasoning, the same enthusiasm for the new undertaking, the same calm courage, and the same vision of future success. Meredith served at different times as secretary, vice-president, and president of the convention. On special occasions in the convention and in churches, he was much in demand as a preacher. Of his sermons William Carey Crane, an eminent theologian of his time, said that they "did not sway men so much by touching appeals as by presenting the truth to them with irresistible power." His sermons were the product of a great intellect as well as a devout heart.

He was keenly interested in the education of young people. So far as the records show, Paschal wrote, when Meredith came to the state in 1817, he was the only minister with a classical education. One of the three purposes of the convention, stated in the constitution that Meredith drew up, was "the education of young men called of God to the ministry." Wake Forest Institute (now Wake Forest University), which opened in 1834, received his staunch support. In its first year he was offered the chair of mathematics and moral philosophy; in 1838 he was elected president of the board of trustees. In his concern for the education of young women, Meredith was far ahead of his time. In 1838, as chairman of a committee, he offered a resolution urging the convention to establish "a female seminary of high order . . . modeled and conducted on strictly religious principles but . . . as far as possible free from sectarian influence." The convention adopted the resolution but took no steps towards carrying it out. Sixty-one years later, in September 1899, the Baptist Female University opened its doors; in 1909 it was renamed Meredith College in honor of the proposer of that 1838 resolution.

Since the organization of the convention, there had been discussion of the need for a periodical to serve as a link between the convention and the churches and to unify Baptists across the state. Thomas Meredith began to meet that need when, in January 1833, he issued the first number of the *Baptist Interpreter*. This monthly paper was so well received that he was encouraged to publish a weekly. The *Biblical Recorder*, replacing the *Interpreter*, made its first appearance in January 1835; in 1838 Meredith gave up his pastorate in New Bern and moved to Raleigh in order to devote his full time to the *Recorder*. The weekly paper, still published in Raleigh, continues to be the journal of the North Carolina Baptist State Convention.

Meredith's ill health and the *Recorder*'s serious financial difficulties were obstacles that made the greatness of his work all the more remarkable. J. D. Hufham, one of the younger leaders of the convention, wrote of him: "To it [the *Biblical Recorder*] he devoted himself with perfect singleness of heart. To the work he brought a vigorous, well-trained intellect, courage both moral and physical to an extraordinary degree; great decision of character, which took small account of obstacles or opposition; and patience which held him to his undertakings where others would have given up." Elsewhere Hufham commented on the chief characteristics of his style—simplicity and strength. "One might read through whole columns of his editorials without finding a single obscure sentence." Both in his editorials and in his answers to questions from correspondents, his keen mind and sound judgment are evident. There are also occasional touches of the humor that, according to a close friend, made him a delightful companion.

In the early, formative years of the convention, the years of Meredith's editorship, his constructive leadership was of great value. He dealt well with sharply divisive issues that arose in the convention and in the churches. Among the most controversial were slavery (which he regarded as an evil of the greatest magnitude), the antimissionary movement, temperance, the break with the Triennial Convention located in Philadelphia, and the formation of the Southern Baptist Convention.

Meredith was instrumental in preventing a disastrous cleavage in the Baptist denomination in North Carolina after Alexander Campbell, founder of the Disciples of Christ, made a trip through the state. Campbell's denomination differed with Baptists on the question of immersion, holding that it was essential to salvation, not a symbol of salvation. Meredith's series of articles in the *Recorder* on Campbellism was the most powerful influence in restoring unity. His ability to deal with controversy drew frequent comment. William Carey Crane said that in controversy he "wielded a Damascus blade." He wrote with vigor and uncompromising conviction, yet with fairness to his opponent. He showed the "tact and ingenuity" for which another contemporary praised him. Campbell, his most formidable opponent, wrote in his own paper, the *Millenial Harbinger*, that Meredith "wrote like a gentleman" and commended his "courtesy and good manners."

In later generations he has been acclaimed the greatest single influence in Baptist history in North Carolina. Thomas Skinner, himself influential in Baptist affairs, considered him "undoubtedly the ablest man who has yet appeared among us." J. W. Moore, author of the *History of North Carolina*, declared: "In the history of North Carolina Baptists Meredith surpasses all others in importance." J. W. Bailey, himself editor and the son of an editor of the *Biblical Recorder*, wrote of Meredith's influence on North Carolina Baptists: "In his twenty years as editor he brought them into unity of faith and work; he set their standards, cast their mold of thinking, and fixed the purpose of their lives and of the lives of hundreds of thousands who came after them."

In 1819 Meredith married Georgia Sears, and the couple had eleven children: Laura, Claudia, Marcus, Bettie, Cordelia and Cornelia (twins), John, Luther, and three who died in infancy. His wife and six of his children survived him. The funeral service was held on 18 Nov. 1850 in the Baptist Church of Raleigh, and he was buried in the Raleigh City Cemetery. Meredith College has two portraits of Meredith; one, copied by his granddaughter, Ada Tolson Ralls, from a portrait by Anne Peale, hangs in the boardroom of the presidential suite in the Livingston Johnson Administration Building. The other, together with a portrait of his wife, is part of the Meredith Historical Collection in the Julia Hamlet Harris Room of the Carlyle Campbell Library.

SEE: *Baptist Interpreter*, January 1833–December 1834; *Biblical Recorder*, 1835–51, 2 Jan. 1935; J. D. Hufham, "Four Able Baptists," *Baptist Historical Papers* (1898); M. L. Johnson, *History of Meredith College* (1972); North Carolina Baptist State Convention, *Minutes* (1830–51); W. B. Sprague, *Annals of the American Pulpit* (1860); Trustees of Meredith College, *Minutes* (1909).

MARY LYNCH JOHNSON

Merrick, John (7 Sept. 1859–6 Aug. 1919), black businessman, community leader, and founder of the North Carolina Mutual Life Insurance Company, was born in Sampson County, the son of a slave mother; his father is unknown. At age twelve he moved with his mother to Chapel Hill, where she worked as a domestic while he labored in a local brickyard and learned to read and write in one of the Reconstruction schools. After six years in Chapel Hill, his mother married and left the South. Merrick remained in North Carolina and became a brick mason in Raleigh, where he worked on the construction of Shaw University.

The uncertainty of his trade forced him into a Raleigh barbershop as a bootblack, but he quickly advanced to barbering and acquired a partnership in the business when it moved from Raleigh to Durham in 1880. By 1892 Merrick had assumed full ownership of the business and expanded it to include five barbershops in Durham, three for whites and two for blacks. In the meantime, with the encouragement of the Duke family and other white business leaders, he had begun a real estate business devoted largely to constructing housing for the waves of black migrants seeking employment in Durham's burgeoning tobacco industry. More significantly for his future, Merrick had become an organizer for a fraternal insurance society, the Royal Knights of King David.

With that experience, Merrick in 1898 took the lead in launching the North Carolina Mutual and Provident Association (renamed the North Carolina Mutual Life Insurance Company in 1919), which became the largest black business in the United States. With its attendant enterprises, the firm earned Durham a reputation as the "Capital of the Black Middle Class." Merrick served as president of the North Carolina Mutual from its founding until his death. The success of the company and its offspring, most notably the Mechanics and Farmers Bank (1908), brought him national fame as a black representative of the New South and as vindication for the philosophy of Booker T. Washington. He eschewed direct politics and instead called for self-help and racial solidarity, all in the optimistic context of a developing southern economy and skillfully built patron-client relationships with the white community. Benjamin Newton Duke and John Sprunt Hill, two of Durham's leading white industrialists, summarized the popular meaning of Merrick's career as a "connecting link" between the old and the new life of the South and the Negro, "between the old life of discontent, idleness and poverty and the new life of satisfaction, industry and success," a career that could "point the way out of the warfares between labor and capital, [and] racial conflicts."

In the black community Merrick was no less a symbol of racial progress, holding out the hope of separate development within the biracial structure of the New South. In his later years he became something of a patron of charitable causes, not only stimulating white philanthropy, but also providing personal support for St. Joseph's African Methodist Episcopal Church, Kittrell College, Lincoln Hospital, the Durham Colored Library, and other Afro-American institutions.

Merrick married Martha Hunter of Raleigh. In their Victorian home on Durham's Fayetteville Street, they reared five children: Geneva, Mabel, Martha, John T., and Edward. Merrick's widow survived until 1939; his son Edward joined the North Carolina Mutual in 1907 and served primarily as vice-president and treasurer until his retirement in 1957. In 1943 the U.S. Navy commissioned a merchant ship out of the Wilmington naval yards as the SS *John Merrick*.

SEE: R. McCants Andrews, *John Merrick: A Biographical Sketch* (1920); William Jesse Kennedy, Jr., *The North Carolina Mutual Story: A Symbol of Progress, 1898–1970* (1970); Walter B. Weare, *Black Business in the New South: A Social History of the North Carolina Mutual Life Insurance Company* (1973).

WALTER B. WEARE

Merrimon, Augustus Summerfield (15 Sept. 1830– 14 Nov. 1892), lawyer, U.S. senator, and chief justice of the North Carolina Supreme Court, was born in Transylvania County at Cherryfields, the home of his maternal grandparents. He was the oldest of ten children of Mary Evelyn Paxton and Branch Hamline Merrimon, a Methodist minister born in Dinwiddie County, Va. His mother was the daughter of William and Sarah Grace McDowell Paxton; Sarah Grace (Sally) was the daughter of Charles McDowell, one of the victors at the Battle of Kings Mountain.

During his formative years Merrimon was influenced by many events. After his family moved to Hooper's Creek, about fourteen miles from Asheville, he became accustomed to hard work. He plowed the farm and worked in his father's sawmill. His hands became so twisted from these tasks that he could not place his palms flat on a table. Aunt Anis, a black maid and cook, cared for Merrimon, and he grew up playing with her son. Merrimon's mother, coming from a family of achievers, impressed on him the need to be great, but he always doubted his ability to do so. Her death when he was eighteen caused him grief for many years. Although Merrimon lived under the influence of his father's preaching, he never felt that he was good enough to be a Christian and did not join the church until a few days before his death.

Merrimon's education consisted of informal schooling, boarding school, and reading law. His father emphasized the importance of learning and required him to read aloud at night. Miss Minerva Cunningham, who lived with the family, started Merrimon's instruction. He also attended irregularly the classes of A. T. Livingston, who taught at a schoolhouse on the Merrimon farm. Young Augustus prided himself on studying *Salem Town's Analysis of the Derivative Words in the English Language* while he plowed. For one year he attended James Norwood's Asheville Male Academy, where he distinguished himself as a grammarian and became Norwood's assistant for a few months. Merrimon wished to attend college, but his father was unable to send him. For a year he read law, together with Zebulon B. Vance,

under John W. Woodfin of Asheville before being admitted to the bar in January 1852. During the former period, Merrimon and Vance became closely acquainted.

While reading law, Merrimon courted Margaret Jane Baird (b. 8 Sept. 1834), the daughter of Israel and Mary Tate Baird. They were married on 14 Sept. 1852. Her maternal grandparents were Samuel and Elizabeth Tate of Pennsylvania; her paternal grandfather was Bedent Baird, the brother of Zebulon and Andrew Baird, New Jersey natives who pioneered in western North Carolina. Zebulon B. Vance was her cousin.

Before and during the Civil War, Merrimon held various minor offices. After serving as solicitor of Buncombe County, he was elected to the legislature of 1860–61. There his strong Union-Whig background led him to oppose an arms bill and to speak against secession. When his state was about to secede, however, he volunteered on 3 May 1861 as a private in the Rough and Ready Guards from Buncombe and served in the Fourteenth Regiment. In June he accepted a captain's commission in the commissary and served at Hatteras, Ocracoke, Raleigh, and Weldon. In the fall of 1861 Judge Robert S. French appointed him solicitor of the mountainous Eighth District, a position he continued to hold after election by the legislature in 1862. Union sympathizers soon seized the town of Marshall because of its Confederate bent, plundering stores and committing acts of violence. Leaders in Buncombe raised one thousand men under military authority to pursue and punish the marauders. After a "violent contention" with these leaders, Merrimon carried his point that the civil authority should prevail. He then captured and prosecuted the marauders. When the Clay and Cherokee courts met in 1865 and 1866, hundreds of armed men who had been on opposite sides in the war waited for a pretext to attack one another, and about sixty of them engaged in a fray in Clay County. To avert bloodshed, Merrimon had the sheriff in each county swear in about sixty men from either faction who were ordered to shoot the first person to riot. Merrimon's position required great tact and courage.

During Reconstruction he achieved increasing recognition in state politics. Although he was an unsuccessful candidate for the convention of 1865, the 1866 legislature elected him judge of the Eighth District. Twice the military ordered him to quash indictments, but he resigned the judgeship in 1867 rather than submit to military orders. Moving to Raleigh, he formed a lucrative law partnership with Samuel F. Phillips. In 1868 Merrimon became chairman of the state executive committee of the Conservative party but failed to win a seat on the state supreme court. From 1868 to 1870 he became closely associated with Josiah Turner, Jr., editor of the *Sentinel*, and wrote many editorials for the paper. As legal counsel for George W. Swepson, he drafted the railroad bills whose passage Swepson obtained by bribery. During the Kirk-Holden war, Merrimon was among the first to apply for writs of habeas corpus to free imprisoned citizens. At the impeachment of Governor William Woods Holden, he cross-examined witnesses for the prosecution and won a statewide reputation for grasping the details of the case. When the legislature called for a constitutional convention in 1871, he sought election as a delegate, but both he and the convention were defeated.

In 1872 Merrimon reluctantly ran for governor on the Conservative ticket with the understanding that the party would support his bid for the U.S. Senate if he lost the race. Defeated by a narrow margin, he permitted his friends to nominate him for the Senate. Before the legislature met, Zebulon B. Vance pledged a majority of Conservatives to his own candidacy. Merrimon's supporters refused to be bound by the Conservative caucus committed to Vance, and they voted with the Republicans for Merrimon. Merrimon had no personal involvement in the manner of his election, which caused bitter feelings within his party. In the Senate Merrimon made speeches opposing the civil rights bill, attacking the Republicans for tyranny and misrule in Louisiana, proposing the expansion of greenbacks but the eventual return to specie, and urging establishment of a national bank to assure the equal regional distribution of banking capital. He served on the post office and claims committees.

Declining to run for reelection, Merrimon established a law firm with Thomas C. Fuller and Samuel A. Ashe in 1873. On 29 Sept. 1883 Governor Thomas J. Jarvis appointed him to the state supreme court. Six years later, on 14 Nov. 1889, Governor Daniel G. Fowle appointed him chief justice, a position to which he was elected in his own right in 1890. He served as chief justice until his death. Merrimon had all of the qualities of a great trial judge. In the supreme court he gave his attention to settling practice under the code. His decisions appear in volumes 89 through 110 of the *North Carolina Reports*.

Merrimon's contemporaries described him as courageous, courteous, punctual, thorough, guided by his conscience, honest and simple, and an "exceedingly handsome man" with a robust figure. The apparent cause of his death was diabetes, and he was buried in Oakwood Cemetery, Raleigh. He was survived by six children. Branch and William lived in Greensboro, Mary married Senator Lee S. Overman, Maggie married John Kinney of Raleigh, Maude married J. L. Cunninggim of Nashville, Tenn., and Charles lived in New York.

SEE: Moses Amis, *Historical Raleigh* (1913); Samuel A. Ashe, ed., *Biographical History of North Carolina*, vol. 8 (1917 [portrait]); *Congressional Record* (1873–79); *Cyclopedia of Eminent and Representative Men of the Carolinas of the Nineteenth Century*, vol. 2 (1892); *DAB*, vol. 7 (1934); Jerome Dowd, *Sketches of Prominent Living North Carolinians* (1888); Ernest Haywood, *Some Notes in Regard to Eminent Lawyers* (1936); Weymouth T. Jordan, comp., *North Carolina Troops, 1861–1865: A Roster*, vol. 5 (1975); Maud L. Merrimon, *Augustus Summerfield Merrimon: A Memoir* (1894); *North Carolina Reports* 89–110 (1883–92); Raleigh *News and Observer*, 15–16 Nov. 1892; Raleigh *Sentinel*, various issues, 1872; Zebulon Vance Papers (Southern Historical Collection, University of North Carolina, Chapel Hill); John H. Wheeler, ed., *Reminiscences and Memoirs of North Carolina and Eminent North Carolinians* (1884).

JOHN L. BELL, JR.

Merritt, Hiram Houston, Jr. *(12 Jan. 1902–9 Jan. 1979)*, physician and educator, was born in Wilmington, the son of Hiram H. and Dessie Cline Merritt. After attending the local schools, he spent a year at The University of North Carolina (1919) before transferring to Vanderbilt, where he received an A.B. degree in 1922. He was graduated from the medical school of Johns Hopkins University in 1926 and pursued further training in New Haven, Boston, and Munich, Germany.

Merritt began his teaching and research career in Boston, where he was visiting neurologist at the Boston City Hospital (1934–42), consulting neurologist at the Peter Bent Brigham Hospital (1939–44), and assistant professor of neurology at Harvard University (1942–44). Moving to New York City, he became professor of clini-

cal neurology at Columbia University in 1944 and was promoted to chairman of the department in 1948, a position he held for twenty years. In 1958 he became acting dean of the medical school and vice-president of medical affairs for the university. At the time of his death, he was Moses Professor Emeritus of Neurology, dean emeritus, and vice-president emeritus of medical affairs.

The author of several widely used textbooks on neurology and of many articles published in scientific journals, Merritt is best known as the principal discoverer of phenytoin (dilantin), now commonly used as an anticonvulsant. He also helped build Columbia-Presbyterian Medical Center as a major training facility for neurology. Thirty-eight of his former students became heads of neurology departments and other institutions.

Merritt was a member of numerous professional associations and the recipient of many honors, including an honorary A.M. from Harvard (1942), an Sc.D. from the New York Medical College (1967), and an Sc.D. from Columbia (1971). He received the North Carolina Award from his native state in 1967, and after treating Antonio Salazar, the premier of Portugal, he was awarded a grand officership in the Portuguese Order of Santiago.

Houston Merritt married Mabel Carmichael in 1930; they had no children. At the time of his death, he resided in Bronxville, N.Y. Dr. Merritt endowed a distinguished professorship of neurology and the H. Houston Merritt Electron Microscopy Laboratory, for use by faculty and students, at the University of North Carolina at Chapel Hill.

SEE: *American Men of Science* (1966); *Biographical Dictionary of the American Psychiatric Association* (1968); *University [of North Carolina] Report* (May 1979); *Who's Who in America*, 39th ed. (1976).

CLAIBORNE T. SMITH, JR.

Meserve, Charles Francis *(15 July 1850–20 Apr. 1936)*, educator and author, was born at Abington, Plymouth County, Mass., the son of Charles, a shoemaker and farmer, and Susan Smith Blanchard Meserve. His forebear, Clement Meserve, a native of the Isle of Jersey, English Channel, came to America in 1673. A brother of Charles Francis was a longtime master of Bowdoin School in Boston. Meserve attended Waterville Classical Institute (later Coburn) for three years before enrolling at Colby College in Waterville, Maine, in 1873. He was graduated with an A.B. degree in 1877 and received an A.M. degree in 1880; Colby also awarded him an LL.D. degree in 1899.

Meserve began his professional career in Massachusetts as principal of the high school in Rockland (1877–85) and of Oak Street School in Springfield (1885–89). He then served as superintendent of the Haskell Institute, U.S. Training School for Indians, in Lawrence, Kans., from 1889 to 1894. In the latter year he became president of Shaw University in Raleigh; his predecessors were Henry Martin Tupper (1831–93), who headed the institution from 1865 to 1893, and Nicholas Franklin Roberts (b. 1849), interim black president for several months. Meserve remained president until 1919, at which time emphasis was placed on training teachers, clergymen, and physicians; thereafter, he was president emeritus. Meserve Hall on the campus was named for him.

A Baptist, Meserve was licensed to preach but was not ordained. From 1894 to 1897 he served on the board of directors of the North Carolina State School for the Deaf, Dumb, and Blind. A member of the Raleigh Natural History Club for thirteen years, he served as its vice-president and president (1931) and delivered several papers to the membership. In addition, Meserve was a member of Phi Beta Kappa and addressed educational groups. He was president for life of the Meserve Family Association as well as instrumental in founding Capon Springs Conference at Capon Springs, W.Va. He was the author of *Abington's Part in the Building of a Great Commonwealth* and several pamphlets on Indian affairs. Meserve was a Republican.

On 19 Dec. 1878 he married Abbie Mary Whittier, of Bangor, Maine, who died in Brookline, Mass., on 6 Oct. 1898, leaving one child, Alice Whittier Meserve. On 10 May 1900 he married Julia Frances Philbrick, of Waterville, who died in 1928. In 1907 his daughter Alice served as professor of Latin at Meredith College in Raleigh, and in 1936 she was a member of the faculty of Peace Institute (later College). Meserve was buried in Pine Grove Cemetery, Waterville, Maine.

SEE: Alumni Secretary, Colby College (Waterville, Maine), to Grady L. E. Carroll, 12 Nov. 1974; Moses Amis, *Historical Raleigh* (1913); Samuel A. Ashe, ed., *Biographical History of North Carolina*, vol. 7 (1908); Hugh Victor Brown, *A History of the Education of Negroes in North Carolina* (1961); Grady L. E. Carroll, *They Lived in Raleigh* (1977); Wilmoth Carter, *Shaw's Universe* (1973); Josephus Daniels, *Editor in Politics* (1941); Frank E. Emory, ed., *Paths toward Freedom* (1976); Mary Lynch Johnson, *History of Meredith College* (1972); Ernest Cummings Marrimer, *History of Colby College* (1963); Raleigh *News and Observer*, 21 Apr., 1 May 1936; Elizabeth Culbreth Waugh and Editorial Committee, *North Carolina's Capital: Raleigh* (1967).

GRADY L. E. CARROLL

Metcalf, Zeno Payne (1 May 1885–5 Jan. 1956), scientist and teacher, was born in Lakeville, Ohio, the son of Abel Crawford and Catherine Fulmer Metcalf; he grew up on the family farm with six brothers. Throughout life he demonstrated an intense interest in birds, insects, and all forms of animal life and in trees, flowers, and other plant life. He received an A.B. degree from Ohio State University in 1907. Graduate studies at Harvard University led to the D.Sc. degree in 1925.

A prolific writer and hardworking scientist, Dr. Metcalf spent all of his professional life in North Carolina except for the year he was an instructor in entomology at Michigan State University. He came to the state in 1908 as an employee of the North Carolina Department of Agriculture. Four years later he moved two miles west to the campus of the North Carolina College of Agriculture and Mechanic Arts, where he was entomologist on the staff of the Agricultural Experiment Station and professor of zoology and entomology at the college. He served the college as chairman of numerous committees, head of the Department of Zoology and Entomology, director of instruction for the School of Agriculture (1923–44), director of graduate studies in agriculture (1940–43), associate dean of the graduate school of the Consolidated University (1943–50), and William Neal Reynolds Professor until his death. In 1955 he received the annual O. Max Gardner Award from the trustees of the Consolidated University as the faculty member (representing all branches of the university) most deserving of the award that year.

Metcalf was known nationally and internationally for his achievements. He was the author of nine books and nearly a hundred research papers. As evidence of his broad interest in all of the biological sciences, he was at one time or another a member of thirty-six learned and professional societies. Three of these—the Entomological Society of America, the Ecological Society of America, and the American Microscopical Society—elected him president. He served on the editorial boards of four national journals. In North Carolina he was active in the North Carolina Academy of Science and its president in 1921. During the late twenties he was an influential leader in public debates and addresses that helped prevent legislation that would have restricted the teaching of evolution in the public schools and colleges.

Internationally, Metcalf became recognized as the world's authority on the classification of a large group of insects, the order *Homoptera*. For over forty years he collected specimens from all parts of the world, read thousands of descriptions of species, visited museums in the United States and Europe, and began work on a forty-two-volume series of books summarizing all knowledge of the *Homoptera*, with descriptions of the families, genera, and species. Completion of the series was interrupted by his death in 1956, but the project was so well planned and sufficiently advanced that assistants were able to finish it. The university provided funding and secured grants from the National Science Foundation and other agencies.

As director of instruction in the School of Agriculture for twenty-one years and in charge of graduate studies for ten years, he encouraged high standards of scholarship and research; this, along with his emphasis on basic science in all curricula, laid the foundation for the future North Carolina State University. Metcalf was a strong influence in the transition of the college from a mediocre land-grant institution to one of the leading universities in the agricultural and biological sciences and in technological areas.

In Raleigh he participated in many civic and community affairs. As an active member of the Kiwanis Club for many years, he served one term as president. He was an elder of the First Presbyterian Church, where funeral services were conducted on 7 Jan. 1956, followed by burial in Oakwood Cemetery. He was survived by his wife, the former Mary Luella Correll of Wooster, Ohio; one daughter, Katherine (Mrs. Micou F. Browne of Raleigh); and two grandchildren, Martha Luella and Micou Metcalf Browne.

In 1969 an eleven-story dormitory at North Carolina State University was named Metcalf Hall, and a portrait of Metcalf was placed in the main social room of the building.

SEE: Raleigh *News and Observer*, 21 Feb. 1933, 5 Jan. 1947, 12 Mar. 1955, 6 Jan. 1956; *Who's Who in the South and Southwest* (1950); *Who Was Who in America* (1960).

CAREY H. BOSTIAN

Metts, John Van Bokkelen (17 Dec. 1876–14 Oct. 1959), military officer, was born in Wilmington, the son of Captain James I. and Cornelia Cowan Metts. He attended the Tileston Normal School and then Cape Fear Academy in Wilmington until age sixteen; later he took army extension courses. Metts spent two years in the wholesale grain business with his father before joining the Walker Taylor Insurance Company in Wilmington. After five years he sold his interest in that firm and established his own general insurance business. During this period his principal hobby was the National Guard. In 1894 he enlisted in the Wilmington Light Infantry (later a part of the National Guard) as a private, rising through the ranks to captain in 1903 and lieutenant colonel in 1907. He was also active in civic affairs and at one time served on the New Hanover County Board of Commissioners.

Metts was called into active federal service in June 1916 and served on the Mexican border, where he was commissioned colonel in 1917. Afterwards his regiment trained at Camp Sevier, S.C. At this time he sold his Wilmington business, as it appeared he would be in the army for an indefinite period. While Metts was at Camp Sevier, the 30th Division was organized and his regiment became the 119th Infantry of the 60th Brigade. He commanded his regiment throughout World War I, participating in three major operations: the Ypres defense sector, Ypres-Lye offensive, and Somme offensive. For this service he was awarded the Distinguished Service Medal, receiving special recognition for the combat action of his regiment in breaking the Hindenburg Line in September 1918.

When the 119th was demobilized, Colonel Metts continued in active service with the Operations Branch, War Department, General Staff, and as commanding officer of the Panama Replacement Depot at Jackson Barracks, New Orleans. There he left federal service to become adjutant general of North Carolina under Governor Thomas W. Bickett. Metts moved to Raleigh in 1920 and resided there until his death.

As adjutant general, his first duty was to reorganize the National Guard. "This tremendous undertaking was carried forward by General Metts with energy, determination and sound judgment, producing exceptionally satisfactory results." In June 1926 he also assumed command of the 60th Brigade, 30th Division, as a brigadier general of the line, a post he held until 1936. When the Works Progress Administration was created, he saw the opportunity to obtain National Guard armories and provide suitable housing facilities for many of his units. With no funds at his disposal, he was able to have plans and specifications prepared, and with the cooperation of local authorities he was responsible for the construction of twenty-eight armories.

Metts believed that the efficiency of the National Guard was due largely to the fact that politics was kept out of it. He frequently said: "You cannot mix politics with the military service and maintain discipline and efficiency."

In addition to his duties as adjutant general, Metts in 1940 was appointed state director of selective service by the president on the recommendation of Governor Clyde R. Hoey; he served throughout World War II in this capacity. When the entire National Guard entered into active federal service, he began to organize the North Carolina State Guard as a protective force for the state. When the war was over, he had the monumental task of reorganizing the National Guard for the second time. In 1949 he was promoted to the rank of major general. After serving the state as adjutant general for thirty-one years, under nine governors, he resigned on 31 July 1951.

During his military career, Metts was president of the Adjutant Generals' Association of the United States and served on the executive council and several standing committees of the National Guard of the United States. He was a recipient of the Medal for Merit for Selective Service, awarded by President Harry S Truman; the North Carolina Daughters of Confederacy Medal to an outstanding son of a Confederate veteran; the Distinguished Service Medal of the National Guard Association of the United States (1955); and the North Carolina Distinguished Service Medal (1956).

In 1906 he married Josephine Budd of Petersburg, Va. They had two children, Josephine Budd Metts Huntt and John Van B., Jr., both of whom remained in the Wilmington area. Metts was buried in Oakdale Cemetery, Wilmington.

SEE: John L. Cheney, Jr., ed., *North Carolina Government, 1585–1979* (1981); *North Carolina Biography*, vol. 3 (1929, 1941); *Who's Who in the South and Southwest* (1952).

JOSEPHINE METTS HUNTT

Mewborne, James Marion (22 Mar. 1848–28 Oct. 1924), farmer, Farmers' Alliance leader, state senator, and public servant, was born in Vance Township, Lenoir County, the son of Levi and Susan Parrott Mewborne. He became prominent during the Farmers' Alliance movement and held a number of positions at both the state and local levels. In 1889 Mewborne succeeded William H. Worth as business agent of the Lenoir County Alliance. In the same year he was elected a member of the three-man executive committee of the North Carolina Farmers' State Alliance and remained in that post until he became president of the order in 1893. Reelected president in 1894, he served until 1895. In 1892–93 he was a lecturer for the Second Congressional District.

Politically ambitious, Mewborne was the Farmers' Alliance Democratic candidate for Congress from the Second Congressional District after illness forced William J. Rogers of Northampton County to withdraw. Mewborne's late entry into the race and questions concerning his loyalty to the Democratic party resulted in his defeat by the black incumbent, Henry P. Cheatham.

Mewborne's liberal leanings led him to join the People's party in 1892. He served in the state senate in 1895, the year the Fusionists, a coalition of Populists and Republicans, won control of the legislature. Elected commissioner by the North Carolina Board of Agriculture, he took office on 15 June 1897 and served until 1 Jan. 1898. On that day, he became superintendent of the state penitentiary and held the position for one year. When the People's party collapsed, Mewborne affiliated with the Republican party, which he served for years as county chairman. In 1910 he directed the census for the Second Congressional District. After 1900, however, he concentrated largely on his farming activities.

Deeply religious, Mewborne had strong moral and political convictions which he expressed in impassioned words. He was described by contemporaries as a "Christian gentleman." A lifelong member of the Christian church, he belonged to the Wheat Swamp congregation. After his second marriage, he moved to Kinston and taught the adult Sunday school class in the Gordon Street Church of Christ.

Mewborne and his first wife, Eliza Palmer, were the parents of two sons, J. Hyman and Noah Palmer, and two daughters, Mary Glenn (Mrs. A. C. Bizzell) and Susie (Mrs. James J. Rogers). His second marriage, to Pattie Parrott, produced three sons, Edward Bruce, James Marion, Jr., and John Franklin, who survived their father. Mewborne was buried in Maplewood Cemetery, Kinston.

SEE: Board of Agriculture Minutes, 1887–99 (North Carolina State Archives, Raleigh); Elias Carr Papers (Manuscript Collection, East Carolina University Library, Greenville); John L. Cheney, Jr., ed., *North Carolina Government, 1584–1974* (1974); Goldsboro *Caucasian*, 23, 30 (portrait) Aug. 1894; *Journal* of the North Carolina Senate (1895); *Kinston Free Press*, 24, 31 July, 30 Oct., 20

Nov. 1890, 28 Oct. 1924; John Franklin Mewborne (Kinston), interview, 29 May 1981; North Carolina Farmers' State Alliance, *Proceedings* (1887–94); Raleigh *News and Observer*, 29 Oct. 1890, 30 Aug. 1924; Raleigh *Progressive Farmer*, 27 Aug. 1889, 28 Oct. 1890, 20 Jan. 1891, 9 Aug. 1892, 22 May 1894; Raleigh *State Chronicle*, 24, 30 Oct. 1890; "Report of the Superintendent," no. 20, *Public Documents of the State of North Carolina* (1899); Seventh Census of the United States, 1850: Lenoir County, N.C., Population Schedule (microfilm of National Archives manuscript copy, East Carolina University Library, Greenville); Lala Carr Steelman, "The Role of Elias Carr in the North Carolina Farmers' Alliance," *North Carolina Historical Review* 57 (1980).

LALA CARR STEELMAN

Michaux, André *(7 Mar. 1746–November 1802)*, French botanist, explorer, and writer, was born at Satory, near Versailles. From an early age he was trained in the agricultural sciences in order to follow in his father's footsteps in managing farmland on the royal estate. In 1769 he married Cecile Claye, who died eleven months later, just after the birth of their son, François André. For the next decade, Michaux devoted himself to an even more intensive study of botany and horticulture. He began his plant-collecting travels in 1779 with trips to England, the Auvergne Mountains, and the Pyrenees. In 1782 he was appointed secretary to the French consul in Persia, but once there, he gave up his post and spent two years studying the plant life of the Tigris and Euphrates valley. Soon after returning to France in 1785, he was commissioned by the French government to study the trees in North America, to send back specimens for the royal gardens, and to ascertain their value for naval construction.

Accompanied by his fifteen-year-old son, Michaux arrived in New York in October 1785. He set up a nursery at Bergen, N.J., where he deposited a wide variety of trees, shrubs, and wildflowers that he had gathered on trips through New Jersey, Pennsylvania, and Maryland. Many of these specimens were shipped back to France and replanted in the gardens of Rambouillet and Versailles. Michaux also included a number of live game birds with these shipments. On a trip to South Carolina he found Charleston a more suitable climate for his botanical collection, and in 1787 he made it his headquarters. He bought a plantation ten miles from the city that served as his nursery and shipping center for the rest of his American stay.

Later the same year Michaux discovered the botanical bounty of the Southern Appalachians and made the first of at least five visits to western North Carolina. Following the route taken by William Bartram, a Philadelphia naturalist who had explored the area in 1775, he entered the state through Georgia and studied the flora along the French Broad River. He returned in 1788, this time entering North Carolina through Charlotte and following the Catawba River up into Burke County before proceeding across the Blue Ridge Mountains.

Michaux also made scientific expeditions to Florida (1788), the Bahamas (1789), and the Hudson Bay (1792). In 1793 the French consul to the United States, Edmund Charles Genet, sent Michaux to Kentucky and Tennessee on a diplomatic mission regarding the transfer of French and Spanish lands in the West, but again his role as a botanist overshadowed his efforts as a negotiator. His last trips to the North Carolina mountains were made in 1794 and 1795. These tours included visits to Roan Mountain, Mount Mitchell (then known as Black

Mountain), Grandfather Mountain, Table Rock, Hawksbill, and the Linville Gorge. He noted in his journal that on the summit of Grandfather (which he mistakenly called "the highest mountain of all North America"), he and his guide sang the new French hymn "La Marseillaise" and cried: "Long live America and the French Republic! Long live Liberty!" During his travels in this area, Michaux came to know and was often a houseguest of such prominent residents as William Wiseman of the Toe River valley, and Joseph McDowell and Waightstill Avery, both of Burke Courthouse (Morganton).

Some of Michaux's most significant botanical discoveries were made in western North Carolina. In the Toxaway area he found one of the rarest wildflowers in North America, the *Shortia galacifolia*. Despite subsequent searches by various botanists, this plant was not seen again until Dr. Asa Gray rediscovered it in 1877. Michaux also identified a rare species of yellow locust and found that the inner bark of its roots yielded a valuable dye, which later came into common use by mountain residents. Probably his most important contribution to western North Carolinians was in making them aware of the commercial value of ginseng, a plant valued by the Chinese for its medicinal qualities. He taught them how to collect it and sell its roots for the Chinese market. The sale of "sang" proved to be a profitable venture for many mountain families, and it continued to be a major cash crop in some areas until recent years. In addition to the valuable information he recorded in his journals, Michaux wrote two books based on his American findings: *The History of North American Oaks*, published in 1801, and *Flora Boreali Americana*, published in 1803 after his death.

The French Revolution deprived Michaux of the financial support the royal government had provided him. By 1796 his resources were exhausted and he was forced to return home to Paris. He sailed from Charleston in August with a vast supply of botanical specimens but was shipwrecked just off the coast of Holland. Though he and most of his plants were saved, a good part of his journal describing his North American travels was lost. On returning to France, he found that most of the American trees he had shipped back during his decade abroad had been destroyed or scattered since the outbreak of revolution. When his efforts to interest his government in sponsoring another trip to the United States failed, he agreed to serve as the naturalist on an expedition to Australia led by Captain Nicholas Baudin, which set sail in October 1800. He abandoned the group on the Indian Ocean island of Mauritania, where he found the tropical vegetation of particular interest. After a six-month stay, he moved on to nearby Madagascar to continue his studies. While there, he became ill as a result of overexertion and died of a fever several months later at age fifty-six.

SEE: *Asheville Citizen-Times*, 9 June 1957; *DAB*, vol. 12 (1933); Shepherd M. Dugger, *The Balsam Groves of the Grandfather Mountain* (1892); Henry Savage, Jr., and Elizabeth J. Savage, *André and François Michaux* (1986); F. A. Sondley, *A History of Buncombe County, North Carolina*, vol. 2 (1930); Reuben Gold Thwaites, ed., *Early Western Travels, 1748–1846*, vol. 3 (1904).

JOHN C. INSCOE

Michaux, François André *(16 Aug 1770–23 Oct. 1855)*, French botanist, explorer, and writer, was the only child of André Michaux. His mother, Cecile Claye Michaux, died just after his birth at Satory, near Versailles. In 1785 he accompanied his father to America and two years later, at age seventeen, took charge of the nursery his father established on a plantation near Charleston. He spent most of his time overseeing its operation, though he traveled with his father on several of his expeditions. In 1790 he returned to France, where he studied medicine for several years. Arriving just as the French Revolution broke out, he also became involved in the republican cause.

In 1801 the younger Michaux was commissioned to return to the United States to continue his father's work in studying and reporting on American plant life. He sailed to Charleston, where he spent the winter of 1801–2 disposing of his father's property and shipping his remaining specimens to France. In June 1802 he left from Philadelphia for a three-and-a-half-month trip through Ohio, Kentucky, and Tennessee that ended in Charleston, where he again spent the winter before returning to France early in 1803. His account of this journey, which focused as much on agricultural developments as on botanical discoveries, was published in Paris in 1804. It was translated into English the next year under the title, *Travels to the West of the Allegheny Mountains*. Though he spent little time in North Carolina, he provided good descriptions of Morganton and Lincolnton, which he passed through on his way back to Charleston.

In 1806 Michaux again set sail for America but was captured by the British and detained for several months in Bermuda. Arriving in New York in May, he spent the next three years studying and classifying trees in the northeastern United States, Quebec, and Nova Scotia. In 1807 he met Robert Fulton and became such a good friend that he was one of two passengers on the *Clermont*'s landmark trip up the Hudson River. After returning to France, he wrote a three-volume work called *The North American Sylva; or, A Description of the Forest Trees of the United States, Canada, and Nova Scotia*. It was published in Paris from 1810 to 1813 and translated into English five years later. Michaux spent most of the rest of his life managing experimental farms owned by the Société Centrale de l'Agriculture near Paris, devoting much of his work to the cultivation and propagation of trees and shrubs grown from seeds he had sent back from America.

Michaux contributed significantly to his father's legacy. He edited and published André's *History of North American Oaks* in 1801. He preserved those journals of his father's American travels that survived his shipwreck off the Dutch coast and presented them to the American Philosophical Society at Philadelphia in 1824, though they were not published until 1889 in the society's *Proceedings*.

Michaux married his housekeeper late in life; they had no children. He died suddenly of apoplexy in Vauréal, France. Much of his fortune was left to the American Philosophical Society and the Society of Agriculture and Arts in Boston; he had been an active member of both organizations.

SEE: *DAB*, vol. 12 (1933); Elias Durand, "Biographical Memoir of the Late François André Michaux," *American Journal of Science* (July 1856); Henry Savage, Jr., and Elizabeth J. Savage, *André and François Michaux* (1986); Reuben Gold Thwaites, ed., *Early Western Travels, 1748–1846*, vol. 3 (1904).

JOHN C. INSCOE

Michel, Frantz Ludwig (*ca. 1680–post-1714*), colonist and explorer, also called Francis Louis Michel, assisted Christoph von Graffenried in establishing a Swiss-German colony at New Bern in 1710. His family, Michel von Schwertschwendi, was prominent in Bern, Switzerland, where his father was a member of the Council and prefect of Gottstatt. Frantz Ludwig seems to have been the older of two sons. His younger brother remained at home in a government career while he undertook military service, probably as an officer in the armies of Louis XIV.

Between 1701 and 1707 Michel made three voyages to America, where he explored parts of Virginia, Maryland, and Pennsylvania. In 1702 he sketched in his journal the first Virginia capitol in Williamsburg and the main building of the College of William and Mary—drawings that proved helpful in documenting twentieth-century restorations. In 1707 he became one of the earliest explorers of the Shenandoah Valley, and he left to posterity a rough map of some principal topographical features.

During one or more of these journeys Michel acted as agent of the government of Bern to seek a tract of land in English America where the canton's paupers (*Landsassen* or squatters) and its Anabaptists (*Wiedertaüfer*), some of whom had been imprisoned for civil disobedience, could be resettled. A company headed by Georg Ritter, a councillor of Bern, was being formed for this purpose. In 1708 Michel was in London. There he met Graffenried and John Lawson, a surveyor who had explored the proprietary province of Carolina.

By 1709 other German-speaking people—refugees from the war-ravaged Palatinate—were pouring into the London area. On 10 May 1710, Graffenried and Michel signed a contract with Georg Ritter and Company under which the two leaders were to resettle about 150 Swiss. They contracted with the British government to resettle some 650 Palatines in the same venture. The colonists were to be guided by Lawson to lands on the Neuse, Trent, and White Oak rivers purchased from the Carolina Lords Proprietors.

Decimated by defections, disease, and Indian uprisings that began in 1711, the project was doomed to failure as a colony, though many of the settlers survived and were assimilated into the English population. Graffenried blamed Michel for allegedly antagonizing the Indians while he was drunk and for leading him to anticipate large revenues from silver deposits Michel said he had found in Virginia and perhaps in Pennsylvania. As financial backing, the colony had only meager Swiss and English transportation funds and vague promises of provisions from the Lords Proprietors.

Michel left no document that speaks in his own defense. But to his credit he forced Graffenried to purchase a small shallop that would bring supplies. In 1712, with the rank of colonel, he led a Swiss-Palatine detachment that joined South Carolina troops in taking the Indian stronghold Fort Nohoroco on Contentnea Creek. A South Carolina account states that he was "much praised . . . on all sides for his skill as an engineer."

Graffenried attempted to transfer the New Bern survivors to land near the Potomac falls in Virginia. However, neither Michel nor the colonists would follow him, and he returned to Switzerland. Meanwhile, in 1714, a group of German miners engaged by the two Swiss made its way overseas and for a few years worked the iron deposits of Lieutenant Governor Alexander Spotswood on the Rapidan River in what is now Orange County, Va. They were the first of many German colonists who settled upland Virginia.

The Swiss soldier did not join the mining families in 1714, and here one loses sight of him. Later, without mentioning any date or place, Graffenried added in a marginal notation to his French-language account of the New Bern venture that Michel "died among the Indians." No portrait of Michel is known to exist.

SEE: Fred J. Allred and Alonzo T. Dill, "The Founding of New Bern: A Footnote," *North Carolina Historical Review* 40 (July 1963); Joseph W. Barnwell, "The Second Tuscarora Expedition," *South Carolina Historical and Genealogical Magazine* 10 (January 1909); William J. Hinke, "Report of the Journey of Francis Louis Michel, from Berne, Switzerland, to Virginia, October 2, 1701–December 1, 1702," *Virginia Magazine of History and Biography* 24 (January 1916); Charles E. Kemper, ed., "Documents Relating to Early Projected Swiss Colonies in the Valley of Virginia, 1706–1709," *Virginia Magazine of History and Biography* 29 (January 1921); Vincent H. Todd and Julius Goebel, eds., *Christoph von Graffenried's Account of the Founding of New Bern* (1920); Elizabeth Chapman Denny Vann and Margaret Collins Denny Dixon, *Virginia's First German Colony* (1961).

ALONZO THOMAS DILL

Micklejohn, George (*ca. 1717–1818*), Anglican clergyman in colonial North Carolina, was probably a native of Berwick-upon-Tweed in the north of England, but no details of his family or early life have been found nor is anything known of his education. However, the title page of a sermon printed in New Bern, which he preached in 1768, notes that he held the degree of doctor of sacred theology. The earliest documented fact concerning him is dated 16 Sept. 1764, when he was ordained. On 12 Mar. 1766 he was licensed by the bishop of London, and later in the year he was sent to North Carolina as a missionary of the Society for the Propagation of the Gospel in Foreign Parts.

Royal Governor William Tryon considered Micklejohn to be a valuable addition to his colony and, after stationing the new missionary briefly in St. Luke's Parish, Rowan County, placed him in charge of St. Matthew's in Hillsborough and the nearby chapels of St. Jude, St. Mary, and "a small Chapel of Ease" at the site of present-day Chapel Hill. In September 1767 he accompanied Governor and Mrs. Tryon and others to Wachovia, where on Sunday the twentieth he preached on Haggai, chapter 2, verse 6, afterwards baptizing several children from the region. Described as "tall, dark, large-boned and gaunt, with harsh features and slow, deliberate manner in the pulpit, and out," he soon gained the esteem of colonial society as well as the royal government. Legend, on the other hand, pictures him as a crank with his congregation and the common people. The Reverend Henry Pattillo, a Presbyterian, even called him a deist.

Prior to 1786 Micklejohn married Elizabeth Lockhart, the daughter of Samuel and Catherine Lockhart, and with his marriage he became allied with a number of prominent families in Orange County. The couple's children, as named in his will, were William, Robert, James, Thomas, George, Elizabeth, and Catherine.

Zealous for the expansion of the Anglican church in the colony, Micklejohn persuaded Governor Tryon to join him in recommending Edward Jones to the bishop of London for ordination to the priesthood. When Jones arrived in London, the bishop refused on the grounds that the recommendations were not sufficient and that he was not personally acquainted with Micklejohn.

Only the intervention of Tryon's influential sister, who resided in London, rescued Jones from privation and eventually obtained his ordination.

When the Regulators in North Carolina began their activities, Micklejohn worked diligently to assist them in obtaining redress from their grievances without having to resort to violence. In 1768 he acted as a courier on several occasions, carrying messages between the rebels and royal authorities. In the Regulator documents he was respectfully referred to as "our Rector," even though there were many Dissenters and others in the Regulator movement who were not communicants of the Church of England. While attempting to achieve a peaceful settlement, Micklejohn remained strongly opposed to violence in any form and did not abandon in the least his loyalty to the British Crown. When Tryon assembled the militia in Hillsborough to restore order, the parish minister was requested to preach to the troops. Accordingly, he delivered a discourse that was soon published under the title, *On the important Duty of Subjection to the Civil Powers: A Sermon Preached before his Excellency William Tryon, Esquire, Governor, and Commander in Chief of the Province of North-Carolina, and the Troops raised to quell the late Insurrection, at Hillsborough, in Orange County, On Sunday September 25, 1768.* The governor was so pleased with the dynamic homily that he persuaded the colonial Assembly to have one hundred copies printed and distributed in the colony and a few sent to officials in England.

Despite his efforts on behalf of peace, Micklejohn was unable to bring the opposing sides to terms. In 1775 he dutifully opened the Provincial Congress with prayer. When the American Revolution began, he remained loyal to the Crown, and tradition says he was among the Tories taken at the Battle of Moore's Creek Bridge. Nevertheless, his name does not appear among the list of prisoners. Instead, he probably was among the Loyalists rounded up in Orange County a short while later. After lengthy negotiations he was paroled and unhappily endured the remainder of the war attempting to minister to a church that was rapidly declining. In 1793 he moved to Granville County, where he purchased a home on Grassy Creek from his friend, Thomas Person. He ministered to congregations at St. John's, Williamsboro, and other localities; was appointed by the legislature to a board of trustees that tried unsuccessfully to establish an academy in Granville County; and was nominated but not elected to the position of professor of humanity at The University of North Carolina. He was disappointed in 1790 when a convention he presided over in Tarborough failed in its attempt to organize the Diocese of North Carolina of the Protestant Episcopal church. He was appointed a delegate to the Episcopal convention of 1792 in New York but did not attend.

In 1803 Micklejohn sold his land in the state and later moved to Mecklenburg County, Va., where he attended St. James's Church but apparently had no clerical connection with it. He seems never to have become reconciled to the separation from England. On one occasion, when requested to conduct a school for young children, he is said to have retorted that he would have nothing to do with the little Democrats for it had always been difficult to control them, and since the Revolution it would be impossible.

Micklejohn's will was probated on 15 Feb. 1819. He was supposedly buried near Speed's Chapel on Dockery Creek, near Smith's Cross Roads in Mecklenburg County, Va.

SEE: Walter Clark, ed., *State Records of North Carolina*, vols. 11 (1895), 22 (1907), 24 (1905); William W. Manross, comp., *The Fulham Papers in the Lambeth Palace Library* (1965); William S. Powell, ed., *The Correspondence of William Tryon and Other Selected Papers*, 2 vols. (1980–81); William S. Powell, James K. Huhta, and Thomas J. Farnham, eds., *The Regulators of North Carolina* (1971); William L. Saunders, ed., *Colonial Records of North Carolina*, vols. 7–8, 10 (1890); Durward T. Stokes, "Different Concepts of Government Expressed in the Sermons of Two Eighteenth Century Clergymen," *Historical Magazine of the Protestant Episcopal Church* 40 (March 1971).

DURWARD T. STOKES

Middleton, Edwin Lee (*10 Sept. 1866–14 Feb. 1928*), educator and Sunday school administrator, was born near Warsaw in rural Duplin County, the son of David John and Lucy Jane Nicholson Middleton. The family was English, and the first of the direct line who came to America was Robert Middleton, who migrated to Virginia in 1663. Robert's son moved to North Carolina, and later his son (the third American generation) took a grant of land in what is now Duplin County. It was there that David John lived and married Mrs. Nicholson, the widow of a Methodist minister.

One of seven children (six sons and a daughter), Edwin Lee grew up in the years of economic and social confusion following the Civil War. His father was an active Baptist, a member first of the Kenansville church and later of the Johnsons church. He indoctrinated his children in the values of the church and all of them became Baptists. The Middletons provided the best education possible for their children: tutors in the home and select private schools in the community.

In 1884, at age eighteen, Edwin Lee enrolled in Wake Forest College and four years later was graduated with honors with a bachelor of arts degree. Choosing education as his profession, he taught successively in established schools in Wilson, Durham, and Cary (1888–1908). During those years he acquired a reputation as a good student himself, and through his meticulous teaching developed the same qualities in many of his students. He expressed great pride in the large number of his former pupils who went on to college and who entered the major professions of teaching, medicine, the law, and the ministry.

Even before his college days, Middleton was an active church member. Especially interested in a budding program in North Carolina Baptist churches known as Sunday schools, he concentrated his efforts on building the valued instructional emphases, as well as directing the organizational pattern of this new adjunct to local church life.

With such a background, he was the logical choice of the North Carolina Baptist State Convention to be its first Sunday School secretary. For twenty years Middleton effectively led the denomination's program in North Carolina, establishing a standard Sunday school in almost every Baptist church in the state. A leader in this expanding movement southwide, he made extraordinary progress in developing Sunday schools in rural communities. He placed great emphasis on teacher training, encouraging thousands to complete the Convention Normal Course through class and home study.

In conjunction with these efforts, Middleton soon developed an active interest in church architecture. The records indicate that during one year alone, he assisted 670 Baptist churches in North Carolina, providing plans and consulting with their contractors and building committees. He regarded this work as an essential part of building good Sunday schools in order to provide them with adequate physical facilities that would be both attractive and comfortable.

After working in the Sunday school movement for fifteen years, he wrote a book entitled *Building a Country Sunday School* (1923), which became a manual for those interested in implementing his ideas for the expansion and promotion of Sunday schools. He touched every county and every Baptist association in North Carolina with his message, and although he remained loyal to his rural brethren, his efforts found a vast harvest in towns and cities across the state.

Although he was not an ordained minister, Middleton traveled widely in North Carolina, preaching, teaching study classes, conducting conferences, and visiting local churches that had asked for his help. He had no time for civic affairs as such but devoted himself with singleness to promoting Sunday schools wherever there was a need and he could get a hearing.

Notwithstanding his concentration on these activities, Middleton was a leader in every aspect of organized Baptist life in North Carolina. For many years prior to his death he served as statistical secretary of the Baptist State Convention. In that "behind-the-scenes" post, he plotted the numerical and financial growth of the denomination each year, compiling his reports from a study of the convention's minutes for the preceding twelve months. It was said that his records not only were accurate but also were more promptly produced than in any other state in the Southern Baptist territory.

While teaching in Durham, he married Mary Eva Rigsbee, who came from a family of religious leaders who were prominent in the life of the city and state and devout members of the First Baptist Church, Durham. The Middletons had six children. The oldest and the youngest two died in infancy. Three grew to maturity: Lucy Kate (Mrs. Robert W. Taylor, Jr.), Mary Rachel (Mrs. James Stanley Brown), and Robert Lee, who married Sarah Edwards of Raleigh. Robert Lee Middleton was for many years head of the Accounting Department of the Sunday School Board of the Southern Baptist Convention in Nashville, Tenn., and himself a Sunday school teacher and author of note.

After twenty years of service to Baptist Sunday schools, Middleton became ill and died in the Baptist hospital in Winston-Salem at age sixty-one. He was buried in Raleigh, where he had lived since 1908.

SEE: *Encyclopedia of Southern Baptists*, vol. 2 (1958); John Milburn Price, *A Survey of Religious Education* (1958); B. W. Spilman, "Edwin Lee Middleton," in John Milburn Price, ed., *Baptist Leaders in Religious Education* (1943).

C. SYLVESTER GREEN

Midgett, John Allen, Jr. (*25 Aug. 1876–9 Feb. 1938*), chief warrant officer, U.S. Coast Guard, was born at Chicamacomico (now Rodanthe) of English ancestry. He was the son of Phoebe O'Neal and John Allen Midgett, Sr., officer-in-charge (keeper) of New Inlet Life-Saving Station (formerly Loggerhead Inlet), located between Oregon Inlet and Chicamacomico on North Carolina's Outer Banks. Midgett was reared on Cape Hatteras Island near the famed "graveyard of the Atlantic"—Diamond Shoals—and attended the village school through whatever grades were taught at that time. He acquired the remainder of his formal education in a private academy in Elizabeth City.

Returning to his native community as a very young

boy, he grew up strong in stature, absorbing the lore and lure of the sea, knowing no fear of the vast ocean but learning a deep respect for it. With the Midgett life-saving tradition behind him, it is no wonder that he, too, chose the U.S. Life-Saving Service as his life's work, enlisting from North Carolina in 1898 and serving through the merger of the Life-Saving Service with the U.S. Coast Guard until his death. Prior to his service at Chicamacomico Station, he served at the Little Kinne-keet and Gull Shoal stations. After the *Mirlo* rescue, the U.S. Navy sent him to the Philadelphia Navy Yard, probably to act briefly as a Coast Guard consultant concerning the German submarine activity off the East Coast. This is supposition, since information of that nature is strictly classified.

No man in the U.S. Coast Guard became more widely known than Midgett after his heroism one August afternoon in 1918. Chief Boatswain Midgett, while in charge of Chicamacomico Coast Guard Station, was in command of a lifeboat that went to the aid of the British tanker *Mirlo*, which had been torpedoed by a German submarine offshore from Midgett's station. The ship's cargo of gasoline and oil spread over ten miles of ocean, burning as it spread. The crew of the stricken tanker abandoned ship in three boats. One capsized as it was being lowered; another was so crowded as to be unman-ageable. The daring crew of the Chicamacomico Coast Guard Station and its commanding officer pulled the survivors of the capsized boat from the blazing oil, lo-cated and took the other two boats in tow, and landed forty-two men safely ashore through a burning ocean of raging, stormy surf. Midgett's simple sentences, in their brevity, are best captured in his official report of the epi-sode in the Coast Guard annals. This report gives an un-forgettable picture of a deed of daring that takes first rank in the saga of the U.S. Coast Guard Service.

In Coast Guard history, one name—Midgett—con-tinually appears. The Midgetts have been labeled "Mighty Men," catalogued and described as legendary, heroic, loyal, proud, and, above all, American. Among them, Chief Warrant Officer Midgett had a profound in-fluence on the Coast Guard's history and was an inspira-tion to the young boot and old salt alike. On 2 July 1972, to acknowledge the contribution by the famous Outer Banks family and to honor John Allen Midgett, Jr., the North Carolina Navy League Council, the state of North Carolina, and the U.S. Coast Guard proclaimed "Mid-gett Day." In remembrance of the chief warrant officer, the Coast Guard named its newest cutter *Midgett* and exhibited the 378-foot ship at Morehead City on Midgett Day. This class of cutter is named after either past secre-taries of the Treasury or Coast Guard heroes. The cutter is primarily a search-and-rescue vessel, but it plays an integral part in the Coast Guard's many other roles in navigation, such as serving as a floating landing pad for helicopters and, in time of war, as an antisubmarine vessel.

In December 1920 Midgett received a gold medal for gallantry in lifesaving from the British government and a silver cup from the British Board of Trade. In 1930 he and the members of the *Mirlo* rescue crew—Zion S. Midgett, Leroy S. Midgett, Arthur V. Midgett, Clarence E. Midgett, and Prochorous O'Neal (married to a Mid-gett)—were awarded the American Cross of Honor.

John Allen was ambitious and actively interested in politics. An independent by tradition, environment, and conviction—voting for "the man" rather than the par-ty—this brave and modest man had many friends both Democratic and Republican. He was a close friend of Franklin Roosevelt and most of the congressmen during the Roosevelt years; many congressmen left their Wash-ington seats to attend his funeral in Rodanthe in 1938.

Midgett sprang from deeply religious Methodists; he was noted for his honesty, courage, and kindness. Like all the "Mighty Midgetts" before (and after) him, he had a great capacity for taking Life by the scruff of the neck and shaking her into doing his bidding. He advised justly, assisted readily, withstood provocations pa-tiently, defended courageously, and was a friend un-changeably. A leader on his native Cape Hatteras, he took an interest in education and in community im-provements such as roads and better transportation on the Outer Banks. He was a Thirty-second-degree, Scot-tish Rite Mason, with membership in the Wanchese Ma-sonic Lodge.

He married Jazania Spencer Payne of Chicamacomico, and the couple had four children: Nora M. Herbert, Bethany M. Gray, Herbert, and Ellery C. (a captain in the U.S. Navy and later a captain in the U.S. Merchant Marine).

John Allen Midgett, Jr., died a "landsman's" death in the Public Health Hospital at Norfolk, Va., as the result of complications suffered in an auto accident during the holidays of Christmas 1937. Had he lived until August 1938, he would have been sixty-three, and that month would have marked the forty-second year of his active service in the Coast Guard. The next year, as a warrant officer, he would have retired, and his period of service would have remained a record for a long while. He, his wife, and their daughter Nora were buried in the Man-teo Cemetery on Roanoke Island.

SEE: *Coast Guard News*, releases 90-72 (30 May 1972), 98-72 (13 June 1972), 92-72 (3 July 1972); U.S. Coast Guard Academy, *Alumni Bulletin* 31, no. 3 (May–June 1969); Nell Wise Wechter, *The Mighty Midgetts of Chicamacomico* (1974); Don Wharton, "The Mighty Midgetts of Hat-teras," *American Mercury* (August 1957).

NELL WISE WECHTER

Midgett, Levene Westcott (*29 Nov. 1891–21 Jan. 1973*), chief boatswain's mate, U.S. Coast Guard, was born at Chicamacomico (now Rodanthe) of English ancestry. His father was Joseph Midgett, a member of the old U.S. Life-Saving Service; his mother was Orenda Sparrow Midgett of Rodanthe. He was the only son among six children.

Levene Midgett began his service career as a surfman at Gull Shoal Station in 1917 and in three years rose to the rank of boatswain's mate, first class. In 1924 he transferred to Chicamacomico Coast Guard Station, ris-ing to the rank of chief boatswain's mate in 1928. That year he was assigned to Bogue Inlet for two months; from Bogue he was transferred to Cape Fear. Reassign-ment to Oak Island followed, and about one and one-half years later he was sent to Hatteras Inlet Station as officer-in-charge.

While at Hatteras Inlet, on 9 Dec. 1931, Midgett re-ceived a radio message that a fishing vessel, the trawler *Anna May* of Hampton, Va., had gone aground. Crews and a surfboat were launched on the south side of the cape; they proceeded about five miles to sea and made several attempts to get around the shoal, but because of high seas they were forced to return to the beach. The crew then hauled the boat across to the north side of the cape and launched at 2:30 P.M., going as close as possible to Diamond Shoals, but were unable to see the *Anna May*. The surfboat returned to the beach at 5:00 P.M. At 6:00 A.M. on 10 December, a second surfboat was launched and proceeded towards Outer Diamond Shoals, where it found the trawler aground. The Hatteras Inlet lifeboat arrived at 7:30 A.M. By 8:30 A.M., the mast fell and the vessel broke into pieces. After many harrowing attempts, the Cape Hatteras Station lifeboat succeeded in rescuing two men. Midgett and his crew from Hatteras Inlet recovered the three remaining survivors. Coast Guard annals state that "these servicemen effected the rescue at great risk to their own lives, both because of the terrible storm that caused the grounding of the vessel and because of the treacherous shoals." On 17 Dec. 1935 Midgett and his rescue crew, along with the other coastguardsmen who had assisted, were awarded the Silver Lifesaving Medal by the U.S. Treasury Department. Midgett's medal was inscribed with the words: "To Levene W. Midgett for bravely rescuing several men from drowning, Dec. 10, 1931."

In 1933 he transferred from Hatteras Inlet to Creeds Hill for a brief tour of duty and then to temporary duty at the Cedar Point and Portsmouth units of the U.S. Coast Guard on the New England coast. In 1936 he was assigned to Oregon Inlet. After two years, he was assigned to Chicamacomico Station, in his home community of Rodanthe, where he served as officer-in-charge until his retirement on 31 Dec. 1953 with a long list of memorable rescues to his credit.

He championed the use of the DUCK amphibious vehicles in the area. A thirty-seven-foot motor yacht with two men and two women aboard ran aground in a violent wind and rainstorm in Oregon Inlet, fifteen miles north of Chicamacomico, and was in danger of breaking up in the surf. The Coast Guard rushed a motor surfboat and lifeboat to the scene, but neither could get near enough to the grounded vessel to assist because of the shallow water. Midgett and one crew member from his station arrived at the scene in the station's "DUCK," which drove into the surf and saved the yacht and its occupants.

Midgett helped to keep alive the custom of observing "Old Christmas," on 5 January, in Rodanthe—perhaps the only place in the New World where two Christmases are celebrated. Service, duty, heroism, and courage best describe this "Mighty Midgett" of Chicamacomico. He had the ordinary education of others like him on the Outer Banks during the early 1900s. Like the traditional Midgett lifesavers before him, his classroom was the Atlantic Ocean, where he became a self-taught man who was plain, gentle, just, cautious, and resolute. He wore his heritage proudly and with no sign of boastfulness. He would have been the first to josh away as foolishness the idea that he was heroic. Yet his gallant record is inscribed in the archives of the U.S. Coast Guard, a record with a proficiency rating of 3.8 and a conduct rating of 4.0 for his thirty-seven years of service.

On 17 Jan. 1915 he married Lucretia Midgett of Rodanthe. Both were active in the affairs of the Fair Haven Methodist Church in their community. There were three children: Levene, Jr., Mrs. Laura M. Scarborough, and Mrs. Eveln M. Stowe, both daughters having married coastguardsmen. Levene, Jr., served three years in the U.S. Coast Guard prior to his death. Midgett was a member of the Manteo Masonic Lodge, No. 521, and of American Legion Post No. 26; for two years he served as president of the Dare County Wildlife Club. He is remembered for the great celebration on Hatteras Island in September 1952, when the North Carolina State Highway Department completed the paving of the road that linked the seven villages of the Outer Banks and forever ended their isolation. Through his leadership and the efforts of his committee, hundreds of "off-is-

landers" rode the converted LST ferries across Oregon Inlet to attend the celebration in the little village of Rodanthe.

Midgett died at age eighty-two in the Veterans Hospital, Hampton, Va. He and his son were buried in the family cemetery at Rodanthe.

SEE: "Chief Boatswain's Mate Levene Midgett, USCG," biographical sketch, and "Levene Midgett," historical data (U.S. Coast Guard Headquarters, Public Affairs Division, Washington, D.C.); Raleigh *News and Observer,* 14 Sept. 1952; Nell Wise Wechter, *The Mighty Midgetts of Chicamacomico* (1974); Don Wharton, "The Mighty Midgetts of Hatteras," *American Mercury* (August 1957).

NELL WISE WECHTER

Midgett, Little Bannister, III *(30 May 1852–24 Jan. 1928),* keeper of Chicamacomico and New Inlet stations, U.S. Life-Saving Service (1879–94), and chief boatswain's mate and officer-in-charge, Chicamacomico Coast Guard Station (1894–1916), was born at Clarks (now Salvo, N.C.) of English ancestry. He was the son of Dorothy Payne and Little Bannister Midgett II.

Young Midgett, who was living on the Outer Banks and coming of school age at the time of the general upheaval of southern institutions during the Civil War, was penalized in obtaining a formal education. All of his life he felt this limitation, blaming it on the "treasonable neglect of the Confederacy to maintain schools during the Rebellion." As he grew up, however, it became apparent that his lack of education would never hamper him in his chosen work. In his teens and early twenties, he worked as a surfman and as a surf fisherman. Both vocations were difficult and dangerous. He was an apt pupil, learning the rigors of the sea, particularly that dangerous part of the ocean, "the graveyard of the Atlantic," opposite the shores on which he lived. Already ingrained within him was the Midgett tradition of lifesaving, handed down by his grandfather and father before him.

In the 1870s the U.S. Life-Saving Service expanded its operations to include the North Carolina coast, constructing seven stations and placing the Outer Banks in the Sixth District. At that time, the stations went by number. According to the service's records, Midgett served for two seasons as a surfman in Life-Saving Station No. 20. On 7 Aug. 1879 J. W. Etheridge, superintendent of lifesaving stations in the Sixth District, sent a letter to Sumner Kimball, general superintendent of all lifesaving stations in the United States, recommending Midgett as keeper of No. 18, stating that "this man is considered to be the best surfman on the coast of North Carolina." Station No. 18 was Chicamacomico Station, built, together with two other stations on Hatteras Island, under the Congressional Enactment of 1878. In 1878 Midgett had been named contractor and supervised the building of this station. On 13 Oct. 1879 he was appointed keeper of Chicamacomico at four hundred dollars a year. He served there until 1888, when he transferred to New Inlet. In 1894 he was sent back to Chicamacomico, where he was serving when the Life-Saving Service and the Revenue Cutter Service formally merged and became the U.S. Coast Guard in 1915—a union that Midgett denounced to the day he died as "a shotgun wedding."

Midgett was a mighty man with an oar. He had an instinctive knowledge of the sea and how to use an oar in a surfboat. His logbook, in which he wrote most often in private, reflects a simplicity and directness that never shows a consciousness of his own heroism. His feats in a surfboat are legend. Of all the "Mighty Midgetts," he safely can be called the Paul Bunyan, because so many traditions have grown out of his life. A proud, yet humble man, he was descended from a long line of Outer Banks Midgetts who were not afraid of anything in the sea or out of it. It would be difficult to list all the shipwrecks in which he participated as a lifesaver. Perhaps no one will ever know for sure the exact number of lives he saved. In 1881 he rescued six survivors from the rigging of the stranded *Thomas J. Lancaster*, which broke up in a hurricane off Chicamacomico. When the *George L. Fessenden* broke into pieces off the Outer Banks in 1898, Midgett fired his Lyle gun, placing the line almost in the hands of the sailors hanging onto the boom. However, the seamen were unable to grab it because the vessel suddenly disintegrated, killing two crewmen with debris and knocking the others into the churning waters. Midgett, with his surfmen, heaved lines and succeeded in dragging three survivors from the surf.

In 1899 "San Ciriaco," the name the Puerto Ricans gave to the hurricane of 1899, spawned in the southern oceans near the equator, bred on the islands of the Caribbean, and spent most of its mature life off the Outer Banks of North Carolina. During the terrible days of that hurricane, numerous ships met their end and many lives were lost and saved. Midgett and his crew were busy night and day. When the *Aaron Reppard* wrecked, they were able to save only three of its company. Ship after ship fell apart. Midgett's logbook records the names of the vessels. Tirelessly, he and his surfmen worked, watched, and waited for opportunities to launch surfboats and to use the Lyle gun when possible; sometimes they even jumped into the surf to reach a drowning man. Midgett's philosophy was the traditional one of the Outer Banks lifesavers: "Regulations say you have to go out; regulations do not say anything about coming back." He is remembered for his honesty, his confidence that superseded fear, his love for his fellowman, and his forbearance and compassion. He left behind him, in other Midgetts, the conviction and the will to carry on the great tradition of lifesaving for which the U.S. Coast Guard is famed.

Ambitious and interested in politics, Midgett was a Republican by tradition. He was active in the Methodist church in Chicamacomico, serving in many official capacities during his lifetime. He was a Master Mason and belonged to an Elizabeth City fraternity.

He married Sabrina Midgett of Chicamacomico on 11 Jan. 1874. They had four sons and six daughters. Three of his sons—Etheridge, Dan, and Thomas—chose the U.S. Coast Guard as a career; two of his daughters married coastguardsmen. Midgett died in Manteo, where he and his wife were buried in Mount Olivet Cemetery.

SEE: General Services Administration, National Archives and Records Service, Washington, D.C.: Nomination File of L. B. Midgett, 1879, Qualification File, 1879, from Assistant Inspector to Superintendent of Life-Saving, 6th Dist., October 1879, and Appointment File, 1879, Department of Transportation, U.S. Coast Guard, Public Affairs Division, Washington, D.C.; Ben Dixon MacNeill, *The Hatterasman* (1958); David Stick, *Graveyard of the Atlantic* (1952) and *The Outer Banks* (1958); Nell Wise Wechter, *The Mighty Midgetts of Chicamacomico* (1974).

NELL WISE WECHTER

Milburn, Frank Pierce (*12 Dec. 1868–22 Sept. 1926*), architect and designer of numerous structures in most states south of the Mason-Dixon Line, was born in Bowling Green, Ky. His father, Thomas Thurmond Milburn, was a building contractor who emigrated from Scotland just after the Civil War.

Educated at Arkansas University and the Arkansas Industrial University at Fayetteville, Ark., Milburn lived from 1884 to 1889 in Louisville, Ky., where, in association with his father, he offered the services of architect and builder. In this manner Milburn and his father built the Clay County Courthouse at Manchester, Ky. From 1890 to 1893 Milburn worked in and around Kenovia, W.Va., and then moved to Winston, N.C., where he designed the Forsyth County Courthouse and Wachovia Bank building and the Mecklenburg County Courthouse at Charlotte. During the first fifteen years of practice, he designed nineteen railroad stations, including Union Station, Durham, in 1901 (demolished 1967); twenty-six county courthouses; fifteen residences; nine college buildings, of which five were for The University of North Carolina (Milburn ultimately designed thirteen halls on the campus); and churches, offices, banks, schools, and jails.

Stylistically, he was eclectic, as were his contemporaries, using one of the classic styles for governmental and college buildings and Gothic for religious structures; for other buildings, he employed a mixture of styles usually termed Queen Anne, the composition and arrangement of parts being the architect's artistic expression. He also followed in the footsteps of such nationally famed architects as H. H. Richardson, Louis Sullivan, Richard Morris Hunt, McKim, Mead, and White, and Frank Lloyd Wright.

Milburn enlarged the state capitols of Tallahassee, Fla., and Columbia, S.C., and projected another at Frankfort, Ky., and the enlargement of the North Carolina capitol at Raleigh; neither of the latter proposals was accepted. Cities in North Carolina containing Milburn buildings include Asheville (Buncombe County Courthouse, thought by Milburn's son to be his best design), Chapel Hill, Charlotte, Durham, Elizabeth City, Gastonia, Goldsboro, Greensboro, Henderson, Oak Ridge, Raleigh, Salisbury, and Winston-Salem. Many of his designs were published in a series of books, copies of which are in the Library of Congress and at The University of North Carolina. Entitled *Designs from the Work of Frank P. Milburn*, editions date from 1901, 1903, and 1905; some are undated and one dates as late as 1922 in association with Michael Heister, each publication adding information, illustrating more designs, and invariably containing a portrait. Heister joined Milburn as a partner when he moved to Washington, D.C., in 1902 to become architect of the Southern Railway Company; Milburn's son, Thomas Yancey, who was graduated from The University of North Carolina in 1915 and studied architecture at the University of Pennsylvania, joined the firm sometime before 1920.

During thirty-six years of practice, Milburn designed at least 250 major structures in addition to domestic architecture of a residential scale. He died in Asheville, N.C. Obituaries appeared in the 23 Sept. 1926 editions of the Washington *Evening Star* and the *Charlotte Observer*.

In 1890 Milburn married Lenora Lyttle, the daughter of Judge David Yancey Lyttle. They had two children. Thomas Yancey, born in Staunton, Ky., became president of the architectural firm after his father's death; the firm had an office in Durham, where he retired in 1952.

The second child, Fay C., born in Barbourville, Ky., in 1896, lived in St. Petersburg, Fla.

SEE: Archibald Henderson, *The Campus of the First State University* (1949); George Lougee, "Rails, Rust, and Station Dust," *Durham Morning Herald*, 4 Mar. 1962; *Nat. Cyc. Am. Biog.*, vol. 12 (1904); John C. Proctor, *Washington Past and Present*, vol. 3 (1932); Lawrence Wodehouse, "Frank Pierce Milburn (1868–1926): A Major Southern Architect," *North Carolina Historical Review* 50 (July 1973).

LAWRENCE WODEHOUSE

Miller, Alexander Calizance (or Calezance) *(ca. 1780–2 May 1831)*, planter and teacher, was born in France before the Revolution, served under the Prince de Condé at the Battle of Düsseldorf, and escaped to Philadelphia in 1797. His parents are unknown, but there are indications that they perished in the Reign of Terror. His French name was Alexandre Ferdinand Leopold Calizance de la Marque, according to one family tradition, Louis Leopold Calezance de la Marc, according to another, and de la Marche, according to a third; there is a notable Calasanz family in Catalonia. Miller adopted his surname from the captain of the ship that brought him from Rotterdam.

The penniless emigré made his living by exercising the genteel skills with which he had been brought up—teaching drawing, piano, and violin—first in Philadelphia and then in Warrenton, N.C., where other French refugees had settled. By 1805 Miller was teaching in the Falkener Seminary, the first boarding school for young ladies in that section of the country. He encouraged Jacob Mordecai of Richmond to open his female seminary in Warrenton in 1808. Mordecai promised, in a public broadside, to offer the students "Vocal and Instrumental Music, by an approved master, of distinguished talents and correct deportment." Miller continued at Mordecai's school until 1812, leaving a strong and lasting impression on all the Mordecais.

Meanwhile, Miller was acquiring influential friends, beginning with the Philadelphia-connected merchant, John Bradley, of Wilmington, who introduced him to leading lights of the Cape Fear area. General and Mrs. Benjamin Smith of Smithville, Dr. John Lightfoot Griffin, General-to-be Joseph Gardner Swift of the U.S. Army Engineers, Judge John Hill, George Burgwin of the Hermitage, and General and Mrs. Thomas Brown of Bladen County all were charmed by what Swift called his "remarkable personal beauty and elegance of manner." Miller painted the portraits of several. His European military experience brought him the rank of major in the North Carolina militia in 1811, no doubt unhindered by his father-in-law, General Thomas Brown, who was appointed to command the detached militia of the state when the second war with Britain broke out.

On 4 July 1811 Miller married Mary Brown, the general's daughter and John Bradley's niece, at Ashwood, one of the Brown plantation homes on the Cape Fear in Bladen County; Joseph G. Swift was the attendant at his marriage as Miller had been at Swift's, and each eventually named a son for the other. For the rest of their lives the Millers resided at Ashwood, where Alexander was a planter; the 1830 census reported that he owned twenty-one slaves. The plantation was located near the residence of Governor John Owen, who had married General Brown's other daughter, Lucy.

Alexander and Mary Miller were communicants of St. James's Episcopal Church, Wilmington, where their children were baptized. A Mason, he died at Ashwood after a wasting illness; he probably was buried in Carver's Creek Cemetery near General Brown's Oakland plantation. The children who grew to adulthood were Thomas Calizance, a prominent Unionist lawyer of Wilmington and owner of Orton plantation, who married Annie W. Davis; Dr. Joseph Swift, of Wilmington, who married Ann Empie Wooster; and August Alexander, a childless Bladen County planter. Miller descendants live in North Carolina and California.

There are indications that Ellen Mordecai was referring to Alexander Miller in his Warrenton days when she wrote in her fanciful reminiscences of "Hastings" (Warrenton): "Amongst the beaux present was one very handsome man, a foreigner who said he 'was not what he appeared' and thus investing himself in mystery became an object of universal interest among the ladies, while the 'harsher sex' had but little patience with him. He spoke most touchingly of his fallen fortunes, titles, and dignities; half hinted that the Montmorency blood flowed in his veins, said that his name was assumed, but that nothing would induce him to divulge the real one, so of course the girls were all dying to know it. He spoke of his mother as having been one of the most lovely women he had ever seen. . . . He was accomplished; that is he drew prettily and played well on the piano and violin. When he pleased he could be fascinating and when he did not he could be provokingly wayward; he was so admired by the fair sex that it was no wonder he was spoiled."

SEE: William E. Craig, "The Mysterious Frenchman: Alexander Calizance Miller in America, 1797–1831," *Lower Cape Fear Historical Society Bulletin* 29 (October 1985); Harrison Ellery, ed., *Memoirs of Gen. Joseph Gardner Swift* (1890); Ida B. Kellam and Elizabeth F. McKoy, *St. James Church Historical Records*, vol. 1 (1965); Lula W. Mathews, Leora H. McEachern, and Curry K. Walker, *St. James Church Historical Records*, vol. 2 (1976); Mordecai Family Papers (Southern Historical Collection, University of North Carolina, Chapel Hill); Claude H. Snow, Jr., "Thomas Brown," in William S. Powell, ed., *Dictionary of North Carolina Biography*, vol. 1 (1979); James Laurence Sprunt, *The Story of Orton Plantation* (1977); Esther Whitlock [Ellen Mordecai], *Fading Scenes Recalled; or, The By Gone Days of Hastings* (1847).

WILLIAM ELLWOOD CRAIG

Miller, Banner Isom *(20 Aug. 1917–23 Nov. 1976)*, meteorologist, geophysicist, and an authority on tropical storms, was born in Lansing, Ashe County, in the northwestern corner of North Carolina. He was graduated from high school in Boone, received a B.S. degree from Appalachian State Teachers College there in 1938, and taught high school in Pinehurst during 1938–39. From 1939 to 1942 he was a weather observer, briefer, and analyst successively at Charlotte, Atlanta, Ga., Washington, D.C., and Brady, Tex. When the National Weather Service (now the National Meteorological Center) was formed in 1942, Miller was the first employee to report for duty.

During World War II he was a meteorologist at the forecast station at Elizabeth City, N.C. (1943–45), from which lend-lease aircraft were flown to Europe. He next was an international aviation forecaster in Baltimore (1945–46) and at LaGuardia Field, N.Y. (1947–48).

At the end of the war Miller pursued graduate study at New York University, where he received the M.S. degree in 1947. He served as principal assistant in the San Juan, P.R., Weather Bureau Forecast Office between 1948 and 1952 and in the San Antonio, Tex., office from 1952 to 1956. In the latter year he moved to Miami, Fla., as a hurricane research forecaster at the National Hurricane Center, where he served for four years. During that time he continued his graduate studies, receiving a Ph.D. degree from the University of Chicago in 1963. Still in Miami, he held a series of positions involving the investigation and prediction of hurricanes. From 1971 until his retirement in 1975, he was chief of research and development at the National Hurricane Center. There he developed numerical models for hurricane prediction and analysis, statistical prediction of the course of hurricanes, their structure and dynamics, energy transformations in tropical weather systems, and air-sea interactions. Miller was the first to discover why hurricanes weaken over land—the low-level inflow into a hurricane over land is chiefly a moist-adiabatic process causing a reduced energy source. This discounted the previous belief that increased friction caused the weakening.

Miller wrote a number of technical reports published by the U.S. Department of Commerce and in the journals and proceedings of such organizations as the American Association for the Advancement of Science and the American Meteorological Society. He also was the principal author of *Hurricane Forecasting*, a Weather Bureau manual. With Gordon E. Dunn he was coauthor of *Atlantic Hurricanes*, published by the Louisiana State University Press in 1960 and revised in 1964. In 1968 he received the Silver Medal from the Department of Commerce for his pioneering work in developing statistical hurricane prediction models.

His first wife was Sue Rice, whom he married in 1947. In 1973 he married Ailsa Eliza Lewis Luza. There were no children. A Presbyterian, Miller maintained a home in Boone as well as in Florida. He died in Miami Springs, Fla.

SEE: American Meteorological Society, *Eleventh Technical Conference on Hurricanes and Tropical Meteorology* (1977 [portrait]); *Nat. Cyc. Am. Biog.*, vol. 59 (1980 [portrait]); *Winston-Salem Journal*, 25 Nov. 1976.

MARK D. BARDILL

Miller, Helen Topping (*8 Dec. 1884–4 Feb. 1960*), novelist, was born in Fenton, Mich., the daughter of Isaac Wallace and Maria Augusta Chipman Topping. She was the niece of John Dewey, the philosopher. Helen began writing stories as a child and had one published in *St. Nicholas* when she was fifteen. After graduating from Michigan Agricultural College (later Michigan State University) in 1905, she taught school in Michigan for two years. She moved with her family to Morristown, Tenn., in 1908 and lived there until 1910, when she married Frank Roger Miller, a journalist and Chamber of Commerce official.

After her marriage she lived for several years in Macon, Ga., where she taught for a time at Mercer University, meanwhile writing short stories, serials, and poems for several national magazines. From 1924 to 1942 she made her home at Arrowhill, near Asheville; at different times during this period she also maintained homes in Washington, D.C., and Dallas, Tex. In 1942 the Millers bought a century-old home—which she renamed Arrowhill Farm—near Morristown, Tenn., where she lived for the remainder of her life. Her husband died in 1944.

Mrs. Miller's first book-length novel was *Sharon*

(1931), a light romance that achieved modest success. It was followed by similar ones, such as *White Peacock* (1932), *Blue Marigolds* (1933), and *Splendor of Eagles* (1935). In all, she wrote over 40 works of light fiction. By 1949 she reported that she had written and published more than 30 books, 11 serials, and 314 short stories.

After 1945 Mrs. Miller varied her light romances with historical fiction. The first of these was *Dark Sails: A Tale of Old St. Simons*, a novel of the South Carolina coast in the nineteenth century. This was followed by *The Sound of Chariots: A Novel of John Sevier and the State of Franklin* (1947) and *Rebellion Road: A Civil War Novel* (1954). In the latter case, she completed a novel begun by her brother, John Dewey Topping, but left unfinished at his early death.

Still a third type of fiction appeared in the 1950s with Mrs. Miller's successful stories of Christmas at the homes of famous men. This series began with *Christmas at the Hermitage: A Tale about Rachel and Andrew Jackson* (1955), followed by others such as *Christmas with Robert E. Lee* (1958) and *Christmas at Mount Vernon* (1957).

An Episcopalian and a lifelong Republican, she was a member of the Authors League of America, the Daughters of the American Revolution, and the Tennessee Press Writers Club. She died at her home in Tennessee. The Millers had two children: John Wallace (1913) and Frank Eugene (1917).

SEE: David J. Harkness, *Tennessee in Literature* (1949); *New York Times*, 5 Feb. 1960; *North Carolina Authors: A Selective Handbook* (1952); Martha E. Ward, *Authors of Books for Young People* (1979); Harry E. Warfel, *American Novelists of Today* (1951); *Who Was Who in America*, vol. 3 (1960).

E. D. JOHNSON

Miller, John Fulenwider (*25 Dec. 1834–9 Jan. 1906*), physician, was born in Rutherford (now Cleveland) County of Scotch-Irish descent. His father, William John Twitty Miller, was a prominent physician and planter who served in the state legislature; his mother, Elizabeth Fulenwider Miller, was a native of Lincoln County. John spent his childhood on a plantation in the foothills of southwestern North Carolina, where he obtained his earliest schooling in nearby Shelby. Later he attended Cokesbury High School in South Carolina and then The University of North Carolina (1854–55). He received medical instruction from his father before taking his first course of study at the Medical College of the State of South Carolina and his second course at the Jefferson Medical College of Philadelphia, from which he received a medical degree in 1858.

Returning to North Carolina, Miller practiced medicine with his father until the outbreak of the Civil War, when he promptly enlisted in the Cleveland Guards as a private on 22 Apr. 1861. After one month's service he was appointed assistant surgeon of the Twelfth North Carolina Regiment. Promoted to surgeon of the Thirty-fourth North Carolina Regiment in June 1862, he served in this post until August 1864, when he was commissioned an examiner of hospitals for the Army of Northern Virginia. In December 1864 he was appointed chief surgeon of the Department of Eastern North Carolina and Southern Virginia and attached to General L. H. Baker's staff. He was serving in this capacity when, in 1865, General William T. Sherman's column under the command of General O. O. Howard found him at Louisburg, tending the wounded. Choosing to surrender rather than leave the wounded in Howard's care,

Miller became a prisoner of war. He received his parole in Goldsboro on 12 May 1865.

After the war he settled in Goldsboro and maintained a private practice in general medicine until 1 Jan. 1888, when he assumed the duties of superintendent of what became Cherry Hospital, a state institution for insane blacks at Goldsboro. He held this position until his death eighteen years later. That he was a most capable director is evident from the history of the Goldsboro institution and from the reports of the Examiners of State Institutions.

Miller's single contribution to medical literature was embodied in his article published by the *North Carolina Medical Journal* in 1896, entitled "The Effects of Emancipation upon the Mental and Physical Health of the Negro of the South." He also presented papers on the same topic before the Medico-Psychological Association at Asheville in 1896 and the Tri-State Medical Society in Charleston, S.C., in 1902. Some considered Dr. Miller a pioneer writer on the insanity of the Negro, whereas others believed he was a representative of that segment of the scientific community that helped foster concepts of racial inferiority. In attempting to explain the alleged increase in black insanity after emancipation, he stated that while the Negro could live in comfort "under less favorable circumstances than the white man, having a nervous organization less sensitive to his environments, yet it is true that he has less mental equipoise, and may suffer mental alienation from influences and agencies which would not affect a race mentally stronger."

A devout Methodist, Miller was frequently a delegate to the annual conference of his church and became president of the Advocate Publishing Company, the literary organ of the North Carolina Conference. After suffering slightly for some time from heart disease, he died at his home on the hospital grounds at Goldsboro. He was buried in Willowdale Cemetery.

On 21 Sept. 1863 he married Sarah Lavinia Borden of Goldsboro; she died on 8 Aug. 1901. Their family included five sons, John, Charles, Hugh, Frank, and Robert; and three daughters, Mary, Bessie, and Louisa.

SEE: Samuel A. Ashe, ed., *Biographical History of North Carolina*, vol. 1 (1905 [portrait]); John Spencer Bassett Papers (Manuscript Department, Duke University Library, Durham); John S. Haller, *Outcasts from Evolution* (1971); North Carolina Medical Society, *Transactions* (1906).

SUSAN TUCKER HATCHER

Miller, Julian Sidney (27 Nov. 1886–28 July 1946), newspaper editor, was born in the New Hope Church community of Fairfield County, S.C., the son of the Reverend Robert Grier Miller, D.D., and his wife, Roberta Emmons. His father was one of the most prominent ministers in the Associate Reformed Presbyterian church. While Julian was still a small child, his family moved to the Sardis Church community, near Charlotte in Mecklenburg County, where his father served as pastor of the Sardis Church for nearly forty years. From 1902 to 1903 he attended The University of North Carolina, then transferred to Erskine College in Due West, S.C., from which he was graduated in the class of 1906.

Soon afterwards Miller traveled to Butler, Pa., where he found employment on the local newspaper. After a short time, however, he returned to Charlotte and in late 1906 joined the staff of the *Charlotte Observer*. He worked for the *Observer* until 1915, when he was appointed editor of the *Charlotte News*. Meanwhile, on 13

Jan. 1913, Miller had married Fannie Belle Faulkner of the Sardis Church community. They became the parents of three sons (one of whom was killed in World War II) and two daughters.

In 1931 Miller stepped down as city editor and editor of the *Charlotte News* to become the director of public relations for federal relief in North Carolina during the administration of Governor O. Max Gardner. He served briefly before his appointment in 1933 as associate editor of the *Charlotte Observer*. In 1935, on the death of Colonel Wade H. Harris, Miller was named to succeed him as editor. He served in this capacity until his own death.

Over time Miller became widely recognized for his contributions as editor, editorialist, and public servant. In 1930 he was awarded a doctor of laws degree by Erskine College as one of its most distinguished alumni. As his prominence grew, so did the importance of his editorials. A number of them—republished in other papers and as pamphlets and articles—wielded much influence. For example, he warned of the impending global crisis of World War II when many still believed it was a "phony war"; he urgently appealed for the increased support of orphanages; he called for continued support of the New Deal; and he especially wrote in favor of improving and expanding public education. A Democrat, Miller was chairman of the Governor's Commission on Education in 1938–39, served many terms on his local county board of education, and was appointed to the State Board of Education in 1943.

Among his other accomplishments, Miller was elected vice-president (1939) and president (1944–45) of the North Carolina Press Association; served as president of the Charlotte Community Chest (1938–40) and of the North Carolina Conference of Social Service; and was a member of the promotion committee of the Southern Conference on Human Relations in Industry, a trustee of Erskine College, and an honorary member of the Omicron Delta Kappa chapter at Davidson College. A powerful public speaker, he used this ability particularly in campaigning for any movements promoting the advancement of the educational system of North Carolina. For the last two years of his life, Miller was less active due to poor health caused by a heart condition. He died of a heart attack in Lumberton while returning to Charlotte from a vacation with his family.

SEE: *Charlotte Observer*, 29 July 1946; Jack Claiborne, *The Charlotte Observer* (1986); Daniel L. Grant, *Alumni History of the University of North Carolina, 1795–1924* (1924); *Greensboro Daily News*, 30 July 1946; Julian Sidney Miller, "Bleeding to Death" (reprint of an editorial in the *Charlotte Observer* [n.d.], in the North Carolina Collection, University of North Carolina, Chapel Hill), and "The South Is Still Solid," *Review of Reviews* (1936); *The Uplift*, 3 Aug. 1946; *Who Was Who in America*, vol. 2 (1950).

MICHAEL WESLEY HICKMAN

Miller, Oscar Lee (7 July 1887–10 Dec. 1970), orthopedic surgeon and teacher, was born on a small farm in Franklin County near the community of Carnesville in northeastern Georgia, the oldest of ten children of John Clarence Calhoun (1850–1913) and Florence McWhorter Miller (1868–1939). As a youth he helped on the family farm, attended rural schools, passed a teacher's examination, and taught school for several years. After attending the University of Georgia for two years, he studied medicine at Atlanta College of Physicians and Surgeons, receiving the M.D. degree in 1912, shortly before the medical college became a part of Emory University. He completed his internship and residency at the Piedmont Hospital, Atlanta, where he came under the stimulating influence of Dr. Michael Hoke, a distinguished pioneer of orthopedic surgery in the South. Miller received further training at Massachusetts General Hospital and Children's Hospital in Boston before returning to Atlanta in 1915 to join Hoke in orthopedic practice.

In 1917 Miller volunteered for service in the army during World War I. He became a captain and orthopedic inspector for camps in five southern states. After the armistice he returned to orthopedic practice and teaching with Dr. Hoke. In 1918 Miller married Rose Evans of Thomasville, Ga.

Miller moved from Georgia to North Carolina in 1921, when he was chosen first surgeon-in-chief and director of the North Carolina Orthopaedic Hospital for crippled children, then under construction in Gastonia. Under his direction this institution grew in a few years from its initial capacity of 50 beds to 150. It also developed a national reputation for effective treatment in the days before antibiotics and immunization, when wards were crowded with children suffering from the ravages of osteomyelitis, tuberculosis of the bones and joints, and infantile paralysis, and when few hospitals could offer facilities for the prolonged treatment required by these crippling maladies.

In addition, Miller in 1923 opened, in nearby Charlotte, a private office that grew to become the well-known Miller Clinic. He also played a large part in the development of statewide orthopedic services for the medically indigent. In the mid-twenties such care was provided by the orthopedic hospital at Gastonia and its monthly eastern clinic in Goldsboro, and by clinics in a dozen other communities operated with the help of the State Department of Vocational Rehabilitation. This work was greatly expanded when the federal Social Security Act of 1935, with the guidance of the U.S. Children's Bureau, provided grants-in-aid to the states to support public clinics and hospitalization for crippled children. With the cooperation of many other individuals and groups, Miller assisted the Crippled Children's Division of the State Board of Health in establishing a system of monthly orthopedic clinics throughout North Carolina. After Duke University established its medical school, Miller cooperated with its first professor of orthopedics, Dr. Alfred Rives Shands, Jr., in the training of students and resident physicians. Not a formal lecturer but an experienced and judicious clinician, Miller taught effectively by precept and energetic example. In 1932 he moved to Charlotte after turning over the North Carolina Orthopaedic Hospital to Dr. William McKinley Roberts, who had been its first resident orthopedist and who remained its second surgeon-in-chief until his death in 1973.

Miller published more than 170 articles on clinical orthopedics and related subjects and was active in a number of professional organizations. He was a member of the American Orthopaedic Association and the American Surgical Association as well as several international groups. He served as chairman of both the Southern Medical and the American Medical associations. As president of the American Academy of Orthopaedic Surgeons in 1941, he was instrumental in introducing the academy's extensive annual program of postgraduate instructional lectures for the continuing education of its members. For twelve years Miller was a consultant to the National Foundation for Infantile Paralysis. He served for ten years on the National Advisory Committee of the social security program for crippled children

and for three years was chairman of the committee. In 1943, as orthopedic consultant for the Children's Bureau, he inspected medical schools and hospitals in Mexico, Central America, and South America, where he promoted the organization of crippled children's services and inter-American orthopedic exchange fellowships. In connection with this work he received a citation from Frances Perkins, Secretary of Labor.

Miller was one of ten doctors on the medical advisory committee that helped found Charlotte Memorial Hospital and for a number of years was chief of its orthopedic service. He served the Myers Park Presbyterian Church in Charlotte as a ruling elder for more than thirty years. He was a Thirty-second-degree Mason, a Shriner, and an honorary life member of Oasis Temple.

Beginning in 1965, Miller's health deteriorated slowly until his death in Charlotte at age eighty-three. Buried in Forest Lawn Cemetery, Charlotte, he was survived by his wife, Rose Evans Miller, and their four children: Mrs. B. Gales McClintock of Greenwood, S.C.; the Reverend John Neel Miller of Greenville, N.C.; Dr. Oscar Lee Miller, Jr., a biologist with the National Laboratory at Oak Ridge, Tenn.; and Dr. Robert Evans Miller, who continued the orthopedic tradition of his father in Charlotte.

SEE: *Charlotte News*, 11, 14 Dec. 1970; *Charlotte Observer*, 28 June 1940, 6 July 1941, 12, 15 Dec. 1970; Charles J. Frankel and R. Beverly Raney, "Oscar Lee Miller, 1887–1970," *Journal of Bone and Joint Surgery* 53-A (1971 [portrait]); Kays Gary, "A Vigorous Life of Healing," *Charlotte Observer*, 24 Sept. 1981; Maude Miller Hayes, *John Clarence Calhoun Miller Family* (1961); Julian E. Jacobs, "Oscar Lee Miller, M.D.," *American Academy of Orthopaedic Surgeons Bulletin* (December 1962); "In Memoriam: Oscar Lee Miller, M.D.," *North Carolina Medical Journal* 32 (1971).

R. BEVERLY RANEY
DOROTHY LONG

Miller, Robert Johnstone *(11 July 1758–13 May 1834)*, clergyman, was born in Baldovie, Scotland (near Dundee), the son of George and Margaret Bathier Miller. The family adhered to the "Jacobite" Episcopal church of Scotland, and Miller attended a classical school in Dundee in preparation for the ministry. However, in 1774 he immigrated to America at the urging of an older brother, who was a prosperous merchant in Charlestown, Mass. Miller soon enlisted on the American side in the Revolutionary War, seeing action on Long Island and in the battles of White Plains and Brandywine. After the war he settled in Virginia and preached on a Methodist circuit for one year.

In 1786 Miller moved to Lincoln County, N.C., where the climate better suited his health, but he also had connections with Burke County, which he represented in the 1788 constitutional convention as an anti-Federalist. Having left the Methodists because he disapproved of their separation from the Church of England, he became a lay reader at White Haven, a church that generally conformed to Anglican practice, located one mile south of Lowesville. Miller established cordial relations with Lutherans in the area, approving of the liturgical nature of their worship. Seeking a firmer ecclesiastical basis for his pastoral duties, he was ordained by a group of Lutheran ministers assembled at St. John's Lutheran Church in Cabarrus County on 20 May 1794. He also served as a lay reader for Episcopal services.

Miller's chief religious loyalties were with the Protestant Episcopal church, the successor to the Church of England in the United States. On 28 May 1794 he attended an Episcopal convention in Tarboro, where the Reverend Charles Pettigrew was elected bishop of North Carolina. But Pettigrew never actually assumed that office and the Episcopal church in North Carolina remained largely unorganized until 1817. Until then, Miller served in Lutheran rather than Episcopal churches. He traveled in Virginia, Tennessee, and South Carolina as a missionary for the Lutheran Synod of North Carolina and preached to congregations in Burke, Iredell, Lincoln, and Rowan counties. In 1787 he had married Mary Perkins, the daughter of John Perkins of Lincoln County, and in 1806 he moved to a farm, which he named "Mary's Grove," located two miles from Lenoir. They had seven sons and three daughters.

On 1 May 1821 Miller was ordained to the priesthood at an Episcopal convention in Raleigh, and on 17 June he resigned from the Lutheran Synod of North Carolina. Thereafter until his death he worked to establish the Protestant Episcopal church on a firm basis in western North Carolina. He was buried at Mary's Grove.

SEE: Samuel A. Ashe, ed., *Biographical History of North Carolina*, vol. 4 (1906); G. D. Bernheim and George H. Cox, *The History of the Evangelical Lutheran Synod and Ministerium of North Carolina* (1902); D. L. Corbitt, ed., "The Robert J. Miller Letters, 1813–1831," *North Carolina Historical Review* 25 (1948); Edward W. Phifer, Jr., *Burke: The History of a North Carolina County* (1982); *Sketches of Church History in North Carolina: Addresses and Papers by Clergymen and Laymen of the Dioceses of North and East Carolina* (1892); Willard E. Wright, ed., "The Journals of the Reverend Robert J. Miller, Lutheran Missionary in Virginia, 1811 and 1813," *Virginia Magazine of History and Biography* 61 (1953).

JOHN B. WEAVER

Miller, Robert Morrison, Jr. *(20 Apr. 1856–11 Oct. 1925),* textile manufacturer and capitalist, was born in Pleasant Valley, Lancaster County, S.C., the son of Robert Morrison and Ann Elizabeth Cureton Miller. His father was a planter, large slave owner, and merchant in South Carolina who served as a major in the Confederate army. After moving his family to Charlotte in 1866, he entered the wholesale and retail merchandising business, bringing flour and meat by railway car from the West.

Young Miller was graduated from Finley High School in Lenoir and in 1876 received a bachelor's degree from Davidson College, where he won a medal for declamation. He and his brother, Roland A., were associates in their father's business, R. M. Miller and Sons, for six years. At that point Robert left the company to establish, with D. A. Tompkins, a mill machinery firm that was to become a key factor in Charlotte's development as a cotton manufacturing center. Ten years later, in 1892, he and Tompkins became pioneers in the spinning of fine cotton yarns in the South at the Atherton Cotton Mills. By 1898 Miller had progressed to even finer yarns at his newly built and model Elizabeth Mills, two miles outside of Charlotte. He had served as vice-president and treasurer of the first two businesses and was president and treasurer of his new mill. During his career, he held similar positions in many other companies including the Chester and the Catawba mills, Millerton Homes, the Buford Hotel, and Buford Homes.

In addition, Miller was a longtime chairman of the tariff and legislative committee, board member, and presi-

dent (1905–6) of the American Cotton Manufacturers Association; an organizer and president for the first five years of the state's Cotton Manufacturers Association (later the North Carolina Textile Association); and an officer in other regional and national trade organizations, including the Cotton Manufacturers Publishing Company. He was a director of two Charlotte banks and of the Federal Reserve Bank; a member of the Charlotte Cotton Exchange and of the Charlotte Board of Trade, and a member and president of the Charlotte Chamber of Commerce; a member and officer of manufacturers' clubs in Charlotte and in Philadelphia; a supporter of the scholarship program in the textile department of North Carolina College of Agricultural and Mechanic Arts (now North Carolina State University); a member and president of the Mecklenburg War Records Association; and president of the Davidson College General Alumni Association for several terms.

Before his death Miller had retired from all of his positions of responsibility except that of vice-president and director of Union National Bank in Charlotte and head of the Port Terminal Special Study Commission. He had been appointed to the latter post by Governor Cameron Morrison, on authority of the General Assembly, to determine the feasibility of establishing and maintaining ocean ports and terminals on North Carolina's coast. Miller, who suffered from a chronic heart condition, died while he and his wife were vacationing in Atlantic City, N.J.

On 6 Feb. 1890 Miller married Estelle Ross, the daughter of John Patterson and Sara Oliver Ross of Charlotte. Their only child, Sara Elizabeth, became the wife of David Wills Hunter, who was connected with the Saco-Lowell Shops in Boston and afterwards resided in Rock Hill, S.C. The only other surviving relative was his sister, Mrs. Lilias B. Miller Wheeler of Danville, Va. He was buried in Elmwood Cemetery, Charlotte.

SEE: Samuel A. Ashe, ed., *Biographical History of North Carolina*, vol. 8 (1917 [portrait]); *Charlotte Observer*, 11 Feb. 1908, 12 Oct. 1925; *Davidson College Alumni Catalogue*, Class of 1876; E. Everton Foster, ed., *Lamb's Textile Industries of the United States*, vol. 2 (1916 [portrait]); *North Carolina Biography*, vol. 3 (1956); *Prominent People of North Carolina* (1906 [portrait]); Marjorie W. Young, ed., *Textile Leaders of the South* (1963).

CLARA HAMLETT ROBERTSON FLANNAGAN

Miller, Smith *(30 May 1804–21 Mar. 1872),* congressman, was born near Charlotte in Mecklenburg County. In 1813 he moved with his parents to Pakota in Gibson County, Ind. After receiving only limited schooling, he engaged primarily in farming.

Active in politics, Miller won a seat in the Indiana State House of Representatives, where he served in 1835–39 and again in 1846. He was a member of the Indiana Senate in 1841–44 and 1847–50 and a delegate to the Indiana state constitutional convention of 1850. Miller moved into national politics with his election as a Democrat to the Thirty-third and Thirty-fourth Congresses (4 Mar. 1853–3 Mar. 1857). In 1860 he was a delegate to the Democratic National Convention in Charleston, S.C. After serving in Congress, Miller returned to his farm in Pakota. He died nearby and was buried in the Robb Cemetery.

SEE: *Biog. Dir. Am. Cong.* (1950); *Who Was Who in America*, historical vol. (1967).

MICHAEL WESLEY HICKMAN

Miller, Stephen Franks (22 Nov. 1805–22 Oct. 1873), author, lawyer, and journalist, was born in Jones County seven miles from Trenton, the son of James Miller. When he was seven, he attended a school at the end of Parsons Lane, in Jones County, where he was taught by John Alonzo Attmore. At age seventeen, Miller left the farm where he had been raised and moved to New Bern. There he worked as a clerk for Samuel Simpson, with responsibility for the warehouse and wharf connected with Simpson's shipping interests, until 1824, when he moved to Georgia.

Miller studied law and was admitted to the bar at age twenty-two. He then practiced law in Twiggs County, Ga., until the Georgia legislature elected him solicitor general of the Southern Circuit. After serving in that post for four years, he moved to Livingston, Ala., where he practiced law and occasionally wrote for newspapers. In 1840 he became editor of a Whig journal, the *Independent Monitor*, a position he held until 1847. He published an article, "The Heads of the Alabama Legislature," in 1843. In 1847 Miller moved to New Orleans, La., and became statistical editor of *DeBow's Review* and an associate in the editorial management of the *Daily Commercial Times*.

Because of failing health, Miller moved to Oglethorpe, Ga., in 1849. While he was living in Oglethorpe, his two-volume work, *The Bench and Bar of Georgia*, was published in 1858. Soon afterwards, he sent copies to President David L. Swain of The University of North Carolina for the university library—these volumes are now located in the library's North Carolina Collection. During these years, Miller also wrote *Wilkins Wyler; or, The Successful Man* (1860), *Memoir of the Late General Blackshear* (1858), and "Recollections of New Bern of Fifty Years Ago," which appeared in Stephen Pool's *Our Living and Our Dead* (1874). For a while during the Civil War, he was editor of the *Southern Recorder* in Milledgeville, Ga.

In addition, Miller was the author of many essays, tracts, and literary addresses and reportedly maintained a library of pamphlets and documents bound in fifty volumes. He assisted William Garrett with the compilation of *Reminiscences of Public Men in Georgia* (1872); in the preface, Garrett acknowledged that Miller's pamphlet collection had been invaluable in writing the book. While gathering information on various collections in 1901, the Alabama Historical Society was told by some of Miller's relatives that his library had been destroyed.

Miller was married as a young man and had a son, D. James A., who later lived in Wilmington, N.C. His first wife died in 1860, and in 1862 he married Jane J. Windsor. Miller died in Columbus, Ga., after having been basically an invalid for twenty-five years. Volume 4 of *Appleton's Cyclopedia of American Biography* (1888) and the *National Cyclopedia of American Biography* (1899) wrongly state that Miller died in 1867.

SEE: *Appleton's Cyclopedia of American Biography*, vol. 4 (1888); C. C. Clay Papers, Georgia Portfolio, and James D. B. DeBow Letters and Papers (Manuscript Department, Duke University Library, Durham); William Garrett, *Reminiscences of Public Men in Georgia* (1872); Stephen F. Miller, *The Bench and Bar of Georgia* (1858) and "Recollections of New Bern of Fifty Years Ago," in Stephen Pool, ed., *Our Living and Our Dead*, vol. 1 (1874); *National Cyclopedia of American Biography* (1899); *Publications of the Alabama Historical Society*, misc. collections, vol. 1 (1901); Benjamin Yancey Collection and Gaston Papers (Southern Historical Collection, University of North Carolina, Chapel Hill).

PATRICIA J. MILLER

Miller, Thomas (d. ca. 1685), acting governor, Council member, secretary, and customs collector, was in North Carolina (then called Albemarle) by 1 Mar. 1672/73. On that date he contracted for shipment of a large quantity of tobacco from Albemarle to England and for his own passage.

In his contract Miller was identified as an apothecary of "Balley Samson in the County of Waxford in Ireland." In other documents related to the shipment, he was identified as a merchant. He seems to have had a fair education and to have had influential connections with the Lords Proprietors of Carolina, with whom he apparently was associated as early as 1669. His behavior, however, did not reflect gentle birth. He was given to vulgar, offensive remarks, and as an official he was abusive and domineering.

In the spring of 1673 Miller sailed from Albemarle on the brigantine *Good Hope of Albemarle*, bound for England with his tobacco, which he expected to sell in either England or Ireland. The voyage, however, was interrupted in New England, where Miller instituted court action against the master and part owner of the brigantine, Robert Risco. In his suit, Miller charged that the *Good Hope* was not seaworthy, and he accused Risco of not acting in good faith and other misdoings. In the trial, held in Suffolk County, Mass., a jury found for Risco. Miller appealed the verdict, but the higher court upheld the lower court. By the time the suit was settled, it was mid-fall. Miller apparently abandoned his trip to England and sold his tobacco in Massachusetts, for he was back in Albemarle in November.

Miller was soon in court again, this time as defendant. In November 1673 he was brought before an Albemarle magistrate on the charge of making treasonable remarks about the king and his family. The charge was dismissed, on the ground of insufficient evidence, by a magistrate who, in dismissing the case, remarked that Miller was always saying such things as those charged but meant nothing by them. The case, however, had political aspects of a local nature, for Miller was prominent in the political faction led by Thomas Eastchurch, who was then seeking to oust the acting governor of Albemarle, John Jenkins, and take his place. The charge against Miller was brought by one of Jenkins's supporters, while the magistrate in the case belonged to the Eastchurch-Miller faction.

About two years later Miller made another appearance in court, having been charged with blasphemy as well as treasonable remarks. In March 1675/76 he was indicted on those charges and imprisoned pending trial. In May he was taken to Virginia for trial on the order of Sir William Berkeley, who was one of the Lords Proprietors of Carolina as well as governor of Virginia. Miller was acquitted in a trial held by Berkeley and the Virginia Council. After his acquittal, Miller sailed for England. In London he joined Thomas Eastchurch, who had gone there earlier, and the two presented to the Proprietors their version of Albemarle affairs.

In November 1676 the Proprietors issued commissions appointing Eastchurch governor of Albemarle and naming Miller a Council member and register, or secretary, of the colony. In addition to his commissions from the Proprietors, Miller obtained from Crown officials an appointment as customs collector for Albemarle.

In the spring of 1677 Miller and Eastchurch left England to assume their respective offices in Albemarle. They interrupted their voyage at Nevis, where Eastchurch met a wealthy woman and married her. Wishing to remain longer at Nevis, Eastchurch sent Miller to govern Albemarle in his stead, giving Miller a commission naming him president of the Council and acting governor. In so doing, Eastchurch ignored the fact that he had not qualified as governor of Albemarle and consequently had no legal authority to issue such a commission.

Miller reached Albemarle in mid-July 1677. He was opposed with arms by a group of colonists, whose long-standing hostility towards him was intensified by the belief that his commission from Eastchurch was invalid. Miller called out the militia, but few responded, so he hired a guard composed chiefly of Virginians who had participated in the recent Bacon's Rebellion and had fled to Albemarle to escape punishment. Supported by his guard, Miller assumed office as governor. Almost immediately he increased his opposition by abusing the power he had seized. He further antagonized the colonists in his role as customs collector, for he and his assistants zealously collected the detested "penny-per-pound tax" on tobacco, about which their predecessors had been lax.

Among the abuses alleged against Miller were the institution of illegal court procedures through which heavy fines were laid on those who had formerly opposed Eastchurch; illegal imposition of restrictive election procedures and eligibility rules that barred election of his opponents to the Assembly; charging the cost of his armed guard against the public treasury; and levying unusually high taxes, which the colonists considered ruinous.

In early December 1677 Albemarle colonists rose against Miller and imprisoned him and most other officials in his government. After electing a new Assembly and Council, they set up a court to try Miller for his alleged offenses. The trial, however, was interrupted by the arrival of a proclamation from Thomas Eastchurch, who had reached Virginia on his way to Albemarle. On learning of recent events in Albemarle, Eastchurch had decided to remain in Virginia and send a proclamation to Albemarle. In his proclamation, he ordered Miller's release and return to office, but Miller was returned to prison instead. Soon afterwards Eastchurch became ill and died in Virginia. Miller remained in prison for nearly two years, during which time the Albemarle colonists governed themselves.

By August 1679 the Proprietors had restored de jure government in Albemarle. Under authority of the new government Miller was brought before the Palatine's court, which heard testimony against him and remanded him to prison to await further proceedings. That trial, like the earlier one, was never completed, for Miller, with the aid of friends, escaped from prison and fled to Virginia, where he took passage to England.

Miller arrived in England in December 1679. On reaching London, he began a flow of complaints to customs officials and others against Albemarle colonists. His chief target of complaint was John Culpeper, whom the Albemarle colonists had appointed to replace Miller as customs collector. Culpeper, who happened to be in England when Miller arrived, was arrested on Miller's complaint and indicted on a charge of treason for participating in Miller's overthrow and for assuming the office of customs collector. Miller also effected the arrest of Zachary Gillam, a New England trader then in London, whose arrival in Albemarle with a shipload of arms had facilitated the 1677 uprising. The charges against Gillam were soon dismissed, and Culpeper, after a longer trial, was acquitted. Contrary to Miller's expectation, the Lords Proprietors testified at Culpeper's trial that Miller had seized power in Albemarle unlawfully and had committed many illegal acts, so that neither his overthrow nor Culpeper's part in it was treasonable.

Although Miller failed to secure the conviction of

Culpeper and Gillam, he was rewarded for his efforts. In response to numerous petitions from him, treasury officials ordered monthly payments to Miller for more than a year. In all, he received more than £244 for his maintenance and as compensation for "his great sufferings" in Albemarle. A series of petitions for reappointment to a customs post also was effective. In March 1680/81 Miller was appointed customs collector of Poole, and in July 1682 he was transferred to a more lucrative post at Weymouth.

Miller's renewed career as customs collector was also brief. By 14 May 1684 he had been removed from office and imprisoned for mishandling funds. He died in prison before October 1685. Available records do not show whether he ever married.

SEE: Timothy Bigg, "A Narrative of the Transactions . . . in . . . Albemarle . . .," 1678, British Records, and *Miller v. Risco* Papers (North Carolina State Archives, Raleigh); Mattie Erma E. Parker, "Legal Aspects of Culpeper's Rebellion," *North Carolina Historical Review* 45 (April 1968); Mattie Erma E. Parker, ed., *North Carolina Higher-Court Records, 1670–1696* (1968); Herbert Richard Paschal, "Proprietary North Carolina: A Study in Colonial Government" (Ph.D. diss., University of North Carolina, 1961); Hugh F. Rankin, *Upheaval in Albemarle: The Story of Culpeper's Rebellion, 1675–1689* (1962); William L. Saunders, ed., *Colonial Records of North Carolina*, vol. 1 (1886).

MATTIE ERMA E. PARKER

Miller, Thomas (d. 1694), Council member and justice of county court, settled in North Carolina (then called Albemarle) before 6 Feb. 1683/84. By that date he was a member of the Albemarle Council, a position that he held, at least intermittently, through 1689. From February 1683/84 through October 1685 he also sat as a justice of the county court of Albemarle, then the highest court of law in the colony.

Miller, who lived in Pasquotank Precinct, had four sons: Thomas, Jr., William, Richard, and Nathaniel. His wife's name is unknown. He died before 16 July 1694, when his will, made the previous February, was probated. He bequeathed all of his land and most of his movable property to his son Thomas, leaving legacies of money to his other sons, who appear to have been mariners shipping out of Virginia ports.

Thomas, Jr., who also was a mariner, had lived in Albemarle only intermittently before his father's death, but he returned and settled on the plantation on Pasquotank River that he had inherited. He served as associate justice of the General Court from 1712 to 1721 with the possible exception of the years 1717 and 1720, for which records are incomplete. He died before 27 July 1727, when his will was probated. If he had a wife and children they apparently died before 1722, when he made his will, for he left his entire estate to one William Wilson, whose wife's mother appears to have been related to him.

SEE: Act of Assembly against "Probious" Language, 1689, and Council Order for Election of Burgesses in Chowan, 10 July 1689, in Colonial Court Records, box 192 (North Carolina State Archives, Raleigh); Albemarle Book of Warrants and Surveys, 1681–1706, Albemarle County Papers, 1678–1714, Land Grants to Francis Tomes in Perquimans County Deeds, book A, Wills of Thomas Miller, Sr., probated 16 July 1694, and Thomas Miller, Jr., probated 27 July 1727 (North Carolina State Archives, Raleigh); J. Bryan Grimes, ed., *Abstract of North Carolina Wills* (1910); J. R. B. Hathaway, ed., *North*

Carolina Historical and Genealogical Register, 3 vols. (1900–1903); Mattie Erma E. Parker, ed., *North Carolina Higher-Court Records, 1670–1696* and *1697–1701* (1968–71); William S. Price, Jr., ed., *North Carolina Higher-Court Minutes, 1709–1723* (1977); William L. Saunders, ed., *Colonial Records of North Carolina*, vol. 3 (1886).

MATTIE ERMA E. PARKER

Miller, William (*1783/84–10 Sept. 1825*), governor, legislator, and diplomatic agent, was born in Warren County, the second son of Thomas Miller, Jr., and his first wife, who appears to have been a daughter of Allen Love of Brunswick County, Va. His grandfather, Thomas, moved to North Carolina sometime between 1766 and 1771; his father, the younger Thomas, was co-partner in a firm of merchants and owned extensive land and slaves in both Virginia and North Carolina. At age nine, when his father died, William Miller inherited a plantation of 930 acres. Having apparently attended the Warrenton Male Academy conducted by the Reverend Marcus George, Miller enrolled at The University of North Carolina in 1802 but did not remain until graduation. By 1809 he was living in Warrenton, where he owned property and probably was practicing law. About this time he may have met his future wife, Lydia Anna (or Lydiana) Evans, of Chesterfield County, Va., as she was a student in 1809–10 at Jacob Mordecai's Warrenton Female Academy.

Governor David Stone named Miller attorney general in 1810 to serve several months to complete the term of Oliver Fitts, also of Warren County, who resigned. Miller also served four terms (1810–13) in the General Assembly and as speaker during two of them. Elected to a fifth term, including the speakership for a third time, he resigned before assuming his duties after his election as governor.

Miller was governor for three terms (1814–17). This placed him in a position of considerable importance, as he served during the War of 1812, when he backed the war measures of President James Madison. It was also during his term that the Antonio Canova statue of George Washington was commissioned for the state capitol. Miller supported the first tentative steps towards a system of public education when he advocated creation of the Literary Fund for that purpose. He lent his efforts to improve transportation in the creation of a similar fund for internal improvements, and he favored humanizing the penal code. The organization of the first North Carolina Supreme Court in 1818 followed Miller's recommendation of Judge John Hall as one of the first two justices to organize such a tribunal.

In 1816, while he was governor, Miller married Lydia Anna Evans and they moved into the new Executive Mansion at the southern end of Fayetteville Street in Raleigh. At the expiration of his third term, they moved to Warrenton; Mrs. Miller died in March 1818 at Oaklands, the home of her father near Petersburg, Va. Their only child, William, Jr., was dead by 1824. Miller returned to Raleigh to represent Warren County in the senate during the 1821–22 session, and in March 1825 he was named by President John Quincy Adams to succeed the late Thomas N. Mann as diplomatic agent to Guatemala. Unfortunately Miller, like his North Carolina predecessor named to this post, died en route. After three days of illness from yellow fever, Miller died at Key West, Fla.; he probably was buried at sea, as the secretary of the legation accompanying him did not report his death to the State Department until the ship reached Havana eleven days later.

There is a portrait of Governor Miller, with a view of the then state capitol visible in the background, in the Philanthropic Society hall at The University of North Carolina.

SEE: Kemp P. Battle, *History of the University of North Carolina*, vol. 1 (1907); John L. Cheney, Jr., ed., *North Carolina Government, 1585–1979* (1981); Daniel L. Grant, *Alumni History of the University of North Carolina, 1795–1924* (1924); W. R. Manning, *Diplomatic Correspondence of the United States concerning the Independence of Latin-American Nations*, vol. 1 (1925); *Nat. Cyc. Am. Biog.*, vol. 4 (1895); Raleigh *Register*, 7 June 1816, 13 Mar. 1818, 15 July, 21 Oct. 1825; Manly Wade Wellman, *The County of Warren, North Carolina, 1586–1917* (1959).

MARY HINTON DUKE KERR
CHARLES H. MCARVER, JR.

Millie-Christine. *See* **McCoy, Millie-Christine.**

Millis, James Edward (*23 June 1884–13 Oct. 1961*), industrialist and civic leader, was born in Guilford County, the son of pioneer industrialist James Henry Millis and his wife, Cornelia Walker. He attended Jule Weatherly's private school in High Point and the Bingham Military Academy in Asheville. In 1920 he entered The University of North Carolina, where he remained for two years, part of the time as a special student concentrating on banking, finance, and accounting.

In 1905 Millis joined his father's company, the High Point Hosiery Mill, as a bookkeeper. In 1927 he was instrumental in the creation of the Adams-Millis Corporation, which merged the textile interests of the Adams and Millis companies, including Piedmont Mills Company, Kernersville Knitting Company, High Point Hosiery Mills, and Pointer Hosiery Company. Millis became secretary-treasurer in 1928 and president in 1935. In 1941 he also became chairman of the board of directors, a position he held until his death. He resigned as president of Adams-Millis in 1952 and was succeeded by his son, James Henry.

Under the elder Millis's direction the company continued to grow and diversify, becoming one of the largest hosiery manufacturers in the world. Millis was known not only for his successful attempts to expand the technological skill necessary to produce modern textiles, but also for his concern for the safety and welfare of his employees.

Millis also served as president of the Thomasville and Denton Railroad and director of the Wachovia Bank and Trust Company. During World War II he was a member of the War Labor Board. He served two terms on the High Point City Council as well as two terms as a Guilford County commissioner. He helped to establish the WUNC-TV network and served as a member of the board of trustees of The University of North Carolina. He was active in the improvement of both High Point and Brevard colleges and was awarded the honorary degree of doctor of textile science by North Carolina State College in 1946. For many years he taught Sunday school at Wesley Memorial Methodist Church and worked with the local Boy's Club and the community chest. He was a Thirty-second-degree Mason, a member of the Elk's Lodge and the Rotary Club, and an avid quail hunter.

Millis married Helen Brooks in 1911, and they became the parents of four children, two of whom, Mrs. J. Harris (Helen) Covington and James H., survived him. He was buried in Oakwood Cemetery, High Point.

SEE: *Greensboro Daily News*, 14 Oct. 1961; Holt McPherson, *High Pointers of High Point* (1975 [portrait]); *North Carolina Biography*, vol. 3 (1941).

CAROLYN A. SIEVERS

Millis, James Henry (*23 July 1849–16 July 1913*), manufacturer, merchant, banker, and businessman, was born in Guilford County of English ancestry. His father was James Nicholson Millis, a successful businessman and farmer; his mother was Elizabeth Armfield Millis, a descendant of James Armfield, who arrived in Philadelphia in 1713, the first of the Armfields in America. James Henry spent his boyhood on the family farm, which is now the Sedgefield community between Greensboro and High Point. At seventeen he expressed a desire to embark on a business career, in which his parents encouraged him notwithstanding his young age.

Millis went first to Asheboro, where for three years he worked in the store of the distinguished North Carolinian, Dr. J. M. Worth, who later became state treasurer. On Worth's advice, he went to Greensboro to associate himself with Odell, Ragan and Company and after two years moved to High Point, where he spent the remainder of his life.

In 1876 he organized the mercantile firm of Ragan, Millis and Company, which for many years was the largest business of that kind in the High Point community. The firm opened a branch in Asheville and for several years was the South's largest shipper of dried fruit.

In 1892 Millis became interested in manufacturing, organizing the Home Furniture Company, of which he was secretary-treasurer. He also established the High Point Overall Company and the Highland Cotton Mills and was a stockholder in various other firms that made his city a manufacturing and marketing center. For a period he was secretary-treasurer of Snow Lumber Company, then the South's largest supplier of woodwork.

Millis was not one to confine his talents to his personal interests alone. He also promoted and was an official in one of the first local building and loan associations in North Carolina. The success of later building and loan institutions in his home town was due in large measure to the confidence and experience he infused into the first one.

In 1876 he married Cornelia A. Walker, who died nine years later. After her death, he plunged into business and political activities even more vigorously. For ten years he served as chairman of the Guilford County Board of Commissioners, a post later held by two of his sons: James Edward, a business and manufacturing leader, and Henry Albion. One daughter died young, while the other married W. J. Armfield, Jr., a pioneer banker at Asheboro, whose sons were active in the development of Burlington Industries.

Millis was fifty when he became a prime mover in organizing the High Point Hosiery Mills, a complex of plants that grew into the Adams-Millis Corporation, later the largest manufacturer of hosiery in the world. He was president of that company until his death.

One of the builders of High Point, with significant impact on Guilford County and the state of North Carolina, Millis was more instrumental in helping young men get a start in business than any of his peers in High Point. He died at age sixty-four and was interred in the Millis mausoleum at Oakwood Cemetery, High Point.

SEE: American Historical Society, Inc., *North Carolina* (1927); Samuel A. Ashe, ed., *Biographical History of North Carolina*, vol. 8 (1917); *Greensboro Daily News*, 17 July 1913.

HOLT MCPHERSON

Mills, Columbus (*20 June 1808–10 Dec. 1882*), physician and regional political leader in western North Carolina in the counties bordering South Carolina, was the son of Eleanor Morris and William Mills, a pioneer settler of western North Carolina. He was the great-grandson of Colonel Ambrose Mills, a Loyalist officer executed after the Battle of Kings Mountain. Columbus Mills represented Rutherford County in the state senate in the session of 1846–47. He was elected by the General Assembly to a two-year term on the Council of State in 1852 (when his home county was reported as being Cleveland) but resigned in July 1854 when Rutherford County returned him to the senate. He was reelected and served until 1857, when he once more was chosen a member of the Council of State (with his home again recorded as Cleveland County). Mills served on the Council of State until 1860. In April of that year he was a delegate from North Carolina to the Democratic National Convention, held in Charleston, S.C.

While a member of the General Assembly in 1855, Mills was instrumental in having Polk County created from portions of Rutherford and Henderson counties. The county seat, Columbus, was incorporated in 1857 and named for him. The town of Mills Spring, incorporated in 1885 (now known as Mill Spring but no longer active as a municipality), was also named in his honor.

Although details of Mills's schooling are unknown, he clearly was well educated. His articles appeared in the *New York Post*, and he was a friend of the South Carolina writer, William Gilmore Simms. He contributed mountain lore to Simms, and Mills himself appears as a character in Simms's "How Sharp Snaffles Got His Capital for a Wife."

On 17 June 1861, at age fifty-three, Mills volunteered his services to the Sixteenth Regiment of North Carolina Troops and was named regimental surgeon; he resigned in March 1863. During much of the war he served as provost marshal and on one occasion ordered a detail of Confederate cavalry to seize two brothers who were hiding refugees and deserters from the Confederate army. Soon afterwards a band of renegades attacked the Mills home, from which the doctor and his family barely escaped.

Mills had large farming interests and before the Civil War owned between sixty and seventy slaves. After the Grange was organized in March 1873 as a cooperative means of resolving some of the farmers' problems in the state, Mills was elected its first president. His antebellum home stood two miles east of Tryon in Polk County; many years later it was enlarged and converted into Mimosa Inn.

Mills married Susan A. Thompson of Spartanburg, S.C., but they had no children. They were both buried in Spartanburg.

SEE: John L. Cheney, Jr., ed., *North Carolina Government, 1585–1979* (1981); Walter Clark, ed., *Histories of the Several Regiments and Battalions from North Carolina in the Great War, 1861–1865*, vols. 1, 4 (1901), and *State Records of North Carolina*, vol. 15 (1898); Clarence W. Griffin, *History of Old Tryon and Rutherford Counties, North Carolina, 1730–1936* (1937); *Harper's Magazine* 41 (October 1870); Weymouth T. Jordan, comp., *North Carolina Troops, 1861–1865: A Roster*, vol. 6 (1977); A. R. Newsome, ed., "Letters of Lawrence O'Bryan Branch, 1856–1860," *North*

Carolina Historical Review 10 (January 1933); Stuart Noblin, "Leonidas LaFayette Polk and the North Carolina Department of Agriculture," *North Carolina Historical Review* 20 (April 1943); Sadie S. Patton, *Sketches of Polk County History* (1950); Stephen B. Weeks Scrapbook, vol. 8 (North Carolina Collection, University of North Carolina, Chapel Hill).

WILLIAM S. POWELL

Mills, John Haymes *(9 July 1831–15 Dec. 1898)*, educator and founder of orphanages, was born in Halifax County, Va., the son of John Garland and Martha Williams Haymes Mills. The Mills family descended from Sir John Mills of England. John H. Mills's great-great-grandfather, John Mills, settled in Hanover County, Va. Mills's father, John Garland, the fifth son of Robert and Mary Mills, was born on 12 Mar. 1804; he was a farmer and a Baptist minister in Hanover County, Va. John H. Mills grew up as a sturdy farmer's boy in a slaveholding family. After his education at a local academy, his father decided that Mills would attend Wake Forest College. Mills made himself a trunk, got aboard a batteau, and went down the Dan and Roanoke rivers to Gaston, where he took the train for Wake Forest.

At college the six-foot-two-inch "Jack" participated in debates and was graduated with honors and a B.A. degree in 1854. Three years later he received an M.A. degree from Wake Forest. He taught in an academy in Milton, and when this proved unprofitable, he moved to Melrose Academy near his home in Halifax, Va. In January 1855 Mills began teaching mathematics in Oxford Female Seminary, Oxford, under Dr. Samuel Wait. Wait retired in 1858, and since the institution was in debt, the trustees sold the buildings and grounds to Mills. He was president of Oxford Female Seminary from 1858 to 1866 through the trying Civil War period. In 1866 he sold the property and for one year conducted his school at St. John's College, which had been built in Oxford by the Masons of the state but since then abandoned.

In 1867 he purchased the *Biblical Recorder* in Raleigh. An early biographer said that during his editorship, from 1868 to 1873, Mills's discussion of issues was strong and he often disposed of his adversary in a short paragraph or even in one epigrammatic sentence. The *Recorder* had few long editorials and certainly not a dull one under his administration. He made a live paper that enjoyed a wide circulation, not only among Baptists but also among people of other faiths.

While editor of the *Biblical Recorder*, Mills traveled throughout North Carolina observing the hardships that had resulted from the Civil War. These privations had fallen mainly on women and children, particularly indigent orphans. As Mills saw the wretched condition of the orphaned children and remembered the orphaned boy who had grown up with his family in Virginia, he felt compelled to help them. When the Grand Lodge of Masons met in Raleigh to decide what to do with the buildings of St. John's College in Oxford, he pleaded with the lodge to establish an orphanage on the site. As a result of his efforts, the lodge set aside two thousand dollars and the legislature in 1873 made a small appropriation, thus making it possible for the facility to open with Mills as its first manager. This was the first orphanage in North Carolina.

Mills "struggled for 11 years against poverty, indifference, and sometimes hostility." His health was broken and he resigned. After resting for a short time at his farm near Thomasville, he began to agitate for the formation of a Baptist orphanage. Although the Baptist

State Convention opposed his proposal at its annual meeting in 1884, the North Carolina Baptist Orphanage Association was formed that year and Mills began traveling across the state to raise money. On 12 Jan. 1885 he became the general manager of the Baptist Orphanage of North Carolina, established at Thomasville, and on 14 July 1887 he began publishing *Charity and Children*, the institution's newspaper. Mills introduced the cottage unit system at the orphanage; he also established a school and a church. In 1895 he retired to his farm near Thomasville.

In June 1898 Mills gave specific directions regarding his funeral and burial. In December he was taken ill and died a few days after his brother had visited him. Following a Masonic funeral service, Mills was buried in a plain white oak coffin in the Rich Fork cemetery.

On 28 Feb. 1856 he married Elizabeth N. Williams, a teacher at the Oxford Female Institute. They had one child, Martha (Mrs. J. D. Newton).

SEE: I. G. Greer, "John Haymes Mills," *Encyclopedia of Southern Baptists*, vol. 2 (1958); J. D. Hufham, "J. H. Mills," *Wake Forest Student* 18 (1899 [portrait]); John Haymes Mills Biography Folder (Baptist Historical Collection, Wake Forest University, Winston-Salem [portraits]); Raleigh *Biblical Recorder*, 10 Apr. 1856, 11, 25 Jan. 1899, 23 Sept. 1908; Bernard Washington Spilman, *The Mills Home: A History of the Baptist Orphanage Movement in North Carolina* (1932); *Wake Forest Alumni Directory* (1961).

JOHN R. WOODARD

Mills, Luther Rice *(17 Aug. 1840–18 Aug. 1920)*, educator, was the youngest of five children of the Reverend John Garland and Martha Williams Haymes Mills of Halifax County, Va. Ordained to the ministry in 1825, the elder Mills served as pastor of rural Baptist churches in the region, while earning a good livelihood for his family as owner-manager of a sizable plantation tended by numerous slaves.

Young Mills received the rudiments of an elementary education under the tutelage of his father prior to enrolling at Wake Forest College in 1857. He was awarded an A.B. degree in 1861, graduating at the head of his class. Afterwards he served in the Confederate army (1861–65), attaining the rank of lieutenant. Captured on the retreat from Richmond (1864), he spent the last months of the conflict as a prisoner on Johnson's Island.

On his release from prison in mid-June 1865, Mills returned to Halifax County. Earlier dreams of pursuing graduate studies in mathematics at the University of Virginia and at Cambridge University had to be deferred as he assumed the management of the family estate, operating it with the help of former slaves, who had chosen to remain as "tenants" following their emancipation, and with such day laborers as he could hire for the work. His sense of duty to a widowed mother—together with an unexpected joy derived from his success at the enterprise—found Mills resolved to devote his time and energy to maintaining the family farm.

In January 1867, however, he yielded to the invitation of President Washington Manly Wingate to return to Wake Forest to teach mathematics. Here he remained for the next forty years, serving as adjunct professor (1867–71) and professor of mathematics (1871–1907), bursar of the college (1876–1907), and agent for the Board of Education (1876–80). The latter, a college-based agency of the Baptist State Convention, was charged with the task of working to "assist promising and indigent young ministers seeking to prepare themselves for the more efficient preaching of the gospel." As a result of ill health, Mills retired from the classroom in June 1907.

As a teacher, Mills was comprehensive and exacting. The young men who sat in his classes soon discovered that whether or not they learned was largely their responsibility. He believed that a teacher should not have to coax a student to study. Nonetheless, the records of many former students—especially those who pursued higher branches of mathematics at universities—attest both to the thoroughness of the work accomplished in his classroom and to his ability to inspire students to do their best.

It was as bursar, however, that Mills probably made his most important contribution to Wake Forest. He is said to have been well ahead of his time in his knowledge of accounting principles and in the skills of business management. His thrift, his prompt payment of bills, and his determination to hold expenditures within the limits of the institution's sources of revenue increased its financial credit. Such practices also won the confidence of the individuals who were able to provide equipment and funding for the college. Knowledge of the value of common stocks and other securities—together with his study of fluctuations in the market—made him a trusted adviser to the board of trustees. Reportedly, his judgment regarding investments proved to be remarkably sound.

Mills married Anna Lewis, of Tarboro, on 14 Jan. 1869. They had five children: Kate (m. Claude Kitchin), Luther Rice, Jr., John Garland, Lucy (m. John Alexander Wray), and Anna. Mills was buried in the town cemetery at Wake Forest. A portrait hangs in the reading room of the Ethel Taylor Crittenden Collection in Baptist History, Wake Forest University.

SEE: Luther Rice Mills, "Forty Years in the Wilderness," *Bulletin of Wake Forest College*, October 1907, January 1908; George Washington Paschal, *History of Wake Forest College*, vols. 1–3 (1935–43); *Wake Forest Student*, "Mills Memorial" vol. (November 1920).

R. HARGUS TAYLOR

Mills, Quincy Sharpe (15 Jan. 1884–26 July 1918), editor, author, and World War I officer, was born in Statesville, the only child of Thomas Millard and Nannie Sharpe Mills. His father was a merchant and his mother a teacher. Both parents were natives of Statesville and were descendants of sturdy pioneer stock; they grew up in the poverty-stricken days of Reconstruction after the Civil War. Quincy was nurtured on his grandmother's tales of the bravery of his forefathers in their struggles against the Indians, the Redcoats, and the Yankees. Soon reading became a part of his life, and he was an eager student in the schools of his day.

In the fall of 1899 he entered the Oak Ridge Preparatory School, where he completed the two-year course in one year, making an average grade of 99.5. His diploma qualified him for admission to The University of North Carolina, but since he was only sixteen, his parents persuaded him to stay at home for a year. In June 1901 he became ill with typhoid fever and was forced to wait until September 1902 to enroll in the university. His four years there were a delight to him. He was the editor of three student publications and a correspondent for two newspapers. Initiated into Phi Beta Kappa, he won medals and honors in all his work. In sports, he starred on the tennis team and excelled in cross-country running.

A charming account of his junior-year summer vacation, entitled *Footing It through the Blue Ridge*, first appeared in serial form in the *Charlotte Observer*. Many of his "Verses, Grave and Gay," short stories, skits, and plays were published.

Immediately following his graduation in 1907, Mills went to New York to seek his fortune in the newspaper world. By his own efforts he obtained a job in the office of the New York *Evening Sun* as a reporter. In a short time he became city editor, remaining in that post until he volunteered for military service when the United States declared war on Germany in 1917. He had already taken officers' training courses at Plattsburg, N.Y., during his vacations since the war began in 1914. From 1914 until his enlistment, a period of twenty-seven months, he wrote 250 editorials on the European conflict and America's lack of preparedness for its deepening involvement. Intensely patriotic, he felt it was his duty to fight in his country's battles against the forces of evil.

Mills was commissioned a lieutenant and sent to France. He died of wounds received at the Battle of Château-Thierry (3–4 June 1918) in an attack on the German lines that successfully blocked the enemy's advance.

A biography of Mills, *One Who Gave His Life*, written by James Luby, senior editor of the *Evening Sun*, was published in 1923; it also includes letters that Lieutenant Mills sent from France. A second volume, *Editorials, Sketches, and Stories*, containing Mills's short stories and editorials, was published in 1930.

Mills was recognized by journalists as a specialist on state and city political affairs; he wrote constantly of the inner workings of party politics. The range of his interests was worldwide and his vision deep and penetrating. Many causes claimed his pen, and he championed them all with his keen intellect and tireless concern for a better city: more parks and playgrounds, better schools, less pollution, and more adequate transportation. His early twentieth-century concerns were the same as those of the waning days of the century. His philosophy of government, his desire for a good life for all people, his love of freedom, and his willingness to give his life for the principles in which he believed stand as a lasting tribute to the young soldier-writer who made the supreme sacrifice for his beloved country.

SEE: Daniel L. Grant, *Alumni History of the University of North Carolina, 1795–1924* (1924); James Luby, *One Who Gave His Life* (1923); Quincy Sharpe Mills, *Editorials, Sketches, and Stories* (1930).

KATHERINE NOE KNOX

Milner, James (*ca.* 1735–9 Dec. 1772), attorney, was a native of Scotland. After residing for some years in Sussex County, Va., he moved to North Carolina about 1766. Milner settled in the town of Halifax, where he began to practice law. In 1769 he purchased a lot in Halifax and in the short time before his death, he amassed considerable property in and surrounding the town. He appears to have lived on a plantation just south of Halifax, known as Green Hill. On his arrival in Halifax, Milner became a member of the Royal White Hart Lodge. Gaining the confidence of Joseph Montfort, who had been made provincial grand master for North Carolina in 1768, he was appointed deputy grand master in 1770.

According to the *Colonial Records*, he had some claim against Herman Husband, the Regulator leader, and won a suit against him in the court of Orange County. As a result of the suit, Milner gained title to a two-hundred-acre farm Husband owned in Guilford County. The question arises whether Husband incurred this debt by having Milner act for him in some capacity.

Milner became well known during his residence in Virginia, as much of the information about him is derived from notices that appeared in the Williamsburg paper, the *Virginia Gazette*. According to this source, in the fall of 1772 he was elected to the Assembly of North Carolina and a great ball was held in Halifax town to celebrate this event. Shortly afterwards, he was thrown from his horse and died of a fractured skull. After his death a rumor began to circulate that counterfeit currency had been found in his possession. Many friends sent in testimonials, printed in the *Virginia Gazette*, denying the rumor. Among these was a letter from the Reverend William Willie, Milner's former clergyman in Virginia, who stated that he had been present in Halifax when the effects of the deceased were examined and no counterfeit money had been found. At the time Willie was the popular rector of Albemarle Parish in Sussex. (Willie Jones and Willie Mangum, both prominent North Carolinians from Sussex County families, were named for the parson.)

Obviously a man of ability, Milner did not live long enough to make his mark in North Carolina. However, as the majority of his friends, such as the Scottish merchants in Halifax, were Tories when the American Revolution broke out, it is likely that he would have cast his lot with them.

The inventory of Milner's estate is one of the most remarkable recorded in North Carolina in the colonial period. In addition to a library of 621 volumes and other personal property, the inventory lists scientific instruments such as a microscope, solar telescope, magnet, and prism glass. The library was of unusual breadth, covering books on music, literature, law, and medicine. A few volumes, containing Milner's elaborate book plate depicting his coat of arms, are in the North Carolina Collection of the University of North Carolina at Chapel Hill. By will, Milner left his old friend, the Reverend Mr. Willie, all his books in Greek and Hebrew. He was buried in the colonial cemetery in Halifax, his gravestone bearing the earliest date of any there.

SEE: John B. Boddie, *Births, Deaths, and Sponsors, 1717–1778, from Albemarle Parish Registers of Surry and Sussex Counties, Virginia* (1958); Thomas C. Parramore, *Launching the Craft: The First Half Century of Free Masonry in North Carolina* (1975); William L. Saunders, ed., *Colonial Records of North Carolina*, vol. 8 (1890); Claiborne T. Smith, Jr., and Stuart H. Smith, *A History of Trinity Parish, Scotland Neck, and Edgecombe Parish, Halifax County* (1955).

CLAIBORNE T. SMITH, JR.

Mims, Edwin *(27 May 1872–15 Sept. 1959)*, educator and teacher of American and English literature, was born in Richmond, Ark., a village near Little Rock, the son of Andrew Jackson, an Arkansas merchant, and Cornelia Williamson Mims. At age thirteen Edwin was sent to Webb School at Bell Buckle, Tenn., and in 1892 he was graduated from Vanderbilt University with a bachelor of arts degree. After receiving a master of arts degree in 1893, he remained at Vanderbilt an additional year as a Fellow in English. He spent the academic year 1896–97 in graduate study at Cornell University and was awarded a Ph.D. degree in 1900.

Mims's long and distinguished career is generally remembered in association with Vanderbilt University, but he spent the first decades of his professional life in North Carolina. From 1894 through the school year 1909 he was professor of English at Trinity College (now Duke University), and from 1909 to 1912 he held a similar appointment at The University of North Carolina. In the fall of 1912 Mims returned to Nashville and Vanderbilt, yet he retained warm and lasting relationships with North Carolina friends, including Frank Porter Graham and Edgar W. Knight.

From 1912 until his so-called retirement in 1942, Mims was chairman of Vanderbilt's English department and from 1928 to 1942 he was also chairman of the humanities division. At a dinner honoring him upon retirement, Mims announced that he would now be "professor-at-large." This was literally true because he remained active as an author, teacher, and lecturer almost until the time of his death. Retirement meant only that he was free to widen his sphere of influence. In early June 1949, at age seventy-seven, Mims delivered an address to a Vanderbilt alumni group on Friday and was its dinner guest in the evening, attended a Duke University alumni banquet in Durham on Saturday evening, addressed a large group of his former Trinity College students on Sunday, and was in Chapel Hill on Monday to attend a reception and the graduation exercises at The University of North Carolina.

Professor Mims was the author of *Sidney Lanier* (1905), *The Advancing South* (1926), *Adventurous America* (1929), and *Chancellor Kirkland* (1940). After retirement came *Great Writers as Interpreters of Religion* (1945), the *History of Vanderbilt University* (1946), and *Christ of the Poets* (1948).

It was in the classroom, however, that Mims exercised his greatest influence. Generations of Vanderbilt students committed to memory countless passages of great literature—both prose and poetry—and, furthermore, they understood the contents. Mims had a gift for reading poetry aloud and firing his students with a love for literature. Also, at a time when scholarly writing was emphasized in English departments and set as a standard for promotion, Mims made the decision to give equal recognition to creative writing. Vanderbilt appears to have been the first institution in this country to have adopted such a policy, and it was undoubtedly one of the reasons why writing flourished there in the 1920s more than in other colleges.

Mims frequently taught at other institutions during the summer sessions—among them, George Peabody College for Teachers, Johns Hopkins University, University of Virginia, University of Southern California, Carnegie Tech, University of Texas, and Duke. In 1935–36 he was Carnegie Visiting Professor at St. Andrew's University (Scotland), Trinity College (Dublin), the universities of London and Wales, and the University of the Southwest (Exeter, England). He also was in demand as a lecturer, and before the public he displayed the same zest for literature that made his classes notable.

After retirement, in addition to his writing, Mims taught for short periods at Emory University, Rollins College (Winter Park, Fla.), the University of Florida, Florida State University, and Stetson University (De Land, Fla.). For one year he was a special lecturer for the New School for Social Research in New York City, and for two years he was a lecturer for Phi Beta Kappa and the American Association of Colleges and Universities.

His effectiveness as a teacher is evident in the tributes paid him by former students, many of them men and women who had become leaders in the business and professional world. In the field of creative writing, few teachers have been privileged to have influenced so many writers as did Dr. Mims. Among his students were Donald Davidson, Robert Penn Warren, Cleanth Brooks, Andrew Lytle, Allen Tate, Merrill Moore, and Jesse Stuart. John Crowe Ranson was not a part of this group but was closely associated with its members and with Mims.

Less known is the story of Mims's work with the Southern Association of Colleges and Schools, which in its early years was called the Association of Colleges and Secondary Schools of the Southern States. In 1895 he was appointed a delegate to the first meeting and seven years later was the association's president. For a number of years thereafter, he was a member of the executive committee.

Mims was a member of the Methodist church. In 1902–3 he served with the joint hymn book commission of the Methodist Episcopal Church, North and South. In June 1898 he married Clara Puryear, of Paducah, Ky., the daughter of a tobacco broker of that city. They had four children: Edwin, Catherine Puryear, Thomas Puryear, and Ella Puryear.

Edwin Mims was an untiring humanist, educator, and professor of English who, for over six decades, was a vital force in higher education in the South. He was a member of the faculty of three leading southern universities and a lecturer on countless campuses. In the summer of 1959 he was preparing a collection of essays on higher education when a fall, resulting in a fractured hip, confined him to a nursing home for the last weeks of his life. Funeral services were held at Nashville's West End Methodist Church, with burial in Woodlawn Memorial Park.

SEE: Edgar H. Duncan, "Edwin Mims: Professor-at-Large," *Vanderbilt Alumnus* 34 (June 1949); "Memorial Resolutions . . . Edwin Mims, Class of '92," *Vanderbilt Alumnus* 45 (December 1959); Nashville *Banner*, 16 Sept. 1959; Nashville *Tennessean*, 16–17 Sept. 1959; *Nat. Cyc. Am. Biog.*, vol. 49 (1966); *New York Times*, 17 Sept. 1959; *Who Was Who in America*, vol. 3 (1969).

J. ISAAC COPELAND

Mitchell, Anderson (13 June 1800–24 Dec. 1876), lawyer, judge, and legislator, was born at the family farm near Milton, Caswell County, the son of David, Jr., and Ann Anderson Mitchell. He attended Bingham School in Orange County and was graduated from The University of North Carolina in 1821. He served as a tutor in 1821–22 and received an M.A. degree in 1824.

Admitted to the bar, Mitchell was elected to the House of Commons from Ashe County in 1827 and 1828 and to the state senate in 1829. In 1830 he moved to Morganton and began to practice law. In the same year he was appointed attorney for The University of North Carolina Board of Trustees, a position he held until his resignation in 1834.

In 1831 Mitchell moved to Jefferson, where he became clerk of the superior court; he served until his relocation in Wilkesboro in 1835. In 1840 he won another seat in the state senate. In 1842 he was appointed to the Twenty-seventh Congress to fill the unexpired term created by the death of Lewis Williams. Defeated for reelection by Governor David S. Reid, Mitchell resigned his office to continue his law practice.

Mitchell was elected again to the House of Commons in 1854 and 1856. Moving to Statesville in 1859, he was elected once more to the state senate the following year. In 1861 he was chosen a delegate to the Secession Con-

vention of 20 May and voted against the Ordinance of Secession.

Until the end of the Civil War, Mitchell remained a devoted member of the Whig party. In 1866, however, he accepted an appointment to the Wilkes County Superior Court under William Woods Holden, the provisional governor, and was elected to the post on the 1868 Republican ticket. In subsequent years he was reelected as a Democrat, although he preferred to be called a Whig.

Mitchell's years as a superior court justice were perhaps the finest of his public career. Distinguished by his integrity and respected for his courtroom skills, he found that the postwar atmosphere of Wilkes County presented a special challenge. Roving bands of Confederate and Union deserters and rising Ku Klux Klan activity threatened to push the county into anarchy. But by dispensing justice without favoritism or malice, he helped bring order to the state's troubled western counties and diminished the influence of the Klan. Similarly, Mitchell's injunction forbidding payment of the state militia during the Kirk-Holden war of 1870 helped end that divisive conflict and clearly demonstrated that he would not allow political pressure to influence his interpretation of the law.

Mitchell resigned from the court in 1875. He died the following year, at age seventy-six, after an illness. Over six feet tall but frail from childhood, Mitchell maintained his sharpness of mind until his last year. He never married. He attended the Presbyterian Church of Statesville and was buried there.

SEE: Nancy Alexander, *Here I Will Dwell: The Story of Caldwell County* (1956); *Biog. Dir. Am. Cong.* (1961); D. M. Furches, "Judge Anderson Mitchell," *North Carolina Journal of Law* 2, no. 8 (August 1905); Daniel L. Grant, *Alumni History of the University of North Carolina, 1795–1924* (1924); J. G. de Roulhac Hamilton, *Reconstruction in North Carolina* (1914); Thomas Felix Hickerson, *Happy Valley* (1940); University of North Carolina Papers (Southern Historical Collection, University of North Carolina, Chapel Hill); Wills, Estate Records, and Marriage Bonds of Caswell County and Jonathan Worth Papers (North Carolina State Archives, Raleigh).

ALLEN JERNIGAN

Mitchell, Elisha (19 Aug. 1793–27 June 1857), educator, geologist, Presbyterian minister, and explorer, was born in Washington, Conn., the oldest son of Abner, a farmer, and Phoebe Eliot Mitchell. Abner was a descendant of Matthew Mitchell, who had emigrated from Yorkshire to Massachusetts in 1635 and then moved to Connecticut in 1637. Mitchell's maternal great-grandfather was Jared Eliot, the prominent minister, intellectual, and scientist whose family had also lived in Connecticut since the 1630s. Prepared for college by the Reverend Azel Backus at his school in Bethlehem, Conn., Elisha Mitchell was graduated from Yale University in 1813 in the same class as George E. Badger, Thomas P. Devereux, and Denison Olmsted. At Yale he studied under Professor Benjamin Silliman, who later published a number of Mitchell's scientific articles in the *American Journal of Science and Arts*, which Silliman edited from 1818 to 1838.

After leaving Yale, Mitchell taught first at Union Hall Academy, conducted by Dr. Lewis E. A. Eigenbrodt in Jamaica, Long Island, and then served as principal of Union Academy in New London, Conn. In 1816 he returned to Yale as a tutor, and the following year he took a brief theological course at Andover, Mass. He was licensed to preach by the Congregationalist Western Association of New Haven County, Conn. Also in 1817 the Reverend Sereno E. Dwight, son of Timothy Dwight of Yale and chaplain of the U.S. Senate, recommended Mitchell for a teaching position in Chapel Hill to William Gaston, then serving both in the U.S. House of Representatives and on the board of trustees of The University of North Carolina.

In January 1818 Mitchell arrived in Chapel Hill to take up his duties as professor of mathematics and natural philosophy. At the same time his former classmate at Yale, Denison Olmsted, was appointed professor of chemistry, geology, and mineralogy. When Olmsted returned to Yale in 1825, Mitchell was chosen to take his place; he taught chemistry, geology, and mineralogy at the university for the next thirty-two years. He also took over and completed the geological survey of North Carolina that Olmsted had begun.

In 1821 Mitchell was ordained by the Presbytery of Orange in Hillsborough; he continued to combine preaching with his education and scientific interests for the remainder of his life. His theological views were clearly expressed in 1825 in a controversy with John Stark Ravenscroft, first bishop of the Episcopal Diocese of North Carolina, in which Mitchell supported Calvinist doctrine, arguing that Scripture was the only source of religious truth and rejecting the use of tradition as an aid to religious interpretation.

At Chapel Hill, Mitchell's students apparently found him a witty and challenging lecturer and enjoyed his courses. In addition to his teaching, he officiated at chapel services, both on week nights and on Sundays; served as bursar and accountant for the university; and, after 1835, acted in place of President David L. Swain when Swain was away from Chapel Hill. As bursar, Mitchell was in charge of grounds and buildings belonging to the university and worked to increase the variety of flowers, shrubs, and trees on the campus. He also complained that he had more than his share of responsibility for discipline because he lived closer to the college buildings than other members of the faculty. The University of Alabama awarded him an honorary doctor of divinity degree in 1838, and he was a corresponding member of the Boston Society of Natural History.

Mitchell expressed definite opinions on the issues of his day. His journal indicates his distaste for Jacksonian democracy, and in North Carolina he supported the efforts of those who were determined to overcome the Rip Van Winkle image the state had acquired and to promote material progress. In 1834 he urged North Carolinians to support the establishment by the state of a tax-supported system of common schools, not only because he believed that educated citizens were essential to the improvement of society, but also because such schools would provide jobs for women as teachers. Mitchell's interest in the education of women is also evident from the classical education he prescribed for his own daughters.

Having been appointed by Governor William A. Graham to survey a turnpike westward from Raleigh to Buncombe County, Mitchell reported in 1846 that such a turnpike was necessary to encourage trade, increase travel, and connect the eastern and western sections of the state. He also supported the temperance movement and the organization of temperance societies as a means of achieving social progress. His belief in the importance of material improvement was also evident in his descriptions of the mountain regions in western North Carolina, which he visited while working both on the geo-

logical survey and on his own research. He deplored the isolation in which mountain people led their lives, which, he argued, led to male laziness, female degradation, and economic stagnation. He looked forward to the day when improved transportation, education, and the development of villages and towns would bring the benefits of civilization to the area.

On the question of slavery, he supported the southern point of view. After coming to Chapel Hill, he acquired slaves himself and, in 1848, preached a sermon arguing that slavery was a system of property holding under God's law and as such was no worse than any other form of property ownership.

Mitchell is best known for his measurement of the Black Mountain in the Blue Ridge and his claim that one of its peaks was the highest point in the United States east of the Rocky Mountains. He first noted in 1828, in the diary he kept while working on the geological survey, that he believed the Black Mountain to be the highest peak in the area. In 1835 and again in 1838 he measured the mountain, showing the highest peak to be higher than Mount Washington in New Hampshire's White Mountains. In 1844 he returned with improved instruments and measured the highest peak at 6,708 feet, 250 feet higher than Mount Washington. By that time local people were referring to the peak as Mount Mitchell. However, Mitchell's claim was challenged in 1855, when Senator Thomas Clingman, arguing that Mitchell had measured the wrong peak, insisted that the one he had climbed and measured stood at 6,941 feet. As a result of the ensuing controversy, Mitchell returned to the Black Mountain in 1857 in a final attempt to prove Clingman wrong and justify his own previous measurements. On 27 June, leaving his son and guides, he started out alone, was caught in a thunderstorm, and apparently fell down a waterfall and drowned in the pool below.

Elisha Mitchell was buried first in Asheville on 10 July 1857. The following year arrangements were made for reburial on top of Mount Mitchell, and on 16 June 1858, with formal ceremonies and addresses by the Right Reverend Bishop James H. Otey of Tennessee and President David L. Swain, Mitchell's remains were buried on the peak. Today his grave is marked by a memorial plaque and observation tower, and the surrounding area has been established as a state park.

In 1881–82 the U.S. Geological Survey upheld Mitchell's measurement of the highest peak on the Black Mountain and officially named it Mount Mitchell. In 1883 the Elisha Mitchell Scientific Society was founded in his memory at The University of North Carolina.

On 19 Nov. 1819 Mitchell married Maria Sybil North, of New London, Conn., whom he had met when he was teaching at Union Academy in 1815. They had seven children: Mary Phoebe (m. Richard J. Ashe), Ellen Hannah (m. Dr. Joseph John Summerell), Margaret Eliot, Matthew Henry (died in infancy), Eliza North (m. Richard S. Grant), Charles Andrews, and Henry Eliot (died in infancy).

Photographs are available in the photographic files of the Division of Archives and History, Raleigh, and in the North Carolina Collection at the University of North Carolina at Chapel Hill.

SEE: Samuel A. Ashe, ed., *Biographical History of North Carolina*, vol. 1 (1905); Kemp P. Battle, *History of the University of North Carolina*, vol. 1 (1907); Hope Summerell Chamberlain, "Life Story of Elisha Mitchell, D.D., 1793–1857," 1945 (typescript, North Carolina Collection, University of North Carolina, Chapel Hill); Charles Phillips, ed., *A Memoir of the Rev. Elisha Mitchell, D.D.* (1858); Raleigh *Register*, 3 Nov. 1835; David Lowry Swain Papers (North Carolina State Archives, Raleigh).

ELGIVA D. WATSON

Mitchell, John *(14 Jan. 1826–3 Mar. 1906)*, Baptist clergyman, educator, benefactor of denominational causes, colporteur of religious tracts, and missionary in the Confederate army, was born in Bertie County, the son of Mary Thomas and James Saunders Mitchell, a state senator in 1842. He was graduated from Wake Forest College in 1852 and for the remainder of his life was associated with the school in one way or another. He continued his education at various theological institutions. In 1855 he returned to Wake Forest as financial agent and directed the raising of funds for an endowment. He next undertook a preaching mission and served as pastor of churches in Greensboro, Hillsborough, and Asheville. For two periods he was pastor at the Ahoskie Baptist Church.

Mitchell was keenly aware of his family's tradition in the fields of Christian education and charitable giving. He contributed generously to the Mills Home Baptist Orphanage in Thomasville and provided funds to erect one of its buildings, which later was named in his honor. He was one of two primary donors in the construction of Wake Forest College Hospital and made numerous other gifts to the college in funds and services. In addition, he was a frequent contributor to Chowan College, of which he was a trustee. Because of his generosity to Chowan College, a cottage there was reserved for his use. He also served as a trustee of Wake Forest College.

Baptist historians applied the title "the Beloved Disciple" to Mitchell because of his work and gifts; he was further described as devout, tolerant, and kind, with the tranquility of an Aquinas. Following his active ministry, Mitchell served as secretary of the Baptist Board of Education and finally returned to his father's plantation in Bertie County, where he died. He never married.

SEE: Edgar V. McKnight and Oscar Creech, *A History of Chowan College* (1964); Mitchell family genealogy (possession of John R. Jordan, Jr., Raleigh); J. Roy Parker, ed., *The Ahoskie Era of Hertford County* (1939); George W. Paschal, *History of Wake Forest College* (1935); Charles B. Williams, *History of the Baptists in North Carolina* (1901).

JOHN R. JORDAN, JR.

Mitchell, William Watson *(20 Dec. 1810–12 Sept. 1897)*, lay leader and benefactor of Baptist causes, planter, and civic leader, was born in Bertie County, the son of William and Rena Mitchell. As a young man he moved from Bertie to adjoining Hertford County, where in 1830, with slave labor, he built an imposing house on a 1,500-acre plantation, which was also cultivated by slave labor.

Chowan College in Murfreesboro became the principal object of his bounty for half a century, and its survival during the Civil War and Reconstruction is attributed to him. In 1848 he was one of the group that gathered at Mulberry Grove, the home of Dr. Godwin C. Moore in Hertford County, and set in motion the organization that became Chowan College. He was a member of its board of trustees for twenty-eight years and chairman for nineteen years.

While Chowan College was his greatest interest, Mitchell also contributed large sums of money and

property to Wake Forest College, the Baptist Orphanage in Thomasville, and the Southern Baptist Theological Seminary, as well as to individual Baptist churches. It was his personal gifts to Chowan College, however, that enabled it to remain open during and immediately after the Civil War. Mitchell worked diligently to improve the quality of the college and to expand its campus. In 1854 he was instrumental in bringing Dr. William Hooper to the institution as president. Formerly an Episcopal priest, Hooper had become a Baptist minister and educator and served as president of Wake Forest College in 1847–48. A graduate of The University of North Carolina who had also studied at Princeton Theological Seminary, he brought progressive changes to Chowan College. Hooper left in 1862 to head the Fayetteville Female Seminary.

Mitchell was chairman of the county court of Hertford County and was chief magistrate of the county for twenty-five years. He built and maintained a neighborhood school and in 1846 was elected to the county board of superintendents of public schools. A frequent delegate to the Baptist association, he was a generous contributor to the Ahoskie Baptist Church, of which he was a member.

The first of his three marriages was to Martha C. Williford in 1832; she died three weeks after the wedding. His second wife was Martha E. Mitchell, daughter of John and Winnifred Saunders Mitchell and sister of James Saunders Mitchell, who represented the Bertie district in the state senate in 1842. They became the parents of Nancy Emily, Mary Jane, Elizabeth Winnifred, and Sara Martha. Following the death of his second wife, Mitchell married her niece, Mary Elizabeth Winnifred Mitchell, the daughter of Senator Mitchell. They became the parents of seven children: James Saunders II, John Pipkin, Admira Hazeltine, Pauline Agnes, Betty Elva, William Judson, and Charles Emerson.

A portrait of Mitchell hangs in the main building of Chowan College.

SEE: *Ahoskie Herald*, 22 July 1968; *Biblical Recorder*, 13 Oct. 1897; Interviews with members of the Mitchell family by the author; Edgar V. McKnight and Oscar Creech, *A History of Chowan College* (1964); Mitchell papers (possession of John R. Jordan, Jr., Raleigh); J. Roy Parker, *The Ahoskie Era of Hertford County* (1955); Charles B. Williams, *History of the Baptists in North Carolina* (1901); B. B. Winborne, *Colonial and State History of Hertford County* (1906).

JOHN R. JORDAN, JR.

Mixon, Forrest Orion *(16 Apr. 1900–28 Oct. 1956)*, Baptist clergyman, denominational leader, and college president, was born at Early Branch, Hampton County, S.C., the tenth of eleven children of William Pearson and Sallie Shuman Mixon. His father, a farmer, descended from John Mixon, who, as an indentured servant, emigrated from southern England to eastern Virginia in 1649 or 1650. His maternal grandfather and great-grandfather were Baptist ministers who served churches in eastern South Carolina.

As a teenager Mixon worked in a mercantile business owned by his oldest brother, and during World War I he served for a year in the merchant marine. Following the war, he became involved in Sunday school work in his community and in 1922 determined to become a minister. After one year of preparatory work at Spartan Academy in Groce, S.C., he was ordained into the ministry of the Baptist church and admitted to Furman University, which awarded him an A.B. degree with honors in 1926. That fall he entered Southern Baptist Theological Seminary, in Louisville, Ky. In 1929 he received a Th.M. degree and accepted the seminary's invitation to become a teaching fellow in the department of church history. In that capacity he continued his studies, earning a Ph.D. degree in 1932. Furman University awarded him an honorary D.D. degree in 1947.

In 1929 Mixon married Daisy Lou Major, of Belton, S.C., then a student at Southern Baptist Theological Seminary, from which she earned an M.R.E. degree in 1931. They later had two children: Forrest Orion, Jr., and Carole Lynn Mixon Hale.

During all of his student years, Mixon was engaged in pastoral activities, serving churches in South Carolina and Kentucky. These included Jackson Church, Jackson Mill, S.C.; Long Branch, Bethany, and Bushy Creek Baptist churches near Greenville, S.C.; First Baptist Church, Augusta, Ky.; and First Baptist Church, Bagdad, Ky. After completing his residential work at seminary in 1931, he served for three years as pastor of Westminster Baptist Church, Westminster, S.C., and from 1934 to 1943 he was pastor of the First Baptist Church, Tifton, Ga.

In 1943 Mixon moved to Raleigh to become pastor of Tabernacle Baptist Church, then the largest Baptist church in the state. While in that position, he helped to initiate and support a movement to encourage members of the downtown Baptist churches to move out and establish neighborhood churches throughout suburban Raleigh. From this movement emerged Forest Hills, Ridge Road, St. John's, and Longview Gardens Baptist churches. He also became deeply involved in the work of the North Carolina Baptist State Convention, serving as a member of its general board from 1947 to 1951 and as president in 1949 and again in 1950.

On 23 July 1951 the trustees of Chowan College invited Mixon to become president of the college. Because of declining enrollment and financial problems, this Baptist institution had found it necessary to assume junior-college status in 1937 and had been forced to suspend operations from May 1943 to September 1949. When the trustees approached Mixon in the summer of 1951, the school was again without funds, faculty, and students; several of the trustees believed that a second suspension of operations was inevitable. Nevertheless, Mixon accepted the post and in September opened the school with 131 students. From then until his death, he worked untiringly to establish the college on a secure footing. During his tenure, Chowan doubled its student enrollment, erected six new buildings on campus, established a graphic arts department, and completed the steps necessary for accreditation by the Southern Association of Colleges and Schools. Accreditation was awarded two months after his death.

Mixon died of a heart attack at his home in Murfreesboro. He was buried in Montlawn Cemetery, Raleigh.

SEE: *Biblical Recorder*, 30 June 1943, 1 Dec. 1948, 4, 18 Aug. 1951, 3, 10 Nov. 1956; *The Chowanian* (Chowan College student newspaper), November 1956; *Encyclopedia of Southern Baptists*, vol. 3 (1971); Edgar V. McKnight and Oscar Creech, *A History of Chowan College* (1964); F. O. Mixon family papers (possession of Mrs. F. O. Mixon, Murfreesboro); John Leslie Mixon, *The Mixon-Mixson Family*, vol. 1 (1972); *North Carolina Baptist State Convention Annual*, 1937, 1946–51, 1956 (portrait).

CHARLES L. PAUL

Moffitt, Elvira Worth Jackson Walker *(3 Dec. 1836– 1 June 1930)*, patriot, club member, editor, and writer, was born in Asheboro, the daughter of Martitia Daniel and Jonathan Worth, who later became state treasurer and then governor of North Carolina. On her father's side, she was descended from English Quakers who had settled on Nantucket Island, Mass., in 1665. Her mother, a native of Virginia, was the niece of Judge Archibald D. Murphey of Hillsborough. Jonathan Worth met his bride while reading law under Murphey. Elvira grew up in Asheboro and was educated by young ladies from New England who taught in the Randolph Female Academy, founded by her father and four other men in 1839. She later attended the Edgeworth Seminary in Greensboro.

She married Samuel Spencer Jackson of Pittsboro while he was studying law in Chapel Hill and tutoring in Greek at The University of North Carolina, from which he had been graduated in 1854. On completion of his law studies, the young couple settled in Asheboro where he joined his father-in-law in the practice of law.

Although her father worked diligently to keep North Carolina in the Union, when the Civil War began Elvira plunged wholeheartedly into the war effort. Together with other women of the town, she helped sew tents and articles of clothing from material manufactured by the cotton mills along Deep River. This was merely the first of three wars in which she was active—during the Spanish-American War she helped to establish the Soldiers' Aid Society in Raleigh, and during World War I she was a leader in the War Relief Society of Richmond, Va.

When her husband died in 1875, Mrs. Jackson was left with a ten-year-old son, Herbert Worth. Two years later she married Samuel Walker, a leading merchant of Asheboro, but after only four months she was again a widow. Six years later Eli Moffitt, a prosperous farmer of Moore County, became her third husband. After his death in 1889 she moved to Raleigh to make a home with her only son, who was a founder and chief officer of the Commercial National Bank of Raleigh. A young newspaper editor, Josephus Daniels, had married her niece, Addie Worth Bagley, and for a time this young couple lived with Elvira and her son.

In Raleigh she was able to give full rein to her patriotic fervor. She affiliated with the Daughters of the Revolution, becoming state regent for the years 1906–10; on her retirement, she was named honorary state regent for life. During the twenty years that the society published the *North Carolina Booklet*, she was either coeditor, biographical editor, or a member of the advisory committee as well as a prolific contributor to its pages. An early member of the North Carolina Literary and Historical Association, she served as vice-president in 1909. The Johnston-Pettigrew Chapter of the United Daughters of the Confederacy made her its honorary president for life. She organized the Wake County School Betterment Association and was a charter member and first contributor to the State Confederate Monument Society. In 1903 she organized a group of women, called St. Luke's Circle of King's Daughters, to aid infirm and indigent sick and to found St. Luke's Home. She was an active member of the Roanoke Colony Memorial Association and was instrumental in securing a congressional appropriation for a painting of the baptism of Virginia Dare for installation in the capitol.

As the founder of the Woman's Club of Raleigh, she was made a life member at a subsequent anniversary dinner held in her honor. She wrote a history of the club movement in North Carolina, which was placed in the cornerstone of the Woman's Club's new building, erected in 1915. As an organizer of the North Carolina Peace Society, she was twice appointed, by two governors, to represent the state at the national meeting. The Stanhope Pullen Memorial Association owed its existence primarily to her efforts, and the Stanhope Pullen Gate, which stands at the entrance to the grounds of North Carolina State University, was one of her projects. Further, she was instrumental in having a bronze tablet to "Ladies of the Edenton Tea Party—1774" placed in the rotunda of the state capitol.

In 1909, when her son, Herbert Worth Jackson, was made president of the prestigious Virginia Trust Company, she followed him to Richmond and lived in his home on West Franklin Street for the remainder of her life. She was immediately invited to become a member of the Association for the Preservation of Virginia Antiquities. Elvira Moffitt personally launched the movement to organize the Matthew Fontaine Maury Memorial Association of Richmond, and a few months before her death she was asked to preside at the unveiling of a monument in Richmond to America's first and foremost oceanographer. She also worked successfully for the installation of a memorial window in the Old Blandford Church, Petersburg, Va., to commemorate the 23,000 Confederate dead who were buried there.

Her native Asheboro was never far from her thoughts. After World War I she bombarded the local newspaper and its editor, Congressman William C. Hammer, with a continuing stream of letters urging that a public library be built as a memorial to the soldiers of Randolph County who had served in that conflict.

Mrs. Moffitt died in her home in Richmond at age ninety-four. Her funeral was conducted at the First Presbyterian Church, Raleigh, and she was buried in Oakwood Cemetery.

SEE: Samuel A. Ashe, ed., *Biographical History of North Carolina*, vol. 8 (1917 [portrait]); Josephus Daniels, *Tar Heel Editor* (1939); Elvira Moffitt (Richmond), interviews, 1926, 1927; Elvira Moffitt Papers (Southern Historical Collection, University of North Carolina, Chapel Hill); Raleigh *News and Observer*, 16 Apr. 1925, 2, 15 June 1930; Richard L. Zuber, *Jonathan Worth: A Biography of a Southern Unionist* (1965).

WILLIAM UNDERWOOD

Moir, James (ca. 1710–February 1767), colonial clergyman, was sent to Edisto Island in South Carolina as a missionary of the kirk of Scotland prior to 1739. In that year, he decided to take Anglican orders and went to London to be ordained. On 12 June 1739 Commissary Alexander Garden in Charleston wrote to the bishop of London that the Reverend Mr. Moir would not be acceptable to the Anglican congregation at Edisto, attributing the objection to prejudice excited against him by the Presbyterians. Accordingly, the bishop assigned Moir to the Cape Fear section.

Having received the king's bounty (passage money paid by the king), Moir arrived in North Carolina and was assigned to St. James's Parish, Wilmington, in 1739. After 1742 he officiated in St. Philip's, Brunswick, as well. Missionaries supported by the Society for the Propagation of the Gospel in Foreign Parts were required to send reports to the secretary of the organization in London twice a year. Moir's reports—the most voluminous of any missionary—were filled with complaints regarding officials and the recalcitrance of his parishioners. His complaint that when living in Bruns-

wick, he had to live in the garret of his schoolhouse, with a single slave to cook his meals, is a reminder that colonial clergymen often were also schoolteachers.

Moir suffered from intermittent fevers or malaria, and in 1747, with official permission, he transferred to Edgecombe Parish, Edgecombe County, thinking that a move slightly northwards would improve his health. In 1759 Halifax County was formed from the northern section of Edgecombe. However, Edgecombe Parish remained in the new county division and the parish in what remained of Edgecombe County was given the name, St. Mary's. Moir chose to officiate in the new parish of St. Mary's. In 1760 he was one of the commissioners appointed to lay out the town of Tarboro and was one of the first lot holders. Joseph Blount Cheshire, Jr., bishop of the Diocese of North Carolina (1893–1932), sensed his influence in the naming of the principal streets of the new town for the patron saints of England, Scotland, and Wales. The streets of Halifax town, laid out the same year, were also so named. The present Calvary Church, Tarboro, was built on a lot owned by this early clergyman.

In 1762 Moir moved to St. George's, Northampton County, where he remained until the end of 1765. While in Northampton he seems to have visited Bertie and Hertford counties and his old charge of St. Mary's with some regularity. Moir's final communication to the Society for the Propagation of the Gospel in London, written from Suffolk, Va., and dated 13 Oct. 1766, describes a trip he took for his health to New York, Boston, and Rhode Island. He closed by saying: "My constitution is so crazy that I despair of being in a condition to officiate in such large parishes." He was no doubt referring to the charges he had held in North Carolina. After Moir's death, Governor William Tryon commented: "his death . . . defeated the Society's direction to have him fixed in some parish."

During his stay in North Carolina, Moir carried on a personal feud with Governor Arthur Dobbs, who wrote in 1764: "He lives upon a plantation penuriously and unhappily and lays out his salary as missionary for retirement." A close reading of the records, however, will show that Moir left solid accomplishments behind in the parishes where he served. He never married. On his death he left an estate of a thousand acres in Edgecombe to his brother Henry, the rector of the parish of Auchterlool in the county of Fife, Scotland.

SEE: Henry W. Lewis, *Northampton Parishes* (1951); William Manross, comp., *Fulham Papers in the Lambeth Palace Library* (1965); William L. Saunders, ed., *Colonial Records of North Carolina*, vols. 4–6 (1886–88); C. T. Smith and Stuart H. Smith, *Trinity Parish, Scotland Neck, and Edgecombe Parish, Halifax County* (1955).

CLAIBORNE T. SMITH, JR.

Monk, Archibald (ca. 20 Aug. 1788–7 June 1869), political leader and educator, was born on Monk's Branch of Dunhams Creek, Moore County, the oldest of eleven children of James and Catherine Monk, both natives of Scotland. His father, veteran of a stint in the North Carolina Continental Line during the American Revolution, was for many years a precentor at Union Presbyterian Church near the Monk farm.

Educated at Moore County Academy and at Fayetteville Academy, Monk in 1815 opened a dry goods store in Fayetteville in partnership with David D. Salmon of Sampson County. He informed the Fayetteville public in August 1818 that he would "attend to the Renewal of

Notes in any of the Banks of this place" on the condition that the interested parties furnish him "with the requisite sum of money." By 1820 he had moved to Sampson County, where he operated a general store in Piney Grove District with his brother, Cornelius H. Monk. He soon relocated in Westbrooks District and acquired extensive landholdings on both sides of the public road that ran from Clinton to Smithfield. He also became the owner of a general store from which the agricultural community in which he lived derived its name, Monk's Store (now Monks Crossroads). By the time of the Civil War, Monk's plantation was the largest producer of cotton in Westbrooks District.

Civic responsibility early absorbed Monk's attention, and he expended time and energy on behalf of his neighbors and county in numerous ways. With unfailing regularity he served as witness to wills and deeds, executor of wills, administrator and auditor of estates, guardian of minors, poll keeper, overseer of roads, patrol committeeman, and justice of the peace. Monk "read" medicine and traveled about his area on horseback tending to the sick from a saddlebag full of medical books and supplies. Politics and education, however, proved to be the fields in which he made his most outstanding contributions as a public servant.

In 1829 Monk was elected to his first term in the General Assembly as a representative of Sampson County; he remained in the House of Commons until 1835. As a legislator he was active in various committees and wrote numerous bills and resolutions. He gave special consideration to public education, serving on the committee on education during five sessions. Monk's support of state aid for internal improvements was a logical corollary to his belief in the imperative of public education in North Carolina. In the legislative session of 1832–33, he worked on the committee on internal improvements and later guided a Sampson County committee to help promote a broad program of expansion, notably railroad construction. He proceeded to break with the Democratic party when it became clear that President Andrew Jackson opposed distribution of federal funds to the states for internal improvements.

One of the founders of the new Whig party in Sampson County and that party's most influential spokesman in the area, Monk was defeated by a Democrat when he ran for the state senate in 1835 and again when he sought election to the lower house five years later. He did have the satisfaction of keeping Westbrooks District faithfully in the Whig column from 1835 to the end of the antebellum period. Whether as a delegate to Whig state conventions or as a party committeeman or assistant elector, Monk pressed the cause of every Whig gubernatorial and presidential candidate in North Carolina.

Notwithstanding his strong Whig affiliation in a Democratic county, Monk effectively promoted public education locally after his terms in the House of Commons. The Whig-controlled General Assembly finally succeeded in passing a comprehensive common school law early in 1839. That summer Monk was counted among those citizens named by the Sampson County Court of Pleas and Quarter Sessions to comprise a committee to launch the common schools in the county. Immediately elected chairman of the board of county superintendents, he continued in that capacity until 1865. Under Monk's zealous and efficient leadership, Sampson County developed one of the most progressive school systems in North Carolina. In 1859 he proudly informed Calvin H. Wiley, state superintendent of common schools, that Sampson County "goes ahead of any of the adjoining counties in the cause of education." Unfortunately, the progress achieved by his many years of dedication to the common schools was mostly undone by the Civil War.

Monk had diverse interests to complement his political and educational commitments. Long an active Mason, he was the first secretary of Hiram Lodge No. 98 in Clinton, organized with his assistance in 1827. Like his parents he was a Presbyterian, and on a visit to Moore County in 1843, he too became a member of Union Church. The post office established at Monk's Store in 1848 had Monk, the community's leading citizen, as its postmaster. Two years later his respectable stature earned him a place at the district meeting in Wilmington to select one Whig and one Democratic representative to attend a convention in Nashville, Tenn., to try to resolve the controversy then raging over the territorial extension of slavery. By the time he made his will in 1856, Monk could state that his handwriting was so well known in Sampson County that he had no need for any witnesses. As befitted a son of a soldier of the American Revolution, he lent his best efforts the next year to raising money for the erection of a monument on the battlefield at Moore's Creek Bridge. He retained his position as postmaster at Monk's Store under the Confederate government when North Carolina seceded from the Union. Receiving a presidential pardon after the Civil War, he resumed his postmastership under the federal government, only to lose that job with the advent of Reconstruction.

On 5 Aug. 1824 Monk married Harriet Hargrove, the daughter of Aaron and Jane Carr Hargrove of Piney Grove District, by whom he had nine sons and two daughters. He died at his home at Monk's Store of an intestinal disorder and was buried next to his wife in the family cemetery on his plantation. In 1979 his house was moved to Newton Grove, where it was restored as the centerpiece of Heritage Place in Weeks Park.

In appearance Monk was of medium height and build, with brown hair and eyes. At least one daguerreotype of him reveals a strong but narrow face etched with age and character. A number of his informative common school reports and letters are in the Reports of Chairmen of County Superintendents of Common Schools (1841–46), the Common School Reports of the Superintendent of Public Instruction (1852–64), and the Calvin H. Wiley Papers—all in the North Carolina State Archives, Raleigh—and in the Calvin H. Wiley Collection in the Southern Historical Collection at the University of North Carolina at Chapel Hill.

SEE: Charles H. Bowman, Jr., "Archibald Monk: Public Servant of Sampson County," *North Carolina Historical Review* 47 (October 1970); Fayetteville *American*, 10 Nov. 1815; Fayetteville *Carolina Observer*, 13 Aug. 1818; *Fayetteville Observer*, 6 Nov. 1849; *Journal of the House of Commons* (1829–35); Sampson County Court of Pleas and Quarter Sessions Minute Docket, 1819–57 (North Carolina State Archives, Raleigh).

CHARLES H. BOWMAN, JR.

Monk, John Carr (*19 Feb. 1827–10 Sept. 1877*), physician and religious leader, was born in Westbrooks District, Sampson County, the second of eleven children of Archibald and Harriet Hargrove Monk. He received his elementary education in a one-room schoolhouse on his father's plantation and then attended nearby Spring Vale Academy. Following his graduation in 1846, he taught in the Sampson County common schools for four years.

The encouragement of friends in the medical profession in Clinton led Monk to matriculate at the University of Pennsylvania, where he was awarded a doctor of medicine degree in 1852.

Returning to Sampson County, he actively supported the Whig party and various local and state projects for internal improvements. He also took a keen interest in Masonic affairs, first as a member of Hiram Lodge No. 98 and then of Mill Creek Lodge No. 125. Monk served in the latter lodge at different times as junior warden, senior deacon, and worshipful master. In 1855 he began acquiring property in Newton Grove, thenceforth his permanent residence. Confident of his good judgment, Monk's neighbors frequently called upon him to be a witness to wills and deeds and to be the executor of wills. The dedicated physician was long a familiar figure about the countryside, sometimes traveling as far as forty miles in his horse-drawn buggy to attend patients in Sampson, Johnston, and Wayne counties.

Politics increasingly drew Monk's attention as the Civil War approached. Sampson County Whigs who gathered in Newton Grove in October 1860 selected him to go to Salisbury to meet with other concerned individuals to try to devise a means of strengthening the cause of the Union in North Carolina. Four months later he was a Unionist candidate for a proposed state convention to consider secession. Although he was not elected, he did have the satisfaction of seeing the convention rejected by voters across the state. When the General Assembly itself called for the election in May 1861 of delegates to a convention, Monk again took the field, this time as Sampson County's sole Unionist candidate; Westbrooks District gave him his only votes.

The advent of secession did not dampen Monk's political spirits. In September 1861 he was appointed a delegate for Sampson County to the convention to nominate a candidate to represent the Third District in the Confederate Congress and also to name an elector for the district in the forthcoming presidential election. Monk enlisted on 3 Mar. 1862 as surgeon to the Twenty-fifth Militia Regiment, Sixth Brigade, and saw fighting firsthand when the Battle of Bentonville took place in 1865 a few miles from Newton Grove.

After the war Monk joined the Republican party and continued his involvement in community affairs. The economic dislocation of the times prompted the enterprising doctor to augment the income from his medical practice by establishing a dry goods store and drugstore on his Newton Grove property. Located in the same building was the post office, where Monk once held the postmastership for ten months. His prestige was such that in 1868 he was elected the first Sampson County trustee of The University of North Carolina under the new state constitution of that year. Throughout the county he was known for his personal integrity, strong individuality, and jovial disposition.

For many years Monk belonged to Goshen Methodist Church, but the ejection there in 1870 of Negro members caused him to rethink his religious views. Early the next year he happened to receive a shipment of medical supplies from New York City. Wrapped around one of the items was a copy of the *New York Herald* containing a sermon of Archbishop John McCloskey about the unity of belief in the Roman Catholic church. Monk was so impressed by the archbishop's words when he read them that he wrote a letter "To Any Catholic Priest" in Wilmington requesting further information about Catholic doctrines. The letter reached the hands of Bishop James Gibbons, who promptly recommended various books for Monk to study. The correspondence that opened between the two men ended in Monk's conversion to Catholicism. Gibbons baptized the doctor and his family in St. Thomas's Church, Wilmington, in October 1871.

In spite of an initial hostility to Monk's new faith on the part of many people in the Newton Grove area, the first Catholic priest arrived there in 1872 and preached outdoors to a sizable group of curious farmers. Gibbons himself came in due course to preach and to baptize several converts. On that occasion Gibbons and Monk decided that regularly scheduled visits by a priest were warranted. The crowds that turned out for those visits grew so large that it became necessary to erect a temporary shelter for their accommodation and to make plans for the construction of a permanent church and a schoolhouse. Monk donated money and land for the buildings, and work on them soon commenced. St. Mark's Church was consecrated by Gibbons in August 1874, and a parochial school was opened within a year. By 1877 the congregation of St. Mark's numbered about one hundred people. Twenty years later three hundred Catholics attended services at the church, a fact that inspired Gibbons to refer to the first convert as "the Monk who fathered three hundred children." As a result of Monk's conversion, Newton Grove today is the most solidly Catholic rural community in North Carolina.

In May 1855 Monk married Euphemia Alice Eason, the daughter of John and Elizabeth Williams Eason of Meadow District, Johnston County, by whom he had three daughters. He died of apoplexy at his home in Newton Grove and was buried in the Catholic cemetery behind the church that he founded.

A man of medium height and weight with brown hair and eyes, Monk wore a close-cropped beard that accentuated his piercing gaze, the intensity of which is captured in daguerreotypes and a charcoal portrait. In the outdoor drama, *Echoes from the Grove*, presented during the Newton Grove centennial in August 1979, Monk and his father figured conspicuously. References to and letters from Monk appear in the St. Thomas's Church Baptismal Register, St. Mary's Rectory, Wilmington; the Diary of James Cardinal Gibbons, Archives of the Archdiocese of Baltimore, Md.; and the Griffith John McRee Papers and the University of North Carolina Papers, Southern Historical Collection, University of North Carolina at Chapel Hill.

SEE: Charles H. Bowman, Jr., "Dr. John Carr Monk: Sampson County's Latter Day 'Cornelius,'" *North Carolina Historical Review* 50 (January 1973); Diary of James Cardinal Gibbons (Archives, Archdiocese of Baltimore, Md.); J. T. Ellis, *The Life of James Cardinal Gibbons, Archbishop of Baltimore, 1834–1921*, vol. 1 (1952); *Fayetteville Observer*, 4 Mar., 23 May 1861; *Fayetteville Times*, 18 Aug. 1979; *Goldsboro Messenger*, 13 Sept. 1877; C. H. Hamlin, *Ninety Bits of North Carolina Biography* (1946); Griffith John McRee Papers and University of North Carolina Papers (Southern Historical Collection, University of North Carolina, Chapel Hill); St. Thomas's Church Baptismal Register (St. Mary's Rectory, Wilmington); Sampson County Estates, Dr. John C. Monk (North Carolina State Archives, Raleigh).

CHARLES H. BOWMAN, JR.

Monk, Thelonious Sphere (*10 Oct. 1917–17 Feb. 1982*), jazz musician and composer, was born in Rocky Mount, the son of Thelonious and Barbara Batts Monk. When Monk was four, his mother took him and two other children to New York, while his father remained in the South. In the early 1930s the family moved into a small apartment in Manhattan, the city where Monk spent most of the remainder of his life. His residence through most of this time was an apartment on West 63rd Street.

Largely self-taught as a musician, Monk started his musical activities by age six, and at ten he began playing an old piano that belonged to his grandparents. Additional valuable experience was obtained when he accompanied his mother's singing at their local Baptist church in New York. One of his first jazz idols was Louis Armstrong, while major influences on his early musical development included Earl "Fatha" Hines, Art Tatum, Fats Waller, James P. Johnston, Willie Smith, Jimmy Yancey, and especially Duke Ellington. As a teenager in Harlem during the depression, Monk developed his highly personalized style of skewed melodies and oblique harmonic progressions. During the late 1930s he played the piano with traveling evangelist shows and in brief gigs around New York City, eventually settling in 1939 with Keg Purnell's quartet.

Monk's emergence as an accomplished jazz pianist occurred during his association with Minton's Playhouse at the Hotel Cecil on 118th Street in Harlem, where in 1940 saxophonist Henry Minton converted a run-down dining room into a jazz club that featured avant-garde improvisation and freewheeling jam sessions. Kenny Clarke organized the first band at Minton's Playhouse, with Monk as the pianist of the group. It was at Minton's and at the Uptown Club that Monk thus became part of the small group of musical innovators whose harmonic and rhythmic explorations spawned the angular breakaway from conventional jazz known as "bebop" or "bop." Although this episode in American jazz has become somewhat romanticized, most of the musicians involved in the events apparently did not consider that they were doing anything unusual or self-consciously creative but merely "playing a gig" for fun and money.

In the early years, particularly at Minton's Playhouse, Monk worked with such leading jazz figures as trumpeter John Birks "Dizzy" Gillespie and alto-saxophonist Charlie "Bird" Parker, as well as Charlie Christian, Joe Guy, and Nick Fenton. At other times during the 1940s he was a member of bands headed by Lucky Millinder (1942), Kenny Clarke (1942), Scotty Scott (1943), Coleman Hawkins (1944), and Cootie Williams (1944). Between 1947 and 1952 Monk produced a series of recordings on the Blue Note label, a collection that remains among the most significant and original in modern jazz.

Although his asymmetrical and complex musical ideas exerted a profound influence on an entire generation of jazz musicians, Monk himself had slipped into virtual obscurity by the early 1950s. His career suffered a major setback during this time, when his cabaret card, a prerequisite for employment in establishments serving liquor, was revoked for six years due to an allegedly unjustified charge involving drug violations. Thus, from 1951 to 1957 Monk was only rarely able to obtain paying jobs in New York.

In the middle and late 1950s, however, he reemerged with new popularity, aided by critically acclaimed recordings with John Coltrane and Sonny Rollins. In 1954 he produced important albums with Rollins, Percy Heath, Art Blakey, Julius Watkins, Miles Davis, and Milt Jackson. The turning point came in 1957, when Monk released his album *Brilliant Corners*, the first Riverside issue containing his original compositions. Later that year, through the assistance of the Baroness de Koenigswarter, Monk was able to obtain a cabaret card, thereby permitting him to resume paid engagements in New

York City. In the summer of 1957 Monk brought together at the Five Spot Cafe a quartet including himself, John Coltrane, Wilbur Ware, and Shadow Wilson. This now legendary engagement, which continued through New Year's Eve 1957, paved the way for Monk's rediscovery as a major figure in modern jazz.

Monk appeared on CBS-TV in December 1957 in the "Sound of Jazz," while in April and May 1958 he was engaged at the Village Vanguard. Subsequently, he was chosen as the outstanding international jazz pianist in 1958, 1959, and 1960 and was elected to *Down Beat* magazine's Hall of Fame. Monk appeared in the Randall's Island Detroit Jazz Festival and at Town Hall in 1959, at Philharmonic Hall in 1963, and at Carnegie Hall in 1964. During the last half of the 1960s, he led a quartet that toured widely at clubs, festivals, and concerts around the world. In 1971 and 1972 Monk toured Europe performing with a group called the Giants of Jazz, which included Sonny Stitt and Monk's old colleague, Dizzie Gillespie. Semiretired after the tour due to health problems, Monk later performed a concert of his music at Carnegie Hall on 6 Apr. 1974 for the New York Jazz Repertory Company and at the Newport Jazz Festival in New York in 1975. He received a special tribute from President Jimmy Carter in 1978 during a jazz concert at the White House.

Monk created more than seventy jazz compositions, of which his early ballad, "Round Midnight," remains perhaps his best-known piece. Other recognized works included "Epistrophy," "Blue Monk," "Off Minor," "Straight, No Chaser," "Well, You Needn't," "Four in One," "Ruby My Dear," "I Mean You," "I Should Care," "Misterioso," "Evonel," "Criss Cross," "Hackensack," "Trinkle Tinkle," "We See," "Locomotive," "Reflections," and "Crepescule with Nellie." He also composed the musical score for the film *Les Liaisons Dangereuses* and appeared in the movie *Jazz on a Summer's Day*. At various times in his career he recorded for Blue Note (1947–52), Prestige (1952–55), Riverside (1955–59), Columbia, Everest, Jazzland, and Savoy.

A major reason for the uniqueness of Monk's contribution is that, to a greater extent than any other musician of his time, he created music that originated completely from within jazz. Most other important composer-pianists have borrowed, with varying degrees of successful assimilation, from formal European music, thus giving the listener an unconscious feeling of ease and familiarity with their work. With Monk's compositions there is no such convenient handle to the music; they create a distinctly different impression from that experienced in listening to most other modern jazz works.

His compositions are angular, complex, and difficult to play. One critic characterized his music as possessing "dissonances and rhythms that often give one the sensation of missing the bottom step in the dark." Monk's melody and harmony lines are so integrated structurally that it is almost impossible for soloists to improvise on the chord sequences alone. His original themes, characterized by rhythmic displacements and irregular structures, are considered among the most unusual of jazz forms, while his compositions often possess melodies of great harmonic charm. Monk usually based his writing on conventional, formalized twelve and thirty-two bar structures, such that the distinctive aspect of his work rests in the melodic originality and harmonic substructures. His rhythmic virtuosity is characterized by mastery of displaced accents, shifted meters, shaded delays, anticipations, silence, and pauses, yet his work remains highly structured and ordered, typically providing a striking sense of emotional and artistic completeness in each piece. Although his compositions are regarded as his most important contribution to jazz, Monk's extraordinary mastery of piano technique, with the stark somber quality and unique dynamics of his playing, made him among the most influential and popular figures in jazz.

Monk was a distinguished-looking man, over six feet tall and massively built, who usually dressed rather elegantly and sported a black Vandyke beard, bamboo-framed sunglasses, and a skullcap, which combined to give him a ferocious appearance, despite being known as a kind and gentle person. He died in Englewood, N.J., following a stroke. He was survived by his wife, Nellie, and two children, Thelonious, Jr., and Barbara "Booboo" Monk. Portraits appear in many articles in *Down Beat*, in his obituary notices, and in Valerie Wilmer's *Face of Black Music* (1976).

SEE: John Chilton, *Who's Who of Jazz* (1978); Leonard Feather, *The Book of Jazz* (1965) and *The Encyclopedia of Jazz* (1966, 1976); Joe Goldberg, *Jazz Masters of the Fifties* (1980); *Greensboro Daily News*, 20 Feb. 1982; Paul Jeffrey, personal contact; Raleigh *News and Observer*, 18 Feb. 1982; *Time* magazine, 1 Mar. 1982; Martin Williams, *Jazz Masters in Transition* (1980) and *The Jazz Tradition* (1970); *Winston-Salem Journal*, 18 Feb. 1982.

MARCUS B. SIMPSON, JR.

Montfort [read: Mumford], **Joseph** (d. 25 Mar. 1776), colonial legislator, public official, and provincial grand master of Freemasons, is said to have been the grandson of Colonel Thomas Montfort of Old Point Comfort, Va. In 1752 he moved to North Carolina and made entry in Lord Granville's land office for 419 acres on Quankey Creek, Halifax (then Edgecombe) County, which was surveyed for him in February 1753. Moving with him from Virginia and settling near him on Quankey Creek were various relatives, including his sister Sarah (1717–1800) and her husband David Stokes (parents of John and Montfort Stokes), and Montfort, Joseph, and John Eelbeck.

Montfort's land entry ripened into a grant on 1 Nov. 1753; two weeks later he married Priscilla Hill, one of the daughters of Colonel Benjamin Hill of Bertie County. By this marriage Montfort gained two influential brothers-in-law: Colonel Alexander McCulloch of Elk Marsh, Halifax County (cousin of the half blood to James Iredell and cousin once removed to Henry Eustace McCulloh), and John Campbell of Lazy Hill Plantation, Bertie County (the rich merchant-planter for whom Governor Arthur Dobbs named the town of Campbellton). Shortly afterwards, Montfort was appointed clerk of the Edgecombe County court. On the division of that county in 1759, he became clerk of the court of Halifax County, then clerk of the Halifax District Superior Court as well. Montfort represented Halifax County in the General Assembly in 1762 and 1764. In the latter year he was, with others of his kin, made a commissioner for the town of Halifax, as well as appointed provincial treasurer for the Northern District of North Carolina. Thereafter he represented the town of Halifax in all five assemblies held from 1766 to 1774. The town elected him a delegate to the Second Provincial Congress (April 1775), but ill health prevented his attendance.

Governor Josiah Martin, when he was engaged in a struggle with Montfort for possession of the land office records of Earl Granville during 1773 and 1774, attributed a most unengaging character to Montfort: "[there is] a certain slyness, and mysteriousness about the man

. . .—in short he is a character nobody pretends to understand. He is well received by all, esteemed by very few, and considered a Problem by everybody." These words were written in ill-feeling and must be weighed accordingly. At the same time, however, the motivation behind several important passages of Montfort's life remains shrouded in mystery.

When in the late 1750s a quarrel sprang up between Montfort's brother-in-law, Colonel Alexander McCulloch of Elk Marsh, and Francis Corbin, principal agent in Lord Granville's land office, it would have been logical for Montfort to take up McCulloch's cause. Probably he did. But the fact remains that when McCulloch's extralegal posse seized Corbin in Edenton in January 1759, forcibly brought him to the Enfield jail, and obliged him to post a £2,000 penalty bond to reform the Proprietary land office, Montfort came to Corbin's aid and stood surety for his bond. No doubt it is significant that after Corbin was dismissed from office three months later, Montfort was, in November 1759, given entrée to the land office by his appointment as an entry taker as well as deputy collector of quitrents within the Proprietary. Four years later he became vice-auditor to the Proprietary. It was in the latter capacity that he came into possession of Lord Granville's records, the retrieval of which caused Governor Martin so much trouble. After attempting for a year to detach the records from Montfort's grasp, Martin finally got them by promising in May 1774 to continue Montfort in the office of vice-auditor and, presumably, by acceding to his demand for grants totaling approximately 7,000 acres of choice land.

Nor is there a satisfactory explanation for Montfort's opposition to Governor William Tryon during the Regulator campaign. When called upon for funds to outfit Tryon's office, John Ashe, treasurer of the Southern District, had paid the drafts requested by Tryon and, when his funds were exhausted, had issued notes on the faith and credit of provincial revenues. When Tryon drew upon Montfort, however, the northern treasurer is said to have refused to honor the drafts on the grounds that he had no funds on hand for contingencies. Montfort's recalcitrance in this matter may have been grounded in his experience during the 1768 investigation into the production of counterfeit money at New Bern in which James Davis's journeymen printers, Samuel R. Hall and James Mansfield, were involved. Since only the two provincial treasurers (Ashe and Montfort), the master printer (Davis), and his journeymen (Hall and Mansfield) had access to the plates, paper, and press, all came under suspicion. Montfort's enemies promptly mounted a canard against him. Although forced to admit that there was no proof of his complicity in the counterfeiting, they kept alive suspicions against him for the remainder of his life through their insinuations both to Governor Tryon, who perceived Montfort to be opposed to his administration, and to Governor Martin, who felt the effects of Montfort's opposition over custody of Lord Granville's records. Montfort took no public measures to acquit himself, but he is said to have watched for his accusers secretly, having resolved to make them repent their temerity through legal prosecution. As there were no prosecutions for slander, it remains impossible to identify by name Montfort's enemies in the colony or to determine the grounds for their enmity. It is possible that their identity could shed light on the early history of freemasonry in North Carolina.

It is assumed that Montfort was originally a member of a lodge of freemasons operating near the home of Alexander McCulloch of Elk Marsh. The Marsh Store Lodge was organized under the name "White Hart

Lodge" but when and under what authority is unknown. When Montfort and his kinsmen and associates decided to take the town of Halifax in hand and make it blossom in 1764, they not only moved into town and built residences there, but they also petitioned for a charter to establish a lodge of freemasons. On 1 Nov. 1764 Cornelius Harnett of St. John's Lodge, Wilmington, issued a warrant of constitution for Royal White Hart Lodge, Halifax, which he signed as grand master. (The assumption is that Harnett held a deputation from Benjamin Smith of Charles Town, who had been inducted as grand master of North Carolina and South Carolina early in 1762.)

At its first meeting in April 1765, the new lodge appointed a committee to meet with a committee from White Hart Lodge at Elk Marsh in order to make equitable division of all monies and matters between the two lodges. (It is probable that White Hart Lodge at Elk Marsh collapsed during the Revolution or sometime thereafter, for in 1794 its treasurer was required to surrender the jewels and apparatus of the parent lodge to the Royal White Hart Lodge in Halifax.) In June 1765 Montfort was elected treasurer, then master of Royal White Hart Lodge; for the remainder of his life he appears to have been preeminent in the life of the lodge. At the end of 1767 the lodge authorized the purchase of elegant glassware from England and four one-gallon punch bowls of Bow china, presumably to be ordered by Montfort on his forthcoming journey with Alexander McCulloch to England. While in England, Montfort secured a new charter for Royal White Hart Lodge under authority of the duke of Beaufort, grand master of England, which he presented to the lodge on his return in May 1768. No doubt the new charter gave the lodge more prestige than the one issued by Cornelius Harnett in 1764.

It may have been at this time that Montfort put into motion the machinery for securing for himself a deputation as provincial grand master for North Carolina. The first hurdle was cleared with the deputation of Edgerton Leigh as grand master of South Carolina, publication of which was made on 8 Mar. 1770, for Harnett's deputation would have come to an end with the termination of Benjamin Smith's tenure as grand master of North Carolina and South Carolina. Presumably as a result of a correspondence Montfort initiated with officials in England, he received a deputation as provincial grand master on 14 Jan. 1771. At the critical place for stipulating jurisdiction, his deputation was worded: "Provincial Grand Master of and for America." The phrase "of and for America," rather than "of and for North Carolina in America," led to a rather unnecessary but long-lived debate in Masonic circles. The minutes of the Grand Lodge of England for 6 Feb. 1771 record his deputation as "Provincial G. M. for North Carolina." The fact that Montfort granted a warrant for a Virginia lodge, in the absence of a grand master for that province, does not actually suggest a continental jurisdiction for him. Continental jurisdiction had been attached by the grand masters of England to the grand masters of Massachusetts since 1733, and Massachusetts had exercised the function by warranting over thirty lodges in eight of the colonies between 1733 and the time of Montfort's deputation.

Although the records of the grand lodge established by Montfort have not been recovered (and are not known to have survived), Masonic historians have been able to discover a part of its history. It appears that Montfort created a new order of precedence for the North Carolina lodges and, by so doing, left a controversy that ripened after his death. He issued a new

charter to the eleven-member St. John's Lodge at New Bern on 10 Jan. 1772 and is said to have issued a new one to the Royal White Hart Lodge, Halifax, on 10 Mar. 1772. During the next three years Montfort granted warrants of constitution to six other lodges: St. John's, Kinston; Royal Edwin, Windsor; Dornoch, Bute County; Royal William, Winton; Royal Arch, Cabin Point, Va.; and Unanimity, Edenton. It is noteworthy that he seems never to have issued warrants for lodges in either the Piedmont region or the Cape Fear area of North Carolina. This suggests that he was able to extend his jurisdiction only to those counties lying in the northern inner coastal plain, where his personal influence or that of his family connections prevailed. In the absence of evidence, it is unclear whether this fact should be attributed to opposition to Montfort from within freemasonry circles, to his political guile, or merely to his increasingly failing health.

Montfort appears to have suffered from a pulmonary ailment that threatened his life during the winter months. In March 1774 he was declared to be past all hope of recovery, in March 1775 he was again so ill that he was unable to attend the Provincial Congress in New Bern, and in March 1776 he succumbed to his malady.

Fifteen years after Montfort's death a dispute over precedence erupted among St. John's Lodge in Wilmington, St. John's Lodge in New Bern, and the Royal White Hart Lodge. In 1791 the Grand Lodge of North Carolina restored St. John's Lodge, Wilmington, to its premier position and assigned second place to Montfort's Royal White Hart Lodge on the basis of Harnett's 1764 warrant to the lodge. St. John's Lodge, New Bern, could produce no warrant of constitution earlier than Montfort's warrant of 1772 and thus was ranked third. Two years later the quarrel broke out anew between St. John's Lodge, New Bern, and the Royal White Hart Lodge. The former claimed precedence after Wilmington (to which, in all fairness, it was entitled by age). New Bern, however, abandoned its claim in 1795, when it became obvious that the lodge could not provide documentary evidence of its antiquity and that the other lodges in the state were prepared to close ranks against it.

Montfort's portrait, owned by the Grand Lodge of North Carolina, reveals a handsome, pale man with a penetrating but introspective look and a mysterious half smile on his lips. He was survived by his wife, Priscilla Hill, and three children: Henry, Mary (Mrs. Willie Jones), and Elizabeth (Mrs. John Baptista Ashe).

SEE: Samuel A. Ashe, ed., *Biographical History of North Carolina*, vol. 6 (1907); Hennig Cohen, *The South-Carolina Gazette, 1732–1775* (1953); Granville Papers (Marquis of Bath, Longleat, England); Granville Proprietary Records (North Carolina State Archives, Raleigh); Albert G. Mackey, *Encyclopedia of Freemasonry* (1917); Mrs. John N. Martin, "Stokes Notes," *William and Mary Quarterly*, 2d ser., 8 (April 1928); Thomas C. Parramore, *Launching the Craft: The First Half Century of Freemasonry in North Carolina* (1975); York County, Va., Register of Deeds and Bonds, vol. 3 (1713–29), Yorktown.

GEORGE STEVENSON

Montgomery, John (d. May 1744), chief justice, attorney general, and Assembly member in colonial North Carolina, was appointed attorney general on 23 Aug. 1723 during the administration of Governor William Reed, although, according to *North Carolina Government, 1585–1979*, there is no evidence that Montgomery actually served at this time. Reappointed attorney general on 30 Nov. 1730, he was suspended from office on 30 Sept. 1734 by Governor George Burrington. Burrington appointed John Hodgson to succeed Montgomery; however, Hodgson served only for the two months left in Burrington's term, if he actually served at all. Either Montgomery was restored to office by Burrington's successor, Governor Gabriel Johnston, or he never left the post. Montgomery remained attorney general until he was commissioned as chief justice by the Crown in March 1741. While attorney general, he was appointed (1732) deputy inspector and comptroller general for quitrents for the colony.

He also served as Tyrrell County representative to North Carolina's Third, Fourth, and Fifth Assembly (1738–41). As a legislator, he demonstrated leadership as chairman of the Committee of the Whole and of an important committee dealing with the transportation of the king's troops. In addition to his service in the Assembly, he was a justice of the peace for Chowan County for two terms (March 1735 and 1739).

Montgomery continued as chief justice until his death. His will was probated in Chowan County before Governor Johnston on 22 May 1744. He devised his estate to his wife, Anne Laster; the will made no mention of any children or other relatives. Montgomery was succeeded by Chief Justice Edward Moseley.

SEE: Robert J. Cain, ed., *Records of the Executive Council, 1664–1734* (1984) and *1735–1754* (1988); John L. Cheney, Jr., ed., *North Carolina Government, 1585–1979* (1981); J. Bryan Grimes, ed., *Abstract of North Carolina Wills* (1910); William L. Saunders, ed., *Colonial Records of North Carolina*, vol. 3 (1886).

MARSHALL HURLEY

Montgomery, Walter Alexander *(17 Feb. 1845–26 Nov. 1921)*, associate justice of the North Carolina Supreme Court, attorney, and Confederate officer, was born in Warrenton, the son of Thomas Alexander (7 May 1818–3 Nov. 1873) and Darian Dawson Cheek Montgomery (15 Jan. 1823–12 Nov. 1849). His grandfather, William Montgomery, at age twenty-one, emigrated from Northern Ireland to New York City in the late eighteenth century. After working as a merchant and silversmith on Maiden Lane in New York, he moved to Hertford County, N.C., about 1800. William soon settled in Warren County and, on 14 Jan. 1809, married Charlotte Jordan, the daughter of Marcellus and Martha (Nancy Ann) Ward Jordan.

Young Montgomery was only sixteen when he enlisted in 1861 as a private in Company E, First North Carolina Cavalry. A month later he was discharged because of physical disability. Within ten days, on 21 August, he enlisted again, this time in Company A, Second North Carolina Volunteers, which became Company F, Twelfth North Carolina Infantry. He was promoted to sergeant late in 1862 and to second lieutenant on 8 Nov. 1864. Montgomery participated in all of the battles fought by the Army of Northern Virginia—from Hanover Courthouse (1862) to the surrender at Appomattox. He was wounded twice: at Chancellorsville and during the first day's fighting at Gettysburg. On 9 Apr. 1865 he was paroled at Appomattox Court House, Va.

Returning to Warrenton, Montgomery continued his classical studies at the Warrenton Male Academy before studying law under former Attorney General William Eaton, Jr. On 14 Jan. 1867 he received his license to practice in the county court and became county attorney. He

was also editor for I. H. Bennett of the *Warrenton Courier*. On 14 Jan. 1868 he received his superior court license, and during that year he edited a newspaper of his own, called *The Living Present*. In 1873 Montgomery and his wife went to Memphis, Tenn., where he practiced law until 1876. He then returned to Warrenton and resumed his former practice. In 1893 he moved to Raleigh and practiced until January 1895, when he was elected associate justice of the state supreme court.

Montgomery served as associate justice for ten years. His work and opinions on the bench are contained in twenty-two volumes of the *North Carolina Supreme Court Reports*, beginning with volume 116. His most eloquent censure of a litigant appears at the end of *Bearden v. Fullum* (129 N.C. 479). His most celebrated case was *Nicholas v. Gladden* (117 N.C. 497), which was cited seventeen times in the next eighteen years. After January 1905, when his term expired, Montgomery practiced law in Raleigh and was appointed standing master in the old U.S. Circuit Court for the Eastern District of North Carolina. His opinions were direct and to the point, marked by accuracy, clear reasoning, and absence of the spectacular.

On 27 Sept. 1871, in Roanoke, Va., Montgomery married Lizzie Holman Wilson (b. 12 May 1850, Warrenton; d. 1 Jan. 1944, Raleigh), the daughter of Dr. Thomas Epps Wilson (7 Feb. 1817–15 Aug. 1876), who married Janet Mitchel (17 Jan. 1828–24 Oct. 1899) on 14 July 1847. Janet was the daughter of Peter Mitchel, of Scotland, and his wife, Elizabeth Holman Person, whose parents were Elizabeth Holman and William Person III. She was the granddaughter of Colonel William Person II and his wife, Martha Eaton, and the great-granddaughter of Colonel William Person (1700–1778) and of William Eaton. The Eaton and Person families were among the first to settle in present-day Warren County.

Walter Montgomery and his wife had four children: Walter A., Jr. (3 Aug. 1872–6 Jan. 1949), who married Gertrude Smith on 8 Aug. 1900 in Fayetteville, Ark.; Thomas (26 Aug. 1873–28 July 1874); Epps Wilson (28 Jan. 1877–24 July 1890); and Elizabeth Mitchel (b. 2 May 1882), who lived in Raleigh.

Both Montgomery and his wife were Episcopalians, but after the war, he joined the Baptist church. Judge Montgomery was a Populist. A portrait was presented to the Supreme Court on 30 Oct. 1923, with an address by Thurston T. Hicks. Montgomery died in Raleigh and was buried in Oakwood Cemetery.

SEE: Thurston Titus Hicks, *Address Presenting a Portrait of Judge Walter A. Montgomery to the Supreme Court of North Carolina at Raleigh, October 30, 1923* (1923); Weymouth T. Jordan, comp., *North Carolina Troops, 1861–1865: A Roster*, vol. 5 (1975); Lizzie W. Montgomery, *Sketches of Old Warrenton* (1924); *North Carolina Biography*, vol. 5 (1919); *Proceedings of the North Carolina Bar Association* (1923); Warren County Deed Book (North Carolina State Archives, Raleigh).

PANTHEA M. TWITTY

Montgomery, Walter Alexander *(3 Aug. 1872–6 Jan. 1949)*, educator, was born in Warren County, the son of Walter A. and Lizzie Holman Wilson Montgomery. He attended Wake Forest College and received bachelor's, master's, and doctor of philosophy degrees from Johns Hopkins University. His first teaching position was in the city schools of Asheville, but in 1906 he joined the faculty of the College of William and Mary to teach Latin and Greek. This was followed by seven years at Richmond College, after which he returned to William and Mary as head of the Greek and Latin department.

For a time Montgomery also served in the National Bureau of Education in Washington, D.C., and between 1919 and 1921 he published studies on various aspects of education in Italy, Japan, Spain, Canada, Belgium, Great Britain, India, and Latin America. Among his other publications were scholarly works in his field of interest, including one on Johannes Gutenberg and the invention of printing from movable type and a Latin grammar. Montgomery was active in the preservation of historic buildings and sites in Virginia, and he wrote and acted in pageants depicting historical events. His wife was the former Gertrude Smith of Fayetteville, Ark., and he was survived by a daughter, Mrs. M. S. Niminger. He was buried in Cedar Grove Cemetery, Williamsburg, Va.

SEE: *Chapel Hill Weekly*, 14 Jan. 1949; Montgomery family notes (in possession of E. C. Hicks, Jr., Wilmington); National Union Catalog (Library of Congress); Raleigh *News and Observer*, 14 Sept. 1929.

WILLIAM S. POWELL

Montgomery, William (*29 Dec. 1789–27 Nov. 1844*), physician, state legislator, and congressman, was born near North Buffalo Creek in northeastern Guilford County three miles from Bethel Church. One of four children of Scotch-Irish parents, William and Hannah Forbus Montgomery, he studied medicine with an old German physician and received his M.D. degree from Princeton University, where he joined the school's Whig Society in 1804. Montgomery first established a medical practice in Randolph County and helped lay off the town of Liberty (incorporated in 1889). He later moved to Albright in Orange (later Alamance) County near present-day Burlington.

While practicing medicine, Montgomery found time to run for political office as a Democrat. He was elected to the North Carolina Senate for nine terms, serving from 1824 to 1827 and from 1829 to 1834. In 1835 he was one of two Orange County representatives to the state's constitutional convention. In the same year he defeated Daniel A. Barringer of Wake County for a seat in the U.S. House of Representatives from the Eighth Congressional District. Despite strong Whig sentiment in his own county, the congressman held his office until 1841, when he retired from politics.

Considered by his contemporaries to be a man of inflexible political principles and a loyal Jacksonian, Montgomery, as state senator, introduced a resolution condemning the U.S. Bank, championed a bill to give voters in each county the right to elect their own sheriff, and called for a reduction in the tariff of 1832. As a congressman he continued his opposition to high tariffs and supported the Independent Treasury Bill of 1837.

Montgomery was married twice. From his union with a Miss Gray, he had four children: William, Hugh, Patterson, and Hannah. On 24 Apr. 1814 he married his second wife, Sarah Albright, the daughter of the local postmaster, Daniel Albright. She bore him ten children: Nancy Elizabeth, Sara, Daniel A., Delilah, James Rudy, Mary Ann, Martha Harriet, Cornelia, Barbara Maria, and William Van. Both Daniel A. and William Van became physicians, and Daniel also was elected to the state legislature.

Montgomery was buried at "the Brick Church" in Albright.

SEE: William S. Hoffmann, *Andrew Jackson and North Carolina Politics* (1958); Hugh T. Lefler and Paul Wager, eds., *Orange County, 1752–1952* (1953); Henry Thomas Shanks, ed., *Willie P. Mangum Papers*, vols. 1–3 (1950–53); Sallie Walker Stockard, *The History of Alamance* (1900).

RICHARD A. SHRADER

Moody, James Montraville (*12 Feb. 1858–5 Feb. 1903*), lawyer and congressman, was born in Cherokee County. He possibly was the son of Henry L. and Elizabeth Moody, who are listed in the 1860 census of Haywood County as the parents of "Monterville B.," ten months old and born in Tennessee, as were his parents and a brother. Given the carelessness of many census takers and the unusual given name, the latter may be the subject of this sketch. It is recorded that when James Montraville was quite young, his parents acquired a farm on Jonathan Creek in Haywood County and moved there. He attended whatever schools in the area were available, then completed a course of study at the Waynesville Academy. Afterwards he attended a collegiate institute at Candler in Buncombe County.

Returning to Waynesville, Moody studied law for about five years and was admitted to the bar in 1881. In 1885 he was elected mayor of Waynesville, and in 1886 he became solicitor of the Twelfth Judicial District. In 1892, as a Republican, he was an unsuccessful candidate for lieutenant governor. Two years later he was elected to the North Carolina Senate and served for one term.

At the beginning of the Spanish-American War in 1898, Moody became one of the earliest volunteers. With the rank of major, he was made chief commissary of the U.S. Volunteers and served on the staff of Major General J. Warren Keifer, commander of the First Division of the Seventh Army Corps. After the war he returned to Waynesville to resume his legal career and soon had an extensive practice. Nominated as a Republican candidate for Congress in 1900, he was elected and served from 1901 to 1903. He was nominated in 1902 for a second term but was defeated by a mere 183 votes. Moody contested the election but died before the matter could be resolved. Returning home in January 1903 because of illness from pneumonia, he died just a month before his term expired and a week before his forty-fifth birthday.

Moody married Margaret E. Hawkins, and they were the parents of six children: James M., Jr., Jessie, Mary, Elizabeth, Keifer, and Margaret. He was buried in Green Hill Cemetery, Waynesville.

SEE: W. C. Allen, *Centennial History of Haywood County and Its County Seat, Waynesville, N.C.* (1908?); *Biog. Dir. Am. Cong.* (1971); *Report of the Fifth Annual Meeting of the North Carolina Bar Association* (1903); U.S. Congress, *Memorial Addresses on the Life and Character of James M. Moody* (1903 [portrait]).

WILLIAM S. POWELL

Moore, Aaron McDuffie (*6 Sept. 1863–29 Apr. 1923*), black physician, businessman, and humanitarian, was born in Columbus County. His parents belonged to the third generation of Negro-Indian-Caucasian families who had owned land in this area as free farmers since the early nineteenth century. Moore, like his nine brothers and sisters, alternately worked on the family farm and attended the county elementary school. After completing the eighth grade he attended normal schools in Lumberton and Fayetteville, returning to his home community for a time as a teacher. In 1885 he enrolled in the newly built black college in Raleigh, Shaw University, and was accepted into its school of medicine, the Leonard Medical School. He completed the four-year program in three years, passed the North Carolina medical board examinations, and in 1888 settled in Durham as the city's first black physician.

Moore married the daughter of John C. Dancy, one of North Carolina's leading black political figures, and became involved in politics himself as a candidate for Durham County coroner. But even in the late 1880s, well before North Carolina's white supremacy campaigns, he found the white majority of Durham hostile to his efforts in direct politics, so he, like other black leaders of the New South, redirected his energies to self-help, racial solidarity, and the formation of all-black institutions. In 1895 he helped organize a community pharmacy, and from that time on he participated in a wide range of black business activities, most notably as medical director and cofounder with John Merrick of the North Carolina Mutual Life Insurance Company. Organized in 1898, the North Carolina Mutual became the largest black business in the United States and brought Durham considerable fame as the "Capital of the Black Middle Class." On Merrick's death in 1919, Moore became president of the company, serving until his own death in 1923.

In the meantime he maintained his medical practice, never sacrificing his primary identity as physician and community servant. Indeed, he is remembered more for his service and philanthropy than for his business efforts, a distinction that lost its meaning in terms of the racial self-fulfillment that Moore had in mind. With Merrick's help in raising money from the white community, Moore founded Lincoln Hospital in 1901 and the Durham Colored Library in 1913. Beginning in 1914 he became absorbed in the rural education movement for the black school children of North Carolina. He personally financed a campaign to point up the need for such schools and then successfully petitioned for state funds and a matching grant from the Rosenwald Foundation.

Moore spent another part of his life working for the Baptist church. At Durham's White Rock Baptist Church he was chairman of the board of deacons, a member of the board of trustees, and superintendent of the Sunday school for twenty-five years. Beyond Durham he served as president of the Baptist State Sunday School Convention. His work for the Lott Cary Foreign Missionary Convention took him to Haiti, where, with funds he had raised in the United States, he founded the Haitian White Rock Baptist Church. He also raised funds for missionary work in Africa. Moore served as trustee for the Baptist orphanage in Oxford and as chairman of the board of trustees for Shaw University, his Baptist alma mater to which he willed five thousand dollars.

His wife, Cottie Dancy Moore, survived until 1950. Their two daughters, Mattie and Lyda, married executives of the North Carolina Mutual. Mattie died prematurely in 1929; Lyda lived in Durham and carried on her father's legacy of social service as founder and editor of the *Negro Braille Magazine*.

SEE: William Jesse Kennedy, Jr., *The North Carolina Mutual Story: A Symbol of Progress, 1898–1970* (1970); Walter B. Weare, *Black Business in the New South: A Social History of the North Carolina Mutual Life Insurance Company* (1973).

WALTER B. WEARE

Moore, Alfred (*21 May 1755–15 Oct. 1810*), lawyer, rice planter, Revolutionary soldier, legislator, attorney general, superior court judge, and associate justice of the U.S. Supreme Court, was born in New Hanover County, the son of Anne Grange and Maurice Moore, a superior court judge. Descended from one of the most distinguished families of the Lower Cape Fear, he was the grandson of Colonel Maurice Moore, principal leader in the migration of the aristocratic Goose Creek planters of the Charles Town area to the Cape Fear in the mid-1720s and founder of Brunswick town in 1726. Alfred was the grandnephew of "King Roger" Moore, lordly proprietor of Orton plantation and the largest slaveholder (with 250 slaves) in colonial North Carolina. His father was one of the colony's ablest judges and a forceful spokesman for colonists' rights against the oppressive British measures of the 1760s. Maurice Moore's spirited challenge to the constitutionality of the Stamp Act and intemperate conduct in preventing its enforcement led to his removal as judge by Governor William Tryon; he was vindicated, however, when the home government in London ordered his reinstatement in 1768. He held the position when the celebrated letter, bearing the signature of "Atticus" and directed to Governor Tryon as he was leaving North Carolina in 1771 to become governor of New York, was penned and attributed to Moore.

Having been educated himself in New England, the judge sent Alfred to Boston for schooling at the early age of nine (probably because of Moore's recent remarriage following the death of Alfred's mother). After several years of study, Alfred returned home before the Revolution, read law in his father's office, and was admitted to the bar in April 1775. Soon afterwards he married Susanne Elizabeth Eagles of Brunswick County, and they had several children.

On 1 Sept. 1775 he was made a captain in the First North Carolina Continental Regiment, commanded by his uncle, James Moore. Alfred saw military action first against the Scottish Highlanders at Moore's Creek Bridge in February 1776 and later against the British forces in the June 1776 defense of Charles Town. He resigned from the army on 8 Mar. 1777, after the death of Judge Moore (ironically, Maurice and James Moore died in the same house on the same day, 15 Jan. 1777), to care for his father's family. Returning to his plantation, Buchoi, in Brunswick County, he resumed the practice of law and engaged in rice planting. While no longer a regular soldier, he became active as a colonel of militia and was very effective in harassing the British forces under Major James Craig, who captured Wilmington in January 1781 as a supply base for Lord Cornwallis's army to the west. Craig retaliated by sending a detachment to Buchoi, where it plundered Moore's house, burned the outbuilding, and carried off the stock and slaves. Craig's attempts to kill or capture Moore failed, and his offer to restore Moore's property and give him amnesty if he would return to the plantation and forego any further military action was spurned by Moore. Although the war left his plantation in disarray and his personal fortune considerably diminished, the immediate postwar period brought rather rapid recovery; by 1790 he owned forty-eight slaves.

In 1782 Moore began his lengthy career as a public servant, first as state senator from Brunswick County. Later in the year, following the resignation of James Iredell, the General Assembly appointed him attorney general of North Carolina. Moore served with distinction for the next eight years. Displeased over the Court Act of 1790, which created the office of solicitor general with the same power and pay as the attorney general, and believing he could not satisfactorily conduct the state's legal work without injuring his private business or his health, Moore resigned as attorney general on 9 Jan. 1791 and retired to Buchoi.

His retirement was short-lived, for in 1792 Moore represented Brunswick County, as a Federalist, in the Assembly and in 1795 he engaged Timothy Bloodworth, a Republican from New Hanover County, in a lively contest for election to the U.S. Senate; Moore lost by one vote. In 1798 the Assembly elected him judge of the superior court. In October 1799, after the death of James Iredell, George Washington's appointee to the U.S. Supreme Court from North Carolina, President John Adams, in recognition of Moore's legal eminence (which only William R. Davie shared before the state's bar), appointed him to replace Iredell. Iredell and Moore were the only North Carolinians ever to serve on the nation's highest bench. Although Moore remained on the Court for five years, he delivered an opinion in only one case, *Bas v. Tingy* (4 Dallas 37, 1800), in which he stated that a "limited, partial" war existed with France, a position supported by the other judges.

Recognition of Moore's mature judgment was also evidenced by his appointment to various delegations or commissions over the years. In 1786 he was appointed by the governor as a delegate to the Annapolis convention, called to determine whether the Articles of Confederation needed to be amended; however, he, along with the other North Carolinians, did not attend. Later, in 1798, President Adams designated him as one of three commissioners to make a treaty with the Cherokee; Moore withdrew from the negotiations before the treaty was signed on 2 October. Ever a public-spirited citizen, he tended to support any worthy cause, such as the formation of the state university—he was one of the original trustees (1789–1807) and contributed sizably to its support.

Always of frail physique, Moore was forced by increasing ill health to retire from the Supreme Court in 1804, thus ending his long and fruitful career. He died and was buried with full military honors at Belfont, the plantation of his son-in-law, Major Hugh Waddell, in Bladen County. Later his remains were moved to the churchyard of St. Philips at Brunswick town. Perhaps Samuel A. Ashe summed up the role of Moore best: "Taking him all in all, he was one of the most masterful men who have adorned the annals of North Carolina."

SEE: Samuel A. Ashe, ed., *Biographical History of North Carolina*, vol. 2 (1905); Walter Clark, ed., *State Records of North Carolina*, vols. 16, 18–19 (1899–1901); *DAB*, vol. 13 (1928); *Journal* of the North Carolina Senate and House of Commons (1794–95, 1798); Raleigh *Register*, 1 Nov. 1810; William L. Saunders, ed., *Colonial Records of North Carolina*, vol. 10 (1890).

JAMES M. CLIFTON

Moore, Bartholomew Figures *(29 Jan. 1801–27 Nov. 1878)*, attorney, was born in Halifax County, the sixth child of James Moore of Virginia and his second wife, Sally Lewis Lowe of Edgecombe County. His father, the son of James and Selah Williams Moore of Southampton County, Va., was a veteran of the American Revolution. His mother was the daughter of Colonel Exum and Elizabeth Figures Lewis and the widow of the Reverend William Lowe. Exum Lewis was a native of Edgecombe County and his wife came from Virginia.

Moore received his early education under John Bobbitt, principal of a school near Louisburg. In 1820 he was graduated with an A.B. degree from The University of North Carolina, which also awarded him an honorary LL.D. in 1868; he served as a trustee of the university from 1840 to 1868 and from 1871 until his death. After studying law under Thomas N. Mann of Nash County, Moore began to practice there in 1823.

During his first years as an attorney in Nash, Moore was notably unsuccessful. As a result of further study, however, he became exceptionally well versed in both statute and common law. In 1824 he supported William H. Crawford of Georgia for president, being opposed to Jacksonian democracy and subscribing to the philosophy of the Old Republicans. When the Whig party was formed, he cast his lot with Henry Clay and the Whigs. In 1828 he lost his first bid for a seat in the House of Commons. In 1835 Moore moved to a farm near Halifax, where he enjoyed a profitable legal practice as well as success in politics. A member of the 1835 constitutional convention, he also served in the House of Commons in 1836, 1840, 1842, and 1844. His defeat in 1838 by one vote was attributed to his support of a bill to give state aid to the construction of the Wilmington and Weldon Railroad (then called the Wilmington and Raleigh). In the legislature he advocated revision of the statutes, internal improvements, public education, and care of the mentally ill and orphans. He did not seek reelection in 1846 because of the need to be out of the state.

In 1848 Moore moved to Raleigh, where he continued his highly successful legal practice. In May of that year Governor William A. Graham named him attorney general following the resignation of Edward Stanly, and in December the legislature elected him to the position. Moore served until May 1851, when he resigned to accept an appointment on the commission to revise the statute law. He, with Asa Biggs and R. M. Saunders, undertook a codification of the statutes, which resulted in the *Revised Code of North Carolina . . . 1854*.

Bartholomew F. Moore's reputation as an attorney was founded primarily on his brief and argument in *State v. Will*, decided in 1834. This case, which Moore argued for the defendant, was significant in determining the relationship between master and slave. The court held that slaves had the right to protect themselves against unlawful violence from an overseer—as in this particular case—as well as from a master.

Moore loved North Carolina, but as war approached, he found himself unable to support secession, even though he felt the South had a legitimate grievance. He made his views known in letters to the press and to individuals and in conversations. In December 1860 he wrote to his daughter Lucy deploring the possibility of secession, and on 17 Jan. 1861 he told her that there was nothing new "except the madness of the South." On 15 Apr. 1861, in still another letter, he said: "Civil war can be glorious news to none but demons, or thoughtless fools, or maddened men."

When the Confederate States court opened in Raleigh, Moore appeared as he had previously done in federal courts. Confederate Judge Asa Biggs, formerly a federal judge, ordered the attorneys present to take an oath of allegiance to the Confederate government. In his sketch of Moore as recorded in the proceedings of the centennial of Christ Church, Samuel A. Ashe related that "Mr. Moore took his green bag, in which he always carried his court papers, his walking-stick and his hat, and withdrew from the courtroom, never to return." He continued to practice in state courts, however, where no such oath was required. Moore's only support of the Southern cause was through his service on the Board of Claims.

Later, in his will, Moore explained that he could not

support the Civil War without sacrificing all self-respect. "With this horrible picture of anarchy and blood looming before my eyes, I could not, as a patriot, consent to welcome its approach to 'my own, my native land.' And truly was I happy, when I saw the sun of peace rising with the glorious promise to shine once more on states equal, free, honored and united: And although the promise has been long . . . delayed by an unwise policy, and I, myself, may never see the full orbed sun of liberty shine on my country and every part of it, as once it did, yet I have strong hopes that my countrymen will yet be blessed with that glorious Light."

At the end of the war Moore, former Governor David L. Swain, and William Eaton were called to Washington to advise President Andrew Johnson on North Carolina affairs. On 22 May 1865 Johnson told them about his plan of reconstruction, a plan Moore regarded as unconstitutional. Moore also opposed the idea of the president appointing a governor who would, in turn, call a convention. He believed that existing legislatures should be permitted to call conventions, thereby preserving legal continuity. A state convention, so called, could then repeal its secession ordinance and restore its relationship to the federal government. On 23 May, during a second meeting with President Johnson, Moore and his colleagues found a second North Carolina delegation present; this group, led by William Woods Holden, approved the president's plan. Johnson asked the North Carolinians to suggest a nominee for provisional governor and then left the room. When asked to take the chair, Moore refused to discuss the matter further and left, accompanied by Swain and Eaton. Those remaining nominated Holden, who was appointed.

Nevertheless, Moore was elected to the 1865 convention as a representative from Wake County. He drew up the ordinance declaring the 1861 secession ordinance null and void, supported the position that all state offices be declared vacant, but sought delay on repudiation of the war debt. A telegram from Johnson demanded instant repudiation of the debt; Moore, opposing federal intervention, urged the convention to refuse, but he was outvoted.

Governor Holden called upon Moore, W. S. Mason, and R. S. Donnell to suggest needed amendments to the laws regarding freedmen. Moore drew up the code—the most liberal legislation proposed by any Southern state on the subject, though it did not give blacks the right to vote or equal legal rights. With few amendments, the ordinance was adopted by the 1866 General Assembly.

In May 1866 the convention met again to consider a state constitution, but the document drafted by Moore and adopted by the convention was rejected by the people. He also was defeated in his bid for a seat in the 1866 General Assembly. Moore was unsympathetic with the conservatives who controlled North Carolina politics between 1866 and 1868 and even more opposed to the radicals. He was pessimistic about the 1868 constitutional convention and about the new constitution itself. Like nearly all old (prewar) Democrats, he felt that members of the constitutional convention were unqualified and "outsiders."

When, during Reconstruction, Chief Justice Richmond M. Pearson and others of the judiciary actively supported the Republican party, Moore, as "father of the bar," drew up a formal protest; the document, signed by him and 107 other lawyers, was published in the Raleigh *Daily Sentinel* of 19 Apr. 1869. As a result, on 8 June the Supreme Court issued an order barring those protesters who practiced before the high court from appearing there again. The rule was subsequently discharged after the offending attorneys indicated that they

had no intention of holding the court in contempt. Moore himself commented on this matter in a letter of 5 July to his daughter: "I expect that you have been somewhat troubled at the war between the Bar and the Supreme Court Bench wherein I am made the most prominent actor. . . . I had no purpose to degrade once more. God knows that my only object was to purify and elevate it. The conduct of the individuals composing the court was unbecoming the judge according to my judgement."

Writing to his daughter on Christmas Day, 1870, Moore observed that the impeachment of Governor Holden "was demanded by a sense of public virtue and due regard to the honor of the state. He [Holden] is an exceedingly corrupt man and ought to be placed before the public as a public example of a tyrant condemned and punished."

After the war Moore practiced for the most part in the federal courts. His U.S. Supreme Court practice was extensive. In 1871 he and his son-in-law, John Thomas Gatling, established a law firm in Raleigh.

On 2 Dec. 1828 Moore married Louisa Boddie, the daughter of George Boddie of Nash County; she died on 4 Nov. 1829. On 19 Apr. 1835, ten days before her nineteenth birthday, he married Louisa's sister, Lucy Williams Boddie (1816–87). They had eleven children: Mary Louisa (1836–43), Bartholomew F., Jr. (1838–90), Lucy Catherine (1839–1908; m. first, P. T. Henry, and second, B. A. Capehart), George B. (1841–95), Sarah Louisa (1844–91; m. John Thomas Gatling), Annie M. (1845–1915; m. Joseph Parker), James (1848–49), Ellen Douglas (1850–1923; m. J. P. Leach), Ben Malton (1853–1913), Van B. (1855–1917), and James (1858–1938).

Moore amassed a considerable estate, including real property, securities, and personal property of value. In his will, dated 12 Aug. 1878, he provided for his children and certain other relatives, left one hundred dollars to each of his former slaves living in North Carolina, and remembered in a tangible way The University of North Carolina, the Grand Lodge of North Carolina, the Oxford orphanage, and Christ Episcopal Church in Raleigh. He was a member of both the Masonic order and Christ Church.

His death followed months of poor health and an enfeebled condition. The Raleigh *Observer* for 28 November declared: "Ripe in years, full of honors, rich in the confidence and regard of his fellow citizens everywhere, he has ended a long career of unremitting and signally successful labor without a taint upon his honor or a blot upon his escutcheon." After funeral services at Christ Church on 28 November, Moore was buried in Oakwood Cemetery underneath a large oak tree near the lake.

SEE: Samuel A. Ashe, ed., *Biographical History of North Carolina*, vol. 5 (1905 [portrait]); Samuel A. Ashe, "Reminiscences and Personal Sketches of Christ Church," *Centennial Ceremonies . . . Christ Church. . . .* (1922); *DAB*, vol. 7 (1934); Moore-Gatling Papers (Southern Historical Collection, University of North Carolina, Chapel Hill); Genealogy of the B. F. Moore family and other family recollections (possession of Bart F. Moore, Raleigh); Daniel L. Grant, *Alumni History of the University of North Carolina, 1795–1924* (1924); *In re B. F. Moore*, 63 N.C. 397 (1869); Bartholomew F. Moore Papers, Wake County Wills, Estate Papers, and Tax Lists (North Carolina State Archives, Raleigh); Raleigh *Observer*, 28, 30 Nov. 1878; *State v. Negro Will, Slave of James S. Battle*, 18 N.C. 121 (1834); Tombstone inscriptions, Oakwood Cemetery, Raleigh.

MEMORY F. MITCHELL

Moore, Clifton Leonard (*28 Sept. 1900–12 July 1966*), judge, was born in Pender County, the second of six children of William David and Ida Murray Moore. He was raised on a farm and as a boy helped his family with the chores, as did most boys in rural eastern North Carolina.

Moore attended the public schools of Pender County and was graduated from Burgaw High School as valedictorian of his class. In 1923 he received a bachelor of arts degree from The University of North Carolina. While in Chapel Hill, he was named to the Order of the Golden Fleece and the Phi Beta Kappa scholarship society. He was instrumental in founding and was the editor of a literary publication entitled *The Prospector*, which was an outgrowth of the university's English 21 class to promote creative writing in the South. Moore received his legal education at George Washington University in Washington, D.C., from which he was graduated in 1927.

In the same year he was licensed to practice and began work in his native Pender County. Moore's rise in the legal profession was steady. Shortly after returning home, he became attorney for the town of Burgaw. He was attorney for the Pender County Board of Commissioners from 1932 to 1943 and served as judge of the Pender County Recorder's Court from 1933 to 1938.

Moore is best remembered as solicitor for the Eighth Judicial District, a post he assumed in 1943. At the time, the Ku Klux Klan was engaging in numerous illegal activities in Columbus County, one of the counties in Moore's district. Moore successfully prosecuted ninety-three Klansmen and thus ended the terror and intimidation they had inflicted upon the people of that community. At his urging, the legislature enacted the "Moore Act," designed to end secret political and military organizations in the state.

Moore continued as solicitor until 1954, when Governor Luther Hodges appointed him a judge of the superior court. On 2 Feb. 1959 Governor Hodges elevated him to the North Carolina Supreme Court to fill the vacancy created by the death of Justice Jefferson D. Johnson. In 1960 Judge Moore was elected to a full eight-year term on the Supreme Court; he served until his death six years later at North Carolina Memorial Hospital in Chapel Hill.

He also served as mayor of the town of Burgaw, chairman of the Pender County Democratic Executive Committee (1928–38), and member of the Democratic executive committee from the Eighth Judicial District. He was a member of the Burgaw Methodist Church, Rotary International, and King Solomon Lodge No. 138, as well as of the North Carolina and American Bar associations.

Moore married Hazel Swinson of Goldsboro, and the couple had two children: Clifton L., Jr., and Mary Hazel Wilson. A portrait of Judge Moore hangs in the superior courtroom of the Pender County courthouse in Burgaw.

SEE: Mattie Bloodworth, *History of Pender County, North Carolina* (1947); John L. Cheney, Jr., ed., *North Carolina Government, 1585–1979* (1981); Daniel L. Grant, *Alumni History of the University of North Carolina, 1795–1924* (1924); *Pender Chronicle*, 20 July 1966; William S. Powell, ed., *North Carolina Lives* (1962); *Who's Who in the South and Southwest* (1967).

GARY E. TRAWICK

Moore, Enoch William (*11 June 1868–25 Oct. 1952*), businessman and inventor, was born in Rockingham County, the son of James Wright and his second wife, Emily Branson Moore. James W. Moore's first wife was Marinda Branson, who in 1855 opened a school near their home known as the Margarita Seminary, for which she wrote a series of textbooks, *Dixie Readers*, published by her brother Levi. James inherited a mill complex on Belews Creek that included a gristmill, sawmill, machine shop, and foundry and smithy. The family enterprises manufactured a wide variety of items including wagons, furniture, coffins, gunstocks, and tobacco boxes.

Educated in the local schools, Enoch Moore attended Trinity College where he excelled in physics, particularly the practical application of electricity. While on summer vacation he constructed a dynamo and, using the waterpower at the creek, installed an electrical lighting system in his father's mill—the earliest use of electricity in this region. After college, Moore began his career by installing an electric plant in Reidsville for the Southern Electric Light and Construction Company; later he constructed plants throughout the Southeast. He became manager of the Augusta Gas, Electric Light, and Railway Company and eventually established the Moore-Edenfield Electric Manufacturing Company to make motors and generators.

At the turn of the century Moore moved to Pittsburgh, Pa., where he became vice-president and general manager of the West Penn Traction and Water Power Company. In 1916 he founded Mooreco Enterprises, which pioneered in the construction and development of electric furnaces. He designed the Lectro-Dryer and the electric vacuum furnace, both of which are used throughout the world. He eventually secured 130 patents.

On 28 Mar. 1922 Moore married Ruth Danley (d. December 1972), and they had one daughter, Grace Danley Moore (b. 27 Mar. 1923). He was buried in Pittsburgh. His nephew, Thomas Moore Price, a native of Rockingham County, became vice-president of the Iron and Steel Division of Kaiser Industries. A civil engineer, Price supervised major construction projects for Kaiser and discovered an important iron ore depository in Australia that bears his name—Mount Tom Price.

SEE: Henry Anderson, "Belews Creek Made Electricity Long, Long Ago," *Duke Power Magazine* 55, no. 1 (February 1970); Harold Coy, *The Prices and the Moores* (1944); *Madison Messenger*, 29 June 1950; Charles Dyson Rodenbough, ed., *The Heritage of Rockingham County, North Carolina* (1983).

LINDLEY S. BUTLER

Moore, Gabriel (*1785–6 Aug. 1844*), congressman, U.S. senator, and governor of Alabama, was born in Surry (later Stokes) County of English ancestry, the son of Matthew and Letitia Moore; Letitia was the daughter of Samuel and Ann Dandridge Redd Dalton. His parents arrived from Louisa County, Va., about 1774 with their five oldest children. The family purchased land and took up grants at the foot of Sauratown Mountain on the Dan River. A year after the birth of their eighth child, Gabriel, the Moores completed a brick dwelling that came to be known as Moore's Castle. This home, which appears to have been built by Moravian artisans, was the finest private residence built in the Dan River valley at this early date, and it was standing in the 1980s.

In addition to his farming interests, Matthew Moore in 1793 began to develop an ironworks on Double Creek. At his death in 1801, his will directed that the proceeds from the sale of his Providence Iron Works be used for the education of his three youngest sons, Gabriel, Tucker Woodson, and Matthew Redd. Part of Gabriel's education must have been under Edward Hickman, who operated a school in the area; according to Matthew's will, Gabriel was at school, presumably away from home, at the time of his father's death. However, there is no documentation of his graduation from The University of North Carolina, as tradition maintains.

Apparently through the influence of older brothers and sisters, Gabriel was drawn to Tennessee and then into that portion of the Mississippi Territory along the Tennessee River that became Alabama. He was commissioned an attorney on 12 May 1808 by Governor Nathaniel Williams of Mississippi. Moore became heavily involved in land speculation, beginning at the Federal Land Sale at Nashville on 18 Dec. 1808, joining a number of men of wealth and education from Georgia and Virginia. He opened a law practice in Madison County in the little town of Twickenham, founded at the Big Spring, which in 1811 became Huntsville. In 1811 Gabriel became a representative in the Mississippi territorial legislature, where he served throughout the War of 1812, preferring politics to the military. From 1815 to 1817 he was speaker of the house. On 3 Mar. 1817 the act establishing the Alabama Territory was approved, and on 10 Jan. 1818, when the first session of the Alabama territorial legislature met at St. Stephans, Gabriel Moore was elected speaker of the house.

During this session Moore married Mary Parham Caller, the daughter of James and Winifred Duke Caller of St. Stephans; James Caller, a native Virginian, was a prominent citizen of Washington County. This marriage was shrouded in bitterness, since it ended in divorce within a year (17 Nov. 1818). Because of the ensuing legal proceedings, Moore did not serve in the second territorial legislature. Moreover, during that time he fought a duel with his wife's brother, leaving the brother wounded. Moore did not remarry.

The statehood Enabling Act was signed in the spring of 1819. When the constitutional convention met at Huntsville on 5 July, Gabriel Moore was one of the eight delegates from Madison County. The first General Assembly met at Huntsville in October, and Moore, elected a state senator, became president of the senate. On 4 Mar. 1821 he won a seat in the Seventeenth Congress, defeating Colonel Silas Dinsmore of Washington County; he continued to serve through the Twentieth Congress, which ended on 3 Mar. 1829.

At that time Moore was an acquaintance and adherent of Andrew Jackson, and his style of politics was much like the general's. An opponent said grudgingly, "Moore was a skillful electioneer, and courted the lower stratum of society." He also came to know John C. Calhoun, who as secretary of war placed a high priority on the Muscle Shoals canal on the Tennessee River west of Huntsville, a project that had Moore's support and earned Calhoun the beginnings of friendship from Moore. In the campaign of 1827, Moore was opposed by Clement C. Clay, the first chief justice of Alabama, whose background closely paralleled that of Moore. At his defeat by Moore, Clay was deeply embittered and he bore a lasting hatred for his opponent.

In 1829 Gabriel Moore was elected without opposition as the fifth governor of Alabama. His administration pressed forward with internal improvements, the completion of the Muscle Shoals canal, and the beginning of the railroad from Tuscumbia to Decatur. In 1830, by the Treaty of Dancing Rabbit Creek, the Choctaw Indians ceded the last of their land in Alabama and Mississippi for lands in the West. Moore furthered the cause of the University of Alabama, which opened its doors on 18 Apr. 1831, just one month after he left office.

Encouraged by his stay in Congress, Moore had apparently set goals beyond the state level. The legislature, which still chose its senators, elected Governor Moore to the U.S. Senate, by a vote of 49 to 40, over Colonel John McKinley. He resigned the governorship on 3 Mar. 1831 and a day later became senator.

Alabama was then a strong Jackson state, and Moore went to the Senate with much backing from the Jackson men. He himself showed an early preference for Vice-President Calhoun, and after a year he broke with the Jackson forces over the nomination of Martin Van Buren as minister to England. In Alabama the Jackson forces were furious, and they attempted to "instruct" Moore on a pro-Jackson line. For several years he remained neutral, balancing Senate factions with the sentiment at home. But by 1834 he had joined several southern senators—John Black and George Poindexter of Mississippi and Willie P. Mangum of North Carolina—in open opposition to Jackson. On the issue of "expunging" they all were similarly instructed by their pro-Jackson legislatures, and each ignored the instructions and voted against the president. In 1835 the Alabama legislature asked Moore to resign. The Whig party was beginning to unite much of the anti-Jackson national feeling, and Moore was now counted as a Whig. Moore defended his actions in the Senate, rejecting completely the concept of instruction. His record in the Senate had been independent and progressive, but it had not succeeded in substantially changing the pro-Jackson politics of Alabama.

In 1836 Moore, realizing the degree to which his support had eroded, did not offer himself for reelection to the Senate but instead ran for Congress. He was decisively beaten by Reuben Chapman. Adding further insult, he was replaced in the Senate by his hated enemy, Clement C. Clay.

Public defeat was followed by financial ruin at the hands of his nephew, Benjamin T. Moore, who in handling his interests while Gabriel was in Washington, had swindled him out of most of his property. A bitter legal battle did not regain his estate.

The Whig party, gaining strength nationally, was led by many of Moore's close political allies. He repeatedly urged them to push his appointment to various patronage jobs, such as collector of customs at Mobile, consul at Havana, marshal of northern Alabama, and chargé d'affaires in Texas. All such attempts failed. In 1844 he left Huntsville, determined to start again in Texas. On the way, he died at a wagon station near Caddo, Tex. Moore was buried on the plantation of Peter Swanson.

There are two known portraits of Gabriel Moore. One, a miniature at about age twenty-five, painted by William H. Scarbrough, is in the possession of the Alabama State Archives. A second miniature, done probably while he was in the Senate, was owned by Mrs. S. L. Boatwright of Bryan, Tex.

SEE: T. H. Benton, *Thirty Years' View*, 2 vols. (1854–56); *Biog. Dir. Am. Cong.* (1941); C. G. Bowers, *The Party Battles of the Jackson Period* (1924); William Garrett, *Reminiscences of Public Men of Alabama* (1872); J. E. Saunders, *Early Settlers of Alabama* (1899).

CHARLES D. RODENBOUGH

Moore, George (1715–78), planter, legislator, and public official, was born in South Carolina, the only child of Roger and Mary Moore, although he had a half brother,

William, and three half sisters, Sarah, Mary, and Anne, who were the children of Roger and Katherine Rhett Moore (1705–45). His paternal grandparents were James (1650?–1707?), who went to South Carolina from Barbados in 1674, and Margaret Berringer Moore (b. 1660), the daughter of Colonel Benjamin of Barbados and Margaret Foster Berringer. Young George's family moved to New Hanover County, N.C., in 1723.

George Moore was the father of twenty-eight children. His first wife, whom he married on 19 Mar. 1739, was Mary Ashe (1723–61), the daughter of John Baptista Ashe (who was the brother of Governor Samuel Ashe). Between 1742 and 1761 they had fifteen children, eight of whom died young. On 3 Sept. 1761, following the death of his wife earlier in the year, Moore married Sarah Jones, the daughter of Thomas Jones. She bore him thirteen children, but, according to a notation in Moore's copy of the *Book of Common Prayer*, only six survived to maturity.

Moore served the first of a number of terms in the colonial Assembly in 1744, was reelected to a second term, and then served continuously from 1755 to 1762. The journal indicates that Moore was an active member and that he was concerned about the welfare of his constituents as well as others in the colony. He served on a number of committees and was frequently chairman. Often he was designated to take bills from the Assembly to the Council for final action. On one occasion when Governor Arthur Dobbs recommended him for a seat on the Council, he declined it.

In 1746 Moore was one of the commissioners appointed to run the southern line of the Granville District, and in 1748 he was one of the commissioners charged with building a fort (later named Fort Johnston) at the mouth of the Cape Fear River. In 1753 he obtained authorization from the Council to resurvey a three-thousand-acre tract in Duplin County granted to his father in 1727 because he could not trace the lines as described in the grant.

On 19 Feb. 1766, in the midst of the Stamp Act crisis in the colony, Moore and Cornelius Harnett delivered a letter to Governor William Tryon, signed by Speaker of the House John Ashe, Alexander Lillington, and Thomas Lloyd, warning the governor of an impending march on his house and seeking to know if the governor wanted an armed guard placed around the house. Tryon declined, but his action gave the local men a clue as to what his reaction might be to their threats.

Throughout most of his adult life, Moore was known as George Moore of Moore Fields because he held an extensive tract of land lying north of Wilmington. His residence, Kendall, was at Rocky Point, some fifteen miles from the port town in an area that served as a center of influence in the years just prior to the American Revolution. Many prominent families of the time lived nearby. Moore also owned numerous slaves and had a summer residence on the sound.

SEE: Robert J. Cain, ed., *Records of the Executive Council, 1735–1754* (1988); John Cheney, Jr., ed., *North Carolina Government, 1585–1979* (1981); Walter Clark, ed., *State Records of North Carolina*, vol. 17 (1899); William L. Saunders, ed., *Colonial Records of North Carolina*, vols. 4–6 (1886–88); *South Carolina Historical and Genealogical Magazine* 37 (January 1936); James Sprunt, *Chronicles of the Cape Fear River* (1914).

JOHN LEONARD RIGSBEE

Moore, Godwin Cotton *(7 Nov. 1806–16 May 1880)*, physician and political and religious leader, was born in Hertford County, the oldest of three children of James Wright and Esther Cotton Moore. The elder Moore had moved to Hertford from Nansemond County, Va., on his marriage to Esther. Godwin's maternal great-grandfather, Arthur Cotton, is said to have settled near the village of St. Johns in what is now Hertford County on his marriage to Elizabeth Rutland, the daughter of James Rutland. He was the builder of Mulberry Grove, the brick plantation house that young Moore later inherited.

Godwin Moore was prepared for college at the Hertford Academy, Murfreesboro (then operated by Thomas O'Grady), and at the Bingham School, Hillsborough, entering The University of North Carolina in 1822. His studies were interrupted prior to completion of his junior year. Subsequently, he studied medicine with his brother-in-law, Dr. N. P. Fletcher, in Brunswick County, Va. He then enrolled in the Medical College of the University of Pennsylvania, receiving the M.D. degree in 1828. Afterwards Moore attained considerable success as a general practitioner in Hertford, Northampton, and Bertie counties.

Although he was a Democrat residing in predominately Whig territory, Moore was elected to represent Hertford County in the House of Commons in 1831 and in the senate in 1842. He lost bids to serve as a delegate to the state convention in 1835 and to the U.S. House of Representatives in 1837. In later years, he served successive terms in the state house of representatives (1866–67 and 1867–68).

Deeply concerned with religion and education, Moore made his most significant contributions in these two areas. For thirty-six years he was the influential moderator of the annual sessions of the Chowan Baptist Association, an organization that consisted of sixty-eight churches in northeastern North Carolina at the time of his death. He was elected to numerous leadership posts in the Baptist State Convention of North Carolina, including membership on its board of managers (1842–44), vice-president (1847–54), and trustee (1849–67). He was also a member of the board of trustees of Wake Forest College (1838–60).

In connection with his work among the Baptists of the Chowan Association, Moore is credited with being the leading spirit behind the founding and early operation of Chowan Baptist Female Institute (now Chowan College). As the first chairman of the institution's board of trustees (1848–67), he was given much of the responsibility for securing and maintaining adequate facilities and instructional staff. He contributed liberally to the financial support of the school during its fledgling years and was instrumental in devising methods that saved the debt-plagued institution from early bankruptcy.

In the late spring of 1832 Moore married Julia M. Wheeler, the daughter of John Wheeler of Murfreesboro. They had eight children: John Wheeler, James Wright, Esther Cotton (Mrs. Richard Thomas Weaver), Charles Richard (died in infancy), Thomas Longworth, Julia Wheeler (died in childhood), William Edward, and Sallie Wood (Mrs. Samuel James Calvert).

SEE: Samuel A. Ashe, ed., *Biographical History of North Carolina*, vol. 8 (1917); Edgar V. McKnight and Oscar Creech, *A History of Chowan College* (1964); John Wheeler Moore, "Early Baptist Laymen of North Carolina: Godwin Cotton Moore," *Biblical Recorder* 24 (June–12 Aug. 1891).

R. HARGUS TAYLOR

Moore, Hight C (*28 Jan. 1871–24 May 1957*), clergyman, writer, and editorial executive, was born at Globe,
Caldwell County, the son of Patterson and Nancy Ann
Moore (first cousins), both of a long line of the Moore
family that settled in North Carolina about 1767. He was
named for an uncle, Hight C Moore. The "Hight" came
from his grandmother's family name, and the "C" (not
an initial) was an abbreviation of another family name,
most likely "Seay."

Young Moore attended free and subscription schools
in Globe Valley (1876–81) and Globe Institute (1882–87).
Early in 1888 he entered Wake Forest College, where he
was graduated with a bachelor of arts degree in 1890.
His studies emphasized English composition and literature, classical courses in Greek and Hebrew, and the English Bible. Following graduation, he served for three
months as principal of Cove Creek Academy in Watauga
County. On 1 Nov. 1890 he became pastor of the First
Baptist Church in Morehead City, the beginning of a
succession of North Carolina Baptist pastorates over
more than thirteen years, interrupted only by a fall semester (1893) at Rochester Theological Seminary, Rochester, N.Y. He went next to Brown Memorial, Winston-
Salem (1893–94); First Baptist Church, Monroe (1894–
98); First Baptist Church, New Bern (1898–1903); and
University Baptist Church, Chapel Hill (1903–4).

During his years as a pastor, Moore attracted denominational attention by his superior performance in the
pulpit and by his facility as a writer. He edited *The Evangelist* during his pastorate at Monroe and the *Atlantic
Messenger* while he was in New Bern; at the same time,
he wrote Sunday school lesson expositions for the *Biblical Recorder*. Those efforts provided a background for his
first professional connection with the North Carolina
Baptist State Convention, with headquarters in Raleigh.
Moore became state Sunday school secretary in 1904
and served for three years. Afterwards he was field secretary of the Sunday School Board of the Southern Baptist Convention (1907–8), stationed in Raleigh.

Late in 1908 he became editor of the *Biblical Recorder*,
Raleigh, serving until 31 July 1917. Then he went to
Nashville, Tenn., as coeditorial secretary and managing
editor of all the publications of the Sunday School
Board of the Southern Baptist Convention. From 1927
until his retirement in 1943, he was editorial secretary
and in that capacity edited more than seventy separate
periodicals. On his retirement he established his residence at Ridgecrest, the site of the Ridgecrest Baptist
Assembly of the Southern Baptist Convention, which he
had helped organize in 1907. He lived at Ridgecrest until
his death and was buried in the Ridgecrest Cemetery.

Moore was the recipient of two honorary degrees:
doctor of divinity, Wake Forest College (1915); and doctor of literature, Baylor University (1920). He was assistant recording secretary (1898–1907) and statistical secretary (1905–7) of the North Carolina Baptist State
Convention, then junior recording secretary (1914–19)
and senior recording secretary (1920–46) of the Southern
Baptist Convention. In addition, he was an ex officio
member and secretary of the executive committee of the
Southern Baptist Convention for thirty-two years (1914–
46), treasurer of the executive committee and of the convention for four years (1929–33), and chairman of the
convention's Committee on Arrangements for more
than twenty-five years (1921–46). Moore was a longtime
member of the Editorial Section of the International
Council on Religious Education (secretary-treasurer,
1924–26) and a member of the Committee on Improved
Uniform Lessons (1924–46).

During his early years in Raleigh, he was a trustee of
Shaw University; in Nashville, he was a trustee of the
American Baptist Theological Seminary. His connections
with both the North Carolina Baptist State Convention
and the Southern Baptist Convention gave him ex officio
memberships on all of the major committees and boards
of both groups.

Moore was a prolific writer. His manuscripts and
memorabilia, totaling over thirteen thousand items, are
in the Southern Baptist Historical Collection in the
Dargan-Carver Library, Nashville, Tenn. He was the author of fifty published volumes, three major pamphlets,
more than a dozen series of articles in periodicals, and
uncounted expository studies of the weekly Sunday
School lesson in such publications as the *Biblical Recorder*, *The Teacher*, and *Kind Words*. (A complete bibliography is available in the North Carolina Baptist Collection, Wake Forest University Library, Winston-Salem.)

His first published work was "Seaside Sermons"
(1892) and his second was "Select Poetry of North Carolina" (1894). An avid traveler, Moore visited every state
in the United States, Canada, Mexico, Europe, Asia,
and Africa. Much of his observations appeared in his
writings. He was a continuous student of the Bible, and
in addition to his weekly commentaries, he wrote thirty-
five yearly volumes, entitled, "Points for Emphasis," a
pocket-size analysis of the Sunday school lessons for
each Sunday in those years (1918–53). In the early days
of radio, he gave a broadcast of the weekly lesson over
station WSM, Nashville.

On 2 May 1893 Moore married Laura Miller Peterson,
a native of Goldsboro. The oldest child of Captain Joseph Eppy and Mary Catherine Parker Peterson, she
was educated at Chowan College, Murfreesboro, and
the Oxford Female Seminary, Oxford. The Moores had
one son, Joseph Peterson, born in Winston-Salem on 3
May 1894.

SEE: Clifton J. Allen, "Hight C Moore: An Apprecia-
tion," *Baptist History and Heritage* (January–March 1971);
The Circle, staff publication of the Baptist Sunday School
Board, Nashville, Tenn., 1 Feb. 1941, December 1943,
December 1951; Data File (North Carolina Baptist Collec-
tion, Wake Forest University Library, Winston-Salem);
Data File (Southern Baptist Historical Collection, Dar-
gan-Carver Library, Nashville, Tenn.); *Encyclopedia of
Southern Baptists*, vol. 3 (1971); R. L. Middleton, *A Dream
Come True* (1957); J. M. Price, ed., *Baptist Leaders in Reli-
gious Education* (1943).

C. SYLVESTER GREEN

Moore, James (*1737–15 Jan. 1777*), brigadier general in
the North Carolina Continental Line, was born in New
Hanover County, the son of Maurice Moore (d. 1743), a
prominent planter, and his second wife, Mary Porter.
James was the brother of Revolutionary leader Maurice
Moore (ca. 1735–77) and of Rebecca Moore, who married
General John Ashe. He lived at his plantation near a
bend in the Cape Fear River known as Rocky Point, fifteen miles north of Wilmington. The fertile land was
first claimed by his father and had been quickly settled
by the Moores and other prominent pioneer families.

Active in the local militia, Moore was captain of the
company at Fort Johnston in 1758. Governor Arthur
Dobbs appointed him to command a company raised
during the French and Indian War. Moore represented
New Hanover County in the provincial House of Commons from 1764 to 1771 and in 1773, serving on various
committees.

During the Stamp Act disturbances in 1766, he was
one of the leaders of the Cape Fear mob that marched to
Brunswick. Governor William Tryon reported that

Moore went to the governor's house as a delegate of the armed mob to get the comptroller of the customs, William Pennington, who had taken refuge in Tryon's home. The governor refused to allow Pennington to leave, but when the armed force grew larger, Pennington resigned his commission and publicly swore not to execute any provision of the Stamp Act.

When Tryon led militia to the backcountry in 1768, Moore was appointed colonel and given command of the governor's artillery. Three years later when the Regulators were defeated at the Battle of Alamance, he was again colonel and commanded the artillery company.

Moore was an early supporter of the Revolutionary movement. In June 1770 he called a meeting of the Wilmington Sons of Liberty, which appointed a committee, chaired by Cornelius Harnett, to enforce the nonimportation agreement on the Lower Cape Fear. On 21 July 1774 an extralegal meeting of freeholders in Wilmington elected Moore to the committee that called upon other counties in the province to elect delegates to the First Provincial Congress. He was an active member of the New Hanover Safety Committee and of the Wilmington area committee that collected a shipload of provisions for Boston after passage of the Boston Port Act. In August 1775 New Hanover County elected him to the Third Provincial Congress. Meeting at Hillsborough, the congress organized two regiments for the Continental army and appointed Moore to command the First Regiment, which assembled at Wilmington.

In February 1776, when Loyalists composed primarily of Highlanders assembled at Cross Creek, Moore commanded the Whig forces charged with preventing the Highlanders' rendezvous with British soldiers on their way to Wilmington. Skillfully maneuvering his troops, Moore blocked the Loyalists' access to the coast and forced an engagement on ground of his choosing. Although he reached Moore's Creek Bridge a few hours after the 27 February battle, his direction of the campaign had ensured the Whig victory.

On 1 Mar. 1776 the Continental Congress appointed Moore brigadier general and gave him command of Continental forces in North Carolina. Moore and the troops under his immediate command remained in Wilmington to guard against the British vessels that did not leave the Lower Cape Fear until October. When Major General Charles Lee was recalled to the northern theater in September, Moore was given command of the Southern Department, and in early January he marched his brigade to Charles Town. Without funds to pay the North Carolina troops and purchase blankets and clothing, Moore divided his time between Charles Town and North Carolina, where he sought additional men and supplies.

In February 1777 the congress ordered Moore to march the North Carolina regiments stationed in the Carolinas north to join General George Washington. His plans to proceed as quickly as possible were hampered by the shortage of clothing and equipment and by the inability of commissaries to secure food along the proposed route.

Moore's frail constitution had been undoubtedly weakened by the winter operations, and he died in Wilmington of what was diagnosed as a "fit of Gout in his stomach." He was survived by his wife, Ann Ivy Moore, and four children.

Janet Schaw's assessment of his character in 1775 typifies the response of both friend and foe: "a man of . . . most unblemished character . . . and a virtuous life . . . his popularity is such that I am assured he will have more followers than any other man in the province." At the time of his death few Revolutionary officers had been as successful as he in strategy, in the organization of undisciplined military forces, and in relations with the Continental Congress and Revolutionary state governments. Death robbed North Carolina of its most obvious choice for high command in the Continental army.

SEE: Evangeline McLean Andrews, ed., in collaboration with Charles McLean Andrews, *Journal of a Lady of Quality* (1921); Samuel A. Ashe, ed., *Biographical History of North Carolina*, vol. 2 (1905); Walter Clark, ed., *State Records of North Carolina*, vol. 11 (1895); *DAB*, vol. 7 (1934); Hugh F. Rankin, "The Moore's Creek Bridge Campaign, 1776," *North Carolina Historical Review* 30 (January 1953), and *The North Carolina Continentals* (1971); William L. Saunders, ed., *Colonial Records of North Carolina*, vols. 6–10 (1888–90); Mabel Louise Webber, "The First Governor Moore and His Children," *South Carolina Historical and Genealogical Magazine* 37 (January 1936).

GEORGE TROXLER

Moore, James Osborne (31 Oct. 1909–1 Sept. 1988), attorney and public official, was born in Wellston, Ohio, the son of James Osborne and Cordelia Richards Moore and the descendant of several noted families from the two Carolinas. Following the death of his parents, he moved to Charlotte when he was sixteen. In 1933 he was graduated from The University of North Carolina with a law degree.

Moore joined a Charlotte firm and soon was judge pro tem of Mecklenburg County Recorder's Court. In 1941 and 1942 he was district price attorney for the Office of Price Administration, and later during World War II he served in the Pacific as signal officer on an aircraft carrier. After returning to Charlotte, he cofounded one of the state's first multispecialty law firms. He also became president of the city's Family and Children's Service Bureau. His concern for children was further demonstrated by his long years of service on the executive committee and as attorney of Thompson Orphanage in Charlotte.

He received tokens of appreciation for his service to the Episcopal Diocese of North Carolina, to the North Carolina Child Care Association, and to the North Carolina Bar Association, where he worked on the appellate rules study commission. In addition to his contributions in these areas, he was a member of the Judicial Conference of the federal Fourth Circuit.

Long active in historical research, Moore was the author of *A Colonial Family on the Southern Frontier*, published soon after his death.

In 1936 he married Jane Margaret Morrison of Charlotte, and they had two sons, James O., Jr., who died young, and Roger A., and three daughters, Allison, Jane, and Brandon. Moore was buried in Elmwood Cemetery, Charlotte.

SEE: *Charlotte Observer*, 2 Sept. 1988; Information supplied by Mrs. Jane M. Moore (Charlotte); William S. Powell, ed., *North Carolina Lives* (1962).

CHARLES B. GAULT

Moore, John (ca. 1753–ca. 1781), Loyalist officer, was born in Tryon (now Lincoln) County. His father was Moses Moore, a native of Carlisle, England, who, after migrating to Virginia in 1745 and marrying a Miss Winston from Jamestown, settled eight miles west of Lincolnton. Since Tryon County was a frontier area, young Moore journeyed east to the more genteel Granville County when he was old enough to begin his education. On completion of his formal instruction he subsequently returned to Tryon County and acquired, through a series of transactions with his neighbors, extensive landholdings in present-day Lincoln, Gaston, and Mecklenburg counties.

Early in the American Revolution Moore declared his allegiance to King George III, a move for which his property was confiscated by the General Assembly on 29 May 1774. In February 1779, when leading a group of Loyalists to Georgia, he was attacked and defeated at Kettle Creek by Colonel Andrew Pickens. After narrowly escaping to the British forces in that vicinity, Moore was said to have aided in the defense of Savannah. December 1779 found him with British troops near Moseley's Ferry on the Ogeechee River.

On 7 June 1780 Moore, referring to himself as a lieutenant colonel in Colonel John Hamilton's corps of North Carolina Loyalists, arrived back at his father's house. On 10 June he met in the woods on Indian Creek with approximately forty Tories. After recounting Lord Cornwallis's siege and capture of Charles Town, Moore instructed the group to "hold themselves in readiness," promising that as soon as the country could provide subsistence, Cornwallis would march in. On hearing that a small Whig force led by Major Joseph McDowell was nearby, Moore appointed 13 June 1780 as the day for all Loyalists to meet at Ramsour's Mill. On the designated day some 200 men, including Major Nicholas Welch, met Moore. By the twentieth the ranks had swelled to nearly 1,300. Though nearly that many men were under Moore's command at Ramsour's Mill, almost one-fourth of them were unarmed.

Late in the evening of 20 June 1780, General Griffith Rutherford's Whig force of four hundred men attacked the encamped Tories. The Tories, wearing green pine sprigs in their hats, were such easy targets for the Whigs (who identified themselves by white clumps of paper in their caps) that soon after the first shots were fired Rutherford's force overran the mill. But as soon as the action began, the unarmed Tories fled to a small creek behind the mill. Realizing the battle was lost, Moore and Welch joined them and planned their escape. Under the guise of a white flag of truce (asking for a halt in the fighting to tend to the wounded and bury the dead), Moore and Welch ordered their troops to escape as fast as they could.

Thus surviving another narrow escape, Moore and thirty men joined the British forces in Camden, S.C. In Camden, his force lost three men killed and fourteen wounded in General Horatio Gates's defeat. However, Moore probably did not participate in this action for he was, at this time, threatened with court-martial for disobeying orders in attempting to embody the Loyalists "without order or caution" before the time designated by Cornwallis. Though never brought to trial, he was treated with disrespect by British officers and still under threat of court-martial.

John Moore had his third narrow escape at the Battle of Kings Mountain. Afterwards he joined Captain Thomas Waters's Tories, who were defeated by Colonel William Washington at Hammond's Store, S.C., on 28 Dec. 1780. Legend claims that Moore sailed to Carlisle, England, and was never heard from again. A more reliable source is probably the statement of a North Carolina Loyalist—published in the *Political Magazine* of London (April 1783)—that Moore was captured by Colonel Wade Hampton near the Wateree and hanged. He left no family.

SEE: Walter Clark, ed., *State Records of North Carolina*, vols. 16, 19, 21 (1899–1903); Lyman Draper, *King's Mount and Its Heroes* (1929); Record of Deeds (County Courthouse, Lincolnton); W. L. Sherrill, *Annals of Lincoln County* (1937); John H. Wheeler, *Historical Sketches of North Carolina* (1851).

BRADFORD M. SHELBY

Moore, John Wheeler (23 Oct. 1833–6 Dec. 1906), historian, was born at Mulberry Grove, his father's plantation in Hertford County, the oldest child of Dr. Godwin Cotton and Julia M. Wheeler Moore. The Cottons and the Moores had long been prominent in the affairs of the region. Godwin Moore is credited with having been the main force behind the establishment of Chowan Baptist Female Institute (now Chowan College) at Murfreesboro in 1848. Moore's mother's family was from Murfreesboro, where his grandfather and namesake, John Wheeler, had been a successful merchant.

Moore's earliest education consisted of private tutoring at home. He was prepared for college at Buckhorn Academy in the Maneys Neck section of Hertford County under the direction of John Kimberly. In July 1849 he matriculated as a freshman at The University of North Carolina, where he became a member of the Philanthropic Society. Moore was graduated with a B.A. degree in 1853.

Returning to Hertford County, he married and began to study law at home. After admission to the bar in 1855, he moved to Anniesdale, a home he had built on the outskirts of Murfreesboro, and began to practice law in that town. During the decade preceding the Civil War, Moore was extremely active in the Democratic party. Nominated for a seat in the state senate in 1856, he lost the election but he did serve as a presidential elector in 1860.

On the outbreak of the Civil War, Moore was commissioned as a staff officer in the Second Regiment of North Carolina Cavalry. In February 1862 he was promoted to major and given command of the Third North Carolina Battalion, a light artillery unit consisting of three batteries. The battalion was immediately ordered to assist in the defense of Richmond and remained with the Army of Northern Virginia until December 1862. At that time, Moore's outfit returned to eastern North Carolina and saw action at Goldsboro, New Bern, and Wilmington. For the remainder of the war, the three batteries were stationed in the Lower Cape Fear River until the retreat of the Confederate forces at the fall of Fort Fisher. Afterwards, the battalion took part in the Battle of Bentonville and surrendered at Greensboro.

After the war, Moore resumed his legal practice in Murfreesboro. However, when Anniesdale burned in 1866, the family was forced to move to Maple Lawn, his wife's ancestral home in lower Hertford County.

Although Moore had long engaged in literary pursuits, the move to Maple Lawn marked the beginning of an active period of historical research. At the urging of his friend Chief Justice W. N. H. Smith, he began the compilation of a *School History of North Carolina* in 1876. The book, published in 1879, was an immediate success and served for years as the standard school history of the state. Moore's next project was a series, entitled "Sketches of Hertford County," that appeared serially in the Murfreesboro *Inquirer* in 1877 and 1878. He then decided to expand his idea of a state history into a two-volume octavo edition, which was published in 1880 as the *History of North Carolina, from the Earliest Discoveries to the Present Time*. Moore drew heavily from the works of previous historians such as Francis X. Martin, Hugh Williamson, Francis L. Hawks, David L. Swain, John H. Wheeler, and Joseph Seawell Jones. Like the school history, this work was highly acclaimed.

In 1881 he published *The Heirs of St. Kilda*, a novel based on the plantation culture of his youth. Unfortunately, Moore's florid, romanticized style of fiction received scant attention. However, the same year marked the beginning of the most ambitious project of his career, as he was commissioned by the state to prepare a *Roster* of the North Carolina soldiers who had served in the Civil War. The magnitude of the task was exacerbated by the scarcity of records within the state. Fortunately, Secretary of War Robert T. Lincoln granted him access to the Confederate archives, which had been taken to Washington, D.C. Here he found the returns of all North Carolina regiments except the Sixty-eighth. Moore's *Roster* represented the first attempt by any Southern state to list its Confederate soldiers.

A devout Baptist, Moore spent the last years of his life preparing a history of the Baptist church in North Carolina. This work was never published; the manuscript is at Wake Forest University.

On 23 Sept. 1853 Moore married Ann James Ward, the daughter of James and Elizabeth Jones Ward. They were the parents of twelve children: Arthur Cotton, Elizabeth Jones (m. W. L. McGhee), Charles Godwin, Julia Wheeler (m. William S. Yeates), Helen Manly, Philip St. John, John Wheeler, Jr., Annie Ward, James Ward, Godwin Cotton, Rutland Ward, and Isabella Campbell. Helen, Annie, James, Rutland, and Isabella died in infancy.

Moore died of a heart attack at Maple Lawn and was buried there in the family cemetery. A portrait of him is owned by a descendant.

SEE: Edwin A. Alderman and Joel C. Harris, eds., *Library of Southern Literature*, vol. 15 (1910); Samuel A. Ashe, ed., *Biographical History of North Carolina*, vol. 8 (1917); Daniel L. Grant, *Alumni History of the University of North Carolina, 1795–1924* (1924).

JAMES ELLIOTT MOORE

Moore, Joseph (*29 Feb. 1832–9 July 1905*), scientist, educator, Quaker minister, and college president, was born in Washington County, Ind., the son of John Parker and Martha Cadwalader Moore and the grandson of Joseph and Peninah Parker Moore, who migrated from eastern North Carolina to Indiana in 1819. After attending county schools, he entered Friends Boarding School in Richmond, Ind., in 1853. Moore began teaching at age eighteen in a county school, then at Blue Ridge Seminary, and in 1852–53 at still a third school. He served as assistant teacher while a student at Friends Boarding School from 1853 to 1859. Entering Harvard University in 1859, he studied under Louis Agassiz, earning a B.S. degree in 1861. He was awarded an honorary M.A. degree by Haverford College in 1869 and an honorary LL.D. degree by Indiana State University in 1882.

Recorded as a Quaker minister on 22 Feb. 1865, Moore became one of the denomination's most influential traveling clergymen, particularly as a scientist who interpreted all knowledge—both natural and moral—as having a unitary, divine source. After spending four years at Friends Boarding School (which had become Earlham College in 1859) as a science professor, he accepted an appointment in late 1865 as superintendent of education for the Baltimore Association of Friends. In that capacity, he supervised a Reconstruction program in North Carolina, combining the rebuilding of its educational program with the total life of the Society of Friends, most of whom were farmers.

According to Governor Jonathan Worth, Moore became a major influence in North Carolina in surveying postwar conditions, rebuilding schools, training teachers, organizing Bible as well as public schools, and using his "magic lantern" as a visual aid in teaching geography, zoology, and astronomy throughout the state. He combined his assets and interests as scientist, teacher, minister, and even "showman" to encourage the development of education in North Carolina in one of its most critical periods. His teacher training program at Springfield Normal School near High Point—believed to be one of the earliest in the state—helped to prepare for the establishment of the State Normal and Industrial School (now the University of North Carolina at Greensboro).

Moore went back to Richmond, Ind., to serve as president of Earlham College from 1868 to 1882; meanwhile, he continued to teach in his special scientific areas. Always involved in the collection of specimens, he received a year's leave of absence in 1875–76 to visit the Sandwich Islands in Hawaii, arriving home with barrels of new exhibits for his constantly growing museum.

Returning to Greensboro, N.C., Moore served the state's best known Quaker institution, the New Garden Boarding School, from 1883 to 1888. He spent the first year traveling to raise funds and support for the expanding program envisaged for this "Friends School in North Carolina." During the next four years he was its principal, preparing the curriculum and faculty for its transition into a four-year liberal arts college, Guilford, in 1888. He was offered its first presidency, but chose to return once again to Earlham, where he could devote the remainder of his life to the sciences and to the important museum that later was given his name. He had already become recognized, in the words of Agassiz, as "the best scientist west of the Alleghany Mountains."

Moore had also become one of the most creative and influential educators during the Reconstruction era, both in North Carolina and Indiana, his two ancestral home states. At a time of growing opposition between science and religion, his career as a leading scientist and museum curator, combined with that as educator, administrator, and Quaker minister, made him one of the major positive forces in both private and public education.

In 1862 he married Deborah Ann Stanton of Springboro, Ohio. She died in 1864 after the birth of a son. In 1872 he married Mary Thorne of Selma, Ohio, and they had three daughters and a son. Moore's portrait hangs in the School of Religion at Earlham College.

SEE: Anna Moore Cadbury, "Life of Joseph Moore," 1934 (typescript, Guilford College Library, Greensboro); Royal J. Davis, "A Biographical Sketch—Joseph Moore," *Earlham College Bulletin* 2 (1 Aug. 1905); Dorothy Gilbert, *Guilford: A Quaker College* (1937); Opal Thornburg, *Earlham: The Story of a College* (1963).

J. FLOYD MOORE

Moore, Louis Toomer (*17 May 1885–30 Nov. 1961*), journalist, author, and local historian, was born in Wilmington, the son of Colonel Roger and Susan Eugenia Beery Moore. He was a lineal descendant of James Moore, colonial governor of South Carolina; of Roger Moore, builder of Orton plantation; and of Maurice

Moore, one of the founders of the town of Brunswick. After attending Wilmington schools, he studied at The University of North Carolina in 1902–3 and again in 1905–6, when he enrolled in the law curriculum. While on campus, he was on the staff of the *Tar Heel* and was Chapel Hill correspondent for the *Raleigh Post*, mainly handling sports news.

Moore began his professional career as associate editor of the *Wilmington Evening Dispatch*, remaining in that position from 1906 to 1919, when he entered private business. In 1921 he became manager of the Wilmington Chamber of Commerce and one of the city's most enthusiastic boosters; he served in that capacity for twenty years. Moore played a significant role in the work with the Corps of Engineers, resulting in the deepening and development of Wilmington's port; he also worked for the extension of the inland waterway. As chairman of the New Hanover County Historical Commission from 1947 until his death, he assisted the State Department of Archives and History in placing some twenty highway historical markers in the Wilmington area. Moore also wrote numerous articles for the press on local historical sites and personages and was in great demand as a speaker to civic, religious, and fraternal organizations.

Among his writings was a pamphlet, *Beautiful Oakdale*, about unusual and historical graves in the local cemetery. Other works included *A History of the Carolina Yacht Club* and *Wilmington: Historical City*. His book, *Stories Old and New of the Lower Cape Fear*, was reprinted a number of times, and the profits from its publication provided a revolving fund to support the publication of other works of local history.

Moore was chairman of the Two Hundredth Anniversary Pageant commemorating the founding of Wilmington, and he was one of the six founders of the Lower Cape Fear Historical Society. His collection of local historical material was added to the North Carolina Collection in the Wilmington Public Library, where it has been widely used.

On 21 Nov. 1916 he married Florence Hill Kidder, and they became the parents of Florence (Mrs. John O. Dunn), Margaret (Mrs. William E. Perdew), and Anne (Mrs. Zack H. Bacon, Jr.).

SEE: Daniel L. Grant, *Alumni History of the University of North Carolina, 1795–1924* (1924); Louis T. Moore Collection (Wilmington Public Library, Wilmington); *North Carolina Biography*, vol. 3 (1941); *Who's Who in the South* (1927).

MARGARET MOORE PERDEW

Moore, Maurice (1682/1686–1743), soldier, legislator, and planter, was born in the Goose Creek section of Berkeley County, S.C., the son of James and Margaret Berringer Moore. His father was governor of South Carolina from 1700 to 1703.

Maurice Moore made his first appearance in North Carolina in 1712. He arrived as a captain in a troop of soldiers under the command of his older brother, Colonel James Moore, to assist North Carolina in the war against the Tuscarora Indians. Colonel Moore, with his force of thirty whites and over eight hundred Indians, defeated the Tuscarora after several months of bitter fighting. Shortly afterwards he returned with his troops to South Carolina, but Captain Maurice Moore remained in the Albemarle section for the next ten years.

Only two years after the defeat of the Tuscarora, the Yamassee Indians and their allies attacked white settlements in South Carolina, threatening the extinction of

many of them. On receiving a call for help from the governor of South Carolina, the governor of North Carolina responded by sending two companies of volunteers, one of which was under the command of Colonel Maurice Moore. In the summer of 1715 Moore began his march to South Carolina. While passing through the Cape Fear section, he learned that the Cape Fear and Waccamaw Indians planned to ambush his troops. Because of the warning Moore not only avoided the ambush but also decisively defeated the Indians. His victory over the Cape Fears at this time opened up the southern part of North Carolina for future settlement. On reaching South Carolina, Moore and his troops played a significant role in bringing the Yamassee War to a successful conclusion. His most important contribution was to persuade the Cherokee not to join with the Creeks against the whites. Members of the South Carolina Assembly expressed their appreciation in a resolution of thanks "for his service to this Province, in his comeing so cheerfully with the forces brought from North Carolina to our assistance, and for what further services he and they have done since their arrival here."

Exactly where Maurice Moore lived in the Albemarle section is uncertain, but it is known that in the Vestry Act of 1715 he was named a vestryman for Perquimans Parish. He appears to have been active in the political affairs of North Carolina shortly after settling there. In 1718 he and his brother-in-law, Edward Moseley, strongly suspected that Governor Charles Eden and Chief Justice Tobias Knight were involved in the piratical acts of Edward Teach (Blackbeard). To verify their suspicions, they broke into the secretary's office and seized the public records. They failed to prove their accusations against Eden and Knight, who were exonerated by the colonial Council. Moore and Moseley were tried by the General Court for breaking into the secretary's office and each was given a fine.

On 28 Mar. 1723 Moore was sworn in as a member of the governor's Council, having been appointed by Joseph Blake, Jr., one of the Lords Proprietors. He served on the Council until his election to the House of Burgesses in 1725. At the November session of that year, Moore was elected speaker of the house. In 1734 he won a seat in the House of Burgesses from New Hanover County; he continued to represent that county until his death.

During the years 1725–34 Moore did not participate in political affairs. Instead, he was engaged in acquiring lands in the Lower Cape Fear and in attempting to establish a permanent settlement in that section of the colony. He had become acquainted with this region when going to the assistance of South Carolina in 1715. As early as 1724, he had secured from Governor George Burrington patents for more than seven thousand acres of land in that section. To encourage settlement, Moore, in 1725, "appropriated and laid out a certain Parcel of Land, containing Three Hundred and Twenty Acres, on the Southwest side of Cape Fear, for a Town" that he named Brunswick in honor of the royal family. The site was about fifteen miles from the mouth of the Cape Fear River. Over the next several years Moore's two brothers, Roger and Nathaniel, arrived from South Carolina to take up lands in the region. Friends and relatives of his from the Albemarle section also acquired large holdings there.

In the fall of 1731 Governor Burrington persuaded the Council to order Maurice Moore, Edward Moseley, and John Porter to appear before it to give an exact account "of Every Tract they hold" on the Cape Fear and "by what Title they Claim the same." Burrington maintained that these gentlemen "Claim Such great quantities of Land . . . that new Comers Cannot find Lands to take up." The governor was not completely objective in his accusation, since at the time he and Moore were engaged in a dispute over certain land boundaries. Maurice Moore appeared before the Council in January 1732 and stated that he owned about fifteen thousand acres in the Cape Fear region, for which he produced documentary proof. In addition to the lots he retained for his own use in the town of Brunswick, his principal holdings were in the Rocky Point section on the northeastern branch of the Cape Fear, where he built his home.

Moore was active in public affairs until the end of his life. In the spring of 1743 the governor of South Carolina requested permission of the government of North Carolina to raise a regiment of one thousand men in that colony for the defense of Georgia and South Carolina in case of a Spanish attack. The request was granted, and Colonel Maurice Moore was commissioned to command the regiment. While raising troops to assist South Carolina, Moore died near Edenton. The place of his burial is unknown.

Moore married first Elizabeth Lillington, the daughter of Alexander Lillington and the widow of Samuel Swann. They had four daughters: Mrs. Thomas Jones, Mrs. John Porter, Mrs. Francis Corbin, and Mrs. George Minot. His second marriage was to Mary Porter, by whom he had one daughter and two sons: Rebecca (Mrs. John Ashe), Maurice, Jr., and James.

SEE: Robert J. Cain, ed., *North Carolina Higher-Court Minutes, 1724–1730* (1981), *Records of the Executive Council, 1664–1734* (1984), and *Records of the Executive Council, 1735–1754* (1988); Walter Clark, ed., *State Records of North Carolina*, vol. 23 (1904); Lawrence Lee, *The Lower Cape Fear in Colonial Days* (1965); William S. Price, Jr., ed., *North Carolina Higher-Court Minutes, 1709–1723* (1974); William L. Saunders, ed., *Colonial Records of North Carolina*, vols. 2–4 (1886); James Sprunt, *Chronicles of the Cape Fear River* (1916); Alfred M. Waddell, *A History of New Hanover County* (1909); Mabel L. Webber, comp., "The First Governor Moore and His Children," *South Carolina Historical and Genealogical Magazine* 37 (January 1936).

LAWRENCE F. LONDON

Moore, Maurice, Jr. *(1735–77)*, jurist, was the son of Colonel Maurice and Mary Porter Moore. He was born in New Hanover County and at an early age was sent to New England for his education. By 1757 he was back in North Carolina and was elected to the lower house of the Assembly from the town of Brunswick. Moore represented his borough in the legislature during 1757–59, 1762, 1764, 1766–68, 1770–71, and 1773. In December 1757 Governor Arthur Dobbs recommended him for membership on the royal Council, citing him as an assemblyman who showed "a good disposition to support his Majesty's Interest." During the next six years the governor attempted unsuccessfully to obtain a permanent upper-house seat for the young man. On 24 Apr. 1760 Dobbs made an emergency appointment of Moore to the Council to ensure a quorum. Moore willingly resigned a lower-house seat to accept the socially prestigious Council chair, and he served there dutifully for a year until a commissioned councillor arrived to displace him. Once back in the Assembly, he sought a leading role there, including the speakership, but it always eluded him.

In January 1763 the governor and the Council made Moore an associate justice of the superior court at Salis-

bury. Except for his two-year suspension beginning in 1766, Moore served as judge in superior courts until their collapse late in 1772. Therefore, by 1765 he was one of the leading young political figures in the colony.

Like many of his friends and associates in the Lower Cape Fear region, Moore was displeased by passage of the Stamp Act in the summer of 1765. Demonstrations against the act occurred in Wilmington on 19 and 31 October. On 16 November Dr. William Houston, the stamp distributor for North Carolina, was compelled to resign his office by a mob of three to four hundred people in Wilmington. Among the leaders of this demonstration was James Moore, Maurice's brother, who was later a general in the American Revolution. Sometime during the summer of 1765, Maurice Moore wrote a pamphlet entitled *The Justice and Policy of Taxing the American Colonies in England*. In it he argued that England had no right to tax the colonies because they were not represented in Parliament. He not only rejected the theory of virtual representation but also contended that Parliamentary representation was based on certain kinds of tenure rather than residence in a particular shire. In the case of North Carolina, such tenure had been conferred by the Charter of 1663. Moore's pamphlet demonstrated a thorough reading in constitutional law and history as well as tightly reasoned arguments. His prominence as an opponent of the Stamp Act led Governor William Tryon to suspend Moore from his judgeship early in 1766. Tryon characterized the pamphleteer's influence as local: "He is a leading man in this river [Cape Fear] though he enjoys no great share of popularity in other parts of the province."

After repeal of the Stamp Act, tempers in the colony cooled. In March 1768 Tryon restored Moore to his judgeship, citing his proper conduct since the suspension. The justice thus returned to the bench during one of the most crucial periods in the life of the colony—the Regulator troubles. During Tryon's first expedition into the backcountry in the summer of 1768, Moore served as colonel of a troop of Gentlemen Volunteer Light Dragoons. In September he joined Martin Howard and Richard Henderson at the Salisbury Superior Court, where several Regulators were tried. Most of these men were acquitted, but at least two leaders were convicted. For a brief time there was an uneasy calm in the backcountry, but on 13 Mar. 1770 Moore reported to the governor that sheriffs in many western counties could neither collect taxes nor serve writs because of Regulator agitation.

As unrest continued to grow in the backcountry, Moore chaired a committee of the legislature on 10 Dec. 1770 that called for stern measures to curtail the Regulators. Shortly after this action, Samuel Johnston introduced the notorious Riot Act, which served as one of the legal bases of the Battle of Alamance. On 20 December, the General Assembly expelled Herman Husband, a Regulator leader, from its membership for publishing a libelous letter from James Hunter to Moore printed in the *North Carolina Gazette* on 14 December. The letter purported to answer an earlier letter from Moore (which does not now exist) in which he blamed Hunter and Husband for most of the backcountry agitation. Soon after Husband's expulsion, open violence flared in several western counties.

Significantly, Moore requested that Tryon allow him to join his associates for the March superior court term in Salisbury. By 18 Mar. 1771 the justices reported that it would be unwise to attempt to hold the Hillsborough session of the court because of the volatile situation there. Regulators gathered around Salisbury at the time said they were willing to have Martin Howard hold court in the backcountry, but not his associates Richard Henderson or Moore. While some of this bias was because Henderson and Moore were commissioned by the despised Tryon and Howard by the king, many Regulators evidenced a special hatred for Moore and expressed their desire to flog him. When the three justices were summoned to Hillsborough on 30 May 1771, they sentenced to death twelve Regulators taken at the Battle of Alamance (only six were executed) and backcountry resistance ended. By August of the following year, Moore joined with Howard and Henderson in urging an end to prosecution of Regulators. If Moore was the author of the Atticus letter attacking Tryon in the *Virginia Gazette* of 7 Nov. 1771, then he had acquired even earlier a distaste for further punishment of the Regulators. Francis X. Martin attributed authorship of the Atticus letter to Moore in his 1829 *History of North Carolina from the Earliest Period* and many subsequent historians have accepted his verdict, though Martin offered no documentation for his statement.

With the general collapse of the colony's court system in 1772, Moore accepted a role as judge in Governor Josiah Martin's specially commissioned courts of oyer and terminer. However, Moore contributed to the demise of this temporary scheme when he pointed out technical irregularities in the court's commission at the summer term of 1774 in Wilmington. As the Revolution drew near, Moore seemed to be a firm supporter of the Patriot cause and served as a delegate to the Provincial Congress convened in Hillsborough on 20 Aug. 1775. While there, he was active on several committees and signed the 23 August resolution protesting taxation while affirming loyalty to the king. Although elected to the congress at Halifax on 12 Nov. 1776, he did not attend.

Moore's wife was Anne Grange. Two of his sons, Alfred and Maurice, served in the Patriot army, and the latter was killed at Brunswick early in 1776. Moore's daughter, Sarah, was the wife of General Francis Nash, and his brother, James, was a Patriot general.

Yet there is some evidence that Moore was not wholly committed to the Revolution. On 9 Jan. 1776 he wrote Governor Martin stating his belief that the people of North Carolina would welcome a return to the status quo before the Stamp Act. He urged the governor to call an Assembly to discuss the matter. Martin answered the letter two days later, suggesting that he and Moore meet personally to discuss the matter, but they never did. To what extent Moore was vacillating in his support for the Revolution is unclear. He may have written the 9 January letter after informing the Wilmington Committee of Safety. In any case, like many Americans, he hesitated to undertake a full-scale war with the mother country. In a career replete with some puzzling contradictions (his desire for high office but his opposition to the Stamp Act, his support of the Regulator expeditions but his distaste for further punishment of them, his role in the Provincial Congress but his 9 January letter), Moore exemplified the irony of an ambitious man devoted to political order but caught up in a Revolutionary situation.

Local tradition holds that Maurice and his brother James died on the same day (15 Jan. 1777) in the same house, but there is some doubt about that claim. Apparently, Maurice died sometime between January and April 1777. His son Alfred became a justice of the U.S. Supreme Court in 1799.

SEE: Don Higginbotham, *The Papers of James Iredell*, 2 vols. (1976); William S. Price, Jr., *Not a Conquered People: Two Carolinians View Parliamentary Taxation* (1975); William L. Saunders, ed., *Colonial Records of North Carolina*, vols. 6–9 (1888–90).

WILLIAM S. PRICE, JR.

Moore, Peter Weddick (24 *June 1859–15 Apr. 1934*), educator, was born near Faison in Duplin County, the son of Weddick and Alecy Thompson Moore, both slaves. His father allegedly was killed by the Ku Klux Klan during Reconstruction, and the task of rearing the five children fell to his mother. Although uneducated, she strongly believed in schooling, and she was deeply religious; it is likely that Moore received from her the perseverance and ideals that characterized his personal and professional life.

It is believed that he attended a school established in the neighborhood by the Freedmen's Bureau. He then studied at the Philosophian Academy, in nearby Sampson County, conducted by Burke Marable, under whose guidance Moore developed independence and ambition. The young man devoted himself to study with great purpose. At age twenty he was certified to teach in a one-room school near Clinton. He supplemented his earnings by raising cotton as a tenant, and with the money he saved he enrolled in Shaw University in Raleigh in the fall of 1880. President H. M. Tupper recognized Moore's ability as well as his need for support and in 1882 appointed him a student instructor. Moore also worked in a brickyard on campus and in a nearby foundry.

A classmate noted that Moore was "well informed on all current events" and that science and mathematics were his favorite subjects. He received an A.B. degree in 1887; later Shaw awarded him both M.A. and LL.D. degrees in recognition of his contributions to education in the state.

After leaving Shaw, Moore taught for about a year in Bertie County and then was named assistant principal of the State Normal School in Plymouth, where he remained for four years. In 1891, on the recommendation of Major S. M. Finger, state superintendent of public instruction, Moore was made principal of the new State Normal School for the Colored Race (now Elizabeth City State University). Here he remained for the rest of his life.

The General Assembly had appropriated nine hundred dollars for the school but made no provisions for either a building or a site. With the aid of the citizens of Elizabeth City and the board of trustees (whose members were all white), Moore and his assistant, J. H. Turner, soon obtained the Rooks Turner Building on Body Road Street and the school opened on 4 Jan. 1892 with sixty pupils. With enrollment increasing each year, the school moved to a larger facility in 1894 and then to its present site in 1912.

Moore was concerned not only with the academic training of his students but also with their spiritual and moral well-being. In addition to intensive and thorough training in subject matter, he stressed "the excellence and dignity of right living." He insisted on upright conduct and always conducted himself in such a manner that his students might learn from his example. As soon as funds were available he added an industrial program, believing that "[t]rained cooks and educated farmers are needed as well as professionally trained teachers." Moreover, some work with the hands, as well as academic exercises, became a required part of the daily routine. He wrote that "industrial education not only increases learning capacity, but promotes fidelity, accuracy, honesty, persistency and intelligence. The capacity to make a living becomes enlarged into the capacity to make a life." He made every effort to provide training that would "help to avoid that which is superficial and furnish in its stead those fundamental qualities that make character."

In addition to his administrative duties, Moore did much of the teaching, supervised the practice school, and handled all disciplinary problems. Around 1921 his health began to fail, and the position of dean was created; John H. Bias was then hired to relieve him of more minor duties. After a few years, however, Moore's health declined further, and it became evident that he could not carry out the responsibilities of his office much longer. At the commencement exercises of 25 May 1928, he was named president emeritus and granted a salary and a well-furnished house for life. After his retirement, at his insistence, he continued to teach courses in classroom management.

For many years Moore conducted the Teachers' Institute in eastern North Carolina and served as president of the North Carolina Negro Teachers' Association, of which he was a charter member. Twice the governor of North Carolina appointed him to represent the state at the National Educational Congress. In 1922 he was also requested to attend an interracial conference in Atlanta.

Indicative of Moore's perception and understanding was his reaction to the political campaign of 1900 for the adoption of an amendment to the state constitution, the effect of which would be to disfranchise blacks. "[T]his disfranchising amendment . . . will be a blessing in disguise," he stated. "It will mean the enfranchisement of the literate members of my race. Many of us are trammeled and we cannot exercise that political freedom which is so essential to the uplifting of any people. Hugging the delusion incident to emancipation, my race is all too gregarious. . . . Our leaders are now subjected to the hectoring of the illiterate of our race. . . . I entertain an abiding confidence that this disfranchising amendment will bring forth an educational awakening, the like of which has never been witnessed in North Carolina [which will] prepare all men, irrespective of race, to exercise the rights of suffrage intelligently . . . upon political principles [and not] be actuated by partisan prejudice."

One observer noted that Moore's greatest work was "the cementing of the ties between the white and . . . colored [races]." Moore himself noted that he had made it a rule of his life never to permit himself to do anything offensive to any person. After his death, the mayor of Elizabeth City attributed to him the absence of racial strife in the city. Another observer wrote that Moore "rose from slavery to a position as educator and statesman, and dedicated his life to the service of both races." To the many people who knew him, it was said, he would always be remembered by his admonition to "be somebody."

In 1889 Moore married Symera T. Raynor of Windsor, and they became the parents of two daughters: Ruth Lawrence and Bessie V. He was buried in Oak Grove Cemetery, Elizabeth City.

SEE: Elizabeth City *Daily Advance*, 16 Apr. 1934; Evelyn A. Johnson, *History of Elizabeth City State University: A Story of Survival* (1978); N. C. Newbold, *Five North Carolina Negro Educators* (1939); Mrs. Bessie Moore Wesley (Raleigh), personal information.

CHARLES INGRAM

Moore, Robert Lee (*8 Sept. 1870–16 Dec. 1949*), teacher, administrator, and Christian layman, was born in Globe Valley, Caldwell County, the son of Jesse Daniel and Mary Ann Berry Moore. A fifth-generation descendant of the Moores who settled Globe Valley, he attended local schools near his home and later Globe Academy, where he studied under R. L. Patton and W. F. Marshall, teachers who had a strong influence on his life. He entered Wake Forest College as a junior in 1888 and completed a bachelor of arts program in two years. His program was interrupted, however, by the need to earn money for expenses. After his first year of study he taught for two years, first at Globe Academy, then at Valle Crucis, and finally for a year and a half at Amherst Academy in Burke County. In the fall of 1891 he returned to Wake Forest and was graduated the following June. In 1927 the college awarded him an honorary doctor of education degree.

While at Wake Forest, Moore had a deep religious experience, announced his decision to be a Christian, and joined the local Baptist church. Although he never became a minister, he gave generously of his time, money, and talents in support of the church and its denominational programs. Through the years he served as Bible teacher, Sunday school superintendent, deacon and clerk of his church, and officer and leader in the local association. In later years he was a trustee of Wake Forest College and of the North Carolina Baptist Orphanage, as well as a member of various committees of the North Carolina Baptist State Convention.

After his graduation from Wake Forest, Moore returned to Amherst Academy and served as principal for five years. There he found among his students his future wife, Edna Corpening. They were married on 11 June 1895. Two years later Moore was offered a position as president of Mars Hill College, and the young couple moved to the mountain community where they would invest their lives in the cause of education for the area's youth. They had a son and a daughter; a third child died in infancy.

When Moore went to Mars Hill in June 1897, conditions at the so-called college would have discouraged most people. Its two brick buildings (one owned in part by the Masonic lodge) were both in need of repair and one unfinished wooden structure maintained a heavy debt. The grounds were unkempt. For several years the school had been running a deficit for current expenses, and the trustees had often found it necessary to raise money or pay salaries out of their own pockets. Frustrated and weary with their endless trials, the trustees offered to lease the institution to Moore with the understanding that he find the students, hire the teachers, raise the money, and run the school. Whatever profits there might be at the end of the year would constitute his salary. Moore accepted the offer—and the challenge.

Later in the summer, after a period of study at The University of North Carolina, Moore returned to Mars Hill, prepared a small catalogue, and began traveling over the region, talking to prospective students and promoting the college generally. When the school opened in the fall, one hundred and eighty students enrolled. Forty-one years later, at the time of Moore's retirement, the student body had grown to seven hundred; the faculty had increased from three to thirty-six; instead of two buildings, there were more than a dozen; and the original four acres had been expanded into a campus of more than a hundred acres. The school was an accredited junior college recognized for its superior academic program.

These accomplishments required great sacrifice and dedication. During the early years the task was difficult, and many times the college's income was in foodstuffs, wood, or labor. Mrs. Moore shared in the work needed to feed, house, and teach the students. She dried and canned fruits and vegetables, conserving the extra food brought as payment on tuition and fees. She served as the school's housemother, dietitian, nurse, and business manager. The Moores took students into their home, and when a residence hall was available, they moved into the dormitory and lived there for almost thirteen years, caring for the students as houseparents. They shared their linens and blankets with those who had none or too few. Their own china and wedding silver were used in the common dining room, and for years the only practice piano was the one in their living room.

It was Moore's policy never to turn away any boy or girl who wanted an education. Student expenses were kept at a minimum, and for several years room and board were provided for five dollars a month. Through all the years of his administration he fought to keep fees down, and Mars Hill never ceased to respond to the cry of the poorest who were worthy and wanted to "improve themselves." Moore did not believe in giving money to students, however, for giving did not develop character and "qualities of resourcefulness, industry and independence in the beneficiaries," whereas offering them an opportunity to make their own way frequently achieved those goals. Acting on this philosophy, he found work for those who needed to earn all or part of their expenses. They were employed to cook and serve meals under supervision in the kitchen, to cut wood and build fires, and to look after the buildings and grounds. A large percentage of the students paid their expenses in this manner.

With determination and business acumen, Moore met operating expenses without deficits and, through sacrifice and savings, raised funds for additional land, new buildings, and needed equipment. He allowed himself a salary of only three hundred dollars a year (reports say his income fell as low as twenty-five dollars during the first few years), returning all other profits to the institution. When the trustees resumed control of the college in 1915 and he was placed on a regular salary, he would never agree to a sum higher than that paid any faculty member—and he continued to return much of that to the college in gifts.

If, however, the school were to survive and become a significant citadel of education in western North Carolina, much more money was needed than what the Moores could hope to save out of the regular college income. The trustees of the college were not a dependable source of support, for, with a few exceptions, they lacked the vision, faith, and courage to undertake the improvements and expansion of facilities that President Moore felt were necessary. Moreover, demands for payment of debts incurred during former administrations continued to plague the school; at times these had to be paid out of some small pittance the Moores had been able to save for themselves. The Southern Baptist Home Mission Board, through its Department of Mountain Missions and Schools, in cooperation with the North Carolina Baptist State Convention, provided some relief, but the greatest assistance came in the form of gifts from an ever-increasing number of individual supporters. Moore's unwavering commitment to education for mountain youth and his integrity as president and administrator attracted the attention of several men who had money and were willing to invest in a sound project. The contributions of one benefactor amounted to a hundred thousand dollars within a few years. Others were equally generous with their gifts.

In 1915, when the college had become financially sound, President Moore turned it over to the board of trustees. In 1921 he separated the high school work from the two-year college program and reorganized the college curriculum to meet standards required for accreditation by the Southern Association of Colleges and Secondary Schools. One of the conditions for accreditation was an assured income beyond student tuitions and fees, and Moore launched a campaign to build an endowment fund adequate to meet this stipulation. He led the school through the Great Depression of the thirties without cutting salaries, except for his own, and without curtailing the academic program. In 1935, as the depression began to ease, he initiated a campaign to raise money for two new dormitories and the renovation of a number of older buildings. Meanwhile, the college bought land for an athletic field and hired a man to landscape and care for the campus.

Throughout his administration Moore was committed to academic excellence and the ideals of the Christian faith. He maintained that the teacher was the keystone of any good school and he chose his faculty with care, selecting teachers on the basis of their character and commitment to service as well as their academic qualifications. He believed that the college should train future leaders of the Baptist denomination, especially young ministers. In cooperation with the local pastor, the Reverend J. R. Owen, he helped organize periods of study under qualified teachers for ministers already in service. The first of these pastors' schools was held during the summer of 1934; later they were taken over and sponsored by the Baptist State Convention. In addition to the pastors' schools, Moore, with Dr. Walter N. Johnson of Salisbury, organized a churchman's retreat for Christian leaders of all races. This multiracial conference was housed in one of the dormitories, and the participants ate their meals together in the college dining room. Long before the beginnings of racial integration, ministers and Christian laymen of several faiths were learning the meaning of brotherhood in these Mars Hill retreats.

In spite of his full-time schedule at the college, Moore found time to work in the community. He led the movement to improve county public schools; largely due to his efforts, the first public elementary school in the Mars Hill area was built in 1904. In 1925 he was influential in getting a public high school for the community. For two years (1903–5) Moore served as county superintendent of schools, and for a number of years he was a member of the county school board. To improve the general level of instruction in the schools, he set up teachers' institutes at the college during the summer. He worked to secure better roads for Mars Hill and the county, and he actively supported all efforts on behalf of good government.

In 1938, after forty-one years of service, Moore gave up his duties as president, but for a number of years he continued to teach almost a full load, to serve on college committees, and to keep up with more than six thousand alumni. He also remained active in the local Baptist church as senior deacon and teacher of a large class of young men. Finally declining health forced him to give up his work at the college. After several months of illness, he died and was buried in the Mars Hill Cemetery. Mars Hill College, with much of the character he gave it, is a monument to his life. His portrait hangs in the Memorial Room of the Robert Lee Moore Memorial Auditorium on the campus.

SEE: *Asheville Citizen*, 2 Oct. 1936, 28 May 1937, 19 May, 17 Dec. 1949; *Asheville Times*, 26 May 1938; *Biblical Recorder*, 27 May 1931, 31 Mar. 1943, 11 Jan. 1950; *Charity and Children*, 22 Dec. 1949; Clarence Dixon Creasman, *Robert Lee Moore* (1950); John Angus McLeod, *From These Stones: Mars Hill College, the First Hundred Years* (1955) and *From These Stones: Mars Hill College, 1856–1968* (1968); Mars Hill College, *The Hilltop*, 14 Dec. 1934, 28 May 1937, 14 Jan. 1950; *Mars Hill College Quarterly* 46 (August 1950); Presidents' Papers: Robert Lee Moore (Mars Hill College Archives, Mars Hill).

EVELYN UNDERWOOD

Moore, Roger *(August 1694–1751)*, colonial official, was born in the Goose Creek section of Berkeley County, S.C., one of ten children of the prominent planter James and Margaret Berringer Moore, the stepdaughter of Sir John Yeamans. One of his brothers, James, served as governor of South Carolina. As befitted his station in life, Roger married a daughter of William Rhett, a leader in South Carolina society.

In 1724 Roger Moore began taking a notable interest in development of the Lower Cape Fear region of North Carolina, joining with his brothers, Colonel Maurice and Nathaniel, to seek land grants in the area. By 1727 Roger had accumulated more than seven thousand acres and had built a fine plantation house called Kendall on the Cape Fear River; four years later he owned nearly twenty-five thousand acres. Moore was instrumental in the establishment of Brunswick town and was a staunch supporter of that community in its struggle with Newton (later Wilmington) for supremacy as a port of entry on the Cape Fear. As a member of the royal Council, he engaged in the fierce political intrigue that surrounded this matter in the late 1730s.

Moore held a number of provincial and local offices in the colony. He was assistant justice of the General Court in 1732, a justice of the peace for New Hanover County in 1734, a commissioner for the boundary with South Carolina in 1735, and a member of the royal Council from 1734 until his death. Because of his grand manner and his reputation as a generous host, Moore was often referred to as "King Roger." By 1748 he had built a one-story plantation house called Orton at a magnificent site overlooking the river near Brunswick town. He was buried on the grounds.

At his death in 1751 (his will was probated in May), Roger owned more than 250 slaves and nearly 60,000 acres of land. He was survived by his wife and five children.

SEE: J. Bryan Grimes, ed., *North Carolina Wills and Inventories* (1912); Lawrence Lee, *The Lower Cape Fear in Colonial Days* (1965); William S. Price, Jr., " 'Men of Good Estates': Wealth among North Carolina's Royal Councillors," *North Carolina Historical Review* 49 (1972); William L. Saunders, ed., *Colonial Records of North Carolina*, vols. 3–4 (1886).

WILLIAM S. PRICE, JR.

Moore, Roger *(19 July 1839–21 Apr. 1900)*, civic and church leader and Confederate officer, was born in Wilmington, the son of Roger and Ann Sophia Toomer Moore. He was a descendant of James Moore, colonial governor of South Carolina and of "King Roger" Moore, founder of Orton plantation. In 1871 he married Susan Eugenia Beery, the daughter of Captain Benjamin Beery of Wilmington. They were the parents of nine children, seven of whom survived infancy: Anne, Parker Quince, Henry Roger, Edwin Yeamans, Robert Jefferson, Louis Toomer, and Mary Ella.

In the spring of 1862 Moore entered military service as a member of Laurence's Partisan Rangers and subsequently was assigned to the Third North Carolina Cavalry. When Laurence's rangers were divided into two companies, Moore was promoted from the ranks to the captaincy and commanded the second company; subsequently, he was made commissary of the Third Cavalry. A year later he was promoted to major and in 1864 to lieutenant colonel, having previously taken command of the regiment following the capture of Colonel John A. Baker. While with the Third Cavalry, he participated in the battles of Kinston and New Bern and the cavalry engagements on the Blackawatts; he then saw action with General James Longstreet in the Suffolk area, resulting in approximately twenty-three encounters with the enemy.

After the surrender at Appomattox Moore returned to Wilmington, where he first engaged in the grocery trade and then went into the brokerage business, subsequently becoming the agent for Paterson, Dawning, and Company. Finally he opened a building supply firm called Roger Moore Sons Company.

His civic record included frequent service as alderman of Wilmington, chairman of the New Hanover County Board of Commissioners, president of the Wilmington Produce Exchange, member of the board of directors of the Seaman's Friends Society, and chairman of the Board of Hospital Managers and of the county auditing board. He was also director of the Associated Charities, chief of the volunteer fire department, and chairman of the board of trustees of the YMCA. As a member of Grace Street Methodist Church, he filled all positions open to laymen.

Moore befriended a young Chinese seaman, Charlie Soong, introduced him to the Methodist faith, and helped obtain his release from the U.S. ship on which he was serving. He then told his old friend from Civil War days, Julian S. Carr, of Soong's intense desire for an education. Carr made it possible for Soong to attend Trinity College in Durham and Vanderbilt University in Tennessee. After returning to China, Soong succeeded in business and lent his influence towards the spread of Christianity. One of his daughters became the wife of Chiang Kai-shek, while the other married Sun Yat-sen.

In the tragic Wilmington race riot of 1898, Moore was called on to be chargé d'affaires until the military could arrive. After forty-eight sleepless hours he was able to return home. No sooner had he arrived than a delegation called on him, requesting that he rush to the jail to prevent a lynching of some of the men held there. It was believed that Moore was the only Wilmingtonian who could control the mob, and this he did. He stood in front of the jail door for twelve hours, daring anyone to harm the outsiders (prisoners who were not from the area), whom he shipped out on the first northbound train the following day. He died a little over a year later at age sixty-two and was buried in Oakdale Cemetery, Wilmington.

SEE: Clement A. Evans, ed., *Confederate Military History*, vol. 4 (1899); Moore Family Bible (possession of Mrs. Zack Bacon, Jr., Raleigh); Louis T. Moore, *Stories Old and New of the Cape Fear Region* (1956); Newspaper clippings (possession of Mrs. William Sissom, Wilmington).

ANN MOORE BACON

Moore, Stephen *(30 Oct. 1734–29 Dec. 1799)*, merchant, army officer, and congressman, was born in New York City, the seventeenth child of Colonel John and Frances Lambert Moore. His grandfather, John Moore, left England in the 1680s to pursue a legal career in the king's service, settling first in Charles Town, S.C., where he became secretary of the colony. In 1687 he moved to Philadelphia and there filled a number of public offices, including those of attorney general of the province and collector of customs.

Colonel John Moore chose a mercantile career and moved to New York, where he amassed a fortune in real estate while following his father's lead in public service. He was a member of His Majesty's Council, commander of a New York regiment of militia, alderman of the city, and vestryman of Trinity Church, where he and many of his family were buried. Among the considerable lands in both Philadelphia and New York that he left at his death was a mansion in New York City at the corner of Moore and Front streets (not, however, built by Peter Stuyvesant, as some have said) and much adjacent land. He also left an estate on the Hudson River at West Point, devised to his youngest son, Stephen. This property consisted of a large house and over two thousand acres, known as Moore's Folly.

Nothing is known of Stephen Moore's childhood or education. Though family tradition says he took a degree at Oxford, the rolls of that institution do not include his name. As his brother Thomas attended Westminster School and his youngest sister, Ann, was said to have been educated in England, Stephen probably received an English education. In 1754 he was apprenticed to John Watts, contractor for army supplies and a New York merchant, training Moore would use throughout his life. After volunteering for the French and Indian War in 1756 and receiving a lieutenant's commission the following year, he was appointed provision contractor for the British army. When the war ended, he was rewarded with the post of deputy paymaster general in Canada.

To his service in Canada belongs the legend that he carried urgent dispatches from Governor-General Sir Frederick Haldimand in Montreal to Governor-General Jeffrey Amherst in New York. He is said to have accomplished the journey within ten days by traversing, on snowshoes and skates, the snow-covered ground and thinly iced waterways of the most direct route between Montreal and New York, then impassable for horse and rider.

Moore left military service to enter the lumber trade. Always attracted to merchandising, he, with his partner Hugh Finlay, then postmaster of Quebec, speculated unsuccessfully and went bankrupt. It is noteworthy that all of Stephen's brothers who lived to maturity were irresistibly drawn to mercantile careers and lost their fortunes in the end.

On Christmas Day, 1768, at Quebec, Moore married Griselda Phillips (18 Feb. 1748/9–15 Jan. 1820), the daughter of Captain John and Griselda Levi Phillips of Boston. Although he continued to live in Canada until 1770, his name in the town reports of neighboring Cornwall indicates that Moore's West Point estate was his official residence during the decade 1765–75.

The increasingly uncomfortable political climate for Loyalists in New York (Stephen was the only Revolutionary Moore), financial difficulties, and the realization that his capital and experience could be turned to greater profit in the developing lands of the South were possible reasons for his decision to move in 1775. Why he chose to settle first in Granville County, N.C., and then in neighboring Caswell County (after returning to New York to arrange his affairs for a permanent move) is unknown. But in January 1777 he bought a plantation on Flat River. Continuing to acquire more adjoining acreage, he named the estate Mount Tirzah; it was high land over the river and fertile, unlike his Hudson River prop-

erty. Both his brother Charles and Griselda's brother Thomas chose to make the move with Stephen and his family.

Political upheaval reached him even on the southern frontier. In 1779 he was appointed a lieutenant colonel in the militia. After raising and equipping a regiment, he had no time to train it adequately before joining General Horatio Gates in the Battle of Camden, S.C., in 1780. He was captured at Camden and sent to the prison ship *Forbay* in Charles Town harbor. Exchanged a year later, he returned to Mount Tirzah in June 1781. Because of his absence while in military service, his election in 1780 to the General Assembly from Caswell County can have been only nominal. He was, however, nominated in both 1786 and 1787 as a representative to Congress. Finally elected, he served one term in the Third Congress in 1793.

Before that he had served as commissioner for specific taxes (1781), superintendent commissioner of Hillsborough District (1782), and deputy quartermaster general of the army (1783–92). Though only a lieutenant colonel in the regular army, he must have been promoted to brigadier general in the militia, for he issued muster notices and signed deeds under that rank, and his tombstone, though showing inaccurate dates, was probably correctly inscribed "General Stephen Moore."

Despite his fertile plantation, a mercantile business (he operated a general store that served a large area), and a mill on Flat River, Moore's financial condition was not secure until 1790. His father's extensive estate had been lost in the Revolution, the real estate in New York City had been burned to the ground in 1776, and his own West Point estate had suffered in the hands of both Tories and Americans—the house had been occupied repeatedly (the last time by Americans when it served temporarily as George Washington's headquarters) and the land despoiled. In 1790 Moore successfully petitioned the government to buy West Point, long recognized as important to the security of New York, and received $11,085 for it. Thereafter he enjoyed moderate prosperity until his death, which occurred, according to family tradition, while he was visiting his friend Richard Bennehan at Stagville.

A lifelong Episcopalian, Stephen Moore had participated in efforts to establish a church in his neighborhood and had been named vestryman and warden in the planning stages; because of insufficient support, the church was never built. He was consequently buried in the Moore family graveyard near his house, built in 1778 and still standing. He left considerable acreage, the mill, the store, and thirteen slaves to his widow and eight surviving children.

The Moores had ten children: John Robert (b. 12 Nov. 1769 in Quebec; m. Sarah Bailey), Phillips (b. 12 July 1771 in New York; m. first Rebecca Moore and second Elizabeth Dudley, the daughter of Thomas Dudley), Frances (b. 5 Nov. 1773 at West Point; m. Jesse Dickins), Ann (b. 12 Jan. 1777 in Granville County; unmarried), Mary (b. 21 Sept. 1778 at Mount Tirzah, where all the younger children were born; m. Richard Stanford), Marcus (b. 27 Nov. 1780; died in childhood), Portius (b. 15 Oct. 1782; m. first Frances Webb and second Lucy Pulliam), Cadmus (b. 31 June 1787; died in childhood), Samuel (b. 15 June 1789; m. Elizabeth A. Stanford), and Sidney (b. 15 Dec. 1794; m. Polly P. Reed).

Portraits of Stephen Moore and his parents came into the possession of Dr. Alexander Stanford, Rich Square, Eden, N.C.

SEE: John L. Cheney, Jr., ed., *North Carolina Government, 1585–1979* (1981); Walter Clark, ed., *State Records of North Carolina*, vols. 17–20 (1899–1902); *Collections of the New-York Historical Society*, vol. 24 (1892); L. Effingham DeForest and Anne Laurence DeForest, *William Henry Moore and His Ancestry* (1934); Edward Vernon Howell Papers, Stephen Moore Papers, Stephen Moore Family Bible, and Webb-Moore Papers (Southern Historical Collection, University of North Carolina, Chapel Hill); Virginia Reavis Lyle, *Person Patchwork* (1971); Agnes Miller, *Owner of West Point* (1952); John Moore, "Memoirs of an American Official in Service of the King," *Journal of American History* 4 (1910); Stephen Moore Estate Papers and Person County Estates Papers (North Carolina State Archives, Raleigh); *North Carolina Journal*, 16 Jan. 1793, 9 Feb. 1795, 1 Aug., 24, 31 Oct. 1796; John Alton Price, *A Biographical Sketch on the Life of Col. Stephen Moore of New York City and Mount Tirzah, North Carolina* (1958); Stuart T. Wright, *Historical Sketch of Person County* (1974).

JEAN BRADLEY ANDERSON

Moore, Thomas Longworth (*22 Feb. 1842–17 May 1926*), Confederate diplomat, was born at Mulberry Grove plantation in Hertford County, the son of Dr. Godwin Cotton and Julia M. Wheeler Moore. His father, a prominent planter and physician, was active in politics and the affairs of the Baptist church. Thomas was a younger brother of historian John Wheeler Moore.

After being educated by private tutors on the family estate, Moore was appointed to the U.S. Naval Academy at Annapolis on 30 Sept. 1857. With the outbreak of the Civil War, however, he resigned from the academy as an acting midshipman on 19 Apr. 1861.

Moore returned to Hertford County for a short time and helped to train troops in Murfreesboro. Entering the Confederate navy as an acting midshipman on 12 June, he served first on the CSRS *United States* and then aboard the privateer schooner *Dixie*. In 1862 he became an acting master and was transferred to the CSS *Florida*. He was later promoted to second lieutenant and then to first lieutenant.

In 1863 Moore was ordered abroad and sailed from Charleston to join the Confederate envoy in Paris as naval attaché. The mission was unsuccessful in its attempts to gain diplomatic recognition of the Confederacy by the French. He remained in Europe and at the end of the war was attached to the staff of Commander James D. Bullock in London. On 27 Aug. 1865, in Baden-Baden, Germany, Moore married Rose Standish Ludlam. Her father, Henry Ludlam, was a wealthy Southern sympathizer who had elected to leave his home in Baltimore and live in Europe during the war.

Returning to the United States, Moore settled in Richmond, Va., where he was employed at the post office. Following the death of his wife, he married Kate Ward on 14 Apr. 1873 at Newport, Ky. In 1877 he was farming at Warrenton, Va., but later moved back to Richmond. Unfortunately, his marriage ended in a scandalous divorce case in which he accused his wife of adultery.

Afterwards Moore left Virginia and became a civil engineer for the city of New York, where he supervised municipal projects for over twenty-five years. His most important achievements were the Croton Dam and Reservoir and the Moore Aqueduct. Retiring because of his advancing age, Moore moved to Portsmouth, Va., to live with his niece. He died there and was buried in neighboring Norfolk.

By his marriage to Kate Ward, he was the father of one son, Godwin Ward, who committed suicide while still in his teens.

SEE: *Register of Officers in the Confederate States Navy, 1861–1865* (1931); Southall and Bowen Papers (Southern Historical Collection, University of North Carolina, Chapel Hill); *The War of the Rebellion: A Compilation of the Official Records of the Union and Confederate Armies*, ser. 2, vol. 7 (1899).

JAMES ELLIOTT MOORE

Moore, Thomas Overton (*10 Apr. 1804–25 June 1876*), cotton and sugar planter and governor of Louisiana, was born in Sampson County, the first of ten children of James and Emma Jane Overton Moore. He was a descendant of Roger Moore of Charles Town, S.C. After attending local schools he left North Carolina in the early 1820s to live with his grandfather, General Thomas Overton, near Nashville, Tenn., and in 1824 he moved to Rapides Parish in central Louisiana to live with an uncle. There he learned large-scale planting and became an overseer of the plantation. Moore began buying land, and following his marriage to Bethiah Jane Leonard in November 1830, he became a planter, eventually acquiring over two thousand acres, including a plantation given to his wife by her parents. The couple's first two children died in infancy, the third lived to be seven, and the fourth to be five; the fifth, Emma Jane, survived and left descendants.

In 1842 Moore entered local politics, and in 1848 he became a state senator. In the legislature he supported a bill to establish a "seminary" that evolved into Louisiana State University. In 1852 he was a delegate to the state Democratic convention. Returning to the legislature, he became an advocate of several popular causes including support for the seminary. In 1859 Moore was nominated for governor and reluctantly consented to become a candidate. He did not campaign for the post and, in fact, left the state to visit relatives in North Carolina and Tennessee and to make a trip to Washington, D.C., and Baltimore. He was overwhelmingly elected, and it was to him as governor-elect that U.S. Army Major William T. Sherman reported in November 1859, when he arrived to become the seminary's first superintendent.

Inaugurated on 23 Jan. 1860, Moore soon faced a crisis as the Civil War approached. He wanted to hold his state in the Union "if any honorable way" could be found, but the course of events led the Louisiana Secession Convention to vote on 25 Jan. 1861 to secede. The governor moved from Baton Rouge to New Orleans, where he could more effectively serve the state, but with the advance of Federal forces, state records and archives were removed from Baton Rouge to Opelousas. At a session of the legislature there, Shreveport was named the state capital. During the war Louisiana was invaded and parts of the state soon fell into enemy hands. Governor Moore's administration was concerned over the fact that Confederate officials failed to help protect the state.

When his term of office ended in January 1864, Moore returned to his home, but Federal officials put a price on his head and he fled to a plantation he owned in Houston County, Tex. There he met other refugee officials from Louisiana, Arkansas, and Missouri, some of whom joined Moore in going to Mexico City. From Mexico Moore went to Cuba, where in November 1865 he was granted a parole by President Andrew Johnson. Returning to his Louisiana plantation, he discovered that his home had been destroyed by the Federal army and that his plantation had fallen into ruin. He and his wife lived in an overseer's house, and there in January 1867 he received word that President Johnson had granted him a full pardon.

Although his health was failing, he was a delegate to the state Democratic convention in Baton Rouge in 1874. He became seriously ill early in 1876 and died in the spring. An Episcopalian, he was buried in Mount Olivette Church cemetery, Pineville, La.

SEE: Jefferson Davis Bragg, *Louisiana in the Confederacy* (1941); Claude Hunter Moore, *Thomas Overton Moore: A Confederate Governor* (1960); Van D. Odom, "The Political Career of Thomas Overton Moore: Secession Governor of Louisiana" (master's thesis, Louisiana State University, 1942); Ida Annie Torrans, "A Rhetorical Analysis of Two Speeches by Thomas Overton Moore" (master's thesis, Louisiana State University, 1959); G. P. Whittington, "Thomas O. Moore: Governor of Louisiana, 1860–64," *Louisiana Historical Quarterly* 13 (January 1930).

EZRA ADAMS

Moore, Walter William *(14 June 1857–14 June 1926),* Presbyterian clergyman and educator, a native of Charlotte, was of Scotch-Irish ancestry. His father, Isaac Hudson Moore, died when he was less than six years old; his mother, Martha Parks Moore, lived until 1925. After attending school in Charlotte, Walter enrolled in the Finley High School at Lenoir. He received an A.B. degree from Davidson College in 1878 and was graduated from Union Theological Seminary, then at Hampden-Sydney, Va., three years later.

On 30 Aug. 1881 Mecklenburg Presbytery ordained him and designated him as stated supply of the Swannanoa and Oak Forest Presbyterian churches. From this field he went to the pastorate of the Presbyterian church at Millersburg, Ky., where he preached for a time in 1882–83. In the latter year he returned to Union Seminary as a teacher of Hebrew. He was assistant instructor (1883–84), adjunct professor (1884–86), and associate professor (1886–89) before becoming a full professor in 1889. Moore became the first president of the seminary in 1904 and assumed the duties of lecturer in Hebrew in 1915. In the spring of 1926 he resigned the presidency on account of ill health.

Moore played a large role in moving Union Seminary from Hampden-Sydney to Richmond, Va., in 1898. He was influential in expanding the institution's physical plant and in enriching its curriculum. Following overtures from him, James Sprunt of Wilmington arranged for the establishment of the Sprunt Lectureship in 1911. Under the guidance of President Moore, the seminary inaugurated a graduate department in 1915.

Active in the affairs of the Presbyterian Church of the United States, Moore was widely recognized as its leader during the first quarter of the twentieth century and served as moderator of the General Assembly in 1908. He was a special lecturer at McCormick Theological Seminary in 1895, delivered the Stone Lectures at Princeton Seminary in 1897, and was Reinicke lecturer at the Episcopal Theological Seminary of Virginia in 1898. In 1919 he was Sprunt lecturer at Union Seminary in Virginia, and in 1921 he delivered the Otts Lectures at Davidson College. Moore was a prime mover in the founding of the General Assembly's Training School for Lay Workers, which opened in Richmond in 1914.

He edited *The General Catalogue of Union Theological Seminary* in 1907 and again in 1924. He was the author of *A Year in Europe* (1904), *The Indispensable Book* (1910), and *Appreciations and Historical Addresses* (1914). Moore received honorary degrees from Central University (D.D., 1885), Davidson College (LL.D., 1892), and Austin College (LL.D., 1924).

In 1886 he married Loula S. Fries of Winston-Salem,

and they had four children: Lisette Fries (Mrs. Andrew R. Bird), Walter Vogler, Francis Hudson, and Mary Louise. Moore died in Richmond and was buried in Salem Cemetery, Winston-Salem. His portrait is at Union Theological Seminary in Richmond.

SEE: *Christian Observer,* 30 June 1926; J. Gray McAllister, *The Life and Letters of Walter W. Moore* (1939); Walter W. Moore Papers (Union Theological Seminary Library, Richmond, Va.); *Union Seminary Review* 38 (October 1926).

THOMAS H. SPENCE, JR.

Moore, William Armistead *(20 July 1831–20 Dec. 1884),* lawyer, judge, and Confederate officer, was the oldest of seven children of Susan Jordan Armistead and Augustus Moore of Edenton; he had four brothers and two sisters. His father, a graduate of The University of North Carolina, was also a lawyer; he was appointed a judge of the superior court in 1848 but resigned the same year. Although a native of North Carolina, William A. Moore is identified as a carpetbagger in several histories of Reconstruction.

After graduating from Edenton Academy, he attended The University of North Carolina from 1848 to 1851. Before he could graduate his father died suddenly, and he returned home to take charge of the estate. Soon afterwards he began to study law. When Moore's eyesight deteriorated, his mother read law books to him. He ranked first in the group examined for admission to the bar by Judge Richmond M. Pearson in 1852.

Moore practiced law until 1861, when he began his short military career. He was colonel and commander of the Fifth Regiment of North Carolina militia, which consisted of four companies of about 200 men. In November 1861 his regiment was ordered to the coast to participate in the defense of Roanoke Island, but it saw no action in February 1862, when Union forces attacked and seized the island. General Henry Wise escaped with 150 men and Moore's militia, which had no arms. His troops helped to block the entrance to the Dismal Swamp Canal, the back door to Norfolk, before Wise sent them home. Encamped at Centre Hill in Chowan County after Roanoke Island had fallen, Moore intercepted a Confederate major and countermanded his orders to burn Edenton because of its Union sentiment. One source indicates that Moore served on General Daniel H. Hill's staff during the Seven Days' Battle near Richmond, that he helped to care for the wounded, and that rheumatism forced him to retire from active service, but no corroborating evidence has been found.

Initially a Democrat, Moore later joined the Republican party. After attending the Democratic National Convention in Baltimore in 1860, his political career progressed slowly. Unpardoned in 1865, he could not vote and took no part in politics. In 1868 the Conservative party placed his name on the executive committee for the First District. Believing the state constitution of 1868 to be a good one, Moore declined the nomination and requested that his name be stricken. Nevertheless, the Conservatives kept his name on the committee and published it across the state, an action Moore considered "an outrage." He firmly believed that the war had settled the issue of states' rights and that his first allegiance was to the United States. Thereafter he affiliated with the Republican party.

During Reconstruction Moore held various public offices. In 1869 he was elected to complete an unfinished term in the North Carolina House of Representatives, then won a seat for a full term (1869–70) and served as speaker for the last two weeks. In April 1871 the governor appointed him a judge of the superior court to complete an unfinished eight-year term. In August 1874 a Republican opponent won this judgeship in a special election called by the legislature, but Moore retained his seat when the state supreme court declared the election unconstitutional.

When the Democratic legislature of 1870–71 assigned a committee to investigate Republican fraud relating to state bonds, Moore came under suspicion. He testified that while he was in New York City in 1869, George W. Swepson had encouraged Tar Heels of both parties to buy North Carolina's special tax bonds on the open market so that their price would rise. Moore had no funds for margin, so Swepson lent him North Carolina railroad bonds for that purpose. When Jay Gould's attempts to corner the gold market led to the panic in September, Moore lost the bonds because his margin was inadequate. No charges were brought against him for this speculation.

Moore died suddenly from paralysis and was buried in St. Paul's churchyard in Edenton. He never married.

SEE: Richard Dillard, *The Civil War in Chowan County* (1916) and *Historical Reminiscences: Centre Hill* (1918); J. G. de Roulhac Hamilton, *Reconstruction in North Carolina* (1914); "Hargrove v. Hilliard," *North Carolina Reports* 72 (1875); William A. Moore, *Law and Order versus Ku Klux Violence* (1870); North Carolina Census of 1850, Town of Edenton, Chowan County (North Carolina State Archives, Raleigh); Thomas C. Parramore, *Cradle of the Colony: The History of Chowan County and Edenton, North Carolina* (1967); Bettie Freshwater Pool, *Literature in the Albemarle* (1915 [portrait]); Raleigh *Daily Standard*, 1870; Raleigh *News and Observer*, 28 Dec. 1884; *Report of the Commission to Investigate Charges of Fraud and Corruption* (1872); John B. Respers, *To the People of the Second Judicial District* (1874); *The War of the Rebellion: A Compilation of the Official Records of the Union and Confederate Armies*, ser. 1, vol. 9 (1899); John H. Wheeler, ed., *Reminiscences and Memoirs of North Carolina and Eminent North Carolinians* (1884).

JOHN L. BELL, JR.

Moore, William John *(4 Apr. 1837–post-1901)*, Methodist clergyman and supporter of Livingstone College, was born at South Creek, Beaufort County, the son of free black parents. His father, Alfred, purchased twenty-five acres at a place in the county called Keysville. Following his mother's death the previous year, the family moved to Washington, N.C., about 1847.

Unhappy with a stepmother, young Moore shipped on a schooner and from 1848 to 1862 worked as a sailor. While ashore for three winters, he attended night school. He took his sister, Mary Susan, to New York in 1854, but she died of smallpox two years later. In 1855 he is reported to have "embraced" religion. While sailing between New York and Washington, Moore was married in the latter town in 1858 and thereafter worked out of New York until 1862. In that year he sailed from New York for the West Indies and on the return voyage was captured near Portsmouth Island, N.C. Taken to his old home in Beaufort County, he was obliged to work as a cook for the Tar River Navigation Company. After the fall of New Bern to Union forces, work ceased on the Tar River and Moore and his father engaged in shad net fishing. Taken aboard U.S. gunboats, the younger Moore served for a year as a steward on a steamer.

Later in Washington, he said, he "got religion." After a Union chaplain in the town organized the Methodist Episcopal Church, North, Moore was made secretary. When Washington was evacuated, he and other blacks were taken to New Bern and settled at a place soon known as James City. Their church was reorganized, became affiliated with the A.M.E. Zion church, and Moore, having been licensed in August 1863, became its preacher. Ordained a deacon in 1864, he became an elder in 1865 and was appointed to serve a church in Fayetteville. In turn, he was assigned to the town of Beaufort and then for a period to Granville County. Afterwards he served in Salisbury, Statesville, Charlotte, Wilmington, and New Bern; in time he became a presiding elder.

Moore was cited for his diligence in organizing sixty-eight congregations, building eleven churches, and improving many others. He licensed fifty-four local preachers, lent financial support to establish the *Star of Zion*, and was among the first to make a contribution towards the creation of the institution that is now Livingstone College in Salisbury, incorporated in 1879 and opened the following year. He was a member of its first board of trustees and received an honorary doctor of divinity degree in 1892. Moore was still living as late as 20 June 1901, but no record has been found of his death.

SEE: James W. Hood, *One Hundred Years of the African Methodist Episcopal Church* (1895); William John Moore, *My Silver Anniversary* (1899); William J. Walls, *The African Methodist Episcopal Zion Church: Reality of the Black Church* (1974).

WILLIAM S. POWELL

Mordecai [read: MOR-de-kee]**, Alfred** *(3 Jan. 1804–23 Oct. 1887)*, U.S. Army major, engineer, and teacher, was born in Warrenton, the son of Jacob and Rebecca Myers Mordecai. He was the ninth of thirteen children who included Moses, a member of the North Carolina bar; Samuel, a merchant in Richmond and author of a history of that city; Solomon, a physician in Mobile, Ala.; and George Washington, of Raleigh, a lawyer, railroad president, and president of the Bank of North Carolina.

Jacob Mordecai owned and operated the Warrenton Female Seminary, and Alfred received his early education from members of the teaching staff, chiefly those of his own family. He was well prepared when he received his warrant to the U.S. Military Academy on 24 June 1819. In his third year he was appointed acting assistant professor of mathematics, a post that he held until 1 July 1823, when he was graduated first in his class and commissioned second lieutenant in the U.S. Army Corps of Engineers. He remained at the academy as assistant professor of natural and experimental philosophy in 1823–24 and as principal assistant professor of engineering in 1824–25.

On 12 July 1825 Mordecai left West Point to become assistant engineer in the construction of Forts Monroe and Calhoun, which were built for the defense of Hampton Roads, Va. In 1828 he was transferred to Washington, D.C., as assistant to the chief engineer of the U.S. Army. Promoted to the rank of captain of ordnance in 1833, he was placed in command at the Washington Arsenal as assistant ordnance officer. In 1833 the secretary of war, General Lewis Cass, instructed him to prepare a bill, requested by the House of Representatives, reducing into one act all of the acts of Congress relating to the army. In producing the draft of this bill, Mordecai made an abstract of all the laws then in force. This was printed under the title, *A Digest of the Laws Re-*

lating to the Military Establishment of the United States (1833), and became a useful army reference.

Mordecai was on leave in Europe in 1833–34. On his return he commanded the Frankford, Pa., arsenal until 1838, when he was appointed assistant to the chief of ordnance in Washington. In 1839 he became a member of the Ordnance Board, which met annually and on which he sat for the remainder of his military career. For a nine-month period in 1840, he was a member of a commission sent by this board to visit the arsenals and cannon foundries of Europe in order to report on the latest artillery improvements there. After settling in at the Ordnance Office, Mordecai began preparing a much-needed ordnance manual for the use of ordnance officers and the army in general. Despite the interruption of his official trip to Europe, *The Ordnance Manual for the Use of Officers of the United States Army* was published in 1841. He prepared a second edition in 1850.

In 1842 he was made assistant inspector of arsenals and was engaged in constructing and experimenting with ballistic pendulums and gunpowder. In 1844 he was placed in command of the Washington Arsenal, where he continued this work, the results of which were published in 1845 under the title *Report of Experiments on Gunpowder*. This report, which was subsequently translated into French and German, is the document by which Mordecai is best known in this country and in Europe. He remained in command at the arsenal during the Mexican War and in recognition of the value of his work—both illustrated and tested in the Mexican battles—was brevetted major on 30 May 1848 "for meritorious conduct particularly in the performance of his duties in the prosecution of the war with Mexico." Earlier, in 1843, Mordecai had been appointed to the West Point Board of Visitors.

In 1853 Mordecai was selected by Secretary of War Jefferson Davis for a secret mission of international diplomacy. He traveled with a small entourage into Mexico to investigate the Gardiner claims, paid out under protest by the Mexican government, as set forth in the peace treaty following the Mexican War. This claim was proven fraudulent and $500,000 was refunded to Mexico. In 1855–57 he was sent, along with Captain George B. McClellan, as a member of a military commission to act as an observer during the Crimean War. His observations were published by order of Congress in Senate Executive Document No. 60 (1860).

In 1857 he was put in command of the Watervleit Arsenal near Troy, N.Y., and in 1860 he was also a member of the board to revise the course of instruction at West Point. With the advent of the Civil War, Mordecai resigned his commission in May 1861 and retired to private life in Philadelphia, unwilling "to forge arms to be used against his aged mother, brothers and sisters in the south." Prior to his resignation he had requested some other position but was refused.

His daughters were teachers in Philadelphia, where he taught mathematics until the war ended. In 1865 he became assistant engineer for the Mexico and Pacific Railroad in the construction of trunk lines from Vera Cruz through Mexico City to the Pacific. When the railway operations were suspended in 1866, he returned to the United States. From 1867 until his death, Mordecai was secretary and treasurer of the Pennsylvania Canal Company, which comprised the canal and coal companies controlled by the Pennsylvania Railroad. A portrait of him now hangs in the room he occupied at that company.

On 1 June 1836 he married Sara Hays of Philadelphia, and they were the parents of eight children: Laura,

Rosa, Alfred, Frank, Miriam, Emma, Augustus, and Gratz. Young Alfred, like his father, was a graduate of West Point. Unlike his father, however, he fought for the Union forces in the Civil War and retired from the army in 1904 as a brigadier general.

Mordecai died in Philadelphia. He had been one of the first Americans of the Jewish faith to choose the army as a career.

SEE: John H. B. Latrobe, *Alfred Mordecai* (pamphlet, n.d.); James A. Padgett, ed., "The Life of Alfred Mordecai as Related by Himself," *North Carolina Historical Review* 22 (January 1945); Harry Simonhoff, *Jewish Notables in America* (1956); Roger J. Spiller, ed., *Dictionary of American Military Biography*, vol. 3 (1984).

MATTHEW STEVEN KARRES

Mordecai, [Miss] Ellen *(10 Nov. 1790–6 Oct. 1884),* teacher and author, was born in Richmond, Va., the fourth child and second daughter of Jacob (1762–1838) and Judith Myers Mordecai (1762–96). During her infancy the family moved to Petersburg, Va., and in 1792 to Warrenton, N.C., where her father was a merchant. After the death of her mother less than three years later, Ellen and her sister Rachel were sent to Richmond to live with their maternal grandmother, the widow of noted New York silversmith Myer Myers. There they received their early education from their aunts, Judah Myers and Richea Myers (later Mrs. Joseph Marx). In 1798 their father married his late wife's half sister, Rebecca Myers (1776–1863).

In 1809, when Ellen was nineteen, she and Rachel and their brother Solomon assisted their father in opening his successful and popular Mordecai Female Seminary in Warrenton. In addition to teaching, Ellen also had the duty of supervising—day and night—the young boarding students who lived in their home. As described in her memoirs, this regimen included keeping the "Neat List . . . inspecting the rosy digits of the little urchins." This rigorous schedule eventually impaired her health, and she spent the fall and winter of 1817–18 under the care of physicians in Richmond and Petersburg, Va., and Wilmington, N.C. During her absence, Rachel wrote of her: "she is a sort of central point to every individual of the family, and we seem at a loss when she is absent for something to which all may tend with the certainty of finding it fixed and furnished with ample resources for complying with every demand made upon it."

When, in 1818, her father closed the Warrenton school and retired to Richmond, Ellen moved there with the family and continued to instruct her young half sisters. Later she taught, in their own homes, her nieces and nephews, including the children of her brother, attorney Moses Mordecai of Raleigh. She became the proverbial welcome and useful "visiting aunt," spending weeks or months at a time in relatives' homes when needed. The possibility of her teaching at St. Mary's in Raleigh was discussed when the school opened in 1842, but the relationship did not materialize. During the 1840s and early 1850s she lived in New York City as governess to the children, successively, of a Dr. Francis, Rubson Maury, Denning Duer, and others.

In the late 1850s Ellen spent several winters in the Mobile, Ala., home of her favorite brother, Dr. Solomon Mordecai (1792–1869). During these visits she was instrumental in convincing him to embrace Christianity, as she herself had done earlier. He was baptized in a Methodist church in Mobile; she had become a communicant of the Episcopal church in Petersburg in 1838. Out of her experience and the spiritual conflict in deciding to abandon her family's Jewish faith, she wrote *Past Days* (1841) and *The History of a Heart* (1845). A reference in an 1848 letter indicates that one of these volumes was published abroad in a foreign language. Some of her shorter pieces were printed in the *New York Review,* and at least one article about Albert Nyanza appeared in the periodical, *The Land We Love* (1868). A third book manuscript, written between 1845 and 1847, was rejected by several New York and Philadelphia publishing houses, including Harper Brothers, John S. Taylor, and Appleton. For this memoir, entitled "Fading Scenes Recalled; or, The By Gone Days of Hastings," she used the pseudonym Esther Whitlock, the maiden name of her paternal grandmother, Mrs. Moses Mordecai (ca. 1745–1804). The work was, in her words, "founded altogether on real life" recollections of the family's years in Warrenton (Hastings), although the names of characters were largely fictitious.

Ellen's sister Rachel, from 1815 until her death in 1838, corresponded regularly with the Irish novelist Maria Edgeworth. Afterwards, Ellen continued the association, retaining copies of the letters of all three women in her voluminous personal journals and in her correspondence portfolios. Also extant are hundreds of Mordecai family letters, many of them Ellen's, intended to be read aloud and circulated among various relatives. Exceptions to that practice were the "Christian letters," so called by their writers, who instructed recipients to keep their contents private so as not to offend other family members who remained in the orthodox Jewish faith.

Ellen never married, having yielded in 1823 to family pressures to refuse the proposal of John D. Plunkett, a Roman Catholic and the son of her sister Caroline's husband by an earlier marriage. In regard to his sisters' having grown up in the only Jewish family in their town, her brother George later wrote: "There is no one thing I have felt more sensibly than the peculiarly disagreeable and unfortunate situation of our sisters in this respect. They are either obliged to lead a life of seclusion and celibacy, marry a man whom they cannot admire or esteem (for few there are of that class at least of our acquaintance who are at all estimable) or they must incur the certain and lasting displeasure of their parents by marrying out of the pale of their religion. . . . It does seem very unreasonable in them to require their daughters to do what no one can do—control their affections and direct them in a particular channel."

Ellen died at Buck Roe Farm near Hampton, Va., a seaside resort, within a month of her ninety-fifth birthday. Her remains were interred in the Mordecai family section of Oakwood Cemetery, Raleigh.

SEE: Little-Mordecai Papers and Pattie Mordecai Collection (North Carolina State Archives, Raleigh); Edgar E. MacDonald, *The Education of the Heart: The Correspondence of Rachel Mordecai Lazarus and Maria Edgeworth* (1977); Mordecai Family Papers and George W. Mordecai Papers (Southern Historical Collection, University of North Carolina, Chapel Hill); Mordecai Family Register (copy made by Margaret Mordecai Blomquist, Durham); Jacob Mordecai Papers (Manuscript Department, Duke University Library, Durham); Raleigh *News and Observer,* 7 Oct. 1884; Esther Whitlock [Ellen Mordecai], "Fading Scenes Recalled; or, The By Gone Days of Hastings" (manuscript, Southern Historical Collection, University of North Carolina, Chapel Hill).

ELIZABETH DAVIS REID MURRAY

Mordecai, [Mrs.] Ellen Mordecai (*12 Apr. 1820–26 Feb. 1916*), author, was born in Mordecai House, Raleigh, the daughter of Moses (1785–1824) and his first wife, Margaret (Peggy) Lane Mordecai (ca. 1786–1821). She was named for her father's sister, author and teacher Ellen Mordecai (1790–1884). When Ellen was less than two years old her mother died, and she was raised by three aunts who lived in the home, one of whom, Anne Willis (Nancy) Lane, her father married in 1824. In the same year, her father died; his half brother, George Washington Mordecai (1801–71), became the guardian of Ellen, her brothers Henry and Jacob, and her half sister Margaret.

Her early education was begun in the Richmond home of her paternal grandfather, Jacob Mordecai (1762–1838), by her aunts Ellen and Rachel, who from 1809 to 1818 had assisted Jacob in conducting the popular Mordecai Female Seminary in Warrenton. Next she spent several years in the Warrenton school, reopened by her aunt, Caroline Mordecai (Mrs. Achille) Plunkett. For one year she was tutored at home by a governess "from the North," as she described her, a Miss Quincy. In her teens she attended Miss Hawkins's seminary in Philadelphia. She became, as a later writer said, "a thorough French scholar, possessing a knowledge of many of the master-pieces in that language," and "her thorough acquaintance with the polite literature of England and America was a source of wonderment and admiration to all who knew her."

After 1840, when her brother Henry became the owner of Mordecai House, Ellen lived with their stepmother in a home (since demolished) called Will's Forest in an area off Glenwood Avenue now marked by Devereux and Will's Forest streets.

On 4 Feb. 1850 she married Samuel Fox Mordecai (b. 19 Dec. 1828), the son of her uncle, Dr. Solomon (1792–1869), and Caroline Waller Mordecai (b. 1805) of Mobile, Ala., where they lived for a time. Their daughter, Margaret Lane, was born there on 25 Nov. 1850.

The family had a farm at Scotland Neck on the Roanoke River, where they spent the summer of 1852. On 22 August Samuel died of what was variously diagnosed as pneumonia or consumption. The widow and daughter went to live with the sisters of Ellen's father in Richmond, Va. Four months later her second child, Samuel Fox II, was born on 12 Dec. 1852. Her own former guardian and uncle, George W. Mordecai, became guardian of the two children.

About 1854 Ellen and the children returned to Raleigh, where for twenty years they lived at the northeastern corner of Wilmington and North streets in the house later owned by Episcopal Bishop Theodore B. Lyman. In the late 1860s and early 1870s she taught school. About 1874 construction was completed on the new house she built at the corner of Person and North Boundary streets. Later owners moved the house about 1934 to 318 North Boundary Street, where it subsequently housed several apartments, was used as an antique shop, and in the 1970s became a private home again. It is listed in the *Historic Oakwood Walking Tour* guide as the Ellen Mordecai House.

Known for her personal charities, Mrs. Mordecai helped to support several indigent individuals by having regular orders of groceries delivered to them. A *News and Observer* obituary noted that "the former slaves owned by her family found her a kind and sympathetic helper in time of need." Her granddaughter wrote that "her original wit and humor, her kindness, her benevolence, her charm, made her beloved by all—high and low, young and old."

Samuel Fox Mordecai II attended private schools and the University of Virginia; he received a law degree from Trinity College, Durham, where he was dean of the School of Law from 1904 until his death on 29 Dec. 1927. He married in 1875 Elizabeth (Bettie) Grimes (1853–1946), the daughter of Confederate General Bryan Grimes of Grimesland, and they had three daughters and six sons. His sister Margaret married Calhoun Tyler Morel (1845–98), a Georgia railroad official, and had four daughters and two sons. She died in Savannah, Ga., on 11 Sept. 1927.

In the last years of her life, "Granny" Ellen moved from Raleigh to Durham to live with her son and his family on the Trinity College campus. There, at age eighty-six, having lost her eyesight, she dictated to her granddaughter Anne Valleau Morel (1875–1961) her reminiscences, particularly of her childhood at Mordecai House. These, together with a letter to a great-grandson, Mrs. Morel published as *Gleanings From Long Ago* (1932). In 1974 the Raleigh Historic Properties Commission, Inc., and the Mordecai Square Historical Society, Inc., reprinted the volume with an introduction and index for the use of students interested in its wealth of material on nineteenth-century life.

Mrs. Mordecai died in her ninety-sixth year at her son's home. Her funeral was conducted at Christ Church, Raleigh, where she had been a communicant since age nine. She was buried in the Mordecai family section of Oakwood Cemetery, Raleigh. At her death Robert L. Gray, editor of the *Raleigh Times*, described her as "a woman whom all the city loved for the gentleness and sympathy of a life that at one time or another touched that of almost every person in it" and as one "who never gave up her books [and] who wrote with the sprightliness of a girl." The *News and Observer* added that "age never dimmed her intellect, or marred the delight which she always felt in the society of . . . relatives and friends."

SEE: Levi Branson, *Branson's North Carolina Business Directory* (1867–68, 1869, 1872); Christ Church (Raleigh) Parish Register; Mordecai Family Papers and George W. Mordecai Papers (Southern Historical Collection, University of North Carolina, Chapel Hill); Mordecai Family Register (copy made by Margaret Mordecai Blomquist, Durham); Jacob Mordecai Papers (Manuscript Department, Duke University Library, Durham); Pattie Mordecai Collection and Little-Mordecai Papers (North Carolina State Archives, Raleigh); Raleigh *News and Observer*, 28 Feb. 1916 (portrait); *Raleigh Times*, 28 Feb. 1916; Wake County Tax Lists (North Carolina State Archives, Raleigh).

ELIZABETH DAVIS REID MURRAY

Mordecai, George Washington (27 Apr. 1801–19 Feb. 1871), attorney, planter, financier, entrepreneur, and railroad and banking executive, was born in Warrenton. His father, Jacob Mordecai (1762–1838), had come to North Carolina as a merchant by way of Philadelphia, New York, and several Virginia locations. His mother, Rebecca Myers Mordecai (1776–1863), was Jacob's second wife and a half sister of his first wife, Judith Myers Mordecai (1762–96). Children of the first marriage included Raleigh attorney Moses; Samuel, merchant of Petersburg and Richmond, Va., and author of *Richmond in By-Gone Days*; Solomon, physician of Mobile, Ala.; Rachel (Mrs. Aaron Lazarus); Ellen, author; and Caroline (Mrs. Achille Plunkett). The last-named four assisted their parents in operating the Mordecai Female Seminary, a prestigious boarding school conducted at their Warrenton home from 1809 to 1818. There, George received a classical education and later briefly taught. His younger brothers and sisters, who also were educated by their family, included Alfred, career army officer and engineer; Augustus, merchant and agriculturist of Raleigh and Richmond; and Julia, Eliza Sarah Kennon (Mrs. Samuel Hays Myers), Emma, and Laura.

In 1818 George Mordecai moved to the Raleigh home of his brother Moses, under whom he studied law. He completed his studies at age nineteen but had to wait until he reached the required age of twenty-one to receive his law license. In the interim he went by horseback to Louisville, Ky., to oversee the family's investments in the tobacco business. Admitted to the bar on 18 June 1822, he practiced in county and superior courts in Wake and other eastern counties until the 1840s, when his health and growing business and philanthropic pursuits caused him to give up circuit riding. Young bar candidates read law with him in preparation for their own practices.

On the death of Moses on 1 Sept. 1824, George became the guardian of his half brother's four children from two marriages. As adviser to the widow Anne Willis (Nancy) Lane Mordecai, he supervised the extensive Lane-Mordecai plantations while continuing his own law practice and that of Moses. He later became the guardian of Samuel Fox Mordecai II, his great-nephew, after the death of Samuel's father in 1853.

Mordecai was a leader in railroad pioneering in North Carolina. He was a subscriber to and an incorporator of the Experimental Rail Road (1832–40) that hauled granite from a local quarry to Union Square for building the 1840 state capitol. He was an incorporator and first president (1836–40) of the Raleigh and Gaston Railroad (later Seaboard) and traveled to England on business for the company during the winter of 1838–39. After the state acquired the road, he was again an incorporator and served a second term as president in 1851–52 under the reorganization, remaining a director for the rest of his life. When the North Carolina Railroad was chartered in 1849, he was appointed a commissioner to create its capital stock and was himself the largest subscriber in the railroad, completed in 1856. He had aided in attempts to build a Raleigh and Columbia (S.C.) Railroad in the 1840s. At the outbreak of the Civil War, he was one of the commissioners who solicited subscriptions for the Chatham Railroad (later Raleigh and Augusta), which was designed to link Raleigh with the Chatham coal fields. A frequent delegate to internal improvements conventions in his own and adjoining states (1849–50 and 1856–57), he also solicited subscriptions for the Fayetteville and Northern Plank Road in 1851.

During the closing decades of the antebellum period, Mordecai was involved in the banking interests of the state. In 1849 he was elected president of the Bank of the State of North Carolina, succeeding his future father-in-law, Duncan Cameron, and in 1859 he also became president of the Bank of North Carolina. Marshall De Lancey Haywood noted that shortly before the surrender of the Confederacy in 1865, Mordecai converted into gold some $500,000 of the bank deposits, which he secreted from possible confiscation by Union forces and later prorated among the depositors to whom the funds belonged.

In 1833 he had established with his brother Augustus and James McKimmon the dry goods business of Mordecai and McKimmon. After 1838 the firm continued under McKimmon's name in a large brick commercial building constructed by Mordecai and Gavin Hogg in

1835 on the site of the burned Casso's Inn in Raleigh. He also served as vice-president of the North Carolina Mutual Insurance Company, chartered in 1849; as organizing chairman in 1858 and longtime director of the Raleigh Gas [Light] Company; and as president of the North Carolina branch of the DeSoto Insurance Company from its organization in 1869 until his death.

Not until after the death of his respected orthodox father in 1838 did Mordecai take the formal steps to convert from the Hebrew faith of his family to Christianity. He was baptized the following year in Raleigh's Christ Episcopal Church and for the rest of his life participated in its affairs. A memorial window in the sanctuary commemorates his contributions to church and community. One of his first church-related activities was aiding in the establishment of St. Mary's School in the buildings of the former Episcopal school for boys. He served Christ Church as vestryman, senior warden, and member of the building committee for the new (present) stone structure consecrated in 1854.

As coexecutor of the will of John Rex in 1839, Mordecai handled details of the estate settlement, which resulted many years later in the establishment of Rex Hospital in Raleigh. Governor Charles Manly appointed him to the board of commissioners for building Dorothea Dix Hospital for the insane; Mordecai served as secretary of the board from 1848 until 1856, when the hospital opened.

In 1861 he was a candidate for delegate to the Secession Convention but lost the election by six votes, along with former governors Manly and Thomas Bragg. During the Civil War Mordecai assisted in purchasing provisions for the Confederacy and was treasurer of the Wayside Hospital Association. His pardon is dated 12 Aug. 1865.

After the war Mordecai assisted the Raleigh Memorial Association in establishing the Confederate Cemetery, and in 1869 he was an incorporator and first president of Oakwood Cemetery. The adjacent cemeteries occupy land made available by his nephew, Henry Mordecai.

On 1 June 1853 he married Margaret Bennehan Cameron (20 Mar. 1810–12 Mar. 1886), the daughter of Rebecca Bennehan and Judge Duncan Cameron of Raleigh and Orange County. After their marriage, the Mordecais lived in the Camerons' Raleigh home on Hillsborough Street, where they both died. The couple's only child, a daughter born in 1855, died in infancy. Mrs. Mordecai, a lifelong member of Christ Church, survived her husband by fifteen years. All three were buried in the Mordecai section of Oakwood Cemetery, to which other family graves had been moved from a private burial site near the Moses Mordecai home at 1 Mimosa Street. Mordecai House, as it became known, was acquired by the city of Raleigh in 1967; with assistance from numerous organizations and individual volunteers, it was opened to the public in 1972 as a historic site and center of Mordecai Historic Park.

SEE: Christ Church (Raleigh) Parish Register; Walter Clark, comp., *History of the Raleigh and Augusta Air-line Railroad Co., Known Originally as the Chatham Railroad Co.* (1877); Marshall De Lancey Haywood, "Biographical Sketch of George Washington Mordecai," in Charles L. Van Noppen Papers (Manuscript Department, Duke University Library, Durham); Little-Mordecai Papers, North Carolina Rail Road Papers, and Will of John Rex, 14 Nov. 1838, in Wake County Wills (North Carolina State Archives, Raleigh); Memory F. Mitchell and Thornton W. Mitchell, "The Philanthropic Bequests of John Rex of Raleigh," *North Carolina Historical Review* 49 (July, October 1972); Mordecai Family Register (copy made by

Margaret Mordecai Blomquist, Durham); George W. Mordecai Papers and Mordecai Family Papers (Southern Historical Collection, University of North Carolina, Chapel Hill); Gratz Mordecai, "Notice of Jacob Mordecai, Founder and Proprietor from 1809 to 1818 of the Warrenton (N.C.) Female Seminary," *Publications of the Jewish Historical Society*, no. 6 (1897); Jacob Mordecai Papers (Manuscript Department, Duke University Library, Durham); *Nat. Cyc. Am. Biog.*, vol. 10 (1900); *North Carolina Private Laws, 1832–1833, 1835, 1848–1849,* and *1866–1867*; Raleigh *Daily Sentinel*, 21, 23 Feb. 1871; Raleigh *Register*, various issues, 1836–59.

ELIZABETH DAVIS REID MURRAY

Mordecai, Jacob (11 Apr. 1762–4 Sept. 1838), merchant and educator, was born in Philadelphia, the oldest son of Moses and Esther Whitlock Mordecai. His father, a Jew and a native of Germany, migrated to New York in 1760 and later moved to Philadelphia, where he became a merchant. He was a signer of the Non-Importation Act of 1765. Jacob's early formal education, which he received at private schools in Philadelphia, was slight, but it was supplemented by what he learned at home and in the synagogue and by what he taught himself as he grew older. He early gained a reputation for being a thorough and highly literate scholar. Deeply religious, he eventually mastered the Hebrew language and became a recognized authority on Jewish literature and Old Testament interpretation. As sergeant of a youthful rifle corps, he had the honor in 1774 of escorting the First Continental Congress from Frankford into Philadelphia.

Mordecai learned the mercantile business in the countinghouse of David Franks; in 1781 he moved to New York and went into business for himself. In 1792, following brief mercantile ventures in both Petersburg and Richmond, Va., he established his residence in Warrenton, N.C., where he became a dealer in tobacco, cotton, grain, and other commodities. Although he and his family were the only Jews in Warrenton and among the few in North Carolina, and he was a strict observer of the laws and customs of his religion, Mordecai encountered no discrimination and soon became a popular and respected member of the community. In 1797 he was elected master of the Masonic lodge in Warrenton, a post he held for at least three years.

For fifteen years his business flourished, but in 1807 heavy losses in tobacco speculation forced him into bankruptcy. As a result, he was obliged to accept a position as dormitory and dining hall steward at the Warrenton Male Academy in order to support his growing family. In 1809, at the request of a group of influential townspeople, he opened a boarding school for girls. Known first as the Mordecai Female Seminary and later as the Warrenton Female Academy, the school offered instruction in English, writing, mathematics, history, geography, Greek, Latin, and composition—all usually taught by members of the Mordecai family—as well as drawing, plain and ornamental needlework, music, and dancing. Throughout the ten years (1809–18) that Mordecai was proprietor and principal of the academy, he, his oldest daughter, Rachel, and his son Solomon bore the main burden of instruction, Rachel being especially helpful to her father. Daughters Caroline and Ellen also became members of the teaching staff. Jacob Mordecai and Solomon wrote several of the textbooks used in the school. By 1811 the academy had acquired a reputation throughout the Southeast for giving girls a thorough and lasting education.

The academy was a financial as well as an educational

success, and by 1818 Mordecai had accumulated a modest fortune. Moreover, he had grown tired of his arduous life as an educator and decided to retire to a farm. In December he sold the academy and the following April moved his family to Spring Farm, a plantation he had purchased near Richmond, Va. He later resided in Richmond, where he died at age seventy-six.

Mordecai's first wife was Judith Myers of New York. Following her death in 1796, he married her half sister, Rebecca. Of his numerous children, six sons and seven daughters lived to maturity. His oldest son, Moses (b. 1785), became a prominent member of the North Carolina bar. His second son, Samuel, who served as business agent of the Warrenton Female Academy during his father's tenure as principal, became a successful businessman in Richmond and wrote a history of that city. His third son, Solomon, studied medicine in Philadelphia and moved to Mobile, Ala., where he became a popular physician. His fourth son, George Washington Mordecai (1801–71), a longtime resident of Raleigh, was a highly successful lawyer, railroad president, and banker. His fifth son, Alfred (1804–87), a graduate of West Point, rose to the rank of major in the U.S. Army but resigned his commission at the beginning of the Civil War rather than bear arms against either his Northern or Southern relatives and became a mathematics teacher in Philadelphia. From 1865 to 1866 he served as assistant engineer of the Mexico and Pacific Railroad, and from 1867 until his death he was secretary and treasurer of canal and coal companies owned by the Pennsylvania Railroad Company. The youngest of the Mordecai sons, Augustus, was a farmer near Richmond. Emma (1812–1906), the youngest daughter, spent much of her long life in educational and religious work.

Mordecai's opinions on political and economic issues were seemingly compatible with those of the Southern wing of the Whig party, which emerged on the national scene during the last years of his life. His portrait, oil on canvas, painted by Wesley Jarvis in 1826, portrays an erect, elderly gentleman with white hair, blue eyes, and a clear complexion wearing a black coat, black silk vest, and white stock. As of 1963, it was owned by Jacob's great-great-grandson, William Grimes Mordecai, of Raleigh.

SEE: Caroline Cohen, *Records of the Myers, Hays, and Mordecai Families from 1707 to 1913* (1913); Stanley L. Falk, "The Warrenton Female Academy of Jacob Mordecai, 1809–1818," *North Carolina Historical Review* 35 (July 1958); Laura MacMillan, comp., *The North Carolina Portrait Index, 1700–1860* (1963); Lizzie Wilson Montgomery, *Sketches of Old Warrenton, North Carolina* (1924); Mordecai Family Papers, George Washington Mordecai Papers, and Cameron Family Papers (Southern Historical Collection, University of North Carolina, Chapel Hill); Gratz Mordecai, "Notice of Jacob Mordecai, Founder and Proprietor from 1809 to 1818 of the Warrenton (N.C.) Female Seminary," *Publications of the Jewish Historical Society*, no. 6 (1897); Jacob Mordecai Papers (Manuscript Department, Duke University Library, Durham); James A. Padgett, ed., "The Life of Alfred Mordecai as Related by Himself," *North Carolina Historical Review* 22 (January 1945).

W. CONARD GASS

Mordecai, Moses (*4 Apr. 1785–1 Sept. 1824*), attorney, planter, and first of the name to live in Raleigh (where his name was given to the historic Mordecai House), was born in New York City, the oldest child of Jacob (1762–1838) and Judith Myers Mordecai (1762–96) and

the grandson of noted New York silversmith Myer Myers. His brothers and sisters included Samuel, merchant of Petersburg and Richmond, Va., and author of *Richmond in By-Gone Days* (1856); Solomon, physician of Mobile, Ala.; Rachel (Mrs. Aaron Lazarus), noted for her correspondence with Irish writer Maria Edgeworth; Ellen, author of *Past Days* (1841) and *The History of a Heart* (1845); and Caroline (Mrs. Achille Plunkett). From his father's second marriage to Judith's half sister Rebecca Myers (1776–1863), Moses's half brothers and sisters included George Washington, attorney, planter, financier, entrepreneur, and railroad and banking executive of Raleigh; Alfred, career army officer and engineer; Augustus, merchant and agriculturist of Raleigh and Richmond; and Julia, Eliza Sara Kennon (Mrs. Samuel Hayes Myers), Emma, and Laura.

When Moses was a child, his parents moved in 1792 via several Virginia locations to Warrenton, N.C., where his father engaged in mercantile pursuits. There his mother died and his father remarried; also in Warrenton, with the aid of Moses's brother and three sisters, Jacob conducted (1809–18) the prestigious Mordecai Female Seminary. Educated primarily by his parents, and after his mother's death by her half sisters, Judah Myers and Richea Myers (later Mrs. Joseph Marx), the daughters of Myer Myers of Richmond, Moses also studied under Marcus George in the Warrenton Academy. Apparently his study of law was self-conducted, although he received some instruction from Judge Oliver Fitts of Warren County.

Obtaining his license to practice in the North Carolina courts on 30 Sept. 1807, he began "riding the circuit" in Nash, Franklin, and Northampton counties. In 1808 he took over the practice of Judge Fitts when Fitts became attorney general. Over the next several years Mordecai's circuit expanded to include Johnston, Wayne, Halifax, Pitt, and Edgecombe counties, as well as superior courts in Raleigh and New Bern. In 1811 he declined the position of clerk in the State Bank but a few months later accepted appointment as engrossing clerk in the state house of representatives.

As early as 1812 he was a Mason, a member of Hiram Lodge No. 40 in Raleigh, and on a committee for constructing—with the Grand Lodge of North Carolina—a hall at the corner of Morgan and Dawson streets, the site given by Theophilus Hunter of Wake. In late 1815 he purchased a house in Raleigh on what was then Halifax Street; thereafter, he made Raleigh his home. His profession proved profitable, and with the aid of his brother Samuel he made lucrative investments by which he acquired the beginnings of a considerable estate. In 1822 a sizable inheritance from a wealthy client and family friend, Mrs. Mary Sumner Blount of Tarboro, significantly increased his fortune. At the time of his death, Mordecai's estate included about four thousand acres of land and thirty slaves.

Meanwhile, on 9 Dec. 1817, at the Wake County home of her grandfather, Major John Hinton, he married Margaret Lane (ca. 1786–1821), the daughter of Henry and Mary (Polly) Hinton Lane. She was also the granddaughter of Joel Lane and the great-granddaughter of Colonel John Hinton, all of Wake County. Mordecai thus came into possession of the Henry Lane House (ca. 1785), located north of the capitol and at the time outside the Raleigh city limits, the nucleus of a three-thousand-acre plantation that he managed and substantially expanded. Again with the aid of his brother Samuel, Mordecai furnished the house, which came to be known as Mordecai House, with New York–made furniture and accessories sent via Petersburg. His wife's three sisters and two of his own half brothers lived with the Mordecais. One of the latter, George Washington Mordecai, read law with Moses and took over some of his older brother's practice. After Moses's death, he remained at the Raleigh home as guardian of Moses's children and adviser to his widow.

Moses was the first president of the Wake Agricultural Society, formed in 1823 in response to the efforts of the short-lived first State Board of Agriculture to establish such societies in every county. Three decades later his son Jacob was a vice-president of a new county agricultural society created under the successful state organization of 1852.

The children of Mordecai's first marriage were Henry (25 Mar. 1819–22 Sept. 1875), planter and state legislator, who married a cousin, Martha Hinton, daughter of Ransom and Mary Willis Hinton; Ellen (12 Apr. 1820–26 Feb. 1916), author, who married her first cousin, Samuel Fox Mordecai, son of her father's brother Dr. Solomon and Caroline Waller Mordecai; and Jacob (26 Nov. 1821–3 Aug. 1867), also a planter and state legislator. Moses's first wife died on 11 Dec. 1821, and on 6 Jan. 1824 he married her sister, Anne Willis (Nancy) Lane (ca. 1794–4 Jan. 1854). He did not live to see the birth of their only child, Margaret Lane (10 Oct. 1824–10 Mar. 1910), later Mrs. John Devereux.

His family attributed his persistent ill health to his three- and four-month circuits in the "low, unhealthy" eastern North Carolina counties and to the hardships of the constant horseback travel. In the summer of 1823 he spent some time in Saratoga, N.Y., "taking the waters" for his health. The following summer he went to Sweet Springs, Va., in an attempt to recover, but after lingering several weeks he died. Some months later his remains were taken to the family cemetery near Mordecai House; in the 1860s they were moved to the Mordecai section of Oakwood Cemetery, Raleigh, where his two wives and all their children eventually were buried.

Born into an orthodox Jewish family, Moses remained in that faith throughout his life. His widow and three of his children were baptized in Christ Episcopal Church on 5 May 1833.

Bartholomew Figures Moore described Mordecai as "one of the best and most successful lawyers who ever appeared before the courts of the State." Numerous anecdotes were circulated about him. One of the most accepted ones concerns a client who tried to thank him for winning his acquittal in court, whereupon the short-statured attorney, already astride his horse outside the courthouse, raised his crop as if to strike the man and shouted, "Get out of my way, you scoundrel. You know you're as guilty as h———!" Another, undoubtedly true, was recounted by his sister Ellen after a stage trip from Raleigh to Richmond in 1822: "Moses made us laugh with his bluntness of manner. He does not like Virginia, thinking of the character of the state what I believe it is—in no small degree, inclined to *puff* and make a *great show*, when there is but little real substance. We were in a very genteel sitting room but the servant, woe to his remissness, had only placed *one* candle on the sideboard. The next time he entered the room with hasty officiousness, to attend to our wants, Moses (little man) walked up to him with a hasty step and said in as few words as may be, 'Waiter, in Carolina when we have *two* candles we light them both—and when we have but *one*, we cut it in two and light both pieces.' 'Yes sir, yes sir, yes sir, have it in a minute sir'—and away he scampered. And in one moment 'there was light.' "

Moses provided funds in his will for a new house for his widow. She decided, however, to enlarge the eighteenth-century home; in 1825–26 state architect William Nichols designed the neoclassical facade and four front

rooms and halls. According to the Raleigh *Standard*, it "was the earliest specimen of that order of architecture among us." The house was successively the property and residence of Moses's son Henry; Henry's daughters, Mary Willis (Mrs. William Armstrong Turk, 1858–1937) and Martha (Miss Pattie, 1860–1949); and finally their nephew, Burke Haywood Little (1880–1968), who represented the fifth generation of the family to reside there. In 1967, some months before Little's death, the city of Raleigh purchased the property for preservation as a historic site and, with assistance from numerous organizations and individuals, opened the house and surrounding Mordecai Historic Park to the public in 1972.

Several portraits of Moses Mordecai are extant. Two, which hang in the Mordecai House, are a William Garl Browne copy (1857) of a portrait, possibly by John Wesley Jarvis (prior to 1824), and a profile by Charles B. J. F. de St.-Memin (ca. 1805).

SEE: John L. Cheney, Jr., ed., *North Carolina Government, 1585–1979* (1981); Christ Church (Raleigh) Parish Register; Mordecai Family Papers and George W. Mordecai Papers (Southern Historical Collection, University of North Carolina, Chapel Hill); Mordecai Family Register (copy made by Margaret Mordecai Blomquist, Durham); Jacob Mordecai Papers and Hinsdale Family Papers (Manuscript Department, Duke University Library, Durham); Pattie Mordecai Collection and Little-Mordecai Papers, Wake County Tax Lists, and Wake County Wills (North Carolina State Archives, Raleigh); *North Carolina Public Laws*, 1822; *North Carolina Standard*, 8 Feb. 1854; Raleigh *Register*, 12 Dec. 1817, 28 Feb., 30 May 1823.

ELIZABETH DAVIS REID MURRAY

Mordecai, Samuel Fox II (*12 Dec. 1852–29 Dec. 1927*), lawyer and legal scholar, was born in Richmond, Va., the son of Ellen M. (1820–1916) and Samuel Fox Mordecai (1828–52), who were first cousins. His family had long and prominent ties to North Carolina. His great-great-grandfather, Moses Mordecai (1707–81), was a German-born Jewish merchant who pursued a career in England and America. His great-grandfather, Jacob Mordecai (1762–1838), was a merchant in Virginia and North Carolina who founded a school for girls in Warrenton (1809) before moving to Richmond in 1818. Two of Jacob Mordecai's thirteen children, Moses (1785–1824) and Solomon (1792–1869), were Samuel Fox's grandfathers. The former, an attorney, married in succession two granddaughters of Joel Lane, a founder of the city of Raleigh, and they lived in a historic house that still bears his name. Solomon Mordecai was born in Warrenton but later moved to Mobile, Ala., where he was a physician.

Mordecai was educated in private schools in Virginia and North Carolina, and he attended the University of Virginia. In 1875 the North Carolina Supreme Court admitted him to the bar. In November of the same year he married Elizabeth D. (Bettie) Grimes, the daughter of General Bryan and Elizabeth Hilliard Davis Grimes of Grimesland. They became the parents of nine children, one of whom died in infancy.

From 1875 to 1904 Mordecai practiced law in partnership with Richard H. Battle in Raleigh and frequently argued cases before the state supreme court. He served as a trustee of the Olivia Raney Library and was nominated for the state legislature in 1887 but was not elected. In 1897 he published his first volume of legal scholarship, *Mechanics' Liens*. This was followed in 1899 by *Negotiable Instruments Law in North Carolina*.

In July 1900 Mordecai was named an assistant professor of law at Wake Forest College, where he lectured with considerable success for the next four years. In 1904 brothers James B. and Benjamin N. Duke pledged an annual contribution of six thousand dollars to support the establishment of a law school at Trinity College in Durham. On the basis of his excellent reputation, Samuel Fox Mordecai was named senior professor and soon afterwards dean. It was at Trinity and its successor institution, Duke University, that he made his most memorable contributions to legal education.

After the Trinity College School of Law opened in the fall of 1904, Mordecai visited several prominent law schools in the Northeast, including Harvard, which was then using the new "case method" of instruction with great success. Trinity adopted this method, although Mordecai's own dynamic lectures formed the core of the school's program and provided the basis of its growing reputation. From the beginning Trinity enforced high standards of admission and achievement; in 1906 it became only the second southern law school to be accepted by the Association of American Law Schools. In 1911 the college awarded Dean Mordecai an honorary doctor of laws degree.

He and his faculty wrote and published their own texts for their courses of instruction. Among Mordecai's works were his *Law Lectures* (1907, 2d ed. 1915) and *Law Notes* (1912–13 and 1914–19), which were widely cited and recognized as authority on the laws of North Carolina. His other writings included *Lex Scripta* (1905), *Case Book on Remedies* (with A. C. McIntosh, 1910), *Questions and Answers on Real Property* (1912), and *Questions and Answers on Second Blackstone* (1923).

Mordecai was without peer as a teacher. Never concerned with mere numbers, he deliberately kept enrollments low, and his students were noted for their ability, character, and devotion to their mentor.

He was perhaps as famous for his wit and erudition as for his legal ability. His bearded visage was well known on the Trinity campus, and although his colorful language occasionally gave a first impression of coarseness, his personal charm and learned discourses endeared him to the college community. He was a lover of animals and had many pets, especially dogs, the most celebrated of which was a dachshund named Pompey Ducklegs, who could allegedly chew tobacco with the aplomb of his master. Mordecai delighted in writing clever prose and mediocre poetry, the best of which he collected and published in *Mordecai's Miscellanies* (1927).

Raised as an Episcopalian, Mordecai was not much given to formal religion. In jesting reference to his family heritage, his church, and his affiliation with Wake Forest and Trinity, he would describe himself as "Methodist, Episcopal, Baptist, Jew." His true beliefs were summed up in the lines he often quoted: "And what doth the Lord require of thee but to do justly, to love mercy, and to walk humbly with thy God?" A member of Zeta Psi and a Democrat, Mordecai died after a series of strokes and was buried in Oakwood Cemetery, Raleigh. A portrait hangs in the Duke University Law School.

SEE: Margaret Mordecai Blomquist, *Recollections of Papa* (1982); *Durham Morning Herald*, 30 Dec. 1927; Mordecai Family Papers and Samuel Fox Mordecai Papers (Manuscript Department, Duke University Library, Durham); *Samuel Fox Mordecai: Presentation of a Portrait by the Alumni of the Duke University School of Law* (1932); *Who's Who in America* (1927).

MARK C. STAUTER

Moreau. *See* **Said, Omar Ibn.**

Morehead, Eugene Lindsay (16 Sept. 1845–27 Feb. 1889), banker and industrialist, was born in Greensboro, the son of Governor John Motley and Ann Eliza Lindsay Morehead. He entered The University of North Carolina in 1861 at age sixteen and remained until 1863, when he enlisted in the Junior Reserves and was ordered to Smith Island at the mouth of the Cape Fear River to help provide for the defense of the port of Wilmington. Morehead was assigned to brigade headquarters with the rank of lieutenant. He saw action in defense of Fort Fisher late in 1864 and participated in the Battle of Bentonville in March 1865. At the end of the war he resumed his studies at the university and was graduated in 1868 near the head of his class.

Returning to Greensboro, Morehead was employed in a bank of which his uncle, Jesse Lindsay, was president. Until 1874 he worked in banking and engaged in the tobacco business with another relative. He lived in Savannah, Ga., from 1874 until 1879, probably in order to expand family business connections, although it is not clear exactly what he did. In 1879 he returned to North Carolina and settled in Durham, a thriving new center of business, where he became a banker and participated in various industrial undertakings. He served on the board of town commissioners and on the board of education, sometimes as president of the latter, when he saw the successful implementation of a system of graded schools.

In addition to his own Morehead Banking Company, which encouraged the industrial development of Durham, Morehead was active in the Faucett Durham Tobacco Company, the electric light and power company, the street railway, the Durham waterworks, the Durham Land and Security Company, the Durham Fertilizer Company, and the Fidelity Bank, among other firms. He also served the First Presbyterian Church of Durham as an elder and a teacher of the adult Bible class. In brief, he participated in almost every phase of Durham's business, civic, and educational life.

On 7 Jan. 1874 Morehead married Lucy Lathrop of Savannah, Ga. They were the parents of three children: Margaret Warren (Mrs. Rufus Lenoir Patterson), Eliza Lindsay (Mrs. John F. Wily), and Lathrop. After becoming ill in the fall of 1888, Morehead went to New Orleans for medical treatment. He died the following year at age forty-four and was buried in Maplewood Cemetery, Durham.

SEE: Alumni Records, University of North Carolina, Chapel Hill; Samuel A. Ashe, ed., *Biographical History of North Carolina*, vol. 2 (1905); Julian S. Carr, *Memorial Address on the Life and Character of Col. Eugene Morehead* (1889); Stephen B. Weeks Scrapbook, vol. 2 (North Carolina Collection, University of North Carolina, Chapel Hill).

C. SYLVESTER GREEN

Morehead, James Turner (11 Jan. 1799–5 May 1875), lawyer, legislator, and congressman, was born in Rockingham County, the son of John and Obedience Motley Morehead. He attended the Reverend David Caldwell's school in Guilford County and was graduated from The University of North Carolina in 1819. Afterwards he studied law in Virginia, was licensed, and established a practice in Greensboro. He was frequently a town commissioner and in 1832 drew up regulations for the government of Greensboro, many of the provisions of which pertained to public health and were advanced for the times.

Morehead served five terms in the state senate between 1835 and 1842 and in the U.S. House of Representatives as a Whig during the years 1851–53, after which he declined to be a candidate for reelection. In addition to practicing law, he also had farming interests and operated the Troublesome ironworks. Although Morehead strongly opposed secession, his four sons were Confederate officers; after the war he retired to private life and occupied himself with his business affairs.

He married Mary Teas Lindsay, and they were the parents of four sons, Robert Lindsay, John Henry, James T., Jr., and Joseph Motley, and two daughters, Annie Eliza (Mrs. Theodore Whitfield) and Mary Harper. His wife died when the children were still young, and he lavished great care and devotion on them as they grew. Morehead was buried in the Presbyterian churchyard in Greensboro.

SEE: *Biog. Dir. Am. Cong.* (1961); Bettie D. Caldwell, comp., *Founders and Builders of Greensboro, 1808–1908* (1925); John L. Cheney, Jr., ed., *North Carolina Government, 1585–1979* (1981); Daniel L. Grant, *Alumni History of the University of North Carolina, 1795–1924* (1924); *Greensboro Daily News*, [September?] 1965 (North Carolina Collection, University of North Carolina, Chapel Hill); *Who Was Who in America*, vol. 1 (1967).

WILLIAM S. POWELL

Morehead, James Turner, Jr. *(28 May 1838–1 Apr. 1919)*, lawyer, legislator, and Confederate officer, was born in Guilford County, the son of James T. and Mary Lindsay Morehead. After attending the private school of Dr. Alexander Wilson in Alamance County, he was graduated from The University of North Carolina in 1858 and immediately entered Judge Richmond M. Pearson's law school at Richmond Hill, Yadkin County. He was licensed to practice in county courts in 1859 and in superior courts in 1860.

In 1861 Morehead enlisted in the Guilford Grays and was elected lieutenant. He rose through the grades to become colonel of the Fifty-third Regiment, with which he served with distinction throughout the Civil War. Morehead was wounded three times—at Gettysburg, Fisher's Hill, and Hare's Hill—and captured on 25 Mar. 1865, remaining a prisoner until the end of the war.

Returning to Greensboro, he resumed his law practice and was soon recognized as an outstanding trial lawyer. During Reconstruction he was a conservative leader and counselor and devoted his efforts to liberating the state from the dominance of numerous outsiders who had attained positions of influence at the end of the war. In 1865–66 he represented Guilford County in the state senate, where he introduced a bill—which became law—to restore to married women their common-law right of dower. He served again in 1871–72 and 1872–74; in the latter years he was speaker of the senate. He returned to the legislature for a final term in 1883.

Morehead, a Presbyterian, never married.

SEE: Bettie D. Caldwell, comp., *Founders and Builders of Greensboro, 1808–1908* (1925); John L. Cheney, Jr., ed., *North Carolina Government, 1585–1979* (1981); Jerome Dowd, *Sketches of Prominent Living North Carolinians* (1888); Daniel L. Grant, *Alumni History of the University of North Carolina, 1795–1924* (1924); *North Carolina Bar Association Proceedings, 1919* (1920); J. T. Tomlinson, *Assembly Sketch Book, Session 1883* (1883).

WILLIAM S. POWELL

Morehead, James Turner *(5 Aug. 1840–19 Apr. 1908)*, industrial entrepreneur and Confederate officer, was born in Greensboro, the son of John Motley, governor of North Carolina (1841–45), and Ann Eliza Lindsay Morehead. Educated in local schools, he entered The University of North Carolina in 1857 and was graduated in June 1861 with first honors.

Morehead enlisted at Wentworth in the Rockingham Rangers, which was mustered into the Confederate army as Company D of the Fifth North Carolina Cavalry (Sixty-third Regiment) at Kinston on 13 Sept. 1862. His initial rank was second lieutenant, to date from 1 Aug. 1862. On 18 October he was transferred to the regimental staff as adjutant with the rank of first lieutenant. At Bristoe Station, Va., on 11 Oct. 1863, Morehead was wounded by a bullet that struck his mouth and neck. He was furloughed and eventually joined the Invalid Corps on 19 Oct. 1864, serving as provost marshal at Greensboro. After brief service in North Carolina, most of the regiment had joined the Cavalry Corps of the Army of Northern Virginia by June 1863. The regiment engaged in a series of skirmishes, cavalry-screening actions, and the major campaigns throughout the summer and fall of 1863 in both eastern Virginia and the Shenandoah Valley. The action at Bristoe, where Morehead was injured, was part of a successful flanking movement of the Army of Northern Virginia to force the Army of the Potomac to retreat.

In December 1864, while recuperating in Greensboro, he married Mary Elizabeth Connally (1842–1917), also a Greensboro native. Afterwards the Moreheads moved to Leaksville to manage Governor Morehead's extensive business enterprises, which included over two thousand acres, a dam and power canal, a gristmill, a cotton-spinning factory, and a woolen factory. On the death of the governor in 1866, Turner Morehead inherited the Leaksville property. In the postwar Reconstruction era he was an apostle of diversified economic development, setting an example by expanding his mills, forming a development company called the Spray Water Power and Land Company, and promoting railroad construction, particularly the North Carolina Midland, the Western North Carolina, and the Cape Fear and Yadkin Valley. By 1884 he had completed construction of the Danville, Mocksville, and Southwestern (Danville and Western) Railroad from Danville to Leaksville for the purpose of serving his various business interests.

In politics Morehead sympathized with the Conservative-Democrats, and at the height of the Reconstruction trouble he served two terms in the state senate (1870–74). In 1875 he was elected a delegate to the state constitutional convention. In the General Assembly, he worked for the impeachment of Governor William Woods Holden and supported legislation favorable to economic development. He advocated the revival of a state geologic and natural resources survey, and in 1891, when the survey was renewed, he was appointed a member of the Board of Control.

Partly to recoup monetary losses from the business recession of 1888, Morehead secured investors for the development of a process for making aluminum. In 1891 he hired Thomas L. Willson, a chemist from Canada, who began experimenting with the reduction of aluminum from a mixture of aluminum oxide and carbon under extreme temperatures. For this purpose the Willson Aluminum Company constructed an electric arc furnace on the canal in Spray, the first such furnace in the United States. Morehead also asked his son, John Motley Morehead III, a recent graduate in chemistry from The University of North Carolina, to serve as Willson's assistant. On 2 May 1892 the company accidentally discovered a new chemical compound, calcium carbide, which released a gas when placed in water. No gas analysis apparatus was available, so the compound was sent to Chapel Hill, where Professor F. P. Venable identified it as acetylene gas. No practical use for the gas and compound was immediately found, and Turner Morehead went bankrupt in 1893, when his aluminum operation proved unprofitable.

He went to New York and in 1894 formed the Electro-Gas Company to manufacture and sell carbide and acetylene, which was now being viewed as an enriching agent to substitute for oil in the manufacture of water gas. Further experimentation at the plant in Spray led to the development of ferrochromium and ferrosilicon alloys for use in the processing of steel. These processes were used in the production of armor plate and armor-piercing shells during the Spanish-American War, bringing Morehead financial security. He expanded his operation by securing power sites on the James River in Virginia and the Kanawha River in West Virginia. His various patents on chemical processes and metal alloys, as well as his development of industrial sites in the latter two states, eventually led after his death to the formation of Union Carbide Corporation, one of the great industrial corporations in the world.

Morehead had one son, John Motley, III, chemist, industrialist, and noted philanthropist, and four daughters: Mary Kerr, Eliza Lindsay, Lilly Connolly, and Emma Gray. Characterized as a "Sunday Presbyterian" by his son, he attended the First Baptist Church in Leaksville with his wife, who was a member and very active in church activities. In 1884 Mrs. Morehead served on the church building committee for the present sanctuary. Portraits of the Moreheads are in the Morehead Planetarium in Chapel Hill. They were buried in Lawson Cemetery, Leaksville.

SEE: Samuel A. Ashe, ed., *Biographical History of North Carolina*, vol. 2 (1905); John L. Cheney, Jr., *North Carolina Government, 1585–1979* (1981); First Baptist Church Records, Eden; Louis H. Manarin, comp., *North Carolina Troops, 1861–1865: A Roster*, vol. 2 (1968); John Motley Morehead III, *The Morehead Family of North Carolina and Virginia* (1921) and "Address before the International Acetylene Association, Chicago, 27 Oct. 1922."

LINDLEY S. BUTLER

Morehead, John Lindsay *(19 Oct. 1894–9 Nov. 1964)*, textile executive and principal officer of the John Motley Morehead Foundation at The University of North Carolina, was born in Marietta, Ga., the son of John Motley and Mary Garrett Morehead. His father later became a Charlotte banker and served in the U.S. Congress. He was a descendant of John Motley Morehead, the prominent early nineteenth-century governor of North Carolina for whom Morehead City was named, and a cousin of John Motley Morehead III, benefactor of The University of North Carolina. Following graduation from Woodberry Forest School in Virginia, John Lindsay entered The University of North Carolina in the fall of 1911. After one year at Chapel Hill, he transferred to the University of Virginia, from which he received a B.S. degree in 1916. During World War I he became a second lieutenant in the U.S. Army Air Corps.

From his Charlotte office, Morehead directed the operations of the Leaksville Woolen Mills, of which he was president and chairman of the board from 1929 until his death. He had joined the Leaksville operation in 1917 as general superintendent, shortly before enlisting in the army. Morehead was also a director of the Chatham Manufacturing Company, the Charlotte Federal Reserve Bank, and the Business Foundation of The University of North Carolina. He was a lifelong Republican and an active Episcopalian.

When his elderly cousin, John Motley Morehead III, established the multimillion-dollar Morehead Foundation at Chapel Hill in the late forties, he turned over its operation to John Lindsay. Patterned after the Rhodes Scholarship at Oxford, the Morehead awards provided exceptionally generous stipends to young men of outstanding ability and promise who planned to enroll at Chapel Hill. For the remainder of his life, John Lindsay Morehead worked enthusiastically to make the Morehead awards among the most prestigious in U.S. collegiate circles. He took great personal interest in the individual Morehead scholars and through the years helped broaden the scope of the program. As a token of its appreciation for "the architect of the Morehead scholarship plan," The University of North Carolina awarded him an honorary doctor of laws degree in 1960.

When Morehead died in Charlotte at age seventy, eight Morehead scholars served as pallbearers at his funeral. He was buried in Charlotte's Elmwood Cemetery. After his death, a resolution drawn up by the Morehead Foundation trustees stated in part: "While this Foundation is the sole creation of the generosity and benevolence of John Motley Morehead, its organization and its rich achievements are in great part the result of the loving and untiring efforts spread upon it by John Lindsay Morehead. Since its inception, the Morehead Foundation occupied a primary position in his affections, and he labored diligently in its behalf. It was the vision, the ability, the integrity, and the devotion of John Lindsay Morehead that built the Morehead Foundation."

On 14 June 1919 Morehead married Louise Nickerson of Maryland. The couple had three daughters: Mary Nickerson (Mrs. Hugh Gwyn Chatham), Jean Motley (Mrs. Peter Alexander Larkin), and Louise Lindsay (Mrs. Alan Dickson). Mrs. Morehead died on 11 July 1976 as a result of an automobile accident.

SEE: *Chapel Hill Weekly*, 11 Nov. 1964; *Charlotte Observer*, 10 Nov. 1964; *Durham Morning Herald*, 10 Nov. 1964; *The John Motley Morehead Foundation Annual Report* (1965); *New York Times*, 10 Nov. 1964; Raleigh *News and Observer*, 10 Nov. 1964; *Who's Who in America*, vol. 33 (1964–65).

EDWARD FRENCH

Morehead, John Motley *(4 July 1796–27 Aug. 1866)*, governor and railroad promoter, was born in Pittsylvania County, Va., the son of John and Obedience Motley Morehead. The family moved to Rockingham County, N.C., when John Motley was two years old. He was educated by Dr. David Caldwell at his school near Greensboro and at The University of North Carolina, from which he was graduated in 1817. Morehead then studied law with Archibald D. Murphey and was admitted to the bar in 1819. Afterwards he began practicing law in Wentworth, the county seat of Rockingham County.

Morehead soon became involved in local politics and represented Rockingham County in the House of Commons during the 1821 session. After moving to Greensboro and beginning to practice there, he represented Guilford County in the house during the sessions of 1826–27 and 1827–28. His next political involvement was as a delegate to the North Carolina Constitutional Convention of 1835, where he ably represented Guilford

County's interests in the successful attempt to equalize political representation between the eastern and western counties of the state.

In the 1830s Morehead became a promoter of internal improvements, particularly the development of transportation to the western part of the state. His advocacy of this cause made him a leader in the North Carolina Whig party, which strongly supported internal improvements as one of its fundamental tenets. Morehead won the governorship in 1840 and again in 1842, defeating in turn Democratic candidates Romulus M. Saunders and Louis D. Henry. As governor he supported internal improvements legislation, including state aid to railroad development, the building of highways, and the improvement of navigation, but his efforts were thwarted by a Democratic majority in the General Assembly. He did succeed in establishing a school for the deaf in Raleigh to which blind students were later admitted. The successor of this school, now exclusively for the sight impaired, bears his name.

After his two gubernatorial terms, Morehead continued his interest in developing the transportation resources of North Carolina. He became president of the North Carolina Railroad and a promoter of the Atlantic and North Carolina Railroad and the Western North Carolina Railroad, devoting most of his time in the 1850s to these endeavors. In 1858–59 he reentered politics as Guilford County's representative in the House of Commons, and in 1860–61 he represented the county in the senate. In February 1861 he served as a delegate to the abortive "Peace Conference" held in Washington to stave off a civil war. Morehead resigned from the senate after North Carolina joined the Confederacy and was one of the state's delegates to the Confederate Provisional Congress during 1861–62. This service terminated his formal political career.

On 6 Sept. 1821 he married Ann Eliza Lindsay of Guilford County. They had eight children, including James Turner and Eugene Lindsay. Morehead died at Alum Springs, Rockbridge, Va., and was buried in the yard of the First Presbyterian Church, Greensboro.

SEE: Samuel A. Ashe, ed., *Biographical History of North Carolina*, vol. 2 (1905 [portrait]); R. D. W. Connor, *North Carolina: Rebuilding an Ancient Commonwealth, 1584–1925*, vols. 1–2 (1929); *DAB*, vol. 13 (1934); Thomas E. Jeffrey, "Internal Improvements and Political Parties in Antebellum North Carolina, 1836–1860," *North Carolina Historical Review* 55 (April 1978); Burton Alva Konkle, *John Motley Morehead and the Development of North Carolina* (1922); C. C. Weaver, *History of Internal Improvements in North Carolina* (1903).

H. THOMAS KEARNEY, JR.

Morehead, John Motley, II (20 July 1866–13 Dec. 1923), textile manufacturer, congressman, and state political leader, was born in Charlotte of Scottish ancestry. The grandson of Governor John Motley Morehead, he was one of four children of John Lindsay and Sarah Phifer Morehead. His maternal grandfather was William Fullenwider Phifer, one of the most prominent planters in the state. In Charlotte, Morehead attended city schools and the Carolina Military Institute. He was graduated from The University of North Carolina with an A.B. degree in 1886 and continued his studies at the Bryant and Stratton Business College in Baltimore.

Morehead spent two years as a clerk in the Commercial National Bank of Charlotte, followed by two years in the leaf tobacco business in Durham. In 1893–94 the partnership of his father and uncle in the James Turner

Morehead Company, a textile firm named after his uncle, was dissolved and some of its properties were sold to the Spray Water Power and Land Company. John Motley Morehead II became a partner in the new James T. Morehead Company and chief executive officer of the Leaksville Woolen Mills, which he continued to operate until his death. The Leaksville mill has been noted as the oldest woolen mill in continuous service in the South. In 1898 Morehead doubled its capacity by building additional facilities and machinery. In later years, he constructed another factory in Mecklenburg County; this had twice the capacity of the parent plant in Spray.

Until 1908 Morehead was politically active as a Democrat. However, changing his affiliation, he ran as the Republican candidate for the Fifth North Carolina District in the congressional election of 1908. He won the contest, becoming a member of the Sixty-first Congress (1909–11). Morehead refused to seek a second term and instead served as chairman of the state Republican executive committee. In 1916 he was elected to the National Republican Committee but resigned shortly afterwards. Later he lost his bid for a seat in the U.S. Senate (1918) and, as a candidate from the Ninth Congressional District, in the U.S. House of Representatives (1919).

Like his forefathers, Morehead was an active Presbyterian and he attended the First Presbyterian Church in Charlotte. He also was a member of the University Club in Washington, D.C., and the Southern Manufacturers Club. In addition to his involvement in the Leaksville Woolen Mills, he served as vice-president of the Thrift Manufacturing Company and as stockholder and director of the Highland Park Manufacturing Company, both in Charlotte. An ardent baseball fan, he officiated as an umpire when Charlotte belonged to an interstate league.

On 5 Apr. 1893 he married Mary Josephine Garrett. They had three children: John Lindsay, Garrett, and Catherine Garrett. Morehead died in Charlotte at age fifty-seven and was buried in the Morehead plot in Elmwood Cemetery.

Lloyd Bronson painted a portrait of Morehead in 1906. A reproduction exists in the family history written by John Motley Morehead III.

SEE: Lindley S. Butler, *Our Proud Heritage* (1971); *Charlotte Observer*, 14 Dec. 1923; *Greensboro Daily News*, 14 Dec. 1923; John Motley Morehead III, *The Morehead Family of North Carolina and Virginia* (1921); Randolph Picton Rixey, *The Rixey Genealogy* (1933); James R. Young, *Textile Leaders of the South* (1963).

CATHERINE L. ROBINSON

Morehead, John Motley, III (3 Nov. 1870–7 Jan. 1965), chemical engineer, inventor, industrialist, and philanthropist, was born in Spray, the only son of James Turner and Mary Elizabeth Connally Morehead. He was the grandson of Governor John Motley Morehead. Graduated from The University of North Carolina in 1891 with a B.S. degree in chemical engineering, he was a member of Phi Beta Kappa.

On leaving Chapel Hill, young Morehead promptly became a chemist for the Willson Aluminum Company, which his father and Thomas L. Willson had founded at Spray, hoping to exploit a new process for the production of aluminum. There James Turner Morehead installed one of the first electric arc furnaces in the United States and on 2 May 1892, while operating it, stumbled onto the first large-scale commercial means of producing calcium carbide, although this point has sometimes been disputed. The elder Morehead later explained: "I didn't know it was calcium carbide. Calcium carbide had never existed. I got a lump of the stuff [slaked lime and tar] about the size of a coconut, and when we put it in water, it gave off clouds of smoke. I didn't have any gas-analyzing equipment, so I sent a piece down here [Chapel Hill] to Dr. F. P. Venable [chairman of the Chemistry Department], and he analyzed the gas and said it was acetylene gas. I analyzed and found we had calcium carbide." He said that Union Carbide had been "born at Spray."

Acetylene gas had been a laboratory curiosity for fifty years. Though Willson Aluminum failed to produce aluminum, it did perfect a practical aluminum alloy, but in 1892 the market for that was limited, nor was there a market for calcium carbide. When the company's operations were drastically curtailed, Morehead's father arranged for him to work in a New York bank. After a brief stay, John Motley went to Westinghouse Electric in Pittsburgh and was graduated from its "expert's course" in 1895. The next year Westinghouse placed him with Consolidated Traction Company of New Jersey.

Meanwhile, in 1894 Morehead's father and Willson had taken fruit jars of carbide to New York and had interested "some capitalists" in forming the Electro-Gas Company to exploit carbide and acetylene. They sold all except the chemical rights to calcium carbide for some cash and stock. Later they produced the first chromium alloy in the country and the first ferrochrome for armor plate steel just in time for the Spanish-American War. (Union Carbide bought out the Willson-Morehead electroalloys business in 1906.) In 1897 John Motley Morehead became associated with the American Calcium Carbide Interest as a construction engineer, supervising the building of plants for the manufacture of calcium carbide and/or acetylene gas in the United States and in various foreign countries. During 1899 he designed an apparatus for analyzing gases, which soon became standard equipment in industrial laboratories, and in 1900 he published his *Analysis of Industrial Gases.*

The Peoples Gas Light and Coke Company of Chicago had taken over Electro-Gas in 1898 and eventually formed Union Carbide. Morehead, while still serving as engineer for Carbide Interest, became chief chemist and engineer of tests for Peoples Gas Light and Coke and moved to Chicago in 1902. Holding both positions, he served as design and construction engineer in charge of the research and development of new processes. In 1910 he completed a course in acetylene welding and cutting at the German Government Imperial School for Machine Building, Cologne.

In 1915 Morehead married Genevieve M. Birkhoff. When the United States entered World War I, he volunteered and, although overage, was commissioned a major in the army. Detailed to the War Industries Board as chief of the Industrial Gases and Gas Products Section, he served under Bernard Baruch. On demobilization, he moved to Rye, N.Y., to be near the Carbide Corporation's laboratories at Niagara Falls and Long Island. In the event his services were needed to review the production of high explosives, he was retained in the reserve for five years.

Morehead served three terms as mayor of Rye between 1925 and 1930, when President Herbert Hoover appointed him minister to Sweden. There, in 1931, he was awarded the gold medal of the Royal Swedish Academy of Sciences, the only foreigner ever to be so honored. Also in 1931 he and his cousin, R. F. Patterson, presented the Morehead-Patterson Bell Tower to The University of North Carolina.

Morehead's wife died on 16 Apr. 1945 in Rye. In the same year he created the John Motley Morehead Foun-

dation at The University of North Carolina. Envisioned were the Morehead Scholars Program, patterned after the Rhodes scholars of Oxford University; the Morehead Building and Planetarium; and the Genevieve B. Morehead Memorial Art Gallery. Morehead saw the foundation as a way to help make his alma mater one of the best universities in the nation.

On 11 May 1948 Morehead married Mrs. Leila Duckworth Houghton. Just a year later he presented the completed Morehead Building to the university. In 1961 he made an additional gift of 50,000 shares of Union Carbide stock to the Morehead Foundation, and his wife, Leila, who died on 22 Oct. 1961, left a bequest of $500,000. Other benefactions in the state included the Morehead stadium and chimes at the Tri-City High School, Leaksville-Draper-Spray [now Eden], and an endowment for the benefit of the Morehead Hospital, Rockingham County.

In 1964 he planned, had built, and gave to Rye, N.Y., a new city hall that he thought was more compatible with the colonial atmosphere of the city than the one projected, for which municipal bonds were to have been sold. He listened to the dedication ceremonies on 5 December by radio from his hospital bed where he was confined with a broken hip, the result of a fall while hurrying from his Union Carbide office to catch his train for Rye. He died a month later. As the major stockholder in Union Carbide, he left the bulk of his estate to the Morehead Foundation. He had no children.

In 1926 The University of North Carolina awarded him an honorary doctorate. Later he also received honorary degrees from Uppsala University in Sweden, Wake Forest, and Davidson.

A contemporary observed: "John Motley Morehead was a man who knew what he wanted and was persistent in getting it." His life exemplified his philosophy as he expressed it at the annual dinners with the graduating Morehead scholars, many of whom called him "Uncle Mot." Of his career he said, "Work is the main road to success," and of his fortune, "Money doesn't bring happiness, but it helps quiet nerves."

SEE: *Chapel Hill Weekly,* 3 Mar. 1958; *Daily Tar Heel,* 25 Sept. 1961; *Durham Morning Herald,* 6 June 1960; *Greensboro Daily News,* 9 Dec. 1962; John Motley Morehead III, *The Morehead Family of North Carolina and Virginia* (1921); *New York Times,* 17 Apr. 1945, 23 Oct. 1961, 25 Nov. 1964, 8, 10 Jan. 1965; Raleigh *News and Observer,* 7 Jan. 1965; Trustees of the Morehead Foundation, *John M. Morehead: A Biographical Sketch* (1954); Union Carbide, "John Motley Morehead: A Retired Union Carbide Executive," 23 July 1963 (mimeographed); Louis R. Wilson, *Louis Round Wilson's Historical Sketches* (1976).

ADA P. HAYLOR

Morgan, Lucy Calista (20 Sept. 1889–3 July 1981), founder of the Penland School of Handicrafts, was born in the Cartoogechaye community of Macon County, the daughter of Alfred and Fannie Eugenia Siler Morgan. She received her earliest education in Hickory at a private school operated by her aunt; afterwards she attended Central Michigan Normal School in Mt. Pleasant, Mich., and became a certified teacher. For several years she taught school in Michigan, Illinois, and Montana, and in the summer of 1916 and 1917 she studied at the University of Chicago. She also worked briefly for the Children's Bureau of Chicago.

From 1920 to 1923 she was principal of the Appalachian School, operated at Penland, N.C., by the Episcopal church. With the decline of that institution, she founded in 1924 a community handicraft program that was later known as the Penland School of Handicrafts. In preparation for this step, she went to Berea College in Kentucky to observe and study the craft activities and training it offered. Through the Penland School, Lucy Morgan aroused the pride of North Carolina mountain people in their traditional crafts and revived skills in weaving, metalwork, wood carving, and jewelry and pottery making which had almost disappeared. A ready market was found for the unique and attractive pieces produced by the local people and the students who soon arrived to learn these crafts. "Miss Lucy," as she was called, conducted tours of the Scandinavian countries to acquaint Americans with crafts there; she also arranged for the exchange of students between her school and similar schools in Finland. Penland was incorporated in 1929 and came under the direction of a board of trustees in 1938. In time it became the largest and the best-known institution of its kind in the United States.

On the eve of World War II, more than sixty looms were in operation at Penland and the school attracted students from many parts of the nation. For her work there Lucy Morgan received honorary degrees and awards of various kinds. On one of these occasions she was characterized as being a teacher, philosopher, humanitarian, and creative artist. On her retirement as director on 1 Sept. 1962, she was succeeded by William J. Brown, who held degrees in the fine arts. Never married, Miss Lucy was survived by a brother and a sister. A member of the Democratic party and the Episcopal church, she was buried in St. John's churchyard, Cartoogechaye.

SEE: *Asheville Citizen-Times*, 12 June 1955, 5 Apr. 1956, 30 Aug. 1962, 4 July 1981; *Charlotte Observer*, 16 June 1940; *Greensboro Daily News*, 4 July 1981; Lucy C. Morgan, with LeGette Blythe, *Gift from the Hills: Miss Lucy Morgan's Story of Her Unique Penland School* (1958); William S. Powell, ed., *North Carolina Lives* (1962); *Who's Who in the South and Southwest* (1952).

WILLIAM S. POWELL

Morgan, Mark (22 Oct. 1837–19 Jan. 1916), Confederate soldier, industrial pioneer, banker, legislator, and philanthropist, was born on a farm near Lillington, Harnett County, the youngest son of Reese (or Reece) (1804–47) and Mary Mathis (1805–92) Morgan. Reese was the son of John Morgan, of Welsh and Scottish ancestry, who emigrated from Pennsylvania (some say Virginia) to the Cape Fear region after 1780; he probably was related to Mark Morgan, settler in Orange County, eponym of Morgan Creek in Chapel Hill, and benefactor of The University of North Carolina, although the relationship has never been established. Reese and Mary gave their sons biblical names. The oldest was David and the fourth, Benjamin; the others were Matthew, Mark, Luke (died in infancy), and John. This pattern was broken for their daughters Maria, Catherine, and Cleopatra.

When Mark was seven, Reese's health failed. Though the child was extremely bright and loved school, he gave it up to take a twelve-hour-a-day job at the Rockfish Manufacturing Company (now Hope Mills), near Fayetteville, where his father had been employed. Mark carried spools and water and acted as bobbin boy to earn fifty cents a week. When Reese died, Mark was already a valued employee. He displayed remarkable mathematical and mechanical abilities and a willingness to work and to assume responsibility. Morgan learned

all aspects of textile manufacturing, made improvements in the mill's machinery, and often forged his own tools for a special job. At twelve he was a spinner and at twenty-four, a supervisor of spinning. With the outbreak of the Civil War in 1861 he, along with other employees of the cotton mill, was "frozen" to the job by Governor John W. Ellis. But Morgan (first lieutenant) and brothers John (sergeant) and Matthew (private) were active members of the Rockfish Liberty Guards. This company was placed under the command of Major Francis S. Childs in Fayetteville and saw intermittent action throughout the war.

On 3 Sept. 1863 Morgan married Margaret Lauder Cameron (1834–1916), a schoolteacher and the daughter of Angus and Katherine Cameron of Johnsonville, Harnett County. They had four children: Marcus Lauder (m. Eugenia Morrison), Lena (m. Eugenia's brother, William H. Morrison, and, after his death, A. A. Malloy), Ida Malloy (died at age two), and Margaret (m. Dr. K. A. Blue and, after his death, A. F. McGuire). When Marcus was born (24 Feb. 1865), Morgan's company had just been called to duty to destroy bridges in the path of General William T. Sherman's army. Taken prisoner, Morgan was paroled by a kindly Union officer on 9 March. Arriving home, he found his house burned, all furniture destroyed except the bed supporting his wife and infant son, and no food anywhere. With fifty dollars in gold and some Confederate currency, the exhausted soldier walked seven miles back to Fayetteville, where he bought nineteen pounds of cornmeal for nineteen dollars. On his return, he learned that the Episcopal priest had brought a gift of bacon from his own meager supply. Sherman burned Rockfish Mill but spared Beaver Creek because it was attached to a gristmill needed to grind Yankee corn. Morgan spent the ensuing months rebuilding Beaver Creek Mill, but late in 1866 he accepted Colonel T. M. Holt's offer of the superintendency of Granite Mills on the Haw River in Alamance County. Here he invented and built by hand a governor for waterwheel gates to turbines, which became a standard device as long as waterpower was used for milling.

Described as five feet seven and slender, with brown hair, neat, short beard, low-pitched voice, and level gaze from piercing hazel eyes, Morgan exhibited a quiet confidence. A later photograph shows him to be stocky, the sadness and strain of the war years finely etched on his face. But he was not wholly solemn—his wit was dry and homespun. The oil portrait hanging in the boardroom of Morgan Mills reveals an undeniable twinkle in his eye. His granddaughter Margaret (Mrs. C. I. Clark, Jr.) remembers how, as a child, she was entertained by his original bedtime tales—one favorite was about a donkey, whose "Hee Haw" he imitated to perfection. He sang in church choirs from an early age and encouraged musical evenings among his mill employees, often playing the fiddle himself.

Morgan built Granite Mills into a leader, but illness forced him to resign in 1870. In 1872, when his health improved, he became superintendent of Colonel Charles Malloy's Laurel Hill Cotton Mill near Laurinburg. He put this mill into top condition and in 1875 and 1880 bought shares in the business, which was renamed Malloy and Morgan. Three additional mills were built: Richmond Cotton Factory (after 1893, Richmond Mill), Ida Yarn Mill (named for Morgan's deceased daughter), and Springfield Cotton Mill, all on the same Gum Swamp stream. After 1880 he also acquired mill interests in McCall, S.C.; became one of the area's leading cotton farmers; helped build the Cottonseed Oil Mill at Gibson, N.C., and establish the First National Bank of Laurinburg; and was named vice-president of the Scotland County Savings Bank and president of Red Springs Cotton Seed Oil and Fertilizer Company. Following the deaths of his son Marcus (1900) and son-in-law William Morrison (1906), both associated with him in the business, Morgan, almost seventy, again shouldered the full burden of the mills and carried on as president until his death.

Having had little formal schooling himself, he became a steadfast champion of education. Besides making private loans to poor, worthy young people for their schooling, Morgan, a staunch Episcopalian, was elected to the board of trustees of Red Springs Seminary (Presbyterian), forerunner of Flora MacDonald College, and in 1904 gave money to build Morgan Hall on campus. His daughter Margaret was the first graduate of the college. In 1905 he built and deeded to the North Carolina diocese an Episcopal church in downtown Laurinburg (now St. David's in Azure Court). The same year he was elected to the North Carolina General Assembly by one of the largest majorities ever returned in the county. He retired after one term. Following a brief illness, he died at his home near Richmond Mill. Funeral services were conducted at the Ida Mill Presbyterian Church before a Masonic burial in the family cemetery nearby.

SEE: Samuel A. Ashe, ed., *Biographical History of North Carolina*, vol. 2 (1905); William Ibbetson Davis, "Mark Morgan: Industrial Pioneer of North Carolina," *The Cotton History Review* 1, no. 2 (April 1960); "History of Morgan Mills, 1867–1958" (manuscript owned by James L. Morgan); *Laurinburg Exchange*, 27 Jan. 1916 (portrait); Malloy and Morgan Papers (Manuscript Department, Duke University Library, Durham).

ERMA WILLIAMS GLOVER

Morgan, Perry (7 Oct. 1884–22 Oct. 1955), Baptist youth leader, was born in Meadow Township of Johnston County, the son of William James and Negelena Barefoot Morgan. They had sixteen children (eight daughters and eight sons)—Minnie, Geronia, Allinia, Sophronia, Naomi, Ethel, Ruth, Nebraska, Philastus, Jasper, Perry, William, Bright, James, Jada, and Harold. The Morgans were "God-fearing" and attached much importance to membership in their rural Baptist church.

In 1890, at age six, Perry Morgan entered the public school at Holly Grove, where he was a student for eight years. He later went to Turlington Institute at Smithfield (1900–1901) after one year at Benson High School. In 1902 he qualified for a provisional teacher's certificate and then taught for four years, first in Johnston County (1902–3) and then in Harnett County (1903–6). Entering the civil service on 2 June 1906, he became a rural mail carrier; working out of the post office at Dunn, he served three separate routes simultaneously. Twelve years later he opened a mercantile business (groceries and feedstuff) in Dunn (1 Jan. 1918–1 Apr. 1920) before embarking on a thirty-five-year career as a professional leader of Baptist youth.

Early in life Morgan had begun teaching a class in his home church Sunday school and for years he served as superintendent. On occasion he was lay pastor of a nearby church, and he spent much of his time each week doing pastoral chores. Having qualified as a magistrate (he was never an ordained minister), he performed marriages and generally ministered to the people of the community. It was with that background, although with very limited formal education, that he was called in 1920 to be secretary of the Baptist Young People's Union of North Carolina. In that post Morgan distinguished himself for his patient, intelligent work among young people and for his development of a strong, inclusive program to train young people in denominational activities.

Speaking of Perry Morgan, a friend one day recalled a story about the famous evangelist Dwight L. Moody. A brash young preacher, fresh from his college graduation, approached Moody and scathingly rebuked him for his poor grammar and his obvious lack of education. Moody replied, "Young man, I use all the grammar I know for the Lord. Do you do as much?" Perry Morgan had Moody's gift, but he was remarkably fluent; moreover, his vast knowledge of the Scriptures and his sincere presentation of the Christian challenge belied any lack of formal schooling. He read widely and became an avid interpreter of principles for good living and faithful service.

In January 1928 Morgan became Sunday school secretary of the North Carolina Baptist State Convention, a position he held for eight years. For the next twelve years (1936–48) he was manager of the Ridgecrest Baptist Assembly, an adjunct of the Southern Baptist Convention. In 1949 he became business manager of the Ridgecrest Camp for Boys, retiring in the late summer of 1954 a few weeks before his seventieth birthday. He then moved to Raleigh and lived with his son, James P., and his wife.

Morgan also served as statistical secretary of the Baptist State Convention for five years and concurrently was director of summer assemblies at Mars Hill and Morehead City and of training schools in local churches throughout the state on a continuous basis. He was a deacon in his local church (Dunn's Tabernacle, Hayes-Barton in Raleigh, and Ridgecrest) and superintendent of the Sunday school. For most of that forty-six-year period, he taught an adult Bible class.

For sixteen years Morgan edited a column in the *Biblical Recorder*, the weekly journal of North Carolina Baptists, and was a contributor to the volume, *North Carolina Baptists at Work, at Home, and Abroad*. For two terms he was president of the Southern Baptist Sunday School and Training Union Field Workers Association. He traveled widely throughout the South on denominational business and was twice a delegate to the Baptist World Alliance (Toronto, 1928; Berlin, 1934). Friends have pointed out that Perry Morgan "knew more Baptists by name in North Carolina than any man in the State at any time in its history."

On 23 Dec. 1908 he married Susan Elizabeth Bell, of Dunn, and they had two children: Margaret, who died in infancy, and James P. The son followed his father in denominational work, both as a local educational director of Baptist churches and later as secretary of the Baptist Training Union of the North Carolina Baptist State Convention. Morgan died in Rex Hospital, Raleigh, just a few days after turning seventy-one. Following a memorial service at the Tabernacle Baptist Church, Raleigh, interment was in the Greenwood Cemetery, Dunn.

SEE: *Biblical Recorder*, 29 Oct. 1955 (portrait); Data File, Baptist Historical Collection (Wake Forest University Library, Winston-Salem); Data File, Southern Baptist Historical Collection (Dargan-Carver Library, Nashville, Tenn.); *Encyclopedia of Southern Baptists*, vol. 2 (1953); Little River Baptist Association Minutes, 1955; *North Carolina Baptist State Convention Annual* (1955 [portrait]).

C. SYLVESTER GREEN

Morgan, Samuel Tate (15 May 1857–16 Apr. 1920), manufacturer of chemical fertilizer, was born in the Fishdam district of Wake County (now a part of Durham County), the son of Samuel Davidson and Talithia Adaline Tate Morgan. Samuel, a farmer, died in 1865. Morgan's early life was spent in comfort on his father's farm. He was educated at Bingham Military School and at nearby Horner Military School. Leaving school in 1874, he began to assist his widowed mother on her plantation. Five years later he moved to the village of Durham, where Julian S. Carr, William T. Blackwell, and the Dukes were gaining national attention with Bull Durham smoking tobacco and Duke's Mixture. There is some evidence that Morgan knew the Duke family from his early years. At first he entered the grain and provision business and also handled chemical fertilizers.

He began his lifework in 1881 with the organization of the Durham Fertilizer Company, which grew into the Virginia-Carolina Chemical Company, chartered in New Jersey on 12 Sept. 1895. The original authorized stock was for $6,500,000. By 1916 the outstanding common stock stood at $27,984,400 and the preferred at $20,000,000. Also by 1916 its output was the largest of any fertilizer company in the world, and the corporation controlled 135 affiliated plants scattered generally over the southeastern United States. Morgan was able to expand the Virginia-Carolina Chemical Company by means of aid from the Dukes. In 1897 Benjamin N. Duke sought assistance for Morgan through Senator Jeter C. Pritchard to reduce the duty on burlap as proposed in the Dingley Tariff Bill. Shortly afterwards, Duke purchased 3,050 shares in Morgan's company. In addition, early in January 1900 Duke supplied approximately $100,000 to increase the capital of VCC, as the company was generally known. Later in the year, however, he decided not to aid Morgan in the purchase of sulfur mines because of his involvement in many other projects, although he believed Morgan's plan to be "a good thing" for the company. Morgan wrote Duke in 1898 that he was going to buy up some plants in South Carolina and Georgia "which with what we have would give us control of the Fertilizer business in the South and enable the Co. to make enormous profits." Morgan laid the matter before James B. Duke and his associates. No available record shows Duke's reaction, but when Morgan died, James B. Duke and several high officials of the American Tobacco Company served as honorary pallbearers. The great profit from stock in the VCC ended with the agricultural depression of the early 1920s and the death of Morgan—almost simultaneous events.

Moving the headquarters of his company to Richmond, Va., in 1896, Morgan soon became immersed in various businesses in that state such as the Merchants National Bank, the Virginia Trust Company, and the Old Dominion Trust Company. His wealth placed him on many other directorates, including those of the Texas and Pacific Railroad, Southern Cotton Oil Company, Mechanics and Metals National Bank of New York, and Charleston Mining and Manufacturing Company. He enjoyed membership in such clubs as the Westmoreland, the Commonwealth Club, the Deep Run Hunt Club, and three groups in New York: the Calumet, the Manhattan, and the New York Yacht Club. Morgan lived in Richmond but maintained an elaborate country place, Meadowbrook, near Curle's Neck, Va.

On 5 Sept. 1875 he married Sally F. Thompson, the daughter of George W. Thompson of Wake County. They had three children: Alice Blanche, Maude Crenshaw, and Samuel Tate, Jr. Morgan, a member of the Baptist church, was a Democrat in name. He was buried in Hollywood Cemetery, Richmond.

SEE: Samuel A. Ashe, ed., *Biographical History of North Carolina*, vol. 5 (1906); Paul B. Barringer, *The Natural Bent* (1949); Benjamin Newton Duke Papers (Manuscript Department, Duke University, Durham); *Report of Federal Trade Commission on the Fertilizer Industry* (19 Aug. 1916); Richmond *Times-Dispatch*, 17–18 Apr. 1920.

NANNIE M. TILLEY

Moro. See **Said, Omar Ibn.**

Morris, Arthur Joseph (5 Aug. 1881–18 Nov. 1973), founder of the Morris Plan Bank and developer of consumer credit, was born in Tarboro, the son of Joseph and Dora Livingston Jacobs Morris. A graduate of the University of Virginia in 1899, he received the LL.B. degree in 1901 and in the same year began practicing law in Norfolk, Va. On 5 Apr. 1905 he married Bertha Myers, and they became the parents of four daughters: Mrs. Earle H. Kincaid, Mrs. E. C. Walton, Mrs. C. Rogers Hall, and Mrs. E. G. Childers.

In 1910 he originated "the Morris Plan" system of consumer banking when he opened his first bank in Norfolk. Three years later, in New York City, he established the first bank holding company in America, the Industrial Finance Corporation, as the parent company of 110 Morris Plan banks in thirty-seven states, organized by Morris with a needed change of laws engineered by him in most of those states. He also originated the concept of insuring consumer loan borrowers and formed the Morris Plan Insurance Society in 1917. In 1921 he organized the Industrial Acceptance Corporation, the first acceptance corporation to discount exclusively automobile dealer paper on a nationwide basis. Morris was the founder of the Bank of Commerce in New York City. He served as chairman of the board of these various corporations and of the New York Morris Plan Bank as well as a director of many others.

Morris's concept of offering consumer credit on a nationwide basis enabled manufacturers and distributors of all types of consumer goods to bring the American economy to a level far above that of any other nation, thereby permitting a corresponding increase in the country's standard of living. Although conservative and old-line bankers initially scorned the idea, banks across the country came to regard consumer credit as an integral and essential part of their function in broadening their services to the public.

Morris belonged to the American Bar Association, American Bankers Association, Virginia State Bar Association, and Association Bar City of New York. A member of the Academy of Political Science and of Phi Beta Kappa, he received an honorary LL.D. degree from the University of Miami in Florida. In recognition of his service as the founder and developer of consumer banking, the American Bankers Association presented Morris with a bronze plaque reproducing his likeness in bas-relief, the first such event in the association's history. The University of Virginia School of Law designated its library the Arthur J. Morris Law Library.

A resident of Ossining, N.Y., he died at North Tarrytown and was buried in the Sleepy Hollow Cemetery. He had been a member of the Republican party and of the Presbyterian church.

SEE: *Appleton's Cyclopedia of American Biography*, vol. 10 (1924); *New York Times*, 20 Nov. 1973; Raleigh *News and Observer*, 21 Nov. 1973; *Time*, 3 Dec. 1973; *Who Was Who in America*, vol. 6 (1976).

THOMAS C. BOUSHELL

Morris, Ellwood (*1814?–3 Apr. 1872*), civil engineer, was born in Pennsylvania. Nothing is known of his parents other than the fact that in 1846 his father, also a civil engineer, was an assistant to Charles Ellet, Jr., engineer and president of the Schuylkill Navigation Company. At age eleven, while a student, Ellwood was living in Bucks County in the household of John D. James, a sixty-one-year-old farmer, conceivably a relative. The Philadelphia city directories for 1843 and 1844 list him as a "conveyancer" of 22 Prune Street (now Anchor Court, near the waterfront). From 1844 to 1847 Morris was a member of the board of managers of the Franklin Institute in Philadelphia (secretary, 1844). He wrote numerous articles on various engineering subjects that were published in the *Journal of the Franklin Institute*. During this period he also was engaged in locating and building the Baltimore and Ohio Railroad. The directories for 1845–47 list him as a civil engineer at the Prune Street address. According to the 1850 census of Schuylkill County, however, Morris was an "agent" living in the household of Elijah Airgood, a thirty-two-year-old canal lock tender.

On 27 Apr. 1859 the state-owned Cape Fear and Deep River Navigation Company of North Carolina appointed Morris chief engineer. A Raleigh newspaper described him as a distinguished civil engineer, "widely known as a scientific writer on matters in the line of his profession, and as chief engineer in various railroads and canals." His experience with hydraulic works, it was reported, "fit him in a pre-eminent degree for the improvement of river navigation." With crews of blacks, including some hired slaves, as well as white laborers hired locally and in Pennsylvania, Morris proceeded to make the Cape Fear River navigable from Wilmington to Averasboro. He submitted frequent reports to Governor John W. Ellis, as well as regular statements of his expenses. The governor and officers of the company visited the work site a number of times during 1859, 1860, and the spring of 1861, when the project was completed.

Various railroad officials also called upon Morris to examine their lines and make recommendations for necessary work. Early in February 1861 he returned home on furlough. Afterwards he informed Governor Ellis that he had been offered an important post with the Lackawanna and Bloomsburg Railroad in Pennsylvania but declined it because he considered himself obligated to North Carolina.

North Carolina's secession from the Union on 20 May 1861 seems to have had no effect on Morris's decision to remain in the state. Earlier, he had switched the scene of his work from the inland waters to the coast and prepared a report on the importance of Ocracoke and Hatteras inlets. Sometime before 20 May he was referred to as Colonel Morris, a title that continued to be applied to him as long as he remained in North Carolina. From 29 April until the end of August 1861, he was busily engaged in supervising the construction of forts and coastal defenses along the Outer Banks. Morris designed and built Fort Oregon, and when a council of war in September resolved to evacuate it, he objected. Both Fort Oregon and Fort Ocracoke, he maintained, were well built, located, and equipped, and they could be held. He did not prevail, of course, and so in August 1861 Federal forces took possession of the sounds of North Carolina, an action later termed "one of the most important events of the war."

In order to gain access to the coal fields along Deep River, the state chartered the Chatham Railroad and appointed Morris the chief engineer responsible for locating and constructing it. By 1 Nov. 1861 he was in Fay-

etteville. He worked well and accurately, and in 1862 and 1863 he reported regularly to Kemp P. Battle and Henry A. London, officers of the line. Work on laying out the route was completed by the fall of 1863. On one occasion he took time out to advise the mayors of Fayetteville and Wilmington concerning the defense of their towns; afterwards he went to Charleston, S.C., for the same purpose but was not well received. Battle noted later that Morris became homesick in 1863 and wanted to go home to visit his aged parents; an assistant, Henry A. Brown, was capable of continuing the work on the railroad. Morris himself, however, wrote that he wished to go to a neutral port, preferably to an English possession, so that he could take steps to secure about $35,000 that he had left in the North; he might lose the money if he remained in the South and did not protect it. Confederate authorities refused to issue him a passport, but with Battle's intervention he obtained documents permitting him to pass through the lines to Newark, N.J.

Morris finally left the state in August 1864. Just before his departure, he asked Battle to care for his cat and pet chickens. After the war, in 1867, he wrote from Camden, N.J., his mother's home, that he had received a cool reception from his Northern neighbors because he had remained in the South. The U.S. Post Office even refused to deliver mail to him. Before leaving North Carolina, Morris assured his friends that he was going for personal—not political—reasons, and that he would return to continue his professional work. He then anticipated that the war would last for some time: "I hope, & always have hoped, that the South would succeed in her objects, because I believe the northern people are *wrong* & *misguided* in this War." Morris counted himself more loyal to the South, he wrote Henry A. London on 5 Mar. 1862, than many there who attacked him for being a Northerner.

On 28 June 1865 Morris wrote a cordial letter to his old friend Kemp P. Battle, thanking him for his efforts the previous August that enabled him to return home. He had found his mother well although feeble, and she also sent her thanks to Battle. Two years later, in May 1867, Morris sent Battle a very long, sympathetic letter about conditions in the South and the reaction of Northern newspaper editors. Morris hoped that white Southerners would remain united politically and that reasonable blacks would join them in establishing a stable government and society.

The 1870 census of the North Ward of the city of Camden lists a household headed by fifty-six-year-old Ellwood Morris, a civil engineer, and twenty-one-year-old Elizabeth Morris, a native of England, whose occupation was "keeping house." Mary Ann Morris, aged sixteen and a native of Pennsylvania, completed the family except for Mary McCue, aged twenty-five and a native of Ireland, who was a domestic servant.

Morris died of dropsy (edema) in Camden at age fifty-nine. His home at 509 Cooper Street, built about 1840, was torn down soon after 1922 to clear the site for an office building.

SEE: John G. Barrett, *The Civil War in North Carolina* (1963); Battle Family Papers and London Family Papers (Southern Historical Collection, University of North Carolina, Chapel Hill); *Camden* (N.J.) *Democrat*, 6 Apr. 1872; Camden, N.J., *West Jersey Press*, 3 Apr. 1872; Robert C. Moon, *The Morris Family of Philadelphia*, vol. 5 (1870); Charles B. Stuart, *Lives and Works of Civil and Military Engineers of America* (1871); Noble J. Tolbert, ed., *The Papers of John Willis Ellis*, 2 vols. (1964); U.S. Census, Bucks and Schuylkill Counties, Pa., 1850, and Camden County, N.J., 1870; War Department Collection of Confederate Records, entry 181 (National Archives Record Group 109 [Staff File], Washington, D.C.); *War of the Rebellion: A Compilation of the Official Records*, ser. 1, vol. 51, part 2 (1897).

WILLIAM S. POWELL

Morris, Naomi Elizabeth *(1 Dec. 1921–11 Sept. 1986)*, lawyer and judge, the daughter of Edward Eugene and Blanche Beatrix Boyce Morris, was born in Spring Hope but the family moved to Wilson when she was a year old. She was graduated from Atlantic Christian College (1943) and from The University of North Carolina Law School (1955), where she was fourth in her class. During World War II she worked for the U.S. Army Signal Corps in Washington, D.C. Before entering law school she was a secretary in a law firm; after receiving her law degree, she joined a firm in Wilson.

In 1967 she was appointed judge of the North Carolina Court of Appeals and the following year she was elected to a full term. Reelected in 1974, she was appointed chief judge of the Court of Appeals, effective 2 Jan. 1979. Naomi Morris was only the second woman in the state to hold such a high judicial position. She retired in December 1982 and returned to her old law firm in Wilson.

During her career Miss Morris received an honorary degree from Atlantic Christian College as well as numerous awards and citations. Active in many state and national professional and political organizations, she was also a trustee of Atlantic Christian College and of the Wilson School of Nursing and a member of the board of associates of Meredith College. A member of the First Baptist Church in Wilson, she was survived by a sister.

SEE: *Chapel Hill Newspaper*, 24 Mar. 1981; *North Carolina Manual* (1981); Raleigh *News and Observer*, 29 July 1979, 7 Jan. 1982, 30 Jan. 1983, 13 Sept. 1986.

WILLIAM S. POWELL

Morrison, Alexander *(1717–28 Jan. 1805)*, physician, author, and Loyalist, was born at Skinidin, Isle of Skye, Scotland. His father was descended from a long line of Highland Scottish physicians; his mother was the daughter of Iain Breac MacLeod, chief of the MacLeod Clan. Morrison entered King's College (now a part of the University of Aberdeen) in 1739 and became a physician. James Macpherson, the alleged translator of the Ossianic poems, visited Morrison in Skinidin in the summer of 1760 and gave him some of the poems he had collected. With the assistance of Morrison and the Reverend A. Gallie, both considered good Gaelic scholars, Macpherson arranged his poems and prepared a version of *Ossian: The Son of Fingal* (1762). Both Gallie and Macpherson were alumni of King's College. Morrison also was coauthor with Macpherson of a volume entitled *Antiquities of Scotland*.

In 1772 rising rents forced Morrison and his family to leave their lands in Scotland and join an emigration of some three hundred Scots to North Carolina. He settled near Carthage. In February 1776 Scottish Loyalists gathered at his home to initiate the recruitment of troops to support the Crown in the Revolutionary War. Morrison raised and commanded a company and was appointed deputy quartermaster general for the Tory forces, only to be captured at Moore's Creek Bridge. A report of the Patriot committee to inquire into the conduct of insurgents and suspected persons, undated from Halifax, stated that Morrison "did actually take up arms, and lead forth to war, as captain of a company[,] thirty-five

men." He was imprisoned at Halifax with James Hepburn, Chaplain John Bethune, Allan MacDonald of Kingsborough and his son Alexander, and other Highland neighbors. Morrison was one of the signers of a petition from a Philadelphia prison requesting permission to return to their families and promising not to support the enemies of America. William Hooper, a North Carolina delegate to the Continental Congress, endorsed this petition for humanitarian reasons.

Paroled in 1777 and exchanged the following year, Morrison was captured at sea in 1779 and jailed at Portsmouth, N.H. Again exchanged, he returned to Scotland in 1779 and soon was able to send for his family in North Carolina. His claim for compensation from the British government in 1783 documented a substantial loss of property in North Carolina—real and personal—and the fact that by this time he was "a cripple from the damps of the Gaols." He died at Greenock, Scotland, at age eighty-eight.

SEE: Peter John Anderson, ed., *Roll of Alumni in Arts of the University and King's College of Aberdeen, 1595–1860* (1900); Walter Clark, ed., *State Records of North Carolina*, vol. 11 (1895); *DNB*, vol. 7 (1909); *The Gentleman's Magazine*, February 1805; Loyalist Claims and English Records (North Carolina State Archives, Raleigh); Blackwell P. Robinson, *A History of Moore County*, vol. 1 (1956); William L. Saunders, ed., *Colonial Records of North Carolina*, vol. 10 (1890).

VERNON O. STUMPF
THOMAS C. PARRAMORE

Morrison, Cameron *(5 Oct. 1869–20 Aug. 1953)*, governor, U.S. senator, and congressman, was born near Rockingham, Richmond County, the son of Daniel M. and Martha Cameron Morrison. Daniel, a Confederate veteran who became a staunch Republican during the postwar years, was at one time or another a farmer, carpenter-contractor, deputy sheriff of Richmond County, and postmaster of Rockingham.

Cameron Morrison attended the public schools of Rockingham and the academy of N. C. McCaskill in Ellerbe Springs. After completing his formal education, he had various jobs in and around Rockingham for several years. He subsequently read law under the supervision of Judge Robert P. Dick of Greensboro and in 1892 was licensed to practice. Morrison remained in Rockingham until 1905, when he moved to Charlotte, his permanent residence for the remainder of his life.

He first became active in Richmond County politics while still not of voting age. Due largely to paternal influence, he was in his youth an avowed Republican. In August 1890 Morrison, then only twenty, was elected to the executive committee of the state Republican party. The following year, however, he resigned, renounced the Republican party, and became a Democrat. In the bitterly contested white supremacy campaigns of 1898–1900, he won recognition as a leader of the "Red Shirt" movement. The unruly and boisterous Red Shirts specialized in harassing Republican candidates and in intimidating black voters. According to Morrison, his followers never "bullied or beat" blacks—just scared them.

During his early political career, Morrison served as mayor of Rockingham in the mid-1890s and won a seat in the state senate in 1900. Thereafter, until his elevation to the governorship, he held no other public office. But he continued to be active in state politics, serving often as a delegate to state Democratic conventions. Throughout this period, he was allied with the party's conservative faction headed by Senator Furnifold M. Simmons.

With the support of the Simmons organization, Morrison won the Democratic gubernatorial nomination in 1920. In the hard-fought primary campaign, his opponents were the incumbent lieutenant governor, O. Max Gardner, and former congressman Robert Newton Page. Morrison subsequently defeated Republican John J. Parker in the general election.

Impulsive, emotional, and "bluff and hearty in his bearing and manner," Morrison was easily one of the more colorful public figures in the North Carolina of his day. But there was little reason to suspect that as governor he would provide anything other than unimaginative, routine leadership. His administration, however, proved to be one of the most constructive in the state's history.

Inaugurated on 12 Jan. 1921, Morrison promptly endorsed the goals of both the Good Roads and educational reform movements. In response to his demands, as well as to pressure from the Good Roads organizations, the General Assembly enacted the historic Highway Act of 1921, enlarging the powers of the Highway Commission and providing for a $50 million bond issue with which to initiate the construction of a 5,500-mile state highway system. In 1923 the legislature, at the behest of the governor, authorized an additional $15 million in road bonds. Substantially completed by the end of Governor Angus McLean's administration (1925–29), the successful and popular highway program begun during the Morrison era was an important factor in North Carolina's emergence in the 1920s as a modern commonwealth.

While best known today as the state's "Good Roads Governor," Cameron Morrison took equal pride in his contributions to enhance educational and charitable institutions. Under pressure from both the governor and citizens' groups, the 1921 General Assembly committed North Carolina to an ambitious six-year, $20 million expansion program at the overcrowded state institutions of higher learning and at the dozen or so state-operated insane asylums, reformatories, sanatoriums, and schools for the deaf and blind. Moreover, in 1921 the operating budgets for these facilities, as well as for the State Board of Health, were significantly increased.

During the administration of Morrison's predecessor, Governor Thomas W. Bickett (1917–21), public education in North Carolina had experienced a genuine revival. With Morrison's active support, the legislatures of 1921 and 1923 expanded the school programs of the preceding administration. Appropriations for the Department of Public Instruction were considerably enlarged, a loan fund for schoolhouse construction was increased from $1 to $10 million, and the county tax structure was reformed to compel more generous local support for the schools. Morrison, on the other hand, performed a disservice to public education when in 1924 he publicly endorsed the antievolution crusade and used his influence as ex officio chairman of the State Board of Education to ban the use of high school biology textbooks that discussed the theory of evolution.

Morrison took a special interest in policies designed to stimulate the economic well-being of the state. His "Live-at-Home" program of 1922 encouraged crop diversification among farmers, and his half-million-dollar fisheries program of 1923 sought to promote the commercial fishing industry. In 1923 he recommended the establishment of a State Department of Commerce and Industry, but the General Assembly rejected his suggestion.

Far and away the most controversial of Governor Morrison's proposals relating to economic development was one calling for a $8½ million bond issue to finance the construction of state-owned port terminal facilities at one or more coastal towns and to establish a state-owned ship line between these points and the seaports of the industrial Northeast. Morrison argued that implementation of his ship and port terminal plan would stimulate commercial development of the state's eastern seaboard, encourage the growth of a seaport in North Carolina rivaling those of Norfolk and Charleston, and compel railroads operating between the state and the great commercial centers of the North to reduce their freight rates. Denounced by many prominent leaders in the state as "socialistic" or as economically unsound, the ship and port terminal proposal was defeated in a referendum in 1924 by an electorate already disturbed by the enormity of the state's debt.

During the Morrison administration North Carolina's bonded debt increased from approximately $12 million to $107 million. This indebtedness alarmed fiscal conservatives and led to frequent warnings that North Carolina was rapidly spending itself into bankruptcy. But at no time in the years that followed did the state default on the bonds issued during this period. On the other hand, a deficit, arising from the failure of the governor and the General Assembly to support a sufficient increase in taxes, occurred in the state's current operating fund during the Morrison administration. The State Budget Commission calculated the amount of the accrued deficit to be $9.4 million as of 30 June 1925, $1.3 million of which was attributed to the earlier Bickett administration. During the term of Governor Angus W. McLean (1925–29), this deficit was funded, state taxes were increased slightly, and in 1929 McLean was able to bequeath a $2.5 million surplus to his successor, O. Max Gardner.

While decidedly a traditionalist in his views on the Negro, Morrison made a sincere effort as governor to improve race relations in the state. In 1921 he summoned a conference of prominent black and white citizens, out of which evolved the North Carolina Commission on Interracial Co-operation. More significantly, he took a vigorous stand against lynching. Due largely to Morrison's policy of dispatching troops to a locality at the slightest hint of impending violence, no lynchings occurred in North Carolina during the last three and one-half years of his term. "I want to let the world know," he declared in 1922, "that lynchings have ended in North Carolina."

Although Morrison was later a U.S. senator (1930–33) and a congressman (1943–45), he is best remembered, and rightly so, for his progressive achievements as governor. To be sure, he was either indifferent to, or opposed outright, such old-style progressive reforms as workmen's compensation legislation, child labor laws, and woman suffrage. But he did favor enlarged state services and economic development schemes. Thus he supported increased appropriations for education, public health, and care of the handicapped and advocated the highway, fisheries, and port terminal programs. That North Carolina acquired a reputation in the 1920s as the South's most progressive state may be attributed in large measure to the policies of his administration.

By all accounts Morrison possessed many admirable qualities as governor, such as boldness, determination, and vision. But he was also inclined to be intemperate and disputatious. Sensitive to criticism, he was frequently at odds with two of the most influential newspapers in the state, the *Greensboro Daily News* and the Raleigh *News and Observer*.

On the expiration of his term in January 1925, Cameron Morrison, dejected by criticism of his spending policies and by the defeat of his port terminal plan, retired to Charlotte. Having recently married the widow of George Washington Watts, the millionaire Durham financier, he could now afford a life of relative ease. He remained active in state politics, however, virtually until his death twenty-eight years later.

Morrison was among those Democrats in North Carolina who, while rejecting the leadership of Senator Furnifold M. Simmons, elected to support the 1928 national ticket headed by Governor Alfred E. Smith of New York. Two years later he backed Josiah Bailey, once a harsh critic of the Morrison administration, in Bailey's successful primary campaign against Senator Simmons. Later in 1930, when the state's junior senator, Lee S. Overman, died, Governor O. Max Gardner appointed Morrison to Overman's vacant Senate seat.

Seeking election to a full Senate term, Morrison entered the Democratic senatorial primary of 1932. Although endorsed by most of the state's leading Democrats, he was defeated in the primary by Robert R. Reynolds of Asheville. Ten years later, in 1942, Morrison was elected to Congress from the newly created Tenth Congressional District. In the House he generally supported the wartime domestic and foreign policies of President Franklin D. Roosevelt. His last attempt at public office came in 1944, when he and several lesser candidates were defeated by Clyde R. Hoey for the Senate seat vacated by Reynolds.

In 1952 Morrison, then eighty-two but still vigorous, headed the North Carolina delegation to the Democratic National Convention in Chicago. Although initially opposed to the nomination of Adlai E. Stevenson, he later campaigned in North Carolina on behalf of the party's nominee.

In 1905 Morrison married Lottie May Tomlinson of Durham. The couple had four children, only one of whom, Angelia (Mrs. James J. Harris), survived infancy. Mrs. Morrison died in 1919, and in 1924 Morrison remarried, taking as his second wife Mrs. Sara Virginia Watts, the widow of George Washington Watts. Cameron Morrison died while vacationing in Quebec City, Canada. He was buried in Elmwood Cemetery, Charlotte.

SEE: Cecil K. Brown, *The State Highway System of North Carolina* (1931); Burke Davis, "Life and Times of Cameron Morrison," *Charlotte News*, 18–22 Nov. 1947; Nathaniel F. Magruder, "The Administration of Governor Cameron Morrison of North Carolina, 1921–1925" (Ph.D. diss., University of North Carolina, 1968); Cameron Morrison Papers (North Carolina State Archives, Raleigh); *North Carolina Biography*, vol. 5 (1919); Elmer L. Puryear, *Democratic Party Dissension in North Carolina, 1928–1936* (1962); William H. Richardson, comp., and David L. Corbitt, ed., *Public Papers and Letters of Cameron Morrison: Governor of North Carolina, 1921–1925* (1927).

NATHANIEL F. MAGRUDER

Morrison, Fred Wilson *(29 Oct. 1890–2 Mar. 1985)*, attorney, educator, and public official, was born in Pioneer Mills, Cabarrus County, the son of Columbus H. and Palmyra (Pallie) S. Pharr Morrison. He received both bachelor's and master's degrees from The University of North Carolina in 1913 and later earned a doctor of philosophy degree from Columbia University. After serving as principal of the New Bern High School in 1913–14, he was superintendent of the Chapel Hill school system from 1914 to 1924 except for service in 1918 during World War I.

In 1924 Morrison went to Greensboro, where he became a member of the education department at the North Carolina College for Women. After two years, at the request of Governor Angus W. McLean, he took a leave of absence (but, in fact, did not return) to serve as executive secretary of a special education commission (1925–27) to study and report on the administration and financing of the state's public schools. After this project was completed, the next governor, O. Max Gardner, prevailed upon Morrison to undertake a similar examination of the State Tax Commission. He also served as secretary of the commission named to plan the consolidation of three of the state's institutions of higher education into the University of North Carolina system. Governor Gardner convinced Morrison that he should study law, and this he did in the evenings of 1929–33, passing the state bar examination early in 1933.

In the interim, however, during the period of the Great Depression, the governor named Morrison director of relief with authority to distribute North Carolina's share of the $300 million loaned to the states by the federal government for unemployment relief. Among the projects under his direction was the assignment of about 5,000 men in the state to work with the U.S. Forest Service, the U.S. Department of Labor, and the army in the early stages of creating the Great Smoky Mountains National Park.

After the expiration of his gubernatorial term, Gardner chose to practice law in Washington, D.C., and he invited Morrison to join him. Among Morrison's early assignments in this new position was as Gardner's assistant counsel for the Rayon Industry of the United States. While Gardner divided his time between New York and Washington, Morrison remained in the Washington office.

Throughout his life Fred Morrison was a shy and private person, yet he had a great concern for people, especially North Carolinians. Among his earliest benefactions were scholarships established at the Woman's College of the University of North Carolina in honor of his mother. He next provided scholarships at the University of North Carolina in Chapel Hill in honor of his father. The firm of Gardner and Morrison offered its services without charge in securing a satisfactory outcome of the bequest that brought the Ackland Art Center to The University of North Carolina. Morrison also was instrumental, as an attorney, in directing others to benefit the university. He was a generous donor towards the establishment of Educational Television at The University of North Carolina. In 1977 he endowed the Fred W. Morrison Southern Studies Fund to enable The University of North Carolina Press to expand its program of publishing books on the South. Morrison and his wife contributed generously towards the acquisition of land for the expansion of the Fort Raleigh National Historic Site on Roanoke Island and in support of the outdoor drama, *The Lost Colony*. Other of Morrison's benefactions, unpublicized at his request, may come to light in the future.

Morrison married Emma Neal McQueen of Laurinburg, and they were the parents of a daughter, Myra. He was buried in Salisbury.

SEE: *Chapel Hill Newspaper*, 3, 5 Mar. 1985; Daniel L. Grant, *Alumni History of the University of North Carolina, 1795–1924* (1924); Raleigh *News and Observer*, 6 Aug. 1932, 3, 9 Apr. 1933, 1 Jan. 1943, 8 Jan. 1945, 1 June 1952, 10 Sept. 1961

WILLIAM S. POWELL

Morrison, Robert Hall *(8 Sept. 1798–13 May 1889)*, first president of Davidson College and for sixty-five years an active Presbyterian minister, was born in the Rocky River section of Cabarrus County, the son of William—Revolutionary soldier, farmer, and miller—and Abigail McEwen Morrison, both of Scottish descent. He attended the Rocky River Academy and was thoroughly schooled by the Reverend John Makemie Wilson, D.D., the local minister. Morrison entered The University of North Carolina in 1816 as a sophomore and was graduated with honors in the class of 1818. This was a distinguished class in which James Knox Polk took first honors. Subsequently, Morrison taught school and studied theology with Wilson and the Reverend John Robinson of the Poplar Tent Presbyterian Church. Their example did much to lead him into the Christian ministry.

After briefly attending Princeton College (which awarded him an honorary A.M. in 1824), Morrison was licensed by the Concord Presbytery and accepted a call from Providence Church in Mecklenburg County. In 1822, after two years at Providence, he relocated in Fayetteville, where he served a church and established the *North Carolina Telegram*, the first religious gazette in the South. In 1827 Morrison returned to Mecklenburg County as pastor of the venerable Sugar Creek Presbyterian Church and a smaller Charlotte congregation. This arrangement continued until 1833, when he became full-time minister at Sugar Creek.

Meanwhile, Morrison had become deeply interested in founding a denominational college in the "Western region." Like many other devout Christians, he had come to believe that secular institutions, such as his alma mater, were increasingly unsuited to prepare an educated clergy. Accordingly, in March 1835 he proposed that the Concord Presbytery found a "Manual Labor School"; from this suggestion grew the plan to establish Davidson College, named for Revolutionary hero General William Lee Davidson. Later that year Morrison prepared a feasibility study and proposed a tentative curriculum. Then he and the Reverend Patrick Jones Sparrow, of Salisbury, were assigned the unenviable task of raising the requisite funds. They secured $30,000, and on 10 Apr. 1836 the Presbytery laid the chapel cornerstone. Morrison addressed a large audience on "the importance of learning generally, and especially of a learned ministry to the happiness of a community, and the security of a free and religious government." The trustees first offered the presidency of the new institution to Samuel B. Wilson, of Fredricksburg, Va. After he declined it, the trustees selected Morrison.

When Morrison took up residence at Davidson in February 1837, the campus consisted of the president's home, one professor's home, a steward's hall, and sixteen small, crowded dormitories set amid a sylvan environment. During the first session (spring 1837), about sixty students enrolled and three professors, including Morrison, did all the teaching. Later a manual labor system—which Morrison warmly supported—was instituted. Under the program, each student was required to work on some mechanical or agricultural project for three hours on weekdays, with wages to be applied against his bill for room and board. This system resulted in widespread discontent and malingering. The period of labor was soon reduced to two hours and after three years was abandoned altogether. A student in these early years remembered President Morrison as a versatile teacher and a powerful preacher. However, personal tragedy and illness sapped Morrison's morale and strength. Two young daughters died of diphtheria in April 1838, and, though he faced this calamity with characteristic fortitude, the loss was a heavy blow. Morrison himself soon developed a serious throat ailment

that affected his speech. In January 1839 the Davidson trustees authorized an extended leave, while urging him to retain the presidency. When northern specialists and rest did not cure the malady, Morrison resigned in 1849 and retired to his Lincoln County farm, where he resided until his death.

Fortunately, the growing Morrison family was easily accommodated in Cottage Home, a three-story farmhouse in eastern Lincoln inherited from Mrs. Morrison's father, General Joseph Graham. With four hundred acres here and several hundred in western Tennessee, there were no inordinate financial problems. The Morrison progeny fondly remembered Cottage Home as stimulating socially and intellectually. By 1842 Morrison had recovered sufficiently to become pastor of the Unity church, which his family attended. In time he also preached regularly at Machpelah and Castanea Presbyterian churches. He served all three—widely different in level of education and social status—for approximately forty years. Although he rarely left his home community, Morrison was one of the best-known preachers in North Carolina. In addition to preaching and studying theology, he was interested in scientific agriculture generally and silk production in particular. Nevertheless, his farm income was largely dependent on such staples as corn, wheat, cotton, and livestock.

While Morrison took no active role in public affairs, he was unusually well informed on current issues. A Union Whig, he opposed secession, but, as many like-minded Southerners, he felt obliged to support the Confederacy. He and his wife, Mary Graham Morrison (1801–64), had eight daughters and four sons, many of whom were deeply involved in the Civil War. The Morrison children included Isabella Sophia (1825–1904), wife of Confederate Lieutenant General Daniel Harvey Hill; Major William Wilberforce (1826–65); Harriet Abigail (1828–97); Mary Anna (1831–1915), second wife of Lieutenant General Thomas J. (Stonewall) Jackson; Eugenia Erixene (1833–58), wife of Brigadier General Rufus Barringer; Sarah (1834–38); Elizabeth Lee (1837–38); Susan Washington (1838–86), wife of Major Alphonso Calhoun Avery; Laura Panthea (1840–1920), wife of Colonel John Edmunds Brown; Captain Joseph Graham (1842–1906); Robert Hall (1843–1922), M.D.; and Alfred James (1849–76), who had a promising but brief career as a Presbyterian minister.

Although Robert Hall Morrison's long life was punctuated by personal grief, he never despaired or lost his faith. He died at age ninety-one, well-loved and venerated, and was buried at Machpelah Church in Lincoln County.

SEE: Eugenia Lore and Robert Hall Morrison, *The Morrison Family of the Rocky River Settlement of North Carolina* (1950); Franklin Brevard McDowell, *The Broad Axe and the Forge* (1897); Neill R. McGeachy, *A History of the Sugar Creek Presbyterian Church* (1954); Robert Hall Morrison Collection (Southern Historical Collection, University of North Carolina, Chapel Hill); J. G. Ramsay, "The Administration of the Rev. R. H. Morrison, D.D.," in *Davidson College Semi-Centenary Addresses* (1887); Jethro Rumple, *The History of Presbyterianism in North Carolina* (1966); Cornelia R. Shaw, *Davidson College* (1923); Charles L. Van Noppen Papers (Manuscript Department, Duke University Library, Durham); Max Williams, ed., *Papers of William A. Graham*, vols. 5–6 (1857–65).

MAX R. WILLIAMS

Morson, Hugh (*19 July 1850–29 Mar. 1925*), educator, was born near Fredericksburg, Va., the son of Dr. Hugh, a surgeon in the U.S. Navy, and Rosalie Lightfoot Morson; earlier Morsons emigrated from Scotland. Morson prepared for college at the academy of Judge Coleman of Fredericksburg. Entering the University of Virginia in 1869, he obtained diplomas in chemistry, moral philosophy, Latin, Greek, and modern languages in 1871 but did not earn a titled degree. During the latter year he tutored in the family of Colonel Thomas Carter of King William County, Va. In 1874 Morson moved to Hillsborough, N.C., where he taught Latin and Greek and was assistant principal in the military academy of Horner and Graves.

In 1877 he began teaching in Raleigh in the school of the Reverend J. M. Atkinson, a Presbyterian clergyman, and his son-in-law, Major Charles D. Scott. The next year Morson assumed leadership of the Lovejoy Academy (named for Jefferson Madison Lovejoy, a native of Vermont), on Burke Square, with John Fray, a former Confederate army officer, marking the onset of the Raleigh Male Academy. When construction of the Executive Mansion began on Burke Square, the academy moved into a new building (completed in 1891) on a block diagonally southeast from the old site, bounded by Jones, Bloodworth, Edenton, and East streets. The partnership with Fray ended with Fray's death in 1885. Captain Claude B. Denson, another former Confederate army officer, then became joint master, and for thirteen years the Morson-Denson Academy was considered to be the leading school for boys in Raleigh because of its high scholastic standards. After Denson's death, Morson maintained the Raleigh Male Academy until he assumed the principalship of Raleigh High School when it opened on 18 Sept. 1905. The new public high school first occupied six rooms in the Centennial School on lower Fayetteville Street. By 1920 Morson was principal emeritus, but he continued to carry a full load of classes as a Latin teacher. When his health failed in 1924, he relinquished all duties and took a leave of absence.

At the Raleigh Male Academy, Professor Morson, a strict disciplinarian, was assisted one year by Charles Lee Smith, later president for one year of Mercer University in Macon, Ga. When the Raleigh High School moved to Morgan Street in 1908, Morson was assisted by Mrs. J. M. Barbee, Miss Eliza Pool, Mrs. M. B. Terrell, Miss Daisy Waite, and C. S. Teeble. Frank P. Graham, later president of The University of North Carolina, began his teaching career as an English instructor in the Raleigh High School (1909–11). Distinguished North Carolinians who had studied under Morson's direction included U.S. Senator Josiah W. Bailey, Joseph B. Cheshire, Jr., Charles E. Johnson, attorney William T. Joyner, and surgeon Dr. Hubert A. Royster, all of whom attended the Raleigh Male Academy; J. Melville Broughton, governor and U.S. senator, and Marshall De Lancey Haywood, librarian and local historian, who were students at the Morson-Denson Academy; and Dr. Ivan M. Procter, gynecologist, who attended the Raleigh High School.

In 1879 Morson married Sallie Todd Field (1852–1932) of Front Royal, Va. They resided in the Oakwood section of Raleigh and were the parents of four children: Harriet (1880–1966), Hugh Alexander (1881–1956), William Field (1885–1964), and John Lightfoot (1888–1969). Morson was a member of the Church of the Good Shepherd, where he served as junior warden (twenty-five years), senior warden, secretary of the vestry, and Sunday school teacher. He also was secretary of St. John's Guild and a founding spirit of St. John's Hospital, Raleigh's first hospital. He was buried in the family plot at Oakwood Cemetery.

On 2 Sept. 1924, a new high school, designed by C. Gadsden Sayre and located at 301 East Hargett Street, was named in his honor. The initial act of the parent-teacher organization, formed in 1925, was to present the school with an oil portrait of Morson. In 1955, when the city school system was reorganized, Hugh Morson High School became a junior high school; in 1965 the building and lot were purchased by the federal government and the school was discontinued.

SEE: Mrs. J. M. Barbee, *Raleigh Public Schools* (1943); Josephus Daniels, *Tar Heel Editor* (1939); Marshall De Lancey Haywood, *Builders of the Old North State* (1968); Hugh Morson Junior High School Library Files; Ivan Procter, *The Life of Ivan Marriott Procter* (1964); *Raleigh Magazine* (Wake Bicentennial Issue, 1971); Raleigh *News and Observer*, 30 Mar. 1925; *Raleigh Times*, 5 Mar., 14 May, 3 Sept., 27 Nov. 1965, 18 Sept. 1973; Tombstone inscriptions, Oakwood Cemetery, Raleigh; University of Virginia Matriculation Book (University of Virginia Library, Charlottesville).

GRADY L. E. CARROLL

Moseley, Edward *(ca. 1682–July 1749)*, colonial official, may have been the single most important political figure in the first half of the eighteenth century in North Carolina. He was a man of great and varied skills: politician, surveyor, book collector, vestryman, planter, and attorney. While several important families participated in North Carolina politics during Moseley's career—the Pollocks, Swanns, and Moores, for instance—none of them produced any single figure who could match Moseley's influence or durability.

Moseley apparently was born and educated in London. William Byrd says of him in *The Secret History of the Dividing Line*: "Plausible [Moseley] had been bred in Christ's Hospital and had a tongue as smooth as the Commissary, and was altogether as well qualified to be of the Society of Jesus." Of Moseley's early life little is known except that in December 1697, at age fifteen, he was apprenticed from Christ's Hospital (an orphanage) "in the Practice of Navigation" to serve on the ship *Joseph* under Jacob Foreland in the Bilbao trade. In May 1703 he was in Charles Town, S.C., cataloging books sent there by Thomas Bray of the Society for the Propagation of the Gospel in Foreign Parts. About a year later he immigrated to the Albemarle region of North Carolina and in 1705 made a "good match" by marrying Henderson Walker's widow, Anne. Settling in the northeastern portion of Chowan Precinct, Moseley began carving out a sizable place for himself in North Carolina politics and society.

An enumeration of Moseley's major offices in the colony is impressive. He was a justice of the peace and vestryman for Chowan in 1705; a member of the Proprietary Council during 1705–7, 1709–11, and 1723–24; speaker of the Assembly in 1708, 1722–23, and 1731–34 (he served as an assemblyman in virtually every session from 1708 to 1734, when he was not serving on the Council); a member of the royal Council from 1734 until his death; surveyor general in 1706; treasurer for the whole province from 1715 to 1735 and then for the southern district until his death; judge of vice admiralty in 1725; chief justice of the General Court from 1744 to 1745; and a member of the boundary commissions with Virginia in 1709 and 1728 and with South Carolina in 1737. In 1743 he was named baron of the Exchequer.

As speaker of the Assembly in 1708, he engineered the seating of delegates favorable to Thomas Cary in his struggle with William Glover for control of the governorship. Despite his Anglican connections, Moseley remained a supporter of Cary throughout the rebellion that took his name. Indeed, in 1713 Thomas Pollock wrote that Moseley "was the chief contriver and carry-er on of Col. Cary's rebellion." Throughout his career Moseley was frequently in conflict with certain factions in the colony, particularly those associated with long-settled families like the Pollocks. Late in 1718 he combined with Colonel Maurice Moore in an effort to discredit Governor Charles Eden and his associate Tobias Knight because of their relations with Edward Teach, the notorious Blackbeard. Moseley and Moore guided the overland expedition under Ellis Brand of Virginia to Bath County in an effort to trap Teach ashore. In December 1718 they broke into the house of Secretary John Lovick in an attempt to examine Council records for incriminating evidence against Eden and Knight. When Moseley and Moore were tried the following year, the event was a sensation. Moseley was fined and barred from public office for three years, but both Eden and Knight suffered irreparable damage to their political reputations.

Significantly, Moseley moved from Chowan to Rocky Point on the northeastern branch of the Cape Fear in 1735. He had taken as his second wife (on the death of his first) Ann Sampson, the stepdaughter of James Hasell, who had ties to that region. Moseley was also clearly attracted by the rapid development that had begun in the Lower Cape Fear late in the 1720s. Finally, in November 1734 he had accepted elevation to the royal Council and thus resigned his long leadership of the lower house. As a master tactician, Moseley knew that his voice would carry more weight for the Lower Cape Fear in the Council than it could in the Albemarle-dominated Assembly.

Moseley was soon embroiled in conflicts in the Council. He sided with the Moores against Governor Gabriel Johnston in the battle for supremacy between Newton (later Wilmington) and Brunswick town as ports of entry on the Lower Cape Fear. Apart from his past association with Maurice Moore, Moseley had been angered during 1735 by the governor's criticism of his part in the blank patent controversy under Governor Sir Richard Everard. Throughout his career as a royal councillor, Moseley consistently supported measures he believed to be favorable to growth in the Lower Cape Fear.

Few accounts of Moseley permit us a glimpse of his character. Despite the generally unfavorable portrait of him by William Byrd in the *Secret History*, Byrd readily concedes that Moseley was the man to whom the North Carolina commissioners looked for leadership as well as the man whom the Virginians had to persuade when any substantive conflict arose. Interestingly, while Byrd refers to the other North Carolina commissioners as Judge Jumble, Shoebrush, and Puzzlecause, he calls Moseley, Plausible. Attesting to Moseley's skill as a surveyor is the magnificent map of North Carolina published in 1733 that bears his name.

Moseley's association with books in South Carolina long remained a part of his life. In 1723 he donated seventy-six volumes (primarily theological works and church history) to Edenton to serve as the basis of a public library. At his death, his personal library exceeded four hundred volumes. He died possessing plantations in Chowan, Edgecombe, New Hanover, and other counties with a total acreage of over thirty thousand. He also owned at least ninety slaves. Moseley was survived by his wife, five sons, and a daughter.

SEE: William Byrd, *Prose Works: Narratives of a Colonial Virginian* (1966); Walter Clark, ed., *State Records of North Carolina*, vols. 22–23 (1904–7); J. Bryan Grimes, ed., *North Carolina Wills and Inventories* (1912); Charles T. Laugher, *Thomas Bray's Grand Design* (1973); *Present State and List of the Children of his late Majesty King Charles II; His New Royal Foundation, in Christ's Hospital* (1766); William S. Price, Jr., *North Carolina Higher-Court Records, 1702–1708* (1974) and *North Carolina Higher-Court Minutes, 1709–1723* (1977); William L. Saunders, ed., *Colonial Records of North Carolina*, vols. 2–4 (1886); Stephen B. Weeks, "Libraries and Literature in North Carolina in the Eighteenth Century," *Annual Report of the American Historical Association* (1896).

WILLIAM S. PRICE, JR.

Moseley, William Dunn (*1 Feb. 1795–4 Jan. 1863*), first governor of Florida, was born at Moseley Hall in Lenoir County, the son of Matthew and Elizabeth Herring Dunn Moseley. A descendant of colonial official Edward Moseley, he was graduated from The University of North Carolina in 1818 and received an M.A. degree in 1821. In 1817 he served as a tutor at the university, but after his graduation he studied law, was licensed to practice, and opened an office in Wilmington. Like many young lawyers of the time, while trying to establish a practice he farmed and taught school. Moseley represented his native county in the state senate continuously from 1829 to 1837 and served as speaker for the four terms between 1832 and 1835.

After ending his legislative service in North Carolina, Moseley moved to Jefferson County, Fla., where he had purchased a plantation. In 1840 he was elected to the Florida territorial house of representatives, and four years later he won a seat in the territorial senate. In 1845 he was elected the first governor of the state of Florida, taking office on 25 June. Among his duties were the establishment of a state government, overseeing the state's role in the War with Mexico, and resolving conflicts between white settlers and Seminole Indians. It was also during his administration that the federal government built Fort Jefferson on one of the coral keys off the southern coast of his state and Fort Clinch in Fernandina. Constitutionally limited to a single term, Moseley returned to his plantation in 1849. Two years later he settled in the town of Palatka, where he stayed the remainder of his life.

In 1822 Moseley married Susan Hill, and they became the parents of six children. After his death a portrait, painted from a daguerreotype, was presented by two of his daughters to be hung in a state portrait gallery in the Florida capitol.

SEE: John L. Cheney, Jr., ed., *North Carolina Government, 1585–1979* (1981); Daniel L. Grant, *Alumni History of the University of North Carolina, 1795–1924* (1924); Robert Sobel and John Raimo, *Biographical Dictionary of the Governors of the United States, 1789–1978*, vol. 1 (1978); Stephen B. Weeks Scrapbook, vol. 7 (North Carolina Collection, University of North Carolina, Chapel Hill); John H. Wheeler, ed., *Reminiscences and Memoirs of North Carolina and Eminent North Carolinians* (1884).

WILLIAM S. POWELL

Moses, Edward Pearson (*24 July 1857–12 Nov. 1948*), educator, was born in Knoxville, Tenn., the son of John L. of Exeter, N.H., and Susan Williams Moses of Knoxville. Threatened by Union forces during the Civil War, the family moved to Exeter when Edward was seven, and for the next four years he was educated in the town's excellent public school system. Later in life he would say that he wished every child in the South could have the same "fine education" he had received in Exeter. After the war his family returned to Knoxville, where, at age seventeen, he was graduated from East Tennessee College (later the University of Tennessee) with both B.A. and M.A. degrees. He immediately began teaching in the Knoxville public schools, where he was influential in the establishment of a graded system and new methods of instruction—particularly the use of phonetics in spelling lessons. At age twenty Moses became principal of the Boys' High School of Knoxville (1877–81).

Moving to North Carolina, he was superintendent of public schools in Goldsboro (1881–85) and then Raleigh (1885–95 and 1898–1907). Although successful in both systems, he is noted especially for his innovations and achievements in Raleigh.

Over the years, North Carolina's public school system had suffered from the lack of financial and political backing. When Moses arrived in Raleigh, the city's system was just beginning to gain support—a new elementary school was opened at the time of his installation. Continuing the momentum, he made similar advancements throughout the next two decades. By the end of his term in 1907, five graded schools and one high school had been purchased or built in Raleigh. Moses introduced the graded school and the nine-month school term to the Raleigh system, as well as new ideas in teaching. He believed that reforms in education should begin at the elementary level and in this regard was influenced by the work of J. H. Pestalozzi, a Swiss educator.

Between 1895 and 1898 Moses was a professor of pedagogy at Winthrop College in South Carolina before he was recalled to Raleigh. After his return, he initiated an industrial arts program in the city schools. He also served as superintendent of the Summer Normal School at The University of North Carolina and as vice-president of the North Carolina Teachers' Assembly (1885–86). He promoted the idea of the North Carolina Historical Commission and was influential in having a resolution passed for its establishment. In addition, Moses was one of the first members of the Watauga Club, formed "to encourage free discussion and promote the educational, agricultural, and industrial interests of the state." He wrote books for the teaching of reading and spelling, including *Moses' Primer*, *Moses' Phonic Readers*, and *First Reader with 4,000 Words for Spelling by Sound*.

A pioneer in the institution of public libraries, Moses was especially supportive of libraries for children. After the school term in 1907, he moved to Tampa, Fla., where he contributed to the administration of the public library system. He then lived in Chapel Hill briefly before finally settling in Nashville, where he became influential in the establishment of the Great Smoky Mountains National Park.

Moses influenced the major educators of North Carolina, including P. P. Claxton, Edwin A. Alderman, James Y. Joyner, and Charles Duncan McIver. Claxton dubbed him "the modern Pestalozzi." In 1945 he received an honorary doctor of law degree from The University of North Carolina.

His wife was Carrie Dosser of Jonesboro, Tenn. They had five daughters and one son. His oldest daughter, Susan Williams, became a Latin teacher at Newcomb College of Tulane University in New Orleans.

SEE: Jennie M. Barbee, *Historical Sketches of the Raleigh Public Schools* (1943); Charles William Dabney, *Universal Education in the South* (1936); *Prominent People of North Carolina* (1906); Douglas L. Wellons, "Historical Development of the Raleigh Public Schools" (M.A. thesis, University of North Carolina, 1942).

AGNES R. BURHOE

Moss, Robert Verelle, Jr. *(3 Mar. 1922–18 Oct. 1976)*, educator, social activist, and president of the United Church of Christ, was born in Wilson, one of four children of Robert Verelle and Constance Bost Moss. Throughout a career marked by fruitful association with a variety of national and international organizations and committees, Moss remained deeply committed to the unity of the Christian church and to the struggle for racial equality and human rights. A leading modern Protestant ecumenist, he was a regular champion of liberal views, believing that the church had an obligation "to pioneer—to move ahead of society."

Moss received a B.A. degree from Franklin and Marshall College, Lancaster, Pa., in 1943 and a B.D. degree from nearby Lancaster Theological Seminary two years later. In 1954 he was awarded a Ph.D. by the University of Chicago Divinity School. A member of Phi Beta Kappa and of Phi Gamma Mu, he later received numerous honorary degrees—among them the D.D. from Franklin and Marshall (1960), Findlay (1967), and Lakeland (1969) colleges and the L.H.D. from Catawba (1971) and Drury (1972) colleges.

In 1946 Moss was ordained to the ministry in the United Church of Christ in Hickory Hill, N.C. In the same year, on 20 June, he married Junia Evelyn Keppel; they became the parents of three sons: John K., Robert V., III, and Timothy I. That autumn Moss became an instructor in religion at Franklin and Marshall College, and in 1949 he was named an assistant professor. In 1951 he moved to the Lancaster Theological Seminary of the Evangelical and Reformed church as a professor of New Testament science. When Moss became president of the latter institution in 1957, at age thirty-five, he was one of the nation's youngest chief administrators of a divinity school. While affiliated with the seminary he wrote three texts designed for the use of Protestant lay workers enrolled in interdenominational leadership education schools, part of a series planned by the National Council of the Churches of Christ, which represented thirty-nine Protestant denominations. His works were titled *The Life of Paul* (1955), *We Believe* (1957), and *As Paul Sees Christ* (1958).

During his twelve years as seminary president, Moss was involved—both in this country and abroad—in the formation of interdenominational religious policy and the struggle for social justice. In 1961 he was a delegate to the World Council of Churches meeting in New Delhi, India, and the following year he served as a member of the International Congregational Council and as one of thirty-two Protestant observers at the Second Vatican Council. A vice-president of the National Council of Churches, he also chaired the council's Commission on Faith and Order. He was a member of the American Association of Theology Schools (president, 1966–68) and cochairman of the Roman Catholic–Presbyterian and Reformed Dialogue Group.

In 1969 Moss became president of the United Church of Christ on the first ballot, his election bringing solidarity to the 1.8 million-member denomination. The United Church was the product of the union of the Evangelical and Reformed church and the General

Council of the Congregational Christian churches, begun in 1957 and completed in July 1961 at Philadelphia with the adoption of a constitution. This merger represented the first joining of American denominations with different backgrounds and forms of government.

On the occasion of his election to the first of two consecutive four-year terms as president of the United Church, Moss gave voice to his commitment to racial and economic justice, a cause that often generated heated opposition. He expressed his awareness of the separation of much of white America and organized religion alike from the poor, black, and powerless people of the world and urged recognition of and unity with the "dispossessed." He encouraged his denomination to "pursue relentlessly and with singleness of purpose absolute equality for the black man and his right to determine his own destiny."

Equally committed to amnesty for conscientious objectors to the Vietnam War, with the full support of his son John, who was disabled while serving as a marine in Vietnam, and to the care of veterans who became victims of drug abuse, Moss also regularly urged Presidents Nixon and Ford to pardon war resisters and noncriminal deserters. In 1969 he was a member of a National Council of Churches delegation to Canada charged with developing channels of assistance for those who had fled there to escape the draft. From 1969 to 1973 he headed the National Council's Special Ministries to the Vietnam Generation. And at a Los Angeles, Calif., meeting of the World Council of Churches in 1973, he urged "total amnesty for all those in legal jeopardy" in order to "heal the wounds" of Vietnam.

His general devotion to social justice and the alleviation of oppression in all its forms led Moss in 1970 to advocate the calling of women to "highly visible" positions of responsibility in all religious bodies; as a result of his pressure, the following year the United Church of Christ created its Task Force on Women. In 1973 Moss headed the first official delegation from an American church to the churches of East Germany, becoming the first American to preach in the German Democratic Republic. In the year of his death he led a group of twenty-five leaders of the United Church on a tour of the Far East to study oppression in Indonesia, martial law in the Philippines, and the division of the Christian church in Japan. He also made a side trip to protest the South Korean government's arrest of twenty-seven Christians of that nation. Thus until the end, when he succumbed to cancer in Montclair, N.J., at age fifty-four, Moss maintained an active personal and institutional concern for dispossessed people and a dedication to the realization of social justice in the world.

SEE: *Asheville Citizen*, 23 Oct. 1976; *New York Times,* 26 Oct. 1976; Raleigh *News and Observer*, 1 July 1969; *Time*, 8 Nov. 1976; *Who's Who in Religion, 1975–76* (1975); *Yearbook of American Churches* (1976).

KATHERINE F. MARTIN

Mott, John James *(7 May 1834–29 Jan. 1919)*, "Iron Duke" of the Republican party in North Carolina during the last half of the nineteenth century, physician, and hydroelectrical pioneer, was born in Hillsborough, where his father, the Reverend Thomas Smith Webb Mott, was serving as an Episcopal priest. The elder Mott was a member of a prominent family of Nova Scotia, and his wife, Susan Amanda Phillips Mott, was a woman of strong character. Three of their sons became practicing physicians. Later the Reverend Mr. Mott taught school on Lower Creek, near Lenoir in Caldwell County, where John James grew up and began his education.

Young Mott attended Catawba College (then in Newton) and was graduated from Jefferson Medical College in Philadelphia. In 1856 he began practicing medicine at Beattie's Ford and, on 8 July, married Theodosia Carolina Hendrix of Wilkes County. They had nine children, one of whom, Marshal L., became district attorney for the Indian Territory.

An enthusiastic Whig in pre–Civil War days, John James Mott was elected to the legislature from Catawba County during Andrew Johnson's Reconstruction in 1866 and 1867. He joined the Republican party when it was organized and remained loyal to it except during the Free Silver campaign of 1896, when he became national chairman of a Free Silver party and voted for William Jennings Bryan.

In 1868, in a hard battle and with Republican support led by Todd R. Caldwell, he was elected president of the eastern branch of the Western North Carolina Railroad, replacing Colonel Samuel McD. Tate, a Democrat. Two years later Mott moved to Statesville and in 1872 was named collector of internal revenue for the large Sixth District in place of Samuel H. Wiley of Salisbury. It was from that office and as chairman of the state Republican committee from 1876 through 1886 that he strengthened his hold on state politics and became known by friend and foe as the Iron Duke of the Republican party.

While the states to the south were surrendering even the presence of a Republican organization, Mott was contesting North Carolina inch by inch with his political enemies. In 1872 he helped in the election of Caldwell as governor and of Augustus S. Merrimon as senator over Zebulon B. Vance. Ten years later he organized the "liberal" movement as an outgrowth of the anti-Prohibition campaign of 1881 that he had directed. Largely by implicating the Democrats in the Prohibition movement, he brought several leading Democrats into the Republican ranks, including Dr. Tyre York of Wilkes, who in 1882 defeated William M. Robbins of Statesville in the race for the U.S. House of Representatives when he had been considered unbeatable.

Mott wielded the patronage afforded by the Western North Carolina Railroad and the collectorship of internal revenue with an iron hand, and as chairman of the state Republican committee he insisted on concentrating on local elections and not wasting energies on hopeless statewide contests such as judgeships. Twice he came close to seizing control of the legislature by such tactics. In the 1890s he welcomed the fusion with the Populists and heartily united with them in an attempt to wrest control of the state from the Democrats.

After his term in the legislature of 1866–67, Mott was never again elected to a government office, although it is suspected that if the Republicans had taken control of the legislature, he would have been candidate for the U.S. Senate. When the Fusionists took over in 1895, he sought his party's nomination but lost to Jeter C. Pritchard. Mott had opposition in his own party. His policy of concentrating on local offices to the exclusion of statewide races, although successful, created a conflict with Logan Harris, a black leader of Raleigh, and with other Raleigh leaders in 1886, the year Mott lost the chairmanship of the Republican party. Even in Statesville there were two Republican factions, with David M. Furches, Republican candidate for governor in 1892 and later chief justice of the North Carolina Supreme Court, active in the opposing faction.

In 1907 Mott sold his farm east of Statesville to his

son-in-law and moved to Radford, Va. During the next few years he bought up land along the New River and its tributaries, and in 1911 he organized and became president of the Dominion Power Company, a million-dollar corporation. Later he purchased a new home in Statesville, spending part of his time in Radford and part in Statesville. He died in Radford and was buried in Oakwood Cemetery, Statesville.

SEE: Samuel A. Ashe, ed., *Biographical History of North Carolina*, vol. 4 (1906); Gordon B. McKinney, *Southern Mountain Republicans, 1865–1900* (1978); Statesville *Landmark*, 31 Jan. 1919.

HOMER M. KEEVER

Mountflorence, James Cole (*ca. 1745–post-5 July 1817*), Patriot, lawyer, and land agent, was a native of France. He was educated at the University of Paris, where he "studied for two years Philosophy and for eight years Mathematicks," and served as an officer in the French army "for more than nine years." By the summer of 1778 he was in North Carolina and had been appointed captain of what was to be a regiment of French volunteers in the North Carolina Continental Line. But by the end of August the state had abandoned plans for the French regiment, since only a few straggling French sailors had been recruited.

In September 1778 Mountflorence obtained letters of introduction from Governor Richard Caswell to General George Washington and President Henry Laurens, recommending him for an appointment in the Continental army. The governor found it necessary to allow Mountflorence and two other French officers £100 each "to enable them to proceed to General Washington's camp." In December Mountflorence informed Caswell that he had abandoned "all thoughts of prosecuting my Military designs" because of a long illness and concern for the support of his wife. He was teaching a school at New Bern and seeking an appointment as "french interpreter" to the state.

On 4 Sept. 1780 Mountflorence joined the staff of Brigadier General Jethro Sumner, who was commanding North Carolina militia near Charlotte. When Sumner resigned in October, offended by the legislature's appointment of General William Smallwood of Maryland to command the state militia, Mountflorence continued in service as a brigade major to General William R. Davie, who soon became commissary general responsible for the supply of General Nathanael Greene's army. Mountflorence proved to be an energetic and capable supply officer, serving both as assistant commissary general and assistant quartermaster general to the state until the two departments were abolished in May 1782. Growing discontent in the state with deputy commissary officers and quartermasters who made unreasonable requisitions and impressments led the legislature to abolish the offices. No doubt Mountflorence shared some of the responsibility. Governor Thomas Burke, writing to Mountflorence in March 1782, had commended his "diligence and activity," yet refusing to support his plans for seizing the property of suspected Tories.

While a supply officer, Mountflorence traveled from the coast to the western portion of the state gathering provisions from the county commissioners appointed to collect the specific tax payable in grain, pork, and other commodities. In 1781 and 1782 he was quartermaster general for the Salisbury district. Like other officers, he suffered from irregular pay and inflation. In February 1782 the state quartermaster general, Robert Burton,

told the governor that Mountflorence was an "active and useful officer" in the Quartermaster Department but that he was "very bare of cloathing." Burton asked permission for Mountflorence to draw shirting, stockings, and cloth for a coat from the state stores at Halifax.

In the short sketch of his public life that Mountflorence prepared some years later, he noted that he was an officer throughout the American war. Soon afterwards he was licensed to practice law in the inferior courts of North Carolina and then in the superior courts of law and equity of the U.S. government in the Territory South of the Ohio. For a time he also was military deputy surveyor in the Cumberland settlements, and among other duties he located western lands to be issued to officers and soldiers of the Continental line in reward for their service.

Mountflorence's experience in the region beyond the mountains led him to believe that the Spanish were exerting a strong influence among the Indians in that region, and he went to Charleston, S.C., to discuss the matter with authorities there. During his stay he contributed articles on this subject, under the pseudonym FABIUS, to the *South Carolina Gazette*, and these were reprinted widely throughout the nation. The *Columbian Magazine* either reprinted some of them or published original contributions from Mountflorence regarding the Spanish. As a lawyer with special knowledge of the area, he also discussed the right of the United States to navigate the Mississippi River.

Moving to Nashville (afterwards in Tennessee), he speculated in town lots, engaged in the river trade, and practiced law. Mountflorence "circulated extensively, and flourished grandly" in Nashville society and was long remembered for his lavish dinner parties. In November 1789 he represented Davidson County (Tenn.) in the Fayetteville convention that ratified the federal Constitution. Mountflorence voted against making ratification conditional on the approval of five proposed amendments and for unqualified ratification of the Constitution. He also helped to write the act by which North Carolina ceded its western territory to the federal government, and in 1791 he was sent to Philadelphia to describe the region to Secretary of State Thomas Jefferson. According to Mountflorence, he was nominated as a candidate for Congress, but the popularity of one of his opponents was too great to overcome.

In 1791 Mountflorence contracted with some members of the Blount family to go to France, where he would assist them in trade and the sale of their western lands. He left for France in January 1792 and returned to America early the following year, bringing some purchasers of his own land. In 1793 he went back to France and continued his efforts to sell western lands and to find markets for American goods. In 1796 Mountflorence reported that he had never made the first sale of Blount lands. Although he wrote of proposed contracts with the French government and promised markets for flour and indigo, his ventures never materialized.

By 1796 Mountflorence was an assistant to Fulwar Skipwith, the U.S. consul general in Paris. He remained in Paris as a contact for Charles Cotesworth Pinckney, the American minister to France, following Pinckney's expulsion in June 1797. When Pinckney returned to Paris along with John Marshall and Elbridge Gerry, Mountflorence was Pinckney's private secretary and an intermediary in the negotiations that culminated in the XYZ affair. Ordered out of France along with the American ministers, Mountflorence was obliged to sell his furniture and other property in great haste and at a loss. He then went to The Hague, where he became private secretary to William Vans Murray, U.S. minister to the Batavian Republic. He returned again to Paris as Murray's private secretary when Murray, along with Mountflorence's old friend William R. Davie and Chief Justice Oliver Ellsworth, negotiated the convention of 1800. On one occasion in Paris, Davie was invited to accompany Mrs. Mountflorence to a concert.

Although he was residing in France (except for the time he sought refuge in The Hague), Mountflorence described himself as an American citizen. He was concerned that a number of American citizens were privateers, attacking other U.S. shipping while flying the flag of France, and he publicized the names of those who were known to him.

Mountflorence was the author of at least four short published pieces, two in English and two in French, which suggest something of his interests and his involvement in disputes. The earliest was *American Vessels captured and carried into the ports of France since July, 1796*, printed in Paris in 1798. In 1805 there were two, both published in Paris, pertaining to Fulwar Skipwith: *Mémoire pour James C. Mountflorence, citoyen des Etats-Unis, résident en france depuis plus de douze ans, demandeur: Contre Fulwar Skipwith, citoyen des mêmes états, leur agent commercial à Paris, y demeurant depuis et avant l'année 1794, défendeur* and *Précis pour m. Mountflorence, citoyen des Etats-Unis: Contre m. Skipwith, agent commercial des Etats-Unis*. Finally, there was a four-page piece headed *His excellency, the Hon. James Monroe, Esq., President of the United States of America*. It was dated in manuscript from Paris, 5 July 1817, and took the form of a letter to the president seeking punishment of Isaac Cox Barnet, U.S. consul at Paris, for his conduct towards Mountflorence.

SEE: *American State Papers*, class 1, vol. 2 (1832–61); *Annals of the Congress of the United States*, 5th Cong., 1797–99, vol. 2 (1851); *Catalogue Général des Livres Imprimes de la Bibliothèque Nationale* 70 (1933); Walter Clark, ed., *State Records of North Carolina*, vols. 15–16, 22 (1898–1907); Alice Barnwell Keith, ed., "Letters from Major James Cole Mountflorence. . . . ," *North Carolina Historical Review* 14 (July 1937); Alice Barnwell Keith and William H. Masterson, *The John Gray Blount Papers*, 3 vols. (1952–65); James Cole Mountflorence, *A Short Sketch of the Public Life of Major J. C. Mountflorence* (n.d.; an apparently unique fragment is in the North Carolina Collection, University of North Carolina, Chapel Hill); *North Carolina Journal*, 23 Feb. 1795, 8 Feb. 1796; Papers of the Continental Congress (microfilm, Library of Congress, Washington, D.C.); A. W. Putnam, *History of Middle Tennessee; or, Life and Times of Gen. James Robertson* (1858); Blackwell P. Robinson, *William R. Davie* (1957); Treasurer's and Comptroller's Papers: Military Papers (North Carolina State Archives, Raleigh).

GEORGE TROXLER

Mouzon, Edwin DuBose *(19 May 1869–10 Feb. 1937)*, Methodist clergyman, educator, and author, was born in Spartanburg, S.C., the son of Samuel Cogswell and Harriet Peurifoy Mouzon of Huguenot ancestry. In 1888 he was licensed to preach and the following year was graduated from Wofford College. Moving to Texas in 1889, he was ordained deacon and elder and became pastor of a church at Bryan; afterwards he served churches in Austin, Galveston, Abilene, Fort Worth, and San Antonio as well as in Kansas City, Mo. Mouzon was instrumental in organizing a theology department at Southwestern University, Georgetown, Tex., where he was professor of theology in 1908–10. Influential in the establishment of Southern Methodist University, he served as acting dean of its School of Theology. From 1911 to 1931 he was a delegate to the decennial Ecumenical Methodist conferences in Toronto, London, and Atlanta.

At the General Conference of the Methodist Episcopal Church, South, meeting in Asheville, N.C., in 1910, Mouzon was elected bishop. He presided over most of the church's annual conferences from 1910 to 1937, as well as serving Texas Methodism (1910–20), Tennessee Methodism (1922–26), the Upper South Carolina and South Carolina annual conferences (1926–30), and Methodism in North Carolina (1926–34). Residing in Charlotte, he was the first bishop to preside over eight consecutive sessions in the state. In 1934 he was assigned episcopal duty in Virginia, West Virginia, the Baltimore Conference, and Washington, D.C., while still living in Charlotte. It was observed that in all of his contacts he was never hasty in making decisions, was sensitive to the needs of his ministers, and never uttered a bitter word towards those who differed with him.

Bishop Mouzon pioneered the "open cabinet" system of ministerial appointments, whereby the bishop consulted with his cabinet, clergymen, and churches in question. In 1910, by action of the General Conference, the Methodist Episcopal Church, South, adopted the cabinet system. In 1930 Mouzon presided over the organization of the newly autonomous Brazil Methodist church, and he also held conferences in Cuba, Japan, and Korea. He was instrumental in the merger of Davenport and Greensboro colleges as well as in the merger of Weaver and Rutherford colleges. While he was bishop in North Carolina, the Brevard Institute property was accepted by the North Carolina Conference and reopened as Brevard College.

In 1923 Mouzon and two other Methodist bishops endorsed a movement to secure the membership of the United States in the League of Nations. He also opposed the candidacy of Alfred E. Smith for president of the United States, and he spoke out against the Ku Klux Klan. In 1929 he gave the Lyman Beecher Lectures at Yale University; on other occasions, he delivered the Fondren Lectures at Southern Methodist University and the Cole Lectures at Vanderbilt University.

Mouzon participated in the campaigns of 1936 and 1937 to raise funds for missionary work. In addition, he served as chairman of the Southern Commission on Church Union and was active on committees and commissions of the movement until his death. (On 10 May 1939 the Methodist Episcopal church, the Methodist Episcopal Church, South, and the Methodist Protestant church merged.)

In 1918, following the death of his wife the previous year, Mouzon wrote *Does God Care?* In 1923 he published a booklet, *So-Called Fundamentalism*, enumerating eight objections to fundamentalism. Enlarging this work, he issued it as a book-length treatise, *The Fundamentals of Methodism*. He stood up to attacks by fundamentalists and, thinking that many Methodists were ignorant of their theological bases, expressed the belief that Methodism was a religion of the spirit. Bishop Mouzon was granted honorary degrees by Southwestern University, Southern Methodist University, and Duke University.

In 1890 he married Mary Elizabeth Mike, and they were the parents of six children: Harriet Peurifoy, Julia Elizabeth, Edwin DuBose, Mary Josephine, James Carlisle, and Olin Terrell. In 1919, two years after his first wife's death, the bishop married Mrs. Mary Pearl Langdon. He died at his home in Charlotte and was buried in

Oakland Cemetery, Dallas, Tex. There are portraits of him at Southwestern University and at the Mouzon Memorial United Methodist Church, Charlotte.

SEE: *Christian Century*, 24 Feb. 1937; Elmer T. Clark, *Methodism in Western North Carolina* (1966); *Greensboro Daily News*, 11 Feb. 1937; Methodist Church, *Journal of the Western North Carolina Conference* (1937); Raleigh *News and Observer*, 11 Feb. 1937; *Southern Christian Advocate*, 18 Feb. 1937; Lee F. Tuttle, *Profiles of Twentieth-Century Pulpit Giants* (1984); *Who's Who in the South* (1927); *Who Was Who in America*, vol. 1 (1981).

GRADY L. E. CARROLL

Mouzon, Henry, Jr. *(18 May 1741–25 Aug. 1807)*, mapmaker and civil engineer, was the grandson of Louis Mouzon, a Huguenot immigrant to South Carolina who obtained warrants for land in Berkeley County in 1705 and 1708. Early in the second quarter of the eighteenth century, Henry Mouzon, Sr., moved north across Santee River to a plantation at Pudding Swamp in Craven County (now Williamsburg County), S.C., where his son, Henry, Jr., was born. After his father's death in 1749, young Mouzon was sent to France for his education, and presumably while in that country he learned engineering.

Mouzon received his first public commission of real consequence in 1771 when he, along with Ephraim Mitchell (subsequently the surveyor general of South Carolina), was appointed by Governor Lord Charles Greville Montague to survey the boundaries of the civil districts of South Carolina. In the following year Mouzon prepared "A Map of Part of the Counties of Mecklenburg and Tryon Lately Added to the Province of South Carolina," occasioned by the location and survey of the westward extension of the boundary between North Carolina and South Carolina earlier in 1772. In January 1773 he advertised "Proposals for Engraving by Subscription, a Map of St. Stephen in Craven County . . . embellished with a curious Representation of the Process of manufacturing Indico. . . ."

At the same time, Mouzon was projecting plans for another map, for he and Mitchell appear to have agreed to incorporate corrections made during their surveys of 1771 in a new map of South Carolina. They jointly advertised their proposals for the execution of a new map in May and June 1774. Mitchell, however, must have withdrawn from the project, causing Mouzon to abandon the plan to create an original map of the colony. Instead, Mouzon produced a map of both North Carolina and South Carolina by consolidating James Cook's 1773 map of South Carolina with John Collet's map (chiefly the work of William Churton) of North Carolina. Mouzon drew on his recent surveys in order to show district lines in South Carolina with greater accuracy and to delineate the 1772 western extension of the boundary between the two colonies. Concurrently, he projected the major rivers and watercourses so as to correct the faulty perspective in the maps of Cook and Collet, corrected the soundings along the North Carolina coast, and placed the names of the North Carolina counties so they would agree more completely with their physical boundaries (though those boundaries were not drawn).

"An Accurate Map of North and South Carolina" was the masterpiece of Mouzon's life. It was published by Sayer and Bennett in London in 1775 and in a French edition by one of the royal geographers, George L. LeRouge, in Paris in 1777. In these forms it was used by American, British, and French forces during the Ameri-

can Revolutionary War. A reissue, using the original engraver's plates, was published in London by Laurie and Whittle, successors to Sayer and Bennett, in 1794. Mouzon's map remained the authority for North Carolina until Price and Strother's map was published in 1808.

Shortly after the British army moved its offensive to the southern colonies, Mouzon became involved in local armed resistance to the British. After the fall of Charles Town in May 1780, an American battalion was formed in Williamsburg District, Mouzon accepted a commission as captain over one of the companies, and the battalion was attached to Francis Marion's brigade. Banastre Tarleton is said to have singled out Mouzon for exemplary punishment, and on 1 Aug. 1780 Mouzon's mansion house and fourteen outbuildings at Pudding Swamp were burned by British forces. Six weeks later, at the Battle of Black Mingo, Mouzon was wounded so badly that he was crippled for life. It is assumed that this injury terminated his promising career as an engineer. In 1772 Mouzon had conducted surveys to determine the proper bed for a canal connecting Santee and Cooper rivers, but there is no evidence that he conducted similar projects after the war. The toll bridge across Black River that bore his name and that was vested in him in 1805 for a term of five years was presumably constructed to his plans and under his supervision; if so, it was his single engineering feat during the later half of his life.

By his wife, Susannah Taylor, Mouzon had eight children: Peter, William, Samuel R., Henry, Sarah, Mary, Susannah V., and Ann. He was buried in the Mouzon burying ground near his home on Pudding Swamp.

SEE: William Willis Boddie, *History of Williamsburg* (1923); Hennig Cohen, *The South Carolina Gazette, 1732–1775* (1953); William P. Cumming, *The Southeast in Early Maps* (1958).

GEORGE STEVENSON

Mull, Odus (or Otis, Odes) McCoy *(18 Sept. 1880–27 Nov. 1962)*, lawyer, legislator, and educational leader, was born on a farm in Township Ten, Cleveland County, the son of Housten (or Houston) E. and Margaret Ann Carpenter Mull. In 1795 his great-grandfather, Jacob Mull, had migrated from Pennsylvania to Burke County, where he became a planter. John Mull, grandfather of Odus, was a planter and merchant and also operated a tannery. Housten E. Mull, Odus's father, died in 1881, leaving the young child in the care of his twenty-two-year-old mother in a log home on a rocky hillside where farming was difficult. Her subsequent marriage to Julius E. Smith made it possible for the youth to be educated.

Odus attended Belwood Institute (1892–96) and Piedmont High School (1896–98), both located near his home. Intending to continue the family tradition of farming, Mull, in a year of hard labor, produced four bales of cotton for which he received $98.67 or 4½¢ per pound. As a result of this discouraging experience, he decided to go to college. In 1899, after teaching briefly in the public schools for $25 a month, he entered Wake Forest College, where he became captain of the baseball team and a campus leader. He was graduated in 1902 with a B.A. degree and, after completing the two-year law course in one year, received an LL.B. degree *magna cum laude* in 1903. Mull immediately began practicing law in Shelby, becoming a partner of two brothers, James L. and E. Yates Webb.

Mull's senior thesis at Wake Forest, in which he

signed his name Odes McCoy Mull, was entitled "The Isolation of the South." It deplored the South's lack of influence in national affairs, a situation that he believed could be corrected by the development of industry and educational facilities in the region. During the next half century Mull was himself able to contribute substantially to the achievement of this goal.

In 1907 he served his first term as a Cleveland County member of the state house of representatives. He returned to the legislature in 1919, 1929, 1939, 1941, and 1947, serving as speaker in 1941. During the 1919 session he was coauthor of the important Mull-McCoin Bill, the first law authorizing state and county cooperation in road building. In the same session he secured passage of a bill establishing vocational education in North Carolina. Beginning in 1928, when he was elected to the first of two two-year terms as chairman of the state Democratic executive committee, Mull exerted a widely felt influence over political affairs in North Carolina. That year he bore the brunt of O. Max Gardner's successful campaign for election as governor.

Two years later Mull discontinued the practice of law to become general manager and financial adviser of the Cleveland Cloth Mills, one of the businesses with which he and Gardner were associated. By this time he was one of the leading landowners and agriculturists of Cleveland County. Mull was a member of the board that built Shelby Hospital and chairman of the county chapter of the American Red Cross. From 1915 to 1928 he was city attorney for Shelby, and for several years he was chairman of the county Democratic executive committee. In 1936 he resumed the practice of general civil and corporation law, serving also as a director and counselor of several textile mills and as an attorney for several banks. He was a member of the Sigma Chi fraternity, the Shelby Kiwanis Club, and the local, state, and national bar associations.

Throughout his career Mull was active in the affairs of the Baptist denomination in the county and state. He served the First Baptist Church of Shelby as chairman of the board of deacons, superintendent of the Sunday school, and teacher for thirty years of the O. M. Mull Bible Class. Despite the importance of his role in the "Shelby dynasty," along with Gardner, the Webbs, Clyde R. Hoey, and Lee B. Weathers, editor of the *Shelby Daily Star*, Mull is better remembered for his key leadership in establishing the Bowman Gray School of Medicine of Wake Forest University and in moving Wake Forest College from Wake County to Winston-Salem.

In 1935 the Council on Medical Education of the American Medical Association voted not to recognize two-year medical schools in the future. Although this particular action was rescinded, the preferred solution to the plight of the two-year schools was expansion to four-year status. In 1937 Governor Hoey appointed a medical school commission consisting of Mull and six others to study needs and make recommendations to the next General Assembly. When it appeared that state funds to expand the two-year school at The University of North Carolina were lacking, Mull told the commission: "If you will give me about a month, I will go around the state and see if I can get the money from private sources." In the fall of 1938 he informed the commission that the person in charge of "a large charitable trust fund had expressed a willingness to make a commitment to the medical school, provided it could be located in the home city of the donor." He was referring to James A. Gray of Winston-Salem and the Bowman Gray Foundation. After the commission voted four to two to recommend that a four-year school be built in Chapel

Hill, Mull arranged a conference attended by himself; Gray; Thurman D. Kitchin, president of Wake Forest; and Coy C. Carpenter, dean of Wake Forest's two-year medical school. Mull explained to Gray what had happened at the meeting of the commission and requested that the same offer be made to Wake Forest. The details of the gift were soon worked out, and in 1941 the medical school began operating in Winston-Salem as a four-year school. Mull was a member of the building committee for the medical school and also of the committee in charge of enlarging the North Carolina Baptist Hospital.

In about 1944 Mull, a trustee of Wake Forest, conferred with J. S. Lynch, president of the hospital board of trustees, about obtaining income from the Z. Smith Reynolds Foundation of Winston-Salem for the college. In a subsequent meeting in Shelby, Mull, Judge E. Yates Webb, and C. J. Jackson, a representative of Wake Forest, formulated plans—to present to North Carolina Baptists—to move the college to Winston-Salem and receive financial support from the foundation. After approval by the Baptist State Convention in 1946, the plans were implemented. The Wake Forest trustees made Mull permanent chairman of the committee charged with raising funds, erecting buildings, and moving the college. Fourteen buildings costing more than $20 million had been completed when the move was made in June 1956.

On 17 Sept. 1955 a portrait of Mull painted by Walter Keul was presented to the Bowman Gray School of Medicine. The state's press described Mull's achievements at length, referring to him as one of the last survivors of the "famed 'Shelby Dynasty'" and as "Mr. Baptist" of North Carolina. He was characterized as a friendly person, with a genuine desire to serve others. A deep, powerful voice and a fluency with words in the spellbinding tradition had contributed to his success. In 1957 Wake Forest College awarded him a doctor of civil law degree.

On 12 June 1907 Mull married Montrose Pallen McBrayer of Shelby. They had one child, Montrose McBrayer, who married Earl Meacham. She died on 24 May 1972, leaving two children, Montrose Pallen and Otis Mull Meacham. Mull was buried in Shelby's Sunset Cemetery.

SEE: Coy C. Carpenter, *The Story of Medicine at Wake Forest University* (1970); John L. Cheney, Jr., ed., *North Carolina Government, 1585–1979* (1981); *North Carolina Biography*, vol. 5 (1941); "Odus M. Mull," *Magazine of Sigma Chi* (May 1957); Odus McCoy Mull Papers (Baptist Historical Collection, Wake Forest University, Winston-Salem); Raleigh *News and Observer*, 18 Sept. 1955; *Shelby Star*, 27 Nov. 1962; Winston-Salem *Journal-Sentinel*, 18 Sept. 1955.

HENRY S. STROUPE

Mullen, James Madison (*10 Sept. 1845–2 Jan. 1931*), jurist and legislator, was born in Pasquotank County, the son of James Whedbee and Susan W. Clary Mullen. His niece Emily, the daughter of Antoinette Mullen and George Gilliam, married Sterling Gary of Halifax. During her long life she and her stepdaughter, Nannie Gary, did much to preserve both the history and the historic sites of that town.

Mullen attended the Hertford Male Academy but left his studies in February 1862 to join the Confederate army, enlisting in the Virginia battery of Captain S. Taylor Martin, of Major Francis S. Bogg's battalion of light artillery. In October 1863 he was transferred to Captain

L. H. Webb's North Carolina battery in the same battalion and so served until the end of the war. In 1890, in an address before the A. P. Hill Camp of Confederate Veterans meeting in Petersburg, Va., Mullen related his experiences during the fifteen days preceding General Joseph Johnston's surrender at Hillsborough. Withdrawing from the town of Weldon, where they had been assigned to guard the Wilmington and Weldon Railroad, the members of Webb's battery passed through the counties of Warren, Franklin, and Nash before General Laurence S. Baker, the commanding officer, arranged their surrender to General William T. Sherman. In this speech, later published in *War Talks of Confederate Veterans*, Mullen made interesting observations on the reaction of the civilian population in this part of North Carolina to the collapse of the Confederacy.

In 1866 Mullen was appointed register of deeds for Perquimans County, an office he held for two years. Having studied law in his leisure time under Thomas G. Skinner of Hertford, he was admitted to the bar in January 1869 and settled in the town of Halifax to practice. A successful attorney, he represented Halifax County in the state senate for the term beginning January 1885. In July 1886 he moved to Petersburg, Va., and formed a partnership with Richard B. Davis, at the same time retaining his North Carolina practice in Halifax and Northampton counties. In 1888 he was elected attorney for the city of Petersburg, serving for six years. In 1894 Mullen succeeded David Meade Bernard, Jr., as judge of the Hustings Court of Petersburg, a post he held until his death.

During his thirty-six years on the bench, he won the respect and affection of the bar; he was especially revered by the younger members, in whom he took a keen interest and to whom he showed great courtesy and consideration. A portrait of Judge Mullen hangs in the courthouse in Petersburg. An active member of St. Paul's Episcopal Church in that city, he was buried in Blandford Cemetery, Petersburg.

On 13 Oct. 1875 Mullen married Evelyn A. Grigg, the daughter of Wesley and Augustina Wells Grigg of Petersburg. They had four children who survived to maturity: James, Thomas Wilson, Grizelle, and Clary Sutton.

SEE: American Historical Society, *History of Virginia*, vol. 4 (1924); George S. Bernard, ed., *War Talks of Confederate Veterans* (1892); Robert A. Brock, ed., *Virginia and Virginians*, vol. 2 (1888).

CLAIBORNE T. SMITH, JR.

Mumford, George (*d. 31 Dec. 1818*), congressman, legislator, farmer, merchant, and dealer in real estate, was originally from the Fayetteville and Cumberland County area. His father, Robinson (or Robeson) Mumford, owned a tobacco warehouse in Fayetteville and was clerk of the Cumberland County Court of Pleas and Quarter Sessions and sheriff. His mother's given name was Margaret.

In 1792 George Mumford purchased 590 acres of the 640-acre grant of Squire Boone on Elisha and Dutchman creeks in Davie (then Rowan) County. He lived at different times in Davie, Cumberland, Orange, and Rowan counties. From 1809 to 1814 he operated a store in or near Mock's Old Field (now Mocksville). In 1815 his wife opened a school for young ladies in their home at Milton in Rowan County.

Mumford was a member of the North Carolina House of Commons in 1810–11. He was one of the first directors of the Salisbury branch of the State Bank of North

Carolina in 1811. Sometime prior to 1817, he was appointed principal assessor of the Tenth Collection District of North Carolina.

Elected as a Democrat (Jeffersonian Republican) to the Fifteenth Congress, Mumford served from 4 Mar. 1817 until his death. Although at first there was a question as to his eligibility because of the tax assessor job, an investigative committee ruled that his office had expired before he took his seat in the House. His term in Congress was during the "Era of Good Feelings"—a period characterized by the absence of two-party strife following the disappearance of the Federalist party. Mumford, a progressive, was one of two North Carolina congressmen who supported the internal improvements portion of Henry Clay's celebrated American system. He died in Washington, D.C., of diphtheria and was buried in the Congressional Cemetery.

SEE: *Biog. Dir. Am. Cong.* (1950); James S. Brawley, *The Rowan Story* (1953); McCubbins Papers (Rowan County Library, Salisbury); Martin Collection (Davie County Library, Mocksville); Lois S. Neal, *Abstract of Vital Records*, vol. 1 (1979); Raleigh *Register*, 8 Jan. 1819; J. K. Rouse, *North Carolina Picadillo* (1966); James W. Wall, *History of Davie County* (1969); John H. Wheeler, ed., *Reminiscences and Memoirs of North Carolina and Eminent North Carolinians* (1884).

JAMES W. WALL

Mumford, Lawrence Quincy (*11 Dec. 1903–15 Aug. 1982*), librarian of Congress, was born in the community of Hanrahan in Pitt County, the son of Jacob Edward and Emma Luvenia Stocks Mumford. Raised on a farm, he knew the hard work required to grow tobacco, cotton, and corn. In high school he won awards as an orator and a debater and received a scholarship to Trinity College (renamed Duke University before he was graduated). Entering Trinity in 1921, Mumford maintained his superior academic record and won honors not only in debating and public speaking but in drama as well. He worked for three years as a student assistant in the library and after graduation joined the library staff while he pursued a master's degree.

From the Duke University library, Mumford went to New York in the fall of 1928 to enter the Columbia University School of Library Service. At the end of the one-year course he accepted a position at the New York Public Library, where he worked from 1929 to 1945, rising to the position of executive assistant and coordinator of general services. In 1945 he became assistant director of the Cleveland, Ohio, Public Library, and from 1950 to 1954 he was director. During these years he took occasional leaves of absence for special work elsewhere, such as lecturing on library science and directing the processing department at the Library of Congress. While in Cleveland he taught library science for eight years at Western Reserve University.

In 1954 he was appointed librarian of Congress. The first professionally trained person to be named to that post, Mumford set about to regain the confidence and support of Congress for the library. At the same time he increased the efficiency of its operation and improved the organization of its staff. Under his direction, the Library of Congress enhanced its position of leadership in the profession, encouraged creative projects, and offered an even wider range of professional services to the nation's libraries as well as to government officials, scientists, scholars, and others with a need for information. The Madison Building, an addition to the Library of Congress, stands as a monument to his service to the nation.

Quincy Mumford was long active in the Association of Research Libraries and played leading roles in numerous other national organizations. He was president of the American Library Association from 1954 to 1955 and a member of the advisory committee for the publication of the papers of George Washington and Woodrow Wilson. He also was a member of the Federal Council on Arts and Humanities and served on the board of trustees of the John F. Kennedy Center for the Performing Arts, of the Historic American Buildings Survey, and of the National Trust for Historic Preservation. For countless other groups he was a trustee, a member of the advisory board, or a director or assisted in some other capacity. In 1963, when North Carolina observed the tercentenary of the granting of the charter of Carolina to the eight Lords Proprietors, Mumford was a member of the Carolina Charter Corporation. He contributed to numerous professional and scholarly journals and often spoke easily and effectively before various audiences. In addition to his earned degrees, he was the recipient of ten honorary degrees.

In 1930 Mumford married Permelia Catherine Stevens, and they became the parents of a daughter, Kathryn. Permelia Mumford died in 1961, and eight years later he married Betsy Perrin Fox.

SEE: Greenville *Daily Reflector*, 26 Aug. 1982; *Illinois Libraries*, vol. 36 (May 1954); *Librarians of Congress, 1802–1974* (1977); *Publisher's Weekly*, 3 Sept. 1982; *Who Was Who in America*, vol. 8 (1985).

WILLIAM S. POWELL

Munroe, John Peter (29 Mar. 1857–14 Oct. 1940), physician and medical educator, was born in Cumberland County, the youngest of seven children of Peter and Isabella Jane Cameron Munroe. His father, of Scottish ancestry, was a well-known architect and builder of churches and civic buildings in North Carolina. Following early education at the Raeford Institute, Munroe in 1878 enrolled at Davidson College, where he became a member of Sigma Alpha Epsilon fraternity, was elected to Phi Beta Kappa, and received a bachelor of arts degree in 1882. After teaching for two years in a private school with Dr. Alexander Graham and for one year at Raeford Academy in Fayetteville, Munroe enrolled in the University of Virginia, where he received a doctor of medicine degree in 1885. On completing his internship at St. Luke's Hospital in Richmond, Va., he returned to North Carolina and engaged in private medical practice in Durham for three years.

In 1890 Munroe moved to Davidson College to serve as college physician, succeeding Dr. Paul Brandon Barringer. Barringer, who had organized the medical preparatory department, had resigned as director in 1899 to accept an appointment at the University of Virginia. On his arrival at Davidson, Munroe became chief of the two-year medical curriculum. Under his direction, the curriculum was expanded into a three-year program and the school was reorganized and incorporated as the North Carolina Medical College in 1893. Munroe taught anatomy, physiology, medicine, obstetrics, surgery, pathology, and neurology as well as serving as president of the Medical College. In 1896 and 1901 new buildings were constructed to serve as a college infirmary, operating suites, and teaching amphitheaters. In 1902 the senior class began attending clinical instruction at the Presbyterian and Good Samaritan hospitals in Charlotte,

and in 1903 the curriculum was further enlarged to include a full four-year course of study, including internships at Presbyterian Hospital beginning in 1905. In 1907 the entire Medical School was moved from Davidson to Charlotte, where it remained until its merger with the Medical College of Virginia in Richmond during the fall of 1914, following an unfavorable report in 1910 by the Flexner Commission.

From 1915 until his retirement in 1939, Munroe returned to the private practice of internal medicine and neurology, first in Charlotte, where he organized the Munroe Clinic in 1923, and later after returning to Davidson from 1938 to 1940.

Active in the Presbyterian church, Munroe served for several years as director of music at the Davidson Presbyterian Church and played a central role in establishing the Presbyterian Hospital and Charlotte Sanitorium. He also organized two cotton mills, serving as president of the Dellberg Linden Cotton Mills at Davidson until 1923 and as director of the American Trust Company of Charlotte. Munroe belonged to the Kiwanis Club, Good Fellows Club, Scottish Rite Masons, and Shriners and was an elder of the First Presbyterian Church of Charlotte. He was president of the Mecklenburg County, Tri-State, and North Carolina medical associations; a member of the Southern and American medical associations; and a Fellow of the American College of Physicians. He served as contributing editor to the journal, *Medical Clinics of North America*, and published a number of original studies in the fields of neurology and internal medicine. From 1916 to 1925 he was chairman of the executive committee and business manager of the Charlotte Sanitorium; he later served as president of the sanitorium. In recognition of his work in medical education, Davidson College awarded him an honorary doctor of letters degree in 1919.

Munroe never married. He was buried in the family plot at Davidson, where he died shortly after retirement.

SEE: American Historical Society, *North Carolina* (1927 [portraits]); R. H. Lafferty, *The North Carolina Medical College* (1946); *Southern Medical and Surgical Journal*, vols. 102–3 (1940–41).

MARCUS B. SIMPSON, JR.

Murchison, Claudius Temple (17 Apr. 1889–19 Aug. 1968), college teacher, economic adviser, and author, was born in Hickory, the son of Claudius Murat and Alice Penelope Temple Murchison. Preparatory education in the Hickory public schools qualified him to enter Wake Forest College in September 1907; he was graduated with a bachelor of arts degree *summa cum laude* in 1911. Wake Forest awarded him an honorary doctor of laws degree in 1936.

After graduation he spent five years in and around New York, primarily as a graduate student in economics at Columbia University. There he earned membership in Phi Beta Kappa and completed his residence requirements for a doctor of philosophy degree. During his last year at Columbia (1915–16), he was a lecturer in economics. In the fall of 1916 he became assistant professor of economics at Miami University in Oxford, Ohio. Returning to New York City, Murchison taught for two years at Hunter College (1918–20) and for one year at New York University (1920–21). He received his doctorate from Columbia in 1919, when his incisive and comprehensive study (an outgrowth of his doctoral thesis) was published under the title, *Resale Price Maintenance*.

Murchison's writings on economics and his addresses before various business gatherings attracted the attention of the administration of The University of North Carolina. In 1921 he joined the faculty as associate professor of economics and the next year he became a full professor. He taught at Chapel Hill until June 1934. Murchison spent much of his time in North Carolina advising various manufacturing organizations, especially those concerned with textiles and related areas.

Regarded as a rational, farsighted, and even prophetic analyst of business factors, Murchison in 1934 was tapped for the post of director of the U.S. Bureau of Foreign and Domestic Commerce. Concurrently, he served as a member of the executive committee of the Commercial Policy Commission of the United States, as well as a member of the board of directors of the Export-Import Bank of Washington.

After an extremely busy year, when his public appearances and governmental activities catapulted him into national prominence, he accepted the presidency of the Cotton Textile Institute of America and was its major economic adviser for fourteen years (1935–49). Murchison also served as a member of the Cotton Mill Advisory Commission to the War Production Board (1942–45) and to the Office of Price Administration (1943–46). In 1954 he was an adviser to the U.S. delegation to the International Cotton Conference.

Murchison held membership in Alpha Chi Rho fraternity, the American Economic Association, the American Statistical Association, and the Merchants Club of New York City. He was a lifetime affiliate of the Protestant Episcopal church. Beginning in 1935, his principal residence was in the Georgetown section of Washington, D.C., and later in Arlington, Va. During his semiretirement after 1949, he lived in Wellfleet, Mass.

One of the early accomplishments of Murchison's work with the Cotton Textile Institute was the execution of a two-year quota agreement with Japanese spinners in January 1937, a feat *Time* magazine hailed as "a solution both surprising and superb." Murchison's ultimate success in Osaka was apparent in an article in the *New York Times* (August 1936), in which he pointed out that the multiplication of Japanese imports (from one million to seventy-five million yards in three years) was a long-feared menace to American manufacturing because of Japan's cheap cottons, especially bleached goods.

When Murchison accepted the latter appointment by President Franklin D. Roosevelt in 1934, he had only recently published his searching study *King Cotton Is Sick*, written at Chapel Hill. His intimate knowledge of cotton growing in the Deep South, plus his avid study of its related economics, equipped him to sit in with State Department officials as they drafted reciprocal trade agreements with Cuba, Belgium, Brazil, Haiti, Sweden, and Colombia.

In the spring of 1936 Murchison began to develop his strategy for negotiating the treaty with Japan. He started with Assistant Secretary of State Frances Bowers Sayre, and together they elicited the interest of Ambassador Saito of the Japanese Embassy. On 24 December he left for Japan with a party of American manufacturers, and ten days after their arrival the treaty was signed, giving "stability where formerly there existed the threat of immeasurable and overwhelming competition." This was only one of many such national and international agreements he effected. What protection and prosperity today's textile industry enjoys owes much to the quiet, "long-headed" efforts of this dignified, courteous, friendly, pipe-smoking southern gentleman who always did his homework and who dreamed of and

worked for a sound economy first—in his own textile trade and correlatively in all American business.

Murchison was a prolific writer. In addition to his many articles for publications of the textile industry, he published and was quoted frequently in the *New York Times*, the *Wall Street Journal*, *Time*, *Business Week*, and *Nation's Business*. In his later years he added two books, *Japan and the World Cotton Goods Trade* (1952) and *World Trade and the United States* (1953). He was coauthor of the volume, *Management Problems* (1931), while teaching at Chapel Hill.

By his first wife, Constance Waterman, whom he married on 24 June 1916, Murchison had three children: Nancy Croom, Cameron, and David Claudius. His second wife was Esther L. Devine, whom he married on 21 Aug. 1951. He died in Wellfleet at age seventy-nine, survived by his wife and the two sons by his first marriage.

SEE: E. I. Olive, *Wake Forest Alumni Directory* (1961); Raleigh *News and Observer*, 20 Aug. 1968; "Spinners' Treaty," *Time*, 8 Mar. 1937; *Who Was Who in America*, vol. 5 (1973).

C. SYLVESTER GREEN

Murchison, David Reid (5 Dec. 1837–22 Feb. 1882), merchant, civic leader, and Confederate officer, was born a few miles west of Fayetteville at Manchester, Cumberland County. He was the son of Duncan (20 May 1801–24 Apr. 1870) and Fannie Reid Murchison and the grandson of Kenneth McKenzie Murchison and Dr. Thomas Reid, both of whom emigrated from Scotland. He attended the University of Virginia but left in 1856 to join the firm of Bauman and Murchison in New York City as a bookkeeper. Returning to North Carolina in 1858, he became a partner in the firm of Eli Murray and Company in Wilmington.

At the outbreak of the Civil War, Murchison, as a private in the Wilmington Light Infantry, participated on 15 Apr. 1861 in the capture of Fort Caswell at the mouth of the Cape Fear River. A few months later, with R. B. McRae and T. H. McKoy, he raised a company of which he was first lieutenant. This company of 108 men was probably one of the largest from Wilmington. Assigned as Company C, Seventh Regiment, North Carolina State Troops, it saw action in the Seven Days' Battle around Richmond, Fredericksburg, Sharpsburg, Manassas, and other places. In April 1863 Murchison was transferred to the Fifty-fourth Regiment as captain and assistant quartermaster; later he became inspector general of the Commissary Department of North Carolina.

After the war he resumed his partnership with Eli Murray and the firm became Murray and Murchison. He soon left the firm and in July 1866, with John D. Williams, his brother-in-law George Williams, and his brother Kenneth McKenzie Murchison as partners, established the firms of Williams and Murchison in Wilmington, J. D. Williams and Company in Fayetteville, and Murchison and Company in New York. David Murchison was also a member of the first board of directors of the Bank of New Hanover, organized in 1872; receiver and later president of the Carolina Central Railroad Company; first president of the Produce Exchange; president of the Wilmington Compress and Warehouse Company; and president of the Express Steamboat Company, plying between Wilmington and Fayetteville. At his untimely death, the Wilmington Chamber of Commerce and the Produce Exchange suspended business and attended the funeral in a body.

With his brother Kenneth, Murchison gave the colonial parish church and graveyard of St. Philip's, Brunswick County, to the Episcopal Diocese of East Carolina. It is now a part of Brunswick town, a State Historic Site. They also owned the Caney River hunting preserve, which included Mount Mitchell.

On 11 Jan. 1872 he married Lucy Wooster Wright (30 June 1850–12 Oct. 1913), the daughter of Joshua Grainger and Mary Ann Walker Wright. They had one daughter, Lucile Wright, who married Walter Marvin. Mrs. Marvin gave the Murchison home on South Third Street, Wilmington, to the Episcopal Diocese of East Carolina; it is now the diocesan headquarters.

Murchison was a member of St. James's Episcopal Church. He died in New York City, where he had gone for medical treatment, and was buried in Oakdale Cemetery, Wilmington.

SEE: Samuel A. Ashe, ed., *Biographical History of North Carolina*, vol. 1 (1905 [portrait]); Weymouth T. Jordan, comp., *North Carolina Troops, 1861–1865: A Roster*, vol. 4 (1973); Oakdale Cemetery Records (Raleigh); St. James's Church Records (Wilmington); James Sprunt, *Chronicles of the Cape Fear River* (1914); Wilmington *Morning Star*, 28 Apr. 1870, 14 Jan. 1872; Wilmington *Weekly Star*, 3 Mar. 1882.

LEORA HIATT MCEACHERN

Murchison, Kenneth McKenzie (*18 Feb. 1831–3 June 1904*), merchant, banker, businessman, and Confederate officer, was born at Manchester, Cumberland County, the son of Duncan (20 May 1801–24 Apr. 1870) and Fannie Reid Murchison. His grandfathers, Dr. Thomas Reid and Kenneth McKenzie Murchison, for whom he was named, both emigrated from Scotland. After graduation from The University of North Carolina in 1853, young Murchison engaged in business in New York City and Wilmington until the outbreak of the Civil War. Returning home, he helped to organize a company in which he served as second lieutenant. This became Company C, Eighth Regiment, and in his absence was captured at Roanoke Island. He immediately raised another company, from which he was promoted colonel of the Fifty-fourth North Carolina Regiment, or Hoke's Brigade. Murchison fought in the battles at Fredericksburg, Chancellorsville, and Winchester and served until captured at Rappahannock Station on 7 Nov. 1863. He was imprisoned at Johnson's Island, Lake Erie, until July 1865.

After the war Murchison returned to New York. In June 1866, with John D. Williams, his brother-in-law George Williams, and his brother David Reid Murchison as partners, established the firms of Williams and Murchison in Wilmington, J. D. Williams and Company in Fayetteville, and Murchison and Company in New York City. Kenneth Murchison lived in New York but generally spent the winters in North Carolina. In 1880 he bought Orton plantation on the west side of the Cape Fear River below Wilmington. Within the boundary of the plantation was the colonial parish church and graveyard of St. Philip's, which he and his brother David gave to the Episcopal Diocese of East Carolina. It is now a part of Brunswick town, a State Historic Site. They also owned the Caney River hunting preserve, which included Mount Mitchell.

Kenneth Murchison was the founder of the Murchison National Bank, owner of the Orton Hotel, and one of the largest stockholders in the Coal, Cement, and Supply Company and had many other business inter-

ests in Wilmington. After retirement in his later years, he spent most of his time at Orton.

Murchison married Catherine (Kate) Elliott Williams (5 Apr. 1836–18 Jan. 1912). He was survived by his wife and five children: Luola (m. James Sprunt), Kenneth McKenzie, Jr. (m. Aurelia deMauriac), Jane (m. Frank Ellis), Jessie Williams (m. Shirley Carter), and Marian E. (m. Charles H. Hurkamp). A Presbyterian, he died in Baltimore while visiting his daughter, Mrs. Carter, and was buried in Oakdale Cemetery, Wilmington.

SEE: Samuel A. Ashe, ed., *Biographical History of North Carolina*, vol. 1 (1905 [portrait]); Weymouth T. Jordan, comp., *North Carolina Troops, 1861–1865: A Roster*, vol. 4 (1973); Ida B. Kellam Records and Oakdale Cemetery Records (Wilmington); James Sprunt, *Chronicles of the Cape Fear River* (1914); Wilmington *Morning Star*, 5, 7 June 1904.

LEORA HIATT MCEACHERN

Murdoch, Francis Johnstone (*17 Mar. 1846–21 June 1909*), Episcopal clergyman, teacher, and manufacturer, was born in Buncombe County, the son of William and Margaret Nixon Murdoch. His parents immigrated to America from Ireland in 1842, settling first in Pennsylvania and later moving to North Carolina, where they purchased a farm in Buncombe County. Young Murdoch received his preparatory education at Colonel Stephen Lee's school in Asheville and in 1860 entered the South Carolina Military Academy (later The Citadel). At the beginning of the Civil War, he enlisted for a six-month period in Company E, First North Carolina Volunteers, known as the Bethel Regiment. Afterwards he returned to the Military Academy, where he remained until the end of the war. As a cadet he took an active part in the defense of Charleston, rising to the rank of lieutenant.

After the war Murdoch taught for several years in a school run by the Reverend Jarvis Buxton, rector of Trinity Church, Asheville. While teaching, he studied for Holy Orders under Dr. Buxton's direction and served as a lay reader at Trinity Church. On 17 Sept. 1868 Bishop Thomas Atkinson ordained Murdoch a deacon in St. Luke's Church, Salisbury. In October he became deacon-in-charge of St. John's, High Shoals, Gaston County, and in that capacity conducted occasional services in several other missions in the county. He was ordained to the priesthood by Bishop Atkinson on 8 May 1870 in St. Paul's Church, Edenton, where the diocesan convention was being held that year. Following ordination, Murdoch took charge of the missions in Buncombe, Haywood, and Rutherford counties. On 29 June 1872 he became rector of St. Luke's Church, Salisbury, where he remained until his death.

At St. Luke's, Murdoch began a long and fruitful career in the Episcopal church, not only in the parochial field but also at the diocesan and national levels. In a few years the number of communicants at St. Luke's more than doubled, a parochial school was established, and an active Sunday school program was inaugurated. Murdoch was noted for his zeal in promoting missions. In 1876 he was instrumental in organizing an association of clergymen, called the Evangelist Brotherhood, "for the purpose of carrying on Parochial missions" and became its warden. Over the next three decades he was tireless in his efforts to establish new missions not only in his home county, Rowan, but in the neighboring counties as well. His first mission church was St. Matthew's, a small wooden building erected about 1880, located six miles west of Salisbury; in 1912 this simple structure was replaced by a larger brick church, given in memory of Murdoch by his widow and his sister Margaret. He was directly responsible for establishing seven other missions in Rowan County and assisted in the formation of missions in Concord, Cooleemee, and Proximity.

Murdoch also had a strong interest in Christian education. He promoted the establishment of the Church School for Boys in Salisbury, sponsored by the Convocation of Charlotte, and served as its treasurer. His primary concern, however, was to educate young men for the ministry. Realizing that many able men in the Diocese of North Carolina were financially unable to attend a regular seminary, he invited them into his home to study theology under his direction. By the time of his death, he had prepared eleven men for the ministry. Two of them, the Reverend Robert Bruce Owens and the Reverend Sidney S. Bost, became prominent clergymen in the Diocese of North Carolina.

Murdoch was recognized by his contemporaries as an outstanding scholar and a profound thinker and preacher. One of his fellow priests remarked that he was "a theological college in himself." Over the years he collected a library of several thousand volumes in the fields of biblical studies, theology, and church history.

Active in the work of the Diocese of North Carolina, Murdoch served on many committees of the diocesan convention and was a clerical trustee of the University of the South, Sewanee, (1884–1909) and of St. Mary's School, Raleigh (1898–1909). He represented his diocese as a clerical deputy to every General Convention from 1889 to 1907 and was a member of the convention's Committee on Christian Unity for fifteen years. At a special diocesan convention in 1893, he was nominated assistant bishop of the Diocese of North Carolina by the Reverend Joseph Blount Cheshire, Jr. After thirty-nine ballots, Murdoch was defeated by the man who had nominated him. Murdoch's contributions to his church and his intellectual attainments were recognized by the University of the South in 1890, when it awarded him the degree of S.T.D.

Among the talents of this many-sided man was his ability as a business organizer and executive. In 1887 Murdoch was one of a group of citizens who organized the Salisbury Cotton Mills for the purpose of giving employment to the needy people of the county. He was elected secretary and treasurer of the company. Murdoch was also a moving spirit in the formation of the Rowan Knitting Company and the Vance Cotton Mill, serving as president of the latter until his death. Seeing the need for more homes in his community, he organized the Salisbury Perpetual Building and Loan Association and was made its first secretary and treasurer. His success in these ventures enabled him to provide financial assistance to many young people, particularly those who sought a higher education.

Murdoch married Eliza J. Marsh of Salisbury on 14 May 1884. They had two children: Francis Johnston and Margaret Nixon (m. Charles Bell). Murdoch was buried in Chestnut Hill cemetery, Salisbury.

Three years after his death, Margaret Murdoch, of Charleston, S.C., established a trust fund of $20,000 in memory of her brother. The income from the trust was to be used for "the education and training of young men for the ministry" of the Episcopal church. It was to be administered by trustees under the name of the Francis J. Murdoch Memorial Society for the Increase of the Ministry. The trustees of the society, appointed by the bishop of the diocese, continue to carry out the provisions of the trust.

SEE: James S. Brawley, *The Rowan Story, 1753–1953* (1953); Theodore Buerman Papers (Southern Historical Collection, University of North Carolina, Chapel Hill); *Carolina Churchman*, December 1912, June 1953; *Carolina Watchman*, 22, 29 June 1909; Archibald Henderson, *The History of St. Luke's Parish and the Beginning of the Episcopal Church in Rowan County* (1924); *Journals of the Diocese of North Carolina* (1867–1909, 1937); *North Carolina Biography*, vol. 4 (1928); William S. Powell, *St. Luke's Episcopal Church, 1753–1953* (1953); Charles L. Van Noppen Papers (Manuscript Department, Duke University Library, Durham).

LAWRENCE F. LONDON

Murfree, Hardy (5 June 1752–6 Apr. 1809), Patriot and state official, was born at Murfree's Landing (now Murfreesboro), the son of William and Mary Moore Murfree. As an officer in the North Carolina Continentals during the Revolutionary War, Murfree won acclaim by leading a column of infantry in a successful attack on Stony Point, a British bastion on the Hudson River. Throughout the war he was a valuable soldier, serving as major and then lieutenant colonel.

After the war he was appointed state inspector of revenue and commissioner of confiscated property in the Edenton District. His interest in internal improvements led to service with a commission to promote the opening of Nag's Head Inlet and to his efforts to have a canal cut from the Roanoke to the Meherrin River. In 1787 he sponsored a successful petition to have the state incorporate the town of Murfreesboro, which he laid off on lands of his father. He was an original member of the Society of the Cincinnati and a Federalist member of the convention of 1789, when North Carolina belatedly ratified the federal Constitution. An active Mason, he founded American George Lodge No. 17 at Murfreesboro in 1789.

His wife, Sally Brickell, having died in 1802, Murfree moved with his children in 1807 to Tennessee, where he had been granted large landholdings as compensation for his services in the war. He died suddenly at his unfinished home, Grantlands, and was eulogized in a Masonic funeral oration by Felix Grundy. In 1811 the state of Tennessee named its new capital, Murfreesboro, in his honor. His son, William Hardy, was a North Carolina congressman, and his great-grandchildren included the novelists Fannie Noailles Dickinson Murfree and Mary Noailles Murfree ("Charles Egbert Craddock").

SEE: Samuel A. Ashe, ed., *Biographical History of North Carolina*, vol. 2 (1905); W. L. Murfree, "Colonel Hardy Murfree of the North Carolina Continental Line," *North Carolina Booklet*, vol. 17, no. 3 (January 1918); John H. Wheeler, ed., *Reminiscences and Memoirs of North Carolina and Eminent North Carolinians* (1884).

THOMAS C. PARRAMORE

Murfree, William Hardy (2 Oct. 1781–9 Jan. 1826), attorney and congressman, was born at Murfree's Ferry (now Murfreesboro), the son of Hardy and Sally Brickell Murfree. He was graduated from The University of North Carolina in 1801. After reading law for a year at Edenton, Murfree opened a law practice in Murfreesboro, where he was also a partner in a mercantile enterprise.

Murfree entered politics in 1805, when he was a successful candidate for the state House of Commons. He served a second term after his reelection in 1812. In the latter year he also served as Democratic elector in the

Edenton District for the Madison and Gerry ticket. In 1813 he was elected to the first of two terms in Congress, during which he "had the reputation of a true republican." Reviving the idea of his father for a series of canals to connect western agricultural regions with Atlantic ports, Murfree in 1814 introduced in Congress an extensive plan of internal improvements similar to that later championed by Archibald D. Murphey. His project included the connection of the larger towns of North Carolina and South Carolina with Norfolk and Savannah. Nothing came of the proposal, though it created considerable interest in the South Atlantic states and won the endorsement of Nathaniel Macon.

By 1820 Murfree had grown discouraged about the prospects for commercial development in eastern North Carolina. After arranging his affairs in the state, he followed his father's footsteps to Tennessee, settling in 1823 on lands inherited from Hardy Murfree. Like his father, however, Murfree survived the change of residence for only a short time. He died at his home in Nashville, leaving his wife of eighteen years, Elizabeth Maney Murfree, and a son, William Law.

SEE: *Biog. Dir. Am. Cong.* (1961); W. E. Dodd, *The Life of Nathaniel Macon* (1913); John H. Wheeler, *Historical Sketches of North Carolina from 1584 to 1851* (1851).

THOMAS C. PARRAMORE

Murphey, Archibald DeBow (1777?–1 Feb. 1832), attorney, legislator, jurist, and manuscript collector, was born near Red House Presbyterian Church in Caswell (then Orange) County, one of seven children of Archibald and Jane DeBow Murphey. His father, a native of Pennsylvania, moved to the Red House community in 1769 and purchased about five hundred acres on Hyco Creek; there he constructed a frame house consisting of two rooms with an attic and a cellar. This simple structure was a curiosity in a community of predominantly log residences and was generally referred to as Murphey's Castle. In the community the elder Murphey met and married Jane DeBow, a native of New Jersey, whose parents had preceded him to North Carolina; he farmed, served with American forces in the Revolutionary War, and was clerk of court in Caswell County from 1780 to 1816. He was a man of some learning; his surviving books carry a plain printed bookplate reading: "A. Murphey, Caswell, N.C."

Archibald D. Murphey did not discuss his childhood in his rather voluminous extant writings, but it is known that he attended David Caldwell's "college" at Greensboro before entering The University of North Carolina in 1796. At Chapel Hill he excelled in his studies, won the confidence of his teachers, and was graduated with honors in 1799. Murphey was immediately hired as tutor in the preparatory department, and the following year he was appointed professor of languages, one of only three members of the entire faculty. He also served as librarian and clerk to the faculty. In 1801 he resigned and moved to Hillsborough to live with and study law under William Duffy. In the same year he married Jane Armistead Scott, the daughter of John Scott of present-day Alamance County.

Licensed to practice law, Murphey purchased his father-in-law's home, the Hermitage, near the Hawfields community, and over the next decade built up an estate of about two thousand acres, including a gristmill and a sawmill near the present town of Swepsonville and an eighty-gallon distillery nearby. He also acquired a large number of slaves, whom he appears to have treated with more than ordinary consideration. Soon he en-

larged his home and built in the yard a law office, which served as a convenient place to keep his farm and legal accounts as well as a meeting place for his clients. His wagons frequently made trips to Petersburg, carrying flour, whiskey, and other produce. During this period Murphey invested heavily in other properties, including Lenox Castle at Rockingham Springs. These properties, acquired with borrowed money, taxed his resources and, coupled with his wife's continued illness, impaired his career.

Much of Murphey's legal work centered around the county seat at Hillsborough, where he built a solid reputation as a lawyer. Turning to public service, he was a member of the state senate from 1812 to 1818, and while in that office he made his greatest contributions to the state. Recognizing North Carolina's backwardness, he proposed bold programs for progress, especially in regard to education and internal improvements. In 1817 he submitted his celebrated report advocating a publicly financed system of education. Noting that "one of the strongest reasons which we can have for establishing a general plan of public instruction, is the condition of the poor children of our country," Murphey argued that the state could not expect to progress dramatically until it elevated the educational status of its population. His plan encompassed primary schools, academies, and the university; when he had finished it on 29 Nov. 1817, he wrote his friend Thomas Ruffin: "I bequeath this Report to the State as the Richest Legacy that I shall ever be able to give it."

Two years later Murphey submitted his "Memoir" on internal improvements, in which he recommended a vigorous program to open rivers and canals and construct roads. He wrote: "If North Carolina had her commerce concentrated at one or two points, one or more large commercial cities would grow up; markets would be found at home for the productions of the State; foreign merchandize would be imported into the State for the demands of the market; our debts would be contracted at home; and our Banks would be enabled to change their course of business."

Murphey's proposals for public expenditures for education and for a bold system of land and water transportation were largely ignored by his fellow legislators. North Carolina, soon to be characterized as the "Rip Van Winkle State," was not yet ready for such advanced ideas.

In 1818 the General Assembly elected Murphey to a judgeship in the superior court. The extensive travel involved in the position and Murphey's need to give more attention to his business affairs, however, led to his resignation after only two years on the bench. He resumed his law practice but became increasingly interested in compiling a history of the state. This undertaking was plagued by the deterioration of his physical and financial condition. A lottery was authorized by the General Assembly for the support of Murphey's history, but the proceeds were insufficient to be of substantial help and the history was never written. Murphey was, however, the state's first major collector of manuscripts, and his papers, even though scattered after his death, were of great value to later historians.

Throughout his life Murphey overextended himself financially. Although he apparently was in an enviable monetary position by 1812, within eight years his property was heavily mortgaged and he was unable to pay his debts. One crisis after another occurred as rheumatism wracked his body and as his investments—some in the internal improvements schemes that he championed—proved unsound. The ultimate indignity came in 1829, when, despite the fact that as a legislator he had sought to abolish imprisonment for debt, he himself was incarcerated in Greensboro for twenty days because he could not pay off a note.

Archibald D. Murphey's vision of the future surpassed that of his generation. Measured only against his contemporaries, he was an apparent failure, for few of his proposals were immediately carried out. However, his agitation for public education helped bring about the establishment of the State Literary Fund in 1825 and the first public school act seven years after his death. His zeal for the preservation of the history of the state infected others such as David L. Swain and John H. Wheeler, and the materials that he had collected are still used a century and a half later. And his proposals for overland and water transportation, though somewhat outdated with the coming of railroads, continued to emphasize the need for North Carolina to cast off its dependence on Virginia and South Carolina for markets. Thus Murphey was far more than a dreamer. He was, indeed, a prophet of an awakened state.

Murphey died at age fifty-five, leaving five children who reached adulthood: William Duffy, Victor Moreau, Cornelia Anne, Peter Umstead, and Alexander Hamilton. He was buried in the cemetery at the Presbyterian Church in Hillsborough.

SEE: Samuel A. Ashe, ed., *Biographical History of North Carolina*, vol. 4 (1906); R. D. W. Connor, *Ante-Bellum Builders of North Carolina* (1914); *DAB*, vol. 7 (1934); William Henry Hoyt, ed., *The Papers of Archibald D. Murphey*, 2 vols. (1914); H. G. Jones, *For History's Sake* (1966); Margaret E. Kerche, "The Life and Public Career of Archibald D. Murphey" (Ph.D. diss., University of North Carolina, 1948); Herbert Snipes Turner, *The Dreamer: Archibald DeBow Murphey* (1971).

H. G. JONES

Murphy, George Moseley (1 June 1903–7 Dec. 1968), chemist and educator, was born in Wilmington, the son of James Moseley, a clerk in a dry goods store, and Katie Bappler Murphy. After receiving a B.S. degree in chemistry (1924) and an M.S. degree (1925) at The University of North Carolina, he taught for two years at Clemson College before enrolling for his Ph.D. at the University of Pennsylvania. Transferring to Yale in 1928, he earned a doctorate under Herbert S. Harned in 1930. His interest in the application of quantum mechanics to chemistry led him to seek a postdoctoral appointment in 1930 with the distinguished physical chemist, Harold C. Urey, at Columbia University, where he was an instructor from 1932 to 1936.

At Columbia, Murphy conducted experiments and theoretical studies on the fractional distillation of liquefied hydrogen, and with Urey and Ferdinand G. Brickwedde he was the codiscoverer of deuterium, or heavy hydrogen, in 1931. This isotope of hydrogen is rare, for less than one part in six thousand of naturally occurring hydrogen is deuterium. Its existence was postulated by Urey, and its properties—some of which had to be known in order to find it—were predicted on the basis of quantum mechanical calculations. The discovery was a scientific feat of the first magnitude, for which Urey received the Nobel Prize in 1934. In a very few years heavy water, with two atoms of deuterium instead of ordinary hydrogen, would become of immense importance in the development of atomic energy for the war effort because of the ability of the deuterium nucleus to absorb neutrons emitted during the fission of uranium atoms in nuclear reactor elements. As a label, deuterium

has proved to be a crucial tool for unraveling the mechanisms of many biochemical processes and for understanding many details of chemical bonding and reactivity. It has been the key to the development of artificial trace markers for calibration of analytical procedures for environmental analysis and other studies.

Murphy's contributions, however, came in the discovery of the isotope and the first applications of deuterium to understanding the spectra of small molecules. After more than half a decade with Urey, he returned to Yale in 1936, combining his research interests in the mathematical theory of chemistry, spectroscopy, and thermodynamics. From 1943 to 1946 he was a division director of the Manhattan Project at Columbia University, working on aspects of atomic energy development. A great love of opera was among the factors that persuaded him to stay in New York at the end of World War II. In 1946 he joined the faculty of New York University, becoming chairman of the chemistry department in 1958, associate dean of the Graduate School of Arts and Sciences in 1960, acting dean later, and finally distinguished professor in 1968, a few months before his death in Columbia Presbyterian Hospital after a long illness.

His interests in mathematical aspects of chemistry led to the publication with Henry Margenau of *Mathematics of Physics and Chemistry* during World War II. This textbook, which went through a number of editions, was both a companion to every physical chemist of the next generation and a model for the present generation of textbooks on mathematics for scientists. Murphy also was coeditor of chemical dictionaries and a treatise on the separation of uranium isotopes. Late in life he wrote a short reminiscence of the discovery of deuterium (*Isotopic and Cosmic Chemistry* 1 [1964]).

In May 1934 he married Mary Daggett, whose father, Parker Daggett, had been head of the electrical engineering department at The University of North Carolina and was then at Rutgers University. They had two children, Margaret and William.

SEE: Maurice M. Bursey, *Carolina Chemists* (1982); *Chapel Hill Weekly*, 11 Dec. 1968; *Chemical Engineering News*, 13, 27 Jan., 3 Feb. 1969; *New York Times*, 8 Dec. 1968.

MAURICE M. BURSEY

Murphy, James Bumgardner (4 Aug. 1884–24 Aug. 1950), research physician, the son of Dr. Patrick Livingston and Bettie W. Bumgardner Murphy, was born in Morganton, where his father was a psychiatrist at the state hospital. An older brother, William Alexander, was graduated from The University of North Carolina with an A.B. degree in 1901 and became a prominent physician in New York. James Murphy attended Horner Military Academy in Oxford and was graduated from The University of North Carolina with a B.S. degree in 1905. On receiving a medical degree from Johns Hopkins in 1909, he spent a year at the Pathological Institution of New York State.

Having decided on a career in research, Murphy entered the Rockefeller Institute in 1910 as an associate in pathology and bacteriology. Here he remained for his entire professional career, with a short hiatus for military service during World War I, later becoming an associate and life member of the institute. During the war, with the rank of major in the U.S. Army Medical Corps, he served as assistant to the surgeon general and rendered distinguished service under General William C. Gorgas. On his return to civilian life, he eventually became head of the laboratory for cancer research at the

Rockefeller Institute, a position he held until a few months before his death.

Murphy's research dealt chiefly with the effects of X-ray on the human body, the role of lymphocytes in establishing immunity to transplanted cancer, the discovery of growth-inhibiting substances in normal tissues, and various aspects of the agents that produce malignant tumors. He was active in the fight against cancer and served on many national and international boards in this regard. A prolific contributor to scientific journals, he was widely regarded as a lecturer and teacher. Murphy was the recipient of many honors, including the Belgian Order of Leopold and the Chinese Order of Merit. In 1927 he received an honorary degree from the University of Louvain and an Sc.D. from The University of North Carolina; Oglethorpe University awarded him a D.Sc. in 1938.

In 1919 Murphy married Ray Slater of Boston, a direct descendant of Samuel Slater, an Englishman who immigrated to New England at the end of the eighteenth century and is credited with founding the American cotton-spinning industry. The couple had two sons: James Slater and R. Livingston. James S. Murphy was graduated from Johns Hopkins in 1945, and like his father, became a research physician at the Rockefeller Institute; by his wife, Margaretta Fitler of Philadelphia, he was the father of four children.

After a short illness, Murphy died at Bar Harbor, Maine, not far from his summer home at Seal Harbor. During the summer months he had been active in medical and civic affairs in Maine.

SEE: *Concise Dictionary of American Biography* (1977); Daniel L. Grant, *Alumni History of the University of North Carolina, 1795–1924* (1924); James B. Murphy File (North Carolina Collection, University of North Carolina, Chapel Hill); *New York Times*, 25 Aug. 1950; *Who's Who in America* (1950).

WILLIAM P. STEVENS

Murphy, John (1785–21 Sept. 1841), lawyer, planter, and politician, was born in Robeson County, the son of Neil Murphy (a recent immigrant from Scotland) and the former Miss Downing. While he was still a child, the family moved to South Carolina. Later he taught school in order to pay expenses at South Carolina College (now the University of South Carolina), where he was president of the Clariosophic Society and was one of the academic leaders of his class. Graduating in 1808, he was elected to the board of trustees of South Carolina College in 1809 and again in 1813, the first alumnus to be elected to that body. After studying law, he was admitted to the bar and served as secretary of the South Carolina Senate from 1810 to 1818.

Murphy moved to Alabama in 1818, settling in Monroe County. He was admitted to the state bar but gave much of his attention to the supervision of his plantation and to politics. In 1819 he represented Monroe County at the Alabama Constitutional Convention and served on the Committee of Fifteen, which prepared the original draft of the Constitution. He was elected to the Alabama House of Representatives in 1820 and to the Alabama Senate in 1822. In the senate, where he served until 1824, he took a particular interest in the state bank and education.

In 1825 and again in 1827, Murphy was elected governor of Alabama without opposition. A member of the North Carolina faction, which was well-entrenched in Alabama politics, he had been handpicked by Governor

Israel Pickens, a fellow North Carolinian. Throughout his two terms, Murphy supported the state bank and encouraged the improvement of education, particularly the planning of the University of Alabama. When the Bank of the United States began plans to establish a branch at Mobile in 1826, he protested vigorously on the grounds that creation of the branch would be an invasion of the sovereignty of the state. In 1828 he denounced the Tariff of Abominations. Conceding that a tariff was justified up to a point, he denied that one was justified if it excluded "general and active intercourse with other nations." He recommended adoption of a "temperate remonstrance" calling attention to the injurious effects of the tariff. In 1829 he again advised that judicious and temperate efforts be continued to secure "the constitutional repeal" of the "obnoxious" measure.

Following his two terms as governor, Murphy returned to his plantation in Clarke County. In 1831 he ran unsuccessfully against the ever-popular Dixon Hall Lewis in a race for the congressional seat representing the Mobile District. During the campaign, he supported the Jackson administration and opposed nullification on the grounds that it was subversive to the Union as established under the Constitution.

Elected to the U.S. House of Representatives in 1833 in a race against James Dellet, Murphy served in the Twenty-third Congress. He made no major contributions on Capitol Hill, but when a controversy erupted between the state of Alabama and the national government growing out of the latter's attempt to remove settlers from the Creek lands, Murphy served as a conciliator. Following discussions in Washington, he assured Governor John Gayle that the national government "never intended to expel all the people from the ceded Creek territory."

In 1839 James Dellet defeated Murphy in the contest for the congressional seat he had formerly held. An ardent supporter of the Democratic party, Murphy was active during the presidential campaign in 1840 and served as an elector.

Murphy's first wife was Sarah Hails of South Carolina. In 1832 he married Mrs. Sarah Darington Carter of Clarke County, Ala. One of his sons, Duncan, later served in the California legislature; another son, Murdock, was the first pastor of the Government Street Presbyterian Church in Mobile. Murphy's other children were John, Jr., and Mary Sue. At one time, Murphy served as master of the Grand Lodge of Masons in Alabama. He died at his plantation and was buried at a cemetery near Gosport. His portrait hangs in the main corridor of the Alabama state capitol at Montgomery.

SEE: Thomas P. Abernathy, *The Formative Period in Alabama, 1815–1828* (1965); *Biog. Dir. Am. Cong.* (1950); Willis Brewer, *Alabama: Her History, Resources, War Record, and Public Men* (1872); William Garrett, *Reminiscences of Public Men in Alabama for Thirty Years* (1872); Theodore H. Jack, *Sectionalism and Party Politics in Alabama, 1819–1842* (1920); *Journal of the House of Representatives of the State of Alabama* (1820); *Journal of the Senate of the State of Alabama* (1822–29); John C. Stewart, *The Governors of Alabama* (1975 [portrait]); Thomas M. Williams, *Dixon H. Lewis* (1910).

JOHN M. MARTIN

Murphy, John Albert (24 Jan. 1837–d. after 1892), clergyman and poet, the son of John and Mary ("Molly") Livengood Murphy, was born in Davidson County on his father's farm between Abbott's Creek and

Rich Fork. The 1850 census lists three children in the family: Daniel K., 21, a teacher, and Hanna B., 17, and John A., 13, both students. He attended a log school at Reedy Run, three miles from his home, until 1853, when he entered Catawba College, then located in Newton. In the fall of 1857 he was accepted on trial by the St. Louis Conference, Methodist Episcopal Church, South, and was assigned to the Independence, Mo., circuit. He was ordained a deacon in 1859 and was a pastor for twenty-two years, attaining the position of presiding elder in the Boonville District by 1866. Articles by him appeared in the *St. Louis Christian Advocate*. In 1879 he transferred to the North-West Texas Conference and was assigned first to the Waco District and then to Fort Worth where he remained at least until 1884 when he became a member of the itinerant ministry. He was living in Austin in 1885.

His long poem, *Cosmostoria*, published in book form (151 pages) in 1878 in Chicago, has been compared to John Milton's *Paradise Lost*. He also was the author of numerous shorter poems including "The First Fallen Soldier of 1861," honoring North Carolinian Henry Wyatt, the first soldier killed in the Civil War, "Progressive Perfection," "Our Silver Wedding," and "Texas," composed on the occasion of the laying of the cornerstone of the Texas capitol on 2 Mar. 1885. His "Get Into Some Good Library and Read" was published in S. Pollock Linn's *Golden Gleams of Thought* in 1882, and four other poems appeared in the July 1892 issue of the *Magazine of Poetry*. In June 1885 Trinity College conferred an honorary master's degree on Murphy and in 1889 Catawba College awarded him an honorary doctor of divinity degree.

Murphy's wife was Louisa Jane Yokeley of Davidson County.

SEE: Sam H. Dixon, *Poets and Poetry of Texas* (1885 [portrait]), Thomas W. Herringshaw, *Local and National Poets of America* (1892); Lucian Lamar Knight, *Biographical Dictionary of Southern Authors* (1929); W. H. Lewis, *The History of Methodism in Missouri. . . from 1860 to 1870* (1890); S. Pollock Linn, *Golden Gleams of Thought* (1882); *Minutes of the Annual Conferences of the Methodist Episcopal Church, South* (1858–62, 1870–84); D. J. O'Donoghue, *Poets of Ireland* (1892).

WILLIAM S. POWELL

Murphy, Patrick Livingston *(23 Oct. 1848–11 Sept. 1907)*, psychiatrist, served for almost twenty-five years as superintendent of the Western North Carolina Hospital in Morganton. He was the son of a wealthy Sampson County couple, Patrick and Eliza A. Faison Murphy. His father was a successful lawyer and businessman who served in the state legislature during the Civil War; his mother was a member of a family prominent in Sampson and Duplin counties. His parents provided Murphy with an education in the best schools and academies of the time. He attended the Male Academy at Clinton, Colonel Tew's Military Academy in Hillsborough, and the Bingham School. The outbreak of the Civil War postponed his further formal education. In 1864 and 1865 he taught at The Oaks and at Mebane. After the war Murphy began the study of medicine under a preceptor, his family physician, before attending one course of lectures at the University of Virginia (1869–70). The following year he completed a second course of lectures at the University of Maryland and was graduated in March 1871.

For a short time Murphy practiced medicine in his native Sampson County, but he soon moved to Wilming-

ton, where he joined Dr. William J. Love in general practice. Murphy came to dislike the routine of private practice and decided to seek experience that would allow him to compete for the superintendency of the Western North Carolina Asylum for the Insane, then under construction. Consequently, in March 1879 he accepted the position of assistant physician of the Western Virginia Asylum, at Staunton, where he remained for three years. The training he received at Staunton and the recommendation of his superiors led to his election in December 1882 as superintendent of the Morganton asylum.

Assuming his duties in January 1883, Murphy guided the hospital through a quarter century of growth and innovative therapy. Under his administration, the Morganton hospital's capacity grew from 150 patients to well over 1,000. Murphy opposed the idea that custodial care for the insane was of primary importance. He considered an asylum to be a place of treatment for the sick and conducted a successful campaign to have the word "hospital" substituted for "asylum" in the titles of all state mental institutions. Murphy also abandoned the use of traditional restraint devices such as the straitjacket and instituted a program of occupational therapy. This therapy consisted of outside work of benefit to the hospital as well as the patient; as a result, the Morganton institution became an almost self-sufficient community with its own farm, dairy, and gardens. Later, Murphy introduced the colony system of patient care, whereby cottages were built away from the main hospital building to serve both as the intermediate phase of treatment for patients soon to be discharged and as a desirable alternate to inpatient care for those considered incurable. In 1895 he began a training school for psychiatric nurses at the hospital.

A highly respected member of state and national medical groups, Murphy belonged to the North Carolina Board of Medical Examiners from 1884 to 1890. In 1897 he was elected president of the state medical society. He served on the executive council of the American Medico-Psychological Association, the forerunner of the American Psychiatric Association. He also served for one term as a director of the state school for the deaf.

Murphy married Elizabeth (Bettie) Waddell Bumgardner in 1878, and they had four children: Malinda McCorkle, William Alexander, James Bumgardner, and Robert. He was buried on the grounds of the Morganton hospital.

SEE: Samuel A. Ashe, ed., *Biographical History of North Carolina*, vol. 6 (1907); J. K. Hall, "Psychiatry—In Retrospect and in Prospect," *Southern Medicine and Surgery* (November 1938); Howard A. Kelly and Walter L. Burrage, *American Medical Biographies* (1920); Pamphlet of proceedings and addresses connected with the presentation of an oil portrait of Murphy to the state library at Raleigh (North Carolina Collection, University of North Carolina, Chapel Hill); *Proceedings of the American Medico-Psychological Association* (1910); *Transactions of the Medical Society of the State of North Carolina* (1908 [portrait]).

SUSAN MILNER

Murphy, Spencer *(29 July 1904–30 Nov. 1964)*, journalist and editor of the *Salisbury Post*, was born in Jamestown, the son of Walter (Pete) Murphy, for many years a major figure in North Carolina politics, and his wife, Maude May Horney. A Salisburian in everything except place of birth, he was a member of one of the town's oldest families. His great-great grandfather, James Murphy, a native of Glasgow, Scotland, settled in Salisbury shortly before the American Revolution. On the maternal side, he was a descendant of Richard Warren and John Howland, signers of the Mayflower Compact.

From 1921 to 1925 Murphy attended The University of North Carolina, where he was a member of Sigma Nu fraternity, the Order of the Golden Fleece, and the Carolina Playmakers. He founded the *Carolina Buccaneer*, a campus humor magazine, and served on the editorial boards of the *Tar Heel* and the *Carolina Magazine*, a campus literary journal. In his junior year he was named assistant editor of the 1924 *Yackety-Yack*, the college yearbook, and because of a staff emergency, took over as editor-in-chief. He was also editor-in-chief of the 1925 edition.

On receiving his A.B. degree, Murphy returned to Salisbury and joined the staff of the *Salisbury Post* as a reporter. Though offered positions with larger newspapers in other states during his career, he chose to remain in his home place. In 1936 he became editor of the *Post*, and in 1956 he was named executive editor.

Murphy's editorials won wide acclaim, many being reprinted in the state's major newspapers. In 1941 the North Carolina Press Association, in the first year of its contest, awarded him first prize for an editorial. He won first place again in 1946 and in 1952. During this period, the *Post* was the only newspaper with a circulation under 20,000 to place first in the editorial division, and Murphy was the only three-time editorial winner. In 1957, when the contest had been divided into two categories according to circulation figures, he took first place in the smaller newspaper division. Murphy also wrote articles for other newspapers; numerous magazines, including *The State*, the *Saturday Evening Post*, and *Literary America*; and trade journals. Other writings appear in both poetry and fiction anthologies.

In 1945 the *Salisbury Post* was nominated for a Pulitzer Prize for a story on the plight of a local widow and her children (the Pinion case) that Murphy had brought to the attention of the national news media. In 1948 the *Christian Advocate* of Chicago awarded him its top prize for an Easter editorial. In 1950 he received national recognition when the Freedom Foundation of Valley Forge awarded him a bronze medal for an editorial entitled "On the Ramparts." He won scroll citations from the same organization in 1951.

A man of character, integrity, and intelligence, Murphy held the respect and love of countless people in all walks of life. He was known for his great generosity, humor, courtesy, and, above all, a gentleness that pervaded all that he did. At his death, the editor of the *Winston-Salem Journal* wrote: "As one of the 'Young Turks' of North Carolina journalism in the late 1920s and early 1930s, he did much to help re-orient the political and social thinking of North Carolinians. Through the years as columnist and editor he established a reputation as an independent thinker."

Newspaper activities, although always at the heart of his endeavors, consumed only a part of his energies. He was an indefatigable worker for "good causes" designed to give humanity a better existence. His interests were diversified, embracing such fields as better race relations, music, and fine literature. As president of the North Carolina Symphony Society from 1946 to 1949, Murphy worked tirelessly for its fund-raising campaigns. He once successfully appealed to the joint appropriations committee of the legislature for a substantial increase in its recommended allotment for the group, which by 1943 had become the first state-subsidized symphony orchestra in the nation.

In 1946 Murphy was appointed to the board of trustees of the North Carolina College at Durham to fill the unexpired term of his father. He was reappointed in 1949 and served until 1953. In addition, he served on the board of The University of North Carolina Alumni Association from 1946 to 1949 and was named Rowan County chairman of the Morehead Foundation in 1952. A member of the national board of the Citizens Committee for United Nations Reform in 1946, he was president of the North Carolina chapter.

Never a joiner in the usual sense, Murphy belonged to numerous organizations dedicated to assist the people of his community and state. He served on the executive committee of the North Carolina Social Hygiene Society (1947–49); the advisory boards of the North Carolina Good Health Association (1947), North Carolina Labor Commission (1948–51), and North Carolina United World Federalists (1948–50); and the Governor's Committee on Highway Safety (1952). He also was a trustee of the North Carolina Library Association (1950–53) and director of the North Carolina Conference for Social Service (1959).

On 1 Sept. 1925 Murphy married Katherine DeBerry Fisher, and the couple had one daughter, Mary Marshall (Mrs. Seth S. Murdoch). He died in Salisbury at age sixty and was buried in City Memorial Park Cemetery.

SEE: *Greensboro Daily News*, 2 Dec. 1964; *Salisbury Post*, 9 Jan. 1955, 30 Nov., 1–2, 6, 17 Dec. 1964; *Who's Who in the South and Southeast* (1950); *Winston-Salem Journal*, 3 Dec. 1964.

MARY M. MURDOCH

Murphy, Walter (Pete) (24 Oct. 1872–12 Jan. 1946), lawyer and state legislator, was born in Salisbury, the son of Andrew, a local merchant, and Helen Long Murphy. He was the grandson of John Murphy, also a Salisbury merchant, and the great-grandson of James Murphy, a native of Glasgow, Scotland, who settled in Salisbury shortly before the American Revolution. On his maternal side, he was descended from local settlers of the 1750s and was a grandson of Dr. Alexander Long, Jr., a member of the class of 1813 at The University of North Carolina.

Murphy attended The University of North Carolina from 1888 to 1890, when he withdrew for two years. Returning in 1892, he enrolled in the law school. After receiving his law license in 1894, he established a practice in Salisbury. During the Spanish-American War, he served briefly in the navy.

Throughout his adult life, Murphy was an indefatigable campaigner for the Democratic party. Stumping tours carried him into all of the state's one hundred counties and, at the behest of the national committee, into other states as well. He was for several years a member of the executive committee of the state Democratic party, twice a delegate to the Democratic National Convention (1908 and 1932), and once (1908) an elector-at-large. Murphy had two brief excursions into federal service. He served once as special assistant to the commissioner of internal revenue during the administration of President Woodrow Wilson, and he assisted in the establishment of the Federal Deposit Insurance Corporation in the Southeast under President Franklin D. Roosevelt.

In the General Assembly, Murphy represented Rowan County in the sessions of 1897, 1903–7, 1913, 1917, 1921–27, 1933, and 1937–39. He was speaker of the house during the extra session of 1913 and the regular session of

1917. In 1945 he was appointed liaison officer of the house and senate, a post especially created for him by the legislature in recognition of his long and outstanding service to the state. Although he never held a higher elective office, he became one of the best-known men in North Carolina, as well as one of the most influential. His gifts as a political orator and as an extemporaneous speaker of uncommon wit and his colorful personality combined to build him a far-reaching reputation while he was still in his twenties.

Murphy's celebrated memory for names, dates, faces, and facts served him well, both as a politician and as a student of history. While serving as reading clerk of the senate in 1899, he always called the roll from memory, sometimes in reverse alphabetical order. Because of his personality, he was often introduced as the "most popular man in the state." As a member of the General Assembly, Murphy backed increased state support for education, including the normal schools for blacks, for good roads, for the physically and mentally handicapped, and for assistance to war veterans, widows, and orphans. His attitude towards higher education was undoubtedly influenced by his lifelong ties with the university at Chapel Hill, where he served on the board of trustees and as a member of its executive committee for forty-four years, from 1901 until his death. When he was speaker in 1913, the university asked for its largest appropriation up to that time. After passage of the bill, Murphy returned to his home in Salisbury; in his absence, the bill was called back to the floor and was defeated.

The *Raleigh Times* in 1963 quoted a former house member, J. Wilbur Bunn of Wake County, on this incident: "Walter Murphy came back to Raleigh. I was sitting twenty feet from the man when he spoke and pleaded for the survival of the University of North Carolina. He had tears in his eyes and was mopping his face with his hand. When he finished his speech, at least ninety per cent of the representatives voted for the bill. It was the most thrilling experience I witnessed while here."

Securing every dollar possible for the state's institutions headed Murphy's legislative interests. At his death it was noted that many people had called "Walter Murphy, late of Rowan, 'the prince of parliamentarians' ever since he managed to get a $3,000,000 appropriations bill for state institutions through the house of 1917, without a dissenting vote."

In the 1920s Murphy took a vigorous stand against attempts to ban by law the teaching of the theory of evolution in the public schools and state-supported institutions of higher learning. In North Carolina, the acrimonious controversy on evolution reached a peak with the Poole Bill of 1925. Introduced in the General Assembly by David Scott Poole of Raeford and supported by powerful sectarian forces in the state, it would have prohibited teaching "as a fact Darwinism or any other evolutionary hypothesis." In the house debate, Murphy joined such able legislators as Henry Groves Connor, Jr., of Wilson, and Sam Ervin, Jr., of Morganton, in denouncing the antievolutionists. Murphy's eloquent address has been credited with having "clinched" the death of the antievolutionary movement in the legislature of 1925. The Poole Bill was rejected in the house by a vote of 67 to 46. Later that year The University of North Carolina awarded Murphy an LL.D. degree.

A steadfast Democrat, Murphy once ensured his own defeat by the voters of Rowan County rather than compromise his loyalty to the party. In 1928 he favored Senator James A. Reed of Missouri for the Democratic presidential nomination. But when the Democratic National Convention nominated Governor Alfred E. Smith of New York—whose candidacy was anathema to much of the South—Murphy campaigned on behalf of Smith and harshly denounced Senator Furnifold M. Simmons, the state's most influential Democrat, for refusing to do likewise. A candidate himself for the legislature that year, Murphy advised his constituents not to vote for him unless they could also vote for Smith. On election day, both he and Smith were repudiated at the polls. In 1930 Murphy supported Josiah W. Bailey in the heated Democratic senatorial primary in which Bailey defeated the once-powerful Senator Simmons.

For many years Murphy was interested in obtaining for the state a suitable memorial to be placed at the Gettysburg Battlefield in Pennsylvania in memory of North Carolina's Civil War dead. He was disappointed at what he regarded as the "pitiful pittance" allotted by the legislature for this purpose. After considerable effort by Murphy, the noted sculptor, Gutzon Borglum, was commissioned to construct a monument. Murphy made the dedicatory address at its unveiling on 3 July 1929. Public recognition for his work in behalf of Civil War veterans came in 1933, when he received the honorary appointment of inspector general of the North Carolina Division of United Confederate Veterans.

For thirty years Murphy was the state's foremost advocate of a "square deal" for blacks and fought for better educational opportunities for Negroes when Jim Crow was still firmly entrenched. Buildings were named for him at what is now North Carolina Central University, where he was a member of the board of trustees, and at North Carolina Agricultural and Technical University. He was the author of the "Murphy Law," which pushed North Carolina far ahead of other southern states in education for blacks.

Murphy never made the same speech twice. He appeared to absorb every fact that he encountered, cataloguing each in its allotted place in his memory, from which he could summon it at will. His library held more than three thousand books, and he was an authority on Napoleon. Many believed that Murphy knew more about the history of North Carolina than any of his contemporaries. The legislature of 1945 suggested that he write a history of the state, but approaching illness prevented him from such an undertaking. On the day of Murphy's death, the *Salisbury Post* observed: "It is commonly believed that a substantial total of the state's history vanished with Pete Murphy, and that a wealth of anecdote and reminiscences which only he could have committed to paper, go with him to the grave."

While a student in Chapel Hill, Murphy was cofounder of the *Tar Heel* and was its first business manager and second editor. He also founded the Psi chapter of Sigma Nu fraternity and became its first eminent commander. Moreover, he acted as personal secretary to university president, George T. Winston. For four years Murphy, who was six-feet-two and weighed two hundred pounds, played football at the university and was "centre rush" on its 1892 "all time wonder team." He once was said to have witnessed nearly seven hundred football games, most of them involving The University of North Carolina.

Murphy was cofounder of the *Alumni Review* in 1912 and served as president of the Alumni Association in 1922. He belonged to numerous civic and patriotic organizations, including the Masonic order, Elks, and Kiwanis. Murphy was a member of St. Luke's Episcopal Church in Salisbury. On 18 Mar. 1903 he married Maude H. Horney, a member of a Quaker family of Jamestown, N.C. She never participated in her husband's public life but was his constant inspiration and adviser at home. They were the parents of two children: Spencer, who became editor of the *Salisbury Post*, and Elisabeth, who married Peter Henderson. Following his death in Salisbury, Murphy was buried in City Memorial Park Cemetery.

SEE: *Daily Tar Heel*, 15 Jan. 1946; Willard B. Gatewood, *Preachers, Pedagogues, and Politicians: The Evolution Controversy in North Carolina, 1920–1927* (1966); *Greensboro Daily News*, 15 Jan. 1946; Elmer L. Puryear, *Democratic Party Dissension in North Carolina, 1928–1936* (1962); Raleigh *News and Observer*, 13, 20 Jan. 1946; *Salisbury Evening Post*, 12 Jan. 1946, 10 Feb. 1963, 29 Apr. 1975; *The State Magazine*, 11 Apr. 1953.

NATHANIEL F. MAGRUDER
MARY M. MURPHY MURDOCH

Murray, James (*9 Aug. 1713–1781*), colonial official, merchant, and planter, was a native of Unthank, Roxburghshire, in the valley of the Ewes, Scotland, the oldest son of John and Anne Bennet Murray, the daughter of the laird of Chesters. After his father's death, James was apprenticed to a London merchant who was engaged in the West Indian trade. Apparently due to his acquaintance with Governor Gabriel Johnston, Murray embarked for North Carolina on 20 Sept. 1735. After a brief stay in Charles Town, S.C., he arrived on the Cape Fear early in 1736 and resided for several months at Brunswick town.

Murray quickly became involved in the economic and political life of North Carolina. He feuded with the Moore family at Brunswick, possibly due to his friendship with Governor Johnston, and then moved to the rival Newton settlement (Wilmington), championed by the governor. In Wilmington, he opened a mercantile business on Front Street and purchased a five-hundred-acre plantation on the Cape Fear River. With Johnston's support, Murray became a justice of the peace for New Hanover County (1737), a deputy naval officer for the port of Brunswick (1739), and a member of the governor's Council (1739). On the Council he joined forces with William Smith, Robert Halton, and Matthew Rowan in their factional disputes with fellow Council members Roger Moore, Edward Moseley, Nathaniel Rice, and Eleazer Allen.

After a five-year absence in Great Britain (1744–49), Murray resumed an active role in provincial affairs. In 1750 the people of Wilmington elected him a town commissioner, and the following year he was appointed associate justice of North Carolina and commissioner of Fort Johnston. In 1753 Murray became secretary and clerk of the Crown, and in 1754 he was elevated by seniority to president of the governor's Council. During 1755 he held the post of deputy paymaster of the forces sent to the Ohio under Colonel James Innes during the French and Indian War.

With the appointment of Arthur Dobbs as governor in 1754, Murray's role in the provincial government came into question. Governor Dobbs became involved in a bitter dispute with Murray and his cousin, John Rutherfurd, and in 1757 the governor suspended the two men from their seats on the Council. Dobbs accused Murray and Rutherfurd of various crimes, including the charge that Murray had illegally issued unlimited private paper currency that was to be accepted by the colony in payment of quitrents. In communications with the Board of Trade, Dobbs attacked Murray "and his junto," which he contended was attempting to organize a party in the Assembly to undermine the governor and advance Murray's popularity.

It was true that Murray had ambitions of becoming acting governor on the death of the aged governor. In 1761 he privately admitted that if he were reinstated to the Council and no lieutenant governor were appointed, then he hoped to succeed Dobbs as governor. If this possibility did not materialize, Murray planned to leave North Carolina and reside in a healthier climate. In 1762 he was restored by the Privy Council as senior member of the governor's Council; but two years later, shortly before Dobbs's death, William Tryon arrived in North Carolina as lieutenant governor of the colony. Frustrated in his design to become governor, Murray left the province in 1765 and joined relatives in Boston, where he became involved in various business ventures including the operation of a sugarhouse.

As a North Carolina planter, Murray had enlarged and developed his Point Repose plantation, located on the Cape Fear River between Hood Creek and the plantation of Matthew Rowan. Here he grew rice, silk, and indigo; owned a sawmill capable of cutting 100,000 feet of lumber annually; manufactured tar; and became involved in tanning and currying operations. Between 1755 and 1759 he had constructed a "grand and splendid" brick mansion built from bricks produced on the plantation. Due to the death of his wife and children, he became disillusioned with plantation life and turned the operation of Point Repose over to his nephew, Thomas Clark, who became a Revolutionary War brigadier general.

During the American Revolution, Murray remained loyal to Great Britain. When the British evacuated Boston in 1776, Murray fled to Halifax, Nova Scotia, where he died four years later. His North Carolina property, including Point Repose plantation, was confiscated by the state as Tory property. Brigadier General Thomas Clark, the son of Murray's sister, claimed the plantation in compensation for debts owed him by Murray. In 1783 the state awarded the property to Clark, who lived there until his death in 1792.

Murray was married twice. His first wife was Barbara Bennet, a cousin, whom he married in Scotland in 1744. Of their six children, four died in childhood, probably at Point Repose. His two surviving daughters were Elizabeth (m. Edward Hutchinson Robbins of Milton, Mass.) and Dorothy (m. the Reverend John Forbes). After Barbara Bennet Murray died at Point Repose in 1758, Murray married Mrs. MacKay Thompson, a widow, in 1761.

SEE: Evangeline Walker Andrews, ed., *Journal of a Lady of Quality* (1923); Samuel A. Ashe, ed., *Biographical History of North Carolina*, vol. 3 (1906); Walter Clark, ed., *State Records of North Carolina*, vols. 19, 22–23 (1901–7); James Murray Papers (North Carolina State Archives, Raleigh); William L. Saunders, ed., *Colonial Records of North Carolina*, vols. 4–6 (1886–88); Nina M. Tiffany, ed., *Letters of James Murray, Loyalist* (1901 [portrait]).

DONALD R. LENNON

Murray, William David (*9 Sept. 1908–29 Mar. 1986*), football coach and athletic administrator, was born in Rocky Mount, one of eight children of Orion D. and Emma Whiteman Murray. He attended the Hill Street Graded School and Rocky Mount High School. During his senior year he was an all-state football back, coached by Jimmy Simpson, a former Trinity College player.

Murray entered Duke University in the fall of 1927. He starred on the freshman football team that year and on the varsity team, coached by Jimmy DeHart, from 1928 to 1930. While a senior he rushed for 1,030 yards, was voted the team's most valuable player, and made the all-southern team as a halfback. Murray also ran track, and during his senior year he helped coach the freshman basketball team. He was voted best all-around member of his freshman class and was president of the men's Student Government Association as a senior. At commencement he received the Robert E. Lee Award as Duke's outstanding senior.

In the spring of 1931 Murray became the principal and coach of all sports at the Methodist Children's Home in Winston-Salem; he also taught history and geography. In ten years as football coach at the home, he compiled a record of 69 wins against only 9 losses and 3 ties.

In 1940 Murray left Winston-Salem to become head football coach at the University of Delaware. Coaching through the 1950 season, with a three-year interruption during World War II, he achieved a record of 49 wins, 16 losses, and 2 ties, with undefeated seasons in 1941, 1942, and 1946. At Delaware he also served as athletic director (1940–45); director of the Division of Student Health, Physical Education, and Athletics; and president of the faculty club.

In 1951 Murray returned to Duke as the head football coach, succeeding Wallace Wade, who had left to become commissioner of the Southern Conference. He coached at Duke for fifteen seasons, only two of which were losing seasons. His teams won the Southern Conference championship in 1952 and the Atlantic Coast Conference championship in 1954, 1960, 1961, and 1962. In 1953 and 1955 Duke was cochampion of the ACC. Murray was voted Southern Conference coach of the year in 1952 and ACC coach of the year in 1954, 1960, and 1962. His Duke teams were ranked in the final wire services' top twenty eight times and played in three bowl games: a 34–7 victory over Nebraska in the Orange Bowl after the 1954 season, a 48–21 loss to Oklahoma in the Orange Bowl after the 1957 season, and a 7–6 Cotton Bowl victory over Arkansas following the 1960 season. His twelve Duke All-Americans included Mike McGee, winner of the 1959 Outland Trophy as the nation's best lineman. Murray won 93 games, lost 51, and tied 9 at Duke.

After the 1965 season, Murray left coaching to take a position as executive director of the five-thousand-member American Football Coaches Association. His duties included scheduling clinics, printing yearbooks, making public appearances, and coordinating the association's annual midsummer All-Star game. Murray had long been active in coaches' organizations. At the University of Delaware, he was president of the Middle Atlantic States Collegiate Athletic Conference (1947–49) and a member of the executive council of the Eastern College Athletic Conference. At Duke, he was active in the American Football Coaches Association and served as president in 1962. While executive secretary of that organization, he was chairman of its ethics committee. He was also on the board of directors of the National Football Hall of Fame. Murray maintained his residence in Durham, discharging his AFCA duties by telephone, correspondence, and travel. He retired in 1982.

On 30 Aug. 1930 he married a fellow Duke student, Carolyn Kirby of Decatur, Ga. She was one year behind her husband and left without a degree. After returning to Duke, she received her degree in 1959 and then taught school for several years. The couple had three daughters: Joy, Marilyn, and Carol. Murray was active in Durham civic and charitable enterprises, particularly Easter Seals. He was a member of Epworth United Methodist Church, Durham, and the Fellowship of Christian Athletes; in the late 1960s he was president of the national FCA.

Murray was a member of the National Football Hall of Fame, the North Carolina Sports Hall of Fame, the Duke Sports Hall of Fame, the University of Delaware Hall of Fame, and the Helms Athletic Foundation Hall of Fame. For his contributions to college football he won an award from the Touchdown Club of New York (1968) and the prestigious Amos Alonzo Stagg Award from the American Football Coaches Association (1972). In 1985 the AFCA dedicated its *Guidebook to Championship Football Drills* to Murray. He died in Durham and was buried in Maplewood Cemetery.

SEE: Bruce A. Corrie, *The Atlantic Coast Conference, 1953–1978* (1978); *Durham Morning Herald*, 30 Mar. 1986; Glenn E. (Ted) Mann, *A Story of Glory: Duke University Football* (1985); Ronald L. Mendell and Timothy B. Phares, *Who's Who in Football* (1974); William D. Murray File (Duke University Sports Information Department, Durham); Raleigh *News and Observer*, 19 Sept. 1954 and scattered issues.

JIM L. SUMNER

Murrow, Edward Roscoe (25 Apr. 1908–27 Apr. 1965), news broadcaster and government official, originally named Egbert, was born near Centre Quaker Meetinghouse in Guilford County on Polecat Creek, the youngest of three sons of Egbert Roscoe and Ethel Lamb Murrow, strict Quakers. Even so, the elder Murrow enlisted in the army during the Spanish-American War and was sent to Vancouver Barracks across the Columbia River in the Washington Territory near Portland, Oreg. Following this service he returned to Guilford County and married. After a few years, when their son, Egbert [Edward], was "a little fellow," the Murrows moved to the state of Washington, where some relatives had taken up residence many years before. They lived there for a year or so, then returned to Guilford County. In 1913 they moved back to Washington, settling at Blanchard in the northwestern corner of the state.

Numerous explanations have been given for the final move, some of them remembered for many years but never published. Low farm prices, asthma attacks suffered by Ethel Murrow, and the lure of the Pacific Northwest, however, were strong reasons. In 1925 the family moved to Beaver Camp, a logging camp in the Olympic rain forest four miles from the Pacific Ocean. Here, when he was seventeen, Murrow worked as an axman with a logging crew. Somewhere along the way, the young man dropped the name Egbert and became Edward or Ed to the crew and his friends. It was not until 1944, however, that he legally changed his name.

Having saved some money and with the help of his brothers, Murrow entered Washington State College at Pullman in the fall of 1926. Intending to major in business administration, he discovered a kindly and capable teacher of speech, Ida Lou Anderson. She was from Tennessee, and in her Murrow found a kindred spirit. Active in sports, debating, drama, and campus politics, he held several student jobs, became class president, and was top ROTC cadet. Among his honors and accomplishments was election to Phi Beta Kappa. Through his activities with the National Student Federation of America, Murrow attended a convention in Palo Alto, Calif., where he took the floor to criticize students for being unduly concerned with "fraternities, football and fun" as the Great Depression began to take effect. He made such a good impression that he was elected national president of the NSFA for 1930–31.

Following graduation in June 1930, Murrow was commissioned a second lieutenant in the inactive reserve. He left immediately for New York, where the offices of the NSFA were located, and soon afterwards went to Europe to attend an international students' meeting in Brussels. There he associated with young people from across Europe and learned firsthand of the problems created by the aftermath of World War I. Back home again, he spoke at meetings across the nation and assisted in an exchange program with foreign students.

In New York, Murrow persuaded the Columbia Broadcasting System, then only a little over two years old, to broadcast a program, "The University of the Air," for the NSFA. For the program he succeeded in recruiting, live, such people as Einstein and Tagore and, by the then-novel transatlantic wireless, such notables as Ramsay MacDonald from Great Britain and President von Hindenburg from Germany.

While president of NSFA, Murrow boarded the train in North Carolina to go to a convention in New Orleans. On the way down he met Janet Huntington Brewster, from Middletown, Conn., who was traveling to the same meeting as a delegate from Mount Holyoke College. They were married in the fall of 1934, and their first and only child, Charles Casey, was born in London on 6 Nov. 1945.

In 1935 Murrow became "director of talks" and education for CBS, still a small network with only a hundred stations. Two years later he was sent to Europe to broadcast special events—the coronation of King George VI and festivals and ceremonies of various kinds. In March 1938, while in Vienna, he transmitted his observations of Hitler's annexation of Austria. Direct journalism was born on this occasion and so was Murrow's rise to fame. In turn, he became CBS's European director, war correspondent (1939–45), and vice-president and director of public affairs. Stationed in London during much of World War II, he described in the first person German bombing raids on the city with the sound of sirens and explosions in the background. His moving and graphic terms, broadcast from the heart of London, contributed to the growth of American concern about the war and sympathy for Britain. His wife, Janet, also broadcast her observations of life among the mass of people in England. To the British Murrow became a hero, and in time he was made a Knight Commander of the British Empire.

Initially, of course, Murrow's medium was radio, but with the advent of television he became an even more notable figure. Among the programs that he developed were "Person to Person," "See It Now," "Small World," and "CBS Reports." All of these drew large and devoted audiences, as did his lectures on international relations across the United States and in Europe. Edward R. Murrow played a particularly crucial role in alerting the nation to the significance of Senator Joseph McCarthy's groundless "witch-hunt" for Communists in the government.

Resigning from CBS, Murrow became head of the U.S. Information Agency in 1961. He served in the post until 1964, when ill health forced his retirement. An inveterate cigarette smoker, he developed lung cancer which apparently spread to his brain. At his insistence, he was taken from a New York hospital to his rural home in Pawling, N.Y., where he died two days after his fifty-seventh birthday. His ashes were scattered across his farm.

Murrow's contributions to the nation were recognized by the awarding of numerous honorary degrees, including that of LL.D. by The University of North Carolina in 1946. He received the Freedom House Award (1954), an Emmy award (1956), and the President's Medal of Freedom (1964). He was the author of *This is London* and many articles in educational journals.

SEE: Edward Bliss, Jr., "Remembering Edward R. Murrow," *Saturday Review*, 31 May 1971; *DAB*, vol. 7, supp. (1981); Alexander Kendrick, *Prime Time: The Life of Edward R. Murrow* (1969); Charles Kuralt, "Edward R. Murrow," *North Carolina Historical Review* 48 (April 1971); Letter from Vera Hamilton (4 Mar. 1980), an unsigned letter (4 Mar. 1980), and letter from Lawrence W. Routh (15 Mar. 1980), all from Greensboro (possession of William S. Powell); R. Franklin Smith, *Edward R. Murrow: The War Years* (1978); Ann M. Sperber, *Murrow: His Life and Times* (1986); *Who Was Who in America*, vol. 4 (1968).

WILLIAM S. POWELL

Myers, Albert Gallatin (15 Jan. 1880–15 Apr. 1976), banker, insurance executive, and textile manufacturer, was born in Chesterfield County, S.C., the sixth of ten children of Stephen Huntley and Winifred Crump Myers. In 1889 his family moved to Charlotte. This marked the end of his schooling and the start of a long and successful business career. His first job was as errand boy and janitor in a store, where he earned twenty-five cents a day. At eighteen he went to work as a clerk at the Merchants and Farmers Bank. He had become head bookkeeper when he left in 1905 to be one of the organizers of Gastonia's Citizens National Bank. Although essentially self-educated, Myers rose to be vice-president, president (1921), and chairman of the board (1953) before retiring from the bank in 1967 as honorary chairman. A close business friend quoted him as saying that the purpose of a bank is not only to make money, but also to serve people. He was remembered by many for his generosity in helping others and his willingness to cancel debts when borrowers were unable to repay loans during the depression.

In 1907 Myers was one of the founders of the Jefferson Standard Life Insurance Company. He was elected chairman of the executive committee and held this position until his retirement in 1970. He was also on the board of the Jefferson-Pilot Corporation and a member of the North Carolina Advisory Board of the Liberty Mutual Insurance Company of Boston. Because of his experience and contacts in banking, Myers was able to enter the textile industry. In 1914 he and a business associate took over a financially troubled Kings Mountain textile mill, paid off all its debts in two years, and built Myers Mill, Incorporated. During the early 1930s Myers organized twenty-three failing Gastonia mills into Textiles, Incorporated, guided the enterprise through the depression years, and developed it into the largest combed yarn-producing corporation in the world. As president and chairman of the board of this company, he became a leader in the textile industry.

During his active business career, Myers served on the board of directors of numerous organizations and in many cases as an officer. Among them were the Piedmont and Northern Railroad Company, North Carolina Transportation Advisory Board (late 1920s), Gastonia Mill Supply Company, North Carolina Textile Foundation, Flint Manufacturing Company, Rex-Hanover Mills Company, Piedmont Iron Works, Cocker Machine and Foundry Company, Commercial Real Estate and Investment Company of Gastonia, North Carolina Cotton

Manufacturers Association, Ragan Spinning Company, Southern Advisory Committee of the National Association of Manufacturers, American Cotton Manufacturers Institute, Southern Combed Yarn Spinners Association (president, 1928), and North Carolina Textile Manufacturers Association. He was appointed to the War Production Board in 1942 and was chairman of the North Carolina State Ports Authority (1945–53) when major construction was begun at the Morehead City and Wilmington ports.

Myers also was active in educational, religious, and community affairs. Perhaps because of his family's poverty and his lack of opportunity for a formal education, he encouraged others to seek higher education. This was done primarily through the Myers-Textiles Foundation, which he started in 1953 for the children of employees of Textiles, Incorporated. Grants and scholarships exceeding $500,000 had been given to more than one hundred students by the time of his death. His interest in education was recognized by his election to membership on the board of trustees of the Consolidated University of North Carolina (1931–33) and to membership on the Duke University National Council (appointed 1954). He was awarded the honorary degree of doctor of textile science by North Carolina State College (1949), was elected to honorary membership in Duke University's chapter of Omicron Delta Kappa (1953), was named "Man of the Year" by the North Carolina State College chapter of Phi Psi (honorary textile society) (1956), and received a doctor of laws degree from Belmont Abbey College (1957). An active Mason, he was for a time potentate of Oasis Shrine Temple. One of his favorite projects was the Shrine Hospital for Crippled Children in Greenville, S.C. Myers was a member of the Newcomen Society and a Democrat in politics.

In his own community of Gastonia, he was a steward in the Methodist church, president of the chamber of commerce, and chairman of the city school board. One of several portraits of him is in the Myers Center at Gaston College, Dallas, N.C.

On 26 Jan. 1916 Myers married Elfrieda Nail of Charlotte, and they had two children: Albert Gallatin, Jr., and Frieda Farrar Myers Shelton. He died at his home in Gastonia and was interred at Gaston Memorial Park.

SEE: *Charlotte News*, 15 Apr. 1976; *Charlotte Observer*, 16 Apr. 1976; *North Carolina Biography*, vols. 4 (1956), 5 (1919); *Southern Textile News*, 29 Jan. 1968; *Who's Who in America*, vol. 34 (1966–67); *Who's Who in the South and Southwest*, vol. 1 (1947).

SOPHIE S. MARTIN

Myers, William Rayford (*17 Dec. 1818–23 Feb. 1901*), business and community leader, was born in Anson County, the son of Absalom and Sarah Pickett Myers. His mother was descended from the Raiford family, of Cumberland and Anson counties, for whom he was probably named, with a change in spelling. He was prepared for college at Pleasant Retreat Academy in Lincolnton. His father provided him with funds to enter The University of North Carolina, but instead he chose to go to Texas, where he joined the army of the Republic of Texas in its war against Mexico. He served for about four months in the early part of 1837, for which he received a bounty warrant of 1,280 acres. After returning to North Carolina, he read law in Hillsborough under William A. Graham, later governor of the state.

In 1843 Myers settled in Charlotte, where he was soon elected solicitor of the county court. He held this office

for several years while continuing to build a successful law practice. However, he gradually gave up his legal career as he became more involved in business affairs and in the management of a substantial estate inherited by his wife. From about the beginning of the Civil War, he considered his occupation to be that of a farmer.

His participation in public affairs during the 1850s included serving as a city commissioner a number of times and in the state legislature as a member of the House of Commons (1854–55) and of the senate (1856–57). Myers, a Democrat, strongly opposed secession, but after seeing that this course was inevitable, he acceded to the wishes of the majority and urged others to join in defending their native section against the North. At the beginning of the Civil War, he was one of the organizers of vigilance committees to protect the community from incendiary fires. Soon volunteering for military service, he equipped Company G, Thirty-fourth North Carolina Infantry, and was commissioned its captain in September 1861. He remained in the Confederate army only until the following April, when the regiment was reorganized and he was not reelected. Nevertheless, according to the widespread custom for those who had been commissioned Confederate officers, he was referred to as "colonel" for the rest of his life.

Myers was active in promoting Charlotte's growth as a business community for almost half a century. In the field of banking, he was a member of the first board of directors of the first locally owned bank—the Bank of Charlotte—which opened in 1853. In 1880 he was vice-president of the First National Bank of Charlotte. Also identified with the development of railroads in the state, he served as president of the Atlantic, Tennessee, and Ohio Railroad Company in the late 1870s and early 1880s. This was one of the several small lines absorbed by the Richmond and Danville Railroad, which, by a later merger, became part of the Southern Railway System. Myers is credited with winning support for a petition to the legislature to pass a stock law, a necessary condition for the building and use of good roads to improve his county's internal transportation.

He also was concerned with enriching his community in ways other than material. The year after he moved to Charlotte, Myers was one of the organizers of St. Peter's Episcopal Church when its status changed from that of a mission to a parish in 1844. He was elected to its first vestry and appointed secretary. In 1857 he was one of the original stockholders who raised money for the establishment of the Charlotte Female Institute, which evolved into present-day Queens College. In the area of education, he is best remembered for a gift in 1867 of eight acres of land for the campus of Biddle Institute, a college for young black men (now Johnson C. Smith University).

During the latter part of the nineteenth century, Myers and his family were among the most affluent residents in Charlotte, and they were apparently generous in sharing their wealth in ways that gave pleasure and help to others. The Myers home, built about 1850, was described by contemporaries as being beautifully situated, elegant, and equipped with many conveniences rarely seen at that period. Not only was it the center of much hospitality for relatives and friends, but also—during the Civil War—it was a haven for refugees fleeing to Charlotte when the Northern forces took over the capitol at Richmond in April 1865. At this time it was one of the homes made available to members of the Confederate cabinet.

On 15 Dec. 1846 Myers married Sophia Springs, the daughter of Captain John Springs III and Mary Laura

Springs (who was his cousin) of York District, S.C. They had eight children: John Springs, Sophia Convert Jones, William Rayford, Leroy Springs, Richard Austin, Mary Pickett Hunter, Elizabeth Nichols Myers, and Baxter Springs. Myers was buried in Elmwood Cemetery, Charlotte.

SEE: *Charlotte Observer*, 24 Feb. 1901, 28 Feb. 1950, 8 Feb. 1975; John L. Cheney, Jr., ed., *North Carolina Government, 1585–1979* (1981); Walter Clark, ed., *Histories of the Several Regiments and Battalions from North Carolina in the Great War, 1861–1865*, vol. 2 (1901); Weymouth T. Jordan, comp., *North Carolina Troops, 1861–1865: A Roster*, vol. 9 (1983); John Wheeler Moore, comp., *Roster of North Carolina Troops in the War between the States*, vol. 2 (1882); *North Carolina Biography*, vol. 5 (1919).

SOPHIE S. MARTIN

Myrover, James Henry (Harry) (*23 June 1843–23 Jan. 1908*), teacher, newspaper reporter, editor, publisher, and Confederate officer, was born in Fayetteville, the son of Henry L. and Urbanna Cooper Myrover. He attended Donaldson Academy in Fayetteville and Caleb Howell's Quaker school in Alexandria, Va., before entering the University of Virginia, where his education was interrupted by the Civil War. On 6 June 1861 he enlisted for six months in the First Regiment of North Carolina Infantry as a private. He was mustered out in November at the end of his enlistment, but on 1 Mar. 1862 he enlisted as a sergeant in the Thirty-sixth Regiment. Myrover was wounded at Goldsboro Bridge in December, promoted to first sergeant in March or April 1863, and transferred in the same rank to the Thirteenth Battalion, North Carolina Light Artillery, on 4 Nov. 1863. There he was named second lieutenant to rank from 1 Dec. 1863; on 1 Nov. 1864 he was promoted to first lieutenant. After extensive service, particularly across eastern North Carolina, and again suffering a wound, he was paroled at Greensboro on 29 Apr. 1865.

Returning home, he participated in political activities during Reconstruction, with the goal of returning North Carolina to the control of the Democratic party. At the same time, he embarked on a newspaper career that later earned him a reputation for excellence across the state. In 1865 Myrover began printing a daily, *The News*, and from July 1866 to 1868 his father (whose occupation was listed in the 1860 census as grocer) joined him in publishing the weekly *Fayetteville News*. For a time Benjamin Robinson, the husband of Myrover's sister Celia, was co-owner of this paper with the younger Myrover. With his brother, George G. Myrover, the *Daily Gazette* was established in 1873 and continued until 1892. Between 1881 and 1884 James published the *Carthage Gazette*, and in October 1883 he became assistant editor of a Fayetteville weekly, *The Sun*. Although he spent most of his life in his native city, Myrover worked for varying periods on newspapers in New York City and in Greensboro (after 1888); he was employed by the *Charlotte Observer* for about a year in 1892. In addition, he served as correspondent for numerous other papers, including those in Durham, Wilmington, Winston, and Richmond, Va. His contributions frequently were of a historical nature.

For a time Myrover also taught in the Fayetteville graded schools. In fact, the 1870 census recorded his occupation as schoolmaster, and he was superintendent of schools in 1893–94. He was a member of the board of managers of the Howard School, which evolved into Fayetteville State University.

Myrover wrote the history of the Thirteenth Battalion for Walter Clark's *Histories of the Several Regiments and Battalions from North Carolina in the Great War, 1861–1865* (1901), and he was the author of a *Short History of Cumberland County and the Cape Fear Section* (1905), sponsored as a promotional piece by the Bank of Fayetteville. In addition, he contributed biographical sketches to all but the first of the eight volumes of the *Biographical History of North Carolina*, edited by Samuel A. Ashe and published between 1905 and 1917. In 1906, when serious consideration was being given to tearing down the Market House in the center of Fayetteville to make way for a new post office, Myrover rallied wide support to save that historic structure.

According to the 1870 census, he and his wife Maria, aged twenty-five, were the parents of a four-year-old son, James Goelet. Maria Goelet Myrover, of Washington, Beaufort County, died many years before her husband. Their son, who worked for a Savannah, Ga., newspaper, also died before his father. Myrover himself later was a part of the household of his elderly mother. He died suddenly after a brief illness; his funeral was conducted in the First Presbyterian Church, and he was buried in Cross Creek Cemetery, Fayetteville.

SEE: Walter Clark, ed., *Histories of the Several Regiments and Battalions from North Carolina in the Great War, 1861–1865*, vols. 1, 4 (1901); Cumberland County Census, 1860, 1870, 1880, 1900, and Marriage Bonds (North Carolina State Archives, Raleigh); *Fayetteville Observer*, 27 (daily), 30 (weekly) Jan. 1908; Louis H. Manarin, comp., *North Carolina Troops, 1861–1865: A Roster*, vols. 1, 3 (1966, 1971); John A. Oates, *The Story of Fayetteville and the Upper Cape Fear* (1981).

WILLIAM S. POWELL

Nadal, Edward Morse (*2 Oct. 1843–13 Apr. 1896*), teacher, pharmacist, and founder of the North Carolina Pharmaceutical Association, was the only child of Captain Peter Edward and Sarah Morse Nadal of Washington, N.C. After settling in Wilson about 1858 with his mother and stepfather-uncle, Anthony Nadal, he attended the Horner School at Oxford for a year or more before enlisting on 14 May 1862 under Captain Joseph J. Lawrence of "The Wilson Partisan Rangers," who were known by 11 July 1864 as Company F, Sixteenth Battalion, North Carolina Cavalry.

As a sergeant Nadal was captured at Fort Harrison on 30 Sept. 1864 and soon was incarcerated in the overcrowded Federal military prison at Point Lookout, Md. Paroled on 15 Feb. 1865 at Boulware's Wharf on the James River, he proceeded to Camp Lee near Richmond and scouted with the cavalry until receiving news of General Robert E. Lee's surrender. His parole was secured from the Federal forces stationed at Goldsboro from then until the end of Reconstruction. During this period, while teaching in the Wilson Male and Female institutes, he was active in the local Ku Klux Klan. In 1873 he joined the Masonic order, rising to senior warden, master, and knight templar; he also became an active member of the then-popular Independent Order of Odd Fellows.

From 1874 to 1878, while teaching mathematics at the Wilson Collegiate Institute and basic courses at "the free school" for poor children several weeks each summer, Nadal served as Wilson County surveyor. One of his projects was to lay out the original area of Maplewood Cemetery. About that time he also became associated with the firm of Moses T. Moye, Drugs and Seeds, successor (ca. 1875) to Dr. Joseph J. Lawrence and the brothers Cullen and Jesse Battle, which was known by 1880 as Moye and Nadal and after 1883 as E. M. Nadal, Wholesale and Retail Druggist, on Tarboro Street.

On 17 May 1880 Nadal circulated a letter among North Carolina pharmacists urging them to support the establishment of a state pharmaceutical association and passage of "a law requiring that Druggists shall have a license from the State Board of Medical Examiners." Nearly one hundred pharmacists attended the convention held in the senate chamber at Raleigh on 11 Aug. 1880 and elected Nadal by unanimous vote to serve as their first president. Governor Thomas J. Jarvis appointed him to the North Carolina State Board of Pharmacy on 27 Apr. 1881, while the General Assembly formally incorporated the new North Carolina Pharmaceutical Association by an act of 12 March. The first *Nadal's Almanac* was published at Wilson in 1884.

Nadal remained on the state board until 1890. He also served as chairman of the committee on the pharmacopoeia revision in 1889, delegate to the American Pharmaceutical Association in 1888 and 1890, and member of various important committees such as that of the examining board. While serving on the committee on papers and queries, he wrote and presented at least one paper. Soon after Governor Elias Carr had honored Nadal with the commission of major of the Second Regiment of the North Carolina State Militia, the pharmacist was fatally stricken by peritonitis.

About 1871 Nadal married Margaret M. (Maggie) Fentress (2 Nov. 1850–31 Dec. 1907), and their only surviving child was Ernest Fentress (3 Jan. 1872–11 July 1922). The families of Anthony and Edward Nadal were among the first Presbyterians in Wilson and helped organize the Wilson Presbyterian Church on 5 July 1885.

Nadal was buried in Maplewood Cemetery, Wilson.

SEE: Josephus Daniels, *Tar Heel Editor* (1939); *Proceedings of the Convention of Druggists, Held in Raleigh, N.C., August 11, 1880* (1880); *Wilson Advance*, 16 Apr. 1896.

HUGH BUCKNER JOHNSTON

Nash, Abner (ca. 1740–2 Dec. 1786), Patriot and second governor of the state of North Carolina, was born at Templeton Manor, his family's plantation near Farmville in Prince Edward County, Va. His father, John Nash, the son of Abner Nash of Tenby, County Pembroke, Wales, had immigrated to Virginia about 1730. His mother, Ann Owen Nash, was the daughter of Sir Hugh Owen, second baronet of Orielton. Where young Nash received his education is unknown, but his later ability as writer and orator testifies to a superior classical training. He was qualified to practice law before the Prince Edward County bar in 1757, and in 1761 and 1762 he represented that county in the Virginia House of Burgesses.

In 1762 or early 1763 Nash moved to Hillsborough (then Childsburgh), N.C., with his younger brother Francis. An older brother, Thomas, had settled in Edenton four years earlier. Abner remained in Hillsborough long enough to acquire some town lots, dam the Eno River, and build the town's first mill. By 1764 he had moved to Halifax to practice law. Here he resided for about twelve years, representing the town in the House of Commons in 1764 and 1765. From 1770 to 1771 he was Halifax County's representative in the house. During the session of 1770, a bill was introduced to establish a seminary of learning at Charlotte. Nash was appointed one of the first trustees of Queen's Museum (later Queen's College).

While in Halifax, he married Justina Davis Dobbs, the widow of Governor Arthur Dobbs. When Dobbs's executors—his two sons by a former marriage—failed to pay their father's bequest to the youthful widow, Nash brought suit. An attachment was issued. The defendants obtained an injunction, which the provincial chancery court made perpetual. In response to an appeal by Nash, the Privy Council in London reversed the decision. This suit, known as the "Martin court quarrel," caused a bitter controversy between Governor Josiah Martin and the Assembly, with the result that all courts of law, except those held by single justices of the peace, were closed for a time in the province. This event gave much impetus to the Revolutionary movement in North Carolina.

Justina Nash died in 1771, leaving three small children. Within a year, Nash moved to New Bern and married Mary Whiting Jones, of Chowan County, the daughter of Harding and Mary Whiting Jones. The Nash plantation, Pembroke, located on the Trent River above New Bern, became a center of hospitality. Here the family lived until the American Revolution, when they were forced to flee before the British advance under Major James H. Craig in August 1781. The house was burned and with it all the family's possessions, records, and papers.

An ardent Whig, Nash had been an early leader in the opposition to Governor Martin, who spoke of him as "an eminent lawyer, but an unprincipled character" and recommended him, among others, for proscription. After Martin fled the colony in 1775, Nash took an active part in the interim government, serving on the Committee of Safety, as a member of the Provincial Council (1775), and as a delegate to all four Provincial Congresses. During the session of 1776, he prepared the resolution that announced North Carolina's stand for freedom and independence. He became the first speaker of the House of Commons of the new state.

In March 1777 Nash was again elected to the House of Commons from New Bern and became speaker. In 1778, while representing Craven County, he was elected to the Continental Congress but declined to serve. In 1779 he represented Jones County in the North Carolina Senate, succeeding Allen Jones as speaker. In 1780 he was elected second governor of the new state.

His term of office as governor, extended by act of the legislature until 25 June 1781, was an unhappy one from the start. The fall of Charles Town, the disastrous defeat at Camden, and the depleted resources of the state all gave heart to the Loyalist faction, estimated to have been half of the state's population. Governor Nash, finding the General Assembly and his own Council too dispersed and unwieldy to be of much help in guiding a state at war, requested a Board of War of three members. He soon bitterly regretted this request. Early on the members proved inadequate for their task and later actively opposed the governor, intercepting his correspondence with the generals in the field and flouting his authority as commander in chief.

The mounting problems of providing and equipping an army, the tensions between governor and Board of War, and the loss of his home and possessions all took their toll of Nash's never-robust health. He declined nomination for a second term in 1781 and became a member of the Continental Congress in 1782, serving as regularly as his health would allow until his death "of consumption" in New York City while attending the Congress. He was buried in St. Paul's churchyard there. Later his remains were reinterred in the family vault at Pembroke.

His children by his first marriage were Abner, Jr., who died young; Margaret, who married Thomas Haslin; and Justina, who never married. By his second marriage, he was the father of Ann, who never married; Eliza, who married Robert Ogden IV; Maria, who married George W. B. Burgwin; Frederick, who married Mary Goddard Kollock; and Francis, who died young. His widow later married David Witherspoon of Craven County.

Had he lived, Nash's short but distinguished career might have been even more notable: he was being considered for the position of president of the Congress. A few days before Abner died, William Grayson wrote to James Monroe: "Mr. Nash . . . is talked of generally, and nothing but his death or extreme ill health will, I am persuaded, prevent his election."

His son Frederick later wrote of his father: "He went into the War of the Revolution a wealthy man, and came out of it worth nothing—the latter I *know* by painful experience."

SEE: Walter Clark, ed., *State Records of North Carolina*, vols. 14, 16, 19 (1896–1901); J. G. de Roulhac Hamilton, *Presentation of the Portrait of Governor Abner Nash to the State of North Carolina* (1909); Frank Nash, "Governor Abner Nash," *North Carolina Booklet* 22, nos. 1–4 (1922–23); William S. Powell, *North Carolina through Four Centuries* (1989); William L. Saunders, ed., *Colonial Records of North Carolina*, vols. 6–9 (1888–90).

JAQUELIN DRANE NASH

Nash, Arthur Cleveland (*21 Oct. 1871–26 Sept. 1969*), architect, was born in Geneva, N.Y., where his father, Francis Philip Nash, was a professor of romance languages at Hobart College. His mother, Katharine Cleveland Coxe Nash, was the daughter of the Right Reverend Arthur Cleveland Coxe, the Episcopal bishop of western New York. Young Nash attended Phillips Exeter Academy and was graduated from Harvard in 1894. After a year at the Massachusetts Institute of Technology, he left for the Beaux Arts Institute, in Paris, where he studied for five years in Jean-Louis Pascal's atelier. In Paris, he received medals in architecture, archaeology, and modeling and was awarded a diploma in 1900.

After teaching briefly at Cornell, Nash moved to New York City, where he was a practicing architect until 1920. During those years he built a number of houses in New York and New Jersey, a gymnasium and science building at Hobart College, a dormitory at Smith College, and a clubhouse in Greenwich, Conn.

In 1922 he became architect for The University of North Carolina, working in association with the builder, T. C. Atwood, and with the consulting architectural firm of McKim, Mead, and White of New York. He contributed to the new library (now the L. R. Wilson Library) and designed Venable Hall (1924), Kenan Stadium and Field House (1927), Graham Memorial (1929–31), and a number of dormitories, including Spencer, Aycock, Graham, Lewis, and Everett. In 1930 Nash designed Memorial Hall, which was built in the same year to replace an older auditorium. He also remodeled some of the older buildings: South Building with its new south portico, Person Hall, the Playmakers Theatre, the hall and stairway of the president's house, and Hill Hall. Nash designed the Carolina Inn adjacent to the campus.

His influence was felt strongly in the town of Chapel Hill. For the main street he advocated the colonial style, which a number of merchants used for their storefronts. Nash felt this style had the necessary "dignity, repose and cultivation" appropriate for a scholarly town. He

designed several fraternities and private houses in Chapel Hill, including his own home on Cameron Avenue and the Leavitt House on Franklin Street. Elsewhere in the state, he designed the John Sprunt House in Wilmington and restored the Lawrence Stallings House near Leasburg in Caswell County. In Raleigh, he designed the Revenue Building, the Fairground Building, and additions at Peace Institute and did some renovations at the state capitol.

In 1930 Nash retired and moved to Washington, D.C., but continued as consulting architect to the university until 1953. In connection with architect H. Raymond Weeks, he contributed design ideas to a number of later buildings, including the public health and medical building; Woollen Gymnasium and Bowman Gray Swimming Pool; Lenoir Hall; Alderman, McIver, Stacy, and Whitehead dormitories; Wilson Hall; the women's gymnasium unit; the naval armory and Navy Hall (later the Monogram Club); the North Carolina Memorial Hospital complex; and additions to the Carolina Inn, Wilson Library, and Venable Hall.

When the North Carolina chapter of the American Institute of Architects wanted to nominate Nash for consideration as a Fellow, he turned it down. He felt that others also deserved credit for his work, citing as an example William M. Kendall, chief representative of McKim, Mead, and White, who had done the detailing of the library. The overview of the campus, however, was Nash's and the results of his efforts were highly praised. Robert B. House spoke of Nash as "an artist in discerning the quality and tone of the ancient campus and blending the new harmoniously with the old." House suggested that his greatest contribution was "the symmetrical spacing of structures with plenty of room for light and air around each edifice." At the June 1954 commencement in Chapel Hill, Nash was awarded an honorary doctor of laws degree.

At Grace Episcopal Church in New York City on 12 Aug. 1914, Nash married Mary Screven Arnold, a distinguished portrait painter. Among those who sat for her were R. D. W. Connor (first archivist of the United States), Bishop Joseph Blount Cheshire, North Carolina Supreme Court justices Henry G. and George Connor and W. A. Hoke, Bishop Henry St. George Tucker (presiding bishop of the Episcopal church), and General Mark W. Clark. The Nashes were the parents of a daughter, Katharine Cleveland, who married Edward E. Caldwell.

Nash died at his daughter's home in Baltimore and was buried in Mount Auburn Cemetery, Cambridge, Mass.

SEE: "A Brief Discussion of Campus Architecture at the University of North Carolina" (manuscript in possession of Mrs. E. E. Caldwell, Chapel Hill); *Chapel Hill Weekly*, 21 Dec. 1928, 23 Jan. 1931, 1 Oct. 1969; *Harvard College, Class of 1894, Twenty-fifth Anniversary Report* (1919) and *Fiftieth Anniversary Report* (1944); George S. Kogh, ed., *American Architects Directory* (1955); Arthur Nash, "Campus Architecture: Survey and Prospects," in Archibald Henderson, *The Campus of the First State University* (1949); Arthur Cleveland Nash Papers (Southern Historical Collection, University of North Carolina, Chapel Hill, and Mrs. E. E. Caldwell, Chapel Hill); *New York Times*, 27 Sept. 1969; Louis R. Wilson, *Historical Sketches* (1976) and *The University of North Carolina, 1900–1930: The Making of a Modern University* (1957).

MARTHA B. CALDWELL

Nash, Francis *(1742?–7 Oct. 1777)*, lawyer and Revolutionary general, was born in Amelia (now Prince Edward) County, Va., the son of John and Ann Owen Nash. Between 1725 and 1730 his parents, both natives of Tenby, Pembrokeshire, Wales, had immigrated to Virginia, where John Nash purchased five thousand acres at the confluence of the Appomattox and Bush rivers near present-day Farmville. An older brother, Thomas, was also born in Wales; another brother, Abner, was a North Carolina statesman and congressman. Nothing is known of Francis Nash's education, but sometime before 1763 he moved to North Carolina and settled in Childsburgh (renamed Hillsborough in 1766), where he invested in a store and set up a law practice. In 1763 he was appointed clerk of the superior court of Orange County and soon afterwards became clerk of the inferior court of the county, both very lucrative positions.

Nash represented Orange County in the colonial Assembly in the sessions of 1764–65 and 1771 and in the First Provincial Congress in 1774, as well as the borough of Hillsborough in the Assembly in 1773, 1774, and 1775. He also was the Halifax borough representative in the Third Provincial Congress in 1775. In 1768, as a part of the early complaints of the Orange County Regulators, he was wrongfully accused of receiving illegal fees but was exonerated. In 1771, as a captain of militia, Nash participated in the Battle of Alamance against the Regulators.

Presumably in 1770 he married Sarah (Sally) Moore, the daughter of Judge and Mrs. Maurice Moore. They became the parents of two daughters: Anna (called Nancy), probably born in 1771, who died at age thirteen; and Sarah (Sally), born in 1773, who married rice planter John W. Waddell of the Cape Fear area. On 3 Mar. 1784 the Orange County court apprenticed Francis Nash (aged thirteen?), the illegitimate son of the late Francis Nash and a barmaid at the Blue House in Hillsborough, to Roswell Huntington, the silversmith. Young Nash soon ran away and apparently went to Tennessee.

In the summer of 1775 the Provincial Congress directed that two regiments be raised, and Francis Nash was appointed lieutenant colonel of the first. Following the promotion of the regimental commander, James Moore, Nash became commander and was promoted to colonel in April 1776. Under his command, the regiment was present at the unsuccessful British attack on Charles Town, S.C., on 25 June.

Returning to North Carolina, Nash's regiment in November 1776 was ordered to join the Continental army operating under General George Washington in the northern states, but these orders were rescinded because of threatened British and Indian attacks on Georgia. Nash, who had been commissioned brigadier general by Congress on 5 Feb. 1777, was again ordered north in March. With the illness and death of General James Moore, Nash assumed command of the entire North Carolina brigade of nine regiments. In June the brigade arrived at Philadelphia, remaining there until Washington and the Continental army marched from the vicinity of New York to Delaware to oppose a British invasion of Pennsylvania via Chesapeake Bay. The British objective was Philadelphia, the American capital. On 11 Sept. 1777 the two armies collided at the Battle of Brandywine, Pa., in which the Americans were defeated. Nevertheless, Nash and his North Carolinians rendered signal service in helping stem the British advance.

With the capture of Philadelphia by the British on 26 September, Washington, regrouping his army, attacked the British-Hessian forces at Germantown, near Phila-

delphia, on 4 October, and was again defeated. In this action General Nash received a hip wound from a cannonball that proved fatal. He died three days later at the home of Adam Gotwals, on the Forty Foot Road, near Kulpsville, Pa., and was buried on 9 October at the Towamencin Mennonite Meeting graveyard beside three other officers who had also perished from wounds received at Germantown. Washington and his generals attended the funeral. Two monuments, one erected in 1844 and the other in 1936, mark the spot. His dying words were reported to have been: "From the first Dawn of the Revolution I have been ever on the side of liberty and my country." General Nash quickly came to be recognized as a North Carolina hero, and his death inspired renewed support in the state for the Revolution.

SEE: Samuel A. Ashe, ed., *Biographical History of North Carolina*, vol. 3 (1905); John L. Cheney, Jr., ed., *North Carolina Government, 1585–1979* (1981); Eting and Simon Gratz Collections (Historical Society of Pennsylvania, Philadelphia); John C. Fitzpatrick, ed., *Writings of Washington* (1932); Hugh F. Rankin, *The North Carolina Continentals* (1971); Revolutionary War Records (National Archives, Washington, D.C.); Alfred M. Waddell, *General Francis Nash: An Address Delivered at the Unveiling of a Monument to General Nash* (1906).

JOHN F. REED

Nash, Francis (Frank) *(29 Jan. 1855–10 July 1932)*, lawyer, assistant attorney general, local historian, and author, was born at Floral College, Robeson County, the son of the Reverend Frederick Kollock Nash, a Presbyterian minister, and his second wife, Anne Maria McLean. He was the grandson of Chief Justice Frederick and Mary Goddard Kollock Nash, great-grandson of Governor Abner Nash and Mary Whiting Jones, and great-grandnephew of Revolutionary general Francis Nash.

Orphaned at an early age, Frank Nash and his sister Mary went to live at the Nash-Kollock school in Hillsborough, where he received his early schooling from his aunts, Sally and Maria Nash. (These early years in his grandfather's old home are perceptively described in *Ladies in the Making* [1964], an account of the Nash-Kollock school written, at Frank Nash's suggestion, by his second wife, Ann Strudwick Nash.) He later attended Ralph Henry Graves's preparatory school at Graham.

After brief employment in a Petersburg, Va., tobacco factory, he went to work in a wholesale grocery in Tarboro, reading law at night with Judge George Howard and Joseph Blount Cheshire (later Episcopal bishop of North Carolina). In 1877 he was licensed to practice and joined Judge Howard's office as a partner. Nash was elected mayor of Tarboro in 1881 and served for four years. He also was presiding judge of the Edgecombe County criminal court from 1882 to 1886. Two successive breakdowns in health forced him to retire almost entirely from his legal practice, and in 1894 the Nashes returned to Hillsborough, where Frank Nash remained for twenty years.

Although writing as an avocation was not new to him (he had in 1890–91 published a series of articles on "Judicial Evolution" in the Albany *Law Journal*), Nash now began to write in swift succession a series of historical romances—"Belleville," a story of the Reconstruction period (1897–98); "The McTravis Sketches" (1898); "A Lawyer's Mistake" (1899); and "Wiolusing," a sequel to "Belleville" (1900–1901). At his death he left a lengthy manuscript of the romance, "Love's Revenge." Like various other members of his family, Nash wrote gracefully, distinctively, and seemingly without effort. His literary output, excluding legal opinions, was a massive one, covering an exceptionally wide range of materials—genealogy (in which he became increasingly interested in later years), Hillsborough and Orange County history, local biography, and religious and political essays. His *Hillsboro: Colonial and Revolutionary* (1903; reprint, 1953) brought together a valuable series of articles printed originally in the *Charlotte Observer* and republished in the *North Carolina Booklet*. It remains the only publication of its kind on Hillsborough history. In addition, Nash published a portion of a projected Orange County history, contributed a notable group of twenty-three biographical articles (chiefly on early Hillsborough figures) to Samuel A. Ashe's *Biographical History of North Carolina*, and prepared five additional sketches for a supplement to Ashe that remains unpublished. Also unpublished is the greater portion of his extensive collection of materials for a history of the Strudwick family, as well as a sizable group of unrelated articles and addresses on dueling, Prohibition, church history, and other topics.

Nash did much of his Hillsborough writing in "a little columned two-room office, shaded by mimosa trees," standing at the head of old Cedar Walk and used for decades by the Nash and Strudwick families. He had inherited "The Office" (still standing) from his aunt, Maria Nash, and in later years used it as a combined dwelling house and office.

From May 1907 to May 1911 Nash served as mayor of Hillsborough, and during his term the town's first concrete sidewalks were laid and plans for a public library began to evolve. From 1910 to 1914 he was attorney for Orange County. An ardent Presbyterian and a vigorous prohibitionist, he served as an elder in the Hillsborough Presbyterian Church and for years led the antiwhiskey ("anti-jug") forces in his county. He also was president of the North Carolina Sons of the Revolution, a charter member of the North Carolina Bar Association, second vice-president (1913–14) of the American Bar Association, and chairman of the Democratic executive committee of Orange County.

In 1915, at age sixty, Nash was elected state senator from the Eighteenth District. In 1918 he was appointed assistant attorney general for North Carolina, a post he filled with distinction until 1931. As Judge John J. Parker observed, "He was a sort of Supreme Court himself," largely owing to the many opinions he had to write in the enforced absence of Attorney General J. S. Manning.

Nash was married twice. His first wife was Jessie Powel Baker of Tarboro (1857–9 July 1896), the third daughter of William S. and Sally Baker, whom he married on 27 Nov. 1878. The couple had three daughters: Susan, Sally, and Catherine Staton. In 1920 he married his cousin, librarian-author Ann Spotswood Strudwick (5 Aug. 1878–20 Sept. 1969), the daughter of lawyer Robert Strudwick of Meadowside, near Hillsborough, and his second wife, Rosaline Brooke Spotswood of Petersburg, Va.

In 1931 Frank Nash was appointed clerk of the North Carolina Supreme Court, but he died in Raleigh the following summer. Both he and Ann Strudwick Nash were buried in the new town cemetery in Hillsborough. The only known photograph of Frank Nash appears in the sesquicentennial publication of the Hillsborough Presbyterian Church, *One Hundred and Fifty Years of Service* (1966).

SEE: A. H. Graham, "Frank Nash," *North Carolina Bar Association Report*, 34th annual session, vol. 34 (1932);

Hillsborough Presbyterian Church, *One Hundred and Fifty Years of Service, 1816–1966* (1966 [portrait]); Ann Strudwick Nash, *Ladies in the Making* (1964); Francis (Frank) Nash Papers (Southern Historical Collection, University of North Carolina, Chapel Hill); Frank Nash, *Hillsboro: Colonial and Revolutionary* (1953); *North Carolina Booklet* 6 (October 1906).

MARY CLAIRE ENGSTROM

Nash, Frederick *(9 Feb. 1781–5 Dec. 1858)*, fourth chief justice of North Carolina, was born in the former colonial governors' palace at New Bern, the son of Governor Abner Nash and his second wife, Mary Whiting Jones. Young Frederick grew up with his brother and three sisters at Pembroke, the Nash plantation on the Trent River near New Bern. His father's death in 1786 and his mother's death thirteen years later left young Frederick as the head of his family. He studied under the Reverend Henry Patillo at Williamsboro and under the Reverend Thomas Irving at New Bern. In 1799 he was graduated as salutatorian from Princeton College. Returning to New Bern, Nash studied law under Edward Harris and was admitted to the bar in 1801. He represented New Bern in the House of Commons in 1804 and 1805.

In 1803 he married Mary Goddard Kollock of Elizabethtown, N.J. Seeking a healthier climate after the loss of their first child, they moved from New Bern to Hillsborough in 1807. Nash represented Orange County in the House of Commons in 1814, 1816, and 1817 and the town of Hillsborough in 1828–29. In 1814 he was speaker of the house.

Nash was elected a superior court judge in 1818 and held the office until 1826, when he resigned to resume his lucrative private law practice. In 1836 he again won election to the superior court, serving until Governor John Motley Morehead elevated him to the North Carolina Supreme Court in 1844 to complete the term of Judge William Gaston. This interim appointment was confirmed when the legislature elected him Judge Gaston's successor.

In 1852, on Judge Thomas Ruffin's resignation, Nash became chief justice of the supreme court; he continued in this office until his death six years later. According to his friend, Dr. Kemp P. Battle, "He proved himself a sound and able judge, and his lofty character, in which all the virtues were harmoniously blended, his great popularity gained by his unfailing courtesy and kindly heart, continued and strengthened the public confidence in the court."

Elected a trustee of The University of North Carolina in 1807, Nash remained an active supporter of the university, from which he received an LL.D. degree in 1853. Although raised in the Episcopal church, he and his wife became ardent Presbyterians around the turn of the century. For nearly fifty years they were among the leaders of the Presbyterian church in North Carolina. Nash suffered his last illness on returning from a meeting of the synod in New Bern. He was buried in the old Presbyterian cemetery in Hillsborough.

Nash and his wife had seven children: Susan Mary (m. Isaac Read III), Ann Eliza (m. Dr. Edmund Strudwick), the Reverend Frederick Kollock, Henry Kollock, Shepard Kollock, Sally, and Maria. Sally and Maria, who never married, ran the Nash-Kollock school in Hillsborough.

Two incidents in his early youth were cherished by Judge Nash. When President George Washington visited New Bern in 1791, he was honored by a reception and ball at the old palace. Mrs. Abner Nash presented her ten-year-old son to the president, who took him on his knee and spoke kindly to him, recommending to the boy his uncle, General Francis Nash, as an example for his life. Eight years later, when his mother was dying, she placed her hand on her son's head and said to her attending physician: "Dr. McClure, here is a son who has never given me one moment's pain." His friends believed that these two incidents, combined with the early burden of family responsibility, helped to form the serious and responsible man he later became.

A portrait of Judge Nash hangs on the wall of the supreme court chamber in Raleigh.

SEE: John H. Bryan, "Memoir of Hon. Frederick Nash, LL.D," *North Carolina University Magazine* 9 (December 1859 [portrait]); John L. Cheney, Jr., ed., *North Carolina Government, 1585–1979* (1981); Francis Nash Collection (North Carolina State Archives, Raleigh); Francis Nash Papers (Southern Historical Collection, University of North Carolina, Chapel Hill); "Social Reminiscences of Distinguished North Carolinians," *The Land We Love* 5 (1865).

JAQUELIN DRANE NASH

Nash, Justina Davis Dobbs. *See* **Dobbs, Justina Davis**.

Nash, Leonidas Lydwell (2 Aug. 1846–11 July 1917), Methodist clergyman and author, was born in Chase City, Mecklenburg County, Va., the son of Hugh W. and Martha Jane Mullen Nash. He attended local public schools and for one year studied at a military school. In 1857 he moved with his parents to Franklin County, N.C. The Civil War denied him an opportunity for further education, and in 1864 he enlisted in the Junior Reserves. Nash saw service in guarding the railroad at Weldon and later was employed in the trenches around Petersburg. There is some suggestion that he served briefly as a private in the Twenty-fifth North Carolina Regiment, although surviving records do not mention him. He became ill from exposure in Virginia and was sent to a hospital in Raleigh. The war ended before he was able to return to duty. Back home, in 1866, he married Sarah F. Marks and they became the parents of a daughter, Rosa, who later married Wilmington merchant E. N. Penny.

During his recuperation, Nash determined to make the Christian ministry his lifework. He was an avid student of the Bible and had also devoted some time to reading law and studying medicine. After an examination by Methodist clergymen, he was accepted as a substitute minister for service in the Bath Circuit, Beaufort County, for two years. His wife died in 1872, shortly before he entered the ministry. In 1873 he married Louise Taylor of Beaufort County.

Nash formally joined the Conference of the Methodist Episcopal Church, South, in 1874 and continued his work in the Bath region. When his field of service expanded, he served a number of churches in eastern North Carolina. One of the largest of these was in Raleigh; although he found it in a declining condition, he was able to increase membership and to build a new sanctuary. Nash also served a large congregation in Wilmington, where he successfully reduced a large debt and made provisions for the payment of the outstanding portion. It was here that he edited a weekly newspaper, the *Atlantic Methodist*, whose income helped decrease the church's debt.

Several of Nash's sermons were printed for wider distribution. *Regeneration* was published in 1897, and *Baptism: The Nature, Mode, and Subjects* was issued without a date. A widely acclaimed biblical scholar, he also was the author of several books, including *Spiritual Life* (1898), *Early Morning Scenes in the Bible* (1910), *The Christian Family* (1915), and *Recollections and Observations* (1916).

During his later years, Nash resided in Hamlet and served the Conference as an evangelist. He traveled widely and held meetings and revivals on request. This was particularly satisfying for him as he enjoyed personal contacts. He also served on examining committees to approve the ordination of young men, and his fair but penetrating questions were long remembered.

By his second wife, Nash was the father of two sons: Marvin and Hugh. He was buried in Oakwood Cemetery, Raleigh.

SEE: *Charlotte Observer*, 13 July 1917; *Journal of the Methodist Episcopal Church, South* (1917); Stephen B. Weeks Scrapbook, vol. 8 (North Carolina Collection, University of North Carolina, Chapel Hill); *Who Was Who in America*, vol. 1 (1942).

WARREN L. BINGHAM

Nash, Sally (Sarah) Kollock (21 Jan. 1811–4 June 1893), **and Maria Jane Nash** (19 Nov. 1819–29 Apr. 1907), Hillsborough educators and founders and principals of the Nash and Kollock Select Boarding and Day School for Young Ladies (1859–90), were born in Hillsborough, the daughters of North Carolina Supreme Court Chief Justice Frederick and Mary Goddard Kollock Nash. They were the granddaughters of Governor Abner and Mary Whiting Jones Nash of New Bern and of printer-publisher Shepard and Susan Arnett Kollock of Elizabethtown, N.J.

Little is known of the formal education of the Nash sisters, both of whom were middle-aged when they opened the Nash-Kollock school in 1859. Maria had attended Miss Mary (Polly) W. Burke's School on East Queen Street in Hillsborough. Sally had taught briefly in the Burwell School and in a short-lived local venture about 1858. She had also reputedly studied drawing for a short time in New York. Both women, however, had spent their lives in close juxtaposition with the remarkable Kollock family of Elizabethtown and Princeton, an acknowledged leader of American Presbyterianism, and with the equally remarkable Nash family of Virginia and North Carolina, a leader of colonial planter aristocracy. Although Sally and Maria Nash "spent their entire lives from birth to death in the old gray unpainted house on Margaret Lane" in Hillsborough, as Ann Strudwick Nash remarked, they were far from being provincial.

Two unrelated events—the closing of the Burwell School in 1857 and the death of Chief Justice Nash in 1858—impelled the sisters to begin a school of their own in the old Nash home. They enlisted the aid of their younger cousin, Miss Sarah (or Sara) J. Kollock (7 Nov. 1826–26 June 1907), a tiny lady of spectacular appearance and hair-trigger temper, and the trio of spinsters, all with totally different personalities, began a surprisingly effective partnership that terminated only with their deaths.

In spite of the fact that the new school opened on the eve of the Civil War, it was immediately successful. The impeccable church and family connections of the Nash women attracted both Presbyterian and Episcopal "young ladies" from old plantation homes up and down the eastern seaboard, even from Kentucky and New Orleans. Inevitably, the Nash-Kollock school was virtually a carbon copy of the earlier Burwell School, with the same strong Presbyterian atmosphere and curriculum and similar living arrangements.

Although both Nash sisters were listed officially as principals of the school, it was always understood that the elder, Miss Sally, was the court of final decision. Besides teaching Bible and arithmetic, Sally met the public, conducted general school exercises, and supervised the servants and the operation of the dining room. Miss Maria taught English grammar and composition, her particular forte; Miss Sarah taught French and saw to all clerical work, advertising, and so forth connected with the school; and an assistant, a Miss Goodridge, taught history and geography. Music, painting, and drawing were taught by a succession of imported masters who used Chief Justice Nash's old law office as a studio. (Still standing, it is a National Register House owned by the Hillsborough Historical Society.)

If the Nash-Kollock school appears to have had a larger and more cosmopolitan student body than the Burwell School, it seems also to have expanded its musical offerings considerably beyond those provided earlier by the Burwells. Five pianos were in use, and the annual *soirée musicale* at Masonic Hall received highly favorable newspaper reviews.

From the beginning, the Nash and Kollock ladies had welcomed to the school a few small boys, cousins from the Nash and Strudwick families. When the school finally closed its doors in 1890, Sarah Kollock, still active, operated for some time—in the old law office—a small day school of her own for Hillsborough boys and girls. Maria and Sarah died within a few weeks of each other. All three women were buried in the Nash-Strudwick plot in Hillsborough's Old Town Cemetery. In 1926 a memorial plaque to the Misses Nash and Miss Kollock, "Being dead, yet liveth," was placed by their students on the interior south wall of the Presbyterian church. At the same time, simple stones were placed at the unmarked graves of Maria and Sarah.

No catalogue of the school was ever issued, nor were any formal records kept. In 1964 Ann Strudwick Nash, widow of Francis (Frank) Nash, following a suggestion of her late husband, published her own collected first-hand memories of the Nash-Kollock school under the title, *Ladies in the Making*. Her sympathetic eyewitness account of the day-by-day operation of the school is the only sustained record of any of Hillsborough's numerous nineteenth-century schools.

SEE: Mary Claire Engstrom, *The Old Town Cemetery, 1757* (1966); Ann Strudwick Nash, *Ladies in the Making* (1964); Francis Nash Collection (North Carolina State Archives, Raleigh); Francis Nash Papers (Southern Historical Collection, University of North Carolina, Chapel Hill).

MARY CLAIRE ENGSTROM

Neilson, Archibald (*ca. 1745–1805*), Loyalist official and merchant, was a friend and associate of Governor Josiah Martin, Janet Schaw, Andrew Miller, James Iredell, and Samuel Johnston. It is believed that he was born into a gentry family in Dundee, Scotland, the home of Governor Gabriel Johnston and his brother Samuel. Little is known of his early life except that he was employed by a Mr. Grenville in the West Indies. (If this is a reference to George Grenville, Neilson's employment could have been about 1765.) While in the West Indies, he may have met the Martin family. In 1788 Neilson wrote John Wilmot: "I had long been honored

with the particular friendship of the deceased Governor Martin on his being appointed to the government of North Carolina and, as I was at that time a young man without fixed line of employment, he in warmest and most friendly manner invited me to join him in his province. I accordingly joined him and lived with him in the most confidential manner. I was, so far as consisted, privy to the measures of his government, in forwarding many of which he did me the honour of calling on my services."

Neilson arrived in the province in 1771 and lived at various times in the governor's palace at New Bern; he also worked as a merchant trader, probably in Edenton. He owned two houses, two slaves, and some furniture and books, which he had to leave behind when he left the colony during the early months of the American Revolution. His valet was humiliated and forced to abide by the rules set by the Wilmington Safety Committee.

Although no record has been found indicating where Neilson was educated, his correspondence reflects his erudition, the vigor of his thought, and his comprehension of government and human nature. Griffith McRee concluded that Neilson was "undoubtedly, one of the most highly cultivated men of his day and region, and though an adherent of government, highly esteemed by [James] Iredell and [Samuel] Johnston." Neilson declared to Iredell that he was a friend of liberty and just authority but an enemy of anarchy.

When Governor Martin named Neilson as clerk of the courts, the Assembly contested the appointment. The governor also gave him an agency for the Granville Grant. In January 1775, on the death of the deputy auditor, Isaac Edwards, Martin appointed Neilson to that office. In October, when it was learned that Samuel Johnston, the naval officer, had accepted the post of moderator of the Provincial Congress, Martin suspended Johnston and gave Neilson his place. Despite the honor of these offices, Neilson never realized any of the emoluments because the progress of the American Revolution had destroyed the value of both of these offices.

As the Revolution accelerated after Martin dismissed the last royal Assembly, Neilson was a source of strength and help to the governor. In May 1775 he arranged for a ship to take Mrs. Martin and the children to the safety of her father's estate on Long Island. Shortly afterwards, Neilson and Martin left the palace in New Bern and rode in a coach through open country to Cross Creek and then down the Cape Fear River to Fort Johnston near Wilmington. Later Neilson joined the governor on the *Cruizer*. He served the governor in several ways, including as a personal secretary. He remained aboard the *Cruizer* until 10 Nov. 1775, when he left for England on the *George* with Janet Schaw and the John Rutherfurd children, Frances, John, Jr., and William Gordon, who were going to Scotland to attend school.

Miss Schaw recorded in her journal some of Neilson's activities during the summer and autumn of 1775 and their voyage to Portugal and England. She noted that Neilson had seen much of the world and that he was highly educated and conversant with many languages.

In January or February 1776 Neilson went to London and applied for a commissaryship or a similar post with the British army in North America. His application was turned down, but when he offered to go to New York as a volunteer, the Treasury granted him a temporary relief. A crisis developed when Neilson's brother died in Dundee, for Neilson was obliged to return home and assume responsibility for an aged mother, two sisters, a sister-in-law, and nine minor children. He renewed his profession as a merchant to supplement the income from the family lands and remained in Dundee for the rest of his life.

Neilson's name appears in fugitive correspondence about trade and in the records of the Loyalist Claims Commission. In 1783 he was awarded a yearly allowance of sixty pounds, which he received regularly until his death. He never married.

SEE: Evangeline Walker Andrews and Charles McLean Andrews, eds., *Journal of a Lady of Quality* (1927); Walter Clark, ed., *State Records of North Carolina*, vols. 11, 15 (1895–98); Letters (Manuscript Collection, Scottish Record Office, Edinburgh); Loyalist Papers (North Carolina State Archives, Raleigh); Griffith McRee, *Life and Correspondence of James Iredell*, vol. 2 (1976); Neilson to James Iredell, Edenton, 8 July 1775 (Manuscript Department, Duke University Library, Durham); William L. Saunders, ed., *Colonial Records of North Carolina*, vols. 9–10 (1890).

VERNON O. STUMPF

Nelson, Ernest William (*5 Feb. 1896–20 Sept. 1974*), educator and historian, was born in Brockton, Mass., the son of William and Elizabeth Nelson. After completing his elementary and secondary schooling in Brockton, he entered Clark University, Worcester, Mass., in the fall of 1912 and was graduated with honors and a bachelor of arts degree in 1916. He served for four years in the U.S. Army and earned a master of arts degree from Clark in 1920.

During the session of 1920–21 Nelson was a resident Andrew D. White Fellow in European history at Cornell University, Ithaca, N.Y., and the next year (1921–22) he was an Andrew D. White Traveling Fellow at the University of Paris. After further graduate work at Cornell (1922–23), he taught history at the University of South Dakota, Vermillion. He was awarded a doctor of philosophy degree by Cornell in 1925 and taught there during the following session. In September 1926 he joined the faculty of Duke University, where he was professor of history for forty years (1926–66).

On his retirement in 1966, Nelson lived with a son, Duncan M., in Sudbury, Mass. After his death in Sudbury, a memorial service was held in Concord, Mass., on 23 Sept. 1974, with interment in the same city.

After going to Duke, Nelson taught in the summer session of the University of Chicago (1929) and was a Fellow of the American Council of Learned Societies (1930–31) for travel and study in Italy. His interest in Italy began during his military tour of duty, when he spent considerable time in that country as well as in Germany, Switzerland, and France. He also taught in the summer session of 1947 at the University of Michigan, Ann Arbor.

At Duke, Nelson established a reputation as a cultural historian. His major field of interest was Italian Renaissance history. It has been written of him that "he was of the old school of teaching, molded in the European tradition which emphasizes the language, literature, and art of a people, not just the record of past events. His special interests were in Renaissance civilization, the history of liberty and ideas of tolerance, church-state relationships, Italian origins of modern diplomacy and balance-of-power relationships. His cluttered office across the hall from the music room in the East Duke Building held a large collection of books, prints, letters and photographs embodying almost every aspect of the cultural history of Europe."

In the classroom, Nelson was a constant stimulus to his students, many of whom pursued further graduate work and ultimately became teachers and writers of history. Of gentle manner, he was an unobtrusive scholar and avid reader. He continually interpreted modern events in the light of the philosophy and facts of history.

The volume of his own writings was much less than the volume he inspired. From his year of travel and study in Italy, he produced several chapters for major historical works, including "Heresies and the Inquisition," in the *Guide to the Study of Medieval History* (1931); "The Theory of Persecution," in *Persecution and Liberty: Essays in Honor of George Lincoln Burr* (1931); and "The Origins of Modern Balance-of-Power Politics," in *Medievalia et Humanistica* (1943). A frequent contributor to the *Journal of Modern History*, he wrote numerous book reviews for that and other scholarly journals.

Nelson held membership in the American Historical Association, Mediaeval Academy, Southern Historical Association, American Association of University Professors, Clark University Scholarship Society, and Phi Beta Kappa honorary society. His outstanding extracurricular activity at Duke was the organization (1945) of the Duke Chamber Arts Society, a sponsorship that established a lasting tradition at Duke through its annual series of popular programs of chamber music.

In 1927 Nelson married Rowena Morse of Ithaca. They had four children: Elizabeth Burr, Duncan Morse, William Evan, and George Anthony. They were divorced in 1943, and he never remarried.

SEE: Data File (Office of Information Services, Duke University, Durham); *Duke Alumni Register* (January 1975); *Durham Morning Herald*, 22 Sept. 1974.

C. SYLVESTER GREEN

Newbold, Nathan Carter (*27 Dec. 1871–23 Dec. 1957*), educator, public servant, and longtime director of the Division of Negro Education in North Carolina, was born in Pasquotank County, near Elizabeth City, and lived his entire life—except for periods of educational residence—in the state. His parents, both members of old-line North Carolina families, were William and Sarah Trueblood Newbold. His paternal grandfather, William Newbold, was for many years sheriff of Pasquotank County. Young Newbold attended elementary school in Pasquotank and Perquimans counties and received his high school education at Bethel Hill Institute in Person County. He was graduated from Trinity College (now Duke University) in 1895.

At Trinity, Newbold determined to become an educator. After graduation he served as principal of Leasburg Academy, near Semora, and then as coprincipal of La Grange High School, near Kinston. He next became, in succession, superintendent of schools in Asheboro, Roxboro, and Washington, N.C. At intervals during this period Newbold pursued graduate work at a variety of institutions, beginning with The University of North Carolina. Subsequently, he studied at the University of Tennessee, Columbia, and Harvard.

But it was as an administrator, and not as a scholar, that Newbold made his greatest contribution. In 1913 he moved from Washington to Raleigh to become North Carolina's first state agent for Negro schools, a position created by funds from the General Education Board. In this capacity, Newbold undertook the delicate task of enlarging educational opportunities for North Carolina blacks at a time when such opportunities were almost nonexistent. In 1920, following a state educational survey, he outlined to the State Board of Education a plan to create an entire Division of Negro Education. The plan was approved, funds—$15,000—were appropriated by the General Assembly, and Newbold was named division director, serving for thirty-seven years. Under his leadership, Negro education in North Carolina experienced remarkable growth in the 1920s, and the idea of publicly supported black schools became more widely accepted. Newbold also worked closely with philanthropic organizations to expand educational opportunities for blacks; as a result of his efforts, funds from the General Education Board, as well as from the Slator, Rosenwald, and Jeanes funds, were utilized efficiently and effectively.

Working quietly and avoiding controversy insofar as possible, Newbold acquired a reputation as an effective advocate of Negro education. As time went on, especially in the years after World War II, he received considerable criticism from various groups and individuals who were dissatisfied with the racial climate in North Carolina. Yet he never permitted criticism from any source to deter him from his goal: the expansion of black educational opportunities within the structure of a separate but equal state racial philosophy. Newbold continued to serve as director of the Division of Negro Education until his retirement in 1950 at age seventy-nine.

He also participated in other path-breaking interracial endeavors. A founding member of the North Carolina Commission for Interracial Cooperation, he was long active in the work of that organization. He also served as director of the Division of Cooperation in Education and Race Relations, a project sponsored by the State Department of Public Instruction, Duke University, and The University of North Carolina. The purpose of this united effort was to disseminate information about Negro life and history, stressing the positive achievements of southern blacks. Books were purchased for university libraries, courses in Negro life were taught in various colleges and universities, and a number of similar programs were initiated.

Newbold held membership in numerous professional organizations, commissions, and advisory boards. He was an honorary member of Phi Beta Kappa and Omicron Delta Kappa fraternities, a life member of the North Carolina Education Association and the National Education Association, a trustee of Payne College, Augusta, Ga., and a member of the State Textbook Commission. A lifelong Democrat, he participated in President Harry S Truman's White House Conference on Child Health and Protection. He also served on a number of boards of Negro colleges as adviser.

A devout churchman, Newbold was a member of the Commission on Cooperation and Council for the Methodist Episcopal church and was long active in the affairs of his home church, Edenton Street Methodist Church in Raleigh. On 2 Mar. 1905 he married Eugenia Lou Bradsher of Roxboro. The couple had four sons: William Bradsher, Nathan Carter, Jr., Arch Bradsher, and James Satterfield. Newbold died four days before his eighty-sixth birthday and was buried in Burchwood Cemetery, Roxboro.

SEE: *Asheville Citizen*, 24 Dec. 1957; Papers of the Director, Division of Negro Education, Department of Public Instruction, 1921–50 (North Carolina State Archives, Raleigh); Raleigh *News and Observer*, 10 July 1950, 24 Dec. 1957; *Trinity Alumni Register* 10 (April 1924).

A. M. BURNS III

Newby, Gabriel (*d. 1735*), colonial official, appears in North Carolina records as early as 1695, when he was residing in Perquimans Precinct. Like many other people in that area, he was a Quaker. In 1703 Newby served in the lower house of the General Assembly. In November 1707 he joined the Proprietary Council during William Glover's presidency as one of the Lords Proprietors' deputies. From that vantage point he supported the efforts of Thomas Cary to assume executive control in the colony. Newby served on the Council during Cary's presidency from July 1708 until January 1711, when Cary and his supporters were ousted. Thereafter, Newby disappeared from provincial politics.

At his death early in 1735, Newby owned at least nine hundred acres of land and several slaves. His will mentions three sons and a wife named Mary.

SEE: J. R. B. Hathaway, ed., *North Carolina Historical and Genealogical Register*, 3 vols. (1900–1903); Secretary of State Papers and Wills (North Carolina State Archives, Raleigh).

WILLIAM S. PRICE, JR.

Newland, William Calhoun (*8 Oct. 1860–19 Nov. 1938*), lawyer, legislator, and lieutenant governor, was born near Marion in McDowell County. The Newland family had immigrated to the American colonies from Wales, and William Newland's grandfather had moved to North Carolina from Pennsylvania. Newland's father, Dr. Joseph C. Newland, was born in 1816 near Lenoir and attended Louisville Medical College. He practiced medicine in McDowell County until 1873, when he moved his family to Lenoir. William Newland's mother was Laura Conley Newland, a native of Caldwell County.

Young Newland attended Finley Academy in Lenoir, then secured an appointment to West Point through Congressman R. B. Vance. After three years, he resigned from the academy and returned home to study law. He apprenticed himself to Judge C. A. Cilley and was admitted to the bar at age twenty-one.

Joseph Newland, a partisan Democrat, named his son in honor of John C. Calhoun. William Newland seems to have inherited his father's interest in politics as well as his party preference. He was elected mayor of Lenoir while still in his twenties and was reelected twice. In 1890 he was elected solicitor in the Eighth District. Nine years later he won a seat in the lower house of the North Carolina General Assembly and in 1903 was reelected. In 1904 Newland was nominated for Congress but lost; four years later he was elected lieutenant governor under William Walton Kitchin. Avery County was created during Newland's tenure, and its county seat, Newland, was named in his honor.

During his active years Newland attended most of the national conventions of the Democratic party, and in 1920 he nominated for the presidency Senator Furnifold M. Simmons as North Carolina's favorite son.

Newland also participated in various civic and governmental functions. By appointment of the North Carolina legislature, he was a member of the Penitentiary Commission; he served as a trustee of the Caswell Training School for the Feeble Minded; and for a time he was a trustee of Davenport College. While in the legislature, Newland introduced the bill establishing Appalachian State Teachers College. He successfully guided the bill past firm opposition, and at the time of his death he was chairman of the school's board of trustees.

Newland was a member of the Masonic lodge, the Independent Order of Odd Fellows, and the Knights of Pithias. He was a Sunday school teacher and active in the Methodist church.

In 1884 he married Jessie Hendrey of Wilmington, and the couple had four children. Towards the end of his life, Newland suffered complications from kidney and heart disease. He died in Grace Hospital in Banner Elk.

SEE: Appalachian State Teachers College Alumni Association, *Hall of Fame*, 5 May 1962 (portrait); John L. Cheney, Jr., ed., *North Carolina Government, 1585–1979* (1981); *McDowell News* (Marion), 1 Aug. 1968; *North Carolina Biography*, vol. 4 (1929 [portrait]); Raleigh *News and Observer*, 19 Nov. 1938; D. F. Sinclair, *Biographical Sketches of the Members and Officers of the General Assembly of North Carolina* (1889).

DAVID H. TYNER

Newlin, John (*8 Apr. 1776–6 July 1867*), merchant, industrialist, land speculator, abolitionist, and Quaker leader, was born in the southeastern part of present-day Alamance County. He was in the sixth generation of descendants of Nicholas and Elizabeth Paggott Newlin, who emigrated from Mountmellick, Ireland, to Chester County, Pa., in 1683. His grandparents, John and Mary Pyle Newlin, bringing his father John, moved to North Carolina in 1768. His mother was Deborah Lindley Newlin, the daughter of Thomas and Ruth Hadley Lindley, natives of Ireland, who had moved to the same neighborhood from Pennsylvania. All of his ancestors and relatives were Quakers.

On 19 Apr. 1810 John Newlin married Rebecca Long. They made their home at the homestead of Newlin's grandfather, Thomas Lindley, near Spring Friends Meeting House, where John operated a mercantile business, a tanyard, and a leather business that made shoes and harnesses. It is said that he employed about twenty laborers in this work. Reputedly, he became the largest landowner in present-day Newlin Township.

Newlin's most noted venture was a textile mill at the site that became Saxapahaw. It was located on the eastern bank of Haw River, where in 1844 he and his sons James and Jonathan formed a partnership known as John Newlin and Sons. They erected a one-story brick building, fifty by two hundred feet, and in 1848 began the production of yarn for sale locally. In 1859 they enlarged the building by constructing two additional stories and added weaving and dyeing to their operations. Following the death of John Newlin in 1867, his sons took their cousin, George Guthrie, into the business, but in 1873 they sold the mill to Edwin M. Holt.

John Newlin was opposed to slavery and expressed this view by joining the Manumission Society of North Carolina, serving as a lobbyist during sessions of the General Assembly, and working with individuals to liberate their slaves. One of his efforts in the interest of manumission involved him in a long series of lawsuits. Mrs. Sarah Foust Freeman had come into possession of twenty-five to forty slaves through the will of her first husband. Before her second marriage, she and her prospective husband signed an agreement that left her in complete control of her slaves and other property. She and her first husband had discussed the possibility of freeing the slaves. After her second marriage, Newlin worked out an agreement with Mrs. Freeman by which he would take the slaves to free territory and there execute a deed of manumission for each of them. In her will she devised all her slaves to Newlin on his promise to carry out their plan for freeing them. On the death of

Mrs. Freeman in 1839, persons claiming to be her heirs attempted, through a series of lawsuits, to break the will and secure possession of the slaves. Three of the suits went to the North Carolina Supreme Court. The last of these was in 1851, twelve years after Mrs. Freeman's death. During the years of those lawsuits, the litigation prevented Newlin from taking the slaves out of the state. A decision of the court finally cleared the way for him to take them to Ohio and set them free.

The Saxapahaw cotton mill was built during the period of litigation. It has been reported that Newlin used slave labor to dig a mile-long race from the dam to the mill, but such action on the part of a Quaker has been questioned. During the actual litigation no one accused him of using the slaves for his own profit, but there can be little doubt that he used them to cover the cost of their upkeep during the decade they were in his charge.

Further evidence of his stand against slavery may be seen in his service with several groups that went to Raleigh during legislative sessions to try to influence legislators to remove some of the obstacles to the manumission of slaves.

Newlin's interest in education was reflected in his appointment in 1834 as the first-named member of a committee to raise money for the erection of a building to accommodate New Garden Boarding School and to supervise its construction. The school began in August 1837 and half a century later became Guilford College.

John and Rebecca Long Newlin had ten children: James, Oliver, Jonathan, Cyrus, William, Mary Ann, Deborah, Thomas, Gulielma, and Nancy. He died at age ninety-one and was buried near his home in the Quaker cemetery at Spring Friends Meeting House.

SEE: Ben Bulla, "Early History of Saxapahaw," *Burlington Daily Times News*, centennial issue (May 1949); Helen Cottergill, *Documents on Slavery: Judicial Cases Concerning American Slavery and Negroes*, vol. 2 (1926); Julian Hughes, *Development of the Textile Industry in Alamance County* (1965); Hugh T. Lefler and Paul W. Wager, *Orange County, 1752–1952* (1953); *Minutes of North Carolina Yearly Meeting of Friends* (1820–67); *Minutes of Spring Monthly Meeting of Friends* (to 1867); *Minutes of Western Quarterly Meeting of Friends* (1820–67); Memory F. Mitchell, "Off to Africa with Judicial Blessing," *North Carolina Historical Review* 53 (July 1976); Algie I. Newlin, *The Newlin Family: Ancestors and Descendants of John and Mary Pyle Newlin* (1965); Andrew Warren Pierpont, "The Development of the Textile Industry in Alamance County" (Ph.D. diss., University of North Carolina, 1953); Sallie Stockard, *The History of Alamance* (1900); H. M. Wagstaff, ed., *Minutes of the North Carolina Manumission Society, 1816–1834* (1934).

ALGIE I. NEWLIN

Newnam, Thomas (*d. 1723*), Anglican clergyman, was born in England and moved to North Carolina in 1722 as a missionary of the Society for the Propagation of the Gospel in Foreign Parts. He began his work in South West Parish in Chowan Precinct. This included present-day Bertie County and the southern shore of Albemarle Sound. In 1722 the Assembly of North Carolina passed an act dividing this parish into South Parish and Society Parish and stipulated that both parishes "make good their agreement with the Rev. Mr. Newnam."

On 29 July 1722 Newnam wrote to the London authorities in some detail, describing his arduous duties and the vast area he had to cover to attend to his parishioners. This included two Sundays a month at Esquire

Duckenfield's, a Sunday at "Eden Town," where the vestry planned to build a church, and occasional visits to the South Shore; Meherrin, which was forty miles away; and a place called Roanoke, which was eighty miles distant. In a letter of 6 Apr. 1723, John Ashe informed the Reverend William Bull that Newnam was the only settled minister in North Carolina. On 9 May Newnam reported to the society secretary that, although he and his family had suffered from fever, he was setting off for Bath County, where three hundred children awaited baptism.

Newnam died the following fall. Sometime before his death he had moved from Bertie to Edenton, since he described himself in his will, dated 21 Sept. 1723, as a missionary of the Society for the Propagation of the Faith, residing in Edenton. His widow Frances was the sole legatee in his will, probated two months later.

After Newnam's death, Nathaniel Duckenfield wrote to the bishop of London urging a speedy replacement. He said that although Newnam had lived in the area only half a year, he was held in so high a regard that not only did the parish give the widow the whole year's salary of sixty pounds, but also the Assembly gave her forty pounds out of the public treasury.

SEE: J. Bryan Grimes, ed., *Abstract of North Carolina Wills* (1910); E. L. Pennington, *The Church of England in Colonial North Carolina* (1937); William L. Saunders, ed., *Colonial Records of North Carolina*, vol. 2 (1886); Stuart H. Smith and C. T. Smith, Jr., *The History of Trinity Church, Scotland Neck, Edgecombe Parish, Halifax County* (1955).

CLAIBORNE T. SMITH, JR.

Newnan, Daniel (ca. 1780–16 Jan. 1851), Georgia planter, general, and congressman, was born in Salisbury. Daniel, his brothers John, Hugh, and Montgomery, and sisters Elizabeth (Gaither), Polly (Payne), Jenny, and Nancy survived Dr. Anthony Newnan, their physician father, who died in 1805. Their mother, Mary Montgomery Newnan, was the daughter of the wealthy Hugh Montgomery, who died in 1780.

The scion of this prestigious family attended The University of North Carolina in 1796 but later, because of some indiscretion, fell under a parental cloud. Confident that the young man would turn out all right, a staunch friend of the Newnans, John Steele, helped Daniel get a junior commission, dated 3 Mar. 1799, in the Fourth Infantry Regiment, U.S. Army. Soon promoted to first lieutenant, the impetuous Daniel nevertheless resigned from the regulars in a letter that reached the War Department from Fort Wilkinson, Ga., on 1 Jan. 1802. Eventually he settled in the general vicinity of Milledgeville, which became the capital of Georgia about 1805.

Commissioned lieutenant colonel in the Georgia militia, he exercised statewide responsibility as adjutant general and inspector general from 13 Dec. 1806 to 10 Nov. 1817. With the outbreak of the War of 1812, he personally led "Newnan's Command" of Georgia volunteers into East Florida. In the Creek War of 1813–14, while campaigning in Alabama under Brigadier General John Floyd, Newnan distinguished himself but was felled by three balls on 27 Jan. 1814 and had to be evacuated to his own plantation in Putnam County, Ga. Mending rapidly, he rallied the state against the threat of British invasion from the harassed coastal islands. On giving up the adjutant generalship, he was immediately commissioned major general to command the Third Division of Georgia militia.

Politically a follower of Governor John Clark, General Newnan was elected from Putnam County to the lower house of the legislature of 1820–21, in which he served on a militia committee and reported for the agriculture and internal improvements committee. Clark appointed him one of the state commissioners to help effect the Creek Treaty of Indian Springs, signed on 8 Jan. 1821, but could not get the Monroe administration to make him agent to the eastern Cherokee. On 12 Dec. 1823 the legislature chose Newnan to be principal keeper of the state penitentiary, a job he held nearly a year under Governor George M. Troup, Clark's successor and adversary. Resplendent in uniform in March 1825, when Milledgeville welcomed Lafayette, Major General Newnan resigned his commission on 14 November and the next day was elected by the Clark-dominated legislature to the position of secretary of state. He served in that capacity until November 1827, when Troup left office.

In the national election of 1828 Newnan, now identified as a resident of Baldwin County, headed the unsuccessful Clark slate of presidential electors. Next heralded to be from Henry County, where he may have had a plantation at or near McDonough, he did succeed in winning election to the Twenty-second Congress (4 Mar. 1831–3 Mar. 1833). In the first session of the House, he sat on the committee on post offices and post roads and in the second session, on the committee on Revolutionary claims. During his stay in Washington, the tariff issue helped fragment the set factions in Georgia, and soon a Union party and a States' Rights or Nullification party emerged. As a candidate for the latter, Newnan failed to be reelected in 1834. Governor William Schley, though a Union man, recognized Newnan's availability and, by an executive order of 2 Jan. 1837, reconstituted him adjutant general of Georgia, an office he headed as colonel until 25 Dec. 1837 and thereafter as brigadier general until 22 Dec. 1840.

Much of Newnan's personal life is untold. Records of his native county in North Carolina are said to contain a letter that he wrote on 1 Nov. 1813, from Eatonton, Ga., to Captain John Fulton of Salisbury. In case of death in the Creek War, Newnan wanted everything left to his own small children, with a double portion to Mary, presumably Newnan's wife. In 1820 the Newnan household in Putnam County—besides Newnan and wife in their prime—consisted of three boys aged between ten and twenty-six, two girls aged between ten and twenty, and about a dozen slaves mostly engaged in agriculture. What happened to members of the family is conjectural, but the aging general lived out his final years in a rural setting several miles east of Rossville, Walker County, Ga., just below Chattanooga and the Tennessee line. At the census of 1850, he was recorded as a seventy-year-old farmer, with only eighteen-year-old Hamilton Montgomery with him.

In 1853, after Newnan's death, the community of Newnan Springs, where he had lived, was shunted into the new county of Catoosa. In 1927 the citizens of Newnan Springs and of the distant city of Newnan, named for him, joined forces to place a bronze tablet to mark his grave in a cemetery near modern Newnan Springs Methodist Church.

SEE: *Biog. Dir. Am. Cong.* (1971); Daniel L. Grant, *Alumni History of the University of North Carolina, 1795–1924* (1924); W. Edwin Hemphill, ed., *The Papers of John C. Calhoun*, vols. 5–8 (1971–75); George Rockingham, *Sketches of Some of the First Settlers of Upper Georgia, of the Cherokees, and the Author* (1926); Jethro Rumple, *A History of Rowan County, North Carolina* (1929); H. M. Wagstaff, ed., *The Papers of John Steele*, 2 vols. (1924); George White, *Historical Collections of Georgia* (1854).

H. B. FANT

Newnan, John *(ca. 1773–1833)*, physician, was born in Salisbury, the son of Anthony Newnan, also a physician, and his wife Mary, the daughter of Hugh Montgomery, a merchant and landowner of Wilkes County. John was educated at the Salisbury Academy and in 1790 went to Philadelphia for medical training. His inaugural dissertation for the degree of doctor of medicine was on the topic of general dropsy (edema); dated 8 May 1793, it was dedicated to Dr. Benjamin Rush and to the Reverend Samuel E. McCorkle, who had been president of the Salisbury Academy.

For some years Newnan practiced in Salisbury, where, on 12 Feb. 1798, he married Margaret Chambers, the daughter of Maxwell and Margaret Chambers. The Newnans had four children. In the first decade of the nineteenth century, the family moved to Tennessee and settled near Nashville.

Records of Newnan's professional career are limited. He applied to teach chemistry at the newly formed University of North Carolina in 1796; his letter was received by the trustees, who deferred consideration until their next meeting, at which it apparently was not mentioned. In 1798 Newnan organized a convention of doctors. He wrote a paper, published in 1807, describing a tracheotomy to remove a bullet and noting the subsequent recovery of the patient.

He was elected to the American Philosophical Society in 1797 and became a corresponding member of the Massachusetts Historical Society in 1802. In his later years he published, in *The Tennessee Administration Advocate* (1828?), an article passionately supporting John Quincy Adams and denigrating Andrew Jackson. He also was the author of *A Commentary on the Roman and Spanish Statute of Frauds and Perjuries*, published in Nashville in 1829. His last known writing is an essay, purportedly on forensic medicine, challenging the will of his brother-in-law, Otho Chambers. Entitled *The Case of John Newnan and Others vs. William Chambers and Others* and printed in Nashville in 1835, it refers to "the insane OTHO CHAMBERS" and to "the illegitimate alience" of D. F. Caldwell. The illogical intensity of the last two compositions suggests a man of unpredictable thought and action. A contemporary described Newnan as a "man of extremely erratic habits."

SEE: Dorothy Long, "Early North Carolina Medicine," *North Carolina Medical Journal* 14 (September 1953); John Newnan, *The Case of John Newnan and Others vs. William Chambers and Others* (1835) and *Inaugural Dissertation on General Dropsy* (for the degree of doctor of medicine, University of Pennsylvania, 8 May 1793) (1793); *Tennessee Administrative Advocate* (copy of article in North Carolina Collection, University of North Carolina, Chapel Hill); H. M. Wagstaff, ed., *The Papers of John Steele*, 2 vols. (1924).

ROSAMOND PUTZEL

Newsom, Dallas Walton *(24 Oct. 1873–21 Feb. 1949)*, educational administrator, county manager, scholar, and poet, was born in Littleton, Warren County, the son of Marion Eaton and Annie Soule Heptinstall Newsom. His grandparents, both maternal and paternal, were prominent landowners and agriculturalists of Halifax County. His maternal grandfather, the Reverend John

Wesley Heptinstall (1812–90), was also a local preacher of the Methodist Episcopal Church, South.

Newsom was the oldest of eight children, four boys and four girls. Throughout his life he recalled "the beauty, the happiness, and the freedom" of his early home. He attended the private schools of his aunt, Mrs. E. A. C. Jackson, and of the Reverend J. M. Rhodes before entering the "Bagley Academy" (Littleton High School and Business Institute), where he was graduated in 1894. During his high school days, he taught Latin and mathematics (1892–93) and later English grammar and classes in business practices, telegraphy, penmanship, and pen art.

In the fall of 1895 Newsom entered Trinity College (now Duke University), Durham, from which he was graduated with a bachelor of arts degree in 1899. His favorite subjects were philosophy, English, and Greek. Based on his superior scholastic record at Trinity, he was later tapped for membership in Phi Beta Kappa. A campus leader, he was a member of "9019" (a secret scholastic society) and Sigma Upsilon (literary) and a charter member of Alpha Phi chapter of Kappa Alpha (social). In his senior year he was class president and chief editor of *The Trinity Archive*, the campus literary magazine. He held many offices in the Hesperian Literary Society and won its orator's medal (1898).

Near the end of his first year at Trinity, Newsom was asked by Dr. John Carlisle Kilgo, president of the college, to be his private secretary. After a week's vacation at home, he returned to Durham in June and began a lifelong friendship with President Kilgo, whom he provided continuous service over many years, and a twenty-seven-year association in the business of Trinity College.

It was President Kilgo who recommended Newsom for a special position in Havana, Cuba, where Newsom spent the year of 1900 as private secretary to the comptroller of customs in the U.S. Customs House. Returning to Trinity in 1901, he became registrar of the college and six years later was named treasurer, a post he held until 1923. He served simultaneously as recording secretary to the board of trustees and as a member of the officers' finance committee.

Opening a real estate and insurance sales and service office in Durham in 1923, Newsom spent the next seven years in private business. During the same period he served as secretary-treasurer and then president (1928) of the Durham Real Estate Board and as a director of the State Board of Realtors.

Active in many local movements and institutions, he was a trustee of the Durham Public Library, Southern Conservatory of Music, and Louisburg College (executive committee); a director of the South Atlantic Publishing Company, Home Building and Loan Association, Hood System Bank, Durham Bond and Mortgage Company (president), Durham Lions Club (charter member), Durham Chamber of Commerce (chairman of the industrial committee), and Hope Valley Country Club; chairman of the annual campaign of the Durham Community Chest; and a member of the advisory committee of the Salvation Army.

In 1924 Newsom was appointed to the Durham County Board of Commissioners and later was elected to three more terms. He expanded that interest through membership in the State Association of County Commissioners (chairman, legislative committee). In 1925 Governor Angus W. McLean named him to the Governor's Commission for a Survey and Study of County Government, assigned to project the modernization of county governments. After the recommendations of the commission were enacted into law by the General Assembly (1927), Newsom was appointed one of five members of the Governor's County Government Advisory Commission (1927–31) to help put these reforms into effect.

In 1930 the Durham county commissioners decided to inaugurate the office of county manager and asked Newsom to take the post. Even three years later, Durham "was one of only three counties in the nation with the managerial plan of government."

Until his death eighteen and a half years later, Newsom's administration of county affairs attracted nationwide attention. No movement for the betterment of the county and the area escaped his notice. The Raleigh-Durham airport became a reality (1943) through his cooperative efforts. All phases of the county's work—education, welfare, law and order—were his continuous concern, and his leadership in stabilizing the financial structure of the county remained impressive decades later.

His deep religious faith sustained him throughout life, giving him courage and composure in all situations. At Duke Memorial Methodist Episcopal Church, South, he served for years as a member of the Board of Stewards, a member and assistant teacher of the Pastor's Aides Class, and—along with his wife—a member of the choir. In 1919 Newsom was campaign director and centenary publicity director for the North Carolina Conference in the great centenary movement of the Methodist church of America and Canada to raise $125 million for use in a world program of evangelistic, educational, and medical work—the church's "answer to the crying need for world reconstruction" after World War I.

While immersed in the administrative and business details of his profession and community, Newsom maintained a deep inner life. He always found joy in returning home after a day's work to the companionship of his family and his beloved books. A calm, gentle, and reflective person, he would sit late at night on his front porch or by an open fire to savor a period of meditation.

Through all his years he wrote poetry that was seasoned with great truths and vibrant with a basic imagery and rhythm. Among his published works are two books of poems: *Song and Dream* (1922) and *Along the Silent Ways* (1973). The latter volume was affectionately edited by his daughters and published in commemoration of the one hundredth anniversary of his birth. It contains a biographical sketch and a large body of his poetry, most of which was written during his later years.

He also was the author of a *History of Duke Memorial Methodist Church from 1886 to 1932* (1933) and *Chapel Talks* (1922) by President John Carlisle Kilgo, transcribed from notes taken by Newsom years earlier. In a lengthy paper relating his philosophy of life, entitled "The Philosophy of a Layman," Newsom pondered "the mysterious nature of the universe, man and his Creator, and the meaning of human life" and "the intricate and perplexing questions that lift themselves upon the horizon of every thinking man's mind." He wrote: "For man to search for God is the most exalted business of the human mind. . . . Man's chief business in the world is to seek and to know God. All other things are but the scaffolding."

Music, too, held an important place in his life. While in high school, he studied piano, and during his college days and afterwards he studied voice under Mrs. Gilmore Ward Bryant of the Southern Conservatory of Music in Durham. He also studied violin at the conservatory. The records indicate that he sang in a male quartet at Trinity College. For a time he directed the choir of the

Main Street Methodist Church, which later became Duke Memorial Methodist Episcopal Church, South. In January 1920 he became director of the first official college choir of Trinity College.

On 14 Sept. 1905 Newsom married Tempie Battle, of Whitakers, Edgecombe County, the seventh of nine children of Marcus Josiah and Susan Ella Garrett Battle. They had four children: Dallas Walton, Jr., Routh Battle, Dorothy (Mrs. Robert Stanley Rankin), and Tempe Garrett (Mrs. Frederick Morgan Prouty).

Newsom died in Durham. The funeral service was held at Duke Memorial Methodist Church, with interment in the old section of Maplewood Cemetery, Durham.

SEE: *Durham Morning Herald*, 22 Feb. 1949; *Durham Sun*, 22 Feb. 1949; Dallas Walton Newsom, *Along the Silent Ways* (1973); *North Carolina Biography*, vol. 3 (1929).

C. SYLVESTER GREEN

Newsome, Albert Ray *(4 June 1894–5 Aug. 1951)*, historian, archivist, and teacher, was born at Marshville, the son of Richard Clyde and Julia Ross Newsome. Studious from boyhood, he was graduated from The University of North Carolina in 1915 with the highest academic record in his class. From 1915 to 1918 he taught in the public schools of Elizabeth City and Washington, N.C. In the summer of 1919, after eight months in the U.S. Naval Reserve, he joined the history staff of Bessie Tift College in Forsyth, Ga. In the autumn of 1921 he entered the University of Michigan as a graduate student and part-time instructor. Two years later, after having completed the residence requirements for a Ph.D. degree, he joined the faculty of The University of North Carolina, where he was an assistant professor of history until 1926.

In the summer of 1926 Newsome was appointed secretary of the North Carolina Historical Commission (later the Department of Archives and History), which had been established on a solid basis by R. D. W. Connor during the first decade of the century. Generously gifted and superbly trained for both editorial and archival work, he edited the *North Carolina Historical Review* with skill and thoroughness as he built an already good Historical Commission into an outstanding one. The excellence of his archival and editorial work soon attracted national as well as local attention, and he was elected president of the National Conference of Historical Societies (1928–29) and chairman of the Public Archives Commission of the American Historical Association (1932–34). In 1932 he published *The Preservation of Local Archives: A Guide for Public Officials*, and in the mid-1930s he played a key role in the establishment of the Society of American Archivists, serving as its first president from 1936 to 1939.

When, in 1934, the position of archivist of the United States was created and President Franklin D. Roosevelt asked R. D. W. Connor, then head of the history department at The University of North Carolina, to serve as first archivist of the United States, Newsome accepted an invitation to return to Chapel Hill and assume Connor's duties as head of the department and professor of American history. Newsome ran the history department until 1950, when poor health compelled him to give up all administrative duties. During these fifteen years he not only guided a growing department firmly and played a central role in the making of policy throughout the university, but he also served for several years both as editor of the *James Sprunt Studies in History and Political*

Science and as historian of the North Carolina Department of the American Legion and did considerable research and writing. His publications included *The Presidential Election of 1824 in North Carolina* (1939); *The Growth of North Carolina* (1940), and *North Carolina: The History of a Southern State* (1954), in collaboration with Hugh T. Lefler; and numerous articles for the *North Carolina Historical Review*, the *American Archivist*, the *Dictionary of American Biography*, *Public Documents*, and the *Encyclopedia Britannica*.

Newsome was regarded as a superior teacher, and his students frequently spoke of his lectures as models of organization, thoroughness, and clarity. A sensitive, gentle, and sincere person, he was never too busy to talk with a colleague or a student who had a problem.

On 4 June 1917 he married Frances Vaughn, and the couple had two daughters: Jennie Wells and Julia Frances. Newsome was an Episcopalian and a Democrat. He died in Chapel Hill and was buried in the town cemetery.

SEE: *Biennial Report of the North Carolina Historical Commission* (1926–36); *Charlotte Observer*, 18 June 1939, 12 Jan. 1941; *Durham Herald-Sun*, 20 Oct. 1940, 22 Jan. 1941; *Greensboro Daily News*, 25 Dec. 1940; History Department Records, boxes 1, 4–10 (University of North Carolina Archives, Chapel Hill); Letters of J. M. Broughton and A. J. Maxwell (clipping files, North Carolina Collection, University of North Carolina, Chapel Hill); Raleigh *News and Observer*, 12 Dec. 1940, 12–17 Jan., 14, 23 Feb., 16, 20–21, 23, 30 Mar., 3, 6, 21 Apr. 1941, 21 July 1942, 6–7 Aug. 1951.

CARL HAMILTON PEGG

Newton, George *(December 1765–4 Dec. 1840)*, educator and Presbyterian minister, was the youngest of seven children of Ebenezer Newton and his wife of Shrewbury District, York, Pa. The family moved to North Carolina before the American Revolution and on 10 Jan. 1774 sold some land in Mecklenburg County. In 1778 George Newton took an oath "to bear faithfull and true allegiance to the State of North Carolina." There is some evidence to suggest that he also served in the war.

Because of the destruction of local records, little is known of Newton until 1797. In the autumn of that year he arrived in the newly chartered town of Asheville to begin a classical school for boys, with which he was associated until 1814. His school came to be highly regarded, and it attracted pupils from several adjacent states. Named Union Hill, it was chartered by the General Assembly in 1805. In 1809, when it occupied a new brick building, its name was changed by legislative act to Newton Academy. An early effort to establish a female seminary with funds coming from a lottery was not successful. Among Newton's students were David Lowry Swain, governor and president of The University of North Carolina; B. F. Perry, governor of South Carolina; Waddy Thompson, of South Carolina, congressman and minister to Mexico; and numerous other state and local officials.

The academy building was also the site of religious services on Sunday, with Newton officiating. He was only a licentiate when he began his teaching career, but when local congregations were organized by visiting missionaries in 1794, he received a call to become the pastor of churches at Swannanoa, Bee Tree, Reems Creek, and Asheville. He was readily ordained after preaching a prepared sermon on a stated passage of Scripture and passing an examination on the chro-

nology, history, and government of the Presbyterian church. Traveling on foot and on horseback, he kept a schedule of services at the various places, but two or three Sunday afternoons each month were reserved for worship at the academy building by his largest congregation.

Late in 1813 or early the following year, Newton consented to go to Bedford County, Tenn. There he generally repeated the process that he had followed in North Carolina, operating schools and nurturing Presbyterian congregations. His Mount Reserve Academy (later called Bethsalem Academy) was the first-known school in the new county. Having established several schools and Presbyterian congregations, Newton moved to Shelbyville, Tenn., where he spent the final years of his life.

Newton's first wife, Mary McCall (or McCaule), whom he married in Orange County, N.C., in 1794, died in 1828. His second wife, Ann, died on 5 July 1831. Sometime before December 1833 he married Helen M., who survived him. His children, all by his first wife, were William, Jane McCall, John, Ebenezer James, Alexander, and Elizabeth.

A portrait of Newton, painted by his great-granddaughter, was unveiled at the Newton School in Asheville, site of the old Newton Academy, on 14 Apr. 1954.

SEE: *Asheville Citizen*, 11, 14 Apr. 1954; Daniel K. Bennett, *Chronology of North Carolina* (1858); Ora Blackmun, *A Spire in the Mountains* (1970); Foster A. Sondley, *A History of Buncombe County*, 2 vols. (1930); Foster A. Sondley and T. F. Davidson, *Asheville and Buncombe County* (1921).

BERTHA FREEMAN

Ney, Peter Stewart *(d. 15 Nov. 1846)*, schoolmaster who died near Salisbury, is believed by many to have been the Napoleonic marshal, Michel Ney, living in hiding to escape persecution. His gravestone at Third Creek Church, Rowan County, describes him as "a native of France . . . and soldier of the French Revolution . . . under . . . Napoleon Bonaparte" and sets his birth at 1769, the year Michel Ney was born.

At least three books, written by North Carolinians, argue that Peter Stewart Ney was Marshal Ney, but evidence gathered during the 1940s and 1950s by William Henry Hoyt (1884–1957), of Greenwich, Conn., establishes that the conditions under which Marshal Ney was executed at Paris in 1815, and the verifications prepared at that time, made it impossible for the execution to have been simulated or another person substituted for the marshal. Since Marshal Ney died in 1815, the Peter Stewart Ney who lived until 1846 must have been a different person. Who was he?

According to testimony recorded by Hoyt, and also by those with whom he disagreed, Peter Stewart Ney said occasionally that he had been born in 1787 in Stirlingshire, Scotland, not far from the ruined castle of the Scottish hero, Sir James Graham, and that his mother's maiden name was Isabella Stewart. Following these clues, Hoyt discovered that on 3 Feb. 1788, one John McNee and his wife, Isbal Stewart, baptized an infant named Peter at Fintry Parish, Stirlingshire, about three and a half miles from the Graham castle ruins. This seems confirmatory. But Hoyt was frustrated in his efforts to trace the subsequent life of Peter McNee so as to connect it with that of the Peter Stewart Ney who in March 1820 declared his intention to become a U.S. citizen, was employed in 1827 by Archibald DeBow Murphey, and later became a schoolmaster. In short, the early life of Peter Stewart Ney remains almost entirely unknown. He was not, however, the marshal.

SEE: René Arnaud, "Mort et résurrection du Maréchal Ney," *Annales politiques et littéraires* 106 (1935); Legette Blythe, *Marshal Ney: A Dual Life* (1937); William Henry Hoyt Papers (Southern Historical Collection, University of North Carolina, Chapel Hill); Commandant H. Lanrezac, "Les légendes du Maréchal Ney," *Bulletin de la Société des amis de la Sarre*, no. 8 (1932); Nino Paul-Albert, *Histoire du cimetière du Père de Lachaise* (1937); J. Edward Smoot, *Marshal Ney before and after Execution* (1929); *South Atlantic Quarterly* 59 (Summer 1960); James A. Weston, *Historic Doubts as to the Execution of Marshal Ney* (1895).

GEORGE V. TAYLOR

Nichols, John *(14 Nov. 1834–22 Sept. 1917)*, printer, labor leader, and congressman, was born near Eagle Rock, Wake County. Until he was fifteen, he worked on his widowed mother's farm and acquired what education he could in neighborhood old-field schools. He then went to Raleigh to serve an apprenticeship in the printing office of a weekly newspaper. Sleeping alone in the office at night, Nichols started reading the *New York Weekly Tribune*, which arrived as an exchange but was routinely thrown away. He soon became a quiet abolitionist, and at nighttime in the office, in violation of state law, he taught some slave men and boys to read.

Young Nichols devoted himself seriously to any task at hand and, with a natural aptitude for the business, in time came to be recognized as one of the best printers in the state. After completing his apprenticeship, he entered Lovejoy Academy, working as a foreman at the newspaper before and after school and on Saturdays to pay his expenses. In 1857 Nichols moved to Beaufort, where he became owner and editor of the independent *Beaufort Journal*. He soon was made superintendent of state printing in Raleigh, a post he filled until 1866, when he entered the business of book and job printing.

During the Civil War Nichols, a Freemason, and other members of the order did what they could to ease the plight of Union prisoners who were fellow Masons, held in the vicinity of Raleigh, by providing food and physical comforts. While Federal troops occupied Raleigh after the war, he printed songs and poems for them and sold them his accumulated Confederate money, which they used in gambling at cards.

Nichols was a member of the Radical Republican element that advanced William Woods Holden to the governorship in 1868. In 1869 he was named president of the newly organized Raleigh Mechanics Building and Loan Association. In 1872 he was appointed principal of the State Institution for the Deaf and Blind, perhaps as a political reward, but also because the facility offered training in printing. He served in this position from 1873 to 1877. All the while he was senior member of the firm of Nichols, Gorman, and Neatherly Printing House in Raleigh. (Gorman, however, had died in 1865.) For a brief time Nichols also was revenue stamp agent in Durham. In 1877 he was given the political post of Raleigh postmaster, a position also sought by former governor William W. Holden. Nichols continued as postmaster until 1885.

At various times during his busy life, he found opportunities to serve the Knights of Labor, which boasted a membership of 1,500 in the Raleigh area. With the inauguration of a Democratic president, Grover Cleveland, Nichols's political appointments came to an end, but at about the same time he was elected state master work-

man of the Knights. On the strength of that organization in his district, Nichols found encouragement to stand for Congress. Running as an independent, because, he said, neither of the established parties really represented the people, he was accused of "negrophilism" and "the vile propaganda of social equality." Nevertheless, he was elected and served one term in the House of Representatives (1887–89).

As a member of the Knights of Labor, Nichols publicized the problems of the working class and called for federal and state laws to reduce working hours, to end child labor, and to recognize organized labor. He supported national regulation of railroads and currency, federal bankruptcy laws, and stricter immigration laws. In Congress he favored the Blair Bill, which would have appropriated federal funds to aid education. He also advocated a protective tariff to benefit American labor and industry.

Afterwards, Nichols served as chief of the Division of Files and Records in the Treasury Department in Washington. Returning to Raleigh in 1893, he took a job with the Internal Revenue Office. His holograph will, dated 1913 and devoid of legal jargon, is something of a literary masterpiece. Among other things, Nichols wrote: "That I have made mistakes in life and provoked the enmity of some, no one realizes better than myself. But now entering my 80th year I can truthfully say that I entertain 'Enmity to none but Charity for All.' "

In December 1855 Nichols married Virginia Caroline Gorman, and they became the parents of three daughters—Bettie, Annie, and Grayce—and a son, who apparently predeceased his parents. Nichols was survived by his daughters and a grandson, John Nichols, Jr., living in Pennsylvania in 1913. Among his bequests were several portraits.

SEE: *Biog. Dir. Am. Cong.* (1961); Jerome Dowd, *Sketches of Prominent Living North Carolinians* (1888); Brent H. Holcomb, comp., *Marriages of Wake County, 1770–1868* (1983); Melton McLaurin, "The Knights of Labor in North Carolina Politics," *North Carolina Historical Review* 49 (July 1972); Elizabeth Reid Murray, *Wake: Capital County of North Carolina*, vol. 1 (1983); Raleigh *News and Observer*, 4 Sept. 1888; Horace W. Raper, *William W. Holden: North Carolina's Political Enigma* (1985); Wake County Wills (North Carolina State Archives, Raleigh); Stephen B. Weeks Scrapbook, vol. 1 (North Carolina Collection, University of North Carolina, Chapel Hill).

WM. A. BLOUNT STEWART

Nichols, William *(ca. 1777–12 Dec. 1853)*, architect and builder, was born in Bath, County Somerset, England, and probably received his early training in England. Arriving in North Carolina in 1800, he was a resident of New Bern by 1805. There he practiced as an architect and builder and may have designed the New Bern Academy building (erected about 1806–10). Nichols moved to Edenton, where he extensively renovated St. Paul's Episcopal Church (1806–9) and had a part in the design and construction of the Palladian mansion at Hayes (ca. 1815–17) and other structures, possibly including Beverly Hall (ca. 1810).

By 1818 Nichols had relocated in Fayetteville. In addition to designing and building public and private structures in that town, he built (ca. 1822) the first local public water supply system, of which he was president and, until 1832, part owner. Most of his Fayetteville buildings undoubtedly were destroyed in the fire that devastated much of the town in 1831. One surviving structure that he probably designed is the Sandford House, built about 1818 as a residence; later it was taken over by the U.S. Bank and then the Woman's Club. As an engineer, Nichols in 1818 gave advice on opening the Cape Fear River to navigation above Fayetteville.

Also in 1818 he was hired to survey the statehouse in Raleigh (built between 1792 and 1796) and advise the General Assembly on needed repairs. After urging extensive improvements in the structure, he was appointed as full-time state architect to plan and execute them. Between 1820 and 1824, Nichols largely rebuilt and greatly improved the building. In the process, it became the second statehouse (Pennsylvania's was the first) to combine the central portico, domed rotunda, and balanced wings housing the two branches of the legislature, which soon became the standard formula for such buildings.

Nichols extended the central pavilions of the east and west fronts to give the ground plan a cross shape, added a third story, fronted the new east and west wings with pseudoporticoes, each consisting of four engaged Ionic columns standing on a rusticated stone basement and carrying a pediment, and stuccoed the brick walls of the structure in imitation of stone. Internally, he formed at the center of the building a rotunda, which he carried up through the roof and capped with a low dome, lighted by a glazed cupola. The rotunda housed Antonio Canova's celebrated statue of George Washington, whose installation Nichols supervised in 1821. The House of Commons was given a semielliptical seating plan (probably derived from the House chamber in the U.S. Capitol) and the Senate a circular seating plan, the members' area being defined in each chamber by a screen of Ionic columns. A classically detailed courtroom was formed on the first floor. While the exterior was essentially Palladian, the interior of the remodeled statehouse must have been a significant early example of neoclassic civic architecture.

In 1825 Nichols designed and, as general contractor, built on Union Square, southeast of the statehouse, a small brick state treasurer's office, which was pulled down about 1840. While in Raleigh, he also directed repairs on the Governor's Palace. He designed (and, in some instances, built) private structures, including the original frame sanctuary of Christ Church (erected in 1829) and the two-story southern section of the Mordecai House (1826) with its two-tiered, pedimented portico, a Palladian design feature that he also used on the Sandford House in Fayetteville.

The University of North Carolina engaged Nichols to design and erect what is now the southern two-thirds of Old West Dormitory (1822–23) and concurrently to add a third story to its pendant, Old East. Thus he established the symmetrical, north-oriented campus plan that prevailed until the end of the century. He also designed and began constructing Gerrard Hall (erected between 1822 and 1837) as a chapel and an assembly hall, which featured a colossal four-columned, pedimented Ionic portico on its southern flank. All three buildings, although modified, survive in form and function. Nichols made alterations to South Building and other university structures during the same period. His work on the campus ended in 1827.

Other North Carolina buildings designed by Nichols include the surviving Eagle Masonic Lodge (built between 1823 and 1825) in Hillsborough and, according to Governor David L. Swain, courthouses for Davidson and Guilford counties. Swain said that Nichols, the first North Carolina architect-builder to operate statewide, "was a skillful and experienced artist, and made the public greatly his debtor for a decided impulse given to architectural improvements throughout the State, in private as well as in public edifices."

Probably in search of a more profitable area of operation, Nichols moved to Alabama in 1827. There he designed at Tuscaloosa a state capitol (built between 1827 and 1829) that was very similar in plan to his remodeled North Carolina statehouse but grander in scale and finer in finish than the older structure. Abandoned as the capitol in 1846, this building housed a school until it burned in 1923. For the University of Alabama, also at Tuscaloosa, Nichols in 1828 designed the original buildings, ordering them in a quadrangle with a rotunda at its head after the manner of Thomas Jefferson's plan for the University of Virginia. Most of Nichols's University of Alabama buildings were burned by Federal soldiers in 1865, the only survivors being the Gorgas House (built between 1828 and 1831), the Observatory, and the monumental President's Mansion (completed in 1841).

The North Carolina statehouse burned in 1831. The legislative act providing for construction of the capitol (as the successor building has always been known) directed that it be an enlarged version of the statehouse. Nichols and his son, William, Jr., were engaged by the commissioners for rebuilding to provide the initial plan, and the younger Nichols arrived in Raleigh in the spring of 1833 to work with the commissioners. In July 1833 the Nichols plan was approved by the commissioners, the two architects were paid, and their connection with the capitol ended. No drawing illustrating the Nichols design has been found, but from contemporary descriptions, it clearly was a further refinement on a larger scale of the cruciform plan that William Nichols had devised for North Carolina in 1820–24 and improved upon for Alabama in 1827–29. The Nicholses determined the ground plan, general dimensions, and massing of the capitol and the disposition of the principal functions within it. Their successor architects, Town and Davis of New York (August 1833–35) and David Paton (1835–40), modified and greatly refined but could not fundamentally alter the basic design.

William Nichols's fourth state capitol design was his 1835 plan for altering and enlarging the former Charity Hospital on Canal Street in New Orleans to serve as the Louisiana state capitol. His fifth and final state capitol was that at Jackson, Miss., which he designed and built between 1836 and 1839. Another grand variation on his basic statehouse scheme, it drew praise from Talbot Hamlin as "expressive of much that was best in the creative thinking and the sensitive aesthetic feeling of its time." It is the only one of Nichols's five statehouses that stands largely as he designed it (though much of the interior is a recent re-creation, not his original work). His other structures in Jackson included the state penitentiary (completed in 1840) and the handsome Greek Revival Governor's Mansion (completed in 1842), recently restored and still in use. For the University of Mississippi at Oxford, he designed the Lyceum (completed in 1848) and other buildings.

William Nichols became a naturalized citizen in 1813. His first wife was Mary Rew, whom he married in Craven County in 1805; his second wife was Sarah Simons, whom he married in Chowan County in 1815. Nichols had at least two children, William, Jr., and Samuel, both of whom married North Carolina residents. Nichols died and was buried in Lexington, Miss. In his obituary, the *Mississippian* said of him: "He has left enduring monuments of his genius, and will long be remembered for many excellent qualities as a man and a citizen."

SEE: Gertrude S. Carraway, *Years of Light* (1944); Cecil D. Elliot, "The North Carolina State Capitol," *Southern Architect* 5, no. 6 (June 1958); Talbot F. Hamlin, *Greek Revival Architecture in America* (1944); Ralph Hammond, *Ante-Bellum Mansions in Alabama* (1951); Henry-Russell Hitchcock and William Seale, *Temples of Democracy: The State Capitols of the USA* (1976); Legislative Papers, 1818–25 (North Carolina State Archives, Raleigh).

JOHN L. SANDERS

Nicholson, Timothy (*2 Nov. 1828–15 Sept. 1924*), Quaker humanitarian, was born near Belvidere in Perquimans County, the second son of Josiah and Anna White Robinson Nicholson, whose forebears had long been prominent in the area. His paternal ancestors emigrated from Cumberland, England, to Marblehead, Mass., before 1650, and his third great-grandfather, Christopher Nicholson, was one of the first Quakers in North Carolina. His great-grandfather, Thomas Nicholson, was a noted missionary, author, and pre-Revolutionary opponent of slavery.

Reared in a rural atmosphere stressing hard work and upright behavior, young Nicholson received his earliest formal education at a local subscription school and at Belvidere Academy. In 1847 he went to Friends School in Providence, R.I., to complete his studies. Returning to North Carolina, he reluctantly abandoned his intention of farming to become a teacher and principal at Belvidere Academy in 1849. In the same year he was appointed county surveyor of Perquimans. In 1855 Pennsylvania's Haverford College appointed him head of its preparatory department; after holding that position for four years, he served for two years as Haverford's superintendent and business manager. In 1861 he moved to Richmond, Ind., where he operated a bookstore and later founded Nicholson Printing Company. His success in business was widely recognized, and he became an organizer of the American Book Trade Association.

During his sixty-three years in Indiana, Nicholson was a progressive leader both in Friends' work and worship and in such areas of social concern as education, penal reform, public welfare, temperance, peace, and woman suffrage. Renowned for his sympathetic understanding, practical judgment, tireless energy, and moral courage, he held executive positions in many religious and secular organizations. Friends appointed him elder, clerk of Whitewater Monthly Meeting, clerk of Indiana meeting of ministers and elders, clerk of Indiana Yearly Meeting, and member of numerous committees. (His brothers held similar positions among Friends—John in Maryland, Josiah in North Carolina, and William in Kansas.)

Nicholson participated in the establishment of a uniform discipline and Declaration of Faith for all American Friends and was a founder of the Five-Year Meeting of Friends in 1902. He was active in state, national, and international Sunday school associations and was a cofounder of the Indianapolis *Morning Star* for the expression of Quakers' views. For forty-nine years he was a trustee of Earlham College, devoting much attention to its management and finances. In the 1860s and 1870s he also served on the Richmond Public School Board and on the board of trustees of Indiana State Normal School. As secretary of Indiana Yearly Meeting's committee on prison reform, of which he was a member from 1867 to 1909, and as a member of the Indiana Board of State Charities from 1889 to 1908, Nicholson played a notable part in securing the humane improvement of the state's prisons, poorhouses, and hospitals.

He was president of the State Conference of Charities and Corrections in 1896 and of the national conference in 1902. Believing that Prohibition would reduce many social ills, he worked against the liquor interests and was president of the Indiana Anti-Saloon League from 1898 until his death.

From his early efforts to have Friends released from the Civil War draft through his fund-raising activities for world relief after World War I, he worked earnestly for peace. It was principally through his efforts that the conscientious objectors' exemption was added to the national Militia Bill of 1903. A Republican, Nicholson was a steady opponent of government corruption and inefficiency at all levels. State and national leaders sought his advice or felt his influence, and he became one of the best-known Quakers in America. Earlham College awarded him an honorary doctorate of laws in 1922, and the press hailed him as "Master Quaker," "Dean of Booksellers," and Indiana's most useful public servant. His public writings included an autobiographical sketch and several short works on religious and social topics.

On 11 Aug. 1853 he married Sarah Newby White (1827–65), and on 30 Apr. 1868 he married her sister, Mary Symons White (1839–1911). His children were Marianna (Mrs. David E. Buffum), John, Josiah, Thomas, Sarah Ellen, Walter, Sarah (Mrs. William V. Coffin), and Eliza (Mrs. John H. Johnson). Nicholson died in Richmond and was buried in Earlham Cemetery.

SEE: *American Friend*, 25 Sept. 1924; *DAB*, vol. 7 (1934); Willard Heiss, ed., *Abstracts of the Records of the Society of Friends in Indiana: Part One* (1962); William W. Hinshaw, *Encyclopedia of American Quaker Genealogy*, vol. 1 (1936); Indiana Biography and Indiana Clipping File (Indiana State Library, Indianapolis); Zora Klain, *Quaker Contributions to Education in North Carolina* (1924); Perquimans County Court Minutes, 1849 (North Carolina State Archives, Raleigh); *Richmond* (Ind.) *Palladium and Sun-Telegram*, 15 Sept. 1924; James Savage, *A Genealogical Dictionary of the First Settlers of New England*, vol. 3 (1861); Walter C. Woodward, *Timothy Nicholson: Master Quaker* (1927).

RAYMOND A. WINSLOW, JR.

Nicholson, William McNeal (*27 Sept. 1905–8 Sept. 1974*), medical educator, was born in Bath, the son of John T. and Annie K. Nicholson. After graduation from a local high school, he entered Duke University in the fall of 1923 and was graduated with a bachelor of arts degree in 1927. He subsequently entered Johns Hopkins Medical School, Baltimore, where he received a doctor of medicine degree in 1931.

Remaining at Johns Hopkins, Nicholson served first as resident house officer (1931–32), then as assistant in pathology (1932–35). From 1933 to 1935 he was the John J. Archbold Fellow in Medicine at Johns Hopkins Hospital. In 1935 he returned to Duke as an instructor in medicine, and in 1952 he was promoted to full professor. Early he became chief of the Metabolism Clinic and director of postgraduate education. For eight years (1960–68) he was assistant dean of the Duke School of Medicine, in charge of continuing medical education. He remained professor of medicine and endocrinology until his death.

Nicholson enjoyed membership in numerous professional organizations, including the American Clinical and Climatological Association, American College of Physicians (Fellow), American Diabetes Association, American Medical Association, American Society for

Clinical Investigations, Durham-Orange County Medical Association (president, 1952–53), North Carolina Medical Society, and Southern Medical Association (secretary [1946–47] and chairman [1948], Medical Section). He was certified by the American Board of Internal Medicine. Nicholson was a member of several fraternities: Phi Beta Kappa (scholarship), Alpha Omega Alpha (social), and Sigma Xi (science). A longtime chairman of the editorial board of the *North Carolina Medical Journal*, he contributed scholarly and comprehensive oversight as well as articles on his medical research and observations.

When Nicholson began his forty-year career at the Duke School of Medicine, the school and Duke Hospital were in their formative years; he provided a complementary scholarship and medical skill that did much to establish both institutions as leaders in medical education and service. He was the author of more than thirty articles appearing in professional journals and was in constant demand as a consultant. Nicholson was particularly proud of the large number of successful physicians and specialists who had trained under him at Duke.

On 30 Nov. 1926 he married Eunice Stamey. They had three children: Anne Katherine, William McNeal, Jr., and Samuel Thorne. He died several weeks before his sixty-ninth birthday. Funeral services were held in Durham, with interment in Maplewood Cemetery.

SEE: Data File (Office of Information Services, Duke University, Durham); *Durham Morning Herald*, 9 Sept. 1974.

C. SYLVESTER GREEN

Nisbet, John *(1738–1817)*, general merchant, Patriot, and state legislator, was born in New Jersey, one of six children of John and Sarah Nisbet. In 1750 his parents moved from New Jersey to that part of Rowan County that later became Iredell.

Nisbet was a member of the Rowan County Committee of Safety in 1774. Fifteen years later he became the first member of the state senate from Iredell County, serving in 1789 and 1790. Nisbet also was a delegate to the Fayetteville convention of 1789 that approved the U.S. Constitution for the state. In 1790 he was one of the commissioners chosen to lay out the town of Statesville as the seat of the new county of Iredell.

After operating a general store in Salisbury, he opened one at his plantation four miles northwest of Statesville. He later had a store in Statesville, but when it burned he did not replace it.

Nisbet married Mary Osborne, the daughter of Colonel Alexander Osborne, and they became the parents of eight children: James, Nancy, Sarah, Elizabeth, Alexander, John, Milus, and Jane. The mercantile interests of the family continued through three generations.

SEE: John L. Cheney, Jr., ed., *North Carolina Government, 1585–1979* (1981); Walter Clark, ed., *State Records of North Carolina*, vols. 21–22 (1903–7); *First Census of the United States, 1790* (1908); John Nisbet Papers (Southern Historical Collection, University of North Carolina, Chapel Hill); William C. Pool, "An Economic Interpretation of the Ratification of the Federal Constitution in North Carolina," *North Carolina Historical Review* 27 (April, July, October 1950); John H. Wheeler, *Historical Sketches of North Carolina from 1584 to 1851* (1851).

E. THOMAS SIMS

Nissen, John Philip *(12 Mar. 1813–17 Dec. 1874)*, wagon manufacturer, was born at Friedland in Forsyth County, the son of Christian and Salome Vogler Nissen. He was the grandson of Tycho Nissen, who was born in Denmark in 1732 and arrived in Salem in 1770.

At age twenty-one, J. P. Nissen started a small wagon factory in the village of Waughtown and managed the business until after the Civil War, when two of his sons, George E. and William M., began to operate the firm under the name of the George E. Nissen Wagon Works. At the peak of production, this company produced about ten thousand wagons a year. John Israel Nissen, another son of J. P. Nissen, also established a wagon factory, which he later sold to his brother, Christian Francis (Frank). The George E. and J. I. Nissen wagon factories were consolidated in 1910 and continued to operate under the Nissen name until 1925, when the firm passed into other hands.

William M. Nissen, the most successful son of J. P. Nissen, became a millionaire and made a large investment in the eighteen-story Nissen Building, erected in 1927 on the corner of Fourth and Cherry streets in Winston-Salem.

John Philip Nissen married Mary Ann Elizabeth Vawter (1813–84) on 1 Oct. 1835 and became the father of twelve children: Martha, Jane, George Elias, John Israel, Mary Elizabeth, Reuben B., Christian Francis, Harriett E., Louis H., Alice A., William M., and Samuel Jacob. He was buried in the cemetery at Friedland Moravian Church.

SEE: Roxie Sides, comp., Nissen Family Records (Moravian Archives, Winston-Salem); Winston-Salem *Journal-Sentinel*, 23 Aug. 1953; Winston-Salem *Twin-City Sentinel*, 9 Oct. 1965.

FRANK P. CAUBLE

Nixon, Alfred *(26 May 1856–26 Mar. 1924)*, local official and historian, was born in Lincoln County near Beattie's Ford, the son of Robert and Millie Womack Nixon. He was descended from William and Elizabeth Black Nixon, who moved from Charlotte County, Va., to Lincoln in 1780. The family was Scotch-Irish and originally emigrated from Ireland. Alfred spent his youth on his father's farm and received his earliest education in local schools before attending Rock Springs Seminary, conducted by D. Matt Thompson, in the new community of Denver. He received a B.S. degree from The University of North Carolina in 1881.

After graduation he returned to Lincoln County and engaged in farming and teaching. In 1882 he married Iola Jane Robinson, a descendant of Francis Asbury. Nixon was sheriff of the county from 1883 to 1892, and at other times he was county surveyor, superintendent of public instruction, clerk of superior court (1892–1924), and mayor of Lincolnton. He never lost an election.

In 1891 The University of North Carolina's class of 1881 held a reunion. Before leaving Chapel Hill as seniors, members of the class had agreed to honor the first son of any member of the class, and at the 1891 reunion young Kemp Battle Nixon, the son of Alfred and Jane Nixon, was declared the winner and awarded a silver cup.

A Presbyterian from childhood, Alfred Nixon became a Sunday school teacher, elder, and clerk of the church. He was the lay representative from the Kings Mountain Presbytery to the General Assembly of the Southern Presbyterian Church in New Orleans. Joining the Masonic order in 1878, he was master of the Lincolnton

Lodge for several years and held other high positions. He was a popular speaker at reunions, club gatherings, church rallies, and school entertainments. As a personal friend of many Confederate veterans, he often spoke at their reunions.

As a local historian, he wrote on many subjects, and his contributions were widely published in newspapers and pamphlets. He prepared a number of family histories including those of the Finger, Hager, Hauss, and Mauney families. Nixon was the author of several church histories, a brief county history, and many lengthy obituaries. He also compiled and published a roster of Confederate soldiers from Lincoln County. His *Cross Woodis: Character Sketch* (1905) dealt with a black man who had a reputation as a conjurer. For his *Annals of Lincoln County*, William L. Sherrill drew on the writings of Nixon.

Nixon and his wife were the parents of nine children.

SEE: Kemp P. Battle, *History of the University of North Carolina*, vol. 2 (1912); Daniel L. Grant, *Alumni History of the University of North Carolina, 1795–1924* (1924); *Lincoln County News*, 27–28 Mar. 1924; *North Carolina Booklet* 9, no. 3 (July 1909); William L. Sherrill, *Annals of Lincoln County* (1937); Mrs. John M. Turley (Lincolnton), interview, 19 July 1975.

MICHAEL EDGAR GOINS

Nixon, John (*ca. 1623–92*), Council member, speaker of the Assembly, and governor of the Hudson's Bay Company, first was in North Carolina (then called Albemarle) as commander of a vessel trading between England and the American colonies. Nothing is known of his parents or his birthplace, but he was known personally to some of the Lords Proprietors of Carolina, particularly Anthony Ashley Cooper, Earl of Shaftesbury, and Sir John and Sir George Colleton. At some unspecified time, according to his own statement, he was in the East Indies. In 1668 and subsequently he brought letters and other documents from the Proprietors to Albemarle officials. By May 1671 Nixon had settled in Albemarle and was a member of the Council. He remained on the Council until 1675, when acting governor John Jenkins was forcibly ousted and his government was overthrown by a faction led by Thomas Eastchurch.

In July 1677 Nixon again became a Council member, taking office under a commission issued by the Proprietors the previous November and delivered in July. The government then was headed by Thomas Miller, a prominent supporter of Eastchurch. Although the Proprietors had commissioned Eastchurch governor, he had stopped in Nevis on his way home from London and had sent Miller to govern in his stead, having issued to Miller a commission of doubtful legality. Miller's oppressive measures as acting governor, the colonists' doubts as to the legitimacy of his claim to office, and other situations resulted in the overthrow of Miller and his government in December 1677 in an uprising now called Culpeper's Rebellion. Nixon, like other Council members, was imprisoned at the beginning of the uprising, but he either escaped or was released and went to London.

By August 1679 Nixon was back in Albemarle serving as a Council member in the government headed by John Harvey, whom the Proprietors had recently appointed. He also sat on the Council in November. As he had been named governor of the Hudson's Bay Company on 23 May of that year, he was in Albemarle for only a brief time, perhaps primarily attending to personal matters.

He served from the trading settlement of Moose Factory in northeastern Ontario, Canada, until he was replaced on 31 Jan. 1683. His record there was not particularly distinguished, as his concerns were largely related to improving relations with the natives and expanding trade to benefit the company. It was under his leadership, however, that Charlton Island was occupied and some buildings were constructed on the island. His inability to get along with others and his age were sometimes the causes of complaints against him.

The scant surviving records in North Carolina do not reveal when he returned to the colony, but he was again living in Albemarle on 4 Feb. 1688, when he made his will, witnessed by some of his neighbors. In 1689 he was elected to the Assembly and served as speaker. He died before 8 Aug. 1692, when his will was probated.

Nixon's public career raises questions about his political affiliations and motives. In a period of bitter factional rivalry and fierce animosities, he served in the government of first one faction and then the other. His participation in the government of Thomas Miller has been interpreted as evidence that he had joined the Eastchurch-Miller faction, but that interpretation is open to question. The Proprietors may have appointed Nixon to the Council because they knew him personally, not because of a recommendation by Eastchurch, who was in London when the appointment was made. Apparently most of the other Council members were appointed then as well. Likewise, Nixon may have accepted the commission because of his friendship for the Proprietors rather than because of any loyalty to Eastchurch and his party. In August 1679, when Miller was brought before a court on charges of treason and blasphemy, Nixon testified against him, although in 1673, while a Council member and judge in John Jenkins's government, he had dismissed similar charges against Miller for insufficient evidence. Perhaps Nixon was not a partisan of either faction, but from friendship and loyalty for the Proprietors worked with whatever government was in power, attempting to use his influence to promote the Proprietors' interest as he saw it.

Nixon lived in Pasquotank Precinct, where he owned three hundred or more acres of land. He was a master mariner and in the 1670s was commander of the bark *Patience*, then trading between the West Indies and the mainland colonies. Although there is no evidence as to his religious views, he may have tended towards Quaker beliefs. His second wife appears to have been a Quaker, and many of his Pasquotank neighbors, including a relative, Zacharias Nixon, were devout followers of that faith.

Nixon was married twice and had a daughter by each wife. His first wife, Elliner, and their daughter, Africa, appear to have come to the colony with him or to have joined him soon afterwards. His second wife, Em, was the mother of his younger daughter, Ann, who was still a minor when Nixon made his will. After Nixon's death, Em married Edward Mayo, a Quaker. She died about 1701. Apparently Ann Nixon died about the same time or soon afterwards, for court records of 1706 concerning a plantation formerly owned by Nixon indicate that Africa and her husband, Samuel Pike, were the heirs. As Nixon had named only Em and Ann in his will, presumably Ann as well as Em was then dead and Africa inherited under the common law.

SEE: *Dictionary of Canadian Biography*, vol. 1 (1966); J. Bryan Grimes, ed., *Abstract of North Carolina Wills* (1910); J. R. B. Hathaway, ed., *North Carolina Historical and Genealogical Register*, 3 vols. (1900–1903); North Carolina

State Archives, Raleigh, particularly Albemarle Book of Warrants and Surveys (1681–1706), Colonial Court Records (box 192, folder on House of Burgesses, 1679–1742), Council Minutes, Wills, Inventories (1677–1701), and Will of John Nixon (1692); Mattie Erma E. Parker, ed., *North Carolina Higher-Court Records, 1670–1696* (1968); William S. Powell, ed., *Yᵉ Countie of Albemarle in Carolina: A Collection of Documents, 1664–1675* (1958); William S. Price, ed., *North Carolina Higher-Court Records, 1702–1708* (1974); Hugh F. Rankin, *Upheaval in Albemarle: The Story of Culpeper's Rebellion, 1675–1689* (1962); William L. Saunders, ed., *Colonial Records of North Carolina*, vols. 1–2 (1886); Ellen Goode Winslow, *History of Perquimans County* (1931).

MATTIE ERMA E. PARKER

Nixon, Nicholas Nichols *(24 July 1800–29 Oct. 1868),* planter and pioneer in the commercial production of peanuts in the South, was born on the family plantation on Topsail Sound, seven miles northeast of Wilmington. He was the sixth child of Nicholas F. and Ann Nichols Nixon.

Nixon very early embarked on a successful career as a planter. Although he inherited land from his father and eventually acquired a plantation near Laurinburg and another near Salisbury, his major interest was the historic Porter's Neck plantation, which he acquired over a fifteen-year period (1839–54). This 1,282-acre plantation on Topsail Sound became the center of his peanut operations. The Nixon family spent its summers at Porter's Neck, where the whitewashed plantation buildings were reported to be in "good order" and "exceedingly pretty." In the winter, the family lived at the Nixon residence on Chestnut Street in downtown Wilmington so that the children could attend school in the town.

In the antebellum period, five-sixths of the commercially grown peanuts in the United States were produced in a small area around Wilmington. The commercial development of this crop was due largely to the pioneering activities of Nixon at his Porter's Neck plantation. Here he developed techniques and practices of peanut farming that became the standard of cultivation for many years.

He began his first experiments with the crop about 1818, and, as he later recalled, it took him some thirty years of "toil and experience" to produce a commercial crop successfully. Numerous agricultural experts who visited his farm before the Civil War reported that he used a system of crop rotation in which a peanut crop succeeded rye, oats, or millet on a field that was then left to lie fallow for a year. Since Nixon devoted about three hundred acres annually to growing his peanut crop, this meant that about nine hundred acres at Porter's Neck plantation were involved in the production of peanuts. Throughout the 1850s and until his death, he was the nation's largest peanut producer. It was on Nixon's plantation in 1856 that Thomas L. Colville, a Wilmington mechanic, constructed a stationary, steam-driven thresher, the first successful peanut picker ever invented.

Nixon made his most significant contribution to the development of the peanut industry in February 1868, when he was prevailed upon to write a long paper for the *Southern Cultivator* on the cultivation of the peanut. Drawing on his unparalleled knowledge of this crop, he wrote what became one of the most widely reprinted articles in the southern agricultural press in the post–Civil War period. It contained nearly all that was then known about the cultivation of peanuts.

Nixon's farming activities recovered quickly from the effects of the war as the peanut market boomed. In 1867 it was estimated that he would produce between 13,000 to 15,000 bushels and that he would receive from two to four dollars per bushel for his crop. At the time of his death, it was noted that "few men of his age rallied as he did from the disastrous effects of the late war, and entered more promptly upon a course of successful labor and enterprize."

In addition to his extensive farming operations, Nixon operated at various times a sawmill, a gristmill, and a number of turpentine stills. He served on the board of the Wilmington and Manchester R. R. Company and on the boards of a number of other companies involved in internal improvements; he also was a director of various public institutions. For many years he was a magistrate of New Hanover County. In 1848 he was elected on the Democratic ticket to the North Carolina House of Commons from New Hanover County, and in 1850 he was elected to the state senate from the Sixteenth District, after which he does not appear to have entered the political arena again. He served as senior warden of St. John's Episcopal Parish from its organization in 1853 until his death and educated all of his daughters at St. Mary's School in Raleigh.

Nixon married Elizabeth Ann Morris (12 Mar. 1807–2 Dec. 1875), by whom he had six daughters. All of them lived to maturity and married. Nixon died in his Wilmington residence and was buried in Oakdale Cemetery.

SEE: *Carolina Farmer*, January 1869, June 1872; Correspondence with C. M. Davis and R. B. Davis (grandsons) and Mrs. E. M. McEachern; Ebenezer Emmons, *Report of Professor Emmons on His Geological Survey of North Carolina* (1852); F. Roy Johnson, *The Peanut Story* (1964); New Hanover County Records (New Hanover County Courthouse, Wilmington); *North Carolina Planter*, August 1860; *Southern Cultivator*, March 1868; *Wilmington Journal* (weekly), 6 Nov. 1868.

HERBERT R. PASCHAL

Nixon, Robert *(d. 4 Dec. 1794),* Baptist minister, local official, and saddler, perhaps a grandson of the Richard Nixon who died in Craven County in 1746, appeared in the Onslow County records as a witness to deeds as early as 1743. In 1753 he was referred to as a saddler by trade. In 1754 he enrolled in the New Topsail Company, commanded by Captain John Ashe, during the French and Indian War.

Nixon's first wife appears to have been the daughter of Charles Ryall (or Royall), of New River, who died about 1754 or 1755. At the time Nixon made his will, his wife was named Sarah.

In 1776 Nixon was allowed the sum of ten pounds "for his vigilant services as chaplain to the Onslow Detachment of Militia." In 1776 and again in 1777, he was made a justice of the peace for Onslow County.

As a minister, Nixon first served as an elder of the Separate Baptists and later as an elder in the Kehukee Baptist Association, being designated as pastor of three congregations in Onslow County. In 1786 he was referred to in the deed records as pastor of a church that met on the "Southwest Branch" of New River and of one that met near the "Lower Ferry" on New River. A deed in 1790 referred to him as pastor of the church that met on the Little Northeast Creek of New River. At least two of these congregations still exist.

According to Baptist historian Cushing B. Hassell,

Nixon had the care of a Baptist church on Newport River in Carteret County and one on New River in Onslow County, which were received into the Kehukee Association in 1788. Nixon also was pastor of the White Oak Church in Jones County. Serving all these congregations at the same time, Nixon acquired a reputation for his zeal and piety.

Nixon's will was probated in January 1795. Mentioned are his wife Sarah; sons Charles Augustine (or Augustus), Robert, Jr., Nathan, and Daniel; and three surviving daughters, Sarah Fields, Rebecca, and Mary Cox. A son-in-law, John Lester, is apparently listed as a devisee in the room of a deceased daughter.

SEE: Lemuel Burkitt and Jesse Read, *A Concise History of the Kehukee Baptist Association* (1850); Cushing B. Hassell, *History of the Church of God* (1948); George W. Paschal, *History of North Carolina Baptists*, vol. 1 (1930).

TUCKER REED LITTLETON

Noble, Marcus Cicero Stephens (15 Mar. 1855–1 June 1942), educator and author, was born at Louisburg, the son of Albert Morris and Mary Ann Primrose Noble. He was ten years old when the Civil War ended, and as a result of the confusion of the times, the family changed its residence several times. The elder Noble was a captain in the First North Carolina Regiment. Reportedly, when Federal forces struck New Bern, the Nobles moved to Louisburg, later went as refugees to Clayton, and finally located in Selma, where they were founding settlers of the town. In later years, Noble liked to tell a story from his youth. When Union General William T. Sherman was on his march from the east to Raleigh and Durham, he stopped briefly in Clayton, and one of his officers was at the Noble home. Sherman came to see the officer and there took ten-year-old "Billy" (as Noble was called) on his knee. They exchanged friendly banter, in which the lad expressed himself fearlessly to the great enemy general.

Noble had limited preparatory schooling in Selma and then was graduated from the Bingham School at Mebane. In 1875 he entered Davidson College, where he received a good grounding in the classics for a year before transferring to The University of North Carolina for two more years of study (1877–79). His graduation thesis, "The Imperative Mood," written under the direction of Dr. George T. Winston, was entirely in Latin. Many years later, Davidson College awarded him an honorary doctor of laws degree.

Immediately after leaving Chapel Hill, Noble returned to the Bingham School as commandant of cadets and instructor for three years. From 1882 to 1898 he was superintendent of schools of the city of Wilmington. His administration of the Wilmington schools was distinctive and expansive. Winning the support of local citizens, he projected many innovative ideas for public school development; among them was the erection of the first separate high school building in the city. With frequency he was heard around the state.

Noble's logical presentations of progressive educational principles and practices attracted such wide attention that in 1898 he was invited to return to The University of North Carolina as professor of pedagogy. In 1913 he was named dean of the School of Education, an administrative post he held for nine years. He also was director (then called superintendent) of the university's summer school under President Edwin A. Alderman and subsequent administrations.

During those years between 1898 and 1913, Noble teamed with North Carolina's great educators—Edwin A. Alderman, Charles Duncan McIver, Edward Moses, P. P. Claxton, J. Y. Joyner, Alexander Graham, and others—to lay a foundation for the masterful emphasis in education that had evolved from the leadership of Charles Brantley Aycock and others of his day. One of the projects on which Noble worked very hard was the holding of teachers' institutes in all parts of the state. One reporter wrote: "These institutes lasted a week, and on the last day or two the people would gather from the whole countryside round-about and these meetings would resolve themselves into a sort of educational revival." The impact of the leadership of those "youthful crusaders" for better education completely refocused public education in North Carolina and produced the impetus for growth and excellence in the decades that followed.

In 1921 Noble asked to be relieved of his administrative duties in the School of Education, and for the next thirteen years he devoted his time to teaching and writing. In 1931, for his comprehensive study, *A History of the Public Schools of North Carolina*, he won the Mayflower Cup, an award for the best book written by a North Carolinian in that year. He diligently worked on the second volume in the years immediately prior to his death. In addition, he was the editor of three textbooks: *Williams' Reader for Beginners* (1893), *Davies' Standard Arithmetic* (1886), and the North Carolina supplements to Matthew F. Maury's *Manual of Geography* (1895). Noble also was the author of *The Battle of Moore's Creek Bridge* (1904) and *The Teaching of County Geography* (1915). His textbooks were widely used in high schools and colleges of the state. His numerous articles, particularly on North Carolina history, appeared in state and national journals and periodicals.

A portrait of Noble was presented to The University of North Carolina in 1941. On that occasion, Clyde A. Erwin paid tribute to the veteran educator and spoke of the twenty years before the turn of the century when he was a pioneer in the cause of public education.

Two "monuments" to Noble were established at the Chapel Hill campus. One was the Emerson athletic field, provided through a substantial gift of Isaac E. Emerson, who told the trustees that he was making the gift largely because of his personal friendship for Noble. The other was the Extension Division, conceived by Noble to take educational opportunities and facilities to the people of the state, thereby serving its whole educational program in countless ways. Noble had heard that such a program was offered by the University of Wisconsin, and he went there at his own expense to study the plan and procedures involved. His recommendations to President Edward Kidder Graham won hearty approval, and the Extension Division became an operating adjunct of increasing value "as a means of drawing the University and the People of the State closer together."

Noble was a longtime leader of the State Teachers' Association (later known as the North Carolina Education Association), serving as president for one term (1913–14) and remaining its mentor through the years. He was also active in the work of the North Carolina Historical Commission and was its chairman for several years. Noble was a trustee (1899–1940) and president of the board (1907–40) of the Agricultural and Technical College of North Carolina at Greensboro, a member of the first board of trustees of the institution that became the University of North Carolina at Greensboro, and a member of the State Board of Education Examiners (1897–1904).

Although he retired from teaching in 1934, he continued to speak out in support of improved education and both publicly and privately advocated that lawmakers and citizens generally authorize increased taxes for this purpose. For thirty-three years he was a director of the Bank of Chapel Hill, and almost until the day of his death he spent a portion of each day at his office there.

Noble was described as an unabashed optimist, a great teacher, human and friendly, and one who always welcomed an opportunity to serve. A popular commencement speaker, he "rode the circuit" until his early eighties. He had an uncanny ability to remember names and made a hobby of keeping in touch with his former students.

On 26 Aug. 1885 he married Alice J. Yarborough of Wilmington, and they became the parents of two children: Alice, a staff member and editor at The University of North Carolina School of Pharmacy, and M. C. S., Jr., onetime executive assistant director of the North Carolina Department of Revenue. Noble died at his home in Chapel Hill and was buried in the family plot in Wilmington.

SEE: *Alumni Catalogue of Davidson College, 1837–1924* (1924); *Asheville Citizen*, 24 Mar. 1956; *Chapel Hill Weekly*, 5 June 1942; *North Carolina Biography*, vol. 5 (1941); William S. Powell, ed., *North Carolina Lives* (1962); *Uplift*, 3 June 1944; Stephen B. Weeks Scrapbook, vol. 5 (North Carolina Collection, University of North Carolina, Chapel Hill); *Who Was Who in America*, vol. 2 (1950); Winston-Salem *Journal-Sentinel*, 24 Mar. 1935.

C. SYLVESTER GREEN

Norcom, James, Sr. *(29 Dec. 1778–9 Nov. 1850)*, physician, was born in Chowan County, the son of John and Miriam Standin Norcom. He received his early education at schools in Chowan County—among them, the Edenton Academy, of which he later served for many years as a trustee. At seventeen he began to study medicine in Philadelphia, where he was both a private student of Benjamin Rush and a matriculant at the medical school of the University of Pennsylvania. The medical school faculty, which, in addition to Rush, included such eminent physicians as Caspar Wistar and William Shippen, emphasized instruction by means of clinical observation as well as lectures; and Shippen, at least, made use of dissection. Norcom was awarded the M.D. degree in 1797 after a defense of his *Inaugural Thesis on Jaundice, Containing Observations on the Liver, and Some of Its Diseases* (1799), which ran to forty-nine printed pages.

Norcom entered the practice of medicine at Edenton, where he became one of the earliest clinical investigators of diseases prevalent in eastern North Carolina. Although Edenton was then the home of several long-established physicians, he soon gained a large practice and a wide reputation as a skillful diagnostician. As a result of overwork, however, his health broke and he became apprehensive that he might contract tuberculosis. He traveled to Philadelphia and consulted his former teachers, particularly his mentor Rush, who prescribed a long sea voyage, especially to the East Indies. Norcom took Rush's advice and spent about three years traveling to various parts of the world, including the Far East. He practiced medicine aboard ship and among the natives of the places he visited and studied the distinctive characteristics of the climate, people, and diseases of the different areas.

His health restored, Norcom returned to Edenton, where, except for a brief period of service as an army surgeon in the War of 1812, he practiced medicine until the last day of his long life. His practice was both lucrative and extensive. He was often called in as a consultant in puzzling or serious cases from distances of over one hundred miles. His personal practice embraced the counties of Chowan, Perquimans, Pasquotank, Camden, Gates, Washington, Bertie, Hertford, and Martin until advanced age prevented him from traveling over such a wide area.

Like his preceptor Rush, who taught his students to "bleed as long as you can get blood; if you can't get blood get water; if you can't get water get wind," Norcom made frequent use of the lancet. His practice was largely confined to medicine, as he had few opportunities for surgery; most of the operations he performed would be classified as minor surgery. He was nevertheless eminently successful in the adjustment and treatment of fractures and reductions and in the management of dislocations. Although Norcom wrote much on medical subjects, only a few of his articles were published, including essays on tetanus, the winter epidemic of 1816, cholera, the endemic summer and autumnal fevers of eastern North Carolina, scarlatina, and influenza. Appearing in such medical journals of the day as the Philadelphia *Medical Museum*, the *Eclectic Repertory*, and the *American Medical and Philosophical Register*, his writings received the approbation of the medical profession.

During most of his life Norcom made and recorded careful observations of weather, temperature, and barometric pressure and compared his records for different years, relating them to the varieties of illness occurring most frequently during the same periods. From these studies he drew certain conclusions concerning the ecology of disease, especially epidemics, and often made accurate predictions as to the character and type of the ailments of an approaching season. Not only was Norcom at home with medical literature, but also he was a serious student of literature and science in general, being particularly fond of the natural sciences, and his opinion was sometimes sought on literary matters. His letters to his family and friends indicate that he was a keen observer of people and social groups and that he was a social, economic, and political conservative and a stern but loving father to his nine children.

As a physician he did much charity work, declaring himself unable to "turn a deaf ear to the sufferings of the indigent . . . even in its connection with vice and infamy." Nevertheless, he managed to accumulate a great deal of wealth during one period of his life, though he left a small estate. A large portion of his income was consumed in the education of his children, much was given to philanthropic causes, and a great deal was used to pay off the debts of others for whom he had stood as surety.

In 1801 Norcom married Mary Curtis, from whom he was divorced about 1805. They had one son, John (1802), who became a physician in Washington, N.C. On 24 July 1810 Norcom married sixteen-year-old Mary (Maria) Horniblow, by whom he had eight children: James, Jr. (1811), who became a prominent planter in Chowan County; Benjamin Rush (1813); Mary Matilda (1822); Elizabeth Hannah (1826); Caspar Wistar (1828), who went to California to practice medicine during the gold rush; H. Standin and Abner, twins; and William Augustus B. (1836).

In politics Norcom was a Whig. An active churchman, he was long a member of St. Paul's Episcopal Church, Edenton. In the autumn of 1850, while making a house call to a patient at night, he fell down a flight of steps, hitting his head against the post and losing consciousness. The physicians called to his aid followed the approved medical procedure of the day for such cases and bled him copiously in both arms—"bled him to death," his granddaughter later declared. He never recovered. He was buried in the cemetery of St. Paul's Church, Edenton. He had practiced medicine for over fifty years.

Norcom's portrait is reproduced in the two-volume *Medicine in North Carolina: Essays in the History of Medical Science and Medical Service, 1524–1960* (1972), edited by Dorothy Long, which also contains a partial list of Norcom's published writings.

Norcom has been identified as the "licentious master" who subjected the slave, Harriet Jacobs, to "unrelenting sexual harassment." This is recounted in Jacobs's autobiography, *Incidents in the Life of a Slave Girl* (1987), edited by Jean Fagan Yellin.

SEE: Carl Binger, *Revolutionary Doctor: Benjamin Rush, 1746–1813* (1966); George W. Corner, ed., *The Autobiography of Benjamin Rush* (1948); Guion G. Johnson, *Ante-Bellum North Carolina: A Social History* (1937); James Norcom and Family Papers (North Carolina State Archives, Raleigh); W. F. Norwood, *Medical Education in the United States before the Civil War* (1944); *Transactions of the North Carolina Medical Society* (1852, 1917); John H. Wheeler, ed., *Reminiscences and Memoirs of North Carolina and Eminent North Carolinians* (1884).

W. CONARD GASS

Norman, Jeremiah (17 Oct. 1771–30 Oct. 1843), pioneer minister of the Methodist Episcopal church in Virginia, Georgia, North Carolina, and South Carolina, was born in Tyrrell County, the son of Mary Norman, whose maiden name is unknown. Evidence is virtually conclusive that his paternal grandparents were Jeremiah and Priscilla Long Norman and that his father was one of their two sons, Thomas or Joshua. Mary Norman was a widow when she died in 1787, leaving her personal property, which included no slaves, to be divided among her surviving eight children—Zeruiah, Kiziah, Susanna, Priscilla, Joel, James, Simeon, and Jeremiah—and the children of her daughter, Mrs. Daniel Garrett, who apparently died before her mother. The legacies consisted of useful household goods, indicating that the Norman family enjoyed a comfortable, though not luxurious, rural life.

Although the details of Jeremiah's schooling are unknown, the journal that he kept from 1793 to 1801 is evidence that he was fairly well educated, was an avid reader of the classics and theological literature, and had received musical training. His religious background was undoubtedly Anglican, as he always showed great respect for "the old Church" and for the Protestant Episcopal church, but he became an enthusiastic member of the Methodist Society. In 1792 he decided to enter the ministry of the Methodist Episcopal church and was assigned by its officials to the Russell Circuit, in Virginia, which included territory in Botetourt and Bedford counties.

Disillusioned after a year's experience as an itinerant, Norman returned to eastern North Carolina. Through 1796 he occupied himself by teaching a singing school and a reading school and preaching when invited to do so in Tyrrell, Martin, and adjacent counties. He maintained his fellowship with the Methodists, met Bishop Francis Asbury, and in 1797 journeyed to Charleston, S.C., in the company of the Reverend Jesse Lee, who had preached the first Methodist sermon in that city a few years earlier.

At the Methodist Conference in Charleston, Norman decided to return to the itinerancy of his church and was assigned to the Bush River Circuit in South Carolina in 1798. Later that year, because of his progress in the new station, the episcopacy sent him to Augusta, Ga., to serve as a pioneer Methodist missionary. Another emigrant from North Carolina, the Reverend Adam Boyd, was already in that city attempting to revive an Anglican parish, and Norman supported the Episcopalian as much as he could while concentrating on his missionary project. By the end of a year, he had established the Augusta Methodist Circuit. Since then, Norman has been known as the father of Methodism in the Augusta area.

In 1799 Norman was assigned to the Broad River Circuit in South Carolina and in 1800 to the Bladen Circuit in North Carolina, after which he left the itinerancy and became a local preacher for the remainder of his life. During this period, he attended the General Conference of the Methodist church in Baltimore, where he associated with most of the Methodist clergy of the time. He continued to praise his friend, Bishop Asbury, but was somewhat critical of Bishop Thomas Coke when he met him.

Sometime after 1800 Norman married Elizabeth Woodberry, the daughter of the affluent Richard Woodberry of Marion District, S.C. They had three children, whose names are unknown, before Elizabeth died. Prior to 1817 Norman married Mary Haynes of Bladen County and became the father of Sarah Bailey, Carolina Emily, and Thomas James. The family lived in Bladen on Mrs. Norman's plantation, Brompton, which was also the site of the unfinished building begun by royal governor Gabriel Johnston for his official residence. All members of the Norman family were buried in a private cemetery on this farm. Jeremiah's tombstone contains the simple epitaph, "50 years a Methodist minister."

In addition to relating Norman's contributions to southern religious life as a dedicated Christian minister, the journal that he kept has historical significance. The clergyman's descriptions of the rigors and discouragements encountered by the Methodist itinerants give a clear picture of the hardships they endured, and his vignettes of people and places, such as Tryon Palace and Brunswick, are intriguing to students of history.

SEE: Elmer T. Clark, I. Manning Potts, and Jacob S. Payton, eds., *The Journal and Letters of Francis Asbury* (1958); Deeds, Births, Marriages, and Wills (Bladen County Courthouse, Elizabethtown, Tyrrell County Courthouse, Columbia, and Marion County Courthouse, Marion, S.C.); W. L. Grissom, *History of Methodism in North Carolina*, vol. 1 (1905); Jeremiah Norman Journal (Southern Historical Collection, University of North Carolina, Chapel Hill).

DURWARD T. STOKES

Norton, John William Roy (11 July 1898–18 Mar. 1974), public health administrator, was born in rural Scotland County, near Laurinburg, the son of Lafayette and Iola Josephine Reynolds Norton. He was graduated from Trinity College, Durham, in 1920 after majoring in economics and English. During the next two years he served as principal and athletic coach at the Laurinburg high school. Returning to Trinity, he studied law during the session of 1922–23 but decided not to pursue that course. After another year as principal and coach in a different Scotland County school, he entered the two-year School of Medicine at The University of North

Carolina, receiving a certificate in 1926. In 1928 he was graduated from the Vanderbilt University School of Medicine.

After his internship and a year of residency in Detroit, Norton became chief of the medical department of a clinic in Fort Smith, Ark., for the year 1930–31. Returning to North Carolina, he was superintendent of health for the city of Rocky Mount until 1935, when he enrolled in Harvard University's School of Public Health under the guidance of Dr. Milton J. Rosenau. After receiving a degree in public health, he became assistant director of county health work with the North Carolina State Board of Health; a year later he was named assistant director of preventive medicine. When Dr. Rosenau joined the public health faculty at The University of North Carolina, Norton went to Chapel Hill as professor of public health administration.

Norton served briefly as a private and a second lieutenant in World War I, but with the advent of World War II he became a medical officer. At first he was in charge of camp sanitation at Fort Bragg; later he saw service in North Africa and Italy and in London. Eventually attaining the rank of colonel, he was reassigned to the United States and placed in charge of the sanitation facilities in all army installations in seven northwestern states. After the war, he served for several years as chief health officer of the Tennessee Valley Authority. In 1948 he became North Carolina's state health officer, a post he filled ably for seventeen years. Under his leadership, successful attacks were made on tuberculosis and Bang's disease, and an informative program of planned parenthood was developed. From time to time Norton served as visiting professor of public health administration at The University of North Carolina. He also served on numerous professional boards and committees and wrote instructive articles and pamphlets, some of which were distributed nationally. Among the latter were papers on rabies and diphtheria control, suggestions for planning a public health program, and public health aspects of civil defense.

Norton was active in many local, state, and national professional organizations, many of which he served as an officer, and he received a number of awards and citations. A member of the Methodist church, he often served as a steward and a Sunday school teacher. In 1938 he married Juanita Harris Ferguson, of Jackson, Miss., and they were the parents of three children: Geraldine (Mrs. Charles Aquadro), Jean (Mrs. Henry Dickman), and Lafayette Ferguson. Norton was buried in the family cemetery near Laurinburg.

SEE: *American Men of Science*, 11th ed., vol. L–O (1966); Data Sheet, 1968 (State Board of Health, Raleigh); William S. Powell, ed., *North Carolina Lives* (1962); Raleigh *News and Observer*, 13 Sept. 1938, 2 July 1948, 16 Mar. 1952, 14 Oct. 1962, 19 Mar. 1974; *Who's Who in America*, vol. 34 (1966–67); *Who's Who in the South and Southwest* (1950).

C. SYLVESTER GREEN

Norwood, John Wall (29 Jan. 1803–24 July 1885), attorney, scientific agriculturist, and member of the General Assembly, was the oldest son of Robina Hogg (30 Dec. 1772–18 May 1860) and Superior Court Judge William Norwood (15 Jan. 1767–29 Jan. 1842) of Poplar Hill, Hillsborough. He was the grandson of Leah Lenoir Whitaker (1737–1831) and John Wall Norwood (1728–1802), Franklin County planter, and of Elizabeth McDowell Alves (d. 1801) and James Hogg (d. 1805), Scottish merchant and planter.

Young Norwood was graduated from The University of North Carolina with an A.B. degree in 1824 "in the group of third honor men" and received an A.M. degree in 1827. Although there appears to be no record of his preparatory schooling or legal training, it is likely that he attended the Hillsborough Academy and read law with Frederick Nash. He promptly began practicing law in Hillsborough and built a handsome Greek Revival office (now razed) just off Court Square.

In 1826 he married Annabella Giles (31 May 1805–28 Mar. 1876), of Wilmington, the daughter of William Giles of Wilmington and his wife Annabella Fleming of Bladen County, but both their lives were clouded for many years by her recurrent bouts of ill health. They had eight children: Hasell, William Giles, Annabella Giles, Robina, John, Margaret Yonge, James Hogg, and Alves. Throughout their marriage the Norwoods lived at Poplar Hill, the Eno River home of John Wall's parents and grandparents, inhabited by Hoggs and Norwoods for almost a century.

In 1832 Norwood was listed as one of the eighteen attorneys (county escheators) for The University of North Carolina, all of whom were considered to be exceptionally able lawyers and notable friends of the university. In 1834 he became treasurer of the Hillsborough Presbyterian Church, succeeding its longtime treasurer, silversmith William Huntington. In 1835 Norwood was confirmed a ruling elder in the church, serving until his death, and from 1865 to 1884 he also was clerk of the Session. Like his older sister, Eliza Alves Norwood Bingham, John Wall Norwood had turned away from the family's traditional Episcopal affiliation.

He served as trustee or patron of three Presbyterian schools. In 1839 he was one of the active trustees of the Bingham School at the time of the so-called "Croom conspiracy." In the 1840s he was listed as a patron or trustee of the Burwell School, which his daughters attended, and in 1848–49 he served as trustee and secretary of the board of the Caldwell Institute in Hillsborough. On 31 May 1843 he joined thirty other University of North Carolina graduates to form the first alumni association.

In the 1840s, after the death of his father, Norwood undertook a complete restoration of Poplar Hill, including the house and surrounding lawns and gardens. A collection of old roses was brought from Wilmington, new beds were laid out, and new hedges were planted. At about this time, Norwood joined forces with such powerful stockholders in the new North Carolina Railroad as former governor William A. Graham, Cadwallader Jones, Sr., and Paul C. Cameron to exert considerable influence in locating the railroad along the Hillsborough route rather than through Chapel Hill.

The reactivation of the State Agricultural Society in 1852 under the leadership of Thomas Ruffin, Robert A. Hamilton, Frederick Hill, and John W. Norwood virtually amounted to a second absorbing career for Norwood. He made countless speeches before farmers' groups, pleading for better land use and promoting the annual agricultural fair in Orange County.

Norwood ventured into public life in 1856, when he was elected a representative of Orange County in the General Assembly. He served until 1858. In 1872 he was elected senator for Orange. One of his speeches, *Speech of Senator J. W. Norwood, Delivered in the Senate, Jan. 27th, 1873, on the Amnesty Bill*, was published in pamphlet form. Another published speech, delivered on 20 Oct. 1871 before the State Agricultural Society at its annual fair, brought together the key recommendations he had made tirelessly for years: enrichment of the soil by the use of decaying vegetable matter, rotation of crops, and prevention of erosion. He himself demonstrated these sound land practices at Poplar Hill. Norwood also called for the creation of a State Board of Agriculture and for courses in agricultural education to be taught in the schools. One of his sons, James Hogg, later became known for his experiments in meadow grasses.

During the Civil War, Norwood and Paul C. Cameron acted as superintendents of relief for the families of Orange County soldiers and used Norwood's law office as their headquarters. In August 1864 the superintendents reported that between 1,500 and 2,000 Orange County citizens had fought in the Confederate army. After the war, Norwood joined with W. A. Graham, Thomas Ruffin, James Webb, Jr., H. K. Nash, and others in an effort to suppress the activities of the Ku Klux Klan.

Norwood died at Poplar Hill at age eighty-two. He was buried in the Hogg-Norwood plot in Hillsborough's Old Town Cemetery.

SEE: Kemp P. Battle, *History of the University of North Carolina, 1789–1912*, vol. 1 (1907); J. G. de Roulhac Hamilton, ed., *Papers of Thomas Ruffin*, vols. 1–3 (1918–20); Thomas Felix Hickerson, *Echoes of Happy Valley* (1962); Session Books of the Hillsborough Presbyterian Church (typescript), 1834–84, and William Norwood Tillinghast Papers (Manuscript Department, Duke University Library, Durham).

MARY CLAIRE ENGSTROM

Norwood, William (15 Jan. 1767–29 Jan. 1842), attorney and planter, borough representative in the General Assembly, and superior court judge, was born in Bute County near the site of modern Louisburg, Franklin County, the oldest of eight children of planter John Wall Norwood (1728–1802) and his second wife, Leah Lenoir Whitaker (1737–1831), widow of William Whitaker and sister of General William Lenoir. He was the grandson of Thomas Lenoir (d. 1763) and his wife Mourning Crawley (b. 1707) of Brunswick County, Va., and Edgecombe County, N.C. (John Wall Norwood's first wife was Lydia Ledbetter [1732–64], by whom he had two sons.)

Essential records of the John Wall Norwood family appear to have been lost in a fire that destroyed the Franklin County home of Colonel John Branch and his wife Elizabeth Norwood (b. 1770), the oldest sister of William Norwood. William L. De Rosset's *Sketches of Church History in North Carolina* (1892) reported that "distinct memories and associations in the Norwood family connect Mr. [George] Micklejohn and John Norwood, of Franklin Co., who was a most zealous and faithful lay reader. . . . After Mr. Norwood's son, the late Wm. Norwood, had removed to Hillsboro, his was one of the families Parson Micklejohn regularly visited."

There seems to be no certain record of William Norwood's formal education and legal training, but his preserved license to practice law in the superior courts of Granville County, dated 18 Oct. 1794, was "given at Hillsborough" before Samuel Ashe and John Williams. Records of the transfer to him, on 10 Aug. 1796, of Hillsborough town Lot 68 and the highly significant conveyance to him, on 6 Oct. 1798, of Edmund Fanning's home Lots 23 and 33 (which Norwood prudently held undisturbed for another quarter of a century) indicate that he had early settled in Hillsborough and begun his successful law practice well before the close of the eighteenth century. It is also known that early in his practice he enjoyed a fair amount of business in Guilford County and adjoining counties.

In 1800, at age thirty-three, he married Robina Hogg

(30 Dec. 1772–18 May 1860), a native-born Scotswoman and the youngest of five children of the eminent Scottish merchant, James Hogg (d. 1805) and his wife Elizabeth McDowell Alves (d. 1801). The Norwoods lived with Robina's ailing parents at their second home on the south bank of the Eno, variously known as Bluffs of Eno, Poplar Lawn, and finally Poplar Hill. There they had eight children: Eliza Alves, John Wall, James Hogg, William, Walter Alves, Jane Burgess, Joseph Caldwell, and Helen Mary. Because of James Hogg's precarious health after a stroke, William Norwood purchased in two separate parcels in 1803 and 1804 his father-in-law's large and valuable estate on the Eno, originally bought, after considerable difficulty, from the heirs of Colonel Francis Corbin and William Churton.

From the outset, Norwood was a highly respected member of the Orange County bar and the Hillsborough community. In February 1803 he contributed one hundred dollars towards finishing South Building on The University of North Carolina campus. In 1806 he represented the borough of Hillsborough in the House of Commons, and in 1807 he was reelected. Essentially a reserved and private man, Norwood seems never to have been seriously attracted to public life nor to have reached out for public office. Unlike his younger colleagues Frederick Nash and Thomas Ruffin, he never accepted law students. A simple red brick law office, still standing on Court Street in downtown Hillsborough, is thought to have been William Norwood's.

Also in 1806, he joined with Duncan Cameron, John Steele, William Duffy, and other eminent lawyers in vigorously opposing the new Judiciary Act of 1806, which established superior courts in every county, thereby reducing the importance of such old court towns as Hillsborough. A public dinner of appreciation was held for the Orange County lawyers who had opposed the bill.

Norwood served as a trustee of the Hillsborough Academy (1816), backed a stamp issue in its favor, and steadily supported it in various ways. In 1826 he served as chairman of the academy's nine-man board. Although an Episcopalian by birth and heritage, he rented a pew in the new Presbyterian church of 1815–16, then the only church in the town and the first church erected after the American Revolution. In 1824 Norwood, Thomas Ruffin, Francis Lister Hawks, Walker Anderson, and Jonathan Sneed formed a reorganized Episcopal vestry to build a second St. Matthew's (Episcopal) Church on land informally donated by Ruffin. William Norwood was elected the first junior warden of the reorganized church. In 1825 he also served as second vice-president of the active Orange County Sunday School Union and joined in presenting a memorial to the General Assembly requesting aid for twenty-two Orange County schools for the poor.

In 1820 Archibald DeBow Murphey exerted personal influence to have Norwood, then fifty-three, appointed to his place on the bench as a superior court judge. "He will be a pleasant man to the Bar," wrote Murphey, "and acceptable to the People." On 22 Nov. 1820 Governor John Branch offered Norwood the temporary appointment, and he served in the post for sixteen years. Of particular note was the celebrated case of *Hoke v. Henderson* in 1833, tried at Lincoln Superior Court. The case was appealed to the state supreme court, but Judge Norwood's ruling was sustained. Increasing ill health and general debility finally forced him to resign in 1836 at age sixty-nine. He died at Poplar Hill six years later.

Although Norwood's will devised a family burying ground to be laid out and plotted "in the cedar grove on the river . . . in the old garden" behind Poplar Hill, this was not done, and he was buried in the Hogg-Norwood plot in Hillsborough's Old Town Cemetery. No portrait of William Norwood is known to exist.

The William Norwood Tillinghast Papers (located at the Duke University Library), a remarkable collection of weekly letters written by Robina Norwood from Poplar Hill to her daughter, Jane Burgess Tillinghast, at Fayetteville covering a period of some thirty years, provide numerous vignettes of Norwood's later life at Poplar Hill.

SEE: Walter Alves Papers, James Hogg Papers, and Hogg and Norwood Family Papers (Southern Historical Collection, University of North Carolina, Chapel Hill); William Lord De Rosset, *Sketches of Church History in North Carolina*, edited by Joseph Blount Cheshire (1892); Mary Claire Engstrom, Survey of Poplar Hill Estate, 1967 (typescript); J. G. de Roulhac Hamilton, ed., *Papers of Thomas Ruffin*, vol. 1 (1918); Thomas Felix Hickerson, *Echoes of Happy Valley* (1962); William Henry Hoyt, ed., *The Papers of Archibald D. Murphey*, 2 vols. (1914); Orange County Deed Books 5, 7, 11–12, and Will Book F-116 (Orange County Courthouse, Hillsborough); Levi M. Scott, "The Bench and Bar of Guilford County," *Publications of the Guilford County Literary and Historical Association*, vol. 1, pt. 2 (1908); William Norwood Tillinghast Papers (Manuscript Department, Duke University Library, Durham).

MARY CLAIRE ENGSTROM

Norwood, William (1806–29 July 1887), Episcopal clergyman, was born in Hillsborough, the son of Judge William Norwood and his wife Robina Hogg, the daughter of James Hogg. He received an A.B. degree from The University of North Carolina in 1826. Deciding to enter the ministry, he studied at the General Theological Seminary in New York with funds provided by the Diocese of North Carolina and was graduated in the class of 1831. It is highly likely that Norwood was ordained deacon in the summer of 1831 by Bishop Richard Channing Moore, of Virginia, who supervised the Diocese of North Carolina in the interim between the death of Bishop John Stark Ravenscroft and the election of Bishop Levi Silliman Ives.

As deacon, Norwood assisted at the first service Bishop Ives performed in his diocese—held at Warrenton on 24 Sept. 1831. For the remainder of that year and in 1832, Norwood served as a missionary in the vicinity of Northampton and Bertie counties. His work at Northampton Courthouse eventually led to the organization of the Church of the Savior in Jackson.

Norwood was ordained priest by Bishop Ives on 20 May 1832 at St. Paul's Church, Edenton, during the annual diocesan convention. Late that year he began to devote two Sundays a month to Scotland Neck in Halifax County; he was also a missionary in Tarboro. It is no doubt a tribute to the ability of the young clergyman that Trinity Church, Scotland Neck, and Calvary Church, Tarboro, were organized and admitted to the diocese in the spring of 1833. In Scotland Neck, he found a wife, Winifred Blount Hill, the daughter of Thomas Blount and Rebecca Norfleet Hill. In 1833 Mrs. Hill, a zealous churchwoman, erected the first church building of Trinity Parish at her own expense. In the early spring of 1834 Norwood became rector of Emmanuel Church, Warrenton, and of old St. John's, Williamsboro. He continued in that capacity until late 1836, when he accepted a call to assist the Right Reverend Richard Channing Moore at the Monumental Church in the city of Richmond.

In July 1836, before moving to Virginia, Norwood performed the marriage of Horace Greeley and Mary Cheyney, a schoolmistress who was then employed by a private school in Warrenton. Greeley, later a prominent journalist and statesman, became an intimate friend of the clergyman and visited Norwood in Richmond when he came south to post bond for Jefferson Davis after the Civil War.

At the time Norwood went to the Monumental Church, which has been referred to as the "Mother Church" of the Episcopal denomination in Richmond, Richard Channing Moore was rector as well as bishop of the Diocese of Virginia. On the death of the bishop in 1841, Norwood became rector. Because the Monumental Church had outgrown the needs of the congregation, plans were made almost immediately for a larger and more centrally located edifice. The cornerstone of the new church, St. Paul's, was laid on 10 Oct. 1843 and dedicated two years later. The rector and congregation of the Monumental Church moved into the new building in a body, carrying with them the parish records. St. Paul's Church, a handsome building in the classical style, located on the west side of Capitol Square, soon became a Richmond landmark. Unfortunately, Norwood's health began to fail and in late 1849 he resigned the rectorship of the new church.

By 1854 he had recovered sufficiently to assume the charge of Christ Church in the Georgetown section of Washington, D.C., where he remained until 1861. Returning to Richmond, he served as rector of historic St. John's until 1862. His last parish, Emmanuel at Brooke Hill, then north of Richmond, was one of the diocese's new churches. In the words of Elizabeth Wright Weddell, the historian of St. Paul's, Norwood had the unique distinction of having been the rector of Richmond's three historic churches and at the time of his death was personally known to almost every citizen. In recognition of his distinguished career, he was awarded a doctor of divinity degree by his alma mater, The University of North Carolina, in 1856.

Norwood and his wife were the parents of seven daughters and four sons. Of the sons, John Jones (1842–1919), who became an Episcopal clergyman, was rector of Trinity Church, Scotland Neck (1872–74), which his father had helped organize many years before. William Norwood was buried in the churchyard of Emmanual Church, Richmond, his last charge. A portrait of him in vestments, by William Garl Browne, hangs in the parish house of St. Paul's. The parish house itself occupies the site of the house built by Norwood while he was rector of the church. In 1923 the parish dedicated the Norwood Room in memory of Norwood's daughters, Rebecca Hill (1833–1919) and Mary Louise (1850–1923). Rebecca Hill Norwood founded and, for many years, was president of the women's auxiliary of St. Paul's Church.

SEE: Joseph Blount Cheshire, *An Historical Address Delivered in Saint Matthew's Church, Hillsboro, N.C., on Sunday, August 24, 1924* (1925); Stuart Hall Hill Manuscript Notebooks, vol. 1 (North Carolina Collection, University of North Carolina, Chapel Hill); *Journals of the Annual Convention, Diocese of North Carolina* (1829–37); Stuart N. Smith and Claiborne T. Smith, Jr., *The History of Trinity Church, Scotland Neck* (1955); Elizabeth Wright Weddell, *St. Paul's Church, Richmond, Virginia: Its Historic Years and Memorials*, vol. 1 (1931); Stephen B. Weeks Scrapbook: History and Biography of North Carolina, vol. 3 (North Carolina Collection, University of North Carolina, Chapel Hill).

CLAIBORNE T. SMITH, JR.

Nowicki, Matthew *(26 June 1910–31 Aug. 1950),* architect and teacher, was born in Chita, Russia, the son of Zygmunt Nowicki, a Polish ambassador in Russia at the time. The elder Nowicki afterwards was Polish consul general in Chicago (1921–25), where Matthew, who had begun his studies in Warsaw, continued his education and attended the Chicago Art Institute. Returning to Poland, he studied at the School of Design in Gerson-Warsaw and was awarded a master of architecture diploma from the Polytechnic of Warsaw in 1936. Before graduation he received prizes for his designs of a mosque in Warsaw and for low-cost residential housing.

In 1936, with Stanislowa Sandecka, whom he married the same year, Nowicki established a commercial art firm, designing book covers and posters as well as book and magazine illustrations. From 1936 to 1943 he was senior assistant at the School of Architecture of the Polytechnic and during that period received numerous prizes and awards, including second prize for the Polish Pavilion at the New York World's Fair (1939) and, jointly with his wife, the Gold Medal for their graphics at the Paris Exhibition. In 1938 he won a prize and the building commission for the administration building at Lodz as well as for the casino at Druskieniki. A district sports center in Prague and a hotel in Augowstow were both completed in 1939. Private homes as well as low-cost apartments were also among his commissions. From 1942 to 1944 Nowicki was a professor at the Technical School of the Municipality of Warsaw. For a time during World War II, he served as a lieutenant in the Polish army and with the underground forces.

After the war, as Polish cities were being rebuilt, he was involved in town planning. In 1945–46 he was cultural attaché to the Polish Consulate in Chicago, and in 1947 he was Poland's representative to the committee for the United Nations building. Nowicki was a member of the faculty of the Pratt Institute, Brooklyn, N.Y., until 1948, when he was named acting head of the Department of Architecture at the School of Architecture and Landscape Design of North Carolina State University in Raleigh.

Since he was not yet licensed as an architect in North Carolina, Nowicki served as a "consultant" to Raleigh architect William Henley Dietrick, preparing preliminary sketches for the interior of the Carolina Country Club, the state archives building, and the North Carolina State Fair Grounds and Dorton Arena—all in Raleigh. He also collaborated on a California shopping center design and was a consultant in the planning of a new capital, Chandigarh, in East Punjab, India. Nowicki was widely acclaimed as one of the world's leading architects; the arena at the North Carolina fairgrounds has been cited as an outstanding example of his promise. His death at age forty was widely mourned.

As he was returning from a trip to India in connection with plans for the new capital, Nowicki was killed in an airplane crash in Egypt. Memorial services were held in the Sacred Heart Cathedral, Raleigh.

Nowicki and his wife, Stanislowa Sandecka, were the parents of two sons: Paul (1941) and Peter (1950). With a degree in architectural engineering, Stanislowa taught engineering at State College. After her husband's death, she went to the University of Pennsylvania to teach architecture.

SEE: Lewis Mumford, *Roots of Contemporary American Architecture* (1952); *New York Times,* 1 Sept. 1950; North Carolina State University Archives (North Carolina State University Library, Raleigh); Laura Pilarski, *They Came from Poland* (1969); Raleigh *News and Observer,* 1, 6 Sept.,

3 Oct., 12 Nov. 1950, 21 May 1942, 15 Oct. 1989; Bruce H. Shafer, *The Writings and Sketches of Matthew Nowicki* (1973).

WILLIAM S. POWELL

Nussmann, Adolph *(July 1739–3 Nov. 1794),* first resident Lutheran clergyman in North Carolina, was born in Münster, Westphalia, the son of Joan and Joanna Maria Hilleke Nussmann. On 12 July 1739 he was baptized a Roman Catholic in the Liebfrauen Church, Münster. As a young man he became a Franciscan friar, but, "through the study of philosophy" and "a more intimate acquaintance" with the Evangelical or Lutheran church, he "was led to serious reflection." Later, "at the University of Göttingen and also in his work at the Teacher's Seminary in Hanover," he became "more and more confirmed . . . in the doctrines and convictions of the Evangelical Religion."

In 1772 "about sixty families, adherents of the Augsburg Confession" in North Carolina, sent two delegates to Europe in search of a resident pastor and a schoolteacher. The delegates, Christopher Rintelmann of Zion (Organ) Church, Rowan County, and Christopher Layrle of St. John's, Mecklenburg (now Cabarrus) County, went first to London and then to Hanover, where the Consistory selected Nussmann as pastor and Johann Gottfried (John Godfrey) Arends as schoolteacher. Before his departure, Nussmann received "written pastoral instructions" from the founder of the Teacher's Seminary, Gabriel Wilhelm Goetten, as well as "a considerable number of Bibles, hymnals, catechisms and other books." In London, Nussmann preached at the German Court Chapel to "the general satisfaction" of its "enlightened members." He also overcame the objections of Dr. Johann Casper Velthusen, a prominent Lutheran theologian, who admitted to some "hesitations" regarding the appointment of so recent a convert from Catholicism. Velthusen and the other members of the Court Chapel became "very fond" of Nussmann during the time he awaited a ship for Charles Town, S.C., and to reduce the drain on his funds, "gave him his meals at their own tables." As he prepared to depart, Velthusen gave him "a special gift" for his personal use from George III and Queen Charlotte.

Nussmann and Arends arrived in America in 1773. At first, Nussmann settled in Rowan County and divided his time between Zion (Organ) Church, on Second Creek, ten miles southeast of Salisbury, and St. John's, Salisbury. He also visited St. John's Church, Mecklenburg (now Cabarrus) County. Some members of Zion Church, however, turned against Nussmann when they discovered that he had been a Roman Catholic. At the end of his first year, therefore, he left the pastorates of Zion and St. John's, Salisbury, in the hands of the schoolteacher Arends and established his home on Buffalo Creek, about a mile and a half east of St. John's Church, Mecklenburg County. The church on Buffalo Creek received him "at once in the most friendly manner." Nussmann wrote the church's first constitution, which required the pastor to "accept with heart and mouth" the various "Symbolical Books of our Evangelical Church." Besides St. John's, Nussmann served a congregation with an "admixture of members of the Reformed Church," located six miles southwest of that on Buffalo Creek, and, later, an "Evangelical Congregation near Peintchurch," three miles southeast of Salisbury. "Thus," he wrote, "I made my living during this time, although sometimes rather meagerly, and with much hard work."

In 1774 Nussmann married Elizabeth Rintelmann, the daughter of Christopher Rintelmann. After her death, he married Barbara Layrle, the daughter of Christopher Layrle. Elizabeth was the mother of his son Paul and his daughters Margaret and Elizabeth, and Barbara was the mother of his sons John and Daniel and his daughters Catherine and Barbara.

The outbreak of the American Revolution interrupted all communication with Europe, cutting Nussmann off from Velthusen and the Consistory of Hanover. Isolated from his friends abroad, he corresponded with the Reverend Henry Melchoir Muhlenburg in Pennsylvania and became more closely associated with the Reverend Frederick Daser of Charles Town, S.C. During the war, Nussmann conducted services as regularly as conditions permitted and continued the educational work of the parish schools. In 1783 the main school at St. John's had an enrollment of seventy-two children, and two smaller schools recorded enrollments of thirty-six and twenty, respectively. Two years later, the General Assembly added Nussmann to the board of trustees of the Salisbury Academy.

In 1786, almost fourteen years after his departure from Europe, Nussmann wrote the first of several letters to Dr. Velthusen at the university in Helmstedt, Brunswick. "With sadness," he told Velthusen, "I observe every day something lacking, now here, now there, and now everywhere." Nussmann "urgently requested" Velthusen to send "at least two preachers," young men with "determination, courage, and a genuine apostolic spirit." Even more urgently, he requested "an entirely new catechism for the young people of North Carolina," one that "would stand up under the severest test." Finally, he asked Velthusen to send him "books suitable for the establishment of a church and school library."

Velthusen believed Nussmann's demands to be "so just and so urgent" that, he wrote, "it was merely a question of how we might in the best manner achieve that which was expected from us." With several colleagues, Velthusen organized the Helmstedt Mission Society, and within two years, three preachers—Christian Eberhard Bernhardt, Carl August Gottlieb Storch, and Arnold Roschen—had joined Nussmann and Arends in North Carolina. With the help of wealthy Germans, Velthusen and his associates also prepared and published at least eight textbooks for use in the parish schools, including the "Helmstaedt" or "North Carolina Catechism." In addition, Velthusen sent many other books for use in the church libraries and for distribution to the poor.

Nussmann worked in "brotherly harmony" with his new colleagues. In 1791 they elected him chairman of their first "semi-annual Assembly." First alone, and then as the senior member of an expanding group of ministers, Nussmann "had supervision over an area of some seven hundred square miles," which included approximately twenty widely scattered congregations in twelve or more present-day counties. In 1794 "a gangrenous ulcer of the breast" ended his life at age fifty-five. "What this unusual man had been in health," wrote Storch, "he remained during the most violent pain." Nussmann was buried in St. John's churchyard, Cabarrus County.

SEE: G. D. Bernheim, *History of the German Settlements and of the Lutheran Church in North and South Carolina* (1872); G. D. Bernheim and George H. Cox, *The History of the Evangelical Synod and Ministerium of North Carolina* (1902); Biographical Data on Lutheran Ministers (Lutheran Archives, North Carolina Synod House, Salisbury); William F. Boyd and Charles A. Krummel, eds., "German Tracts Concerning the Lutheran Church in North Carolina," *North Carolina Historical Review* 7 (January, April 1930); *Life Sketches of Lutheran Ministers: North Carolina and Tennessee Synods, 1773–1965* (1966); John Baxter Moose, "Adolph Nussmann: Pioneer Lutheran Preacher in North Carolina," *Lutheran Church Quarterly* 13 (October 1940); Jacob L. Morgan, Bachman S. Brown, and John Hall, eds., *History of the Lutheran Church in North Carolina, 1803–1953* (1953); Joseph Stewart, ed., "Extract from a Letter by Pastor Storch in North Carolina, Dated Salisbury, Jan. 20–Feb. 25, 1796," *North Carolina Historical Review* 20 (July 1943).

GARY G. ROTH

Nye, Edgar Wilson (Bill) *(25 Aug. 1850–22 Feb. 1896)*, journalist and humorist who spent his last years near Asheville, was born in Shirley, northern Maine, the oldest of three sons of Franklin and Elizabeth Loring Nye. His father, a lumberman, was a descendant of one of the earliest (1635) settlers of Lynn, Mass. In 1852 the family moved to a settlement on the St. Croix River in Wisconsin and took up farming. Bill Nye later described his boyhood home as "one hundred and sixty acres of beautiful ferns and bright young rattlesnakes." He received a common-school education ("between Indian massacres," he later wrote) and prepared himself for the law. He taught school briefly and began his writing career as a correspondent for local Wisconsin newspapers. In 1876 he moved westward on his own and settled in the city of Laramie in the new Wyoming Territory.

Here Nye passed his bar examination and became a justice of the peace for a short time, but his real work began as a humorous contributor to the *Laramie Daily Sentinel*. His sketches of western life became widely known and were reprinted as far west as San Francisco and south to Texas. In 1881 he founded his own paper, the *Laramie Boomerang*, which he edited for three years. He quickly achieved a national reputation with his humorous articles, and three collections of them were published: *Bill Nye and Boomerang* (1881), *Forty Liars and Other Lies* (1882), and *Baled Hay* (1884). For health reasons, he was advised to seek another climate. He lived briefly in Greeley, Colo., and Hudson, Wis., before going east to accept a position on the *New York World* in 1886.

Over the next decade Nye joined the top rank of American humorists: his columns were syndicated nationally, he contributed to the leading magazines, and his work even became well known abroad. During this period and for the rest of his life he was a popular lecturer across the nation, at first alone and then in the company of poet James Whitcomb Riley. Nye and Riley were one of the most popular lecture teams of that time; Riley's sentiment and pathos contrasted well with Nye's wit and satire.

Bill Nye first visited the Asheville area in 1886 and was impressed with the scenery and climate, writing: "You will find enough climate in twenty minutes to last a week" and "the two chief products of Western North Carolina are smoking tobacco and climate. If you do not like the climate you can help yourself to the smoking tobacco." In a mountain hollow he came upon what "seemed to be a kind of laboratory, for I could see here and there the earmarks of the chemist." Then a shaggy mountaineer appeared and "showed me a new beverage that he had been engaged in perfecting. . . . I took some of it to show that I confided in him. . . . The fluid must have been alcoholic in its nature, for when I regained consciousness I was extremely elsewhere. . . . I hardly knew how I got home, but I finally did get there, accompanied by a strong leaning toward Prohibition."

In 1891 he moved permanently to Arden, ten miles south of Asheville. He was in poor health due to attacks of meningitis, yet he continued to write and give lectures. The citizens of Asheville welcomed their famous new resident with a gala banquet on 29 Dec. 1891. He and Zebulon B. Vance were the featured speakers, and the audience, according to newspaper reports, "wept with laughter" during the evening. His house, or "shatto" as he called it, was located at Buck Shoals on the east side of the French Broad River. He wrote of it: "George Vanderbilt's extensive grounds command a fine view of my place." Here in his last years he welcomed many distinguished visitors and wrote often of the attractions of western North Carolina. He died at Buck Shoals of meningitis. Services were held at Calvary Episcopal Church, Fletcher, N.C., of which he was a member. He was buried in the churchyard, where a memorial monument was erected in 1925.

Tall and spare of build, bald with wire-frame glasses and a stooping posture, Nye was a favorite target of caricaturists; his image was known to millions of Americans in the early 1890s. His humor was in the school of Mark Twain, Artemus Ward, Josh Billings, and other humorous journalists of the time. Like them, he depended on broadness and exaggeration, but his satire, in which he often used himself as a foil, was gentle rather than cutting. He was also a talented pen-and-ink artist and often illustrated his articles with sketches.

On 7 Mar. 1877 he married Clara Frances Smith of Chicago. The couple had four children: Bessie, Winifred, Max, and Frank Wilson. The latter wrote an excellent biography, with excerpts from his father's writings, in 1926.

One tribute at his death, written by a young Houston reporter, William S. Porter, has become notable in its own right. The man who would later become O. Henry said of him: "His was a child's heart, the scholar's knowledge and the philosopher's view of life."

SEE: *Asheville Citizen*, 11, 18 Mar. 1951, 26 Jan. 1969; Walter Blair, *Native American Humor* (1937); *DAB*, vol. 7 (1962); Frank Wilson Nye, *Bill Nye: His Own Life Story* (1926); *The State*, 30 Dec. 1939.

JAMES MEEHAN

Oates, John Alexander (*2 June 1870–12 Feb. 1958*), editor, lawyer, and educator, was born in Piney Grove Township, Sampson County, the son of John Alexander and Mary Jewell Ashford Oates. His father was sheriff of Sampson County during the Civil War and subsequently a county commissioner, a state senator, and, at the time of his death in 1901, the mayor of Dunn. Oates was the grandson of David Cogdell and Laruhama Fleming Oates and the great-grandson of John and Susan Cogdell Oates. These and other ancestors were of predominantly English and Scottish origin. His maternal grandmother spoke Gaelic.

Oates attended Faison Academy (1876–79), public schools (1879–84), and Clinton Academy (1884–87). After teaching for a time in the public schools of Sampson County, he enrolled at Wake Forest College for the academic year 1888–89. However, Oates "kept up with his class at home" and "taught a large school" until March 1889, when he took up residence at Wake Forest. After twenty months of college he returned home, where in 1891 he became principal of Autryville School. During the year 1894–95 he was again registered at Wake Forest

but went to the campus only twice before taking his examinations. He received an A.B. degree in June 1895. In the summer of 1910 Oates attended the Wake Forest Law School—the only time he ever spent in a school of law. On 29 Aug. 1910 he was licensed to practice law by the North Carolina Supreme Court.

Meanwhile, on 1 Jan. 1892 Oates had become managing editor of the *North Carolina Baptist*, a weekly denominational newspaper founded in Fayetteville one year earlier by the Reverend T. B. Newberry. Before the end of 1892 Oates became editor and proprietor, moving to Fayetteville to the house on St. James Square where he lived for the rest of his life. Under the slogan, "The saloon must go," he made Prohibition "the most potent moral issue in the State." While chairman of the temperance committee of the Baptist State Convention of North Carolina, Oates invited religious and social organizations to send representatives to a statewide temperance convention, held in Raleigh in 1902, at which the Anti-Saloon League of North Carolina was organized. Oates was corresponding secretary of the league until 29 Aug. 1907, when he succeeded Josiah W. Bailey as secretary. Having decided to use the league as his principal forum, Oates discontinued the *North Carolina Baptist* with the issue of 27 Nov. 1907. In it he wrote: "For fifteen years I have pressed hard the battle for temperance in North Carolina. I hope now, as the struggle waxes hotter and the crisis draws nearer, that I may be able to give more of my time and my talents to this cause which is so close to me." He sold his subscription list of 7,400 to the *Biblical Recorder* for six thousand dollars.

Led by Heriot Clarkson, president, and Oates, chairman of the executive committee, the Anti-Saloon League persuaded Governor Robert B. Glenn to ask the legislature, which met in special session on 21 Jan. 1908, to allow the people to vote on the issue. The two houses agreed. Oates managed the vigorous campaign that followed, using Glenn as the leading speaker.

On 26 May 1908, by a margin of 113,612 to 69,416, North Carolina became the first southern state to adopt statewide Prohibition. Two days later the Raleigh *News and Observer* said of Oates, "he has done gloriously." As the "General of the campaign" he "has won a victory more lasting for good in North Carolina than has been won in this generation." His health shattered by the campaign, Oates spent the summer of 1908 recuperating at Virginia health resorts and the Johns Hopkins Hospital.

From 1910 until 1950, when his eyesight failed, Oates practiced general civil law in Fayetteville. Among the clients of his firm were the Seaboard Air Line Railway, Metropolitan Life Insurance Company, Continental Casualty Company, and Davison Chemical Corporation. After discontinuing the *North Carolina Baptist*, Oates, in partnership with James A. Parham, published *The Fayetteville Index* from 1909 to 1912. From 1909 to 1927 he was a director of the National Bank of Fayetteville.

For half a century Oates was active in public affairs and the Democratic party, holding many different elective and appointive positions. Before the turn of the century, he had become a member of the Fayetteville Board of Aldermen. In 1903 he was elected chairman of the Cumberland County Board of Education, continuing until 1913, when he resigned to become the first judge of the Cumberland County Recorder's Court. Although he served as judge only for a year, he was usually addressed as Judge Oates for the rest of his life. From 1911 to 1928 he was chairman of the Fayetteville School Board. Elected to the state senate for the 1917 session, he sought unsuccessfully to increase the state school term from four to six months. From 1925 to 1933 he was a director of the state School for the Blind and Deaf. Beginning in 1935, he served eight years as a member of the state School Commission. This was followed by four years on the state Welfare Commission. During World War I he was the federal food administrator for Cumberland County and chairman of the county council of defense. In World War II he was a government appeals agent in the Selective Service System.

At an early age Oates became superintendent of the Sunday school of the First Baptist Church, Fayetteville, continuing for the next forty years. After this he taught the Oates Bible class in the Sunday school. From 1906 until his death he served as deacon. From 1898 to 1908 he was clerk of South River Baptist Association, and from 1915 to 1917 he was president of the Baptist State Convention of North Carolina. On 23 May 1906 Oates was elected a trustee of Wake Forest College, serving continuously until 31 Dec. 1948. He was president of the board for nine years, including the World War II period when decisions were made to admit women, establish a four-year medical school in Winston-Salem, and move the other schools of the college to Winston-Salem. R. C. Lawrence regarded Oates's work as a Wake Forest trustee as his "greatest single service." Other denominational activities included the chairmanship in the 1930s of the convention's debt commission, which helped Meredith College recover from a heavy burden of indebtedness. At various times he was a trustee of Dell School, Buies Creek Academy, and Southern Baptist Seminary. He was founder and chairman of the executive committee of the Baptist Seaside Assembly near Southport.

Oates's hobbies were farming and the study of history, especially the history of the Scots in America. He was general chairman of the Cape Fear Valley Scottish Festival, which began in 1939 as an annual event. In 1950 he published *The Story of Fayetteville and the Upper Cape Fear*, a nine-hundred-page book that won the Smithwick Award given by the North Carolina Society of County and Local Historians. On 19 June 1953 he was the Raleigh *News and Observer's* "Tar Heel of the Week." Cumberland County made him chairman of the arrangements committee for the 1954 celebration of the two-hundredth anniversary of its founding. Additional memberships included the Cumberland County Bar Association, the Fayetteville Chamber of Commerce, and the Junior Order of United American Mechanics.

On 20 May 1897, in Winston, Oates married Emma Estelle Cain Dodd, of Fayetteville, who died on 28 Feb. 1928. On 17 June 1931, in Fayetteville, he married Isabelle Charters Crowder of Crowder's Crossing, Ga. By the second marriage he had two children: John Alexander III, M.D., of Nashville, Tenn., and Mary Ashford Oates Burton of Fayetteville.

Oates died in Winston-Salem and was buried in Cross Creek Cemetery, Fayetteville. His widow subsequently married P. L. Lindley of Fayetteville.

SEE: *Annual of the Baptist State Convention of North Carolina* (1958 [portrait]); R. C. Lawrence, "John Alexander Oates: Prince of Cape Fear," *Biblical Recorder*, 17 Feb. 1943; *Nat. Cyc. Am. Biog.*, vol. 47 (1965 [portrait]); *North Carolina Biography*, vols. 2 (1929), 6 (1919); *North Carolina Manual* (1917); John Alexander Oates Papers (Baptist Historical Collection, Wake Forest University, Winston-Salem); Raleigh *News and Observer*, 19 June 1953; Margaret Jane Tharrington, "John A. Oates: Crusader for Statewide Prohibition" (M.A. thesis, Wake Forest University, 1973).

HENRY S. STROUPE

O'Berry, Annie Land *(28 May 1885–4 Feb. 1944)*, administrator of the North Carolina Emergency Relief Administration, president of the Rural Rehabilitation Corporation, and a leader in women's clubs, civic affairs, and the Democratic party, was born in Edgecombe County to V. W. and Mary Dawson Mayo Land. Her father, a Virginian by birth, was a veteran of the Civil War, and her mother was a descendant of the Lees of Virginia and the Mayos of Virginia and Ireland. Annie lived on the family plantation, enjoying outdoor sports, until she was thirteen, when her parents died; she then went to live with her sister in Littleton.

She attended Littleton College and later was graduated first in her class from Peace Institute in Raleigh. After college she made her home with her brother, Edward M. Land, an attorney in Kinston. On 14 Dec. 1909 she married Thomas O'Berry, whose father, Nathan O'Berry, was a prominent citizen and lumberman in Goldsboro. Her father-in-law served as treasurer of North Carolina from 1929 until his death in 1932. Her husband founded an insurance agency in his hometown and later served in the North Carolina House of Representatives (1933 and 1935) and the state senate (1941–48).

Soon after moving to Goldsboro with her husband, Annie O'Berry became very active in civic groups and women's clubs. Among the many positions that she held, she was first chairman of the antituberculosis committee in Wayne County and president of the city charity organization. By 1920 she had become interested in women's club work, associating with Gertrude Weil of Goldsboro and many others. She especially promoted beautification of the city, charity efforts, and civic involvement of women. Rising rapidly through the local and state offices in the North Carolina Federation of Women's Clubs, she was president of the organization from 1927 to 1929. During her administration she stressed education and a program to obliterate adult illiteracy. Her sister-in-law, Marie Long Land (Mrs. Edward M.), who by then had moved from Kinston to Statesville, followed her as president from 1929 to 1931.

Annie O'Berry later held positions as a member of the executive committee of the General Federation of Women's Clubs in the United States. Meanwhile, as a result of her involvement in other civic projects, Governor Angus W. MacLean named her to the state Commission to Study County Government (1926) and to the State Historical Commission (1928). In 1930 Governor O. Max Gardner appointed her vice-chairman of the state executive committee of the Democratic party.

While working with the charity organization in Goldsboro, she personally investigated relief cases in her hometown and took a course in social work at Columbia University to better equip herself for this effort. When Kate Burr Johnson resigned as commissioner of charities and public welfare in 1930, Annie O'Berry sought to replace her. However, she lost the position to Annie Kiser Bost because of concerns about Mrs. O'Berry's health.

During the early years of the Great Depression, her father-in-law helped her raise five thousand dollars to assist white-collar persons who were victims of the depression but not destitute enough for regular relief. Because of this work and her important political connections, Governor J. C. B. Ehringhaus, in August 1933, chose her to head the new North Carolina Emergency Relief Administration, created by the Federal Emergency Relief Administration under Harry Hopkins. After the name of the organization was changed to the Civil Works Administration in the winter of 1933–34, she continued as director. She also remained administrator of the NCERA until 1935, when its work was transferred to either the newly created Works Progress Administration or the State Board of Charities and Public Welfare. Mrs. O'Berry sought unsuccessfully to be named administrator of the WPA for North Carolina, a post that went to George A. Coan, Jr., since WPA positions were a patronage of U.S. senators rather than state governors. She continued until her death to hold the nominal position of president of the North Carolina Rehabilitation Corporation, an agency that had been created under the NCERA to lend money to farmers to buy land; it continued to receive payments on those loans for more than a decade.

After the demise of the NCERA, Mrs. O'Berry became less active in state affairs as she experienced repeated illnesses. She died in a hospital in Baltimore, Md., where she had gone for an operation, and was buried in Willow Dale Cemetery, Goldsboro.

The O'Berrys had no children, but Annie O'Berry had raised her nephew, Virginius Boddie Perry, whom she treated like a son.

One of the few women emergency relief administrators in the United States, Mrs. O'Berry demonstrated the ability of women to handle what was considered a complex, dirty, and difficult task. She was responsible for providing relief to thousands of North Carolinians, negotiating with labor groups, and dispensing in little more than two years over $52 million in relief funds on projects as varied as a state symphony orchestra, highway and airport construction, beautification projects, and basic sustenance to disabled and destitute persons who were unable to work on the relief projects.

SEE: Census of 1900, North Carolina, vol. 32, ED 33, sheet 18, line 19; *Charlotte Observer*, 26 May 1940; Emma R. Edwards, "History of the Goldsboro Business and Professional Women's Club," 1960 (mimeographed, North Carolina Collection, University of North Carolina, Chapel Hill); *Goldsboro Daily Argus*, 1909–10, 1920 passim.; *Goldsboro News*, 1927, 1929; *Goldsboro News Argus*, 1930, 1932, 1943–44 passim, 12 June 1957, 4 July 1976; *Greensboro Daily News*, 16 Nov. 1930; J. S. Kirk and others, *Emergency Relief in North Carolina* (1936); Marriage Register for Lenoir County, N.C.; Thomas S. Morgan, "A Step toward Altruism" (Ph.D. dissertation, University of North Carolina, 1969); *North Carolina Clubwoman* (March 1944); Raleigh *News and Observer*, 1930–35 passim, 6 Feb. 1944; Lou Rogers, *Tar Heel Women* (1949); Harriette Hammer Walker, *Busy North Carolina Women* (1931); Gertrude Weil Papers (North Carolina State Archives, Raleigh).

THOMAS S. MORGAN

O'Brien, William Thomas *(21 Sept. 1854–27 Jan. 1906)*, machinist, was born in Lynchburg, Va., of Irish ancestry. His father was John O'Brien, a laborer, who came to the United States in 1846; his mother was Katherine McLaughlin O'Brien, who also came from Ireland. Brought up in poverty, O'Brien left school at age fourteen and for two years worked in a Lynchburg tobacco factory. At sixteen he was apprenticed to a machinist in Lynchburg and served in that capacity for four years. During the next seven years he worked as a journeyman machinist in several large cities, including Baltimore, Philadelphia, Kansas City, Denver, and St. Paul. For a time he worked on the War and Navy Building in Washington but resigned to become foreman of the machine shops of the Glamorgan Company in Lynchburg.

Early in 1881 O'Brien accepted a position with the Bonsack Cigarette Machine Company, also of Lynchburg. His assignment was to install and correct minor defects in the operation of the cigarette machine invented by James A. Bonsack. Almost immediately he was sent to install two cigarette machines in the factory of W. Duke Sons and Company in Durham, N.C., and to instruct the Duke employees in their operation. He remained with the Dukes about six months and then, in 1882, went to Chicago and St. Louis to install and service other Bonsack machines.

Returning to the Duke factory in 1883, he overhauled the machines that were not performing well. The Dukes, recognizing his mechanical ability, offered to hire him on a permanent basis. O'Brien was reluctant to leave Bonsack, where he worked for a salary; the Dukes, with limited resources, wanted to employ him on a contract basis at three cents per thousand cigarettes. In 1883 he accepted the Duke offer. About seven months later, the machines were greatly improved by numerous small changes O'Brien had devised. Business expanded, and soon O'Brien was making money faster than the Dukes. He eventually went to his employers and suggested a change so that the Dukes could earn their proportionate share. As a result, O'Brien became superintendent of the Duke cigarette plant in Durham in 1897. Though he contributed nothing to the basic development of the cigarette machine, O'Brien did create a number of refinements that led to its successful operation. In this way, he played a major role in making possible the formation of the original American Tobacco Company.

O'Brien also participated in the business development of Durham, serving as a director of the Durham Loan and Trust Company, the Erwin Cotton Mills, and the Durham Savings Bank. He was an alderman of the city from 1902 to 1904. A Republican, he served in various capacities in the North Carolina Republican party and was a delegate to the Republican National conventions of 1896 and 1904.

In 1883 he married Catherine Biggins, and they became the parents of four children: William Joseph, John Joseph, Thomas Joseph, and Mary Joseph. He and his wife, both Roman Catholics, made generous donations for the establishment of the Immaculate Conception Catholic Church in Durham. O'Brien also donated to numerous charitable organizations and supported moving Trinity College (later Duke University) to Durham. He died in Durham and was buried in Holy Cross Cemetery in Lynchburg, Va.

SEE: Samuel A. Ashe, ed., *Biographical History of North Carolina*, vol. 3 (1906); Mrs. Mary Joseph O'Brien Milburn (Durham), personal information; *North Carolina Biography*, vol. 3 (1929); W. J. O'Brien, interview, Durham, 26 June 1936; Records of Immaculate Conception Catholic Church, Durham; *Southern Tobacco Journal*, 25 Oct. 1897; Mrs. Joseph B. Wingfield, Librarian of Jones Memorial Library, to Nannie M. Tilley, 17 Feb. 1976.

NANNIE M. TILLEY

Ochiltree, William Beck *(18 Oct. 1811–27 Dec. 1867)*, lawyer and public official, was born in Fayetteville. The only person of this name recorded in the 1810 census for the county was Elizabeth Ochiltree, whose household consisted of four females and one slave, but no male. Young Ochiltree went first to the Florida Territory and then to Alabama, where he studied law. After practicing for a time in Alabama, he moved to the Republic of Texas in 1839, continuing his law practice. In 1842 he was appointed judge of the Fifth Judicial District, a position that also made him an ex officio judge of the Texas Supreme Court. During the administration of President Anson Jones (1844–45), Ochiltree served first as secretary of the Treasury (1844) and then as attorney general (1845).

Ochiltree wrote a series of articles for the San Augustine (Tex.) *Red-Lander* opposing the annexation of Texas to the United States. During the annexation and constitutional convention of 1845, he served as a delegate from Nacogdoches County and participated in the writing of the Texas state constitution of the same year. After the convention he again served as a judge but resigned to return to private law practice.

While working to bring about a two-party system in Texas, Ochiltree was a leader of the state's Whig party. He ran unsuccessfully for the U.S. Congress from the Eastern District of Texas in 1851 and finished second in the gubernatorial race in 1853. Two years later, he was elected a member of the sixth Texas legislature. Ochiltree also served as a delegate to the Texas Secession Convention in 1861 from Harrison County, to which he had moved in 1859. He went to Montgomery, Ala., in 1861 as a delegate and member of the Provisional Congress of the Confederate States of America but resigned and returned to Texas to organize an infantry regiment for General John G. Walker's Division. Ill health in 1863 forced him to resign his commission, and he returned to Texas. He died in Jefferson, Tex., four years later.

SEE: Randolph Campbell, "The Whig Party of Texas in the Elections of 1848 and 1852," *Southwestern Historical Quarterly* 73 (July 1969); *Dictionary of the Texan Conventions and Congresses, 1832–1845* (1941); James D. Lynch, *The Bench and Bar of Texas* (1885); Dallas (Tex.) *Morning News*, 30 May 1897.

L. TUFFLY ELLIS

Odell, James Alexander (*4 Nov. 1841–10 Feb. 1930*), merchant and business leader, was born at Cedar Falls, Randolph County, the son of James, a farmer, and Anna Trogden Odell. After completing his studies at Middleton Academy in his native county, Odell opened a general merchandise store at Cedar Falls in 1865. In 1868 he moved to High Point, where he started and operated a similar store. In 1872 Odell, his brother, John M., who became a prominent textile manufacturer in Concord, and W. H. Ragan founded a general merchandise store in Greensboro. Gradually they shifted to hardware, and in 1884 the Odell Hardware Company, one of the largest of its kind in the South, was incorporated. Odell served as president of the firm until 1912, when he retired and assumed the duties of chairman of the board of directors, a position he held until his death.

With John M. Odell and Julian Carr, he also founded the Durham Cotton Manufacturing Company; the first cotton mill in Durham, it opened in 1884 with 224 looms and 8,600 spindles. James A. Odell was president of the company for two years, then a stockholder and a director. In addition, he was vice-president of the Odell Manufacturing Company in Concord and the Five Cent Savings Bank of Greensboro, director of the Piedmont Bank, president of the Mount Airy Granite Company, stockholder and director of the Kerr Bag Manufacturing Company of Concord, and stockholder of the Morgan and Hampton Company in Nashville, Tenn. Odell was a founder of the J. M. Odell Manufacturing Company of Bynum and the People's Bank. He was a director of the Greensboro Insurance Company (later a part of the Jefferson Standard Insurance Company) and of the Greensboro Loan and Trust Company (later the Greensboro Bank and Trust Company).

A Democrat and a Mason, Odell served on the Greensboro Board of Aldermen and was active in the municipal reform and temperance movements. When Greensboro College nearly collapsed financially in 1882, he and several others became guarantors for the college; later he gave the school substantial gifts of money. A member and lay leader of the West Market Methodist Church in Greensboro, he gave the church its initial endowment of fifty thousand dollars. He also served as treasurer of the Board of Finance of the North Carolina and Western North Carolina Conferences of the Methodist Episcopal Church, South; as a delegate to the denomination's General Conferences in 1890, 1894, and 1902; and as a member of its Book Committee.

In 1865 Odell married May J. Prescott, the daughter of James and Repsy Prescott. She died on 26 Dec. 1918. They had no children. He was buried in Green Hill Cemetery, Greensboro.

SEE: Samuel A. Ashe, ed., *Biographical History of North Carolina*, vol. 2 (1905 [portrait]); Robert F. Durden, *The Dukes of Durham, 1865–1929* (1975); *Greensboro Daily News*, 11 Feb. 1930; *North Carolina Biography*, vol. 3 (1929); A. Davis Smith, *Western North Carolina: Historical and Biographical* (1890); *Who's Who in the South* (1927).

TOM E. TERRILL

Odell, John Milton (*20 Jan. 1831–22 July 1910*), merchant and business leader, was born in Randolph County, the son of James, a farmer, and Anna Trogden Odell. After attending Middleton Academy, he taught school for several years, served for a year in the Confederate army (Company M, Twenty-second North Carolina Infantry), and then began his business career as a clerk in the Cedar Falls Manufacturing Company store. Later he joined the firm's successor organization, the Cedar Falls Company. In 1869 he left Cedar Falls and helped form Odell, Curtis, and Company, a mercantile and hardware company in Concord.

In 1872 Odell sold his interest in the Concord firm and moved to Greensboro. There, with his brother, James Alexander Odell, and W. H. Ragan, he opened Odell and Company, a general merchandise store. They gradually shifted to hardware, and in 1884 the concern became the Odell Hardware Company, one of the largest hardware retailers in the South. In the interim, John M. Odell served as a charter member and a director of the National Bank of Greensboro, organized in 1876. In 1877 he bought the McDonald Cotton Mills, which had been built in Concord in 1839, incorporating the firm in 1878 as the Odell Manufacturing Company. As its president, he moved back to Concord permanently in 1880. By 1888 the Odell Manufacturing Company was the largest plaid mill in the South.

Odell was a principal organizer and sometime president of the Durham Cotton Manufacturing Company, the J. M. Odell Manufacturing Company at Bynum, the Salisbury Cotton Mills, the Pearl Cotton Mills in Durham, the Southern Cotton Mills in Bessemer City, and the Cannon Manufacturing Company, the Magnolia Mills, and the Kerr Bag Manufacturing Company in Concord. In his later years he gave most of his attention to the Odell Manufacturing Company, the Kerr company, the Southern Cotton Mills, the concern at Bynum, and the Magnolia Mills. He was also president of the Concord National Bank and the Concord Electric Light Company.

Odell was a Whig-turned-Democrat. He supported the Methodist Episcopal Church, South, of which he was a member, as a Sunday school teacher and a philanthropist. His first wife, whom he married on 9 Mar. 1859, was Rebecca Kirkman, the daughter of Robert Kirkman of Randolph County. They had three children: William R., James T., and Ollie Makepeace Durham. Mrs. Odell died on 13 June 1889. Odell's second wife, whom he married on 4 Aug. 1891, was Mrs. Addie A. White, the daughter of R. W. and Sarah Anne Phifer Allison. Odell was buried in the Odell mausoleum in Concord.

SEE: Samuel A. Ashe, ed., *Biographical History of North Carolina*, vol. 2 (1905 [portrait]); *Charlotte Observer*, 22–23 July 1910; Jerome Dowd, *Sketches of Prominent Living North Carolinians* (1888); Robert F. Durden, *The Dukes of Durham, 1865–1929* (1975); Gary R. Freeze, "Model Mill Men of the New South: Paternalism and Methodism in the Odell Cotton Mills of North Carolina, 1877–1908" (Ph.D. diss., University of North Carolina at Chapel Hill, 1988); A. Davis Smith, *Western North Carolina: Historical and Biographical* (1890); Marjorie W. Young, *Textile Leaders of the South* (1963).

TOM E. TERRILL

Odum, Howard Washington (*24 May 1884–12 Nov. 1954*), American sociologist, was born near Bethlehem, Ga., the son of William Pleasants and Mary Ann Thomas Odum. He was graduated from Emory College, Oxford, Ga., in 1904. Young Odum taught in a rural school in Mississippi, collected materials on Negro life for two dissertations, and "commuted by muleback" to the University of Mississippi, in nearby Oxford, from which he received a master's degree in the classics in 1906. Here he later became a colleague of Professor T. P. Bailey, a recent graduate of Clark University, who aided Odum in the transition to the social sciences and helped him secure a fellowship with G. Stanley Hall at Clark. Odum earned a doctoral degree from Clark University in social psychology (1909) and from Columbia University in sociology (1910). His two dissertations on black studies were published: the first was on religious traits in folk songs, and the second was on black social life.

Returning to Georgia, Odum taught at the University of Georgia and at Emory University. In 1920 he moved to The University of North Carolina, where he spent thirty-four productive years. It was Harry W. Chase, a fellow student at Clark and the new president of The University of North Carolina, who brought Odum to Chapel Hill as Kenan Professor of Sociology and head of the recently formed Department of Social Welfare. Odum established the journal, *Social Forces*, and the Institute for Research in Social Science and promoted a new Department of Planning (1947).

Resuming his writing, Odum cultivated four related areas: race, region, social planning, and folk sociology. His selected writings, *Folk, Region, and Society* (1964), a volume edited by Katharine Jocher and others, has a biography and a bibliography. Recording changes in values and attitudes over forty-five years of Negro life and culture with humane scholarship, Odum did much to improve race relations. His *Rainbow Round My Shoulder* (1928) was a work of literary artistry, a semipoetic account of a black Ulysses. Two other volumes appeared in his "trilogy." The development of his thought—its complexity and its unity—was illustrated as Odum moved from the Negro and Negro folk song to the folk society, from the South as a section and region to regionalism and regional-national planning, from folkways to technicways to stateways, and from social values to social action.

At the request of President Herbert C. Hoover, Odum secured foundation backing for a national study of social trends, persuaded W. F. Ogburn to direct it, and served as assistant director. *Recent Social Trends in the United States* was published in two volumes in 1933. Later he noted the lack of systematic treatment of diverse areas. In regionalism, Odum was at his best. His perceptive study of the South, *An American Epoch* (1930), was preliminary to his *Southern Regions* (1936). In this full-scale analysis, he used cultural indices to delimit the South as an ecological unit in order to demonstrate both the immaturity and the potentials of southern development. Odum sought new standards for the South in race relations, industrialization, and regional planning. Regional planning involves regional-national equilibrium. With Harry Moore, Odum wrote *American Regionalism* (1938), depicting the nation's eight regions. Odum, who believed the South was pursuing an absolute sectionalism, advocated a regional approach.

Odum married Anna Louise Kranz (1888–1965), also a student of Stanley Hall at Clark University. They had three children: Eugene, a distinguished professor of zoology at the University of Georgia; Howard Thomas, professor of zoology at the University of Florida; and Mary Frances (Mrs. Phillip Schinan) of Chapel Hill.

Odum was a builder and "a scholar in the grand manner" who became a public figure. He brought over $650,000 in funding to The University of North Carolina, and his ready access to foundations was the wonder of all who knew him. Under his direction, the Institute for Research in Social Science published 87 books and 322 articles, many in *Social Forces*. Odum's own output consisted of 22 volumes and some 200 articles. In the throes of production, he slept little and made full use of his great energy. Called a "promoter," Odum selected younger men and attended to the funding and publication of their projects. No man for the ivory tower, he placed emphasis on using as well as obtaining knowledge.

He advised public officials and participated in setting up organizations devoted to regional development. Certain projects that later succeeded had been outlined earlier in his published work and correspondence, indicating that his fine imagination was capable of anticipation.

Many honors came to Odum, including the presidency of the American Sociological Association in 1930. He received honorary degrees from Emory University (LL.D., 1931), the College of the Ozarks (Litt.D., 1935), Harvard University (LL.D., 1939), and Clark University (L.H.D., 1941). His work in race relations brought Odum the Catholic Conference of the South's award in 1943 and the Bernays Award in 1945. Resolved not to leave the South permanently, he held various visiting professorships for brief periods. In 1953 Odum received the O. Max Gardner Award for the faculty member "who in the current year has made the greatest contribution to the welfare of the human race." A select herd of Jersey cattle that he kept won one of the few awards of Master Breeder from the American Jersey Cattle Association. His whimsical comment that his bulls were worth more than his books was widely quoted.

Many who feared the impact of his new ideas never realized the true conservatism of his thought. To students who advanced simplistic explanations, Odum replied: "That is true, but what else is true?" "Academic statesman of the South at its best," Odum at his death was called the "Eli Whitney of the Modern South" by the *Washington Post*, which said he inspired a revolution.

Odum retired in June 1954 at age seventy and died the following November. His last words, said to a good friend visiting him in the hospital, were: "Everything is going to be all right."

SEE: Wayne D. Brazil, *Howard W. Odum: The Building Years, 1884–1930* (1988); *International Encyclopedia of the Social Sciences* (1968); Howard Washington Odum Papers (Southern Historical Collection, University of North Carolina, Chapel Hill); George B. Tindall, "The Significance of Howard W. Odum to Southern History: A Preliminary Estimate," *Journal of Southern History* 24 (August 1958); *Who Was Who in the South*, vol. 3 (1966).

RUPERT B. VANCE

Oertel, Johannes Adam Simon (3 Nov. 1823–9 Dec. 1909), artist and Episcopal clergyman, was born in Fürth, near Nuremberg, Bavaria, the son of Thomas Friedrich and Maria Magdalena Mennensdorfer Oertel. Expecting to become a missionary, he began to study under a Lutheran pastor, but he demonstrated such clear artistic talent that he was persuaded to study art. As a pupil of a Munich engraver, J. M. Enzing-Müller, he was influenced by the painting of Wilhelm von Kaulbach.

In 1848, with his parents and two brothers, Oertel moved to Newark, N.J., and began offering lessons in drawing. In 1851 he married Julia Adelaide Torrey, one of his pupils, and in the same year made plans for a series of four paintings that would depict the redemption of mankind. This was to be the great work of his life, and for nearly half a century he pursued this goal. During the period 1852–57 he was employed in engraving banknotes and painting portraits, and in 1857–58 he prepared designs for the painted ceiling of the U.S. House of Representatives. For a brief time during the Civil War he was with the Army of the Potomac, preparing to paint several war scenes. Later in the 1860s, while living in Westerly, R.I., he painted a picture known originally as *Saved; or, An Emblematic Representation of Christian Faith.* Afterwards known as *The Rock of Ages*, it was widely reproduced and distributed around the world. A faulty copyright entry denied Oertel the revenue that he might otherwise have received from this work.

Oertel worked in a variety of mediums. In addition to engraving and drawing, he painted in oil and watercolors, modeled figures, and carved wood. His subjects were human figures, animals, landscapes, flowers, and marine and still life. During a productive period of forty-six years, for nine of which he kept no records, he produced almost 1,200 major works.

After leaving Rhode Island, Oertel moved to Tarrytown, on the Hudson River, N.Y. While there, he and his family met a young art student, Laura Norwood, from Lenoir, N.C., who was an Episcopalian. Oertel had recently been confirmed in the Episcopal church and served as a lay reader before his ordination as deacon in June 1867. Miss Norwood impressed upon him the great need for an Episcopal clergyman in her home community. She also described a comfortable setting in which he might express his artistic talents and perhaps even find it possible to work on his projected masterpiece.

In 1869 Oertel, his wife, and their children moved to Lenoir, where he served St. James's Church and two nearby missions: the Chapel of Peace and the Chapel of Rest. In 1871, at Bishop Thomas Atkinson's urging, Oertel was ordained to the priesthood. Afterwards he established a school for girls in Lenoir where he, his wife, and daughter were employed as teachers. When the Episcopal church in Tarrytown bought a new organ, it sent the old one to St. James's. Oertel worked it over and installed it; he also carved a handsome reredos for the church in Lenoir, which is still in place. Concerned about the poor in his community, Oertel ordered groceries and supplies in large quantities from New York and generously distributed them to the needy. To supplement his meager income, he often traveled to Wilmington, Charlotte, and elsewhere in North Carolina as well as to Rock Hill, S.C., to paint portraits, leaving his wife and daughter to operate the school. For a few months in 1874 he was in charge of St. James's Church while the rector was away.

In 1876 Oertel was obliged, largely for financial reasons, to leave Lenoir and paint wherever he could find commissions: Florida, Washington, D.C., Sewanee and Nashville, Tenn., and St. Louis, Mo. In 1876 he completed the painting of a North Carolina centennial flag, commissioned by ladies of the state, to be displayed at the Centennial Exposition in Philadelphia. Returning to North Carolina in 1879, he was rector of Grace Church, Morganton, for eighteen months. In the period 1889–91 he was an instructor of fine arts at Washington University in St. Louis.

For the last eighteen years of his life, his sons made it possible for him to work without concern for earning a living, and it was during this period that he completed the "Redemption" series that he had so long anticipated. *The Dispensations of Promise and the Law, The Redeemer, The Dispensation of the Holy Spirit*, and *The Consumation of Redemption* were given to the University of the South at Sewanee, Tenn. In 1902 Oertel received an honorary doctor of divinity degree from the University of the South. His paintings and carvings are owned by the National Gallery, the Church of the Incarnation, and the National Cathedral in Washington, D.C., and by churches in New York City; Glen Cove, Long Island, N.Y.; Lenoir, N.C.; St. Louis, Mo.; Jackson, Tenn.; Emmorton, where Oertel served briefly as rector, and Belair, Md. His popular engraving, *Pulling Down the Statue of George III by the "Sons of Freedom" at the Bowling Green, City of New York, July, 1776* (1859), is often reproduced.

Oertel was buried in Vienna, Va., where he had been living with one of his sons. He and his wife were the parents of four children: Henry B., Eugene Theodore, John Frederick, and Mary Magdalene.

SEE: *Charlotte Observer*, 1 May 1927; *DAB*, vol. 13 (1934); Thomas Felix Hickerson, *Happy Valley: History and Genealogy* (1940); *The Home Magazine* (Minneapolis, Minn.), 4 Sept. 1904; Thomas Lenoir Papers (Manuscript Department, Duke University Library, Durham); *Lenoir News Topic*, 19 Feb. 1945, 27 Oct. 1971; *North Carolina Churchman*, February 1953; Mrs. J. A. Oertel, *Hand in Hand through Happy Valley* (1881); J. F. Oertel, *A Vision Realized: A Life Story of Rev. J. A. Oertel* (1917); D. M. Stauffer, *American Engravers* (1907).

WILLIAM S. POWELL

O'Hara, James Edward (26 Feb. 1844–15 Sept. 1905), congressman, Halifax county commissioner, black politician, educator, and lawyer, was born in New York City, the son of an Irish seaman and a West Indian woman. At age six, he moved with his parents to the West Indies. It is said that he was a resident of St. Croix, Virgin Islands (at the time a Danish possession), St. Thomas, Virgin Islands, and Jamaica. Eventually, he returned to New York and, in the fall of 1862, accompanied a group of missionaries to eastern North Carolina, then occupied by Federal troops at the onset of the Civil War.

After he embarked on a teaching career in his adopted state, O'Hara's abilities as an educator became well known among his fellow blacks and served as an impetus for his political career. During the early years of Reconstruction, he was called upon to perform secretarial work at various meetings in which black leaders participated. O'Hara served as secretary for the North Carolina Freedman's Convention of 1866. The following year he was secretary for the North Carolina Republican conventions of March and September, the executive committee of the state Republican party, and the Wayne County Republican Convention. (In 1867, as a resident of Wayne County, he applied for U.S. citizenship.) His clerical work in politics continued when he served as engrossing clerk for the North Carolina Constitutional Convention of 1868 and for the North Carolina House of Representatives in 1868 and 1869.

Having studied law at Howard University in Washington, D.C., O'Hara was admitted to the bar in 1873, and he immediately established a busy practice in Enfield, Halifax County. Throughout Reconstruction, he was active in Republican party politics in North Carolina. He became a member of the Halifax County Board of Commissioners, serving as chairman from 1872 to 1876.

Halifax County was a part of the Second Congressional District, which became known as the "Black Second" because of the large Negro population in that part of eastern North Carolina. In 1874 O'Hara failed to win his party's nomination for the congressional seat from the Black Second, which went to John Adams Hyman, North Carolina's first black congressman. This defeat was offset the following year, when O'Hara was chosen to represent Halifax County in the North Carolina Constitutional Convention of 1875. During the convention, he opposed Conservative party efforts to discontinue popular elections at the county level.

With the new constitution preventing local popular elections, O'Hara had no chance to regain his position on the Halifax County Board of Commissioners. This setback led him once again to seek the Republican nomination for the Second District's congressional seat. After winning the nomination in 1878, he was defeated in a contested election by Conservative William Hodge (Cap'n Buck) Kitchin of Scotland Neck. Although he failed to receive his party's nomination in 1880, O'Hara finally won the Black Second congressional seat in 1882. The opposition Democrats had not placed a candidate in the field, hoping to widen the Republican party's factional differences by allowing the Republicans to fight it out among themselves. Moreover, infighting growing out of the state Prohibition campaign of 1881 had weakened the Democrats. O'Hara had backed the anti-Prohibitionists' cause, a stand that strengthened his support among black voters.

O'Hara was the second black to represent North Carolina in the U.S. House of Representatives, serving in the Forty-eighth and Forty-ninth Congresses (1883–87). Unlike Hyman, who preceded him, O'Hara was an extremely active and capable congressman during both his terms. He was an untiring worker, especially in behalf of his North Carolina constituents—black and white. O'Hara sought appropriations for the improvement of waterways and roads, public education, animal husbandry, and public buildings in his state and district. As a member of the House Committee on Invalid Persons, he worked to obtain appropriations for the relief of Civil War victims, both veterans and their relatives, and sought to alleviate the sufferings of Negroes in the aftermath of the war. In matters pertaining to his race, he attempted to obtain equal rights for blacks in public places and equal accommodations in public transportation. O'Hara's votes in Congress reflected, for the most part,

an unbiased and intelligent consideration for the betterment of his nation, his state, and his district. He did not appear to allow party politics to hold sway over his principles.

Having won his second term in Congress by defeating Democrat Frederick A. Woodard of Wilson County, O'Hara failed to garner the necessary votes in his third attempt, losing to Democrat Furnifold M. Simmons of Craven County in 1886. Simmons took advantage of existing divisions among the Republicans, who had held two conventions and nominated two candidates: O'Hara and Israel B. Abbott, another black. An ugly racial contest developed when Abbott, claiming to be a pure-blooded Negro, questioned O'Hara's right to represent his race in view of his mixed blood. O'Hara tactfully refrained to respond, but the opposition Democrats seized upon the split among the Republicans and won the election.

Throughout the congressional campaign of 1888, O'Hara actively supported George Allen Mebane, a black, who ran against the successful Republican candidate, Henry Plummer Cheatham. Cheatham, who became North Carolina's third black congressman, was accused of having close ties with the Democrats, whereas O'Hara strongly favored a "pure" Republican party. In the 1890s he adamantly opposed the Fusionist movement, when the new Populist party joined forces with the Republicans.

From the time O'Hara entered public life, he urged his fellow Negroes to obtain a good education. At political meetings, fairs, and other public gatherings, he continually stressed the need for better teachers and public schools to assist blacks in rising above a servile status. He deplored the fact that North Carolina lacked good teachers, believing that this was one of the chief reasons for the backwardness of the state's educational system. His interest in education extended beyond public schools, for he was among the first of his race to advocate a state university for Negroes in North Carolina.

On leaving Congress, O'Hara returned to his law practice in Enfield. After 1890 he moved with his wife, the former Elizabeth E. Harris, to New Bern. There his son, Raphael, joined his law firm. New Bern remained O'Hara's residence until his death.

SEE: *Biog. Dir. Am. Cong.* (1961); *Congressional Record*, 48th-49th Cong. (1883–87); Goldsboro *Carolina Messenger*, 1874–76; Goldsboro *Messenger*, 1874–84; *Journal of the Constitutional Convention of the State of North Carolina at Its Session of 1868* (1868); *Journal of the Constitutional Convention of the State of North Carolina Held in 1875* (1875); New Bern *Daily Journal*, 1882–1905; Benjamin Perley Poore, comp., *The Political Register and Congressional Directory: A Statistical Record of the Federal Official, Legislative, Executive, and Judicial, of the United States of America* (1887); Raleigh *Register*, 1884; *Senate Report*, no. 693, 46th Cong., 2d sess.; Tarborough *Southerner*, 1876–1900.

JOSEPH E. ELMORE

O'Kelly, Berry (ca. 1861–14 Mar. 1931), merchant, realtor, banker, and philanthropist, was called at his death "the most prominent leader of the Negro race in Wake County and outstanding as an educator and religious chieftain of his race." He was born in Orange County to a slave mother, Frances Stroud, who died soon after his birth. Relatives of hers, who raised him, gave him the family surname and reputedly the first name of an uncle. He later moved to Wake County to live with other relatives who had been among the first settlers of Method, a small post–Civil War community west of Raleigh. These included an uncle, William Patterson, and a first cousin, Nelson O'Kelly. He acquired his education in an early postwar public school in Orange County and in the village school at Method, then called Mason Village.

As a youth O'Kelly began doing general chores and driving for a white family in Raleigh. At about age twenty-two, he became a clerk in the store that had opened in Mason Village in 1873; by then it was owned by C. N. Woods, one of its organizers. With a hundred dollars saved from his earnings, O'Kelly bought an interest in the store, which was renamed Woods and O'Kelly, and acquired sole ownership when Woods moved to Oklahoma in 1889. He continued to travel by horse and buggy to buy produce, eggs, butter, and chickens to sell and became a commission and wholesale merchant. Situated alongside a spur track of the Southern Railroad, which also paralleled the highway then linking Raleigh and Durham, the store prospered not only as the principal supplier to Method residents but also as the unloading facility for goods sought by affluent residents of Raleigh. Eventually the business owned two large warehouses, and O'Kelly's trade included transatlantic shipments of goods to ports in Africa and other foreign points.

In October 1890 the U.S. government established a post office in the Mason Village community, changing its name to Method and naming O'Kelly its first postmaster.

O'Kelly's business enterprises in Method and in Raleigh were extensive. In the early 1900s he established the Peoples Investment Company, of which he was president. About 1910 he formed a partnership with John T. Turner, proprietor of a grocery store in Oberlin, another postwar Negro village west of Raleigh, and they organized the Raleigh Shoe Company at 15 East Hargett Street downtown. The partnership continued until about 1925, after which the business was O'Kelly's alone, with Turner's son Jerome managing the store. At about the same time O'Kelly purchased and remodeled a brick commercial structure near the corner of South Wilmington and East Hargett streets. Known as the O'Kelly Building, it leased space to other black-operated businesses such as cleaning and tailoring services and a building and loan association. From this and nearby buildings were operated businesses in which O'Kelly was owner and/or officer. Among them, he was president of the Acme Realty Company, board chairman of the Eagle Life Insurance Company, and principal stockholder in the *Raleigh Independent*, a Negro newspaper published between 1917 and 1926.

O'Kelly was also active in banking. When the Durham-based Mechanics and Farmers Bank established an office in Raleigh, he headed the stock sales committee and negotiated the purchase of a building site for the bank, which opened in January 1923. In 1928 he became vice-president and manager of the Raleigh branch; later he was named chairman of the local board. In the bank holiday of 1929, only two banks in Raleigh remained open: the Wachovia Bank and Trust Company and the Mechanics and Farmers Bank.

Over the years O'Kelly acquired considerable property. Weathering the financial crisis of 1929, his real estate holdings at the time of his death two years later had a valuation of $145,855—a figure that the *News and Observer* particularly noted when the estate papers were made public. Included were large tracts in and near Method and about thirty-seven parcels of land in Raleigh.

O'Kelly wielded strong political influence, demonstrating more than once his ability to secure black votes for bond elections and other causes. In 1911 Raleigh and Wake County leaders, with his assistance, were successful in having a major western highway from Raleigh routed through Cary rather than Leesville. In the mid-1910s he helped secure passage of a bond creating a new road district between Raleigh and Cary. He also persuaded the county commissioners to locate one section of the new pavement in such a way as to avoid bypassing Method and isolating its churches and school, as well as the O'Kelly store and warehouses. At the time of his death, Raleigh attorney J. M. Templeton, Jr., wrote: "Not only those of his own race, but all movements for civic progress had his support and his influence . . . extended beyond his own color and was felt in school and road elections in western Wake during the last two [1911–31] decades." Admittedly neither Republican nor Democrat, O'Kelly was said by his friend and business colleague, Charles R. Frazer, Sr., to have believed in "the best man for the job" and to have organized a civic and business league to fight the practice of ward heeling.

In his later years O'Kelly's chief interest was in promoting education, especially for blacks. As chairman of his school committee, he set about upgrading the small school in Method that had opened soon after the Civil War. In 1914 it became a county teacher-training and industrial school, one of only three in North Carolina, and was named the Berry O'Kelly Training School. O'Kelly contributed heavily of time, money, and real estate to improve the campus and curriculum and raised additional funds by obtaining small gifts from others in the community. He was instrumental in consolidating the school with three other small rural Wake County schools and transforming it into a boarding school that drew pupils from throughout the state. In 1919 it was one of the first Negro schools to establish a nine-month term, and by 1923 it was one of only three black public schools accredited by the state. All five members of its first graduating class that year entered college. By the 1927–28 school year, the campus included eight buildings. O'Kelly succeeded in enlisting the aid of foundations, beginning with the Slater Fund in the 1910s. While participating in the annual Tuskegee Conference held by Booker T. Washington, O'Kelly met philanthropist Julius Rosenwald, of the Sears Roebuck Foundation, who made gifts to the school in the 1920s. Visiting Wake County in 1928 to dedicate a new auditorium at the O'Kelly school, Rosenwald noted his pleasure in being associated with "my friend, Berry O'Kelly, the man who has really made this school possible." With the gradual improvement of Negro schools in other counties, the number of boarding pupils at Method decreased, and the boarding department was eventually eliminated. Following educational changes resulting from desegregation in the 1950s, both high school and elementary grades on the campus had been phased out by 1966. O'Kelly was also a trustee of Kittrell College.

Although opposed to the principle of separate state fairs for blacks and whites, O'Kelly once served as president of the North Carolina Negro State Fair and secured Booker T. Washington as speaker. O'Kelly was a member of the State Interracial Commission and served on its executive committee, a member and auditor of the Raleigh Union Society, and a life member of the National Negro Business League, which he and Booker T. Washington had founded. He was a Mason and an Odd Fellow and served on the executive committee of their local organizations.

A member and major supporter of St. James's African

Methodist Episcopal Church in Method, O'Kelly was a trustee, a steward, and a teacher in the Sunday school; he was a lay member of the North Carolina General A.M.E. Conference.

His first wife was Chanie Ligon (4 July 1863–7 July 1902), the daughter of one of the earliest Method settlers, Lafayette Ligon, for whose family Ligon Street was named. She left no children. In 1923 O'Kelly married Marguerite Bell (1893–1967), of Bayonne, N.J., who had been a teacher in the Method elementary school since 1921. Their daughter Beryl (b. 5 Nov. 1929) married Joseph Brooks, of Long Beach, Cal., where she became a school principal. Beryl Street in Method was named for her, as O'Kelly Street had been named for her father. O'Kelly's widow later married Algernon Thomas White (1887–1955), who had been his secretary and business partner in the Method community enterprises and who succeeded him as postmaster there. White's son John Owen and his wife Harveleigh M. White, the third and fourth postmasters, became civic leaders in Method.

The Method community underwent a series of changes beginning in 1960, when it was annexed to the city of Raleigh. In 1969 the one-hundred-unit "RICH" housing project opened on part of the Berry O'Kelly Training School site. The O'Kelly store buildings were demolished after his death.

O'Kelly became ill in mid-February 1931 and died in St. Agnes's Hospital four weeks later. Funeral services were conducted from the auditorium of the school named for him, followed by burial in the nearby churchyard of St. James's A.M.E. Church at 608 Method Road.

SEE: Thomas Byrd and Jerry Miller, *Around and about Cary* (1970); E. A. Cox, "The Berry O'Kelly Training School: A Tribute and a History," *North Carolina Teachers Record* 2 (May 1931); L. M. Mason, "Historical Sketch of . . . Method" (Charles N. Hunter Papers, Manuscript Department, Duke University Library, Durham); *Norfolk* (Va.) *Journal and Guide*, 11 July 1925, 21 Mar. 1931; Berry O'Kelly High School, *The Student's Guide* 1 (January 1925); Raleigh *Carolinian*, 28 Oct. 1961; Raleigh *News and Observer*, 15 July 1928, 15, 26 Mar. 1931, 21 Oct. 1964, 24 Jan. 1967; Elizabeth Davis Reid, guest ed., "Black Studies," *Raleigh* [Magazine] 3 (December 1971); Wake County Deeds (Wake County Courthouse, Raleigh); Richard Barry Westin, "The State and Segregated Schools: Negro Public Education in North Carolina, 1863–1933" (Ph.D. diss., Duke University, 1966).

ELIZABETH DAVIS REID MURRAY

O'Kelly, James (pre-1741–16 Oct. 1826), clergyman, was an early Methodist itinerant who seceded from the Methodist church and headed a movement that became the southern Christian church. In 1931 this denomination and the Congregationalists formed the Congregational Christian church. A merger between the latter denomination and the Evangelical and Reformed church in 1957 resulted in the formation of the United Church of Christ.

Of Irish ancestry, O'Kelly was born either in Ireland or in the colony of Virginia. Nothing is known of his early life except that, according to his statement, he was born of poor parentage. He married Elizabeth Meeks, reportedly on 25 June 1759, and in 1787 they were listed among the homeowners of Mecklenburg County, Va. About 1797 the O'Kellys moved to Chatham County, N.C., and were living there when the minister died. They had two sons, John and William. John was apparently a farmer. William represented Chatham County in the North Carolina legislature in 1805 and in four later

sessions. He was elected to the state senate in 1818 and died the following year while still in office. He left many known descendants.

In 1775 James O'Kelly joined the Methodist Society in Virginia, and three years later his name first appeared in the records of the Virginia Methodist Conference as a minister on trial. At the same meeting, he was assigned to assist Beverly Allen in the New Hope Circuit in North Carolina. His popularity and influence as a preacher grew rapidly in the area that he traveled.

When the American Revolution began, O'Kelly attempted to obey the instructions of John Wesley and remain neutral. However, after he had been robbed, falsely accused, half starved, twice captured, and generally mistreated by the British forces, he became an outright Patriot. He related that he stood his draft, engaged in exhausting military marches, and served in the army during the hostilities.

The Methodist itinerants were not ordained clergymen but evangelists within the Church of England. Consequently, the sacraments of the church could be administered to the members of the society only by official Anglican priests. Because of the Revolution, there were few such ministers to serve the needs of the increasing number of Methodists. As a result, when the Virginia Methodist Conference met in 1779, O'Kelly joined with eighteen of his fellow circuit riders in approving a decision to appoint a committee from among their number to administer the sacraments and to ordain ministers. This action was condemned as illegal by Francis Asbury, who had assumed leadership of the Methodists during the war. As a result of his decision, the Methodist Episcopal church was organized at the celebrated 1784 Christmas conference in Baltimore, with Thomas Coke and Francis Asbury ordained as bishops and James O'Kelly and his fellow evangelists ordained as ministers.

A period of intense activity followed during which Asbury appointed O'Kelly district superintendent in a Virginia area, where the minister soon became one of the most efficient cohorts of the bishop. Tributes to his rise in stature as a preacher were paid by his colleagues, including Freeborn Garrettson, John Kobler, James Meacham, Richard N. Venable, Philip Gatch, and William McKendree. Among his actions was a fearless denunciation of slavery; as a testimony to his conviction, on 5 Mar. 1785 he manumitted the only slave he ever owned. Four years later, he wrote and published a condemnation of the institution entitled *Essay on Negro-Slavery*.

Despite his ministerial success and his close association with Asbury, O'Kelly began to have misgivings about the increasing autocracy of the bishop. While the southern clergyman had acquiesced in the elevation of Asbury to the bishopric, he did not wish to see the rise of an infallible hierarchy and he feared that individual ministers were in danger of losing the right to express a voice in their affairs. He was offended when the venerable Wesley's name was dropped from the American General Methodist Conference rolls, and he opposed the formation of a Bishop's Council in 1789, although he was made a member of that body.

Rising dissension came to a head at the General Conference held in Baltimore in 1792. O'Kelly proposed that legislation be passed giving each clergyman the right to accept or protest his appointment to territory by the bishop. After lengthy and acrimonious debate of the issue, the Conference defeated O'Kelly's proposal by a majority vote. Feeling that he could not accept this ruling and its implications, O'Kelly, together with several ministers of similar convictions, left the Conference and returned to Virginia. As efforts were continued to reach a compromise, the Virginia ministers petitioned Asbury to meet with them to discuss the government of the church. The bishop's refusal was delivered to the Methodists when they met for their conference at Mannakintown in 1793. Despairing of any remedy for what he considered to be an impossible situation, James O'Kelly then seceded from the Methodist Episcopal church, accompanied by a number of his ministerial colleagues and their parishioners.

On 4 Aug. 1794 the secessionists met in Surry County, Va., to organize their own church. The name "Republican Methodists," denoting opposition to an episcopal form of government, had been used for two years previously. Because of its similarity to Thomas Jefferson's growing political party, this appellation was abandoned, although a small group continued to use it for a number of years. The decision was made that "Christian" was an appropriate name for the church. Furthermore, the organizers declared that the Bible was a sufficient creed, and they recognized the right of individual interpretation of the Scriptures. Government was to be by majority vote in the local congregations as well as in the annual conferences. The Surry meeting was the beginning of the southern Christian church, which was never connected with the Christian church headed by Barton W. Stone. (In 1922 it united with the New England Christians, who were followers of Abner Jones and Elias Smith.)

The formation of the new church group, often referred to as "O'Kellyites," touched off the publication of a veritable shower of pamphlets—by both the Methodists and the Christians—containing charges and countercharges of heresy, personal ambition, illegal actions, and the flagrant use of falsehoods. O'Kelly added fuel to the fire in 1798, when he published *The Author's Apology for Protesting against the Methodist Episcopal Government.* The next year he wrote a pamphlet, entitled *An Address to the Christian Church under the Similitude of an Elect Lady and Her Children,* urging all Christian denominations to consider a general ecumenical plan. This idea, which was far ahead of its time, was generally either ignored or ridiculed. After its author published *A Vindication of the Author's Apology, with Reflections on the Reply* in 1801, the battle subsided. The following year, a reconciliatory meeting took place between O'Kelly and Asbury.

The founder of the new church devoted his remaining years to the task of building a denomination. This did not prove to be easy, as many disagreed with his views. He firmly believed that the Holy Trinity was composed of Father, Son, and Holy Spirit as three distinct persons and not one tripartite God. While he respected freedom of choice in the mode of baptism, he strongly preferred sprinkling to immersion, and he would agree to no written man-made creed for the church. In addition, O'Kelly vigorously opposed the increasingly popular institution of slavery as unchristian. In support of his efforts, he published *Hymns and Spiritual Songs Designed for the Use of Christians* (1816), *The Divine Oracles Consulted; or, An Appeal to the Law and Testimony* (1820), *Letters From Heaven Consulted* (1822), and *The Prospect Before Us, By Way of an Address to the Christian Church* (1824).

No portrait or accurate physical description of O'Kelly has been found. *The Ordination of Francis Asbury,* which hangs in Lovely Lane Museum, Baltimore, includes every person known to have been present on the occasion. The artist, Thomas Coke Ruckle, who had no description of O'Kelly, solved his problem by positioning the figure in front of him so as to obscure almost all of O'Kelly's face and figure. Nevertheless, there is abundant testimony to the magnetic personality and influence of the minister. His friends and admirers donated land and built a church for him near his Chatham County home and named it O'Kelly Chapel. The clergyman preached in this church as long as he was physically able and was buried in its adjacent cemetery when he died. The Christian church erected a fitting marker over his grave; another impressive memorial stands in the center of the campus at Elon College. However, the greatest memorial to James O'Kelly is the church that he founded, which survived and grew slowly but steadily into a denomination.

SEE: Eli Washington Caruthers, *Revolutionary Incidents and Sketches of Character Chiefly in the "Old North State"* (1954); Elmer T. Clark, J. Manning Potts, and Jacob S. Payton, eds., *The Journal and Letters of Francis Asbury,* 3 vols. (1958); Charles Franklin Kilgore, *The James O'Kelly Schism in the Methodist Episcopal Church* (1963); Wilbur Ernest MacClenny, *The Life of Rev. James O'Kelly* (1910); *Minutes of the Annual Conferences of the Methodist Episcopal Church, for the Years 1773–1828,* 3 vols. (1840); James O'Kelly Collection (Church History Room, Elon College); Records of Chatham County (Chatham County Courthouse, Pittsboro); Records of Mecklenburg County, Va. (Mecklenburg County Courthouse, Boydton).

DURWARD T. STOKES

Olds, Frederick Augustus (12 Oct. 1853–2 July 1935), historian, newspaper columnist, lecturer, and editor, probably was born in North Carolina. He was the son of Louis and Pauline Evans Olds, natives of Pitt County. His father, an attorney, was a graduate of Randolph Macon College, and his mother was a graduate of Salem College. Following the death of his mother, he was raised by a relative in Hillsborough and attended school in Cary before enrolling in the Virginia Military School. In the 1870s Olds moved to Raleigh to enter the insurance field, and for six years he served as secretary of the chamber of commerce.

Recognizing that his interests were in newspaper work, he became a reporter for the Raleigh *News* and later was city editor of the Raleigh *News and Observer.* In 1874 he enlisted as a private in the National Guard. In 1877 he was appointed to the staff of Governor Zebulon B. Vance, and when the State Guard was organized in the same year, he was named state ordnance officer and quartermaster general, serving until 1891." At that time, the old State Arsenal was located on Capitol Square. Olds came to be referred to as "Colonel" Olds.

Perhaps his greatest contribution to the state was in the preservation and dissemination of North Carolina history. Olds was an early advocate of "social history"— history about and for the people. Newspaper editor Samuel A. Ashe, who began promoting state history through his editorials, no doubt inspired his young reporter to begin his own endeavors in that area. During the administration of Governor Alfred M. Scales, Olds started collecting land grants, marriage bonds, wills, early court proceedings, and inventories of estates, as well as portraits and photographs of North Carolina governors and other noted citizens. These were deposited in the State Library, then housed in the old supreme court building. The records and artifacts, arranged chronologically beginning with the first settlements and including portraits of Sir Walter Raleigh and Queen Elizabeth, the John White drawings, and the baptism of Virginia Dare, eventually filled two display cases in the library. The compilation, in time, was considered to be an outstanding historical collection. By 1930 it was estimated to contain some 30,000 items. Records from the state's counties and several generations of citizens were made available to the public for research and learning. Colonel Olds, after several years of collecting, was belatedly put on the state payroll at a nominal salary.

Olds received numerous requests for information and advice in the preparation of historical pageants and the preservation of such historic sites as the Constitution House in Halifax and the Philip Alston House in Moore County. He was a member of many boards and commissions such as those dealing with the Battle of Alamance, the sesquicentennial of the Battle of Guilford Court House, and the Andrew Johnson House. Frequently he was asked to contribute historical articles to the *News and Observer* and the *Progressive Farmer*. For many years he also wrote for the *Orphan's Friend and Masonic Journal*, *Uplift*, *Prison News*, *Carolina Motor News*, *Manufacturers Record*, and other journals as well as for the state's newspapers. He compiled an *Abstract of North Carolina Wills* and published a popular booklet, *Story of the Counties of North Carolina*. To spread the word of North Carolina's history, he also lectured at State College summer sessions, at normal school institutes, and in the public schools. One listener commented: "He knew how to brush his enthusiasm off on others."

Serving as a modern-day Pied Piper to children all over North Carolina was probably his greatest joy. Olds worked with Boy Scouts and Girl Scouts, formed "Sunshine Clubs," and took school groups on tours of Raleigh and other interesting locations in the state. His methods were sometimes regarded as unorthodox, but his overall purpose was to entertain as well as to instruct. His greatest delight was "to weave around each object displayed a romantic halo" that pleased those who heard him, even if it became necessary, as at least one newspaper suggested, for teachers to clarify historical discrepancies. Olds also conducted tours for convention delegates and visiting dignitaries (such as King Albert of Belgium, Marshal Foch, Sir Esme Howard, and Lady Alicia North, a descendant of Lord North, who gained fame during the American Revolution).

During his lifetime he received awards from numerous civic, educational, and patriotic organizations. The Fred A. Olds Hall of History and a Raleigh public school named in his honor were evidence of an appreciation of his contributions to the community. Later generations of historians regarded him as an "incurable romanticist," forgetting his "magnificent contribution to the people of the state as a vigorous, crusading writer, a great lover of the people of his state and its traditions." On his eighty-first birthday, Olds commented: "I have had plenty of fun, but I am not through yet by a long way." Nevertheless, he died shortly afterwards and was buried in Oakwood Cemetery, Raleigh.

Olds married Mrs. Kate Cannon Primrose in 1878, and they were the parents of two sons: Douglas, who died in 1906, unmarried; and Frederick Charles, whose son of the same name lived in Albuquerque, N.Mex. Mrs. Olds died in 1905.

SEE: M. R. Dunnagan, "Colonel Frederick Augustus Olds" (manuscript, North Carolina State Archives, Raleigh); Raleigh *News and Observer*, 3 July 1935; *Raleigh Times*, 18 Apr. 1932, 10 July 1955; Harry S. Warren, "Colonel Frederick Augustus Olds and the Founding of the North Carolina Museum of History" (M.A. thesis, East Carolina University, 1988).

BETH G. CRABTREE

Olive, Eugene Irving (*7 Dec. 1890–6 Mar. 1968*), clergyman and college administrator, was born in south-

western rural Wake County, the son of William Johnson and Ellen Bland Olive. He received his early education in the Wake County schools and at Buies Creek Academy, from which he was graduated in 1906.

That fall he entered Wake Forest College and in 1910 was graduated *cum laude* with a bachelor of arts degree. In the latter year he was ordained in the Baptist ministry. As an undergraduate, Olive wrote for college publications, was active in the local literary society, and became a member of Omicron Delta Kappa (leadership fraternity). After graduation he spent five years as a public schoolteacher in Cumberland County, where he also preached in Baptist churches.

In the late summer of 1915 he entered the Southern Baptist Theological Seminary, Louisville, Ky., receiving a master of theology degree in 1918. Olive then served as pastor of the First Baptist Church, Dunn (1918–21); First Baptist Church, Mount Airy (1921–24); University Baptist Church, Chapel Hill (1924–33); First Baptist Church, North Wilkesboro (1933–40); and Wake Forest Baptist Church (1940–47). At Wake Forest, he also was chaplain of Wake Forest College, of which he had been a trustee (1934–40), and began a successful ministry in Christian higher education that continued for the rest of his life. While at Mount Airy, Olive attended the Baptist World Alliance in Stockholm, Sweden (1923), and spent some time touring the Continent and the United Kingdom.

For one year (November 1941–November 1942) he was editor of the *Biblical Recorder*, the weekly journal of North Carolina Baptists, and for eighteen months (1945–46) he was on leave from the Wake Forest pastorate to solicit financial support for the expansion of Wake Forest College on its old campus. As much or more than any other denominational leader in the state, Olive was instrumental in appraising and implementing the offer of the Z. Smith Reynolds Foundation to move Wake Forest College from its century-old site at Wake Forest, N.C., to the new and modern Reynolda campus in the western section of Winston-Salem (1956).

Olive had resigned his pastorate in Wake Forest in mid-1947 to become director of the college's public relations and alumni activities. In that post he managed innovative files and organizations of alumni, not only in North Carolina but also in adjacent states. He was, in effect, assistant president of the college because of the precarious health of President Thurman D. Kitchin. Olive represented the college at many of the conferences and committee meetings held to consider the offer of the Reynolds Foundation. These discussions culminated in a special session of the North Carolina Baptist State Convention's Council on Christian Education held at the Wake Forest campus on 11 Apr. 1946, at a subsequent special joint session of the council, and at the convention held in Greensboro on 30 July.

As plans for the new campus began to materialize, Olive moved to Winston-Salem (1952), and, while continuing his aggressive alumni leadership, was virtually the administrator of the college. Those who knew of his work praised him for his leadership and wise planning during those formative years of the new campus operation.

Olive also played a key role in the trustees' decision to invite Harold Wayland Tribble, of Andover Newton Theological Seminary, Newton Center, Mass., to become the new head of the college. Tribble, who had received an honorary doctor of laws degree from Wake Forest in 1948, became president in mid-1950, succeeding Dr. Kitchin, who had retired that spring after serving for twenty years.

It was Olive who initiated and negotiated the sale (1953) of the old Wake Forest campus to the Southern

Baptist Convention as the site of the projected South-eastern Baptist Theological Seminary. His next four years of combined service as director of public relations and of alumni activities centered around enlisting the support of graduates and friends for the new campus. His efforts led to a successful conclusion in 1956, when the new Reynolda campus in Winston-Salem was occupied. From 1955 until his retirement in 1961, Olive devoted himself almost exclusively to alumni affairs, while continuing to edit the *Wake Forest Magazine* and to make many other valuable contributions to the college.

In addition, he wrote frequently for the *Biblical Recorder*, for various publications of the Sunday School Board of the Southern Baptist Convention, and for periodicals of the American Baptist Publication Society. His capping work was the compilation and editing of the comprehensive *Wake Forest Alumni Directory* (October 1961), which contained an alphabetical and geographic roster of students from 1834 to 1960 and a listing of recipients of honorary degrees during the same period.

On 29 June 1926 Olive married Iva Lanier Pierson of Raleigh. They had one daughter, Emily Caroline (Mrs. W. C. Rankin). After his retirement, he continued to live in his home on the Reynolda campus of Wake Forest College and spent much of his time implementing a program (insurance and other areas) for retired ministers, especially alumni of Wake Forest College.

Those who appraised Olive's more than half-century connection with Wake Forest spoke of his loyalty and energy in behalf of the college. It has been said that "he was more widely known and more universally beloved than any individual connected with the College in the Twentieth Century." He died in Winston-Salem and was buried in Forsyth Memorial Park.

SEE: *Biblical Recorder*, 16 Mar. 1968; Data File (North Carolina Baptist Collection, Wake Forest University Library, Winston-Salem); *Encyclopedia of Southern Baptists*, vol. 3 (1971); S. T. Habel, *Centennial Monograph Celebrating the First One Hundred Years of the Baptist Church at Chapel Hill* (1954); Raleigh *News and Observer*, 7 Mar. 1968; *Winston-Salem Journal*, 7 Mar. 1968; Winston-Salem *Twin-City Sentinel*, 7 Mar. 1968.

C. SYLVESTER GREEN

Olive, Hubert Ethridge, Sr. *(25 Aug. 1895–5 Mar. 1972)*, superior court judge, legislator, and Baptist layman, was born in Randleman of English-Irish ancestry, the sixth child of Andrew Jackson (24 Oct. 1894–18 Feb. 1911), a farmer, and Emma D. Beckwith Olive (29 Dec. 1854–25 Mar. 1945). He was the grandson of Henderson (1826–65) and Martha Jane Ragan Olive (1827–92). Young Olive attended the public schools of Thomasville. Enlisting in the army in 1917, he served for a year in France with the 317th Field Artillery of the 81st Division, popularly known as "the Wildcats." He was honorably discharged as a first lieutenant in 1919. While he was in Europe, he enrolled at Toulouse University for four months.

Returning to America, Olive attended Mars Hill College and Wake Forest College, where he received a law degree. As an undergraduate, he played football for four years. He remained a student in spirit throughout life, exercising a well-disciplined mind and a thirst for knowledge; he held membership in Phi Delta Phi legal fraternity. In 1922 he began a law practice in Lexington; later he was a judge of the town's lower court. In 1933 Olive was elected from Davidson County to the North Carolina House of Representatives, where he ably

served his constituents. He was a convincing orator and received many important house committee assignments. From 1934 to 1935 he was department commander of the North Carolina American Legion.

In the election of 1936, Olive served as Clyde R. Hoey's primary campaign manager. In 1937 he was appointed by the governor to the superior court bench and later was reappointed by Governor J. Melville Broughton for two more terms, serving for eighteen years. From 1947 to 1949 he was chairman of the State Board of Elections. In 1955 he was named resident judge of the Twenty-second District Court (composed of Davidson, Iredell, Alexander, and Davie counties) at its formation. In 1956 he was elected to the post and served for six more years.

A spectacular personality in the courtroom, Olive had a powerful, resonant voice, a great abundance of thick white hair, and a massive six-foot frame (he wore a size fourteen shoe). Under his judgeship, court was held in a dignified, authoritative manner without any impudence or horseplay. Olive felt that the court existed for the sole purpose of ensuring that justice would be done. In 1947 he returned to his law practice, but because of his judicial ability, he was drafted to serve as an emergency judge on numerous occasions. Olive was a participating jurist for the North Carolina Bar Association and a member of the North Carolina State Bar.

A contender in the Democratic gubernatorial primary of 1952, he was defeated by a narrow margin (294,170 to 265,675) by William B. Umstead of Durham. The primary cost him $61,579. He served on the board of trustees of Wake Forest College for many years and was its chairman for six terms. Over the years he was active in the alumni affairs of Wake Forest, giving able leadership as time would permit. He was president of the Wake Forest General Alumni Association during the crucial years when the college moved from Wake Forest to Winston-Salem. Prior to 1956 he was appointed chairman of the financial drive to match the $7.5 million offered by the Z. Smith Reynolds Foundation to implement the move.

Olive was an outstanding civic and political leader in the state and in his home community of Lexington. Committed to the work of the First Baptist Church in that town, he served as chairman of the Board of Deacons, as a committeeman in many capacities, and for forty years as a teacher of the Olive Men's Bible Class. Indeed, he was considered one of the most competent, willing, and scholarly laymen of his day. His fellow citizens highly respected his integrity and judgment. Olive knew when to be silent and when to be eloquent.

In 1921 he married Charlotte Ann Southerland, the daughter of Dr. Robert Edgar and Valeria Virginia Williams Southerland of Henderson. They had three children: Virginia (m. Louis S. Hartzog), Hubert, Jr. (m. Catherine Sloxer Hodgin), and Charlotte Ann. His son became a lawyer in Lexington. Olive died suddenly in Pinehurst while attending a judicial conference. He was buried in Forest Hill Memorial Park, Lexington. A portrait of him hangs over the judge's bench in the Davidson County courthouse, and another is located at Wake Forest University.

SEE: John L. Cheney, Jr., ed., *North Carolina Government, 1585–1979* (1981); *The Heritage of Davidson County* (1982); *Men of Achievement in the Carolinas* (1952); Raleigh *News and Observer*, 13 Aug. 1947, 23 Jan., 10 June 1952, 27 Feb. 1962, 6 Mar. 1972.

IRMA RAGAN HOLLAND

Olmsted, Denison *(18 June 1791–13 May 1859),* teacher and physical scientist, was born in East Hartford, Conn., into a family of early New England settlers. He was the fourth child of Nathaniel Olmsted, a respected farmer of moderate means and a descendant of John Olmsted, who emigrated from Essex, England, to Connecticut in 1632. His mother was Eunice Kingsbury Olmsted (1755–1846), the daughter of Denison Kingsbury of Andover, Conn. His father died when Denison was a year old. In 1800 his mother remarried and the family moved to Farmington, Conn. During several winters Olmsted lived with the family of Governor John Treadwell, who befriended and tutored him. His mother strongly influenced his religious and moral training and encouraged his interest in learning.

After clerking in a country store, Olmsted was prepared for college by James Morris of Litchfield South Farms and later by the Reverend Noah Porter in Farmington. He entered Yale College in 1809 and was graduated high in his class in 1813 with a B.A. degree. A classmate was Elisha Mitchell, with whom he continued a personal and professional association. For the next two years Olmsted taught in a private school for boys in New London, Conn.; in 1815 Mitchell took charge of a girls' school in the same town, where both men met their future wives. In 1815 Olmsted became a tutor at Yale and, intending to enter the ministry, studied theology with President Timothy Dwight. He obtained an M.A. degree in 1816, when he presented a plan for a state-supported seminary for schoolmasters, a forerunner of the normal school.

In November 1817 Olmsted and Mitchell joined the faculty of The University of North Carolina, Olmsted as professor of chemistry, a newly created position, and Mitchell as professor of mathematics, to fill the vacancy created in December 1816 by the second election of Joseph Caldwell as president of the university. The two appointments were recommended by Congressman William Gaston, a longtime trustee; Gaston had learned of the two young men from the Reverend Sereno Dwight, chaplain of the U.S. Senate and the son of President Dwight of Yale. As he was poorly prepared to teach chemistry, Olmsted received leave for a year's private study with Benjamin Silliman, professor of chemistry and natural history at Yale. This opportunity completely reoriented Olmsted's career. Also during this time (1818), he married Eliza Allyn of New London. He began teaching at Chapel Hill in the fall of 1819. Meanwhile, Mitchell had assumed his duties in January 1818. Following his marriage in 1819, Mitchell and his wife lived for a time in the Olmsted household.

Olmsted seems to have begun at once to investigate North Carolina geology. In 1820 he published a work on the red sandstone and coal of the Deep River area, and in 1822 he contributed two papers on the state's rocks and minerals. In 1821 he had proposed to the Board of Internal Improvements that he undertake a survey of the geology and useful minerals in North Carolina during his vacations, requesting only $100 to cover traveling expenses. The board turned him down. At the end of 1823, however, the legislature directed the Board of Agriculture to have a geologic and mineralogical survey made; the sum of $250 per annum for four years was appropriated and Olmsted was employed to do the work. He examined chiefly the Piedmont and in 1824 and 1825 wrote two reports totaling about 100 pages; l,500 copies of each were printed. He also prepared a manuscript geologic map of the state, dated November 1825, which was never printed. This was the first geologic examination of a state undertaken at public expense. When

Olmsted left North Carolina at the end of 1825, the survey was continued by Elisha Mitchell, who also succeeded him as professor of chemistry, mineralogy, and geology.

Though brief, Olmsted's contribution to knowledge of North Carolina geology was significant. William Maclure's work in 1809, covering the eastern half of the country, had differentiated in North Carolina only three groups of rocks. Olmsted, on the other hand, mapped and described eight subdivisions. Most significant was the delineation of the "Great Slate Formation" in the central Piedmont and the two sandstone belts. He traced belts of iron ore, limestone, and plumbago (graphite), reported building stones, and throughout emphasized useful mineral products. He employed Charles E. Rothe, a Saxon mining engineer, to prepare a report on the gold mines, which was published with Mitchell's work. Olmsted's practical outlook is further indicated by his pamphlet on the preparation of mortar, which he read to the Agricultural Society in 1821, and by his experiments on making illuminating gas from cottonseed, a method later improved and patented in July 1827.

In 1825 Olmsted accepted the chair of mathematics and natural philosophy (physics) at Yale College, though this again involved a drastic change in field. He did not feel fully competent in higher mathematics and requested that this be deleted from his job description, which was finally done in 1835, when he became professor of natural history and astronomy. Olmsted occupied this position for the next twenty-five years.

In 1829 his wife died, leaving five sons and two daughters. Two years later he married Julia Mason of Rensselaer County, N.Y., by whom he had one daughter. His four oldest sons were graduated from Yale and started promising careers in science and medicine, but all died of consumption between 1844 and 1853.

Olmsted wrote several widely used and profitable textbooks. The first was his two-volume *Introduction to Natural Philosophy,* appearing in 1831 and 1832, followed in 1833 by an abridgment entitled *School Philosophy.* In 1839 he published an *Introduction to Astronomy* for college use and two years later an abridged *Compendium of Astronomy* for schools. He wrote *Letters on Astronomy, Addressed to a Lady* (1841) at the request of the Massachusetts Board of Education. Finally, his *Rudiments of Natural Philosophy and Astronomy* for elementary schools appeared in 1844; this was also issued in an edition with raised letters for use by the blind. Some of these texts went through five to one hundred editions; more than 200,000 copies were sold.

Olmsted was an industrious and successful teacher of astronomy, meteorology, and physics. He used experimental demonstrations during his lectures and introduced laboratory work in his classes. Continuing his interest in the common schools, he addressed meetings of teachers, published papers on teaching methods and qualifications, and appeared before the legislature on school matters. In 1840 he was a member of the Connecticut Board of Commissioners for Common Schools. He and Professor Silliman gave lectures at night to mechanics and others who could not study during the day. He delivered public lectures and contributed articles to the press on scientific concerns.

Although Olmsted regarded himself primarily as a teacher, he was also an internationally recognized investigator in meteorology and astronomy. He published many scientific papers, including those on the thermometric observations made by Dr. Joseph Caldwell in 1820–22, his thoughts on the causes of hailstorms

(1830), and the behavior of lightning (1850). By his detailed observations of the famous meteor shower of 13 Nov. 1833, he established the periodicity of such falls and their origin by matter from outside the earth's atmosphere revolving around the sun, perhaps derived from comets. He also set forth his ideas on the zodiacal light, suggesting a possible relationship to meteors. He and Professor Elias Loomis of Yale were the first American observers of the return of Halley's comet in 1835. After studying the aurora borealis for more than twenty years, he published (1856) a detailed description and analysis of this phenomenon, in which he clearly showed it to be secular and of cosmic rather than earthly origin.

Olmsted wrote memoirs of Sir Humphrey Davy, Eli Whitney, E. P. Mason, John Treadwell, W. C. Redfield, Timothy Dwight, and others, reviewed various publications, and contributed religious essays. He was active in the programs of the American Geological Society and the American Association for the Advancement of Science. New York University awarded him an honorary LL.D. degree in 1845.

He died at his residence in New Haven, Conn., after a two-month illness and was buried in that city. He was survived by his wife, three children, and a brother.

SEE: Kemp P. Battle, *History of the University of North Carolina*, vol. 1 (1907); *DAB*, vol. 14 (1934); F. B. Dexter, *Biographical Sketches of Graduates of Yale College*, vol. 6 (1912); *First One Hundred Years of American Geology* (1924); C. S. Lyman, "Biographical Sketch of Professor Denison Olmsted," *American Journal of Science* 28 (1859); George P. Merrill, "Contributions to a History of American State Geological Surveys," *U.S. National Museum Bulletin* 109 (1920); *Nat. Cyc. Am. Biog.*, vol. 8 (1900); Denison Olmsted, *Report on the Geology of North Carolina*, parts 1 and 2 (1824–25); "On the Recent Secular Period of the Aurora Borealis," *Smithsonian Contributions to Knowledge*, vol. 8 (1856); Charles Phillips, *A Memoir of the Rev. Elisha Mitchell* (1858); Gary Lee Schoepflin, "Denison Olmsted, 1791–1859: Scientist, Teacher, Christian" (Ph.D. diss., Oregon State University, 1977).

JOHN M. PARKER III

Omar Moreau. *See* **Said, Omar Ibn**.

Ormond, Wyriot (or Wyriott), Sr. *(ca. 1707–ca. 1758)*, colonial official, perhaps the son of William Ormond, longtime clerk of court of Beaufort County, was one of Beaufort County's most prominent residents during the mid-eighteenth century. His birthplace is unknown, but the family was of English descent and noted for its "wealth and distinction."

Ormond was a member of the colonial Assembly when it met in Bath in 1744. Also in that year he was granted 940 acres of land in Beaufort County. The family home, located two miles north of Bath, was reported standing early in the twentieth century. Ormond represented Beaufort County or Bath in the Assembly for a number of terms and was a member at the time of his death; he was succeeded by his son. In 1746 he was a member of the committee to "settle the seat of government," and three years later he was appointed an agent for Bertie, Chowan, Currituck, Pasquotank, Perquimans, and Tyrrell counties in a dispute over representation. Also in 1746 Ormond was identified as an attorney-at-law in Beaufort County, and the next year his commission as "King's Attorney" was read in the Bertie County court. In 1754 he became one of three special tax receivers for Beaufort, Carteret, Craven, Hyde, and Johnston

counties. The following year he was appointed the receiver of tonnage duties for the port of Bath.

Ormond had at least three sons: Henry, Roger, and Wyriot, Jr. Henry, a bachelor, was murdered in his sleep by some of his slaves in about 1770, and Wyriot, Jr., died in 1773. Roger, who served in the colonial Assembly and the Provincial Congress and on the Committee of Safety for the New Bern District, died in 1775.

SEE: Robert J. Cain, ed., *Records of the Executive Council, 1735–1754* (1988); J. Bryan Grimes, ed., *Abstract of North Carolina Wills* (1910); Lida Tunstall Rodman, "Historic Homes and People of Old Bath Town," *North Carolina Booklet* 2, no. 8 (10 Dec. 1902); William L. Saunders, ed., *Colonial Records of North Carolina*, vols. 4–5 (1886–87).

JERRY COTTEN

Ormond, Wyriot (or Wyriott), Jr. *(d. 1773)*, colonial official, was a resident of Beaufort County and succeeded his father, Wyriot Ormond, Sr., in the colonial Assembly. He had two brothers, Henry and Roger.

In 1762 he was elected to the Assembly as the borough representative from Bath; his election was contested but resolved in his favor. During this term and again in 1764, he served on the propositions and grievances committee. In 1766 Ormond was appointed a port commissioner for Bath, and two years later he became receiver of duties on spirituous liquors for the town. In 1770 he sat on a committee that drafted a bill establishing inferior courts of pleas and quarter sessions. The following year he was licensed to practice law by the court of Bertie County and was a member of the commission that laid out the town of Martinsborough (later renamed Greenville). In 1772 he was clerk of Beaufort County.

By his wife, Elizabeth Penelope, Ormond was the father of two daughters, Nancy and Sarah. His will, proved on 1 Dec. 1773, left the bulk of his estate, including six slaves, to his wife and young daughters. He left firm instructions concerning the daughters' education. There is evidence that Ormond died young and probably after an illness of a few months.

SEE: John L. Cheney, Jr., ed., *North Carolina Government, 1585–1979* (1981); Walter Clark, ed., *State Records of North Carolina*, vols. 23–24 (1904–5); J. Bryan Grimes, ed., *Abstract of North Carolina Wills* (1910) and *North Carolina Wills and Inventories* (1912); William L. Saunders, ed., *Colonial Records of North Carolina*, vols. 8–9 (1890).

JERRY COTTEN

Orr, Louis *(19 May 1879–18 Feb. 1966)*, painter and etcher, was born in Hartford, Conn., the son of John Henry and Carolina Louise Naedele Orr and the grandson of J. W. Orr, a well-known New York City engraver and printer. He was a pupil of Walter Griffin at the Hartford Art School (1903–5) and afterwards studied as a scholarship winner at the Art Students League in New York. In 1906 he went to Paris, where he attended the Académie Julian and studied under Jean-Paul Laurens. Orr first painted in oils and watercolors, but dissatisfied and unsuccessful with his efforts, he turned to etching, a medium that had long interested him. Working from intuition, he taught himself and developed his own unique method for etching. For a time he served as art editor of the *Paris Herald*. On 10 July 1913 Orr married Gabrielle Chaumette. For the rest of his life he resided periodically in Paris (in the 1930s, at 5 Rue Mazarine), where he died.

At the start of World War I, having applied to the

French government for work that would assist France, Orr made etchings of Rheims Cathedral under German artillery fire. For these and other etchings, he was made a member (1918) and an officer (1930) of the French Legion of Honor. His were the first works by a living artist acquired by the French government for the Louvre National Museum and the first original etchings by an American artist purchased for the permanent collection in the Louvre's chalcography department. Among these works are three of *Rheims Cathedral under Bombardment*, *Le Pont Neuf, Paris*, the centennial portrait entitled *Louis Pasteur in His Laboratory*, and six others. His works also appear in the Luxembourg Museum and the Bibliothèque Nationale in Paris.

By the time he returned to the United States after the war, Orr was regarded as preeminent in his field and was lionized by East Side art dealers. He completed many commissions in this country, among them the Municipal Group, Springfield, Mass.; college buildings at Dartmouth, Duke, Pittsburgh, Princeton, University of Virginia, Wellesley, and Yale; *The National Capitol at Washington*, commissioned by Yale University as the William Howard Taft Memorial Etching and used in all important American embassies throughout the world; the Phoenix (Arizona) Insurance Company headquarters; and the United Nations Building, presented in 1959 to member governments as "the official representation of the international organization's mid-Manhattan Exhome." In the United States, his works are represented in the Albright Art Gallery, Buffalo, N.Y.; the New York Public Library; the Oakland (Calif.) Museum; the State Bank, Hartford; and the Yale University Art Museum. An important collection of his French etchings is owned by the Department of Foreign Languages and Literatures at East Carolina University.

In June 1939, on a sojourn in the United States that would be prolonged by World War II, Orr acceded to a request to execute the most outstanding work of his career—a series of etchings on North Carolina. The request came from Greenville native Robert Lee Humber, a fellow expatriate with whom Orr had become acquainted in Paris and who had recently returned from Europe because of the war. An international lawyer and business executive and later a leader in the founding of the North Carolina Museum of Art, Humber first had to overcome Orr's reluctance to concentrate for years on a single geographic area and to forego the high prices he was accustomed to receiving for his works in the capitals of the world. But largely by underwriting the cost of the project himself, he convinced Orr to accept a commission that would result in the artist's magnum opus—fifty etchings of uniform dimensions depicting North Carolina scenes (13¼" × 15¾") plus a larger state capitol (ca. 17" × 21"). Orr worked exclusively on this commission for twelve years (1939–51).

The first year of this ambitious project he devoted largely to research and planning. He examined approximately 4,000 to 5,000 photographs in the North Carolina Department of Conservation and Development and discussed the undertaking with Christopher Crittenden, director of the Department of Archives and History, and R. D. W. Connor, professor of North Carolina history at The University of North Carolina. He also traveled about 6,000 miles around the state to become familiar with its numerous cultural centers and historic sites. Sometimes he was a guest of people in the area he visited, as when he stayed with Mr. and Mrs. James Sprunt at Orton plantation near Wilmington.

After he and Humber decided on the subjects for the series, ranging from the Wright Brothers' Memorial at Kitty Hawk to the Biltmore House near Asheville, Orr would visit a selected site and, using pencil and paper, make a freehand drawing at the time of best light and shade. If the subject were a building no longer in existence, such as the old statehouse or Tryon Palace, he would base his drawing on older pictures. Later he would etch his intricate drawing into the surface of a plate from which the etchings would be made. The etching process often took months, with the oversized state capitol alone engaging him from about November 1940 to April 1941. Although he made the freehand drawings for the series in North Carolina, he did the actual etchings at his apartment on the Connecticut estate of a former president of the Hartford Life Insurance Company. Orr devised steel-faced plates for the etchings, a technique he developed especially for the North Carolina series, permitting each successive etching to have the same degree of sharpness as the first one.

The printer contracted to pull the etchings from the plates was a Mr. White of New York, known at the time as perhaps the outstanding U.S. printer of etchings. In an effort to keep the cost of the prints affordable, however, an inexpensive paper was chosen; it has proven to be of inferior quality, with the result that many etchings now need conservation.

When Orr completed the commission, Humber himself oversaw distribution. At Orr's insistence, he sold selections from the series in ten albums of five etchings each, except for the large state capitol, which was sold separately. Orr felt he could not afford to sell one etching for ten dollars, the price Humber proposed so that institutions with limited resources and individuals with moderate means could acquire selections from the series. But he rationalized that he could sell one for fifty dollars and, because the buyer liked his work so much, give the other four in the album to the purchaser without charge. This plan reconciled Orr to the modest prices and enabled Humber to make the project a cultural undertaking rather than a commercial enterprise. Humber eventually declined an offer from The University of North Carolina Press to take over distribution of the series; the press wanted to charge one hundred dollars per album, a price he felt would prohibit many from acquiring the works. Now available only rarely on the secondary market, the etchings currently sell for hundreds of dollars apiece.

It has been estimated that a total of 7,934 etchings were produced, with as few as 122 etchings of some scenes and as many as 230 of others (the number depending on the market demand for each album). In addition to individual albums, 91 complete sets were purchased, of which 23 were placed in college and county libraries around the state for public viewing. Although the etchings are not numbered, they are all signed by the artist.

As Humber noted, Orr could see beauty where others could not and captured this beauty in his etchings. He was a superb draftsman who noted the minutest detail, "recording even the slightest deviation in the angles of roofs, the exact number of sawteeth in a pediment, and the elaborate ornamentation of a cornice." He was a master of lights and shadows, pursuing them "down fluted columns, under the eaves of buildings, and around the . . . edges of shrubbery and leaves." He also possessed "an unrivaled technique for interpreting texture, whether it be wood, brick, or stone, especially the mellowed patina that comes with age." Largely for these reasons, the director of a leading museum observed that the three greatest etchers of all times were Rembrandt in the seventeenth century, Piranesi in the eighteenth, and Orr in the twentieth.

Executed by one of history's three finest etchers, Louis

Orr's North Carolina series represents, as Humber remarked, the most important artistic work on any state in the Union. It captures "the architectural splendor of North Carolina in all its phases," reflecting the excellence of the state's underestimated architecture as well as the refinement of its social life and the rich cultural heritage of its people. The series also reveals the artist's affection for his subject, an affection he once expressed in a letter: "The South always, from childhood, intrigued me; I love North Carolina and if the Etchings express some of this sincere admiration, then I have not been chasing a mirage."

Selections from the series can be seen in many private collections throughout the state, especially in the east. Complete sets of the etchings are owned by the Greenville Art Center, the Kinston Arts Council, the State Library of North Carolina in Raleigh, and the public libraries in Asheville, Burlington, Charlotte, Durham, Fayetteville, Gastonia, Greenville, Hickory, Rocky Mount, Smithfield, Wilmington, and Winston-Salem. Colleges and universities owning complete sets include Davidson, Duke, East Carolina, North Carolina State, the University of North Carolina at Chapel Hill (Ackland Museum and North Carolina Collection), and the University of North Carolina at Greensboro.

SEE: Elizabeth Copeland, "The North Carolina Etchings of Louis Orr," *North Carolina Libraries* 23 (Summer–Fall 1975); Peter Hastings Falk, *Who Was Who in American Art* (1985); John L. Humber to W. Keats Sparrow, 24, 30 Oct. 1988; Robert Lee Humber, "History of the Etchings on North Carolina by Louis Orr," *North Carolina Libraries* 23 (Summer–Fall 1975); Brian N. Morton, *Americans in Paris* (1984); *New York Times*, 20 Feb. 1966 (obituary); Glenn B. Opitz, ed., *Mantle Fielding's Dictionary of American Printers, Sculptors, and Engravers*, 2d ed. (1963); LeLand M. Park, "The Orr Etchings: An Addendum," *North Carolina Libraries* 23 (Winter 1975); *Who Was Who in America with World Notables*, vol. 4 (1961–68).

W. KEATS SPARROW

Osborn, Charles (21 Aug. 1775–29 Dec. 1850), abolitionist and Quaker minister, was born in Guilford County, the son of David and Margaret Stout Osborn and the grandson of Matthew and Isabel Dobson Osborn of Sussex County, Del. Little is known of Osborn's early life. At age nineteen he moved with his parents to Knox County, Tenn., and in 1798 he married Sarah Newman. Before her death in 1812, they had seven children: James, Josiah, John, Isaiah, Lydia, Elijah, and Elihu. In 1813 Osborn married Hannah Swain, who survived him by twenty-eight years. By his second wife, Osborn had nine children: Narcissa, Cynthia, Gideon, Charles N., Parker B., Jordan, Benjamin, Sarah S., and Anna.

About 1806 Osborn became a Quaker minister, his lifework and the animating force for his humanitarian interests. As was the wont of the Quaker ministry in the nineteenth century, Osborn traveled extensively to preach at Quaker meetings. From 1806 to 1840, the active period of his ministry, he visited most existing meetings in the United States and Canada and a considerable number in Great Britain and on the Continent. The peripatetic Osborn was also involved in the significant Quaker migration from North Carolina, through Tennessee, to the Old Northwest. In 1816 he left Tennessee to settle in Mount Pleasant, Ohio, before departing for Wayne County, Ind., in 1819, where he helped to lay out the town of Economy in 1825. Osborn returned to Ohio in 1827, but by 1830 he had resettled in Wayne

County, Ind. In 1842 he moved to Cass County, Mich., and in 1848 he established his last residence, in Porter County, Ind.

Osborn's early perambulations through North Carolina and Tennessee awakened him to the travail of slavery, and he became a confirmed foe of the institution while still a young man. Coming to maturity at a time when the Society of Friends was throwing off worldly ways for a return to the inner kingdom, Osborn inherited a rich and vigorous reform tradition. His contacts with northern and English reformers reinforced his reform convictions. Although he supported a host of humanitarian concerns, he devoted most of his energies to the slavery issue. A compelling speaker and an indefatigable organizer, he was instrumental in founding several antislavery societies in the South and the West.

As early as 1815 Osborn joined other transplanted North Carolina Quakers at Lost Creek Meeting, Tenn., to establish the Tennessee Manumission Society, an organization that prospered through the 1820s as a result of his cautious petitions for gradual, compensated emancipation. Also in 1815 he carried his antislavery message to Mount Pleasant, Ohio, where his moral example and inspiration convinced Benjamin Lundy, then in the seedtime of his own antislavery witness, to form the Union Humane Society, Ohio's first antislavery society. The next year Osborn agitated for emancipation in Guilford County, N.C. There he exercised a powerful, although transitory, influence in pushing the Manumission Society of North Carolina towards a more resolute stance in behalf of abolition. He also founded several local antislavery groups, all of which were short-lived. Contrary to the arguments of George Julian, none of these early societies advocated immediate abolition, each preferring—in varying degrees of intensity—compensated, gradual abolition and colonization. Osborn demurred on the last point.

In August 1817, at Mount Pleasant, Ohio, he began publishing *The Philanthropist*, a weekly forum for the discussion of slavery, war, Indian suffering, and related evils. Osborn's chief editorial contribution to his paper was a searching analysis of African colonization, which he branded impractical financially and wrong morally. In this he anticipated the Garrisonian criticism of colonization as an iniquitous design to expatriate free blacks and, through its assurance of compensation to slaveholders, as a means to retard true abolition and to dupe reformers into acknowledging the slaveholder's right to property in his slaves.

In 1818 Osborn sold the paper to Elisha Bates and went to Indiana. In Wayne County, he embraced the peculiarly Quaker doctrine of Free Produce, which exhorted the public to abstain from consuming the products of slave labor. By boycotting slave products, Free Produce advocates like Osborn sought to forge an economic weapon to strike at slavery and, at the same time, to cleanse themselves of any contamination from the hated institution. Wayne County became the focus of Free Produce activities in the West, and Osborn, along with fellow native North Carolinian and Quaker, Levi Coffin, was a leading proponent of the cause.

Osborn's growing preoccupation with abolition conflicted with the conservative temperament of many Indiana Quakers. The Society of Friends, brittle and partially fragmented after years of internal dissension over social policy and polity, was in Indiana convulsed by disputes between reform radicals of the Osborn stripe and conservatives who wanted Friends to eschew politics and to confine their reform attention to the Society of Friends. In 1842 the conservative faction expelled Osborn and his associates from the Meeting for Sufferings of the Indiana Yearly Meeting. A schism ensued. Osborn and about two thousand like-minded Friends seceded from the Indiana Yearly Meeting to form the Indiana Yearly Meeting of Antislavery Friends in 1843. Although the seceders never received official sanction from any other Yearly Meeting, Osborn used the separation to force the antislavery issue upon the Society of Friends. With Levi Coffin, the most prominent seceder, he tirelessly prepared addresses, memorials, and defenses for radical antislavery action. In one of his last acts, Osborn drafted an 1849 memorial to Congress condemning the government's involvement in slavery by its reluctance to prohibit slavery in the territories and abolish it in the District of Columbia. This memorial reflected Osborn's partial digestion of the militant Garrisonian strain of abolition and his growing impatience with northern tolerance for slavery. He died the following year as he was preparing a blast against the Fugitive Slave Act.

No portrait of Osborn is known to exist, although his posthumously published *Journal* gives a revealing intellectual and spiritual likeness of the Quaker abolitionist.

SEE: *DAB*, vol. 7 (1934); Merton L. Dillon, *Benjamin Lundy and the Struggle for Negro Freedom* (1966); Thomas E. Drake, *Quakers and Slavery in America* (1950); *Free Labor Advocate*, 1841–48; Ruth A. Ketring, *Charles Osborn in the Anti-Slavery Movement* (1937); Randall M. Miller, "The Union Humane Society," *Quaker History* 61 (1972); Minutes of the Indiana Yearly Meetings of Antislavery Friends (Earlham College, Richmond, Ind.); Minutes of the Manumission Society of North Carolina (Quaker Collection, Guilford College Library, Greensboro); Chase Mooney, *Slavery in Tennessee* (1957); Ruth Ketring Nuermberger, *The Free Produce Movement: A Quaker Protest against Slavery* (1942); Charles Osborn, *Address to All Who Profess to Desire the Abolition of Slavery* (1850), *Journal of That Faithful Servant of Christ* (1854), and *A Testimony Concerning the Separation Which Occurred in the Indiana Yearly Meeting of Friends* (1849); *The Philanthropist*, 1817–18.

RANDALL M. MILLER

Osborne, Adlai (*4 June 1744–14 Dec. 1814*), lawyer and political and educational leader, was the son of Alexander Osborne, of New Jersey, a prominent frontiersman of Rowan County, N.C., and a member of the 1761 colonial Assembly, and Agnes MacWhorter Osborne, the daughter of Hugh MacWhorter of New Castle, Del. Before the spring of 1749 he migrated with his parents from either Delaware or New Jersey to the headwaters of the west branch of Rocky River, then in Anson County, N.C. Alexander quickly attained political office and acquired land. Belmont, the Osborne home, became the religious (Presbyterian) and educational center of the developing community. Adlai and his cousin Ephraim Brevard attended Crowfield Academy nearby, then went to a private school in Prince Edward County, Va. In 1768 both Adlai and Ephraim were graduated from Nassau Hall (Princeton). They returned to North Carolina, where Adlai studied law and married, on 30 Jan. 1771, Margaret Lloyd, the daughter of Major General Thomas F. Lloyd of Orange County.

Osborne early began an active public life in Rowan County. He signed an anti-Regulator petition during that uprising, against which his father and father-in-law assumed commanding positions. On 30 July 1772 he was appointed clerk of the Rowan Court of Pleas and Quarter Sessions, and he soon established a law office in Salisbury. As hostilities towards the British grew in the Piedmont, Osborne became more involved in the Revolutionary movement. He was appointed a member of the Rowan Committee of Safety (November 1774) and served as its clerk; with William Kennon, he seized lawyer John Dunn, a suspected traitor, to send him south. On 9 Sept. 1775 he was appointed lieutenant colonel of minutemen in the Salisbury District. The public magazine was lodged at Belmont for four years—until Osborne was appointed a commissioner to erect one with public funds. During this period (1774–77), he was also clerk of the Salisbury District Court of Oyer and Terminer for its duration.

When his parents died in July 1776, Osborne, the only son of six children, inherited a great estate (his father had received various state grants totaling more than 8,000 acres). Through the 1770s and 1780s he used his increased resources to buy and sell town lots in Salisbury and Charlotte to good advantage.

Osborne was a commissioner of forfeited estates for Rowan County (1780–82), inspector of money for the Newington District (1780), and private secretary of Governor Alexander Martin (1780). He was nominated, but not elected, a delegate to the Continental Congress in 1782. In August–September of that year he attempted a move to Georgia, where he had obtained an appointment as register of probates in Chatham County. Due to the unsettled financial conditions prevailing, the move was aborted. Remaining in Rowan, he was elected a delegate to the Continental Congress of November 1784 but, as many did, resigned the commission a year later.

With the formation of Iredell County, in which Belmont was situated, Osborne was appointed attorney for the state in that county (1789–96) and was one of its five delegates to the Fayetteville convention (November 1789), where he voted for ratification of the U.S. Constitution. He did not, however, relinquish his offices in Rowan, serving as county trustee (treasurer, 1795–1802) and de jure clerk of the Rowan County court until 1809, although he stopped attending in 1802. His inactivity, the general disorder of the office and books, and his arrearages in fines and forfeitures prompted an investigatory committee to issue a reluctant though stern censure in May 1809. He resigned the office of de jure clerk the next day.

In the 1790s Osborne turned his attention to land trading, in which he engaged with evident success in Mecklenburg and Iredell counties. In June 1798 he, David Caldwell, and Abner Sharpe of Iredell entered into a speculative partnership to subdivide 19,000 acres they had acquired in northern and western Iredell County. This continued with moderate activity until 1805. From 1795 to 1803 Osborne represented the trustees of The University of North Carolina as attorney in the Salisbury and Morgan districts and as commissioner of confiscated property in the Salisbury and Fayetteville districts. Both positions kept him busy collecting and selling escheats and recovering debts.

A trustee of the university from its inception (1789), Osborne served on committees to read William R. Davie's educational plan and to report on the building plan for the university. He was a trustee until his death. Four of his sons were graduated from the university. He had previously been a trustee of Liberty Hall Academy in Charlotte (1777–80), of which his uncle, Alexander MacWhorter, was president.

Osborne spent his last years at Belmont. Known for its large library (over one hundred volumes) and second-floor ballroom, this centrally located plantation (twenty miles from Charlotte, Statesville, and Salisbury) of excellent bottomland was, in 1800, worked by twenty-five slaves who raised corn, wheat, oats, barley, cattle, hogs, sheep, flax, and cotton. A dairy and an orchard were also tended. Osborne died at Belmont and was buried in Centre Churchyard near Mount Mourne. His wife and eleven children survived him.

SEE: Samuel A. Ashe, "Adlai Osborne" (Charles L. Van Noppen Papers, Manuscript Department, Duke University Library, Durham); *Charlotte Observer*, 31 Mar. 1935; Walter Clark, ed., *State Records of North Carolina*, vols. 13 (1896), 15–22 (1898–1907), 25 (1906); R. D. W. Connor, *A Documentary History of the University of North Carolina, 1776–1799*, 2 vols. (1953); Archibald Henderson, "Adlai Osborne: A Memorial Tribute," in *Program of the Sixth Annual Convention of the Lloyd Clan* (1941?); Iredell County Estate Records (North Carolina State Archives, Raleigh); James McLachlan, *Princetonians, 1748–1768: A Biographical Dictionary* (1976); Adlai Osborne Papers (Southern Historical Collection, University of North Carolina, Chapel Hill, and North Carolina State Archives, Raleigh); Rowan County Court of Pleas and Quarter Sessions and Wills (North Carolina State Archives, Raleigh); William L. Saunders, ed., *Colonial Records of North Carolina*, vols. 8–10 (1890); *Statesville Landmark*, 24 July 1914.

D. W. ADAMS

Osborne, Alexander (1709–11 July 1776), frontiersman, was born in New Jersey but spent his early years in Lancaster, Pa. He moved to North Carolina about 1749 and settled on the headwaters of Rocky River in Anson (now Iredell) County. There he built a log house named Belmont on his thousand-acre land grant, which in 1753 fell in Rowan County when that county was cut off from Anson. Like many of the Scotch-Irish who emigrated from Ulster in 1725–68 to settle on the frontier, Osborne possessed industrious habits, integrity, and a love of freedom. Religion and education were very important in his life.

His residence, Belmont (which was later rebuilt and also referred to as the Red House), was one of the earliest places of worship for Presbyterians in Rowan County before Centre Church was erected; it became the central meetinghouse of worship for a large area. Hugh McAden, the first Presbyterian missionary in North Carolina, spoke of being "at Osborne's"; the Centre Church was called "Osborne's Meeting House." Belmont also was the center of the military, educational, social, and civil life of the area. Osborne contributed to the establishment of Crowfield Academy (ca. 1760) near Belmont within the bounds of Centre congregation. This was a classical school where young men prepared for Princeton. His own son, Adlai, went from Crowfield to Princeton and on to an outstanding career in North Carolina. Alexander Osborne is known to have had a "well stocked library and a room for dancing on the second floor." His name is on a petition from Rowan County to Governor Josiah Martin in regard to amending the Marriage Act so that Presbyterian ministers could conduct marriages.

Osborne represented his district as a member of the Council of the province in New Bern (1749 and 1759) and Brunswick (1762). He was a member of the Provincial Assembly meeting in Wilmington on 21 Mar. 1761. In 1749 he was appointed magistrate for Anson County. He also served as justice of the peace in Anson and, though a Presbyterian, as vestryman of St. George's (Episcopal) Parish. As one of the original justices,

Osborne held the first court in Rowan County. He remained on the court for many years, often presiding over its sessions.

Active in military affairs, Osborne constantly helped to protect the settlers from Indian attack. He served in the Fourth Rowan Foot (1754–55, 1758, and 1767). On 21 Aug. 1754, serving as a commissioner to the Indians, he and fellow commissioner James Carter met with King Hagler of the friendly Catawba tribe and many of his chiefs and warriors. On 29 August they signed a treaty pledging to build the Catawba a fort for the protection of their old men, women, and children in times of war. During the French and Indian War, Osborne served as captain of a company. He was in direct communication with Governor Arthur Dobbs and advised him about the exposed condition of the frontier. Had it not been for the protection of the Catawba fort and Fort Dobbs, built for the settlers' safety, together with a special company of rangers and patrollers, the settlers no doubt would have been the victims of many Cherokee attacks. For taking part in this war against the Cherokee, which virtually destroyed their power to make war, Governor Dobbs commissioned Osborne colonel of a regiment of foot in 1756.

In 1768 Colonel Osborne led an organized force to Salisbury to aid Governor William Tryon in suppressing the Regulators. There, at a review of troops on 20 Aug. 1768, he read a letter from four Presbyterian ministers counseling harmony and submission on the Regulators' part. Osborne himself spoke in support of the government and of the liberties and properties of the inhabitants that were in danger if "these insurgents" were able to overturn the Hillsborough Superior Court. He thanked the governor for the trouble he had taken to preserve peace in the province. Continuing his involvement in the Regulator campaign, he went on to Hillsborough to attend a Council of War and was appointed by Governor Tryon to carry a proclamation of pardon for the insurgents to Salisbury. The proclamation was to be read at the head of the brigade and to be attached to the courthouse door on 2 Oct. 1768.

By 1771 Osborne and the Rowan militia had changed sides. He was active in the first movements towards independence and was a prominent member of the Rowan Committee of Safety. Not living to enjoy the independence he had worked for, he and his wife died within two days of each other, she on 9 July 1776. They were buried in Centre Church graveyard in Iredell County.

Osborne married Agnes MacWhorter, the daughter of Hugh (d. 1748) and Jane MacWhorter, who immigrated to America from County Armagh, Ireland, and settled in New Castle, Del., in 1730. Agnes's brother was Dr. Alexander MacWhorter, president of Queens Museum in Charlotte before the Revolution. The Osbornes left six children: one son, Adlai, who married Margaret Lloyd of Orange County; and five daughters (Jean, Mary, Rebecca, Agnes, and Margaret), who married members of prominent families in their area. Alexander Osborne was an ancestor of Adlai Stevenson, vice-president of the United States, and his grandson, Adlai E. Stevenson, an ambassador to the United Nations.

SEE: Autobiography of Col. E. A. Osborne (North Carolina Collection, University of North Carolina, Chapel Hill); *Charlotte Observer*, 31 Mar. 1935; Chalmers Davidson, *Piedmont Partisan* (1969); William Henry Foote, *Sketches of North Carolina, Historical and Biographical: Illustrative of the Principles of a Portion of Her Early Settlers* (1846); Archibald Henderson, *North Carolina: The Old North State and the New*, vol. 1 (1941); C. L. Hunter,

Sketches of Western North Carolina (1877); Mrs. Alexander Duncan Moore, letter, 2 Dec. 1872 (possession of Mrs. J. Philo Caldwell); Robert W. Ramsey, *Carolina Cradle* (1964); Rowan County Will Book A (Rowan County Courthouse, Salisbury); Jethro Rumple, *History of Rowan County* (1881); William L. Saunders, ed., *Colonial Records of North Carolina*, vol. 4 (1886); Cornelia Rebeckah Shaw (Librarian, Davidson College), personal information, 1923; *Statesville Landmark*, 14 July 1914.

MARIE OSBORNE CALDWELL

Osborne, Edwin Augustus *(6 May 1837–12 Oct. 1926)*, Civil War hero, Episcopal priest, and founder of Thompson Orphanage, was born in Moulton, Lawrence County, Ala., one of eleven children of Ephraim Brevard and Nancy Smith Osborne. He was named for his father's brother, Edwin, and for General John Augustus Young. Thought to have descended from a family who emigrated from England to New England as early as 1645, his great-grandfather, Alexander, was born in New Jersey but moved to North Carolina about 1754, first settling in Salisbury and later in Iredell County; a colonel of the militia for Governor William Tryon against the Regulators, he was also a justice of the county court and a leader of the rangers to protect settlers from Indians. His grandfather, Adlai, was appointed clerk of Rowan County by the Crown, an office that he held throughout the Revolution and afterwards until 1809; a good friend of education, he was one of the first trustees of The University of North Carolina. His father, a physician who fought with Andrew Jackson, was one of the few to escape the Indian massacre at Fort Mims and was with Jackson at the Battle of New Orleans. Originally from North Carolina, Ephraim moved to Alabama and practiced medicine for a time; from there he went to Arkansas and later to Hill County, Tex., where he died a successful physician and a wealthy slave owner. Osborne's youngest brother, Polk, was a member of the North Carolina state legislature and started the street-car lines in Charlotte. Nancy Smith Osborne was the daughter of a rice planter who moved to Virginia early in the nineteenth century. Her brothers were well-to-do slave owners in Alabama, Mississippi, Arkansas, and Texas.

Born in Alabama in a double log house, Edwin Augustus Osborne grew up accustomed to slaves, but he recalled that as a ten-year-old in Arkansas he "witnessed savagery and brutality toward slaves never before seen." Said to have been a delicate youth, Osborne was an avid reader, especially of the Bible. He first attended a small school in Texas five miles from home and boarded with a family related by marriage. His chances for further education were very poor; his plan was to study at home, work for a while, and then go to school. He became an expert horseman, breaking and training wild horses and helping herd cattle. After working at various jobs and traveling in the state, Osborne appealed to his widowed Aunt Peggy, Margaret MacWhorter Davidson, who owned a large plantation in Mecklenburg County, N.C. Noted for her generosity, she immediately invited him to her home, arranged for him to enter a preparatory school, Statesville Military Academy, and paid for his education there. He entered the academy in 1859 and remained until the Civil War broke out. When he joined the Confederate army, his aunt gave him money to buy a good horse and saddle as well as a valuable slave boy.

Elected captain of Company H, Fourth Regiment, North Carolina Troops, Osborne fought at Yorktown, Williamsburg, and Seven Pines, where he was wounded in 1862. In the Maryland campaign, he saw action in the Battle of South Mountain and at Sharpsburg, where he was wounded again. His regiment then proceeded to Chancellorsville, Gettysburg, Spottsylvania and the Wilderness, where he received another injury, and Appomattox. Promoted to major, lieutenant-colonel, and finally colonel, he left his regiment only to recover from his frequent wounds. In 1865, during one of those periods of recuperation, he met and married his second cousin, Fannie Swann Moore, a descendant of colonial governor James Moore of South Carolina and General Maurice Moore of Revolutionary War fame.

A few weeks after the wedding, while attempting to rejoin his regiment, he learned that General Robert E. Lee had surrendered. The Fourth Regiment had earned a fine reputation in the war, especially at Sharpsburg and again at the Battle of Seven Pines, where Osborne exhibited exceptional personal courage and gallantry. Awaiting support that never came and facing evident destruction, Company H, the "Hunting Creek Guard" from nothern Iredell, under Major Osborne, charged the enemy with such determination that the entire regiment followed, driving back the enemy and capturing six pieces of artillery. Wounded within a few rods of the breastworks, Osborne forced a Union soldier to carry him beyond the breastworks to the point where his troops had advanced. Many observers witnessed his valiant behavior in battle on various occasions. On 19 May 1864 at Spottsylvania Court House, as commander of a division line of pickets against two enemy lines, he led his men out of a difficult situation; while charging and repulsing the Federalists, he was shot through the right hand, losing two fingers. At the end of the war he was left with nothing but his horse. Ill with fever, he went to Statesville, where his wife was staying with her mother.

After the war Osborne taught school in Statesville and subsequently in Charlotte, where, having studied law, he was admitted to the bar. In 1867 he was appointed clerk of the superior court. Known for his ability, industry, and efficiency, he was reelected twice, holding the position for ten years.

In 1874 he left the Presbyterian church, became a member of the Protestant Episcopal church (the denomination of his wife), and decided to enter the ministry. Ordained deacon on 3 June 1877, he was named rector of Calvary Church, Fletcher. Osborne remained in the mission area of Henderson, Buncombe, Rutherford, Polk, and Haywood counties until his ordination as priest on 29 May 1881.

In 1884 he was appointed to the charge of St. Mark's mission (in Mecklenburg County) and St. Paul's (Monroe), neither of which had a church building. Under his leadership, two churches were constructed and both congregations prospered. He also added a black congregation, St. Michael's and All Angels, in Charlotte. Shortly after returning to the Mecklenburg area, Osborne conceived the idea of establishing an orphanage. The rector of St. Peter's Episcopal Church, the Reverend B. S. Bronson, held in trust the deed to some property formerly used by a private school that had failed; he donated the property to the diocese, stipulating that it be used as an orphanage and that Osborne be appointed its first superintendent. Visiting groups around the state at his own expense, Osborne appealed for funds. As a result of his efforts, on 10 May 1887 the Thompson Orphanage and Training Institution opened its doors with ten children. It was named for Lewis Thompson, who had given money for the failed school.

When war broke out with Spain, Osborne—thinking

that his war experience would be of special use—resigned his position to serve as chaplain of the Second Regiment of North Carolina Volunteers. He remained on active duty throughout the war.

After the conflict, he became secretary of the Executive Missionary Committee of the diocese and for a short time was chaplain of St. Mary's School in Raleigh. From 1899 to 1902 he served as archdeacon of the Diocese of North Carolina and then, when the diocese was divided into two convocations, as archdeacon of the Charlotte Convocation. He was a deputy to the General Convention from 1907 to 1910 and for a time served on the diocesan committee on canons. Osborne's particular interest was the mission field rather than the pastorate of established congregations. In 1908 he was appointed chaplain to the bishop and attended the Pan-Anglican Congress in London.

Noted for his gentle spirit, chivalry, bravery, and idealism, Osborne gained the affection and esteem of the community. Very much affected by his Civil War experiences, he wrote poetry in a diary that he had kept during the war. Years later he reflected that one year, on the first day of July, he had noticed a feeling of sadness coming over him, then remembered that it was the anniversary of Gettysburg. For a time Osborne was the chaplain of the Mecklenburg Camp of Confederate Veterans.

The Osbornes had six sons (Alexander Duncan, James Walker, Adlai, Francis Moore, Edwin Augustus, and Ephraim Brevard) and two daughters (Mary Lloyd and Josephine Ashe). Fannie Swann Osborne died in 1925 shortly after their sixtieth wedding anniversary. Edwin Augustus died at age eighty-nine after a period of declining health. He was buried in Elmwood Cemetery, Charlotte.

SEE: Samuel A. Ashe, "Edwin Augustus Osborne," in Charles L. Van Noppen Papers (Manuscript Department, Duke University Library, Durham); *Charlotte Observer* 7 May, 13 Oct. 1926; Margaret Davidson Will (North Carolina State Archives, Raleigh); Diocese of North Carolina, *Journal* (1927); "History of Thompson Orphanage," *Messenger of Hope of Thompson Orphanage* 7 (May 1930); Weymouth T. Jordan, comp., *North Carolina Troops, 1861–1865: A Roster*, vol. 4 (1973); Edwin Augustus Osborne, Diaries and Autobiography (Southern Historical Collection, University of North Carolina, Chapel Hill); William S. Powell, "N.C. Church History," *North Carolina Churchman*, September 1952; *Prominent People of North Carolina* (1906); John G. Young Diary (North Carolina State Archives, Raleigh).

DOROTHY H. OSBORN

Osborne, Francis (Frank) Irwin *(29 May 1853–20 Jan. 1920)*, lawyer and politician, was born in the U.S. Mint building, Charlotte, where his father, James W. Osborne, was superintendent. His mother was Mary Ann Irwin Osborne, the daughter of John and Mary Patton Irwin of Charlotte. In Charlotte Frank Osborne attended school and was prepared for college by his cousin, Fred Moore. He was graduated from Davidson College in 1872. The following year he studied mathematics, Greek, and Latin at the University of Virginia. He then entered the law school of Richmond M. Pearson at Richmond Hill, Yadkin County, where he read law for two years. He was admitted to the bar in 1875.

Osborne formed a partnership with T. H. Brem, Jr., in Charlotte and gained a wide reputation for studiousness and incisive presentations. At age twenty-five he was elected mayor of Charlotte. Later in the year, on 13 Nov.

1878, he married Mary Dewey, the daughter of Thomas Webber and Bessie Lacy Dewey of Charlotte.

In 1882 Osborne was elected solicitor of the Sixth Judicial District (Mecklenburg). He served through the district reorganization, which changed the Sixth to the Eleventh District, until 1892. His reputation for honesty, clarity, and fairness led to his nomination by the Democratic party and subsequent election as attorney general of North Carolina in 1893. In his bid for reelection in 1896, he was defeated by the combined Populist-Republican forces. Osborne won a seat in the state senate from Mecklenburg County in 1898 and served in the term of 1899. A member of nine standing committees, he was elected to represent the upper house on a committee formed to hear and analyze Governor Daniel L. Russell's reasons for asking two railroad commissioners to resign. Osborne read the concluding report before a joint session of the legislature, which voted to exonerate S. Otho and James Wilson, the two commissioners, of any wrongdoing in the "Round Knob Hotel affair."

Though there was talk of Osborne running for governor in 1899, he returned to his law firm, Osborne, Maxwell, and Kearns. In 1901, on the impeachment of Chief Justice David Moffatt Furches and Associate Justice Robert Martin Douglas of the North Carolina Supreme Court, Osborne was a counsel for the defendants. Although a Democrat, he felt that the two Republican judges were victims of an attempted political purge. In his summation and closing words, considered the most brilliant speech of the trial, Osborne charged his fellow Democrats in the legislature with political partisanship in their accusations. The judges were acquitted. It is said that, because of this defense of the judges, Marcus Hannah of Ohio recommended Osborne to President Theodore Roosevelt for federal appointment. On the death of Judge Thomas G. Fuller, Roosevelt appointed Osborne a judge of the U.S. Circuit Court of Private Land Claims, which met in Santa Fe, N.Mex., and Denver, Colo., in 1901. The purview of the court extended back from present claims to early Spanish titles, which involved an extensive review of records. Osborne served in this capacity until 1904, the designated length of the court.

Afterwards he returned to private practice in Charlotte, where he worked for the remainder of his life, except for a summer in New York City where he collaborated with his younger brother, James W., on some of his legal cases. Frank Osborne had been a partner of W. C. Maxwell in Charlotte for many years, but he spent the last ten years of his life in partnership with Norman Cocke of Charlotte. He was the general attorney for the Southern Power Company and the Southern Public Utilities Company and affiliates, one of the largest utility companies in the South.

Judge Osborne's portrait was hung in the Mecklenburg County courthouse in Charlotte. He was tall, lean, and fair-haired. A quietly dignified, courteous man, he was a student of history and literature and pursued a scholarly jurisprudence. His most intimate friend in Charlotte was Joseph Caldwell, editor of the *Charlotte Observer*. Osborne was also an inveterate poker player and enjoyed competing for high stakes. He died in Charlotte and was buried in the Osborne plot in Elmwood Cemetery. Four of his seven children lived to adulthood and survived him.

SEE: A. L. Brooks and H. T. Lefler, eds., *The Papers of Walter Clark*, vol. 1 (1948); Mrs. W. A. Capron (Asheville), interview; *Charlotte Observer*, 22 Feb. 1920; Josephus Daniels, *Editor in Politics* (1941); *Journal of the Senate of the General Assembly of the State of North Carolina, Ses-*

sion 1899 (1899); *North Carolina Biography*, vol. 6 (1919); *North Carolina Yearbook and Business Directory* (various issues); *Trial of David M. Furches and Robert M. Douglas on Impeachment by the House of Representatives for High Crimes and Misdemeanors* (1901); Charles L. Van Noppen Papers (Manuscript Department, Duke University Library, Durham).

D. W. ADAMS

Osborne, James Walker (*25 Dec. 1811–10 Aug. 1869*), lawyer, politician, and businessman, was born in Salisbury, the youngest of four children of Edwin Jay and Harriet Walker Osborne. His father, an eloquent and gifted lawyer, was the son of Adlai Osborne of Iredell County. His mother was the daughter of James and Magdalene Margaret DuBois Walker of Wilmington. When Harriet Osborne died in 1815, the four children were sent to various relatives to be raised. James lived with his paternal uncle and aunt, Robert and Margaret O. Davidson, who, though childless, reared many of their nephews. Their farm, Hollywood, on the horseshoe bend of the Catawba River (Mecklenburg County), was known for its abundance.

Osborne attended a school conducted by the Reverend S. C. Caldwell, then, through the aid of Elisha Mitchell, entered the sophomore class of The University of North Carolina. He was graduated in June 1830, before his nineteenth birthday, and received an M.A. degree from the university in 1839. After studying law in Hillsborough with his cousin, William A. Graham, he was admitted to the bar in 1833. From 1836 to 1838 he was solicitor for Mecklenburg County.

On 5 Apr. 1842 Osborne married Mrs. Mary Ann Irwin Moore, the widow of Thomas J. Moore of South Carolina and Mississippi and the daughter of John Irwin, a merchant and banker in Charlotte.

His political career initiated, Osborne, a Whig, was a candidate for state senator from Mecklenburg in 1840 but lost to J. T. J. Orr by sixty-six votes in a general Democratic victory. An able political observer, orator, and debater, he was chosen first presidential elector at large in the Clay campaign of 1844. Politically he allied himself with the "Federal Whigs," William A. Graham and John Motley Morehead, and through the influence of Graham, his mentor and friend, he was appointed by President Millard Fillmore as superintendent of the U.S. Mint at Charlotte, serving from 1849 to 1853. Osborne reluctantly entered the campaign of 1853, running against Democrat Burton Craige for the Seventh District congressional seat. He advocated distributing the proceeds of public land sales and opposed the indefinite extension of the U.S. boundaries. The Whig party's decline (by then it was practically defunct) and the concern for southern rights helped ensure Craige's victory.

A supporter of internal improvements throughout his career, Osborne was a principal speaker at the first public meeting held at Charlotte (1848) to arouse sentiment for railroad construction and corresponded with political leaders to emphasize this need. He wrote an informed report on the geographic features, natural resources, products, and potentials of the North Carolina Piedmont. This knowledge and the mint superintendency led him to invest heavily in mining. In 1854 he acquired the Rudisil gold mine, then the premier mine of the state, and owned or invested in the Bush Hill mine, the Dunn mine, the Williams mine, and the Brem mine in Chesterfield, S.C. He also invested in the Western Plank Road.

A Whig without a party, Osborne, in 1856, allied himself with the Democrats. In 1859 Governor John W. Ellis appointed him judge of the superior court, an office he held for six years. In 1861 Osborne served as a delegate from Mecklenburg to the Secession Convention, where he voted for secession. During the Civil War, he resided in Charlotte or at his aunt's farm on the Catawba River. At this time he was a partner in the Mecklenburg Salt Works, directed by Professor W. C. Kerr of Davidson College, which manufactured salt from the South Carolina coast.

After the war, Osborne formed a law partnership with Rufus Barringer in Charlotte. He was an elector in the Seymour-Grant campaign of 1868. In that election, as a Democrat, he won a seat in the state senate, representing Mecklenburg County until his death.

Osborne was known for the depth and diversity of his knowledge. He was said to have been an adroit military tactician while also well-versed in Christian theology; he served as a ruling elder in the Presbyterian church for twenty years. He corresponded with David L. Swain, James D. B. DeBow, Peter Force, and Benjamin Lossing on various historical topics and often expressed his intention to write a history. He was a trustee of the Charlotte Female Academy and of Davidson College from its incorporation until his death. (Osborne, William A. Graham, and Joseph H. Wilson were attorneys for the college in its attempt to secure the Maxwell Chambers bequest.)

In addition to his other economic pursuits, Osborne had landed interests in Louisiana, Alabama, and North Carolina. Despite the monetary advantages of his inheritance and marriage, his nine-hundred-volume library, which was sold, and other assets could not cover the $20,000 in debts that remained at his death.

Osborne was the father of seven children. Three sons lived to adulthood and became lawyers. His wife was known to be high-minded, well read, and an exceptionally shrewd businesswoman. Four portraits of Judge Osborne are known to exist. He died in Charlotte and was buried in Elmwood Cemetery.

SEE: J. B. Alexander, *The History of Mecklenburg* (1902); Samuel A. Ashe, ed., *Cyclopedia of Eminent and Representative Men of the Carolinas of the Nineteenth Century*, vol. 2 (1892); Peter Force and William Force Papers and Mecklenburg Declaration Papers (Southern Historical Collection, University of North Carolina, Chapel Hill); J. G. de Roulhac Hamilton, *The Papers of William Alexander Graham*, vols. 1–4 (1957–61); Minutes of Mecklenburg County Court of Pleas and Quarter Sessions, 1860 Census, Mecklenburg County, Mecklenburg County Deeds, Wills, and Estates, David L. Swain Papers, and Zebulon B. Vance Papers (North Carolina State Archives, Raleigh); *North Carolina Whig*, 20 Apr., 4 May 1853; *Western Democrat*, 17 Aug. 1869; John H. Wheeler, ed., *Reminiscences and Memoirs of North Carolina and Eminent North Carolinians* (1884).

D. W. ADAMS

Osborne, James Walker (*5 Jan. 1859–7 Sept. 1919*), lawyer, was born in Charlotte, the fourth and youngest son of James Walker and Mary Irwin Osborne. The widow of Thomas J. Moore, his mother was a woman of strong and vigorous mind, widely read in literature and profoundly interested in public affairs; she was a devoted companion to her children. Among his Scotch-Irish ancestors were Colonel Alexander Osborne and Adlai Osborne. Edwin Augustus Osborne was a cousin.

Young Osborne attended Davidson College, where he

was active in debating societies and athletic events. In 1878 he won the Fowle Medal, given for the best oration delivered by a member of the junior class. He was graduated from Davidson the following year, and as one of the commencement speakers he chose as his topic "The Mediaeval Knight"—evidence of his gift for public speaking. Also an excellent student, he showed even then the enormous energy, both mental and physical, that characterized him throughout life.

Entering Columbia College law school, Osborne paid his way by giving lessons as a tutor. After graduation in 1885, he opened a small law office, serving chiefly sailors and longshoremen. From the beginning he was successful and enthusiastically immersed himself in the life of his adopted city.

An ardent Democrat, by heredity and by principle, he early assumed an active role in New York politics. Appointed to the staff of DeLancey Nicoll, district attorney of New York County, Osborne gained distinction and within two years was one of the most trusted and successful trial assistants in the office. For eleven years he conducted many of the most important criminal prosecutions in the county, perhaps the best known of which were the cases of Roland Burnham Molineux and Albert T. Patrick. At Molineux's first trial, the defendant was convicted of murder, but the judgment was reversed by the court of appeals; at his second trial, he was acquitted. Patrick, himself a brilliant lawyer, was convicted, and the sentence was affirmed. After a legal battle of several years, however, the sentence was commuted to life imprisonment by Governor Francis W. Higgins; later Patrick was pardoned by Governor John A. Dix.

On 8 Jan. 1896 Osborne married Lelia Grey Van Wyck, the daughter of Judge Augustus Van Wyck. The couple had one son, James W.

In 1902 Osborne resigned as prosecutor and joined the firm of Osborne, Hess, and Churchill. On the dissolution of that firm, he resumed private practice with his old firm, Osborne, Lamb, and Garvan (formerly Osborne, Lamb, and Petty). In 1905 he was the Democratic candidate for the office of district attorney for New York County. He lost in a close race to William Travers Jerome, an independent Democrat, who had been nominated on the Fusion ticket.

For the rest of his life Osborne remained in private practice, accepting a number of public retainers in which he rendered notable service. In 1909 he was appointed a special attorney general of the state of New York and assigned to investigate and prosecute the American Ice Company for violating antitrust statutes. After long and bitter litigation, he obtained a conviction and the imposition of the maximum penalty. In 1910 he appeared as counsel for Senator Benn Conger of the New York State Senate in the prosecution of Senator Jothan Allds before the senate on the charge of taking a bribe to influence his actions as a legislator. Despite Allds's powerful financial and political backing, Osborne conclusively proved his guilt. The senator's conviction earned high praise for Osborne and resulted in the destruction of a corrupt lobbying influence and a general raising of ethical standards in the legislature.

The following year Osborne was counsel for the committee of the New York Senate that investigated political and social conditions in Albany; afterwards, conditions in that city markedly improved. In 1913 he was named special attorney general to investigate conditions and the treatment of prisoners in the state prison at Ossining; a vigorous and effective inquiry disclosed many abuses and led to a demand for prison reform and the appointment of Thomas Mott Osborne as warden of Sing Sing prison.

Osborne's last service to the state in a public capacity came in 1917, when District Attorney Edward Swann appointed him a special assistant in the investigations of alleged Rockaway land frauds, the Ruth Cruger murder case, and alleged motorcycle police graft, unearthed during the Cruger murder investigation. As a result of Osborne's work, indictments were found in all cases.

Thorough and painstaking in preparation, logical and forceful in the presentation of evidence, and masterly in cross-examination, Osborne became one of the best-known and ablest lawyers in New York City. His eloquent and persuasive addresses to the jury earned him a reputation as a Demosthenic orator.

In addition to his professional activities, Osborne was a devoted student of literature and history, particularly of medieval England and France. He was passionately fond of chess and was an excellent amateur player. In spite of failing health, he continued to participate in sports; indeed, he was a remarkably active man. An individual of high ideals, he was one of New York's most distinguished and picturesque citizens. He died in his apartment in New York City and was buried in Greenwood Cemetery.

SEE: Samuel A. Ashe, ed., *Cyclopedia of Eminent and Representative Men of the Carolinas of the Nineteenth Century*, vol. 2 (1892); Association of the Bar of the City of New York, *Year Book* (1920); *DAB*, vol. 7 (1934); Davidson College Catalogue (1879); New York County Lawyers' Association, *Year Book* (1920); *New York Times*, 8 Sept. 1919; Stephen B. Weeks Scrapbook, vol. 8 (North Carolina Collection, University of North Carolina, Chapel Hill).

DOROTHY H. OSBORN

Osborne, John Chevor (d. 5 Mar. 1819), physician, printer, publisher, Masonic leader, and merchant, was born in Middletown, Conn., the son of an eminent physician. He settled in New Bern, N.C., as a young man.

In 1792 Osborne was a steward of St. John's Masonic Lodge and its treasurer of 1793–94. He served on the lodge's committee of laws and correspondence, which was instructed to "form an address to our Grand Master Wm. R. Davie, Esq., and Congratulate him on his appointment as Chief Magistrate of the State of North Carolina." Osborne wrote the script, went over it with the other committeemen on 11 Jan. 1799, and obtained their approval before relaying it to Davie, whose appreciative reply was read to the lodge on 20 March.

At the same time, the committee was requested to "form an address to our Worsh'l Grand Sen'r. Warden J. L. Taylor and Congratulate him in the above manner on his Late Appointment as one of the Judges of Law & Equity in No. Carolina." Osborne also was on a 1799 committee of three "to draw up a Subscription for the building of a lodge upon the lotts purchased by the brethren." He was a liberal contributor towards the cost of constructing the Masonic Temple.

In 1802 he was elected grand marshal of the Grand Lodge of North Carolina. While still holding that office, he was chosen to formally present to the lodge on 6 Mar. 1805 the purchased portrait of its worshipful master, Francis Lowthrop, painted by William Joseph Williams. A decade previously Williams had painted a similar portrait of George Washington in Masonic regalia for the Alexandria-Washington Lodge, Alexandria, Va.

In 1800, when there was an outbreak of "contagious fevers" a mile and a half below New Bern, Dr. Osborne was one of three physicians named as "health examiners."

To supplement his income as doctor, printer, and publisher of the *Newbern Gazette*, established in April 1798 and continued until sometime between July 1799 and May 1800, Osborne also operated a store. In 1799 an item in his newspaper advertised "Currants for sale at the store of John C. Osborn and Co." His "Soothing Syrup" was praised, "as all mothers within reach considered it a blessing to them for their children."

At the second annual meeting of the first, short-lived North Carolina Medical Society on 1 Dec. 1800, in Raleigh, Osborne was elected president. For its 1801 meeting, also held in Raleigh, he delivered the opening address: "A cursory narrative of the progress of the science of Medicine, from the earliest ages." He remained president until the organization ceased to function sometime after 1804.

From 16 Apr. 1799 to 25 Apr. 1807, when he sold it to Francis Hawks, Osborne and his family resided in a frame house on Hancock Street. In the 1980s it was entered in the National Register of Historic Places as one of the few gambrel-roofed structures in the region, having remained "remarkably unchanged from its period of occupancy by the Hawks family, prominent in North Carolina for three generations."

In 1807 Osborne moved from New Bern to New York to become professor of the Institutes of Medicine at Columbia University. He also was a trustee of the New York College of Physicians and Surgeons. After contracting tuberculosis, he went to the Virgin Islands for his health but died on the day he landed.

Osborne married Elizabeth Barron, the daughter of Major David Barron, of New Bern, a successful merchant and distinguished Patriot. She was the granddaughter of Major Thomas Graves, Episcopal churchwarden and the 1760–62 representative of Craven County in the Assembly. Their son, Samuel, died in 1804. Elizabeth Osborne apparently died before her husband moved to New York, for in 1816 Osborne was married to Louise Payne of New York City.

SEE: Clarence S. Brigham, *History and Bibliography of American Newspapers, 1690–1820*, vol. 2 (1947); Gertrude S. Carraway, *Crown of Life* (1940); Marshall De Lancey Haywood, *Builders of the Old North State* (1968); Minutes of St. John's Lodge, AFAM (New Bern); Lois Smathers Neal, comp., *Abstracts of Vital Records from Raleigh, North Carolina, Newspapers, 1799–1819* (1979); *New Bern Mirror*, 1 Mar. 1963.

GERTRUDE S. CARRAWAY

Osteneco (Judd's Friend) (1705?–1777?), the second warrior of the Overhill Cherokee and a member of the Wolf Clan, was known to the colonials as Judd's Friend (sometimes Judge's Friend) because early in his career he had saved a trader named Judd from Cherokee wrath. He appears in the South Carolina records as one of "the two Tacites," or great warriors, of Tellico in Monroe County, Tenn. His name signifies "The Pigeon."

As a great warrior of Tellico, he was one of the principal supporters of the South Carolina–sponsored spurious "Emperor," Ammonscossitte, or the "Young Emperor of Tellico." When in 1751 the Tellico coterie of headmen decided to treat with South Carolina to obtain the removal of a trade embargo occasioned by disorders arising from the Creek-Cherokee war, Osteneco was the agent sent to enlist the support of the Cherokee Lower Towns. The headmen of Chota, the legitimate Overhill

capital, frustrated this move. Despite Chota opposition, Osteneco persisted and went to Charles Town, where he won Governor James Glen's agreement to hold a conference on the condition that the Tellico headmen would bring the recalcitrant Chota headmen to Charles Town. The Chota headmen, inspired by the "Little Carpenter," hoped to break the South Carolina trade monopoly by obtaining trade in Virginia and refused to attend. The Tellicos went ahead with the conference and agreed to halt visits of the northern Indians, who had inspired the disorders, and to deliver up the troublemakers if Glen would remove the embargo and negotiate a Creek peace. But since the Cherokee were slow to implement the treaty terms, Governor Glen did not make a Creek peace for them or fully restore the trade.

Disillusioned with South Carolina, the Young Emperor went to Virginia to seek trade but failed to obtain it. In this circumstance he lost the confidence of the Tellicos and of South Carolina. The Tellicos then accepted Chota leadership. Osteneco, to be nearer the seat of power, moved to the Overhill town of Tomatley and became a member of the Chota council.

Osteneco tended to be a rival of the Little Carpenter. When in 1755 the Little Carpenter was preventing Cherokee warriors from participating in the conflict between England and France in the Ohio Valley in order to obtain better terms for trade, Osteneco recruited Overhill warriors to go to Virginia's aid in the Sandy Creek expedition against the French-allied Shawnee in the winter of 1755–56. After this expedition failed, he went to Williamsburg, Va., for his reward. There he was entertained by Governor Robert Dinwiddie, who was happy to treat with a Cherokee who was less truculent than the Little Carpenter. He returned to the Overhills with Colonel Andrew Lewis's expedition to build the Virginia fort near Chota agreed to by the Little Carpenter and other headmen at the Treaty of Broad River in March 1756. When Virginia failed to garrison the fort and to commence the promised trade, Osteneco's prestige fell somewhat. Nevertheless, in the ensuing tensions, in which Old Hop, the Cherokee first man, began a correspondence with the French, Osteneco favored the English, and when Captain Raymond Demere built Fort Loudoun for South Carolina near Chota, Osteneco befriended him. He again led Overhill forces to support the Virginia frontier, where he was active against the French until his recall late in 1757 on the occasion of a misunderstanding that had led to the imprisonment in Winchester of several Cherokee deputies on their way to visit the Six Nations in New York.

In the stressful years of 1758 and 1759, when the Cherokee were murdered by Virginia frontiersmen, Osteneco opposed the Little Carpenter's efforts for peace and supported the great warrior, Oconostota, in demands for war on the English. In the war with South Carolina that followed, Osteneco planned and led the attack on Fort Loudoun that led to its fall.

Even after English and colonial forces had devastated the Cherokee country in campaigns of 1760 and 1761, Osteneco refused to consider peace. But he was finally prevailed upon to visit Colonel Adam Stephens's Virginia forces, which were poised to strike the Overhill towns, and saw for himself that resistance was useless and that good terms could be had—even better than those obtained by Little Carpenter at Charles Town. He therefore set himself up as the proprietor of the Virginia peace and escorted Lieutenant Henry Timberlake of the Virginia forces to Chota with the final terms of the treaty. When these were ratified at Chota, Osteneco accompanied Timberlake to Williamsburg to seal the peace with Governor Francis Fauquier. On the way he stopped at Shadwell, the home of Peter Jefferson, which he had visited before. Osteneco was the Indian chief best known to Thomas Jefferson, who had seen him at his father's house and who now visited him at his camp near Williamsburg. During his interviews with Fauquier, Osteneco demanded to be sent to England; for, he said, he desired to know whether the Little Carpenter, who had been in England in 1730, spoke the truth. It would appear that Osteneco sought again to undermine the Little Carpenter by absorbing to himself the glory of having talked personally with the king of England.

In early May 1762 Osteneco, accompanied by Timberlake and William Shorey as guides and interpreters and a few of his countrymen, set sail for England. Arriving in early June, the Indians were a sensation. Fauquier had given Timberlake an introduction to Lord Egremont, who was to look after the Indians and obtain an audience with the king. Osteneco's party lodged in a London tavern, the proprietor of which began to charge admission to the visitors who flocked to see the Indians. To escape this sort of thing as much as possible, Timberlake took his charges to various public entertainment gardens, where again they were the center of attention. On one occasion, Osteneco was given so many free drinks that he had to be dumped into a coach and hauled away. However, he did review the Grenadier Guards, was entertained at the tables of various lords and gentlemen, and finally was given an interview with the king. Osteneco prepared to smoke the pipe of peace with King George, but the king did not smoke and the Indian was made to see that a man so close to God could not smoke with mere mortals. During the two-hour meeting, Timberlake interpreted the king's remarks as the professions of friendship he thought the Cherokee had come to hear.

Despite unseemly episodes, the visit to England was a diplomatic and social success, and the Indians set sail from England vastly impressed by English wealth, energy, and power. Osteneco reached Charles Town in October 1762; thereafter, he was devoted to the English Crown and to its agent, John Stuart, His Majesty's superintendent of the southern Indians.

Osteneco's devotion to the Crown was instrumental in frustrating the efforts of certain Creeks to involve the Cherokee in the Pontiac conspiracy developing in the North. Sympathetic to this conspiracy was Oconostota, the great warrior of the Cherokee who had been well treated by the French during the Cherokee war with South Carolina and who deeply resented the English for having held him hostage for a short time in 1759. Since Oconostota would not meet directly or treat with the English, Osteneco as second warrior was the highest-ranking Cherokee warrior attending Stuart's conference of the southern governors and southern Indians at Augusta, Ga., in November 1763. At this meeting, pledges of peace were obtained, a new trade agreement was made, and Stuart and the southern governors agreed to mark a boundary between the Indians and the whites beyond which there would be no settlements and no trespass. Osteneco did not speak at the conference, but he did support all the propositions made by the Little Carpenter and regarded himself, with the Little Carpenter, as a prop of peace with the whites.

Osteneco continued to oppose Oconostota's talks with war-minded Creeks, asserting that if the Creeks went to war against the English, the Cherokee would join the English against them. In late 1764 he led a Cherokee war party to the Mississippi to waylay French trader convoys carrying goods and ammunition, to support northern Indian hostility, to the frontier. He destroyed a small convoy and brought back two French prisoners. After quarreling over the prisoners, Oconostota finally released one and Osteneco sent the other to Charles Town.

In 1765, when Oconostota—angry at English trespasses on Cherokee hunting grounds—proposed to precipitate war by killing the traders among the Cherokee, Osteneco joined the Little Carpenter in thwarting the great warrior and preserving the peace.

During the next two years he led Cherokee parties to supervise the survey of the boundaries between the Carolinas and the Cherokee. Thus, in June 1767 he was the principal Cherokee at Governor William Tryon's survey of the North Carolina boundary. The occasion was festive with many great speeches, the firing of salutes, and the drinking of fine wines, but Osteneco did warn of rogues—both white and Indian—who would not respect the boundary, the whites hunting for deer and the Indians hunting for horseflesh. The line, marked by blazes on trees, was completed only to the top of Tryon Mountain but proclaimed as far as Chiswell's mines in Virginia.

In 1768 Osteneco joined the Cherokee headmen in protesting settlers' disregard of the boundary line and attended Stuart's conference at Hard Labour, S.C., where the Cherokee agreed to the boundary from Chiswell's mines to the mouth of the Great Kanawha in the Ohio River.

In the spring of 1769 he visited Virginia and North Carolina, stopping to see Governor Tryon at New Bern. He returned by way of Charles Town, where he agreed to alter the Virginia line to include white settlements west of the Kanawha but continued to protest white invasion of the Cherokee hunting grounds.

In 1774 Osteneco became embittered against the frontiersmen when a settler at Watauga wantonly killed one of his relatives who was escorting survivors of a wreck on the Tennessee River back to Watauga. However, in 1776 he supported Stuart's effort to prevent the Cherokee from going to war against the frontiersmen until the British—now engaged in the Revolutionary War—could launch a major attack on the south. The young Cherokee warriors, disregarding Osteneco and their elders, plunged into war and met disaster. The colonials retaliated with large expeditionary forces from South Carolina, North Carolina, and Virginia, ravaging the Cherokee country. Oconostota and the Little Carpenter made a peace that ceded to North Carolina and to South Carolina large areas of the Cherokee country; the Cherokee also agreed to remain neutral in the war between the Americans and the English. The Cherokee who refused to accept the treaty and desired to continue fighting withdrew to the Chickamauga Creek area of northwestern Georgia. When last heard from, in 1777, Osteneco was in the Chickamauga region sending messages to Stuart at Pensacola, demanding goods and ammunition with which to carry on the war. Presumably he died shortly afterwards.

SEE: John R. Alden, *John Stuart and the Southern Colonial Frontier* (1966); John P. Brown, *Old Frontiers* (1938); Colonial Office Transcripts (Library of Congress, Washington, D.C.); David H. Corkran, *Cherokee Frontier: Conflict and Survival, 1740–62* (1962); Gage Papers (Clements Library, Ann Arbor, Mich.); W. L. McDowell, Jr., ed., *Colonial Records of South Carolina: Documents Relating to Indian Affairs* (1958); South Carolina Council Journals (South Carolina Department of Archives and History, Columbia).

D. H. CORKRAN

Otey, James Hervey (27 Jan. 1800–23 Apr. 1863), teacher, missionary, and first Protestant Episcopal bishop of Tennessee, was born at Mount Prospect, the family home at Liberty, Bedford County, Va. He was the son of Isaac and Elizabeth Matthew Otey. Although his parents were not active church members, his mother was a descendant of Tobie Matthew (1546–1628), bishop of Durham and archbishop of York. Otey was graduated from The University of North Carolina in 1820 and remained for the 1820–21 term as a tutor of Greek and Latin. In 1821 he married Eliza (Betsy) Pannill, the daughter of a widow who kept a boardinghouse for students in Chapel Hill. As a tutor Otey was called upon to lead chapel services, but his lack of experience caused him considerable concern until a friend named Piper (perhaps the Alexander Piper who joined others in giving land on which the university was located) offered him a copy of the Episcopal *Book of Common Prayer*. His use of it led to an understanding and appreciation of the church.

From Chapel Hill Otey and his wife went to Franklin, Tenn., where he established Harpeth Academy, a school for boys, near the end of December 1821. It was not long, however, before they were back in North Carolina and Otey was principal of the Warrenton Academy (1823–25). As was the practice in the case of alumni who followed a promising professional career, The University of North Carolina awarded Otey an M.A. degree three years after graduation. While in Warrenton, he was baptized by the Reverend William Mercer Green, his classmate at the university, and confirmed by the Right Reverend John Stark Ravenscroft. In 1825 Bishop Ravenscroft admitted Otey to the diaconate, and in 1827 he elevated him to the priesthood at St. Matthew's Church, Hillsborough.

Assigned to the mission field of Tennessee, Otey returned to Franklin, south of Nashville near the center of the state. Before the end of 1827 he had organized another school as well as St. Paul's Church in Franklin and Christ Church in Nashville. For eight years, as one of only two Episcopal priests in the state, he served as missionary, pastor, and teacher. In 1829 Bishop Ravenscroft visited him and in Nashville organized the Diocese of Tennessee. The church grew and in 1833, with five priests and one deacon, Otey was elected bishop. In recognition of this new step in his life, Columbia College in South Carolina awarded Otey an honorary D.D. degree in 1833. He was consecrated in Philadelphia on 14 Jan. 1834.

As a frontier bishop, Otey rode thousands of miles each year rendering service not only across the long state of Tennessee but also in Florida, Louisiana, Mississippi (of which he was formally designated provisional bishop until his friend, William Mercer Green, became bishop in 1850), Arkansas, and the Indian Territory. Because of growing physical infirmities, Otey was encouraged by his friends and assisted financially to take a year off. From April 1851 to March 1852 he visited England, where he was well received and participated in a number of religious services. After returning home—to be a little nearer the center of his territory and to make travel by water more accessible, although he had been relieved from service in parts of the vast region he formerly served—he settled in Memphis.

Over the years Otey was responsible for the establishment of five schools, and he conducted one in his home from 1825 to 1852. One of his educational ambitions was to see an institution of higher education established in the South from which men trained in literary and theological subjects would go out to serve the people of the region. His idea took root, and on 4 July 1857 an organizational meeting was held at Lookout Mountain near Chattanooga. Otey was elected chairman and in time also chancellor of the new institution. Chartered in 1858, the University of the South had the promise of $500,000 and the cornerstone was laid in the fall of 1860. The approaching conflict intervened, and work did not resume until after the Civil War.

As a Whig, Otey was active in trying to avert war. Futile though his efforts were, he wrote the U.S. secretary of state urging that steps be taken to restore peace. In services he conducted during the war, taking a neutral stance, he used a section of the *Book of Common Prayer* that did not contain the customary prayer for the president.

Otey's attachment to North Carolina remained strong throughout his life, and he was often in the state. He returned to conduct the service for his old teacher and friend, Elisha Mitchell, at the reinterment of Mitchell's remains atop the mountain that bears his name. Bishop Otey delivered the commencement sermon in Chapel Hill in 1857, and he attended the commencement of 1859, when both he and President James Buchanan were awarded honorary LL.D. degrees.

A number of his sermons were published, and he was the author of *Doctrine, Discipline and Worship of the American Branch of the Catholic Church, Explained and Unfolded in Three Sermons* (1852). Otey was the father of nine children. He died in Memphis. His remains were held in a receiving vault until after the war, when he was buried in St. John's churchyard at Ashwood near Franklin, Tenn.

SEE: Kemp P. Battle, *History of the University of North Carolina*, vol. 1 (1907); Charles L. Coon, *North Carolina Schools and Academies, 1790–1840* (1915); Ellen Davies-Rodgers, *The Romance of the Episcopal Church in West Tennessee, 1832–1964* (1964); Thomas F. Gailor, "James Hervey Otey—First Bishop of Tennessee," *Historical Magazine of the Protestant Episcopal Church* 4 (March 1935); Daniel L. Grant, *Alumni History of the University of North Carolina, 1795–1924* (1924); Frank McClain, *James Hervey Otey of Tennessee* (1956); James Hervey Otey Papers (Southern Historical Collection, University of North Carolina, Chapel Hill).

WILLIAM S. POWELL

Outlaw, David (14 Sept. 1806–22 Oct. 1868), lawyer, legislator, and congressman, was born near Windsor, Bertie County, the son of Ralph and Elizabeth Cherry Outlaw. His maternal grandfather was Solomon Cherry, a captain in the Revolutionary War and a member of the General Assembly. Two of his uncles were William Walton Cherry (1806–45), a legislator, and Joseph Blount Cherry (1816–82), a planter, lawyer, and public official—both of Bertie County. A cousin, George Outlaw (1771–1825), was a legislator and congressman from Bertie County.

David Outlaw attended private schools and academies of the county before entering The University of North Carolina in 1820 at age fourteen. After he was graduated in 1824 with an A.B. degree, he began to read law under Judge William Gaston of New Bern. He was admitted to the bar in 1827 and established a practice in Windsor.

In 1831 Outlaw was elected to the General Assembly, serving until 1834. In 1835 he was chosen as a Whig delegate to the state constitutional convention in Raleigh. For a time, Outlaw lived in Raleigh and edited the Raleigh *Star*, a newspaper used to communicate Whig ideas. When his father died in 1836, Outlaw, as the oldest son, moved back to Windsor to help with family matters. From 1836 to 1844 he was solicitor of the Edenton Circuit. In 1844 Outlaw was a delegate to the Whig National Convention in Baltimore. During this time he was colonel of the Bertie County regiment of the state militia. In 1845 he was an unsuccessful candidate for Congress from the Edenton District; the victor, Judge Asa Biggs of Williamston, won by 145 votes. Two years later, in the 1847 election, Outlaw defeated Biggs by 724 votes and became a member of the House of Representatives. He was reelected in 1849, defeating General Thomas J. Person of Northampton County by 511 votes, and again in 1851, when his opponent was Colonel William F. Martin of Elizabeth City. In the election of 1853, Dr. Henry M. Shaw of Currituck County defeated Outlaw by a mere 87 votes.

In Congress, Outlaw was a quiet listener but very persuasive when he did speak. Using simple language, Outlaw impressed his colleagues with his forceful voice. During the period 1847–53, he strongly opposed the bill establishing territorial governments in Oregon, New Mexico, and California on the grounds that the bill was not a compromise between the North and the South. Rather, he believed, the measure was unfair to the South. Similarly, Outlaw was against the acquisition of any Mexican territory by conquest for fear the action would create sectional difficulties and jeopardize the Union. As a congressman, he strived to maintain peace between the North and the South.

After his defeat in 1853, Outlaw returned to Windsor and was again elected to the General Assembly in 1854, 1856, and 1858. In 1860 and 1866 he won a seat in the state senate.

Outlaw was a tall man, measuring six feet two and one-half inches. He was very slender, with red hair, fair skin, and hazel eyes. Being very nearsighted, he wore glasses.

On 7 June 1837 Outlaw married Emily Turner Ryan, of Tennessee, the widow of Joseph Ryan of Bertie County. He had two stepdaughters (Harriet and Emily Ryan) and four children of his own (Elizabeth, Annie Peyton, David, and George). Outlaw always felt loyal to the local Episcopal church, since his wife and children were members of the congregation. He was buried in the Episcopal church cemetery in Windsor.

SEE: *Biog. Dir. Am. Cong.* (1961); Pulaski Cowper, "Colonel David Outlaw," *Wake Forest Student* 15 (March 1896 [portrait]); Daniel L. Grant, *Alumni History of the University of North Carolina, 1795–1924* (1924); J. G. de Roulhac Hamilton, ed., *The Papers of Thomas Ruffin*, vol. 2 (1918); John Nichols, *Directory of the General Assembly of the State of North Carolina for the Session Commencing November 19, 1860* (1860); David Outlaw Papers (Southern Historical Collection, University of North Carolina, Chapel Hill); David Outlaw, *Speech of Mr. David Outlaw of North Carolina on the Army Appropriation Bill: Delivered in the House of Representatives of the United States, August 3, 1848* (1848) and *Speech of Mr. David Outlaw of North Carolina on the Presidency and the Fugitive Slave Law: Delivered in the House of Representatives of the United States, June 10, 1852* (1852); John H. Wheeler, *Historical Sketches of North Carolina from 1584 to 1851* (1851).

REBECCA B. LITTLETON

Outlaw, George (*25 Oct. 1771–15 Aug. 1825*), merchant and legislator, was the only child of Ralph, Jr., and his second wife, Mary Knott Outlaw, whose plantation lay a few miles north of Windsor, Bertie County. The immediate ancestors of Ralph Outlaw had migrated from Norfolk County, Va., to Chowan Precinct and thence to Bertie. The surname "Outlaw" has been traced to thirteenth-century origins in Bedfordshire, England.

Educated by private teachers and in the common schools, young Outlaw was engaged in farming and in the mercantile business before his election to represent Bertie in the state House of Commons in 1795. Thereafter, he maintained rather prosperous plantation and mercantile interests while serving frequently in the General Assembly. He was a member of the House of Commons during the sessions of 1795–98 and 1819. He represented Bertie in the state senate in the sessions of 1799, 1802, 1806–8, 1810–14, 1817, and 1822.

Characterized by kind, genial manners and a generous disposition, Outlaw—a Jeffersonian Republican—presided as speaker of the state senate for the sessions of 1812–14. In the latter year, he was a nominee for governor but was defeated by William Miller. Outlaw's political career was climaxed with his election to the Eighteenth Congress to fill the unexpired term of Hutchings Gordon Burton after Burton's election as governor of North Carolina. Declining to stand for reelection, Outlaw retired to his home in Bertie following a brief tenure in Congress (19 Jan.–3 Mar. 1825).

It is probable that Outlaw's service in the General Assembly was due more to his strength of character, depth of piety, and general popularity—especially among his fellow Baptist constituents in northeastern North Carolina—than to his talents as a statesman. His popularity is evidenced by the fact that he frequently was chosen to preside over the annual sessions of the Chowan Baptist Association, a union of churches that spanned the geographic region from the Roanoke River to the Atlantic. In his capacity as moderator of the association, Outlaw signed a letter of 20 May 1806 to Thomas Jefferson expressing the deepest gratitude for the civil and religious liberties enjoyed "under the administration of the government over which you, Sir, at present preside." Jefferson's response, dated 24 Jun. 1806, noted gratification for the confidence expressed in him and his administration, together with the request that Outlaw assure the churches of "my prayers for the continuance of every blessing to them now and hereafter; and accept yourself my salutations and assurance of great respect and consideration."

Outlaw was married twice. His first wife was Elizabeth Bryan, the daughter of Joseph and Mary Hunter Bryan, by whom he had four children: Joseph Bryan, George Bryan, Harriett (m. Jonathan R. Leggett and then Anthony W. Putney), and Mary Bryan (Polly) (m. William Dossey). Elizabeth Bryan Outlaw died on 28 July 1816. On 19 Jan. 1818 Outlaw married Frances Mackey Smith, the widow of Henry Harrison Smith, by whom he had three more children: William Thomas Mackey, Frances (died in adolescence), and Julia.

Outlaw died of typhoid fever and was buried in the family cemetery in Bertie County.

SEE: *Biog. Dir. Am. Cong.*, (1950); Biographical sketch appended to "Minutes of Cashie Baptist Church (Windsor)," January 1827; John L. Cheney, Jr., ed., *North Carolina Government, 1585–1979* (1981); *Minutes of the North Carolina Chowan Baptist Association, Holden at Cashie Meeting House, 2, 3, and 4 of May 1807*; Albert Timothy Outlaw and Abner Henry Outlaw, *Outlaw Genealogy* (1972); John H. Wheeler, ed., *Reminiscences and Memoirs of North Carolina and Eminent North Carolinians* (1884).

R. HARGUS TAYLOR

Overman, Lee Slater (*3 Jan. 1854–12 Dec. 1930*), lawyer, legislator, and U.S. senator, was born in Salisbury, the son of William H. and Mary E. Slater Overman. He was educated in the private schools of Salisbury and at Trinity College, from which he was graduated in 1874. For the next two years he taught in Winston at one of the state's first public schools. In 1876 Trinity awarded him a master of arts degree.

Overman worked in the 1876 gubernatorial campaign of Zebulon B. Vance and after the election became Governor Vance's private secretary. Following Vance's departure for the U.S. Senate two years later, Overman stayed for one year as private secretary to Governor Thomas J. Jarvis.

While working for Vance, Overman read law under J. M. McCorkle of Salisbury and Richard H. Battle of Raleigh. He was admitted to the North Carolina bar in 1878 and won his first case the following year before the North Carolina Supreme Court. Returning to Salisbury in 1880, he opened a law office and became president of the Salisbury Savings Bank.

Overman supported the Prohibition amendment in the statewide referendum of 1881. The next year he was elected to the state house of representatives. Reelected in 1884, 1886, 1892, and 1898, he served as speaker of the house for the 1893 session. Overman favored discontinuation of state aid to railroads and in 1895 was instrumental in the leasing of the North Carolina Railroad Company, of which he had been made president in 1894, to the newly formed Southern Railway Company. He served as a presidential elector for the state at large in 1900 and was president of the state Democratic conventions of 1900 and 1901.

As the Democratic caucus's candidate for U.S. senator in 1895, Overman lost to Jeter C. Pritchard, the nominee of the Republicans and the Populists. The state legislature appointed Overman to succeed Pritchard in 1902. He was reappointed in 1909, elected in 1914, and reelected in 1920 and 1926. In 1914 he was the first U.S. senator from North Carolina to be elected by popular vote.

Although a political conservative, Overman supported most of the measures of the Wilson administration, including the Federal Reserve Act, the income tax law, and federal assistance to farmers. He wrote and sponsored the Overman Act of 1918, which gave the president extraordinary powers to coordinate government agencies in wartime. During Woodrow Wilson's terms, Overman served as chairman of the Joint Inaugural Committee and chairman of the Rules Committee (1913), was acting chairman of the Judiciary Committee, and was a ranking member of the Appropriations Committee. He was chairman of a committee to examine the activities of Capitol Hill lobbies in 1913 and chaired investigatory subcommittees on German and Bolshevist propaganda in 1918 and 1919. Overman also worked for the creation of a Department of Labor and for passage of the Clayton Anti-Trust Act. He favored the extension of foreign trade and consistently opposed pork-barrel legislation. Through Josephus Daniels, President Wilson persuaded Overman to cast the deciding vote for the confirmation of Louis D. Brandeis for the U.S. Supreme Court.

According to suffragists Carrie Chapman Catt and Nettie Rogers Shuler, Overman "sounded the keynote" of the southern resistance to woman suffrage. Based on his concern that a deleterious effect of the woman suffrage movement would be the extension of the Fifteenth Amendment to illiterate black women and his belief that woman suffrage should be a state—rather than a federal—decision, Overman was uncompromising in his opposition to the amendment.

In the presidential campaign of 1928 Overman supported Alfred E. Smith, but North Carolina's electoral votes went to Herbert C. Hoover, the Republican candidate. The bitter fight among North Carolina Democrats that year over the Smith candidacy saw Overman and the senior senator from North Carolina, Furnifold M. Simmons, on opposite sides of the issue.

During his almost twenty-eight years on Capitol Hill, Overman served on sixteen standing committees. He was a noted constitutional authority and was known in the Senate as the "grand old man of the South." In Senate eulogies he was characterized as "dignified, courtly, and courteous" and "unyielding on a question of principle." At the time of his death, he was tied for second in seniority in the Senate behind Simmons.

A lifelong Methodist and friend of public education, Overman served on the board of trustees of Duke University and The University of North Carolina. Both schools awarded him an honorary LL.D. degree, as did Davidson College.

On 31 Oct. 1878 Overman married Mary Paxton Merrimon, the daughter of Augustus Summerfield Merrimon, a U.S. senator and chief justice of the North Carolina Supreme Court. They had three daughters: Margaret Gregory, Kathryn Hambley, and Grace Snow. Another daughter and a son died in infancy.

Overman died at his apartment in Washington's Shoreham Hotel after suffering a stomach hemorrhage. As he had requested, the funeral service was conducted in the chamber of the U.S. Senate. Burial was in Chestnut Hill Cemetery, Salisbury.

SEE: Samuel A. Ashe, ed., *Cyclopedia of Eminent and Representative Men of the Carolinas of the Nineteenth Century*, vol. 2 (1892); *Biog. Dir. Am. Cong.* (1961); Carrie Chapman Catt and Nettie Rogers Shuler, *Woman Suffrage and Politics* (1923); *DAB*, vol. 14 (1946); Joseph L. Morrison, *Josephus Daniels: The Small-d Democrat* (1966); *Lee S. Overman Memorial Addresses in the Seventy-First Congress* (1931); Lee Slater Overman Papers (Southern Historical Collection, University of North Carolina, Chapel Hill); Raleigh *News and Observer*, 9 Apr. 1920, 28 Oct. 1928, 12 Dec. 1930; *Who Was Who in America*, vol. 1 (1942).

BRENDA MARKS EAGLES

Owen, Allen Ferdinand (*9 Oct. 1816–7 Apr. 1865*), lawyer, Georgia legislator and congressman, and U.S. consul to Havana, was born in rural Wilkes County, N.C. His family moved to Georgia when he was four. The census of 1830 for Upson County, Ga., reveals that his father was no longer living. The teenaged boy's Virginia-born mother, Mary Owen, headed a household of three children and thirteen blacks, one of whom was a freeman. Although both Thomaston and Franklin academies existed in his county, young Owen, coming from an apparently affluent background, is thought to have had the advantage of private tutors. His college and professional training, seemingly disjointed, included some contact with the University of Georgia and graduation with the class of 1837 from Yale College, where he is said to have entered as a sophomore.

Owen attended Harvard Law School between 23 Aug. 1837 and 3 Jan. 1838 and again from 3 May to 25 Oct. 1839. The Charleston, S.C., office where he read law and must have gained some practical insight was that of James L. Petigru, the famous South Carolina Unionist. In St. Philip's Church, Charleston, on 18 Dec. 1837,

Owen married Emmeline Matthews, the daughter of South Carolinian Robert A. Matthews. On 23 Oct. 1839, the final year that Owen attended Harvard, the Circuit Court of the United States at Boston admitted him to practice as an attorney and counselor.

In 1840 Owen settled in Talbotton, Ga., the seat of Talbot County, adjacent to Upson. He represented Talbot County in the legislature in 1843 and 1845 and was appointed clerk of the Georgia House of Representatives in 1847. Elected to Congress, he took his seat in December 1849 as a member of the Whig party. In the notable contest in which Georgia Democrat, Howell Cobb, was elected speaker, Owen and his fellow Georgia Whigs, Robert Toombs and Alexander H. Stephens, consistently voted against Cobb. At the beginning of the second session of the Thirty-first Congress, Owen became ill in Washington and remained so through nearly all of December 1850. With adjournment in March 1851, he accepted appointment under the Fillmore administration as consul to Havana in Spanish-controlled Cuba.

Embarking from Charleston with his family on 1 May 1851, Owen warned Secretary of State Daniel Webster that rumors of an intended filibuster from the United States filled the air. Indeed, the slippery Cuban patriot, Narciso Lopez, on 3 August, launched from New Orleans a third and final expedition. Because Spanish authorities intercepted and summarily executed a number of American citizens who were among the Lopez adventurers, and because Owen had followed the "steady aim and conduct to not intermeddle with the politics of Cuba," he was blamed for gross inattention to the interests of his countrymen. Owen attempted in vain to justify his course through a communication to an American newspaper. In November 1851 Secretary Webster reacted by naming a replacement, and the following month Owen returned to the United States with his family.

He resumed his role as attorney and community leader in Talbotton and, with the demise of the Whig party, became a Democrat. Governor Joseph E. Brown appointed him a delegate to the Southern Commercial Convention held in Montgomery, Ala., in May 1858. At the census of 1860, Owen reported a personal estate of $12,000, including eight slaves. His wife, familiarly called Emma, was thirty-five. Their oldest child, Robert, about nineteen or twenty, was no longer with them. There were two daughters at home: Susan Hamilton, seventeen, and Mary A., sixteen. The four younger children were Charles, fifteen; Allen Richard, nine; Edward, born in Cuba, eight; and Franklin, five. Also now recorded with the household at Talbotton was Owen's mother, Mary, aged seventy-three, with a personal estate of $6,000, including ten slaves.

In time, Owen suffered a partial paralysis of his right side. While on a visit to relatives in a nearby county, he died at Upatoi just as the Civil War was drawing to an end. He was buried at Oak Hill Cemetery, Talbotton.

SEE: I. W. Avery, *History of Georgia from 1850 to 1881* (1881); *Biog. Dir. Am. Cong.* (1961); Johnson J. Hayes, *The Land of Wilkes* (1962); *Journal of the House of Representatives of the United States, Being the First of the Thirty-first Congress* (1849–50); *Journal of the House of Representatives of the United States, Being the Second of the Thirty-first Congress* (1850–51); Lucian L. Knight, *Georgia Landmarks, Memorials, and Legends*, vol. 2 (1914); John H. Latane, *A History of American Foreign Policy* (1928); Mrs. Stahle Linn, Jr., "Wilkes County, North Carolina: Wills, Deeds, Tax Lists, etc." (typescript, National DAR Library, Washington, D.C.); Stephen F. Miller, *The Bench and Bar of Georgia*, vol. 1 (1858); Carolyn W. Nottingham and Evelyn Hannah, *History of Upson County, Georgia* (1930).

H. B. FANT

Owen, Benjamin Wade (4 June 1904–7 Oct. 1983), traditional potter, was born and raised near the Westmoore community in northwestern Moore County, the son of Rufus and Martha McNeill Owen. As a member of a large clan of potters, Owen learned to make pottery alongside his brothers Charlie (b. 1901) and Joe (1910–86) at the family shop. Between the seasonal demands of farming, their father provided informal but practical training in all phases of the craft. As Owen recalled: "I'd help him knead up his clay—weigh it out and knead it up—and help him lift his jars off. And when he'd be doing something else—putting on handles on something else—I'd be trying to make me some little jugs and pitchers to sell." By the time he was sixteen, he was a proficient potter and did some work as a journeyman at other shops. Like the other potters in this region, he produced lead-glazed earthenware pie dishes and flowerpots, as well as salt-glazed stoneware jars, jugs, pitchers, churns, and milk crocks, all familiar, utilitarian forms used in local homes and on farms.

Owen's life took a dramatic turn in 1923, when Jacques Busbee offered him a job at the newly established Jugtown Pottery. Together with his wife Juliana, Busbee sought to revitalize the native pottery industry by introducing new forms and glazes and developing new markets outside of the region. Since he was not a potter himself, Busbee had to rely on the skilled hands of local men. He soon found that the members of Rufus Owen's generation wanted no part in such innovations and had no desire to make "toys," as they scornfully referred to the smaller and more decorative wares. And so Busbee hired the younger potters, first Charlie Teague (1901–38) and then Ben Owen: "He came to my house and wanted to know if I'd come down and try. He wanted some young potters that he could show and tell. The older potters, he said, was harder to get it in their heads what he wanted."

The fusion of Jacques Busbee's vision with Ben Owen's skills eventually earned an international reputation for the Jugtown Pottery. Busbee patiently educated the young man in the ceramic traditions of the Orient, most notably works from the Han, T'ang, and Sung dynasties of China. He took Owen to museums in New York and Washington, D.C., and provided sketches, photographs, pictures, and even a tea bowl to study and imitate. Owen found that "it didn't take me long to get on to it," but he soon learned that he had to finish these pieces much more carefully than the old utilitarian wares. "It had to be just right or he wouldn't have it. . . . He wanted it to be just like the picture or the model." Busbee did not neglect the old forms—Owen continued to turn jugs, jars, pitchers, pie dishes, and ring jugs—but now the Jugtown repertory included equal numbers of Han vases, Sung bowls, Korean bottles, and Persian jars. Likewise, Owen learned about new glazes—white, mirror black, Chinese blue—to go with the old lead, salt, and frogskin types. In all, the collaboration of the two men produced a classic pottery unlike that made anywhere else, a blend of old and new founded on the principles of restraint and simplicity that were inherent in both the native folk and Oriental traditions.

Jacques Busbee died in 1947, but Ben Owen remained at Jugtown until 1959, when the business was sold to John Maré. After a disagreement with the new owner,

Owen left and founded the Old Plank Road Pottery, where he continued to produce the same forms and glazes until his retirement in 1972. During this final phase of his career, he stamped his pottery with his own name: Ben Owen/Master Potter. Fittingly, Owen's work has been widely exhibited in North Carolina, the United States, and abroad. Permanent collections may be found in such institutions as the Mint Museum, Charlotte; the North Carolina Museum of Art, Raleigh; the Smithsonian Institution, Washington, D.C.; the Metropolitan Museum of Art, New York; and the Louvre, Paris.

Although severely crippled by arthritis late in life, Owen had the pleasure of watching his son and grandson revive his work. From his marriage to Lucille Harris on 27 Mar. 1937, there were two children: Benjamin Wade, Jr., and Jane. Son Wade worked at the Old Plank Road Pottery but then moved on to other occupations such as farming and teaching. However, in late 1982, he and his son, Benjamin Wade III, reopened the shop as the Ben Owen Pottery and began producing a full line of old North Carolina forms and Oriental translations, most of them based closely on the earlier work of the master. In his last years, Ben Owen was able to teach and encourage his grandson, thus extending the tradition he had learned as a boy. He died of a heart attack after a bout with pneumonia and was buried at the nearby Union Grove Baptist Church, the final resting place of many generations of North Carolina potters.

SEE: *Ben Owen Pottery* (1974) (exhibition catalogue, North Carolina Museum of History); Jean Crawford, *Jugtown Pottery: History and Design* (1964); *Jugtown Pottery: The Busbee Vision* (1984) (exhibition catalogue, North Carolina Museum of Art); Benjamin Wade Owen, "Reflections of a Potter," *The State of the Arts* (April 1969), newsletter of the North Carolina Arts Council; Charles G. Zug III, *Turners and Burners: The Folk Potters of North Carolina* (1986).

CHARLES G. ZUG III

Owen, Guy (*24 Feb. 1925–23 July 1981*), teacher and writer, was born of Welsh and English ancestry in the Elkton community near Clarkton (called "Clayton" in his fiction) in Bladen County ("Cape Fear County"), the oldest of four sons of Margaret Ethel Elkins and Guy Owen, Sr. His brothers were James Eugene (d. 1965), Charles Cowan, and Ronald Earl. John Owen, governor of North Carolina (1828–30), was a brother of their great-great-great-grandfather.

During Guy Owen's childhood, the family lived for a while in Florida and South Carolina but returned to Clarkton during the depression. As a boy, he stayed in the home of his grandfather, James Samuel Elkins, a tobacco grower, whom the impressionable youngster accompanied to auctions in the Clarkton warehouses. He also clerked at his father's crossroads general store and on idle days listened to the local menfolk swap yarns. After graduating from high school in 1942, he spent the summer months as a welder in the Wilmington shipyards; then in the fall he became a freshman at The University of North Carolina. Three years as an army private in France and Germany followed, whereupon he reentered the university, receiving a B.A. in 1947 and an M.A. in English in 1949. He taught at Davidson College from 1949 to 1951. Back in Chapel Hill, Owen pursued courses leading to a Ph.D., which he received in 1955 with a dissertation on the Elizabethan playwright, Thomas Middleton. During 1954–55 he was a member of the Department of English at Elon College. He then ac-

cepted an associate professorship at Stetson University in De Land, Fla., moving there with his wife, Dorothy Meadows Jennings, whom he had married in April 1952. They had two sons: William James and John Leslie.

At Stetson, Owen wrote short stories and poems, began a long work of fiction, and taught creative writing. He founded *Impetus* (1958–64), a modest journal, which, although originally intended to print the best work of his students, soon opened its pages to writers everywhere. *Cape Fear Country and Other Poems* (1958), a lyrical tribute to the people and environs of Bladen County, was his first book. Then came *Season of Fear* (1960), a novel of the 1930s set in a rural community very like those of his native region. Its protagonist, an aging, slow-witted, slovenly farmer, works hot, dry days in the tobacco fields. At night he is alternately torn between prayers to a red-bearded Christ and his gnawing desire for a homely, "slough-hipped" girl in the neighborhood. The struggle within one person between religion and sex is an ancient theme in literature. Though the tragic *Season of Fear* was well received in both America and England, Owen decided that his next fiction would be comic. He spent the year 1961–62, on a leave of absence from Stetson, at White Pines Farm near Pores Knob in the Moravian Falls section of Wilkes County. At this home place of his wife's family, he took over an abandoned post office as writer's studio and completed the first draft of a novel about a flim-flam charlatan operating along the banks of the Cape Fear River. He spent several more summers there revising the manuscript.

Meanwhile, in 1962, Owen accepted an invitation to join the faculty of North Carolina State University. His courses in creative writing and American literature were popular with students, who time and again honored him with best-teacher awards. *Impetus* was transferred to Raleigh and became the *Southern Poetry Review*, for which he was general editor (1964–78). For seven years (1966–73) he was coeditor of the *North Carolina Folklore Journal*.

In *The Ballad of the Flim-Flam Man* (1965), a picaresque novel in the tradition of Melville's *Confidence Man* and Mark Twain's *Huckleberry Finn*, attractive old swindler Mordecai Jones is joined by young, guitar-playing Curley Treadaway, AWOL from Fort Bragg, in a series of hilarious adventures in and around "Cape Fear County." Right and left they fleece those who are greedy and willing to deceive others; but as Curley says, "You can't con an honest man." Almost immediately the book was purchased by Twentieth Century–Fox and made into a successful motion picture (1967) with George C. Scott and Michael Sarrazin. Owen's next novel, *Journey for Joedel* (1970), won the Sir Walter Raleigh Award for the best work of fiction by a North Carolinian and was nominated for the Pulitzer Prize. According to Owen, who always considered it his best book, the theme of the novel was a child's "initiation into the moral ambiguity of the adult world." It is the story of thirteen-year-old Joedel, half Lumbee Indian, half white, during the span of a single summer day in the middle of the depression years. On a trip to the tobacco market with his father, Joedel faces a number of tests that examine his readiness to pass from boyhood to manhood. *The Flim-Flam Man and the Apprentice Grifter* (1972) continues the frolicsome, wily capers of Mordecai and Curley, as do some of the selections in *The Flim-Flam Man and Other Stories* (1980).

More than forty short stories by Owen were published in such diverse periodicals as the *Carolina Quarterly*, *Sandlapper*, and *Fantasy and Science Fiction*. *The Guilty and Other Poems* (1964, chapbook) and *The White Stallion and*

Other Poems (1969), which was awarded the Roanoke-Chowan Cup for the best book of the year by a North Carolina poet, included only a portion of his verses appearing over the years in anthologies and publications such as the *Saturday Review, Poetry, College English,* and the *New York Times,* but mostly in "little magazines" like *Voices* and *Epos.*

Owen's critical and scholarly articles treated such writers as Stephen Crane, Robert Frost, Erskine Caldwell, F. Scott Fitzgerald, William Faulkner, Thomas Wolfe, and others. He edited *Modern American Poetry: Essays in Criticism* (1972) and coedited *Southern Poetry Today* (1962), *Essays in Modern American Literature* (1963), *New Southern Poets* (1975), *Contemporary Poetry of North Carolina* (1977), and *Contemporary Southern Poetry* (1979). Among his many honors was a Bread Loaf scholarship (1960), the Henry H. Bellamann Foundation Award (1964), a Yaddo fellowship (1968), and the North Carolina Award (gold medallion) for Literature (1971). Beginning in 1964 he was director of the North Carolina Poetry Circuit, whose purpose was to bring poets to meet with students and give readings on college campuses. Later he participated in the "poetry in the schools" project. In his dedication to the cause of southern poetry, in his commitment to its promotion, he was ever on the move throughout North Carolina and the South, lecturing and conducting literary workshops in cities and small communities, in public schools, and in colleges and universities, where his mission was to encourage both beginning and emerging writers. This evangelical assignment he carried out up to within a few months of his death from cancer. He was buried in the family plot in the Clarkton Cemetery. Owen was a member of the Community United Church of Raleigh and a registered Democrat.

SEE: John Carroll, ed., *Kite-Flying and Other Emotional Acts: Conversations with Twelve Southern Writers* (1972); Vic Dalmas, "Guy Owen and the World of Cape Fear County," *St. Andrews Review* (Winter–Spring 1975); Patricia Anne Finch, "Cape Fear County: The Novels of Guy Owen" (M.A. thesis, University of North Carolina, 1970); Guy Owen Papers (Southern Historical Collection, University of North Carolina, Chapel Hill); "Guy Owen Special Issue," *Pembroke Magazine,* no. 13 (1981).

RICHARD WALSER

Owen, James (*1784–4 Sept. 1865*), legislator, state official, U.S. senator, and promoter, was the oldest son of Thomas and Eleanor Porterfield Owen of Bladen County. He was the brother of Governor John Owen. Following his formal education at the celebrated Bingham School in Pittsboro, James took over the farming interests of his father at Milton plantation on the Cape Fear River, which he inherited at Thomas Owen's death in 1806. He was elected to the state House of Commons in 1808. After leaving that office in 1811, he was active in the state militia, in which he served as an adjutant general during the War of 1812. Evidently successful as a planter, he continued to add to his inheritance in land and slaves. In 1817 he won a seat in the U.S. Senate. Returning to North Carolina in 1819, he devoted the remainder of his life to his farming and business interests.

Appointed collector of customs at Wilmington, Owen divided his time during the 1820s between his plantation and his official duties. A devoted Presbyterian, he was a leading member of Fayetteville's First Presbyterian Church and an officer in the Fayetteville chapter of the American Bible Society. In 1835, having become interested in a project to bring a railroad to Wilmington, Owen sold his plantation and moved his family to the

city. As a member of the railroad's board of directors, he took a hand in altering the original plan for building the line between Wilmington and Raleigh, settling instead upon a route to Weldon. Linked at Weldon with lines reaching major northern markets, the Wilmington and Weldon's 161½ miles of rails made it the longest line in the world at its completion in 1840. When Edward B. Dudley resigned that year as president of the railroad to become governor of the state, Owen succeeded him. The heavy costs of completing the final portions of the line, however, had apparently drained Owen's own financial resources, and he was able to retain little of his property after resigning as head of the railroad in 1841.

For long periods during his later life, Owen was frequently absent from Wilmington, giving his attention mainly to a plantation he owned in Alabama. He was in Wilmington, however, on several notable occasions, as when he served on reception committees for Henry Clay in 1844 and James K. Polk in 1849 and 1854. Owen remained spasmodically active in the political and religious life of the Wilmington area, having joined the First Presbyterian Church when he moved there. He also was in Wilmington at the outbreak of the Civil War but appears to have moved during the war to the plantation—Owen Hill—of his late brother, just opposite Milton on the Cape Fear River. He died and was buried at Owen Hill, having outlived his wife, Eliza Mumford Owen, by twenty-four years. He was survived by five of his seven children. His remains were later reinterred in Oakdale Cemetery, Wilmington.

An interesting association was that of James Owen with his Moslem slave, Omar Ibn Said, known to the Owen family as "Moro." Owen purchased Omar, then a fugitive runaway, at the Fayetteville jail in 1810 and continued as his master until the servant's death in 1864. Through the Owens, Omar, a product of Koranic schools in Senegal, was converted to Christianity and became a regional celebrity as a result of his scholarly habits and dignified decorum.

SEE: *Biog. Dir. Am. Cong.* (1950); *North Carolina Presbyterian* (Fayetteville), 23 July 1859; Owen family papers and genealogical typescripts (possession of Mrs. L. N. Trammell, Atlanta); "Owen Hill: Home of the Owens," *Bladen Journal,* 11 Nov. 1971.

T. C. PARRAMORE

Owen, John (*August 1787–9 Oct. 1841*), farmer, politician, and governor, was born in Bladen County of Welsh ancestry, the son of Eleanor Porterfield and Colonel Thomas Owen, one of the leaders of the Battle of Elizabethtown in August 1781. General James Owen was his brother. His father was born in Chester County, Pa., but moved to Bladen with his family when he was a child. In addition to his service in the American Revolution, for which he received military honors, Thomas Owen was a member of the Provincial Congress at Hillsborough, was elected justice of the Bladen County Court of Pleas and Quarter Sessions, and served many terms as state senator both before and after the war. He died in 1803.

John Owen was a student at The University of North Carolina in 1804 and later served as a trustee of the university for over twenty years. As a young man he married Lucy Brown, the daughter of General Thomas Brown, and they lived at Owen Hill, a plantation up the Cape Fear River from Elizabethtown, where he spent most of his life. They became the parents of a daughter, Lucy, who married Haywood W. Guion, a lawyer.

Before his election as governor, Owen served Bladen

County in a number of capacities. In addition to presiding as judge of the inferior courts, he won a seat in the North Carolina House of Commons in 1812 and 1813. He was also state senator in 1819 and 1827. Owen was elected governor by a joint ballot of the General Assembly in 1828 and 1829. For personal reasons he chose not to accept the office a third time. His term ended on 18 Dec. 1832, when he was succeeded by Montfort Stokes. Later Willie P. Mangum defeated him by one vote in his bid for the U.S. Senate.

Owen's two years as governor were marked by his special interest in education and transportation. He submitted a plan for a public school system based on improvements begun in New York and the New England states. He also urged that the rivers of North Carolina be cleared for better transportation, and in 1829 he obtained an appropriation for the construction of a canal and locks at Weldon and the opening of a channel from Albemarle Sound to the ocean. During his administration the election of sheriffs and clerks of county courts was given to the voters instead of the justices.

John Owen's retirement from the governorship did not end his public service to Bladen County and the state. As a delegate to the constitutional convention of 1835, he opposed disfranchising free Negroes and supported a proposal to abolish religious tests as a qualification for officeholders. He also served as president of the Whig National Convention in Harrisburg, Pa., in 1839. During the convention he was offered the nomination of vice-president with William Henry Harrison running as president. Had he chosen to run, he would have become president on the early death of Harrison. However, he declined the nomination on the grounds that it was not proper for him to accept such an offer from a body over which he was the presiding officer. He died in Pittsboro, where he was buried.

SEE: Samuel A. Ashe, *History of North Carolina*, vol. 2 (1925), and ed., *Biographical History of North Carolina*, vol. 8 (1917); Beth G. Crabtree, *North Carolina Governors: 1585–1974* (1974); Daniel L. Grant, *Alumni History of the University of North Carolina, 1795–1924* (1924); John H. Wheeler, *Historical Sketches of North Carolina*, (1851).

GUY OWEN

Owen, John Fletcher (30 May 1895–10 Mar. 1976), psychiatrist, was born in Sampson County, near Roseboro, the son of John Fletcher and Eugenia Herring Owen. Both his parents died before he was nine, and he made his home with his mother's sister, Elizabeth Herring (Mrs. E. J.) Crumpler in Roseboro. After attending the local schools, Owen went to Wake Forest College, where he received the degree of bachelor of science in medicine in 1918. In the fall of that year he enrolled in the third-year class of the Jefferson Medical College, Philadelphia, from which he was graduated with the degree of doctor of medicine in psychiatry in 1920.

During the next six years, Owen served an internship at Bryn Mawr (Pa.) Hospital, specialized in neuropsychiatry in field assignments with the U.S. Public Health Service, and completed a one-year residency at Cook County Hospital, Chicago, with an additional six months in Philadelphia and eighteen months at Cherry Point, Md. He then served successive residencies at the Chicago State Hospital and the State Hospital of Massachusetts at Medfield. These special residencies provided further training and research in his branch of medicine, even then comparatively new. Reportedly, all seven of these institutions offered him a permanent staff appointment, but he chose to return to North Carolina,

where he joined the staff of the Dorothea Dix Hospital, the state hospital of North Carolina at Raleigh, in the summer of 1926. Within a few years Owen, in addition to maintaining his heavy schedule of staff duties, became associate superintendent of the hospital. He served in that capacity until 18 Aug. 1942, when he was named superintendent, succeeding Dr. Julian W. Ashley, who retired.

Three years later, Owen elected to enter private practice in Raleigh (1945–58). At age sixty-two, he became head of the Psychiatric Hospital Unit of North Carolina Central Prison, Raleigh. He remained in the post until his retirement in 1973.

His search for knowledge sent Owen to law school in the 1930s (he had originally wanted to be a lawyer). After attending night classes for several years, he passed the bar examination in 1939. He never practiced law but had the unique dual background of medicine and law to guide him in his use of psychiatry in correctional institutions.

Dr. Owen was one of the few physicians certified by the American Board of Psychiatry. At the time of his selection to the top post at Dorothea Dix, it was written of him: "He is well qualified for his work and is one of the outstanding psychiatrists in the South. . . . He has taken many postgraduate courses and kept consistently up to date with the treatment of the mentally sick. He contributes regularly to the *North Carolina Medical Journal*." His abstracts of medicolegal articles were widely printed.

A profile of Owen, produced by feature writer Ann Pelham, appeared in the Raleigh *News and Observer* on 2 June 1975. It is a sensitive, revealing portrait of an innovative pioneer in the fields of psychology and psychiatry. The piece focuses on the motivations of a well-trained, modest—even shy—individual who always worked hard, delved into new fields of learning, and counted himself happiest when he was helping those who had been neglected and untreated largely because of the lack of knowledge and impetus in the treatment of the mentally ill. Unquestionably, Owen's forty-four years in psychiatric practice in North Carolina did much to magnify and stabilize this branch of medical science.

During his retirement, Owen learned Italian and Spanish—"just for the enjoyment"—and read current magazine articles and books dealing with medicine and law. In the summer of 1974 he suffered a detached retina and resorted to listening to cassettes of both language lessons and published articles. He had a real talent for music and enjoyed playing the organ at his home on Fairview Road in Raleigh.

Owen married Mary Harrison. He died at his Raleigh home. A funeral service was held at St. Michael's Episcopal Church, with interment in Oakwood Cemetery, Raleigh.

SEE: Information sheets (Alumni Association, Jefferson Medical College, Philadelphia, and Wake Forest University, Winston-Salem); Raleigh *News and Observer*, 16 July 1942, 2 June 1975, 11 Mar. 1976; A. G. Tolley, M.D. (Dorothy Dix Hospital, Raleigh), personal correspondence.

C. SYLVESTER GREEN

Owen, Thomas (1735–2 Nov. 1806), Revolutionary officer, was born of Welsh ancestry in Chester County, Pa., but moved to North Carolina with his father when he was about five. The family may have lived first in Granville County but soon was established in Bladen County. Nothing is known of Owen's early training and education, but over time he acquired three thousand acres of land and in 1790 owned thirty-seven slaves. In August 1775 he was elected a justice of the Bladen County Court of Pleas and Quarter Sessions, and on 9 Sept. 1775 he was made major of the local militia company.

During the American Revolution he was promoted to colonel of state troops, and at the Battle of Camden on 16 Aug. 1780 he earned a reputation for bravery. A year later he saw action at the Battle of Elizabethtown, where the Tories were routed and their commander, John Slingsby, was killed. A contemporary who knew him well said: "Tom Owen was a warm-hearted friend, generous to a foe, and as brave a soldier as ever wore a sword."

Owen represented Bladen County in the Third Provincial Congress in 1775 and in the Fifth Provincial Congress in December 1776, when the state constitution was adopted. He early demonstrated his Revolutionary sentiments as a member of the county safety committee. Owen also served in the House of Commons in 1777 and in the state senate in 1778–79, 1779–80, 1784–85, 1787, and 1790. Intermittently during the war, he was a member of a legislative committee to consider ways of bringing the Tories of the Cape Fear section "to justice" and of a committee concerned with obtaining material from the Wilcox Iron Works on Deep River in Chatham County. On one occasion he was reimbursed for expenses in connection with taking four Continental army deserters to headquarters. At the Hillsborough convention of 1788, when North Carolina declined to approve the new U.S. Constitution, he was a delegate from Bladen County. Reelected to the Fayetteville convention of 1789, he voted with the majority to adopt the Constitution.

Owen's wife was Eleanor Porterfield, the daughter of James Porterfield and the sister of Captain Dennis Porterfield, who was killed at the Battle of Eutaw Springs, S.C., in September 1781. Thomas and Eleanor Owen were the parents of John, governor of North Carolina; James, a general and congressman; and Mary, who married Elisha Stedman.

SEE: Samuel A. Ashe, ed., *Biographical History of North Carolina*, vol. 8 (1907); Bladen County Wills (North Carolina State Archives, Raleigh); Walter Clark, ed., *State Records of North Carolina*, vols. 12 (1895), 19–22 (1901–7); William L. Saunders, ed., *Colonial Records of North Carolina*, vols. 9–10 (1890), 12 (1895); John H. Wheeler, *Historical Sketches of North Carolina from 1584 to 1851* (1851).

WILLIAM S. POWELL

Owen, William (*d. May 1734*), colonial official, was appointed an assistant justice of the North Carolina General Court by Governor George Burrington in October 1732. He quickly appealed to Burrington, who was seeking able allies in his quarrels with leading families of the colony. In January 1733 the governor elevated Owen to the royal Council as his own emergency appointment. Three months later both Nathaniel Rice and John Baptista Ashe of the Council protested Owen's appointment because a majority of the councillors had not concurred in it. Burrington ignored their protests, and his enemies soon characterized Owen as "a very weak and ignorant man of bad (not to say) infamous) Character."

Owen attended his first Council meeting in March 1733. In the following months, the governor made him a justice of the peace for Beaufort and Hyde precincts. Owen returned the governor's favor by voting consis-

tently for Burrington's position in the Council. However, by May 1734 Owen was dead.

Described as a bachelor, Owen in his will named his sister, Elizabeth Owen, as his "only next of kin." His uncle and "principal creditor," Thomas Walker, was the administrator of his estate.

SEE: J. R. B. Hathaway, ed., *North Carolina Historical and Genealogical Register*, vol. 3 (July 1903); William S. Price, Jr., " 'Men of Good Estates': Wealth among North Carolina's Royal Councillors," *North Carolina Historical Review* 49 (January 1972); William L. Saunders, ed., *Colonial Records of North Carolina*, vol. 3 (1896).

WILLIAM S. PRICE, JR.

Owen, William Hayes (*ca. 1807–ca. 1877*), teacher, was born in Virginia, the son of John and Rebecca C. Owen. His family moved to Oxford when he was a child. Owen was graduated with honors from The University of North Carolina in 1833. He remained at Chapel Hill as tutor in ancient languages until January 1835, when he resigned to establish the Leasburg Classical School. When his expected replacement declined the tutorship, he was persuaded to return to his post; a year later he was also appointed university librarian. In 1838 he received an A.M. degree from the university, and in 1843 he was one of the organizers of the alumni association.

Owen was named professor of ancient languages at Wake Forest College in 1843. On assuming his duties in January 1844, he also established and operated for four years a girl's boarding school, with his mother as matron and two of his sisters, Mary and Sallie, as teachers. During his fifteen years at Wake Forest, he served much of the time as secretary of the faculty. When President John B. White contemplated resigning in 1852, Owen was elected acting president, a post to which he was reelected in December 1853, when White did resign. Owen served as acting president until June 1854.

At the commencement of 1858, the trustees asked Owen to resign—in part, because of the long-standing and undesirable influence that his able but intemperate brother, Hugh, had been exerting on the college students. Owen blamed his dismissal on "very unprofessional practices," which may have included the wish by some Baptists to rid the faculty of this Methodist professor. He terminated his connection with the college at the end of the fall term of 1858–59.

By February 1859 Owen was in Hillsborough teaching in a school that he and Ralph Henry Graves operated as a partnership. In January 1862 he became an assistant at the Beulah Institute, a boy's preparatory school established in Madison by the Beulah Baptist Association and conducted by the Reverend Lewis H. Schuck, a former student of Owen at Wake Forest. Sometime after February 1863, when the school closed as a result of the Civil War, Owen moved to Tennessee, where he continued to teach in private schools until his death in late 1876 or early 1877. During the war he was the author of a tract advocating abstinence of alcoholic beverages, entitled *Soldiers, Conquer Your Great Enemy!*

Owen's service as librarian won him recognition from Kemp Plummer Battle, historian of The University of North Carolina, as "the most active of the early librarians." The "uncommon" dignity of his manner led the students at Chapel Hill to give him the title "Judge." Both Battle and Wake Forest students agreed that Owen had limited intellectual abilities, but they praised him for his command of his subject, his reputation as a teacher, and his character as a person. Owen taught at Wake Forest longer than any other full professor before the Civil War, and, in the opinion of George Washington Paschal, "in all probability contributed more to the education of the students of that period than any of his colleagues." He enthusiastically supported the young college, and he contributed several letters and articles to the *Biblical Recorder* commending the school to the Baptists.

SEE: Kemp Plummer Battle, *History of the University of North Carolina*, vol. 1 (1907); *Biblical Recorder*, 25 July 1877; Charles L. Coon, *North Carolina Schools and Academies, 1790–1840: A Documentary History* (1915); George W. Paschal, *History of Wake Forest College*, vol. 1 (1935); John L. Sanders, ed., "Journal of Ruffin Wirt Tomlinson," *North Carolina Historical Review* 30 (January 1953); U.S. Census, 1850 (North Carolina State Archives, Raleigh); Calvin H. Wiley Papers (Southern Historical Collection, University of North Carolina, Chapel Hill).

ROBIN BRABHAM

Oxley, Lawrence Augustus (17 May 1887–2 July 1973), social worker and civil servant, was born in Boston, Mass., the son of William Junius Brutus and Alice Agatha Martin Oxley. His parents sent him to Prospect Union Preparatory School in Cambridge, and he later received special tutoring from Harvard University instructors.

During World War I Oxley enlisted in the army and rose in rank from private to first lieutenant. He served as a special investigator for the Infantry Morale Branch of the War Department Commission on Training Camp Activities for Negro Troops. From 1919 to 1941 he retained his reserve commission and became an active member of the American Legion.

Oxley's postwar activities led him gradually to North Carolina and increasingly responsible service there. After serving as assistant industrial secretary at the Harlem YMCA in New York City in early 1919, he spent the rest of the year surveying social conditions in black urban communities in the Midwest and South as a field representative of the War Camp Community Service. His work as executive secretary of the National Student Council of the Protestant Episcopal church placed him in contact with St. Augustine's College, Raleigh, where he served as instructor of social sciences, starting in 1920. While in that position Oxley came to the attention of Kate Burr Johnson, head of the North Carolina State Board of Charities and Public Welfare, who asked him to head the new division of Negro Welfare in 1925.

Funded for six years by the Laura Spelman Rockefeller Memorial Fund, North Carolina's statewide welfare program for blacks was the first of its kind in the nation. As director of this program, Oxley worked through established black organizations to help them improve community life. When he assumed the post in 1925, there was only one black social worker in the state, and not a single black community had been organized for welfare work. Furthermore, the state had no facilities for training black delinquents, no orthopedic care for black children, no training for mentally retarded blacks, no statewide parent-teacher organization for blacks, and no training institution for black social workers. There also had been no systematic study of black social problems in North Carolina, so Oxley himself conducted and published studies on social problems and capital punishment and supervised other studies.

Under his leadership, social work for blacks made great strides. The Morrison Training School for delin-

quent and underprivileged black boys, a black children's ward at the North Carolina Orthopedic Hospital in Gastonia, a training school for girls at Efland, an industrial school for dependent children in Winston-Salem, and the Bishop Tuttle Training School for social workers in Raleigh were all established after Oxley's work began. In addition, he supervised the organization of some thirty-five counties for welfare work among blacks and placed social workers in twenty-three counties. This work was so impressive that Tennessee, Pennsylvania, Missouri, Michigan, Ohio, and Georgia followed North Carolina's lead in establishing statewide welfare programs for blacks.

The advent of the depression offered new opportunities for Oxley to serve the state. In 1931 he organized the black communities for unemployment relief, a project that was recognized as one of the most effective in the nation. This work and his involvement in the presidential campaign of 1932 helped him obtain the directorship of a New Deal program in North Carolina, the Division of Negro Relief under the Federal Emergency Relief Administration. Impressed with his performance as director, Secretary of Labor Frances Perkins called Oxley to Washington, D.C., in 1934 to serve as a conciliator in industrial labor disputes.

Even more important than this position was Oxley's involvement with the "Black Cabinet," a group of nine black appointees in the Roosevelt administration who had served as unofficial advisers in the 1932 presidential campaign. Although Oxley was on the periphery of this group, he made valuable contributions, arguing successfully for the same minimum wage for blacks as for whites on the grounds that blacks were as intelligent and industrious as whites. He also sought equal employment opportunities for blacks, and he urged blacks to shift to those occupations most likely to grow in demand. Oxley remained with the Department of Labor in a variety of positions—all concerned with the improvement of employment opportunities for blacks—until his retirement.

After retirement, Oxley continued to pursue his intense interest in political and social issues. His activities in Washington, D.C., ranged from presiding over the Pigskin Club for fifteen years to serving a sixteen-year trusteeship of St. Paul's College, consulting with the U.S. Senate Committee on Aging, serving as a field representative for Senior Citizens for Kennedy in the presidential campaign of 1960, and working with the Boy Scouts. He was also active in the NAACP, the National Urban League, the Episcopal church, and the National Conference of Christians and Jews. In 1972 Oxley was honored by the city of Washington for meritorious public service. St. Augustine's College awarded him the degree of doctor of humane letters (1967).

Oxley married Mamie Elizabeth Hill, and they had two daughters: Dora Alice Clara (16 Aug. 1908–1950) and Edna Gertrude Oxley DesVerney (b. 24 Jan. 1910) of New Rochelle, N.Y. He was survived by one daughter, five granddaughters, and six great grandchildren.

SEE: Ralph J. Bunche, *The Political Status of the Negro in the Age of FDR* (1973); *Ebony* (February 1966 [portrait]); John B. Kirby, *Black Americans in the Roosevelt Era* (1980); *New York Times*, 28 Nov. 1935, 10 Oct. 1937, 30 Sept. 1960, 28 Oct. 1973; Raleigh *News and Observer*, 25 Aug. 1930, 18 Jan., 14 Nov. 1931; Wiley Britton Sanders, *Negro Child Welfare in North Carolina: A Rosenwald Study* (1933); *Washington Post*, 5 July 1973; *Who's Who in Colored America* (1941–44, 1950); Raymond Wolters, *Negroes and the Great Depression: The Problem of Economic Recovery* (1970).

JOHN L. BELL, JR.

THE EDITOR

William S. Powell is professor emeritus of history at the University of North Carolina at Chapel Hill. Before joining the history faculty he served for twenty years as curator of the North Carolina Collection.

Powell has published over seventy books and articles on North Carolina, including a pictorial history of the University of North Carolina at Chapel Hill, and *The North Carolina Gazeteer*, which won an award of merit from the American Association for State and Local History in 1969. His *North Carolina through Four Centuries* won the 1989 Mayflower Cup for Nonfiction.

THE CONTRIBUTORS

About seven hundred people have written biographical sketches for the *Dictionary*. Contributors include scholars, genealogists, journalists, local historians, and students. They are from almost every state in the country as well as France, England, and Canada. Many contributors traveled at their own expense, several to England and Scotland, to do their research. Some long-accepted "facts" about North Carolina history have been proven false by these researchers' meticulous investigations, and much new and valuable information has come to light.